DATE DUE

OCT 13 2009	
APR 23 2013	

BRODART, CO.   Cat. No. 23-221-003

Feminists Who Changed America

1963—1975

EDITED BY

Barbara J. Love

FOREWORD BY

Nancy F. Cott

University of Illinois Press • Urbana and Chicago

Design and composition by Truus Teeuwissen.
Cover photo © Bettye Lane, used with permission.

⊗ This book is printed on acid-free paper.

Library of Congress Cataloging-in-Publication Data
Feminists who changed America, 1963–1975 / edited by Barbara J. Love ;
with an introduction by Nancy F. Cott.
p.   cm.
Includes index.
ISBN-13: 978-0-252-03189-2 (cloth : alk. paper)
ISBN-10: 0-252-03189-X (cloth : alk. paper)
1. Feminists—United States—Biography.
2. Feminism—United States—History—20th century.
I. Love, Barbara J., 1937–
HQ1412.F46   2006
305.42092′273—dc22 [B]   2006020759

Contents

Photo essay follows page 256

FOREWORD

How did the women's movement begin in the 1960s? At the time, to young women like myself, it seemed to come out of nowhere, riveting one's awareness to women as a subject sex. Suddenly women's stories demanded attention. Women became the most interesting people in the world.

Yet it did not come out of nowhere. The great upsurge had been building for decades, its near antecedents being in gender equality efforts in labor unions and leftwing activism during and after World War II, as well as in the longer campaign to write equal rights into the U.S. Constitution. Sociologist Helen Mayer Hacker's 1951 article, "Women as a Minority Group" (taking its inspiration from Gunnar Myrdal's far more celebrated *An American Dilemma* of 1944 on racism in the U.S.), was a straw in the wind.

The 1950s was a decade of tumult and contradiction. Despite the domestic façade, and while Americans were marrying younger than ever before, having their children earlier, and having more children, paid employment of adult women was the rising norm. The expectation of a one-paycheck family was observed in the breach, as men's wages did not keep up with the cost of all the goods included in the "American way of life." The proportion of married women working for pay increased faster during the 1950s than in any decade before, so that by 1960, more than sixty percent of the female labor force was made up of married women. Thirty percent of white wives, and almost half of African American wives, were employed. Since childbearing followed marriage so quickly in these years, the increase in married women at work meant an increase of mothers at work, too.

These women in the 1950s and early 1960s experienced the double burden of employment and household management with very little social support except sympathetic relatives and neighbors. Meanwhile, underground currents were running among the majority of married women who were *not* counted in the labor force. Women's magazines of the 1950s were peppered with articles bearing titles such as "Blues and How to Chase Them," "What Do You Do When Worries Get You Down," and "I Can't Stand It Anymore!" recognizing the frustrations and psychological tensions mining the home front.

Growing numbers of college-educated women especially felt the pinch of the housewife role. In the late 1950s, women were little more than a third of college students (their proportion reduced because the GI Bill propelled so many male World War II veterans into higher education), and most women in coeducational colleges did not complete their degrees. But student bodies had grown so large in the postwar expansion of higher education that even at one-third of the whole, college women were more numerous than ever. And women's enrollment was rising. Among young housewives, there was a much larger pool of those who had been to college and were likely to feel a mismatch between their youthful aims and their current occupations. *The New York Times* picked up the restlessness of this group in a 1960 article titled "Road from Sophocles to Spock Is Often a Bumpy One."

Policymakers were not deaf to such potentially seismic rumblings. The immediate background for the feminist lives and activities in this directory included President John F. Kennedy's Commission on the Status of Women (1961) headed by Eleanor Roosevelt; the fifty state-level commissions on the status of women that the President's Commission spawned; and both the principles and the limitations of the federal Equal Pay Act of 1963 and Title VII of the Civil Rights Act of 1964 (fatefully amended to prohibit sex discrimination as well as race discrimination in employment), and its Equal Opportunity Employment Commission.

The background must also include, at a minimum, Rosa Parks' historic refusal to obey Jim Crow and her women friends' engineering of a bus boycott in Montgomery, Alabama, in 1955; the lunch-counter sit-ins launched by the new Student Nonviolent Coordinating Committee in 1960; the Port Huron statement and the founding of Students for a Democratic Society; the Freedom Rides undertaken by the Congress of Racial Equality in 1961 and 1962; the protest activities of Women Strike for Peace that moved President Kennedy to sign a limited nuclear test ban treaty; the Freedom Summers that brought Northern student volunteers to Mississippi to register voters in 1963 and 1964. Journalist Betty Friedan's *The Feminine Mystique* (1963), identifying "the problem that has no name," signaled a new era; like a rock thrown into the water, its impact rippled in widening circles.

The women's movement in the mid-1960s thus strode across prepared ground. With anti-war protest politicizing millions of Americans who came to oppose the growing U.S. war in Vietnam, new women's organizations burst on the scene. In 1966, Betty Friedan joined with civil rights activist and lawyer Pauli Murray, government official and lawyer Mary Eastwood, public relations executive Muriel Fox, union organizer Dorothy Haener, sociologist Alice Rossi and other professionals, businesswomen, union leaders, government officials, and academics to create the National Organization for Women (NOW). Its statement of purpose announced that "the time has come for a new movement toward true equality for all women in America, and toward a full equal partnership of the sexes, as part of the world-wide revolution of human rights now taking place within and beyond our national borders." The second national gathering of NOW overcame internal controversy to endorse eight ambitious aims: the Equal Rights Amendment; the right of women to control their reproductive lives (in effect, a call for abortion as needed); enforcement of employment discrimination laws; maternity leave rights for employed women; better tax deductions for parents' childcare expenses; establishment of childcare centers, equal and unsegregated education; and job-training incentives for women below the poverty line equal to those offered to men in President Johnson's "war on poverty" programs.

Varied as that program was, it did not reach all women. Youthful radical women whose political views were born in civil rights struggles led by the Student Nonviolent Coordinating Committee (SNCC) and in New Left groups such as Students for a Democratic Society (SDS) came to their own awakening. In 1967, women at the anti-war radicals' National Conference for New Politics exploded in fury at male elitism, and formed new and separate "women's liberation" groups. They put into practice SNCC's self-determination credo to "look to your own oppression"—that is, to start close to home in order to create a more just world.

With moral urgency and egalitarian idealism, women's liberation groups shared discussion of individual discontents, and found that common themes surfaced. Using a personalized approach to organizing that had been relied on in both SNCC and SDS, radical women called this small-group approach "consciousness-raising." In small groups, participants came to see that their own difficulties were not theirs alone—"merely personal"—but rather were related to structural inequalities that required social change on a large scale, to be corrected. Recognizing that "the personal is political" meant energizing people and motivating collective action.

With increasing momentum, organizations sprouted and splintered: the National Welfare Rights Organization (1966), the Women's Equity Action League (1968), The Third World Women's Alliance (1968), Bread and Roses (1969), the Boston Women's Health Book

Collective (1969), Chicago Women's Liberation Union (1969), Redstockings (1969), Hijas de Cuauhtemoc (1971), Asian Sisters (1971), the Combahee River Collective (1973), the National Black Feminist Organization (1974), and the Coalition of Labor Union Women (1974), to name a few. Electrifying texts woke up countless other women—in 1970 alone, for example, *The Black Woman: An Anthology*, edited by Toni Cade; *Sisterhood Is Powerful: An Anthology of Writings from the Women's Liberation Movement*, edited by Robin Morgan, *The Dialectic of Sex: The Case for Feminist Revolution* by Shulamith Firestone; and *Sexual Politics* by Kate Millett.

As small groups multiplied (their consciousness-raising technique diffusing far beyond its radical origins), and "zap" actions inspired more public protests, feminist theory and new institutions gathered momentum, intending to re-envision and re-value the politics and the needs of female bodies and minds. In bursts of creative energy, by inventing neologisms such as "sexism" and tirelessly analyzing patriarchy, by founding women's health clinics and rape crisis centers and establishing women's studies courses, by rediscovering women composers, writers and sports heroes and championing single mothers, the women's movement aimed to comprehend sexual difference anew and to end gender hierarchy.

More fully than a composite history could, the 2,200 biographies in this volume reveal the panoply of individuals, innovations, groups, protests, publications, services and institutions that made up the women's movement and bear its legacies into the future. The movement's impact was cultural, legal, political, social—and at least as much conceptual as material. While diversity and internal conflict characterized the movement from its beginning, and multiplied as numbers grew, whether feminist, womanist, pro-woman, or simply for women's rights, proponents compelled the rest of the world to change perspective, and even if haphazardly or briefly, to see things through women's eyes. The invention of new vocabulary such as "sexism" was a sign. What had been unspeakable now had to be heard.

Like any great, hydra-headed, controversial, world-changing movement with outspoken and courageous leaders, the women's movement attracted derision and has been always subject to reductive portrayals. It deserves better. It aimed at nothing less than new understandings of justice and injustice. The biographies herein provide a precious resource for the future. Read them for a hedge against forgetting, a vital collective portrait, and a deep well of inspiration.

Nancy F. Cott
Director, Schlesinger Library on the History of Women in America,
Radcliffe Institute for Advanced Study and
Trumbull Professor of American History, Harvard University

INTRODUCTION

This book *had* to be written. The 2,220 biographies in this reference work must be available for anyone who wants to understand *why* the second wave women's movement succeeded so quickly and pervasively. More than any other social revolution in history, ours grew from the struggles of thousands of individuals to erase thousands of separate forms of discrimination in every sector of society.

Not only did this book need to be written, it needed to be written soon, in our lifetime when most of the subjects could provide first-hand accounts.

It was clear to me that feminists who had written books on our history, or had become high-level public officials, or had founded powerful feminist organizations will be remembered over time. But there are countless other women and some men who contributed to improving women's lives. What about the women who took their employers to court to overcome job discrimination? Or those who helped other women obtain safe abortions when abortions were illegal? Or those who published radical feminist newspapers and newsletters across this country? What about the women who forced changes in the credit laws so that no bank would ever again tell a woman that, yes, she could have a mortgage— but only if her husband or father signed the contracts? And those who forced authorities to pass and implement laws punishing rape and domestic violence, or those who created safe shelters for victims? And the list goes on.

Veteran Feminists of America, my partner in this project, has recognized and honored the contributions of second wave feminists through numerous events since its founding in 1992. VFA has helped us to celebrate and remember our great victories and how very far we have come, and how rewarding the struggle has been. It has helped us resolve our differences within the movement and focus on what we have in common: a lifetime dedication to improving women's lives. Each VFA program has provided a valuable historical record. But a more comprehensive, enduring history was needed to tell the world about the thousands of feminists who made a difference. Maybe, I thought, a book.

How is this book different from other books?

First, *Feminists Who Changed America, 1963 – 1975* is the result of years of work by dozens of feminists—activists, scholars, and authors—who generously contributed their time and talent to its creation. It is truly a collective effort, supported by many feminist groups and individuals.

Second, this reference work focuses on individual feminists and their contributions to the women's movement. Generally, books about our movement have concentrated on organizations and events, their successes and failures. The change-making people behind the events have not usually been discussed. One reason is the distaste for leadership and a commitment to anonymity that persisted among radical feminists, so that leaders and authors sometimes failed to identify themselves.

Third, this book is different because it is so inclusive. The foremost criterion for selection was being a changemaker. Feminists in this book played a role in changing the landscape for women in social, political and economic arenas.

There is a preponderance of NOW people in this book, as well there should be. That organization started the movement, and has been the major force for change over the years. But we went out of our way to make sure that those who founded or were active in radical feminist groups, which challanged social structures and took the movement in new directions, employing different strategies and tactics, are well-represented.

Apart from work in feminist organizations, many individuals forced change within their own spheres of influence—in academia, government, corporations, unions, religion, education, music, art, sports, psychology, philosophy, science, literature, finance, the military and every male-dominated institution in America.

In all cases, feminists active on the local level were hard to find. There have been very few community-level studies. Yet we all know the enormous role that grass-roots organizers played in women's history.

We wanted to make sure that the movement is represented here by those who made it happen, in as many areas of society as we could. We sought out and encouraged African American and Chicanas to participate in this project, realizing that they had suffered double oppression and were fighting battles for women within their own ranks. We attempted to trace women from all ethnicities and origins. Labor union women and poor women who fought to improve women's lives needed to be found, and we had some success there as well.

Lesbian feminists made a huge contribution to the second wave women's movement. This fact, documented by the biographies in this reference book, was concealed in the late 1960s and early 1970s because of discrimination against gays and lesbians in society, and an uneasiness in some quarters that the visibility of lesbians would damage the women's movement and its specific campaigns. But lesbians, living independently and claiming control over their own lives and bodies, were natural participants and leaders in this movement. Lesbians participated in the women's movement in greater numbers than their percentage in the general population. Lesbian feminists' contributions to women on all fronts should be acknowledged and celebrated, and not ignored or written out of history.

Fourth, every attempt was made to use primary sources—the subjects themselves—for the information in the book. Even when individuals had written autobiographical books, or had Web sites with their biographies on them, we insisted that a hallmark of this project be first-hand accounts. With few exceptions, each feminist told us her or his story. We edited their stories to address space restrictions and style, and told them in the third person.

These individuals' perspectives are recorded here. To our delight, feminists understood the value of providing primary source information. Second wave feminists have already experienced the angst of seeing incorrect secondary information about them in various publications and on the internet; they are grateful for a chance to set the record straight. Others are pleased to have their contributions recorded for the first time.

We sought approvals of the biographies from the individuals themselves after their biographies had been written and edited, and then made requested changes—a process that added two years to the creation of this book. **When (ABS) appears at the end of an entry, that biography has been Approved By Subject.**

Because of this unusual format, we expect that some readers will disagree with some of the statements that appear in individual biographies. In some instances, a claim made by a feminist may be inaccurate from another's point of view; sometimes that is the result of different experiences or political viewpoints. The content of biographies has been checked and verified by the feminists themselves, wherever possible. Accuracy is key to this project; it is embodied in each person's own personal story.

For those biographies with an ABS designation, the information was either initiated by the subject or confirmed by the subject as accurate. For biographies without the ABS, we may have worked from material sent in by the subject, but were unable to locate the subject to obtain his/her approval after we finished our editing. We relied on secondary sources for biographical information *only* when absolutely necessary.

Sources of information on deceased feminists included obituaries, accounts from feminists and relatives, and books covering the period. For deceased feminists we tried to get approvals on biographies from family, friends or colleagues; those approvals are not noted in the text.

For each feminist with a primary listing in this book there is a folder on file at the Sophia Smith Collection, Smith College, Northampton, MA, containing the source of information used in the writing of the biography, along with approval documents and correspondence.

Regarding claims made by biographees, when someone says she was "first" at something, that is her belief. Because women strode successfully into almost every place where they had been denied entry, we take claims of being "first" seriously. It is possible, with so much happening in different geographical areas, that some women were moving simultaneously on an issue without knowledge of each other. We report it here as we were told. In a different type of work, a cautious editor would have said "among the first." That kind of editing would greatly diminish the personal quality of experience these feminists shared with us. Readers will understand that we have not assumed the role of arbiter in recounting these personal histories told through the prism of several decades of memory, even if it were possible to verify such claims independently.

In keeping with our agreement that subjects approve their own biographies, we did not include information that subjects wanted excluded—for example, age. To our surprise, a number of subjects did not want their birth dates published, so we left them out, even though those dates are public information. Ageism is a new battle for these brave women who have been fighting sexism since the 1960s or earlier.

Fifth, this book includes archival information where available. The location of papers donated by many people in the book is noted at the end of each biography. This will be helpful to scholars who want to find out more.

Most of the individuals in the book are unsung heroes, about whom the wider world has never heard before. Let us hope that future biographers will shed still more light on their lives and deeds.

Why the dates 1963 – 1975?
This book honors changemakers in the second wave movement beginning in 1963, when Betty Friedan's book, *The Feminine Mystique*, was published and spurred countless women into action. But some historians say the true second wave movement began in 1966 when the National Organization for Women was founded. The year 1975 was somewhat arbitrarily chosen as the final year for inclusion in our book because 1963 – 1975 were the years of involvement by the greatest number of feminists. A feminist had to have entered the women's movement by 1975 to qualify for inclusion.

During 1963 – 1975, many participants in the women's movement thought of themselves as a "second wave" of feminism comparable to the long struggle for the right to vote that began in 1848 and culminated in 1920. Their daughters' generation in the 1990s began to call themselves a "third wave," signaling both the continuation of feminist activism through many decades and its necessary evolution. As we go to press, we know that the concept of a second wave has been rejected by some scholars who prefer to see the women's movement as one wave. Many of us who participated in the creation of this book still view ourselves as second-wave feminists.

By any name, 1963 – 1975 was a period of explosive activism when pioneer feminists—visionaries and builders—embarked anew on what has resulted in massive changes for women and girls in America.

How did we find the pioneer feminists?

I started handing out questionnaires in 1999 at the Berkshire Conference on the History of Women in Rochester, NY. Noted feminist historian Sara Evans was the very first person to fill out a questionnaire; that was a good sign, I thought. From there questionnaires were taken to conferences and events held by national NOW, the Feminist Majority, the National Women's Studies Association and Veteran Feminists of America. Questionnaires were also available on the Pioneer Feminists Project Web site and the Veteran Feminists of America Web site.

The majority of pioneer feminists were found through networking—pioneer-get-a-pioneer. Veteran Feminists of America board members were extremely helpful in this outreach phase. I also pored through books covering feminist events of the 1960s and 1970s to see which key players had not been reached or had not responded through networking, and then with the help of three genealogists found and contacted many of them. Along the way I worked with various women's history archives to see who should additionally be included and to obtain biographical information of the deceased.

Of course, inevitably, there are thousands of others who made contributions but are not included, either because we could not find them or failed to secure sufficient information about their involvement in the movement. We apologize to them and their families. Their names and stories also have to be remembered and honored.

How did we write the biographies?

The focus was on contributions to the women's movement between 1963 – 1975. In writing and editing the biographies, we tried to capture the spirit of the feminists, not just the facts. Most of the biographies are "a good read" to the extent possible in the limited space allowed. Readers should know that if certain facts are not included, such as education or archives, that does not mean the biographee did not have a higher education or a designated archive for their movement papers. It merely means that the editor assigned to that individual's biography did not have that information or selected other information she considered more representative of the subject's life and feminist contributions. Spouses/partners are mentioned only when those individuals were part of the feminist activity covered in the biography.

We regret that space restrictions for this book required us to heavily edit the biographies of the subjects, many of whom deserve a book of their own to tell their inspiring stories of success and failure confronting patriachy. To save space we also opted to use abbreviations for frequently-mentioned organizations. Abbreviations for well-known and not-so-well-known organizations mentioned in this book are explained on pages xxv – xxviii.

How did these feminists change America?

The ways are too numerous to mention in a brief summary. The biographies include the feminists who shaped our revolution through theory; fought endlessly over decades for the Equal Rights Constitutional Amendment; fought for control over our own bodies; overcame discriminatory practices in pay and promotions; made it possible for pregnant women to keep their jobs; greatly increased job opportunities by integrating Help Wanted advertising; passed legislation to ensure that girls have access to sports, science and math programs; introduced new approaches to healthcare; experimented with non-hierarchal structures; formed health groups and health centers so that women's needs could be met in a woman-focused environment; introduced non-sexist language in children's textbooks; helped women obtain the right to their own property, their own credit, and use of their own names; fought for tax deductions for home and childcare expenses; established child care centers; worked privately and publicly for partnership marriages with shared responsibilities; established women's studies and women's history programs so that women became a recognized and respected focus of study; changed the way women are regarded in areas of psychology, philosophy, politics, art and religion; addressed unfair and discriminatory treatment of women and children in poverty; established respectful treatment of rape victims and punishment of rapists. Feminists in the second wave women's movement overcame discrimination on many fronts, even while knowing that their efforts to address inequities and injustices could lead to humiliation, harassment, dismissal, or worse.

It was not only the concrete victories these feminists fought for and won—and sometimes did not win—that substantially changed women's lives; the culture of our nation and the world were changed as well. And women themselves have changed. We are not the people we were before 1970. Women have come to expect full equality, and that is the greatest difference of all.

Before the second wave women's movement, women were called "girls." The media talked about how we looked, dressed and cooked rather than about our accomplishments; and we were assumed to be incapable of almost everything. Girls were warned that if they spoke up or showed their strength or intelligence, boys wouldn't like them. Women who did so were labeled abrasive, unladylike, masculine, or crazy. Pregnant women were fired for being pregnant, and desperate pregnant women often risked their lives by using wire coat hangers to abort the fetus.

The unhappiness that women felt and that Betty Friedan described in 1963 as "the problem that has no name" now has a variety of names, but in those days we had to create the language needed to express the problem: "unpaid housework," "lack of positive female role models," "unequal education, training, opportunity and pay," "displaced homemaker," "sexism," "sexual discrimination," "sexual harassment," "sexual abuse," "domestic violence," "date rape," "sexual dissatisfaction," and "the feminization of poverty," to name a few. A problem that has no name is easily ignored; once a problem has a name, it becomes visible and can be addressed.

There is a great deal more work to be done. Far too many women still do not have equal opportunity, held back by attitudes, rules, power structures, laws, customs, and institutions. There is a move to roll back many of the victories in many quarters, including a politically connected right wing. While we do have much further to go, the feminists included here, their friends and colleagues have contributed to a better life for women in America and in the world. Many of the feminists active early in the second wave are still active in the movement today addressing unfinished business and working to hold onto gains made over generations.

We who fought in the early years of the second wave women's movement learned from and were inspired by our foremothers' vision, bravery and commitment. It is my hope, and the hope of dozens of others who worked on this reference book, that young feminists today and in the future will know the contributions each of us made and that this knowledge will nurture them in the continuing struggle.

Whether you, the reader, are a feminist, journalist, historian, researcher, or relative of someone included in *Feminists Who Changed America, 1963 – 1975*—or just want to know more about the social revolution that some historians have termed "the most important happening of the Twentieth Century"—I hope you will be informed and inspired by these first-hand accounts.

Barbara J. Love, Editor

P.S. If you are a pioneer feminist from the second wave and are not included in this book, you can still be part of the Pioneer Feminists Project and have your information on file at The Sophia Smith Collection for historians to consult, and be part of other re-lated events in the future. Please go to Google and enter "Pioneer Feminists Project" to secure a questionnaire and send it to me at 82 Deer Hill Avenue, Danbury, CT 06810, or email me at BJLove@msn.com The Pioneer Feminists Project does not end with this book. We will continue collecting questionnaires and biographies as long as they are submitted to us, and will keep updating the database on the Web site as well.

ACKNOWLEDGMENTS

Dozens of individuals worked on *Feminists Who Changed America, 1963 – 1975* for over seven years. Interest in collecting biographies grew organically, like the women's movement itself. Feminists around the country heard about the project and spread the word, did research and wrote biographies. Others provided advice and helped us make needed connections with hard-to-locate feminists.

In 1999, I embarked on this venture, naming it the Pioneer Feminists Project. I visualized the project as a database. Eileen McDermott of New York NOW borrowed my computer and entered data. Carol Taylor, Claire Friedland and Naomi Penner entered biographical information. Elayne Snyder and Celine Sullivan helped in planning. Jacqui Ceballos, president of Veteran Feminists of America, provided names of feminists in VFA to get us started. Gloria Steinem offered encouragement and helped me through red tape to put an office together. Sherrill Redmon, director of the Sophia Smith Collection, agreed to house the back-up material at that prestigious archive. All very promising, but not enough yet to accomplish the enormous task ahead.

Heavy technology problems and scarcity of volunteers bogged down the project for many months until VFA chair Muriel Fox put together a dedicated outreach committee of four board members: Virginia Watkins (Minnesota), committee chair, who vowed to stay on until the project was over, and did; Heather Booth (Washington, D.C.), who brought years of consulting experience with progressive groups to the effort; Judith Meuli (Los Angeles), a national leader who put us in contact with many West Coast feminists; and Grace Welch (Long Island, NY), a good friend and can-do feminist who took on challenging special assignments.

Muriel and I contacted well-known feminists to support our work by lending their names to the Advisory Board, and everyone we asked agreed.

A new and impressive second beginning

It was clear that this work could not be accomplished without Veteran Feminists of America. This partnership was nurtured by goodwill, generosity and a shared excitement about the importance of preserving our history. As a board member of VFA I welcomed the organization's official adoption of this project as one of its priorities. I am happy to say that part of the royalties from the sale of each book will go to Veteran Feminists of America for its enduring work.

More than any other single person, I am indebted to Muriel Fox. Her enthusiasm and support were enormously important to this project. In addition, she provided guidance and valuable contacts that helped the project gain momentum. Muriel often anticipated needs, paving the way for a smooth outcome. My mentor 35 years ago when I published *Foremost Women in Communications*, Muriel once again showed her faith in me by standing behind this project and taking an active role in its creation.

Jacqui Ceballos also deserves special thanks. She did whatever she could to provide information, spread the word and encourage participation. For many months we were in contact on a daily basis.

The Advisory Board was key to estabishing early credibility for this project. I owe a lot to these pioneers, many of whom provided sage advice when needed.

I am indebted to Nancy Cott, professor of American History at Harvard University and director of the Schlesinger Library on the History of Women in America, for the excellent essay she wrote as Foreword; to Sara Evans, whom I relied upon for her knowledge and insights into second wave history. Thanks also go to literary agent Charlotte Sheedy for putting me in touch with potential publishers; and to Joan Catapano, editor in chief, University of Ilinois Press, who enthusiastically took on this book and skillfully guided me through the pre-publication process.

Over two dozen conscientious project editors wrote biographies with an approach that combined data with personal warmth. Those who contributed immeasurably include Valerie Harms (Montana), an old friend and talented writer; Joan Michel (New York City), a long-time VFA contributor and editor; Zoe Nicholson (Los Angeles), a mighty inspiration and gifted writer; and Ann Wallace (Connecticut), who became a partner in this project during the tough times.

David Dismore (Los Angeles), Yolanda Retter (Los Angeles), and Yvette Scharf (Connecticut) are three researchers who must be given credit for finding dozens of feminists who needed to be included in this book. All were asked to locate specific feminists, find biographical information, birth and death dates—frequently with 24 hours' notice. And all came through every time.

Web tech Elle Douglass (New Jersey) created a much-needed Web site for the Pioneer Feminists Project, which she updated with new names and their status in the book on a monthly basis. The Web site became a valuable tool for feminists to determine who was and was not yet in the book.

The photographers who donated their works to this reference book must be thanked for all the work they performed over the years. Because of their professionalism and generosity, some of the stirring images they recorded are available to posterity through the photo pages of this book. Very special thanks are due to Bettye Lane (New York City), who offered whatever we wanted from the moment she heard about the project. JEB (Joan E. Biren) (Washington, D.C.), Cathy Cade (Oakland, CA), Diana Davies (North Hampton, MA), Dori Jacobson-Wenzel (Chicago), Lynda Koolish (San Francisco) and Judith Meuli (Los Angeles) supplied their best and most representative images of the women's movement of the time.

Diane Brenner, a professional indexer, volunteered to create the index for this book and completed this laborious task in a short time frame.

Others who contributed to the creation of this work include Margie Adam, Dolores Alexander, Toni Armstrong, Jr., Rosalyn Baxandall, Charlotte Bunch, Patricia Carbine, Estelle Carol, Joan Casamo, Cynthia Clark, Linda Clarke, Jan Cleary, Rebecca Davison, Mary Eastwood, Carol Giardina, Sonia Pressman Fuentes, Aileen Hernandez, Elizabeth Homer, Patrice Ingrassia, Barrie Karp, Kate Lindemann, JoAnne Myers, Lynn Shapiro, Alix Kates Shulman, Donna Smith, Susan Tucker, and Laura X. Natasha and Albert Konstorum generously provided computer programming assistance.

Numerous archives were helpful in this project. I especially want to thank Sherill Redmon and her staff at The Sophia Smith Collection, Smith College. They were there in the beginning and when needed, which was often. Other distinguished archives I relied on were the Schlesinger Library, Radcliffe College; the Sallie Bingham Center for Women's History and Culture, Duke University; Newcomb College Center for Research on Women; The Wisconsin Historical Society; the Michigan Women's Hall of Fame; UCLA Chicano Studies Research Center Library; the Chicago Women's Liberation Herstory Project; Redstockings

Women's Liberation Archives for Action; The Lesbian Herstory Archives, and the Walter P. Reuther Library.

While much of the work on this book was done by volunteers, there were still many costs associated with technology, editing, design, production and clerical help. Donors came through to assist, and heroically helped at the end when my own funds were exhausted. I want to note in particular the first major donor, Lynda Simmons, a great friend who believed in me as well as the importance of the project when it was still just an idea; and Kathleen Polutchko, who chose the Pioneer Feminists Project as the designated recipient of a small trust left by her mother, the late Betty Harragan, a brave feminist whom I am proud to have known. I also want to thank Elizabeth Angelone, Merrill Lynch (Connecticut), who understood the financial challenges I faced with this project and helped me meet them. Sheila Tobias, who gave me encouragement with a donation way back in 1999, used her considerable reputation to appeal to other donors.

The Ms. Foundation for Education and Communication played a key role in contributions. When Pat Carbine offered the Ms. Foundation's services to accept donations and provide a 100 percent pass-through, I was thrilled and grateful. This meant extra work for the foundation with no financial benefit to them. But it surely added more stature to our venture.

Those who worked daily on the book—the staff—are Koryne Etemi, office administrator and so much more; Deb Schwab, a highly capable copy editor, and Truus Teeuwissen, a very creative graphic designer with editorial expertise. This book could not have been created without the commitment of these three people over a long period of time.

On a personal note, I would like to thank my mother, the late Lois Townsend, who taught me "first to thine own self be true." She stuck to it even when she found out my own self was a rebel with a cause.

Last, but actually first, special thanks and gratitude go to my partner, Donna Smith, for her support during this great journey.

EDITORS AND ADVISORY BOARD

DONORS

We thank the following people who gave generously to support the creation of this book:

Bette Orovan Adelman, Esq.

Elizabeth Angelone in memory of Patricia Angelone

Kay V. Bergin

Heather Tobis Booth in memory of Hazel Weisbard Tobis

Patricia Burnett

Virginia Carter and Judith Osmer in memory of Toni Carabillo

Mariam K. Chamberlain

Arlene Colman-Schwimmer

Mary Courtney and Joanne DePaola

Elizabeth B. Dater

Carole De Saram in honor of Doris Rush

Elliott Detchon and Ann Wallace

Eleanor Thomas Elliott in memory of Dorothy Q. Thomas

Donald T. Evans and Scott A. Mas

The Hon. Barbara Hackman Franklin

Merle Hoffman

Mary Anne Krupsak in memory of Bella Savitzky Abzug

Sally Herman Lunt

Judith Meuli and Stephanie Palmer in memory of Toni Carabillo

Joan Nixon in memory of Bella Savitzky Abzug and Mim Kelber

Kathleen Andrea Olson in memory of Wilma Scott Heide

Helen Z. Pearl in honor of Sheila Tobias

Kathleen Harragan Polutchko in memory of Betty Lehan Harragan

The Hon. Roberta Ralph in honor of Equal Rights for Women

Marlene Sanders

Muriel Siebert

Lynda Simmons

Donna Smith in memory of Mary Ida Rarick Smith

Kappie Spencer in honor of Carol Spencer

Sheila Tobias

Diane H. Welsh

Peg Yorkin in memory of Toni Carabillo

AAAS	American Association for the Advancement of Science
AALC	Association of American Law Schools
AARP	American Association of Retired Persons
AAUP	American Association of University Professors
AAUW	American Association of University Women
AAWCJC	American Association of Women in Community and Junior Colleges
ABA	American Bar Association
ABS	Approved By Subject (Feminist in this book approved of his/her biography)
ACLU	American Civil Liberties Union
AFGE	American Federation of Government Employees
AFSC	American Friends Service Committee
AFSCME	American Federation of State, County and Municipal Employees
AFT	American Federation of Teachers
AFTRA	American Federation of Television and Radio Artists
AHA	American Historical Association
AIAW	Association for Intercollegiate Athletics for Women
AIM	American Independent Movement; American Indian Movement
AIR Gallery	A gallery in New York City for women artists
ALSSA	Airline Stewards and Stewardesses Association
AMWA	American Medical Women's Association
ANA	American Nurses Association
APA	American Philosophical Association; American Psychiatric Association; American Psychological Association
APSA	American Political Science Association
ARM	Abortion Rights Mobilization
ASA	American Sociological Association
AU	Americans United
AWARE	Arming Women Against Rape and Endangerment; also Association for Women's Active Return to Education
AWC	Art Workers Coalition
AWP	Association of Women in Psychology
AWVV	Aid of Women Victims of Violence
BPW	Business and Professional Women
BWE	Black Women Enterprise
BWHC	Boston Women's Health Collective
BWL	Baltimore Women's Liberation

BWOA	Black Women Organized for Action
CAA	College Art Association
CALM	Custody Action for Lesbian Mothers
CAP	Community Action Programs
CARASA	Coalition for Abortion Rights and Against Sterilization Abuse
CCLU	Connecticut Civil Liberties Union
CCWHP	Coordinating Committee on Women in the Historical Profession, now known as CHW, Committee of Women Historians
CEDAW	Convention for the Elimination of All Forms of Discrimination Against Women
CESA	The Committee to End Sterilization Abuse
CETA	Comprehensive Educational and Training Act
CFMN	Comision Femenil Mexicana Nacional (National Mexican Feminist Commission)
CHW	Committee of Women Historians
CICCR	Consortium for Industrial Collaboration in Contraceptive Research
CIPA	Committee for Independent Political Action
CISPES	Committee in Solidarity with the People of El Salvador
CLAW	Chicago Legal Action for Women
CLGR	Coalition for Lesbian and Gay Rights
CLUW	Coalition of Labor Union Women
CONRAD	Contraceptive Research and Development Program
CORE	Congress of Racial Equality
COYOTE	Call Off Your Old Tired Ethics
CPD	Continuing the Peace Dialogue
CR	Consciousness Raising
CSU	California State University
COWLI	Coalition on Women's Legal Issues
CUNY	City University of New York
CWA	Communications Workers of America, also Community of Women Artists
CWEALF	Connecticut Women's Educational and Legal Fund
CWL	California Women Lawyers, also Columbia Women's Liberation
CWLU	Chicago Women's Liberation Union
CWSS	Center for Women's Studies and Services
CWVA	Conference for Women in the Visual Arts
DA	District Attorney
DACOWITS	Defense Department Advisory Committee on Women in the Services

DAR	Daughters of the American Revolution	**LFL**	Lesbian Feminist Liberation
DFL Party	Democratic-Farmer-Labor Party	**LGBTQ**	Lesbian, Gay, Bi-Sexual, Transsexual, Queer and Questioning
DOB	Daughters of Bilitis	**LIPS**	A lesbian action multi-action political group (Washington, D.C.)
EEGO	East End Gay Organization		
EEOC	Equal Employment Opportunity Commission	**LLDEF**	Lambda Legal Defense and Education Fund
ERA	Equal Rights Amendment	**LWC**	Lutheran Women's Caucus
EVE	Education, Volunteer, Employment	**LWV**	League of Women Voters
EWG	Executive Women in Government	**LWVUS**	League of Women Voters of the United States
FCC	Federal Communications Commission		
FEW	Federally Employed Women	**MALDEF**	Mexican American Legal Defense and Education Fund
FRN	Feminist Radio Network		
FSP	Freedom Socialist Party	**MATE**	Married Americans for Tax Equality
FWF	Fort Wayne Feminists	**MCC**	Metropolitan Community Churches
GAA	Gay Activists Alliance	**MEA**	Michigan Education Association
GAAG	Guerilla Art Action Group	**MELUS**	The Society for the Study of the Multi-Ethnic Literature of the United States
GGSCC	Grassroots Group of Second Class Citizens		
GLBTQ	Gay, Lesbian, Bi-Sexual, Transsexual and Questioning	**MLA**	Modern Language Association
		MOMA	Museum of Modern Art (NYC)
GLC	Greater London Council	**MORAL**	Modern Oklahomans for the Repeal of Abortion Laws
GLF	Gay Liberation Front		
GLSEN	Gay, Lesbian, and Straight Education Network	**MPA**	Magazine Publishers of America
		MWBE	Minority Women Business Enterprise Program
HERA	Hoosiers for Equal Rights		
HERS	Higher Education Resources Services	**NAACP**	National Association for the Advancement of Colored People
HEW	Department of Health, Education and Welfare		
		NAAFA	National Association to Advance Fat Acceptance
HUAC	House Un-American Activities Committee		
ICPD	International Conference on Population and Development	**NABF**	National Alliance of Black Feminists
		NACCS	National Association of Chicano (Chicana) Studies
ICPR	International Committee for Prostitutes Rights		
		NACW	National Association of Commissions for Women
ICWP	International Center for Women Playwrights		
IFBPW	International Federation of Business and Professional Women	**NAM**	New American Movement
		NAPECW	National Association of Physical Education for College Women
IFUW	International Federation of University Women		
		NARAL	National Abortion and Reproductive Rights Action League
ILGWU	International Ladies Garment Workers Union		
		NASCW	National Association of State Commissions for Women
ILO	International Labor Union		
IPPF	International Planned Parenthood Federation	**NAWBO**	National Association of Women Business Owners
		NBFO	National Black Feminist Organization
IPRA	International Peace Research Association	**NBWC**	National Black Women's Caucus
ISA	International Sociological Association	**NCAA**	National Collegiate Athletic Association
IWD	International Women's Day	**NCADV**	National Coalition Against Domestic Violence
IWMF	International Women's Media Foundation		
IWY	International Women's Year	**NCASA**	National Coalition Against Sexual Assault
LACAAW	LA Commission on Assaults Against Women	**NCCJ**	National Conference of Christians and Jews
LAW	League of Academic Women	**NCGO**	National Coalition of Lesbian and Gay Organizations
LDEF	Legal Defense and Education Fund (NOW LDEF now called Legal Momentum)		
		NCJW	National Council of Jewish Women

NCNW	National Congress of Neighborhood Women
NCTE	National Council of Teachers of English
NEA	National Education Association; also National Endowment for the Arts
NEH	National Endowment for the Humanities
NELA	National Employment Lawyers Association
NEWMR	New England Women's Music Retreat
NEWSA	New England Women's Studies Association
NGLTF	National Gay and Lesbian Task Force
NGO	Non-governmental organization
NHWL	New Haven Women's Liberation
NIH	National Institute of Health
NIMH	National Institute of Mental Health
NLGLA	National Lesbian and Gay Law Association
NLRB	National Labor Relations Board
NNHW	National Network of Hispanic Women
NOBEL	National Organization of Black Elected Legislative Women
NOMAS	National Organization for Men Against Sexism
NOW	National Organization for Women
NSF	National Science Foundation
NTPF	National Task Force on Prostitution
NWCC	National Women's Conference Committee
NWHN	National Women's Health Network
NWHP	National Women's History Project
NWLC	National Women's Law Center
NWP	National Women's Party
NWPC	National Women's Political Caucus
NWSA	National Women's Studies Association
NYALR	New Yorkers for Abortion Law Repeal
NYFAI	New York Feminist Art Institute
NYPAC	New York Political Action Committee
NYRF	New York Radical Feminists
NYRW	New York Radical Women
OAS	Organization of American States
OAW	Organization for the Advancement of Women
OBOS	*Our Bodies, Ourselves* book and Women's Health Information Resource Center
OEF	Overseas Education Fund
OEO	Office of Economic Opportunity
OFCC	Office of Federal Contract Compliance
OFCCP	Office of Federal Contract Compliance Programs
OLOC	Old Lesbians Organizing for Change
OWL	Older Women's League
PCSW	Permanent Commission on the Status of Women

PPFA	Planned Parenthood Federation of America
PROW	Puerto Rican Organization for Women
R2N2	Reproductive Rights National Network
RC 32	Research Committee 32 on Women in Society
RCADV	Rockland County Against Domestic Violence
RW	Radical Women (Socialist feminist organization)
SACU	Society for Anglo-Chinese Understanding
SAGE	Senior Action in the Gay Environment (now Services and Advocacy for Gay, Lesbian, Bisexual and Transgender Elders)
SCLC	Southern Christian Leadership Conference
SDS	Students for a Democratic Society
SDSU	San Diego State University
SEIU	Service Employees International Union
SEWSA	Southeastern Women's Studies Association
SHARE	Self Help Experience for Women with Breast and Ovarian Cancer
SMHA	Southern Mutual Help Association
SMU	Southern Methodist University
SNCC	Student Nonviolent Coordinating Committee
STWR	Stewardesses for Women's Rights
SUNY	State University of New York
SWIP	Society for Women in Philosophy
SWS	Sociologists for Women in Society
TWWA	Third World Women's Alliance
TWWO	Third World Women's Movement
UAW	United Auto Workers
UCC	United Church of Christ
UFW	United Farm Workers
UNESCO	United National Educational, Scientific and Cultural Organization
UNIFEM	United Nations Development Fund for Women
UNRRA	United Nations Relief and Rehabilitation Agency
UNU	UN University
UUA	Unitarian Universalists Association
VFA	Veteran Feminists of America
WAAC	Women's Affirmative Action Coalition
WAC	Women's Action Coalition
WAGE	Women's Alliance to Gain Equity
WAMS	Women Against Male Supremacy
WAND	Women's Action for New Directions
WAO	Women's Action Organization
WAR	Women Artists in Revolution; also Women Against Rape
WARM	Women's Art Registry of Minnesota

WARS	Women's Abortion Referral Service	**WID**	World Institute on Disability
WASABAL	Women Artists and Students for Black Art Liberation	**WILPF**	Women's International League for Peace and Freedom
WASS	Women Against Sexual Slavery	**WIPF**	Women's International Peace and Freedom
WAVAW	Women Against Violence Against Women	**WISE**	Women in Science and Engineering
WAVPM	Women Against Violence and Pornography and Media	**WITCH**	Women's International Terrorist Conspiracy from Hell
WCA	Women's Caucus for Art, founded in 1972 as an offshoot of the American Art Association	**WLALA**	Women Lawyers Association of Los Angeles
		WLF	Women's Liberation Front
		WLM	Women's Liberation Movement
WEAL	Women's Equity Action League	**WNBA**	Women's National Book Association
WEEA	Women's Educational Equity Act	**WOW**	Women of Westchester, also Women's One World Cafe
WEDO	Women's Environment and Development Organization	**WPC**	Women's Political Caucus
WFH	Wages for Housework	**WRAP**	Women's Radical Action Project
WHEP	Women's Health Education Project	**WREE**	Women for Racial and Economic Equality
WHIP	Women's Health Information Project	**WREI**	Women's Research and Education Institute
WHO	World Health Organization, also Whores, Housewives and Others	**WSP**	Women Strike for Peace
WIA	Women in the Arts	**WUB**	Women's Union of Baltimore
WIC	Women in Communications		

Feminists
Who
Changed
America
1963 — 1975

Aalfs, Janet Elizabeth (1956 –) Before she was 16, Aalfs had read her older sister's copy of *Sisterhood Is Powerful*; with her mother had participated in activities that led to the establishment of a women's center in New Bedford, MA; and had some of her poems published in Southeastern Massachusetts University's women's center newsletter. As a first-year student at Hampshire College (1974), Aalfs joined the women's center and enrolled in women's studies at the University of Massachusetts (which shared classes with Hampshire and other area colleges). After coming out, Aalfs helped found a women's writing group, then two lesbian writing groups, Calypso Borealis and the Tuesday Night Lesbian Writers Group, as well as Orogeny Press, which published one fiction/poetry anthology and three books of lesbian poetry. In 1978, she began practicing martial arts and was a founding member of Valley Women's Martial Arts and the Institute for Healing and Violence Prevention Strategies, as well as the National Women's Martial Arts Federation. She has served as a director of VWMA/HAVPS since 1982 and was a board member and instructor of NWMAF since 1980. Aalfs holds a B.A. and M.F.A. Archives: The Sophia Smith Collection, Smith College, Northampton, MA. (ABS)

Aalfs, Joann (1923 –) A graduate of Bennington College (1945), Aalfs studied at the Union Theological Seminary in New York City and served with her husband in various Presbyterian ministries, including Salem, NY, and Kasur, Pakistan, 1951–1952. In New Bedford, MA, in 1963, Aalfs and other mothers got together and organized political rallies and social events and eventually found a meeting space in the YWCA. They started the Women's Awareness Group and a small newsletter, "Rough Draft," which put their own stories in a larger context. Aalfs worked with a small group of women starting the New Bedford Women's Center (1972), worked with Women and Violence (1976–1977), and Southeastern Massachusetts University Women's Center (1972–1978). In 1980, Aalfs escaped what she describes as an abusive marriage and took refuge at the Battered Women's Shelter in Springfield, MA. In 2004, she and other lesbians in New Bedford and Northampton were finding ways to make community more of a reality in their everyday lives. Aalfs, born in St. Paul, MN, has four children. Archives: New Bedford Women's Center and The Sophia Smith Collection, Smith College, Northampton, MA. (ABS)

Aarli, Helen (1926 –) joined Chicago Women's Liberation Union in 1970. The next year, she established a consciousness raising group of "older women" (self-defined) within CWLU who decided that rape would be their issue. Later joined by some law students and a local attorney, Renee Hanover, the group realized that to change the picture for rape victims, they had to confront three institutions: the hospitals, the police and the courts. They were successful on all counts: a hospital that had not previously accepted rape victims eventually did; the police changed a rape manual they were using that was highly biased against the victim; and the courts began providing special training for attorneys handling rape cases and included female lawyers. In 1974, Aarli's group established Chicago Legal Action for Women and became lay advocates for women who could not face the court scene alone. They also started a rape crisis line in Chicago. In addition, Aarli inspired Lee Phillips, who hosted a noon television show in Chicago, to make the film "The Rape of Paulette," the true story of a young African American woman who was gang-raped after daring to go out dancing alone. Prior to joining the women's movement, Aarli was active in fair housing. Working within her community and with assistant U.S. Attorney Thomas Todd, she participated in a successful anti-discrimination suit brought against a real estate board in Chicago in the 1960s. Aarli, who is a retired teacher and intergenerational program director, has two children and holds two master degrees. (ABS)

Abbott, Sidney Afton (1937 –) says her childhood as an "Army brat" opened her eyes to the reality that different groups of people have different opportunities. She joined NOW in 1969 and was one of the first to speak out on behalf of lesbian rights on panels at the New York NOW chapter and at Columbia University. One of the Lavender Menace, a group that "came out" at the Second Congress to Unite Women and protested the treatment of lesbians in the early women's movement, she co-authored (with Barbara Love) *Sappho Was a Right-on Woman: A Liberated View of Lesbianism* (Stein & Day, 1971). In the mid 1970s she joined Love to lobby for a NOW national task force to address lesbian issues. Although a lesbian task force was eventually established, NOW originally named it the sexuality and lesbian task force, with Abbott serving as co-chair with a heterosexual woman. At the highly politicized NOW Philadelphia national conference in 1976, Abbott used Robert's Rules to bring a resolution to the convention floor at a "time certain" that gave the task force 1 percent of the total NOW budget. One of only two resolutions to get to the floor, it was passed. Abbott served as a founding member of the board of directors of the National Gay Task Force (now known as the National Gay and Lesbian Task Force). She led a successful effort to increase the number of lesbian board members to equal that of gay men. Abbott was named by the Manhattan borough president to be the first openly gay person on a community planning board, and served as a program analyst in two departments of New York City government. She served as co-chair of NYPAC. She has also been active in local politics on the North Fork of Long Island, NY. A journalist and technical writer, Abbott attended Smith College for three years and graduated from the University of New Mexico in 1961. She attended graduate school, studying urban planning, at Columbia University. Archives: The Sophia Smith Collection, Smith College, Northampton, MA. (ABS)

Aber, Ita (1932 –) Born in Montreal, Canada, Aber says her first exposure to feminism came from her mother, an early feminist and the founder of the Milk Fund of Canada, and her grandmother, who was an early suffragist in Canada. A multimedia artist, textile conservator and Jewish Art historian, Aber was a founding member of the New York Feminist Art Institute. Her work has been exhibited widely in the United States and Canada. Beginning in 1972, and for 20 years thereafter, she taught needlework to women at the Jewish Museum, NY; Cooper-Hewitt Museum, NY; Embroiderers Guild, various chapters; the Valentine Museum, Richmond, VA; and the Pomegranate Guild of Judaic Needlework, which she founded. This effort was focused on encouraging women to express themselves, their femaleness and respect for their labor. Aber became politically active in 1964 through her involvement with the Reform Democratic movement to abolish laws restricting abortion in New York State. She was among the founding group of Women Strike for Peace, was an early supporter of efforts to clean up the Hudson River, and has worked over the years to be involved with conservation and environmental groups. She has actively supported the ERA, the rights of working women and older women, and minority rights. Aber is a graduate of Empire State College, and has an M.A. equivalent in Jewish Art. She has three children. Archives: Archives of American Art, New York, NY. and the National Museum of Women in Art, Washington, D.C.   (ABS)

Abod, Jennifer (1946 –) An activist in New Haven (CT) Women's Liberation (1969 – 1979), Abod was a co-founder of and singer in New Haven Women's Liberation Rock Band (1970 – 1976). Highly political in nature, the band once played in front of the White House for a women's liberation march on Washington, and at Niantic State Prison, where Erica Huggins was incarcerated. With Chicago Women's Liberation Rock Band, the group recorded Mountain Moving Day (Rounder Records, 1972), which meant that feminists could dance to feminists making music. With Virginia Blaisdell, Abod was a contributor to an article by Naomi Weisstein called "Feminist Rock: No More Balls and Chains," published in 1972 in *Ms.* magazine. She was also a co-writer of "The Liberation of Lydia," the first feminist radio soap opera (1970), and was the first woman in Connecticut to host a nightly AM radio talk program, "The Jennifer Abod Show," which she ran for four years (1977 – 1980). Abod was a founding member of Women's Health Advocates. She, with Esta Soler and Laura Ponsor Sporazzi, interviewed many women in drug treatment programs in the Northeast, resulting in a critical look at how women were treated, "The ABC's of Drug Treatment for Women" (*Stash Capsules: The Student Association for the Study of Hallucinogens*, May 1976). In 1988, Abod created Profile Productions to produce and distribute media featuring feminist activists and cultural workers, particularly women of color and lesbians who influence broad constituencies. She completed her first feature video documentary in 2002, "The Edge of Each Other's Battles: The Vision of Audre Lorde," screened in national and international venues beginning in 2003. Abod has a B.S. from Southern Illinois University, an M.S. from Southern Connecticut State College, and a Ph.D. from Union Institute and University. Archives: The Sophia Smith Collection, Smith College, Northampton, MA.   (ABS)

Abod, Susan Gayle (1951 –) was a member of Chicago Women's Liberation Rock Band—as a singer, bass player and songwriter. In 1972, the group recorded an LP, Mountain Moving Day, with New Haven Women's Liberation Rock Band. Abod attended the first Champaign Women's Music Festival and later produced several women-only concerts in Chicago. She recorded on Casse Culver's 3 Gypsies album (1976) and on two of Willie Tyson's, titled Debutante (1977), and Willie Tyson (1979). She performed with Tyson and Robin Flowers at the Michigan Women's Festival, and went on several tours of the East and West Coasts. In 1982, she completed a six-week solo tour in Europe, organized by the German women's music distributors, singing in women's shelters, bookstores, rape crisis centers, women's bars and women's centers. Diagnosed with Chronic Fatigue Immune Dysfunction Syndrome and Multiple Chemical Sensitivities in 1986, she nonetheless was able to contribute to the creation of the play, "Alive with Aids," for which she wrote and performed "In the Moment" and "Soliloquy." She wrote and produced an hour-long video documentary, "Funny You Don't Look Sick: Autobiography of an Illness," about her own and other women's experiences with these illnesses. The video took three years to complete and premiered at the Museum of Fine Arts Boston in 1995. In 2004, she produced/recorded a solo CD of her original songs, which Outmusic nominated Best Female Debut CD.   (ABS)

Abramovitz, Mimi (1941 –) moved to New Haven, CT upon graduating from the University of Michigan in 1963 and became involved in the civil rights, anti-war and women's movements, and worked with the American Independent Movement. With other women, she formed New Haven Women's Liberation, where she focused on Welfare rights, organizing anti-Vietnam War rallies to Washington, D.C., and unionizing Yale University clerical workers. Abramovitz earned her M.S.W. (1967) and her D.S.W. (1981) from the School of Social Work, Columbia University. Since 1981 she has taught social welfare policy at Hunter School of Social Work, CUNY, in both the M.S.W. and D.S.W. programs. Continuing her commitment to low-income women, she co-founded the Welfare Rights Initiative at Hunter and focused her research on gender and the U.S. Welfare state. Abramovitz is the author of *Regulating the Lives of Women: Social Welfare Policy From Colonial Times to the Present* (South End Press, 1988); *Under Attack, Fighting Back: Women and Welfare* *in the U.S.* (Monthly Review Press, 1996); and *Dynamics of Social Welfare Policy* (with Joel Blau) (Oxford University Press, 2004). Her book *Under Attack, Fighting Back* was named Outstanding Book on the subject of human rights in North America by the Gustavus Myers Center for the Study of Human Rights (1977). In 2004, the Commission on the Role and Status of Women presented the Feminist Scholarship Award in her honor.   (ABS)

Abrams, Diane Schulder (1937 –) As a student at Columbia Law School (1961 – 1964), Abrams knew her chosen career path, public interest law, was not popular and that there were few women in criminal law. Nonetheless, after clerking for one year in the chambers of the Hon. Dudley B. Bonsal, Abrams went to work for the Legal Aid Society, Criminal Branch, in New York. Because of her work there, she met a professor, Peggy Dobbins, who had been arrested for throwing a stink bomb at the Miss America Pageant in Atlantic City. Dobbins invited Abrams to weekly CR meetings where Abrams met a number of law students who wanted to create a course on women and the law. From this came Abram's outline for the first course on women and the law taught in the United States. Abrams herself taught this course in 1969 at the University of Pennsylvania Law School and New York University Law School. Her course is taught in many law schools in the U.S. In the mid to late 1960s, Abrams worked for civil liberties/constitutional law attorney Leonard Boudin, whom she assisted in the defense of Dr. Benjamin Spock, who was then on trial for conspiracy. From the late 1960s to early 1970s, Abrams worked as a matrimonial lawyer representing women because, she says, "Wives in divorce cases often did not have a lawyer whom they could rely on and trust." In 1974, she married Robert Abrams, who served as New York State attorney general from 1978 – 1993. In all of his state-wide races, Diane Abrams was chair of the women's issues group. Abrams, who has two children, has also worked as a real estate broker with Brown Harris Stevens in NYC.   (ABS)

Abrams, Rosalie M. Gresser (1921 –) In 1971, Abrams founded the Orange County Feminist Repertory Theater. The theater provided a forum for issues that weren't touched by larger theaters in Orange County, CA. In 1969, Abrams founded the first chapter of NOW in Orange County, serving as VP in 1970 and president in 1971. Also in 1971, Abrams wrote the first full-length version of the play "Myth America: How Far Have You Really Come?," both as an educational vehicle and a means of raising funds to build the NOW chapter. In 1972, the play was performed for the first CA NOW state conference in Sacramento. In 1973, Abrams and her husband guaranteed the rental payments of the first pro-choice feminist women's health clinic in Orange County by signing the lease. "We have, along with other NOW and church members, defended the Orange County and Los Angeles clinics from being burned and destroyed, by staying overnight, sleeping in our cars, and securing the doors with our bodies." In 1976, Abrams wrote an original show for the Bicentennial about Martha Mitchell and performed it for the fifth annual CA NOW conference in Fresno. In 1977, she presented a scroll to two members of the Women's Federation at Peking University; the scroll sends greetings from Orange County NOW to the women of China. Abrams, who taught mini-courses on feminist issues at various schools and colleges, was named "feminist consultant" by the chairman of the psychology department at Fullerton College (1975). Abrams remains a political activist and plans to resume her theater group. She holds a B.A. (1971) and M.A. (1975) from California State University, Fullerton, and has two children.   (ABS)

Abzug, Bella Savitzky (1920 – 1998) Sometimes called "Battling Bella," Abzug was passionate and outspoken on women's equality, peace, the environment and civil rights in the U.S. and globally. She served three terms in the U.S. Congress (1971 – 1977), where she was considered a brilliant strategist. She was the first Jewish woman to serve in the House of Representatives, defeating Democratic incumbent Leonard Farbstein in a bitterly fought primary battle using the slogan "This woman's place is in the House—The House of Representatives." From 1990 on she worked to address environmental issues, and social and economic injustice to women in undeveloped nations around the world. Born in New York City to Russian-Jewish immigrant parents, Abzug was recognized early as a leader and elected president of her high-school class (Walton HS in the Bronx) and president of the Student Self-Government Association at Hunter College, where she received a B.A. in 1942. Rejected by Harvard Law School because of its males-only policy, Abzug attended Columbia University Law School on scholarship and received her law degree in 1945. She specialized in labor law and civil liberties and defended people who were victims of the Joe McCarthy-inspired witchhunt. As chair of the subcommittee on government information and individual rights, Abzug held hearings on illegal and covert activities by federal agents. In six years on the public works committee, she brought $6 billion to New York, especially for public transportation. She was a founder of Women Strike for Peace and was its national legislative coordinator from 1961 – 1970, and led thousands of women on expeditions to Congress and the White House on behalf of a nuclear test ban. She is best known for her contributions to women: in the 92nd Congress alone, Abzug and Martha Griffiths introduced more than 20 bills relating to women. Abzug was a co-founder of the NWPC and became co-chair in 1971; she was also a founder of the Congressional Caucus on Women's Issues. Abzug also introduced the first gay rights bill in Congress in May 1974. President Carter appointed her presiding officer of the National Commission on the Observance of IWY, which organized the National Women's Conference in

Houston (1977). Abzug gave up her congressional seat in 1976 to run for the U.S. Senate, narrowly losing to Daniel Patrick Moynihan. She ran unsuccessfully against Ed Koch for mayor of New York City in 1977. President Carter appointed her co-chair of the national advisory committee for women, but dismissed her after she and others protested cuts in programs for women. Abzug worked extensively with the U.N. on women's issues and environmental issues. She participated in the U.N. Women's Conference in Mexico City (1975), Copenhagen (1980), Nairobi (1985) and Beijing (1995). Along with Mim Kelber, her long-time friend and political partner, Abzug founded Women USA Fund Inc. (1980), and its program Women's Environment and Development Organization (WEDO) (1990). In 1994, Abzug was inducted into the National Women's Hall of Fame in Seneca Falls, NY. In 1996, she was a *Ms.* magazine Woman of the Year honoree. Among her writings are *The Gender Gap: Bella Abzug's Guide to Political Power for American Women* (Houghton Mifflin, 1984), written with Mim Kelber. She was married to Martin Abzug, a stockbroker and novelist who actively supported her public achievements, and had two children. Archives: Butler Library, Rare Books and Manuscripts, Columbia University, New York, NY.

Aceves, Lilia Valentina (1930 –) (also known as Lillian Acuna Aceves) has worked for decades to organize and empower Mexican/Chicana women so that they can make a positive difference in their communities. In 1954 she was part of the co-op nursery movement (Ramona Gardens Co-Op Nursery, Heights Co-Op Nursery, East Los Angeles, CA). In 1965 she was appointed by the Los Angeles county supervisor to represent the low-income community on the board that received anti-poverty funds for the county and city of Los Angeles. Thereafter, Aceves worked in community non-profit organizations that dealt with civil rights, minority rights, poverty and politics. In October 1970, Aceves was among a group of Chicana leaders invited to a workshop by Francisca Flores, who had initiated the League of Mexican American Women in the early 1960s. During the workshop, which was part of the Mexican-American Issues Conference in Sacramento, the women organized a Mexican-American women's organization called Comision Femenil Mexicana Nacional (CFMN/ National Mexican Feminist Commission) to empower Mexican/Chicana women and address issues that were not being addressed by the women's movement or the Chicano movement. In 1971, the group met at the Issues Conference and decided there was a need for a Chicana Center. They subsequently opened the Chicana Service Action Center; Aceves became the director. The Center subsequently incorporated and is a successful employment training center. The childcare centers, Centro de Ninos, also incorporated and operate two daycare centers in Los Angeles. In June 1997, Comision Femenil de Los Angeles presented Aceves with a Lifetime Commitment Award at its 25th anniversary meeting. Aceves, who has

three children, holds a B.A. from California State University, Los Angeles, and a J.D. from Peoples College of Law. Archives: Comision Femenil Mexicana Nacional, Inc. has its archives at the University of California, Santa Barbara; Comision Femenil de Los Angeles has its archives at the UCLA Chicano Studies Research Center.   (ABS)

Ackelsberg, Martha A. (1946 –) (also known as Martha A. Mendelson) was a founding member of the New York Women's Health Collective (1970), and taught classes on the anatomy and physiology of reproduction as part of the group's series on women and their bodies. She also served as an abortion counselor (via telephone) for New York Women's Abortion Project. In 1971, she spearheaded a movement among graduate students at Princeton University, dept. of politics, to change the way names were reported to potential employers, making the job search more gender-neutral. In 1972, Ackelsberg cofounded Ezrat Nashim, the first modern organization of Jewish women committed to establishing equality for women within the Jewish community. In March of that year, she attended (with 10 other women) the convention of the Rabbinical Assembly of America, the organization of conservative rabbis, to make public their demands and issue the statement, "Jewish Women Call for Change." It was reported by the news media and served as a basic organizing agenda for many years. Ackelsberg later helped organize, teach and read Torah at the First National Jewish Women's Conference in NYC (1973), and in 1974 delivered a plenary address at the First National Conference of Jewish Women and Men. After joining the faculty at Smith College, Ackelsberg taught one of the first courses on women and gender (1973 – 1975). A professor of government and women's studies, she continues to be active in establishing women's studies at Smith College, and is involved in a variety of Jewish feminist ventures. Ackelsberg, who earned her B.A. from Radcliffe College (1968), and an M.A. (1970) and Ph.D. (1976) from Princeton University, also contributed to the anti-Vietnam War movement, and has demonstrated for gay/lesbian rights.   (ABS)

Acker, Joan R. (1924 –) A researcher, writer and lecturer, Acker came to the women's movement with experience in the peace, labor and civil rights movements. She was a founder and CEO of the Center for the Study of Women in Society at the University of Oregon in 1973, which is still operating today (2006). From 1981 – 1983, she was a member of the Oregon State task force on comparable worth, through which she raised the pay of low-wage women's jobs in the state system. A sociologist, Acker has written widely on the issues of class, gender and pay equity. Her most recent book is *Class Questions: Feminist Answers* (Rowan & Littlefield, 2006). Acker, who has three children, holds a B.A. from Hunter College, an M.A. from the University of Chicago, and a Ph.D. from the University of Oregon.   (ABS)

Ackerman, Ellen – See Lee, Pelican

Ackerman, Judith – See Freespirit, Judith

Adam, Margie (1947 –) is one of the earliest singer/song-writer/activists whose music helped release the tidal wave of artistic expression and political energy that women's music generated in the early 1970s. She gave her first public performance at a women-only music festival organized by Kate Millett in 1973 at Sacramento State. By spring 1974, word had spread through the nascent network of women musicians that a National Women's Music Festival would be held in Champaign-Urbana, IL. Meg Christian, Cris Williamson and Adam filled the evening with a new kind of experience—one that would become known as Women's Music. Says Adam, "For me, Women's Music is an entry point for a transformative experience of feminism." Adam is one of the touring artists whose post-production gatherings nurtured the network of musicians, distributors, producers, bookstores and radio show programmers who disseminated this cultural union of feminist thought and spirit. In 1977, Adam led 10,000 delegates at the Houston National Women's Conference in a three-part rendition of her song, "We Shall Go Forth!," which now resides in the Smithsonian Institute's Political History Division. Adam's interest in building a diverse audience for Women's Music led her to work with many feminist and progressive organizations. In 1980, the NWPC sponsored her on a 20-city tour for the ERA and feminist candidates. From 1975 – 1984 Adam and manager/producer Barbara Price worked together to promote Women's Music through mainstream media while producing Adam's music on Pleiades Records: Margie Adam. Songwriter, Naked Keys (piano solos), We Shall Go Forth! (live) and Here Is A Love Song. Committed to challenging the music industry, they set standards for quality recording, promotional materials and concert productions within the independent music scene while working with all-women crews. After a "radical's sabbatical" from 1984 – 1991, Adam returned to her work as a singer/songwriter/activist. Subsequent recordings on Pleiades Records include Best of Margie Adam, Another Place, Soon and Again (piano solos) and Avalon, recorded in 2001. She worked as associate producer on two films released during 2000 – 2003: "Radical Harmonies: A History of Women's Music" and "No Secrets Anymore: The Times of Del Martin & Phyllis Lyon." Adam is a 1971 graduate of the University of California, Berkeley. (ABS)

Adams, Jane (1943 –) A veteran of the Southern civil rights movement, Adams was the first woman elected national secretary of SDS in 1967. In 1967 and 1968 she published articles in *New Left Notes* urging that women demand equality and not be intimidated by male chauvinism. At the 1967 SDS national convention she and other women introduced the first resolution advocating women's liberation. (ABS)

Adams, Whitney — As a member of NOW's national board when she was 25 years old, Adams served as national coordinator of NOW's FCC task force. In 1973, she and Joan Nicholson, national coordinator of NOW's task force on the image of women, proposed revisions to the National Association of Broadcasters Television Review Board and the Radio Review Board to the ways women and the women's movement were presented by the media. These revisions were presented in extensive testimony before both boards by Toni Carabillo, NOW VP-public relations. Adams' work with the FCC was "an enormous coup," according to Betty Newcomb. "New FCC regulations required all broadcasters to survey the public before license renewals [every three years] regarding their coverage of women and minorities."

Adamsky, Cathryn Ann (1933 – 2007) (also known as Cathryn Levison) became a feminist at the University of Chicago in the mid 1960s, where she helped gather data for a class action charging the university with sex discrimination. In 1971, Adamsky went to Indiana-Purdue at Fort Wayne to teach in the psychology department. She was the organizing force behind the creation of a department of women's studies at IPFW, and taught the first course, on the psychology of women. She also did research on the sexism of language, which was used in courses thereafter. IPFW became the first campus in Indiana to offer a major in women's studies. In addition, Adamsky helped develop the Association for Women in Psychology, coordinated the first AWP conference (1973), and served as spokeswoman (1978 – 1982). At the same time, she was part of the Fort Wayne Feminists and helped establish Sisterspace, a storefront bookstore/coffeehouse. She also trained speakers to work for the ERA; was instrumental in the establishment of the first battered women's shelter in Fort Wayne; and was part of the community feminists who protected the first abortion clinic in the area. Believing that all issues are women's issues, Adamsky invited lesbians to speak to her students; was involved in the labor movement; and participated in anti-war, anti-pollution and anti-segregation causes. The first woman in her family to attend college, she graduated from Clark University with honors and earned a Ph.D. from the University of Rochester. She has two children. (ABS)

Adelman, Bette Orovan (1936 –) entered Vassar College in 1953, but did not complete her undergraduate education until 1971, when she graduated from the University of Illinois. During that time she had married, divorced, married again and given birth to five children. It was an arduous time that sensitized Adelman to the need for change in the way women and minorities, who historically had been denied equal access to education and employment, were treated. She received a master's degree in public administration in 1977, and in 1985 a J.D. from Arizona State University College of Law. In 1982, Adelman became the director of affirmative action at the

State University of New York, College of Arts and Science at Geneseo (NY). Adelman devoted large amounts of time to community organizations that supported women's rights and the rights of minorities and handicapped people. She helped found the Livingston County Women's Network and was elected to national, regional, state and local offices in such groups as the American Association for Affirmative Action, the State University of New York Affirmative Action Council, the Women's Education and Development Committee of the Rochester Area Colleges Consortium, and the local chapter of the American Association of University Administrators. She established the Geneseo Women's Center and served as its institutional coordinator, and has taught in the women's studies program. She has also been a frequent speaker on issues concerning women and was commended for her efforts in affirmative action by New York Governor Hugh Carey in 1981. After receiving her law degree in 1985, Adelman became a staff attorney at the Urban Indian Law Center in Phoenix, AZ, assisting off-reservation Native Americans. Later she engaged in child support enforcement litigation at the office of the Arizona attorney general. After her husband died in 1990, she went into private practice and has since been appointed, and regularly serves as, a judge pro tem in the family law division of the Maricopa County Superior Court. (ABS)

Adelman, Charlotte (1937 –) graduated from the University of Chicago Law School in 1962. In 1963 she opened her own law office after being refused employment because she was a woman. In 1970, Adelman testified on the need for the Equal Rights Provision in the Illinois Constitution before the Bill of Rights committee at the Illinois Constitutional Convention (it passed). And in 1971, she testified before the Illinois Fair Employment Practices Commission regarding guidelines for sex discrimination. As a NOW member, she drafted several proposed Chicago Ordinances, one of which outlawed sex discrimination in public accommodations; another added gender as a category of discrimination in cases heard before the Chicago Commission of Human Rights. From 1973–1986, Adelman was one of several attorneys who staffed a weekly drop-in legal clinic developed to provide free on-the-spot legal consultation at the Loop Center YWCA. In 1977, Adelman drafted an Illinois child support collection law and lobbied for it until 1980 when it passed the legislature and was signed into law by the governor. In recognition of her child support collection work, the University of Chicago awarded her its 1987 Citation for Public Service; Oakton Community College awarded her the Gladys G. Shute Award in 1985; and Pioneer Women, Na'amat, suburban Chicago council, named her 1985 Woman of the Year. Adelman was founding president of the National Association of Women Business Owners, Chicago Chapter (1978–1979); was legal counsel for the Chicago chapter of NOW for a number of years, and was the first female president of the North Suburban Bar Association (1985–1986). Adelman has been a member of the Women's Bar Association of Illinois since 1963, and served as its 70th president in 1984–1985. She arranged for the association to donate its records to the Chicago Historical Society. As WBAI's archivist, Adelman wrote "WBAI 75," the history of the association's first 75 years. She prevailed in the first case filed in Illinois charging sex discrimination. She was co-counsel with Sheribel Rothenberg in Greenfield v. Field Enterprises charging several Chicago newspapers with violation of the 1964 Civil Rights Act by running sex-segregated want ads. Although the judge ruled for the newspapers, the papers integrated the ads in 1972 when the plaintiffs filed a Notice to Appeal. Adelman negotiated a divorce settlement gaining her client one-half of her ex-husband's $1 million Nobel Prize. Adelman is co-author of *Prairie Directory of North America*. She retired from the law in 1999 to focus on environmental issues. Archives: Chicago Historical Society, Chicago, Il. (ABS)

Adelman, Sybil – See Sage, Sybil Adelman

Aiken, Joyce Braun (1931 –) began teaching feminist art at California State University, Fresno, in 1973, on the heels of Judy Chicago, who had created the class—the first feminist art course in the U.S.—in 1970. Aiken was to teach the course for 20 years. In 1974, Aiken's students founded Gallery 25, a women's alternative art gallery in Fresno that helped make Fresno central to the feminist art movement. In 1978, Aiken was elected president of the newly formed Coalition of Women's Art and spent the year in Washington, D.C., lobbying for the rights of women artists. Because of this work, she was chosen One of 80 Women to Watch in the 80s by *Ms.* magazine. In 1986, Aiken curated the Fresno Art Museum's year-long exhibition honoring California women artists (1945 – 1965). It was the first museum in the U.S. to give a full year to showcasing women. In 2001, the WCA honored Aiken with a Lifetime Achievement Award in Visual Arts. In 2004 she was co-chair of Council of 100, an organization within the Fresno Art Museum that honors a distinguished woman artist each year with an exhibition, catalog and lecture presentation. She became director of the Fresno Arts Council in September 2004. Aiken, who has two children, earned her B.A. and M.A. from California State University, Fresno. (ABS)

Aiken, Susan Hardy (1943 –) Director of graduate studies in literature in the English department at University of Arizona, Aiken found that feminist change was just beginning on campus when she arrived in 1973. Aiken became a founding member of the women's studies advisory committee at the university and, in 1974–1975, designed and successfully proposed (with Jo Inman and Sidonie Smith) two courses on women, Women Authors and Women in Literature. Graduate seminars were introduced soon after. From that point forward, Aiken was deeply involved with both feminist scholarship and academic activism to help bring about feminist changes. In addition to her work with the women's studies program and later with the Southwest Institute for Research on Women, Aiken regularly taught and lectured both here and abroad on feminist approaches to literature and culture. She also worked with other feminist faculty on many feminist curriculum-transformation projects sponsored by such agencies as the Ford Foundation, NEH and the Rockefeller Foundation. One, an NEH Curriculum Integration project to introduce feminist scholarship to courses throughout the campus, ultimately resulted in a book that Aiken co-edited: *Changing Our Minds: Feminist Transformations of Knowledge* (State University of New York Press, 1988) and the article "Trying Transformations: Curriculum Integration and the Problem of Resistance" (*Signs 12*, Winter 1987). Aiken also worked with interdisciplinary feminist discussion groups and campus-wide organizations and, throughout the late 1970s and 1980s, inaugurated and led feminist theory reading groups for graduate students. Her essays and books have all dealt with gender issues and feminist theories: *Isak Dinesen and the Engendering of Narrative* (University of Chicago Press, 1990); *Dialogues/Dialogi: Literary and Cultural Exchanges Between (Ex)Soviet and American Women* (Duke University Press, 1994), co-authored with Adele Barker, Maya Koreneva and Ekaterina Stetsenko; and *Making Worlds: Gender, Metaphor, Materiality* (University of Arizona Press, 1998), co-edited with Ann Brigham, Sallie Marston and Penny Waterstone. Aiken, who holds a Ph.D. from Duke University (1971), has two children. (ABS)

Aikey, Mary Eleanor (1928 –) As executive director of the Greater Lansing, MI, YWCA in the 1970s, Aikey was able to help women take charge of their lives by providing job training programs for non-traditional work, displaced homemaker programs for women who had been out of the workforce for some time, employability skills training for low-income women, and help for teenage mothers. Aikey formed resume-writing classes, developed childcare programs to allow women time for job interviews, and organized workshops on healthcare for women. Aikey, who has a B.A. from Manhattan Christian College and an M.A. and Education Specialist degrees from Michigan State University, was executive director at the YWCA in Lansing until the late 1990s. (ABS)

Aldridge, Adele T. (1934 –) A fine artist, book illustrator, graphic designer and Web designer, Aldridge began her major feminist work in 1970 with an interpretation of the "I Ching" from a woman's perspective. In 1971 she published *NotPoems*, a collection of feminist concrete poetry, and in 1972 was a co-founder of Magic Circle Press, presenting *Celebration with Anais Nin*. Active in Connecticut Feminist in the Arts from 1970 – 1975, Aldridge contributed covers and concrete poetry to various literary magazines, including *Aphra*. Aldridge received an A.F.A.

degree from the Parsons School of Design (1956), an A.F.A. (1967) and a Certificate of Advanced Studies (1968) from Silvermine College of Art in New Canaan, CT, and a Ph.D. from the Union Institute University (1981). She has two children. (ABS)

Alea, Patricia Veith (1945 –) (also known as Patricia Nastali and Patricia N. Veith) Activist, writer, editor and mentor, Alea began her feminist work in 1970 when she organized women in Chicago into feminist CR groups. From 1971 – 978 she helped women to organize and publicized issues related to their well-being. She helped form a NOW chapter in rural Wisconsin, which established services for victims of sexual assault and family violence, and supported implementation of Title IX equal opportunity for women. From 1984 – 1988 Alea chaired the Society for the Prevention of Family Violence in Walworth County. From 1989 – 1995 she traveled and spoke at national gatherings on advocacy, mentoring and service by and for women. She was the founding chair (1997 – 2001) of The Living Room Project, a statewide initiative for women supporting pro-choice female political candidates in Wisconsin. In 2003, Alea was program manager and moderator for the first women's executive leadership summit at University of Wisconsin-Madison's School of Business Executive Education Department. She also worked with lieutenant Governor Barbara Lawton on a statewide initiative, Wisconsin Women = Prosperity, to address raising the status of women in all areas of their lives and tying women's well-being to economic progress and prosperity for all. In 2003, Alea was nominated for the Athena Award, which promotes women's leadership and honors outstanding leaders. She conducts workshops on career acceleration for Wisconsin Women in Higher Education and the UW System. Alea holds a B.A. from Creighton University (1967) and an M.A. from the University of Wisconsin, Milwaukee (1977). She has two children. (ABS)

Alexander, Dolores Anne (1931 –) An activist editor and writer, Alexander was working as a reporter on *Newsday* (Long Island, NY) in summer 1966 when the announcement of the birth of NOW was tossed onto her desk. It was a day too late, so Alexander called for an interview with Betty Friedan. After the interview, Alexander signed up every woman in the newsroom for NOW membership, including future NY NOW president Ivy Bottini. When Alexander excitedly told her analyst the news, he said, "You're 50 years too late! Women got the vote in 1920." Undeterred, Alexander helped organize the NYC chapter of NOW (1967 – 1968). A member of the image committee chaired by Patricia Trainor, Alexander focused first on integrating the Help Wanted ads in *The New York Times* as part of a negotiating team that met with *NYT* management. Armed with Title VII of the 1964 Civil Rights Act and questionnaires gathered with Suzanne Schad Summers that demonstrated that women did not look under Help Wanted Male for jobs, the committee contributed to the integration of the want ads at the *New York Times* and, eventually, all newspapers. In 1969 – 1970, Alexander became the first executive director of national NOW and the editor of its newsletter, "NOW Acts." Although not a lesbian at the time, Alexander says she was suspected of being a lesbian by some people in national NOW, and claims national "adroitly moved the national office from NYC to Chicago to avoid lesbian influences." What followed, she says, "was a purge of lesbians, including president Ivy Bottini, from NY NOW in 1971." Alexander left NOW soon thereafter and, with Jill Ward, opened Mother Courage restaurant, a nationally known gathering place for feminists in the West Village. During that time, she also worked with New York Radical Feminists to develop the speakout, a new feminist institution. The restaurant closed in 1977, the same year Alexander was a delegate to the National Women's Conference in Houston. Alexander was later appointed by President Carter to the IWY continuing committee, which was launched at a tea hosted by Roslyn Carter at the White House. In 1979 – 1983, Alexander was co-founder, coordinator and fundraiser for Women Against Pornography. In recent years, she has been active in the nonprofit North Fork (Long Island, NY) women's community helping to provide healthcare for needy lesbians. Archives: Personal papers are at The Sophia Smith Collection, Smith College, Northampton, MA; early NOW papers (1966 – 1970) and Women Against Pornography papers are at The Schlesinger Library, Radcliffe Institute, Cambridge, MA.   (ABS)

Alexander, Ruth Ann (1924 –) began her fight for women in 1970 when she was elected to a five-year term —as the first woman—on the Brookings, SD school board. Her first vote was to permit women teachers to wear pants to school. Alexander later took the board to the South Dakota Human Rights Commission for inequity in athletic opportunity for girls, because it failed to provide girls' teams at the middle school level. In 1977, Alexander assisted her youngest daughter in a case before the Human Rights Commission against the American Legion/American Legion Auxiliary for failing to provide scholarships for female journalists at Girls' State, while providing them for boys at Boys' State. From 1973 – 1978, Alexander served on the Governor's Commission on the Status of Women, and in 1975 organized and ran a conference on women in business in Sioux Falls. In 1977, she was a delegate to both the state convention and the National Women's Conference in Houston. In 1981 – 1990 she taught a course on women in American culture at South Dakota State University. In 1989 and 1990 she played the role of Elizabeth Cady Stanton on the Great Plains summer circuit, introducing this early fighter for women's rights to people from Oklahoma and South Dakota. Alexander, who has an M.A. from the University of Minnesota (1947) and a Ph.D. from Michigan State

University (1952), was head of the English dept. at South Dakota State University from 1981 – 1989. She has three children. Archives: South Dakota State University Library, Brookings, SD.   (ABS)

Alexander, Sandra McCorkle – See de Helen, Sandra.

Alexander, Shana Ager (1925 – 2005) Prize-winning columnist, author and editor, Alexander was a trail-blazing journalist, chalking up many "firsts" for women. In 1961 she became the first woman to be a staff writer at *Life* magazine. In 1969 she moved to *McCall's*, the first woman editor at that publication in almost 50 years. Alexander quit the job in 1971, and 19 years later told the *Chicago Tribune*, "Here was this magazine selling all these products to women, and it had no women in any level of photography or editing. I was a figurehead." In her prophetic October 2, 1972, *Newsweek* column, Alexander declared, "I am not a full-fledged feminist on any issue save one—abortion. [Women] had the vote for over 50 years without really using it, without understanding its power. Through abortion reform they begin to understand." From 1975 to 1979, Alexander joined CBS's "60 Minutes," representing the liberal side of the program's debate segment, "Point Counterpoint." Alexander's best-selling books included *Patty Hearst; Very Much a Lady* and *The Untold Story of Jean Harris and Dr. Herman Tarnower*. Born in NYC, Alexander was a 1945 graduate of Vassar College.

Allan, Virginia R. (1916 – 1999) An educator, businesswoman, civic leader and stateswoman, Allan was U.S. delegate to three U.N. World Conferences, including the Mexico City International Conference on Women (1975), and was president of the Michigan and National Federation of Business & Professional Women's Clubs. In 1969 she was named chair of President Nixon's task force on women's rights and responsibilities. Her work there eventually led to the report "A Matter of Simple Justice," which became a foundation of the Women's Equality Act of 1971. In 1972, Allan was named deputy assistant secretary of state for public affairs, and in 1983 helped develop the United States committee of the United Nations Development Fund for Women, which was created to foster the political, economic and social empowerment of women around the world. She was also director of the Graduate School of Women's Studies at George Washington University (1977 – 1983). A graduate of the University of Michigan, Allan received the university's Outstanding Achievement Award in 1964.

Allen, Carolyn – See Gabel-Brett, Carolyn

Allen, Chude Pamela (1943 –) (also known as Pamela Allen and Pam Parker) organized the first independent women's liberation group in New York City with Shulamith Firestone (1967). During that time, she also traveled around the Midwest and upper South encouraging women to organize. After moving to San Francisco, Allen organized one of the first women's groups in the Bay Area, and with the assistance of her group, Sudsofloppen, wrote *Free Space: A Perspective on the Small Group in Women's Liberation*, published first by a local press in 1969 and then by Times Change Press in 1970. That same year, Allen and six other women founded Breakaway, a women's community school, where she taught a workshop on racism and white supremacy. She also taught similar workshops for the YWCA in San Francisco, Marin County and Santa Cruz. Allen collaborated with her first husband, Robert Allen, on the book *Reluctant Reformers: Racism and Social Reform Movements in the United States* (Howard University Press, 1974), writing the chapter on the woman suffrage movement. In 1972, Allen used her study of racism and woman suffrage as the basis for a talk as the white women's representative at the Women's Presentation of the 1972 Venceremos Brigade in Cuba. After returning from Cuba, she wrote and produced two women's history television shows with Valentine Hertz: "Votes For Women," which aired in 1973, was nominated for a local Emmy award; and "The Uprising of the Twenty Thousand," on the Shirtwaist Strike of 1909. In 1975, Allen was elected to the executive board of the Union Women's Alliance to Gain Equality. From 1977–1979, she was editor of the *Union WAGE* newspaper. In that capacity, Allen wrote the story of the founding president's life, "Jean Maddox: Labor Heroine," which WAGE published as a pamphlet. Other pamphlets Allen helped publish include "Organize! A Working Woman's Handbook" and "Woman Controlled Conception." A founder of the Bay Area Veterans of the Civil Rights Movement, Allen has continued to teach in community schools and to do public speaking. She holds a B.A. from Carleton College and has one child. Archives: The Wisconsin Historical Society has her civil rights and early women's liberation papers. *Union WAGE* papers are in the Labor Archives and Research Center at San Francisco State University. (ABS)

Allen, Donna (1920 – 1999) was the founder of Women's Institute for Freedom of the Press (1972), which published "Media Report to Women" for 16 years. The genesis of this institute was Allen's belief that mass media not only prevented the free flow of ideas, but were controlled by an exclusive group of wealthy men who did not take women or women's issues seriously. Much of Allen's work was geared to getting more women into positions of authority in the media. Besides the Women's Institute for Freedom of the Press, Allen was active in the NWPC, the NWP and NOW. She was a public member of the media committee of the National Women's Conference in Houston in 1977, as well as a delegate at large. In addition to her work for women, Allen worked for military intelligence during WWII, and helped organize farm workers on the West Coast. She is the author of *Fringe*

Benefits: Wages or Social Obligation? (Cornell University Press, 1964), and spoke widely about the economic benefits to be gained from disarmament. Allen received a Ph.D. from Howard University in 1971. She had four children. Archives: National Women and Media Collection, University of Missouri, Columbia, MO.

Allen, Martha Leslie (1948 –) An activist for media democracy and for promoting women's media so that women's voices may be heard, Allen founded and chaired Women's Media Project, Memphis, TN, 1973–1975; was associate director of the Women's Institute for Freedom of the Press (WIFP), 1978–1985; and was director of WIFP from 1985–2003. She helped coordinate seven annual WIPF conferences on Planning a National and International Communications System for Women, most held at the National Press Club in Washington, D.C., from 1978 –1984. Allen was also on the board of directors, NWP, 1996–1999, and on the board of WIFP from 1972 –2003. In addition, she was an organizer of the Women's Leadership Conference, Memphis, in 1973, and organizer and co-chair of NOW's employment rights task force in 1975. Allen has spoken on women and media, and is the editor of the *Directory of Women's Media* (15 annual editions 1975–1989 and resumed again in 2001), published by WIFP, Washington, D.C. She was associate editor, *Media Report to Women*, 1976–1983, and editor and publisher, *The Celibate Woman Journal*, 1982–1988. Allen wrote her Ph.D. dissertation on the history of women's media. As director and president of WIFP, she continues the work of the organization her mother, Donna Allen, founded. Archives: National Women and Media Collection, University of Missouri School of Journalism, Columbia, MO. (ABS)

Allen, Sylvia (1953 –) In 1973, while at the University of California, Santa Cruz, Allen started Keep Abortion Legal. She wrote, printed and distributed fliers and brochures; spoke to diverse audiences; created sample letters to members of Congress to use at letter writing tables; and recruited dozens of volunteers to staff the tables. The result was hundreds of letters per year sent to senators and representatives urging support for women's access to safe, legal abortion. Allen later did crisis intervention and meetings training for local women's groups and lesbian, community service and political organizations. She was also active in the peace movement and the United Farm Workers campaign. (ABS)

Allison, Dorothy (1949 –) A tell-it-like-it-is author, Allison has powerfully addressed themes of class struggle, child and sex abuse, lesbianism as well as feminism. The first child of a 15-year-old mother, Allison experienced severe poverty and emotional deprivation and sexual abuse as she was growing up in Greenville, SC. Despite these childhood traumas, she was the first person in her family to graduate from high school, much less go to college

(Florida Presbyterian College, which she attended on a National Merit Scholarship). A poet and writer of short stories and novels that explore themes of forgiveness, families in trouble and redemption, Allison has become the patron saint of battered women. She joined a feminist collective in the early 1970s, and has said that feminism saved her life, that it was a substitute for religion that made sense. Her first book of poetry, *The Women Who Hate Me*, was published in 1983. Her second book, *Trash* (1988), received two Lambda Literary Awards, for Best Small Press and Best Lesbian Book. With the publication of *Bastard out of Carolina* (1992), a finalist for the 1992 National Book Award, Allison gained recognition and acclaim outside of the lesbian and gay community. Allison says, "It never would have happened if not for the women's movement. When I was 24, I fell in love with militant feminists. They said, 'Well, why not write?'" And she did. Archives: The Lesbian Herstory Archives, Brooklyn, NY. (ABS)

Allness, Aida (1910–1967) was one of 28 founding members of NOW when it was organized at the June 1966 meeting of the Third National Conference of Commissions on the Status of Women in Washington, D.C. Allness was a member of the Wisconsin Commission on the Status of Women. An active Republican living in Viroqua, WI, Allness was on the college faculty at La Crosse (now the University of Wisconsin). She earned a B.A. from Beloit College and taught in Wisconsin high schools before coming to La Crosse State University in 1944; in 1954 she became a full-time history instructor.

Alonso, Harriet (1945 –) A noted professor of history, lecturer and author, Alonso began her feminist career in 1971 when she joined a New York women's group called Half of Brooklyn. The group worked in Brooklyn's Park Slope community addressing women's concerns, especially at the Methodist Hospital GYN clinic. Alonso also participated in the group's antiwar activities, CR groups and study group, where she was exposed to women's history. She earned her M.A. in women's history at Sarah Lawrence and in 1986 her Ph.D. from SUNY Stony Brook. She concentrated on war and peace and women's history—an unusual combination at that time as most women's historians were concentrating on social history. Alonso went on to serve as director of the women's center at Jersey City State College and professor of history at Fitchburg State College in Massachusetts, where she helped found the women's studies minor and institutionalized a huge Women's History Month celebration. In 1999, Alonso became associate dean/director of the City College Center for Worker Education (NYC). At this writing, she continues as a professor of history at City College of New York and the Graduate Center of the City University of New York. Alonso has brought a feminist consciousness to her prolific writing, which includes 26 scholarly papers, three edited volumes and three books:

Growing Up Abolitionist: The Story of the Garrison Children (University of Massachusetts Press, 2002), which won the Warren F. Kuehl Prize from the Society for Historians of American Foreign Relations; *Peace as a Women's Issue: A History of the U.S. Movement for World Peace and Women's Rights* (Syracuse University Press); and *The Women's Peace Union and the Outlawry of War, 1921-1942* (The University of Tennessee Press). (ABS)

Alper, Rika (1947 –) In 1970, Alper went to Cuba with the 2nd Venceremos Brigade to cut sugar cane. Women in the first brigade had rebelled against the traditional division of labor in cane cutting, and had won the right to cut cane with machetes instead of piling cane cut by the men. "This," she says, "was my introduction to women's liberation." When Alper came home, she joined the New Haven Women's Liberation Rock Band, and played for four years at dances, demonstrations and parties for the women's movement and the anti-war movement. Alper helped to form and run the New Haven Women's Abortion Referral Service, which counseled and referred pregnant women, and ultimately started a health clinic. She was active in the civil rights and anti-war movements, and from 1978 – 1990 participated in left-wing political satire theater and music groups. Alper, who has a Ph.D. in Developmental Psychology, has a private therapy practice, and teaches at Montclair (NJ) State University. She has two children. (ABS)

Alpern, Harriet Cooper (1922 –) was a founder of Detroit, MI, NOW in 1969, and because of her PR background handled its media relations. She participated in several actions, including negotiations with a local TV station (an affiliate of ABC) to comply with FCC regulations. As a result, the station agreed to consider women on screen and as camera operators, and to promote women in all aspects of the industry. Alpern was also a member of the committee to examine the images of women and girls in advertising. She created two programs: "What Are Big Girls Made Of?" that dealt with women as sex objects; and "What's Wrong With Wrinkles?" that pointed out the absence of older women even in Mother's Day and Christmas commercials. Her NOW chapter also joined national NOW in a sex-discrimination conference with Bell Telephone, and she says "We all know of the success feminists had in abolishing segregation in the phone industry when we see women in hard hats climbing telephone poles as 'linemen.'" The group also infiltrated a Catholic Bishops news conference, sporting signs reading "Jesus was a feminist." The clerics "barred us from their midst with scornful stares, so we staged our own conference and were encircled by newspaper reporters and television cameras." Archives: The Walter Reuther Library of the UAW, Wayne State University, Detroit, MI. (ABS)

Alpert, Jane Lauren (1947 –) A controversial figure in the women's movement, Alpert made the transformation from an underground revolutionary to a feminist while under indictment for an anti-Vietnam War bombing conspiracy. To avoid prison, Alpert went underground from 1970 – 1974, during which time she wrote "The People of Sam Melville," published in *Letters From Attica* (William Morrow, 1972) and another article, "Mother Right: A New Feminist Theory," published in *Ms.* magazine (1973) that renounced her earlier affiliation with the male-dominated Left and stated her belief that "the origin of feminist consciousness lies in female biology." Although Alpert herself later rejected this theory, it polarized feminists at the time. In 1981, Alpert wrote *Growing Up Underground* (William Morrow). Her conversion from armed revolutionary to radical feminist was provoked, says Alpert, by a "long brewing impatience with the sexism of men in the anti-war movement and an intellectual fascination with questions of gender identity." Alpert led a takeover by women of a counterculture newspaper, *The Rat Subterranean News*, in 1970 and became co-founder and co-editor of *The Women's Rat*. The newspaper remained in all-women's hands for the remainder of its life. In 1972, she was a member of a San Diego CR group, and from 1977 – 1978 of the Women's Anti-Pornography Collective in NYC. Since 1981, Alpert has worked as a management and development consultant to non-profit organizations. She holds a B.A. from Swarthmore College (1967) and an M.P.A. from New York University (1999).   (ABS)

Alpert, Rebecca T. (1950 –) (also known as Rebecca Trachtenberg) During 1971–1976, Alpert was one of the first six women to study for and be ordained to the rabbinate. She spoke on and wrote about women in Judaism, and was involved in founding The Women's Rabbinical Association (later, the Women's Rabbinic Network), an organization for women rabbis. During the years 1983 – 1995, she was a founding member of B'not Esh, a national organization of Jewish feminists; was a board member of the Family Planning Council (Southeastern PA); was active in reproductive-rights work; and published articles on women and Jewish issues. From 1992 – 2002, she was co-director of the women's studies program, Temple University, Philadelphia. She was also a member of the board, Women's Law Project, and published two books and a series of articles on lesbian transformation in the Jewish community. Alpert was part of the anti-nuclear movement in the 1980s and has worked with Women in Black for peace in the Middle East. She has also been a rabbinic spokesperson working against the death penalty in Pennsylvania. Alpert has an A.B. degree from Barnard College (1971); Rabbi, Reconstructionist Rabbinical College (1976); and a Ph.D. from Temple University (1978). She has two children.   (ABS)

AlRoy, Phyllis Delson (1927 –) was part of a Central New Jersey NOW task force that studied sex-role stereotyping in children's readers. She then served as co-author of the booklet *Dick and Jane as Victims*. With Pryde Brown, AlRoy prepared a slide show based on the booklet that showed in detail just how children's readers presented girls as helpless victims and boys as innovative, adventuresome achievers. The slide show was the basis of a program presented at libraries and other groups, and was widely viewed. In addition to this work, AlRoy helped start several CR groups for both women and men, working as part of a task force for Central NJ NOW. She served as treasurer of that chapter for several years, and organized several fundraising events to help pay the rent on the chapter's office, which they called The Woman's Place, in downtown Princeton. A media consultant who has three children, AlRoy holds a B.S. degree.   (ABS)

Alstad, Diana ("Dianne") (1944 –) was a founder of New Haven Women's Liberation (1968) and the Yale Women's Alliance (1969). She also taught the first women's studies courses at Yale and Duke universites. Coming from the anti-war and New Left movements, Alstad shifted her analysis to the core importance of gender as a result of her feminist experiences: "We women in AIM (a local New Left group) created New Haven Women's Liberation, extending Marxist class analysis to women's issues," she explains. But Alstad, Florika, Leah Margulies and Gilda Hymer (now Outremont) were convinced that sexual oppression was more basic than class. So while still remaining deeply involved with NHWL, they created the New Haven radical feminist collective to focus on the gender roots of women's oppression and further develop the theory of patriarchy. The Yale Women's Alliance was formed in 1969—the year Yale admitted women undergraduates. Its most memorable event, says Alstad, was the 1970 Free Women Conference. "Bringing Kate Millett, Naomi Weisstein and Rita Mae Brown into a bastion of male supremacy was exhilarating and a tremendous boost for the New Haven women's movement," she says. The Alliance also picketed Mory's, the men-only dining club Yale used for meetings and job interviews, for two weeks and posted Polaroids of men outside who entered the club. Mory's settled their lawsuit by admitting women. Alstad has been living, teaching and writing with Joel Kramer since 1974, broadening her focus to social evolution, spirituality and survival issues. They wrote *The Guru Papers: Masks of Authoritarian Power* (1993), which decodes the hidden social and spiritual controls underlying patriarchy. Their book, says Alstad, predicted the global "morality wars." Their Internet papers, "Abortion as a Moral Act" and "Abortion & the Morality Wars: Taking the Moral Offensive" (1997) created a new morality-based, pro-choice framework (instead of only rights), she explains. Alstad was a VFA board member (1998 – 2004). She holds a B.A. from the University of Minnesota (1966) and is a Woodrow Wilson Fellow. She did one of the first second-wave feminist dissertations at Yale and received a Ph.D. from Yale in 1971.   (ABS)

Alta (1942 –) A published poet by the mid 1960s, Alta, with the encouragement of her second husband, John

Oliver Simon, founded Shameless Hussy Press in 1969. It was the first feminist press in America in the second wave of feminism. Using a printing press in their garage, Alta began publishing poetry by Susan Griffin, Pat Parker and later Mitsuye Yamada, Jane Cannary Hickok (known as Calamity Jane) and Ntozake Shange, among others. Shameless Hussy was the only feminist press at that time to publish men. Alta reasoned that since 6 percent of the books published in the U.S. were by women, 6 percent of the books she published should be by men. Her *Letters to Women* contained the first blatant lesbian poems most people had seen since Sappho. Alta has published 14 books, 12 by other presses, most notably Crossing Press, which published her collected works, *The Shameless Hussy* (1980), for which she won the American Book Award. By the time Shameless Hussy Press closed in 1989, it had published more than 50 volumes of women's writing. Archives: Shameless Hussy Press archives are housed in Special Collections, University of California Santa Cruz, Santa Cruz, CA. (ABS)

Altenburg, Lois Ivers (1937 –) Teacher, health educator and refugee resettler, Altenburg was the only female chemistry major at Concordia College (1957–1959) and the only female in her medical school freshman class (1959). A board member or president of the LWV of North Dakota or Fargo since 1970, she also served as president of the North Dakota Women's Coalition during state ratification of the ERA (1975), and spearheaded elimination of discriminatory laws in ND (some of which had been on the books since Statehood). Altenburg taught sex education through the YWCA and PTA and led the movement to include sex education in pubic schools in the 1970s. She was board member and president (1974 – 1984) of the YWCA and established a women's shelter and a Woman of the Year Event. Altenburg was also a board member of the Evangelical Lutheran Church's Commission on Full Participation of Women in the Church and led numerous workshops. Altenburg, who has four children, attended Radcliffe College and graduated from Concordia College. She also holds an M.S. in Education. Archives: University of North Dakota in Grand Forks; and North Dakota State University Regional Archives, Fargo, ND. (ABS)

Altman, Yvette (1939 –) (also known as Yvette Scharf) was a volunteer staffer at New Haven (CT) Women's Center (1969). She was a member of The Superintendent's Advisory Committee on Sexism in the Hamden (CT) Public Schools; co-founder and member of CT Women's Political Caucus (1970-1986), CT delegate to first WPC national conference, co-coordinator of CT WPC Women and Power Conference (1971), co-founder of New Haven CT NOW (1972), newsletter editor, member of board CT NOW and member of board Women's Health Services, New Haven, CT (1974-1983). Altman attended the 1978 ERA March in Washington, DC. (ABS)

Alwan, Joy Ann (1946 –) (also known as Joy Ann Mead) A patent attorney, Alwan has used the process of filing EEOC complaints as her means to further both her own life's work and the women's movement. Her first complaint, filed in the mid 1960s against Uniroyal Rubber Company, went nowhere. Alwan was "informed by an African American male at the regional EEOC office that Title VII applied to black men—not to women and certainly not to white women." Although she won her next suit—filed against U.S.S. Lead in 1970 when she applied for a job as chief chemist and was told the company did not hire women—she was laid off within a year because "back then, winning an EEOC complaint provided a job and some back pay, but no protection against retaliation." Employed by Bethlehem Steel in 1975, she applied for a promotion to management and was told that "they had one token female and didn't need another." She again filed an EEOC complaint and was promoted to foreman in the blast furnace, "the ultimate in a hostile working environment. While I was on vacation, my substitute and an electrician were trapped underground and burned to death." After graduating from law school, Alwan took a patent attorney position with the U.S. Department of Energy, only to discover that she was working in an office intensely proud that it had never been forced to promote a woman attorney to management. "The male attorneys also thought it was acceptable to call me a feminazi and tack right wing political and KKK literature on the walls around my office." As a first step to filing suit, she complained to management, only to be told that she wasn't being a good Christian and should learn to turn the other cheek. Alwan continues to monitor and record discrimination abuses as a means to fight unfair and unequal treatment of female employees. She holds a B.S., an M.B.A. and a J.D. (ABS)

Amatniek, Kathie – See Sarachild, Kathie

Amatniek, Sara (1922 – 1996) An award-winning artist and printmaker, Amatniek was an active member of the National Association of Women Artists, Hudson River Contemporary Artists, New York Artists Equity and Women's Caucus for Art. She was also a member of NOW and participated in Redstockings, a radical feminist group formed during the 1960s. Amatniek held a B.A. from Brooklyn College and an M.A. from Columbia University, and trained at the Pratt Graphics Center. She is survived by two daughters, feminist Kathie Sarachild (a founding member of Redstockings) and Joan Amatniek. Archives: Redstockings Women's Liberation Archives for Action, Gainesville, FL.

Ambrose, Jean L. (1932 –) A founding member of NOW in Union County, NJ (1971), Ambrose has worked to establish equality of educational opportunity for women. From 1971 – 1974, she was NJ state chair of NOW's task force on education. She lectured to and gave workshops for teachers' groups, school administrators and school board members about sex discrimination in education, and testified before the NJ Assembly committee on education. During this time she was also a frequent speaker on the right of women to an abortion. In 1971 Ambrose filed discrimination complaints with the NJ Division on Civil Rights against 24 school districts in Central NJ that sex-segregated home economics and industrial arts classes in junior high schools. Thereafter, she worked as a consultant with the NJ Department of Education to desegregate those courses statewide and to address other stereotypical practices in the NJ public schools. In 1972 She publicly challenged the Westfield NJ United Way's discriminatory allocation of funds to the Girl Scouts as compared to the Boy Scouts. Because of the extensive media coverage of this act, the Westfield United Way increased the allocation to the Girl Scouts the next year. Subsequently, the per capita allocation to each was equalized. From 1974–1976 Ambrose taught the senior seminar in women's studies at Rutgers University (Douglass College), and from 1983–1986 co-taught the Women's Rights Litigation Clinic at the Rutgers School of Law-Newark. Ambrose, who has an M.A. from Columbia and a J.D. from Rutgers, published two monographs on discrimination and sexism in education in 1971, and in 1974 published "Analyzing Physical Education for Equality" in the Women's Studies Newsletter, The Feminist Press. Now retired, she was a Rutgers University administrator. She has four children. (ABS)

Amgott, Madeline Karr (1921 –) In 1961, Amgott became the first woman news producer in New York City, working for WABC-TV, The Big News. Says Amgott, "The media powers that be thought the news would go to hell if women produced it. Today they have learned that women work harder and longer and maybe are smarter because line producing has become almost a pink ghetto." She worked with Muriel Fox and Betty Friedan as the press contact for national NOW's founding announcement. Working on "Not For Women Only," she put all major women feminists on Barbara Walters' show in the 1970s. In 1975, Amgott won the Matrix Award in broadcasting and was still producing TV documentaries in 2003. Amgott holds a B.A. from Brooklyn College. (ABS)

Amlong, Karen Coolman (1947 –) (also known as Karen Coolman) joined Broward (FL) NOW in 1972 and marched for the ERA the day she gave birth to her second child. As FL NOW's first state coordinator (1972–1973), Amlong helped start chapters around the state and ran FL NOW's ERA lobbying effort from a storefront office. She was elected to NOW's national board in 1973. In 1974, after being told by a male legislator that she didn't have "a snowball's chance in hell" of ever getting elected, Amlong ran for and was elected as the first woman legislator from Broward County. Says Amlong, "I solicited $5 and $10 donations from NOW members across the coun-

try and stood on street corners with a sign in one hand that said 'It's Time' and usually one of my babies in the other." She served one term, and spoke and voted for the ERA. Her aide, feminist Linda Cox, then ran for Amlong's vacant seat and won. Cox, in turn, was followed by feminist Anne MacKenzie, who became the first woman Speaker Pro Tem of the Florida House of Representatives. In 1976, Amlong went to law school, then began practicing law in 1979. Since that time, she has been heavily involved in employment law involving gender discrimination, and sexual harassment, and family law. Amlong, who has two children, earned a B.A. from Michigan State University and a J.D. from Nova University Center for the Study of Law (1979). (ABS)

Ananda, Zoe – See Nicholson, Zoe

Andersen, Patricia – See Edith, Patricia

Andersen, Ruth G. – See Kirsch, Ruth G.

Anderson, Bonnie S. (1943 –) joined Columbia Women's Liberation in 1969 and served on the curriculum committee, which led to joining a CR group. "That's certainly what changed my life," Anderson says. She then joined the Coordinating Committee for Women in the Historical Profession (CCWHP). By 1974 she had developed several courses in women's studies and women's history. From 1972–2005 she was at Brooklyn College and the Graduate Center, CUNY, as a member of the history dept. and the women's studies program. Anderson coordinated women's studies at Brooklyn from 1984–1989, and became Broeklundian Professor of History in 2000. Her first book was *A History of Their Own*, co-authored with Judith Zinsser, a two-volume work (Harper, 1988). They also co-wrote *Globalizing Women's History: Early Modern and Modern European Women's History*, an AHA Pamphlet in 2001 and published by University of Illinois press in 2005. Alone she wrote *Joyous Greetings: The First International Women's Movement 1830–1860* (Oxford University Press, 2000). From 1988–2000 Anderson worked as a volunteer rape crisis counselor at St. Vincent's Hospital in New York City. Archives: Brooklyn College, City University of New York, Brooklyn, NY. (ABS)

Anderson, Doris D. (1925 –) Of American Indian descent, Anderson has been a fighter for the ERA, for reproductive rights, and the needs of older women. She joined the movement in 1972 when she became a member of WEAL in Dallas. Anderson was also a member of Women for Change in Dallas, and in 1973 joined NOW, where she took part in various activities. A data management technician, she has one child. Archives: DeGoyer Library, Southern Methodist University, Highland Park, TX. (ABS)

Anderson, Mitzi (1939 –) Anderson was active in the civil rights movement and joined marches in Alabama and

Washington before becoming a founder and two-term president of Northern NJ NOW. In addition to serving as president, Anderson edited the newsletter. After feminist groups, including her own NOW chapter, successfully challenged the *The New York Times* to desegregate its help-wanted ads—which had always been separated into Help Wanted Female and Help Wanted Male, with all the better-paying jobs in the male section—Anderson's NOW chapter persuaded local NJ papers such as the *Bergen Record* to follow suit. The chapter also campaigned hard for the ERA. Anderson was the NJ chair for Shirley Chisholm's campaign for President of the United States. From 1975–1980, Anderson was a member of FEW, a federal government feminist organization, and was VP of her chapter in the Department of Energy. Anderson's job with the Department of Energy took her from NJ to Albuquerque and then to Las Vegas, where she is retired from her job as manager of the Las Vegas DOE's department of human resources.   (ABS)

Anderson, Peg Stair (1928 –) has worked to bring more women into government, education and religious bodies. In 1974, she organized a Black Hawk County (IA) WPC, of which she became president in 1975. She was the lone woman on the Cedar Falls board of education during the time of the debate over Title IX implementation, and with the help of other women initiated plans for a women's center at the University of Northern Iowa and a Girls Leadership Camp for high-school girls. During this time, Anderson was also involved with the issue of the ordination of women in the Episcopal Church, serving as a deputy to the General Conventions in 1973, when ordination was defeated, and in 1976 when it was approved. In 1979, Anderson was asked by several women state legislators to head up a statewide campaign to pass an equal rights amendment to the Iowa State Constitution. Although the issue passed the legislature, it had to go to the electorate in November 1980. The women organized a broad-based campaign coalition of women's and political organizations to form IOWA ERA, which Anderson chaired and which involved her in a televised debate with Phyllis Schlafly. Says Anderson, "We lost the election, but we won a large following of newly sensitized women." In 1981, Anderson was appointed to the Iowa Board of Regents and was seen as the women's representative, especially, she says, "after pushing for additional women's toilets at the University of Iowa football stadium." As a regent and a member of the Iowa Commission on the Status of Women (1976 – 1984), Anderson helped organize the Way Up Conferences for Women in Higher Education, which were and still are designed to promote and assist women in seeking administrative positions in colleges and universities. Anderson's other work includes serving as president of Cedar Falls Branch of AAUW (1962–1964); president of Planned Parenthood of Northeast IA (1970–1971); president of United Way of Black Hawk County (1975); member of the state advisory committee to the U.S. Commission on Civil Rights (1975 –1980); and member of the committee on the full participation of women in the church (1986–1988). In 1982, Anderson was inducted into the Iowa Women's Hall of Fame. Archives: Iowa Women's Archives, University of Iowa Libraries, Iowa City, IA.   (ABS)

Andreas, Carol (1933 – 2004) (also known as Andrea Gabriel) A feminist sociologist, Andreas earned a doctorate from Wayne State University in Detroit in 1969. She then taught at the University of Michigan (where she was the only woman among 40 men in the sociology department) and at Oakland University, north of Detroit, introducing a course on sex roles in modern society. Out of this course, Andreas developed one of the first sociology texts on gender roles, *Sex and Caste in America* (Prentice-Hall, 1971). Andreas served as a coordinator of the movement against the Vietnam War in Detroit and helped develop the burgeoning women's movement, participating in several organizations, including a student-led group of new feminist women at Monteith College. She said, "I think I can personally take some credit for linking black union workers with the women's movement and anti-war movement." Unable to secure a divorce in Detroit, Andreas moved to Berkeley, CA, where she taught for several years. She then moved to Chile, participating in the popular movements of the Allende years, which she documented in *Nothing Is as It Should Be: A North American Woman in Chile* (Schenkman, 1976). She lived and taught in Peru for several years, initiating women's studies courses and supporting grassroots movements among women in villages and urban working-class communities. She also published *When Women Rebel: The Rise of Popular Feminism in Peru* (Lawrence Hill Press, 1985), which was based on her experiences and research. She lived and taught in Colorado for several decades, retiring in 1994 from the University of Northern Colorado. She was active in the feminist movement in CO and worked with immigrant workers, publishing *Meat Packers and Beef Barons: A Company Town in a Global Economy* (University Press of Colorado, 1994), which exposed the conditions faced by undocumented workers in the Montfort plant in Greeley. Andreas was also an artist, creating over 200 torn-paper collages, many of which told the stories of women she knew in her life of activism.

Andrews, Sara Sonsol (1929 – 2005) A member of NOW for many years, Andrews served as treasurer of the New York City chapter and chair of its CR committee. She was also chair of the NY State chapter in the 1980s during the administrations of Noreen Connell and Marilyn Fitterman. After learning to drive in her sixties, Andrews traveled around NY State with Connell, visiting NOW chapters in rural areas and inspiring the women to establish their own chapters if one did not exist. Andrews was also involved in the civil rights and peace movements, and was active in Women's Strike for Peace, the WPC and the Downtown Independent Democrats in NYC. A member of a reading group with friends, she founded several discussion groups for feminists in NYC, including one concerned with employment issues. Andrews, who fled from Nazi persecution of the Jews in Italy as a child, earned her B.A. from New York University. She retired as an accountant after having been a comptroller for numerous corporations.

Andrews, Zelle W. (1938 –) Andrews was co-founder and president of Hawaii Women's Liberation (1968); founding member of Hawaii WPC (1970); and co-founder of the Honolulu chapter of NOW (1972). From 1971–1973 Andrews was, by appointment of the governor, a member of the Hawaii State Commission on the Status of Women. The group worked, among other things, to achieve gender-neutral job advertising and for the passage of the national and state ERA. From 1975–1981, Andrews was secretary, then president, of the Westchester (NY) chapter of NOW; chapter delegate to the state organization; president of NY State NOW; and member of the NOW national board in Washington, D.C. In the latter capacity, she headed the Phonathon for ratification of the national ERA in both NY and Washington. From 1980–1985, as a member of the national staff in Washington of the United Church of Christ, Andrews advocated on Capitol Hill for ratification of the United Nations Convention on the Elimination of Discrimination Against Women (CEDAW). In the early 1990s, she continued that advocacy as a national coordinator of the Religious Network for Equality for Women in NYC. From 1994–2000, Andrews served as Westchester, NY, liaison to the lesbian and gay community. She also worked in NYC with Senior Action in a Gay Environment, and was a leader in the effort to get domestic partner benefits for Westchester County employees and a domestic partner registry open to all same-sex couples. In addition, she was a leader in the coalition of civil rights organizations that succeeded in amending the County Human Rights law to include new protected classes: age, marital status, disability and sexual orientation. Active in (the Lesbian and Gay Community Services Center in White Plains, NY, she became president of The Rainbow Alliance of Westchester in 2003. In 1998, she was named Westchester's "Woman of the Year" in recognition of her decades of work for women's rights, and in 2000 was among 10 leaders recognized by the Westchester chapter of the New York Civil Liberties Union for work in helping to create the Westchester County Human Rights Commission. Andrews holds an A.B. (1960) from Wheaton College, Norton, MA, and an A.M. (1968) and Ph.D. (1975) from the University of Hawaii.   (ABS)

Angers, Valerie Marguerite (1939 –) In 1973, Angers was a co-founder, with Joanne Parrent, of the first women's financial institution in the U.S., The Feminist Federal Credit Union. Says Angers, "This was a major accomplishment in that we had to educate the federal government, the chartering body for credit unions, in the concept of feminism. They had never heard the term." Rapidly successful and influential, the Credit Union was visited by bankers eager to learn how the women determined if a potential borrower was a good credit risk. Their success was used in many case studies and was instrumental in the passage of the Fair Credit Reporting Act and the Equal Credit Opportunity Act. In addition to this work, Angers, who is the owner of a medical transcription service, was active in the anti-Vietnam War movement, transporting conscientious objectors to Canada.   (ABS)

Ansley, Fran (1946 –) A teacher of law, Ansley was a member of Bread and Roses in Boston, founded in 1969. She worked and wrote with other members to integrate emerging feminist analysis with other kinds of social theory on race, class and gender. Ansley wrote a chapter on venereal disease for the first edition of *Our Bodies, Ourselves,* helped organize the Bread and Roses office, participated in its actions, and with Meredith Tax compiled a songbook for women to use at mass actions. Ansley was also a member of a women's study and discussion group, Women and Imperialism (1969–1970). Among other activities, the women wrote papers and helped organize an action for International Women's Day. Ansley moved to Tennessee in 1971, where she continues to be active on issues of gender, race and class. She is co-author with feminist Brenda Bell of several articles, and writes and teaches about the impact of globalization on local communities. Ansley, who has two children, has supported civil rights, gay rights and the labor, environmental justice and peace movements. She holds a B.A. from Harvard University (1969), a J.D. from the University of Tennessee (1979) and an LL.M. from Harvard Law School. Archives: Schlesinger Library, Radcliffe Institute, Cambridge, MA.   (ABS)

Anthony, Barbara (also known as Barbara DeFalco and Barbara Blom) As correspondence secretary of Boston NOW (1972–1973), Anthony researched and filed a complaint with bank regulatory agencies alleging gender discrimination in the composition of bank boards of several Boston-area banks. As legislative coordinator (1973–1974), she lobbied for the state ERA; changes in state property laws that discriminated against married women; pregnancy-related benefits; equal rights for gays and lesbians; and reproductive rights for women and teens. She was also a co-founder of the committee to ratify the MA ERA, and co-author of a book explaining the effects of its passage. In 1974–1975, Anthony was coordinator of MA NOW and program chair, MA State NOW Conference. In 1975–1976, she co-founded and co-chaired MA NOW's first task force on lesbian and gay issues, and in 1977 was a marshal in the ERA march on Washington. She was a member and later vice chair of the Northern VA WPC (1978–1985), and organized efforts to pass federal ERA and to support reproductive rights in

Virginia. During that time, she was also a member of Washington, D.C., NOW. As a member of the credit committee of the Washington Women's Bar Association, she co-authored a booklet on credit and financial issues for women. She was also a volunteer at the Transition House battered women's shelter and, as part of Legal Counsel for the Elderly, volunteered her legal services for indigent women in credit and landlord/tenant issues. Anthony was a member of the board of LLDEF (1986–1988). As a member of the board of the MA Women's Bar Association, she testified before the MA Legislature to protect abortion clinic access, and participated in numerous activities to protect reproductive rights and to promote gay and lesbian rights in MA. As a deputy attorney general in MA, Anthony oversaw prosecutions of anti-choice clinic blockaders, and after fatal shootings at Planned Parenthood in Brookline, MA, co-organized a state and federal security committee to take appropriate measures to safeguard patients and clinic workers. From 1997–2000, she represented the MA Women's Bar Association in the joint committees for judicial appointments in MA, and sought to promote the appointment of women and men sensitive to feminist issues to the bench. Since 1999, Anthony has served as regional director of the Federal Trade Commission's Northeast Regional Office in NYC. A frequent speaker and media commentator, she earned her B.S. and M.A. from Northeastern University, Boston, and her J.D. from Suffolk University Law School, Boston, where she is a professor on the adjunct faculty teaching consumer protection law.   (ABS)

Antiga (1932 –) (also known as Mary Lee Geisser) is one link in a five-generation chain of American activists. These include one grandmother working in the Ohio River underground railroad and the other speaking at suffrage events, as well as her daughters, who inspired her to file a case in Minnesota that resulted in equal funds for physical education and sports for girls and boys in the St. Paul public schools. Because the St. Paul school system defaulted and wrote no plan, the judge accepted the plan written by Antiga and her partner, Charlotte Striebel. For Antiga, the apex of this family of feminists was marching in Buffalo, NY, on August 26, 1970, with her mother, Eloise Marian Downing George (1902–1998), to honor the 50th anniversary of woman suffrage. Antiga was a founding member of Buffalo, NY, NOW (1969) and one of the first members of MN NOW. She has been a speaker for The Emma Willard task force on education, and participant in various groups including the MUSE, a feminist arts program, Maiden Rock women's learning institute, Spiderwimmin, a group that organized Wicca rituals around solar holidays, Women's Art Registry of the Midwest, OLOC and the GAGE Foundation. She teaches and speaks on feminism, positive uses and revisions of common language, meditation and ceremonies related to Wicca. She has also produced over 300 works of feminist art in music, visual arts, writing, poetry, singing perform-

ances and quilting. In addition, Antiga, who has been blind since 1985, is a public transportation advocate. Antiga, who has four children, holds a B.A. and M.A. Archives: The Lesbian Herstory Archives, Brooklyn, NY. (ABS)

Antin, Eleanor (1935 –) Emeritus professor of visual arts at University of California, San Diego, Antin has had many museum shows, including the Museum of Modern Art, the Whitney Museum, the Los Angeles County Museum of Art, and Wadsworth Antheneum. Several of her mixed media works, including "100 Boots," "The Angel of Mercy" and "The Adventures of a Nurse," are frequently referred to as classics of feminist postmodernism. Antin has made nine videotapes, and has written, directed and produced numerous narrative films. She won Best Show AICA (International Association of Art Critics) awards in 1999 and 2002; a Guggenheim Fellowship (1997) and the National Foundation for Jewish Culture Media Achievement Award (1998).   (ABS)

Antrobus, Judith S. (1928 –) has been in private practice as a feminist therapist for over 30 years. In 1960, while working toward her Ph.D. in clinical psychology at Columbia University, she wrote the first dissertation in the field of EEG sleep study, then a new science. At that time, and for many years after, she was the only woman pioneer in sleep research. She designed her own research studies (many of which led to significant follow-up studies), and has written about her experiences in this male-dominated world. In the 1970s and 1980s, Antrobus worked as a clinical associate and later as a member of the board of trustees of the Psychological Service Center, a group that provides psychotherapy to those who cannot afford private practice. In that capacity, she arranged for therapists to volunteer their time to mothers and children in an experimental housing situation for the poor and disenfranchised (not a shelter) that provided meals for all and a nursery for the young children—another first. During that time she became the first feminist psychotherapist to supervise doctoral candidates in the clinical psychology program at Columbia University. In 1983, Antrobus founded The Division of Women's Issues of the New York State Psychological Association, serving as president for the first three years. She also served on the Council of Representatives, wrote a regular column in the NYSPA magazine, and has received awards from both DOWI and NYSPA. As a member of the Council of Representatives of the American Psychological Association, she worked on the women's caucus and presented a paper on the effects of abortion. Antrobus has also written reviews for *The Women's Review of Books*. Antrobus has two children.   (ABS)

Anzaldua, Gloria Evangelina (1942 – 2004) A feminist theorist and one of the first openly lesbian Chicana authors, Anzaldua was co-editor, with Cherrie Moraga, of *This Bridge Called My Back: Writings by Radical Women* of Color (Persephone Press, 1981) and editor of *Making Face, Making Soul—Haciendo Caras: Creative and Critical Perspectives by Feminists of Color* (Aunt Lute Books, 1990). The former anthology won the 1986 Before Columbus Foundation American Book Award, while her autobiographical text, *Borderlands/LaFrontera: The New Mestiza* (Aunt Lute Books, 1987), was named one of the 38 best books of 1987 by *Library Journal*. Her work looks at the ways race, class and sexual preference function to define a person, and pointed out that the women's movement's failure to take those factors into consideration perpetuated some forms of discrimination. Her work as an editor grew from the role she was forced to play as interpreter for all women of color for the Feminist Writers Guild, which led to her efforts to expose racism in the women's movement. Anzaldua's numerous awards include the Lamda Lesbian Small Book Press Award, the Lesbian Rights Award, the Sappho Award of Distinction, a National Endowment for the Arts Fiction Award, and the American Studies Association Lifetime Achievement Award. Anzaldua earned her B.A. from Pan American University, her M.A. from the University of Texas, Austin, and was completing a doctorate at the University of California, Santa Cruz, at the time of her death from the complications of diabetes.

Apple, Jacki (1948 –) is an artist, writer, composer, producer and educator. As a young artist in New York in the early 1970s, her works included feminist performance, installation and conceptual artworks dealing with image and identity. The first public piece, Transfer (1971), was a collaboration with Pamela Kraft and was based on the idea that there are four people in every relationship between two people: how you see yourself and how others see you. From 1973–1974, the feminist critic Lucy Lippard organized a traveling conceptual exhibition featuring the works of a number of young feminist artists; Apple and Martha Wilson met through the catalog and subsequently created a collaborative work, Transformance: Claudia, which explored the relationship between media images of women and their own self-images. Performed in December 1973 at the Plaza Hotel in NYC and in the streets and galleries of Soho, Transformance: Claudia was also included in Lippard's book, *From the Center: Feminist Essays on Women's Art,* and exhibited at the Nova Scotia School of Art and Design Gallery, Halifax, Nova Scotia (1974) and in New Zealand. Asked to write about her experiences as a feminist for a catalog for the 2002 exhibition Gloria: another Look at Feminist Art of the 1970s, Apple wrote, "When I went to art school, my teachers were all men and we were told that 'painting was a man's job.'" Apple has taught at Art Center College of Design, Pasadena, CA since 1983. She is a graduate of the Parsons School of Design. Archives: Wesleyan University, World Music Archive, Middletown, CT; work is also being compiled for Fales Library & Special Collections, New York University, New York, NY.   (ABS)

Applebroog, Ida (1929 –) An artist, Applebroog attended the first Feminist Conference at the California Arts Center, Valencia, CA (1970). She was also one of nine women artists who met and worked together at the University of California, San Diego, from 1971–1973. Her work has been exhibited in numerous shows, including Invisible/Visible at the Long Beach Art Museum (1972), Anonymous Was a Woman (a collection of letters to young women artists), Feminist Art Program, California Institute of Arts (1974); and A Woman's Sensibility, also at the Feminist Art Program (1975). She moved to New York City in 1974, and in 1976 had a one-woman show at the Women's Inter-Art Center. In 1977, she published in *Heresies – A Feminist Journal on Art & Politics.* Applebroog, who holds degrees from the New York Institute of Applied Arts and Sciences and the School of the Art Institute of Chicago, has received several grants and awards, including a MacArthur Foundation Fellowship (1998) and the Lifetime Achievement Award from the College Art Association (1995).   (ABS)

Arcana, Judith (1943 –) (also known as Judy Pildes) joined Jane, the abortion counseling service of the CWLU, in 1970 and stayed for two years. Arcana was working there on the day the service was busted, an experience that brought her into intense ongoing contact with the police and judiciary, deepened her political understanding, and raised her consciousness even further. She subsequently took part in two other CWLU activities: the Liberation School, through which she taught classes in women's health and sexuality at various schools and community organizations, and the Prison Project, where she was part of a group teaching similar classes at Dwight, the Illinois state reformatory for women. Arcana also received a fellowship to attend the University of Illinois Medical School Dept. of Preventive Medicine's Preceptorship Program for community health workers. In 1973, Arcana began inventing and teaching courses in women's studies at two local colleges, and was the faculty sponsor for a fledgling women's center at one small college where she taught for six years part-time. From 1976–1984, she was a member of a women's consciousness raising rap group, and in 1977 attended the founding conference of the NWSA where she remains a member. Arcana is the author of *Our Mothers' Daughters* (Shameless Hussy Press, 1979), *Every Mother's Son* (1983), a literary biography of Grace Paley, and *What If Your Mother*, a collection of poems and monologues about abortion. She has also published feminist articles in movement journals, such as *Chrysalis*, and in various mainstream magazines, such as *Cosmopolitan*. Arcana holds a B.A., M.A., Ph.D. and Urban Preceptorship in preventive medicine. Archives: University of Illinois, Chicago, Il.   (ABS)

Arceneaux, Muriel D. (1926 –) As a member of the AAUW and the National Business and Professional Women's Clubs, Arceneaux, a teacher and social worker, began early to work to expand women's legal rights. She lobbied for ratification of the ERA in Louisiana and several other states, and worked to support legislation to strengthen the rights of women in LA. Faced with the ignorance of LA women regarding women's rights, "even trained women lawyers who thought that ERA supporters just resented wearing bras," she organized an affiliate of LA ERA United, published a newsletter, organized informational and how-to workshops, and raised funds for out-of-area lobbying and attendance at rallies and national conferences. She spoke for the advancement of women in traditional and non-traditional jobs, and held workshops for working women on acquiring credit and money management. Arceneaux also lobbied for and financially supported civil rights and environmental groups; worked for and supported women running for political office; and served on the LA State Democratic committee for four years. Archives: Newcomb College Center for Research on Women, Tulane University, New Orleans, LA. (ABS)

Arditti, Raquel Rita (1934 –) came to the United States from Italy in 1965 to do a postdoctoral fellowship at Brandeis University in biochemistry. Originally from Argentina, she had been studying and living there for 10 years. In the Boston area, she joined an anti-war group, Science for the People. Within that group, Arditti began to realize the marginality of women in science as well as the role of science in perpetuating stereotypes about women. She then joined the group's women's caucus and wrote and published feminist articles. In 1969, Arditti was co-author of the booklet "How Harvard Rules Women," published under the sponsorship of the New University Conference. In 1974, Arditti and three other women started the first women's bookstore in the Cambridge/Boston area, New Words, A Women's Bookstore. Closed in 2002, the store has been transformed into the Center for New Words "where women's words count." After joining the Union Graduate School (1974), Arditti began spreading the word about women's studies, and supervised several doctoral dissertations on women's issues, "a revolutionary thing at the time." Since 1975, Arditti has continued her involvement in feminism by writing, editing, teaching and public speaking on women's topics. In 1989 she co-founded the Women's Community Cancer Project in the Cambridge area, a grassroots group committed to changing all aspects of cancer prevention and care as it pertains to women. In 1999, Arditti published a book on the Grandmothers of Plaza de Mayo in Argentina. Says Arditti, "Most recently, my work has focused on women and human rights as a framework that will, I believe, transform our activism and link the local to the global." A graduate college teacher, Arditti has one child and holds a doctorate in the biological sciences. (ABS)

Arenal, Electa (1937 –) is best known for her contributions to the study of Sor Juana Inés de la Cruz; for pioneering work on early modern Hispanic women writers and monastic women's culture; for helping establish CUNY's women's studies programs; and for offering one of the first courses on Spanish and Latin American women writers. She earned the nicknames "la Pasionaria" and "Candela" (firebrand) for her organizing, CR work, and intense engagement with the arts and the urgent political issues of the times. As one of the earliest scholars engaged in re-visioning the field of Hispanic culture, she assisted colleagues and students in reading the literary canon through a feminist lens and in acknowledging gender as a legitimate category of analysis. She presented a foundational and often-cited essay, "The Convent as Catalyst for Autonomy: Two Hispanic Nuns of the Seventeenth Century," at Barnard College's first Scholar and Feminist Conference (1974); and she directed CUNY's Center for the Study of Women and Society and a similar center at the University of Bergen (Norway). Her translations and writing on Central American poets Claribel Alegría and Gioconda Belli were among the first U.S. literary introductions to writings of the Sandinista struggle. Arenal, in collaboration with Stacey Schlau, wrote the landmark *Untold Sisters: Hispanic Nuns in Their Own Works;* and with Amanda Powell the first gender-focused edition of Sor Juana's famous 1691 essay, "The Answer/La Respuesta." Arenal's play, "This Life Within Me Won't Keep Still," based on the lives and works of two 17th century poets, Anne Bradstreet of Massachusetts and Sor Juana of Mexico, previewed at the Modern Language Association convention (1979) and premiered at San Francisco's Fort Mason Foundation. During what Arenal calls "my first life" she was a prima ballerina with the early Joffrey company. (ABS)

Arfer, Irene (1930 –) has been involved in the peace, gay rights and women's movements. She took a course at the Women's Trade Union League in New York City in 1952, and her feminist consciousness grew from there. In the early 1970s, Arfer became part of a CR group in Westchester County, NY, and attended meetings of NYRF at the firehouse on 13th Street in NYC. She participated in speakouts and demonstrations in the city, and in gay/straight dialogues. In addition, working with NOW in Westchester County, Arfer went to numerous churches and community centers to help women start CR groups, and through her Quaker affiliation offered several workshops on women's issues. A retired social worker, Arfer holds a B.S. and M.S.W., and has two children. (ABS)

Ariel (1944 –) (also known as Geri Gray) is an artist, freelance photographer and executive director of the Marshall Ho'o Center of Arizona (martial arts). After graduating from North Texas University in 1972, Ariel went to Los Angeles to join the West Coast women's art movement. She was a member of the cooperative Grandview Galleries in the Women's Building in Los Angeles, and had two of her pieces included in the Woman USA Competition in

Laguna Beach, CA (1973). In 1978, she began a series of installation works based on Jungian archetypes, and in 1979 was a co-founder of The Ladies' Harvest Moon Society (Oakland and Los Angeles). The group established a seven-year tradition of gathering on the full moon of harvest to celebrate the female principle through festivities, art and ritual. In 1983, Ariel began teaching English and art in public schools in Pasadena, Los Angeles and Phoenix. She also began studying Tai Chi Chuan. "The connection," she says, "is that Tai Chi emphasizes the female principle, yin. In Chinese internal martial arts and healing arts, the yang (male principal) always follows the yin." In 1988, Ariel established Two Fishes Swimming, a center for the study of classical Tai Chi Chuan, in Phoenix. Ariel has one child.   (ABS)

Armistead, Betty Jameson (1923 –) Active in politics since 1932, Armistead is known for suggesting that Betty Friedan call the August 26, 1970, strike, 50 years after women got the vote. Armistead sent a letter to Friedan and others on February 22, 1970, proposing the strike and signing the letter "member NOW." The very successful nationwide strike and march on 5th Avenue in New York City brought a wave of new feminists into the women's movement. A historian, Armistead had an EEOC complaint against Florida State University in 1974. Because she could not get a job in education, she wrote a letter to Augustine F. Hawkins, chair of the House Education and Labor Subcommittee on Equal Opportunities, and asked to testify in Congress. In the letter she said: "I am supporting my 13-year-old daughter and myself by being a dishwasher and cleaning woman at a hospital for $85 a week. This is my only income and I am going broke. It does not matter that many leading women in Florida consider me to be the state's authority on the history and statistics of women. I'm rotting." Active in the drive for the ERA and in feminist organizations and government, Armistead was the 1976 Republican nominee for Florida Commissioner of Insurance and State Treasurer. Born in Boston, MA, Armistead is a WWII Army veteran. She holds a B.S. from William and Mary and a M.A.T. from Rollins College, and identifies her career as stockbroker with Merrill Lynch. She has one child. Archives: Schlesinger Library, Radcliffe Institute, Cambridge, MA. (ABS)

Armstrong, Alice (1922 –) A teacher, researcher and consultant, Armstrong has focused her life's work on the problems women face entering the paid workforce, and in the boardroom. In 1972, she was a co-founder, with Ellen Campbell, of the Institute of Managerial and Professional Women (Portland, OR). Over 2,000 women were members in the following 16 years, taking part in conferences, classes for college credit, seminars and workshops. During the late 1970s and early 1980s, Armstrong taught classes at the School of Business at Portland State University. In 1976, she became co-author of *Careers for Women in Management*. In the 1990s, she consulted with the Inter-

national Development Bank in Istanbul, Turkey—with one stated goal being to convince upper management of the important contributions women make as leaders. In 1999, over 200 people gathered at Portland State University to honor Armstrong, who is to be included in the Hall of Heroines being constructed on campus to honor women who have contributed to the recognition and advancement of women in OR. Before being stricken with Alzheimer's disease in the late 1990s, Armstrong had done 10 years of research on her book, *The Great Brain Robbery: The Saga of the Gender Wars*. In 2002, business and economic consultant Peggidy Coffman Yates became co-author. Armstrong, who has five children, earned her B.A. from the University of Arizona; her M.A. from the University of Oregon; and, in 1978, her Ph.D. from the Fielding Institute, Santa Barbara, CA. Archives: Business School library, Portland State University, Portland, OR.

Armstrong, Louise (1937 –) joined the women's movement in New York City in 1972 and began researching father-daughter incest. She is author of the groundbreaking book on incest, *Kiss Daddy Goodnight* (Pocket Books, 1978). Her other books include *The Home Front: Notes from the Family War Zone* (McGraw-Hill, 1983); *Kiss Daddy Goodnight: Ten Years Later* (Pocket Books, 1987); *Solomon Says, A Speakout on Foster Care* (Pocketbooks, 1989); *And They Call it Help, The Psychiatric Policing of America's Children* (Addison-Wesley, 1993); *Of 'Sluts' and 'Bastards': A Feminist Decodes the Child Welfare Debate* (Common Courage Press, 1996); and *Rocking the Cradle of Sexual Politics, What Happened When Women Said Incest* (Addison-Wesley, 1994). She has also published numerous children's books. In addition, Armstrong has written many articles, keynoted numerous feminist conferences, and spoken at universities and to groups nationally and internationally on the issue of violence and sexual violence against women and children. She was on the faculty of the Institute of Children's Literature (1980 – 1987), and chaired a committee on family violence for the National Women's Health Network (1979 – 1984). She is an affiliate of the International Coalition Against Trafficking in Women and Children; is on the advisory board of the Center for the Study of Psychiatry and the advisory board of the National Center for Protective Parents; and has been on the editorial board of *Women and Therapy*. Armstrong believes that violence against women is a feminist issue that has been co-opted by the media and the medical community, resulting in "the pathologizing and individualizing of the victims."   (ABS)

Armstrong Jr., Toni (1954 –) became an activist in 1971 when her high-school term-paper topic on gay liberation was turned down by the school administration and she wrote on women's liberation instead. Since then, she has served the women's and LGBT communities in numerous capacities. She was co-president of Illinois State University Gay People's Alliance (1973 – 1976). From 1995 –

2003, when Armstrong was the youth leadership development coordinator for the Chicago chapter of the Gay, Lesbian and Straight Education Network, she helped students develop more than 40 Gay-Straight Alliance clubs in Chicago area high schools; founded Student Pride, the national network of GSAs; established the chapter's youth scholarship program; launched an e-newsletter linking Chicago and GSAs; and coordinated a monthly LGBT youth segment on Lesbigay Radio. GLSEN Chicago awards an annual Toni Armstrong Jr. Pathfinder Award in her honor. From 2000–2002, she was also a founding member of Color Triangle, the Chicago coalition to end racism in the LGBT community. She was also publisher (1977–1995) of "We Shall Go Forth: Listing of Resources in Women's Music" and later "Women's Music Plus: Directory of Resources in Women's Music and Culture." A concert producer (1978–1982, 1998–present) with Mountain Moving Coffeehouse for Womyn & Children, Chicago, Armstrong played in several openly lesbian-feminist pop bands—most notably Surrender Dorothy and Lavender Jane; was coordinator (1984–1986) of the National Women's Music Festival's Music Industry Conference; served as publisher/editor/photographer/writer (1984–1994) for *HOT WIRE: The Journal of Women's Music and Culture;* and helped start two LGBT newspapers in Chicago, *Windy City Times* and *Outlines*. In 1997, she was inducted into Chicago's Gay and Lesbian Hall of Fame. In addition, Armstrong is the founder (1998) of Leaping Lesbians Chicago Skydiving Club. She holds a B.S. from Illinois State University and an M.A. from Northeastern Illinois University. (ABS)

Arnold, Charlotte S. (1929 –) (also known as Charlotte S. Ginsburg) joined NOW in the late 1960s, and then became a founding member of Pittsburgh's Executive Women's Council. This group forced the formerly all-male Duquesne Club to admit women members, and through its efforts, says Arnold, women began to be invited to serve on corporate boards. Arnold was the first president of Women in the Urban Crisis, a coalition of every national women's group with a chapter based in Allegheny County. In 1969, she became the staff person in Pittsburgh for an organization started by AAUW to uncover the unfair treatment of women prisoners. Arnold went on to start an agency that advocated for women in trouble with the law, helping them to find jobs and training. Arnold, who testified before the United States Senate Judiciary committee about the plight of the female offender, says the agency "was the first program in the country to give women the opportunity to 'serve their sentences' in a facility where their children could live with them." In addition to this work, Arnold was the first woman to serve on the board of the Better Business Bureau in Allegheny County, and was the first chair of the governor's justice commission's juvenile advisory committee. She has received numerous awards and honors, including those from the YWCA, the Merton Center,

Vectors/Pittsburgh and Carlow College. When she retired from The Program for Female Offenders, it was declared "Charlotte Arnold Day" in Pittsburgh. Arnold, who has three children, has also been active with interfaith projects and was a civil rights activist. She was a member of the NAACP and a board member of the Urban League, and demonstrated with the Black Construction Coalition protesting the racist hiring by U.S. Steel. Says Arnold, "I walked arm-in-arm with my black brothers when Pittsburgh 'burned' after Martin Luther King was assassinated." Arnold holds a B.A. from SUNY Albany. (ABS)

Arnold, June Fairfax Davis (1926 – 1982) A "southern belle" who made her debut in 1947 at the Allegro Club ball, Arnold attended Vassar College and received her B.A. (1948) and M.A. (1958) from Rice Institute (now Rice University). Arnold became a powerful voice for lesbian feminists through her writing and activism. After divorcing her husband, she moved with her four children to New York City, where she studied writing at the New School for Social Research. *Applesauce*, her first novel (1967), examines the changes in personalities that occur when people marry. Although it predated by a decade the lesbian feminist audience for which it was intended, the book was rediscovered in 1977 and widely praised. Arnold advocated against lesbians publishing with patriarchal presses. After completing *Applesauce*, she moved to Vermont and, with Parke Bowman, founded Daughters Incorporated. Two of the books it published were her own: *The Cook and the Carpenter* (1973), published under the pseudonym Carpenter; and *Sister Gin* (1975). *The Cook and the Carpenter* recounts, in part, the true story of the takeover by women of an abandoned building in lower Manhattan on New Year's Eve in 1970. Arnold's third book, *Sister Gin*, arguably her most popular work, calls for lesbians to "come in" to a safe place among other women, not to "come out." Arnold was a member of NOW and the Texas Institute of Letters. She was a founder of Feminists in the Arts, and one of the organizers of the first Women in Print conference (Omaha, 1976). Her last novel, *Baby Houston*, was written to re-create her mother's life and life in Houston as a small southern city in the first half of the 20th century. It was published posthumously in 1987.

Aronson, Shepard Gerard (1913 – 2004) A medical doctor, Aronson was a charter member of NOW and in 1966 attended the founding conference in Washington, D.C., with his wife, Muriel Fox. He was the first board chair of New York NOW, from 1967–1968, and in 1972 represented national NOW on David Susskind's national television show "Open End." When asked by Susskind, "But how would you feel if your wife made more money than you?" Aronson replied, "Relaxed." He upheld feminism for men in magazine interviews by Gail Sheehy and Claudia Dreyfus (1967–1968), and was on the medical advisory committee of Planned Parenthood of NY from

1973 – 1975. In 1980, Aronson organized a NY County Medical Society meeting with women's groups on "What's Wrong With Doctor's Attitudes Toward Female Patients." This resulted in a report that was distributed to physicians worldwide and summarized in an article by Nan Robertson in *The New York Times*. Aronson also organized America's first Joint Committee of Nurses & Physicians, with nurses voting equally (1981), and campaigned for greater authority for nurses in U.S. hospitals. He lectured widely on medical/feminists topics, and wrote "Marriage with a Successful Woman: A Personal Viewpoint," published in *Women and Success* (1974). In 1996 Aronson was honored by VFA.   (ABS before death)

Ashley-Farrand, Margalo (1944 –) attorney, mediator and judge pro tem of the Los Angeles Superior and Municipal Courts since 1989, Ashley-Farrand began her activism early in 1971 in Pittsburgh NOW and founded East Hills NOW in 1972. In 1973, she was legal assistant to Sylvia Roberts on Title VII individual and class action suits against the University of Pittsburgh. She was also a lobbyist for the ERA ratification campaign in Pennsylvania and for Title IX enforcement in Pennsylvania schools (1972 – 1974), and served as campaign manager of the East Hills area of Pittsburgh for Shirley Chisholm's presidential campaign (1972). Ashley-Farrand was also a political campaigner for Bella Abzug's mayoral race (1976), and for her congressional campaign (1977). In 1973, Ashley-Farrand was co-coordinator of the Eastern Regional NOW convention. She was a member of the founding board for PA NOW, which wrote the by-laws used as a model by other NOW state organizations and national NOW (1973). In 1972, she represented East Hills NOW in negotiations for a formal agreement with the local television stations to improve both their image of women on air and their employment of women. In 1974 she convened and chaired the Los Angeles Women's Coalition for Better Broadcasting, negotiated agreements with two television stations in Los Angeles, and filed four petitions to deny license renewals to KNXT-TV, KTLA, KTTV and KCOP. In 1973 – 1974, she represented East Hills NOW in negotiations with the chancellor of the University of Pittsburgh to improve the employment status of female staff and professors. As a law student intern, Ashley-Farrand researched Constitutional issues at ACLU of Southern California for a sex discrimination suit against the 1984 Olympics that won for women the right to compete in Olympic marathons and other sports. Ashley-Farrand is founder and coordinator of Shades of Culture Women's Club (2000), and was president, Pasadena Interracial Women's Club (1993 – 994); board member, LWV, Pasadena Area (1993); co-president, Hollywood NOW (1974); convener and president, East Hills NOW (1972 – 1974); and NY NOW media committee and fundraising chair (1976 – 1978). She received her J.D. from Southwestern University School of Law, SCALE Honors Program (1980).   (ABS)

Aspen, Kristan – See Knapp, Kristan B.

Astarte, Pamela Ann (1952 –) (also known as Pamela McDonald and Pamela Lagarde) was a member of the Bread and Puppet Theater from 1970 – 1974. Located in both New York City and Vermont, the collective was an avantgarde, agit-prop, anti-war theater company in which all the women insisted on doing everything the men could do—both the creative work and the loading of trucks and driving of tour buses. Says Astarte, "This may not sound like a big deal today, but back then it was huge!" The group held several important rallies and events in Washington and across the U.S. At one point, traveling through the heartland, they performed a piece that included nudity "in the most respectful way, representing the female form as something quite other than a sexual piece of meat to be used for male gratification. Other pieces done by the group focused on the suffering of the Cambodian and Vietnamese women and their grief and courage in the face of the soldiers' guns. A teacher, Astarte has two children and earned an M.Ed. from Lesley College (1985).   (ABS)

Atkins, Carol M. (1923 –) A writer and poet who entered the women's movement in 1972, Atkins was a founding member of Williamsport, PA, NOW and a convener of Manistee County (MI) NOW. She spent seven years campaigning for the ERA in Pennsylvania, Illinois, Florida and Virginia, and was involved in creating shelters for battered women in Pennsylvania and Michigan. Atkins, who holds a B.A. from the University of Michigan (1945), has written many feminist articles in her capacity as a newspaper columnist. She has three children.   (ABS)

Atkinson, Ti-Grace (1938 –) A radical feminist, writer, theorist and often dissenting voice of the women's movement, Atkinson joined NOW in 1966 and served as the second president of NY NOW. With NOW for two years, Atkinson became frustrated with NOW's elitism and its resistance to taking on abortion as an issue. NOW leaders criticized her for attending radical feminist Valerie Solanas' trial for attempted murder in 1968, even though Atkinson disclaimed any association with NOW in this action. About this time, Atkinson was working on a non-hierarchal structure for NY NOW, which she proposed at a packed meeting in October 1968. When her proposal was rejected, Atkinson immediately resigned her position. She also says her decision to leave was prompted by "NOW's curious position about 'sexual issues.' So it was abortion and lesbianism and probably would have been other issues which arose later around gender identity." Atkinson left with some other NOW members, including Flo Kennedy, and formed The October 17th Movement, named after the day she left NOW. A year later, it was renamed The Feminists. Atkinson and several other women protested at the NYC Marriage License Bureau, accusing the Bureau of "fraud with malicious intent." In addition to anti-marriage actions, she participated in a raid on Grove Press to protest pornography and to support women (including Robin Morgan) fired for union organizing, which resulted in the arrest of Atkinson and eight others. Later, she organized against the women's movement and its cooperation with the U.S. government's persecution of women in the anti-war underground. Atkinson resigned from The Feminists in 1970 because she says, the group, founded on principles of equality, had difficulty with the fact that she was in demand as a speaker at colleges and was frequently singled out by the press. Atkinson has served on the board of Human Rights for Women since 1969 and is the author of *Amazon Odyssey* (1974), a collection of feminist writings. An eloquent speaker with a following, Atkinson was on the faculty of the 1975 Sagaris Collective of feminists organized by Goddard College faculty women in 1975. There she and a group of students and faculty split off and moved to another location, denouncing the Sagaris Collective for accepting $10,000 from the *Ms.* Foundation soon after Redstockings published an attack on Gloria Steinem, which Steinem had not yet addressed. Later Atkinson denounced the women's movement altogether, remarking that women would not truly progress until they were willing to sacrifice privilege and take action to promote positive change. Born in Baton Rouge, LA, Atkinson relocated frequently because of her father's work as a chemical engineer with Standard Oil. As a hobby, Atkinson breeds American Shorthair cats. Atkinson has an academic background in art and philosophy with a focus on "a careful analysis of the phenomenon of women's oppression." She has been trying to "finally" complete her dissertation in the philosophy of logic. In recent years, Atkinson has been doing research and presentations on depleted uranium and the use of it by the U.S.. (ABS)

Atlantis, Dori (1950 –) (also known as Doris Bigger) A founding member of the Feminist Art Program at Fresno State University (CA) under Judy Chicago (1970), Atlantis documented the program with photographs, and worked in collaboration with Nancy Youdelman and Karen LeCocq, Jan Lester and Chris Rush. Her work is included in the book *The Power of Feminist Art*, by Mary D. Garrard and Norma Broude. Atlantis was also one of the "4 cheerleaders" (C.U.N.T.), a performance group that glorified words that had been used to insult women. As of this writing, Atlantis is working as an installation artist in Los Angeles. She has two children and holds a B.F.A. and M.F.A. from the California Institute of Arts. (ABS)

Attie, Dotty (1938 –) was a founder, with five other women, of the AIR (Artists in Residence) Gallery (1971), in New York City. With Womanspace (Los Angeles, 1972) AIR was one of the first two women's alternative galleries. The two galleries became models that were copied across the country. Attie remained a member of AIR until 1988. In addition to exhibiting her own work, she participated in

running the gallery; curated, with other members, several exhibitions of international women artists; organized panels on subjects of interest to women artists; and concentrated on making the art world a friendlier place for women. Attie holds a B.F.A. and has two children. (ABS)

Auslander, Susan B. (1953 –) was a founder of the Wesleyan Math Clinic, with Sheila Tobias, formed to increase women's participation in mathematics and the sciences. From 1975–1978, they ran the clinic at Wesleyan, and also ran conferences for high-school girls to increase their participation in math and science. The author of several articles on approaches to math anxiety, Auslander is coordinator of the Math Science House at Columbus High School, Bronx, NY. Auslander, who has one child, earned her B.A. from Windham College and her M.A. from Wesleyan University. (ABS)

Austin, Dorothy Witte (1918 –) A 1940 graduate of Marquette University, Austin is an award-winning journalist who for many years wrote features for *The Milwaukee Journal* and the *Milwaukee Sentinel*. She attended the NOW organizing conference in October 1966 in Washington, D.C., at the request of Kay Clarenbach. Because Austin attended as a reporter for the *Milwaukee Sentinel*, she did not consider herself a NOW founder. The meeting was not open to the press, and the conference attendees initially proposed to evict Austin from the room, but after discussion agreed to let her stay. She stayed through the entire conference. "Her newspaper articles on women's issues were very important in educating women and the public in general, and incidentally contributed to NOW recruitment," says Mary Eastwood. Austin's honors and awards include Milwaukee Section of the National Council of Jewish Women Faith and Humanities Award (1979), Southeastern Wisconsin Women in Communications Headliner Award (1979), Milwaukee Chapter of NOW Woman of the Year (1983), and the Milwaukee Press Club Media Hall of Fame (1985). Austin retired in 1983, but continued freelance writing, working with NOW in Wisconsin and the County Commission on Aging. (ABS)

Austin, Sue (1947 –) (Also known as Sue Austin Brown) A military wife in 1973, Austin formed the first NOW chapter in the Fort Bragg, NC, area. In 1976, the chapter successfully prepared a grant request and received $5,000 to conduct a series of workshops addressing areas such as female sexuality, battered women, sexism in education and roles and identity. The group also formed a rape crisis line, a self-defense class, and a center for battered wives, and worked to pass the ERA. In 1975, very pregnant with her second child, Austin traveled to Philadelphia to attend the national NOW convention. "We had many good laughs at the FBI following us around whenever we left any meeting that even vaguely spoke about lesbian issues," she says. Austin, who has four children, earned her B.S. from the University of Tennessee (1969) and her M.S. Ed. from the University of Southern California (1973).   (ABS)

Ausubel, Bobbi Gloria (1936 –) (also known as Bobbi Edelson) served as co-artistic director of Caravan Theater for 13 years, beginning in 1963. Described by Rosemary Curb, drama historian, as the first feminist theater in the U.S. in the second wave, Caravan Theater (Cambridge, MA) produced "How to Make a Woman" under the supervision of Ausubel and in a collaborative process in 1968. About the socialization of women, the play was continuously rewritten in the late 1960s and early 1970s to reflect the evolving thinking of the early women's movement. From 1970 – 1972, male/female gender workshops were offered through Caravan Theater. The theater directly influenced the creation of several important women's theaters, including Earth Onion (Washington, D.C.) and Foot of the Mountain (Mpls., MN). From 1976 – 1999, Ausubel, a theater director, teacher and registered drama therapist working with children and adults, was part of Ark Theater, which produced plays on such themes as sexual abuse. Ausubel, who has two children, earned an M.F.A. from Boston University. Archives: Schlesinger Library, Radcliffe Institute, Cambridge, MA.   (ABS)

Avallone, Fran (1937 – 2003) was a prominent reproductive rights advocate who became active in 1973 when she joined the board of directors of Middlesex County (NJ) Planned Parenthood. In 1974 she became chair of the public affairs committee; in 1979 she became president of the board; and from 1984 – 1989 was staff director of fundraising. In 1974 Avallone founded New Jersey Right to Choose and worked with that organization until 1994. During that time she established the Right to Choose Education Fund and established the Right to Choose PAC. Right to Choose brought suit against the state of New Jersey (Right to Choose v. Byrne, 1982) to enable women on Medicaid to have funded abortions, and won. From 1993 – 1994 she was chair of CHOICE NJ, a coalition of 30 statewide pro-choice groups, and co-chair of NJ Women's Health Collaborative, a coalition of pro-choice and women-of-color groups. In 1986, she served as editor of *New Jersey Speaks Out* (now in its 5th edition), a compilation of true stories by women about their abortions, both before and after the 1973 Roe v. Wade decision. In 1992, she wrote "Parental Consent and Notification Laws," which was published in *Taking Sides*, a college textbook. She was also active in pro-choice political campaigns on local, state and national levels. Honors include The Giraffe Project, a national organization that recognizes people who stick their necks out for the common good (1987), the Women of Achievement Award, given by Douglass College and the NJ Federation of Women's Clubs (1992), and the Mary Philbroke Award, given by the NJ WPC (1993). A high-school graduate, Avallone had two children.

Avedon, Barbara (1930 – 1994) (also known as Barbara Avedon Hammer) A TV writer and producer, Avedon invited 15 women to her house in 1967 to take a stand against the Vietnam War. The result was the founding of Another Mother for Peace and the organization's logo, a sunflower with the words "War Is Not Healthy for Children and Other Living Things," created by Los Angeles artist Lorraine Schneider. The logo became an instant classic that was sent as a Mother's Day card, in protest, to Washington legislators. Avedon wrote for many of the leading TV shows and co-created "Cagney and Lacy" on CBS, which won a number of Emmys. Her anti-war work continues through her son, Joshua.

Avery, Byllye Y. (1937 –) For her daughter's 11th birthday, Avery used icing on the cake to wish her daughter "Happy Birthday, Happy Menstruation," which characterizes her bold and passionate commitment to women's health, particularly African American women. Living in Florida in the early 1970s, Avery was part of a referral network for women who wanted to go to New York City to obtain abortions (which were illegal in Florida at the time). In 1974, she was founder, with Judy Levy, Margaret Parrish and Joan Edelson, of the Gainesville Women's Health Center. Established shortly after the Roe v. Wade decision, the clinic developed a partnership approach to patients where medicine was demystified by the sharing information, in a non-authoritarian environment, by patients and healthcare providers. The clinic, which remained open until the late 1990s, provided abortions as well as annual exams and treatment for gynecological conditions. Avery also co-founded Birthplace, an alternative birthing center in Gainesville, in the early 1970s. After leaving Birthplace in 1980, Avery became director of CETA in Gainesville. While serving on the board of the National Women's Health Collective in 1981, Avery began planning the National Black Women's Health Project, now known as the Black Women's Health Imperative. As the organization's executive director (1982 – 1990), Avery saw it grow to an international network of more than 2,000 participants in 22 states and six foreign countries. In 2002, Avery founded the Avery Institute for Social Change to address the health concerns—in particular affordable healthcare—of people of color. Prior to her entry into the healthcare arena, Avery taught special education to emotionally disturbed students and consulted on learning disabilities. Her numerous awards include a MacArthur Foundation Fellowship for Social Contribution (1984); Grassroots Realist Award, Georgia Legislative Black Caucus (1994); Academy of Science Institute of Medicine's Gustav O. Leihard Award for the Advancement of Healthcare (1994); President's Citation of the American Public Health Association (1995); Dorothy Height Lifetime Achievement Award (1995); University of Florida's School of Medicine's Leadership Award (1998); BPW New Horizons Award (1998); and Trailblazer Award, Lifetime Television (2002). Avery holds a B.A.

from Talladega College in Alabama (1959) and a M.Ed. from the University of Florida (1969). In addition, she holds Honorary Degrees from Thomas Jefferson University, SUNY Binghamton, Gettysburg College, Bowdoin College and Bates University. (ABS)

Avery, Kathryn (1920 – 2003) was a behind-the-scenes worker on behalf of women for 20 years. She served on the board of the Women's Party Corporation in many capacities, worked on the ERA campaign, and helped organize the ERA March on Washington in 1977. Born Kathryn Cavan in Seattle, WA, Avery graduated from the University of Washington and later obtained teaching credentials. She married a Naval officer, Walter, and moved to Newport, RI, and then to Washington, D.C. In Washington, in the early 1970s she sold real estate, met Alice Paul, and became active in the NWP. Her husband was also active in NWP and became its second male member. Always involved in the theater wherever her husband was stationed, Avery worked in Washington with the Children's Shakespeare Festivals.

Ayhens, Olive Madora (1943 –) An artist, Ayhens joined a group of women artists in San Francisco/Oakland in 1971. Group members, who met weekly to discuss various topics relating to art and women artists, were in shows together, including a show at the Berkeley Art Center (1972). In 1973, Ayhens exhibited in the show Woman USA, held at the Laguna Beach Art Museum. Ayhens, who has two children, holds a B.F.A. and M.F.A. from the San Francisco Art Institute. (ABS)

Aylon, Helene (1931 –) (also known briefly as Helane) An artist, Aylon was introduced to the feminist movement in 1972 through CR groups. In 1977, the artwork Formations and Formations Breaking spoke against the *Playboy* attitude about the body. Says Aylon, "Formations were formed by pouring oil. The forms took on an oval shape with a membranous skin. I did not want to force this imagery, but to show that it is there already, inherent in nature where the oval egg shape and the nucleus are primordial. In all my work I was juxtaposing feminist centered icons with the icon in the culture. Later, in the early 1980s, it was the juxtaposition of the sac with the SAC (Strategic Air Command)." In 1979, Aylon took part in the first eco-feminist conference at Amherst, MA. From 1973 – 1976, Aylon taught art at San Francisco State University, where projects were oriented toward a feminist approach. Aylon's article "Academia and the Fear of Feminism" was published in 1976 in a San Francisco publication, *Visual Dialogue*. She then taught a course, Performance Art as Anti-War Strategy, at the newly formed Feminist Institute. Aylon has two children. (ABS)

Azara, Nancy J. (1939 –) An artist, sculptor, and spiritual teacher, Azara was a founding member of the New York Feminist Art Institute, and a member of a Redstockings offshoot from 1969 – 1975. She participated in CR and public demonstrations and discussions about the ERA, and went to prisons to hold art-focused CR meetings. She was for many years a member of the AIR Gallery (the first women's cooperative gallery in the United States) and has spent much time exploring the idea of a "women's aesthetic." Her carved and painted wood sculpture is shown internationally. Azara is the author of *Spirit Taking Form: Making a Spiritual Practice of Making Art* (2002). She is co-author of "Working with the Light: Women of Vision" (1996) in *Feminist Foremothers in Women's Studies, Psychology and Mental Health* (1995) with editors Phyllis Chesler, Ester Rothblum and Ellen Cole. Archives: New York Feminist Art Institute, Rutgers University, New Brunswick, NJ. (ABS)

Babson, Averill (1951 –) has been an active participant in the women's movement and the peace movement since 1969, when she participated in marches in both New Haven, CT, and Washington, D.C. She has been a supporter of NOW LDEF and was vice chair of NWPC CT in the mid 1980s. Since 1990 she has been a charter member of the Women's Commission for Refugee Women and Children (International Rescue Fund), and is on the advisory committee for the Children's Defense Fund. She is the author of several articles that have appeared in local papers, *Mothering Magazine* and *The Chicago Tribune*. Babson, who earned a B.A. from Stanford University (1974), has three daughters. (ABS)

Bachenheimer, Beth (1948 –) An artist, Bachenheimer uses historical, satirical, socially conscious and politically conscious subject matter. Her work in the feminist movement started in 1970 – 1972 when she graduated from California Institute of the Arts. She collaborated with other feminist artists in Los Angeles on three rooms in The Womanhouse (1972), which made a strong political statement about women's lives. Bachenheimer's work appears in *The Power of Feminist Art*, by Norma Broude and Mary Garrard (1994) and *Other Visions, Other Voices*, by Dr. Paul Von Blum (University Press). As a result of a back injury in the 1980s, Bachenheimer stopped oil painting on six by four-foot canvases and started creating smaller-scale art, including masks, and taught mask-making at universities. As a Holocaust survivor's daughter, she also created 30 collages from her father's immigration documents for an art book, *Living with Memory*. She received a B.F.A. from the California Institute of the Arts and an M.F.A.V.A., Vermont College, 1996. (ABS)

Bacon, Margaret Hope (1921 –) Bacon's discovery of Lucretia Mott, an anti-slavery and women's rights leader (1793 – 1880), was the beginning of a lifetime of researching, writing and organizing for women's equality. Bacon is the author of *I Speak for my Slave Sister: The Life of Abby Kelley Foster* (1974); *As the Way Opens, The Story of Quaker Women* (1980); *Valiant Friend, the Life of Lucretia*

Mott (1980); *Mothers of Feminism: The Story of Quaker Women in America* (1986); *One Woman's Passion for Peace and Freedom: The Life of Mildred Scott Olmsted* (1993); and *Abby Hopper Gibbons: Reformer and Social Activist* (2000), among others. Bacon was a founding member, Fair Housing of Delaware County; and was a member of WILPF and several environmental and land trust groups. She was also a founding member of Women's Way (1976), which raises money and mobilizes community resources to support programs by and for women; and was a member of the Philadelphia Commission on Women (1980). In 1985 she received an award for presentation of women's history. Bacon, who has three children, holds A.B. degree from Antioch College and an Honorary Degree from Swarthmore College. Archives: Special Collections, Haverford College, Haverford, PA.   (ABS)

Bailey-Mershon, Glenda Mariah (1949 –) Writer, historian, activist and planner, Bailey-Mershon joined the Illinois chapter of NOW in 1974. She has been president, VP/chapter development, chair of the political action committee, and board member, IL NOW Legal and Education Fund, and has chaired committees on women's history. She was a founding member of the Park Forest Women's Conference (1981) and served on its steering committee (1981 – 1984). In addition, Bailey-Mershon was lead editor and co-founder in 1994 of Wild Dove Studio and Press, which sponsored workshops for women writers and became a showcase for their work, and one of the owners of Prairie Moon Feminist Bookstore. She was a founding board member of the Women's Leadership Council, which was designed to bring together women of various parties and organizations for discussions, and helped found the Women's Lobby Day Coalition, which worked to prevent legislation injurious to women and families (Springfield, IL, 1996 – 1998). Bailey-Mershon was part of Remembering Nicole Day, which helped heal divisions over the O.J. Simpson verdict. A member of Chalkers for Choice, she was arrested and convicted ("proudly," she says) for writing pro-choice slogans on a post office walkway. Bailey-Mershon has also been active in the civil rights, anti-war and environmental movements. She is a member of the Writer's Cooperative at Jane's Stories Press Foundation and is on the advisory board for the 40th ACCORD Project, documenting civil rights history. Her published work includes *Bird Talk: Poems* (1999); *The History of the American Women's Movement; A Study Guide* (1998); and *Shaconage/Blue Smoke: Poems from the Southern Appalachians* (2003). Bailey-Mershon, who has two children, holds a B.A. from Knox College (1974), and an M.A. from Governors State University (1977). Archives: University of Illinois, Springfield, Il.   (ABS)

Baird, Bill (1932 –) Called by some media the father of the abortion-rights movement, Baird was central to three U.S. Supreme Court cases that helped legalize birth con-

trol and abortion. Nonetheless, Baird has not been embraced by all major groups fighting for the same cause. Many feminists have derided him as an outcast and a self-promoter. Pro-life supporters have shot at him, bombed his clinic—and even offered to pray for him. He was jailed eight times in five states in the 1960s for merely lecturing on abortion and birth control. His crusade began in 1963. Then clinical director for EMKO, a birth control company, Baird, while doing research at a NYC hospital, heard screaming in the corridor and saw an African American single mother of nine covered in blood from the waist down with an eight-inch piece of wire coat hanger protruding from her uterus. She died in his arms. That year, he distributed birth control foam to women at New York area drug stores and malls, and in 1964 established the nation's first nonprofit birth control/abortion facility (Hempstead, NY), staffed by doctors providing free reproductive healthcare. In 1971, two firebombs struck the Jewish Community Center in New Bedford, MA, just minutes before Baird was scheduled to speak. With his clinic under constant threat, Baird wrote and distributed the nation's first clinic self-defense manual to combat terrorism (1978). In 1979, Baird's clinic, with 50 people inside, was firebombed; in 1980, Baird sued the FBI, claiming it had failed to investigate anti-abortion terrorists. Later (1985), Baird pioneered a 50-foot demilitarized zone and a 500-foot quiet zone to protect clinics. Despite appeals for an end to violence, Baird's clinic was forced to close temporarily due to chemical bombs in 1992. In 1993, it was closed again because of flooding with fire hoses. Believing that there was a clear connection between inflammatory rhetoric and violence, Baird and his co-director of the ProChoice League, Joni Scott, worked with Fr. Frank Pavone, co-founder and director of Priests for Life, to create a document calling for an end to anti-abortion hate speech and violence. In 2002, the agreement between pro-choice and anti-abortion sides was signed, and copies sent by Fr. Pavone to hundreds of diocese and anti-abortion groups nationally. Baird has also worked through the courts to secure women's right to choose. He is the first and only non-lawyer in American history with three Supreme Court victories. In 1972, Baird v. Eisenstadt legalized birth control for individuals (the 1965 Griswold case was for married couples only); and in 1976 – 1979, in Baird v. Bellotti I and II, minors were empowered to obtain abortions without parental veto. Baird, founder and director of the ProChoice League, earned his B.S. from Brooklyn College in 1955, and received its Alumni Lifetime Achievement Award in 2004. Having used his own money to fight for a woman's right to choose, Baird lives today on Social Security.   (ABS)

Bajan, Janet W. (1944 –) was active with NYRF, involved in putting on the prostitution and sexuality conferences. She was book review editor for *Majority Report*. She was on the board of Through the Flower, a non-profit organization that supports feminist art, and serves on the board of the Elizabeth A. Sackler Foundation, created to purchase Judy Chicago's Dinner Party. The foundation then donated Dinner Party to the Brooklyn Museum. Bajan, a stockbroker living in New Mexico, is working with the Brooklyn Museum, which is building a Center for Feminist Art with the Dinner Party as the centerpiece. (ABS)

Bajoie, Diana (1948 –) Politically active in the late 1960s, Bajoie began her formal political career as a Louisiana state representative (1976–1991). In 1992 she became the first black woman senator in the Louisiana State House. Bajoie was a founder and former chair of the Louisiana Legislative Black Caucus and the Louisiana Legislative Women's Caucus. She has also served as president of NOBEL, a national legislative women's organization. Her many accomplishments include the creation of school-based health clinics, the formation of the Minority Health Care Commission, increased healthcare coverage for citizens with mental health disorders, and mandated coverage for mammography and other cancer screenings. Bajoie attended Southern University and A & M College in Baton Rouge, where she earned her undergraduate degree.

Baker, Vaughn (1937 –) was a member of the Louisiana Council for the Humanities and a founding member of the Mayor's Commission on the Needs of Women in Lafayette (mid 1970s). She established a division of the Center for Louisiana Studies called the Women in Louisiana, and helped found the women's art collection at the University of Louisiana at Lafayette. (ABS)

Bako, Yolanda (1946 –) In the early 1970s, Bako was coordinator of New York City NOW's rape prevention committee, and was a founding member of the NYC Women's Anti-Rape Coalition. She was also a founder of the Mayor's Task Force Against Rape under the Lindsay administration; was founder and coordinator (for the first year) of the Center for the Elimination of Violence in the Family; and a founder of the NYC Coalition for Battered Women and the NY State Coalition Against Domestic Violence. She was also a founder of the National Coalition Against Domestic Violence, and director (1982 – 1995) of World Peace Begins at Home. Bako created the first program to train medical students about the trauma of sex crimes at Albert Einstein College (1975), and trained advocates at Jacobi Hospital to accompany rape victims through the ER. She also demonstrated at 1 Police Plaza (NYC) to demand the establishment of a sex crimes unit (1972); was the conceptualizer and producer of Women's Walk Against Rape through Central Park at Night (1976), which became the prototype for subsequent Take Back the Night marches; and organized a demonstration in front of WABC (1976) to chastise the televised remark by Tex Antoine that women should lie back and enjoy rape. A graduate of Evander Childs High School (Bronx, NY), Bako is the author of *How to Start a*

County Wide Task Force on Family Violence. She was also involved in the anti-Vietnam War effort, and served as an NGO representative at the United Nations, 1982–1995. Archives: Schlesinger Library, Radcliffe Institute, Cambridge, MA. (ABS)

Baldauf, Mary (1922 –) founded the Ft. Myers, FL, NOW chapter (1971), and later the Lee County Gray Panthers. Ft. Myers NOW was diligent in fighting sex discrimination in local government, education, law enforcement, media and business. It was also the catalyst for a women's shelter and abortion referrals. Baldauf was married for 24 years and had six children when "my husband traded me in for a new model, just like a car." Fired from a "dead-end job at a telephone company because I started the NOW chapter," she reached an out-of-court settlement based on findings by the EEOC. Baldauf ran for county commissioner in 1972 and 1974, and was arrested in 1984 at Cape Canaveral for civil disobedience. She was a member of the NAACP, the FL WPC, and peace and environmental groups. She retired from Florida Legal Services as a paralegal in 1995. Archives: Records held by her daughter, Laurel Duran, Ft. Myers, FL. (ABS)

Ballantine, Morley (1925 –) An award-winning civic activist and fighter for gender and racial equality in Colorado, Ballantine was a member of the Durango board of the LWV (1955–1965) as well as the state board (1960–1965). She served on the state Anti-Discrimination Commission (1959–1961) and the State Commission on the Status of Women (1973–1975), among others. Over the years she has served Durango in governmental posts in education, the library, historical preservation, land use and fine arts. A founding member of the Colorado Women's Foundation, Ballantine also helped start the Women's Resource Center in Durango (1987). Ballantine and her husband, Arthur Ballantine, purchased the *Durango Herald* in 1952. Ballantine was the editor and publisher of the *Durango Herald* (1952–1975) and has been editor and board chairman since 1983. Ballantine attended Smith College and the University of Minnesota, and at 50 graduated from Fort Lewis College with a B.A. (1975). She holds Honorary Degrees from Simpson College (1980) and the University of Denver (2002). She has four children. (ABS)

Ballard, Ernesta Drinker (1920 – 2005) A life-long activist for equal rights and reproductive rights for women, Ballard was a member of the first elected board of national NOW (1968) and was a founder of Philadelphia NOW. She was also a founder of NARAL Pro-Choice America and served as chair of NARAL's national board. She helped establish many women's organizations, including the Pennsylvania Women's Campaign Fund and Woman's Way, one of the country's first funds to finance organizations and charities that serve women and children. She lobbied for the ERA and raised funds for a number of women and pro-choice candidates. She also fought the Archdiocese of Philadelphia over teaching Girl Scouts about birth control and feminist history; fought for pay equity and equality of opportunity in employment for women in Philadelphia; and marched on Washington for women's rights. She was appointed to the Pennsylvania Commission on Women, helped create the Women's Bicentennial Center, and was named VP of the PA WPC. In addition, Ballard traveled to Nairobi to support women in emerging countries. A horticulturalist and environmentalist, she closed a thriving horticultural business in 1964 to head the Pennsylvania Horticultural Society, which, under her leadership, built the Philadelphia Flower Show into a world-class event, according to the *Lancaster Intelligence Journal*. She was a Fairmount Park Commissioner, helped found the Fairmount Park Historic Preservation Trust, and spearheaded efforts to save and restore some of Philadelphia's greatest landmarks. She was honored by Women's eNews as one of 21 Leaders for the 21st Century. (ABS)

Bambara, Toni Cade (1939 – 1995) (also known as Miltona Mirkin Cade) A prolific writer and documentary filmmaker, Bambara fought all her life for the rights of women, children, minorities and the homeless. Particularly concerned with the rights of African American women, Bambara was a founding force in the development of black women's literature, beginning with the publication of *The Black Woman: An Anthology*, which she edited and to which she contributed (New American Library, 1970). Of her numerous books, her best known is a collection of her short stories, *Gorilla, My Love* (1972). She also served as editor of *Women Writers of the Contemporary South* (University Press of Mississippi, 1984), and of *Black Women Writers at Work* (Continuum, 1983). In 1973, Bambara traveled to Cuba, and in 1975 she visited Vietnam. In both places, Bambara met with women and women's groups dedicated to improving the position of women, including the Federation of Cuban Women and the Women's Union (Vietnam). Bambara moved from NYC to Atlanta in 1974, where she helped found the Southern Collective of African-American Writers. Bambara, who had one child, earned a B.A. from Queens College in 1959. In the 1960s, Bambara worked as a family and youth caseworker for the New York Department of Welfare, and in 1965 earned her M.A. from City College of New York, where she taught. In the last decade of her life, Bambara collaborated with others on several television documentaries.

Banner, Lois W. (1939 –) was a founder of the field of women's history and of the Berkshire Conference of Women Historians' national convention, held in 1972 at Douglass College, Rutgers. A Ph.D. and an academic for over 40 years, Banner was the first woman president of the American Studies Association, and has written many books on the history of women, including *Women in Modern America* (1974); *Elizabeth Cady Stanton: A Radical for Women's Rights* (1980); *In Full Flower: Aging Women, Power and Sexuality* (1992); and *Intertwined Lives: Margaret Mead, Ruth Benedict and Their Circle* (2003). She has two children. See Banner's autobiographical book, *Finding Fran* (Columbia University, 1998). (ABS)

Barchilon, Helen – See Redman, Helen Barchilon

Bargowski, Dolores (1942 –) As a student at Wayne State University, Monteith College, in 1967, Bargowski attended a Students for a Democratic Society meeting where she met Barbara Burris, who shared her belief that women needed to organize for women's rights. Bargowski started a student-led, accredited seminar through Monteith College called Society in Women, which lasted one academic year (fall 1967 – spring 1968). This was the beginning of a group that became Detroit Women's Liberation. The seminar was used as an educational tool and the basis for political action. Bargowski and the seminar participants started the first college chapter of NOW; filed complaints to the EEOC regarding jobs for women; protested discriminatory newspaper ads; organized the first women's teach-in at Wayne State University; and participated in the 1968 Miss America Pageant protest in Atlantic City. After moving to New York City, Bargowski became involved with Women Make Movies (1969 – 1970); The Feminists (1970); and Radicalesbians (1970). As a member of The Feminists, she distributed an analysis of women's oppression and other feminist writings. At NOW's Second Congress to Unite Women (1970), she was part of the group that brought forth the issue of class in the women's movement. She wrote a pamphlet: "Notes Toward a Women's Analysis of Class" (1971). Bargowski moved to Washington, D.C., in 1971 to be part of developing a Lesbian-Feminist Collective community. She wrote for *Dykes for an American Revolution* (1971) and for the *The Furies* newspaper (summer 1972 – 1973) and was a founder of *Quest, A Quarterly Journal of Feminist Analysis* (1973). (ABS)

Barkman, Donna (1934 –) In 1969, Barkman and other mothers of students at the Woodward School in Brooklyn, NY, formed a sex roles committee that met for several years. Barkman was also a member of a CR group that became affiliated with radio station WBAI. From 1972 – 1974, Barkman produced a children's program for the station, "Taking Turns," that featured the reading of books that emphasized strong, active girls. She also conceptualized and produced two recordings for Caedmon Records, Hurray for Captain Jane and Turning Points, that were stories about decisive girls and biographies of accomplished women. In Wisconsin, Barkman was a founding member of Wisconsin Women Library Workers (1975), and worked with them until 1981 on feminist activities such as film festivals and Take Back the Night marches. Throughout the 1980s and 1990s, Barkman was an escort and coordinator of escorts at a Westchester County, NY, women's health facility that was picketed by religious fanatics; volunteered at the Bedford (NY) Correctional Institution, a women's prison, where she worked in the children's visiting room and tutored college students. In addition, Barkman was a phone counselor for a battered women's shelter in Providence, RI. With a colleague, she created and taught a course called Teachers as Women, focusing on women's acculturation and how women often pass sexist values to students. This class was taught at the Bank St. College of Education and many teacher centers around NY State. Barkman, who has three children, is chair of a national children's book award sponsored by the Jane Addams Peace Association that honors books on peace, justice and equality of genders and races. She holds a B.S. from Wisconsin State College, a graduate degree from the University of Wisconsin, and an M.A. from Columbia University. (ABS)

Barnwell, Corinne (1936 –) (also known as Corinne Smith) Active in the civil rights and anti-poverty movements in Louisiana, Barnwell was also an early fighter for the ERA, and one of the early Head Start teachers in New Orleans (1965 – 1966). She also taught English as a Second Language to fourth graders (1966 – 1967). In that role, she saw the hunger and domestic violence that affected very low-income Hispanic mothers and was greatly disturbed by the lack of physical and mental health care for women —black, white or Latina. Consequently, she became a community social worker and spent 25 years working in political and governmental positions. She was Human Rights Coordinator on the staff of the first African American mayor of New Orleans (Dutch Morial) from 1979 – 1986. Barnwell entered the anti-war movement in 1965 and kept up firm opposition to the Vietnam War until 1973. Also in the 1960s, she organized discussion groups on abortion rights in New Orleans. Later, when support in the community increased, she helped found the chapter now called Planned Parenthood of Louisiana and the Mississippi Delta, and worked to reform and expand sex education in the public schools. She served on the PPLA board for 12 years. In 1990, she originated a state-wide teen-pregnancy-prevention information directory at the State Department of Public Health, and helped research and write "Louisiana Programs for Violence Prevention and Victim Support: A Resource Directory" (1994). Barnwell has a B.A from Radcliffe College (1958); an M.A. from the University of California, Berkeley (1963); and a Master of Social Work from Tulane University (1975). Now retired, Barnwell has two stepdaughters (one deceased) and a son. Archives: Newcomb Women's Center, New Orleans, LA. (ABS)

Barovich, Margaret D. (1939 –) was a founder of Florida NOW, as well as first president of South Palm Beach County NOW (1972 – 1973). She was also president (state coordinator) of FL NOW from 1974 – 1976, and was

elected director from the Southeast Region to the national board. Barovich was a member of NOW's national board from 1994 – 1996. Archives: For FL NOW, University of Florida, Gainesville, FL. For SPBC NOW, Florida Atlantic University, Boca Raton, FL. (ABS)

Barrington, Judith Mary (1944 –) Born in England, Barrington was part of a feminist writers group in London (1971). She helped make a "pirate edition" of Robin Morgan's book *Monster* (which Morgan applauds) after Ted Hughes allegedly prevented U.K. publication because it contained a poem blaming him for the death of Sylvia Plath and his next wife, who was also a suicide. Barrington was also involved in an underground activist group that created campaigns against sexist advertising by the U.K. government prior to a national referendum on joining the European Common Market. In 1977, Barrington says she was fired from the Portland State University women's studies department for being a lesbian. At a subsequent National Women's Studies Conference, she joined with other fired lesbians to form a support group that documented their experiences, and published a story in *Off Our Backs*. In the late 1970s, Barrington was the only paid reporter for *Rag Times*, a women's newspaper in Portland. She was also part of a group started by Melanie Kaye Kantrovitz that protested the Rose Festival and its beauty pageant, and helped produce an alternative spoof newspaper about the festival. In 1983, Barrington and her partner, Ruth Gundle, founded The Flight of the Mind Writing Workshops for Women; in 1990 they started Soapstone Inc., a women writers retreat. Beginning in the early 1980s, she published columns in *The Oregonian* newspaper on feminist and lesbian/gay issues. She is the author of three collections of feminist poetry, including *Horses and the Human Soul* (Story Line Press, 2004). Her memoir, *Lifesaving: A Memoir*, won the Lambda Book Award in 2000 and was a finalist for the PEN/Martha Albrand Award for the Art of the Memoir. Barrington has edited a collection of women writers on sexuality, *An Intimate Wilderness*. She holds a B.A. from Marylhurst College and an M.A. from Goddard College. (ABS)

Barrons, Geraldine ("Gerry") Phyllis (1940 –) In 1971, Barrons' life changed when she attended her first NOW meeting. In 1973 seven feminists created New Options Inc. as a consulting firm specializing in affirmative action. Barrons and three of the feminists started New Options Personnel Inc. to provide job counseling, recruitment and placement of women and minorities. New Options received federally funded grants from Detroit for five years (1975 – 1980) as the sole source for placing and counseling women in non-traditional jobs. Barrons was founding president, National Association of Women Business Owners, MI Chapter (1980); was on the founding board, Sojourner Foundation for Women and Girls; was vice chairperson, Small Business Advocacy Council, Women in Business Committee, MI (1980 – 1982); and was on the founding board of Majority Business Initiative, a coalition of women's organizations to ensure women's inclusion in economic development as contractors, decision makers and employees. From 1979–1982 she was chair, women's business development, State Conference on Small Business; and from 1973–1983 was a local and state officer, NOW. She has received numerous awards, including Women of Achievement and Courage, from the Michigan Women's Foundation; Feminist of the Year – Loretta Moore Award, given by the Detroit Chapter of NOW (1999); and the Women Helping Women award from the Sojourner Foundation (1995). Barrons received a B.A. from Ohio Dominican University, and studied theater at The American Musical and Dramatic Theatre in NYC. She has two children. (ABS)

Barrow, Willie Taplin (1924 –) Honored by the VFA in 2004, Barrow began a lifetime of activism in the civil rights movement in the mid 1950s. She worked with Martin Luther King Jr. as an organizer and participated in marches (including the 1965 march on Selma) and sit-ins. In the mid 1960s, she was one of three founding members of Operation Breadbasket. Barrow was later an organizer of the first statewide coalition against hunger, successfully boycotted various corporations, marched for peace and justice, and supported passage of the ERA. She worked on political campaigns that supported women's rights and racial justice in the U.S., and led delegations supporting women's rights to countries around the world. A clinic at Doctors Hospital in Chicago that treats patients with limited resources was named The Rev. Willie Barrow Wellness Center in her honor. In addition, she has a street in Chicago bearing her name, and the Barrow Hall of Justice Museum and Library is being built in her honor. Barrow is actively involved in AIDS research and gay and lesbian rights, and serves on the board of the Rainbow/ PUSH Coalition. (ABS)

Barry, Kathleen (1941 –) is an internationally known feminist, activist and sociologist. Although Barry "grew up poor working class with no plans for college," she eventually earned a Ph.D. from the University of California, Berkeley. She is the author of *Female Sexual Slavery* (1979), which launched an international movement against sexual exploitation of women and trafficking in women. Barry also collaborated with UNESCO (Paris) in developing an international law, The Convention Against Sexual Exploitation. In 1995, her book *The Prostitution of Sexuality: Global Exploitation of Women*, was published. And in 1996, following her work with women in Vietnam, her book *Vietnam's Women in Transition* was published. She is also the author of *Susan B. Anthony: A Biography of a Singular Feminist* (1988). With a Fulbright Award, Barry began a project in Ireland (1995) on Irish women's storytelling. She was also active in early civil rights movements in Syracuse and Detroit (1960–1967); did volunteer teaching in a Mexican-American commu-

nity in Texas (1963–1965); and was a women's advocate, Sacramento State University (1972). In addition, she started a community college women's studies program in Detroit (1969–1970); did abortion counseling and anti-rape work (1968–1972); and in 1970 participated in issuing *Fourth World Manifesto* against leftist males' imperialist assault on feminism. Barry was also part of CR groups, guerrilla theater, street actions and abortion demonstrations in Detroit. (ABS)

Barstow, Anne Llewellyn (1929 –) (also known as Anne Driver) As a faculty member at SUNY in Old Westbury, NY, Barstow was part of the core group that developed the first women's studies program there, in 1971–1972. She contributed the course Women and Religion, an exploration of how Christianity and Judaism have both repressed and empowered women. Later she added roles that women play in Buddhism, Islam, Hinduism and possession religions. She also taught the course at New York University. Because there were no materials to teach the course in 1971, Barstow joined The Feminist Scholars in Religion, a group of academics in New York City who asked feminist questions of religious history and shared Xeroxed manuscripts until a series of books emerged from the group. Barstow also used the pioneering work being done in the women's caucus of the American Academy of Religion and was active in the Coordinating Committee of Women Historians. She was especially drawn to issues of violence against women, which led to her study of persecution of women for witchcraft: *Witchcraze: A New History of the European Witch Hunts* (Harper, 1984), and to editing a book on contemporary violence: *War's Dirty Secret: Rape, Prostitution and Other Crimes Against Women* (Pilgrim Press, 2000). Barstow also published a feminist study of Joan of Arc: *Joan of Arc: Heretic, Mystic, Shaman* (Mellon, 1986). Barstow, who is now retired, has three children. (ABS)

Bart, Pauline (1930 –) Author of *Portnoy's Mother's Complaint*, the first pro-mother dissertation in the women's movement, Bart taught the first undergraduate course on Women in Society in the University of California system (1968). She also taught women's studies and behavioral science for medical students at the University of Illinois, Chicago (1969), and wrote 24 articles primarily about women and health, and women and violence. Bart published *The Student Sociologist's Handbook*, which included all the feminist journals; and with Diana Scully published an analysis of what gynecology textbooks said about women, *A Funny Thing Happened on the Way to the Orifice*. After interviewing members of Jane, the pre-Roe abortion collective, she wrote the article "Seizing the Means of Reproduction." She later published (with Patricia H. O'Brien) the feminist book *Stopping Rape: Successful Survival Strategies* (1985). Bart also helped form the section on sex roles of the American Sociological Association and was its first president, and was a founding mother for Sociologists for Women in Society. Bart, who has a Ph.D. from UCLA, has two children.   (ABS)

Bartczak, Andi Weiss (1948 –) was an officer in three chapters of NOW: Bucks County, PA; New Haven, CT; and Middlesex County, NJ. In 1972, she celebrated Women's Equality Day with other Bucks County NOW members by driving to Washington's Crossing Park. She also organized a rally for the ERA held on the New Haven Green. Bartczak, who has a B.S. from Syracuse University and a Ph.D. from the University of North Carolina at Chapel Hill, works in the environmental movement.   (ABS)

Bartczak, Sue Weiss (1925 – 1995) became active in reproductive rights in Nassau County, NY, in the mid 1960s after a friend nearly died following an illegal abortion. She remained active for the rest of her life. At rallies for abortion rights, Bartczak was able to get the police "to favor her side," says her daughter, Andi Bartczak. She volunteered at Planned Parenthood and escorted patients into abortion clinics for years. Also active in Democratic politics, Bartczak was one of the women whose persistence finally persuaded Governor Mario Cuomo to change his position and support reproductive rights.

Barth, Ilene (1944 –) While an editor of *Columbia College Today,* the Columbia alumni magazine, Barth joined Columbia Women's Liberation (1969) and was a member of a CR group that grew out of CWL. In 1969–1971, a lawsuit was underway demanding that the economic and academic status of women at Columbia be brought into line with the men. After 18 months working at *Columbia College Today,* Barth learned that the top editor was leaving and that he had recommended that she, as the number-two editorial person, be given the top spot. At a meeting with the college dean, Carl Hovde, and several members of the magazine's advisory board (all men), the comment was made that it "has always been a condition that the [top] editor be a graduate of Columbia College." Barth replied that since all the graduates were men, that qualification, by definition, excluded women. She added, "I think the EEOC would be very interested in that." Barth was offered the job, but declined to accept it. Later, when Barth was an editor at *Newsday* (1976), she, along with the other top woman editor, was involved in an equal pay lawsuit against the paper. She now has a small book publishing company, Red Rock Press, which publishes gift books and children's books. Barth, who has three children, attended Vassar College and holds an A.B. degree from the University of Sussex, England.   (ABS)

Barth, Ramona Sawyer (1911 - 2002) The daughter of one minister and the wife of another, Barth was a fiery feminist who once burned Bible quotes that she considered derogatory to women on church pulpits on Mother's Day. She introduced women's studies at the Cambridge (MA) Center for Adult Education and Harvard Extension (1968 – 1970), and in 1970 led a boat excursion to Nantucket Island in honor of the 50th anniversary of woman's suffrage. In 1979, she launched a one-woman drama, "Men, Women and Margaret Fuller," founding the Margaret Fuller Women's History Society, and also lectured in the U.S. and Mexico on women's drama. Barth was the author of *Fiery Angel—The Story of Florence Nightingale* (Glade House, 1945) as well as a monograph on Edna St. Vincent Millay. The founder of the Maine chapter of NOW, Barth also created She Shirts, a Maine T-shirt company highlighting noteworthy women. Barth, who had five children, held a B.S. from Tufts and a Bachelor of Divinity from Meadville.

Bartky, Sandra Lee (1935 –) A professor of philosophy at the University of Illinois at Chicago, Bartky was a member of Chicago Women's Liberation Union and the Circle Women's Union, a local group at the University of Illinois Chicago. Bartky was one of the organizers and initiators of the UIC women's studies program, and developed and taught many women's studies courses. She was also an organizer of the Society for Women in Philosophy, U.S. chapters, as well as in Scandinavia. Western Europe, Canada, Mexico, and Argentina. She published *Femininity and Domination: Studies in the Phenomenology of Oppression* (Routeledge, 1990), and also *Sympathy and Solidarity* (Roman and Little, 2002); and edited, with Nancy Fraser, *Revaluing French Feminism* (Indiana University Press, 1992). Bartky has been active in civil rights and gay rights, as well as peace and environmental issues. She holds a B.A., M.A. and Ph.D. from the University of Illinois, Urbana. Archives: University of Illinois, Chicago, Il. (ABS)

Bartl, Joan (1940 –) was an original member of the Princeton (NJ) NOW group Women on Words and Images. The group's research into sexism and sex role stereotyping for both girls and boys in children's textbooks was published in the early 1970s in *Dick and Jane as Victims: Sex Stereotyping in Children's Readers.* They produced a powerful slide show that brought to life "the rampant sexism that we all grew up with," says Bartl. Other works include "Channeling Children," a study of the sex roles reflected in popular television programs; and research and a slide presentation of "Career Education Materials." Bartl was involved in testimony supporting the passage of Title IX regulations and in bringing educators to the table in recognizing the dangers of restricting children to narrow roles. In addition, Bartl worked through the Princeton YWCA to reform abortion laws and was involved in the desegregation of The Nassau Inn, which had been an all-male public restaurant in Princeton. Bartl was also the first woman in sales in the radio broadcast industry in NJ. She produced two award-winning, all-day, all-female radio shows commemorating woman's suffrage, in 1972 and 1973. Archives: The Women on Words and Images papers are archived at the Margery Somers Foster Library, Rutgers University, New Brunswick, NJ.   (ABS)

Batchelder, Eleanor Olds (1940 –) joined a New York Radical Feminist CR group in 1973, and in 1974 worked on the NYRF Motherhood Conference. Batchelder was also active with the NYRF speakers bureau, and worked on the *Heresies* issue *Women Working Together*, co-writing (with Linda Marks) an article on women's collectives. Batchelder, who came out as a lesbian in 1974, co-founded (with Fabi Romero Oak and Karyn London) the bookstore Womanbooks in New York City in 1975. There, she compiled and published a bibliography on women playwrights, as well as a booklist of in-print lesbian books. Batchelder, who has three children, holds a B.A. from Hunter College and a Ph.D. from the Graduate Center of the City University of New York.   (ABS)

Batchelor, Ruth (1934 – 1992) A songwriter and feminist singer from California, Batchelor started her career writing songs for Elvis Presley. In the 1970s, she decided to write nothing but songs for women, and with that in mind founded a record company, Femme Records. Among the 10 songs on the first recording put out by the company are "Barefoot and Pregnant" and "The Princess," a song about women's economic dependency. She also wrote a march for NOW, believing that a march turns a mob into a parade. As a member of NOW, she made a donation to the organization for each record she sold via mail order. Batchelor had two children.

Batlay, Jenny (1941 –) In the late 1960s, Batlay left France and came to the U.S. to teach French literature. While at Columbia University doing graduate work (1970 – 1976), Batlay compiled a reading list of French woman authors that traced the roots of feminism to a medieval French poetess named Christine de Pisan. Batlay says that the seeds of feminism were already blooming in the Dark Ages in the form of that poetess, who succeeded in achieving financial, emotional and professional independence from men. Batlay taught French at Princeton University in the 1970s, a time when women intellectuals were rarely accepted. Males from the old/all-boy network "found it difficult, even detestable," she states, "to share their turf with 'inferior' females and resented any change in their habits. My list of feminist French authors was not exactly a hit with the male-dominated atmosphere at Princeton." Nevertheless, it was kept in the library and "had a striking impact on those who saw and used it." Batlay's feminist articles include "If Isaac Wasn't Sacrificed, His Sister Probably Was," "Why Do Women Read Sade?: Cultural Anarchy, Intellectual Fallacy, Stylistic Boredom and Delusional Liberty," "Sisters, Concubines, and Mistresses: The Harem in Dick's Fantasies," and "Derrida's Invaginated Text: Mad Libido, Feminicide and the Rape of the Page." In her dissertation on Rousseau's *Reveries*, Batlay discussed Rousseau's femininity as a stylist and thinker, and in the middle 1970s she was one of the founders of the now full-fledged North American Association for the Study of J.J. Rousseau. Batlay has one child.   (ABS)

Baum, Terry (1946 –) Playwright, actress, director and teacher, Baum has been writing plays since 1972 on gay rights and lesbian issues. In 1972, while in graduate school at the University of California, Santa Barbara, Baum founded the Isla Vista Community Theater, which had a feminist theater as one of its components. In 1974, she founded Lilith, a San Francisco women's theater collective. In 1980, in collaboration with Carolyn Myers and Alice Thompson, she created "Dos Lesbos, a Play By, For and About Perverts," which, she says, "was the first lesbian play that many people saw, and inspired one audience member, Kate McDermott, to create *Places, Please,* the first anthology of plays by lesbians" (1985). In 1983, Baum premiered "Immediate Family" at the First Women's Theater Festival in Santa Cruz (CA). Her work "One Fool or How I Learned to Stop Worrying and Love the Dutch" was published in *Tough Acts to Follow* (1990), an anthology of gay and lesbian one-act plays; and her two-person play, "Two Fools," was published in *Intimate Acts,* an anthology of lesbian plays (1997). Baum, who in 1970 worked as Bella Abzug's personal aide in her first campaign for Congress, is the founder of the Pat Bond Memorial Old Dyke Award, given annually to lesbians over 60 in the San Francisco Bay Area. In 2003, she self-published *This Is My Peace Sign,* a book of photos from anti-war demonstrations in San Francisco.   (ABS)

Baxandall, Rosalyn Fraad (1939 –) As a young mother with a son in need of day care, Baxandall helped start Liberation Nursery, the first feminist day care center in New York City, in 1968. After getting the city to support it, she was named by the mayor to the city's task force on day care in 1969. With an M.S.W. from Columbia University (1963), Baxandall (who also received an A.B.D. in sociology from Columbia) taught women's studies at Columbia Strike School (1968) and Queens College (1969), and helped found women's studies courses at SUNY, Old Westbury, NY (1971). She was part of the Panther Support demonstration for jailed women (1969) and participated in abortion demonstrations in NYC and Washington. A conference organizer for Defend the Right to Learn Women's Studies (1969), she also worked with New York Radical Women, Redstockings, WITCH, No More Nice Girls and CARASA. Baxandall is the author of *Words on Fire, the Life and Writing of Elizabeth Gurley Flynn* (1987); co-editor of *America's Working Women, An Anthology of Women's Work, 1620 – 1970* (1976); and co-author of *The Rise and Fall of the Suburban Dream, 1945 – 2000* (2000). She is co-editor of *Dear Sisters: Dispatches from the Women's Liberation Movement,* and the author of numerous articles and book reviews on day care, working women, sexuality and reproductive rights, and class, race and gender in suburbia. She is a professor of American studies at SUNY at Old Westbury and chair of the American studies department, and is on the board of Virago Press and New Feminist Library. Archives: Tamiment Archives, New York University, New York, NY.   (ABS)

Baxter, Annette Kar (1926 – 1983) was a professor of history at Barnard College (1952–1983) and chair of its American studies program from 1967–1983. An early proponent of women's studies, she created one of the earliest college courses in women's history (1966). She also served as co-editor of three large Arno Press reprint series that made formerly out-of-print books on women's history newly available. A staunch supporter of women's colleges, Baxter believed that they not only fostered intellectual confidence in young women but also served educational pluralism. As trustee of Kirkland College from 1968 until its absorption by Hamilton College in 1978, Baxter played a significant role in creating and nurturing both a curriculum and positive educational experience for women. In addition, she contributed six significant essays on important figures in women's education to *Notable American Women* and to the *Dictionary of American Biography*. Baxter died in a fire at her summer home on Fire Island, NY. Her husband, James E. Baxter died with her, but their two children survived. Archives: The Sophia Smith Collection, Smith College, Northampton, MA.

Bayh, Birch (1928 –) A member of the U.S. Senate from 1963–1981 (D-IN), Bayh was the primary author of Title IX of the Education Amendments of 1972, which outlawed sex discrimination in education, and was chief sponsor of the ERA, which passed both houses of Congress but failed to be ratified by two-thirds of the states. Bayh also played a major role in the drafting and passage of the 1964 Civil Rights Act, which through its Title VII prohibited sex discrimination in employment. When he introduced the measure that became Title IX to the Senate, Bayh said, "One of the great failings of the American educational system is the continuation of corrosive and unjustified discrimination against women. It is clear to me that sex discrimination reaches into all facets of education—admission, scholarship programs, faculty hiring and promotion, professional staffing and pay scales. The only antidote is a comprehensive amendment such as the one now before the Senate." Bayh's work benefited minorities as well as women. As ranking member of the Senate Judiciary Committee, he led the successful battle to defeat the Nixon nominations of Judges Haynesworth and Carswell to the U.S. Supreme Court. As a result, the Leadership Conference on Civil Rights bestowed its highest award on Bayh in 1972 for his "unyielding dedication to human equality and civil freedom." In addition, Bayh was the author of the 25th Amendment to the U.S. Constitution, which established the rules for presidential succession, and wrote the 26th Amendment, which gave 18-year-olds the right to vote. Bayh, who has two children, holds a B.S. from Purdue University and a J.D. from Indiana University School of Law. (ABS)

Bazin, Nancy Topping (1934 –) created the women's studies program at Rutgers College, which was the all-male college at Rutgers University until 1971. In 1971, under threat of lawsuits, the college began to admit a few women. Bazin taught her first gender-oriented course to 18 men and three women. Then she created a course on women writers that regularly enrolled 60 students. Bazin also taught the first graduate course in women writers at Rutgers University, and organized the first series of lectures and performances by women at Rutgers College. In 1973, she obtained Faculty Senate approval for a Women's Studies Certificate. In 1974, Bazin became the first director of the university-wide Women's Research Institute. She did not get tenure, despite her book *Virginia Woolf and the Androgynous Vision* (1973), which was among the first feminist analyses of literary works. In 1978, after one year as coordinator of women's studies at the University of Pittsburgh, Bazin was hired by Old Dominion University to create the first women's studies program in VA. She served as chair of the English dept. from 1985–1989. Co-editor of *Conversations with Nadine Gordimer* (1991), Bazin wrote more than 40 articles focusing primarily on curriculum transformation, women's studies and women writers. She received a state teaching award in 1994 and a college research award and the designation of Eminent Scholar in 1996. When Bazin retired in 2000, the Nancy Topping Bazin Graduate Scholarship in Women's Studies was created at Old Dominion University. Bazin is an artist who exhibits her drawings and paintings in galleries and juried shows. (ABS)

Beal, Frances M. (1940 –) Author of the widely reprinted black women's manifesto, "Double Jeopardy: To Be Black and Female," first published in 1969, Beal was a co-founder, with other women involved with SNCC, of the Third World Women's Alliance (1968). Self described as "the radical tradition of the anti-racist movement," the TWWA was adamant in its insistence that black militant men were being "white" and middle class when they enforced middle-class gender roles and expected black women to be "breeders" for the revolution. Beal served as editor of TWWA's newsletter "Triple Jeopardy." She was also a member of the National Council for Negro Women, where she edited *The Black Woman's Voice*. Beal was honored as a "peace and justice activist and writer who has focused her formidable energies on black women and African American politics over the past three decades" by the Women of Color Resource Center. Beal retired from her position as research associate with the American Civil Liberties Union, Northern California Racial Justice Department in 2006. She has been national secretary of the Black Radical Congress and a columnist for the *San Francisco Bay View* newspaper. Beale was born in Binghamton, NY, began college at the University of Wisconsin, Madison, and completed her degree at the Sorbonne in Paris. She has two children. (ABS)

Beare, Muriel Nikki (1928 –) The state of Florida has been the beneficiary of Beare's lifetime of work in changing attitudes, informing the public, safeguarding those in danger, electing women to office, and helping the disabled. She began as a reporter for the *Miami News* and then started the *Women's Almanac* 1975 – 1985. She launched "Women's Powerline" on WKAT Radio with co-hosts Elaine Gordon and Elaine Bloom, both of whom went on to become legislators. Beare was also a founding member of the NWPC, FL WPC, VFA and FL NOW. She served on NOW's national board from 1969 – 1972 and the FL WPC board for over 10 years. She helped eliminate the sex-segregated help-wanted ads at the *Miami Herald*, after being "stonewalled," which led to her induction into the Florida Women's Hall of Fame (1994). She also worked for the Equal Credit Opportunity Act at the federal level and formed Florida Feminist Credit Union, serving as its first president. Working with the NWPC, she helped elect the first black woman, Gwendolyn Sawyer Cherry, to the FL House of Representatives (1970). She lobbied the FL Legislature on women's issues, representing the AAUW, FL WPC, the Florida Nurse Anesthetists Association, Dade Seniors Association and several different women's groups. She never stopped lobbying for the ERA. She also helped draft and lobby for the establishment of the Florida Commission on the Status of Women and Florida Women's Hall of Fame. In addition, Beare helped found Safe Space in Miami; helped reconstitute Refuge House in Tallahassee; and worked to get FL universities to admit women to their law and medical schools. Working with the Metro Dade County Commission on Women, Beare also helped establish the first Metropolitan Dade County Child Care Center. She helped found the Women's Art Caucus in Miami, and in 1973 worked with the local NOW chapter to hold the first Feminist Film Festival and developed a series of discussion groups around the issue of lesbians. Beare attended the United Nations Women's World Congress in Nairobi, Kenya (1985), and in Beijing, China (1990). She owns a PR firm and an antiquarian bookstore, The Historical Bookshelf, and also works with her husband, Lord Richard Beare, raising organic fruit. She has one child.   (ABS)

Beasley, Elizabeth ("Betsy") McCoy (1941 –) became a member of Kansas City NOW in 1969, of the Kansas City WPC in 1973, and of Kansas City Planned Parenthood in 1975. From 1972 – 1973, she lobbied for the ERA in the Missouri Senate. ("In 1971, the ERA passed the Missouri House by an overwhelming vote because the Congressmen were confident that the bill would not pass the Senate. That proved to be true.") Beasley also helped establish a rape crisis center at St. Luke's Hospital (1973), serving on the Mid-America Regional Council Advisory Committee representing KC NOW. In addition, she lobbied for childcare legislation and appeared on cable TV discussing legislation that would authorize free day care for families below the poverty line. She began working for legal access to abortions for all women in 1972, and later served on the board of KC Planned Parenthood. She is a board officer of the Endowment and Education Fund of

the Greater Kansas City WPC, and an administrative associate at the University of Missouri-Kansas City. Beasley, who has two children, earned her B.A. in 1964.   (ABS)

Beck, Audrey Phillips (1930 – 1983) A member of the Connecticut state board of directors of the LWV (1962 – 1965), Beck was elected to the Connecticut House of Representatives in 1969. During her three terms in the House and two terms in the Senate, she sponsored legislation that created the Permanent Commission on the Status of Women, worked for the reform of state laws discriminating against women, and inspired other women to run for office. In the House, she rose to prominence as assistant minority leader from 1973 – 1975, and as the only female chair of a legislative finance committee. She also worked at the national level for the Democratic Party, was a delegate to the Democratic National Convention, and chair of the Democratic state platform committee in 1978. Following her three terms in the House, Beck spent one year as a professor of practical politics at Rutgers University, returning to Connecticut to run successfully for the state Senate. In that body, she served on the state education committee and as assistant majority leader. Although born in Brooklyn, Beck grew up in Norwalk, CT. In 1961, she became a University of Connecticut faculty member and was a member of the Mansfield Board of Finance. Beck, who had two children, earned both a B.A. and M.A. from the University of Connecticut, which she entered in 1948. Archives: Archives and Special Collections, Thomas J. Dodd Research Center, University of Connecticut, Storrs, CT.

Beck, Evelyn Torton (1933 –) has worked to transform the academic world and its curriculum and to foster the rights of women. In 1974, she was a founder of women's studies, Jewish women's studies and lesbian studies at the University of Wisconsin, Madison, where she taught until 1984. In addition, she was a founding member of the feminist organization Women in German (1974), which helped bring women and issues of gender into the German curriculum, and was founding editor of the organization's newsletter. In 1977, Beck was a founding member of the NWSA, and a founding member of its lesbian and Jewish caucuses. In 1984, she became chair of women's studies at the University of Maryland and brought a major, minor, graduate certificate and finally a Ph.D. in women's studies to the university. In 1982, Beck published *Nice Jewish Girls: A Lesbian Anthology* (Persephone Press) and in 1979 was co-editor, with Julia Sherman, of *The Prism of Sex: Essays in the Sociology of Knowledge* (University of Wisconsin Press). Born in Vienna, Austria, Beck brought feminist perspectives to Europe, giving a series of lectures in Hamburg. She has lectured widely on the issues of anti-semitism and gender, especially on the anti-semitism and sexism of the "Jewish American Princess" epithet, which she conceptualized as a form of violence against Jewish women. Beck, who has two children, holds a Ph.D. in Comparative Literature (1969) and a Ph.D. in Clinical Psychology (2004). Archives: The Lesbian Herstory Archives, Brooklyn, NY, and Jewish Women's History Archives, Brandeis University, Boston, MA. (ABS)

Becker, Carolyn – See Berry, Carolyn

Becker, Linnea – See Johnson, Linnea

Beckman, Linda Hunt (1942 –) (also known as Linda Hunt) became active in Bread and Roses in Cambridge, MA, in the late 1960s. She was in a women's history study group with Linda Gordon, Priscilla Long Irons and Lillian Robinson. Later, she was involved in the takeover of a Harvard building that became the university's women's center. Beckman taught part time at the University of Massachusetts-Boston, where she helped organize the women's studies program and was elected to its first governing board. She also developed and taught one of the first women's studies courses there, Women and Men in Nineteenth-Century Literature. In the early 1970s she was involved in the Marxist Feminist Conference. Beckman became the director of women's studies and assistant professor of English at Ohio University in 1983, and ran the women's studies program there for 10 years. A member of National Women's Studies Association, she published book reviews in *Women's Review of Books*. In 1988, Garland Press published *A Woman's Portion: Ideology, Culture and the British Female Novel Tradition* (under Linda C. Hunt). In 2000, Ohio University Press published *Amy Levy: Her Life and Letters,* a biography of an Anglo-Jewish fiction writer and poet, a feminist active in the 1880s. Beckman was involved in many civil rights activities, including the March on Washington and picketing Woolworth's, and was part of anti-Vietnam War demonstrations. Beckman holds a B.A. from Hunter College and an M.A. and Ph.D. from the University of California, Berkeley, and has one child. (ABS)

Bedoz, Ellen – See Shumsky, Ellen

Beebe, N. Lorraine (1910 –) Beebe's feminism was ignited when as a high-school counselor in Michigan (1963 – 1966), she witnessed girls with the highest grades being channeled into stereotypical female careers. From 1966 – 1970, Beebe served in the Michigan State Senate—at that time, the only woman there. In 1967 – 1968, she introduced a bill to create the Michigan Women's Commission, the first statutory women's commission in the U.S. Prior to this, the Governors' Commissions on the Status of Women were by executive order. From 1967 – 1970, Beebe worked with the Michigan Correctional Department to build the first modern women's correctional facility in Michigan, which offered treatment and opportunities equal to what male inmates received. In 1968, she sponsored legislation on sex education in public schools

mandating alternative education for pregnant girls. Beebe founded the Women Against Crime Committee in 1968 – 1969, and in 1969 – 1970 chaired the Michigan State Senate's committee on abortion law reform. In 1970 – 1972, she co-chaired the MI abortion referendum committee. Beebe was a founding member and co-chairwoman of the Michigan WPC (1971 – 1974); chair, Michigan Women's Commission (1972 – 1975); and in 1975 attended the first United Nation's International Women's Conference in Mexico City. She was elected delegate to the National Women's Conference in Houston (1977); was chair, Michigan Abortion Rights Action League (1977 – 1982); and state chair, John Anderson for President campaign (1980). In addition, Beebe was appointed to the President's committee on mental retardation by three presidents—Nixon, Reagan and Carter—serving most of the time as chair. Beebe holds a B.S. from Western Michigan University, Kalamazoo (1932) and an M.A. from Wayne State University, Detroit (1946). She has two children. (ABS)

Beers, Jinx (1933 –) was the founder of *The Lesbian News*, a monthly Southern California newspaper published since the mid 1970s. She served as managing editor for 14 years. She also joined NOW and participated in its lesbian rights task force. She was part of the Briggs Initiative in California and Take Back the Night marches, and served as chair of the last Lesbian Conference sponsored by the task force. Earlier, Beers taught a course titled The Lesbian Experience for three semesters at the UCLA Experimental College. Out of that class Beers helped form The Lesbian Activists group, whose intent was to be available to demonstrate peacefully at a moment's notice whenever action was appropriate. Beers holds a B.A. from the University of California, Los Angeles. (ABS)

Behrens, Martha Clayton Skeeters
– See Skeeters, Martha Clayton

Beiner, Syd (1933 –) A retired teacher of English literature and film history, Beiner was a reporter and book and film critic for the early feminist newspaper, *Majority Report* (1971 – 1974). She was a member of the Radical Feminists (1969 – 1972), joined NY NOW in 1971 "in response to the lesbian purge," and was active in that chapter through 1980. Beiner was editor of the NY NOW newsletter (1972 – 1975) and chair of NY NOW's board in 1975. Beiner is a member of the NOW-East End chapter and the East End Gay Organization. She received a B.B.A from Bernard Baruch College (1955), a B.A. from Brooklyn College (1964) and an M.A. from Hunter College (1970). She resides in Sag Harbor, Manhattan and Delray Beach, FL. (ABS)

Belcher, Jennifer Marion (1944 –) (also known as Jennifer Marion) As a member of the governor's staff in Washington State in 1973, Belcher was part of the

Governor's Commission on the Status of Women, and worked on several programs to increase women's pay and status, including persuading the telephone companies to list women's names separately from their husbands' names. At the same time, Belcher helped create the WA State WPC, and was a founding member of the Thurston County chapter and later state chair. As a member of the Washington State Legislature for five terms, beginning in 1982, she sponsored and passed legislation limiting strip searches of women; establishing spousal rape laws; and increasing penalties for domestic violence. She sponsored the first day care center built on the capitol campus for children of state employees, and worked to establish day-care centers in private businesses. Belcher also chaired a joint select committee of the Legislature to oversee the implementation of comparable worth pay equity. In 1992 she became the first woman to be elected Commissioner of Public Lands. Archives: Washington State Archives Department, Olympia, WA.   (ABS)

Belinoff, Deanne (1941 –) participated in forming Womanspace, the precursor of the Los Angeles Women's Building, which opened in 1973. She was a member of Grandview Gallery, one of the first U.S. women's co-operative galleries. Belinoff earned an M.F.A. from Cal State Long Beach, was awarded two NEA Fellowships, and received a California Arts Council Grant. She served as president of the Los Angeles chapter of the WCA, 1989. She has two children. Archives: National Museum of Women in the Arts, Washington, D.C.   (ABS)

Bell, Sun ("Sunny") (1949 –) Activist, musician, writer, photographer and videographer, Bell was one of the founders of Women Against Rape in Bloomington, IN. This small group helped many women, in particular one who had been raped by football team members. WAR assisted in bringing charges against those involved. Bell is an active musician and award winning songwriter of songs that cover peace, equality, lesbian and gay rights, and environmental issues. Her first CD is Songs from the Wild. She is a published photographer and was chosen to read her poetry for National Women's Month. Her videos have been shown on public television. Archives: One Institute & Archives, Los Angeles, CA.   (ABS)

Bellamy, Carol (1942 –) A lawyer in New York State, Bellamy spent several years as an associate with the law firm of Cravath, Swaine and Moore before becoming a public servant. She became active in politics and was elected to the New York State Senate in 1973, where she served until 1977. In 1978, she was elected the first woman president of the NYC Council, a position she held until 1985. She served for two years on the board of NOW Legal Defense and Education Fund. In addition, she served as a trustee for the New York City Pension System, as a member of the New York Metropolitan Transit Authority, and as first VP of the National League of Cities.

After an unsuccessful run for mayor of New York City, she held high-level executive positions at finance and investment firms for 11 years. Bellamy was named director of the Peace Corps, the first person ever to have been a Peace Corps volunteer before becoming its director. In 1995 she began 10 years as executive director of the United Nations Children's Fund. In January 2005 she became CEO of World Learning, a private, non-profit, international educational organization, and president of the School for International Training. Bellamy holds bachelor's degree from Gettysburg College and a law degree from New York University. Bellamy is a former Fellow of Government at Harvard University's Kennedy School of Government, and an honorary member of Phi Alpha Alpha, the U.S. National Honor Society for Accomplishment and Scholarship in Public Affairs and Administration.   (ABS)

Belzer, Ruth K. (1926 –) Working at the University of Chicago in the 1970s and early 1980s, Belzer put on what was probably the first women's conference there, persuading the university to provide financial support. In the 1980s, she became the executive director of a family foundation and served on the board of Chicago Women in Philanthropy. She later served on the board of what is now known as Women in Philanthropy, and eventually joined the Chicago Foundation of Women, where she remains active. Belzer served as one of the first women officers of her synagogue in the 1970s, and was a stalwart advocate for women as participants in the rituals of synagogue life. She has also worked consistently to advance reproductive rights. Belzer, who has four children, earned her B.A. from Wellesley College and her M.A. from the University of Chicago.   (ABS)

Bement, Susan – See Groves, Susan Stevens

Bender, Rogie (1935 –) With several other women, Bender researched, wrote, published, publicized and sold a booklet, *Dick and Jane as Victims: Sex Stereotyping in Children's Readers* (1972), which clearly showed that male chauvinist conditioning in schools starts in kindergarten. Research was based on the study of 2,760 children's stories from 18 publishers. Their company, Women on Words and Images Consultants, used slide shows, lectures, television and counseling to change sex role stereotyping of children's textbooks, which, says Bender, "did not even represent a traditional reality."   (ABS)

BenDor, Jan (1946 –) Known as the founding mother of the rape crisis center movement in Michigan, BenDor led the establishment of the Women's Crisis Center in Ann Arbor, MI, one of the first in the U.S. Her task force of rape crisis counselors produced the Criminal Sexual Conduct Law Reform of 1974. In addition, some of the nation's first training programs in the treatment of sexual assault and domestic violence survivors for police and hospital personnel and prosecutors were initiated by

BenDor. As president of Ann Arbor/Washtenaw NOW, BenDor led a national boycott of Domino's Pizza (then a major financier of the anti-choice movement). She has worked to dispel myths about adult survivors of incest and sexual assault, and to end sexism in the mental health system. In 1991, BenDor was inducted into the Michigan Women's Hall of Fame. Archives: Wayne State University Law Library, Detroit, MI; and the University of Michigan Bentley Historical Library, Ann Harbor, MI.   (ABS)

Beneria, Lourdes (1938 –) Professor and economist, Beneria can trace her roots as a feminist from her early life in the roadless rural village of Boi, on the Spanish side of the Pyrenees. The youngest of six children, she attended the University of Barcelona during 1956–1960, despite her father's suggestion that it was not necessary for her to have a university degree. Arriving in the United States with a Fulbright scholarship, Beneria first enrolled at New York University and later at Columbia University as a Ph.D. student. In the late 1960s, she met women involved with the Columbia Women's Liberation group and was gradually drawn to the movement through conversations with Harriet Zellner and other feminists. With the arrival of her second child, Beneria and her husband became active in the Columbia Day Care Coalition, which resulted in the creation of the first day care center in NY's Upper West Side. She was also active in feminist and political groups working on anti-war and peace efforts, and in international solidarity work with other women's organizations. During the 1970s she was a member of one of the Marxist-Feminist groups that met regularly in NYC. She was also a member of the Women and Development group (WAD, later Gender and Development, or GAD) that met regularly at her house. Beneria is a professor at Cornell University specializing in gender, Latin American development, and international issues. She is a very active member of the International Association of Feminist Economics, was its president in 2003, and an associate editor of its journal *Feminist Economics*. She has published numerous articles and books on these issues, among them *Gender, Development, and Globalization: Economics as if All People Mattered* (Routledge, 2003). Her autobiographical essay, "In the Wilderness of One's Inner Self: Living Feminism," was published in *The Feminist Memoir Project* (1998).   (ABS)

Benjamin, Betty (1924 – 2004) A social worker who was married to a doctor, Benjamin saw firsthand the kinds of problems that necessitated abortion. During the 1960s, she co-founded the Minnesota Council for the Legal Termination of Pregnancy. In 1971, offered the presidency of both the MN LWV and MCLTP, she chose the latter, serving from 1971–1987, and again in 1992. Under her leadership, MCLTP campaigned for legal abortion by establishing relationships with state legislators, hiring a lobbyist, and building a solid grassroots organization. For some years, the MCLTP office was in Benjamin's home,

and she worked as a full-time volunteer running the organization. An early member of Twin Cities NOW, and active with the LWV and other organizations, Benjamin was honored in 1999 by Minnesota NARAL (formerly MCLTP) with the establishment of a permanent endowment in her name to guarantee the organization's existence for generations to come.

Benjamin, Jessica R. (1946 –) A leader in feminism and psychoanalysis, Benjamin developed new ideas about gender identification. She took part in the first women's group at the University of Wisconsin, Madison (1966 – 1967). With several other women, she initiated the first sit-in against Dow Chemical (1967). After graduating in 1967, Benjamin spent four years in Germany where she was active in the SDS and brought attention to women's issues to "a large collective terrified of feminism." In 1972, she joined New Haven (CT) Women's Liberation, and was active in its abortion counseling collective, the women's self-help health group and the steering committee. Benjamin also taught an introduction to women's studies at Southern Connecticut State College. In graduate school in NYC in 1973, she joined a Marxist Feminist group and began writing her dissertation on social theory and psychoanalysis, which eventually became her groundbreaking book *The Bonds of Love: Feminism and the Problem of Domination* (Pantheon Books, 1988). One of the founders of the journal *Studies in Gender and Sexuality*, Benjamin was also a founding board member of a new association for Relational Psychoanalysis and Psychotherapists for Social Responsibility, a peace group in NYC. She published *Like Subjects, Love Objects: Essays on Recognition and Sexual Difference* (Yale University Press, 1995), and *Shadow of the Other: Intersubjectivity and Gender in Psychoanalysis* (Routledge, 1998).   (ABS)

Benjamin, Roberta F. (1940 –) Benjamin joined the women's movement in the late 1960s in Boston, where she and her cohorts simultaneously headed NOW committees, worked with women in the media to get more female voices on the radio, drafted legislation to prohibit discrimination in public accommodations, and threatened to sue the *Boston Globe* if it didn't stop discriminating in its employment section's listings. A founding member of Boston NOW, Benjamin served as president (1970 – 1971), and was a member of its advisory board until 1973. In addition, she was an organizer of the August 1970 Boston women's march; was a founding member and board member of the MA WPC; served on the MA Governor's Commission on the Status of Women; and was a coordinator of the MA committee to ratify the ERA (1972 – 1976). From 1972 – 1974, Benjamin wrote a regular column on women's issues for *The Real Paper*, an alternative newspaper published in Boston. In 1973 she and eight other women dressed in judicial robes and demonstrated in front of the Supreme Court to dramatize what the Court would look like if it consisted exclusively of women. Benjamin holds a B.A. from Radcliffe College and a J.D. from Harvard Law School. She practices family law in Boston. (ABS)

Bennett, Anne McGrew (1903 – 1986) A feminist theological pioneer, Bennett fostered feminist critical reflection in the Christian tradition. She worked on numerous committees and organizations, speaking and writing on issues related to women's rights in the church and society. Much of her work is collected in *Woman-Pain to Woman-Vision: Writings on Feminist Theology,* edited by Mary E. Hunt (Fortress Press, 1999). She and her husband, John Bennett, were at the Pacific School of Religion, Berkeley, CA, 1938–1943; Union Theological Seminary, NY, 1943–1970; and Pacific School of Religion 1970–1975. Bennett, who had three children, earned her B.S. from the University of Nebraska (1928), and her M.A. from Auburn Seminary (1932). In 1983 she received an Honorary Doctorate of Humane Letters from the Starr King School for the Ministry, Berkeley, CA. In 1986, she and her husband each received the Union Medal, Union Theological Seminary's highest honor. Archives: Archives of Women in Theological Scholarship, Union Theological Seminary, New York, NY.

Bennett, Trude (1946 –) A maternal and child health specialist working on global reproductive health policy, Bennett was working with high-school students for the SDS in New York City in 1968 when she began to see her social reality from a feminist perspective. Moving to Boston in 1969, Bennett helped establish a branch of Teachers for a Democratic Society and Bread and Roses. She worked with the Boston Women's Health Collective and wrote sections for several editions of *Our Bodies, Ourselves.* Bennett was a participant in CR, community discussions, anti-war and anti-imperialist organizing. She went to Cuba in 1970 as part of the Venceremos Brigade, and worked with a feminist caucus among the volunteers. Returning to Massachusetts, Bennett became a psychiatric social worker, developing feminist theory in her practice. She also worked on the staff of *Dollars and Sense* and wrote articles on women's economic issues. Bennett helped start the Seattle (WA) Reproductive Rights Coalition. Later, in New York City, she worked in CARASA, advised students at the women's center of Brooklyn College, and served on the advisory board for a feminist series of the Monthly Review Press. Bennett is a founder of Loi Hua/Women's Promise in Vietnam, whose goal is to create solidarity between American and Vietnamese women and to help victims of Agent Orange. Bennett, who has one child, holds an A.B. from Barnard College (1967), an M.S.W. from Simmons College, School of Social Work (1976), and an M.P.H. (1984) and a Dr. P.H. (1988) from the University of North Carolina, Chapel Hill. She is associate professor in the School of Public Health, The University of North Carolina at Chapel Hill. (ABS)

Benninger, Judith – See Brown, Judith B.

Benson, Francesca (1935 –) (also known as Francesca Stonaker) In 1970, Benson co-founded the University-NOW Day Nursery in space provided by Princeton University (NJ). It was the first full-day childcare center in the area, and is still serving families. Benson was organizer and educational director of this project as a member of the Princeton area NOW. She was also active in civil rights and was a member of the Congress for Racial Equality, Fair Housing Coalition. (ABS)

Benson, Joyce M. (1929 –) A charter member of Duluth, MN, NOW in 1967, Benson served as chair and state board representative (1977–1984), and VP (1982–1984). As a NOW member, she worked for passage of the ERA, and raised funds. In 1974, she served as an abortion counselor at Duluth Community Health Center. In 1982, she was a founder of the Greater Minnesota Women's Alliance, created to initiate and support legislation on women's issues. In 1987, Benson initiated the ordinance establishing the Duluth Sister Cities Commission, and was especially active with its Russian sister city. She helped secure grants for domestic violence and leadership training, and supported women's organizations working together on common issues. As one result, Petrozavodsk, Russia, now has a shelter for women and children. Benson was a board member of the Duluth Women's Commission from 1981–1985, and served as chair from 1981–1983. From 1983–1985, she was VP, board of directors, Women's Health Center. She was a delegate to the United Nations Decade for Women Conference in Nairobi, Kenya, in 1985, and since 1985 has worked with the LWV, as president of the Duluth chapter (2002–2005), and international chair (1996–2005). Benson, who has three children, received her B.A. from the University of Minnesota, Duluth. Archives: University of Minnesota, Duluth, MN. (ABS)

Bentley, Helen Delich (1923 –) A journalist, politician and mentor, Bentley broke the glass ceiling in the federal government when she became chair of the Federal Maritime Commission (1971–1975), the fourth highest appointment for women in the history of the U.S. government at that time. In that position, she was able to mentor the newly arriving, small group of women, such as Barbara Franklin, who were becoming part of the federal government in capacities other than personal secretaries and clerks. Bentley was also a member of the U.S. House of Representatives from 1985–1995. In 1995, she formed her own consulting company. Earlier, as a journalist in the 1940s, Bentley was one of only three women kept on staff at the *Baltimore Sun* after the men returned from WWII. In 1947, she was the first woman journalist ever to cover the national conventions of the AFL and CIO (at that time, separate unions). Bentley earned her B.A. from the University of Missouri in 1944. She holds eight Honorary Doctoral degrees. Archives: University of Baltimore, Baltimore, MD. (ABS)

Benton, Suzanne (1936 –) An artist and sculptor, Benton was one of the first nine members of Connecticut NOW when she joined in 1968. She started Central CT NOW in 1969; founded CT Feminists in the Arts in 1970, and was the convener of the first women's festival in New Haven, Women: Metamorphosis I. In 1971, Benton founded Western CT NOW, and was president (1971 – 1973). A creator of welded masks at a time when women were discouraged from using blow torches, she performed the first mask tale, about Sarah and Hagar from *Genesis*, at Lincoln Center in 1971. From 1974 – 1976 she was national coordinator of NOW's Women in the Arts national task force, and worked on Women's International Year art events through the United Nations. In subsequent years she was a mask maker, workshop leader and performing artist, gathering stories about women throughout the world as she traveled. From 1999 – 2002 she was grant writer, managing director and artistic director, Positive Power: Women Artists of Connecticut. In 1998, she co-founded Dragon Women, a Ridgefield, CT, regional artists discussion and support group. Benton, who was active in civil rights issues from 1963 – 1967 through the LWV, received a B.A. from Queens College (NY) in 1956. She has two children. (ABS)

Berg, Barbara Joan (1949 –) Historian, writer and college teacher, Berg was active in the anti-war movement of the 1960s. She taught seminars on American women's history at Sarah Lawrence College (1976 – 1977) and at Marymount Manhattan College (1978 – 1982). At the Horace Mann School (1992 – 2000), where she was associate dean of students (1993 – 2000) and director of co-education (1997 – 2000), she headed a three-year study evaluating the quality of girls' experiences and education from K through 12. She also interviewed and participated in an oral history project (made into a video) of the experiences of women who graduated from The School Barnard in the 1940s; founded and directed the first Women's Issues Club; and started *Folio 51*, the first journal written by and about women in the history of the school. Berg served as an adviser on Women's Health Day, Mount Sinai Hospital (1981 – 1982), and was a member of the Mayor's Commission on the Status of Women (1981 – 1983). She is the author of *The Remembered Gate: Origins of American Feminism, The City and the Women 1800 – 1860* (Oxford University Press, 1978); *Nothing to Cry About – A Feminist View of Childbearing* (Seaview Books, 1981); *The Crisis of the Working Mother* (Summit Books, 1986); and *The Women's Movement and Young Women Today* (Enslow Publishers, 2000). She has been a member of the Wellesley Center for Research on Women, the AAUW, NOW and VFA. Berg, who has three children, holds a A.B. from the University of Rochester, and an M.A. and Ph.D. from CUNY Graduate Center. (ABS)

Berg, Linda Breslau (1948 –) A political director of NOW (2004), Berg graduated from Georgetown Law School in 1973 and became a VISTA volunteer on the island of Maui in Hawaii. The first woman lawyer to practice on the island, she "became somewhat of a tourist attraction as people wanted to see what a wahini lawyer looked like," she says. Although a District Court Judge told Berg that he did not think women belonged in the courtroom, Berg nonetheless won a court challenge to the height and weight requirements of the Maui police department, which enabled the first woman to become a police officer on Maui. After returning to Washington, D.C., in 1975, Berg joined a small law firm specializing in employment discrimination. She represented a woman who had worked in the U.S. Senate, but was fired for complaining about its discriminatory practices against pregnant workers. After a three-year battle, Berg won the cases in both the D.C. Court of Appeals and the U.S. Court of Appeals for the District of Columbia. The case established important legal rights for women employees on Capitol Hill. Since that time, Berg's career has focused on the rights of women. Berg, who has three children, holds a B.A. from Carnegie Mellon. (ABS)

Berger, Caruthers Gholson (1917 – 1984) An attorney in the Office of the Solicitor, United States Department of Labor, Berger was active in the National Women's Party before 1960. She provided data and arguments for the NWP to submit to Congress to aid in securing passage of the sex discrimination amendment of Title VII of the Civil Rights Bill of 1964. She attended the organizing conference of NOW in October 1966, and worked as a volunteer attorney on nearly all of the early Title VII test cases in the United States appellate courts (with Sylvia Ellison, Mary Eastwood and Marguerite Rawalt). Because of her government position, Berger worked on these cases without signing her name. Berger was a founder and member of the board of directors of Human Rights for Women, established in 1968. Because of a dispute about who would serve on the NOW Legal Defense and Education Fund board (and because cases she was working on were no longer under the auspices of NOW), Berger left NOW in 1968. She is the author of "Equal Pay, Equal Employment Opportunity and Equal Enforcement of the Law for Women," published in the *Valparaiso University Law Review* (1970), as well as numerous papers on sex discrimination in employment and women's constitutional rights for the National Women's Party and NOW. She graduated from Mississippi Synodical College, Holly Springs, and the University of Mississippi Law School. Archives: University of Texas, Austin. Also, case papers are in HRW files, Schlesinger Library, Radcliffe Institute, Cambridge, MA.

Bergin, Kay V. (1921 –) In 1974, Bergin became the first executive director of Connecticut's Permanent Commission on the Status of Women. Under her tenure, a system for intake, analysis and disposition of sex discrimination cases was set up; publication and widespread distribution of materials was undertaken; volunteer task forces were established; and public hearings were held statewide. A significant advance came when the commission was able to delay implementation of the Affirmative Action Plan for State Agencies until the plan was revised to include sex discrimination as well as racial discrimination. A second major gain was to publicize broadly that the ERA was to be on the ballot, which resulted in passage in CT. In 1975, Bergin was named deputy banking commissioner for the State of Connecticut by the late Governor Ella Grasso as part of Grasso's outreach to women in her administration. One of Grasso's important decisions, in which Bergin participated, was to prohibit state employees from traveling in any state that had not passed the federal ERA. In her role as deputy banking commissioner, Bergin published and distributed a definitive tract on equal credit for women. Her testimony on sex discrimination in banking before the U.S. Senate Committee on Banking was widely published and distributed. Bergin was a delegate to the First National Women's Conference in Houston, has served on the board of CWEALF, and is a member of NOW, the WPC, VFA and Emily's List. Bergin, who has one child, holds a B.S. and an M.A.L.S.   (ABS)

Bergman, Ciel Olsen (1938 –) (also known as Cheryl Bowers) In 1988, Bergman legally changed her name from Cheryl Bowers to Ciel Bergman to honor her maternal grandmother, Emma Bergman. A poet, Emma came to the U.S. from Sweden in 1887 hoping to create a life as a writer. While Emma was unable to fulfill her dreams, Ciel was able to fulfill hers. Painter and professor in the department of art at the University of California, Santa Barbara, Bergman taught all her students, of both sexes, to be feminists. She sat on the affirmative action committee of the Academic Senate, hiring and teaching many women. She was also deeply involved as an eco-feminist in environmental movements and activism. Bergman was a founding member of Women Beyond Borders, an ongoing international exhibition. Her work has been exhibited at major galleries and 11 major museums in San Francisco, Chicago, New York City, Brussels and London, England, and in collections including The Metropolitan Museum of Art and The San Francisco Museum of Modern Art. She has two children.   (ABS)

Bergmann, Barbara R. (1927 –) Professor emerita of economics at the University of Maryland and American University, Bergmann is a lifetime member of NOW and served on the board of WEAL in the 1970s. A specialist in economics and social policy, Bergmann introduced feminist topics in her lectures in the early 1970s, including classes on power and discrimination and the economics of sex roles. She testified on a case involving pension inequities by TIAA-Cref, a pension management company for teachers and nurses not covered by state plans. They were sending women pension checks amounting to only 80 percent of what men received on the grounds that women lived longer. Her testimony showed that 87 percent of the women and men could be paired up as dying in the same year, so most women were being disadvantaged compared to men with similar experience. That 1970s fight for equity went all the way to the Supreme Court, where women won. Also in the 1970s, Bergmann served as an adviser to the committee for the U.S. Census. She persuaded the committee to collect data on child support, and to stop automatically designating the husband as the "Head of Household" on the form. Bergmann is the author of numerous scholarly articles on race and sex discrimination and its effect on wages. She has also published several books, including *The Economic Emergence of Women* (Basic Books, 1986) and *America's Child Care Problem: The Way Out* (Palgrave), written in collaboration with Suzanne Helburn. Bergmann, who has two children, holds a B.A. from Cornell (1948) and a Ph.D. from Harvard (1958). She has served in numerous government positions, including as a senior staff member of the President's Council of Economic Advisers during the Kennedy administration.   (ABS)

Berkeley, Ellen Perry (1931 –) was one of nine founding members of the Alliance of Women in Architecture in New York City (1972). Senior editor of *Architectural Forum* from 1967 – 1972, she published "Women in Architecture" in that journal in 1972. Berkeley was also one of seven founding coordinators of the Women's School of Planning and Architecture, 1975 – 1980. She was volume editor of *Architecture: A Place for Women* (Smithsonian Institution Press, 1989) and *At Grandmother's Table* (Fairview Press, 2000), and published chapters on women and the man-made environment in *Modern Social Reforms* (Macmillan, 1974), edited by Arthur Shostak; *Feminist Collage* (Teachers College Press, Columbia University, 1979), edited by Judy Loeb; and *New Space for Women* (Macmillan, 1980), edited by Gerda Wekerle, Rebecca Peterson and David Morley. Berkeley has a B.A. from Smith College (1952); studied architecture at Harvard Graduate School of Design (1952 – 1955), and returned to HGSD with a Loeb Fellowship in Advanced Environmental Studies (1972 – 1973), the first year women were awarded this fellowship.   (ABS)

Berman, Joan R. Saks (1941 –) became active in the women's movement in Chicago in 1967. In 1969, she was a founding member of CWLU and the Association of Women in Psychology. She taught women's studies part-time at Northeastern Illinois University in Chicago from 1972 – 1977, then English as a second language for the Urban Skills Institute of Chicago City Colleges. At that time, she also had a private practice as a feminist psychotherapist. In 1980, she moved to Tuba City, AZ, to work for the Indian Health Service on the Navajo Reservation, where, with the help of Vista volunteers, she set up a battered women's shelter. She moved to Albuquerque in 1984. Archives: CWLU Herstory Project, Chicago, Ill. (ABS)

Berman, Ruth Nemzoff – See Nemzoff, Ruth

Bernard, Jessie Shirley (1903 – 1996) A writer and sociologist, Bernard published 14 sole-authored books, nine co-authored or edited volumes, over 75 journal articles and more than 40 book chapters. She published *The Female World* (1981) and *The Female World From a Global Perspective* (1987); "The Inferiority Curriculum" (1988); and "A Woman's Twentieth Century" (1990). As she entered her sixties, she was among the first women to become feminist scholar activists. A professor of sociology at Pennsylvania State University, she chose to retire at 62 and became a "sociologist at large." Her focus was to increase the understanding of the effects of sexism on women's experience of marriage, parenting, education and economic life. She believed that men and women live in different worlds, and her research, published in *The Paradox of the Happy Marriage* (1971) and *The Future of Marriage* (1972), showed that marriage was good for men, but not for women. A major influence in the creation of the Center for Feminist Research, Bernard was honored on her 85th birthday by the creation of the Jessie Bernard Wise Women Award to recognize "women leaders, activists and scholars whose lives and work demonstrate an advocacy of feminist enlightenment." Archives: The Jessie Bernard Papers: Pennsylvania State University Library, University Park, PA.

Bernard, Shirley (1923 –) The first western regional director of NOW (1970 – 1972) and chair of the Western Regional Conference (1971 and 1972), Bernard was also western membership chair (1967); on the national board (1968 – 1972); and on the national executive committee (1970 – 1972). She was part of the steering committee of NWPC (California, 1971), and chair of the founding California State National Women's Political Caucus Conference (1972). In 1973, Bernard was on the founding steering committee of Women in California Higher Education, and was its president in 1977. She was co-founder of the Fullerton College Commission for Women's Concerns in 1974, and its president in 1975. Bernard has been a singer and actress in the Orange County Feminist Theater from 1969 forward, and has represented NOW on A.M. shows in Los Angeles and other media venues. A co-chair of the Women's Strike of 1970, she wrote her dissertation on this event for her Ph.D. (Union Graduate School, 1975). She wrote two articles, "The Economic Status of Women," published in *Women: A Feminist Perspective*; and "Aggression in Women," published in *The Radical Therapist*. She also wrote The Glib Lib column in *NOW ACTS*, 1969 – 1971. Bernard has one child. Archives: NOW papers: Schlesinger Library, Radcliffe Institute, Cambridge, MA; publications: Social Science Division, Los Angeles Public Library. (ABS)

Bernhard, Betty (1940 –) A professor of theater, Bernhard has worked in the fields of art, music and theater to increase the visibility and participation of women. Her first contribution to the women's movement came in 1970 when she was a founder of a day care center at the University of Oregon, Eugene, one of the first university day care centers in the U.S. Initially, the center's founders received hate mail accusing them of being Communists for raising children communally, and of disrupting the American family. As a Ph.D. candidate in 1976, Bernhard directed Leonard Bernstein's Mass with over 500 people and six departments at the university's field house. In 1983, Bernhard and Susan Keizer, an artist from Portland, OR, created a four-day women's conference on the arts held at Hecta Head Lighthouse on Oregon's West Coast. Active in the Women's Project of the American Theatre Association from its inception, Bernhard has given numerous papers and presentations across the U.S., and has presented feminist work at Women Playwright's Project International Conferences in Buffalo, Greece and Ireland. She has adapted and directed three plays by American women in India. As a Fulbright Scholar in India, she taught and lectured on American women playwrights, and created a video on women who do activist theater in India. On her own campus, Pomona College, Bernhard has directed plays and taught two courses. Bernhard has one child. Archives: Video archives are at Pacific Basin Institute, Pomona College, Claremont, CA. (ABS)

Bernikow, Louise (1940 –) A feminist writer and educator since the early 1970s, Bernikow is the author of seven books, including *The World Split Open: Four Centuries of Women Poets in England and America* (1973), *Among Women* (1980) and *The American Woman's Almanac: An Inspiring and Irreverent Women's History* (1997). She has written articles for feminist publications, *Signs*, *Ms.* and *Aphra*. Bernikow created and taught women's studies at Jersey City State College and Hunter College; was a founder of the Columbia University Seminar on Women and Society; and taught a seminar on women in literature at the Julliard School (1969). Bernikow represented the second wave at the NWSA Generations Conference opener, and has been an activist with WAC and NOW. Bernikow, who did legwork for Bella Abzug's first campaign, also participated in anti-war and civil rights activities, as well as Panthers defense. She lectures on "The Shoulders We Stand On; Women as Agents of Change" at campuses and communities nationwide. (ABS)

Bernstein, Paula (1944 –) An obstetrician/gynecologist with an M.D. from the University of Miami School of Medicine, Bernstein was a member of Louisiana NOW from 1970, and served as chair of the employment committee. She participated in a coalition with African American and Latino civil rights groups in the filing of an antitrust complaint against 45 savings and loans associations, and helped initiate a women's studies program at

UCLA, where she taught a course on women in science. Bernstein, who holds a Ph.D. in chemistry from Caltech, organized a group of Caltech women faculty, students and student spouses in 1969 to develop a childcare center, which is still functioning. (ABS)

Bernstein, Ruth – See Carol, Ruth Etta

Berry, Betty Blaisdell (1922– 2007) joined New York NOW in 1967, became recording secretary in 1968, and that year was appointed chair of the marriage and family committee. From 1968–1973, Berry was national coordinator of the marriage and family relations task force. During that time, she wrote, with NY NOW task force members, NOW's "Position Paper on Marriage and Divorce." In 1970 she wrote "Marriage as a Career," which was published in the first *NOW York Times* under the byline Juliet Capulet. From 1968 – 1973 she edited and published the "Marriage, Divorce and Family Newsletter" for the task force. Berry also edited "Your Marriage, the Law and You" booklets that were distributed in various states, and in 1974 founded and was president of the Marriage and Divorce Press, which published the first private non-profit newsletter on divorce for laypersons. As well as writing and editing, Berry worked for laws concerning marriage, tax deductions for childcare expenses, compulsory financial disclosure and equitable division of property in divorce, individual Social Security benefits for housewives, continued health insurance and Social Security benefits for divorced persons, equal division of property, training and vocational guidance, and compulsory payroll deductions for child support. A charter member of Women's Forum NYC until 1988, a consultant on divorce matters to the National Family Relations Society, and a speaker to Young Republicans on divorce legislation, Berry was also a founding member of VFA. She has a B.A. from Smith College (1944) and an M.A. from New York University (1968). Archives: Schlesinger Library, Radcliffe Institute, Cambridge, MA; Bobst Library, New York University, NY; and The Sophia Smith Collection, Smith College, Northampton, MA, (ABS)

Berry, Carolyn (1930 –) (also known as Carolyn Bishop and Carolyn Becker) A visual artist, writer and poet, Berry was an original member of the Northern California chapter of the WCA (early 1970s) and served as treasurer for several years. During the same period, she became a member of the National Museum of Women in the Arts, and in 1977 was part of a WIA traveling exhibition, Artists Choice. Earlier, in 1974, Berry was a member of Alternative Directions, a group of women artists who met at Sunset Center in Carmel, CA. In 1976, Berry published an article on Vinnie Ream, the first woman in history to get a commission from the U.S. Congress for a statue, in *The Feminist Art Journal*. She also researched and wrote an article on a Northern Cheyenne woman, Comenha, published in 1981 in *Frontiers*. In addition, Berry had articles

published in *Heresies*. She also arranged an exhibition of the works of Gene McComas and, with June Braucht, was able to save McComas' murals from being destroyed in San Francisco. Two projects that Berry worked on were *Dictionary of Women Artists, An International Dictionary of Women Artists Born Before 1900* (G.K. Hall &Co., 1985), and *Ethnic Notions*, by Jan Faulkner. Berry has also been active in the NWPC and the NAACP. Archives: Monterey Museum of Art, Monterey, CA; Rutgers University, Rutgers, NJ; Moore College of Art, Philadelphia, PA; and Archives of the Monterey Jazz Festival, Stanford University, Stanford, CA. (ABS)

Berry, Mary Frances (1938 –) In 1973, Berry was a consultant to the Office of Civil Rights in the Dept. of HEW to advise on how to apply President Nixon's executive order 11375 (1968) requiring contractors to have affirmative action plans which included not just race, but sex for the first time, in higher education. "I was there when we forced Columbia University in response to women's complaints to modify their plan, which they violated," she says. "I told the staff they should debar them from contracts and they did so. The staff applied the order to a number of cases involving women faculty who at the time were only given temporary jobs, while their husbands, no better qualified, received tenured positions." Berry is the Geraldine R. Segal Professor of American Social Thought, professor of history and adjunct professor of law, University of Pennsylvania. She became chair of the U.S. Commission on Civil Rights in 1993, and was reappointed by the President in 1999. She is the author of *The Pig Farmer's Daughter and Other Tales of American Justice: Episodes of Racism and Sexism in the Courts from 1865 to the Present; Why ERA Failed: Politics, Women's Rights and the Amending Process of the Constitution; and Politics of Parenthood: Child Care, Women's Rights* and *the Myth of the Good Mother*. Berry earned a J.D. from the University of Michigan Law School. She has received 31 Honorary Doctoral degrees and numerous awards for her public service. (ABS)

Bersch, Blanche Cion (1934 –) A new lawyer in 1969, Bersch joined the Women Lawyers' Association of Los Angeles. Bersch headed WLALA's legislative committee (1970–1971), then served on its board for several years. The organization worked to get California to ratify the ERA, and also to add wording against discrimination on the basis of sex to all existing civil rights legislation. Bersch then helped draft legislation that would refuse state licenses to businesses that discriminated on the basis of sex, mostly directed to private clubs that needed liquor licenses to operate. As a delegate to the State Bar Conference of Delegates (1971–1976), Bersch worked to draft, review and create strategy for passing numerous feminist resolutions. In 1971, she was a co- founder of a women's caucus comprising most of the women delegates who had met for dinner the evening before the start of the State Bar

Conference to examine the resolutions. They called for refusing state licenses to businesses that practiced sex discrimination, giving married women control over their earnings and other community property, and supporting reproductive choice. Bersch spoke at the conferences for various resolutions, including one in September 1975 that would allow married women to retain their birth names. In the early 1970s Bersch was a spokesperson for feminist causes in Southern California. She participated in organizing the Los Angeles chapter of the NWPC. In 1975, Bersch attended the first United Nations Conference on Women in Mexico City. In 1974, Bersch co-founded, with Bette Bardeen and Karen Kaplowitz, the firm Bardeen, Bersch and Kaplowitz (later Bersch and Kaplowitz), considered the first women's law firm west of New York. As a member of the California Board of Medical Quality Assurance (1975 – 1976), Bersch testified before the CA Legislature to oppose bills that would limit reproductive choice rights. In 1981, Bersch was a founder of the Family Law Center, which became the Harriett Buhai Center for Family Law. Bersch, who has three children, holds a B.A. from the University of Michigan (1955) and a J.D. from the University of San Fernando Valley College of Law (1968). (ABS)

Berson, Ginny Z. (1946 –) was part of the first women's house and collective in Washington, D.C., in the early 1970s. As part of the D.C. women's liberation movement, she was active in Women Against Imperialism and Women Against Racism. A founding member of The Furies collective and newspaper, she wrote frequently about lesbian-feminism and class issues for feminists. She was a founding member of Olivia Records in 1973, which produced and distributed work by women, and taught them how to produce a concert. After leaving Olivia in 1980, she began working in community radio, and was the first paid director of women's programming at KPFA in Berkeley. As senior producer of live national programming for Pacifica Radio, she produced and/or hosted the live national broadcast of several pro-choice rallies in Washington, D.C. Active in the peace movement in late 1960s and early 1970s, Berson has a B.A. from Mount Holyoke College (1967). Archives: The Lesbian Herstory Archives, Brooklyn, NY. (ABS)

Betz, Katherine Ann – See Weesner, Katherine Ann

Biaggi, Cristina (1937 –) An artist and writer, Biaggi has demonstrated, marched, protested and been arrested for women's rights. Born in Switzerland, she also protested and organized in England and Italy, and attended the International Women's Conferences in Nairobi and Beijing. She participated in the Vancouver, New York City, Amsterdam and Sydney Gay Games as a martial artist representing older women. She has spoken on eco-feminism; organized conferences on the Great Goddess; and written articles for women's publications such as *Sojourner* and

Dyke News. Biaggi wrote *Habitation of the Great Goddess* (Knowledge, Ideas and Trends, 1994), *In the Footsteps of the Goddess* (KIT, 2000), and *The Rule of Mars: Reading on the Origins, The History and Impact of Patriarchy* (KIT, 2005). In addition, she has made films on animal rights and older women. Biaggi, who has a Ph.D. from New York University, has four children. (ABS)

Bick, Barbara Ruth (1925 –) joined a small group of Washington women determined to protest the escalation of nuclear weapons testing in the atmosphere. On November 1, 1961, Women Strike for Peace was born. Bick ran its national office for over a decade, and also became the editor of WSP's national and international newsletters, coordinated many of its national actions, and represented WSP at national and international meetings. Bick then moved to the Institute of Policy Studies and in 1975 became an associate fellow there. During her years at IPS, she collaborated with female staff in the struggle against the old boys' network "that dominated the selection of fellows and IPS's intellectual life." Having internalized the maxim "The personal is political," she wrote "Anatomy of An Affair," published in *Ms.* magazine in 1972. Bick also became involved in the mental health movement after her teenage daughter was diagnosed as schizophrenic. In collaboration with Nancy Hartsock, a feminist professor at Johns Hopkins, Bick wrote a critique of Dorothy Dinnerstein's *The Mermaid and the Minotaur*, titled "Parenting & the Human Malaise" and published in the *Monthly Review*. Bick also worked closely with Bella Abzug during Abzug's years in Congress, assisting her various initiatives such as the NWPC, and during the United Nations Decade of Women, beginning in Houston in 1977 and ending in Beijing. Bick was appointed to the first board of the Institute for Women's Policy Research in 1987, where she served for 10 years, serving as an emeritus member from 2001 – 2005. Bick, who has three children, also worked against the Taliban for 15 years and has written a memoir of this activism. (ABS)

Biele, Deborah (1939 –) joined New York NOW in 1969 and served as chair of the women in the media committee in 1970. When the committee challenged the FCC licensing of WABC (because it viewed the station's reporting as biased, and objected to the negative editorializing of the local news anchor), Biele spearheaded a study that identified the ratio of males to females seen on the news and in commercials. In addition, the study characterized the "roles" of women when they were observed as principal characters or spokespersons. Study members compiled data for two solid weeks of airtime. Assisted by the Center for Constitutional Law, the committee successfully solicited the cooperation of women in the news and human resources departments of WABC, gaining access to employment statistics for women at WABC. The result was that WABC and its senior management asked the committee to enter into negotiations with them. The FCC reviewed the information, and WABC lost its license until it came into compliance on employment of more women and in fair reporting of the feminist movement. In addition to her work in media, Biele was co-owner of a Manhattan art studio, and with Maria Melero published the *NOW York Times*. Biele has a B.A and M.A. from SUNY at Stony Brook, NY. (ABS)

Bigger, Doris – See Atlantis, Dori

Bikman, Minda (1941 – 1997) A radical feminist and freelance writer from Chicago, Bikman attended what is considered the first women's liberation meeting. Held in New York City in 1967, the meeting was called by Pam Allen, also from Chicago. "This is a very famous meeting that has assumed legendary status in New York City feminist lore," says Barbara Mehrhof. Bikman joined Redstockings in July 1969. She was one of the first organizers of New York Radical Feminists (October and November 1969); was a member of NYRF's founding "brigade," the Stanton-Anthony Brigade; organized CR groups and fundraisers, including the 1971 Feminist Film Festival; and was a workshop leader at NYRF's rape and prostitution conferences (1970 or 1971). In February 1971 Bikman developed NYRF's legislative program. Also in the early 1970s, Bikman formed Video Women, a collective that taped speakouts and conferences and produced "Marriage: Women Speak Out" from the 1973 NYRF Marriage Conference. She was a founding member of Women Against Pornography in 1979, served on the organizing committee, and was a workshop leader at WAP's 1979 conference. Bikman interviewed Doris Lessing and then wrote "A Talk with Doris Lessing" (*New York Times Book Review*, March 30, 1980) and "Creating Your Own Demand," published in *Putting Questions Differently: Interviews with Doris Lessing 1964 – 1994*, edited by Earl G. Ingersoll (Flamingo, 1996). She also wrote several articles for the *Village Voice*. A graduate of Washington University in St. Louis, Bikman was a copy editor at *Time* magazine, and chair of the affirmative action committee at Time's Newspaper Guild unit.

Bird, Caroline (1915 –) is the author of *Born Female: The High Cost of Keeping Women Down* (Longman Publishing Group, 1968), which analyzed the exploited, brainwashed and underprivileged status of working women. Bird's involvement in the women's movement began before the founding of NOW when she met Alice Paul at a meeting in Betty Friedan's New York City apartment. Through Catherine East, Bird was hired as chief writer for the First National Women's Conference in Houston. Her report, published by the Government Printing Office in 1978, put her in much demand as a speaker and took her to every state in the union. Bird also wrote *Second Careers: New Ways to Work After 50* (Little Brown, 1992); *Everything a Woman Needs to Know to Get Paid What She's Worth* (Bantam Books, 1973); *The Case Against College* (Bantam, 1975); *Enterprising Women* (A Mentor Book, 1976); *What Women Want* (Simon & Schuster, 1979); *The Two Paycheck Marriage* (Rawson, Wade Publishers, 1979); and *Lives of Our Own: Secrets of Salty Old Women* (Houghton Mifflin, 1995). She has done assignments for *New Choices*, a magazine for people over 50. In addition to her writing and to several editorial jobs, Bird worked in public relations for 21 years. A student at Vassar (1931 – 1934), she left to get married. She received her B.A. from the University of Toledo, OH (1938), and an M.A. from the University of Wisconsin (1939). She was Froman Distinguished Professor, Russell Sage College 1972 – 1973) and Mather Professor, Case-Western Reserve University (1977). She has two children. (ABS)

Bird, Rose (1937 – 2000) was the first female deputy public defender in Santa Clara County, CA (1966), the first female to hold a cabinet-level job in CA when she was appointed by Governor Edmund Brown as secretary of the Agriculture and Services Agency (1975), and the first female Justice on the California Supreme Court (1977). In addition, Bird was a founder of California Women Lawyers (1974 – 1975). CWL created the Rose Bird Memorial Award in 2001 to honor those in public service who serve as an inspiration to women lawyers of California. A champion of the underdog and a staunch opponent of the death penalty, Bird worked to support the rights of tenants, farm workers and labor, and consumers. She also established a task force to make California courtrooms free of sexual and racial bias, and wrote a decision banning ladies nights at nightclubs and bars. Bird earned her J.D. from the Boalt Hall School of Law at the University of California, Berkeley (1965).

Biren, Joan Elisabeth (1944 –) (also known as JEB) was an early member of Washington D.C. Women's Liberation, and worked with Sharon Deevey, Charlotte Bunch and others on issues of reproductive rights and feminist CR. She came out as a lesbian in 1965, and "came out (of a closet) to women's liberation in 1970." Following the gay/straight split in D.C. Women's Liberation, Biren and others created a lesbian separatist movement, The Furies, and published *The Furies* newspaper. Biren taught herself photography and supplied photographs for many lesbian and feminist publications. In 1979, she published her first book of photographs, *Eye to Eye: Portraits of Lesbians*. This may be the first book of photographs where women identify as lesbians, with the word "lesbian" in the title. In 1987, her second book, *Making A Way: Lesbians Out Front*, was published. In 1974, Biren was co-founder, with Mary Farmer, of Moonforce Media, which distributed women's films. Moonforce Media organized the first feminist film festivals in Washington, D.C., and also started The Women's Film Circuit, bringing the work of lesbian and feminist filmmakers like Donna Deitch, Barbara Hammer and Jan Oxenberg to audiences around the country. In the 1980s Biren became a filmmaker. Her films include "For Love and For Life" (1988); "A Simple Matter of Justice" (1993); "Removing the Barriers" (1999); "Women Organize!" (2000); and "No Secret Anymore: The Times of Del Martin and Phyllis Lyon" (2003). In 1997, a retrospective of her photographic work, Queerly Visible 1971–1991, was exhibited by George Washington University; it subsequently toured the country. Her work is in permanent collections at the Library of Congress; Schlesinger Library, Radcliffe Institute, Cambridge, MA; the Academy of Arts, Berlin, Germany; the Women's Museum, Dallas; and the National Civil Rights Museum, Memphis. She earned a B.A. from Mt. Holyoke College; an M.A. from American University; and a Probationer B.Litt. from Oxford University. Archives: The Lesbian Herstory Archives, Special Collections, George Washington University, Washington, D.C. (ABS)

Birenbaum, Ellen (1951 –) was one of the original members of Barnard/Columbia Women's Liberation. Following her graduation from Barnard in 1973, she attended medical school, graduating from SUNY at Stony Brook in 1980. She did her residency in internal medicine at Harlem Hospital Center (1980 – 1983). She is the founding medical director of The Robert Mapplethorpe Residential Treatment Facility, a nursing home at Beth Israel Medical Center, NYC, established to provide long term care for substance abusers with HIV/AIDS. (ABS)

Birkby, Noel Phyllis (1932 – 1994) was a filmmaker and architect, and a member of an early important group of lesbian feminist artists, writers and theoreticians who made up a thriving women's culture in New York City. She worked for Davis Brody & Associates, a NYC architectural firm, from 1966–1972, where she was the primary architect on commercial buildings. She left to pursue feminist visions of architecture. In 1972, Birkby was a founding member of the Alliance for Women in Architecture. In 1974, she was one of seven founders of the Women's School of Planning and Architecture in Maine, where women architects developed, fantasized and realized women-oriented spaces. She gave lectures in the U.S. and Europe, and later moved into teaching, a private architectural practice and writing. In the 1980s, Birkby worked in NYC with Gruzen Partner-ship and Lloyd Goldfarb, and taught at the New York Institute of Technology. Birkby was born in New Jersey, where she was a state champion swimmer. She received a Certificate of Architecture from Cooper Union (1963) and an M.A. in architecture from Yale University (1966). She was the first woman to graduate from the Yale School of Architecture. She died of cancer in Massachusetts, surrounded by long-time lesbian feminist friends, SOBs (Sisters of Birkby), who took care of her in her final months. Birkby had a reputation for being a "pack rat," which was demonstrated by the 92 boxes of documentation of the women's movement (films, photos, oral histories, memorabilia, printed material and writings)

that she left at her death. Archives: The Sophia Smith Collection, Smith College, Northampton, MA.

Bishop, Carolyn – See Berry, Carolyn

Bishop, Gene Beth (1947 –) A physician, Bishop has spent a lifetime working for reproductive rights. Living in Boston, MA, in 1969, she helped write for and publish an underground newspaper, The Old Mole. After writing an article about obtaining an abortion (illegal, as at that time there was no other kind), Bishop was "flooded with phone calls from women seeking help." As a member of Bread and Roses (1970), Bishop helped take over a building to use as a women's center. Bishop and others created the Somerville Women's Health Project, a free women's health center, staffed only by women physicians and supported by lay trained patient advocates (1971). It was the first women's free clinic in the country. In addition to this work, Bishop contributed to early versions of Our Bodies, Ourselves, including a chapter on rape. Later, as a physician, she volunteered at the Cambridge Women's Clinic. In addition to fighting for reproductive rights, Bishop has been active in the ongoing struggle for national health insurance. She was both a board member and employee of the Elizabeth Blackwell Health Center for Women, a feminist health center in Philadelphia, now closed. Active in the civil rights movement, she worked during her college years to end the war in Vietnam. In the latter struggle, she was placed on probation at Harvard/Radcliffe for sitting in against recruiters from Dow Chemical, the makers of napalm. Bishop, who has one child, holds an undergraduate degree from Radcliffe College (1968) and graduated from the Stony Brook School of Medicine (1976). Archives: Schlesinger Library, Radcliffe Institute, Cambridge, MA. (ABS)

Black, Cathleen (1944 –) The president of Hearst Magazines and one of the most powerful women in corporate America, Black started out in publishing selling advertising for Holiday and Travel & Leisure magazines and then joined New York magazine in 1970. She helped launch Ms. magazine two years later, becoming its associate publisher. She returned to New York magazine, where, in 1979, she became the first female publisher of a weekly consumer magazine. Black acknowledged in a 2005 interview that Ms. was "probably the most difficult job" because not only was she managing an ad staff for the first time, but the magazine was viewed very skeptically by advertisers, most of whom were men, back in the mid 1970s. But the thrill of helping to put Ms. on the map and to truly make a difference was like "being part of a revolution; you were part of something much bigger and more important than just a magazine," she said. Even though she has been running one of the largest consumer magazine companies for a decade now, with great storied titles like Cosmopolitan, Harper's Bazaar, O the Oprah Magazine and Good Housekeeping, she is also well known for being part of the launch team of *USA Today*, where for eight years she was its president and publisher, again in a trailblazing position for both a woman, media executive and marketer. Black is a graduate of Trinity College (1966) and holds eight Honorary Degrees. (ABS)

Blackham, Ann R. (1927 –) was one of very few women who were sole owners of a real estate company in Massachusetts in 1968, Ann Blackham & Co. Inc. Realtors. From 1965 – 1979 she served as secretary and then VP of the National Federation of Republican Women, and from 1969 – 1974 was a member of the Board of Economic Advisers to the governor of Massachusetts. In 1972, she was a MA judicial selector. A member of the presidential task force on women's rights and responsibilities (1969), Blackham was co-author of "A Matter of Simple Justice," written to further the ERA. From 1971 – 1975, she served as chair of the Governor's Commission of the Status of Women, and from 1971 – 1974 was regional director, Interstate Association of Commissions on the Status of Women. From 1974 – 1978, she was a member of the Defense Advisory Commission on Women in Service, U.S. Department of Defense. She was appointed by four successive MA governors as chair of the Board of Registration of Real Estate Brokers & Salespeople in MA (beginning in 1984). She has been a member of the League of Women Voters since the 1950s and is an elected Republican state committee member. Blackham, who has two children, earned a B.A. (1949) from the College of St. Mary of the Springs (now Ohio Dominican University). (ABS)

Blackmon, Antonia (1932 – 1998) (also known as Barbara Ireton) The founding president of Washington, D.C., NOW, Blackmon presented the ERA resolution at NOW's 1967 national conference, held several NOW press conferences, and opened NOW's first national office. At the request of Alice Paul, Blackmon held the Susan B. Anthony celebration at the NWP's headquarters in the Sewall-Belmont House. Blackmon died of cancer in 1998.

Blair, Linda – See Miller, Linda Blair

Blaisdell, Virginia L. (1940 –) (also known as Virginia B. Fortino) A graphic designer and photographer, Blaisdell contributed to the anti-war and feminist movements through the media and music. From 1969 – 1975, she was a printer and graphic designer for The Advocate Press, a print shop established by the American Independent Movement to produce anti-Vietnam War literature and other materials for the New Haven (CT) radical community. In 1970 she was a member of AIM's women's group (which later became New Haven Women's Liberation). She and other members of NHWL formed the New Haven's Women's Liberation Rock Band to challenge the sexism of rock and roll. Blaisdell played the French horn and later drums for the group, which performed mostly at women's dances and political events. The rock band pro-

duced a record with the Chicago Women's Liberation Rock Band called Mountain Moving Day. It was reissued by Rounder Records (2005) as Papa Don't Lay That Shit On Me. Between 1971 – 1979, Blaisdell and others in NHWL converted the Women's Center bulletin into a monthly magazine titled *Sister*. She was active in AIM, a New Haven anti-war and community organizing group, from 1968 – 1973. Blaisdell received a B.A. from Wellesley College in 1962. (ABS)

Blakely, Mary Kay (1948 –) moved from Chicago to Ft. Wayne, IN, in 1973 and immediately joined the Fort Wayne Feminists. At the time, NOW was considering combining forces with this new group, but decided it was "too radical." Fort Wayne Feminists were "terrifically" involved in the fight for ratification of the ERA, says Blakely, and speaking out for the ERA was how Blakely learned public speaking. In the end, however, Indiana became the last state to ratify the ERA. Blakely helped her mentor, Joan Uebelhoer, run for public office. At the same time, she started writing feminist columns for the *Fort Wayne Journal Gazette*—but not without sparking controversy in that conservative town. On Mother's Day 1975, Blakely wrote about her husband being her "comrade in parenting." That comment engendered three weeks of debate on whether she was a Communist. Next, Blakely became a writer for The New York Times, doing the weekly "Hers" column on women's issues. In 1981, Gloria Steinem asked Blakely to write for *Ms.*, which she has been doing ever since. Blakely joined the University of Missouri Journalism School in 1997 and continues (2006) to teach writing in the magazine sequence. She is on the national advisory board of Women's Enews and the National Writer's Union, and is on the board of directors for the Journalism and Women's Symposium (JAWS). (ABS)

Blanchard, Margaret M. (1938 –) Teacher and activist, Blanchard contributed to *Unlacing: Ten Irish-American Women Poets* (1987), wrote three books on intuition, one book of poetry, and two novels about women's issues: *Hatching* (2001) and *Wandering Potatoes* (2002). She was a member of the editorial collective for *Women: A Journal of Liberation* (1970 – 1979); was one of the founders of the Baltimore Women's Union; and was on the staff of the Women's Growth Center (Baltimore) for three years. She helped organize 9to5: Baltimore Working Women, and at Towson (MD) University, was a three-year faculty member on a project on the scholarship of women. Blanchard has also been active in civil rights, gay rights and peace marches. She holds a Ph.D. from Union Institute & University, Cincinnati. (ABS)

Blatnik, Irene (1918 – 2002) was president of the first ERA coalition (ERA Central Illinois) in 1972, and was co-founder of the national ERA summit formed with the NWP. A primary school teacher who worked to establish fairness in public policy and for legislation that protected women and family life, she was a member of the LWV, and had two adopted children and one foster child.

Blau, Rachel – See DuPlessis, Rachel Blau

Blea, Irene Isabel (1946 –) (also known as Irene Blea Gutierrez and Irene Blea Moreno) joined the women's movement as a student at what was then Southern Colorado State College (1972) and has been active on issues of childcare, education, employment and labor. Calling herself an abused wife (1965 – 1968), she has fought violence against women, and supported reproductive rights. Since 1965, Blea has insisted on female inclusion in the leadership of organizations to which she belonged. Since 1972, she has worked to get women incorporated into university curriculum. She has written over nine classes, 29 nonfiction articles, plus three chapbooks of feminist poetry. She has also taught classes focusing on women in the departments of sociology, women's studies and Chicano studies (1976 – 1998) at various colleges and universities. Blea was one of the founders of the women's studies section of the Western Social Science Association (1979) and the Chicano studies section (1972) and was the first female national president of the National Association of Chicano (Chicana) Studies (1978 – 1979) (now NACCS). She was also one of the founders and chair of the NACS Chicana caucus in the early 1980s, and a founder of the Chicano Mental Health Association in Colorado (1979). Blea protested the Hyde Amendment in the 1970s, worked on Welfare rights, and served on the Denver Art Museum task force to include Chicana/o art in the museum (1980). Blea, who attended the World Women's Conference in Mexico City in 1975, had to pay her own way because, Blea says, Anglo women would not allow her to be a delegate because she spoke out against racism/sexism against women of color in the U.S., and feminists of the time did not recognize racism as a feminist issue. Blea holds a Ph.D. in sociology and is retired as full professor and chair, Department of Mexican American Studies, California State University, Los Angeles. She is working on the rights of older and disabled women. Awards include the Governor's Woman at Work Award, Denver, CO (1985); Outstanding Woman Scholar of the University of Southern Colorado (1985); and the Jesse Bernard Wise Woman Award, Center for Women's Policy Studies, Washington, D.C. (1995). Archives: Benson Latin American Collection, University of Texas, Austin, TX; and Southwest Research Center, University of New Mexico, Albuquerque, NM.   (ABS)

Bleier, Ruth H. (1923 – 1988) was a professor of neurophysiology at the University of Wisconsin, Madison, as well as a founder and faculty member of the women's studies program. One of the first scientists in the world to examine the foundations of the modern biological sciences from a feminist perspective (early 1970s), Bleier demonstrated how science, gender and sexuality, rather than being objective and value-free, change constantly in response to social values and ideas. Her studies culminated in the book *Science and Gender*, published in 1984. That book was followed in 1986 by her edited volume, *Feminist Approaches to Science*. In 1970, Bleier was a founder of the Association of Faculty Women, which challenged administrators to review the status and salaries of female instructors system-wide and to correct inequalities. Under Bleier's leadership, AFW organized graduate students and filed complaints with the civil rights office of the Department of HEW over faculty salary inequities, and with HEW and EEOC over lack of resources for women's intercollegiate athletics. Off campus, Bleier helped start Lysistrata, a feminist restaurant and bookstore. She was active in lesbian-friendly community groups and, as a lesbian herself, stood against the growing lesbian separatism within feminism.

Blessing, Elizabeth (1919 –) A resident of Dallas since the early 1920s, Blessing has been a lifetime member of Munger Place United Methodist Church, where she was the first woman member of the Board of Stewards and the first woman to chair the Commission on Missions. Blessing was Dallas City councilwoman from 1961 – 1965, and the first woman candidate for mayor of Dallas, 1965. Blessing has four children.   (ABS)

Blockstein, Liesl (1931 – 1986) served as president of the Wisconsin WPC in the mid to late 1970s. In 1979, she was named to the board of the Wisconsin Women's Network. Blockstein also served on the board of Community Shares of Wisconsin, which established the Liesl Blockstein Community Grants to fund innovative projects that reflect her vision of advancing social change, economic justice and social welfare.

Blom, Barbara – See Anthony, Barbara

Bloom, Elaine (1937 –) began her public advocacy for women's issues in 1967 when she spoke to the national convention of the National Council of Jewish Women about the need to include abortion law reform among its resolutions. She also began working for the ERA at that time. A member of the Florida State Legislature for over 18 years, Bloom authored over 100 major laws. First elected in 1974, she served two terms (1974 – 1978) representing Northeast Dade County. She returned to the House from Miami Beach and Miami in a special election in March 1986, and served as deputy majority leader (1986 – 1988); chair of the Dade County Legislative Delegation (1990 – 1991); and speaker pro tempore (1992 – 1994). She chaired committees such as healthcare, tourism and cultural affairs, joint legislative auditing, joint legislative management, federal/state appropriations and public transportation. Elected founding chair of the Dade County Commission on the Status of Women, in 1975 she published "Why Dade County Needs A Commission on the

Status of Women" in the *University of Miami Magazine*. Bloom also served the NCJW as president of the Greater Miami Section, Florida state legislation chair and national board member. She was the first woman appointed as a trustee of the Florida International University Foundation, where she also worked as acting director of the Institute for Women. Bloom has received numerous awards from organizations involved in women's issues, education, public safety, economic development and social services. She was named one of Dade County's five most influential women in 1970 and in 1997. The Miami Beach Chamber of Commerce named her its first female Citizen of the Year. Bloom, who has two children, earned her A.B. degree from Barnard College in 1957. Archives: Florida International University, North Miami, FL.   (ABS)

Bloomer, Barbara Ruth (1932 –) While working for Global Missions of the Methodist Church in the early 1970s, Bloomer went to John's Island (Charleston) to help dig wells, fix nursery schools and construct a health clinic. "This was dangerous work," she says, "because the year before some northern whites had been hung for causing 'unrest' in the black community." While she was there, local churchwomen asked her about the situation of women in "the outside world," which gave Bloomer a chance to introduce them to NOW. Back in Lansing, MI, Bloomer joined a NOW group, and was treasurer and then VP for several years. During the 1970s and 1980s, Bloomer marched in Washington for the ERA, reproductive rights, civil rights and employment equality. She has three daughters who, she says, are continuing the struggle for equality.   (ABS)

Bloomer, Ruth Ann (1953 –) As a founder of Traverse City, MI, NOW in 1978, Bloomer held various offices through the 1980s. She was on the board of directors of the Women's Resource Center in Traverse City (1978 – 1980), and worked to help displaced homemakers enter or re-enter the workplace. She established the first sexual assault program in the area, as well as safe houses for women and children. Bloomer also established a non-traditional employment program, working with trade unions and Lansing, MI, women, and helped create a recruiting effort for women in the building trades. She was one of the founders of the Women's Economic Development Organization in Traverse City (1986); founded a women-only golf event to raise funds for women's healthcare needs (1995 – 2003); and helped organize a women-only art exhibit and sale to raise money for the women's cancer fund (2003). Bloomer holds a B.S. from Central Michigan University (1975) and an M.S. from Michigan State (1978). She has one child.   (ABS)

Blum, June (1929 –) is an artist and pioneer in getting New York City women artists and their works exhibited in mainstream museums. Her Female President Light Event (1968 – 1969) helped raise awareness of Long Island, NY, artists and residents. As curator of contemporary art at the Suffolk Museum, Stony Brook, NY (1971 – 1975), she created the exhibit titled Unmanly Arts, the first in-house museum-curated exhibit of women artists (1971 – 1972). She also coordinated Works on Paper, a show for women artists at the Brooklyn Museum (1975). She also created a series of portraits of women prominent in feminist circles. In 1975, Blum formed Women Artists Living in Brooklyn, and was a juror for the exhibit Washington to Washington, held at the National Museum of Women in the Arts. In 1980, Blum formed East Central Florida Women's Caucus for Art, and initiated women's exhibits around the country. Blum, whose works have been exhibited nation-wide, studied at Brooklyn College, Brooklyn Museum Art School, The Pratt Graphic Art Center and the New School for Social Research. She created Women for Art to publish catalogs, and was a member of the New York Professional Women Artists Group. In addition, she was an original artist and member of the all-women Central Hall Artists Gallery.   (ABS)

Blum, Sharon L. (1939 –) joined Detroit NOW in 1972 under the initial organization by Patricia Burnett and Marj Levin, and served on the executive board as secretary (1973 – 1974) with Mary Jo Walsh as president. Blum helped organize the leafleting and picketing of Sears in response to its practice of keeping its largely female staff on a part-time basis in order to avoid pensions, medical benefits and equal pay. She also spoke on the "Editorial Reply" segment of a local TV station in response to a Right to Life speaker, and protested at the Catholic Bishops Conference regarding the lack of women priests and the Church's much-publicized stand against choice. Blum was also an active member in the Detroit area Catholics for a Free Choice.   (ABS)

Blumberg, Joyce – See Kozloff, Joyce

Boccaccio, Shirley Jean (1935 –) Artist, writer and organic farmer, Boccaccio was author/artist of the "Fuck Housework" poster (1971). She was a member of San Francisco NOW from 1970 – 1974, and as head of the speakers bureau and the creative women's task force, organized marches, street theater and press conferences, and did TV appearances "explaining what women want." She wrote three feminist children's books: *Penelope and the Mussels, Penelope Goes to the Farmers Market* and *Penelope and the Earth* from 1971 – 1975, and published two bilingual books for children featuring heroines: *The Valiant Children of Cuale*, of which she was author/illustrator; and *Califia, Queen of California*, written and illustrated by Trina Robbins. She also wrote a semi-autobiographical book, *Buying the Ranch: Book I, Facing Real Life.* Boccaccio has a ranch in Mexico (where everything is grown organically) and three children.   (ABS)

Bock, Lois Ann – See DiCosola, Lois Ann Bock

Boddy, Margaret (1909 – 2003) One of the first women to become a full professor at Winona (MN) State University, Boddy joined a successful equal-pay suit against the state college system when, in the 1970s, she realized that she was not being paid as much as her male colleagues. She also challenged the mandatory state retirement age, and in the 1970s and 1980s lobbied state officials for abortion rights. Boddy ran for the State Senate in District 34, which covered Winona and Houston counties (1982), and was honored by the Ramsey County WPC as a "founding feminist" for starting the Winona County WPC in the 1960s.

Boehning, Karen (1945 –) joined the Chicago chapter of NOW very early in 1969, and served as chapter president in 1971. She co-chaired the 1970 Women's Strike for Equality in Chicago to celebrate the 50th anniversary of women's right to vote, and was an Illinois delegate to the 1971 founding convention of the National Women's Political Caucus. In 1972, Boehning helped organize the first coalition to coordinate Illinois ratification of the ERA, and chaired Chicago NOW's media action committee focused on de-stereotyping the image of women in broadcast programming and advertising. Since 1988, Boehning has been a consultant to women and minority owned foodservice businesses. As state co-coordinator of Illinois WPC and treasurer of ERA Illinois, Boehning continues working on ERA ratification. (ABS)

Boersma, P. Dee (1946 –) A professor at the University of Washington since 1974, Boersma has held various positions in environmental science, zoology, biology and the women's studies program. She was a member of President Nixon's task force on women's rights and responsibilities (1969); was a member/adviser, U.S. delegations to the United Nations Status of Women Commission (1973); and a member of the United Nations World Population Conference, Romania (1974). She also testified at the Senate hearing on the ERA, and was on the organizing committee for the Washington State Women's Convention (1974). As an undergraduate at Central Michigan University, Boersma worked to get rid of dorm hours for women through organizations where she held leadership positions, such as the Association of Women Students and Student Government. Boersma has a B.S. from Central Michigan University (1969) and a Ph.D. from Ohio State University (1974). (ABS)

Boesing, Martha (1936 –) was the founder and artistic director of Minneapolis' At the Foot of The Mountain, the longest running professional women's theater company in the country (1974 – 1984). The company created plays about women's issues and many more about human issues from a woman's perspective. The company performed and worked in Minneapolis, but also toured around the nation. Boesing, the author of more than 40 plays, also performed a series of monologues about the second wave women's movement, "These Are My Sisters,"

at various places around the country. Boesing, who has three children and was active in the civil rights, peace and poverty movements, lives and works in Oakland, CA. She holds a B.A. from Connecticut College for Women (1957) and an M.A. from the University of Wisconsin, Madison (1958). Archives: Smith College, Northampton, MA; and the University of Minnesota, Minneapolis, MN. (ABS)

Boland, Colleen (1928 – 1994) was head of the Air Line Stewards and Stewardesses Association in 1965, and went before the EEOC and other branches of the state and federal governments to fight against the airlines' policies of grounding or terminating stewardesses when they reached the ages of 32 or 35, or on marriage. It was not until 1968 that the EEOC released new guidelines prohibiting that practice. Flora Davis writes in *Moving the Mountain* that by "tackling the age and marriage restrictions, stewardesses assaulted some of society's ingrained assumptions: that marriage was all women really wanted; that it was perfectly natural to judge a woman solely on her looks; and that men somehow had a right to the services of women—and if it could be arranged that the women doing the serving were young, single and attractive, so much the better." Boland had two children and worked in Cleveland as an arbitrator.

Bolden, Dorothy (1925 – 2005) founded the National Domestic Workers Union in 1968, and was an adviser to Presidents Nixon, Ford and Carter. Bolden's father was a chauffeur, her mother a housekeeper. Concerned about the plight of domestic workers toiling 12 hours a day for $35 a week, Bolden asked Dr. Martin Luther King Jr. what could be done about it. King's response—"That's a good job for you"—motivated Bolden to establish the union for household workers. She said in a 1986 *Atlanta Journal Constitution* article that "I was the one who went to Washington to kick up some hell about women not getting the attention they deserved." She said she fought "vicious hard" for maids to be recognized by the Social Security Administration. Eventually her union organized in 10 cities and had 13,000 applicants for job referrals. Her only requirement was that the applicant be a registered voter. After Bolden closed the union office in 1994, she continued her advocacy. Throughout her life Bolden was proud to proclaim that she was a "professional maid." She had six children.

Bolton, Roxcy O'Neal (1926 –) stopped the naming of hurricanes after women only, initially requesting that they be named after U.S. senators instead. The first fundraising VP of NOW, she founded Florida NOW, one of the first women's shelters and a rape crisis center, and was the organizing founder of the first Crime Watch in America. She also succeeded in opening the men-only lunchrooms at Jordan Marsh and Burdine's in Dade County, FL, to women, and helped the National Airlines stewardesses organize a "motherhood" demonstration that led to a contract agreement allowing maternity leave for stewardesses, married or not. (Previously, pregnancy meant a woman would lose her job.) Bolton also helped end discriminatory airline advertising campaigns. A fighter for the ERA, she persuaded U.S. Senator Birch Bayh (D-IN) early in 1970 to hold hearings on the ERA. Those hearings resulted in a national push that brought the ERA to the House floor for the first time ever. In addition, Bolton got the first woman appointed to the Dade County Commission in 1971; and recommended to the Florida attorney general that degrees of rape be established, which passed the Florida Legislature in 1974. In 1985 she established a fund to help homeless women and protest their mass burials in watery trenches. She also founded Women's Park in Dade County (1992). Inducted into the Florida Women's Hall of Fame (1984) Bolton says her Coral Gables home was designated by the State of Florida as a historical site, the Roxcy O'Neal Bolton Home, in 1999. Bolton has three children. Archives: The Roxcy Bolton Collection, Florida State Archives, Tallahassee, FL. (ABS)

Bond, Pat (1915 – 1990) (also known as Patricia Childers) was a comedian, actress, monologist and playwright, and was considered a trailblazer in providing gay and lesbian theater experiences. She attended Catholic School in Davenport, IA, an experience that she described as "a finishing school that finished me." In 1945, she enlisted in the U.S. Army Corps. In 1947, in occupied Japan, a "witch hunt" began in the Army and ultimately 500 lesbians were dishonorably discharged. Many of the women had nervous breakdowns; some committed suicide. Bond escaped harassment because she had married a gay man. When she left the Army, Bond moved to San Francisco where she attended San Francisco State College, then did some acting and bartending. She also trained at the University of Iowa under E.C. Mabie, who founded the first graduate program in theater. In the 1970s and 1980s Bond toured the country performing her four one-woman shows: "Gerty Gerty is Back Back Back," in which she impersonated Gertrude Stein; "Conversations with Pat Bond," about her childhood; "Murder in the WAC,"about the Army witch hunt; and "Lorena Hickock and Eleanor Roosevelt: A Love Story." Every two years since 1992 the Pat Bond Committee gives the Pat Bond Memorial Old Dyke Award, honoring lesbians 60 years and older who have not been recognized. Archives: San Francisco Gay and Lesbian Historical Society, San Francisco, CA.

Bonk, Kathy (1953 –) Executive director, Communications Consortium Media Center, Bonk has used media as her method to help women since the 1970s, when she became involved in the license renewals of Pittsburgh television stations. She also helped with the *Pittsburgh Press* at the Supreme Court case and the integration of Little League at Williamsport (PA). Bonk chaired national NOW's FCC committee, worked in 25 states to bring license challenges and agreements to help hire women in

the media, and filed rulemaking before the FCC to support women in the media. A founder of the Pittsburgh NWPC, she worked on the Shirley Chisholm for President campaign. Bonk also served on the staff of the National Commission on the Observance of International Women's Year, and in 1977 ran the media operations for the National Women's Conference in Houston. Bonk was the communications director of the National Commission on Working Women (1978 – 1979), and director of the Women's Media Project for the NOW Legal Defense and Education Fund (1979 – 1988). From 1988 – 1991, Bonk held a Leadership Fellowship with the W.K. Kellogg Foundation that resulted in the first family planning clinics in Moscow (USSR). She worked with Betty Friedan in Iceland on the 75th anniversary of suffrage, and was the communications director, National ERA Countdown Campaign (1980 – 1982). Bonk earned her B.A. from the University of Pittsburgh. Archives: University of Missouri Journalism School, JAWS Collection, Columbia, MO. (ABS)

Booksh-Wackwitz, Winnie Davis –
See Wackwitz, Winnie

Booth, Heather Tobis (1945 –) developed a political consciousness in high school. After hearing Martin Luther King Jr. speak, Booth dropped out of a school sorority and cheerleading team that discriminated against blacks and girls who weren't "pretty." Within months of arriving at the University of Chicago in 1963, she was active in the Friends of the Student Non-Violent Coordinating Committee (SNCC), organizing South Side freedom schools during a school boycott and protesting unequal school conditions. In 1964, she joined the Mississippi Freedom Project to focus attention on the denial of voting rights to black citizens. Booth entered the women's movement as an undergraduate at the University of Chicago (where she earned a B.A. in 1967 and an M.A. in 1970) when she started Jane, an abortion counseling service, in 1965. That same year, she started one of the first campus women's groups in the country, Women's Radical Action Project, which lobbied for courses on women and against parietal hours and nepotism laws (used to prevent wives from becoming full professors). She helped found the Chicago Women's Liberation Union (1968), and during the Women's Strike of 1970 ("Don't Iron While the Strike is Hot!"), began working with NOW and designed training for its national board, regions and many of its chapters. In 1969 Booth organized Action Committee for Decent Childcare, which won $1 million in state funding for childcare; a change in licensing for day care centers; and a client- and provider-controlled review board. At the same time she helped organize Sojourner Truth day care center. In 1971, Booth helped organize a clerical employees union. In 1973, with funding she won from a labor dispute for organizing these workers, she founded Midwest Academy to train organizers of social change. The first class trained women organizers, including many early NOW leaders, and those from 9to5 and other working women's organizations. From this base she helped to support and/or create a wide range of organizations. Booth was a consultant for the ERA in a number of states, and directed the first state mobilization for the ERA (Springfield, IL). She also helped start Citizen Action (1979), and as co-director and then president, helped build it to nearly three million dues-paying members in 36 states working on issues such as healthcare, toxic waste and consumer concerns. She also worked on political campaigns for candidates who promoted these kinds of issues, and was field director for Carol Moseley Braun's successful Senate races. Booth ran the Illinois Democratic Coordinated Campaign in 1996; directed the Mobilization for Women's Lives, which brought out over one million people around the country; and was the national training director of the Democratic National Committee and then director of NAACP national voter fund directing—the largest African American voter mobilization. She continues organizing for women's rights. She has a husband who also works for social change, and two children. Archives: Chicago Historical Society, Chicago, IL.   (ABS)

Borisof, Lyn Radewagen (1943 –) A feminist organizer, Borisof was a social worker counseling parents and children from 1964–1972. After the birth of her son in 1973, she organized a babysitting co-op with six women and nine children living in Evanston and Wilmette, IL. She later began doing workshops on imagination, friendship and home at the Ethical Humanist Society of Greater Chicago, where she organized a women's group in 2002. She also worked to pass the ERA. Borisof, who has one child, holds a B.A. from the University of Michigan and an M.A. from the University of Chicago.   (ABS)

Borman, Nancy (1947 –) wrote for, edited and published *Majority Report*, the feminist newspaper in New York City from 1971–1979. Although the paper covered all feminist organizations and activities, it had the flavor of the radical feminism prevalent at that time in Greenwich Village, where it was located. Borman founded *Majority Report* with a group from the Socialist Workers Party. The SWP people wanted to emphasize political issues like the Vietnam War, while Borman wanted a feminist newspaper. There was a showdown in May 1971, when the feminists outvoted the SWP group and *MR* became an unfettered feminist newspaper. After Borman participated in the 1970 march down Fifth Avenue in NYC, she joined several women's liberation groups in NY, but says her heart was with NOW until the organization put on a major anti-lesbian campaign (1969 – 1970), at which point she dropped out. She worked on many feminist projects, including the printing and posting of "Wanted" posters of CEOs who discriminated against women. Fluent in German and French, Borman worked for the Department of Public Information of the United Nations,

where she wrote press releases in English and summarized coverage of the U.N. for German newspapers. She retired from the U.N. in 2003 and now (2006) does freelance writing and translating in Vienna, where she lives. Borman holds two B.A. degrees from St. John's University, one in Theology and one in German. Archives: *Majority Report* publications at Schlesinger Library, Radcliffe Institute, Cambridge, MA.   (ABS)

Born, Brooksley Elizabeth (1940 –) (also known as Brooksley Elizabeth Landau) taught some of the first classes on women and the law in the 1970s at Columbus School of Law, Catholic University of America; and Georgetown Law Center, Georgetown University. She helped found the Women's Legal Defense Fund (now the National Partnership for Women and Families) and served on its first screening committee (1972 – 1974), and the Women's Rights Project of the Center for Law and Social Policy (1972), and chaired its advisory board (1972 – 1981). When the Project incorporated as the National Women's Law Center, she served on its board of directors continuously from 1981 to the present and chairs its board. Born established the Rights of Women Committee of the American Bar Association's section on Individual Rights and Responsibilities, and served on its governing council. As a member of ABA, she has been successful in urging it to support the constitutional equality of women, to endorse Congressional and state legislation forbidding sex discrimination, and to advocate the opportunities and interests of women. Born was the first woman on the ABA's Standing Committee on Federal Judiciary (1977 – 1983) and was its first woman chair (1980 – 1983). She revised its standards to allow it to find women and minority candidates qualified for the Bench, and was chair when it found Sandra Day O'Connor, the first female nominee to the Supreme Court, qualified for that appointment. Born served as a member of the ABA's Commission on Women in the Profession, and chaired a task force responsible for a publication urging legal employers and bar associations to provide childcare benefits (2000 – 2003). Born also co-founded and co-chaired the ABA's women's caucus. As an associate and then a partner at Arnold & Porter, Born engaged in pro bono activities furthering the opportunities and interests of women, and chaired the firm's pro bono committee (1990 – 1995). She worked in the civil rights movement, and also supported legal services for the poor. A graduate of Stanford Law School (1964), Born has five children.   (ABS)

Bornstein, Sarah Barbara (1947 –) (also known as Sarah B. Edeiken) Member of CWLU from 1972 – 1977, Bornstein co-chaired a Liberation School for Women workgroup and developed training on how to start a rap group. Her activism and career reflect a persistent focus on employment/labor and reproductive rights for women. She was a member and later chair of the Health Evaluation and Referral Service (1980 – 1987), as well as workgroup and developed training on how to start a rap group. Her activism and career reflect a persistent focus on employment/labor and reproductive rights for women. She was a member and later chair of the Health Evaluation and Referral Service (1980 – 1987), as well as one of the founders of the Chicago Abortion Fund. Since 1977 she has been a member and board chair of Women Employed. She is the administrative director of the Junior League of Chicago. Bornstein holds two master's degrees, one in American History and the other in Industrial Relations. She has one child. (ABS)

Boroson, Florence (1927 –) was an early member of NOW and a founder of the NOW chapter at Stony Brook University in Long Island, NY. From that chapter the mid-Suffolk chapter of NOW emerged (1970s). Boroson was also active in the planning and strategy of a class action suit against State University of New York. Although the suit was ultimately lost, it had "a salutary effect" on hiring practices at Stony Brook and other SUNY campuses. Boroson also led a two-year effort to reclassify the positions of about 30 female professional staff members in the library at Stony Brook. After making their case to the EEOC on campus, the women used the mechanism of a union grievance to pursue their cause. Although the grievance was officially denied, "everything we asked for was granted. For each of the women involved, this meant at least tens of thousands of dollars, as well as a new-found sense of self-respect." Boroson also participated in a community effort to persuade the school district to hire more female teachers. She has been politically active since her teens, and participated in civil rights and peace activities, as well as many political campaigns. Boroson has two children and holds a B.A. degree. Archives: Stony Brook University Library, Stony Brook, NY. (ABS)

Bosque, Beverly – See McCarthy, Beverly Fitch

Bottini, Ivy (1926 –) One of the founders of New York NOW (1966), Bottini was president from 1968 – 1970. In 1969 she held a public forum, "Is Lesbianism a Feminist Issue?" (the first time lesbian concerns were introduced into NOW); and designed NOW's national logo. In 1970, she led the takeover of the Statue of Liberty and hung the "Women of the World Unite" banner across its pedestal. Also in 1970, after conservatives in NY NOW raised the issue of the "lavender menace," Bottini moved to Los Angeles, where she fought anti-gay and lesbian legislation, and where, in 1977, she created the first lesbian/gay radio show on a mainstream network, KHJ Los Angeles. In 1981 she was appointed commissioner for the California Commission on Aging, the first "out" lesbian to hold such a post. In 1982 she joined the AIDS fight, forming the first information-clearing center, AIDS Network, Los Angeles. In 1983 Bottini was a founder of the lesbian/gay police advisory task force of Los Angeles. From 1998 – 1999 she was co-chair of the addiction and recovery city

task force, and established the ad hoc committee, City of West Hollywood, to publicize the issue of partner abuse in the gay/lesbian community. Also in 1999, she was chair of NOW's annual national conference, Pioneer Reunion, in Beverly Hills. In early 2001, Bottini joined with a broad coalition from the lesbian and gay community to form the Alliance for Diverse Community Aging Services, which helps secure affordable retirement and assisted living for lesbian and gay seniors. After she and others formed Gay Lesbian Elder Housing, the group raised $18.3 million and opened a 104-unit apartment complex, called Encore Hall, in Hollywood, CA. Archives: The ONE National Gay & Lesbian Archives, Los Angeles, CA. (ABS)

Boucher, Sandy (1936 –) belonged to a women's collective living in San Francisco (1971 – 1973) that published a newspaper, *MotherLode*. In this "movement house," residents planned demonstrations and responded to emergencies, such as protecting women who were threatened by violent spouses or boyfriends, and getting people out of jail. Boucher was a founding member of the Berkeley Feminist Institute, and beginning in 1978 taught women's writing workshops in the San Francisco Bay Area for 20 years. Also active in the peace movement, Boucher was arrested for demonstrating at Vandenberg Air Force Base against the MX Missile, and spent 11 days in jail (with 400 other women) for demonstrating at the Livermore Laboratories in 1983. She is the author of seven books, including *Turning the Wheel: American Women Creating the New Buddhism*. (ABS)

Boulding, Elise Marie (1920 –) A Quaker peace activist and homemaker with five children in the 1960s, Boulding began networking for women's causes and peace by starting a newsletter for Women Strike for Peace, and serving as international chair of the Women's International League for Peace and Freedom (1967 – 1970). Boulding served as secretary, working group on the study of sex roles in society, for the International Sociological Association (1970 – 1973) and chair (1973 – 1977). She also helped start the International Peace Research Association and affiliate U.S. peace studies organizations, and began an IPRA newsletter, now published in Japan. She has served on American Sociological Association committees on the status of women, and began working with UNESCO in the 1970s on projects concerning women and the culture of peace. She also served on the UNESCO Peace Prize jury. As an adviser and then board member of United Nations University (1970s – 1980s), she helped develop UNU's Household, Gender and Age project. Boulding, who has a Ph.D. from the University of Michigan (1969), has written extensively on women, the family and peace. Archives: Elise Boulding Archives, University of Colorado, Boulder, CO. (ABS)

Bourcier, Lee Ann MacDonald (1952 –) (also known as Lee Ann Magan) Bourcier learned about discrimination against women at an early age when her junior high school would not allow her to take the advanced math and science courses considered suitable only for boys. This awareness grew exponentially during her years at Barnard College, and later when she worked as a volunteer in the Women's Health Clinic in Portland, OR (1976). She entered law school at the University of Washington in 1979 and, after attending a law conference on women's issues at Willamette University Law School, helped organize a conference at the University of Washington in 1980. As a legal intern for the Seattle firm of Mrak and Blumberg (1980), she did groundbreaking research for a sexual harassment suit involving a lumber company that required female applicants to disrobe to demonstrate their musculature. Her work, published in *Remedies for Sexual Harassment in Employment* (by Christine M. Mrak and Lee Ann Magan, September 22, 1980), was distributed at many conferences. In addition to her work for women, Bourcier has been an anti-war activist, and served as co-coordinator of the United Farm Workers lettuce boycott in the Chelsea section of New York City (1972–1973). She also volunteered in campaigns to stop passage of the anti-gay referendums of Lon Mabon and his Oregon Citizens Alliance, and helped form People of Faith Against Bigotry, an ecumenical consortium that lobbied groups to make official statements opposing Mabon's referendums. Bourcier, who has two stepdaughters, graduated from Barnard College in 1973. (ABS)

Bourg, Lorna (1942 –) was co-founder (1969), president (1997) and executive director (1995) of the Southern Mutual Help Association. Her objective was to change the quasi-slave conditions—especially those of women and children—on Louisiana's sugar cane plantations. After some unions and others said there were no women farmworkers, SMHA published *Plantation Portraits – Women of the Louisiana Sugar Cane Plantations*. Bourg created, through SMHA, home ownership opportunities and access to affordable credit and capital, especially for women. In 1972, she co-founded the first medical and dental health clinic for farmworkers in Louisiana, and in 1977 co-founded the first adult education program on the plantations. Also in 1977, Bourg served as LA delegate to the Houston National Plan of Action Convention. Representing LA's rural areas and women, she changed the proposed NPA to include not just "farm wives,"as stated, but "women farmworkers." She subsequently spent years in the Houston National Women's Conference's successor organization, the National Women's Conference Committee. In the middle and late 1960s, Bourg was active in the first Headstart Program, and helped desegregate numerous restaurants with an African American friend, Mae Gage, of Abbeville, LA. In 1992, she began a quest to find the remains of the airmen of the 1958, C-130 Cold War shoot-down, including those of her older brother, Airman First Class Archie T. Bourg Jr. She ultimately secured full military burial honors in Arlington

Cemetery for the loved ones of all 17 families. In 1992, the John D. and Catherine T. McArthur Foundation named her a McArthur Fellow. Bourg holds a B.S. (1965) and an M.S. (1975). She serves on the U.S. Commission on Civil Rights, Louisiana Advisory Committee. (ABS)

Bouvier, Libby (1946 –) An anti-war and civil rights activist in the 1960s, Bouvier participated in several progressive student groups at Cal State/Northridge, including efforts to organize a campus women's center and to raise issues about sexism and the second-class status of the women students. She also worked with a small group of women to publicize efforts to free Angela Davis, and for several years was involved with the Chicano Educational Opportunity Program and its efforts to increase the number of Chicana (women) students who successfully complete college. In 1972, Bouvier moved to Boston and became resident caretaker at the Women's Center for 13 years. With six other women, she started the Boston Area Rape Crisis Center, and also taught courses on U.S. women's history and U.S. women's labor history at the Women's School. In addition, for several years she co-taught Women's History Ovular at the Cambridge-Goddard Graduate School for Social Change. In 1980, Bouvier started the Boston area Women's Movement Archives at the Women's Center, and was a founder of the Boston area Lesbian and Gay History Project (now called The History Project). She was curator (1996) of the Boston Public Library exhibit Public Faces/Private Lives: Boston's Lesbian and Gay History. In 1998, Beacon Press published The History Project's book *Improper Bostonians: Lesbian and Gay History from the Puritans to Playland*. Bouvier has one child and is the archivist for the Massachusetts State courts. (ABS)

Bowdler, Nancy O. (1918 – 1990) Originator of the slogan "Women Are People," Bowdler was vice chair of the legislative committee of Pittsburgh NOW. She was active in the campaign to get the Sex Amendment added to the Pennsylvania Human Relations Act and the Pennsylvania Constitution.

Bowen, Anne (1946 –) A longtime activist in feminist causes, Bowen was working at the Valley Women's Center in Northampton, MA, in the early 1970s, when she contacted Pamela Brandt and Helen Hooke to ask if they would be interested in forming a band for an upcoming women's arts festival. They were interested, and the three received an enthusiastic response from the audience; thus, The Deadly Nightshade—one of the earliest women's bands—was born. In 1974, the group signed a recording contract with RCA. Bowen did guitar, percussion and vocals for the group, which played at a wide variety of commercial venues and women's events from 1972–1977. She also worked for many years at the Women's Action Alliance where she was involved with the National Women's Agenda Project and the operations office of the

Pro-Plan Caucus at the National Women's Conference in Houston (1977). She now lives in Tucson, AZ.   (ABS)

Bowers, Cheryl – See Bergman, Ciel Olsen

Bowers, Ruth McLean (1920 –) served on the board of Planned Parenthood from its earliest years, and helped found Texas Abortion Rights Action League. While serving on the board of NARAL, she helped fund Roe v. Wade, and is responsible for the first abortion clinic in San Antonio, which was created immediately after the Roe v. Wade decision. An advocate of women's education, she served on the board of regents of Texas Women's University for 11 years. Her interest in education includes St. Mary's Hall, a private co-educational college preparatory school in San Antonio, from which she graduated in 1938. She has served on the board of trustees for over 40 years, and was named Trustee Emerita in 1988. She received the Distinguished Alumnae Medal in 1986 and the Founders Day Award in 2003. The Texas WPC named her Woman of the Year for her volunteer and philanthropic help, and she has been active in Emily's List and the International Women's Forum. A graduate of Finch College, she has six children.   (ABS)

Bowles, Gloria Lee (1942 –) In 1972, after passing her Ph.D. exams in comparative literature at Berkeley, Bowles taught a course on women's literature. With a group of undergraduates, assistant professors and staff, she lobbied for a women's studies major at Berkeley. Approval finally came in the fall of 1975. Because there was no money to support the major, Bowles began lobbying, netting a small amount, but sufficient to open the doors in fall of 1976. Bowles served as coordinator from 1976–1983, and as a full-time lecturer until 1985. Her writings include "A Quiet Struggle: Women's Studies at Berkeley" (*Chronicle of the University of California 5,* Spring 2002); "From the Bottom Up: The Students' Initiative" (*The Politics of Women's Studies: Testimony from Thirty Founding Mothers,* edited by Florence Howe, the Feminist Press, 2000); and *Theories of Women's Studies*, edited by Gloria Bowles and Renate Duelli Klein (Routledge, 1983). Bowles earned her B.A. (1964) and M.A. (1966) from the University of Michigan, and her Ph.D. from the University of California, Berkeley (1976).   (ABS)

Bowman, Meg M. (1929 –) A retired professor of sociology at San Jose State University (CA), Bowman was a member of the local NOW chapter, starting in 1972, where she participated in ERA and CEDAW efforts. She was co-chairof the feminist caucus of the American Humanist Association, for 10 years, and chair of the Women's Alliance, First Unitarian Church (1972–2000). She is the editor of several books, including *Sexist Language* (with Rosemary Matson) and *Rise Up and Call Her Name,* by Elizabeth Fisher, and is the author/editor of 10 feminist books, primarily on women's history. Bow-

man, who taught women's studies classes at San Jose State from 1985–1996, became active in OWL in 1995, where she facilitated several programs, including Crone Rituals. She has designed, organized, recruited and escorted several women-focused international tours, including taking 108 persons to the 1985 End of U.N. Women's Decade Conference in Nairobi, Kenya, and 75 women to the 1995 U.N. Women's Conference in China. She has supported scholarship programs for bright, impoverished girls in Kenya, and collected funds to put nine young women through secondary and then post-secondary schools. Active in the civil rights and peace movements from 1948–1960s, she has marched for peace, civil rights and the ERA, and helped raise funds for all three.   (ABS)

Boxer, Marilyn J. (1930 –) A noted historian, Boxer began teaching women's history in 1971, and chaired the country's first women's studies program at San Diego State University (1974–1980). She has published many articles in scholarly journals on women and history, and written *When Women Ask the Questions: Creating Women's Studies in America* (Johns Hopkins University Press, 1998). She was co-author and co-editor, with Jean H. Quataert, of *Connecting Spheres: Women in the Western World, 1500 to the Present* (Oxford University Press, 1987) and a revised second edition, *Connecting Spheres: European Women in a Globalizing World* (Oxford, 2000); and with Quataert was co-editor and contributing author, *Socialist Women: European Socialist Feminism in the Nineteenth and Early Twentieth Centuries* (Elsevier, 1978). Boxer served as a consultant for women's studies, University of California, Irvine (1975); women's history at San Diego County Schools (1974–1975); women's studies, Domi-nican University of California (2004); Title III grant for development of the Women's Center, San Diego City College (1980); and women's studies, University of California, Riverside (1985). She has received numerous awards, including the Susan B. Anthony Award from NOW, San Diego County (1979), and Women of Achievement Award, President's Council of Business and Professional Women's Organizations of San Diego (1987). Boxer is professor of history emerita at San Francisco State College (2005). She earned an A.B. from the University of Redlands (1965) and an M.A. (1966) and Ph.D. (1975) from the University of California, Riverside.   (ABS)

Boyea, Ruthe Wright (1918 –) A member of the U.S. Navy from 1941–1945, Boyea was president of the LWV in 1955. She was founder and director of the women's center at Central Connecticut State College (now called the Ruthe Boyea Women's Center) in 1965, and in 1968 was appointed to the Permanent Commission on the Status of Women. A member of the board of the Connecticut Conference of the United Church of Christ (1965–1972), Boyea was also New England Representative on the national board of the AAUW (1970–1976). In addition, she attended all four U.N. Conferences on the Status of Women (1975, Mexico City; 1980, Copenhagen; 1985, Nairobi; and 1995, Beijing). By the time Boyea left the Navy in 1945, she was responsible for the welfare and morale of a Naval Air Base. Just 21 at the time, she became a feminist "before the word existed" when she realized that whatever job the women of the Navy were assigned, they did with distinction, including air traffic control, hospital and nursing work. Boyea researched women who have served in the military for the 150th anniversary of New Britain, CT, put it into a presentation, and traveled across the state sharing the information. A college professor, Boyea has two children. The recipient of the NAACP Community Service Award in 2004, Boyea holds an undergraduate degree from Boston University and an M.A. from Central Connecticut State College.   (ABS)

Boyer, Elizabeth Mary ("Betty") (1913–2002) Attorney, author, teacher, artist and activist, Boyer received her law degree in 1947 and her master's in law from Western Reserve University's Thomas Bachus School of Law in 1950. She was admitted to the bars of various federal, district and circuit courts, and was admitted to practice before the U.S. Supreme Court. Boyer was the founder and first president of WEAL (1968), and in 1973, with feminist lawyer Marguerite Rawalt, brought the fight against sex-labeled classified job advertising to the U.S. Supreme Court. WEAL was also central to forcing state universities to abandon quotas and discrimination against women, in "desexing" banks, and in passing Title IX of the Educational Amendments, which prohibited sexual discrimination in any educational program receiving federal assistance. Boyer lobbied for the ERA in Washington, and spoke frequently on issues of law and women's employment and education. She also served on a White House Advisory Committee on the Status of Women. In 1976 she wrote "The Legal Status of Homemakers in Ohio." Boyer received many awards over her lifetime. One of the first women ever inducted into the Ohio Women's Hall of Fame, she was honored in 1999 by the VFA. She was a president of the LWV (Cleveland), a member of the National Association of Women Lawyers, and on the Ohio Commission on the Status of Women. She was also a full professor of business law at Cuyahoga Community College, retiring in 1978.

Boyer, Gene Cohen (1925 – 2003) saw her most significant contribution as "a change agent for women in business and as a mentor for feminist women and girls considering business careers and other leadership positions." As a child in an Orthodox Jewish family living in Milwaukee, Boyer questioned the role of women in Judaism, and challenged laws and customs in public life thereafter. As a member of the Status of Women Commission in Washington, D.C. (1966), she took part in the founding of NOW and served as NOW's first treasurer. She also served two terms as finance VP. From 1974–1993, Boyer was a board member of the NOW LDEF, including serv-

ing one term as president. Known for her coalition-building skills, Boyer founded six feminist organizations, including Wisconsin NOW, the Wisconsin Business Women's Coalition, the Wisconsin Women's Network, and the Jewish Women's Coalition. She was also a charter member of the National Association of Women Business Owners. She and her husband, Burton Leonard Boyer, co-owned a multi-store retail home furnishings operation in Beaver Dam, WI, for 32 years. After selling the business, she became a consultant to small business owners and nonprofit organizations. She served by presidential appointment on the Advisory Council to Small Business Development Centers, and on the Governor's Committee on Minority and Women-Owned Businesses. Among her many citations and awards are Woman Business Advocate of the Year by the Small Business Administration (1985); a citation by the Wisconsin Legislature (1986); Wisconsin Stateswoman of the Year by the Wisconsin Women's Network (1997); and the Circle of Excellence Award from the Broward County, FL, Women's Chamber of Commerce (1999). Archives: National files to the Schlesinger Library, Radcliffe Institute, Cambridge, MA. Papers dealing with events in Wisconsin are in the Gene Boyer Legacy Project (open to other feminists papers), Wisconsin Historical Society, Madison, WI.   (ABS before death)

Boylan, Elizabeth – See Wade, Betsy

Boyle, Mary O. (1941 –) An early feminist political organizer and elected official, Boyle joined the Heights (Ohio) YWCA board in 1970. That board worked jointly with the local YMCA, which wanted YWCA income without proportionately sharing facilities and services. The YWCA's women's successful negotiations taught Boyle how women can use their power to get what they deserve. Boyle testified for the ERA before the OH State Legislature, and worked for its ratification in that state until that effort succeeded. In 1972, she was a charter member of the Cleveland WPC, and in 1973 and 1974 managed the successful political campaign of a feminist candidate for the State Legislature. While president of the Cuyahoga WPC in 1974 and 1975, Boyle helped form an OH State WPC. In 1978 she won a seat in the OH House of Representatives, and served three terms. Her maiden speech was in support of Medicaid funding for abortions for poor women. While representing her district, she was able to work on women's issues such as equal pay, the development of women's businesses, and reforming the laws on rape. In 1984, Boyle became the first woman elected Cuyahoga county commissioner, defeating a popular Republican incumbent and subsequently serving for three four-year terms, including three as president. She also represented OH on the board of the National Association of Counties. In 1996, Boyle won the Democratic nomination to run for U S. Senate, becoming the first woman in OH to win a Senate nomination. After losing in the general election, she stayed active in OH politics and community affairs and accompanied President Clinton on his historic peace missions to Ireland. In 2004, she became a Registered Nurse and a community outreach nurse and volunteered at Cleveland's Free Clinic. She is included in the Ohio Women's Hall of Fame. Archives: Ohio Historical Society, Columbus, OH. (ABS)

Boyle, Patricia J. (1937 –) As a county prosecutor in the Wayne County (MI) prosecutor's office, Boyle created a victim's program emphasizing the treatment of rape victims. And as a member of the Michigan Women's Task Force on Rape, she helped draft the reform of MI's criminal sexual conduct law, legislation that has been described as the most successful rape law reform measure in the U.S. To familiarize attorneys, police and judges with the new law, Boyle created and directed training seminars. In 1978, Boyle was appointed to the Federal District Court by President Jimmy Carter. As a Justice of the Michigan Supreme Court (1983 – 1999), she participated in decisions upholding victim's rights. A 1963 graduate of Wayne State University Law School and senior editor of *Wayne Law Review*, Boyle is the recipient of two NOW Feminist of the Year Awards, and was inducted into the Michigan Women's Hall of Fame in 1986. (ABS)

Boyne-Mead, Kay Eggleston (1931 –) was a co-founder of a NOW chapter in Traverse City, MI (1979), and was its president for the first years. She worked for the ERA with fundraisers and marches (Washington, D.C., Detroit, Chicago), and in the 1980s joined a Manistee, MI, chapter of NOW. As a member of Susan B. Anthony Women, Boyne-Mead helped abused women and introduced them to feminist ideals and actions. In 1982, Boyne-Mead was part of the Benzie Area Women's History Project, which created an annual Education Day in March. The group won a Michigan Women's Hall of Fame award. At the age of 70, Boyne-Mead posed for breastcancer survivor photos, which were shown in many venues around the country. An early fighter for civil rights, she has also been an active Democrat and organized six peace marches in Benzie County (MI). Boyne-Mead, who has two children, holds a B.A. from the University of Michigan. Archives: Women's History Project of Northwest Michigan, Traverse City, MI. (ABS)

Brabant, Sarah Callaway (1932 –) Professor emeritus of sociology (retired) at the University of Louisiana at Lafayette, Brabant served on the steering committee that designed and developed the Lafayette Commission on the Needs of Women (1977 – 1980), and was its president from 1977 – 1979. She also served on the steering committee that designed and developed both the Rape Crisis Center and the first battered women's shelter in Lafayette. Brabant was a member of the advisory committee, Salvation Army's Women's Care Shelter, 1979 – 1980; served on the advisory board, University Medical Center Rape Crisis Center (1980 – 1989); and was part of the rape

crisis line escort (1981 – 1984). She was also a member of the board of directors, Faith House (1981 – 1992), and served as its president (1982 – 1983). A member of the Southern Sociological Society, she served on its committee on the status of women (1987 – 1990), and was its chair from 1988 – 1990. Brabant has written widely on sex-role stereotyping and sex bias. She has three children. Archives: Dupre Library, University of Louisiana, Lafayette, LA. (ABS)

Brackenridge, Mary Ann Rossi – See Rossi, Mary Ann

Braderman, Joan E. (1948 –) As a graduate student at New York University in the early 1970s, Braderman led a seminar exploring the history of women directors. In 1972, she published a feature article in *Artforum*, a review of the First International Festival of Films by Women, and joined a CR group and CARASA. At the School of Visual Arts, Braderman taught "the first, or one of the first, courses on women as directors of film and video" (1973), a class she has been teaching in one form or another for over 30 years. In 1974, Braderman was a co-founder of *Heresies*, where she worked on *Issue #1* with May Stevens, Lucy Lippard, Harmony Hammond, Betsy Hess and Arlene Laddin. She also worked on *Issue #9: Women Organized; Women Divided* with some of the same women in 1979. In 1975, Braderman was also a co-founder of New York Socialist Feminists. She has written several articles about feminism and film and produced numerous videos. Some of her best known videos about women and popular culture are "Joan Braderman 'Reads' the *National Enquirer*, or Natalie Didn't Drown" (1983); "Joan Does Dynasty" (1986); "No More Nice Girls" (1989); and "Joan Sees Stars" (1993). In the early 1980s, Braderman was part of No More Nice Girls, an ad hoc group of friends, writers, artists and other feminists who did agit-prop street theater addressing the Reagan administration's attack on reproductive rights. A video artist and professor of video, film and media studies at Hampshire College, Braderman holds a B.A. from Harvard (1970) and an M.A. (1973) and M. Phil., cinema (1977) from New York University. Her videos are distributed by Women Make Movies, the Video Data Bank and London Electronic Arts. (ABS)

Bradway, Norma (1944 – 2004) was one of the founders of the Indianapolis chapter of NOW. In addition she had been a member of the state's first NOW chapter, which started in Muncie. After attending a hearings on federal credit laws, Bradway became interested in women's financial issues and pressured the Indiana legislature to change state laws. Among the issues she championed were the ERA, the Uniform Marital Property Act and the Indiana Commission for Women. She later brought her considerable skills to the issue of domestic violence, becoming the first executive director of the Indiana Coalition against Domestic Violence when it was founded in 1983.

Brady, Judith Ellen (1937 –) (also known as Judith Syfers) was a member of early CR groups in San Francisco in the late 1960s, and in 1970 wrote "Why I Want a Wife," which was part of the public program in SF celebrating the 50th anniversary of women's suffrage. The article was then published in *Motherlode*, a local women's paper on which Brady worked, and in *Ms.* magazine. In 1970, she joined Breakaway, a community school about women led by women in the SF Bay area, where she taught an overview class on the women's movement. She was a member of Women's National Abortion Action Coalition and became one of seven national coordinators (1970 – 1972). "In 1973 I went to Cuba on the Venceremos Brigade, and from then on I have devoted my political work to a much broader scope of issues as it became clear to me that the liberation of women could not be realized until all people were free." For the last 20 years, she has spent most of her political energy on the link between environmental contamination and health, specifically as it relates to cancer. In 1991 she published an anthology, *1 in 3: Women With Cancer Confront an Epidemic* (Cleis Press). She has been a member of Women's Cancer Resource Center (Oakland); National Coalition for Health and Environmental Justice (now defunct); and the Charlotte Maxwell Complementary Clinic (training on the politics of cancer for volunteers). She has two children.   (ABS)

Brandenburg, Judith Berman (1941 – 2003) was associate dean at Yale College, Yale University (1977 – 1985). There, she played a leading role in establishing the women's studies program and chaired a committee that developed grievance procedures for sexual harassment complaints, procedures that were adopted by many other institutions of higher learning nationwide. She later became professor of psychology and education in the dept. of counseling and clinical psychology, Teachers College (Columbia University), and was the first woman to hold the position of VP for academic affairs and dean of the college (1985 – 1994) at TC. Until her death, Brandenburg conducted research at TC on sexual harassment and other women's issues. She is the author of "Confronting Sexual Harassment: What Schools and Colleges Can Do."

Brandt, Pamela Robin (1947 –) was one of three members (with Anne Bowen and Helen Hooke) of The Deadly Nightshade, a self-described "hideously loud rock/country dance band" that originally got together in 1972 in the Northampton, MA, area, where the women had gone to college. Beginning at a benefit concert for the Valley Women's Center, the group played everything from lesbian bars and the National Women's Music Festival to "even the roughest holes-in-the-wall." In 1974, they recorded for the RCA Phantom label, signing the first record contract with veto power over any advertising, etc., that they considered offensive to a feminist sensibility. They went on to make two albums, and several singles— one of which hit the national Cashbox and Billboard Top 100 chart. In 1976, they opened for Billy Joel. Their last performance was the National Women's Conference, Houston (1977). When the Smithsonian Institute requested "relics" from The Deadly Nightshade, it was sent both albums and a "Mr. Big" Appalachian dancing doll that the group used in one of its feminist songs. In 2001, the Country Music Hall of Fame in Nashville also requested artifacts. In addition to her music, Brandt co-wrote two books, *Are You Two Together*, the first gay travel book to be published by a mainstream publisher (Random House, 1991) and *The Girls Next Door: Into the Heart of Lesbian America* (Simon & Schuster, 1996). A graduate of Mount Holyoke College, Brandt continues (2005) to play her bass. She has two stepchildren. Archives: Items at The Smithsonian and Country Music Hall of Fame.   (ABS)

Brannigan, Mary – See Schattman, Mary Ellen

Brannon, Robert (1943 –) was secretary and treasurer of the Association for Women in Psychology (1970). He was an organizer for NYC NOW's Men's CR Groups (1972 – 1973); a panelist on "Equality in Marriage," NY MENSA (1972); and was selected by NIMH as one of 25 participants for the National Conference on Research on Women, Madison, WI (1975). He is co-author of "Eliminating Sexist Language" (APA *Monitor*, 1975), and gave an address, "Does female liberation include male liberation?" at Central Connecticut State College in 1975. He is also co-author of the college gender studies text, *The Forty-Nine Percent Majority: The Male Sex Role* (Addison-Wesley, 1976). In 1986 he was awarded the Outstanding Achievement in Sex Equality in Education Award from the NY State Department of Education. Brannon has a B.A. from Harvard University (1965) and a Ph.D. from the University of Michigan (1975).   (ABS)

Braun, Suzanne – See Levine, Suzanne Braun

Brautigan, Virginia – See O'Toole, Virginia Anne

Bravo, Ellen (1944 –) An activist, author and speaker, Bravo first became involved in the women's movement in Montreal in 1969. In the 1970s, she taught women's studies in southern Maryland and San Diego, CA. She moved to Baltimore, where she did organizing in a low-income community and then in various office jobs. Bravo discovered 9to5 (a grassroots organization founded in 1973 that strengthens women's ability to win economic justice) in 1982 and helped found the Milwaukee chapter. She became head of the national organization in 1993. During those years Bravo was active in organizing low-wage women in a variety of campaigns, including pay equity, sexual harassment, family leave, Welfare reform, and part-time and temp work. Several times she testified before Congressional committees about the needs of the working poor. She has also served on a number of state and federal bodies, including the Commission on Leave appointed by Congress to study the impact of the Family and Medical Leave Act. In 1997 Bravo was the recipient of a Women of Vision Award from the *Ms.* Foundation. In addition, Bravo is the co-author of *The 9to5 Guide to Combating Sexual Harassment* and author of *The Job/Family Challenge: A 9to5 Guide (Not for Women Only)*, and *Taking on the Big Boys: Reflections from the Feminist Trenches*. Bravo is an assistant professor of women's studies at the University of Wisconsin-Milwaukee. She also coordinates the Multi-States Working Families Consortium. (ABS)

Breed, Elizabeth ("Deedy") Collins (1922 –) A former aeronautical engineer at Pratt & Whitney Aircraft (CT), Breed is the publisher of *And Then She Continued*, a book of poems published by the New Haven Women's Poetry Group (1974). She was also involved in setting up the New Haven (CT) Feminist Federal Credit Union, the New Haven Women's Health Center and the Women's Center in New Haven, and was active on the board of the Girl Scouts Council in New Haven. From 1981–2002 she was treasurer and board member of New England Women's Music Retreat, and from 1993–2003 was on the steering committee of Old Lesbians Organizing for Change. Breed, who has three children, earned her M.B.A. from the University of New Haven. (ABS)

Breen, Aviva (1936 –) A retired attorney, Breen lobbied the Minnesota Legislature for passage of the ERA in 1972. As an attorney with a legal services program in 1979, she successfully lobbied for the Domestic Abuse Act, the second in the country providing civil orders for protection. From 1983–2001, Breen was director of the Legislative Commission on the Economic Status of Women for the State of Minnesota. During that period, the group pushed for the Pay Equity Act, which eliminated gender-based wage discrimination in public employment in the state; one of the first parental leave laws in the country; elimination of discrimination in credit to women business owners; establishment of a sliding-scale fee childcare system for low-income families; strengthening of enforcement of child support orders; and funding for programs for battered women. In 1997 and 2003, Breen traveled to Bulgaria to assist in writing and lobbying for laws to support the rights and welfare of women. In 2005, the Bulgarian Parliament passed its domestic violence law "modeled after ours," says Breen. Breen, who has four children, earned her B.S. from Northwestern (1957) and her J.D. from the University of Minnesota (1977). (ABS)

Breines, Winifred (1944 –) An academic with a Ph.D. in sociology, Breines joined the Boston group Bread and Roses in 1969. She has been active in feminist activities and women's studies ever since. A supporter of the civil rights movement, Breines was also active in the New Left and anti-war movements. Archives: Schlesinger Library, Radcliffe Institute, Cambridge, MA. (ABS)

Brelle, Karen Voltz (1945 –) An active feminist since 1971, Brelle was a founder (1976) of Sistermoon feminist bookstore in Milwaukee, "a place to sit, read, explore women's ideas, think, discover, share, be free, and be energized." Brelle also helped establish the women's crisis line, a project of the Women's Coalition of Milwaukee (1972). In 1982, Brelle moved to Northern Wisconsin and founded Ishpiming Retreat Center. Under the name of "Sage," Brelle has published seven books on self-improvement and spirituality. (ABS)

Brennan, Peg (1924 –) Restless as a suburban executive housewife in the late 1950s, Brennan joined the civil rights movement, the anti-war movement, and then—as soon as it arrived—the women's movement. Working in NYC in crisis intervention, Brennan and feminist activist Flo Kennedy purchased property in Nova Scotia and on Fire Island, NY. The two used the places to host numerous political events, while Brennan imported an old British taxi-cab for the two to ride around in. In 1963, Brennan was a co-founder of an anti-war coffeehouse, MacDougal East, at the same time providing safe haven for draft dodgers in her home. By 1968 she had joined a CR group started by Redstockings, purchased a Brooklyn brownstone, and created a feminist household, providing a venue for women musicians, filmmakers, etc. She was a co-founder of the Feminist Party, a member of the Women's Coffeehouse (NYC), and a member of the Feminist Referral Collective, a group of women providing feminist therapy. She also had a small role in the feminist fantasy cult film "Born in Flames," starring Flo Kennedy. Brennan, who has three children, is a member of Senior Action Network, OWL and Gray Panthers. She holds a B.A. from New York University. (ABS)

Brentlinger, Ann F. – See Ferguson, Ann

Breslau, Linda – See Berg, Linda Breslau

Breslin, Madeline Jane (1935 –) was an early member of the Women's Center in Dayton, OH. She helped with some of the proposal writing and did counseling there, then went on to co-found Women Against Rape (WAR). After a few years, WAR became the catalyst for the formation of the Victim-Witness Project in Dayton. Affiliated with the prosecutor's office, the project remains. As an employee of the American Friends Service Committee, Breslin ran the student rights and responsibilities project, where her particular focus was Title IX. In addition to helping several schools obtain equity treatment for women in high-school sports, this project also dealt with school suspensions in the Dayton Public Schools, which were extraordinarily high and affected primarily minority males and females. Breslin also worked with feminist filmmakers Julia Reichert and Jim Klein. Breslin, who has an M.S. in counseling and is a licensed massage therapist, has three children. (ABS)

Bright, Paul (1965 –) The son of feminist Jean Stapleton, Bright grew up in the offices of Los Angeles NOW, making protest signs, folding letters and running errands. Bright remained active through his early twenties, "working conferences, marching, writing letters, fundraising and, most importantly, questioning the sexist traditions in my schools, church and community." He has worked for reproductive rights and against the sexist stereotyping of toy advertising. A resident of Lockhart, TX, Bright is a railroad brakeman. (ABS)

Bro, Greta (1951 –) Bro has dedicated herself to improving women's self-esteem, spirituality and gender issues since the early 1970s, employing a wide range of talents as a healer, teacher, writer, singer/songwriter and dancer. While attending Marlboro College (1969 – 1974), she helped set up a women's center/circle for underprivileged and battered women. Bro's senior thesis, "The Emergence of the Women's Movement in Nineteenth Century America and the Effects it Had on the French and Industrial Revolutions," paved the way for the college's women's studies program. Moving to New Jersey, Bro joined the Goddess collective that produced the biannual journal *Lady Inclination of the Night*, which described the oral history, rituals and traditions of matrilineal culture. In 1977, after moving to New York City, Bro put together (along with her mother, theologian June Bro) a month-long retreat that focused on the many faces of the Mother as she appears in art, writing and inner life. She has continued to arrange retreats and workshops on the healing powers of the Divine Feminine and Goddess heritage, including teaching at Interface Foundation and Lesley College, where she earned an M.A. in counseling psychology and expressive arts therapies in 1984. (ABS)

Broadaway, Carolyn (1946 –) (also known as Carolyn Forrey) received her Ph.D. from Yale in 1971. By 1969, she had come to focus her work on American women writers of the late 19th and early 20th century. With Carol P. Christ, she founded the first CR group in New Haven (1970). In 1972, Broadaway joined the faculty of Empire State College, a nontraditional college of the State University of New York geared to individualized education for adults. There, "unburdened by the constraints of traditional departments and curriculum committees, I was free to offer some of the very first undergraduate courses in women's studies in the nation, including American Women Writers, African American Women Writers, Introduction to Women's Studies, and Issues in Feminism." Her article "The New Woman Revisited," on late 19th century American women writers, was published in the new feminist journal *Women's Studies* (Spring 1974). She developed and chaired a panel, Contemporary Women's Art: Arriving at Women's Heritage, for the American Studies national convention in San Antonio, TX (1975), and presented a paper, "Problems in the Portrayal of the Liberated Woman as Heroine in American Literature," at

that same convention. In 1975, she returned to Yale for a semester as a visiting lecturer in American studies and introduced "two women's studies courses to a curriculum that had been long and staunchly androcentric." A course on American women writers was the first at Yale to focus on women as authors of American literature. At Yale, Broadaway became a fellow of Calhoun College, where she joined with young faculty in African American studies "to challenge the curricular focus on the culture of white upperclass males." Returning to Empire State College, she and colleagues planned and delivered a weekend residential seminar in women's studies in Millbrook, NY. Broadaway, who earned her B.A. from the College of Wooster in 1967, has two children. (ABS)

Brodkin, Karen (1941 –) Professor of anthropology and women's studies at UCLA, Brodkin (who frequently publishes as Karen Brodkin Sacks) graduated from Brandeis in 1963 and earned an M.A. from Harvard (1964) and a Ph.D. from the University of Michigan (1971). In 1967, while at the University of Michigan, Ann Arbor, she wrote "Social Bases of Sexual Equality" (*Sisterhood is Powerful*). In addition, Brodkin wrote "Engels Revisited," which was published in two collections said to have established feminine anthropology: *Woman, Culture and Society,* by Michelle Zimbalist Rosaldo and Louise Lamphere (1974); and *Toward an Anthropology of Women,* by Rayna Reiter (1975). She also wrote *Sisters and Wives* (1978). This work, together with Eleanor Leacock's work, was said to have established Marxist perspectives on feminist anthropology theory. As an activist, Brodkin participated in feminist study groups in Detroit, and taught at Oakland University (Rochester, MI) from 1968 – 1976. Working with a feminist campus group, Brodkin helped women go to Canada for safe abortions and after 1973, to New York once abortion had been legalized. In 1969, creating the first women's studies course on campus, she taught under the rubric of Sociology of Sex Roles. After leaving Oakland and Detroit in 1976, Brodkin taught in the women's studies programs at Clark University and Oberlin College. She directed UCLA's women's studies program (1987 – 1993) and also worked as a research director for the Business and Professional Women's Foundation. Other publications include *My Troubles Are Going To Have Trouble With Me,* co-edited with D. Remy (1984); *Caring By The Hour: Women, Work And Organizing At Duke Medical Center* (1988); *How Did Jews Become White Folks?* (1994); and *Motherhood Is Not An Entry-Level Job* (1998). Brodkin has two children. Archives: The Labadie Collection, University of Michigan Library, Ann Harbor, MI. (ABS)

Brodsky, Judith K. (1933 –) A pioneer in the women's art movement, Brodsky joined a group of women artists, art historians and curators who, in 1973, were planning Philadelphia Focuses on Women in the Visual Arts. She became a member of the steering committee and raised funds to mount this event, the first of its kind. In 1976 she became president of the WCA and organized its first conferences—in Los Angeles, then in NYC. She continued the surveys that showed women were qualified to teach and exhibit at major institutions, but were discriminated against. In response, she began the annual WCA awards to honor women artists and art historians for their achievements. She also organized national exhibitions of women artists in 1976 and 1977. Brodsky, who has two children, holds a B.A. from Harvard University and an M.F.A. from Tyler School of Art, Temple University (1967). Archives: Rutgers University Library, New Brunswick, NJ.　　(ABS)

Brody, Sherry Thomas (1932 –) An artist, Brody joined the Feminist Art Program in the early 1970s, and became the assistant to Miriam Schapiro at the California Institute of the Arts, Valencia. In 1972, she collaborated with Schapiro on The Dollhouse, a three-dimensional construction made especially for Womanhouse (a feminist political art statement). As an instructor at Cal Arts (1972 –1974), Brody conducted workshops to develop subject matter related to the history of women artists. From 1978 –1980, she spoke at various universities about her work and involvement with the women's movement. As part of The Year of the Woman (1995), Brody curated five shows in Los Angeles for women artists. She has participated in several women's shows, including Division of Labor: Woman's Work in Contemporary Art (1995); Sexual Politics: Judy Chicago's Dinner Party in Feminist Art History (1996); and The American Century: Art & Culture 1950 – 2000 (1999). She holds a B.F.A. (University of California, Los Angeles (1968) and a M.F.A. (California Institute of the Arts, 1974). She has two children.　　(ABS)

Broner, E.M. (1927—) (also known as Esther Masserman) Ph.D., professor emerita, Wayne State University, Broner has pioneered Jewish feminism through her works and rituals. She co-authored *The Women's Haggadah*, and lead the New York Women's Seder for 30 years. She is the author of 10 books, fiction and non-fiction, including *A Weave of Women*, a novel about a community of women who use politics and rituals against patriarchy, *The Telling*: a group of prominent NY feminists find spirituality together, *Mornings and Mourning: A Kaddish Journal*, a personal tale of fighting the prohibition against women mourning in the synagogue; *Bringing Home the Light: A Jewish Women's Handbook of Rituals*. She has keynoted feminist and literary speeches in France, Israel, Africa, the States and has spoken frequently for UNIFEM at the United Nations. She won two National Endowment for the Arts in fiction, the Wonder Woman Foundation Award "for courage in changing custom and ceremony." "Higginson," an historical musical, book and lyrics by Broner, and music by Morton Zieve, premiered in 2005. Archives: Brandeis University, Walthan, MA.　　(ABS)

Bronfman, Lois Ann Martin (1941 –) (also known as Lois Ann Martin) Having just received an M.A. in interna-

tional relations from Johns Hopkins, Bronfman applied for a job in the international division of a Detroit bank in 1964. The interviewer's first question was, "Can you type and take shorthand?" Bronfman did not get the job. While studying for a Ph.D. at the University of Oregon, which she received in 1972, Bronfman participated in a variety of feminist activities. She was a founding member of the Oregon WPC, worked on Patsy Mink's brief presidential campaign, and was a member of the Oregon Commission on the Status of Women. Bronfman also wrote one of the first studies on the impact of the equal employment provisions on the employment of women (1972). In subsequent years, she taught the first class on women and politics at Portland State University, and had it placed in the permanent course bulletin. She also volunteered at a domestic violence shelter, and serves on its board. Earlier, Bronfman took part in protests against the Vietnam War, and helped a soldier flee to Canada. Bronfman, who has three children, holds a B.A. from Michigan State (1962) in addition to her graduate degrees.　　(ABS)

Brooks, Betty Willis (1934 –) In California in the 1970s, Brooks joined a task force on women in the United Church of Christ. The group nailed 95 Women's Thesis on a church door, lobbied for more women's leadership, helped ordain the first gay male minister, and fought to change the liturgy. Brooks was instrumental in getting a woman appointed pastor of her local congregation, then left and "moved full-blown with all my religious zeal into the women's liberation movement in the secular world." She attended the national NOW conference in Washington, D.C., and interviewed women for the D.C. Rape Crisis Center. After starting Women Against Sexual Abuse, she began doing anti-rape training and taught workshops on sexuality, sex roles and self-defense. She also founded the second Rape Crisis Hotline in Los Angeles and co-financed a feminist bookstore in Laguna Beach, Persephone's Place. When Brooks was terminated from her part-time teaching job at CSU Long Beach, feminists on campus held a huge rally. Although Brooks was not re-instated in the physical education department, the women's studies department took her in. In 1976, Brooks and several other women founded Califia, a feminist-identified educational experience that was an offshoot of Sagaris. Califia lasted until 1984. In 1982, Brooks was part of a lawsuit against Cal State Long Beach charging that the university had not protected women's right to teach from a feminist perspective. From 1995 to the present, Brooks has read a monthly commentary, "Another Day in the Life of a Feminist," on KPFK radio in Los Angeles. The commentaries were published in "Feast," a quarterly newsletter, in 2000 and 2001. Brooks, who has one child, earned her B.A. from Centenary College, Shreveport, LA (1956); an M.A. from California State University, Los Angeles (1962); an Ed.D. from the Institute for Advanced Study of Human Sexuality, San Francisco (1978); and an M.A. from Immaculate Heart

College Center, Los Angeles (1995). Archives: Library of California State University, Long Beach. (ABS)

Broude, Norma (1941 –) was among the initial organizers of the WCA (1972) and served for several years as its first affirmative action officer. In the early 1970s, while teaching at Vassar and Columbia University, Broude wrote her first piece on feminist art, the article "Degas's Misogyny," presented at the annual meeting of the College Art Association in Washington, D.C. (1975) and published in *The Art Bulletin* (1977). In 1980, she and other artists boycotted the CAA annual meeting, which was scheduled for New Orleans, because Louisiana had not ratified the ERA, and organized an alternative conference called Social Change Takes Courage, at the Corcoran Gallery School of Art, in Washington, D.C. To preserve history, Broude and Mary D. Garrard wrote *The Power of Feminist Art: The American Movement of the 1970s, History and Impact* (Abrams, 1994). A pioneering feminist scholar, Broude is co-editor (with Mary D. Garrard) and contributor to the anthology *Feminism and Art History: Questioning the Litany* (1982), and its sequel *The Expanding Discourse: Feminism and Art History* (1992); and *Reclaiming Female Agency: Feminist Art History After Postmodernism* (University of California Press, 2005). Broude is professor of art history at American University in Washington, D.C., where she has taught since 1975. With Garrard, Broude was the recipient (2000) of the Art History Recognition Award given by the Committee on Women in the Arts of the College Art Association of America. Broude earned a B.A. from Hunter College (1962), and an M.A. (1964) and Ph.D. (1967) from Columbia University. (ABS)

Brown, Betsey J.S. (1929 –) served as part-time director of Women's Career Counseling Agency, begun by volunteers in Morris County, NJ, in 1968. In 1969, she formed a group of volunteers to establish a similar agency in Union County, NJ. As a result of these efforts, a program named Education, Volunteer, Employment was established at Kean College in Union (1970), which offered life-choice and career counseling to women. Brown served as director for the first five years. After leaving EVE, she became a family therapist. Brown has an M.A. from Teacher's College, Columbia University, and an Ed.D. from Rutgers University. Brown has four children. (ABS)

Brown, Elaine D. (1943 –) As chair of the Black Panther Party, Brown was one of the first, if not the first, woman in the U.S. to head a paramilitary, progressive organization. Prior to taking leadership, she was editor of the group's newspaper and served as minister of information. She was instrumental in the 1972 revision of the masculine language of the original 1966 10-point program and platform. The party was singular among black organizations in supporting gay liberation and women's liberation, and Brown has noted, "We were the only black

organization of the time committed to instituting gender parity." Prior to and after joining the party, she worked closely with the Welfare Rights Organization, aimed at guaranteeing decent food, healthcare, clothing, housing and other necessities for poor women. Brown was instrumental in establishing and administering the party's model community school in Oakland, California. Its free community clinics provided, among other services, free Pap smears to poor women. In 1969 and 1971 she recorded two albums of original, politically oriented songs, one for Motown's Black Forum label. The author of A Taste of Power and The Condemnation of Little B, Brown attended Temple University, UCLA, Mills College and Southwestern University School of Law. She has one child. Archives: Emory University, Atlanta, GA. (ABS)

Brown, Helen Gurley (1922 –) wrote *Sex and the Single Girl* in 1962, which captured the zeitgeist of the early 1960s. On the best-seller list for months, the book was eventually made into a movie featuring Natalie Wood and Tony Curtis. Brown's next book, *Sex in the Office* (1964), sold reasonably well. Brown became editor of then-failing *Cosmopolitan* magazine in 1965. She brought dramatic changes to the magazine, which continued to grow circulation for decades. Brown came from humble beginnings in Green Forest, AK, but she excelled socially and academically, graduating as valedictorian in her high-school class and then attending Texas State College for Women for one semester. She returned to Los Angeles to put herself through business school. Brown began working as a secretary, but, given the chance, proved to be an excellent copywriter. By the late 1950s, she had become the best-paid female copywriter on the West Coast. In 1959, at age 37, she found a marriage partner in David Brown, a former magazine and book editor who became a film executive. In 1997, Brown gave up editing U.S. *Cosmopolitan* to become editor in chief of international editions. Brown's feminist career has been marked by controversy. When *Sex and the Single Girl* was published, restrictions on women and sex were still stringent. Feminists criticized the sex-object *Cosmo* girl and Brown's idiosyncratic notions of liberation and sexual freedom. Her dismissal of sexual harassment in the workplace as an issue and her indifference to AIDS as an issue for heterosexual women drew further fire from feminists. Brown nevertheless identifies herself and *Cosmopolitan* as unfailingly feminist. She has worked on behalf of NARAL in support of abortion rights and supported other feminist organizations and causes. Archives: The Sophia Smith Collection, Smith College, Northampton, MA. (ABS)

Brown, Janet Welsh (1931 –) Brown's work contributed significantly to the advancement of women and minorities in the sciences. She started out as an academic, teaching Asian studies and international relations (1956 – 1958) at Sarah Lawrence, when it was an all-women's college. She became an academic, she says, "partly because in my generation teaching was something women could do." Later she taught at Howard University (1964–1968) and Federal City College, now the University of the District of Columbia (1968–1973). Because both colleges were predominantly African American, Brown was in the midst of the civil rights movement, always being challenged. At Federal City she experienced sexism and sex discrimination. After a successful suit against Federal, she moved to the American Association for the Advancement of Science (AAAS) to head the new Office of Opportunities in Science. "The purpose was very vague," she says, "but it was to address under-representation of women and minorities in the sciences." She organized representatives from different professional societies responsible for women and minorities, and together they figured out how to influence policy. She left in 1979. When President Carter appointed her to work on his transition team, her assignment was the transition at the National Science Foundation. She then moved to the Environmental Defense Fund, where she was executive director 1979–1984. She continued to work with environmental groups until her retirement in 1997. She now works a volunteer in affordable housing. Brown remained on the board of the Higher Education Resource Services (HERS) for 30 years (1976–2006). She holds a B.A. from Smith College, an M.A. from Yale University, and a Ph.D. from American University. Archives: The Sophia Smith Collection, Smith College, Northampton, MA. (ABS)

Brown, Judith Benninger (1941 – 1991) An attorney who focused largely on child sexual abuse and human rights in her law practice, Brown was co-author with Beverly Jones in 1968 of the pamphlet, "Towards a Female Liberation Movement," which has been credited with starting the movement and has been published in several feminist anthologies. Brown also founded, with Carol Giardina, Gainesville (FL) Women's Liberation in 1968, said to be the first women's liberation group in the South. She was an emeritus board member of Redstockings, and was instrumental in founding Stop Child Sexual Abuse (1988) in Gainesville. A fighter for civil rights, Brown earned her M.A. from the University of Florida (1968), writing her thesis on black author Zora Neale Hurston. She served on the NAACP education committee and coordinated the Student Group for Equal Rights. Active in the Congress of Racial Equality voter registration project in Gadsden County in 1963, she was arrested and jailed on several occasions during her civil rights work. Brown earned her law degree in 1974 from the University of Florida.

Brown, Rita Mae (1944 –) Best known today as the author (with the cat, Sneaky Pie Brown) of the Mrs. Murphy mystery series, Brown was a charismatic figure in the early lesbian feminist movement. She made waves about lesbian rights when others dared not speak at all, and organized lesbians into a group that became the Radicalesbians. Brown entered the women's movement in

1968, when she became a member of NY NOW; joined Redstockings in 1969; and was a member of The Furies from 1970–1972. Brown was also a member of Women in Media. Author of more than 25 books, Brown's first and most influential is *Rubyfruit Jungle*, a classic, humorous book about lesbian life. She has published articles in *Sisterhood Is Powerful, Out of the Closets, The New Woman* and *Women: The New Voice,* among others. She is the recipient of numerous awards in literature, and was nominated for two Emmys by the American Academy of Television Arts & Sciences. Brown has a B.A. from New York University (1968) and a Ph.D. from the Institute for Policy Studies (1976). Archives: The University of Virginia Library, Charlottesville, VA. (ABS)

Brown, Sue Austin – See Austin, Sue

Browne, Vivian E. (1929 – 1993) A recipient of the New York Feminist Art Institute/Women's Center for Learning Award; the National Association of Business and Professional Women Achievement Award; and an achievement award from the National Council of Negro Women, among others, Browne grew up in Jamaica, Long Island, NY. Although she wanted to be a teacher, she was told by Hunter College that she was "not suitable." Disappointed but not down, she graduated instead with a B.A. in art (1950), and in 1959 received her M.A. from Hunter. She was active in Women's Caucus for Art and the National Conference of Black Artists, and taught at Rutgers University. She had nearly 20 solo exhibitions of her work, with public collections at the Wadsworth Athenaeum in Hartford, CT; Bakersfield Museum of Art, Bakersfield, CA; and Chase Manhattan Bank, NY, among others. In an interview before her death, when she was asked about her future plans as an artist, she said, "I have one big plan and that is to become known as an artist. And not a female and not anything else, you see, an artist. Or, I would say, an artist who is black."

Brownmiller, Susan (1935 –) Described as a midwife of the second wave, Brownmiller is best known for her book *Against Our Will: Men, Women and Rape* (Simon & Schuster, 1975), which traces the history of rape in the law and in warfare. A journalist, Brownmiller began her career in 1959, first with *Coronet* magazine, then with the *Albany Report* and later *Newsweek*. She became deeply involved in the civil rights movement, traveling to Mississippi in 1964 to work with the SNCC. Back in New York City in the late 1960s, she worked in television and magazine journalism and was a writer for the *Village Voice.* Her articles and book reviews appeared regularly in *The New York Times, Rolling Stone, Newsday, Vogue* and *The Nation.* She joined NYRW after the Miss America protest in Atlantic City in 1968, and was an early member of NYRF in Greenwich Village. In March 1970, she orchestrated the take over of the *Ladies' Home Journal* offices. That led to a feminist-written and edited issue of the magazine. After publication of *Against Our Will*, she became an advocate for victims of rape. In 1978, her vision led to the creation of Women Against Pornography. The group was largely responsible for changing the climate of opinion about pornography, which until then had been seen as chic and trendy. Brownmiller's other books include *Shirley Chisholm, A Biography for Children* (Doubleday, 1969); *Femininity* (Simon & Schuster, 1984); *Waverly Place*, a novel (Grove Press, 1989); *Seeing Vietnam, Encounters of the Road and Heart* (HarperCollins, 1994); and *In Our Time: Memoir of a Revolution* (Random House, 1999). Brownmiller attended Cornell University and studied acting in New York. Archives: Schlesinger Library, Radcliffe Institute, Cambridge, MA.   (ABS)

Brumberg, Joan Jacobs (1944 –) (also known as Joan J. Irwin) was active in civil rights, especially equal housing opportunities in the Rochester, NY, area (1963 – 1965). She entered the women's movement in 1972 as a graduate student at the University of Virginia representative to the Coordinating Committee on Women in the Historical Profession. From 1972–1980, she was Upstate New York Women's History Conference program coordinator and taught women's studies at Cornell University. An advocate for girls, Brumberg wrote *Fasting Girls: The Emergence of Anorexia Nervosa as a Modern Disease* (Harvard, 1998), and *The Body Project: An Intimate History of American Girls* (Random House, 1997). Brumberg, who has one child, has a B.A. from University of Rochester and a Ph.D. from University of Virginia. Archives: Kroch Library, Cornell University, Ithaca, NY.   (ABS)

Brumder, Mary Eliz (1941 –) worked with SNCC in Mississippi from 1964 – 1965, then was an anti-war activist, and later joined an early women's rap group in Berkeley (1966 – 1968). She was an abortion rights counselor and a co-founder of an abortion rights group in Chicago in 1969. In the early 1970s, Brumder explored the founding of *Woman/News* with Susan Davis, and was active in NOW, serving as assistant to NOW's board chair. From 1974 – 1977, she was active in Seattle-King County NOW, where she chaired the employment task force, counseled women who had complains, supported plaintiffs, and lobbied and did actions for women's workplace rights. In the late 1970s, Brumder was Washington Feminist Federal Credit Union board chair. She received a law degree from the University of Washington in 1981. In the late 1980s and early 1990s, Brumder began working to stop violence against women. From 1989 – 1991 she developed a program for junior-high and high-school education on abuse in Northwest CT, and from 1992 – 1995 was a volunteer with the Northwest Women's Law Center in Seattle. Brumder works as a mediator with a focus on family law.   (ABS)

Brumer, Miriam (1939 –) is an artist whose painting, construction and drawings have always had an organic character, and are often seen as relating to the female body. Brumer has participated in feminist exhibitions including Unmanly Art at Stony Brook (NY) and Philadelphia Focuses on Women in the Arts. She has been a member of Central Hall, a women's gallery on Long Island, NY. In the early 1970s Brumer wrote about organic imagery for the *Feminist Art Journal*. She has also written book reviews for *Women Artists News*.   (ABS)

Brunstad, Donna (1938 –) Active in the civil rights movement in the mid 1960s, Brunstad began to question the role of women in America. After moving to Connecticut in 1970, she joined NOW and became a founding member of the CT WPC. She also served on the Redding (CT) Democratic Town Committee and became registrar of voters. From that position, Brunstad challenged the all-male delegation chosen to attend the 1972 Democratic National Convention under the newly written McGovern-Fraser Guidelines. As a result of her pressure, the delegation eventually included women, among them herself. She worked on Ella Grasso's first campaign for governor (1974) and then, at Grasso's behest, Gloria Rice Clarke's successful campaign to become CT's first female sheriff. Brunstad moved to Westport, CT, in 1975, where she served on the Democratic Town Committee and the Planning and Zoning Commission. She also worked with and for Gloria Schaeffer (secretary of state); congresswoman Bella Abzug on the Win With Women campaign; Lee Novick of New Haven; and Barbara Mikulski, Maryland's first woman Senator. Brunstad also debated Phyllis Schlafly on behalf of ERA.   (ABS)

Bryan, Gail (1939 –) founded and served as chair (1970 – 1972) of the legislative task force, MA NOW, where she was instrumental in the passage of laws that prohibit sex discrimination. The task force effected state ratification of the ERA and played a pivotal role in legislation that eliminated gender segregation in Massachusetts public schools and public accommodations. In 1970, Bryan, whose married name was Lazenby, tried to legally regain her maiden name. Told by the MA Commonwealth that it was "against the public interest," she initiated legislation that would allow a woman to use her own name. She retrieved her name before the law was changed, at the time of her divorce in 1971. In 1970, Bryan was appointed by the mayor of Boston to the Boston Commission to Improve the Status of Women. As chair of the education committee, Bryan wrote a report that was responsible for closing the substandard women's vocational school and integrating female students into the far superior male school. Bryan, an artist whose portraits of women have appeared widely, was photography editor of *Equal Times*, a newspaper for women, from 1976 – 1977. Her work has been syndicated internationally, appearing in publications such as *Ms., U.S. News and World Report, Health* and *Woman of Power*. Working for *The Christian Science Monitor* in 1981, Bryan focused her writing and images on women from Kenya, Colombia, Brazil, Peru, Alaska, the Amazon, the Alps, China, Nepal and India. From 1986–1993, Bryan served as chair of the education and research committee, board of trustees at The New England Wildlife Center. From 1991–1994, she was director of development for Artists for Humanity, Boston. In 1994, Bryan received the Margaret Rawlings Lupton Award for lifetime achievement for her work in bettering women's lives. Bryan received her A.B. (1960) and M.A. (1961) from Duke University, and her Ph.D./abd (1970) from Brandeis University. (ABS)

Bryant, Barbara S. (1949 –) discovered discrimination in the sixth grade (1959) when she wanted to be a school crossing guard, but was told that only boys were allowed in that role. From 1971–1975, she was a student at California State University in Sacramento working on a master's in social work. There, she served on the women's studies board until 1974 and helped hire a women's advocate for the campus. CSUS also had a gay studies board, the first on any college campus, on which Bryant served from 1972–1975. During that same time, Bryant and three others formed the Sacramento Gay Speakers Bureau. From 1970–1975, she co-wrote successful grants for local city and county funding to the Sacramento Women's Center. In the mid 1970s, Bryant co-founded the Association for Gay Psychologists. In 1975, she moved to the San Francisco Bay area and became a carpenter. She connected with a number of feminist attorneys. By 1977, Bryant herself was in law school, and edited the school's *Women's Law Forum*. She volunteered at Bay Area Women Against Rape, and from 1982–1983 was a staff attorney at a Legal Services office. In the early 1980s, she spent a year as the legal coordinator of the NOW chapter. From 1983–2000, Bryant was a litigator specializing in employment discrimination. She was VP of California Women Lawyers and a committee member of the California State Bar's Women and Law Committee, and a member of several gay and lesbian legal organizations. From 1992–1994, she served on the board of the Women's Philharmonic in San Francisco. Bryant earned a B.A. from the University of California, Berkeley, an M.S.W. from California State University, Sacramento (1975), and a J.S. from Golden Gate University School of Law (1980). (ABS)

Buck, Lynn (1921 –) (also known as Lynn Dillon) An early fighter for peace, Buck helped manage the campaign headquarters for congressman John Dow, a peace candidate running for re-election in the late 1960s. She and another woman challenged and succeeded in breaking the unquestioned power of the "boys in the back room." Returning to graduate school at Stony Brook University, NY, in 1970, Buck chose as her major fields 19th and 20th century American and British literature with—she hoped —an emphasis on women. This was not allowed, says Buck, because "the patriarchs did not consider that appropriate. They said it was just a passing phase." But she did

it anyway, unofficially, adding many books written by women to her reading lists and analyzing how female characters were regarded in fiction and poetry. She landed a job in 1974 teaching a groundbreaking course called Sexism and the Humanities at Suffolk Community College. By 1978, she and others on the SCC faculty pioneered the first women's studies program at a community college in New York. Buck taught women's studies for 13 years, and became faculty adviser for a student journal called *Lilith*. In 1974 she joined East End NOW and became newsletter editor and later telephone respondent and president. Buck served on the board of directors of East End NOW until 1994, when she moved to Baltimore and joined Baltimore NOW. She is a member of the National Women's Studies Association and in 2003 chaired a roundtable on women and aging at the association's annual conference, held in New Orleans. Buck is the author of *Eccentric Circles: An Uncommon Tale of Five Women* (1997); *Amanda's House* (2002); and two volumes of poetry. (ABS)

Buck, Martha (1935 –) became a member of Monmouth County (NJ) NOW in 1971 and participated in demonstrations at Bell Telephone Labs and the ERA march. In 1972 she joined the Essex County (NJ) NOW chapter. As a civil rights investigator (sex discrimination), NJ division on civil rights, Buck participated in a successful case against the Little League in which the Little League was ordered to admit girls. She investigated and found "probable cause" against the Montclair School District and wrote an early affirmative action plan adopted by the district to promote women into administrative positions. From 1974 –1976 she was a national board member of NOW, and from 1976–1977 was executive VP. She participated in planning the First National March for ERA, and was involved in the administration of the Washington, D.C., NOW national offices. From 1982–1989, as a senior labor economist in the research department at the national headquarters of the American Federation of State, County and Municipal Employees, Buck participated in and oversaw all union activity nationwide directed at achieving pay equity for women working in the public sector. Buck, who has a B.S. from Skidmore College and a B.T.S. from Episcopal School for Deacons, was ordained a deacon at Grace Cathedral, San Francisco, in 1997. (ABS)

Buck, Rosalie – See Davies, Rosalie Grace

Buckler, Diane (1956 –) was both a student and a participant in the Feminist Art Program at the California Institute of the Arts, where she earned a B.F.A. in 1978. Her work elevates and illustrates an empowered, intelligent and active vision of the human body, particularly woman's body in her earlier works. Buckler became a lecturer in the women's studies program at UCLA in 1999, and is now concentrating her energies in the studio. She has one child. (ABS)

Bucknell, Susan – See Pogue, Susan

Budapest, Zsuzsanna Emese (1940 –) A spiritual writer/teacher, Budapest was born in Budapest, Hungary, and immigrated to the U.S. in 1959 as a refugee fleeing the Hungarian Revolution. She became a student at the University of Chicago, and later, in Los Angeles, saw women taking part in political demonstrations and speaking truths she had only felt—about private property, and how women need to own their own bodies. Inspired, she became a volunteer at the Los Angeles Women's Center. Budapest, who has always followed the religion of her mother, paganism/Goddess worship (which she considers to be inherently feminist), soon learned that her greatest contribution to women's liberation would be through her spirituality. She used her spiritual healing practices to help heal rape and abuse victims, and founded the Susan B. Anthony Coven Number l. Considered the first feminist witches coven, it became a role model for thousands of other groups across the nation. Budapest was arrested in 1975 for reading Tarot cards to an undercover policewoman. Although she lost the case, it led to the abolishment of laws against psychics nine years later. A prolific writer and teacher, her books include *The Holy Book of Women's Mysteries* (Luna Press, 1975); *The Grandmother of Time* (Harper Collins, 1989); *Grandmother Moon* (Harper Collins, 1991); *Goddess in the Office* (Harper Collins, 1993); *Goddess in the Bedroom* (Harper Collins, 1995), and *Summoning the Fates* (Random House, 2000). (ABS)

Buhle, Mari Jo (1943 –) A feminist scholar whose work encompasses women's history and the intersection of women's history and radical movements in the U.S., Buhle is co-editor (with Paul Buhle) of *The Concise History of Woman Suffrage* (University of Illinois Press, 1978). She is also author of *Women and American Socialism, 1870 – 1920* (University of Illinois Press, 1981) and *Women and the American Left: A Guide to Sources* (G.K. Hall, 1983). In 1998, Harvard University Press published her book *Feminism and Its Discontents: A Century of Struggle with Psychoanalysis*. From 1973 – 1984, Buhle was a member of the reprint advisory board of the Feminist Press, and from 1985 – 1999 was an editor of the Women in American History Series, University of Illinois Press. Among her numerous academic honors and awards, Buhle received faculty development grants from the Center for Research on Women in Higher Education and the Professions, Wellesley College (1978), and the Bunting Institute, Radcliffe College (1978). She also held a Five-Year Fellowship (1991 – 1996) from the John D. and Catherine T. MacArthur Foundation. Although Buhle has spent most of her academic career teaching at Brown University, she also held a guest teaching position at Sarah Lawrence College (1973 – 1974). Buhle holds a B.A. from the University of Illinois, Champaign-Urbana (1966), an M.A. from the University of Connecticut

(1968), and a Ph.D. from the University of Wisconsin, Madison (1974). Archives: The Sophia Smith Collection, Smith College, Northampton, MA. (ABS)

Bulbul – See Guracar, Genevieve Leland

Bulpitt, Mildred Bernice (1926 –) A community college faculty member and administrator, Bulpitt co-founded a chapter of the Association for Women's Active Return to Education (1966 – 1967) in Arizona. From 1968 – 1974, she served as a member of the subcommittee on education, Governor's Commission on the Status of Women, and in 1972 helped organize the AZ chapter of WEAL, serving as its second president. From 1972 – 1974, Bulpitt chaired the Commission on the Status of Women, Maricopa Community College District, and in 1975 was a member of the Arizona State Department of Education task force to develop Title IX guidelines for the public schools. She coordinated an organization of the American Association of Women in Community and Junior Colleges (1973 – 1974) and served as national president (1975 – 1983). From 1979 – 1980, she co-wrote a proposal that resulted in funding for the National Institute for Leadership Development, and served as director of the program for 10 years. In 1984, Bulpitt was a member of the founding board of Arizona Women in Employment and Education. In 1986, she helped organize the first Arizona Women's Town Hall, and chaired the second one in 1987. Bulpitt earned her B.A. from the University of Connecticut (1948); her M.A. from Washington State University (1950); and her Ed.D. from Arizona State University (1970). (ABS)

Bunch, Charlotte Anne (1944 –) Bunch has led a life of service to women, lesbians and oppressed people around the globe. Bunch was the founder of the Washington, D.C., Women's Liberation Movement and Center, 1968 – 1971; organizer of the first national Women's Liberation Movement Conference outside Chicago, November 1968; and co-editor of one of the first anthologies on the women's liberation movement, *The New Women*. Bunch was also one of the founders of The Furies collective in Washington, D.C., and was co-founder and first editor in chief of *Quest: A Feminist Quarterly* (1973 – 1979), a publication that influenced the evolution of feminist theory from an activist perspective. Serving on the board of the National Gay and Lesbian Task Force, she helped organize the lesbian caucus and participated in the pro-feminist caucus for the National Women's Conference in Houston in 1977. Bunch has been involved in international social justice projects and issues since 1966, when she served on the executive committee of the World Student Christian Federation. In 1970 she was part of the Mobilization Committee to End the War trip to North Vietnam and Laos. And she was part of the planning committee for the first conference of Indochinese and North American women, held in Toronto, Canada, 1971. She also participated in preparatory meetings for the United

(ABS) indicates Approved By Subject

Nations Decade for Women in 1975 and 1980. In the early 1980s, Bunch focused her attention on the development of global feminism and an understanding of global issues within the U.S. women's movement. In the late 1980s, as a professor at Rutgers University, she founded and has since directed the Center for Women's Global Leadership, which has initiated and been involved in many international activities. As part of the Center's work in monitoring United Nations activities affecting women and human rights, Bunch has been involved in convening Women's Human Rights Caucuses at many U.N. venues, as well as convening an Expert Group Meeting on Violence Against Women (co-sponsored with the United Nations Division for the Advancement of Women) in 1993, and serving as an independent expert at the Expert Group Meeting on the Development of Guidelines for the Integration of Gender Perspectives into United Nations Human Rights Activities and Programmes in 1995, and at the Oslo Symposium on Human Development and Human Rights held by the UN in 1998. She has supervised the Center's leadership development work including the convening of nine annual (1991–2002) Women's Global Leadership Institutes and two leadership institutes organized with the Network of Women Living Under Muslim Laws (Istanbul, Turkey, 1998; and Lagos, Nigeria, 1999) and one with OSKA in Poland for women in Central and Eastern Europe. As of 2003, Bunch had written or edited 11 books on feminism, global feminism and feminist education; served on 20 boards of directors; and received 15 honors and awards for her work, including induction into the National Women's Hall of Fame, Seneca Falls, NY, October 1996, and the Eleanor Roosevelt Award for Human Rights from the President of the United States, December 1999. She received her B.A. from Duke University in 1966, and is a graduate of the Institute for Policy Studies. Archives: Childhood through the early 1980s, Schlesinger Library, Radcliffe Institute, Cambridge, MA. The mid 1980s to present will be at the Women's Movement Archives of Rutgers, the State University of New Jersey, New Brunswick, NJ. (ABS)

Bunks, Selma – See Miriam, Selma

Buoncristiano, Barbara Ann (1938 –) An administrator at Columbia University in 1970, Buoncristiano saw a sign on the inside of the ladies' room door that read "You've come a long way, baby, or have you?" That, she says, "was the beginning of Columbia Women's Liberation." Within a year, CWL had organized the first major feminist conference in New York City, held at Barnard College. Buoncristiano, with one other woman, did PR for the event. Over the next two years, a few women in CWL formed the Women's Affirmative Action Coalition of Columbia, with Buoncristiano serving as head of the steering committee. The group organized women at every level of Columbia—students, faculty and support staff— and filed a complaint with the Federal Office for Civil

Rights charging Columbia with failure to develop an affirmative action plan. As a result of this action, all of the university's federal contracts were suspended for six months and the university was precluded from bidding on government contracts until it developed an acceptable affirmative action plan. Later, when the university attempted to lay off two dozen maids, almost all of whom had more seniority than the janitors, WAAC obtained an injunction stopping the layoffs. Because of this, Buoncristiano adds, women in maintenance at Columbia became eligible to be security guards, carpenters, air conditioning specialists, etc. In addition to this work, Buoncristiano assisted the late feminist gynecologist Marcia L. Storch in establishing the first feminist practice in New York City (1971) and was invited to join Donna Shalala's Ph.D. program in politics and education at Columbia University, where she served as Shalala's research assistant and feminist adviser (1973). She was also invited by Ruth Bader Ginsburg to take a civil rights course at Columbia Law School. Since 1989, Buoncristiano has held several positions with the New York State Division of Human Rights. Buoncristiano holds a B.S., M.A. and M.P.H. from Columbia University. Archives: Columbia University, New York, NY. (ABS)

Burckhardt, Yvonne – See Jacquette, Yvonne

Burko, Diane (1945 –) was founder and president of Philadelphia Focuses on Women in the Visual Arts: FOCUS. The month-long event in 1974 celebrated women artists, collectors and writers. In 1975, Burko testified at the State Department, which was holding sessions relative to the Year of the Woman. Burko, who remained active in the National Women's Caucus for Art throughout the 1980s, has a B.S. from Skidmore College, and an M.F.A. from the Graduate School of Fine Art, University of Pennsylvania. She has one child. Archives: FOCUS papers are stored at the Philadelphia Museum of Art, Philadelphia, PA. (ABS)

Burnett, Patricia Hill (1921 –) An accomplished portrait painter, sculptor and former beauty queen, Burnett co-founded and chaired Michigan's first NOW chapter in 1969. She was president for two years, served as head of the international committee in the 1970s, and organized the International Feminist Conference in 1974. Since 1975 she has been a member of the National Association of Commissions for Women, where she has served on the executive board of directors and as president. She was also a member of the Michigan Women's Commission, appointed by the governor for four terms, and chaired two terms. Burnett, whose art appears in galleries in the U.S., London, Paris and Rome, was commissioned to do 35 portraits of feminists for the Hall of Fame, Seneca Falls, NY. She is the author of *True Colors – An Artist's Journey From Beauty Queen to Feminist* (Momentum Books, Ltd.). In 1993, she was named Michigan Woman of the Year. A survivor of the fiery days before Roe v. Wade, Burnett identifies as Republican and pro-choice. In 2003, she and Marj Jackson Levin plunged back into the movement, forming Veteran Feminists of Michigan because they saw the gains that they had fought so hard for eroding. Archives: Personal papers, Bentley Library, University of Michigan, Ann Arbor, MI; personal history in the women's movement, Schlesinger Library, Radcliff Institute, Cambridge, MA. (ABS)

Burris, Barbara — Co-founder of a group in 1967 that later became Women's Liberation Coalition of Michigan, Burris is co-author (with Kathleen Barry and Joanne Parrent) of *The Fourth World Manifesto* (1971), an expression of cultural feminism. It was later revised and published in *Notes from the Third Year* and *Radical Feminism*. Burris is a graduate of Wayne State University.

Burstyn, Joan Netta (1929 –) was one of the first scholars to publish on women's issues. In 1968, she completed her Ph.D. dissertation (University of London) on "The Opposition to Higher Education for Women in England During the 19th Century." Her works include *Victorian Education and the Ideal of Womanhood* (Falmer Press, 1980), a book based on a revised version of her dissertation; "Religious Arguments Against Higher Education for Women in England, 1840 – 1890" (*Women's Studies*, 1972); "Education and Sex: The Medical Case Against Higher Education for Women in England, 1870 – 1900" (*Proceedings of the American Philosophical Society*, 1973); and "Women and Education: A Survey of Recent Historical Research" (*Educational Leadership*, 1973). She was associate editor and member of the founding editorial team of *Signs: Journal of Women in Culture and Society* (1974 – 1980), and from 1981 – 1985 served as director of the women's studies program, Rutgers, New Brunswick campus. During that time, the program introduced a bachelor's degree program and graduate programs in women's studies. Since 1986, Burstyn has been a member of the advisory board of the women's studies program at Syracuse University. She served as dean of the School of Education at Syracuse University (1986 – 1989). Burstyn has received numerous grants and awards, including the Marion Talbot Fellow of the AAUW, to study the opposition to higher education for women in 19th century England (1965 – 1966), and an instructional development grant to design graduate level interdisciplinary courses in women's studies at Rutgers (1979 – 1980). In 1984 – 1985, she received a grant from the New Jersey Fund for the Improvement of College Education to retain women in mathematics and science. Burstyn has also been on the fundraising advisory committee, the Feminist Press (1974 – 1981); associate, Columbia University, Seminar on Women and Society (1975 – 1985); and member, steering committee, women's caucus, American Association for the Advancement of Science (1976 – 1978). She is the editor in chief of *Past and Promise: Lives of New Jersey Women* (1990). Archives: E.S. Bird Library, Syracuse University, Syracuse, NY. (ABS)

Burton, Frances E. (1926 – 1998) (also known as Frances E. Glaesemann) A telephone operator in 1947, Burton participated in the first national strike of the Communication Workers of America, San Francisco, protesting pay and benefits. A CWA union steward for over 30 years and a lifelong activist for women's rights and economic justice, Burton joined Twin Cities NOW in 1972, and served on its board during the 1970s.

Burton, Gabrielle B. (1939 –) was a member of the D.C. Women's Liberation Bureau and NOW, and in 1972 went to Florida to work for the Shirley Chisholm campaign. She is the author of *I'm Running Away from Home but I'm Not Allowed to Cross the Street* (Know, 1972), numerous magazine articles, and *Heartbreak Hotel* (Penguin Books), for which she was awarded Scribner's Maxwell Perkins Prize for a First Work of Fiction (1985). Burton is also the recipient of the Women Helping Women Award from NOW (1995). She graduated from Marygrove College in 1960 and earned an M.F.A. from the American Film Institute in 1997. Her highly successful screenplay "Manna From Heaven" was produced by her daughters' company, Five Sisters Productions (2002). (ABS)

Burton, Lyn (1948 –) was the first woman elected at-large to the Student Senate at the University of North Dakota (1968). Her platform included reproductive freedom and support of women's right to live off campus. Burton served as VP and legislative director, Twin Cities NOW (1972 – 1976) and represented NOW on the Minnesota ERA Coalition, which succeeded in ratification in 1972. In addition, Burton worked on the adoption of MN's first childcare law and the Minnesota Act Against Discrimination. She was a founding member and communication director of the Ramsey County WPC (1972) and a co-founder of the Minnesota Association for Women in Housing (1975). In 1986, Burton was named Woman of Today by Minnesota Women's Jaycees. Employed in the field of affordable housing and community development since 1970, Burton entered the United Theological Seminary of the Twin Cities in 1999 to become a Unitarian Universalist parish minister. She is the co-founder of the Unity Church Affordable Housing Advocates, UU Affordable Housing Coalition, and Twin Cities Metropolitan UU Social Justice Advocates. Burton, who has one child, earned her B.A. from the University of North Dakota, Grand Forks (1970) and her M.A. from the University of Minnesota (1983). (ABS)

Busby, Daphne — Busby was the founder of the Sisterhood of Black Single Mothers in 1973 in the Bedford-Stuyvesant section of Brooklyn, NY. It was one of the first post-civil rights organizations devoted exclusively to black single women. Established to help black single mothers complete their high-school equivalency, it built the women's self-esteem and motivated many to attend and graduate from college. The Sisterhood of Black Single Mothers operated home day care, out-of-the-home children's activities, a big sister program for pregnant single women, a monthly newsletter and an exchange for clothes and books.

Bussabarger, Mary Louise (1923 –) was teaching English at the University of Missouri (1960–1982) when she helped add women's studies courses to the curriculum and taught women's studies. She was also active in the creation of the campus Rape Crisis Center and Women's Center, and in 1973 became director of newly opened The Woman's Place, an agency in Columbia, MO, that provided support groups and resources for health services, job referrals and housing, and held an extensive library of feminist and lesbian writings. The Woman's Place also provided services to many women recently released from the state mental hospital. Bussabarger's experiences with these women led to her passion for mental health advocacy. Through her work on several Missouri state mental health boards and councils, she helped reduce the stigmatization and increase political recognition of mental health issues and developed improved mental health services. Also active in politics, Bussabarger joined the NWPC in 1971, became a local chairperson, and attended the national conventions in 1971 and 1973. She also served on the Boone County Central Democratic Committee (1988–2002), and was a Democratic Committeewoman (1988–2002). She is Mental Health Commissioner of Missouri, and continues to be active in local politics. Archives: Ellis Library, University of Missouri, Columbia, MO. (ABS)

Bussie, Fran (1935 –) began her feminist work in the 1970s. She was chair of the Louisiana United ERA (1975) and of the first Governor's Conference on the Status of Women, and served as vice chair of the Louisiana Health Care Authority. She also served on President Jimmy Carter's task force to pass the ERA.

Butcher, Mary Lou (1943 –) A journalist, Butcher began working for the *Detroit News* in 1965. After 11 years of seeing few gains for women in the newsroom, she charged the paper with sex discrimination in 1976, initiating an eight-year battle for women reporters and other women on the editorial staff. In bringing the lawsuit, Butcher also sought to eliminate sexual stereotyping in news assignments. In 1984, the paper paid $330,000 to 90 female employees in a settlement. Butcher used a significant portion of her share to endow an annual Diversity in Journalism award at the University of Michigan. Later, Butcher was co-founder of Women Involved in Giving Support, which combats sex discrimination in the workplace. In 1992, Butcher was inducted into the Michigan Women's Hall of Fame.

Butler, Jessie Haver (1886 – 1985) Butler was a suffragist who was very active in the 1920s. She was educated at Smith College and gave speech lessons to congressional wives and diplomats (including Eleanor Roosevelt) from 1935–1950, and was the speech coach for the General Federation of Women's Clubs. Toward the end of her life, she taught a speakers class for members of Los Angeles NOW, and gave an inspirational speech at the August 1970 march. She was author of the first textbook on public speaking for women, *Time to Speak Up* (1946) and published *Adams Other Wife* (1967). In 1970, Butler served as chair of the task force for childcare centers of Pomona Valley NOW.

Byrd, Florence Cozart – See Stevenson, Florence Byrd

Bysiewicz, Shirley (1930 – 1990) was a founder of Connecticut Women's Educational and Legal Fund (CWEALF) in 1973 and co-author of the legislation establishing CT's Permanent Commission on the Status of Women. As the first tenured woman professor and long-time law librarian at the University of Connecticut Law School, Bysiewicz was selected CWEALF's first president. In both her scholarly and activist work, she mentored waves of women law students, some of whom were choosing the law in the 1970s as a way to be more effective advocates for women's rights. An indefatigable advocate for a woman's right "to be all she can be," Bysiewicz brought her energies to bear on a number of other feminist issues and contributed to many organizations, among them *Alert: Women's Legislative Review*, where she served on its first board. In 2001, CWEALF introduced the Shirley Bysiewicz Legacy Society to carry on her work.

Cadden, Wendy (1945 –) A printmaker, painter and civil-rights and anti-war activist, Cadden was a founder (1969) of the Women's Press Collective, in Oakland, CA, which published works by women authors for 12 years, merging in 1975 with Baltimore's Diana Press. Because of the presence of the press and A Woman's Place Bookstore, says Cadden, "Oakland became a center for other feminist institutions, including the Feminist Health Center, the Oakland Rape Crisis Center and Olivia Records." As a founding member of Gay Women's Liberation in Oakland and San Francisco, Cadden focused on issues of empowerment, domestic violence and gay child custody issues. She has lectured extensively on her personal history and the historical lesbian experience. Her paintings and prints are in numerous collections, including the New Mexico Museum of Fine Arts, Harvard University and the Cabo Frio Print Biennial, Brazil. Cadden holds a B.A. from Antioch College (1968). (ABS)

Cade, Catherine ("Cathy") Elise (1942 –) A photographer and personal historian, Cade published *A Lesbian Photo Album: The Lives of Seven Lesbian Feminists in 1987* (Waterwomen Books). Her work has appeared in numerous shows, including Don't Call Me Honey: Photographs of Women in the Trades (University of California, Berkeley) and DAR, Dykes for an American Revolution (Glide Memorial Church, San Francisco, 1972). Her first contribution to the women's movement was teaching a class, with Peggy Dobbins, on women and sociology at the Free University in New Orleans. In 1968, she was a founder of the New Orleans Women's Liberation Group. After moving to San Francisco in 1970, Cade participated in a CR group at Glide Memorial Church, fought for childcare at women's events, and was part of Breakaway, a women's liberation school, teaching a course on the family with Tanis Walters. After coming out as a lesbian in 1971, she became a photographer and has seen her work published and exhibited in lesbian and feminist media since the early 1970s. In 1987 she joined a co-counseling community, and in 1995 attended the 4th International Women's NGO Forum in Beijing. From that came the founding of Whirlwind Women, a nonprofit that helps disabled women in developing countries build wheelchairs. Cade, who has two children, earned a B.A. from Carleton College (1963) and a Ph.D. from Tulane University (1969). (ABS)

Cade, Miltona Mirkin – See Bambara, Toni Cade

Cain, Patricia Ann (1945 –) was the first woman (other than a spouse or daughter) hired to practice law in Montgomery, AL, and in 1974 became the first woman hired on tenure track at the University of Texas, Austin School of Law. With three other women faculty members from other colleges and departments, Cain formed the Women's Faculty Caucus, which rewrote the draft of the University grievance procedure, then under consideration by the Faculty Senate, to include stronger protection for women faculty who wanted to claim discrimination. From 1975–1976, Cain successfully lobbied the Faculty Senate to adopt the draft. She was then elected to chair the committee that oversaw grievance complaints and, in that capacity, was able to advise many women with claims of discrimination and harassment. In 1975, Cain was elected vice-chair for finance of the TX WPC. While a visiting professor at the University of Wisconsin in 1977, Cain testified before the legislature on legal and policy issues raised by a proposal to stop funding for abortions. From 1977–1989, she was active in Austin politics, helping to campaign and raise money for women candidates. During that time, she was also a participant in the National Conference on Women and the Law. She worked with Texas students to host the conference in 1979 and 1988, and published a short history of the conference in the *Women's Law Journal* in 1997. From 1979 – 1983, Cain served on the board of the Battered Women's Center in Austin. In 1987, she was chair of the section on Women in Legal Education, Association of American Law Schools. A fighter for LGBT issues, she served as a faculty adviser for a fledgling gay law student group at UT in the

1970s. In 1983, she was a founding member of the section on gay and lesbian legal issues of the Association of American Law Schools. This group created the first visible presence of gay and lesbian law faculty in the national organization. Cain served on the executive committee and chaired the section in 1985. She also served on the board of the Lambda Legal Defense and Education Fund from 1985–1992. Cain is active with the NLGLA, and was the program coordinator of the association's annual Lavender Law Conference in 1997. She also helped to found Lesbian and Gay Alumni of Vassar College. Cain has written many articles and books on feminist legal and LGBT issues, including *Rainbow Rights: The Role of Lawyers and Courts in the Lesbian and Gay Civil Rights Movement* (Westview Press, 2000). Cain, who has an A.B. from Vassar and a J.D. from the University of Georgia Law School, is interim provost (2003) and Aliber Family Chair in Law at the University of Iowa. (ABS)

Calderwood, Ann — Born in Oklahoma in the early 1940s, Calderwood was involved with Columbia Women's Liberation (NYC) and was the first editor of the scholarly journal *Feminist Studies*, launched in 1972 after three years of planning. Calderwood published *FS* on her own money and out of her apartment. She published three volumes prior to 1977. Women's studies programs were developing rapidly across the country at that time. In late 1977 the journal was restructured and thereafter run by a collective of academics.

Calio, Louisa (1947 –) (also known as Louise Calio) A poet, writer and performer, Calio says that performances of her works since 1974, such as Rites of Isis, In the Eye of Balance and Feminine Rising, have been her greatest contribution to feminist spirituality, as well as her feminist spiritual writings in publications such as *Studia Mystica, She Is Everywhere* and *Dark Mother*. In Connecticut in the 1970s, she helped create and participated in events such as women-in-the-arts festivals at Albertus Magnus College. In 1976, she became coordinator and later first executive director of City Spirit Artists Inc., where she hired many women artists, some single mothers, into important positions. In 1981 she received the Women in Leadership Award for her contributions to the arts from the New Haven (CT) YWCA. (ABS)

Callow, Laura Carter (1927 –) was elected president of Livonia (MI) LWV in 1968, and in 1969 was appointed to the women's advisory committee of Schoolcraft College. In 1972, she helped found the Northwest Wayne County chapter of NOW (later renamed Western Wayne County NOW), where she worked with chapter members to change Michigan credit laws (1974), on the National Credit Law (1975), and on the establishment of a battered women's shelter. In 1973 she began public speaking throughout MI about the women's movement, especially the ERA. In 1975 Callow was appointed as a representative of the MI LWV to the newly-formed coalition of MI women's organizations, Women Organized to Meet Existing Needs. This group became the nucleus that formed MI ERAmerica (1976). Callow, a founding member, served as co-chair and then chair from 1976 – 1988. From 1977 – 1986, Callow recorded a monthly commentary on various aspects of the ERA and other women's rights issues for "Point of View," a radio program on WJR Detroit. In 1980, Governor Milliken appointed her to the regional White House Conference on Families. In 1987, she was appointed to the Livonia Human Relations Commission, serving as chair from 1994 – 1997. In 1991, she was appointed as MI ERAmerica representative to the ERA Summit, and has served as secretary/treasurer 2001 –). She became MI coordinator to the ERA Campaign. Callow is the recipient of the Alice Paul Award from the Metropolitan Detroit Area chapters of NOW (1977); Women Helping Women Award from Soroptimists International-Livonia (1976); and Salute to Women Award from the Livonia branch of the AAUW (1978). Callow, who has three children, holds a B.A. from Wayne State University (1951). She is a retired teacher. Archives: Documentation of her ERA work is at the Bentley Historical Library, University of Michigan, Ann Arbor, MI.   (ABS)

Calof, Joan (1928 –) worked as a psychotherapist from 1953 to 1996 with a focus on women's mental health. As a senior psychiatric social worker at Hennepin County Mental Health Center in Minneapolis, she responded to the negative attitudes held toward women patients by male leadership by starting the first women's therapy group in 1970. Calof used her husband's last name, Fishman, until her divorce in 1970, when she became one of the few women in her community to take back her original surname. A humanist Jew, Calof was born in Winnipeg, Manitoba. She holds a B.A. in French, English Literature and Psychology, an M.A., and an M.S.W. Since 1992, she has worked as a playwright and performance artist in the Twin Cities. Archives: Letters at Anderson Library's Tretter Collection, LGBT Archive, University of Minnesota, Minneapolis, MN.   (ABS)

Campbell, Ann Chess (1911 – 2000) A social worker, Campbell was a role model for women committed to peace and social justice through coalition building. During her years at Smith College, she actively supported striking textile workers in Massachusetts. She helped organize women into No. 38 Ladies Garment Workers by working in the factory herself and meeting with the Women's Trade Union League. Campbell won the Mary Van Kleek Award, given for the best essay on women workers' history, for an article she wrote about this experience. In Portland, OR, Campbell was a longtime member of and leader in WILPF, the oldest women's peace organization in the U.S. In her 30 years with WILPF, Campbell (among other actions) helped create a revolving bail fund for victims of police harassment and activists arrested for civil disobedience. Campbell graduated from Smith, and earned an M.A. from Columbia University and an M.S.W. from the University of California, Berkeley. In 1988 she received the Social Worker of the Year Award from the OR chapter of the National Association of Social Workers, and in 1992 received the Oregon Peace Institutes Peacemaker Award. Campbell had one child.

Campbell, Jean W. (1918 –) Wanting to create a continuing-ed program for women that would both prepare them for the workplace and accommodate their needs to balance work and family life, Campbell became the guiding force behind the University of Michigan Center for Continuing Education of Women and served as its director from its establishment in 1964 until her retirement in 1985. Campbell also helped develop research on women's education and its uses and was a leader in advocating workplace reforms such as part-time and flex-time schedules. Campbell also represented women's interests on issues such as affirmative action, discrimination in employment and women's studies programs. Campbell, who holds a B.S (1938) and an M.A. (1939) from Northwestern University, was inducted into the Michigan Women's Hall of Fame in 1993.   (ABS)

Campbell, Nancy Duff (1943 –) A co-founder and co-president of the National Women's Law Center, Campbell knew from a young age that she wanted to go to law school so that she could improve civil rights and civil liberties. After graduating from New York University School of Law in 1968, she joined a law reform organization focused on public benefit programs. "It was clear to me that women and children were the ones being hurt by some of the policies in place," she says. In the late 1970s, after teaching law at Catholic University and Georgetown Law Center, she joined the Women's Rights Project of the Center for Law and Social Policy, which became the independent National Women's Law Center in 1981. Campbell's accomplishments include participation in Supreme Court litigation establishing that two-parent families with unemployed mothers are entitled to Welfare benefits; litigation establishing a uniform right to child support enforcement services for custodial parents without regard to income; legislation expanding tax assistance for single heads of household and significantly increasing childcare assistance; and advocacy expanding the rights and remedies of military women. Campbell's many awards include Woman of Genius by Trinity College and a Lifetime Achievement Award from the U.S. Department of Health and Human Services. She was appointed by Congress to the U.S. Commission on Child and Family Welfare. Campbell holds an undergraduate degree from Barnard College (1965).   (ABS)

Candib, Lucy Michelle (1946 –) In the late 1960s and the 1970s, Candib was one of the first feminists in family medicine. During medical school, Candib was part of the group that founded the Somerville (MA) Women's Health Project. One of the original co-authors of *Our Bodies, Ourselves* (Boston Women's Health Collective, 1971), Candib wrote the chapter "Women, Medicine and Capitalism." The author of *Medicine and the Family: A Feminist Perspective* (Basic Books, 1995), Candib has spoken widely on women's health, addressing women's sexuality, violence against women, and women's adult development. Candib has also published numerous scholarly articles on women's health and development. Candib, who has two children, is a faculty physician at the Family Health Center of Worcester, MA. She earned a B.A. from Radcliffe College (1968) and an M.D. from Harvard Medical School (1972). Archives: Schlesinger Library, Radcliffe Institute, Cambridge, MA.   (ABS)

Canfield, Elizabeth K. (1922 –) worked as a volunteer interpreter for Spanish-speaking women at a Los Angeles Planned Parenthood clinic, created and developed an extensive no-cost family planning program for low-income women throughout California, and organized and directed a speakers bureau for the California Committee on Therapeutic Abortion, a public education and law reform group. She created and co-directed the Clergy Counseling Service for Problem Pregnancies, serving as a liaison between clients and service providers in the U.S., Mexico and Japan, and training and supervising clergy members. At California State University and the University of Southern California, she counseled students on family planning, reproductive health, sexuality and pregnancy options. Canfield served as chair of Project Straight Talk, a speakers bureau on gay, lesbian and bisexual issues, which sought to defeat the Briggs Amendment in CA through public education. Canfield is the author of "Young Women and the Sexual Revolution" (*Women's Sexual Development*, Plenum, 1980) and "Am I Normal?" (*The Frontiers of Sex Research*, Prometheus Books, 1979). From 1980 to 2003, Canfield worked as a pregnancy options counselor for Planned Parenthood of New Mexico and served as a public speaker on teenage sexuality, pregnancy, abortion rights and homophobia. Archives: Records on abortion law reform donated to the School of Public Health, University of California, Los Angeles, CA.   (ABS)

Cano, Ursula Gerda — entered the women's movement in 1961. She was a member of WIPF, AAUW and the LWV, and was active in gay rights and the civil rights, peace and environmental movements. In the 1960s, she helped international graduate students via the Experiment in International Living at Indianapolis University, thereby creating "integration" and collaboration of different races from many countries, including Africa, India, Japan, Nepal and Germany. Cano taught in the Modern Language Department of Indiana University-Purdue University Indianapolis; was a bilingual counselor at Chicago State University; and served in various Chicago Public Schools.

She also lectured at Indiana University Northwest and in various Study an International Language groups in Northwest IN. She is a member of OWL.   (ABS)

Cantarow, Ellen (1940 –) was a founding member of Boston's Bread and Roses in 1969. She was active in the New University Conference, a New Left young-faculty and graduate student organization, and the Radical Caucus of Modern Language Association (1968 – 1970). Cantarow was also active in promoting women's studies at Harvard University as a graduate student in comparative literature, and taught women's studies at the State University of New York, Old Westbury, among others, from 1974 – 1976. Cantarow became the feminist columnist of Boston's *The Real Paper* in 1977, and wrote on women's social, economic and political issues for Conde Nast publications and other national publications in the 1970s. From 1988 – 1998 she was associate editor and then senior editor of *The Women's Review of Books*. She was also general editor and co-author of *Moving the Mountain: Women Working for Social Change* (the Feminist Press and McGraw-Hill, 1981). Cantarow participated in the anti-war movement of the 1960s, and has been continuously involved in promoting justice "both through published writing and through activism" for the Palestinian people. She has a B.A. from Wellesley (1962) and a Ph.D. from Harvard University (1971). Archives: Schlesinger Library, Radcliffe Institute, Cambridge, MA.   (ABS)

Cantor, Rusty (1927 –) was a member of Los Angeles NOW in the early 1970s. A member of various CR groups, she supported the ERA and reproductive rights, and worked to stop violence against women. A painter, sculptor and mixed-media artist, Cantor was a member of the board of the WCA for 20 years, beginning in 1984, and served at various times as president of Northern California WCA for a total of 12 years. In 2004, she encouraged the WCA to hold two exhibitions on women and violence, one in Berkeley, CA, at the Nexus Gallery and the other in San Francisco at the California Institute of Integral Studies. Cantor has two children.   (ABS)

Capek, Mary Ellen S. (1941 –) (also known as Mary Ellen Stagg) Capek, who wrote her Ph.D. dissertation on Sylvia Plath (1967 – 1973), taught basic skills classes at Essex County College (Newark, NJ) that included early feminist writing (1969 – 1974). From 1975 – 1983, she ran a continuing education program at Princeton University, getting many women back into school. From 1977 – 1982 she ran the NJ chapter of the American Council on Education's National Identification Program for the Advancement of Women in Higher Education. She helped found and ran the National Council for Research on Women (1981 – 1996), and has been part of and written about the Women's Funding Movement since the mid 1980s. Capek is the co-author of *Effective Philanthropy: Organizational Success Through Deep Diversity and*

Gender Equality (MIT Press, 2005). She is also author of a monograph series for the W.K. Kellogg Foundation, *Women and Philanthropy: Old Stereotypes, New Challenges.* Other published works include "Funding Norm Doesn't Fund Norma: Women, Girls and Philanthropy," a chapter in *The State of Philanthropy 2002; Fostering Effective Funding for Women and Girls: A Next Stage Strategy,* published by Chicago Women in Philanthropy; and "Documenting Women's Giving: Biases, Barriers, and Benefits," a chapter in *Women, Philanthropy and Social Change: Visions for a Just Society,* edited by Elayne Clift. Capek has served on numerous national and state boards and committees, including the Conference Board Work and Family Council, Funders for Lesbian and Gay Issues, the New Jersey Commission on the Status of Women, and Equality New Mexico Foundation. Capek, who has two stepsons, holds a Ph.D. from the University of Wisconsin. Archives: Schlesinger Library, Radcliffe Institute, Cambridge, MA. (ABS)

Caplan, Paula Joan (1947 –) A psychologist, Caplan published three major articles in the 1970s that were considered daring and marginal because they dealt with sex differences from a feminist perspective. The articles were based on her master's thesis about response to school failure and her doctoral dissertation about determinants of antisocial behavior. Since the 1980s, Caplan has done extensive political and social action and public education about women's issues, especially about the harm often done to women in the mental health system. She has been especially concerned about bias in psychiatric diagnosis and problems with psychotropic drugs. A professor and visiting professor at numerous universities and colleges, Caplan was a lecturer in women's studies at the University of Toronto (1979 – 1995). She was also full professor of applied psychology and associate director (1984 – 1985) and then head (1985 – 1987) of the Centre for Women's Studies in Education, Ontario Institute for Studies in Education, University of Toronto. Her books include *Between Women: Lowering the Barriers* (Personal Library, 1981); *The Myth of Women's Masochism* (E.P. Dutton, 1985); *Don't Blame Mother: Mending the Mother-Daughter Relationship* (Harper & Row, 1989); *Lifting a Ton of Feathers: A Woman's Guide for Surviving in the Academic World* (University of Toronto Press, 1993); co-authored with her son, Jeremy B. Caplan, *Thinking Critically About Research on Sex and Gender* (Harper-Collins, 1994); *You're Smarter Than They Make You Feel: How the Experts Intimidate Us and What We Can Do About It* (The Free Press, 1994); *They Say You're Crazy: How the World's Most Powerful Psychiatrists Decide Who's Normal* (Addison-Wesley, 1995); (with Mary Crawford, Janet Hyde and John Richardson) *Gender Differences in Cognition* (Oxford University Press, 1997); and (as first editor, with Lisa Cosgrove) *Bias in Psychiatric Diagnosis* (in press). She received the Woman of Distinction Award, Toronto YWCA (1986), the Veteran Feminist Writers of

America Medal (2002), and Woman of the Year Award, Canadian Association for Women in Science (1991). She was also named Eminent Woman Psychologist, American Psychological Association Division 35 (1996) and nominated for First Toronto Women's Health Awards (1988). She served as spokesperson for the Association for Women in Psychology, 2002 – 2005. Caplan earned her B.A. from Radcliffe College and an M.A. (1971) and Ph.D. (1973) from Duke University. Archives: Schlesinger Library, Radcliffe College, Cambridge, MA. (ABS)

Capra, Joan Ruth (1947 –) was a member of the first women's liberation rap group in Chicago, started by Kathleen Thompson, that founded the first women's center in the city. The center housed a bookstore and counseling center; sponsored concerts, lectures and slide shows; and provided free pregnancy testing. Capra expanded the bookstore from primarily feminist literature to include fiction and non-fiction. As a violinist, Capra performed in the original Family of Woman lesbian feminist band, founded by Linda Shear in Chicago. Capra has an M.A. from the University of California, San Diego. (ABS)

Carabillo, Toni (1926 – 1997) was a feminist leader and historian whose works chronicled the feminist movement. Her commitment to feminism began in the 1960s when, as a writer and graphic designer for a large corporation in Los Angeles, she was dismissed for her involvement in an unauthorized survey of women employees that showed sex discrimination. She became a member of NOW in the 1960s; helped found branches throughout CA; and held various positions, including president of the Los Angeles chapter, national VP, board member, and co-editor of its national newsletter. In 1969, Carabillo co-founded Women's Heritage Corp., which published calendars and almanacs, as well as a series of books on early feminist leaders. She was a major fundraiser and organizer for the ERA ratification campaign in the early 1980s. In 1987, with Eleanor Smeal, Peg Yorkin, Katherine Spillar and Judith Meuli (her partner), she founded Feminist Majority, which was designed to encourage women's empowerment. She was co-author, with Meuli and June Csida, of *Feminist Chronicles, 1953 – 1993* (Graphics Press, 1992), which became a textbook for college-level classes on women's studies. She was also co-author with Meuli of *The Feminization of Power* (Fund for the Feminist Majority, 1988). An erudite, polished speaker, Carabillo made numerous appearances as a feminist advocate on TV and radio, both local and network. She was particularly effective when debating anti-feminist foes on talk shows. At the time of her death, she was national VP of Feminist Majority and had been working on *The Feminist Chronicles of the 20th Century.* Carabillo graduated from Middlebury College in 1948 and earned an M.A. from Columbia University in 1949. Archives: *The Feminist Chronicles,* Schlesinger Library, Radcliffe Institute, Cambridge, MA.

C

Carbine, Pat (1931 –) A founder of *Ms.* magazine (with Gloria Steinem, 1972), Carbine was also its first editor in chief and publisher. Her feminist consciousness had been awakened at *Look*, where she started as an editorial researcher in 1953 and moved up the ranks to executive editor in 1965. Carbine left in 1970 to become editor of *McCalls*, where she hoped to make the magazine "a little more contemporary." Carbine introduced a section called "Right Now" "that dealt with subjects on the minds of women in the 1970s, like, 'Is domestic life all there is?'" Steinem came to her with the idea of a newsletter, but Carbine realized that what was needed to change the image of women and provide women opportunities in publishing was a magazine. The decision to leave *McCalls*, where Carbine had a contract, was hastened by what she calls a "dust up" with *McCalls* management over the *McCalls* Woman of the Year for 1972. Steinem had been selected and was on the cover of 8.5 million copies, but management, thinking Steinem too radical, wanted Pat Nixon. They seriously considered reprinting the cover, but Carbine said she would resign, and "not without public comment." Steinem stayed on the cover. Carbine had another "dust up" with management over reportage on issues potentially upsetting to advertisers. When Carbine saw that *Ms.* was not going to happen without her, she asked *McCalls* to break her contract and management accepted. At *Ms.*, Carbine hired women to sell advertising space, which was unheard of at that time. "A lot of people told us hiring women was a mistake," says Carbine. The women were often insulted, but they prevailed and many went on to become incredible successes. Carbine slowly brought in advertisers not associated with women's magazines—auto manufacturers, financial services and alcoholic beverages. "I believe we helped the marketing and advertising community rethink their approach to women, how they pictured women, and what products we bought," she says. Carbine also served on the board of the Magazine Publishers of America (1973 – 1988), the Advertising Council, and the American Society of Magazine Editors. She was the first woman on the board of MPA and the first woman chair of the Ad Council. For a number of years she was successful in persuading the MPA not to hold its annual conference in Florida, a critical state in the ERA campaign. Carbine holds a B.A. from Rosemont College (1952), and served as a trustee at that college from 1972 – 1996. Archives: The Sophia Smith Collection, Smith College, Northampton, MA. (ABS)

Card, Claudia Falconer (1940 –) A professor of philosophy at the University of Wisconsin, Madison, Card studied the penitentiary system in the U.S. (1974 – 1975), researching women in prison and women's prisons. In 1976, Card joined the Society of Women in Philosophy, subsequently serving more than 25 years presenting papers and hosting conferences. In 1977, she created and taught a university course called Feminism and Sexual Politics. She went on to create and teach courses in les-

bian culture and, in the classics, in feminist theory (late 18th century through the 1930s) and feminist ethics. She presented her coming-out paper, "Lesbian Feminist Ethics" at the University of Minnesota in 1978. In 1979, she began 12 years of work in the university's women's studies program. Her writing includes *Lesbian Choices* (Columbia University Press, 1995), *The Unnatural Lottery: Character and Moral Luck* (Temple University Press, 1996), and *The Atrocity Paradigm: A Theory of Evil* (Oxford, 2002). She is the editor of *Adventures in Lesbian Philosophy* (Indiana University Press, 1994), *On Feminist Ethics and Politics* (Kansas, 1999) and *The Cambridge Companion to Simone de Beauvoir* (Cambridge University Press, 2003). Card was named Distinguished Woman Philosopher of the Year in 1996 by the Society of Women in Philosophy. In 2001, she became the Emma Goldman Professor of Philosophy at the University of Wisconsin. Card is active in several cademic feminist organizations, including the International Association of Women Philosophers. In addition to her work in feminism, Card has been a member of the Environmental Studies Program (1989), the Jewish Studies Program (2000) and the LGBT Studies Program (created in 2003) at the University of Wisconsin. She earned her Ph.D. (1969) and M.A. (1964) from Harvard, and her B.A. (1962) from the University of Wisconsin. (ABS)

Carini, Louise (1921 – 2003) A plaintiff in a landmark sex discrimination case against *The New York Times* in the mid 1970s, Carini came to this country from Italy when she was 10. After graduating from a high school run by the Sisters of Charity, she began taking night classes at City College (NYC), studying both French and accounting. When she went looking for work, however, she swiftly learned an unspoken rule of accounting: jobs for women were nearly impossible to secure. Instead, she became a wartime translator for the government in both French and Italian. In 1951, Carini got a job in the accounting department at *The New York Times*, and then watched as six of the men she trained became her bosses. In 1974, after discussions with Guild leader Edwin R. Egan and attorney Harriet Rabb, Carini joined the federal class action lawsuit Boylan v. *Times*. Seven women, including Carini, stood in for the 550 female employees of *The Times* who, they said, had been passed over for advancement, harassed and otherwise treated in an illegal and unfair manner. The case was settled in 1978. In 1994, Carini, along with the six other plaintiffs, was awarded a citation from the National Women's Hall of Fame.

Carlander, Marilyn J. (1941 –) As a member of a teaching collective, Carlander taught women's studies at University of Illinois, Chicago (1974 – 1990). She was appointed by Mayor Harold Washington to his Advisory Commission on Women, and was one of the founders of the Chicago Area Women's Studies Association and Women United for a Better Chicago. Carlander began developing a women's studies program at UIC as its first full-time employee (administrative assistant) in 1977. Since 1995 Carlander has been a part-time teacher of women's studies at Northeastern Illinois University. She has been a supporter of AIDS research, and "was arrested while participating in a Committee in Solidarity with the People of El Salvador demonstration against U.S. policy/ intervention in Central America." (ABS)

Carlton, Mary Holt (1915 –) A Virginia blue blood, Carlton was attending a 1969 meeting of the Poetry Society of Virginia at the University of Charlottesville, where young co-eds were selling liberation literature. Carlton bought a copy of *No More Fun and Games* and, she says, "was hooked." She was a co-founder, with Zelda Nordlinger, of the Richmond chapter of NOW (1973), and with Nordlinger "worked in various endeavors to advance the humanist ideal." Her accomplishments include assisting in the elimination of sex-segregated classified ads in Richmond newspapers; helping to open the men-only Soup Bar to women in Thalhimer's department store; and single-handedly eliminating separate seating in the Tea Room at department store Miller and Rhoads. Says Carlton, "I had only one national NOW chair, which was to look for and endeavor to eliminate sexism in church literature for children. I also worked for the ordination of women." In addition, Carlton served as treasurer and member of the policy council of the VA WPC. Once described as "the only ERA picket on the State Capitol steps wearing white gloves," Carlton published an intellectual defense of the ERA in the September 1972 issue of *The Virginia Club Woman*. She has also published articles in the *Richmond Quarterly* on women of historical importance. Carlton holds a B.S. and M.S. from the Richmond Professional Institute of William and Mary. Archives: Swem Library, William and Mary, Williamsburg, VA; and Cabell Library, Virginia Commonwealth University, Richmond, VA. (ABS)

Carmody-Arey, Christine (1938 –) (also known as Mary Christine Carmody) marched up Broadway (NYC) in the summer of 1970 to celebrate Women's Equality Day, and has been marching and fighting ever since. She became a charter member (and later president) of Jersey City NOW in the early 1970s, and made disability benefits for pregnant workers her first campaign. She worked on the Hudson County ERA Amendment Coalition, and lobbied to promote passage nationally. She also conducted workshops and facilitated NOW CR groups. In the 1960s, she was part of the peace movement opposing U.S. involvement in Vietnam, and since the 1970s has worked on issues concerning the labor movement. She has a B.A. and M.A. from New Jersey City University. Describing herself as the product of Irish Catholic Republican immigrant parents, she says, "We are a labor, animal rights, civil rights, environmental rights, women's rights family." She has one son. (ABS)

Carol, Estelle Myra (1949 –) A graphic artist, cartoonist, illustrator and activist, Carol was co-founder of the Chicago Women's Graphic Collective in 1970. As part of their feminist/socialist vision, the collective, founded in Carol's apartment, produced and distributed thousands of posters for CWLU. The collective ended in 1983, but its work lives on through the Chicago Women's Liberation Herstory Project, founded in 1999, also in Carol's residence. Carol was a member of the Women's Radical Action Project at the University of Chicago (1968), and helped organize protests against the firing of Marlene Dixon, a feminist sociology professor. Carol was also a founding member of CWLU (1969), where she served on the steering committee, and is coordinator of CWLU's Herstory Project on CWLU's Web site. In addition to her work as a feminist, Carol was a member of the Civil Rights Club at her high school in New York, and as a college student was active in the anti-war and anti-draft movements. While a CWLU member, she traveled to Cuba (1974) as a member of the Venceremos Brigade to learn more about Third World struggles. Around 1985, she partnered with Bob Simpson to produce cartoons for the labor movement that have been widely circulated in the union press. She is active in her local community peace group, the Oak Park Coalition for Truth and Justice. Carol's mother, Ruth Carol, is also a feminist. Estelle Carol, who has two children, earned her B.A. from the University of Chicago, and graduated from the Chicago Typographer's Union typesetting school. (ABS)

Carol, Ruth Etta (1921 –) (also known as Ruth Bernstein) In 1968, with the support of Long Island NOW and Citizens Association For Superior Education, Carol and her husband, Bernard Carol, successfully petitioned Great Neck Junior High School to allow their daughter to take Shop, rather than Home Economics. A nutritionist, Carol later became a research associate serving as the specialist in nutrition for The Prenatal Project at Columbia University Medical School. Despite her impressive degrees (a B.A. from Brooklyn College and an M.A. and Ed.D. from Columbia), Carol was often disregarded. In 1972, when conditions at Columbia's Prenatal Project were becoming unbearable, Carol charged her immediate superior with sex discrimination. After a woman psychologist joined Carol in her accusation of sexism, Carol was asked to resign. Refusing to do so, she was fired. After realizing the consequences of the loss of Carol's services, the university delivered an oral and later a written request for Carol to remain. Although she was discharged 18 months later, Carol continued to advance professionally. Describing the documentation filed with the Contract Compliance Branch of the United States Department of Health, Education and Welfare as one inch thick, Carol says her complaint was just another episode in the women's movement, but the case markedly improved the working conditions of the women in the department. Carol has four children. (ABS)

Carpenter, Liz Sutherland (1920 –) A feminist activist and later an advocate for aging Americans, Carpenter was the first woman executive assistant to a vice president (Lyndon Johnson). In 1963, after the assassination of President John Kennedy, she became press secretary and staff director for Lady Bird Johnson. In 1971, she was a founder of the NWPC, and was a state keynote speaker that year in Florida and Texas. Later, she worked and traveled to push passage of the ERA. She is the recipient of numerous journalism awards. In 1984, the Liz Sutherland Carpenter Distinguished Lectureship was established in the College of Liberal Arts at the University of Texas. With Alan Alda, she received an award from a United Nations committee for service on behalf of equality, and was the recipient of an Award from the Southwest Society on Aging. She was inducted into the Texas Women's Hall of Fame by former Governor Mark White; received the Anne Morrow Lindbergh Award for distinction in health; and served on the advisory committee for President Clinton's Commission on Aging. Carpenter's book *Unplanned Parenthood, the Confessions of a Seventy-Something Surrogate Mother* details the experience of raising her brother's children. Her other books include *Ruffles and Flourishes* and *Getting Better All the Time,* which concerns aging and widowhood, and *Start With a Laugh.* Honored in 1998 by VFA, she has a journalism degree from the University of Texas and two children. Archives: Lyndon Baines Johnson Library, Austin, TX. (ABS)

Carr, Cynthia M. (1950 –) was a member of the *Lavender Woman* newspaper collective in Chicago from the early 1970s until the paper folded in 1976. The women who put out the paper met at the home of Susan Edwards and Leigh Kennedy (now Leigh Smith) to hash out what would be covered, then had marathon weekend sessions to design and layout the pages. "I remember going through a major convulsion over separatism, which split the collective. The separatists left. I was not among them." In 1979, Carr moved to New York City and immediately joined the Heresies collective, where she worked on a journal related to women in the arts. In the early/mid 1980s, Carr was a founding member of No More Nice Girls, a group that focused on abortion rights. (ABS)

Carroll, Berenice A. (1932 –) was a teacher at the University of Illinois at Urbana, Champaign, and active in the anti-war movement when, in 1967, she offered, for the first time, a course on women's liberation through the local "Communiversity." She introduced the first course in women's studies at the University of Illinois in 1970. She was later active in founding and developing women's studies programs at Illinois, Maryland and Purdue universities. She co-founded the Women's Caucus for Political Science and the Coordinating Committee on Women in the Historical Profession in 1969. Also in 1970, she was a co-founder of what, she says, may have been the first women's crisis shelter in the country, A Woman's Place, which opened in Urbana in 1971. Since 1960, Carroll has been active in the peace movement, becoming a member of the national board of SANE in 1962 and raising feminist issues in faculty, community and professional peace groups over many years. In 1970 she was a co-founder of the Consortium on Peace Research, Education and Development and in 1972 was a founding editor of *Peace and Change: A Journal of Peace Research.* Says Carroll, "In May 1970, I was one of a group of professors at UIUC named by the *Chicago Tribune* in an editorial titled 'Why the Crazies Get that Way,' for signing a Faculty for Resistance statement against the war in Vietnam." In 1972 she was arrested in a demonstration at Chanute Air Force Base (charges were eventually dropped). She is author of "Peace Research: The Cult of Power," in which she put forward a theory of the "powers of the powerless," In 1976, she published *Liberating Women's History.* In 1982, Carroll was the oldest member of the Grassroots Group of Second-Class Citizens, which occupied the Illinois State Capitol Building for four days and carried out a series of direct action protests in the last month of the ERA ratification struggle. (ABS)

Carroll, Betty Jean (1930 –) was a member of Dayton Women's Liberation (1970 – 1975), serving in many capacities including treasurer and member of the Women's Center task force. From 1973 – 1978, she was a member of WILPF, serving as VP from 1974 – 1975, and in 1973 became a charter member of the local group of FEW at Wright-Patterson Air Force Base. A member of Freedom of Choice – Miami Valley (1978 – 1982), she served as VP from 1979 – 1980, and coordinated the Twilight Vigil on the Dayton Courthouse Square in 1979 during Abortion Rights Week. Carroll was also a member of Women for Racial and Economic Equality (1987 – 1991), serving on its constitution committee at the national convention in 1990. In addition, she was a charter member of the Dayton chapter of CLUW, a member of NOW and a supporter of Planned Parenthood. Carroll helped open training programs and other new opportunities for women in the federal workforce at Wright-Patterson Air Force Base, beginning in 1973. She organized a women's support group, named Betty's Flock, which met biweekly. Most of the women had filed grievances or EEO complaints that Carroll was handling. At the American Federation of Government Employees national convention in 1974 (Boston), she helped pass a resolution that established the first women's department in any national labor organization in the AFL-CIO. In 1976 (Las Vegas), she offered the resolution that AFGE would never again hold a convention in a state that had not ratified the ERA. And in 1978 (Chicago), she offered the resolution that provided line item funding for the separate women's department. In 1980 (Honolulu), she wrote the resolution and organized the floor action that upgraded the director of the women's department to a seat on the national executive board with pay equivalent to the district VPs. Carroll is writing a series of books for young adults called The Foothill Spirits Series. The books cover the history of Ohio from 1803 – 1937, and all deal with the subjugation of women. Carroll, who has five children, earned a B.A. from Wright State University. (ABS)

Carrsyn, Maureen Doris (1946 –) (also known as Maureen Stickles) was staffing coordinator for the Springfield (MA) Women's Union (1972 – 1977). Founded in 1972 and originally called The Women's Center, the group quickly formed a Rape Crisis Center, including a 24-hour hotline. The group also founded a childcare center, a speakers bureau, a job resource bank and numerous support groups. In 1974, Carrsyn organized an action against Fred Storaska, a self-proclaimed expert on rape who was paid by colleges throughout the Eastern Seaboard to lecture female students on how to prevent rape. The main focus of his lectures was his advice, says Carrsyn, to "lay back and bear it" because fighting back might make the rapist mad. Scheduled to speak at Bay Path Jr. College in East Longmeadow, MA, Storaska responded to statistical challenges about rape offered by Carrsyn's group by having the women ejected from the lecture. A sit-in by 20 members of the Springfield Rape Crisis Center and the Women's Union followed. Carrsyn has an A.A. from Springfield Technical Community College. (ABS)

Carson, Leslie Borgia (1941 –) was co-founder of Summit, NJ, NOW in 1972. A supporter of Emily's List and a member of national NOW, Carson has marched on Washington, initiated community coalitions of women's organizations, and "raised my two daughters as feminists." Carson was a charter member of the National Museum of Women in the Arts and president of the Summit (NJ) branch of AAUW. Carson attended the European Conference of the International Federation of University Women, and has raised money for girls' scholarships and fellowships. She also initiated her AAUW branch's sponsorship of girls softball teams and a girls school in India. A supporter of the peace and environmental movements, Planned Parenthood and NARAL, Carson has a B.A. from the University of Michigan (1963) and an M.A. from Columbia University. (ABS)

Carson, Patricia – See Tavenner, Patricia

Carter, Lyda (1943 – 1997) was committed to improving the lives of women and workers. As president of the Chicago librarian's union, AFSCME Local 1215, Carter helped found CLUW (1974), the first feminist association of women union workers. She was also chair of Direct Action for Rights in Employment; an early member of Women Employed; and a pioneer in the right-to-adoption battle for lesbians and gays. As a response to Anita Bryant's efforts to use the Bible to oppress gays, Carter attended Seminary and became a deacon and parish counselor in the Metropolitan Community Church.

Carter, Myra A.Y. (1929 –) A Scottish actress and writer, Carter joined NYRF in 1972 after moving to the West Village (NYC). She wrote for the group's newsletter and worked on speakouts for marriage, rape and work. By floor procedure, she instigated feminist committees in her three U.S. acting unions—Actors Equity Association, American Federation of Television and Radio Artists, and Screen Actors Guild—saw them into being, but refused to chair them. To open her own field of the professional stage and film to some feminist perspective, she pursued professional press reps and producers to allow her to review works for *Majority Report*. She is a member of the Older NOW committee in Manhattan. (ABS)

Carter, Virginia L. (1936 –) Born and raised in Northern Quebec, Carter served as president of Los Angeles NOW during its explosive growth years, 1970 – 1972. She struggled to find consensus as to the place within the feminist agenda of such issues as the war in Vietnam, lesbianism and CR versus overt public activism. Carter began her career as a research physicist at the Aerospace Corporation (1962 – 1972), a nonprofit adviser to the United States Air Force, Space Division. As L.A. NOW president, Carter's security clearance at the Aerospace Corporation, and thus her career, was placed in jeopardy by the public and heated controversy concerning lesbianism. During her 10 years at Aerospace, she did experiments in vacuum ultraviolet spectroscopy and flew satellite experiments to measure properties of the high atmosphere. In so doing, she became the first woman to have successfully designed and flown a satellite-based experiment. With a B.Sc. from McGill University in Montreal, Canada, and an M.S. from the University of Southern California, Carter is the author of 20 technical papers in the fields of high atmospheric studies and spectroscopy. In 2002 she was granted an Honorary Doctorate in Science from McGill University. In an unusual career change, after meeting Norman Lear through his wife, Frances Lear, Carter became VP of Embassy Television in Hollywood in 1973. Her primary responsibility was to ensure pro-social and accurate feminist content in many hit half-hour comedies being produced by Embassy (a Norman Lear Company). As senior VP, Carter established a Movie For Television division at Embassy. She is the recipient of a number of Emmy and Peabody awards for her work in television. Now retired, Carter serves on the board of the Population Media Center, an NGO that works to reduce population growth and the spread of disease and to elevate the status of women in Third World countries through the design and broadcast of radio or television soap operas. (ABS)

Cary, Sylvia (also known as Sylvia Hartman) A Hollywood screenwriter and marriage and family therapist in California, Cary helped editor Varda Murrell with the newspaper *Everywoman* in the early 1970s, and started a newsletter for the Los Angeles chapter of NOW, which she kept going for several years. Cary, who joined NOW in

1968, also worked on publicity and press releases. Cary was active in all national NOW conventions until 1972. She also worked with others, including some attorneys, to persuade the *Los Angeles Times* to stop its sex-segregated help-wanted ads, both meeting with *Times'* representatives and picketing. She also took part in a number of bar sit-ins, "because fancy places such as the Beverly Hills Hotel wouldn't serve women at a bar. That got good press coverage," she says. Cary appeared on a number of television shows to discuss these actions and other feminist issues. Her four published books include *It Must be Five O'Clock Somewhere,* about addiction recovery and her early experiences in NOW. Cary, who has two children and two stepchildren, is a member of the Scriptwriters Network, Women in Film, International Writers of Southern California and The California Association of Marriage and Family Therapists. (ABS)

Casale, Joan Therese (1935 –) joined San Diego (CA) County NOW in 1973, and from 1973–1975 was editor of its newsletter. In April 1975, she fought the excommunication of NOW members by Catholic Bishop Leo T. Maher for publicly supporting freedom of choice. From 1977–1978, she was president of San Diego County NOW and continued the fight for reproductive choice. Working with NOW, she taught local news media that child molesters are not typically strangers, but men in or close to the family. During that same period, she gave national publicity to the landmark legal ruling by Judge Norbert Ehrenfreund that allowed, for the first time, a married woman to obtain a restraining order against an abusive husband. Says Casale, "His decision was imitated by other judges, enacted into state law, and copied across the country." Carroll waited for years until the right judge came to head the Family Court, but because she was too ill to carry the work herself, she got younger women attorneys to help. She came to San Diego County NOW because, she said, it could get the publicity, and because the decision must be widely known to give other judges the courage to imitate it. Casale is the author of two one-act (produced) plays about women in American history: "Created Equal" and "A Woman's Work Is Never Done." She has a B.A. from Seton Hill College and two children. Archives: Women's History Museum and Education Center, San Diego, CA, has the documents relating to Bishop Maher's excommunication of NOW members. The original San Diego County NOW documents and Casale's personal papers are at San Diego State University, San Diego, CA. (ABS)

Casals, Rosemary ("Rosie") (1948 –) A tennis star, Casals was considered a rebel who believed women had a destiny in professional tennis and deserved equal rights on the courts. The seven-time Wimbledon women's and mixed doubles champion was born in San Francisco and lived in what was called the Western Edition on the poor side of town. She was raised by her great aunt and her uncle, who came to the U.S. from El Salvador. Her uncle played recreational tennis at Golden Gate Park and taught Casals how to play tennis when she was about eight or nine. Once she advanced beyond the junior ranks and into the women's circuit she faced the challenges of being a female, Latina and poor in a traditionally exclusive sport. So that athletes could earn a living doing what they did best, Casals sought to have tennis recognized as a professional sport. She was one of the first women to claim professional status, but was troubled by the vast difference in prize money between male and female players. Although the U.S. Tennis Association ignored her and other women's pleas and boycott threats over this issue, the media and, in particular, Gladys Heldman, editor of *World Tennis* magazine, supported them. In 1973 Casals was a founder of the Women's Tennis Association. Through that organization, she sought sponsors who saw the value of promoting professional women's sports. This pioneering ultimately paid off for both Casals and subsequent female tennis players. With Billie Jean King, Casals has worked for tennis opportunities for disadvantaged girls. In 1995 she was inducted into the Northern California Tennis Hall of Fame; in 1996 she was inducted into the International Tennis Hall of Fame; in 2003 she was inducted into the Bay Area Sports Hall of Fame; and in 2004 into the African-American & Ethnic Sports Hall of Fame. She is owner and president of her own sports promotion company, Sportswoman, Inc. (ABS)

Casamo, Joan M. (1950 –) A feminist singer/songwriter and retired special education teacher, Casamo was a founding member of the board of the Poughkeepsie Women's Center (1971–1973). She participated in feminist and lesbian CR groups from 1971–1994, and wrote and sang feminist/lesbian music at local colleges and centers. She was singer/songwriter/guitarist for The Angel's Trumpet, a cassette tape of original and some traditional songs (1988). In the summer of 1989, Casamo was a member of Kate Millett's writers and artists colony at Millett's farm in Poughkeepsie, NY, and forward has been a long-time friend of the farm. Since 1988, she and her partner, Linda Clarke, used their home in New Paltz, NY as an "annex" to Millett's farm, providing a nurturing, encouraging space for their feminist and lesbian friends and family. Casamo raised her daughter as a single lesbian parent, "before it was popular and supported" (1973–1987). In 2004, The Human Rights Commission of New York State received and began processing a discrimination complaint on Casamo's behalf in an attempt to gain health insurance coverage for her domestic partner, based on sexual orientation and marital status. (ABS)

Casiano, Inez (1926 –) was born in New York City to parents who had come from Puerto Rico "with high expectations and confidence of success." In 1960, she graduated from CCNY Baruch School with a B.B.A. and several years of full-time research experience. In 1963, Casiano was not hired by a male marketing manager of a large cosmetic company for the specified reason that there were "too many women in the company." Casiano joined the Puerto Rican Community Development Project and served on the planning panel for the NYS Pre-White House Conference on the Black Family. In June 1966, the White House conference To Fulfill These Rights was held, and Casiano attended with Dr. Anna Arnold Hedgeman. When Casiano told Hedgeman of her determination to create a women's rights organization, Hedgeman invited her to participate in the October 1966 NOW founding conference. Both were elected to NOW's first board of directors. In March 1967, Casiano resigned from the board when she was appointed executive assistant to the EEOC executive director (a policy position). Casiano moved on to the U.S. Dept. of Labor as social science adviser to the secretary; she then served on a number of national and local boards and commissions; was director, human relations unit, conference office for the 1970 White House Conference on Children and Youth; was an adviser to government agencies; served as NOW link to minority women's groups; was a founder and Washington Capitol area president of the National Conference of Puerto Rican Women; and spoke at public, government, business and university forums promoting cooperation toward social justice. In 1971, Casiano was the first Hispanic woman graduate of the Federal Executive Institute, and at one time held the highest grade of any Puerto Rican woman in the U.S. Civil Service. In 1990, Casiano retired after serving three years as a loan executive in the Arizona Governor's Office of Women's Services. (ABS)

Cason, Sandra ("Casey") – See Hayden, Casey

Cassedy, Ellen D. (1950 –) was a founder in 1973 of 9to5, National Association of Working Women. It started, she says, as a Boston organization of women office workers, and expanded to include chapters across the country, bringing the concerns of "pink collar" workers into the public eye. Cassedy was director of the Boston organization until 1979, and held positions in the national organization until 1985. She also helped create District 925, a nationwide local of the Service Employees International Union that championed the rights of office workers; and helped file suit against three Boston publishers, which led to major changes in employment policies in the industry, says Cassedy. She is co-author of two books on the rights of working women: *The 9to5 Guide to Combating Sexual Harassment,* written with Ellen Bravo (John Wiley & Sons, 1992); and *9to5: The Working Woman's Guide to Office Survival*, with Karen Nussbaum (Viking-Penguin, 1983). Active in the civil rights and antiwar movements, Cassedy was a speechwriter for the Service Employers International Union (1985–1998), and from 1993–1996 was a speechwriter for the head of the U.S. Environmental Protection Agency during President Clinton's first term. She has a B.A. from the University of California, Berkeley (1971). (ABS)

Castaldi, Serena (1943 –) was introduced to women's liberation while visiting New York City in 1970. Returning to her native Italy, she started the first CR group in Milano, L'Anabasi (ancient Greek for "the ascent"). To spread the ideas and vision of women's liberation, she translated a collection of documents she had brought from NYC (and also from Paris, where in 1970 she had met some of the first members of the French WLM). She called the collection "Donne e Bello" ("Women Is Beautiful") and published it independently (1972) as a collaborative project of L'Anabasi. It was one of the first feminist publications to appear in Italy. During this time, L'Anabasi created Soccorso Femminista, where women in distress could find a friendly woman who listened to their concerns, offering comfort, advice and support. Castaldi, with Liliana Caruso, wrote *L'Altra Faccia della Storia Quella Femminile (The Other Side of History, Herstory)* (D'Anna, 1974); *Femminile Pateriale* (Paterial Femininity) (Evangelista, 1978) and *Seeds of Wholeness* (Liride, 1995). Castaldi lives in California. Archives: The Women's Library, Milano, Italy. (ABS)

Castanis, Muriel (1926 –) A sculptor, Castanis was one of the founders of Women Artists in Revolution. She also helped gather names and information for the women who started Women in the Arts, and supported June Arnold in the takeover of the 15th Street building (New York City) for an art museum. Castanis, who is represented by the OK Harris Gallery (NYC), is a high-school graduate and has four children. (ABS)

Castillo, Sylvia — taught the first course on Chicanas at the University of California, Santa Barbara 1973. She was a founder and chair of the National Network of Hispanic Women (1980). Archives: NNHW archives are now with California Ethnic and Multicultural Archives, David-son Library, University of California, Santa Barbara, CA.

Castleberry, Vivian Anderson (1922 –) "I entered the feminist movement before there was a feminist movement. As a journalist and editor of the features section of the *Dallas Times Herald* (1955–1984), I pushed, prodded and prevailed in moving what was a traditional women's section to become a bellwether for the reporting of issues significant to women and the family—abortion, child abuse, custody, women and legal concerns, family and spousal abuse, violence and on and on." Castleberry was a founder of the Women's Center of Dallas, the Women's Issues Network and the Dallas Women's Foundation. She was the founder of Peacemakers, Inc., which sponsored an international women's conference in 1988 that drew 2,000 attendants from 57 countries to work on women's responsibility to create a more peaceful world. She is the author of *Daughters of Dallas* (Odenwald Press). Castleberry, who has a B.S. (1944) and an Honorary Doctorate (1998) from SMU, has five children. Archives: Women of the Southwest, DeGolyer Library, Southern Methodist University, Dallas, TX. (ABS)

Cataldo, Mima (1943 –) In New York City in the late 1960s, Cataldo helped develop several CR groups, and also began photographing street life—an endeavor that led her to see the women's movement as history in the making. In the mid 1970s, she co-taught the first women's studies courses at Syracuse University and helped establish the women's studies program there. In 1983, she photographed the women's peace camp near Seneca Falls. For the next two years, Cataldo analyzed and edited interviews from that time, and collected photos of other women who had participated in the peace camp. This work, *Women's Encampment for a Future of Peace and Justice,* was published in 1987 by Temple University Press. From 1988 – 1994, Cataldo taught psychology, sociology, photography and women's studies courses for local colleges in Upstate NY, and spent a year as a senior research fellow at Victoria University in Wellington, New Zealand, where she continued her work of examining sex differences in non-verbal communication. In 2001, Syracuse University's Light Work Gallery exhibited a retrospective of her photographs of the women's and peace movements. Cataldo is district librarian for the Reed Union School District in Tiburon, CA, where she continues to photograph women and the peace movement. Cataldo, who earned her undergrad degree from the University of Michigan (1966) and her Ph.D. from Syracuse University, has two children. (ABS)

Cavanagh, Joan Margaret (1954 –) Born in Burbank, CA, Cavanagh wrote high-school editorials in support of the ERA and reproductive freedom, and entered the women's movement around 1969. She turned 21 in 1975, just two days before the last Americans left Vietnam. At the time, she was serving 52 days in the Women's Detention Center in Washington, D.C., for an act of civil disobedience against the war. Also in 1975, she spent 30 days at Niantic State Prison in Connecticut for another anti-war action. Two years later she moved to New Haven, CT, and got a job at the Feminist Union, the political arm of New Haven Women's Center. Cavanagh was a founding member in the late 1970s of the committee for education and defense against racism. In the middle to late 1980s, she worked with the New Haven Pledge of Resistance, organizing against U.S. arming of the Nicaraguan contras and the brutal government in El Salvador. Since 1990 she has been a key member of the Connecticut Peace Coalition/New Haven. Cavanagh is an archivist and historical consultant for the Greater New Haven Labor History Association. She was educated at Wesleyan University and Yale University, where she received her Ph.D. in 1996. (ABS)

Ceballos, Jacqueline Michot (1925 –) After graduating from Southwestern College in Lafayette, Ceballos moved to New York City to "pursue an impossible dream in 1946—to be an opera singer." She married a Colombian in 1951, had three children, and moved to Bogota, Colombia, in 1958. There she had a fourth child and formed an opera company. Then a friend gave her a copy of *The Feminine Mystique,* and she knew her discontent wasn't her fault or his fault. "It was society, and society had to change." She returned to NY with her four children in 1967 and attended her first NY NOW meeting that November. She subsequently formed a PR committee, a speakers bureau and, with Anselma dell'Olio, New Feminist Theater. Ceballos served on national and local NOW boards from 1967 to 1973. She urged Betty Friedan to unite with radical women, which resulted in the Congress to Unite Women (1969 and 1970). In 1970, when Friedan announced a national strike on the 50th anniversary of suffrage, Ceballos helped organize the coalition and was NY NOW's strike coordinator. She also conceived of *The NOW York Times,* and fired up radical groups and NOW committees to plan pre-march actions. Offices Ceballos has held include NY NOW's board chair, 1970; president, 1971; and eastern regional director, 1972. That year she ran as a delegate for Presidential candidate Shirley Chisholm and was NOW's representative to the Democratic Convention. In 1973 she helped to initiate the NWPC; in 1974 she co-founded the Women's Forum and was its first executive director. In 1975 she was NOW's delegate to the United Nations IWY Conference in Mexico. Ceballos started two businesses: New Feminist Talent, a speakers bureau with well-known feminists on the roster; and a PR firm, which produced the first feminist education course. In 1989, Ceballos moved to Florida to make commercials, but was called back to NYC by Mary Jean Tully to help with interviews for her Schlesinger Library History of NOW project. In 1992, with the help of Dorothy Senerchia, she organized the first reunion of second wave feminists. Under the name Veteran Feminists of America, the organization held its first reunion in 1993. In 1994, Ceballos returned to Lafayette where she helped re-found the Louisiana Caucus. She works full time as president of VFA. (ABS)

Cervelli, Pat Fineran (1943 –) had been a community organizer/anti-war activist with CIPA in New York City when she joined the women's movement. She participated in weekly CR groups and in several demonstrations before moving (1969) to Oakland, CA, where she and several women formed Bay Area Women's Liberation, which founded the magazine *Tooth and Nail.* Cervelli helped organize an action at the American Psychological Association's annual conference in San Francisco, leafleting a workshop by a psychologist whose premise was that women who were strippers chose this profession because they lacked adequate nurturing as children. She also helped organize an action against the underground newspaper *Dock of the Bay,* which published a pornographic magazine to raise money. Says Cervelli, "We liberated the proofs." In 1970, she worked to organize telephone operators at Pacific Telephone, where she was employed. Moving back to NYC (1977), she joined Redstockings.

From 1977–1990, Cervelli worked at a battered women's shelter in Brooklyn, and helped found Mother Lode Women's Center in Sonora, CA (1980). Cervelli, who has one child, is a medical social worker and on the board of Mountain Women's Resource Center, Sonora, CA. (ABS)

Chaffee, Ellen Earle (1944 –) (also known as Ellie Kilander) was a co-founder of North Dakota's first NOW chapter (1977). She was a member of the ND Commission on the Status of Women (1972–1976); served as its president (1973–1974); and was sponsor of Outstanding Women of North Dakota (1975). In 1972–1973, Chaffee was a coordinator, lobbyist and major provider of testimony for the ratification of the ERA in ND, and was a public speaker on women's rights, feminism and the ERA for over 100 groups and schools (1972–1975). From 1974–1977, she was Title IX coordinator, North Dakota State University, and in 1974 was co-founder, Tri-College Women's Bureau. At the same time, she was the organizer of a major speaker series on women's rights, funded by three agencies in two states. Active in civil rights, Chaffee was a member of the North Dakota State Advisory Board, U.S. Commission on Civil Rights (1974–1975), and the Fargo Civil Rights Commission (1975–1976). A university president, Chaffee earned her B.A. from the University of Kentucky (1966); her M.S. from North Dakota State University (1971); and her Ph.D. from Stanford (1980). She has one child. Archives: University of North Dakota Library, Grand Forks, ND. (ABS)

Chalimonczyk, Donna Mae (1933 –) organized the coordinating council for the ERA in North Dakota, and served as director for the statewide organization. The coordinating council included most statewide women's organizations (with ERA platforms) as members. It also had chair people in all major ND cities that worked as area coordinators. Chalimonczyk developed strategy with council members and carried out a plan for a statewide lobbying corps. The ERA passed in the ND Legislature in 1975. Trained as a radiologic technologist, Chalimonczyk hasn't worked in that field since 1956. She has two children and works as a watercolor artist. Archives: North Dakota State University, Fargo, ND. (ABS)

Chalker, Rebecca (1943 –) A medical writer, professor and women's health activist, Chalker edited early versions of *A New View of a Woman's Body* and *How to Stay Out of the Gynecologist's Office* (1974–1975). She has also worked as an abortion counselor and assisted in abortions. A prolific writer, Chalker is the author of *The Clitoral Truth* (Seven Stories Press, 2000); was senior author of *A Woman's Book of Choices: Abortion, Menstrual Extraction, RU-486* (Seven Stories Press, 2000) and *Overcoming Bladder Disorders: Medical and Self-Help Advice on Incontinence, Cystitis, Interstitial Cystitis, Prostate Problems and Bladder Cancer* (HarperCollins, 1990); and author of *The Complete Cervical Cap Guide*

(Harper & Row, 1987). She has also lectured widely on female sexuality, held workshops and presented papers. From 1966–1967, she was a Peace Corps teacher at The College of Social Work, Tehran, Iran; and since 2000 has been adjunct professor of women's and gender studies, Pace University, New York. Chalker received her B.A. (1966) and her M.A. (1975) from Florida State University, Tallahassee. (ABS)

Chamberlain, Mariam K. (1918 –) has been called the fairy godmother of women's studies because of her work as a program officer in higher education at the Ford Foundation (1971–1981), where she helped develop the field of women's studies. After leaving the foundation (and retiring in 1982), Chamberlain became a resident scholar at the Russell Sage Foundation, where she headed the task force on women in higher education. In 1981, Chamberlain was the founding president of the National Council for Research on Women. She has been a board member of the Feminist Press, the Institute for Women's Policy Research, the Network of East-West Women and the Women's Interart Center. Books she has written or edited include *Women of Color* and *The Multicultural Curriculum* and *Women in the Academe* (Russell Sage Foundation, 1988). She has taught at Connecticut College and the School of General Studies, Columbia University, and Yale University. Chamberlain graduated from Radcliffe College in 1939, and earned a Ph.D. from Harvard University in 1950. During WWII, she served as an economic analyst in the Office of Strategic Services in Washington, D.C. (ABS)

Chambers, Jane (1937 – 1983) was the first openly lesbian playwright produced Off-Broadway. She was also a founding member of the NJ WPC and of The Interart Theatre in New York City, and a member of the planning committee of the Women's Program of the American Theatre Association. A published author of numerous plays, novels and poetry, Chambers was a member of The Writer's Guild East and The East End Gay Organization for Human Rights. Her work is taught in women's studies programs, writing programs and acting programs in colleges and universities throughout the U.S. A graduate of Goddard College, Chambers began her career in the late 1950s as an actress and playwright, working Off-Broadway and in coffeehouse theater. Her plays include "My Blue Heaven," "A Late Snow," "Last Summer at Bluefish Cove," and "KUDZU." Published novels include *Burning* (Jove Press, 1978) and *Chasing Jason* (JH Press, 1987). Chambers received numerous awards during her lifetime, including the Connecticut Educational Television Award (1971), a Eugene O'Neill fellowship (1972), a National Writer's Guild Award (1973), The New York Dramalogue Critic's Circle Award, The Alliance for Lesbian and Gay Arts Media Award, The Robby Award, The Oscar Wilde Award, The Los Angeles Drama Critic's Circle Award and a Proclamation from Los Angeles for Outstanding Theatre.

She also received two Betty Awards (1985 and 1987) and The Fund for Human Dignity Award (1982), among others. In 1983, Women in Theatre (originally The American Theatre Association - Women's Program) created The Jane Chambers Playwrighting Award to encourage the writing of new plays that address women's experiences and have a majority of principal roles for women.

Champagne, Margot J. (1946 –) worked with Patricia Maginnis in the mid 1960s at the Society for Humane Abortion, helping women get to Mexico, lobbying in Sacramento (CA), and doing defense work for doctors arrested for performing abortions. Beginning in 1970 and continuing into the 1980s, Champagne worked for Human Rights for Women as a summer intern, and then joined the board of directors, drafting and filing amicus briefs in the Supreme Court in support of Dr. Milan Vuitch (abortion case) and Bill Baird (right to birth control for single persons). Champagne also drafted and published an employment discrimination handbook for women. In 1972, she was legal counsel to East Bay (CA) women's clinic, in 1973 was on the advisory board, *Women's Rights Law Reporter*. She was later briefly on the board of directors, National Women's Party. Champagne holds a B.A. from San Francisco State University (1969) and a J.D. from Hastings College of the Law (1972). (ABS)

Chapman, Alice Joseph (1918 –) A feminist organizer and ERA activist, Chapman joined the Danbury, CT, chapter of NOW in 1970, where she became president and later president of the state chapter. She worked for CT ratification of the ERA, which succeeded the second time it was brought before the legislature. She was also on the steering committee to pass Question I, a referendum on a CT State ERA, which passed with a vote of over 2:1. Later, Chapman became a board member of the Connecticut All the Way coalition to defeat an attempt to rescind passage of the ERA. In 1975, Chapman was one of six women founders, a board member and the first treasurer of what became the Women's Center of Greater Danbury, Inc. Also in 1975, Chapman started a rape crisis service, which operated out of her home for the first two years. In 1977, this service was coordinated with the police force and the Danbury Hospital and later became a part of the Women's Center. Chapman was elected to represent CT at the 1977 Houston First National Women's Conference to celebrate International Women's Year, and elected to the IWY continuing committee. She was a member of the Danbury Equal Rights and Opportunity Commission, where she helped to author the city's affirmative action program. She also served on the Danbury school system Title IX advisory committee. In 1979, Chapman was elected treasurer of national NOW and spent two three-year terms in Washington, D.C. While in Washington, she attended a conference on the United Nations Decade for Women and, on invitation, a conference on SALT—the Strategic Arms Limitation Talks—for leading women's or-

ganizations in the country. Returning to Danbury, Chapman served two two-year terms as president of the Women's Center, during which time the Center purchased a shelter for victims of domestic violence. Chapman served as treasurer of the Center during the time it bought a building to accommodate its growing services and administrative staff. Chapman, who has six children, is an emeritus board member of the Center. (ABS)

Chappell, Annette (1939 –) (also known as Annette Flower) Chappell was a founding mother of the women's studies program at Maryland's Towson University (1970 – 1974), and taught women's studies courses there. As a co-researcher (with Jane Sheets) in statistical studies on the status of women faculty at Towson, she established methodologies for assessing equity in promotion, salaries, benefits and job assignments. She was also a co-founder (with Elaine Hedges, Sara Coulter and Jane Sheets) of the university's commission on the status of women, and served as a consultant and workshop leader on implementation of Title IX at both high school and university levels. From 1974 – 1977, Chappell was Towson's first affirmative action officer and, in that office, wrote the university's first affirmative action plan and guided it through the process of adoption by the academic senate. She also co-founded the Maryland Association of Affirmative Action Officers; co-founded the Executive and Professional Women's Council of Maryland; served as the first president of the Baltimore County Commission for Women; and assisted in founding the Sexual Assault and Domestic Violence Center of Baltimore County, now known as TurnaRound. Leaving the affirmative action position in 1977, Chappell became dean of the College of Liberal Arts at Towson, where she helped the women's studies program grow and develop, and helped found Towson's national center for teaching and research on women. She retired from Towson University in 1999. Chappell earned a M.Div. degree at the General Theological Seminary in New York and became an ordained Episcopal priest. She serves a small urban parish in Baltimore. In addition to her M.Div., Chappell holds a B.A., M.A. and Ph.D. (ABS)

Chasek, Arlene Shatsky (1934 –) was founding director, Center for Family Involvement in Schools, and the Consortium for Educational Equity, Rutgers University, New Brunswick, NJ. She was lead person/director for the Women Searching for Self study group in Cavalier, ND (1972); the Women's Arts Festival, also in Cavalier (1973); and the Free to Be Career Day in the New Providence (NJ) Schools (1975). Chasek was also chair of the affirmative action committee in the New Providence Schools, and from 1981 – 1985 was director of Futures Unlimited-Career Seminars for girls in grades seven to 12. Chasek is author of *Rutgers Family Science, Family Tools & Technology*, and *Futures Unlimited Planning Guide*. Chasek was also active in the ACLU and Planned Parenthood. She has three children. She holds a B.A. from Cornell University, an M.A. from Columbia University, and an M.A.T. from Teachers College. (ABS)

Chatzinoff, Millie (1925 – 1973) was head of the Long Island, NY NOW marriage and divorce committee. Although she was not an attorney, she analyzed difficult problems in New York State laws, suggested solutions, and had the material translated into legislative language. Part of her work became NOW's Responsible Divorce Reform Bill. The bill did not pass, but because of it, financial forms were created and sold in stationery stores.

Chay (1943 –) (also known as Chay Paule) served as VP of the Oakland chapter of NOW. She also served as editor of *Michigan NOW Times* and editor/publisher of *Michigan Sportswoman*, which she started after noting that, in the early 1970s, women's sports were "deliberately being stifled." Involved in the struggle for Title IX, she was associated with WDET Women's Radio writing for and announcing women's sports. Known simply as Chay, she was a part of numerous marches and conferences, and as a poet/writer produced "reams of info that male publishers wouldn't publish." A supporter of the ERA, Chay was in Springfield, IL, on June 30, 1982, "and cried along with everybody else when the ERA was defeated." Chay also worked on the political campaigns for Sonia Johnson, Geraldine Ferraro, Shirley Chisholm, Barbara Jordan and Bella Abzug. (ABS)

Cherry, Gwendolyn Sawyer (1923 – 1975) Inspired by the passage of the Civil Rights Act, Cherry left teaching after 18 years to study law and earned a J.D., cum laude, from Florida A&M in 1965. She became legal assistant for the U.S. Coast Guard Seventh District, which included Puerto Rico and the Virgin Islands. In 1968, at the urging of Martha Ingle, first president of Dade County NOW, Cherry joined the chapter as legal counsel. She championed Equal Pay for Equal Work in 1969, ratification of the ERA, and legislation supporting childcare. Cherry was the first black woman elected to the Florida State Legislature, where she served from 1970 – 1979. The first major bill she drafted was for childcare support for working women. It was passed after a long struggle. Later, a childcare center was built and dedicated in her name. Cherry was a founding member of the NWPC in Washington, D.C. (July 1971), and of the first NWPC chapter in Miami (September 1971). Her father, W.D. Sawyer, M.D., was a Dade County public health doctor and founder of the Christian Hospital in Overtown in Miami. Her mother, Mary Elizabeth Sawyer, owned the only black hotel in Miami, the Mary Elizabeth Hotel, where black entertainers stayed while visiting in Miami. Cherry had two children. Archives: Black History Museum, Miami, FL.

Chesler, Phyllis (1940 –) is a feminist author, professor emerita and activist. Active in the Northern Student

Movement civil rights movement and anti-Vietnam War movement, Chesler began attending NOW meetings in 1967. She lectured about and taught courses on women's studies at a number of Free Schools; helped women get abortions; and supported one of the country's first women's crisis centers, on Dean Street in Brooklyn. She is a co-founder (1969) of the Association for Women in Psychology. That same year, Chesler received a Ph.D. in psychology from the New School of Social Research (New York City) and began teaching at Richmond College, a branch of City University of New York (CUNY) on Staten Island, as the only female member of the psychology faculty. She turned the women's studies course first into a minor and later a major at Richmond College. In 1971, Chesler and others at CUNY began a class action suit on behalf of women against CUNY, which was won 17 years later. With Vivian Gornick, Chesler created an early feminist salon (1970 – 1971). She was involved in the formation and on the board of Women's Action Alliance. By late 1971 – 1972 she was also dealing with racism and anti-Semitism among feminists. In 1975 she co-led one of the first feminist Passover seders and continued to do so for 18 years. In 1974 – 1975 she co-founded the National Women's Health Network. Despite her groundbreaking feminist work, Chesler had to fight hard for tenure and to keep it, and was investigated several times for (presumably) teaching "man-hating," "witchcraft" and "lesbianism." She did not become a full professor for 22 years. From 1987 – 1999 she served as editor at large for *On the Issues* magazine. Chesler is author of *Women and Madness* (Doubleday and Company, 1972); *Women, Money and Power*, with Emily Jane Goodman (William Morrow & Company, 1976), *About Men* (Simon & Schuster, 1978), *With Child: A Diary of Motherhood* (Lippincott & Crowell, 1979), *Mothers on Trial: The Battle for Children and Custody* (McGraw-Hill, 1986), *Sacred Bond: The Legacy of Baby M.* (Times Books/Random House, 1988), *Patriarchy: Notes of an Expert Witness* (Common Courage Press, 1994), *Letters to a Young Feminist* (Four Walls Eight Windows, 1998), *Woman's Inhumanity to Woman* (Nation Books, 2002), *Women of the Wall: Claiming Sacred Ground at Judaism's Holy Site*, with Rivka Haut (Jewish Lights, 2003), and *The New Anti-Semitism: The Current Crisis and What We Must Do About It* (Jossey-Bass/John Wiley, 2003). Archives: Sallie Bingham Center for Women's History and Culture, Duke University, Durham, NC. (ABS)

Chewning, June Spangler (1925 –) joined the women's movement as a child, learning from her grandmother, who was a suffragist marching to get the vote. As an adult, Chewning discovered that she had her own problems at her government job, "particularly in upward mobility— above the grade that was considered good for a woman." Chewning obtained the names and addresses of federally employed women participating in a 1967 seminar for women executives, because "women executives were not getting the training—only the men were," and sent them invitations to a luncheon in Washington, D.C. (1968). Interest was high, and after several months, FEW (Federally Employed Women) was incorporated, with Chewning as secretary. Its first large event was a management training program. Today, there are some 300 chapters worldwide. During one stint at the Atomic Energy Commission, when Chewning's position was threatened by a young male supervisor intent on scuttling her career, Chewning filed an EEO complaint and turned it into a class action. After 10 years, the case was settled in favor of the class. The action helped establish case law regarding the dates from which compensation can be calculated, and resulted in more than $2.25 million being distributed among the 130 women who had joined the class action. During her career, Chewning also worked as an editor and research analyst at the Library of Congress, as a military intelligence analyst with the Department of Defense, and as an expert in the manpower needs of the nuclear industry. Chewning, who has two children, holds a B.A. from American University, Washington, D.C.   (ABS)

Chicago, Judy (1939 –) Renowned feminist artist, author and educator, Chicago is creator of The Dinner Party, a monumental installation that required the collaboration of over 400 people. It premiered at the San Francisco Museum of Modern Art in 1979 and has since become a feminist icon. It will be permanently installed in 2007 in the Elizabeth A. Sackler Center for Feminist Art at the Brooklyn Museum. Earlier, in 1970, Chicago created the first feminist arts program at California State University, Fresno. The next year, Chicago and artist Miriam Schapiro brought the program to the California Institute of the Arts, where the two team-taught for two years. One outcome of the program was the Womanhouse project (1971 –1972). With art critic Arlene Raven and designer Sheila De Bretteville, Chicago co-founded the Feminist Studio Workshop, located in the Woman's Building in Los Angeles (1973). For the next 25 years, Chicago focused on her studio practice. She also lectured and presented workshops and critiques at universities around the world. Chicago's books include a two-volume autobiography, *Through the Flower: My Struggle as a Woman Artist* (1975) and *Beyond the Flower: The Autobiography of a Feminist Artist* (1996); a two-volume history of the creation of her tribute to the history of women in Western Civilization, *The Dinner Party: A Symbol of our Heritage* (1979) and *Embroidering Our Heritage: The Dinner Party Needlework* (1980); as well as *Birth Project* (1985); *Holocaust Project: From Darkness Into Light* (1993); *The Dinner Party 1996*, a tour of that installation; and *Women and Art: Contested Territory*, co-authored with Edward Lucie-Smith (1999). More recently, she has published *Fragments from the Delta of Venus* (2004) and *Kitty City: A Feline Book of Hours* (2005). Chicago holds a B.A. (1962) and M.A. (1964) from UCLA, and four Honorary Doctorates—from Duke University, Lehigh University, Smith College and

Russell Sage College. Archives: In 1978, Through the Flower, a nonprofit educational corporation, was established to help Chicago complete The Dinner Party and preserve The Dinner Party, the International Quilting Bee, the Birth Project, the Holocaust Project and Resolutions. A large segment of Chicago's individual art will become part of Through the Flower's collection.   (ABS)

Chico, Beverly (1931 –) has been teaching women's history courses in Maryland and Colorado colleges since 1971. Her Women in U.S. History and Women in Western History were the first such classes taught at a two-year college in Maryland. She is the author of *Women's Rights in Spain* (1959); five biographies of women artists, published in *Notable Maryland Women* (1975); and "Woman's Place & Space" (*Social Science Journal*, January 1982). In 1973 she was a member of the steering committee for a series of five women's studies conferences, and was chair of the women's history conference, presented by Women in Higher Education (MD). Since 1973 she has been a reviewer of women's history books for *Choice*, a publication of the American Library Association. In 1975 Chico was a consultant to the WILPF Calendar, and in 1976 was a consultant for Hidden Faces, a Colorado Women traveling exhibition. Chico was an official observer at the 1977 National Women's Conference in Houston, and was women's history consultant for the Girl Scouts, Mile-Hi Council, Colorado, in 1979 and 1980. She was program chair of the first (1980) and second (1981) Women's History Week in CO; president of the National League of American Pen Women in Denver (1986 – 1988); and president of Denver Women's Press Club (1992 – 1993). In 1994 she received the Foremother Award from the Colorado Women's Agenda. Chico, who has four children, holds a B.A. from Boston College (1962), an M.A. from Johns Hopkins University (1965) and a D.A. from the University of Northern Colorado (1979). Archives: Auraria Library, Denver, CO.   (ABS)

Childers, Patricia – See Bond, Pat

Chisholm, Shirley Anita St. Hill (1924 – 2005) Chisholm is best remembered as a candidate for President of the United States in 1972. In 1964, she was the first African American woman elected to the New York State Assembly. Four years later, she became the first African American woman elected to the United States Congress. When she took her seat in 1969, she was committed to dismantling the legal constraints against women, and to greater employment and educational opportunities for women and minorities. The core of her legislative program included bringing domestic workers under minimum wage, reproductive rights, and increased funding for childcare. An early supporter of the ERA, Chisholm's Congressional testimony in 1970 helped galvanize minority women nationally. In 1971, Chisholm was an organizer of the NWPC. She was also an active member of NOW and the Equal Rights Amendment Ratification Council. When she ran for President of the U.S., her primary issues were racial and gender equality, and getting out of the war in Vietnam. She won 28 delegates and received 152 first ballot votes at the Democratic National Convention, and then found many of her issues supported by the nominee for President, George McGovern. Chisholm experienced conflict during her political career as she tried to maintain her standing within the power structure while advancing the gender and race agendas. Notable was her support of Republican John Lindsay for mayor of New York City, whom she saw as the best supporter of her issues. Although her support was undoubtedly a key factor in his victory, it alienated the Democratic Party regulars and weakened Chisholm's presidential bid. Although Chisholm founded the National Political Caucus of Black Women in an effort to unite the interests of feminism and civil rights, many feminist and black leaders stuck with the entrenched political powers during her presidential campaign. Although disillusioned and bitter, Chisholm continued her career in the House of Representatives until 1983. She is the author of several books, including *Unbought and Unbossed*, and is the subject of many books documenting her life and career. In 2004, Brooklyn College, Chisholm's alma mater, renamed the Women's Studies Center in her honor. Archives: Rare Book and Manuscript Library, Columbia University, NY, NY.

Chittick, Elizabeth L. (1908 –) A cohort of Alice Paul, Chittick was president of the National Woman's Party for 19 years (1971 – 1989). She feels she was "destined to be president of the National Woman's Party." She was the first woman civilian administrator of the U.S. Naval Air Station in Seattle, WA (1941 – 1942) and the U.S. Naval Station, Banana River, FL (1942 – 1945). She was the first woman registered representative of the New York Stock Exchange (Bache & Co., 1950 – 1962), and first woman revenue collections officer with the IRS (1965 – 1979). As president of NWP, she saved the Sewell-Belmont House, home of the party, from eminent domain and was responsible for it being declared a National historic Land Site. A tireless worker for the ERA, Chittick was author of "Answers to Questions About the Equal Rights Amendment" (1973) and was a radio and television commentator on the ERA. She planned and led the 1977 parade of 5,000 down Pennsylvania Avenue in Alice Paul's honor in 1977. She was the first woman invited to speak at the podium of the House of Representatives in Oklahoma, in 1978, where she got a standing ovation. The subject was the ERA. Chittick was a delegate to the International Woman's Year conference in Mexico, 1975, and U.S representative, Commission on the Status of Women, World Woman's Conference, in Nairobi, Kenya, 1985. She held many prominent positions on national and international women's commissions and organizations. Losing her eyesight in 1985 was a shock for this activist, but Chittick still keeps up with ERA news. Ballroom dancing helps her cope with her challenge. Born in Bangor, PA, Chittick was educated at Columbia University, New York Institute of Finance and Hunter College. Archives: Records of the National Woman's Party still in Chittick's possession will go to The Smithsonian Institute, Washington, D.C., where earlier NWP files reside. (ABS)

Chmaj, Betty (1930 – 1997) In 1969, Chmaj was the only woman on the American Studies Association council of 27, and almost single-handedly forced ASA to face the "woman question." Enough people followed Chmaj's lead so that in 1969 the ASA executive council passed a resolution: "That the American Studies Association formally states its opposition to discrimination against women in admissions, grants, awarding of degrees, faculty employment, salary and conditions of employment and consideration for promotion, and that it undertake to receive, solicit and publicize information relating to specific instances of such discrimination." In 1971, the committee on the status of women chaired by Chmaj subsidized *American Women and American Studies* (2 volumes), which she edited. The 1972 ASA series of resolutions on the status of women became the model for many other academic organizations. Chmaj taught in the humanities department at California State University, Sacramento (1972 – 1994), and was well known as an early advocate of women's studies at her own institution. She was also one of the founding members of the Sonneck Society's Music and Gender Interest Group.

Christ, Carol Patrice (1945 –) One of the first women graduate students in religious studies at Yale (1969), Christ helped organize a feminist speaker series at Yale Divinity School. She also joined the Yale Graduate Students Alliance; was active in Yale Women's Liberation; and was a founding member (with Marcia Keller, Virginia Walbot and Caroline Whitbeck) of the Yale Graduate, Faculty and Staff group (1971). This group supported the first (unsuccessful) effort of the largely female administrative staff to unionize, and brought HEW to investigate Yale for sex discrimination in 1972. With Caroline Whitbeck, Christ was co-author of a model affirmative action plan for universities that was distributed by WEAL. Christ was also part of Occupation Shit Room, a sit-in at the men-only bathroom in the Divinity School Library's stacks, which led to the integration of the facility. In 1971, Christ attended the first meeting of women theologians at Alverno College and founded the Women's Caucus—Religious Studies associated with the American Academy of Religion and Society for the Study of Bible Literature. She served as its first co-chair and later co-chaired the Women and Religion program unit in the academy (1980s). A paper presented at its first session became the basis for her first book, *Diving Deep and Surfacing: Women Writers on Spiritual Quest* (1980). At Columbia University, Christ taught one of the first feminist courses on women and religion (1973). Readings for this course later became the basis for the anthology *Womanspirit Rising: A Feminist Reader in Religion* (1979), which Christ co-edited with Judith Plaskow. In 1972, Christ and Anne Barstow organized New York Feminist Scholars in Religion. Christ was featured (with Z Budapest and Naomi Goldenberg) on the first documentary of the women and religion movement, made by Gloria Kaufman in the mid-1970s. At that time, Christ became a member of the Goddess movement, and was a co-creator of the conference The Great Goddess Re-Emerging (1978). In California in the late 1970s, Christ co-founded a women's spirituality ritual group. She later moved to Greece. She also co-founded Ariadne Institute, through which she leads Goddess pilgrimages in Crete and Lesbos. Christ is an environmentalist and a founding member of Friends of Green Lesbos. She earned her B.A. from Stanford University (1967); and her M.A. (1969), M.Phil. (1972), and Ph.D. (1974) from Yale University. Archives: Leaders in the Women's and Religions Movements, Union Theological Seminary, New York, NY.   (ABS)

Christian, Barbara (1944 – 2000) Professor of African-American studies at the University of California, Berkeley, at the time of her death, Christian was best known for her study, "Black Women Novelists: The Development of a Tradition" (1980). Her article "The Race for Theory" challenged the domination of those who were primarily interested in theory, rather than the African American writers themselves and their work. She was a significant presence in the debates over the relationship of race, class and gender. In 1972 she was instrumental in establishing the department of African American studies at Berkeley, and from 1978 – 1983 was its chair. In 1978 Christian became the first African American woman to be granted tenure at Berkeley, and was the first to be promoted to full professor (1986). She was also the first African American to win the university's Distinguished Teaching Award (1991). Born in the Virgin Islands, Christian entered Marquette University (WI) at the age of 15, and graduated cum laude in 1963. She received her doctorate from Columbia University in 1970. Christian had one child and a stepchild.

Christie, Jean (1912 –) (also known as Jean C. Claus) Uncomfortable with the traditional model of womanhood presented to girls in the 1920s, and dismayed as an educated adult to be told not even to apply for a job at the National Archives because "women weren't strong enough for the work," Christie began to talk about the situation and became "at least a vocal feminist." In the late 1950s, very happily married with two small children, she nonetheless had never been comfortable adopting her husband's name. After consulting the leader of the Lucy Stone League about possible legal complications (there were none), she resumed her own name. She also resumed her graduate studies and, in 1963, earned a Ph.D.

in history from Columbia. Teaching at Fairleigh Dickinson University (NJ), she initiated a course on women in America, published an article in that field and, with faculty from various disciplines, taught Women: Myth and Reality. She also joined the Coordinating Council on Women in the Historical Profession. As a board member of the Great Neck (NY) Forum, she helped arrange and chaired a meeting on the feminist movement. Christie was also an early member of NOW, and was active in organizations for women for peace. In the 1970s, she retired from Fairleigh Dickinson University as professor emerita, and has taken part in a number of feminist activities. She has two children, one deceased.   (ABS)

Ciarrochi, Lillian T. (1930 –) joined Philadelphia NOW in 1971, becoming treasurer, then executive VP (1975) and president (1977). During the 1970s, the Philadelphia chapter filed suit against the police force, which resulted in the first woman being hired. It also opened up all-male clubs, such as the Union League, to women, and organized a Teachers NOW, which changed curriculum to sex-neutral language. In 1973, Ciarrochi co-chaired the NOW Media Project, which challenged all three local network affiliates' licenses. As a result, they were given a Saturday night show that was directed, produced, taped and acted by NOW members studying communications at local colleges. The chapter also won promotions for women at the three stations. In 1980, Ciarrochi went to Florida for the ERA campaign, and handled all press—statewide, local and national. She was also involved in legislative research and lobbying for the ERA, and was statewide financial manager for the campaign. In late 1982, she went to Washington to handle direct mail for national NOW, and became NOW's controller. Archives: Schlesinger Library, Radcliffe Institute, Cambridge, MA.   (ABS)

Cimino, Edda Mary (1930 –) A south Florida teacher and community leader, Cimino has worked to protect and expand women's rights. She opened the first lesbian- and gay-friendly counseling center in the southeastern United States in 1971, sponsored by the head of the University of Miami Guidance and Counseling Department. In 1972, Cimino helped the minister of MCC, Miami, purge sexism from his sermons. Later, however, she led a permanent walkout of female board members and congregants when women were excluded from a party to honor the church's founder. In 1972, while serving as co-coordinator of the National Coalition of Lesbian and Gay Organizations during the Republican National Convention, Cimino pressed the national media to provide coverage of lesbian and gay issues. In 1973, she wrote and produced a school play, "Ain't I a Woman?" In 1975, at a Dade teachers' union meeting, Cimino originated a motion for equal pay for female high-school varsity coaches. It was tabled, but eventually passed. In 1975, while on the board of the Dade County Coalition for Human Rights, she thwarted the intended outcome of Anita Bryant's Save

Our Children anti-gay referendum. She secured the union "right to privacy," saving the jobs of teachers statewide. In 1995 she produced "Reaching Out," a video to raise consciousness about discrimination against lesbian and gay youth in schools. Praised by the American Library Association, and distributed by Cinema East, it was gifted to local schools and libraries. In 2001, Cimino was presented with the Dade Human Rights Foundation Community Service Award. Archives: Stonewall Library & Archives Inc., Fort Lauderdale, FL.   (ABS)

Cisler, Lucinda (1937 –) was a primary activist for abortion and contraception rights in the early years of the second wave, an architectural designer and planner who worked in many states, and later had a practice in information design. In 1967 Cisler began working full-time to repeal abortion/contraception laws, with Parents' Aid Society, and from 1968 – 1969 was active in NYRW. A member of NOW from 1968–1980, Cisler was a national coordinator of the task force on reproduction and its control (1969 – 1971) and on the national board (1970-1971). In NY NOW she was active on these issues and as chapter VP. Cisler was a founder of the statewide New Yorkers for Abortion Law Repeal (1969), its treasurer, president, and (1970 – 1973) legislative representative. She took part in the 1969 founding conference of NARAL and helped frame its statement of purpose. A member from 1969 – 1980, she was NARAL's first secretary and (1969 – 1979) a board member. A national board member of Zero Population Growth (1969 – 1972), she was a founder of the NYC chapter (1970) and on its advisory council. Cisler also co-coordinated Congress to Unite Women I and II and took part in People to Abolish Abortion Laws, Coalition of Organizations for Abortion Rights, Libertarian Abortion Action Group, and others. She was a founding member (1971) of the *Majority Report* newspaper group, the Alliance of Women in Architecture (1972), and the Association of Libertarian Feminists (1975). Her annotated, categorized *Women: a Bibliography* (1968 – 1970) exemplified the new feminism both as scholarship and in publicizing others' current writings. Without being advertised, 20,000 copies of six editions were sold to readers, groups, and college and public libraries in the United States and abroad, with condensations in several books. *Women: A Bibliography* was a cornerstone resource for the new field of women's studies. Cisler also published widely cited anthology and periodical essays, appeared as a speaker, and co-produced, with James Clapp, the first radio series on abortion (Pacifica, 1968). Among her works of graphic design for the movement were the female equality symbol and the abortion law repeal "alpha." Cisler holds an A.B. from Vassar College; a B.Arch. from Yale; and the M.Arch., M.C.P., and Certificate in Civic Design from the University of Pennsylvania. Archives: Mostly destroyed, 1999. Oral history (with Clapp, 1975) at the Schlesinger Library, Radcliffe Institute, Cambridge, MA.   (ABS)

Claire, Nola (1933 –) (also known as Nola Dorries and Nola Szymalak) convened NY State NOW, was elected its first president, established new chapters, and organized the first two state conferences. Claire was appointed assistant to the president (1974) when Karen DeCrow became NOW's national president. At the first regional conference, Claire developed the NOW policy to include women regardless of their finances. Claire was campaign manager for women running for mayor and sheriff. She was also the first married woman to drop her father's and husband's name legally in New York. While attending Syracuse University, Claire organized Sisters Rising and helped establish the campus women's center and a women's studies class. She also held a "swim-in" to publicize the inequitable funding of the women's athletic department. With professor emerita Marguerite Fisher, Claire brought a class action suit against the university challenging the hiring, promoting of faculty, and fairness in graduate programs. She organized the Syracuse Coalition for the Free Flow of Information in the Broadcast Media with black and Hispanic groups, monitored the local news broadcasts, and challenged the licensing of the ABC affiliate because of its biased treatment of women. With Patsy Scala, Claire produced and hosted "The Time is NOW," a talk show about women, with segments for PBS. Claire testified before the U.S. Senate and House during hearings on FCC regulations. Claire also painted an old school bus purple and pink and stumped across the country in the tradition of the suffragists from the first Women in Politics Conference in Seneca Falls, NY, to the National NOW conference in Los Angeles, speaking to gatherings along the way about underground abortion and the ERA. Claire introduced gender sensitivity training at military bases in central NY. She conferred with Alice Paul and subsequently wrote, with Rose Ann Weinstein, the screenplay "Flying Colors," the story of the final thrust to secure women's right to vote. Claire has two children and holds an undergraduate degree from Syracuse University. Archives: An oral history by Rebecca Drieling is at Arizona State University, Tempe, AZ.   (ABS)

Clapp, Analoyce (1914 – 2004) was one of the 28 women founders of NOW who organized in June 1966 at the Third National Conference of Commissions on the Status of Women in Washington, D.C. She worked for the Office of Minority Business Enterprise, Department of Commerce, in the 1960s. In addition, she wrote feature articles for the *Milwaukee Sentinel*, and in the 1970s was involved in PR work for the University of Wisconsin system and worked in the office of representative Robert Kastenmeier (D-WI) until 1982.

Clapp, James E. (1943 –) In 1968, Clapp quit his job for two years to work full time on women's liberation. He joined NOW and served as a national board member, secretary of the New York City chapter, and co-coordinator (with Cindy Cisler) of the chapter's abortion, contraception, and sex education committee. In one of its early projects, the committee compiled and distributed a list of abortion counseling groups, which helped women to get then-illegal abortions. At the first August 26th march (1970), the committee illegally passed out condoms and contraceptive foam to call attention to the New York law restricting distribution of even nonprescription contraceptives to pharmacies. Clapp was also a founder of New Yorkers for Abortion Law Repeal (NYALR) and served as president for the first two years. Prior to passage of the Cook Bill, which legalized most abortions in New York, both NOW and NYALR polled legislators and led letter-writing campaigns to repeal all special laws on abortion and contraception in the state. Clapp also helped organize a demonstration in Boston when Bill Baird, an early abortion advocate, was arrested for giving contraceptive foam to a woman at a lecture. Clapp holds a B.A. from Grinnell College. In 1974 he entered Columbia Law School, from which he received a J.D. in 1977. He is the author of *Random House Webster's Dictionary of the Law* and other works on law and language. (ABS)

Clarenbach, Kathryn F. (1920 – 1994) was a key figure in the development of second wave feminism in the Midwest. Clarenbach was head of the Wisconsin Commission on the Status of Women. Believing that it would do nothing for women, she put all her effort into forming NOW, and was named temporary chair by Catherine Conroy at the pivotal June 1966 luncheon. At the organizing conference held later in Washington (October 1966), she was elected chair of the board, and Betty Friedan was elected president. In 1970, she began her 15-year chairmanship of the Wisconsin Governor's Commission on the Status of Women, and within months organized an Interstate Association of Commissions. She keynoted the first Women's Conference in 1970 and is credited with getting the WI Legislature to revise laws on sexual assault, divorce and marital property. Clarenbach worked continuously for the movement, and in 1977 was executive director of the National Women's Conference held in Houston. Clarenbach earned her academic degrees in political science from the University of Wisconsin (B.A., 1941; M.A., 1942; Ph.D.; 1946). In 1962, the university chose Clarenbach to establish a program of continuing education for women—a program that launched her leadership in the women's movement in WI and the country. As chair of NOW's national board, Clarenbach is said to have "forged the link between the emergent women's movement and traditional women's organizations." Six weeks before her death from emphysema, she was awarded the VFA's Medal of Honor. Archives: Steenbock Memorial Library, Madison, WI.

Clark, Katrina (1945 –) joined New Haven (CT) Women's Liberation in 1970 and sat on the board of the women's building association until the early 1990s. Clark was one of five women who raised funds from within the

women's community for the building on Orange St. that served as the group's center, and was also involved in renovating the building and staffing the center. The women used the then-innovative approach of creating and renting out apartments on the top floor of the building to finance the needs of the center itself. Since 1973, Clark has been executive director of the Fair Haven Community Health Center. She holds a B.A. from Cornell (1967) and a graduate degree from the Yale University School of Public Health (1971). Clark has two children. (ABS)

Clark, Michele (1945 –) was active in the anti-war movement in the 1960s, and joined the women's movement in 1968. Clark wrote for the Liberation News Service, and was a member of Bread and Roses (Boston) and the Women's Mental Health Collective (1974 – 1989). Clark, who has two children, has an M.Ed. and an M.A. Archives: the Jewish Women's Archive, Brookline, MA. (ABS)

Clarke, Linda Joyce ("Clarkie") (1942 –) From 1970 – 1972, Clarke was a member of the original CR Super-group #1 (the first of 28 CR groups open to all feminists in New York City), and helped establish several other groups in NYC dedicated to lesbian/feminist theorizing. In 1980, she was a co-founder, with Kate Millett and Sophie Keir, of The Farm, a feminist art colony in Poughkeepsie, NY. From 1980 – 1990, she co-ran the farm and was "cook and emptier of ashtrays." Beginning in 1988, Clarke and her partner, Joan Casamo, made an art out of hospitality for their feminist community in the Hudson Valley. In 1993, Clarke wrote a dissertation, *The Bachelor Mind*, a critique of the male philosophical tradition from Plato to Richard Rorty and Charles Taylor. She later worked as an adjunct professor of philosophy. Since 1999 she has written the newsletter "Ravings," dedicated to the earth and her creatures. Casamo and Clarke started a small publishing operation, JL Blue Candle Adventures, in 2005. Their first book, *On a Planet Sailing West* (2006) by Clarke, is based on writings in "Ravings." Clarke earned a B.A. from the University of New Hampshire (1988), an M.Ed. from Bank Street College (1990) and an Ed.D. from Teachers College, Columbia University (1993). (ABS)

Clegg, John Frank (1944 – 1972) attended his first NOW meeting in October 1969 after his wife, Jean Stapleton, attended the September meeting and found that there were men there. Because NOW at that point was meeting in a restaurant once a month and in homes and community spaces the rest of the time, Clegg and his wife volunteered to have a phone installed in their apartment for Los Angeles NOW. Clegg was working on his Ph.D. at the time and was often home during the day, so he would answer the phone—much to the surprise of the callers. Clegg served as corresponding secretary for the chapter, a staff member for "NOW Acts," the national newsletter, and circulation manager for the L.A. chapter newsletter. A member of the speakers bureau, Clegg taught a six-week course in speech for the other members. Elected to NOW's national board in September 1971, Clegg was the only male on that board at the time. With his wife, Jean, Clegg co-chaired a national task force on marriage. He died of Hodgkin's Disease a year after his election to the board. Clegg earned a B.A. from the University of New Mexico, an M.A. from Northwestern University, and a Ph.D. from the University of Southern California.

Clement, Alice R. (1942 –) A researcher, teacher and civil libertarian for women, labor and minorities, Clement helped found the Los Angeles NWPC in 1971, joined NOW in 1970, and taught women's history at several colleges. She was co-founder of the Western Association of Women Historians, and founder of the Historical Institute of Southern California. She also helped found the Women's Center of the University of California, Davis (1969 – 1970), for older women returning to education; participated in every demonstration for the ERA held in Los Angeles; and supported feminist candidates. Awarded Woman of the Year by the California Federation of Teachers in 1988, she spent 30 years in the labor movement on behalf of teachers. Clement, who has two children, holds a B.A. from Trinity College, Washington, D.C.; an M.A. from Duquesne University, Pittsburg, PA; and a Ph.D. from the University of California, Davis. (ABS)

Clemmens, Ginni (1936 – 2003) was one of the founding mothers of the women's music movement. Her round robins at early women's music festivals helped foster the concept of women's music as a participatory event—not simply performers playing for a passive audience. Her album Long Time Friends was in Ladyslipper's first catalog. Clemmens later established her own recording label, Open Door Records, and produced seven albums. She is perhaps best known for her cover of Wild Women Don't Get the Blues, and for a later song, Fat, White Dyke Over Forty. She died in a car accident.

Clendining, Andrea – See Viggiano, Andrea

Clermont, Erin (1943 –) A writer and editor, Clermont was a co-founder of two CR groups in the 1970s. In 1971, she was a member of the committee to free Joan Bird, which raised $100,000 bail for Bird, who was one of the Panther 21. Clermont also collaborated on a feminist soap opera, "Through the Looking Glass." She has been an anti-war activist from Vietnam to Iraq, and supports Amnesty International, animal rights and reproductive rights. She has a B.A. from Syracuse University. (ABS)

Cless, Elizabeth L. (1916 – 1992) Concerned about the ever-growing number of women with good educations who had lost their intellectual edge after trading academia for domesticity, Cless, who was assistant to the dean of the General Extension Division at the University of Minnesota, initiated faculty discussions about possible educational remedies. In 1959 – 1960, New Worlds of Knowledge, an experimental seminar for educated women, was taught by top faculty members from the physical and natural sciences, liberal arts, and the social sciences. The seminar was the successful precursor to the Minnesota Plan for the Continuing Education of Women. That plan, funded by a generous three-year grant from the Carnegie Corporation (and widely copied in the U.S. and abroad), was developed in collaboration with Virginia Senders, a psychologist who had organized the Minnesota Women's Center. The Center provided counseling and vocational services to undergraduate women who found themselves facing new work environments. In 1965, Cless relocated to California and took a position at Claremont Colleges, where she continued her work on behalf of women, including helping to organize one of the first women's studies courses on campus. Cless later helped found the Plato Society at ULCA, a pioneering "learning in retirement" program.

Clohesy, Stephanie June (1948 –) (also known as Stephanie Jagucki) As a student at Alverno College (WI) in 1967, Clohesy discovered the women's movement via student conferences that followed the founding of NOW. From 1972 – 1979 she was a volunteer researcher, writer and reporter for Majority Report, New York City's feminist newspaper. As executive director of the NOW Legal Defense and Education Fund (1977 – 1983), she guided the organization through ERA ratification; fought for an extension period for the ERA; and helped organize NOW LDEF's conference on the future of the family (1979). Clohesy was a board member of NOW LDEF from 1985 – 1990. During that same period, she was a consultant to Argentine women's groups. She was a board member, Women & Philanthropy (1987 – 1993) and of the Woman's Funding Network (1992 – 1999), and was a consultant for STAR to strengthen women's leadership in Bosnia, Croatia, Macedonia, Serbia and Kosovo (1992 – 1998). Clohesy helped to start up and/or strengthen the Nokomis Foundation, the Michigan, New York, Iowa, Cleveland and Central Ohio Foundations for Women, and the Chrysalis Foundation. Active in the peace movement from 1967 forward, she was involved in international peace and civil liberties work in Ireland (1967 – 1975), Argentina (1983 – 1990), Eastern Europe (1992 – 1998), and South Africa (1984 – 2000). Clohesy holds a B.A. from Loyola University, Chicago, and is the author of Smart Growth: A Life Stage Model for Social Change Philanthropy (2002). (ABS)

Clore, Marilee – See Sargent, Mary Lee

Clusen, Ruth Chickering (1922 – 2005) became president of the WI LWV in 1962, and in 1974 was elected national president. In that capacity, Clusen played a lead role in LWV's campaign for ratification of the ERA. Also in 1974, Clusen and the LWV were selected as one of 19 women's organizations asked to meet with President Gerald Ford to discuss issues related to the women's movement. Clusen became nationally known when, during the 1976 presidential campaign, she hosted the LWV-sponsored televised debates between Jimmy Carter and Gerald Ford. In 1975, she served as a member of the U.S. delegation to the U.N. Conference on Women in Mexico City. In 1977, *Ladies' Home Journal* named Clusen Woman of the Year for politics and government. Clusen stepped down as LWV president in 1978. She then served as assistant secretary for the environment for the U.S. Department of Energy until 1981.

Clutz, Signe – See Hammer, Signe

Cobbs Hoffman, Lisa ("Elizabeth") (1956 –) was publications coordinator and a member of the leadership collective of the Center for Women's Studies and Services (San Diego, CA) from 1972 – 1994. She was president of the board (1988 – 1994), and edited all publications, organized publicity, wrote grants and did fundraising. She was managing editor of its newsletter (1972 – 1975); managing editor/founder of *The Longest Revolution: News and Views of Radical Feminism* (1975 – 1983); and editor of *Young Woman's Survival Handbook*, both published by CWSS. From 1980 – 1983, she was an organizer and fundraiser for Project Choice, and from 1979 – 1983 was organizer/editor of the Young Women's Journalism Project, San Diego. Cobbs Hoffman holds a B.A. from the University of California, San Diego, an M.A. and Ph.D. from Stanford University. She has two children. (ABS)

Codish, K.D. ("Kay" or "Kandy") (1945 –) was completing her graduate studies at the University of Paris during the Vietnam War when she launched what became her lifetime commitment to social justice. In 1970 she founded the Theatre of Light and Shadow: A Company of Women (TLS) with friends Ruth Beaumont and Belinda Beezly in New Haven, CT. TLS used its widespread media coverage for over a decade to bring issues such as rape, battering, abortion rights, sexual harassment and later HIV/AIDS to diverse audiences across the country. An avid student of martial arts, Codish (with other TLS members) formed the Women's Self Defense Alliance in the early 1970s. At the same time, she initiated and helped organize the first of many Women's Health Weekends and Take Back the Night Marches in New Haven. As the first director for the Office of Women in Medicine at the Yale School of Medicine, Codish drafted the school's first sexual harassment policies for faculty and convened the school's Permanent Committee on the Status of Women. She was a founding member of the Women's AIDS Coalition as well as director of education and volunteer services at AIDS Project New Haven for many years. Since 1992 through this printing, Codish has headed the New Haven Police Academy as well as the police department's Division of Training and Education. An initial board member of the National Center for Women and Policing, she also advises other police departments throughout the country on recruiting and retaining women and people of color. She is the recipient of numerous awards and honors including NOW's Elizabeth Blackwell Award for ongoing Advocacy for Women and Children; the National Center for Women and Policing Innovations in Police Education. Archives: The Sophia Smith Collection, Smith College, Northampton, MA. (ABS)

Cody, Pat Herbert (1923 –) is the founder of one of the first issue-specific groups that arose out of the women's health movement. Her social activism began in the early 1960s. She and her husband, Fred Cody, were running Cody Books specializing in quality paperbacks in Berkeley, CA, when, in 1961, Cody and other concerned mothers decided to stage a Women's Strike for Peace. They organized visits to local government offices to protest nuclear testing and the country's early involvement in Vietnam. What was to have been a one-day event became Women for Peace, still ongoing in 2006. When the 1964 Free-Speech Sit-ins hit the media, floods of young people came to Berkeley, many of whom needed medical help. A Berkeley Free Clinic was established, with Cody, an economist, as treasurer. In the 1970s, the Berkeley Women's Health Collective was formed. Cody helped gather an older women's support group (1976) that met at the Collective. In 1974, Cody learned the devastating news that her daughter had abnormal, possibly pre-cancerous tissues traced to an anti-miscarriage drug called DES. Cody and a dozen or so health professionals and advocates met at Cody Books and started DES Action, which grew into a national organization over the next decade. Cody continued to run DES Action, which soon became international and still exists (2006). Cody earned a B.A. at Eastern Connecticut State University in 1943 and an M.A. from Columbia University in 1948. (ABS)

Cohen, Harriet (1943 –) After graduation from Queens College in 1964, Cohen went to the Yale Graduate School for City Planning for two years, long before women were accepted as undergraduates at Yale. That landed her in New Haven, CT, where she was involved with the New Left and the American Independent Movement (AIM). She admits to being slow to join the women's movement because, "I didn't think it was for me. I was politically involved and knew how to chair a meeting." But she soon learned that women's liberation did address her needs, and joined New Haven Women's Liberation in 1970. She played the guitar for four years in New Haven Women's Liberation Rock Band. That band played at colleges, women's bars and women's prisons, often playing its own songs. One of its more famous songs was about abortion when abortion was still illegal. (Thirty years later, the group made a recording called Moving Mountains with the Chicago Women's Liberation Rock Band. A CD was released in 2005). In 1978 Cohen was co-chair of

CARASA, and also began her work teaching and coordinating the Women's School of Planning and Architecture. Cohen taught sociology at Quinnipiac College and a course in women's studies. Her career centered around city planning, housing and neighborhood work. In 2002 she became director of programs for the Lantern Group, which builds and operates supportive housing for people with special needs in New York City. She is a single mother with one child. (ABS)

Cohen, Marcia Friedlander (1930 –) Writer, editor and painter, Cohen is perhaps best known as the author of *The Sisterhood: The True Story of Women Who Changed the World* (1988), a history of the women's movement from its birth in the 1960s to the 1980s. She also wrote the first article on unnecessary hysterectomies, published in *Ladies' Home Journal*, and many newspaper articles on the civil rights movement in *The Binghamton* (*NY*) *Sun-Bulletin*, 1960s and human rights issues in the *New York Daily News*. A graduate of Harvard-Radcliffe, Cohen has two children. Archives: Schlesinger Library, Radcliffe Institute, Cambridge, MA. (ABS)

Cohen, Patricia ("Pat") Lee (1943 –) was active in the Women's Strike for Peace (1968). In 1970, she was a founder of the Woodmere Women's Center (Long Island, NY). That same year, she was part of women's CR group in Long Beach, and started the lesbian feminist committee, Nassau County Women's Liberation Center, as well as a lesbian feminist CR group. In 1972, Cohen was part of the Women's Film Co-Op in Northampton, MA, and in 1973 started a lesbian softball team in Long Beach, NY. In 1974, Cohen attended BOCES Automotive Trade School for Auto Mechanics, and worked as an auto mechanic from 1974–1987. She has also worked as a fleet manager (1988–1998), and as an assistant professor at Farmingdale State University. Since 1989, she has been associated with the Michigan Womyn's Music Festival. Cohen, who has one child, holds a B.S. (1990) and an M.B.A. (1994) from Adelphi University. Archives: The Lesbian Herstory Archives, Brooklyn, NY. (ABS)

Cohern, Colleen Wilson (1938 –) A leader in the fight for reproductive freedom, Cohern served as reproductive rights chair for California NOW. She was one of the co-founders of the Feminists Women's Health Center and the self help clinic, the first female group to accompany women for abortion services in Los Angeles County. Cohern traveled around the U.S. teaching women how to do self exams (1969–1972). She was one of the women arrested (1972) at the Center in L.A. for practicing medicine without a license. Cohern had 11 charges and served two years summary probation. She was court-ordered not to work in the Center. She turned her efforts towards CA NOW and was the president of Harbor South Day NOW chapter. She then moved to Northern California and became the founder and president of the Los Gatos/Saratoga

NOW chapter. In CA NOW she was the reproduction chair. Cohern started a campaign button and manufacturing business, with a feminist partner, called the Funky Slogans. It started out with 178 feminist slogans and then went into campaign, cause and gay rights; there are now over 200 feminist slogan buttons in the Smithsonian. The name was changed in 1986 to a Button Factory, which is still in existence. Cohern has two children. (ABS)

Coker, Rosemary Leitz Smithson
– See Smithson, Rosemary Leitz

Cole, Delores Darlene – See Lanai, Delores Darlene

Cole, Johnnetta B. (1936 –) has consistently addressed issues of racial, gender and all other forms of discrimination. Her career as a college and university professor and administrator spans over three decades. Cole made history in 1987 by becoming the first African American woman to serve as president of Spelman College. In May 2004 she became the first African American to serve as chair of the board of United Way of America. Cole is president emerita of Spelman College and professor emerita of Emory University, from which she retired as Presidential Distinguished Professor of anthropology, women's studies and African American studies. Cole began her college studies at Fisk University and completed her undergraduate degree at Oberlin College. She earned a master's degree and a Ph.D. in anthropology from Northwestern University. She is the author of numerous publications for scholarly and general audiences. She co-authored, with Beverly Guy-Sheftall, *Gender Talk: The Struggle for Women's Equality in African American Communities*. She is a fellow of the American Academy of Arts and Sciences and the American Anthropological Association. Cole serves on the board of directors of America's Promise, the National Visionary Leadership Project, and the United Way of Greater Greensboro. She also serves on the board of directors of Merck & Co., Inc., and consultant on diversity matters with Citigroup. She has three sons. (ABS)

Cole, Kay Walker (1939 –) (also known as Kay Cole Petty) Asked to be part of a new electronics company in Texas in 1970, Cole said she would if three conditions were met: that she be allowed to take any job she was qualified for—not simply a secretarial job; that no woman in the company would ever have to kiss her boss to get a raise; and that she be a founder and have a say in how the company was run. The men offering her the position had no problems with items one and three, but were flummoxed by number two. How could it possibly be enforced? Cole said she would enforce it as the one with responsibility for all the women in the company. And she did. During her years at the company, Cole was able to hire and mentor many women, moving them into positions of responsibility that they might otherwise never have achieved. Determined to help women with financial and credit problems, Cole began volunteering at the Women's Southwest Federal Credit Union in 1975. She was elected to the board in 1976, and became president in 1977—and in the process helped save it from extinction three times, she says. Cole, who has two children, is a member of NOW and the VFA. She holds a B.A. from Dallas Baptist University (1980). (ABS)

Coleman, Corrine Grad (1927 – 2004) was a founding member of Redstockings and participated in the first protest of the Miss America pageant in Atlantic City (1968). She was also a leader in the occupation of the editorial offices of the *Ladies' Home Journal* in 1970. Anticipating her own divorce, Coleman wrote guidelines on how to make divorce fair to women, and had an article on divorce published in the *Ladies' Home Journal*. She was a co-founder and editor of *Feelings: A Journal of Women's Liberation*, one of the first literary magazines of the women's movement, and published some of her work there. Her works were also published in *Daring to Be Bad: Radical Feminism in America, 1967–1975*, by Alice Echols (University of Minnesota Press, 1989); *The Brooklyn Phoenix* and the *Village Voice*. A teacher in the NY public school system until she retired, Coleman had four children.

Collins, Laura (1944 –) was a member of NYRF and helped put together its newsletter. She was also a part of the NYC coffee-house women's collective, and worked at Tower Press and Womanbooks. With two other women, she helped to celebrate Susan B. Anthony's birthday by renting a truck with a sound system. One woman gave a speech, doubling on the drum of the Victoria Woodhull Marching Band, and another sang. Collins printed the fliers. Collins also ran in the Gay Games, winning five medals, and has been active in lesbian issues and sports-related events. She is a graduate of Hunter College. (ABS)

Collins, Lorraine Hill (1931 –) used her position on the Belle Fourche, SD, board of education (1969) to further the concerns of women. Her challenges included trying to get the school district to cover pregnancy and childbirth in its insurance plan for employees ("the superintendent of schools said they were not covered because they were 'self-inflicted'") and working to get girls admitted to vocational training programs traditionally reserved for boys. As press secretary in 1974 for a Republican woman feminist trying for a seat in the U.S. Senate, Collins helped articulate various feminist positions, including support for the ERA and the right to choose. In late 1974 Collins was appointed to the South Dakota Commission on the Status of Women. In 1976 she was appointed by the governor to chair the commission, a position she held until 1978, when she moved to Singapore. During her tenure, Collins debated Phyllis Schlafly, who had been brought to the state by anti-ERA forces trying to get the Legislature to rescind ratification. Also during her tenure, the commission developed projects regarding displaced home-

makers, vocational training for girls, sex-role stereo typing and other feminist issues. They developed films and educational materials about women in various nontraditional roles for schools and libraries, and developed a history of women's contributions to the state. In 1977, Collins was co-chair of the planning committee for the state's International Women's Year conference, and was a delegate to the National Women's Conference in Houston. Collins has a B.S. from Cornell College, and three children. (ABS)

Collins, Mary Jean (1939 –) (also known as Mary Jean Collins-Robson) NOW leader, director of the Illinois ERA campaign and deputy director of Catholics for a Free Choice, Collins joined NOW in 1967, was active through 1975, and remains (2005) a member. An officer of the Milwaukee chapter in 1967, she moved to Chicago in 1968 and was elected president of the Chicago chapter. In 1970, Chicago NOW held an employment conference; hosted the national conference of NOW; was involved in activities and pickets related to discrimination in higher education; and sponsored the Women's Strike for Equality, which brought 15,000 people to Daley Plaza in downtown Chicago. Also in 1970, Collins was elected Midwest regional director: In 1972, Chicago NOW entered the fight against AT&T for discriminating against women employees. Again in 1972, the Twin Cities chapter of NOW filed formal charges of sex and race discrimination against General Mills, and urged a boycott of its products. In 1980, Collins was again elected president of the Chicago chapter and helped direct the last days of the ERA campaign. She served for two years, then was elected national action VP in 1982. She served in that capacity until 1985. Collins also served as deputy director of Catholics for a Free Choice from 1985–1993. She is VP and national political director for People for the American Way (2005). Archives: Schlesinger Library, Radcliffe Institute, Cambridge, MA; the University of Illinois, Chicago; and the University of Wisconsin, Madison, WI. (ABS)

Colman, Penny Morgan (1944 –) (also known as Penelope Granger Morgan) A writer and professor, Colman is the author of *Rosie the Riveter: Women Working on the Home Front in WWII* (Crown, 1995). Other books include *Spies! Women in the Civil War* (Betterway Books, 1992); *A Woman Unafraid: The Achievements of Frances Perkins* (Atheneum, 1993); *Girls: A History of Growing Up Female in America* (Scholastic, 2000); and *Where the Action Was: Women War Correspondents in World War II* (Crown, 2002). In 1975, she wrote a one-act play, "Dare to Seek," which focused on Jesus' relationships and interactions with women, and formed an all-woman drama group, The New Image Players, in Oklahoma City, OK. Colman, who has three children, earned her A.B. from the University of Michigan and her M.A.T. from Johns Hopkins University. (ABS)

Colman-Schwimmer, Arlene (1940 –) was an important Los Angeles NOW officer (1969 – 1971), past president (1978 – 1979) of the Women Lawyers' Association of Los Angeles, and a founder/pioneer and life member of California Women Lawyers Association. Dubbed a high-powered women's divorce lawyer, according to *Los Angeles* magazine (February 1988), and later named one of the top lawyers in California, Colman-Schwimmer's clients have included Elizabeth Taylor and Roseanne. After law school, Colman-Schwimmer worked for the U.S. Government Securities and Exchange Commission, then went into private practice in New York. She moved to California in 1968 and finally got a job in general practice. She eventually began her own practice doing sex discrimination work and family law. Eventually her practice became specialized in family law only. She says that being one of seven women in a law school class of 349 "was one of my first feminist activities, but I didn't know it then. The criminal law professor called on the women only to recite on the sex crimes—in order to embarrass us (he claimed it was to harden us). When I asked my criminal law professor how I should get started if I wanted to be a criminal lawyer, he told me to find a husband and have babies. My feminist consciousness and activism began right then." She was an editor of the law review and graduated 7th in the class. Colman-Schwimmer holds a B.A. from Brooklyn College (1961) and a J.D. from Brooklyn Law School (1963). (ABS)

Comer, Constance — was a "restless housewife with a need to change" when she met Jacqui Ceballos, who introduced her to NOW. After joining NY NOW in 1969, Comer began lobbying in Washington, D.C., for the ERA. She sat on the steps of the Capitol in an all-night vigil. Comer was the "priestess" at St. Patrick's Cathedral in the August 26, 1970, Women's Strike for Equality march up Fifth Avenue. She also ran CR groups for NYC NOW. She produced many first day U.S. postage stamp covers commemorating American Black Heritage and sold them city to city. Comer received her B.A. from Sarah Lawrence (1972) and became a New York City high school English teacher. She has three children. (ABS)

Comfort, Connie (1934 –) A peace and civil rights activist in Middletown, CT, in the early 1970s, Comfort was among the women volunteers who, with Alice Williams, started an innovative prenatal and family planning clinic at Middlesex Hospital. During the planning stage, Comfort's leadership and positive approach helped overcome strong opposition from the hospital's ob/gyn doctors. The group then elected Comfort to head the clinic. Opened in 1972, the clinic was an immediate success and became a learning center for women's health-care. It was later taken over by Planned Parenthood, at which time Comfort and the volunteer advocates and teachers were replaced by staff. Comfort and her colleagues then formed the Middlesex County Women's

Health Council, which in the next few years started CR support groups for women experiencing domestic abuse, met with police department representatives to discuss improving responses to domestic abuse, pressured the hospital to offer a less institutional setting for childbirth, and worked with community leaders to promote teaching about contraceptives to teens. By 1975 many of the group's innovative ideas had been adopted and made standard practice. Comfort worked for Wesleyan for many years as the university's principal pre-med adviser, then as general adviser in the Career Counseling Center. Interested in computers, she became the database person for the Connecticut Council for the Humanities. She later took on responsibility for running Wesleyan's Russell House programs, which included prose and poetry reading series and, at the same time, the administration of the Wesleyan Honors Program. Retired (2005), Comfort has started a film series program at the Old Lyme Phoebe Noyes Griffin Library in Connecticut. (ABS)

Conant, Doris S. (1925 –) was a member of the board of directors, Loop Center YWCA, a feminist center in Chicago. She also served on the board of directors of ERA Illinois, and was state chair in 1975. "I tried for two years to form a women's bank in Chicago (1st Women's Bank of Chicago), but it never got off the ground." Conant was a member of the Chicago Foundation for Women, an umbrella organization contributing to a wide range of women's causes. She also helped start and run North Shore Open Housing (1964 – 1967); was a member of various peace movements in the late 1960s; and participated in the Selma to Montgomery march in 1964. Conant, who has a B.A. from the University of Pennsylvania, has three children. (ABS)

Conant, Therese (1926 –) "I was always a feminist but didn't know it," says Conant. "My life previous to being the founder of NOW New Mexico (1968) was uneventful." In 1966, Conant saw an article in *Barrons* about Betty Friedan that "fired me up." Conant didn't want to be the first president of NM NOW, which began with about 30 members coming from women's organizations, so started out as VP. After two years, she agreed to be president and served two terms. Years later, when other chapters came into being, NM NOW became Albuquerque NOW. Under Conant's leadership, NM NOW worked on the naming of hurricanes, which at the time were given only women's names; successfully integrated the want ads at the *Albuquerque Journal* and the *Albuquerque Tribune*; and demonstrated and picketed on Mother's Day for childcare facilities everywhere. "We also demonstrated outside a store whose manager was seducing women and got that man fired, and we did a bit of rabble-rousing at the New Mexico State Legislature around abortion," she adds. Born in Arlington, MA, Conant describes herself as a radical feminist. While she studied sociology at the University of New Mexico after being inspired by the article on Friedan, she made a living as a "professional waiter" and secretary, she says. (ABS)

Conger, Jean Tastrom (1941 –) (also known as Jean Keating) As state president of Delaware NOW in 1972, Conger filed an EEOC class action complaint against every school district in the state, charging sex discrimination in employment from the custodial level up. As a result, back pay was awarded to women, with parity in pay for positions, and a statewide committee was formed that examined textbooks, curriculum and materials for race and sex discrimination; its recommendations were adopted into policy. From 1975 – 1977, Conger was a member of the Delaware State Committee of the U.S Commission on Civil Rights, organizing women inmates at WCI Greenbank to testify about discriminatory conditions in prison. Following the hearings, the women's prison at Greenbank, which had denied women access to healthcare and job training, was closed, and the women were sent to a modern facility with better services. Elected NOW co-director (with Rosemary Belmont Dempsey) of the Eastern Region at the NOW Wonder Woman Regional Conference in Atlantic City, Conger helped organize the first Mother's Day March on the Vatican Embassy in Washington, D.C. Elected national secretary at the 1975 Philadelphia National Conference, she served as credentials committee chair at the NOW Constitutional Convention in Kansas City, and the national conference in Detroit in 1977. From 1977 – 1979, Conger was a member of the NOW political action committee and, along with Ellie Smeal and Eve Norman, drafted the PAC policy and procedures manual. From 1979 – 1982, she was executive assistant to Ellie Smeal, working for passage of the ERA. Conger also worked as volunteer coordinator of the Ginny Foat Defense Fund, helping to raise more than $100,000 for the defense of a NOW leader accused of murder. (Foat was acquitted in two hours.) Active in lesbian and gay rights, Conger was the first executive director of Southern California Women for Understanding (1982 – 1989). From 1992 – 1996, she was executive director of the Los Angeles Women's Foundation, launched a Women's Health Initiative in Los Angeles, and in 1994 co-wrote "How Are Women Doing in LA?," an analysis of women's economic status (1994). Conger moved to Hawaii in 1996, where she works with the Women's Fund of the Hawaii Community Foundation. Conger, who has a B.A. from SUNY Stony Brook and a M.Ed. from the University of Delaware, has three children. Archives: Schlesinger Library, Radcliffe Institute, Cambridge, MA. (ABS)

Conlin, Roxanne Barton (1944 –) Conlin graduated from law school in 1966 and gave her first speech on women's legal rights to a church group in 1968. "I was condemned!" It hardly stopped her. Conlin managed the campaign of Willie Glanton, who became the first African American Iowa State Representative. In 1969, Conlin became the first part-time assistant attorney general for IA, a position from which she had to resign in 1976 because of her "activist advocacy" for women's reproductive freedom. Conlin attended the first convention of NWPC in Houston, advising on its bylaws. In 1972 she was appointed to the first Iowa Commission on the Status of Women, and supported Shirley Chisholm for President, chairing the IA effort. Conlin says she "used parliamentary procedure to bring the Iowa Democratic Convention to a halt, with eventual passage of a platform including ERA and reproductive freedom." Delegates committed to Chisholm were elected to the 1972 National Democratic Convention from IA. Also in 1972, Conlin tried the first sex discrimination case in IA (Huebner v. American Republic Insurance Company). In 1975, she ran for president of the NWPC. From 1976 – 1977, she was a consultant to the U.S. Department of State on International Women's Year, editing and writing booklets on homemakers' rights for all 50 states and the District of Columbia. She was appointed U.S. attorney for the Southern District of IA by President Carter in 1977 and confirmed by the Senate, the second woman in history to hold that position. Conlin founded the Advocacy Institute within the Department of Justice to train government lawyers on trial skills; served as president of the Federal Executive Board, the consortium of 71 federal agencies; and served on the U.S. Attorneys Advisory Committee. In 1981, she resigned to seek the Democratic nomination for governor of IA. In 1982, she won a three-way primary, "but narrowly lost the election for governor." From 1986 – 1988, she chaired the NOW LDEF, and in 1988 became the first woman officer of the Association of Trial Lawyers of America; she wrote and secured passage of a resolution requiring women and minorities in programs and on all committees. She also created a minority caucus with representation on the board of governors and added women's caucus members to it. In 1992 – 1993, she was elected the first woman president of the Association of Trial Lawyers of America, an organization of consumer attorneys. From 1994 – 1997, she was the first woman to chair the Roscoe Pound Institute, established in 1956 by trial lawyers to honor and build upon the work of Roscoe Pound, former dean of the Harvard Law School. In addition to her law degree, Conlin earned an M.B.A. in 1978. She has four children. Archives: University of Iowa, Iowa City, IA. (ABS)

Connell, Noreen (1947 –) was president of the New York City chapter of NOW from 1977 – 1979. With Barbara Rochman, she initiated a job development program that resulted in the creation of 40 Longshore jobs for women. Connell also made lesbian rights a standing committee of NYC NOW. She served as chair of the NYC board for five terms; held several VP positions; and was chair of the employment and childcare committees. From 1984 – 1988 she served as president of NYS NOW. During that time, Connell formed delegations of feminists who traveled to Iceland, Spain, England and Norway to learn how other feminist movements functioned. In 1987 she ran unsuccessfully for president of NOW against Molly Yard. Connell entered the women's movement in 1970, joining NYRF. She also edited a book with Cassandra Wilson on NYRF's 1971 conference and speakout on rape, *Rape: The First Sourcebook for Women* (1974). Also in 1974, Connell co-founded Women Office Workers with Annie Chamberlin and Susanne Paul. She remained on the staff until 1977. Connell was also active in childcare issues. She is the author of "The Politics of Child Care" and "What is Good Child Care," published in the 1978 *Women's Yellow Pages,* and wrote an article for *The Nation* responding "to neo-conservative attacks on the women's movement for not being concerned with childcare and children." Connell was a delegate to the 1977 National Women's Conference and the 1980 White House Conference on Families, and worked on expanding federal funding for childcare centers. As a result of her fight to improve women's employment rights, Connell received the 1984 Coalition of Labor Union Women-NYC Chapter Award. Born in Mexico City, Connell attended Beloit College (1965 – 1969) and then the Graduate Division of the New School for Social Research, where she earned an M.A., and New York University, where she earned an M.A. Archives: Tainement Library, Bobst Library, New York University, New York, NY. (ABS)

Connelly, Jane Marie – See Field, Jane

Conroy, Catherine (1919 – 1989) worked for over four decades in the women's movement and the labor movement. One of the women who met in Betty Friedan's hotel room during the June 1966 Conference on the State Commissions on the Status of Women to discuss the formation of NOW, Conroy was also present the next day at lunch when the initial organizing of NOW began. In addition, she co-founded the Chicago chapter of NOW in 1968 and served as its first president. In the 1970s, she was appointed to President Carter's women's advisory committee. Her first feminist activism began early in her life when she worked for Wisconsin Bell and experienced unfair treatment. In response, she became involved with the Communications Workers of America, helping to organize strikes and negotiate contracts. She was subsequently elected president of Local 5500, a post she held until 1960 when she joined the CWA national staff. In both positions, she fought for women's pay equity, improved working conditions and career advancement for women. In the 1960s, she served as labor representative for the Wisconsin Governor's Commission on the Status of Women. In 1974, Conroy set up the Milwaukee chapter of CLUW, and became the first woman elected to the executive board of the WI AFL-CIO. In 2004, Conroy was honored posthumously by VFA.

Cook, Alice Hanson (1903 – 1998) A social worker, labor organizer and educator, foreign service member and professor, Cook was one of the first scholars to study the plight of working women. As industrial secretary at the YWCA in Chicago (1927 – 1929) and then Philadelphia (1931 – 1937), Cook saw how women struggled to balance work and home. Feeling that education was essential to women's progress, Cook created and taught special summer schools for women workers at Bryn Mawr, PA, and in several locations in the South. She continued her efforts on behalf of women as education director of the Textiles Workers Organizing Committee (1937 – 1939) and as assistant to the manager of the Amalgamated Clothing Workers of America (1940 – 1943). She also worked in Germany (1950 – 1952) as chief of the adult education section of the U.S. Office of Cultural Affairs in Frankfort-am-Main. There, she studied how Germans implement adult and labor education. Cook began her academic career as a researcher at Cornell University in 1952. In 1969, she became Cornell's first ombudsman, a position she held until 1971. She was also a catalyst in opening a Cornell University faculty club to women. Cook's research focused on equal pay and comparable worth, as well as maternity leave and other public policies that could support working women. In 1972, she drew up a Maternal Bill of Rights that would compensate women for loss of employment opportunities and advancement during the years they cared for their children. Also in 1972, Cook was a founding member of the group that later became the advisory committee on the status of women at Cornell University. She was a lifetime member of the committee, which annually presents the Cook Awards to persons who have helped advance the status of women on campus. After her retirement in 1972, Cook was named emeritus professor; she spent the next 26 years until her death writing about and studying the needs of the working woman. She completed her autobiography, *A Lifetime in Labor* (the Feminist Press), shortly before her death. Cook, who had two children, was the recipient of many awards, including the Governor's Empire State Woman of the Year Award (1984). She was also the subject of the documentary "Never Done: The Working Life of Alice Cook" (1993). Cook earned a B.A. from Northwestern University in 1924.

Cook, Barbara Ann (1940 –) joined the AAUW in Olympia, WA, in 1968, and worked for passage of Referendum 20, which would grant abortion rights and mandate abortion services in the state. (Referendum 20 was voted into law in November 1970, and WA remains, in 2004, the only state to have approved abortion rights by public vote.) Cook subsequently became founding chair of the Family Planning Association, and opened the first Thurston-Mason Family Planning Clinic in 1971, of which she was board chair. She also worked with the AAUW to gain passage of the ERA. In 1973, Cook began working for the State Department of Social & Health Services in the family planning program. In 1977, she moved to the State Human Rights Commission, investigating complaints of discrimination. At that time, sexual harassment complaints were considered "personality conflicts," not violations of law. But when the EEOC defined sexual harassment as sex discrimination in 1981, Cook developed a sexual harassment education and prevention program and became an agency spokesperson/trainer on that issue. For the next 15 years, Cook presented sexual harassment training programs to employers, employees and high-school students. Her *Sexual Harassment Prevention Guide* and *Fair Employment Practices Guide* remains in use by Washington State HRC. Cook, who has two children, earned her B.S. from Bowling Green State University. (ABS)

Cook, Blanche Wiesen (1941 –) Activist, historian, journalist and author of *Eleanor Roosevelt*, vols. I and II, Cook became aware of gender issues as a high-school debater and athlete during the 1950s. She and her Flushing (NY) teammates protested the rules by which girls were forced to play basketball, achieved the support of their coaches, and continued to fight for sports equity. At the same time, Cook was part of a Central Park women's softball team (with Elaine Rosenberg, Blue [Doris] Lunden and a group of 1950s bar lesbians dedicated to sports) that later fought for what became Title IX. One of very few women fellows at Johns Hopkins University, Cook became vividly aware of discrimination against women, and began fighting against discrimination of all kinds. At her first teaching position at Hampton Institute (1963), historically a black college, Cook and her colleagues protested various outrages including Virginia's voting restrictions. In 1964, Cook was a founder of The Conference on Peace Research in History, now the Peace History Society, and joined WILPF. Teaching at Stern College for Women, Yeshiva University (1964 – 1967), Cook met Linda Kerber, who brought her into the Berkshire Conference of Women Historians. This group then organized CCWHP (1969), with Cook serving as co-chair with Alice Kessler-Harris in 1972. At the same time, Cook was active in the anti-war movement through WILPF and other organizations. In 1969 Cook became senior editor of the *Garland Library on War and Peace* and reprinted 360 volumes of classics by women and men emphasizing anti-imperialist and peace movements. A radio broadcaster at WBAI Radio Pacifica and syndicated journalist, Cook was one of 10 columnists featured by One Woman's Voice, created by the Anderson-Moberg Syndicate in the early 1970s. During that time, Cook was also active in Marxist-feminist CR groups in NY, lesbian organizations, and peace and justice committees. She is on the board of the Feminist Press. In addition to her books on Eleanor Roosevelt, Cook has published scores of articles, including "Female Support Networks and Political Activism" (*Chrysalis*, 1977) and "Women Alone Stir My Imagination" (*Signs*, 1979). Archives: The Sophia Smith Collection, Smith College, Northampton, MA. (ABS)

Cook, Joan R. (1922 – 1995) was a reporter in the "Metropolitan News" section of *The New York Times*

when, in 1974, she helped organize a sex-discrimination lawsuit against the newspaper. She was one of seven named plaintiffs. The class-action suit, which was settled in 1978, resulted in cash payments for the women and an affirmative-action plan. In 1980, Cook became the second woman to be elected head of the New York Newspaper Guild's *Times* unit.

Cookston, Patricia – See Davidson, Patricia

Coolman, Karen – See Amlong, Karen Coolman

Cooper, Eleanor (1940 –) A leading, frontline advocate for women's and lesbian rights in New York City in the 1970s and 1980s, Cooper founded Lesbian Feminist Liberation in 1971 with a group of women who had split from the male-dominated Gay Activists Alliance. She became an officer of the Women's Center on West 20th Street, which was the home of LFL. Throughout the 1970s Cooper kept the center running and heated, literally shoveling coal for its furnace. In 1977, as a leader of LFL, Cooper formed the Coalition for Lesbian and Gay Rights with GAA, ultimately bringing together 50 gay and lesbian rights groups. She was elected a spokesperson for the group. Cooper was executive director of the Coalition in 1986 when its long battle for a NYC lesbian and gay rights bill ended in victory with the passage of Intro 2 by the New York City Council, which was signed into law by Mayor Ed Koch. In 1987, Cooper represented CLGR in Albany in the fight for hate crimes legislation and a state lesbian and gay rights bill. Hate crimes legislation took another decade to pass. Cooper graduated from the Harriet Sophie Newcomb Memorial College for Women, Tulane University in 1962. (ABS)

Cooper, Janet Rose (1948 –) began fighting for working women as an undergraduate at Mary Washington College. By 1968, rules at the college had been changed to allow women to wear pants—but not women working to pay for their educations by waitressing in the campus dining hall. Cooper and some other women "presented a united front when the dean came to see us," she says, "and we carried the day." After graduating from Howard University School of Law (1973), Cooper interviewed with a labor union but was told by the general counsel that they had never hired a female lawyer. "I answered that maybe it was time," Cooper says, "and he hired me." Working within the union, Cooper was able to help other women move into positions of greater influence. She became the general counsel, and had women in charge of lobbying, PR and publications. Cooper started her own law firm, continuing in employment law and discrimination work. She began serving as president of Federally Employed Women-Legal and Education Fund in 1985. (ABS)

Cooper, Patricia Ann (1949 –) In 1969, Cooper was a founder, with Lucy Wicks, Molly Garrett and others, of the Wittenberg chapter of Women's Liberation. The group offered CR and distributed the very first editions of the *Birth Control Handbook* on the Wittenberg College campus. In 1971, Cooper moved to Cleveland and became involved with Cleveland Women's Liberation. She was a co-founder of Cleveland Women's Counseling, which offered abortion counseling. Because abortion was illegal in Ohio at the time, the group made arrangements for women to travel to NYC. Cooper moved to Washington, D.C., and joined the D.C. Area Feminist Alliance, where she created teaching projects on the history of women workers and women unionists. She earned her Ph.D. in U.S. Women's History at the University of Maryland. In the mid 1980s, Cooper co-founded, with Ellen Rose, the women's studies program at Drexel University in Philadelphia. She later became director of women's studies at the University of Kentucky (1994 and 1998). Cooper was also active in the anti-Vietnam War movement and has been a voice against the war in Iraq. Archives: Wittenberg College Archives, Springfield, OH. (ABS)

Cooper, Sandi E. (1936 –) A professor of history, Cooper was national chair (1971 – 1973) of the Coordinating Committee on Women in the Historical Profession, the first caucus in the national historical academic community. She was also co-chair of the Metropolitan NY chapter of CCWHP (1970 – 1971), and program chair of the Berkshire Conference of Women Historians' conference on women's history, which she helped launch in 1970. Cooper chaired the Berkshire Conference from 1978 – 1980, and served on its executive committee and program committee for 20 years. She was also an original trustee of the NYC Commission on Women. She has two children. Archives: Schlesinger Library, Radcliffe Institute, Cambridge, MA; and the Peace Collection at Swarthmore College. (ABS)

Cooperperson, Ellen Donna (1946 –) (also known as Ellen Donna Cooperman) joined NOW in 1972 and created "Women NOW," a film documentary "about real women and their struggles" that was distributed nationwide. In 1978, she changed her name to Cooperperson after a two-year court battle that reached the NY State Supreme Court. "The court had previously denied my petition in a 15-page decision, saying men have a right to identity—inferring that one of those rights was to name women." Her film, "Yes, Baby, She's My Sir," addresses women and language. In 1978, Cooperperson founded the Women's Educational and Counseling Center at SUNY Farmingdale, which, she says, "for the next 10 years was a mecca for women—17,000 of them used the center to find help with issues from re-entering the job market, to math anxiety." Cooperperson, who has one child, holds an M.A. from Goddard-Vermont College, and a Master Practitioner from the NLP Institute. (ABS)

Cordova, Jeanne R. (1948 –) was president of the Los Angeles Daughters of Bilitis (1970 – 1971). In that capac-

ity, she opened the first lesbian center in Los Angeles and edited the DOB newsletter, which evolved into *The Lesbian Tide*. She was publisher of *LT* until 1980. Cordova was a core organizer of the West Coast Lesbian Conference held at UCLA (1973); was a delegate to the National Women's Conference in Houston (1977), where she helped pass a lesbian affirmative resolution; and was an organizer of the National Lesbian Feminist Organization Conference held in L.A. (1978). She was president of the Stonewall Democratic Club (1979 – 1981), and in 1980 became California state chair of the Destination New York drive, which elected 33 California lesbians and gays as Democratic Party delegates. During these years, she helped grow the National Gay and Lesbian Democratic Caucus and served as a Kennedy delegate to the 1980 National Democratic Convention in New York. She was a founder of the Los Angeles chapter of the Gay and Lesbian Press Association (1983) and a founding board member of Connexus Women's Center/Centro de Mujeres, a Los Angeles lesbian center. Cordova was also media director for STOP 64, a campaign that defeated the AIDS quarantine measure proposed by Lyndon La Rouche (1986). She published the first gay and lesbian telephone book, *The Community Yellow Pages* (1982 – 1999), and founded and published *The Square Peg* (1992 – 1994). A former nun, she is the author of *Kicking the Habit: A Lesbian Nun Story* (1995) and *Sexism: It's a Nasty Affair* (1976), a collection of feminist essays. Cordova has a B.A. (1970) and an M.S.W. (1972) from UCLA, Los Angeles. Archives: June Mazer Collection, Los Angeles, CA. (ABS)

Corea, Gena (1946 –) Figuring out the implications for women of the new reproductive technologies and then organizing resistance to their proliferation are Corea's most significant contributions to the women's movement. While a reporter at *The Holyoke Transcript* (1971 – 1973) in Holyoke, MA, Corea initiated a new section of the paper featuring investigative reporting on women's status in the city. After leaving the newspaper and while working on *The Hidden Malpractice: How American Medicine Mistreats Women* (William Morrow, 1977), Corea wrote and published 75 "Frankly Feminist" columns for *The New Republic Feature Syndicate*. She is also the author of *The Mother Machine: Reproductive Technologies from Artificial Insemination to the Artificial Womb* (Harper and Row, 1985), and *The Invisible Epidemic: The Story of Women and AIDS* (HarperCollins, 1992). With four other feminists (Renate Duelli-Klein, Janice G. Raymond, Jalna Hanmer and Robyn Rolland), she founded the Feminist International Network of Resistance to Reproductive and Genetic Engineering, and together they organized the Women's Emergency Conference on the New Reproductive Technologies, held in Vallinge, Sweden, in 1985. Corea addressed many of the first feminist conferences held in other nations on the dangers of the new reproductive technologies. She was also a co-founder, with Janice

Raymond, of the National Coalition Against Surrogacy. The two held a number of press conferences and testified at many hearings in opposition to the legalized sale of women's bodies for reproductive purposes. Corea earned a B.A. from the University of Massachusetts (1971). Archives: The Sophia Smith Collection, Smith College, Northampton, MA. (ABS)

Corfman, Philip — A graduate of Oberlin College and Harvard Medical School, Corfman was in charge of contraceptive research at the National Institutes of Health when feminism's second wave began to gather momentum. In 1970, he was called to testify at Senate hearings about the birth control pill. When activists disrupted the hearings, pointing out that no women had been invited to testify and questioning why women's concerns about the pill's effects were not being considered, Corfman told the senators that the women were asking important questions. From then on, he was a behind-the-scenes supporter of attempts by the women's health movement to influence federal policy. He shared information, gave advice when asked, and ensured that activists had a place at the table—or at least at the microphone. Corfman went on to work on contraceptive development and approval at the World Health Organization. In 1987, he moved to the FDA to be in charge of the medical review of drugs for contraception, fertility, obstetrics and gynecology. His group was involved in a variety of challenging issues, such as approval of Norplant and Depo-Provera, revisions of oral contraceptives' labeling to facilitate their use by older women and to remove the requirement that a physical exam must be done before a woman could start oral contraceptives, and efforts to make mifepristone, emergency contraception, and once-a-month injectables available to American women. Corfman has served as a consultant or committee member for several organizations, including the International Medical Advisory Panel of the International Planned Parenthood Federation, the American College of Obstetricians and Gynecologists, and the Public Health Service Commissioned Corps, in which he was an officer. He was named by *Ms.* magazine as one of "40 Male Heroes: Men Who've Taken Chances and Made a Difference" (1982), and was one of 30 activists honored for NWHN's 30th anniversary (2005). He has published more than 30 scientific articles. (ABS)

Corinne, Tee A. (1943 – 2006) An artist and writer of erotic fiction, poetry and reviews, Corinne was a co-founder and past co-chair of the Gay and Lesbian Caucus, and a co-founder of the Lesbian and Bisexual Caucus of the Women's Caucus for Art. In 1991, the *Lambda Book Report* named her one of the 50 most influential lesbians and gay men of the decade, and in 1997 she received the Women's Caucus for Art President's Award for her service to women in the arts. In addition, she was a co-facilitator of the *Feminist Photography Ovulars* (1979 – 1981) and a co-founder of *The Blatant Image, A Magazine of Feminist*

Photography (1981 – 1983). Her books include the *Cunt Coloring Book*, first published in 1975 and then reissued as *Labiaflowers* in 1981. Books of her art include *The Southern Oregon Women Writers' Group Picture Book* (1982); *Yantras of Womanlove* (1982), the first book of lesbian erotic photographs ever published; *Women Who Loved Women* (1984); and *Lesbian Muse: The Women Behind The Words* (1989). Her fiction books include *Courting Pleasure, The Sparkling Lavender Dust of Lust, Lovers* and *Dreams of the Woman Who Loved Sex*. She served as editor of *The Body of Love* and *The Poetry of Sex: Lesbians Write the Erotic* (a Lambda Award finalist), and edited and supplied photographs for *Riding Desire* and *Intricate Passions* (winner of a Lambda Literary Award). Her poetry books include *Mama, Rattlesnakes, Key Lime Pie* and *Does Poetry Make a Difference?* She wrote about art for numerous publications, and in 1987 became art books columnist for *Feminist Bookstore News*. She was art book columnist for *Women's Caucus for Art Update* and the "Arts Council of Southern Oregon News-letter." Corinne earned her B.A. from the University of South Florida (1965) and her M.F.A. from the Pratt Institute (1968). Archives: Special Collections, University of Oregon, Eugene, OR. (ABS before death)

Corkery, Arlene - See Raven, Arlene

Cormack, Judith Lightfoot (1937 – 2006) (also known as Judith Lightfoot) became a member of the Atlanta (GA) chapter of NOW in 1969. She was director of the Southern Region (1971 – 1973); chair of the NOW national board (1973 – 1975); and a member of the NOW LDEF board (1973 – 1975). She participated in marches, rallies and campaigns, including Sears, AT&T and the Salvation Army. Cormack also served as NOW liaison to the SCLC (1974 – 1975), and was part of the Democratic Party reform movement in New York City in the 1960s. Asked to summarize her contribution to the women's movement, she said, "Building strong functional organizations addressing relevant issues was essential to successful mainstream feminism." Archives: Schlesinger Library, Radcliffe Institute, Cambridge, MA. (ABS before death)

Cornell, Harriet (1933 –) gave voice to the aspirations and concerns of women and created innovative public policy in her roles as the first woman to chair the Rockland County (NY) Legislature and the only woman to date (2006) to chair the Rockland County Democratic committee. Cornell became politically active in Ann Arbor, MI (1955 – 1958), and then in Rockland County, where she and her husband, Martin, settled. By 1966 she was chair of the women's division of the Rockland County Democratic committee. She was elected Democratic Party chair in 1972 and re-elected in 1974 and 1976. Cornell is VP of the Eleanor Roosevelt legacy committee, a statewide organization dedicated to supporting pro-choice Democratic women who run for local or state offices, and policy chair of the NY State Democratic committee. In Cornell's first year as an elected legislator, she realized that little attention was being paid to the needs of women and families. She sponsored a resolution establishing the Rockland County Commission on Women's Issues, which has enabled thousands of women to have a voice in formulating public policy on domestic violence, access to healthcare, quality, affordable childcare, housing, pay equity, care for the aging and more. Cornell was elected chair of the Rockland County Legislature in 2005, and re-elected in 2006. In 1989, on the heels of the U.S. Supreme Court Webster decision, Cornell formed the Rockland County Pro-Choice Coordinating Council to create awareness of and solidarity in protection of women's reproductive freedom. In 1998 she received the first-ever *Good Housekeeping*/Ford Foundation Award for Women in Government "for her extraordinary efforts, which demonstrate how government can directly improve women's lives." (ABS)

Cornet, Nancy – See Jaffe, Nancy Linda

Cornillon, Susan Huddis Koppelman
– See Koppelman, Susan Huddis

Corso, Mary Elizabeth ("Betti") (1932 –) A founding member of Danbury, CT, NOW (1969), Corso served as the chapter's first treasurer and later as a two-term president. Among other issues, the chapter worked for state ratification of the national ERA and for passage of a state ERA. They picketed for the ERA at the Jefferson-Jackson Day dinner of the Democratic Party and protested a wet T-shirt contest in their area. The women also worked to implement Title IX, getting the local schools to offer shop and home economics equally to girls and boys. In 1975, with other women, Corso helped found the Women's Center of Greater Danbury. Corso served as board secretary, published the center's newsletter, and later became a two-term president. With nine children to care for while attending college and working part-time, Corso remained active in feminist causes. As of 2005, she has returned to the Women's Center board. Corso holds a B.A. from Western Connecticut State University. (ABS)

Corwell-Shertzer, Marion (1931 –) A role model and activist for women in business and education, Corwell-Shertzer was the first management level woman on Ford Motor Company's public affairs staff (1966) and became the first woman manager in every department as she rose through the ranks at Ford. As personnel planning manager, Corwell-Shertzer created and implemented non-gender-specific titles ("production supervisor" instead of "foreman," for example) that are now industry standard. A member of the Michigan Women's Commission for eight years, Corwell-Shertzer created and chaired speak-out forums that gave women the opportunity to discuss and alleviate problems of abuse, employment and child-

care. As a member of the employment committee, she worked to eliminate workplace discrimination throughout Michigan. And as the only woman member of the Andrews University Board of Trustees (1968 – 1976), she helped bring about equal-pay-for-equal-work policies for women at the university. From 1969 – 1970, Corwell-Shertzer served as president of American Women in Radio and Television, where she advocated equal employment opportunities in the broadcast industry. From 1982 – 1984, she was a member of the Defence Advisory Committee on Women in the Services. In 1997, she was inducted into the Michigan Women's Hall of Fame. (ABS)

Coss, Clare Millicent (1935 –) is a psychotherapist, playwright and activist who grew up in New Jersey and New Orleans. Her feminist awakening came at the age of 10 when she played Jo in "Little Women." At Friends Academy, Locust Valley, L.I., her love for the theater continued to blossom. At Louisiana State University, Coss joined a sorority, but ultimately found the Bohemian world on campus more challenging. She graduated from New York University with a master's in theater. Coss's activism began in the early 1960s when she joined WILPF. In the mid 1960s Coss, with Maryat Lee, used sociodrama to create plays at the Soul and Latin Theatre out of young people's experiences. Coss founded a drop-in theater for disaffected, radical youth in Calgary, Alberta, where she lived for a year. Her first play, "Madame USA," had a staged reading at the American Place Theatre in 1969. Coss's plays include "Titty Titty Bang Bang," published in *Aphra*, Fall 1971, and produced by the Women's Theatre Troupe, Vancouver, 1974; and "The Star-Strangled Banner," produced at the Berkshire Theatre Festival Barn, Stockbridge, MA, 1971. She is co-author of a musical, "The Well of Living Waters," a feminist interpretation of women in the New Testament. In 1974, Coss became co-artistic director, with Sondra Segal and Roberta Sklar, of The Women's Experimental Theatre Company. WET's trilogy of plays, "The Daughters Cycle:" "Daughter," "Sister/Sister," "Electra Speaks," were performed at the Women's Interart Center. Coss's other plays include "Growing Up Gothic"; "The Blessing"; "Lillian Wald, At Home on Henry Street"; "Our Place in Time"; and "Emmett, Down in My Heart." In 1996 she edited *The Arc of Love, An Anthology of Lesbian Love Poems* (Scribner), which was a Lambda Literary Award finalist in 1997. She served on the board of Thanks Be to Grandmother Winifred, which gave grants to women 54 years old or older that would benefit women. Coss, who holds an M.S.W. and C.S.W. from SUNY Stony Brook, has been a psychotherapist in NYC since 1976. Archives: The Sophia Smith Collection, Smith College, Northampton, MA. (ABS)

Costanza, Mary E. (1937 –) In 1970, while doing her medical oncology fellowship at Tufts-New England Medical Center, Costanza began volunteering at the Somerville Women's Health Clinic, where she remained until the early 1980s. She also attended numerous feminist meetings in New York City with Ellen Frankfort and others, and wrote the introduction to Frankfort's book, *Vaginal Politics*. Costanza was also involved with the Boston Women's Health Book Collective, and helped them with the breast cancer sections of the new editions of their book. From 1980 – 1990, Costanza was director, division of oncology, at the University of Massachusetts and the University of Massachusetts Hospital. From 1990 – 2003, she was director of the High Risk Breast Cancer Clinic. Since 1993, Costanza has been chair of the gender equity committee at the University of Massachusetts Medical School. Costanza earned her A.B. from Radcliffe College (1958), her M.A. from the University of California, Berkeley (1963), and her M.D. from the University of Rochester School of Medicine (1968). (ABS)

Cotera, Martha (1938 –) Activist, writer, librarian, Cotera and her husband Juan were active in many labor and civil rights movement groups in the 1960s. In 1969, she participated in the Crystal City school walkouts and was a founding member of the new Raza Unida Party. With other women she struggled for the inclusion and visibility of women in the RUP through Mujeres Pro-Raza Unida Caucus, which they founded in 1973. In 1971 Cotera was a founder of the Texas Women's Political Caucus and of the National Women's Political Caucus. She and other Chica-nas have been active in these organizations on and off depending on resolutions of race and class issues. In 1974 she also founded the Chicana Research and Learning Center (Austin), and the Mexican American Business and Professional Women Association. Cotera worked as a librarian in several cities and has served as archives acquisi- tions librarian at the Benson Latin American Collection (University of Texas-Austin) for 30 years. She wrote essays on the differences between Chicana and Anglo feminists that were published as *The Chicana Feminist* (1977). Her groundbreaking work *Diosa y Hembra: History and Heritage of the Chicana in the United States* (1976) offered the first detailed record of Latina women's activism and achievements in the United States. (ABS)

Council, Carol Diane (1948 –) (also known as Carol Rowell) was a member of the ad hoc committee for women's studies at San Diego State University (1969 – 1970). As founder and coordinator, she lobbied the administration, faculty committees and student groups for formal approval (1969 – 1971). Ultimately, all that stood in the way of the first women's studies program in the United States was space for an office. Determined not to be undone by a logistical problem, Council found a small house on the campus that had a boarded-up, dirty and dusty kitchen, but there was no room for a desk. She spied a slender wall cabinet, opened it, pulled down an ironing board, and set her briefcase on it. Final approval of the women's studies program came in 1972, and the press release announcing it was written on that ironing board. Council was coordinator of the program (1971 – 1972), and coordinator of the Center for Women's Studies and Services at San Diego (1971 – 1992). Council organized many actions locally on behalf of women's equality, abortion rights and childcare. She was a contributor to *Sunrise, A Journal of Change* (1970); an editor/reporter for the *CWSS Bulletin* (1970 – 1976) and *The Longest Revolution* newspaper (1976 – 1984); and the author of *Feminism in a New Key: A Key to Organizing* (CWSS, 1972). Also in 1972, she wrote the introduction to *Rainbow Snake: SD Women Poets*. Council holds a B.S. and an M.F.A. Archives: San Diego State University, San Diega, CA. (ABS)

Courtney, Anne Sheffield – See Sheffield, Anne Helen

Courtsal, Frances Chase (1930 –) held the first North Hills, PA, NOW meeting, with the help of Jo Ann Evansgardner, in the early 1970s. Through the years, she served as newsletter editor and handled membership and publicity. A supporter of the ERA and women in sports, she also founded, coordinated and monitored Unitarian Universalists for Equality in the UU Church of the North Hills. The group was successful in removing men's names from rooms in the hall ("no rooms were named for women"), deleting sexist language from the by-laws, and forcing the board to pass a resolution calling for a balance of male and female board members. Courtsal served for eight years as coordinator of the women and religion task force for the Ohio-Meadville District of the Unitarian Universalist Association. A graduate of Wellesley College (1952), she has two children. (ABS)

Cowan, Belita (1947 –) has spent decades working to improve women's healthcare. In 1972 she formed Advocates for Medical Information at the University of Michigan to locate the women who had been given DES as a contraceptive. After interviewing these women, Cowan went on national television saying that the study published in the *Journal of the American Medical Association* that said DES was 100 percent effective and completely safe as a "morning-after pill" was dishonest and deceptive. Also in 1972, Cowan started a leading newspaper of feminist health, *Her-Self*. It was the first publication to report to the public on the dangers of DES, in particular its use as a "morning-after pill." Cowan's research led to her 1975 U.S. Senate testimony at DES hearings held by Senator Edward Kennedy on Capitol Hill. At these hearings, Cowan became the first women's health activist to testify as a medical expert witness. Her work ultimately led the FDA to deny approval of DES as a birth control method because of the safety issues Cowan raised. Also in 1975, Cowan organized a protest held on the steps of the FDA to commemorate women who had died from taking the birth control pill, and to demand stricter regulations of the pill. Believing that there should be a strong women's health movement that functioned as a counterforce to organized medicine and the drug industry, Cowan founded (with Barbara Seaman) the National Women's Health Lobby in 1974. Incorporated as the National Women's Health Network in 1976, the group elected Cowan to its board of directors. In 1978, Cowan became its first executive director, a position she held until 1983. During those years, she had NWHN take legal action against the manufacturers of the Dalkon Shield and Depo-Provera. The group also joined a precedent-setting lawsuit that ultimately forced all drug companies to create patient warning labels for estrogen drugs. Cowan says that she is most proud of her work with NWHN board member Byllye Avery in raising funds for the creation of the National Black Women's Health Project. After retiring from the NWHN, Cowan worked as the health policy adviser to the attorney general of Maryland, focusing on patients' rights and consumer access to Medicare information. She is also author of *Women's Health Care: Resources, Writings, Bibliographies; Health Care Shopper's Guide: 59 Ways to Save Money;* and *Nursing Homes: What You Need to Know.* Cowan was appointed by President Carter to the White House Commission on Women. In 1973, she was given the Uppity Women Unite Award from the Ann Arbor, MI, chapter of NOW. In 1980, she was chosen by *Ms.* magazine as its Woman to Watch in the 80s. Cowan, who has one child, holds a B.S. from Ohio State University (1969) and an M.A. from the University of Michigan (1971). (ABS)

Cowan, Ruth Schwartz (1941 –) joined NOW at the Stony Brook, NY, campus of SUNY in 1969 and was a member until her retirement in 2002. She was "founder, often chair or co-chair, and worked to improve salaries and benefits for women employees." She was a plaintiff (and fundraiser) in a successful sex discrimination suit for professional employees at SUNY (Coser v. Moore, 1974 – 1989), and one of the founders of the women's studies department. Cowan was department director for five years and developed courses (1972) and curricula, including graduate certificate courses. She was also one of the founders of the Benedict Day Care Center (1971) at SUNY. Cowan, who has three children, holds an A.B from Barnard, an M.A. from the University of California at Berkeley, and a Ph.D. from Johns Hopkins. She is the author of *More Work for Mother* (Basic Books, 1983). (ABS)

Cowley, Alice Winifred (1931 –) Early in 1971, Cowley read an article in the *St. Paul Pioneer Press* headlined "Catholics Gird for Fight Against Abortion Reform." In response, she wrote her first pro-choice letter to the editor, and she's been writing and fighting for reproductive choice ever since. She joined the Minnesota Organization to Repeal Abortion Laws (now MN.NARAL), and was responsible for answering "the huge amount of statewide letters." At a hearing at the State Capitol to change abortion law, "a man came up to me. He was very angry and shoved a picture in my face of a fetus in the wastebasket,

yelling 'This is what you're killing!'" In response, and at her husband's urging, Cowley went to the Hennepin (MN) County Coroner's office and secured four photographs of women who had died following illegal abortions. In the early 1970s, Cowley and her husband, who was fire chief, worked, unsuccessfully, to have a woman join the fire department. Cowley is a high-school graduate, and has four children. (ABS)

Cox, Barbara Moore (1942 –) served as executive director of NOW LDEF from 1974 - 1976. Cox's work with NOW LDEF led her to a career in fundraising, "because it quickly became apparent that women weren't going anywhere until we learned how to raise serious money." In 1979, by then an independent fundraising consultant, Cox was recruited by Muriel Fox to organize the first National Convocation on the Future of the Family. Its goal was to take the family issue back from the Right Wing by making clear that fundamental family issues (income, childcare, women's health) were top priorities for feminist activists. Says Cox, "Muriel and I also founded the first corporate fundraising dinner for a women's movement organization—a dinner that continues today and brings in over $1 million annually for NOW LDEF/Legal Momentum." Cox joined the board of NOW LDEF/Legal Momentum in 1990, and in 1993 became chair. Earlier, in her college years (early 1960s), Cox was active on behalf of black civil rights, registering voters and encouraging turnout primarily in Massachusetts. She worked for nuclear disarmament as a board member of the Fund for Peace. Cox holds a B.A. from Smith College and an M.S.W. from Fordham University School of Social Service. (ABS)

Cox, Rita ("Rico") (1935 – 2007) Author and artist, Cox filed state and federal sex discrimination charges against the town of Islip, NY (then her employer), in 1972, winning the state but losing the federal case. She also forced Long Island, NY, *Newsday* to change employment ads from Male Wanted or Female Wanted to Person Wanted, and marched in Washington for the ERA. She was working on "a radical feminist bible to bring back goddess worship and eliminate the violent male gods." (ABS)

Crabtree, Davida Foy (1944 –) has been a passionate and eloquent voice for women for more than three decades while working in campus, parish and statewide ministries in Connecticut. Knowing since 7th grade that she had been called to the ministry, Crabtree entered Andover Newton Theological School in 1967. Seeing that the church was not responding to women's issues, she "pressed hard for it to step forward," almost always in collaboration with other women, though sometimes alone. She co-led the creation of the Women's Theological Center of the Boston Theological Institute; brought the Cambridge play, "How to Make a Woman," to the Andover Newton campus in 1969; became VP at large of the National Council of Churches of Christ in the U.S.

and helped form its first women's caucus; created the women's resource center at Andover Newton; wrote the title chapter in *Women's Liberation and the Church: The New Demand for Freedom in the Life of the Christian Church* (Sarah Bentley Dole, ed., Associated Press, 1970); led the formation of the women's caucus of the national United Church of Christ; developed the first task force on the status and role of women in church and society; was elected to the national executive council of the United Church of Christ (first ordained woman and youngest person to that date); and was ordained to the ministry of the United Church of Christ in 1972 in a service led entirely by women. Crabtree established the Prudence Crandall Center for Women in New Britain, CT, in 1973, a community-based center that brought together women from the CAP agencies, low-income housing projects, the YWCA, churchwomen and the Junior League. It was repeatedly attacked and Crabtree endured death threats. In 1999 she received the President's Award from the Connecticut Coalition Against Domestic Violence. She is chair (2005) of the Council of Conference Ministers of the United Church of Christ nationally.   (ABS)

Craig, May (1889 – 1975) (also known as Elizabeth May Adams Craig) A lifelong feminist, Craig was a World War II correspondent and syndicated columnist for the Maine-based Gannett newspaper chain, a White House press corps reporter and radio broadcaster. Her daily column "Inside Washington" ran for more than 50 years. A leader in Eleanor Roosevelt's Press Conference Association and the Women's National Press Club, Craig was a tireless promoter of initiatives designed to empower women journalists in Washington, D.C. The *bete noire* of sexist politicians and incumbent Presidents, Craig delighted in posing provocative questions on women's rights issues. A regular on NBC-TV's "Meet the Press," Craig pressured representative Howard W. Smith of Virginia, an arch-conservative, to introduce an amendment to put equal rights for women into Title VII of the pending Civil Rights Act (1964). Since the "Southern strategy" was based on the theory that the House would never pass anything "so silly," Smith did just that the next day. He was wrong. Although Craig succeeded in overturning several military rules banning women from planes and ships during her World War II days, she was unable to convince male officials that women could work effectively in rough, outdoor conditions. She wryly predicted, "When I die, the word 'facilities' [will be found engraved on my heart], so often it has been used to prevent me from doing what men reporters could do." Archives: Library of Congress, manuscript division, Washington, D.C.

Crandall, Lona Maurine Setbacken (1908 –2006) In 1972, Crandall became founder and first president of the Sioux Falls, SD, chapter of NOW. In 1975 she attended NOW's national conference, and in 1976 attended its constitutional convention. In addition, Crandall was a member of the SD delegation to the 1977 National Women's Conference in Houston. She also sat on the SD Commission on the Status of Women (1970 – 1978), and worked for passage of the ERA by lobbying, public speaking, and radio and TV broadcasting. She also publicly changed her lifetime Republican Party registration to Democrat when the Republicans removed the ERA from their national platform in 1980. She was honored by the VFA in 2004. Crandall had three children, one of whom is activist Mary Lynn Myers. She earned her B.A. from the University of South Dakota in 1930.   (ABS before death)

Crandall, Mary Lynn – See Myers, Mary Lynn

Crane, Barbara Baumberger (1949 –) has been affiliated with and contributed financially and as a volunteer to women's causes and organizations since her senior year at Wellesley College (1970). From 1989 – 1990, she researched and subsequently published "The Transnational Politics of Abortion" in *The New Politics of Population: Conflict and Consensus in Family Planning* (J.L. Finkle and C. Alison McIntosh, editors, New York: The Population Council, 1994). She also co-taught the first course on international women's reproductive health issues at the Harvard School of Public Health. She was senior policy adviser in the Office of Population of the U.S. Agency for International Development (USAID), and served with U.S. delegations to the International Conference on Population and Development in 1994 and the five-year review of ICPD in 1999. Crane worked with others to ensure women's voices were incorporated in official U.S. policies and reflected in the U.S. position supporting women's reproductive rights and health. Crane also helped ensure that U.S. policies were reflected in the operating programs of USAID, as a more woman-centered approach to reproductive health and family planning. Since 2000, she has served as executive VP of Ipas, a woman-led international non-governmental organization that promotes women's ability to exercise their sexual and reproductive rights and their access to comprehensive reproductive healthcare. In addition to a B.A. from Wellesley, Crane has an M.A. from the Fletcher School of Law and Diplomacy, and a Ph.D. from the University of Michigan. She has two children.   (ABS)

Crannell, Rose Marie (1929 –) was a co-founder and first president of the Albert Lea, MN, chapter of NOW. She demonstrated for the ERA in Springfield, IL, and Washington, D.C., as well as in Minnesota. She was active in the LWV and the AAUW, and served as president of her local American Federation of State, County and Municipal Employees union. Crannell, who has four children, earned her B.A. from the University of Minnesota. She is a retired social worker.   (ABS)

Crater, Flora (1914 –) convened and served as first president of the Northern Virginia chapter of NOW, and convened and served as first coordinator of the VA WPC. In 1972, she led a group of women known as Crater's Raiders to lobby Congress for passage of the ERA. She became an independent candidate for lieutenant governor in 1973; ran for the Democratic nomination for U.S. Senate in 1978; and as a Democratic nominee for House of Delegates in 1982. She served as action coordinator of the Virginia Women's Network, and as vice chair of the Virginia ERA Amendment Ratification Council. She is the founder (1973) and chair of The Woman Activist, Inc., which publishes *The Woman Activist*, and is founder (1976) and chair of *The Almanac of Virginia Politics*. She was recognized as a First Feminist of Virginia by Northern VA NOW, and was honored by women's organizations with a Key to Motivating Women award. She also received the Human Rights Award from the Fairfax County (VA) Human Rights Commission in 1999.   (ABS)

Crawford, Barbara Evans (1931 – 1996) In the mid 1960s, Crawford, then a young nurse, answered an ad in *The Pittsburgh Press* for a salesperson for a Pittsburgh pharmaceutical company. After a few perfunctory questions, the interviewer—who had his feet up on his desk—said, "Well, Mrs. Crawford, I'm not going to hire you. I just wanted to see what kind of woman would apply for a man's job." Devastated and humiliated, Crawford was to spend the rest of her life fighting for equal job opportunities for women and the ERA. She was president of the Greater Pittsburgh Area chapter of NOW, which filed suit against *The Pittsburgh Press* for publishing separate help-wanted ads for men and women. The Pittsburg Human Relations Commission decided in NOW's favor, but the *Press* appealed. Crawford herself prepared the legal briefs required by the higher courts and proofread the court stenographer's transcripts. In 1976, the U.S. Supreme Court upheld the commission's recommendation. In 1972, Crawford and her daughter Deborah went to Florida, knocking on doors and talking to women in the little towns around Tallahassee, and inviting them to NOW meetings about the ERA. In 1978, she participated in the Washington, D.C., march in support of the amendment, and for months afterward organized a weekly busload of Pittsburgh women who went to Washington to press for an extension. Once that was accomplished, Crawford headed to Illinois, which like Florida was holding out on ratification. Weekly bus trips to Springfield, IL, continued until that state voted down the amendment. Crawford also worked in Pennsylvania, persuading the school district in Forest Hills to allow her daughter to take shop classes instead of home economics. As manager of the Marada Golf Course in Findlay, Crawford made sure young women were hired as rangers, taught them how to handle flirtatious golfers, and confronted any golfers she heard making offending comments.

Crawford, Jan (1943 –) A trauma therapist, Crawford became active in the women's movement in NYC in the early 1970s. As a member of the board of NYC NOW (1972–1974), she planned programs that introduced and connected different groups within the feminist movement and stimulated cross-pollination of theory. In 1974, she founded the Feminist Community Coalition, which organized community meetings and provided testimony before Congress on women's issues. She also helped develop NOW's public service ad campaign (1971–1973), trained people in various local chapters to request air and print time, and worked to improve the image of women in the media. During that same time, she appeared on numerous radio and television programs discussing feminist topics, and helped build a coalition between the then-injured lesbian feminist community and NOW. When the Catholic Church's work against the gay rights amendment succeeded in City Hall in the early 1970s, Crawford helped negotiate the takeover of St. Patrick's Cathedral in New York City in protest. Crawford has taught gender and sexuality candidates in Self Psychology, and is the author of "The Severed Self – Gender as Trauma," published in *Ideas Reconsidered, Progress in Self Psychology*, vol. 12, Analytic Press, 1996. She also published "Feeling Our Way" in *Our Right to Love: A Lesbian Resource Book*, edited by Ginny Vida.   (ABS)

Crawford, Lauren R. (1949 –) focused on health and reproductive rights as part of CWLU (1971 – 1976). She taught classes in the Liberation School, organized around abortion rights, fought to save the Chicago Maternity Center, supported the nurses and doctors strike at Cook County and University of Illinois Hospitals, and developed an occupational health and safety organization with labor unions. From 1971–1980, she was part of the staff of the Urban Preceptorship Program, a grant-funded, accredited program for medical, nursing and allied health students and workers, plus community health activists. This group created the Health Evaluation & Referral Service, and programs for community-based free clinics, among other activities. A supporter of civil rights, Crawford spent the summer of 1966 in Chicago as part of Dr. Martin Luther King's movement. In 1971, she joined the Medical Committee for Human Rights. Crawford, who has one child, earned her B.A. and M.A. from the University of Chicago. Archives: Northwestern University, Chicago, IL; and the Chicago Historical Society, Chicago, IL. (ABS)

Crawford, Mary Pegau – See Ruthsdotter, Mary Esther

Crawford-Mason, Clare (1936 –) (also known as Clare Wootten Crawford) was catapulted into the women's movement in 1957 during her senior year at the University of Maryland. Although she had been promised the editorship of the university's newspaper, the offer was rescinded because, as a woman, she was viewed as potentially unstable. In 1962 she became the first married woman to move from copyboy to reporter at a Washington daily newspaper, *Washington Daily News*, and in

1965 became America's first female shop steward for the Newspaper Guild. While pregnant, Crawford-Mason wrote an expose of D.C. maternity clinics' poor treatment of lower-class women (1965). Her article on the easy availability of guns led to the first gun control law in the Western Hemisphere in Montgomery County, MD, a Washington suburb. In 1975, Crawford-Mason produced the first television news documentary on spousal abuse (NBC), and the first national magazine story on the subject (*People*). In 1977, she again produced the first documentary and first national magazine story on child sexual abuse. In l979, she produced the first network news documentary on abortion as a political issue (NBC) and the first national magazine story on the subject (*People*). Her 1980 NBC documentary "If Japan Can, Why Can't We?" introduced W. Edwards Deming to the West and is credited with starting popular awareness of quality, productivity issues and the global marketplace. "Deming's philosophy of management was—though he did not know it—feminist," says Crawford-Mason. "It is the first management philosophy to value the person over the system." Crawford-Mason has won a Peabody Award and two Emmys, and was nominated twice for the Pulitzer Prize by *The Washington Star* and the *Washington Daily News*. She was a founding editor and Washington bureau chief for 10 years of *People* magazine. Crawford-Mason has a B.A. from the University of Maryland and two children. Archives: Schlesinger Library, Radcliffe Institute, Cambridge, MA. (ABS)

Cremonesi, Alma (1941 –) An activist in California (1970–1978) Cremonesi was a member of the support staff of the San Francisco Women's Center (1970–1972) and editor/distributor of the "Bay Area Women's Liberation Newsletter." She was also active in the Feminist Women's Health Center in Los Angeles (1972–1973), and co-wrote the proposal for the national NOW convention calling for housing for women fleeing violence (1973). She was also a founder and fundraiser (1978) of the first safe house in Colorado Springs, CO, the Domestic Violence Prevention Center. She took part in the Women's Liberation Peace March on the Presidio (San Francisco, 1970); attended the First International Women's Conference (1974); and was a member of Flo Kennedy's Hollywood Toilet Bowl Caravan from San Francisco to Los Angeles (1973) to influence the entertainment industry to expand roles for women and to hire more women. Cremonesi was also part of "Free Inez" fundraising events. (Inez Garcia, who had shot her rapist and was sentenced to 20 years in prison, received a new trial and was found not guilty.) Cremonesi helped choose selections to be published and was involved in the printing and distribution of the *Shameless Hussy Press Review* (1971–1978), and was a distributor for the women's newspaper *It Ain't Me Babe.* She was also an organizer and speaker at the rally for the 17th anniversary of Roe v. Wade to stop compromising of pro-choice laws in

Colorado Springs, CO (1990). Author of the article "Preventing Breast Cancer Naturally," Cremonesi is founder and director of The Pikes Peak Lavender Film Festival in Colorado Springs. She holds a B.A. from The Colorado College. Archives: The Sophia Smith Collection, Smith College, Northampton, MA. (ABS)

Crisp, Ann (1923 –) (also known as Glory Ann Crisp) A lawyer from the late 1950s into the mid 1960s, Crisp was "always agitating to change laws to improve the status of women," she says. She wrote and worked to pass legislation that ended the virtual ownership of children by husbands and fathers in Texas. Founding president of Greater Kansas City NOW and a national NOW board member, Crisp worked on various national NOW legal issues from the mid to late 1960s. She also taught law at the University of Missouri, Kansas City from 1970 to the mid 1980s, and edited law books in San Francisco. (ABS)

Crisp, Mary Dent (1923 – 2007) began her career as a political leader in Phoenix in 1961, was elected Republican national committee woman from Arizona in 1972, and then re-elected in 1976. In 1976, Crisp served as secretary of the Republican National Convention. In 1977, she was elected co-chair of the Republican National Committee. At the 1980 National Convention, Crisp warned the party that its opposition to the ERA and abortion would undermine its ability to gain majority party status. When her term as co-chair expired at the close of the convention, Crisp chaired independent candidate John Anderson's National Unity Campaign. In 1981, Crisp formed a political consulting business in which she remained active through the mid 1990s. Founder and former chair of the Republican Coalition for Choice, formed in 1989 in the wake of the Supreme Court Webster decision, Crisp serves on the advisory board of the NWPC, the Pro-Choice Resource Center, Planned Parenthood and the National Museum of Women's History. She held a B.A. from Oberlin and an M.A. from Arizona State University, and was the recipient of Honorary Doctor of Law degrees from Oberlin and Cedar Crest College. Archives: Schlesinger Library, Radcliffe Institute, Cambridge, MA. (ABS)

Cristiano, Roslyn Berkman
– See Payne, Roslyn Berkman

Crittenden, Ann (1937 –) (also known as Ann C. Scott) An author, journalist and lecturer, Crittenden was one of the 12 lead plaintiffs in a class action lawsuit of 120 women alleging sex discrimination at Time Inc. in 1970, one of the first such suits in the nation. They negotiated with management and won broad concessions, breaking down sex segregation at the four Time Inc. magazines. Women—previously restricted to the role of researchers—won the right to be promoted to writer and editor. Management also agreed to hire men as researchers, and to give bylines to reporter/researchers. *Newsweek* had a similar successful suit, and Crittenden became the first female writer *Newsweek* hired after that settlement, in January 1971. In 1972, Crittenden wrote a piece for the first issue of *Ms.* magazine, "The Value of Housework," and 30 years later (2001) wrote "The Price of Motherhood," which analyzed the economic contribution and the systematic devaluation of the work of raising children. Crittenden, who has one child, holds a B.A. and M.A. from Southern Methodist University, as well as a master's degree from Columbia University. (ABS)

Crockett, Ethelene (1914 – 1978) entered medical school at Harvard University when she was 28. She was the first black woman specializing in obstetrics and gynecology in Michigan, where she practiced medicine for 35 years. Crockett was also the first woman to be president of the American Lung Association. She served as director of the Detroit Maternal Infant Care Project from 1967 – 1970, and in 1972 led the fight to liberalize Michigan's abortion laws. Crockett, who worked aggressively for day care centers to assist working women, lectured frequently on family planning and public healthcare. She also helped design and direct the Detroit Model Neighborhood Comprehensive Health Center. The recipient of numerous awards and honors, Crockett was cited by the *Detroit Free Press* in 1971 as one of Detroit's Nine Most Successful Women. In 1973, the Howard University Alumni Federation cited her "For Conspicuous Service to Her Profession and Community," and in 1977, the Detroit Medical Society elected her Physician of the Year. In 1988, Crockett was inducted into The Michigan Women's Hall of Fame. Crockett had three children.

Cron, Marcia Marie (1939 –) In the early 1960s, Cron "made a scene" when she was refused credit in her own name at a dealership—she was single and they wanted her father's signature. When she later married, she kept her own name "even though I did not know anyone else who did it, and had to fight long and hard" for the right to do so. As a businesswoman, she fought for and obtained a liquor license in her name at a time when a married woman in Michigan was not allowed to have a liquor license. "It was my business and I refused to include my husband," she says. This law has now been changed. Cron served on the board of Detroit NOW as speakers bureau chair and treasurer; was treasurer and then VP of the MI NOW board; and was on the board of the Michigan Abortion Rights Action League and the National Association of Women Business Owners. She participated in all NOW conferences in Detroit, Washington, Indianapolis and Chicago, and marched in all ERA marches, parades and demonstrations in the area. She also helped promote Michigan's Public Accommodation Act, which states that women cannot be discriminated against in public places. She "stormed the doors of the Detroit Athletic Club," and as a member of Catholics for a Free Choice was part of the demonstration and press conference when the U.S.

Bishops Conference met in Detroit in 1976. She assisted in writing and delivering a prayer for the bishops at that meeting that was variously described as offensive and blasphemous. Says Cron, "Like everyone, I just did what had to be done." (ABS)

Cronan, Sheila (1942 – 2003) An outspoken leader, Cronan was a member of NYRW, Redstockings and The Feminists. In 1970, she published the article "Marriage," in which she equated marriage with slavery and said "Freedom for women cannot be won without the abolition of marriage." Inspired by her work in the women's movement, Cronan attended Boalt Law School, University of California, Berkeley, and graduated in 1974. Her career in labor law included 25 years as an attorney at the Department of Labor in Washington, D.C.

Crosby, Marlene Suzanne (1940 –) (also known as Marlene Lawrence and Marlene Crosby Mainker) Crosby was president, Summit (NJ) Area NOW (1974 – 1975); VP, Northern NJ WEAL (1976); and founding member, National Women's Health Network, Washington, D.C. (1979). With Carole Picard Fuller, she formed two companies to create products focusing on sexism, racism and ageism, and later cancer and alcoholism, with the main catalyst being career development: Womanpower Projects Inc. (1974) and MCM Associates (1976). Speeches given at Womanpower workshops were collected and published as *Women In Crisis*, edited by Penelope Russianoff (Human Science Press, 1981). In 1979, Crosby and AT&T Long Lines, through MCM Associates, pioneered a project called Spouse Relocation Career Development, an employer-paid benefit to the spouses of company employees transferred to new locations. Initially, most of these "trailing spouses" were wives; eventually, 30 percent were men following their wives to their new management-level positions. In 1978 – 1979, Womanpower Projects began a cancer research project called Looking for Rosie the Riveter. During their factory work in WWII, these women were exposed to many toxins with long latency periods. With the help of epidemiologists and toxicologists, the team obtained valuable cancer statistics on 50 women in NJ. In 1980 – 1982, Crosby opened Center for Women Affected by Alcoholism, which focused on alcoholism, equality in employment and career development. Crosby, who has one child, earned a B.A. from the New School for Social Research and an M.A. from The Fielding Institute, Santa Barbara, CA. Archives: The Rosie the Riveter Project, The Smithsonian Institute, Washington, D.C. (ABS)

Crothers, Diane (1946 –) (Also known as Diane Landerman) worked on voter registration in Fairfield and Birmingham, AL, during the summer of 1967 with an SCLC project headquartered at Mills College. Her mother was born and raised in Mississippi and shared with her daughter her critical perspective as a white woman on segregation and racism. As a direct result of her experience in

Birmingham, Crothers spent the rest of the 1960s involved in the labor movement and later the women's movement in North Carolina and New York. In 1969 she joined Redstockings and then co-founded NYRF. She led discussions to establish rape as a women's issue, and, with NYRF, led discussions on creating a legislative agenda. In 1970–1971, she, along with Ann Boylan, Jeannie Friedman, and Nancy Crothers (her sister) co-founded the *Women's Rights Law Reporter* in the basement of Rutgers Law School. Crothers later became a lawyer, taught civil rights law and women's studies, prosecuted domestic violence cases, and enforced employment-related affirmative action laws. **(ABS)**

Crouch, Dorothy (1940 –) was an active member of NY NOW from 1969–1974. She served on the membership task force, as chair of the board, and in 1972 as president, and later as a member of the advisory council. An entrepreneur, she is founder of Crouch International, which provides publishing-related services to clients on three continents. She held various executive positions at Paperback Library, later Warner Books (1970–1984), ending as VP, general manager. In 1994, she started her own business. In 1997, she was appointed VP licensed publishing for *MAD* Magazine and DC Comics, as well as associate publisher, MAD Magazine, a position she held until retiring from corporate life in 2002. In addition, in the mid 1970s, Crouch was appointed to the American Arbitration Association's Commercial Panel of Arbitrators, where she serves as an arbitrator for AAA. She is author of *Entertaining Without Alcohol* (Acropolis Books, 1985). **(ABS)**

Cruikshank, Margaret (1940 –) was founding director (1975 – 1977) of women's studies at Mankato State University (MN). Since 1975 forward (2006), she has taught women's studies at Mankato, the City College of San Francisco and the University of Maine. She has begun concentrating on classes about women's aging and is the author of *Learning to be Old: Gender, Culture and Aging* (Rowman and Littlefield, 2003). She is also editor of *The Lesbian Path* (Grey Fox Press, 1980); *Lesbian Studies* (The Feminist Press, 1982); and *New Lesbian Writing* (1984). Cruikshank, who lived in San Francisco from 1977 – 1997, took part in various political and cultural activities there and briefly worked for the Gay Educational Foundation in 1978. She has a B.A., M.A. and Ph.D. Archives: The Lesbian Herstory Archives, Brooklyn, NY; June Mazur Collection, West Hollywood, CA; the Gay and Lesbian Collection of the San Francisco Public Library, San Francisco, CA. **(ABS)**

Csida, June Bundy (1923 – 2006) was an active member of Los Angeles NOW since 1970, when she coordinated a search for surviving pre-WWI suffragists to participate in NOW's August 26th Women's Strike for Equality celebration. During the 1970s, Csida held various offices in Los Angeles NOW, including VP, secretary and PR officer. She also assisted NOW's national VP (Toni Carabillo) with media relations, and was a contributor and columnist for the *National NOW Times*. In 1971, she persuaded several Los Angeles TV and radio stations to create and air public service spots for NOW—a first for the organization. In 1992, she co-authored *The Feminist Chronicles 1953 – 1993* with Carabillo and Judith Meuli. She also set up a public forum on the then-startling theme, Rape, the Number One Crime Against Women. The following year, she and her husband, Joseph, also a NOW member, wrote *Rape (How to Avoid It and What To Do About It If You Can't),* the first book-length feminist treatment of this subject. Csida is author of several other books, including *Elizabeth Cady Stanton, The 19th Century Renaissance Woman.* A contributor to the *World Book Encyclopedia Year Book* for 14 years, Csida wrote a *World Book Yearbook* report on the second feminist revolt, tracing the history of women's fight for equality from 1848 through 1972. She also scripted and researched a syndicated radio series, "Show Ms!" a feminist tribute to women musical stars from the 1920s to the 1980s. In 1986 she wrote a tribute to male feminists that was delivered by actor Ed Asner at NOW's 20th anniversary show. **(ABS before death)**

Culbertson, Janet Lynn (1932 –) An artist, college art teacher and eco-feminist, Culbertson drew her Mythmaker series (1974) to confirm the woman heroine as an active protagonist saving the world. This series of 20 works is now in the National Museum of Women in the Arts in Washington, D.C. In 1978, Culbertson worked on the Great Goddess issue of *Heresies,* and in 1979 proposed, with Lucy Lippard and others, the *Heresies* Feminism & Ecology issue, for which Culbertson wrote an article titled "Ecotage." In the 1980s, Culbertson was a panel member, Women's World Ecology Convention, and in 1990 wrote an article for and contributed images to the Canadian magazine *Gallerie: Women Artists.* Culbertson earned her B.F.A. from Carnegie-Mellon University (1953) and her M.A. from New York University (1964). Archives: Women Artists Archives, Rutgers University, New Brunswick, NJ. **(ABS)**

Cumfer, Cynthia ("Cindy") Dee (1949 –) Now a lawyer and historian, Cumfer was in her last term at New College in Sarasota, FL, when she started a gay liberation group and attended her first feminist meetings (1971). In Portland, OR, after graduation, Cumfer became involved in the gay women's liberation movement. In 1972, her collective house and others helped found a gay women's caucus. That same year, Cumfer was a founder of a women's center and a women's bookstore in Portland, and worked in both places for the next 18 months. While there, she helped create the Women's Resources Fund and set up a distribution network for several feminist items produced in Portland. After starting law school in 1974, Cumfer became involved in women's and gay caucuses there and co-wrote a women's self-help divorce manual,

Partings. For several years after graduation in 1977, Cumfer worked in a women-run public interest law firm, the Community Law Project. The firm handled the earliest sexual harassment case and most of the earliest lesbian custody cases in Oregon. Cumfer created a book on how to get your own restraining order, and set up a clinic to help women fill out the forms. In 1985, Cumfer "got what may be the first adoption order for two women in a donor insemination situation in the United States." She later wrote a self-help book for unmarried couples, *The Legal Guide for Unmarried Couples in Oregon,* and wrote a chapter on the same topic for the legal guide for women published by the Oregon Commission on Women. In 1985, Cumfer was a founder of the Lesbian Community Project. Cumfer holds a Ph.D. as well as a J.D.   (ABS)

Cummings, Claire (1941 –) (also known as Claire Ostema) was a member of one of the earliest CWLU CR groups, led by Elizabeth Robson. She also worked briefly on *Womankind,* the paper of the CWLU. Cummings started and ran (1972 – 1976) a feminist day care center, New Morning Children's Center, in Somerville, MA. For 30 years, she taught sociology and women's studies at Newbury College, where she is also involved in organizing women students. Since the mid 1990s, she has worked with *Survival News* and Survivors Inc., an anti-poverty, Welfare rights feminist collective, serving as editor of the paper and co-president of the organization. She published the first article on Welfare reform in *Sojourner* (1997), and nine profiles of women Welfare warrior/activists in *Survival News* (1987 – 2000). She was also active in the civil rights and anti-Vietnam War movements. Cummings, who was born in England, has one child. She earned her B.A. from Roosevelt University, and her M.A. and Ph.D. from Clark University. Archives: Schlesinger Library, Radcliffe Institute, Cambridge, MA.   (ABS)

Cunningham, Elizabeth ("Evelyn") (1916 –) A 1943 journalism graduate of Long Island University, Cunningham was immediately hired by the *Pittsburgh Courier,* then one of America's leading newspapers serving the African American community. She remained at the paper until 1968. While at the *Courier,* Cunningham made a conscious effort to stay away from writing about things women usually had to write about—cooking and weddings. Among other topics, she covered civil rights. After campaigning for Nelson Rockefeller, Cunningham was appointed by the then-governor to head the women's unit of state government (1968). In 1969, she became a member of the task force on women's rights and responsibilities, and later served in various positions in the White House. Cunningham is a founder of The Coalition of 100 Black Women, and has helped forge coalitions of women of all ethnic and racial backgrounds. On August 26, 1970, she marched with her entire staff down 5th Ave. in New York City in the NOW-sponsored Women's Strike for Equality march. Also in 1970, Cunningham attended the founding meeting of the NWPC. In 1973, she supported Shirley Chisholm for President, and in 1997 received the George Polk Award for Outstanding Journalism from Long Island University. Cunningham's civil rights activities include five years as producer and host of "At Home with Evelyn Cunningham" for WLIB-NY. Her first interview was with Malcolm X. Archives: Amistad Collection, Tulane University, New Orleans, LA.   (ABS)

Curran, Hilda Patricia (1938 –) As director of the Michigan Office of Women and Work (1977 – 1991), Curran led statewide hearings in Michigan on sexual harassment and comparable worth, and was central to the establishment of one of the first programs for women in skilled trades and displaced homemakers in the United States. In addition, Curran has served as national president of Big Sisters of America, was a founding member of Women in State Government, a founding trustee of the Michigan Women's Foundation, and one of the founders and eventually president of the Greater Lansing Food Bank, the first of its kind in the U.S. Curran was inducted into the Michigan Women's Hall of Fame in 1998. (ABS)

Curran, Patricia Andrea – See Gozemba, Patricia Andrea

Currie, Arlyce – See Feist, Arlyce Swanson

Cutler, Lynn Germain (1938 –) Children's issues spurred Cutler's interest in the political process. At the appointment of the governor of Iowa, Harold Hughes, she served on the Iowa Commission for Children and Youth in the 1960s. She helped write one of the first battered child laws in the country, and worked for the protection of migrant mothers and their children. She also spent four years with Head Start, helping mothers work their way out of poverty and go to school. In 1974, Cutler was the first woman elected as county supervisor in Black Hawk County, IA. In that capacity, she helped create the first battered women's shelter, put affirmative action hiring policies in place, and instituted childcare and other programs. Cutler was a founding member of the IA WPC (1972). As a county official, Cutler was also one of the founders of the women's caucus in the National Association of County Officials. In 1980, Cutler ran for Congress, the first woman to be nominated in her district. She lost by one point. In 1981, she ran for, and won, the vice chairmanship of the Democratic National Committee. In that capacity, she helped create the Women's Vote Project for the 1984 elections, and started the Eleanor Roosevelt Fund, which helped women running for office at state and local levels. As an officer of the 1984 convention, Cutler produced the event "Winning With Women, Running to Win." In 1985, she co-produced a conference, Business Women and the Political World. Held on the *Mississippi Queen* riverboat, it became a seminal meeting for young women like Mary Landrieu, Carol Moseley Braun and Jane Campbell. After working to elect Bill

Clinton President (1992), Cutler went to work in the Clinton White House as deputy assistant to the President and in the office of the chief of staff. She also worked with the VP's office on women's issues. Since leaving the White House, Cutler has been at Holland & Knight, a national law firm. She is still involved with the Democratic party, and has served as senior adviser, pro bono, to the women mayors caucus of the U.S. Conference of Mayors. Inducted into the Women's Hall of Fame (1996), Cutler has been honored by many Native American groups. She has served on many boards, including the new Museum of the American Indian. She is a member of the Washington Women's Forum, and helps with the Washington Area Women's Foundation. Cutler, who has four children, earned her B.A. (1955) and M.A. (1957) from the University of Northern Iowa. Archives: Library of the University of Northern Iowa, Cedar Falls, IA. (ABS)

Cutler, Wendy Judith (1952 –) At Goddard College in 1971, Cutler took a course on feminist history (taught by Marilyn Salzman-Webb). From that time forward she has identified herself as a feminist and immersed herself in women's culture, literature and politics. At the University of California, Berkeley, in 1972, she joined Bay Area Women Against Rape and for the next two and a half years served as an anti-rape advocate, rape counselor and speaker. A student in the university's School of Criminology, Cutler was able to create her own program in women's studies (with help from Gloria Bowles, who subsequently became one of the chairs of the women's studies department) and graduated with an individual major in feminism in 1974. Earlier, in 1973, Cutler joined the Berkeley-Oakland Women's Union, a socialist-feminist women's organization, where she was active until 1975. There she was involved in political theory building; planning conferences, benefits, fundraisers and educational and study projects; and fomenting revolutionary Socialist-feminist transformation. Cutler is a senior instructor of women's studies at Portland State University and a licensed massage therapist. She holds a B.A. from the University of California, Berkeley, and an M.A. from San Francisco State University. Archives: The Berkeley-Oakland Women's Union has donated its archives to the Bancroft Library's Social Change Collection, University of California, Berkeley, CA. (ABS)

Cutler-Shaw, Joyce Arlene (1932 –) (also known as Joyce Shaw) was part of Nine Women Artists, a group formed in San Diego in 1972. The women worked together for a year evolving a feminist performance work, The Bride. In 1973, Cutler-Shaw joined the Los Angeles Woman's Building, and was also an original member of the Grandview Gallery. Also in 1973, Cutler-Shaw organized a contemporary art course/public lecture series through the University of California, San Diego. Titled Speaking of Art, it was held at the La Jolla Museum of Art. Without announcing it as such, all eight speakers were women, including June Wayne, Miriam Schapiro and Lucy Lippard, among others. In 1974, Cutler-Shaw was the first artist and the first woman artist to exhibit at an installation work in the Los Angeles International Airport. The enormous exhibit, titled The Namewall, was installed overnight with a crew of women artists from the Woman's Building. From 1974 – 1980, Cutler-Shaw developed college art courses with free public lecture series and then public broadcast television interviews on new art, equally presenting women and men. She has participated on panels for the WCA during its annual conferences, as well as panels of the College Art Association. Since 1992, Cutler-Shaw has coordinated Dialogues in Art and Architecture at the Athenaeum Music and Art Library in La Jolla, which, since 2001, have been sponsored by Woodbury University School of Architecture. In addition to this work, Cutler-Shaw is the first artist and first woman artist nationally to have an appointment as artist-in-residence/visiting scholar at a medical school, The School of Medicine of the University of California, San Diego, for a fine art project. Cutler-Shaw, who has three children, earned her B.A. from New York University and an M.F.A. from the Visual Arts Department of The University of California, San Diego. Archives: Special Collections Library, University of California, San Diego. (ABS)

Dailey-Stout, Thelma (1918 –) An African American/Native American, Dailey-Stout entered the women's movement in 1974. She was founding publisher of *The Ethnic Woman* (1977). On the Publisher's Page of the magazine's first issue, Dailey-Stout wrote that the magazine was for "third-world women," the women of African, Latin, American Indian and Asian heritage. She said, "Our potential is unlimited. There are many messages that need to be communicated, many stories to be told, many plans to make, many minds to shape. *The Ethnic Woman* will be your drum, your smoke signal, your link to the sisterhood." Active in labor and civil rights, Dailey-Stout had earlier served as VP of the UAW. As placement director, she was responsible for 30,000 members. Dailey-Stout was a member of the Coalition of Trade Union Women, the Coalition of 100 Black Women, the Congress of Racial Equality and the International Organization of Journalists. Dailey-Stout, who has one biological daughter and who has nurtured several boys and girls, holds a B.A. from Empire State College. She was awarded a Fellowship in women's studies by Sarah Lawrence College. (ABS)

Daly, Mary (1928 –) is a radical feminist philosopher who, with outrageous originality, tackles everything that would diminish women. Daly chose to study philosophy and religion, but after receiving her Ph.D. in religion at St. Mary's College (Notre Dame, IN, 1954), she learned there were no universities in the U.S. that would allow women to study Catholic theology as graduate students. Instead, she went to Europe, where she obtained a doctorate in theology and another in philosophy at the University of

Fribourg in Switzerland. Returning to the U.S., she joined the faculty at Boston College and actively entered the feminist community. She was part of NOW's task force on women and religion, and wrote many books and articles on women, the patriarchal nature of Catholicism and other religions. She also challenged secular systems of thought (such as those based on Freud and Marx), and anything that dulled women. In 1969, she received a "terminal contract" from Boston College, meaning that she would not be rehired after the term of her current contract, because of her 1968 book, *The Church and the Second Sex*. A victory for feminism was won out of that incident when huge student protests (mostly of men because women were not allowed into the College of Arts and Sciences at the time) resulted in Daly being rehired and promoted to the rank of associate professor, with tenure, in 1969. After 1969 Daly continued her stormy career teaching at Boston College, lecturing around the U.S. and Europe, organizing protests and writing fiery radical feminist philosophical books. In 1971 she was invited to preach a sermon at Harvard Memorial Church, and instead preached an "anti-sermon," calling for a walkout from patriarchal religion. Hundreds of women did walk out. In 1999, BC took all of Daly's courses out of the computer and catalog, making registration impossible. BC had been trying to get rid of Daly, allegedly because of her insistence on teaching male students separately from women in her women's studies classes. Her reason for the separation was that the "the dynamic is totally interrupted" if men are present. In 1999, under pressure from right wing Republicans, BC was again determined to get rid of Daly. After a huge protest and prolonged legal battle, Daly finally left the "prison" of Boston College. Her books are *The Church and the Second Sex* (1968); *Beyond God the Father: Toward a Philosophy of Women's Liberation* (1973); *Gyn/ Ecology: The Metaethics of Radical Feminism* (1979); *Pure Lust: Elemental Feminist Philosophy* (1984); *Websters' First New Intergalactic Wickedary of the English Language,* with Jane Caputi (1987); *Outercourse: The Be-Dazzling Voyage* (1992), *Quintessence... Realizing the Archaic Future: A Radical Elemental Feminist Manifesto* (1998), and *Amazon Grace: Re-Calling the Courage to Sin Big* (2005). (ABS)

Damon, Betsy (1940 –) A conceptual humanist artist, she was a founding member of the WCA and of the Feminist Art Studio at Cornell University (1973). Damon organized a three-week conference at Cornell called Woman in the Arts in 1973. She founded a workshop called No Limits for Women Artists in 1984, a support system that became a national organization for women artists. From 1976–1985, she performed such pieces as The 7,000 Year Old Woman, Blind Beggarwoman and Meditation with Stones for the Survival of the Planet. Her Shrine for Everywoman was part of the United Nations Conferences for Women, 1980 and 1985. In 1978, she organized readings, videos, films, performances and discussions for A

Lesbian Show in NYC. A Memory of Clean Water, a 250-foot cast of a dry riverbed, funded by the Mass Council on the Arts, traveled to over 10 museums. With the founding of Keepers of the Water (1991), she began directing public projects about water that bring artist, scientist and citizen together. Her Chengdu, China, event with over 25 Chinese artists was so successful that Damon was invited to design a six-acre water garden along the banks of the Fu River. This garden is a world model of urban possibilities. She now designs and creates projects worldwide. Damon, who holds an M.F.A. from Columbia University, is the recipient of a National Endowment for the Arts Grant (1990), a Jerome Foundation Grant (1994), and a Bush Fellowship (1996). In 2003 she was honored by the VFA at a celebration of feminists in the arts. (ABS)

Dan, Alice Jones (1942 –) (also known as Mary Alice Jones) A professor and psychologist, Dan began her work researching women's health in 1972 as organizer and co-chair of Chicago Women in Research (1972–1985). She was also co-chair of the Illinois Women's Health Conference in the early 1970s, and first president of the Society for Menstrual Cycle Research, founded in 1977. She has published studies on premenstrual symptoms, the effects of stress on menstrual functioning, physical activity in midlife women and the health consequences of menopause. Dan has also edited several books on menstrual cycle research and women's health, including *The Menstrual Cycle* (Springer Press, 1980), *Menstrual Health in Women's Lives* (University of Illinois Press, 1991), and *Reframing Women's Health* (Sage Publications, 1994). A charter member of the National Academy of Women's Health Medical Education, Dan has served on the board of the National Council for Research on Women and the *Journal of Women's Health*. Dan, who has two children, has worked to increase participation of women at all levels in science and engineering. She holds a B.A. from the College of Wooster and an M.A. and Ph.D. from the University of Chicago (1976). (ABS)

Daniell, Rosemary Hughes (1935 –) Writer, teacher and self-described "high-school dropout," Daniell instigated and led writing workshops in women's prisons in Georgia and Wyoming. Since 1981, inspired by her mother's death and unrealized talents as a writer, as well as the women she met while working in Georgia's State Prison for Women, Daniell began Zona Rosa, a series of creative writing workshops for women in the U.S. and Europe. Earlier, in 1969, Daniell wrote "what I believe to be the first trade coverage of the women's movement in the Southeast, 'The Feminine Frustration,'" published in the June 1970 issue of *Atlanta* magazine. She is also the author of *A Sexual Tour of the Deep South* (1975). In it, as in her later books, she says, "I broke the taboo with which I and all the Southern women I knew had been brought up: never to speak directly about anger or sexuality." Other books include *The Woman Who Spilled Words All Over*

Herself (1977) and *Confessions of a (Female) Chauvinist* (2001). A supporter of civil rights, gay rights and the peace movement, Daniell has three children. Archives: Georgia College & University, Milledgeville, GA.　(ABS)

Daniels, Arlene Kaplan (1930 –) was professor, Department of Sociology, Northwestern University (Evanston, IL), from 1975–1995, and director of women's studies there from 1991–1995. She won the Ford Foundation Faculty Fellowship for Research on the Role of Women in Society (1975–1976); was Visiting Scholar, Center for Research on Women, Stanford University (1979–1980); and Visiting Scholar, Center for Women's Studies, University of Oregon (1986). Daniels was a founder and later president of Sociologists for Women in Society. As a feminist editor of the *Journal of Social Problems*, she published many women contributors. She was the first director of The Program on Women at Northwestern University, and started women's studies there. She is the author of numerous articles about women in society, including several on the WEAL. Daniels received a Ph.D. from the University of California, Berkeley in 1960. Archives: Northwestern University, Evanston, IL.　(ABS)

Danielson, Susan Steinberg (1944 –) Danielson's activism began in 1969 when she worked at *Liberation Magazine*. In 1970, when Danielson (an instructor at Lehman College) and her husband (an assistant professor at CUNY) were expecting their first child, he applied for maternity leave to care for the baby and was fired; she, meantime, was granted a maternity leave that she had not asked for. With the help of the Center for Constitutional Law, they filed a class action suit that eventually established the legal basis for parental leaves of absence. She was a signator on Roe v. Wade, served as faculty adviser and coordinator of the first childcare center at Lehman College, and worked with the Women's Collective of the Bronx Coalition. The Women's Collective was proactive and successful in initiatives related to women's health. With support from the American Cancer Society, they organized two or three Pap smear clinics in a storefront on Tremont Ave., then demanded that Montefiore Hospital (NYC) open an abortion clinic. The hospital built a new facility and hired several of the feminists to develop and run it. Danielson, who has a Ph.D. from the University of Oregon (1990), taught women's studies at Portland State University. She was also active in the civil rights and peace movements, and in community and labor organizing. She has three children.　(ABS)

Danzig, Myrna Arlene (1935 –) was a charter member of the Essex County, NJ, chapter of NOW (1972). During a three-year period teaching at Montclair State College (1972–1975), she was a co-organizer of the women's center, the women's studies minor program and the affirmative action program there. She also taught the first women's studies course offered at the school (Women

and Education in Modern Western Society). Danzig went on to teach an introduction to women's studies, and wrote and taught about sexism in education. In 1975, she came out as a lesbian and left her family in NJ to join NYRF and LFL. She also worked at the Women's Coffee House. Danzig, who has three children, holds an M.A.T. from Harvard and an A.B.D. from Rutgers University.　(ABS)

Darcy, Lynne (1941 –) From 1973–1976, Darcy was chair of NOW's national compliance task force. At that time, demonstrations against the steel industry were initiated by Chicago NOW and Southwestern PA NOW, in cooperation with the task force, when it was learned that the steel companies' plan to correct job discrimination in the industry did not include women. Also during Darcy's tenure, the Washington, D.C., NOW chapter in conjunction with the NASA subcommittee on compliance, was successful in opening up NASA opportunities for women, including the opportunity to be astronauts.　(ABS)

Dashu, Max (1950 –) (also known as Max Hammond) An independent scholar, Dashu founded the Suppressed Histories Archives, a global women's history project, in 1970. She built an archive of some 14,000 slides. In 1973, Dashu began teaching women's history in feminist bookstores, coffeehouses and women's centers. From 1980 forward, she has presented hundreds of slide talks at universities, community centers, and other venues around the U.S., as well as Canada and Mexico. In 2000, Dashu created the Suppressed Histories Web site, which includes excerpts from an unpublished sourcebook, *The Secret History of the Witches*. In addition to this historical work, Dashu helped form the first women's center in Cambridge, as well as pagan women's circles (1971–1972). On the West Coast, Dashu worked on the Inez Garcia defense committee (1976) and the Household Worker's Rights organization (early 1980s). A founding mother of the pagan goddess resurgence, she is author of *Witch Dream Comix* (1975). She also acted as historical consultant for the San Francisco Women's Building mural (1994). As an artist, Dashu created covers for feminist magazines, and feminist logos and posters.　(ABS)

Dater, Elizabeth B. (1945 –) A successful investment-management entrepreneur, Dater joined the women's movement in 1969, attending the First Congress to Unite Women and working with the legislative and political committee of NY NOW. In 1969, she co-coordinated the NY NOW bus trip to Washington to lobby every member of the Senate Judiciary Committee for the ERA. This was the first event of the second wave to lobby for and publicize the ERA. She coordinated and participated in many rallies and demonstrations for the ERA in NY. In May 1970, she helped lead a demonstration protesting opposition to the ERA by House Judiciary Committee chair Emanuel Cellar. With Ann Wallace, Dater coordinated NY NOW's public introduction of CR. She and Wallace also gave talks around NY to community groups. Dater was one of the NY NOW members who resigned in 1971 to protest what they considered to be an unfair election of officers and the resulting management of the organization. A security analyst and portfolio manager, Dater joined ForstmannLeff Associates in 2004 and is (2006) chief investment officer for the Growth Equity Group. Dater is the recipient of the Merit Award of Women's Bond Club of New York. She was an early member of the Financial Women's Association and of Women In Need, an organization that provides shelter and counseling to homeless women and children. Dater was also a founder, with Maria Rolfe and Dr. Amy Augustus, of the Women's Economic Roundtable. (ABS)

Dauphinee, JoAnne (1950 –) joined Maine NOW in the 1970s. She served in numerous capacities over the years, including state coordinator. She helped found many NOW chapters, including Farmington, Washington County, Bar Harbor, Brunswick and Bangor. She co-founded ME NOW PAC, and has been treasurer since 1978. Also in 1978, she was a founder of the Coalition to End Medicaid Discrimination, was an organizer and analyst from 1977–1982; and was a founding member of the Maine Women's Lobby. She served on the first and several boards, and committed the Lobby to economic justice issues for poor women. She also co-founded and served on Maine's Alliance to Preserve Reproductive Choice (1982), and several other pro-choice groups, including Communities United for Reproductive Safety. A member of the Maine Coalition for Human Rights (1976), she attended the founding meetings and worked on the first and subsequent lesbian and gay rights bills in the ME Legislature. In 1985, she was a co-founding member of the Maine Lesbian Gay Political Alliance and the Bangor Area Gay Lesbian Straight Coalition, formed after the murder of Charlie Howard (July 7, 1984). She has also worked on some of ME's annual symposiums for LGBT people and was a 2003 volunteer with the Maine Coalition for Equal Rights, working toward referendum confirmation of ME's LGBT rights bill. Dauphinee has served as a delegate to the Democratic State Conventions for several decades. She has lobbied for homemakers' rights, women's rights, the rights of raped and battered women, lesbian and gay rights, women's reproductive rights, childcare, affordable housing and healthcare. She has also been active in civil rights issues, and was a founding member of the AFL-CIO's Women's Caucus of Maine. A playwright of feminist satire as well as serious issues, Dauphinee is the author of "The Lazy Slut Welfare Queen and Her Middle-Aged, Laid-Off Slug Mother" and "The Promise Kreepers." She received the Mable Sine Wadsworth Women's Health Achievement Award and the Maine Progressive's Women's Award. (ABS)

Davidoff, Ida F. (1905 – 2001) In her fifties and faced with an "empty nest," Davidoff was unwilling to extend the role of traditional wife and mother to traditional grandmother. Accepted into a new program on marriage counseling at the University of Pennsylvania, Davidoff, by age 58, had received a doctorate in education from Columbia University; had become an associate professor of psychiatry and psychology at Albert Einstein University; and had opened her own practice in family counseling. Particularly interested in women's issues, she founded A Woman's Place to help train and support women in transition. From her study and her practice, Davidoff threw her support to activist feminists who were fighting gender discrimination in the workplace, in children's socialization and in politics. She came to national prominence when, in her eighties, she was interviewed by Betty Friedan for her book, *The Fountain of Age*, in which Davidoff was quoted as saying, "The older you get, the more you get to be like yourself." A resident of New Canaan, CT, Davidoff was still seeing clients for marriage counseling and was working on a book at 96.

Davidson, Patricia (1931 –) As a board member of Planned Parenthood in 1969, Davidson was invited to speak at her Unitarian Church about abortion and the law in Texas. Shortly thereafter, the church's Women's Alliance formed a committee to study abortion; raised $200 to print and mail pamphlets; drove to Ft. Worth to ask for assistance from a young attorney, Sara Weddington; talked to legislators; and in January 1970 filed an amicus curiae brief in support of Roe v. Wade. "We had, of course, no idea that the case would go down in history. It was simply a moment to stand up and be counted." In 1978, Davidson helped found the Family Place, Dallas' first shelter for victims of family abuse. As of 2003, the Family Place had sheltered more than 11,000 women. Archives: Roe v. Wade papers (given by Ginny Whitehill) are at Southern Methodist University, Dallas, TX; other papers at Every Woman's Story Project, Phoenix, AZ. (ABS)

Davidson, Sara (1943 –) was often the first or only woman in the newsrooms where she worked. She wrote the first piece on women's liberation published in a major national magazine, "An Oppressed Majority Demands its Rights," which she began working on in 1969. The article appeared in *Life*. Says Davidson, "I was attacked by women's lib groups in Boston and New York for working for the 'bourgeois capitalist press.' But *Life* had a circulation of eight million, and the piece had a huge effect, introducing feminism to the mass culture." For a 1973 issue of *Esquire* she wrote "Foremothers," portraits of four early pioneers—Ti-Grace Atkinson, Marilyn Webb, Kate Millett and Susan Brownmiller—and "an assessment of the first CR groups and the terrible bloodletting and fighting among women that shocked all of us," she says. Her 1977 novel, *Loose Change*, about three women growing up in the 1960s, chronicled the start of the women's movement and the sexual revolution, and became an international best seller. She is also author of

Real Property (1980), *Friends of the Opposite Sex* (1984), *Rock Hudson, His Story* (1987) and *Cowboy* (1999). She created two drama series for ABC-TV, "Jack and Mike" and "Heart Beat." The latter was the first ensemble of women on television who had no male superior over them, and featured the first lesbian TV character. Davidson became co-executive producer of "Dr. Quinn, Medicine Woman" and in 1994 was nominated for a Golden Globe. Davidson is (2006) writing a book about how the baby boomers will handle the next part of life. Davidson's work has appeared in numerous publications, including *Harpers, Esquire, The Atlantic, The New York Times* and *Rolling Stone.* Davidson, who grew up in CA, attended the University of California, Berkeley, and the Columbia Graduate School of Journalism. (ABS)

Davies, Diana (1938 –) A musician, theater worker and photographer, Davies became a photojournalist in the 1960s. One of the key photographers who documented the second wave women's movement in several U.S. cities, she also photographed in Africa, The Middle East and Europe. She "uncovered" the civil rights and peace movements, the poor people's and Welfare rights movements, and the farm workers' struggles, and worked with many organizations concerned with social and economic justice. Her work has been published in many books, journals, newspapers and magazines. Davies stopped doing photography (except for photos of friends) in the 1990s in order to work as a graphic artist, painter and illustrator. Having continued throughout her life to participate in and support all aspects of people's theater, she has now written four plays with social justice themes, three of which have been performed to favorable response. She lives in Northampton, MA, where she does artwork, works for social change, and helps feed and clothe the needy. Archives: The Sophia Smith Collection, Smith College, Northampton, MA. (ABS).

Davies, Dorothy ("Dody") Cecilia (1931 –) In the early 1970s, Davies formed and coordinated a coalition panel of AAUW, LWV and NOW members in Willmar, MN, that gave educational presentations in support of the ERA. At the same time, Davies began speaking on the interrelationship of feminism and spirituality, which led to her writing and performing poetry/song lyrics of feminist music written from the secular and Christian feminist perspective. In 1990, her collection *WomanVoice: A Collection of Lyric Poetry,* was published by Songs of Womanspirit. Davies has supported and picketed with the Willmar Eight, a group of women who charged a local bank (Citizens National Bank) with sex discrimination and unfair labor practices, formed their own union (1977) and went on strike. In 1975, Davies wrote a paper identifying and analyzing how institutional religions affect thinking about the ERA. A life-long musician, Davies has two children and earned her B.A. (1953) from the College of St. Catherine, St. Paul. (ABS)

Davies, Rosalie Grace (1939 –) After losing custody of her two children because she was a political lesbian, Davies founded Calm Inc. (Custody Action for Lesbian Mothers) in Narbarth, PA (1974). A litigation support service that lasted 25 years, the group was made up of volunteer lawyers who represented women who had lost or were threatened with the loss of custody of their children. In order to personally provide litigation support to these women, Davies entered Temple University Law School, graduating in 1979 with a J.D. She also holds a B.A. from the University of Pennsylvania (1972). Born in London, England, Davies was also active in the civil rights and anti-war movements. Archives: Center for Lesbian and Gay Rights, Philadelphia, PA. (ABS)

Davis, Barbara – See Hillyer, Barbara

Davis, Caroline Dawson (1911 – 1988) was one of the founders of NOW in 1966 and its first secretary/treasurer (1966 – 1967). She directed the United Auto Workers Women's Department from 1948 – 1973. Davis grew up in a poor Kentucky mining family steeped in religion and unionism. In 1934 she got a job as a drill press operator with Excel Corporation, an automobile parts factory. Inspired by her father, Stephen Dawson, who worked to better conditions for KY coal miners, Davis helped unionize the plant in 1941 and was on the negotiating committee for eight years, serving as chair for five years. She became VP two years after the formation of the local and was the first woman president of a UAW-CIO local; the shop represented by the local was 90 percent male. In 1948, she accepted an appointment by Walter Reuther, president of the UAW International Union, to direct its Women's Department, helping approximately 200,000 women union members obtain equal pay, maternity leaves, better health and safety conditions, training and promotional opportunities. Title VII of the Civil Rights Act of 1964, which prohibited employment discrimination based on sex, caused a split among feminists with regard to the legality of state protective legislation. Davis sided with NOW and organizations that represented business and professional women in arguing that legislation that limited women's employment was superseded by Title VII. This position ultimately prevailed. Davis was an excellent negotiator. (There were no strikes, slowdowns or lockouts during her administration.)

Davis, Elizabeth Gould (1910 – 1974) A librarian, Davis was the author of *The First Sex* (1971), an influential and controversial work that described a prehistory governed by women who were physically, mentally and morally superior to men. This rebuttal of the prevailing myth of feminine inferiority energized numerous feminists. Davis was also the author of *The Female Principle* and *The Founding Mothers.* She died of a self-inflicted gunshot wound in 1974. Contemporary news reports of her death noted that she had been ill, but some say she killed herself because of many book reviews attacking her and her work documenting a matriarchal prehistory.

Davis, Madeline D. (1940 –) was a founder of the Mattachine Society of Niagara Frontier (Buffalo, NY) and Lesbians Uniting. A playwright, singer and historian, Davis was also directly involved in getting the 1972 George McGovern presidential campaign to include a gay liberation plank. With Elizabeth Kennedy and others, Davis helped found the Buffalo Lesbian Community Oral History Project (1978), considered one of the most comprehensive histories of a lesbian community ever undertaken. Davis is co-author (with Kennedy) of *Boots of Leather, Slippers of Gold: The History of a Lesbian Community* (Penguin Books, 1994). She retired as chief conservator and head of preservation for the Buffalo and Erie County Public Library System in the late 1990s.

Davis, Patricia Wood (1935 –) A graduate student at the University of Michigan in the early 1970s, Davis helped organize a CR group. She also wrote and produced a play to raise awareness of women as an oppressed group, and presented it several times in Ann Arbor, MI. Later, in the early 1980s, it was presented at a Unitarian Church in New Orleans. A member of NOW in New Orleans, Davis belonged to a group called Feminist Counselors—lawyers, psychologists and social workers who spoke to university classes and used its letterhead stationery to press legislators and the media on issues important to women. Davis also went to Chicago with other feminists from LA to lobby for passage of the ERA, and made presentations on women's issues at various universities. In the 1990s, Davis became active in the push to prevent domestic violence, and as director of medical social work for the Louisiana Health Department (1991 – 2001) was able to take a leadership role in improving healthcare service to women. Davis, who has three children, holds a B.A. from Women's College of the University of North Carolina; an M.A. from Eastern Michigan University; an M.S.W. from the University of Michigan; a Ph.D. from Tulane University; and an M.P.H. from Tulane University School of Public Health and Tropical Medicine. (ABS)

Davis, Susan E. (1941 –) was a core member of CWLU and NOW in the 1960s, and in 1969 launched *The Spokeswoman*, the first national publication of the women's movement. At the same time, she helped start the Sojourner Truth Child Care Center in Hyde Park, NY, one of the first non-racist and non-sexist childcare centers in the country. In 1970, Davis began work on a national women's newsmagazine, *WomanNews*. She invited eight of Chicago's top women in various fields to help, but at that time venture capitalists did not fund women's deals. They eventually gave the concept to the *Chicago Tribune* to get important news out to serve women. In 1976 the eight women regrouped to create The Chicago Network, one of only two groups in the country then to network

top women within a city. Davis later created Chicago Finance Exchange, which networked the top women in finance in Chicago, and in 1989 created Committee of 200, a national networking group for women business owners. In 1994, she became founding organizer of Capital Circle, the first network of women investors created to invest in women-led companies. Active in civil rights, she helped launch Boston's second black newspaper, *The Bay State Banner* (1965), and launched the first national publication on minority enterprise, *Urban Enterprise*, for the Urban Research Corporation in Chicago (1968). Davis holds a B.A. from Brown University and did graduate work in anthropology at the Harvard Graduate School of Education. She has two children. (ABS)

Daw, Leila (1940 –) Inspired by a CR group in Woods Hole, MA (1970), Daw returned to school and earned an M.F.A. from Washington University, St. Louis, MO. With several other women, she founded the Community of Women Artists (CWA), which later became a chapter of the Women's Caucus for Art. After achieving a tenure-track faculty position at Southern Illinois University, she worked with art historian Pamela Decoteau to create a program for women. In 1980, the Women in Art program funded a series that brought in prominent women artists. Daw has also taught weekend workshops at the New York Feminist Art Institute (later NYFAI/Women's Center for Learning). She was a professor in the Studio for Interrelated Media at Massachusetts College of Art in Boston, 1990 – 2002. In 2004 she completed an installation for the 375-foot long ticketing hall at Bradley (CT) International Airport. In addition to her M.F.A., Daw earned an A.B. from Wellesley College. She has two children. (ABS)

Day, Clara (1923 –) A champion of and advocate for domestic workers, Day was a member of the Illinois Governor's Commission on the Status of Women. She was also a founder and former VP of CLUW, delegate to the National Women's Conference in Houston (1977), and business representative, trustee and director of community services for the International Brotherhood of Teamsters Local 743. In addition, Day was a member of the Chicago Commission of Human Relations. She worked tirelessly to improve women's working conditions and to make childcare available to them, and traveled extensively in both the U.S. and abroad to achieve these goals. (ABS)

De Baptiste, Barbara W. (1936 –) An educator and mentor to countless Connecticut women, De Baptiste has been an advocate for women and children. In the 1960s, she piloted the Head Start program in Waterbury, CT, helping to establish it as an independent agency. She also served as president of the Child Care Centers of Waterbury (CT), creating jobs and opportunities for women and their families. She chaired the career development committee for the Community Action Program in Waterbury and provided training for the Head Start staff.

Under her leadership, the chapter of Western CT Association for the education of young children, which sponsored educational programs for women, was established. During the 1970s, De Baptiste served on the boards of Connecticut Trails Council of Girl Scouts, the Hartford YWCA and Waterbury Youth Services. She was a founder of the Waterbury BPW chapter and district director in the Connecticut Federation of BPW organizations. De Baptiste also chaired community advisory boards for local and statewide television stations and promoted programming to raise awareness of women's issues.   (ABS)

de Bretteville, Sheila Levrant (1940 –) started the first women's design program at Cal Arts in 1971. She later left Cal Arts to start (with Arlene Raven and Judy Chicago) the Woman's Building, a public center for women's culture in Los Angeles. In 1974, she joined with Arlene Raven, Susan Rennie and Kirsten Grimstad to start *Chrysalis*, a journal of feminist studies. For 16 years, she organized exhibitions and taught at the Woman's Building and its Women's Graphic Center. In 1980, her attention shifted from print graphics to public art about people and places generally left out. This led to her creation of an 82-foot long concrete stone and steel mural honoring Biddy Mason (1818 – 1891), an African American midwife, businesswoman and entrepreneur who was one of the first African American women to own property in CA. In 1989, Naomi Schor and Elizabeth Weed started *differences*, a journal of feminist cultural studies, and asked de Bretteville to consult, design and format it, which she did. In 1990, de Bretteville moved to New Haven, CT, to become the first tenured woman on the faculty of the School of Art, Yale University. In addition, she is a member of the collective Not In Our Name/Artists Against the War. de Bretteville, who has one child, holds degrees from Barnard College and Yale University, and has been awarded Honorary Doctorates from the Moore College of Art and California College of Arts and Crafts.   (ABS)

de Helen, Sandra (1944 –) (also known as McCorkle Alexander and Sandra McCorkle Gale) In 1971, de Helen was a member of the Ad Hoc Young Democrats Committee in Anchorage, AK. By going door-to-door, she persuaded many young people to attend the open meeting to elect the precinct chair. "Imagine the surprise on the old party members' faces when all the young upstarts arrived and I easily won the precinct chair. The Ad Hoc Committee had a profound effect on Alaska's state politics that year and the next." In 1973, de Helen entered the University of Missouri at Rolla, one of 500 women among 5,000 men, and was one of only three women economics majors. She was also the first woman to write for the university newspaper in its 105-year history. After one of her biweekly columns made derogatory comments about the male engineers, de Helen received death threats. In Kansas City, MO, in 1976, she taught a free community class in feminist theater where she met Kate Kasten. In

1977, the two founded Actors Sorority and began writing plays. In 1981, de Helen founded Portland (OR) Women's Theatre Company. Active in the anti-Vietnam War movement, de Helen—who is part Cherokee—also worked for the American Indian Movement. She has two children and earned her B.S. from Western Illinois University. Archives: The Lesbian Herstory Archives, Brooklyn, NY, and the ICWP Archives, The Lawrence and Lee Theatre Research Institute, Ohio State University, Columbus, OH.   (ABS)

de Long, Jane – See Mansbridge, Jane

de Pick, Gracia Molina – See Molina de Pick, Gracia

De Saram, Carole (1939 –) started the national movement to end credit discrimination against women (1972 – 1976). She closed a CitiBank branch by joining with many other women to cancel savings accounts previously opened to demonstrate the bank's discriminatory policies. She created the slogan "Give Women Credit Where Credit Is Due." In 1975 she conceived the idea for a Women's Bank and worked with a group of women to form the Feminist Credit Union. After De Saram testified before a Banking Commission hearing using national data compiled from women relating credit discrimination, legislation was passed to end discrimination. De Saram joined NOW in 1970, chaired several committees locally and nationally, became president of the New York City chapter in 1974, and served on the national board. In 1974, she called for a hearing against the New York State Human Rights Commission for not giving unemployment benefits to pregnant women who were fired, with the result that the practice was eliminated. In 1976, she disrupted the U.S./Mexico City Embassy's presentation of U.S. Women Representatives to demonstrate that the conference represented the male mentality on women's issues. De Saram is also known for creative and effective "zap" actions between 1970 and 1972. With the banner "Women Power," she closed down the American Stock Exchange, and, with others, she hung a feminist banner on the Statue of Liberty (1972). De Saram, who has two children, holds a B.A. from Columbia University. Archives: The Sophia Smith Collection, Smith College, Northampton, MA.   (ABS)

de Varona, Donna (1947 –) A swimmer, TV sports commentator and women's sports advocate, de Varona worked tirelessly for Title IX, the 1972 Equal Education Act Amendment that mandated that girls and women attending schools receive the same opportunities and funds that boys and men do. In 1974, de Varona and Billie Jean King established the Women's Sports Foundation, with de Varona the first president; de Varona also served as chair of the 1999 Women's World Cup, an important event in women's soccer. As a child, de Varona's first love was baseball, but barred from playing in Little League because of her sex, she turned to swimming. She set 18 world records, won two Olympic Gold Medals in the Tokyo Olympic Games, and was voted Most Outstanding Female Athlete by Associated Press and UPI. However, long before she reached her prime, de Varona retired to attend college. While her male teammates attended America's best universities on sports scholarships, women of de Varona's era were offered no such opportunities. During her college years at UCLA, she worked with ABC Television Sports. In her broadcasting career, which earned her an Emmy, de Varona helped introduce new programming, including "The Lady is a Champ," the first television special devoted entirely to women's sports. She also served on the President's Council on Physical Fitness, was appointed to President Ford's Commission on Olympic Sports, served on President Carter's Women's Advisory Commission, and was a consultant to the U.S. Senate. De Varona, who has two children, was inducted into the Women's Hall of Fame in Seneca Falls, holds numerous honorary doctorates, and was twice presented with the Gracie Award (2000 and 2001) by American Women in Radio and Television for outstanding radio commentaries that profile women and women's issues in sports. (ABS)

Dean, Nancy (1930 –) A playwright, Dean taught at Hunter College for 28 years, where her field of specialization was Chaucer and Medieval Studies; she also taught Women Centered Literature and women's studies courses. She served as head of the English department and acting coordinator of the women's studies program. Dean co-edited, with Myra Stark, an anthology of contemporary feminist short stories by women, *In the Looking Glass* (Putnam, 1977). Learning that women received less than 1 percent of foundation grants, Dean founded Astraea (1977), a lesbian foundation for all women. Dean has written articles on Chaucer. Her books include *In the Mind of the Writer* (Canfield Press) and a novel, *Anna's Country*, under the pseudonym Elizabeth Lang (Naiad Press, 1981). Her plays include "Larks and Owls," "Returning Home," "Hetty Pepper's Stew," "Blood and Water," "Ophelia's Laughter," "Wrath and Avocados," "Gloria's Visit," and "Which Marriage?" as well as "Murder at the Regatta," "Upstairs in the Afternoon?," "Resort," "That Ilk," and a translation and switch in genders for Moliere's "Misanthrope." "Upstairs?" was produced at Playquest Theatre Off-Off Broadway in 1995 and "That Ilk" at the Hudson Guild Theatre Off-Broadway in 2000. She was playwright in residence for The Actors Alliance for three years (1999 – 2002). She is a member of the Dramatists Guild and Washington Square Playwrights. In 1985, she and Beva Eastman, her partner, founded Open Meadows, a private foundation that funds projects nationally and internationally for women and girls. In 1995, Sisters on Stage honored Dean with an award for playwriting and support for other lesbian playwrights. The award, named after her, will be given annually. Dean and M.G. Soares co-edited *Intimate Acts: Eight Contemporary*

Lesbian Plays (Brito and Lair, 1997). Dean holds a B.A. from Vassar (1952), a master's from Harvard (1953), and a Ph.D. from New York University (1963). Archives: Vassar College, Poughkeepsie, NY. (ABS)

deCaro, Rosan Jordan – See Jordan, Rosan Augusta

DeCrow, Karen (1937 –) A writer and an attorney specializing in Constitutional law, gender and age discrimination, and civil liberties, DeCrow helped found NOW and convened the first NOW chapter in Syracuse, NY, where she served as president in 1967. She was a member of NOW's national board from 1968 – 1974, and from 1974 – 1977 was NOW's national president—the last to serve without a salary. Under DeCrow's leadership, NOW persuaded NASA to recruit women; challenged and changed the Public Accommodation law, persuaded the EEOC to investigate sex discrimination complaints as opposed to race only; and pressured the three major networks to include women and minorities in front of and behind the cameras. Also under her leadership, NOW fought to integrate the Jaycees and similar clubs that had business implications; counseled traditional women's magazines to show a more balanced view of women and their lives; pressured the all-male Ivy League schools to admit women; worked with the Armed Services academies to integrate women into their classes; and brought a lawsuit in NY State to integrate the Little League. Campaigning for passage of the ERA, DeCrow traveled the country and debated Phyllis Schlafly more than 50 times. A supporter of the right to choose, DeCrow spent much of her personal time serving as an escort for women from all over the world who had traveled to NY for legal abortions. (NY State had passed legislation to legalize abortion in 1972, the year before Roe v. Wade.) In 1988, she was co-founder (with Robert Seidenberg) of World Woman Watch. She was also a founder of the Central New York Chapter of the New York Women's Bar Association, serving as its president from 1989 – 1990. DeCrow is the author of *The Young Woman's Guide to Liberation* (Bobbs-Merrill, 1971); *Sexist Justice* (Random House, 1974); and *Women Who Marry Houses: Panic and Protest in Agoraphobia* (with Robert Seidenberg, M.D., McGraw-Hill, 1983). DeCrow has a B.S. from the Medill School of Journalism, Northwestern University (1959) and a J.D. from the College of Law, Syracuse University (1972). (ABS)

Deevey, Sharon (1944 –) (also known as Sharon Deevey Wolfson) In 1969, Deevey co-rented office space for Washington, D.C., Women's Liberation and taught courses at the Institute for Policy Studies, including Watch Out Girlie, Women's Liberation Is Going to Get Your Momma. She was a member of Those Women (1970); a contributor to *The Furies* (1971); and a member of Cassandra Radical Feminist Nurses Network in Cleveland (1983) and Columbus (1985). She has published several articles about lesbian health in nursing journals, and has done research on lesbian aging and bereavement. She has also been involved in minority rights, the rights of older women and gay rights. She became an HIV activist in 1981. Archives: The Lesbian Herstory Archives, Brooklyn, NY. Her lesbian health library is at the Lesbian Health Research Center, San Francisco, CA. (ABS)

DeFalco, Barbara – See Anthony, Barbara

DeFazio, Marjorie DeBol (1933 –) was one of the principal organizers of the 1970 Strike for Equality event. She helped organize two subsequent marches and served as master of ceremonies for two events associated with them. She was a member of the UN Speakers Bureau during the United Nations Year of the Woman. DeFazio was a founder and first elected CEO of the Women's Interart Center, and with Jane Chambers founded the Women's Interart Theater. A poet, playwright and director, DeFazio compiled and edited, with Anne Brady, *Raising Our Voices, Women Up Through the Ages*, poetry about women by women. With Patricia Horan, DeFazio wrote, directed and acted in "What Time of Night It Is ..." the story of the 19th and 20th century feminist movement performed at NOW's national conference in 1973. In 1976, she wrote (with Patricia Horan) and directed "Revolution to Revolution, the undercover story," a history of women's progress in the U.S. as seen through their undergarments, presented at the Hotel Pierre (NYC), with Colleen Dewhurst as narrator. DeFazio, who has two children, holds B.A. (1958) and an M.A. from Hunter College(1987.) (ABS)

Degler, Carl N. (1921 –) A history professor, Degler published his first article on women's history in 1956. At Vassar College in the mid 1960s, Degler edited a book published in 1899 by Charlotte Perkins Gilman, *Women and Economics*, and released it in a new edition in 1966. When Betty Friedan heard about the book, she invited Degler to become a founding member and director of NOW. He was later honored by the VFA at the Seventh Avenue Armory (NYC) in 1998. At Vassar College from 1952–1968, Degler is the author of numerous books and scholarly articles. His books about the history of women, mostly written when he was a history professor at Stanford University (1972–1990), include *Is There a History of Women?* (Oxford University Press, 1975) and *At Odds: Women and the Family in America from the Revolution to the Present* (Oxford, 1980). His book *Neither Black Nor White* (New York, 1971) won the Pulitzer Prize in History in 1972. Degler was on the editorial board of *Signs: Women in Culture and Society* (1974–1984). He earned his B.A. from Upsala College (1942); served in the U.S. Army Air Force (1942–1945); and earned an M.A. (1947) and Ph.D. (1952) from Columbia University. (ABS)

Deihl, Marcia Jeanne (1949 –) A member of Bread and Roses (1970–1971), Deihl taught a course on feminism and the media at Boston's alternative Communiversity

(summer 1970), and did street theater for the ERA in 1973. A musician, she was a member of the New Harmony Sisterhood Band, worked on the songbook *All Our Lives* with Deborah Silverstein and Joyce Cheney (1976), and played with the band for the album Ain't I a Woman (Paredon Records, 1979). Deihl was music editor of *Sojourner* (1985 – 1986). She was a member of the Women's Heritage Commission (1990s), and was part of the Cambridge LGBT Working Group for a City Liaison (2004). She also helped found the Boston Bisexual Women's Network (1983) and the Cambridge Lavender Alliance (1990). Archives: Schlesinger Library, Radcliffe Institute, Cambridge, MA. (ABS)

DeJong, Cheryl R. – See Register, Cheri L.

Del Drago, Maria (1926 – 1978) A pioneer in organizing Latina women, Del Drago was head of continuing education at the University of California, Berkeley. She worked to pass the first all-university-wide wheelchair accessibility ordinance for the University of California system, and served in NOW. Born in Italy to an Italian count (her father) and an opera singer, she was raised in Italy and Brazil. Del Drago, who had two children, took her life in June 1978. She was the subject of *Sita*, by Kate Millett (Random House, 1977), which was described as "a wrenching and intimate autobiography of Millett's passionate and obsessive relationship." A second book, *Elegy to Sita* (1979), was designed by Millett and published in a private edition of 350 copies signed by the author.

DellaVedova, Deanna (1948 –) An activist for 31 years, DellaVedova is president of the Westmoreland (PA) chapter of NOW, VP of Squire Hill NOW, and on the board of NARAL Pro-Choice Pennsylvania. She also served as president of the Westmoreland chapter in 1975 and 1976. She has marched in ERA rallies in Pennsylvania, Washington, D.C., and Chicago; picketed the IRS on April 15 on several occasions; and marched in D.C. in the Gay Pride parade and with the sister of Nicole Brown Simpson to protest violence against women. She also marched in D.C. against the Papal Embassy "to keep the Pope out of my bedroom." A member of Emily's List, she has been active in many political campaigns to elect women to public office. DellaVedova has also been involved in the peace movement; her son served in the Middle East. (ABS)

Dell'Olio, Anselma (1940 –) came to New York City from Rome, Italy, in 1966 and met Ti-Grace Atkinson through an ad for a roommate placed in *The New York Times*. Atkinson subsequently invited Dell'Olio to the founding meeting of NYC NOW. "Feminism allowed me to make the leap from rumbling volcano, always threatening to explode, to rebel with a cause," says Dell'Olio. With a father who was anti-Fascist when the Italian-American community was pro-Mussolini, Dell'Olio says she was destined for the Left. In NYC, she joined and started CR groups, and founded the New Feminist Repertory Theater, which launched with a play by Myrna Lamb, whose work was later produced by Joseph Papp. Dell'Olio became disillusioned with feminism when she was attacked as being a leader at a time when leaderlessness was politically correct. She addressed this issue in an important paper titled "Divisiveness and Self-Destruction in the Women's Movement" (which she delivered at the Second Congress to Unite Women in NYC in 1970). She moved back to Rome to work on a film by Marco Ferreri and decided to stay. In 1987 she unexpectedly married an Italian political print and television journalist, and together they anchored a prime time television show called "Lezioni d'amore." Since her return to Italy she has contributed essays to various U.S. feminist anthologies. Dell'Olio is no longer in or on the Left. She says she is "bemused and disappointed by the fossilization of feminism and its acritical, rabidly anti-intellectual leftism." Although her views on abortion remain the same, she "regrets that feminism has always 'forgotten' to put the 'choice' into 'pro-choice,' and continues to demonize those who feel differently." Dell'Olio has continued to fight for women through an association she co-founded in 2000, Branco Rosa, to encourage women to honor their ambitions, support other women in theirs, and seek high office whether elective or appointed. Dell'Olio contributed an essay to *The Feminist Memoir Project*, and wrote and sold a screenplay based on the life of Frances Xavier Cabrini, to be directed by Liv Ullman. An essay by Dell'Olio is the preface to a book by Noa Bonetti, *Io, Donna Kamikaze,* which examines the lives of the 42 known female suicide assassins. Educated in the U.S. and Europe, she took a degree in translating and interpreting from L'Ecole Internationale des Hautes Etudes d'Interpretariat, Switzerland.   (ABS)

Deming, Barbara (1917 – 1984) An influential theorist of nonviolence, Deming developed an argument for nonviolence free of any religious framework, thus making it easier for non-religious people to accept. There was a feminist facet to her theory as well; nonviolence, she noted, combines masculine self-assertion with feminine sympathy for people. Active in the civil rights and peace movements of the 1950s and 1960s, Deming demonstrated with black protesters in the South, joined the San Francisco to Moscow walk for peace, and traveled to both North and South Vietnam. Following an automobile accident in 1971 that left her in ill-health for the rest of her life, Deming turned to letter-writing as a form of activism and became an articulate voice in the second wave of feminism. She also came out in 1973 and worked to bring her ideas of nonviolence into the developing movement for gay and lesbian rights. In 1983, Deming was one of 54 women arrested at the Seneca Women's Peace Encampment in Upstate New York. Although the crowd was hostile, even threatening, the women protesters remained nonviolent. In 1984, New Society Publishers released the book *We Are All Part of One Another: A Barbara Deming*

Reader, edited by Jane Meyerding. Deming began a career as a film analyst for the Library of Congress. She later became a professional writer. Her best known essay, "On Revolution and Equilibrium," was published in the *Journal Liberation* in 1968. Deming earned her B.A. from Bennington College (1938) and her M.A. from Case Western Reserve University.

Demsky, Hilda Green (1936 –) An artist whose works have been exhibited worldwide, Demsky initially found her entry into the art world blocked. "After experiencing continued rejection in juried art shows," she says, "I began to submit my work using my husband's name—and proclaimed sexist practices at the openings." As an art teacher in NYC schools (1958 – 1971) and at White Plains (NY) HS (1972 – 1993), she practiced non-sexist teaching and promoted women artists in the classroom—an approach that culminated in the Christa McAuliffe Award from the U.S. Dept. of Education for students to study contemporary women artists. A representative on the board of the New York State Art Teachers Association (beginning in 1974), she worked to bring women educators to the forefront of art history and education, and lobbied to have women artists become the keynote speakers at state conferences. Demsky worked in Bella Abzug's successful run for the House of Representatives. Active in Westchester NOW Art Branch, she received the Art Award for Women's International Year from the Mamaroneck, NY, Women's Club (1975). She demonstrated at the Museum of Modern Art to protest sexism in artists whose work was exhibited there, and in 1978 participated in the ERA rally in Washington. As Democratic District Leader in Westchester for 27 years (in the 18th CD), she worked to support women for elected office. Demsky also used art to make statements on the environment, and received a Proclamation from the Westchester County Board for calling attention to pollution of the marine environment. (ABS)

Denham, Alice (1933 –) Author, adjunct professor of English at the City University of New York, and model, Denham says, "I'm the only *(Playboy)* Playmate to have a short story published in the same issue and made into a festival prize-winning movie." As an original NOW member, she helped stage the *Ladies' Home Journal* takeover in March 1970, and presented Media Women demands on ABC-TV. She says she "admitted to an illegal abortion in a full-page ad in *The New York Times* and the *Washington Post*, and was one of the first four feminists to be interviewed on national TV" (CBS, the Walter Cronkite Show, 1970). As a teacher of writing at John Jay College (NY), she represented the college in a landmark 1975 EEOC discrimination suit that won $3,500,000 for the City University of New York women faculty. The author of numerous novels, articles, television and movie adaptations, and short stories, she has published two feminist novels: *My Darling from the Lions* (Bobbs-Merrill, 1968) and *AMO* (Putnam, 1974). She holds a B.A. from the

University of North Carolina (1949) and an M.A. from the University of Rochester (1950). Archives: Library of the University of North Carolina, Chapel Hill.   (ABS)

Denmark, Florence L. (1931 –) A pioneer in the psychology of women, Denmark conducted research that emphasized women's leadership and leadership styles, the interaction of status and gender, women in cross-cultural perspective, women and aging, and the contributions of women to psychology. She taught the first doctoral course in the U.S. on the psychology of women (1970), and was one of the founders and foremothers of the Association for Women in Psychology. She was also one of the organizers and third president of the Division of the Psychology of Women of the American Psychological Association. Denmark served on the APA Council of Representatives and board of directors (1975 – 1977), and became president in 1980. She was co-chair of the first national Ford- and NIMH-funded research conference on the psychology of women (1975), and was a member of the editorial boards of *Psychology of Women Quarterly* (1975 – 1977) and *Sex Roles* (1976). The author and editor of various books and many research articles on the psychology of women, she was Distinguished Lecturer at Hebrew University in Jerusalem (1976), and a Mellon Scholar at St. Olaf College in Minnesota (1977). During this time, she was involved in the Hunter College Women's Studies Collec-tive writing the first textbook on women's studies, *Women's Realities, Women's Choices*. She received her B.A. and Ph.D. from the University of Pennsylvania, and was the first woman in that school's history to graduate with two majors—in both psychology and history. In 2004 she received the American Psychological Association's Gold Medal for Lifetime Achievement in Psychology in the Public Interest.   (ABS)

Denning, Bernadine Newsom (1930 –) has a distinguished career as an educator, civil rights leader and advocate for women. She began as a physical education teacher in 1951 with the Detroit Public Schools, served as Title IV civil rights director and retired as assistant superintendent for community relations. She then became director of the human rights department, City of Detroit. President Jimmy Carter appointed Denning as director of the Office of Revenue Sharing, Department of the Treasury. An active member of numerous women's organizations, Denning started out at age 16 teaching swimming at the "Black" Lucy Thurman YWCA. She rose to the level of national VP and honorary life member of the national board. She was a member of the Michigan Women's Commission from 1975 – 1977, served as vice chair (1976 – 1977), and was appointed chair by governor William Milliken (1981 – 1987). Denning was inducted into the Michigan Women's Hall of Fame in 1989.   (ABS)

Densmore, Dana (1945 –) Scholar, teacher, theorist and publisher, Densmore was a systems programmer at the

Massachusetts Institute of Technology in 1968 when women's liberation was exploding. Her mother, Donna Allen, an activist in the peace and social justice movements, alerted her to the emerging feminist ferment. Densmore, Roxanne Dunbar, Betsy Warrior, Abby Rockefeller and Jayne West began formulating the politics of female liberation, including self-defense. This was the beginning of a rich collaboration that became Cell 16, a group that made a major contribution to women's movement theory. Rockefeller, West and Densmore began serious martial arts training and teaching women. "Of the female liberation groups, we in our Boston group seemed the most deeply radical of the wholeheartedly-ready-to-overturn-and-to-sacrifice-everything groups around," says Densmore. However, she adds, "It's also true that the theoretical work was our major contribution." In 1968, Densmore and Dunbar co-founded the journal *No More Fun and Games*. Densmore is widely known for her essay "On Celibacy," which was published in the first issue. In 1971, Densmore assisted West in founding an independent women's martial arts school. In 1974, Densmore and West co-founded the feminist martial art of Ja Shin Do. Densmore then moved to Washington, D.C., where she opened up a second Ja Shin Do school. She also organized the first continental conference for teachers of women's martial arts and self-defense (1975). Densmore was editor and publisher of the magazine *Black Belt Woman: The Magazine for Women in the Martial Arts and Self Defense* (six issues published 1975 through 1976), and *Continental Direc-tory of Women's Martial Arts Schools and Self Defense Classes*. She became a board member and officer of the Women's Institute for Freedom of the Press in 1972, and has served as senior editor and research director. She also developed a system of self-empowerment for women; built up a private practice of coaching and counseling for those skills; published a journal of self-empowerment theory for students and clients; and developed a system of mind-body integration called Awareness Energetics in which she led workshops around the country. In 1982, Densmore retired from her computer career and moved to New Mexico. From 1987 – 1994 she was on the faculty of St. John's College in Santa Fe; she received her M.A. there in 1993. In 1994 she left St. John's to finish a book and to found the Green Lion Press. She is co-director and chief editor of Green Lion Press, which publishes classic source texts in the history of science and mathematics. She is also on the training committee of the St. John's College Search and Rescue Team and has led nationally advertised wilderness trips for Earth Treks and the Sierra Club. In addition to her graduate degree, Densmore holds a B.A. from St. John's College in Annapolis (1965).   (ABS)

Denton, Pat (1939 –) was a member of New Orleans NOW (1973 – 1986), the LA WPC (1979 – 1983) and the NWPC. As a NOW member, Denton participated in various actions, including jury duty registration. (Women were not eligible for jury duty unless they registered.) She was also an organizer and participant in New Orleans' First Woman's Photography Exhibit: From a Woman's Darkroom (1975), which was put together because women were routinely excluded from photography exhibits. She also participated in and photographed NOW's 1976 ERA march at the State Capitol in Baton Rouge, and in 1979 spoke before the New Orleans city council on behalf of a resolution stating New Orleans' support for the ERA. The resolution passed. From 1982–1983 Denton was a YWCA rape crisis line volunteer. In 1983, as president of the LA WPC, Denton spoke against an anti-choice resolution before the New Orleans City Council. The resolution, which declared that "human life begins at conception," was defeated in a tie vote. In 1983, Denton submitted an amendment to the bylaws of the LA WPC that stated that the group was to "work against discrimination based on ageism, sexual orientation and to ensure reproductive freedom." Although her amendment failed, Denton, who was state president at the time, wrote up and submitted a proposed amendment to the Statement of Purpose in the bylaws of the NWPC that included the same wording and added that every state chapter must include national's entire Statement of Purpose in its own Statement of Purpose. That amendment passed with overwhelming support. Denton dropped her membership in the LA WPC, and at the next NWPC convention, members of the LA chapter were not allowed to be seated because they had not added the words to their state bylaws. The chapter subsequently folded. Over the years, Denton has been an active supporter of political candidates who supported women's issues. She also wrote, directed, edited and produced a video, "Feminist! Are You One?" (1983). In 1998, her photographs were shown at the Hanson Gallery in New Orleans in an exhibit titled Come Out, Come Out Wherever You Are, in honor of National Coming Out Day. She was also a founding member and board member (1980–1999) of the Louisiana Lesbian and Gay Political Action Caucus. Archives: Newcomb College Center for Research on Women, New Orleans, LA.   (ABS)

DePaola, Joanne (1945 –) In 1971, DePaola began working to pass the ERA and joined NYS NOW. She was active in the Northern Westchester chapter and served as co-president for four years (1972–1976). She helped found the Westchester Lesbian Connection (1979), originally a task force of Westchester NOW. Through the mid 1970s, she co-coordinated Westchester Consciousness Raising Clearinghouse, setting up, facilitating and trouble shooting grassroots CR groups. From 1973–1978, she ran groups for female inmates at the Westchester County Jail. DePaola began working to end domestic violence in 1980. With Susan Schechter, author of *Women and Male Violence*, DePaola began creating and implementing support groups for battered women based on the idea that "The personal is political," and that feminist analysis is essential to the anti-violence movement. She has worked to change social services, law enforcement, the judicial system, medical services and education to eliminate violence against women. Says DePaola, "The intersections of racism, sexism and homophobia and how they all must be addressed for change to happen, is the core of the issue." DePaola, a social worker who has three children, is president of the board of directors of the New York State Coalition Against Domestic Violence. She holds a B.A. from Pace University (1979) and an M.S.W. from Fordham University (1981).   (ABS)

DeRise, Mavra – See Stark, Mavra

Destiny, Diane (1938 –) (also known as Diane Manning) In 1972, Destiny says, women were "taking on their own identities" and women artists "were taking their own names—no more married names!" Diane Manning became Diane Destiny. She was a board member of Womanspace, Los Angeles; joined NOW Women in the Arts; and was a member of the Los Angeles Council of Women Artists, Women for CAL ARTS, Double X and Women Writers Workshop. She has lectured on women and art. Her art is in the permanent collection at National Museum of Women in the Arts, Washington, D.C. Destiny has an M.F.A. degree and two children.   (ABS)

Detert-Moriarty, Judith Anne (1952 –) An educator and activist involved in everything from political cartooning to teaching, and from corporate art director to knitting instructor, Detert-Moriarty joined the women's movement in 1970. Over the next 25 years, Detert-Moriarty served as founding board member, task force chair and newsletter editor on the local and state level for various feminist organizations, including NOW, Planned Parenthood, LWV and WPC in Wisconsin and Minnesota. Active in the Democratic Party, supporting women candidates since "Clean for Gene (McCarthy)" in 1968, she was not only the Mower County, MN, Democratic Party secretary (1988), but also the Wisconsin 1st Congressional District 4th Vice Chair (1998–2001), Rock Co. secretary (1988–2000), communications VP and newsletter editor (1988–). Upon the birth of her third child in 1980, she filed a sex discrimination suit against her employer, who had hired a less qualified man 16 years her junior to take her job. Detert-Moriarty settled the suit two years later in her favor. Detert-Moriarty received a B.A. from the University of Wisconsin, Green Bay, in 1991, and in 1997 was nominated for the Distinguished Alumni Award. Other nominations include the YWCA Women of Distinction Award (1996, 1997, 1998), the Rock Co. Hall of Fame (1996) and the Wisconsin Assembly of Local Arts Agencies Prized Curator of the Community (1997).   (ABS)

Dexter, Edwin (1906 – 1994) A Rear Admiral, Dexter was a supporter of NOW because, according to his business partner, feminist activist Betty Berry, "he had a great sense of fairness." Together, Dexter and Berry formed the

Marriage and Divorce Press Inc. and the "Marriage and Divorce" newsletter, the first national clearinghouse for divorce information. Especially effective as a liaison with bar associations, Dexter introduced new ideas to a subscription list of lawyers, legislators, the judiciary, mainstream legal publications and individuals.

Di Leo, Ann – See Wallace, Adriane Ann

Dickinson, Eleanor Creekmore (1931 –) An artist and professor of art, Dickinson is the author of "Gender Discrimination in the Art Field," a compilation of statistics proving gender and racial discrimination against women artists. She began collecting these statistics in 1972, and the material has been widely presented, including as testimony before the State of California Commission on the Status of Women, 1987. In 1974, Dickinson pioneered and developed business classes for college undergraduate artists. She also helped start the National Women's Caucus for Art (1971), and several of its chapters, as well as various "clandestine groups that took actions against museums and galleries that harmed artists." In 2003, she received the Lifetime Achievement Award from the Women's Caucus for Art. Dickinson, who has three children, earned a B.A. from the University of Tennessee (1952), where she was the first woman editor of the yearbook, and an M.F.A. (1982) from the California College of the Arts. Archives: Huntington Archives, Archives of American Art, San Marino, CA; and the Smithsonian Institute, Washington, D.C. (ABS)

DiCosola, Lois Ann Bock (1935 –) An established artist by the 1950s, DiCosola was one of 12 women who in 1969 began planning X-12, an exhibit of works by women artists. The Pioneer Feminist Art Exhibition took place in January 1970 in New York City, and served as a model for later feminist exhibits. DiCosola, who has one child, holds a Fine Arts degree from Prospect Heights (1953), studied for a year at the Museum of Modern Art school (1951) and earned a Bachelor of Professional Studies degree from SUNY. Archives: The Museum of Women in the Arts, Washington, D.C.; and Guild Hall Museum, Easthampton, NY. (ABS)

Diggs, Elizabeth (1939 –) As a graduate student at Columbia University in the late 1960s, Diggs joined SDS and the New University Conference, and was active in the women's caucus and in the women's movement. In 1969 she was a delegate from NUC to Cuba, where she and her group spent five weeks visiting schools, hospitals, block associations and factories. Says Diggs, "As a graduate student, this had a big impact on my political awareness." On the trip, Diggs proposed that the group draw lots for rooms without separating men and women, as a means of showing that they were not sexist. "This scandalized the Cubans," she says, "but we did it. We also asked to be given cigars along with the men when they were passed around at the various meetings we went to. We accepted them happily. I still love a Cuban cigar." Earlier, Diggs went to teach-ins about the Vietnam War. Diggs is (2006) a playwright and professor of dramatic writing in the Goldberg Department of Dramatic Writing, Tisch School of the Arts, New York University. Her plays include "Nightingale," "Close Ties," "Dumping Ground," "Goodbye Freddy," and "American Beef." Awards and honors include playwriting grants from the Guggenheim Foundation and the N.E.A., the Los Angeles DramaLogue award for playwriting, the CBS/FDG prize, the Kennedy Center Fund for New American Plays grant, and runner-up for the Susan Smith Blackburn prize. Also active in the environmental movement, Diggs has one child. She is a graduate of Brown University. (ABS)

Dillon, Lynn – See Buck, Lynn

Dimen, Muriel (1942 –) (also known as Muriel Schein) A feminist therapist, Dimen is known within psychoanalysis as a leader of feminist theories of gender and sexuality, including the queer critique. She joined her first CR group at Columbia University in 1968. A supporter of reproductive rights, Dimen was co-author (with Harriet Cohen) of CARASA's principles of unity. She also served briefly as CARASA treasurer. In 1975, Dimen began teaching a class in sex roles in the anthropology dept. of Lehman College (CUNY), where she was a professor. In 1978, she was a founder of a feminist therapist study group. In 1981, she published her MARHO talk in *Heresies, The Sex Issue*. In 1982, she led a workshop at the Barnard Conference on Sexuality, presenting a paper that became *Surviving Sexual Contradictions: A Startling and Different Look at a Day in the Life of a Contemporary Professional Woman* (Macmillan, 1986). With Jessica Benjamin, Virginia Goldner and Adrienne Harris, Dimen then put together a 10-year-long seminar, "Psychoanalysis and Sexual Difference," at the New York Institute for the Humanities (1986 – 1996). In 2003, her book *Sexuality, Intimacy, Power* (The Analytic Press) was published. Dimen holds a B.A. from Barnard College (1964), as well as an M.A. (1966) and Ph.D. (1970) from Columbia University. She completed her training in psychotherapy and psychoanalysis at New York University (1983). (ABS)

Dinnerstein, Dorothy (1923 – 1992) was co-founder, with Nancy Chodorow, of feminist psychoanalytic theory. Her landmark book *The Mermaid and the Minotaur: Sexual Arrangements and Human Malaise* was released by Harper & Row in 1976 and re-released by The Other Press in 1999. Dinnerstein is also author of *The Rocking of the Cradle and the Ruling of the World* (Souvenir Press, 1978).

Dinnerstein, Myra (1934 –) In 1972, Dinnerstein joined a subcommittee on the status of university women, formed by Kate Cloud at the University of Arizona to investigate the formation of a women's studies program there. After three years of working, studying and investigating, the group had enough momentum to appoint a director of women's studies—Dinnerstein. She remained in that position until 1989. In 1979, a grant from the Ford Foundation facilitated by Mariam Chamberlain led to funding for the Southwest Institute for Research of Women, which was attached to the university's women's program. In 1982, Dinnerstein helped found the Association for Women Faculty, a group focused on issues such as pay equity, tenure and work overload as they related to women. Her book *Women Between Two Worlds: Midlife Reflections of Work and Family* was published in 1992. Dinnerstein, who served as research professor of women's studies at the University of Arizona, was chair of the University of Arizona's Commission on the Status of Women and, for five years, co-chair of the Millennium Committee whose report outlined ways to improve the climate for women and minorities at the university. She retired in 2003 and is now research professor emerita.   (ABS)

Dismore, David Michael (1946 –) "I can't imagine wanting to do anything other than be a full-time feminist," says Dismore. "I first realized this in high school when I learned about the suffragists." He received his B.A. from Arizona State University in 1972. In 1974, Dismore went to a Los Angeles NOW meeting and started on the pursuit of equality for women. His journey took him from the image of women in the media committee to Women Against Violence Against Women, to the ERA extension and ratification drive, which in 1982 included a 4,482-mile cross-country bikeathon. In the mid 1980s he worked for Toni Carabillo and Judith Meuli in their NOW Fulfillment Service selling feminist merchandise through the national newsletter. As full-time archivist for the Feminist Majority Foundation since its founding in 1987, he monitors, videotapes, catalogs and preserves television news stories about feminist issues. Additionally, he transcribes articles and press releases from 1848 to 1973 into a Feminist History E-Mail Archive, which he shares with feminist history buffs, students and researchers. Other Web sites host many of his essays on feminist topics and issues relating to looksism, ageism and sexuality. His Web site gives people new to the movement the basics on any feminist issue so they can argue key talking points. (ABS)

Dittmar, Linda (1938 –) (also known as Linda Slotnick) began her fight for women's rights in the mid 1960s when she and a group of women graduate students at Stanford University's English dept. protested the provost's decision to deny graduate scholarship support to women married to graduate students because female graduate students "do not continue with their careers." As a teacher at the University of Massachusetts, Boston, Dittmar became part of a student/faculty women's group formed in the early 1970s. Related activism includes the founding of the (co-ed, but feminist) New University Conference, in which Dittmar was active; the founding of the Socialist-

feminist-anti-racist journal *Radical Teacher*, to which she contributed essays and whose editorial collective she eventually joined; membership in Boston's Bread and Roses; and a regional Marxist/feminist group in which Dittmar participated. In 1972, Dittmar was teaching Images of Women in Literature and then developed a new course, Women's Image in Film. She added a companion course in the late 1970s, Women Film Directors. She served on UMB's board of the women's studies program, and mentored and supported women students and feminist projects. Her published works include *Multiple Voices in Feminist Film Criticism* (Minnesota UP, 1994, with Diane Carson and Janice Welsch) and *From Hanoi to Hollywood* (Rutgers UP, 1990, with Gene Michaud). Other publications include work on lesbian and queer literature and film.   (ABS)

Ditzion, Joan Sheingold (1943 –) is a founder of the Boston Women's Health Book Collective; co-author of all editions of *Our Bodies, Ourselves* and *Ourselves and Our Children;* and a contributor to *Ourselves Growing Older*. Says Ditzion, "*Our Bodies, Ourselves*, which we thought was subversive in its time, was the first women-centered, consumer-oriented, preventive-health-focused book on women's health, reproduction and sexuality." She also worked on "Beginning Parenthood" for *Ourselves and Our Children* and "Caregiving" for *Ourselves Growing Older*. Since the first publication of *Our Bodies, Ourselves*, over four million copies have sold as of this writing. The book has been translated and adapted into 25 languages, including Braille. Ditzion, who has two children, is a social worker/educator. She holds a B.A., M.A. and M.S.W. Archives: Materials from the Boston Women's Health Book Collective: Schlesinger Library, Radcliffe Institute, Cambridge, MA.   (ABS)

Dixon, Marlene (1936 –) was an assistant professor in sociology and human development at the University of Chicago (1967 – 1969). A prominent radical in the women's movement and in scholarship, Dixon was not rehired when her position came up for renewal. This was seen as both sex and political discrimination, and prompted a protest sit-in by women's liberationists. Dixon then moved to the sociology department at McGill University, Montreal, but met with both overt and covert opposition, again because of her radical views. Her book *Things Which Are Done in Secret* (Black Rose Books, 1976) is an account of the academic witchhunt she endured. Dixon is the author of many articles on women, including "The Rise and Demise of Women's Liberation: A Class Analysis" (1977). She was also a member of Chicago Women's Liberation.

Dobbin, Deborah (1942 – 1997) was born in England and lived in Chicago from 1967 – 1983. She was a very active member of CWLU, living on the South Side of the city and working with a group of women from Hyde Park. She participated in the underground abortion network and worked on the CWLU outreach project, which meant linking people in different parts of the city who were interested in joining the Union. She also played a major role in the CWLU health project and was a member of two communes set up on the North Side, consisting of about 25 people, which minimized problems with childcare and other issues for participants. Dobbin's sister, Jennifer Knauss, was also a member of CWLU. Both women were brought up in England by their mother, Marjorie Dobbin, who, according to Knauss, taught them to insist on equality.

Dobbin, Jennifer L.M. – See Knauss, Jennifer L.M.

Dobbins, Peggy Powell (1938 –) Sociologist, artist, activist, and author, Dobbins co-taught (with Cathy Cade) Sociology of Women at New Orleans Free University in 1966. In New York City in 1967, she was a co-founder of NYRW and delivered their "Litany for Martyred Motherhood" at the Jeanette Rankin Brigade. In 1968, Dobbins was arrested at the Miss America protest; on the trip back from the trial, WITCH was born. With Florika Remetier, Dobbins led the Halloween hexing of Wall Street, and with Naomi Jaffe, the Wall Street work-ins of WITCH women in typing pools in corporate headquarters at Travelers' and AT&T (1968–1969). In 1970, as a member of the Upper West Side Women's Center, Dobbins organized CR groups, a childcare co-op and a sliding scale food co-op. In 1972, she returned to New Orleans and wrote her dissertation, "Unionism, Professionalism and Feminism Among Registered Nurses." In 1974, Dobbins began teaching as an assistant professor of sociology at the University of Alabama, Tuscaloosa, and introduced Sex, Race and Class as an academic course. She and Walda Fishman presented their findings on the sources of the "Right Wing Attack on the Women's Movement" to the women's caucus of the ASA in 1980. After Dobbins was arrested while performing a skit based on her research with Fishman, the university fired her. Dobbins then joined the Communist Party and worked until 1993 as a full-time volunteer to unite the civil rights, labor and women's movements in Alabama, then in Oakland, CA. Dobbins is the author of *From Kin to Class, Speculations on the Origins and Development of Family, Class Society, and Female Subordination* (1981). In Atlanta since 1996, Dobbins concentrates on art forms that continue concepts central to the ideas of women's CR. Dobbins, who has two children, graduated from Wellesley in 1960 and the University of Madrid in 1961. She earned her Ph.D. from Tulane in 1974. (ABS)

Dobkin, Alix (1940 –) (also known as Alix Hood) In the late 1950s, Dobkin was "a teenaged guitar-totin', card-carrying comrade grounding myself in mushrooming crowds of progressive Jews, self-taught musicians and other local subversives." She launched her professional folk singing career in Greenwich Village (NYC) in the 1960s, and then in 1972 came out as a lesbian and "turned to writing and singing for women in general and to building lesbian culture in particular." In 1973, with Kay Gardner, Dobkin produced Lavender Jane Loves Women, "the very first internationally distributed album by, for and about lesbians in the history of the world." Since then, she has focused her music on the lives, concerns and perspectives of women who love women. Dobkin has brought her music and vision to hundreds of women's communities in the U.S. and abroad. Dobkin has a B.F.A. from the Tyler School of Fine Arts of Temple University, Philadelphia. Archives: Schlesinger Library, Radcliffe Institute, Cambridge, MA. (ABS)

Doderer, Minnette (1923 – 2005) Elected to the Iowa House of Representatives in 1964, Doderer was the leading advocate of women's rights during her 25-year career in the state legislature. A magnet for female constituents who had been ignored by her male colleagues, Doderer handled issues no one else had wanted to touch. Her work on rape law reform, the federal and state ERA, juvenile justice, childcare and inheritance tax revision resulted in many laws that improved the legal status of women. As president *pro tempore* of the senate for two years, she attained the highest position ever held by a woman in the IA Legislature. Doderer was one of the founding members of the IA WPC and co-chair of the International Women's Year coordinating committee. In 1977 she was chair of the IA delegates attending the National Women's Conference in Houston. Featured in the book *More Strong Minded Women*, by Louise Noun, Doderer was inducted into the Iowa Women's Hall of Fame in 1979. She was the recipient of numerous awards, including the Reproductive Rights Award, 1998; Business and Professional Women Woman of Achievement Award, 1997; Feminist of the Year Award, 1996; and Iowa City Senior Center Woman of the Year, 1995. Archives: University of Iowa Women's Archives, Iowa City, IA. (ABS before death)

Dodson, Betty Ann (1929 –) Artist, author, sex educator and video producer, Dodson has spent her life "liberating" women by teaching them masturbation skills through workshops, articles, books and videos. In 1968 she had the first one-woman exhibition of erotic art at the Wickersham Gallery (New York City), showing heterosexual couples as equals in the sexual embrace. It "was well received and most of the drawings sold." In 1970, a second exhibition celebrated masturbation; it "was a dismal failure financially and there was a media blackout." In 1971 Dodson came out publicly in *Evergreen*, a national magazine, as "a sex positive feminist who supported masturbation." She began running physical and sexual CR groups for women in 1972, which later became Bodysex Groups and lasted 25 years. In 1973 she worked with Dell Williams on NOW's first sex conference showing a slide-show of female genital imagery, and had a retrospective exhibition in San Francisco at the International Museum of Erotic Art. The museum sold the monograph "Liberating Masturbation," which influenced West Coast sex educators at UC Berkeley to begin using masturbation in the treatment of non-orgasmic women. In 1974 Dodson's article on masturbation was published in *Ms.* magazine. Its popularity led to the publication of *Liberating Masturbation: A Meditation on Selflove.* From 1975 – 1980, Dodson published numerous articles in national magazines, and in 1986 sold *Liberating Masturbation* to Crown Publishing Group. The book was renamed *Sex for One: The Joy of Selfloving.* Dodson is also the author of *Orgasms for Two: The Joy of Partner Sex* (Harmony Books, 2002). A featured guest on many national Cable television talk shows, Dodson's workshops and documentaries continued through the 1990s. In 1992 she received a Ph.D. in sexology from the Institute for Advanced Study of Human Sexuality, San Francisco. Dodson continues to produce erotic sex education videos and maintains a private practice in New York City. Archives: The Betty Dodson Foundation, New York, NY.   (ABS)

Doherty, Sister Austin (1927 –) A member of the School Sisters of St. Francis and a faculty member at Alverno College, Doherty began making presentations throughout Wisconsin on women's issues in 1960. In 1966, she attended NOW's organizing conference and was elected to its first board. In 1967 Doherty, with Catherine Conroy and others, founded a Milwaukee chapter of NOW. Doherty participated in the 50th anniversary of the Women's Bureau of the Dept. of Labor in Washington, D.C. (1970). As co-director of Alverno's Research Center on Women, Doherty organized many feminist conferences, seminars and projects, including Women in Public Life in Wisconsin (1971), Midwest Conference on Women's Studies (1971), Oral and Visual History Project, a series of videotapes and slide/film interviews with WI suffragists (1971 – 1974), The Contribution of Education to Women's Roles, with Claire and Laura Nader (1972), and Social Myths and Sex Roles, with Elizabeth Janeway (1972). In June 1971, Doherty helped organize and served as co-chair of the first conference of women theologians, which marked a historic conceptual leap, incorporating women's experience into the theological process. Active in Milwaukee NOW, Doherty worked to end the sex-segregated employment ads at the *Milwaukee Journal* (1973), and for WI ratification of the ERA. She also hosted the 1974 conference for the Wisconsin Governor's Commission on the Status of Women, Homemaking and the Family: Changing Values and Concerns, held at Alverno College; was an individual delegate to the 1977 National Women's Conference in Houston, and continued to work in WI for women's rights through 1980. In 1992, Doherty was interviewed for several audio- and videotapes for the Women's Oral History Project: "Bridges that Carry Us Over: Midwestern Leaders of the Modern Women's Movement." Doherty holds a B.A. from Alverno College, an M.A. from Marquette University, and an M.A. and Ph.D. from Loyola University. She is director of the Alverno College Institute. Archives: Papers will go to the Alverno College archives and the archives of the School Sisters of St. Francis International Headquarters, St. Joseph Convent, Milwaukee, WI.   (ABS)

Dolan, Merrillee A. (1941 –) attended an Atlanta NOW conference in the 1960s, and was nominated to the board of directors by Jacqui Ceballos; Betty Friedan later appointed her to the women and poverty task force. "As someone who was paying my way at 14," says Dolan, "this issue was dear to my heart. Back in New Mexico, Albuquerque NOW and I began to raise hell and eyebrows." Dolan started a "Sisters in Poverty" newsletter to give guidance on forming coalitions with women on Welfare and similar groups, and lobbied the chief of police to get women on the force and the state penitentiary to get meaningful job training for women. She also picketed for a young woman who was sexually harassed by her boss. (This was before the EEOC recognized sexual harassment as a legitimate issue). As a result, the boss was fired. With four others, Dolan started the first women's studies class at the University of New Mexico (1969).   (ABS)

Donovan, Josephine Campbell (1941 –) A writer, professor, and eco-feminist, Donovan founded, with Suzanne Howard, a women's studies committee at the University of Kentucky (1971), and was the first chair. Donovan also taught her first women's studies course there in 1972. She was the first coordinator of the women's studies program at the University of New Hampshire (1977 – 1980), and was instrumental in the development of a women's studies program at the University of Maine in the 1980s. She is the author of *Feminist Theory: The Intellectual Traditions* (1985) and *Women and the Rise of the Novel* (1999). She is also editor of *Feminist Literary Criticism: Explorations in Theory*, which is considered the first book of feminist critical theory (1975). Donovan is co-editor, with Carol J. Adams, of *Animals and Women* (1995) and *Beyond Animal Rights: A Feminist Caring Ethic for the Treatment of Animals* (1996). She was active in the 1960s antiwar movement, marched in civil rights and gay pride demonstrations, and has supported animal rights. Donovan has a B.A. from Bryn Mawr (1962), and an M.A. (1967) and Ph.D. (1971) from the University of Wisconsin-Madison.   (ABS)

Dooley, Betty Parsons (1927 – 2002) In 1954, Dooley stunned her highly conservative Republican neighbors in West Texas by inviting Eleanor Roosevelt to speak. Fearing a disaster, she nonetheless rented space, prayed for a miracle, and was gratified to see an enormous turnout of "farmers, ranchers, wildcatters and bankers, Baptists and Catholics—they all crowded onto those bleachers. There was a standing ovation from start to finish." In 1964, Dooley was the first woman elected to the board of

Odessa College (1964). In 1971, Dooley left her TX home to become regional director for the Health Security Action Council in Washington, D.C., a consortium of unions working to enact national health insurance. In 1977, she became the first executive director of the Congressional Caucus for Women's Issues, a group of 17 women who, under Dooley's leadership, passed legislation promoting women's health research, economic security, and education and career rights. In 1982, she became founder of, and for the next 20 years served as president of the Women's Research and Education Institute, the caucus's research arm. She was responsible for numerous programs, including the Congressional Fellowships on Women and Public Policy, the center for women in the military, and *The American Woman*, a book series. The eighth edition, *The American Woman: Getting to the Top*, was dedicated to Dooley when she retired from WREI in 1999.

Doran, Judith Dennehy (1942 – 2003) In the 1970s, Doran was president of the Oakland County (MI) chapter of NOW and president of the Women Lawyers Association of Michigan. She was also a founding member of the Women's Bar Association of Oakland County, and the first female president of the Detroit College of Law Alumni Association. When Doran received her J.D. degree in 1972, however, "law firms were still reluctant to hire female attorneys, and nobody would hire her," says her daughter, Ann Gerk. She fought back by opening her own law firm, and used it to fight gender discrimination for the next 30 years. Among other achievements, Doran won employment discrimination lawsuits against Wayne County, Farmington Hills and General Motors, with significant settlements in all three.

Doress-Worters, Paula Brown (1938 –) has written on women and health, reproductive rights, women and poverty and older women. She was a founder of the Boston Women's Health Book Collective in 1969, a co-author and staff member from the 1970s to the early 1980s, and a board member until 1999. She was a contributor to all editions of *Our Bodies, Ourselves*, including *Our Bodies, Ourselves for the New Century* (1998), *Ourselves Growing Older* (1986,1994), and *Ourselves and Our Children* (1978), and continues to serve on the founders committee. Doress-Worters has also contributed articles to academic journals and several anthologies, including *Myths About the Powerless: Contesting Social Inequalities* (Temple University Press, 1996), for which she wrote "Choices and Chances: How a Profit-Driven Healthcare System Discriminates Against Middle-Aged Women," and others on women and elder care, menopause and women and aging. In addition to advocating for women's rights, she has supported civil rights and Welfare rights, and been part of the anti-war movement. She is a writer and resident scholar in women's studies at Brandeis University, where she is documenting the work of 19th century women's rights reformer Ernestine L. Rose

for publication. Doress-Worters, who has two children, received her B.A. in 1962 from Suffolk University, her M.A. from Goddard College, and her Ph.D. from Boston College in 1992. Archives: Schlesinger Library, Radcliffe Institute, Cambridge, MA. (ABS)

Dorries, Nola – See Claire, Nola

Doty, Suzanne (1950 –) was both an employee at NOW's national office and a member of Chicago NOW, where she was active in the early years of its existence and organized the Civic Center rally. As chair of Chicago NOW's ERA committee, Doty led the first bus trip to Springfield, IL, to lobby and demonstrate for the ERA, led Moms for the ERA in a St. Patrick's Day parade, and debated Phyllis Schlafly on WLS radio. In addition, Doty organized many of the actions against Sears, including one in which she picketed the store dressed as Ms. Claus. After receiving her M.B.A. in 1980, Doty moved to Cairo, Egypt, where she spent four years, and then moved to California. She has been active in Soroptimists International of Americas since 1990. (ABS)

Dougherty, Ariel (1947 –) In 1962, Hubert Humphrey offered to sponsor Dougherty as a page in the United States Congress, but she was denied the position because of her sex. In 1969, she started filmmaking, focusing on teaching kids. She joined a film "collective," which became Women Make Movies. The first movie they made (1971) was "Mother America." It was followed by "The Women's Happy Time Commune" (1972). In the winter of 1971 – 1972, Dougherty says, she and her core group "dreamed up the Women's Silver Screen Roadshow to tour women's media across America at open-air screenings," but they could not get funds. Women Make Movies was incorporated as a non-profit entity in 1972 by Sheila Paige and Dougherty. The New York State Council of the Arts funded their community-based media-teaching workshop for women in the Chelsea section of NYC. In 1979 – 1987, Dougherty was development director for Women's Studio Workshop, Rosendale, NY, where she curated a series of women's films and video. She also initiated Teaching Artists to Reach Technological Savvy in 1984, a collaboration with the Women's Building in Los Angeles. Seeing the rise of anti-feminism in the 1980s, she began surveying the health of women's art organizations. This led to the inclusion of women, for the first time, in a special constituency on Re-Authorization of Foundation on the Arts and the Humanities Act of 1988. Archives: Papers, photographs and original videos at Schlesinger Library, Radcliffe Institute, Cambridge, MA. (ABS)

Douglas, Carol Anne (1946 –) was a staff member, in 1972, of *The Second Wave: A Magazine for the New Feminism*, produced by Boston-based Female Liberation. In 1979 she was a member of the D.C.-area Feminist Alliance, and from 1979 – 1981 was a member of the No-

Name Group, a lesbian feminist organization in Washington that met for monthly discussions. Since 1973, she has been a member of *Off Our Backs*, a women's news journal, doing writing, editing and layout. Douglas is the author of *Love and Politics: Radical Feminist and Lesbian Theory* (Ism Press, 1990), and contributed to the anthology *Radically Speaking: Feminism Reclaimed* (Springfield Press, 1996). Douglas has an M.A. from UCLA.   (ABS)

Dowey, Lois M. (1925 –) "My contribution to the movement was to fight for equal pay for female teachers —against the opposition of most of the women—at a flossy prep school in Princeton, NJ." At the time, "one did not speak about money and salaries to other faculty members; it was considered uncouth." Dowey and Eileen Lemonick led the effort, and thanks to federal and state law, they succeeded. Women and their roles became a significant component of the Medieval history Dowey was teaching. She later worked with inner city children, focusing on girls' explorations of their options. She also changed the terms of her marriage, and influenced her husband to support the women newly admitted to the theological school where he was teaching.   (ABS)

Downer, Carol Aurilla (1933 –) A pioneer of the women's self-help movement, Downer joined Los Angeles NOW in 1969. With a reproductive history that included six children, two miscarriages, an illegal abortion and a legal abortion that required her to claim she would commit suicide without it, Downer was a natural for NOW's abortion committee. Lana Phelan, committee coordinator, became her mentor. Although hospital abortions had become legal in California, Downer and Lorraine Rothman understudied in an illegal abortion clinic, where they observed a method that Rothman simplified. The two women also created a procedure called menstrual extraction, which could be used to regulate menstruation, relieve cramps, or when a woman missed her period, not knowing whether she was pregnant. Convinced that women could not be liberated without hands-on knowledge of their bodies, Downer's group began the practice of self-examination. On April 7, 1971, they held a meeting in Venice, CA, at Every Woman's Bookstore, where Downer inserted a speculum into her vagina and invited other women to observe her cervix. Fascinated, the women agreed to meet again to do self-exams and to discuss health issues—and thus a women's medical self-help clinic was born. Downer and Rothman took off across the country spreading the self-help idea and starting clinics as they went. In 1972, Downer and Colleen Wilson were arrested for practicing medicine without a license. Downer went on trial for inserting plain yogurt into a woman's vagina. The publicity from the trial made women's self-help a national issue and Downer was acquitted. In 1973, Downer's group incorporated as The Feminist Women's Health Center and referred women for legal hospital abortions. Later she and her colleagues traveled to other countries giving lectures and demonstrating how self-help clinics work. Downer earned a law degree from Whittier Law School and practices civil law in Los Angeles.   (ABS)

Downing, Christine (1931 –) began teaching at Douglass College, the women's college of Rutgers University, in 1963. In 1968, inspired by her students, Downing began introducing a feminist perspective into her courses on world religions. She also became an active participant in the creation of a women's studies program at Douglass, and was the faculty adviser to the Homophile League, the university's gay and lesbian student group. Downing helped start CR groups, led workshops and lectured at many universities and study centers on gender and sexuality. In 1971, at the annual meeting of the American Academy of Religion, Downing helped gather all the women in attendance ("about 30 compared to the several thousand who now come!") and took the steps that led to the formation of a formally recognized women's caucus and to the establishment of a major disciplinary section on Women and Religion. In 1974, Downing became the first woman president of the organization. In the fall of 1974, she moved to CA and became chair of Religious Studies at San Diego State University and a core member of the faculty of the California School of Professional Psychology. At CSPP, she introduced a course on the psychology of women and served as faculty adviser to female, gay and lesbian students. At SDSU, she helped transform the oldest women's studies department in the nation into a fully academic enterprise. Her many writings include *The Goddess* (Continuum International Publishing Group, 1996), *Psyche's Sisters* (Harper San Francisco, 1988), *Journey Through Menopause* (Crossroad Publishing Company, 1987), *Mirrors of the Self* (St. Martin's Press, 1991), *Women's Mysteries* (Crossroad, 1992), *Gods in Our Midst* (Crossroad Publishing Company, 1993) and *Long Journey Home* (Random House, 2001). In 1994, Downing moved to Orcas Island (off the coast of WA). She teaches (2004) in the Mythological Studies and Depth Psychology programs at the Pacifica Graduate Institute in Santa Barbara and lectures worldwide. Born in Germany, Downing has five children. She earned her B.A. from Swarthmore College (1952) and her Ph.D. from Drew University (1966). Archives: Campbell-Gimbutas Archive, Pacifica Graduate Institute, Carpinteria, CA.   (ABS)

Dreher, Ellen ("Chelsea") (1935 –) is the author of "The Little Prick," a self-published cartoon booklet and sociologic study of "the man." As a member of NYRF, Dreher helped arrange conferences on rape, prostitution and marriage. With Susan Brownmiller and others, she organized CR groups, spoke at colleges and private schools, and got airtime on TV. With Hester Brown, Dreher and her partner, Laura Collins, organized a demonstration for a U.N. chair for women. Dreher participated in the formation of Lesbian Feminist Liberation and The Coffee House Collective on 7th Ave., NYC. A drummer for the Victoria

Woodhull Marching Band, she was part of the first Gay Olympics, women only, in Riverside Park, and the Statue of Liberty action. A member of the Daughters of Bilitis, Dreher helped found the Women's Center on 22nd Street. She was a counselor for 12 years at Identity House (a counseling center for gays and their families). She has also been a volunteer at the Gay and Lesbian Community Center, and Seniors in a Gay Environment. Archives: The Lesbian Herstory Archives, Brooklyn, NY. (ABS)

Drell, Sally Barbara (1948 –) was an assistant to Betty Friedan from 1970 – 1971, editing articles, handling correspondence and occasionally acting as Friedan's driver. During that time, Drell was a NY NOW member, where she helped to compile a database, and a charter member of the 1971 NWPC in Washington, D.C. In Florida she joined the Boca Raton NOW and since then has been an activist on the Equality Day planning committee. She has worked in publicity, participated in media events, been a writer for the newsletter, and done research. Drell has a B.A. from Queens College (NY) and an M.A from New York University. (ABS)

Dresselhaus Mildred S. (1930 –) received a Ph.D. in physics from the University of Chicago in 1958. In 1960 she moved to the Lincoln Laboratory at MIT, then after seven years joined the MIT faculty. When Dresselhaus arrived at MIT in 1960, women comprised just 4 percent of the undergraduate student population. As the mother of four, Dresselhaus faced unique challenges in the workplace that inspired her to assist other women in pursuing scientific careers. In 1970 she co-founded the Women's Forum at MIT, which was established to equalize opportunities for all women at MIT. In 1973 she received a Carnegie Foundation grant to encourage women to study traditionally male-dominated fields, *e.g.*, physics. The same year, she was appointed as the Abby Rockefeller Mauze chair, endowed in support of the scholarship of women in science and engineering. In her 45 years at MIT, Dresselhaus produced several key breakthroughs in physics, including her work in increasing our understanding of carbon nanotubes. She is past president of the American Physical Society, the American Association for the Advancement of Science, and treasurer of the National Academy of Sciences. She is also winner of the National Medal of Science, recipient of 21 Honorary Doctorate degrees, director of the Office of Science at the U.S. Department of Energy under President Clinton, and chair of the American Institute of Physics governing board. She was one of six Americans to receive Heinz Awards on May 24, 2005, hers being under the category called Technology, the Economy and Employment. Dresselhaus began her higher education at Hunter College in New York City and received a Fulbright Fellowship to attend the Cavendish Laboratory, Cambridge University (1951 – 1952). In addition to her Ph.D. she holds a master's degree from Radcliffe College (1953). (ABS)

Drews, Elizabeth Monroe (1915 – 1976) A psychologist and educator, Drews was one of the people working behind the scenes in the formation of NOW in 1966. In the document "How NOW Began," Betty Friedan notes that "Elizabeth Drews and Vera Schletzer were doing pioneer work in educational psychology to broaden the aspirations of women themselves." In 1962 – 1963, Drews was a member of the President's Commission on the Status of Women. She graduated from high school at age 15, then from an Oregon teacher's college at 18. She taught in a one-room schoolhouse in Oregon. Drews earned a Ph.D. from the University of Michigan. She was a professor at the Michigan State University in the early 1960s and Portland State University in the late 1960s. She lived in Michigan when most of her major feminist work was done. She had one child.

Dreyfuss, Cathy Robin (1951 –) was a member of the Libera Collective (1971 – 1973) in Berkeley, CA, which published a feminist literary arts journal of the same name. From 1971 – 1974, she was a member of the Berkeley Oakland Women's Union and was active in organizing and advocating around women's issues of race, poverty and social justice. In the summer of 1980, Dreyfuss was a law student intern at the National Women's Law Center in Washington, D.C., working on Title IX issues, responses to Moral Majority attacks on women, and reproductive freedom. Since 1980, she has been a member of the National Lawyers Guild, serving, variously, as chapter president, regional VP and national VP. Through the NLG, Dreyfuss has participated in organizing and advocacy on women's issues of race, poverty, social justice and reproductive freedom. As an attorney, Dreyfuss has represented primarily indigent clients. She was a member of the California Battered Women in Prison Coalition, working on clemency applications for battered women convicted of murder of their batterers, and on political asylum cases involving human rights violations against women (rape, forced prostitution). Dreyfuss has also participated in organizing and advocacy on issues of peace, social justice, poverty, civil liberties, civil rights, immigrants' rights, and international issues such as ending the Cuba embargo. She has also fought to abolish the death penalty. Dreyfuss is in a women's writing group and working on a documentary about her mother and other peace activists involved in Women Strike for Peace and Another Mother for Peace in Los Angeles in the 1960s. Archives: Papers from the Berkeley Oakland Women's Union will go the BOWU Reunion Committee in Berkeley, CA. (ABS)

Driver, Anne – See Barstow, Anne Llewellyn

Drolma, Lama Shenpen – See Leghorn, Lisa

Drumm, Skip DeeAnna (1938 –) (also known as Evelyn Drum) A member of NOW since 1974, Drumm has been an elected delegate to NOW national conferences each year since 1975; served as president of Somerset County (NJ) NOW (1976 – 1977); and president of Middlesex County NOW (1994 and 1995). From 1980 – present (2004), she has been a NJ NOW state board delegate, and helped plan the NJ NOW Stand UP for Choice rally in Trenton (2000). Drumm helped establish a rape crisis center at Raritan Valley Hospital (1975), and founded and co-facilitated a battered women's support group (1976 – 1979). Drumm chaired the women's bodies women's health NJ NOW committee (1976 and 1977), participated in the White House ERA vigil (1976), and was a delegate from NJ to the National Women's Year Conference in Houston (1977). From 1978–1985, she founded and fa-cilitated a personal growth group for divorced women. She has worked aggressively to support women's right to choose, including infiltrating (1991) the Right to Life and Army of God's Operation Goliath in Dobbs Ferry, NY, a weeklong effort to shut down all the abortion clinics in the area. Drumm posed as an anti-choice rescuer, then funneled information back to the clinic defenders. From 1991–2000, she attended the NJ Right to Life annual con-vention as a mole, and from 1994–1996 attended the NJ committee for life in the same capacity. In 1991, Drumm founded the Amethyst Circle of Sisters, a Dianic Wiccan Coven, and continues to serve as high priestess. In 2000, Drumm attended the LGBT march on Washington. She earned her B.A. (1961) from Westhampton College, University of Richmond. Archives: Political button collec-tion and activity files will go to the National Women's History Museum, Washington, D.C.   (ABS)

DuBois, Ellen Carol (1947 –) was one of a small group of people who planned the formation of the Chicago Women's Liberation Unions (1968 – 1969). DuBois was active in a chapter she formed at Northwestern University and the Liberation School (a project of CWLU), where she taught her first courses in women's history. In 1972, DuBois went to SUNY/Buffalo, where she taught history and women's studies for 16 years. In 1988, she became a professor at the University of California, Los Angeles in women's history and women's studies. Through her re-search, she has become a leading figure in the field of women's history, writing primarily on the history of the women's rights/woman suffrage movement, but also, later on, working to diversify the field through greater racial inclusiveness. She has published numerous books on feminism and suffrage, including *Feminism and Suffrage: The Emergence of an Independent Women's Movement in America 1848 – 1869* (Cornell University Press, 1978); and *Harriot Stanton Blatch and the Winning of Woman Suffrage* (Yale University Press, 1999). She was co-editor, with Vicki Ruiz, of *Unequal Sisters: A Multi-cultural Reader in U.S. Women's History* (Routledge, 1994). A recipient of the 1999 Guggenheim Foundation Fellowship, DuBois received her Ph.D. from Northwestern University in 1975. Archives: Northwestern University

and The Sophia Smith Collection, Smith College, Northampton, MA.   (ABS)

Dubrow, Evelyn (1911 – 2006) was a labor leader, recipi-ent of the President's Medal of Freedom (1999), and a leader of the efforts to pass civil rights and Medicare leg-islation. From 1943 – 1946, she was secretary of the NJ chapter of the American Newspaper Guild, an organizer and political education director for the New Jersey Textile Workers Union of America, and assistant to the president of the New Jersey CIO Council. She was also VP and leg-islative director and executive secretary of the political department of UNITE. Active in the Democratic Party, she was president of the National Democratic Club from 1981 – 1983. Dubrow, who joined the International Ladies Garment Workers Union in 1956, was ILGWU rep-resentative at the Leadership Conference on Civil Rights, for the National Consumers Leagues, and CLUW. In 1994, ILGWU established the Evelyn Dubrow Post-Graduate Scholarship. The recipient of numerous awards, Dubrow was named by *George* magazine as one of Washington's 20 Most Important Political Women Leaders (1996); by *Ladies' Home Journal* as one of the 75 Most Important Women Leaders; and by the Washington Dossier as one of Washington's Mightiest 500.

Dubrow, Marsha (1943 –) A writer and editor, Dubrow has written thousands of articles encouraging all aspects of women's equality. But her most significant contribu-tion was suing her employer, Reuters News Agency, for sex discrimination in 1976 and winning a generous, concilia-tory out-of-court settlement in 1978. The Newspaper Guild used her victory as a landmark case. She also estab-lished a Women's Issues beat at Reuters, and freelanced articles to many magazines, including a cover story, the first, on women's assertiveness training for *New York* magazine in 1975. She also appeared regularly on a weekly PBS-TV show, "Women: New York Edition," from 1977 – 1980. With the NY NOW media reform task force, Dubrow helped write, edit and present presentations to many top ad agencies to persuade them to show a more positive image of women. She also did this with TV net-works, including PBS and local stations. On her own, Dubrow drew up non-sexist language guidelines for AP/UPI stylebooks. As press secretary for the U.S. Senate Commerce Committee, she worked hardest for bills that would eliminate sex discrimination in insurance, among other legislation to benefit women. Dubrow has a B.A. from Adelphi University (1965) and an M.F.A. from Bennington College (2000). Archives: Bennington College, Bennington, VT.   (ABS)

Duke, Barbara Martin (1930 –) (also known as Barbara Martin) joined NOW in 1966/7, and celebrated the 1970 Women's Strike for Equality ("Don't Iron While the Strike Is Hot") with friends in Ft. Worth, TX. After moving to Austin in 1973, Duke became Austin NOW president, TX state president, and then director of the NOW South Central region. She also represented the region on NOW's national board. Duke was co-organizer of the Austin Women's Center and served as its first board president. From 1982–1983, she worked for NOW in the FL ERA campaign, and in 1983 was a lobbyist for the Texas Association Against Sexual Assault. Duke then moved to CA to work as a librarian at UCLA. Since retiring in 1993 and moving to KS, she has lobbied for reproductive rights as president of the Kansas Choice Alliance and as pro-choice coordinator for the KS AAUW. In July 2004, Duke completed a term as co-president of the KS AAUW. She supports the Lawrence, KS, chapter of NOW and the AAUW branch, and is membership chair for the Kansas Choice Alliance. She is also (2006) co-president of the board of the Peggy Bowman Second Chance Fund, which helps KS women who need but can't afford abortions. Archives: University of Texas, Austin, TX.   (ABS)

Dunbar-Ortiz, Roxanne Amanda (1938 –) A professor in the Dept. of Ethnic Studies at California State University, Hayward, since 1974, Dunbar-Ortiz was interim director of the women's studies program at CSUH from 1995–1997. Born poor and reared in rural OK, Dunbar-Ortiz and her six-member family lived in a series of one-room sharecropper cabins. She earned a B.A. from San Francisco State in 1963, and in 1967 formed the first women's liberation group at UCLA. With Dana Densmore, she formed Cell 16 (1968–1971) in Cambridge/ Boston, published its journal, and organized small and large, local and regional meetings. In 1970–1972, she founded the Southern Female Rights Union, organized local, regional and national meetings and conferences, published bulletins, and was involved in cross-racial organizing among women. From 1972–1973, she participated in on-the-job union organizing among women electronic assembly workers in Silicon Valley, CA. Since 1974, she has fought for international human rights for women through the United Nations Decades for Women. In addition to fighting for the rights of women, Dunbar-Ortiz has been involved in the American Indian Movement/International Indian Treaty Council (1975 – 1982); published Treaty Council News; and organized lobbying at the United Nations. She is founder (1981) and director of the Indigenous World Association; represented the Afro-Asian People's Solidarity Movement at United Nations meetings (1978–1985) and published articles in AAPSO's journal. A prolific writer, Dunbar-Ortiz is the author of *Outlaw Woman: A Memoir of the War Years, 1960–1975* (City Light Books, 2002); was an editor, founder and contributor, *No More Fun and Games! A Journal of Female Liberation* (1968–1970); and published "Female Liberation as the Basis for Social Liberation" in Robin Morgan's book, *Sisterhood is Powerful*. She has one child. In addition to her B.A., Dunbar-Ortiz holds an M.A. (1965) and Ph.D. (1974) from University of California, Los Angeles.   (ABS)

Dunlap, Mary C. (1948 – 2003) A civil rights lawyer and, at the time of her death, director of San Francisco's police-watchdog agency the Office of Citizen Complaints, Dunlap was an out lesbian who had twice argued before the U.S. Supreme Court. She taught Women and the Law and Sexuality and the Law at Bay Area (CA) law schools, and was a founder (1973) of the feminist public interest law firm Equal Rights Advocates. Dunlap argued an early women's rights case before the United States Supreme Court on behalf of a pregnant schoolteacher who had been forced to take maternity leave. She also argued the Gay Olympics case before the Court in 1987, and litigated numerous important cases in the early women's movement. After 20 years of practicing law and teaching, Dunlap retired to paint watercolors of landscapes and animals. She also wrote an unpublished memoir, "Fighting Words, Mending Words."

Dunn Dalton, Rosemary (1940 –) joined the Panel of American Women in 1966. Held in Detroit, the meeting was one of many across the country designed to address questions of racism and sexism, and was the beginning of Dunn Dalton's awakening to the issues that would be addressed by the women's movement in the 1970s. After working in the civil rights and Welfare fields, Dunn Dalton graduated from Southern Oregon State College (1975) as a Welfare mother of three. She then organized a Lifelong Learning Program (with another student) to which many women came to learn how to return to work or school. At the end of this graduate project, the college hired Dunn Dalton on a CETA grant, and she began the program Women in Transition (1976) at the college's counseling center. Says Dunn Dalton, "This launched the women's movement in Southern Oregon—the late-blooming state of our nation of sisterhood. Over 500 women a year visited our center, questioning their paths, divorcing their husbands, going back to school, deciding to have children on their own, coming out as lovers in the midst of a meeting on sisterhood issues." A shelter for battered women and their children was launched in 1977, and in 1980 was named The Dunn House, after Dunn Dalton. Another group started by Dunn Dalton at Women in Transition was focused on fathers and daughters. From this came Dunn Dalton's book, *Lamenting Lost Fathers: Adult Daughters Search for the Message of the Father* (iuniverse, 2004). In 1983, Dunn Dalton moved to Boston, where she became chair of the Lesbian, Gay & Bisexual Political Alliance, and where she co-edited the book *Lesbian Psychologies* (University of Illinois Press). In addition to this work, Dunn Dalton was a co-founder of the first women's studies class taught at Southern Oregon State College, where she also taught Feminism as Therapy. She continues to teach at the institution, which became a university in 2002. In addition to her undergraduate degree from Southern Oregon State College, Dunn Dalton earned an M.S. (1976), and an M.S.W. from Boston College (1988).   (ABS)

Dunn, Elizabeth M. (1925 –) "Although I come from a family that gave its women the same educational opportunities that the men got, society made it pretty difficult to capitalize on that education to the same extent that men could," says Dunn. So it was not surprising that on August 26, 1970, she was thrilled to join the march organized by the Eastern Massachusetts chapter of NOW to celebrate the 50th anniversary of the 19th Amendment. Dunn eventually became president of MA NOW (1978 – 1980), fighting for the ERA extension. She joined national NOW as a member of the political staff working for Molly Yard and Ellie Smeal in Washington, D.C., Oklahoma and Florida during the final year of the ERA ratification campaign. "It was while I was compiling a publication called 'Women Can Make The Difference' that I coined the phrase Gender Gap," says Dunn. "It was first cited by columnist Judy Mann in the *Washington Post*, October 16, 1981." At the end of the ERA campaign, Dunn returned to Boston and became State House lobbyist for MA NOW. Since 1972, she has been active in electoral and party politics. Seeing the value of a party position to advance feminist goals, she twice ran for the Democratic State Committee before winning a seat over the opposition of the governor. She has been on the platform committee every two years in order to first promote and then protect the abortion plank, and "have finally even been entrusted with writing it." Dunn has a B.A. from Vassar College (1946) and an M.P.A. from the JFK School of Government, Harvard University (1981). Archives: Schlesinger Library, Radcliffe Institute, Cambridge, MA. (ABS)

Dunn, Jeanne Lynn (1945 –) was a founding member (1969) of The Center for Women's Studies and Services at San Diego State University, the first women's studies program in America. In 1970 – 1971, she participated in the first feminist art exhibition at SDSU, which was held in the university library and included major feminist artists of the region such as Martha Rosler and Eleanor Antin. Dunn was a participant in CR meetings in San Diego and, as a feminist, in anti-Vietnam War protests and campus teach-ins at SDSU. She also helped organize the first Earth Day march in San Diego (1971) and has contributed to various environmental organizations. Dunn, who has two children, holds a B.S. from the University of Wisconsin, Madison, and an M.A. from SDSU. (ABS)

Dunson, Linda – See Werden, Frieda Lindfield

DuPlessis, Rachel Blau (1941 –) (also known as Rachel Blau) Professor, feminist scholar, writer and editor, DuPlessis was active in Columbia Women's Liberation (1969 – 1970). She has been a member of the editorial board of the journal *Feminist Studies* since 1974, and has been involved in feminist scholarship, literary criticism and theory since the early 1970s. She was co-editor, with Ann Snitow, of *The Feminist Memoir Project* (Three Rivers/ Crown Random House, 1998). Her work with *Feminist* *Studies* included helping to facilitate the transition to a collective board, being sole editor for literary criticism and creative writing (1974 – 1982), serving as associate editor for creative writing (1982 – 1987), and other general work. She is the author of countless feminist essays and several books. These include *Genders, Races, Religious Cultures in Modern American Poetry, 1908 – 1934* (Cambridge University Press, 2001); *Writing Beyond the Ending: Narrative Strategies of Twentieth-Century Women Writers* (Indiana University Press, 1985); *H.D.: The Career of that Struggle* (Indiana University Press, 1986); *The Pink Guitar: Writing as Feminist Practice* (Routledge, 1990); and *Blue Studios: Poetry and its Cultural Work* (University of Alabama Press, 2006). She is also a poet. Her scholarly articles have appeared in periodicals such as *The Kenyon Review, Diacritics, MLQ* and *American Literature*, and in anthologies from the seven university presses. DuPlessis holds a B.A. from Barnard College (1963) and a Ph.D. from Columbia University (1970). Archives: Papers related to *Feminist Studies* are at the University of Maryland, College Park, MD. (ABS)

Durden, Betty J. (1923 –) A university administrator, Durden was director of women's programs, College for Continuing Education, Drake University (1969 – 1974), and served as director of human resources and equal opportunity programs there from 1974 – 1988. She organized and chaired Iowa's Commission on the Status of Women (1969 – 1972), and is the author of "An Informal Retrospective of Iowa Governor Robert D. Ray's Commission on the Status of Women." A charter member of the national board of the Interstate Association of Commissions on the Status of Women (1971 – 1973), Durden was also the first woman member of Great Plains States Regional Manpower Advisory Committee (1972 – 1974). A life member of AAUW, Durden served as chair, Continuing Education for Women, Adult Education Association (1971 – 1973). In 1992, she served as chair, statewide campaign committee, ERA IA. Durden was given the Des Moines Women of Achievement Award by the YWCA in 1984. Durden, who has three children, received her B.A., M.S.E. and Ed.D. from Drake University, Des Moines. Archives: Iowa Women's Archive, University of Iowa Libraries, Iowa City, IA. (ABS)

Durgananda, Swami – See Kempton, Sally

Durham, Anne Guerry – See Hoddersen, Guerry

Durham, Christine Meaders (1945 –) began her lifetime of activism as a college student in the 1960s at Wellesley College, attending demonstrations in favor of civil rights and in opposition to the Vietnam War. Durham began her law career in 1969 at Duke University Law School, where she helped organize one of the first women's law caucus groups in the country. In 1970, she was appointed a student member to the new American

Association of Law Schools' committee on women and the law. In 1971–1972, she lobbied for ratification of the ERA in the North Carolina Legislature. She became Utah's first female general jurisdiction trial judge in 1978, and later Supreme Court Justice and then Chief Justice. As co-founder of Women Lawyers of Utah, she worked and spoke extensively in support of women's rights and for the advancement of women in the legal profession. Durham was also a founding member of the National Association of Women Judges in 1979, and its president in the late 1980s. She was active in Democratic Party politics before going on the bench. As of 2003, Durham is committed to helping the disabled achieve parity.   (ABS)

Duzy, Merrilyn Jeanne (1946 –) As an undergraduate at California State University, Northridge, in the early 1970s, Duzy wanted to do a paper on women's erotic art but was unable to find any women in the then-current books on the topic. After five years of work, she published her own book, *The New Art: Female Eroticism*. Her association with the numerous artists whom she interviewed for the book led her to curate several women's erotic art shows, including Erotic Visions: Art by Women, the first all-women erotic art exhibit on the West Coast (1977). That same year, she curated Autobiographies, held at the Palos Verdes (CA) Library. The exhibit's overt sexuality resulted in it being closed down, the artwork confiscated by the police, and heated community debate on censorship in the arts. Also in 1977, Duzy co-curated, with David Stuart, the Dirty Dozen, an exhibit that included six women artists from Southern Califirnia and six from New York City. In the mid 1970s, Duzy began a 15-year association with the WCA and CAA. Duzy served as president of the Southern CA chapter of WCA from 1980–1982, and founded the Florida West Coast chapter in 1983. She served on its board from 1984–1989, and was also a member of the CAA committee on women in the arts in the late 1980s. In 1982, Duzy was part of the Women Artists performance presented by the Southern California WCA, and later produced a series of paintings based on the women's experiences. From there, she created an illustrated slide lecture, "Walking Through History: Women Artists, Past & Present," which she has presented in several U.S. cities, as well as in Israel, France and the Philippines. Duzy holds an M.F.A.   (ABS)

Dworkin, Andrea (1946 – 2005) Herself a victim of rape and abuse, Dworkin said, "The war is men against women." Dworkin wrote prolifically about rape, pornography, prostitution and violence against women. She believed that pornography is a precursor to sexual violence against women. With feminist attorney Catharine MacKinnon, Dworkin drafted a law that defined pornography as a civil rights violation against women and gave women the right to sue the producers and distributors of pornography in a civil court for damages. In 1983, the law was passed in Indianapolis, but was subsequently over-

turned by the Seventh Circuit Court of Appeals in 1985. The Supreme Court of the United States later upheld the lower court's ruling in American Booksellers Association, Inc. v. Hudnut. Her work was very controversial and she was criticized by both ends of the political spectrum. The Right saw her as a threat to family values. Others saw her as a proponent of censorship, which even many feminists felt would be against the interests of feminism. Dworkin's books include *Heartbreak: The Political Memoir of a Feminist Militant* (2002); *Scapegoat: The Jews, Israel, and Women's Liberation* (2000); *Life and Death: Unapologetic Writings on the Continuing War Against Women* (1997); *Letters from a War Zone: Writings, 1976 – 1987* (1988); *Intercourse* (1988); *Right-Wing Women: The Politics of Domesticated Females* (1991); *Pornography: Men Possessing Women* (1981); *Our Blood: Prophesies and Discourses on Sexual Politics* (1976); and *Woman Hating* (1974). Dworkin earned a B.A. from Bennington College (1968). Archives: Schlesinger Library, Radcliffe Institute, Cambridge, MA.

Dykewomon, Elana (1949 –) (also known as Elana Nachman and Elana Dykewoman) Author, editor and activist, Dykewomon's first book, *Riverfinger Women*, was published in 1974 by Daughters, Inc., a pioneering women's press. Like *Patience and Sarah* (written by Isabel Miller), *Riverfinger Women* is a lesbian novel with a happy ending, the first to have Jewish characters. With the publication of her second book, *They Will Know Me By My Teeth* (1976), she changed her name from Nachman to Dykewoman. With her third book, *Fragments From Lesbos* (1981), she changed her name again, this time to Dykewomon. In Northampton, MA, she was a co-founder of The Valley Women's Union, co-chair of the Women's Film Group and founder of Lesbian Gardens (1972 – 1976). In 1987, Dykewomon became editor of the journal *Sinister Wisdom*, which deals with lesbian arts and politics. Her novel *Beyond the Pale* received the Lambda Literary Award for Lesbian Fiction in 1998.   (ABS)

Eagan, Andrea Boroff (1944 – 1993) Author of the first feminist advice book for teenage girls, *Why Am I So Miserable if These Are the Best Years of My Life?* (Lippincott, 1976) and *The Newborn Mother: Stages of Her Growth* (Little, Brown, 1985), Eagan was also author of numerous newspaper and magazine articles on women's health. She served as editor of the National Women's Health Network Series for Pantheon Books and was president of Healthright, a non-profit organization. Active in local and national efforts for abortion rights and other women's issues, Eagan also taught about these issues at New York University, and at La Guardia, Manhattan Community and Hunter Colleges. Eagan served as founding president of the National Writers Union (1983 – 1987), and was a founding board member of The Writers Room in Manhattan. Eagan graduated from Columbia University in 1969.

Earle, Eleanor Grace Lee (1929 –) An R.N. with a bachelor's degree in political science, Earle was the president of the LWV in Wausau, WI. In 1966 she moved to Baton Rouge and became the League president there as well. During her membership she worked to elect Joe Delpit, who was the first African American to serve on the city council. She also worked to seat four women on the local school board. Earle joined NOW, the ERA Coalition and AAUW. She served on the state LWV and AAUW state boards. In addition, she counseled at the Battered Women's Program and served on that board. She has three children. (ABS)

Early, Ann McKenny (1925 –) was a pioneer teacher of women's studies. Appointed to the course curriculum committee at Southern Methodist University (1968), she spearheaded implementation of a two-week segment on women in the year-long course titled The Nature of Man. Concurrently, other women's studies classes developed so that by 1973, the Women's Studies Program was established—one of the first 50 women's study progrms in the country. From 1975 – 1993, Early taught in the program and served on the council, and from 1980 – 1989 she served as director. Early, who has three children, earned her B.A. from Clark University (1946) as a member of the first class to accept women. She earned her M.A.T. from Harvard University (1947). (ABS)

East, Catherine (1916 – 1996) was a federal government career civil service employee and, as described by Betty Friedan, a part of the government's "feminist underground" and "the midwife to the birth of the women's movement." She was technical secretary of the federal employment committee of the President's Commission on the Status of Women in 1963. There she met and worked with several women—Mary Eastwood, Pauli Murray and Marguerite Rawalt—founders or early supporters of what was to become NOW. In 1965 – 1966, East was one of several people who helped persuade Betty Friedan to organize NOW. East served as executive secretary of the Interdepartmental Committee and Citizens Advisory Council on the Status of Women, established after the President's Commission completed its work. In this position she served as a national focal point for receiving and disseminating information pertinent to women to state women's commissions and women's organizations throughout the country. East came to know women leaders nationally, and the information she made available to women helped provided fuel for their activism. East was highly respected by the government officials she worked for and was able to influence the shaping of national policy. From 1975 – 1977, East served as the principal staff of the National Commission on the Observance of IWY. She received VFA's first medal of honor and was inducted into the National Women's Hall of Fame in Seneca Falls, NY (1994). Born in West Virginia, East graduated from Marshall University and attended George Washington University Law School. She had two children. Archives: Schlesinger Library, Radcliffe Institute, Cambridge, MA.

Easton, Dossie Marguerite (1944 –) Writer, therapist, activist, revolutionary queer theorist and founder of several communes, Easton was a psychedelic crisis counselor at the Haight-Ashbury Medical Clinic in 1968. After the birth of her daughter in 1969, she formed two communes, The Church of Morally Regenerate Hedonism and Liberated Ladies at Large, where women raised their "post-Summer of Love" babies. In 1970, Easton developed a women's self-defense course with a Marine hand-to-hand combat instructor, and in 1971 joined and helped organize a free university course on car repair. In 1972, Easton became a volunteer with San Francisco Sex Information, where she remained active for 12 years. From 1973 – 1975, she hosted a weekly radio show on KPOO focusing on sex education, gay and lesbian liberation, feminist medicine, and legal and child abuse issues. After earning her bachelor's degree from the New College (1973), Easton joined the Society of Janus (1974), an S and M group, and became a member of the first board of directors. Easton worked for two years (1979) at Women's Crisis Support and Shelter Services, as both a shelter volunteer and a legal advocate for women prosecuting rapists. From 1984 – 1993, she worked at Sub-Acute Residential Treatment, a halfway house for people coming out of an acute hospitalization. She also completed graduate school and became a licensed marriage and family therapist. Publications include (with co-author Janet Hardy) *The Bottoming Book, The Topping Book, The Ethical Slut*, and *When Someone You Love Is Kinky*. Easton's poetry has appeared in various anthologies under the name Scarlet Woman. Archives: Papers will be donated to the San Francisco LGBT Historical Society, San Francisco, CA. (ABS)

Eastwood, Mary (1930 –) was executive secretary for the civil and political rights committee, President's Commission on the Status of Women, 1962 – 1963. Eastwood, a Justice Department attorney in 1966, and the late Catherine East were largely responsible for persuading Betty Friedan to start NOW. Eastwood was one of the women at the June 1966 meeting in Friedan's hotel room at the Conference of State Commissions on the Status of Women, and was at the lunch table where the initial organizing occurred. She also made the arrangements for the October 1966 NOW organizing conference in Washington, D.C. Eastwood worked anonymously on most of the early Title VII job discrimination test cases with Caruthers Berger, Sylvia Ellison and Marguerite Rawalt. An alternate member for the Justice Department on the interdepartmental committee on the status of women, she worked on recommendations submitted to the EEOC on interpretation of the sex discrimination provisions of Title VII, and served as staff for special task forces of the Citizens Advisory Council on the Status of

Women on family law and reproductive control, and the ERA. Eastwood was a founding member and member of the board of Human Rights for Women, and is a former member of FEW and the NWP. She is also a former executive VP of VFA, drafted VFA's bylaws, and was a member of VFA's nominating committee and the voting procedures committee. In 1980, president Carter named Eastwood acting special counsel of the Merit Systems Protection Board. Archives: Schlesinger Library, Radcliffe Institute, Cambridge, MA; also, some papers are at Wisconsin State Historical Society, Madison, WI.   (ABS)

Edeiken, Sarah B. – See Bornstein, Sarah Barbara

Edel, Deborah (1944 –) was one of the principal founders of The Lesbian Herstory Archives of New York City (1974), the largest and oldest lesbian archive in the world. In addition to working for gay/lesbian rights, Edel has been active in the civil rights, peace and women's movements. A social worker and psychologist, she has a B.A., M.A. and C.S.W. Archives: The Lesbian Herstory Archives, Brooklyn, NY.   (ABS)

Edelheit, Martha Nilsson (1933 –) (also known as Martha Ross Edelheit) A painter, sculptor, filmmaker and teacher, Edelheit was one of the women artists who, in the late 1960s and early 1970s, broke down barriers in the male-dominated art world. In 1965, when her explicitly erotic watercolors and paintings of male and female nudes—genitals showing—were shown at the Byron Gallery in New York City, John Canaday, then the head art critic for *The New York Times,* refused to review "that obscene woman." Edelheit has been exhibited worldwide. In the 1960s and 1970s she worked primarily with female and male nudes. She showed her work in Gedok, American Woman Artist Show in Hamburg, Germany (1972); was part of the Women Choose Women show at the New York Cultural Center and The New School Art Center Erotica Show (1973); and had her work in group exhibitions at the Erotic Art Gallery and the Self Image show at the Women's Interart Center in New York City (1974). In 1975, her work was exhibited in Works on Paper at the Brooklyn Museum, and at the New York Cultural Center and the Queens Museum. For Sister Chapel (a collaborative piece with other women artists), she created a nine-foot by four-foot painting, "Woman Hero," of a female nude painted with tattoos of various female goddesses from Greek and Egyptian legends (1978). Edelheit is a member of Women/Artists/Filmmakers Inc. and the WCA, and is an associate member of Soho 20 Chelsea. She has received, through Women/ Artists/Filmmakers, several grants for filmmaking from the New York State Council on the Arts. Edelheit, who now lives in Sweden, has one child. She holds a B.S. from Columbia University (1957).   (ABS)

Edelson, Bobbi – See Ausubel, Bobbi Gloria

Edelson, Joan (1933 – 1980) was a co-founder, with Judy Levy, Byllye Avery and Margaret Parrish, of the Gainesville (FL) Women's Health Center (1974), and was its first director. The clinic, which took a pro-woman, pro-patient, partnership approach to treatment, offered abortions, annual exams, testing for sexually transmitted diseases, and other gynecological and primary care services. It also served as a vehicle for CR. She left the GWHC to found Alternative Birth Center in Jacksonville, and later became a lay midwife for the remainder of her days in Texas.

Edelson, Mary Beth (1933) Artist and New York City resident, Edelson has founded numerous feminist enterprises over the years, is a lecturer and has written four books. *The Art Of Mary Beth Edelson* covers 30 years of Edelson's oeuvre as well as the feminist movement. From 1968 forward, Edelson states, "the underpinning of my exhibitions and art works rested on feminist subjects." In 1972 Edelson organized the first Conference for Women in the Visual Arts at the Corcoran Gallery of Art, Washington, D.C., where "women across the country met each other for the first time, and established and continued networking." In 1973 Edelson organized a seven-week seminar on feminism for the Smithsonian in Washington, D.C. From 1975 – 1985 she was a member of the AIR Gallery in NYC, the first feminist art gallery. Edelson was a founder of the Heresies Magazine Collective (1976 – 1989), and was active in the Mother Collective. From 1972 forward she has lectured internationally on her artwork and on feminism at museums, conferences and universities. She was active in forming the Women's Action Coalition in 1991, and in 1994 presented Combat Zone: Hq Against Domestic Violence in NYC, a three-month store front that provided self-defense workshops to abused women. In 1996, Edelson spearheaded a group that researched Title IX as a tool for challenging museums to provide equal representation for women in museums. Edelson has been active in the civil rights, peace and eco-feminist movements. Edelson has a B.A. from DePauw University, an M.A. from New York University, and an Honorary Doctorate of Fine Arts, DePauw University. She has two children. Archives: Feminist Archives of the Brooklyn Museum, Brooklyn, NY.   (ABS)

Edgar, Joanne (1943 –) An editor, writer and communications consultant, Edgar was a founding editor of *Ms.* magazine and stayed from 1971 – 1986. She typed the first statement of purpose of the NWPC (1971) and helped staff the National Women's Conference in Houston in 1977. She is the author of "Wonder Woman for President," published in *Ms.* magazine, July 1972; "The Women Who Went to the Summit" (*Ms.,* February 1986); and "Iceland's Feminists: Power at the Top of the World" (*Ms.,* December 1987). Edgar was also active in the civil rights movement in Mississippi in the early 1960s and the anti-war movement during the Vietnam War. She has a B.A. from Millsaps College and an M.I.A. from Columbia

University. Archives: Notes from her years at *Ms.* magazine are in The Sophia Smith Collection, Smith College, Northampton, MA. (ABS)

Edith, Patricia (1945 –) (also known as Patricia Andersen) was a member of the *Ain't I A Woman* newspaper collective from 1969 – 1976. Active in the women's movement in Iowa City, she was involved in both the general and radical lesbian women's communities and lived in four women's and lesbian collectives. Edith also participated in various gay rights, labor and anti-war activities as a member of the women's movement. (ABS)

Edwards, Lee R. (1942 –) From the late 1960s to the mid 1970s, Edwards was part of one of the earliest CR groups in Amherst, MA. From 1970 forward, she participated in various efforts to mobilize and organize women on the campus of the University of Massachusetts, Amherst. With Arlyn Diamond, Edwards conducted a salary review that showed women professors at the university earning significantly less than their male peers. With Diamond and Helen Curtis (then dean of women) Edwards petitioned the trustees to support various efforts to create greater equity for women on campus. These efforts, says Edwards, led to the founding of both the Everywoman's Center and the women's studies program. Edwards was co-editor, with Mel Heath and Lisa Baskin, of "Women: An Issue," published in *Massachusetts Review* in 1972. She was co-editor, with Diamond, of *American Voices, American Women* (Avon Books, 1973) and *The Authority of Experience,* a collection of feminist criticism published by University of Massachusetts Press. In addition, Edwards is author of *Psyche as Hero: Female Heroism and Fictional Form* (Wesleyan University Press). Edwards directed the women's studies program at University of Massachusetts, Amherst (1988 – 1991), and in 1991 became the first woman dean of the faculty of what became the College of Humanities and Fine Arts at UMass, Amherst, MA. (ABS)

Edwards, Susan Hollely (1943 –) was a pioneer gay activist on the Champaign/Urbana campus of the University of Illinois. One of the first women on campus to come out publicly as gay (1970), she developed a theory of lesbian feminism at a time when feminists, fearing male attack, refused to accept lesbians. Her theory led to group discussions and a community of women who supported one another—something she says was nonexistent at that time. The founding of Chicago Lesbian Liberation was an outgrowth of that community. Edwards, who served as the last editor of *Lavender Woman,* which ended in 1975, did public speaking and outreach in the Chicago area, and developed women's studies courses in film, literature and writing at William Rainer Harper College, Palatine, IL. Distressed by the arguments and anger that arose around separatism, Amazon Nation and class warfare, Edwards became a Buddhist practitioner and taught for 15 years at Naropa

Institute (now Naropa University). She is the author of *The Wild West Wind: Remembering Allen Ginsberg* and *The Practical Mystic.* Edwards holds A.B.D. and M.A. from the University of Illinois, Champaign/Urbana. (ABS)

Ehrenreich, Barbara (1941 –) has been involved in the anti-war movement since the 1960s, the women's health movement and the movement for economic justice. She has written and co-written over a dozen books and articles on a wide variety of subjects. Awards and grants include a Ford Foundation Award for Humanistic Perspectives on Contemporary Society, a Guggenheim Fellowship, and a grant for Research and Writing from the John D. and Catherine T. MacArthur Foundation. She has taught at the Graduate School of Journalism, University of California, Berkeley. Among her books are *Nickel and Dimed: On (not) Getting By in America* (Metropolitan Books, 2001); *Blood Rites: Origins and History of the Passions of War* (Metropolitan Books); *Fear of Falling: The Inner Life of the Middle Class; The Hearts of Men: American Dreams and the Flight from Commitment; and The American Health Empire: Power, Profits and Politics* (Random House, 1970). Her works as co-author include *Witches, Midwives and Nurses: A History of Women Healers* (The Feminist Press, 1973), with Deirdre English; *For Her Own Good: 150 Years of the Experts' Advice to Women,* with Deirdre English; *Re-Making Love: The Feminization of Sex,* with Elizabeth Hess and Gloria Jacobs; and *Global Woman: Nannies, Maids, and Sex Workers in the New Economy* (Metropolitan Books, 2002) co-edited with Arlie Hochschild. Her essay in *Harper's,* "Welcome to Cancerland," was a 2003 finalist for a National Magazine Award. Ehrenreich holds a Ph.D. from Rockefeller University. (ABS)

Eichelberger, Brenda (1939 –) was a founding member of the Chicago chapter of the National Black Feminist Organization (1974). A black woman, she lived on the South Side of Chicago where she worked as a counselor at Bryant Elementary School. Eichelberger, who had already started a student group to discuss women's issues, became involved with women's liberation after reading an article on NBFO in the May 1974 issue of *Ms.* magazine. The Chicago chapter of NBFO, which welcomed all black women, held monthly meetings that rotated around the city. It had a newsletter, CR groups and workshops, and provided childcare and transportation. When NBFO faltered, Eichelberger founded and headed the Chicago chapter of the National Alliance of Black Feminists (1976). NABF, which allowed non-black supporters to join, lasted until 1979. In 1977, *Quest* magazine published Eichelberger's article, "Voices of Black Feminism." Eichelberger continues to work as a counselor in predominantly black public schools in Chicago. Archives: National Alliance of Black Feminists, Vivian G. Harsh Research Collection of Afro-American History and Literature, Chicago Public Library. (ABS)

Eisenberg, Bonnie (1947 –) A founder of the first women's liberation newspaper in the U.S. (Berkeley, CA, 1970), and Women's Liberation Basement Press, Eisenberg also organized the first sit-in at the University of California, Berkeley, demanding classes in women's self defense (1970). In 1972, she founded *Marin Women's News Journal,* and in 1980 *Sonoma County Women's Voices.* Eisenberg was projects director of the Sonoma County Commission on the Status of Women, and education/publications director of the National Women's History Project (which launched National Women's History Month). A writer and editor, she was publications director for NWHP, and did promotion for the 150th anniversary of the founding of the women's rights movement (1848 – 1998). With Mary Ruthsdotter, she researched and wrote the video series "Women in American Life," funded by the U.S. Department of Education's Women's Equity Act Program. Eisenberg was also co-author, with Ruthsdotter, of the booklet *101 Ways to Celebrate Women's History,* and many other publications published by the NWHP. (ABS)

Eisenbrandt, Jacqueline June (1950 –) Abused as a child, pregnant and disowned by her family after her second year of college, Eisenbrandt fled her rural Wisconsin home for Milwaukee, choosing life on Welfare rather than give up her child for adoption. Unfamiliar with inner city life, she was raped, assaulted and robbed, but nonetheless managed to graduate from the University of Wisconsin, Milwaukee (1974) and earn a J.D. from Marquette University Law School (1981). After joining Milwaukee NOW in 1973, she participated in actions and on task forces, and marched in support of the ERA. She served as her chapter's representative, traveling to out-of-town meetings and writing reports on those meetings for the chapter newsletter. Eisenbrandt also helped establish childcare services for members during state conferences. As an attorney, Eisenbrandt helped women attain needed services. In addition, Eisenbrandt also volunteered to Sistermoon, a feminist bookstore and gallery; was a VISTA volunteer (1977 – 1978) at an inner-city, parent-run alternative school; and was part of a coalition of alternative schools (1975 – 1978). She has also been involved in anti-war and gay rights actions and marches. (ABS)

Eisenstein, Hester (1940 –) has worked consistently to help establish the field of women's studies. She was a co-founder of the women's studies program at Barnard College, Columbia University. As a member of the Barnard faculty, she participated, with Jane S. Gould and a group of faculty planners, in the development of the Scholar and the Feminist conference series, which began in 1976, and in the design and implementation of the women's studies program, which began in 1978. She served on the women's studies steering committee and introduced the first course at Barnard on feminist theory in 1975, although, she says, "I was compelled to call it Contemporary Feminist Thought, as the curriculum committee informed me that there was no such thing as feminist theory. Ironically, my book of that title, published in 1983 with G.K. Hall, is invariably now referred to as 'Contemporary Feminist Theory.'" Eisenstein was in Sydney, Australia, from 1980 – 1988, and worked as a "femocrat" implementing a government-sponsored affirmative action program for Aborigines, immigrants of non-English speaking backgrounds, and women of all backgrounds. From 1996 – 2000 she was director of women's studies at Queens College, City University of New York. She is the author of several articles and books, including *Gender Shock: Practicing Feminism on Two Continents* (Beacon Press, 1991). Now a professor of sociology, Eisenstein has a B.A. from Radcliffe (1961) and a Ph.D. from Yale University (1967). (ABS)

Eisenstein, Sarah (1946 – 1978) was the principal organizer of the Women's March on the Pentagon (1971). A pioneer researcher in the history of U.S. working-class women, her dissertation, published posthumously, was *Give Us Bread, But Give Us Roses: Working Women's Consciousness in the United States, 1890 to the First World War* (Routledge, 1983). Earlier, she had been active in SDS and the New York City anti-war movement, Mothers for Adequate Welfare, Bread and Roses, and the women's issue of *Leviathan.* She remained active to the end of her life as one of the founding members of CARASA.

Eisler, Riane (1931 –) was a co-founder of the Los Angeles Women's Center (1968 – 1969), and as staff attorney incorporated it as a nonprofit organization. In 1969, she founded the Los Angeles Women's Center Legal Program, the first of its kind in the U.S. In 1970, Eisler co-wrote an amicus curiae brief to the U.S. Supreme Court in the case of Perez v. Campbell, arguing that women should be considered persons under the equal protection clause of the 14th Amendment, thus paving the way for the later case of Reed v. Reed, which finally held that gender-based discrimination is prohibited by the 14th Amendment. In 1971, Eisler introduced the first classes at UCLA on the social and legal status of women. She is the author of *Dissolution: No-Fault Divorce, Marriage and the Future of Women* (McGraw-Hill, 1977), *The Equal Rights Handbook* (Avon, 1978), and *The Chalice and the Blade: Our History, Our Future* (Harper & Row, 1987). Translated into 20 languages, *The Chalice and the Blade* places feminism at the center of the political and social agenda. Other books include *Sacred Pleasure: Sex, Myth, and the Politics of the body* (Harper Collins, 1995), *The Power of Partnership* (New World Library, 2002), and *Tomorrow's Children: A Blueprint for Partnership Education in the 21st Century* (Westview Press, 2000). She was the principal investigator and senior author of "Women, Men and the Global Quality of Life," a three-year study published by the Center for Partnership Studies (1995). Eisler, who has two children, earned her B.A. from UCLA and her J.D.

from the UCLA School of Law. She is president of the Center for Partnership Studies, and founder of the Spiritual Alliance to Stop Intimate Violence. Archives: University of California, Santa Barbara, CA. (ABS)

Elias, Lois Raeder (1926 –) joined NOW in the early 1970s and worked to pass the ERA and pro-choice legislation. She was active in efforts to change women's image in advertising, and pushed to get New York City TV stations to hire women on camera and off. She also insisted on coverage of women in sports. As a member of the National Council of Jewish Women, she worked on NY State issues of choice, and passage of a women's health and wellness bill. She is senior adviser for public affairs at the National Council of Jewish Women, NY section. Elias, who has one child, is a retired media specialist. (ABS)

Elioseff, Jane Woodward (1940 –) joined Eastern MA NOW in 1972 and was immediately put in charge of the image of women in the media task force. In 1973, she began offering feminist counseling and was a founder of Women in Counseling and Therapy, an organization of early feminist mental health providers. Elioseff was a delegate to several regional and national NOW conventions. After moving to California, she became active in the WPC and the LWV in San Diego; in the mid 1980s, she served as the League's affirmative action representative to the San Diego public schools. In 1988, she moved to Texas, and has since been active in human rights and environmental issues. She is a founding member of the Green Party of Texas, serving two terms as state treasurer. Elioseff attended Smith College (1958 – 1959) and earned a B.A. from the University of Texas in 1962. (ABS)

Elkins, Patricia Davis – See Davis, Patricia Wood

Elliott, Beth (1950 –) was an early 1970s lesbian feminist who "viewed lesbian oppression as having to do with our being women first and homosexual second." She was first officer of a local chapter (CA) of Daughters of Bilitis under age 21, and a co-founding member of the Alice B. Toklas Memorial Democratic Club (the first such gay/lesbian club). Elliott was an alternate delegate for Shirley Chisholm in the 1972 California presidential primary. In addition, she was elected to the board of the California committee for sexual law reform, which successfully lobbied for the repeal of the state's sodomy laws. Elliott wrote and performed original songs, including "Ballad of the Oklahoma Women's Liberation Front" and "Teen Love." Since 1975, she has written extensively on anti-lesbian prejudice in the AIDS movement. Elliott also wrote lesbian commentary for the *San Francisco Bay Area Reporter* (1995 – 1998), and in 2003 had a satirical lesbian time-travel novel, *Don't Call It "Virtual"* (Emperor's New Clothes Press). Elliott attended the University of San Francisco. Archives: LGBT Historical Society, San Francisco, CA. (ABS)

Elliott, Eleanor Thomas (1926 – 2006) The daughter of a suffragist, Elliott fought to open doors of empowerment for women and girls. As board chair of Barnard College (1973 – 1976) she led a successful fight in 1973 to prevent Columbia University from "swallowing up" the prestigious all-woman college. She co-founded the trailblazing Women's Health Symposium for New York Hospital, served on the board of NOW LDEF (1983 – 1990), was president of the Maternity Center Association and chaired The Foundation for Child Development. She also campaigned to get more women on corporate boards and ran a program to train women in corporate finance. Elliott received an Honorary Degree from Duke University in 2002 for "advancement of women in education." (ABS before death)

Ellis, Carol Lashine (1948 –) (also known as Carol Lashine) was an early member of New Haven (CT) Women's Liberation, which had CR groups, a newsletter, a rock band and a radio soap opera, "The Liberation of Lydia." Empowered by the movement, Ellis entered medical school and became an internist at a time when women began breaking into medicine in numbers. Ellis, who was also involved in the anti-Vietnam War movement, earned her B.A. from Connecticut College (1969) and her M.D. from the University of Pennsylvania Medical School (1978). (ABS)

Ellis, Kate Ferguson (1938 –) was the first chair (1972 – 1978) of the women's studies program at Livingston College, Rutgers University. She was a member of the planning group of the Barnard College Conference on Sexuality (NYC, 1982), and in 1984 was a member of the founding collective of the feminist anti-censorship task force, participating in debates and demonstrations against the Meese Commission. She was an editor of *Caught Looking: Feminism, Censorship and Pornography* (Caught Looking, Inc., 1984). She is also the author of *The Contested Castle* (University of Illinois Press, 1989), and *Crossing Borders: A Memoir* (University of Florida Press, 2001). Ellis, who has one child, earned a Ph.D. from Columbia University (1972). (ABS)

Ellison, Sylvia (1911 – 1976) A U.S. government lawyer, Ellison worked with Caruthers Berger and Mary Eastwood as a volunteer on Title VII and other women's rights cases in the federal appellate courts, under the auspices of Human Rights for Women. She retired from her position as counsel for appellate litigation and chief trial attorney, U.S. Department of Labor, so that she could represent the women litigants and put her name on the briefs and other court document files. Ellison also served on the board of Human Rights for Women. She graduated from Atlanta (GA) Law School. Archives: HRW files, Schlesinger Library, Cambridge, MA.

Ellquist, Claudia Dianne (1948 –) Lawyer, professor, author and political consultant, Ellquist was "a grassroots organizer who worked toward governance as though the lives of women matter." She was a member of NOW, University of Arizona campus (1970 – 1971) and the AZ WPC (1971 – 1975), and lobbied Arizona legislators for the ERA in 1972. An officer and committee member for both Tucson NOW and AZ NOW, she organized rallies, marches, coalitions, pickets, letter-writing campaigns and led the largest successful recall campaign in AZ history, against the county assessor. From 1990 – 1994, she was a member of NOW's national board. In 1994 she was named a Woman of Courage by Tucson NOW, and in 1999 was named Valiant Woman by Arizona Church Women United.   (ABS)

Elsea, Janet Gayle (1942 –) As president of Arizona State University's faculty association (1975 – 1977), Elsea brought in Sheila Tobias to help organize the women's studies program. Elsea also worked with her counterparts at the University of Arizona and Northern Arizona University to form a statewide faculty women's organization. During that time, Elsea released salary studies to the campus newspaper and to the *Arizona Republic* showing the salary gap between women and male faculty. Although the president of Arizona State University was outraged, Elsea says, she stood by her guns and later became the first woman tenured and promoted in the history of her department. Earlier, Elsea had been the first female Ph.D. candidate in speech communication in 10 years at the University of Iowa (1968 – 1970). She organized the women graduate students into an informal support group. In addition to her Ph.D., Elsea holds a B.A. and M.A. from the University of California, Davis.   (ABS)

Emerson, Thomas I. (1907 – 1991) A Constitutional scholar and professor at Yale Law School, Emerson argued Griswold v. Connecticut in the U.S. Supreme Court in 1965. The culmination of lengthy litigations pursued over many years by Catherine Roraback and Fowler Harper. Besides winning the right for Connecticut women to obtain contraceptives, the Griswold case established the right of privacy and facilitated the outcome of Roe v. Wade. In the 1970s, Emerson testified on behalf of the ERA before Congress and the CT Legislature. He also traveled and spoke throughout the country and co-authored a seminal article on the prospective legal effects of the ERA with Barbara Brown, Gail Falk and Ann Freedman. Emerson served for many years on the Connecticut Permanent Commission on the Status of Women.

Emmachild, Sandra (1946 –) (also known as Sandra Lichenstein) was teaching philosophy at Suffolk Community College (Long Island, NY) in 1970 when she taught the first women's studies course at the college; by 2003, it had developed into an Associates Degree program with over a dozen courses and many faculty. Emmachild also founded The Women's Group and served as its adviser for 14 years. In 1972, she sponsored the

group's first event, a documentary on abortion. She subsequently began efforts to create a childcare center; helped formulate the Suffolk County Chapter of the Long Island Right to Choose Association; and became faculty adviser to the college's first feminist publication, *Lilith*. A supporter of the ERA, she debated with various local political leaders, appearing on local television and radio programs. In 1974, Emmachild organized the first Women's Week at the college, and at International Women's Year, was honored by the college for her service. She also wrote a legal column for the East End NOW newsletter, and legally changed her name to Emmachild to reflect her female heritage, rather than the male. Emmachild, who has one child, holds a B.A. in Philosophy, a B.A. in Classics and an M.A. in Religion.   (ABS)

Emmett, Kathryn (1944 –) graduated from Yale Law School in 1970. Within three years, while practicing law, she was teaching a class on women and the law at Yale. She played a pivotal role in the case that forced Mory's— a private dinner club at Yale that, even after the university went co-ed in 1970, remained closed to female members —to open its doors to women. A group of "remonstrants" challenged Mory's state liquor license on the grounds of its exclusion of female members. Emmett represented the case, Daley v. Liquor Control Commission, at trial and on appeal where it achieved its goal: Mory's had to open its doors to women. The case was widely cited in hundreds of other public accommodations suits. In addition, Emmett represented plaintiffs challenging CT's anti-abortion statues. She was a member of the all-female team of attorneys that brought Abele v. Markle on behalf of more than 2,000 CT women resulting in a judgment holding CT's anti-abortion statutes unconstitutional. Emmett presented the plaintiffs' position and formulated the trimester rationale adopted by the three-judge panel in CT and later adopted by the Supreme Court in Roe v. Wade. She was also one of the attorneys who represented the State of Connecticut in its case against the tobacco industry, focusing in particular on the impact of smoking on pregnant women and children and documenting the lack of services for pregnant women who quit smoking. Emmett was appointed a judge of the Connecticut Superior Court in 1982. In 1985, she became the first sitting judge in CT to give birth. She remained a judge for six years, and 1989 formed one of the state's first all female law firms, Emmett & Glander.   (ABS)

English, Deirdre Elena (1948 –) A writer, editor and teacher, English has taught at the State University of New York and the Graduate School of Journalism at the University of California, Berkeley. She is co-author, with Barbara Ehrenreich, of *Witches, Midwives and Nurses: A History of Women Healers* (1973); *Complaints and Disorders: The Sexual Politics of Sickness*; and *For Her Own Good: 150 Years of Experts' Advice to Women*. She has been a public affairs commentator on San Francisco public radio and television, and is a former editor in chief of *Mother Jones* magazine. English holds an M.A.   (ABS)

Ensler, Eve (1953 –) Playwright, writer and activist, Ensler is perhaps best known as the creator of "The Vagina Monologues," which is based on interviews with more than 200 women. The play became a crusade for Ensler after women who had seen it besieged her with their stories of having been beaten or raped, or who were the victims of incest. Determined to do something about it, Ensler and a group of friends established V-Day: Vagina Day, anti-Violence Day, Victory Day, a global movement to stop violence against women. Earlier, as an undergraduate at Middlebury College, Ensler brought feminists books into the classrooms and speakers to the college, started CR groups, and helped in the fight to win a sex discrimination suit for a feminist professor. In addition to "The Vagina Monologues" and the book version, *The Vagina Monologues: The V-Day Edition,* Ensler is author of *Necessary Targets: A Story of Women and War,* and *The Good Body,* which addresses why women of all cultures feel compelled to change their bodies, looks, and style of dress to fit in or be accepted. Ensler is the recipient of the Guggenheim Fellowship Award in Playwriting, the Elliot Norton Award for Outstanding Solo Performance, the 2002 Amnesty International Media Spotlight Award for Leadership, and The Matrix Award (2002). She is an executive producer of "What I Want My Words To Do To You," a documentary about the writing group she has led since 1998 at the Bedford Hills Correctional Facility for Women. In May 2003, she received an Honorary Doctor of Letters degree from Middlebury College.

Enstam, Elizabeth York (1937 –) A historian with a Ph.D. from Duke University, Enstam has spent a lifetime writing "from a feminist consciousness, and with the purpose of breaking the patriarchal stranglehold on the investigation and interpretation of U.S. history." In 1974, she turned to research, writing and speaking about women to "try to inform local (Dallas, TX) audiences and readers, especially those interested in history, not only about the lives and work of women in Dallas, but also about the significance of their lives to the development of this city." She has published numerous articles on the topic in both local and national publications, and is the author of *Women and the Creation of Public Life, Dallas, Texas, 1843 – 1920.*   (ABS)

Eppstein, Dorothy Jean (1918 –) was a pilot in the Women's Airforce Service in World War II (1943 – 1944), and flew all Army planes. She was then commissioned as a 2nd Lt. in the Airforce Reserves. After raising five children, Eppstein—who is a chemist, counselor and writer, in addition to being a pilot—went back to work. In 1965, she helped launch a women's liberation movement in Kalamazoo, MI, and spoke to conservative groups and schools about women's issues. She also helped found a

NOW chapter in Kalamazoo, led various CR groups, and brought in feminist speakers. Eppstein earned a B.S. from Michigan State University (1940), as well as an M.A. in Teaching (1964), an M.A. in Counseling (1968) and an M.S.W. (1984) from Western Michigan University.   (ABS)

Epstein, Barbara (1944 –) A scholar whose work has focused on social movements, Epstein is considered one of the architects of socialist feminism. As an undergraduate at Harvard/Radcliffe and a graduate student at the University of California, Berkeley (Ph.D., 1973), she was both a student of and a participant in critical movements of her time. She was a member of Bay Area Women's Liberation in the early 1970s. Her books are *The Politics of Domesticity: Women, Evangelism, and Temperance in Nineteenth Century America* (Wesleyan University Press 1981) and *Political Protest and Cultural Revolution: Nonviolent Direct Action in the 1970s and 1980s* (University of California Press, 1991). She is co-editor, with Marcy Darnovsky and Richard Flacks, of *Cultural Politics and Social Movements* (Temple University Press, 1995). For many years, she was on the editorial collective of the journal *Socialist Revolution* (later *Socialist Review*). She is (2006) working on a book on Jewish anti-fascist resistance in the Minsk ghetto during World War II.   (ABS)

Epstein, Cynthia Fuchs (1933 –) was a founding member of NY NOW (1966). In this capacity, she testified before the EEOC on the determination of guidelines for Title VII of the Civil Rights Act. A professor of sociology, she wrote one of the first books in the social sciences on women's exclusion from the professions, *Woman' Place: Options and Limits on Professional Careers* (1970). She is also author of *Women in Law*, the first book in the social sciences on women lawyers (1981), for which she received the 1981 Scribe's Book Award and the Merit Award of the American Bar Association; and *Deceptive Distinctions: Sex, Gender and the Social Order* (Yale University Press, 1988). Epstein has lectured extensively on women in professions, business and politics. She was a consultant to AT&T and General Motors, and conducted a research project on workplace culture for AT&T. She also served as a consultant to the White House under two administrations, and at the National Academy of Sciences on the committee on women's employment and related social issues. She is the recipient of the first American Sociological Association Sex and Gender Award for Distinguished Contribution to the Study of Sex and Gender (1994). Other awards include a Guggenheim Fellowship, the Jessie Bernard Award of the American Sociological Association for Lifetime Work on Gender (2003), and the Merit Award of the Eastern Sociological Society (2004). Epstein, who has one child, received her Ph.D. from Columbia University in 1968.   (ABS)

Erickson, Nancy S. (1945 –) A feminist educator in the legal field, Erickson became a member of New York City

NOW in 1969 and was treasurer in 1970. She was also a member of the NOW education committee headed by Kate Millett, and of the legislative and political committee headed by Charlene Suneson. From 1970–1973, she attended and graduated from Brooklyn Law School. Erickson was co-founder of the first women law students association at BLS, and wrote an article for the *Brooklyn Law Review* on Phillips v. Martin Marietta, the first U.S. Supreme Court case concerning sex discrimination brought under Title VII of the Civil Rights Act. From 1973–1975, she was a volunteer law student and then attorney at the Women's Law Center, founded by attorney Emily Jane Goodman, where she wrote fact sheets for women on legal issues such as women's names, family law and credit. She also wrote *A Woman's Guide to Marriage and Divorce in New York* (Women's Law Center, 1974). As an associate at a law firm, Erickson provided free legal assistance to New York Women Against Rape and Lady Carpenter. As a law professor in NYC from 1975–1980, she was co-founder of Metropolitan Women Law Teachers Association; chair (1976–1977) of the Association of American Law Schools Section on Women in Legal Education; co-founder, Society for the Study of Women in Legal History; and one of the first professors to teach Women and the Law at New York Law School. From 1979–1980, she was one of the first professors to teach that course at Cornell Law School. She was also a volunteer attorney for ACLU, writing briefs in sex discrimination cases, including Ludtke v. Kuhn, in which women reporters sued to get access to athletes after baseball games, and has been a prolific writer on women's issues. In addition to her law degree from Brooklyn Law School (1973), she holds an LL.M. from Yale Law School (1979).   (ABS)

Erkel, Blanche L. (1919 –) As a consumer affairs officer for the Food and Drug Administration in the 1960s, Erkel "monitored the positions of women," as the federal women's coordinator, and was influential in upgrading one woman who was a single mother working as a dishwasher. Planning to quit and accept Welfare because she couldn't afford health insurance, the woman was given an opportunity for an upward mobility program, got a college degree, was hired, and became a public affairs officer for the FDA. "We also hired the first women to be FDA Investigators (1972)," she says. Erkel, who has three children, holds a B.S. from the University of Minnesota and an M.S. from Michigan State University.   (ABS)

Errington, Sue Ellen (1942 –) joined the Muncie-Delaware County (IN) NOW chapter in 1972, and worked on several issues: credit for women in their own names, images of women in the media, the right to abortion, and the ERA. In the mid 1970s, she became the first female Little League baseball umpire in Muncie. In 1976, she was IN NOW state coordinator, was part of the group of NOW members who developed an election strategy to pass the ERA, and worked for a targeted legislative candi-

date. She left her job to work on IN's successful ratification drive in 1977. Errington later became a NOW national board member, participated in the successful campaign to defeat Toledo, OH's anti-abortion ordinance, was in the pilot group of NOW's ERA missionaries to Utah, and spent nine months on the Oklahoma ERA countdown campaign. She is director of public policy, Planned Parenthood of Greater Indiana. Errington, who has two children, earned a B.A. from Indiana University and an M.A. from the University of Michigan. Archives: Ball State University, Muncie, IN.   (ABS)

Ervin-Tripp, Susan Moore (1927 –) An associate professor at the University of California, Berkeley, in the late 1960s, Ervin-Tripp helped found the Association of Academic Women, and was a member of a senate committee that issued a report on the status of women at the university. The report was published in July 1970 during the hearings of the special subcommittee of the committee on education and labor of the California House of Representatives. This resulted in the University of California, Berkeley, senate setting up a standing committee on the status of women and ethnic minorities. Ervin-Tripp twice served as chair of the senate committee. In the early 1970s, she joined the League of Academic Women, which had filed a discrimination complaint with HEW, then chaired by Casper Weinberger, resulting in an Affirmative Action program, an administrator, and a set of statistics on the availability and attributes of applicants and hires, as well as public advertisement of academic positions. Ervin-Tripp was also part of a faculty senate committee that looked into complaints of discrimination against female custodians, and worked on a campus committee to equalize the opportunities for women in sports. In 1974, she wrote a report to the federal government, which was soliciting comments on its proposal for Title IX. Ervin-Tripp, who has three children, participated in several peace movements and is active in the Faculty for Israeli-Palestinian Peace. She holds an A.B. from Vassar College and a Ph.D. from the University of Michigan. Archives (and oral history): Bancroft Library, University of California, Berkeley.   (ABS)

Escalante, Alicia Lara — In the early 1960s, Escalante formed the East Los Angeles Welfare Rights Organization (later known by other names). For more than a decade, the organization worked to influence policy in the area of women and Welfare rights, and helped develop sensitivity training and affirmative action programs and Spanish language materials for the California Department of Welfare. Escalante also worked with organizations such as the Chicana Service Action Center in Los Angeles, providing policy support. In 1969, she helped Católicos Por la Raza organize a Christmas Eve protest in front of St. Basil's Church in Los Angeles. The groups hoped to persuade the Catholic Church to spend less money on elegant churches and more on the poor. As the police pushed the demonstrators back, Escalante lost her youngest child, Alex. When the police would not let her pass, a desperate Escalante "kicked an officer in his privates." He fell over and she was arrested and sentenced to 30 days in the county jail. Her son was found by friends and kept safe. In August 1970, Escalante was an invited speaker at the Chicano Moratorium rally. She later worked for 20 years as a CA State employee in various community-based programs including Indian Health Services, the Equal Opportunity and Civil Rights office and the Deaf Access Program. Born in El Paso, TX, in the 1930s, Escalante raised five children as a single mother while working full-time as an activist for Chicana Welfare rights. (ABS)

Eskenazi, Elayne (1934 –) was active with both NYC NOW and NY State NOW. She served as board member of the NYC chapter and led CR groups for many years. She also served as treasurer of NY State NOW. Eskenazi visited the Bedford Hills (NY) women's prison to lead CR groups; marched on Washington for Roe v. Wade and the ERA; and stood on street corners in New York City to solicit signatures in the "war" against Supreme Court Justice nominee Robert H. Bork. In addition, Eskenazi supported civil rights activist Daisy Bates and marched in many gay pride parades. (ABS)

Estey, Donelle (1947 –) (also known as Donelle Paint) was part of a women artists CR group ("believed to be the first") in the San Francisco Bay area that worked to get recognition for women artists. The group challenged local museums to show women artists' works; started a newspaper, *WEB (West Coast Bag)*; and met until 1974. Estey also participated in the Los Angeles Woman House events and conferences. She holds a B.F.A. and M.F.A. (ABS)

Etelson, Doris Carol (1930 –) considers herself a "pre-pioneer" whose efforts made it possible for the women who followed her in the mid 1960s forward to "find the openings, understand the routes, and have the courage to challenge the status quo." For example, when Etelson was employed by a major corporation, she challenged every barrier to move from one "not for women" job to another, until she broke the glass ceiling to become that company's first female corporate VP in 1975. In her own corporation, she mentored female employees, and in one instance pushed for equality by contracting with a major industrial plant to own and operate one of its facilities—and then employed only women. Etelson also pioneered the lifestyle of a married couple living in two cities to accommodate both their careers. She was a board member of Women in Business of Boston, a founding member of the International Alliance of Women's Networks, and has been a member of the NAACP for the past 50 years. As education chair of the NAACP, she developed and ran the first Career Conference for Minority Students, held in Rockland County, NY. In later years, Etelson moved to Florida, joined the board of The Florida Women's

Alliance, and served as president of WEAL. Etelson, who has two children, holds an M.B.A. and was awarded an Honorary Doctorate from State University of New York for her contributions to women and education. (ABS)

Evan, Dina Bachelor (1942 –) is an author, psychotherapist, teacher and seminar presenter who has worked her entire life for both the equality of women and the rights of the lesbian and gay communities. She has been the chapter chair of NOW in Phoenix, AZ, and Newport Beach, CA, as well as the CA state membership chair. In the summer of 1982, Evan, along with six other women, fasted for 37 days for the ERA in Springfield, IL. She also officiated at the marriage of 10,000 gay men and lesbians on the steps of the IRS at the national march on Washington in a demonstration for equal rights for gays and greater funding for AIDS research. Evan is the author of two books: *Break Up or Break Through* and *The Trouble With Marriage*. She holds a Ph.D. in Psychology and another in Holistic Health, and has four children. (ABS)

Evans, Pat Terrell (1931 –) was a founding member of NOW in Louisiana, and a member of the Commission on the Status of Women. As director of the Louisiana Bureau on the Status of Women, she developed a model non-traditional training program for women; helped pass displaced homemaker legislation; established the first family violence and first rape crisis programs; and helped change rape and community property laws. Evans also established a creative writing and pre-release program for women in prison, and created the first Governor's Conference on Women. She led the Louisiana delegation to the International Women's Year conference in Houston, and conducted political campaigns for women running for office. She also worked for passage of the ERA, planned strategy for the pro-choice initiative, and developed the Bureau on the Status of Women into a multi-million dollar state agency offering service and advocacy for women. Evans, who has three children, holds a B.A. from Southeastern Louisiana University and has done postgraduate work at Harvard University. (ABS)

Evans, Sara Margaret (1943 –) A history professor at the University of Minnesota, Evans entered the women's movement in the late 1960s, working in Illinois with Heather Booth to provide abortion counseling at the Chicago West Side Group and the Hyde Park Group. She then moved to North Carolina, where she was a founder, with Paula Goldsmid, of Group 22, Durham/Chapel Hill, the first women's liberation group in NC. Since 1976, Evans has been an active member and adjunct faculty of the women's studies program at the University of Minnesota. She a founder of the Center for Advanced Feminist Studies (1983) at the university, and director (1986 – 1989). During that time, the Center pioneered projects in curriculum integration, graduate curricula in feminist studies, and post-doctoral studies in feminist

E

theory. From 1987 – 1990, Evans was on the board of the National Council for Research on Women. She is editor of *Journeys that Opened Up the World: Women, Student Christian Movements, and Social Justice, 1950 – 1975* (Rutgers University Press, 2003), and author of *Tidal Wave: How Women Changed America at Century's End* (2003) and *Born for Liberty: A History of American Women* (New York: Free Press, 1989), a selection of the History Book Club. She is also author of *Personal Politics: The Roots of Women's Liberation in the Civil Rights Movement and the New Left* (Alfred A. Knopf, 1979), and *Jenny's Secret Place* (Lollipop Power, 1970), a book for young children. Evans is co-author, with Barbara J. Nelson, of *Wage Justice: Comparable Worth and the Paradox of Technocratic Reform* (University of Chicago Press, 1989). Also active in the civil rights and anti-war movements in NC, Evans holds a B.A. (1966) and an M.A. (1968) from Duke University, and a Ph.D. from the University of North Carolina at Chapel Hill. She has two children. Archives: Duke University, Durham, NC.　(ABS)

Evansgardner, Jo Ann (1925 –) A member of Pittsburgh NOW, Evansgardner formed (with Wilma Scott Heide, Jean Witter, Phyllis Wetherby and her husband, Gerry) KNOW, Inc. in 1968. KNOW is a feminist publishing house that for years was the chief source and/or resource on women for NOW. In 1969, Evansgardner proposed the use of Ms. instead of Miss or Mrs. She was elected to NOW's national board that same year, served several terms, and was co-coordinator of the Eastern Region. She coordinated many actions and projects, including the national demonstration against AT&T. Evansgardner was the first person to work on conflict-resolution within NOW. She was arrested in 1971 for defending a young sculptor, Lorna McNeur, who had climbed up the statue of Father Duffy in New York City and placed a papier-mâché statue of Susan B. Anthony on his head. While living in Houston, Evansgardner started the Houston University chapter of NOW. A longtime member of the NAACP, Evansgardner has been active in civil rights. She holds a Ph.D. from the University of Pennsylvania. Archives: University of Pittsburgh, Pittsburgh, PA.　(ABS)

Everett, Jana G. (1947 –) (also known as Jana Matson) A member of the Women's Liberation Abortion Counseling Group in Ann Arbor, MI (1970 – 1973), Everett was part of a volunteer group that researched legal options available in New York, and obtained information on adoption and keeping a baby. From 1973 – 1974 she helped set up and run a women's crisis center in Ann Arbor, and from 1971 – 1974 was a founding member of the women's caucus in the Political Science Dept. at the University of Michigan, responsible for getting the department to offer more fellowships to women and people of color, and to use inclusive language. Everett and others taught the first women's studies courses at UM (1971 – 1974), and co-taught and co-designed the first Women and Politics

courses at UM. In 1975, in Denver, CO, she was a founding member of the Feminist Credit Union that operated from 1975 – 1977. Everett is the author of *Women and Social Change* in India (St. Martins Press, 1979), and has one child. She earned her B.A. (1969) from Mount. Holyoke College and her Ph.D. (1976) from the University of Michigan.　(ABS)

Everhart, Jane Sandra — After moving to NYC from Tenafly, NJ, Everhart attended her first NY NOW meeting, where she heard a paper read by then-Columbia graduate student Kate Millett (1967) "and became totally hooked." Everhart went on to help plan the NOW picket of *The New York Times* to protest the newspaper's sex-segregated want ads—"a smashing success," she says—and attended many women's rights demonstrations. She also started the first newsletter for NY NOW, and in 1968 arranged for feminists to be on the "The David Susskind Show." She started several CR groups in her West Side neighborhood. In addition, Everhart worked with Betty Berry on the marriage and divorce committee, but her childcare needs were too pressing to wait for Congress to discover working mothers. Everhart explains that she and other young mothers eventually dropped out of the movement to earn a living and support their children.　(ABS)

Evola, Carroll F. (1939 –) was a board member of Detroit NOW. She helped organize a successful action against the Detroit Athletic Club, which did not allow women to enter through the front door, and was also part of a threatened action against local high-end stores that had refused to give women credit in their own names. (When pickets were threatened, the stores backed down and issued credit). Representing Catholics for a Free Choice, Evola was part of the protest action against the Catholic Bishops Conference at Cobo Hall in Detroit.　(ABS)

Ewing, Anne D. (1930 –) (also known as Anne D. Radlow) joined San Diego NOW's education task force in 1970. In that capacity, she helped lobby for Title IX until its passage in 1972. In 1973, Ewing became chair of CA NOW's education task force. Working with the chairs of 24 NOW education task forces, Ewing helped design a detailed questionnaire to evaluate sexism in children's readers being considered for use in public schools. Their report, "Sexism in California Readers," was presented to the CA board of education in 1974, which adopted the readers "shown to be filled with crippling sexism." Threat of a suit by CA NOW led to negotiations and the U.S. commission created to review all textbooks under consideration to eliminate sexism and racism. Elected president of San Diego NOW in 1975, Ewing protested the local Catholic bishop who had declared that any Catholic who supported NOW's position on choice would be excommunicated. In 1977, she was founding president of the San Diego NWPC. Ewing, who has two children, holds a B.A. (1952) and is a professor, researcher and principal planner in San Diego County planning and land use. Archives: San Diego NOW archive, Love Library, San Diego State University, San Diego, CA. (ABS)

Ezorsky, Gertrude (1926 –) Committed to ending academic discrimination against women, Ezorsky was an active member of the City University of New York's Women's Coalition in the 1970s, and participated in the Melani suit, which gave City University women a financial settlement for sex discrimination. Ezorsky was the coordinator of a full-page ad published in *The New York Times* (April 6, 1975) addressed to President Ford that urged that the affirmative action provisions of Executive Order 11246 be enforced on behalf of academic women and minorities. The ad had 3,000 signatures and endorsements by about 100 outstanding academics, including many men. Ezorsky was a founding member of the Society for Women in Philosophy (NY) in the early 1990s, and received the Distinguished Woman Philosopher award from the group (Eastern Division, American Philosophical Association) in 1997. Ezorsky's many published works include *Racism and Justice, the Case for Affirmative Action* (Cornell University Press, 1991), chosen as Outstanding Book on Human Rights by the Gustavus Meyers Center in 1991. Ezorsky, a retired professor of philosophy, earned her Ph.D. from New York University in 1961. (ABS)

Fahey, Shirley Nickols (1935 – 2001) The national co-chair, with Dell Williams, of NOW's heath and sexuality task force in the early 1970s, Fahey served at the University of Arizona College of Medicine for 30 years. She contributed to the programs of the college as a teacher, counselor and curriculum coordinator, but is perhaps best known for her work as associate dean of admissions. In 1972, Fahey and a colleague began teaching Human Behavior and Development to freshman medical students. With a Ph.D. in psychology (University of Florida, 1964), Fahey served on the Western Psychological Association committee on the status of women (1973 – 1975); as a charter member of American Psychological Association Division of Psychology and Women, (1975); as a woman liaison officer for the University of Arizona College of Medicine to the Association of American Medical Colleges (1977 – 2001); and on the Association for Women Faculty, University of Arizona (1981 – 2000, and VP from 1983 – 1984). Fahey was also a reviewer for *Signs: Journal for Women in Culture and Society* (1981 – 1984). Her various papers and addresses include "Where are Equal Opportunities for Women?" American Association of University Women (1974). Born in Omaha, NE, Fahey had two children.

Falk, Edith Sharon (1944 –) was a member of the task force to reactivate the North Dakota Commission on the Status of Women (1972), and was vice chair of Region VII, ND Women's Coalition (1973 – 1974). She was also fiscal officer for the ND National Women's Conference in

Houston (1977), and served as delegate at large. A member of the AAUW, Falk was ND division legislative chair, helping ND pass the ERA (1974 – 1976), and a member of the board of directors, ERAmerica (1975 – 1977). An active Republican, she was program chair of the Bismarck area Republican Women's Club (1976 – 1978), and a delegate to the National Convention of the Republican Federation of Women's Clubs, Atlanta (1977). "In the early days of the movement in North Dakota, there were very few Republican women involved, and even fewer businesswomen. People like me forced others to confront the fact that these were issues of all women," she says. Falk has three children. She holds a B.A. from the University of North Dakota. Archives: University of North Dakota, Grand Forks, ND. (ABS)

Falk, Gail (1943 –) A member of the New Haven (CT) Women's Liberation (1969 – 1971), Falk was a co-founder of the Yale Law Women's Association (1969) and a co-teacher of the first Yale Law School undergraduate seminars on women and the law. She was also co-author of "The Equal Rights Amendment for Women," published in the *Yale Law Review* (1971), and was co-founder of Women v. Connecticut (to legalize abortion). In Charleston, WV, she was a founding board member of the Women's Health Center. She offered legislative testimony on the ERA in the Tennessee and West Viriginia Legislatures, and was an active member of the West Virginia Women's Group (1971 – 1974). In 1970, she wrote a booklet on how to keep your own name. Falk has also been active in the civil rights, peace and labor movements, and has been a longtime fighter for disability rights, beginning in 1977. She has three children, and earned her B.A. from Radcliffe (1966) and her J.D. from Yale Law School (1971). (ABS)

Falk-Dickler, Florence (1939 –) At the second national meeting of NOW, Falk-Dickler stated her concern to Betty Friedan that "women in the future would not benefit from feminist economic and social advances without accessible, affordable, high-quality childcare." Friedan promptly appointed her national coordinator for childcare, a position Falk-Dickler held for six years. Falk-Dickler was also a co-founder of the Northern NJ NOW chapter (1970), and served as head of its childcare committee for 10 years. From 1975 – 1999, she was deputy regional administrator of the Women's Bureau, U.S. Dept. of Labor. After leaving the Department of Labor, Falk-Dickler continued her advocacy for women at the Women's Rights Information Center, Englewood, NJ. She is a member of the National Council of Jewish Women, Bergen County section, and serves on the operating board of Northern NJ NOW and as a women's advocate in the office of assemblywoman Loretta Weinberg. Falk-Dickler has a doctorate degree (Teacher's College, Columbia University, 1981). Her dissertation was on the difficulties women face returning to school after an extended period of absence due to marriage and family obligations. She has two children. (ABS)

Farians, Elizabeth Jane (1923 –) A pioneer theologian, Farians believes that the Christian Church has perpetuated discrimination against women for centuries by saying the practice is divinely inspired. Earning her doctorate in theology in 1958 from Saint Mary's College at Notre Dame, she was one of the first women to try to get a teaching position in theology. Despite being threatened with arrest, Farians integrated the prestigious all-male cleric Catholic Theology Society in 1966. Farians joined NOW in 1966; was the founder of its task force on women and religion in 1967; and was elected to NOW's national board. Following four years of written requests and protests, on August 20, 1970, the women on the task force finally obtained a meeting with a liaison committee of the bishops at their headquarters in Washington, D.C., where the women presented a list of demands to bring women into full equality in the church—a list that generated much media attention. Farians was fired from her university position, she says, "because I was a feminist." Then, she says, she "filed the first case of sex discrimination in higher education." In addition to her theological activities, Farians wrote a comprehensive program for women's studies, and in 1969 created a popular series of women's studies lectures at Loyola University. Farians also worked with Alice Paul on the ERA and testified on its behalf before both Houses of Congress as a theologian. Farians helped start the first NOW chapters in CT, NJ and OH, and brought the NWPC to OH. Archives: Schlesinger Library, Radcliffe Institute, Cambridge, MA. (ABS)

Farley, Lin (1942 –) is credited with coining the term "sexual harassment." Farley was a reporter for Associated Press when she was assigned to a feminist demonstration against AT&T and realized that she belonged with the demonstrators. She became active in the lesbian feminist movement and Lesbian Liberation Front (LLF). While teaching a class on women and work at Cornell University in 1974, Farley and her colleagues became aware that women they knew had either been fired or quit their jobs because they had been made uncomfortable by men. Farley reasoned that this type of behavior must also exist in other areas of employment, not just within academia, and determined to study it. In 1995, Farley and other activists from Ithaca, NY, formed Working Women United (WWU), held the first "Speak-Out on Sexual Harassment," and organized the first survey devoted solely to the issue. The term "sexual harassment" entered general use with the publication of Farley's book *Sexual Shakedown: The Sexual Harassment of Women on the Job* (McGraw-Hill, 1978).

Farley, Tucker Pamella (1939 –) Active in organizing women's liberation at Penn State University and State College in the mid 1960s, Farley pushed for the establish-

ment of Women's Liberation House, a shelter that offered abortion counseling and also ran an underground railroad for abortions. In 1969, Farley organized a women's caucus in the National Workers Education Local, and in 1970 began The New York Women's Labor Project. Farley developed and taught women's studies courses at CUNY Brooklyn, establishing and co-coordinating a degree-granting women's studies program. She also organized the first campus women's center and designed a grant to develop a model education project for adult women in the community. An organizer of the Strategies for Survival conference held at Brooklyn College (1974 – 1975), Farley was also a NY representative at the founding of NWSA and was one of its early leaders; helped found and coordinate NWSA's lesbian caucus; headed the NY WSA, and subsequently served as one of the founding editors of the *NWSA Journal*. Working in the MLA in the late 1960s and early 1970s, Farley, with others, initiated the Commission on the Status of Women in the Profession and the Job Market Commission, which she headed; she subsequently served as liaison from the Lesbian and Gay Caucus of MLA to that commission. When Maidenrock, a national lesbian institute, was held outside Minneapolis in the late 1970s, Farley was the first teacher. She also taught lesbian studies at Barnard College, and organized and participated in the first lesbian theory session offered at the Berks in 1975. She organized the first CUNY-wide lesbian and gay organization, and as its coordinator helped establish the Committee (later the Center) for Lesbian and Gay Studies at CUNY Graduate Center. Archives: The Sophia Smith Collection, Smith College, Northampton, MA; and Brooklyn College, CUNY, Brooklyn, NY. (ABS)

Farrell, Warren (1943 –) An icon of the men's movement, Farrell was active in the feminist movement in the late 1960s and early 1970s, directing NOW's masculine mystique task force and leading the men's portion of the Women's Strike for Equality marches in D.C.. The only man ever elected to the NYC NOW board of directors three times, he became known for conducting men's beauty contests to get men to understand how it feels to be treated as a "sex object", and role-reversal dates to get women to experience the risks of sexual rejection. He first deviated from NOW's stance when he began doing research for *Father and Child Reunion* (eventually published in 2001), which led him to believe that children of divorce should be raised equally by both parents rather than the mom having the option to be the primary parent. In 2003 Farrell ran for governor of California emphasizing the importance of the presumption of both parents' equal involvement after divorce. Farrell's other books include *Why Men Are The Way They Are* (1986) and *The Myth of Male Power* (1993) and *Women Can't Hear What Men Don't Say* (1999). His most recent, *Why Men Earn More* (2005), offers 25 specific ways women can out-earn men in the work place. He has taught at the School of Medicine at the University of California in San

Diego, as well as at Georgetown University, Rutgers, Brooklyn College and the California School of Professional Psychology. He was chosen by the *Financial Times* as one of 100 of the world's top Thought Leaders. (ABS)

Farris, Linda J. – See Kurtz, Linda Farris

Fass, Diane M. (1941 –) was a convener of the NWPC in 1971, and in 1972 was a founder of the Minnesota WPC. She served as coordinator for the national conference in Minneapolis for the Interstate Association of Commissions on the Status of Women (1972), and that year was a representative for the women's advisory committee at an African American meeting at Stillwater State Prison. From 1971–1974, she served, by appointment of the governor, as a member of the women's advisory committee to the MN State Department of Human Rights. From 1972–1974, she was coordinator for childcare programs for use at women's conference sites, and from 1973–1974 was Region 10 representative to the MN State Department of Human Rights sex bias task force. In addition, Fass was VP for legislation, Twin Cities NOW (1972) and from 1971–1972 was a volunteer lobbyist for Twin Cities NOW and the Greater Minneapolis Day Care Association. In 1973, Fass convened Rochester MN NOW. In 1974, Fass was a lecturer on combating gender bias stereotyping at Rochester Community College, and was a community curriculum consultant, reviewer for non-discrimination, women and minorities in Rochester. Fass was a convener of All the Good Old Girls in Rochester, (1978). She was also a member of the International Women's Watch (1993 –1995). In 1997, Fass received the Marvelous Minnesota Woman Award from the MN secretary of state. Fass, who has one child, earned her B.S. from Florida State University, Tallahassee (1963). (ABS)

Faust, Jean Satterthwaite (1930 –) was president of NOW's first chapter, NY NOW, 1966–1967. Starting with no office space, equipment or supplies, Faust used her apartment as the NOW office. Other NOW offices held include VP, 1968; chair of the board, 1969; chair of the EEOC committee, 1967–1970; national legislative co-chair, 1968–1970; and national board of directors, 1968–1969. The struggle to include rights for women in the NY State Constitution occupied much of Faust's first year with NOW. Not supported by other women's groups, the constitutional amendment did not pass. Faust also played a role in the 1968 fight to integrate newspapers' classified sections, an important early victory for NOW. She testified at Congressional hearings in Washington, D.C., on the ERA, and participated in efforts to support a sex discrimination suit brought by women workers against Colgate-Palmolive. Faust also testified at Department of Labor hearings on sex discrimination in employment, and at the Senate hearings on EEOC enforcement (1969). She also helped organize demonstrations against the EEOC for not responding to women's problems and for

denying permission for herself and Betty Friedan to speak at NY hearings. She also worked with media to achieve a more balanced view of women, feminists in particular. During all this time, Faust was attending meetings and conferences as aide to Congressman William F. Ryan. Illness forced her retirement from both jobs in 1970–1971. Faust has a B.A. from the University of North Carolina (1952). Archives: Schlesinger Library, Radcliffe Institute, Cambridge, MA. (ABS)

Faxon, Alicia Craig (1931 –) has written widely on women artists, and has published articles in *Woman's Art Journal*. She made a catalog of the etchings of Mary Cassatt for the Danforth (MA) Museum, and created an exhibition of 19th century women there in 1971. In 1972, Faxon wrote a feminist view of the *New Testament* in *Women and Jesus* (Pilgrim Press, 1973). A professor of art history at Simmons College (1979–1993), Faxon was a member of the women's studies board and created the first history of women artists course there. She joined the Women's Caucus for Art when it was formed in Boston, and remains a member. In 1987, Faxon was co-program-chair of the first WCA conference in Boston and regional editor for Rhode Island of *Art New England* (1994–1998). With Liana Cheney and Kathleen Russo, Faxon wrote *Self-Portraits by Women Painters* (London: Ashgate, 2000), a feminist view on women painters through history to the present. Faxon, who says she has "two feminist sons," holds a B.A. from Vassar College, and an M.A. and Ph.D. from Radcliffe College. Archives: Vassar College, Poughkeepsie, NY. (ABS)

Feather Song, Elsie (1948 –) (also known as Elsie Lojek) Feather Song has worked with media, educational, and legal and spiritual groups to provide physical security for women and to further the causes of women's rights. She was security coordinator for the Women's Peace Encampment, Seneca Army Depot, in 1983, and provided security services and education at NOW meetings in Los Angeles, NYC and Detroit for various events. She has also provided security and safety services for Vanderbilt University Women, and taught seminars on personal safety and pursuing education in non-traditional criminal justice careers. In 1970 and 1980, she was a volunteer media responder and security sentinel at the Hermitage Cherokee Challenge Clans Women Council for Female Education, held in Nashville, TN. She spent three years (1980–1983) at the Women's Peace Encampment, which was trying to divert a nuclear shipment, and was a security and cultural center representative at the Rochester Women's Activities parades and marches in 1969, 1974, 1984 and 1998. Feather Song has a B.A. in Security; is a Native American Educator, Wolf Clan Teaching Lodge of the Seneca Indian Historical Society; and is a Wolf Song Peace Elder. Archives: Native American Education & History, Cherokee Star School, Cherokee, NC; also, National Spiritualist Association of Churches. (ABS)

F

Federbush, Marcia Joyce (1934 –) wrote the first published study of sex discrimination in a school system, *Let Them Aspire! A Plea and Proposal for Equality of Opportunity for Males and Females in the Ann Arbor Public Schools* (Ann Arbor, MI, 1971). She rewrote the handbook of the Michigan High School Athletic Association, which did not include the words "she" or "her," and did include sentences such as "The duty of a coach is to be the kind of man he wants the boys under him to become." Federbush also wrote the first Title IX complaint against a major university (Michigan) solely on the grounds of gross discrimination in athletics (1973). In addition, she gave the speech (1976) to the University of Michigan regents that started the first athletic scholarships at the university. In 1975, Federbush wrote the revenue sharing grant proposal that started one of the earliest infant care centers for the babies of students in the Ann Arbor schools. Earlier, in 1967, she was part of a group that started the Childcare Action Center for students and staff at the university. In 1982, Federbush led a group of Michiganians in filing state and federal civil rights charges against the Michigan High School Athletic Association (and others) for having girls playing their major sports in the wrong seasons; the suit was dismissed because the group did not receive federal funding and "the wrong seasons" was not considered discriminatory at that time. In 1994, she gave the speech to MI's board in control of intercollegiate athletics that persuaded them to keep men's gymnastics, which they were going to cut, in partnership with women's gymnastics, which they were going to keep. Federbush, who has two children, taught fifth and sixth grades, and worked for 15 years at EEOC. She was inducted into the Michigan Women's Hall of Fame in 1988, and has received the International Women's Year Award from the University of Michigan, and the Susan B. Anthony Award from the Ann Arbor/Washtenaw County, MI, chapter of NOW. Archives: State of Michigan Library, Lansing, MI. (ABS)

Federici, Silvia (1942 –) A Marxist-feminist scholar and activist, Federici was one of a small number of feminists who raised consciousness in the U.S. about the value of women's unpaid labor. Believing that neither radical feminists nor socialist feminists have the answer to women's oppression, she was motivated to find a more satisfactory explanation of the roots of the social and economic exploitation of women. Her work was originally inspired by early 1970s work of Selma James, Mariarosa Dalla Costa and others active in the Wages for Housework movement. Together with Dalla Costa and James, she was one of the co-founders in 1972 of the International Feminist Collective, the organization that launched the Wages for Housework Campaign internationally. In 1973 she was a co-founder of the New York Wages for Housework Committee. In the course of this campaign, in 1975, Federici wrote two pamphlets: "Wages Against Housework" and (with Nicole Cox) "Counterplanning From the Kitchen." In 1984, she and Leopoldina Fortunati published *Il*

Grande Calibano: Storia del corpo sociale ribelle nella prima fase del capitale (Milano, Franco Angeli), a book that explores "the transition to capitalism" from a feminist viewpoint. Other publications include feminist essays such as "Reproduction and Feminist Struggle in the New International Division of Labor" (1999); and "Women, Land-Struggles and Globalization: An International Perspective" (2004). In 2004, Federici also published *Caliban and the Witch. Women, the Body and Primitive Accumulation* (New York: Autonomedia), the culmination of work she began in the mid 1970s. Federici has also worked against the death penalty and, in the anti-globalization movement, especially against the World Bank educational policy in Africa. Archives: Marxist Archives, University of Texas, Austin. (ABS)

Feeley, Dianne (1939 –) A socialist feminist, Feeley is the author of "Why Women Need the ERA," a 24-page pamphlet published by Pathfinder Press in 1973 and 1976. She has written articles for *Feminism and Socialism, The Militant* and *The International Socialist Review*. She also helped organize the 1970 rally in San Francisco's Union Square on the 50th anniversary of woman suffrage. As a member of NY NOW, she helped organize teach-ins, classes and conferences, as well as demonstrations on the right to choose, sterilization abuse, the ERA, and women political prisoners. Feeley also debated Phyllis Schlafly (1976) and Meg Katz (1970) on the ERA. Feeley was a Socialist Workers Party candidate for governor of NY State in 1979, and a member of the party's national committee (1976, 1977 and 1978), but was "expelled for freelancing in the women's movement in 1983," Feeley says. (ABS)

Feigen, Brenda (1944 –) became a feminist by default when she entered Harvard Law School in 1966. "Almost immediately, I became furious at the way women were treated. There were only 32 of us in a class of 565, and there were no women faculty. Professors had 'Ladies' Days,' the only days of the year when they would call on us. The squash courts and sole student eating club were off limits. More important, law firms interviewing students on campus for jobs simply announced that they were not hiring women." She was successful in changing all that by June 1969, when she graduated. Feigen has since been honored by women graduates of the law school for forcing Harvard to change. In NYC, Feigen joined a CR group and helped start the Women's Action Alliance and *Ms.* magazine. She directed the ACLU's Women's Rights Project with Ruth Bader Ginsburg, and served as NOW's national legislative VP, focusing on abortion rights and the ERA. In 1971, she was a founding member of NWPC. Her journey through life as a feminist is chronicled in her memoir, *Not One of the Boys: Living Life as a Feminist* (Alfred A. Knopf, 2000). (ABS)

Feist, Arlyce Swanson (1944 –) (also known as Arlyce Currie) joined the women's movement at Yale University

(1970 – 1972). She began an information organization, Free the Children, to educate parents about sex-role stereotyping (1972 – 1975), and helped develop Bananas, a childcare information and referral service that helps parents find childcare, support and children's services (1973 forward). Although her primary focus has been on children, Feist also helped found the unions for non-academic employees at the University of California and at Yale University. She attended the University of Chicago, and has one child and two stepchildren. (ABS)

Feldman, Bella (1930 –) A sculptor and professor, Feldman helped found the women's studies course at the California College of Arts and Crafts (now known as the California College of the Arts) in the 1970s. She also created and taught for 23 years a sculpture course that explored the materials and sensibility normally excluded by the machismo orientation of sculpture programs. The course continues to be offered by the college. When faced with "an arbitrary male replacement" for her job as sculpture professor, Feldman galvanized the campus around her and took the case to the Federal Board of Equalization. She won. Publicity from this battle led to her becoming graduate director, making her able to work for the goal that all graduate students be accepted on a gender-neutral basis. Feldman also organized an informal group, The Ladies Auxiliary of California College of Arts and Crafts, that, in the 1970s and early 1980s, intervened in several cases where women's faculty positions were jeopardized. Feldman has two children. She earned her B.A. from Queens College (NYC) and her M.A. from San Jose State University. (ABS)

Feldman, Margaret Eichbauer (1916 –) A retired (1981) professor of psychology at Ithaca (NY) College, Feldman was listening to a speech on racism in 1969 when she heard the speaker say, "Just as there is discrimination based on race, there is discrimination against women. I am a womanizer myself." Shocked, she said to herself, "What he means is, there is sexism." Feldman began to use the word at parties, lectures and panels, and was credited by Dr. Charlotte Conable, in a book she wrote on women at Cornell, with inventing the word "sexism." In 1970, Feldman helped organize a rally to celebrate the 50th anniversary of woman suffrage, and in 1972 organized a women's political seminar at Ithaca College that was designed to encourage women to run for office. As a professor at Ithaca, she helped plan a women's studies program, and began insisting on the use of non-gendered pronouns. In 1977, Feldman was chair of the committee that planned an event at Eisenhower College in Seneca Falls, NY, in anticipation of the 1977 Houston National Women's Conference. She and her husband, Harold, who taught the first course on women at Cornell, both attended the conference, as well as the 1985 Nairobi conference. Beginning in 1981, she and her husband began the first of five years of three-month stays in Washington,

working for family and women's issues. She also participated in the planning for the 1990 five-year follow-up to the 1985 conference. Feldman has been active in the Democratic Party, has done work related to violence in the family, and with her husband organized a local Gray Panther group in 1981. She has three children. (ABS)

Feldman, Maxine Adele (1944 –) A lesbian feminist singer-songwriter and stand-up comic, Feldman was asked to leave college in 1962 because she was gay, and her parents sat Shiva for her as though she were dead. Feldman returned to college in 1969, attending El Camino College in Torrence, CA. There she helped create a women's center and organized a CR group. Feldman then put an act together, singing feminist and lesbian songs that she wrote and performing as a stand-up comedian. She also recorded a feminist album, Angry At This. Feldman's act was a bridge between the gay and straight worlds and she performed it at many venues, including college campuses. In New York City, Feldman performed in the Women for Women series put on by NOW (1974). Feldman also played at the 1977 National Women's Conference in Houston. Although Feldman has retired from acting, her songs are still performed at women's gatherings. Recently she was included in the documentary film, "Radical Harmonies." (ABS)

Felshin, Jan R. (1931 –) By the late 1960s and early 1970s, Felshin was speaking and writing frequently on feminist topics related to women in sports. She is the author of *Handbook for Girls Sports Organizations* (1961). In her high-school teaching career (1953 – 1956), she fought for competitive opportunities for girls and insisted on equal opportunity for use of sports facilities for girls. At the University of Nevada, Reno (1959 – 1965), when she complained that the men traveled to games by plane, "while we had to drive long distances, I was actually offered the use of the plane." As a member of national organizations concerned with girls' and women's sports, she fought consistently for competition and for equality for women in sports. Asked to name her most significant contribution to the women's movement, she says, "It is the fact that I have always been an out lesbian. I have never been intimidated. In fighting for recognition and acknowledgement of lesbians, I believe I have contributed to the empowerment of all women. I believe our book, *The American Woman in Sport*, co-authored with Ellen W. Gerber, Pearl Berlin and Waneen Wyrick [Addison-Wesley Publishing Co., 1974], was the first to raise the issue of lesbians." Felshin met with Eleanor Smeal in planning PA NOW in the late 1960s, and was a founding member of Pocono NOW. The group "immediately integrated the classified section of *The Pocono Record* and gave pause to local school principals about their treatment of girls in sports and other school activities," she says. In addition to her writing, Felshin has served as a consultant to local and national organizations, including the NOW task force on sports (1974–1975); at West Point, on provisions for the admission of women cadets in 1975; and at the Women and the Law National Convention, where she offered expert testimony on athletics in 1984. Felshin holds a B.S. from Boston University, Sargent College (1952), an M.S. from Wellesley College (1953), and an Ed.D. from the University of California, Los Angeles (1958). Archives: The Lesbian Herstory Archives, Brooklyn, NY.   (ABS)

Ferber, Marianne A. (1923 –) Professor emerita of economics and women's studies at the University of Illinois, Urbana-Champaign, since 1993, Ferber has researched and written on sex discrimination, focusing on the workforce, since 1971. She has been a member of the university's executive committee on women and gender in global perspective since 1997, and a member of the women's studies advisory committee since 2000. Ferber has also served on editorial boards, including *Feminist Economics,* 1993 to date. She is the author of *Women and Work, Paid and Unpaid* (Garland Press, 1987). She is also co-author (with Francine D. Blau) of *The Economics of Women, Men and Work* (Prentice-Hall, 1986), now in its fourth edition with Ann Winkler as the third author; and co-author (with M. Brigid O'Farrell) of *Work and Family: Policies for a Changing Work Force* (National Academy Press, 1991). Ferber, who was born in Czechoslovakia and fled the Holocaust with her family, earned her B.A. (1944) from McMaster University, Canada, and her M.A. (1946) and Ph.D. (1954) from the University of Chicago. She was director of women's studies, University of Illinois, 1980–1983 and 1991–1993, and was Martina S. Horner Distinguished Visiting Professor, Radcliffe, 1993–1995. In recognition of her service to the women's movement, she received the Carolyn Shaw Bell Award (2002) and Doctor of Humane Letters, Eastern Illinois University (2002). Archives: Women and Gender Resources Library, University of Illinois, Urbana-Champaign.   (ABS)

Ferdon, Nona Marie (1928 –) (also known as Nona Springel) In Boston in the early 1970s, Ferdon was a member of NOW and worked as a coordinator for the ERA in MA. In 1972, she founded and co-directed The Boston Psychological Center for Women. Earlier, she had been active in the civil rights and anti-war movements. She took part in the Selma march with Dr. Martin Luther King, worked in Montgomery, AL, doing health education and voter registration, and counseled draft resisters. Ferdon, who has two children, holds a B.A., M.A. and Ph.D. She a semi-retired university professor and clinical psychologist in London, England.   (ABS)

Ferguson, Ann (1938 –) (also known as Ann F. Brentlinger) A professor of philosophy and women's studies, Ferguson began helping students access (then) illegal abortions in 1967. Ferguson was involved in the women's caucus of the New University Caucus (1970–1972); was a member of the women's caucus of the

University of Massachusetts/Amherst Coalition against the Vietnam War (1972); and participated in a 1972 takeover of the ROTC building on campus to protest the racism and sexism of the war policy. Also in 1972, Ferguson was part of a feminist studies committee that worked to create a women's studies program at the University of Massachusetts; and she co-created and co-taught a course on American philosophy from a feminist perspective. Ferguson created other feminist courses and published several articles on feminist theory—one in support of androgyny as a feminist goal (1977), and one on women as a revolutionary class in the U.S. (1979). Her theoretical works led to two books: *Blood at the Root: Motherhood, Sexuality and Male Domination* (Unwin and Hyman, 1989) and *Sexual Democracy: Women, Oppression and Revolution* (Westview, 1991). She is also co-editor, with Bat Ami Bar On, of *Daring to be Good: Feminist Essays in Ethico-Politics* (Routledge, 1998). The author of articles on lesbian sexuality, the feminist sex wars, women and work, and other feminist topics, Ferguson was also a founding member of the Pioneer Valley Women's Union (1973–1977), and was a member of its workgroup, Women Against Nukes. She helped organize a University of Mass/Amherst Women's Conference in January 1974; was part of a university childcare group that demanded that the university keep and expand its childcare services (1973); and attended the National Socialist Feminist Conference in Columbus, OH, in June 1975. Ferguson was active in the civil rights movement from 1961 forward, in the peace movement from 1964 forward, and was a member of the anti-nuclear-power movement in the 1970s in the Pioneer Valley. Ferguson, who has one child, holds a B.A. from Swarthmore College (1959) and an M.A. (1961) and Ph.D. (1965) from Brown University. Archives: W.E.B. Dubois Library, University of Massachusetts, Amherst, MA.   (ABS)

Ferguson, Kathy Ellen (1950 –) gave a Phi Beta Kappa banquet speech at Purdue (1972) calling for the establishment of a women's studies program on campus. "Purdue's president came up to me afterward and told me he had more important things to do than worry about women's studies." Undeterred, Ferguson introduced and taught classes on women and political theory at the University of Minnesota (1974–1975), and wrote the first dissertation in her department on women and feminism. She is the author of several feminist books, including *The Man Question* (University of California Press, 1993); *The Feminist Case Against Bureaucracy* (Temple University Press, 1984); and *Self, Society and Womankind* (Greenwood, 1980). Ferguson, who has two children, has also been active in peace and environmental groups. She has a B.A. from Purdue University (1972) and a Ph.D. from the University of Minnesota (1976).   (ABS)

Ferguson, Mary Anne (1918 –) began teaching at Ohio Wesleyan University, where her husband was a full professor and she was a part time instructor, in 1947. Hoping to improve her position in academia, she completed her Ph.D. at Ohio State University in 1965, and taught at Ohio University for one year. However, even after receiving her Ph.D., no new professional avenues opened for her. Later, "hiring in the academic world improved and my husband and I both got jobs at the newly created University of Massachusetts/ Boston, in 1967. But within a year, I had been demoted from full-time to part-time because of what I later learned was a non-existent nepotism law." As a member of MLA, Ferguson became part of the Commission on the Status of Women in the Professions (1968), where she worked to overcome unfair hiring practices. She also helped start a grassroots network of female English professors, many of whom had been denied tenure and promotion. The commission "definitely had an influence on the gradual liberation of women, many getting tenure. Only in the elite 'research' universities was progress dismally slow," she says. Ferguson attended the first National Conference on Women in Academia and the historic Women as Resources for Society, held at Radcliffe College in 1972. She also compiled a textbook, Images of Women in Liter- ature, an anthology of writings that highlight stereotypes of women in literature, that went through five editions. She was instrumental in founding the women's studies program at UMass/Boston in 1973, which became a department in 1975, one of the earliest in the country. She won two grants, one from the Carnegie Foundation to improve the status of women on campus, 1974 – 1976, and one from NEH, to inaugurate experimental interdisciplinary courses on women, 1973 – 1975. Ferguson was the director of women's studies, and chair of the English department at UMass/Boston until her retirement in 1986. Ferguson, who has three children, received her B.A. and M.A. from Duke University.   (ABS)

Ferguson, Terry (1936 –) was founding chair of the Middletown, CT, chapter of NOW (1971). Focused on securing women's economic rights, including gender equity in insurance, she led workshops on these and other economic issues. She also organized protest demonstrations, rallies and lunch-hour picketing at office buildings such as the Aetna Insurance Building, as well as at courthouses and at the state capitol, and coordinated bussing groups from the mid-state area to marches in Washington, D.C., for the ERA and women's reproductive rights. Ferguson founded and edited the NOW newsletter, "The Waterfall," which became CT NOW's statewide publication. She later served as president of CT NOW. Ferguson, who has five children, holds an M.A. from Northeastern University and a Ph.D. from the University of Connecticut (1979). (ABS)

Fernandez, Shelley (1930 –) served two terms on the board of NOW in the 1970s, and one term as president of San Francisco NOW. She is the co-founder of La Casa de las Madres in San Francisco, and the founder of Our Lady of Guadalupe Health Center (1968). Fernandez was also active in the Third World Women's Movement and the Puerto Rican Organization for Women. She earned a B.A, M.A. and Ph.D., and has one child.   (ABS)

Ferne (1930 –) (also known as Ferne Williams) joined the Essex (NJ) chapter of NOW in 1970. Using only the name Ferne, she worked on the abortion issue, the ERA and many other local and national projects. Ferne became chapter fundraiser because, she says,"I was able to make feminist items and sell them at the many conferences and events on the East Coast. The profits went to the chapter until I got divorced and needed to make a living." She became a feminist entrepreneur and started Ferne Sales Co, which made T-shirts, jewelry, bumper stickers, buttons and many other items that could be sold to help raise the status of women. She has four children   (ABS)

Ferrandino, Marilyn – See Myerson, Marilyn

Ferrante, Donna (1943 –) (also known as Donna Loercher) A member of NY NOW and editor of its newsletter, "The NOW York Woman," from 1968 – 1971, Ferrante was a founding member (1971 – 1974) of the Queens (NY) chapter of NOW and co-president in 1972. She started an education committee to combat sexism in the schools and in children's literature. She is the founder of Feminist Book Mart (1970 – 1977), a mail-order book service specializing in non-sexist and non-racist children's literature, and in women's studies literature. This was the second women's book source in the U.S. (The first was Women's Place, in Berkeley, CA.) Denied a loan from her commercial bank in 1975, Ferrante found herself embroiled in what would result in a class action suit that would continue until 1979. The Small Business Administration denied the loan request not because the Book Mark was a poor credit risk, but because it "was a specialty book store devoted to women," says Ferrante. "We claimed and ultimately demonstrated that the Book Mart offered a wide variety of selections representing many viewpoints to a wide customer base that included men." The case, which the women won, was defended by a law firm including Carol Bellamy. Ferrante and eight other women, under the leadership of Jacqui Ceballos, founded New York Women In Business (1975 – 1977). Ferrante holds a B.A. and M.B.A. from Pace University (NY).   (ABS)

Ferraro, Geraldine Anne (1935 –) was the first female vice presidential candidate on a major party ticket in the U.S. in 1984 when she ran unsuccessfully with Walter Mondale, the Democratic nominee for President of the United States. The daughter of Italian immigrants, Ferraro graduated from Marymount Manhattan College in 1956. While teaching at PS 85 in Queens during the day, she studied law at night at Fordham University, graduating in 1960. In 1974, she became an assistant district attorney in the Investigations Bureau in Queens County. That same year, she married John Zaccaro, but kept her maiden name professionally, which was unusual in that day. In 1974 she became an assistant district attorney in the Investigations Bureau in Queens County. After serving three years as a trial assistant, she created the Special Victims Bureau, which handled all the sexual abuse and domestic violence cases in the county, prosecuted the referrals of child abuse from Family Court, and handled all violent crimes against senior citizens. During that period she also · served as president of the Queens County Women's Bar Association. In 1978, she was elected to the U.S. House of Representatives from the 9th Congressional District in Queens, and was re-elected in 1980 and 1982. In 1980, Ferraro was elected secretary of the House Democratic Caucus and took a seat on the steering and policy committee. In 1984, she was appointed chair of the Democratic platform committee, the first woman to hold that post. In Congress, Ferraro spearheaded efforts to pass the ERA. She also sponsored the Women's Economic Equity Act in 1984. In 1988 she held a fellowship at the Harvard Institute of Politics, and in 1992 ran unsuccessfully for the U.S. Senate. She was appointed ambassador to the United Nations Human Rights Commission by President Clinton and served in Geneva for the 1993 – 1996 terms of the commission. She served as president of the International Institute for Women's Political Leadership from 1987–1990. In 1985, Ferraro wrote *Ferraro: My Story* describing the 1984 vice presidential campaign. She is the author of two other books: *Geraldine Ferraro, Changing History* and *Framing a Life*. She is a former co-host of CNN's "Crossfire" and is a Fox News contributor. Ferraro is senior managing director of The Global Consulting Group, an international investor relations and global communications firm. (ABS)

Ferree, Myra Marx (1949 –) As a graduate student at Harvard University, Ferree joined a small group of women who were part of the Harvard/Radcliffe Catholic student community and helped form a women's self-examination and discussion group (1972). They were also involved in the issue of women's ordination to the priesthood, and supported the new bookstore, New Words. Ferree did several early studies on women in politics and working class women (which became her dissertation in 1975), and attended early meetings of the NWSA. Hired by the University of Connecticut in 1976, she was enlisted by Martha Mednick, first director of the women's studies program, to teach courses and build the program. Ferree served as the director of women's studies in the 1980s. Also involved with the AAUP and the President's Commission on the Status of Women, Ferree did a study of salary inequity among faculty that resulted in major wage adjustments. She served as an expert witness/statistician on an employment discrimination case in the 1980s for CWEALF, and on the Connecticut Chief Justice's task force on gender equity in the courts in the 1990s. Ferree was also involved nationally in Sociologists for Women in Society, helped found its journal, *Gender & Society*, and

served as its president in 2000. Says Ferree, "I have become more a consultant and resource for the movement than an activist, but then I was always better at theory than at actual activism." Ferree holds a Ph.D. from Harvard University (1976). (ABS)

Fichtenbaum, Myrna (1930 –) worked to get Shirley Chisholm elected to Congress from Brooklyn, NY, in the 1950s. In 1960s, she helped organize the committee for a fair trial for the Black Panthers (New Haven, CT); and was secretary of the New Haven NAACP. Fichtenbaum also worked to desegregate schools in New Haven. In the 1970s, Fichtenbaum was a founder of the WPC in St. Louis. She organized the Women's Labor Coalition of St. Louis, and researched and wrote a paper on black women in a 1933 labor struggle in that city, later published as *The Funsten Nut Strike*. She was also an organizer of the fair employment committee of St. Louis to pass the Humphrey-Hawkins bill; served as program chair of the first women's labor conference held in St. Louis; and founded the Coalition of Labor Union Women in St. Louis. In 1976 she wrote a paper, "Breaking the Skill Barrier: Progress and Problems," for the conference Crisis: St. Louis Women. Fichtenbaum has also organized women's workshops on healthcare, Medicare and Social Security. For many years prior to retirement as an investigator, she was president of her local union and represented it at the EEOC. A member of the Gateway OWL Chapter in St. Louis, Fichtenbaum holds a B.A. and has three children. Archives: University of Missouri, St. Louis. (ABS)

Fiedler, Maureen Ellen (1942 –) co-founded and coordinated Catholics Act for the ERA (1978 – 1982). During that time, she worked full-time speaking, writing, fundraising and lobbying, and in 1982 was one of seven women who fasted for 37 days for ratification of the ERA in Springfield, IL. A member of the Sisters of Loretto, Fiedler has worked since 1975 to promote women's equality in the Roman Catholic Church, especially in the priesthood. She has also been active in the peace movement, demonstrating and doing civil disobedience during the Vietnam War, the wars in Central America, and both Iraq wars, and has also worked at times for gay/lesbian rights, civil rights and human rights globally. Fiedler earned her B.A. from Mercyhurst College and her Ph.D. from Georgetown University (1977). (ABS)

Field, Connie Elyse (1947 –) was a founding member of Bread and Roses, Cambridge, MA, in the late 1960s. From 1969 – 1972, she organized workshops and conferences, and spoke on women's issues at various colleges and universities in New England. In 1970, she was project director, Conference on Working Women. A film producer and director, Field produced, directed and edited the feature documentary "The Life and Times of Rosie the Riveter." The feminist film earned 12 international awards for best documentary, was translated into 10 languages, and is one of the few documentaries listed in the National Film Registry of the Library of Congress. Archives: Material from the film is at the Schlesinger Library, Radcliffe Institute, Cambridge, MA; the Library of Congress, Washington, D.C.; and the Academy of Motion Pictures Arts and Sciences, Beverly Hills, CA. (ABS)

Field, Jane (1920 – 1993) (also known as Jane Marie Connelly) was a strong, loyal, witty feminist and catalyst for social change. A copywriter for 20 years, she was ultimately copy group head for J. Walter Thompson in NYC (1964 – 1972). In 1970, she joined the women's movement, heeding a call for help from JWT PR executive Betty Harragan, unknown to Field at the time, who had an employment discrimination suit against the company. Field worked within NOW to gain support for Harragan, who eventually won an EEOC decision. Field became chair of NY NOW in 1971. With Jacqui Ceballos, Dell Williams and Laureen Helen, she founded New Feminist Talent, a speakers bureau, in 1972, and was president from 1972 – 1975. NFT represented 29 feminists who spoke at colleges and universities. In 1976, Field founded the *Hudson Valley* (NY) *Women's Times,* a political primer devoted to issues affecting women. She particularly wanted to educate housewives who voted against the ERA. In her later years, Field, a diabetic, wrote for the LaCrosse (WI) newsletter for the American Diabetic Association. Although Field did not graduate from college, she was a "drop in" at numerous colleges, taking courses relevant to her work and interests.

Fields, Daisy B. (1915 –) is the founder of Fields Associates, an HR consulting firm specializing in women's career-related issues. She was a founding member of FEW (1968), serving variously as national president, executive director and editor of its newsletter. In the 1970s, she served on Flora Crater's team lobbying Congress for passage of the ERA. Since 1972, she has published several articles on sex discrimination in the workplace and women in management, among other topics. She is the author of *A Woman's Guide to Moving Up in Business and Government* (Prentice Hall, 1983). From 1984 – 1988, Fields served as president of the Clearinghouse on Women's Issues, and was editor of its newsletter from 1984 – 2000. From 1985 – 1998, she was VP of The Women's Institute of Washington, D.C., and managing editor of The Women's Institute Press. In that capacity, she was co-author of *The United Nations Decade for Women, Plans of Action, 1975 – 1985,* incorporating the "Convention on the Elimination of all Forms of Discrimination Against Women," published in 1987. In 1991, she edited *Winds of Change: Korean Women in America,* by Diana Yu. Among her numerous activities, Fields has served as chair, advisory board, First Women's Bank of Maryland; commissioner, Maryland Commission for Women (1973 – 1977); commissioner, Montgomery County (MD) Commission for Women (1979 – 1982);

president, Maryland Chapter, WEAL; member of the executive boards of the Federation of Organizations for Professional Women and the National Council of Career Women; member, board of directors, National Woman's Party (1989 – 1997); founding member and PR chair of the National Association of Women Business Owners; consultant, USAID (1990 – 1993). She is the recipient of numerous awards, including FEW's Barbara Tennant Award (1974); WEAL's Special Award in appreciation and recognition of distinguished service to WEAL and the women's equality movement (1978); and the VFA Medal (1998). Archives: Schlesinger Library, Radcliffe Institute, Cambridge, MA. (ABS)

Fiene, Susan (1946 –) A visual artist, Fiene co-founded the Women's Art Registry of Minnesota in Minneapolis in 1973 to share professional information and organize art exhibits of women's work. Yet their greatest efforts went to creating a new way of being an organization—collective sharing and decision-making on a non-hierarchical basis. The Women's Erotic art Show in 1973 was the first attempt to examine one another's work from the perspective of whether there existed a feminist esthetic. In 1976, WARM established the Women's Collective Art Space. An exhibition space that functioned for 14 years, it also served as a cultural center and became the locus of Minnesota's burgeoning art community. Although the gallery has closed, many of its programs continue, including the mentor program that pairs older members with aspiring artists and culminates in an exhibition. Fiene holds a B.F.A. from Virginia Commonwealth University and an M.F.A. from the University of Michigan, Ann Arbor. She lives and works as an artist in St. Paul. (ABS)

Fine, Elsa Honig (1930 –) attended the founding meeting of the Women's Caucus for Art, held in 1972 at the College Art Association meeting in San Francisco. She was active with the WCA for the next 12 years, and in 1978 published *Women and Art: A History of Women Painters and Sculptors from the Renaissance to the 20th Century* (Allanheld and Schram). In 1980, she founded *Woman's Art Journal,* and serves as editor and publisher. Fine, who has two children, earned her B.F.A. from Syracuse University, her M.E.D. from Tyler College of Fine Art, and her Ed.D. from the University of Tennessee. (ABS)

Fine, Maxine (1942 – 2003) An award-winning artist and feminist/lesbian art activist, Fine was a member of the Lesbian Artist's Collective (1970s). Her painting was shown in 1978 at A Lesbian Show, NYC, the first show by lesbian artists in an art world context. In 1980 she co-curated the next lesbian show, The Third Wave, Hibbs Gallery. In 1981, Fine moved to New Mexico, where she exhibited in museums, galleries and community spaces, while continuing to show in NYC. She conceived and directed the "Intergalactic Lesbian Show," a NM monthly cable television program (1989 – 1990). From 1967 to her death, Fine courageously traced her life journey in her art, and in so doing chronicled issues of vital concern to women: her 25-year triumph over breast cancer, and the ambiguities of gender and sexuality newly articulated as political by the LGBTQ liberation movements. Fine was the recipient of the Art Students League Edward G. McDowell Traveling Fellowship for a year of study in Europe and a one-person show (1970), and three national arts awards: the Adolph and Esther Gottlieb Foundation Grant (1998), the Pollack-Krasner Foundation Grant (1999), and the Astraea National Lesbian Foundation for Social Justice Annual Visual Arts Award (2003).

Fineberg, Jean (1946 –) A pioneer in women's rock bands, Fineberg joined Godmother, a NYC group, as their saxophonist/flutist in 1971. She also played with ISIS, an eight-piece all-woman horn band that was signed by Buddha Records. The group's first recording, Isis, contained Fineberg's song "April Fool." Isis toured the country from 1972 to 1976. "I believe we changed a lot of minds about the ability of women to play powerful rock 'n' roll, and to excel on traditionally male instruments such as trumpet, saxophone and trombone. I also believe that the lesbian content of the material was, for many listeners, their first introduction to out-and-proud lesbianism." Fineberg also recorded with the women's trio Deadly Nightshade, as well as Laura Nyro, David Bowie and Melba Liston. Eventually, she would contribute to over 45 albums. In 1980 she and trumpeter Ellen Seeling created the seven-piece fusion group DEUCE to showcase her original compositions, and recorded two albums, DEUCE (released on women-owned Redwood Records) and WindJammer (released on women-owned Pivotal Records). Fineberg is assistant director of the Montclair Women's Big Band (a 17-piece all woman swing band), founded in Oakland, CA, by director Ellen Seeling and producer Barbara Price. She has received two Meet The Composer Grants for original compositions, an NEA grant for jazz composition, an ASCAP special composition award, and an appointment to the San Francisco Arts Commission Cultural Equity Grants Panel.   (ABS)

Fineman, Martha L.A. (1943 –) is an internationally recognized law and society scholar and authority on family law and feminist jurisprudence. A graduate of the University of Chicago Law School (1975), Fineman says, "We were the first class with more than a token number of women. We invented feminist legal theory, as contrasted with just having a concern with women in law." Fineman is a founder and director of the Feminism and Legal Theory Project (1984), and in 1999 joined Cornell Law School as the first endowed Chair in the U.S. in Feminist Jurisprudence. She has served on several government study commissions, and has published numerous articles and books on feminism and feminist topics. Her books include *At the Boundaries of Law: Feminism and Legal Theory* (Routledge Press, 1990); *The Illusion of Equality:*

The Rhetoric and Reality of Divorce Reform (University of Chicago Press, 1991); *The Public Nature of Private Violence* (Routledge Press, 1994); *The Neutered Mother, The Sexual Family and Other Twentieth Century Tragedies* (Routledge Press, 1995); and *The Autonomy Myth: A Theory of Dependency* (The New Press, 2004). She was also co-editor, with Terrence Dougherty, of *Feminism Confronts Homo Economics* (Cornell Press, 2005). Fineman, who earned her undergraduate degree at Temple University (1971), is the recipient of numerous awards for her writing and teaching. Archives: Woodruff Library, Emory University, Atlanta, GA.   (ABS)

Fineran, Pat – See Cervelli, Pat Fineran

Fineson, Luba (1934 –) (also known as Luba Zimmermann) joined NYC NOW in 1972, and in 1973 became chair of the rape prevention committee. With other committee members she created "Rape, Myth and Fact," a presentation shown at synagogues, churches, schools and hospitals, and on radio and television. It was also used at police department conferences in New York City and Newark, NJ. In 1974, Fineson became action VP of NYC NOW, responsible for the committees on childcare, rape prevention, and marriage and divorce. She was involved in support actions for the freedom to choose, fought gender bias at television stations, and campaigned for the ERA. Fineson and others engendered the creation of the Westchester NOW lesbian task force. Through her job as director of central files at the Population Council, Fineson saw the gender disparity in funding for research, and with other female staff formed a women's caucus to monitor and discuss gender discrimination on the job. "I believe they fired me because of my involvement in the caucus," she says. From 1976 – 1985, Fineson was corresponding secretary, Westchester NOW, and from 1978 – 1983 was a board member, Westchester Women's Federal Credit Union. From 1985 – 1990, she was secretary, Philadelphia NOW, and from 1987 – 1994 was a board member of Choice, a Philadelphia research and referral agency for affordable day care. Retiring in 1995, Fineson moved back to New York, and remains active in Westchester NOW, serving from 1997 – 2001 as chapter president. In her profession as a certified purchasing agent, Fineson was the first female purchasing manager at Lehman College of the City University of New York, and the first female director of purchasing and services at Community College of Philadelphia. Fineson, who has two children, holds a B.S. from Syracuse University. Archives: Women's Studies Program, Lehman College, Bronx, NY; and Women's Studies Program, Community College of Philadelphia, Philadelphia, PA.   (ABS)

Fink, Carolyn – See Fish, Carolyn

Finkel, Bruria (1932 –) Artist and teacher, Finkel was a founding member of the Los Angeles Council of Women in the Arts (1970), Womanspace, and the Joan of Art seminar (1971), created to raise the consciousness of women in the arts in California. A participant of numerous demonstrations, she was part of an action at the Los Angeles County Museum of Art, addressing the lack of women artists in its Art and Technology show, and a second action with LACMA's board of trustees, which resulted in the creation of a show featuring women's work. Also active in the civil rights, labor and peace movements, Finkel was part of a group of artists who built a peace tower in 1964 on La Cienega Blvd. and Sunset to protest the war in Vietnam. Finkel has four children. (ABS)

Finlayson, Edith Norman (1925 – 2001) served on the Wisconsin Governor's Commission on the Status of Women and was one of the original 28 women who founded NOW at the Conference of State Commissions on the Status of Women in June 1966. A nurse, Finlayson was a champion of social justice and active in Milwaukee civic affairs. She was a member of the University of Wisconsin System Board of Regents, appointed by former governor Lee Sherman Dreyfus, from 1980 – 1987; chaired the board's education committee; and helped establish the Leon Sullivan Distinguished Professorship at the university. She also served as a board member of the Wisconsin African Relief Effort, and was board chair of the Milwaukee Foundation.

Fiore, Genevieve N. D'Amato (1912 – 2002) Peace activist and humanitarian, Fiore worked aggressively for women's and human rights in Colorado for over four decades. She attended the Mexico City Women's Conference in 1975 and chaired the plan of action committee at the Colorado Women's Conference in 1977. Fiore received the highest number of votes in the state to serve as a delegate to the Houston National Women's Conference (1977). In addition, Fiore was the founder of UNESCO-Colorado. She has three children. Archives: Genevieve Fiore Collection, Avraria Library, Denver, CO.

Firestone, Laya (1947 –) (also known as Laya Seghi) joined Chicago Women's Liberation, West Side Group, in 1967. She helped stage various happenings to raise consciousness about sexism, including confronting Hugh Hefner at a reception for potential Playboy Bunnies at the Playboy Mansion. After the Democratic National Convention of 1968, the Chicago Women's Liberation group helped plan for the first National Women's Liberation Conference, funded in part by the Institute for Policy Studies in Washington, D.C. Firestone, representing Chicago, helped organize the conference. Firestone then participated in several national actions organized by her sister, Shulamith, and other radical feminists from New York. But, she says, "Rather than being stimulated by the political friction, I found myself trying to mediate and make peace between rivals." Firestone is a psychotherapist and certified BodyTalk practitioner in private practice. She holds a B.A. (1980) and M.S.W. (1981) from Washington University. Firestone has three children. (ABS)

Firestone, Shulamith (1945 –) A feminist author and activist, Firestone wrote the feminist classic *The Dialectic of Sex* (1970) when she was 25. The book has been translated into more than a dozen languages and reprinted more than a dozen times. Firestone was a founder of Chicago Women's Liberation, West Side Group, in 1967 and later NYRW, Redstockings and NYRF. She also participated in many other groups. One of the more important radical thinkers in the movement, she founded the first feminist journal in the country, *Notes From the First Year;* was executive editor of *Notes From the Second Year*; and was a consulting editor on *Notes From the Third Year*. In 1997, she published *Airless Spaces*, a series of vignettes about trapped and helpless people (Semiotext(e) Press). Like many other radical feminists, Firestone was an early civil rights organizer and worked with the St. Louis Congress on Racial Equality (1961 – 1963). She holds a B.F.A. from the School of the Art Institute of Chicago (1967).

Fish, Carolyn (1945 –) (also known as Carolyn Fink) is an acknowledged leader in the fight against violence against women. Her activism began in the early 1970s when she attended a planning meeting of Rockland County (NY) NOW. She subsequently joined a CR group, and by 1973 was volunteering for various feminist activities and helping RC NOW conduct it first conference, held at Rockland Community College. She co-coordinated, with Diane Sussman and Susan Staub, the next two conferences, and with Sussman and Staub taught a feminist course on women's health at RCC. In the early 1970s, RC NOW established a crisis hotline. It soon became clear that the major problem facing the women calling was that they were being abused by their partners and had nowhere to turn. As programming chair of RC NOW, Fish convened the first public forum on domestic abuse and violence in the county. This led directly to the creation of the Rockland County Coalition Against Domestic Violence. In 1977, as VP of RC NOW, Fish and Sussman represented the chapter on the Rockland Coalition Against Domestic Violence. Fish subsequently became VP of the Rockland Coalition Against Domestic Violence. The coalition incorporated as the Rockland Family Shelter and opened a battered women's shelter and emergency hotline in 1979. Fish joined the staff as assistant director and became executive director in 1980. Her continuing efforts to involve the community in the struggle against violence against women led to the creation of STOP F.E.A.R., a coalition that has produced progressive policies for the police, judiciary, and the business and medical communities. Fish was a member of the housing committee of governor Cuomo's Commission on Domestic Violence (1983 – 1985); and member of the board of the NYS Coalition Against Domestic Violence (1982 – 1994) and co-president in 1996. From 1996 – 1997, she was a member of governor Pataki's task force to create the NYS Model Domestic Violence Policies for Counties. Fish, who has two children, holds a B.A. from Queens College, CUNY. She has also been active in peace and civil rights efforts, and has supported gay pride events. (ABS)

Fishbein, Helene – See Ince, Helene

Fisher, Elizabeth (1924 – 1982) was a writer and editor/founder in 1969 of *Aphra, The Feminist Literary Magazine* (named after Aphra Behn, 1640 – 1689, one of the first women professional writers). It was the first and longest-lived second-wave literary journal. According to Alix Kates Shulman, "*Aphra* was important not least because, at the time, when women's liberation was impatient with literary writers (considering literature something of a distraction from radical politics) Fisher, who never compromised her commitment to literature, insisted that women's literature could have a key role in challenging male supremacy and raising consciousness." Fisher wrote *Woman's Creation: Sexual Revolution and the Shaping of Society* (Anchor Press/Doubleday, 1979), a feminist account of evolution and history that was nominated for a Pulitzer Prize in 1979. Two more volumes on woman's evolution were planned. The immediate impetus for the book, which took seven years to write, came out of women's liberation. In 1971, when Fisher was to write an article for *Aphra* covering prostitution, she was dissatisfied with her speculations on the meaning of prostitution in a patriarchal society. She agonized and had a "visionary night." She said to herself, "I've just rewritten Engels' *Origin of the Family, Private Property, and The State.*" That was patently untrue at the time, she says in the introduction to her book, "since at that moment I had written nothing, though later on it would be true and untrue." Fisher attended Smith College for one year and dropped out at age 15. In the 1950s, she worked in Rome as a cultural columnist for *The Rome American*. Fisher, who had one child, committed suicide on New Year's Day 1982.

Fisher, Mara (1953 –) A member of NOW in New York City and Brooklyn (1970 – 1971), Fisher facilitated CR groups. As a member of NARAL in NYC (1970 – 1972), she collected signatures on the corner of 8th Street and Avenue of the Americas every Saturday to get abortions legalized. In addition, she participated in all marches for women's rights in NYC and Washington, D.C., through 1975. Fisher, who holds an M.S.W., is a women's spiritual and relationship coach. (ABS)

Fishman, Joan – See Calof, Joan

Fishman, Karen (1948 –) (also known as Karen Wellisch) was founder of the Women's Radical Action Project, University of Chicago (1967). She was a board member and ultimately president of the Sojourner Truth Child Care Center (1972 – 1975), and held various offices in Chicago

NOW, including president (1982 – 1983) and executive director (1983 – 1987). In the 1970s, she was the managing editor, and then editor and publisher of *The Spokeswoman*, a national newsletter covering the women's movement. Fishman, who has one child, is the executive director of Music of the Baroque (Chicago), a professional chorus and orchestra. She holds a B.A. from the University of Chicago (1970). Archives: *The Spokeswoman* archives are at Northwestern University; archives for Chicago NOW are at the University of Illinois, Chicago. (ABS)

Fitterman, Marilyn (1938 –) had five children (two sets of twins) between 1958 – 1962. An illegal abortion in 1964 compelled her to join (1967) a group of activists in Suffolk County, NY, who were fighting to legalize abortion. Although she worked full time and attended college at night, Fitterman became a major lobbyist, organizer and lecturer at the early abortion speakouts, which finally, in 1970, led to legalized abortion in NYS. In 1986 she was elected president of Mid-Suffolk NOW. She is a co-founder of Long Island's NOW PAC, and in 1988 was elected president of NOW NYS. Throughout her four-year tenure, she flooded Albany with NOW-trained lobbyists for state-level economic and reproductive rights legislation. She also organized more than 100,000 New Yorkers to attend the 1989 NOW/NARAL March on Washington for Choice. In 1990, she was elected president of the presidents, or president of National NOW's caucus of state presidents, a think-tank and information exchange for state and national-level activists. Also throughout her presidency, Fitterman led workshops for national NOW on developing and organizing feminist PACs, and won a stunning NYS Legislative victory on the NOW side of no-fault divorce. On the state level, she facilitated the establishment of the largest and most comprehensive women of color task force in NOW's history, and initiated NYS's first anti-stalking bill, which passed in 1999. Fitterman also effectively opposed "criminalization of pregnancy" legislation that would penalize women, mostly disadvantaged and/or minority women, for having exposed fetuses to drugs (both illegal and legal, such as alcohol). Fitterman was editor of NOW NYS's newspaper from 1988 – 1995, and in 1997 received a grant/award from the Thanks Be To Grandmother Winifred Foundation to facilitate completion of her memoirs. She is chair of the East Hampton Anti-Bias Task Force. (ABS)

Fitzpatrick, Therese Marie (1953 –) has been fighting for women's rights since she was in grade school, when she refused to wear a white dress that looked like a bridal gown to her eighth grade graduation. An attorney, Fitzpatrick joined NOW and helped battered women get divorces. She lobbied the Nebraska Legislature on behalf of the NE NOW chapter to enhance women's rights in the divorce process. She has supported gay rights, abortion rights, and parity in education and curriculum, Armed with a law degree, a master's in organizational development, a certificate in women's leadership from the Hubert Humphrey Institute of Public Policy, and a master's equivalent in nonprofit administration. Fitzpatrick, who has one child, worked in Washington as an organizational consultant "to create a workplace where women can bring their whole selves to work." Her current (2006) consulting practice convenes evolutionary salons to focus on conscious social systems. (ABS)

Flack, Audrey (1931 –) is one of the leading Photorealist artists, the only woman in the groundbreaking movement. A graduate of Yale University's School of Art and Architecture, she was involved in early feminist CR groups, feminist art history journals and the college initiative to get women tenure. Flack was one of the first women to be included in the book *History of Art*, revised by Tony Janson. As a painter, sculptor and author, Flack changed the imagery in a male-dominated art world, using heroic imagery and iconic subjects to deal with the human condition from a female perspective. Her still-life painting, *Jolie Madame,* created an uproar when it was exhibited at the Huntington Hartford Museum in NYC in 1970 because it contained traditionally-unacceptable female iconography such as beads, bracelets, china, and roses. Flack has concentrated almost exclusively on sculpture since 1982. Tired of looking at bronzes of generals with swords on horses, Flack has devoted herself to creating monumental bronzes of the female figure. Her four "civitas" goddesses for the Gateway to Rock Hill, SC, won the U.S. Department of Transportation award. (ABS)

Flax, Jane (1948 –) An organizer of the New Haven (CT) Women's Center (1970), Flax was involved in CR, education and demonstrations. She served as a counselor (1972 –1974) at the New Haven Counseling Center, and from 1977–1979 was an editor of *Quest* in Washington, D.C. A professor and psychotherapist, she is the author of *Disputed Subjects* (Routledge, 1993); *Thinking Fragments* (University of California, 1990); and *The American Dream in Black & White* (Cornell University Press, 1998). She is also an editor of and contributor to *Building Feminist Theory* (Longman, 1981). Flax, who has a B.A. from Berkeley (1969) and a Ph.D. from Yale (1974), has one child. (ABS)

Fletcher, Dixie Johnson (1943 –) Living in Memphis, TN, Fletcher joined NOW in 1973 and organized orientation groups for first-timers. She started CR groups, organized a group of Women in Mental Health, and gave women assertiveness training. She also lectured on sexuality, sexism and self-esteem. In 1985, Fletcher led a support group for People With AIDS and helped organize the quilt displays in Memphis. Politically active, she helped organize a peace walk in Memphis with Thich Nhat Hanh, a Vietnamese Buddhist monk, and Dr. Monsuk Patel from the Light Foundation in Wales.

Fletcher, who has two children, retired after 25 years as a school psychologist. She works as a psychotherapist, body worker and energy healer, and returned to college to focus on women's and African American studies. (ABS)

Fletcher, Marilyn Lowen – See Lowen, Marilyn

Flexner, Eleanor (1908 – 1995) was the author of the first scholarly history of the battle to win suffrage for women, *Century of Struggle: The Women's Rights Movement in the United States.* Published by Harvard University Press (under its Belknap Press imprint) in 1959, it was the forerunner of the second feminist revolution sparked by Betty Friedan's 1963 book *The Feminine Mystique.* Friedan, the original "desperate housewife," called *Century of Struggle* "the definitive history of the women's rights movement in the U.S." and acknowledged her debt to Flexner for "many factual clues I might otherwise have missed in my attempt to get at the truth behind the feminine mystique and its monstrous image of feminists." Never out of circulation, *Century of Struggle* has undergone nine printings in English and six other languages. Flexner graduated with honors from Swarthmore College in 1930 and studied history at Oxford University on a yearlong fellowship in England. She focused on social-justice history, as a playwright in the 1930s and as a union activist and supporter of the Congress of American Women, the Foreign Policy Association and the National Association of Colored Graduate Nurses in the 1940s. Flexner moved from New York to Northampton, MA, in 1957 to utilize the resources of Smith College's women's history archive while writing *Century of Struggle.* Her second major book, *Mary Wollstonecraft: A Biography* (Coward, McCann and Geoghegan, 1972) was nominated for a National Book Award in 1973. Archives: Schlesinger Library, Radcliffe Institute, Cambridge, MA.

Florant, Anne (1911 – 1999) A member of NY NOW, VFA and WILPF, Florant also did work for the United Nations, helped organize Chelsea Against Nuclear Destruction United, and worked with theater groups. She served on the national board of WILPF for six years, as both VP and chair of its policy committee; attended national and international congresses and participated in campaign strategy and decision-making; and was a member of the WILPF UN team for 16 years covering human rights. Her interest in human rights began early when, at a time when interracial marriages were rare, she married Lionel Florant, an African American who worked for the State Department and the U.S. Army. When they lived in the South, Florant tried to "pass" as a black woman to make things easier for them. Florant was also an organizer of the Women Fighting Poverty Conference and the renewed celebration of International Women's Day in the U.S. Professionally, Florant worked for many years at Columbia University in the Neuro-Physiology Department, overseeing a large staff, editing reports, reviewing grant applications, and supervising fund procedures. Florant received a posthumous award from NY NOW for her work with WILPF.

Flores, Francisca (1913 – 1996) In 1971, when Chicano cultural nationalists called for preservation of traditional gender roles for the sake of Chicano culture, Flores countered with "Our culture, hell!" She called for self-determination generally for Chicanas, and specifically for women to have control over their own bodies. "If a woman wants a large family, no one will interfere with her right to have one," she said. Flores was a founder of Comision Femenil Mexicana Nacional, an early chicana activist group (1971). Affiliated with the National Mexican-American Issues Conference, CFM invited men to join. Flores always believed that Chicanas working for their specific issues within the general Chicano movement and working together on common issues was imperative to success. A lifetime community activist, Flores was a journalist and commentator who left many valuable writings about the Chicana movement. Archives: A portion of her work is at the California Ethnic and Multicultural Archives, Davidson Library, University of California, Santa Barbara.

Florika (1946 – 1979) (also known as Florika Remetier) A member of NYRW, Florika was a co-founder of WITCH (1968). She was the instigator of the NYRW anti-war demonstration (1968) in which the members dressed as Vietnamese women and handed out leaflets designed by Florika and Paul Simonin to women only as they ran through the crowd ululating. By 1969 Florika was in New Haven, CT, where she was co-founder of the New Haven Women's Liberation Rock Band. She played bass and taught most of the others, some of whom had little musical training. Deeply concerned about the powerful, controlling influence of large corporations on individual lives, Florika wanted to attack capitalism—a position that irritated some feminists who believed that women should concentrate on overthrowing male supremacy. Florika was instrumental in the Halloween "hexing" of Wall Street in 1968, and was co-author of *The Politics of Day Care*. A gifted violinist, Florika, born in Romania, spent much of her early childhood in refugee camps before coming to NYC with her family. Although she experienced prosperity and some fame as a performer with major European orchestras, a major mental breakdown in her adolescence ended that phase of her life and was the beginning of a lifetime fighting depression and suicidal thoughts. Hoping to rekindle her musical career, Florika moved to San Francisco in the early 1970s. After years of struggle, she died of a drug overdose.

Flower, Annette – See Chappell, Annette

Flowing – See Johnson, Margaret Katherine

Foa Dienstag, Eleanor (1938 –) is the author of *Whither Thou Goest: The Story of an Uprooted Wife* (EP Dutton, 1976), which confronted an issue that had never before been looked at from the wife's perspective. A member of the Rochester, NY, chapter of NOW in the early 1970s, she organized and participated in a series of sit-ins, and covered the women's movement and women's issues as a freelance writer. In 1978, divorced and with two children, she moved back to NYC and became a corporate writer. And, she says, "I believe I was the first female speechwriter on Wall Street." In 1983 she formed her own company, Eleanor Foa Associates, providing writing for global and not-for-profit clients. A past president of the American Society of Journalists and Authors, she is also the author of several corporate histories. Born in Naples, Italy, Foa Dienstag graduated from Smith College in 1959. (ABS)

Fonda, Jane (1937 –) A noted actress and later an entrepreneur, Fonda was a high-profile anti-Vietnam War activist whose feminist activity is seen in the roles she has played in Hollywood. Fonda won two Academy Awards (for "Klute" in 1971 and "Coming Home" in 1978) and several Oscar nominations for Best Actress. Her experiences of the sexual exploitation of women by the Hollywood film industry—in particular, when she played the title role in "Barbarella" (1968)—were the beginnings of her feminist consciousness. But it was during the production of "Klute," a psychological thriller about a prostitute being stalked by a killer, that Fonda embraced the women's movement. She began handing out feminist leaflets, along with her anti-war leaflets, as she traveled across the United States, and eventually became involved in such groups as the Georgia Campaign for Adolescent Pregnancy Prevention, which she founded in 1995. She has also provided inspiration and financial support for numerous other projects, including V-Day: Until the Violence Stops, Ms. Magazine Foundation, NARAL, Sexuality Information and Education Council of the United States, and Planned Parenthood Federation of America. At the National Women's Leadership Summit in Washington, D.C. (2003), Fonda delivered a strong feminist speech. She spoke of the need for women to overcome patriarchy—which she sees as damaging not only to women, but to men and boys and the health and future of the world—and replace it with a feminine paradigm. Fonda has three children and attended Vassar College for two years (1955 – 1957). Archives: The Sophia Smith Collection, Smith College, Northampton, MA. (ABS)

Fontana, Lorraine (1947 –) An early activist in the anti-war, anti-racist and anti-imperialist New Left movement, Fontana was a founding member of the Atlanta Lesbian Feminist Alliance (1972 – 1994), and later Dykes for the Second American Revolution, and a member of the short-lived Atlanta Socialist-Feminist Women's Union (1975). Fontana helped establish ALFA's lending library of books by and about women and other oppressed communities, and was active on the newsletter committee and as a regular contributor. After moving to Los Angeles in 1976,

Fontana became a member of three caucuses at The People's College of Law, for women, gay and working-class students. Returning to Atlanta in 1979, she again took up lesbian-feminist activism with ALFA. She often served as an ALFA rep to coalition/partnership projects with others in the growing out-LGBTQ community, and served at the ALFA rep to the newly formed National Anti-Klan Network, now the Center for Democratic Renewal. From 1980–1983 she was a staff person for the National Jury Project, an organization supporting progressive trial lawyers, in its Atlanta office. She later used her legal skills as a paralegal for the EEOC in New York City (1999–2004). She is (2006) a legal assistant for Lambda Legal, and a member of WAND and Queer Progressive Agenda (QPA). Fontana holds a B.A. from Queens College, CUNY, and a J.D. completed at Atlanta Law School, 1981. Archives: Fontana's papers will go to ALFA friend and archivist Elizabeth Knowlton. (ABS)

Fontanella, Rose (1928 –) A graphic artist, antiques dealer, raconteur and comedian, Fontanella was co-creator, with Stephanie Lynne Marcus, of Liberation Enterprises. Launched in Brooklyn, NY, in 1972, the company designed feminist items such as T-shirts, posters, greeting cards, jewelry, stationery, patches, decals, tote bags and tool kits. "With little capital and no knowledge of business, we improvised," they said. In 1975 the two were forced to close up shop—a consequence of the Arab oil embargo and a deep economic recession. Fontanella helped plan and participated in the 1970 Women's Strike for Equality march in NYC. She picketed Brooklyn Family Court in protest of a misogynistic judge (1973); demonstrated against the Miss America pageant; kept score for a survey of sexism and lack of women on ABC-TV; and marched in Washington, D.C., for abortion rights. Fontanella was also a member of Brooklyn, NY NOW, and in 1973 was awarded Brooklyn NOW's Woman of Achievement Award. She has two children. (ABS)

Ford, Betty Bloomer (1918 –) As First Lady of the United States (beginning in 1974), Ford broke precedent both by expressing her political views and by being open about her personal issues. She immediately threw her support to the ERA and to the women's movement in general, and made clear to critics that she was not about to back down, saying "I do not believe that being First Lady should prevent me from expressing my views." Ford's openness about her breast cancer created a surge of awareness among women nationwide of the importance of breast examination and treatment. The same was true of her struggle with alcohol and prescription-drug addiction. She later founded the Betty Ford Center for alcohol and drug rehabilitation. Her book *The Times of My Life* started a trend for subsequent First Ladies to write about their experiences in the White House.

Foreman, Jill - See Hultin, Jill Foreman

Forer, Anne —joined the women's liberation movement in fall of 1967 in NYC. She was a member of NYRW, a group started by Shulamith Firestone. Forer, Kathie Sarachild and Carol Hanisch came up with the idea of CR during the group meetings as a tool to raise their own consciousness. An activist who participated in most of the events of the next few years, Forer dropped out of the women's liberation movement in 1971. Says Forer, "Women's liberation was a genuine grass roots mass movement when it began. Although only a few names are remembered afterwards, the fact is the energy, creativity, movement and liberation came from the large groups of women who attended meetings. This is not a story of individuals, but of what women accomplished when they joined together for their liberation." (ABS)

Forfreedom, Ann (1947 –) co-created and co-taught the for-credit interdisciplinary class on women's status from a feminist perspective at UCLA (1969). The first in the University of California system, the class was a forerunner of women's studies at UCLA. In 1970, she helped establish the Los Angeles Women's Center, where the first feminist women's health center eventually began, and served on its board of directors and at the Venice (CA) Women's Center. Forfreedom, a feminist writer and researcher, co-founded *Everywoman* newspaper (1970) and established the "Herstory" column for the newspaper that year. In 1972, she published *Women out of History: A Herstory Anthology,* and in 1980 co-edited and published *Book of the Goddess.* She has also published a feminist periodical, *The Wise Woman,* since 1980, and is (2005) working on two books, *America's Goddess Liberty,* and *Great Goddess! A World Encyclopedia of Powerful Goddesses.* As a result of her research, she rediscovered and named the 1794 Justice and Liberty State Seal of Maryland; her research article is in the Peale Archive at the National Portrait Gallery, Smithsonian Institution, and in the Maryland Historical Society Library. Forfreedom received the Alice Paul Award for her work as treasurer of the ERA task force of the Sacramento NOW chapter in the 1970s. Born in Germany in a refugee camp, Forfreedom became a naturalized citizen of the U.S. when her parents became naturalized citizens. In 1970, Ann Herschfang legally changed her name to Ann Forfreedom, for feminist reasons. She was also active in the abortion rights movement in 1969, throughout the 1970s, and in the next decades, and taught women's history classes at the Los Angeles NOW center and in community centers in the 1970s. Archives: *Everywoman* newspaper on microfilm at the Women's History Archives, Northwestern University. *The Wise Woman* on microfilm, The Alternative Press Collection and the Underground Press Collection of University Microfilms, Ann Arbor, MI. (ABS)

Formby, Margaret (1929 – 2003) In 1975, Formby established the National Cowgirl Museum and Hall of Fame, a concept that she had spent 19 years developing, in

Hereford, TX. Originally housed in her local library, the collection is now located in Fort Worth, TX. Editor of *Sidesaddle* magazine for the Cowgirl Hall of Fame and a board member for the All Girl Rodeos in Hereford, TX, Formby was the first woman elected to the Texas Tech Rodeo Hall of Fame, and was an inductee in the Cowgirl Hall of Fame in Fort Worth in 1994. In 1997, she was named one of the Texas Plains Girl Scout Council's Women of Distinction. A former president of the Deaf Smith County Chamber of Commerce Women's Division, Formby was one of two women in the state named to a blue ribbon commission to investigate child pornography, and also served on the Texas House Speaker's Committee to research teen pregnancy. A 1950 graduate of Texas Tech University, Formby had four children.

Forrey, Carolyn – See: Broadway, Carolyn

Forst, Mary Claire (1941 –) A lawyer, Forst assisted in the startup of the first Feminist Federal Credit Union in Detroit (1973) by helping to argue the case for getting the federal charter from the National Credit Union Administration. In 1974, she and her partner, Grace Schaefer, moved to San Diego, where they started the California Feminist Federal Credit Union, one of the few FFCUs still operating in 2005. The two also attended Project Repair, which taught carpentry, plumbing and electrical wiring to women, and did a lot of work on what became Las Hermanas coffee house. The two later opened a home repair business, Ladybug Unlimited. In 1975, Forst worked at the Center for Women's Studies and Services in San Diego helping women get non-traditional jobs. She also taught a class on women and the law through a non-traditional San Diego school. In 1975 – 1976, Forst helped produce the first Women's Music Festival on land owned by a woman outside San Diego. In 1976, Forst moved with her partner to Portland, OR, where they started the Portland Feminist Federal Credit Union, which lasted about 10 years. The same year, Forst began working with the Community Law Project, a feminist legal collective, public interest law firm. The women did lesbian custody cases and also brought the first sexual harassment lawsuit in the form of a suit for "outrageous conduct." The women also worked with battered women and defended Women's Night at Mountain Moving Café, and anti-nuclear protesters at the Trojan Nuclear Power Plant. Forst helped start TKO, an organization designed to bridge the gap between gay men and lesbians in Portland, and designed and ran a mediation program for sexual orientation and gender identity issues for the City of Portland. In 1979, Forst became director of Portland Town Council, a gay rights organization, and later worked for the City of Portland. A mediator in private practice, Forst holds a B.A. from Ursuline College and a J.D. from Detroit College of Law. (ABS)

Fortino, Virginia B. – See Blaisdell, Virginia L.

Fox, Gerald (1933 – 1988) As a VP of NY NOW, Fox was the attorney who negotiated with New York newspapers on NOW's behalf for the elimination of sexually segregated help-wanted ads, which was accomplished on December 1, 1968. Fox received his B.A. from UCLA (1954) and his LL.B. from Yale Law School (1957). He had two daughters who are active feminists.

Fox, Mary Frank — joined Sociologists for Women in Society in 1973 during her graduate school years. She became a co-founder of the Michigan chapter of SWS, and later served as publications chair, VP and president of SWS, national. In addition, Fox was a co-founder and a founding associate editor of the SWS journal, *Gender & Society*. She also edited and published the collection, *Scholarly Writing and Publication*, which resulted from her term/experience as publications chair; all royalties from the volume were contributed to SWS. In 2005 Fox is NSF Advance Professor, Georgia Institute of Technology. Her research has focused on gender, science and academia. She was named SWS Feminist Lecturer 2000 (for prominent feminist scholar who has made a commitment to social change) and awarded the 2002 WEPAN (Women in Engineering Programs) Betty Vetter Research Award (for notable achievement in research on women in engineering). Fox earned a Ph.D. from the University of Michigan (1978). (ABS)

Fox, Muriel (1928 –) As a co-founder of NOW in 1966, Fox was "the communicator of the revolution" who introduced the new women's movement to world media. As head of PR for NOW, she helped organize its founding conference in Washington, D.C., wrote and distributed the first press releases, arranged for photos, and helped edit the original Statement of Purpose. In addition to her PR work, Fox served as operations lieutenant to president Betty Friedan. Fox also edited early NOW letters to President Johnson, attorney general Clark, the EEOC and other government groups, and met with government leaders on behalf of NOW. After meeting with John Macy in the White House, Fox wrote the NOW letter that helped persuade President Lynden B. Johson to add women to Executive Order 11246 in October 1967, creating jobs for many millions of women through affirmative action. In 1967, Fox organized NOW's NY chapter, and served on all NOW national boards from 1966 – 1975. She testified to Congress for equalizing pensions (1970), and organized NOW actions for "desexigrating" help-wanted ads (1967), abolishing sexsegregated factory seniority lists (1968), and many other causes. Fox founded and edited the first national NOW newsletter, "Do It NOW" (1970 – 1971), and was a co-founder of the NOW LDEF (1970), serving in various capacities. Among many march participations, she led the 1978 ERA March in Washington in a long white dress, holding the hand of eight-year-old Brooke Schafran; they are commemorated in a popular NOW medal. For NOW LDEF Fox initiated and chaired the

National Assembly on the Future of the Family (1979), the first major conference publicizing how "traditional" U.S. families have changed; the Convocation on New Leadership in the Public Interest (1981); and the Equal Opportunity Awards Dinner (1979 –), which has built feminist bridges to corporate America while garnering millions of dollars for the women's movement. She was founder and president of The Women's Forum (1976), and a founder and early board member of Child Care Action Campaign (1989) and the NWPC (1971). Fox co-chaired, with senator Maurine Neuberger, VP Hubert Humphrey's task force on women's goals (1967). Fox is the recipient of numerous awards, including the Barnard College Distinguished Alumna Award (1985); NYS NOW's first Eleanor Roosevelt Leadership Award; the Matrix Award of NY Women in Communications; Rockland County NOW's Babcock Award (2000); and the first Muriel Fox Award for Communications Leadership Toward a Just Society, established by NOW LDEF. A charter member of the VFA (1992), Fox has been chair of the board since 1993. Fox cherishes her role as a spokes person for feminism. In addition to numerous public speeches and television and radio appearances, she has been a passionate advocate within the movement, helping conflicting factions find ways to work together. She often urged complaining NOW members in the early days: "Don't give up, this movement needs us all." Her current (2006) work as board chair of VFA stresses outreach to present and future opinion leaders. As president of Rockland Center for the Arts in Rockland County, NY, she helped VFA organize a joint "Salute to Feminist Artists." Fox holds an A.B. degree from Barnard College (1948) and has two children. Archives: Schlesinger Library, Radcliffe Institute, Cambridge, MA.   (ABS)

Fox, Roberta Fulton (1943 –) A Florida attorney and NOW member, Fox worked in support of abortion rights from 1970 – 1974. As a member of the FL House and Senate (1976 – 1986), she was a prime sponsor behind the passage of the Florida Equal Education Opportunity Act in 1984. The only female member of the Governor's Commission on Marriage and Family (1974), Fox helped move FL toward an equitable distribution of marital property. From 1988 – 1995, she was a member of the Florida Clemency Review board, reviewing women convicted of murdering a partner (notwithstanding being a victim of battered spouse syndrome). Also active in the peace and civil rights movements, she represented the Gainesville 8 in 1973. Fox holds a B.A. (1964) and J.D. (1967) from the University of Florida. She has a stepdaughter and two nephews whom she calls her children.   (ABS)

Fraad, Harriet (1941 –) was a principal founder, with Polly Gassler and others, of the first women's liberation group in New Haven, CT, in 1968. The group worked on a range of issues, including abortion rights, equal pay, day care at Yale and feminist shelves in bookstores. The women also organized several actions, including a women's support march for Black Panther Erica Huggins. She was also part of the group of women who demanded and finally got the right to have babies delivered by midwives at Yale New Haven Hospital. ("We had to threaten a pregnant women's sit-in before the right was granted.") Fraad also worked to improve New Haven's schools with demonstrations and a child-in at the mayor's office. "We brought hundreds of kids with peanut butter sandwiches and sticky candy into the mayor's office!" A psychotherapist, Fraad has two children and holds a B.A. from Bennington College and an M.A. and Ed.D. from Columbia University. She was also active in anti-Vietnam War marches and in the civil rights movement.   (ABS)

Frank, Barbara Ruth (1943 –) In 1971, while still a graduate student in fine arts, Frank organized a group of women who worked collaboratively on the National Conference for Women in the Arts, Washington, D.C., the first national gathering of feminists in the arts. Museum curators, art critics, art historians and artists showed their work, discussed their professional experiences, and sought ways to break through the existing barriers to succeeding in the male-dominated art world. The event was the forerunner of the Women's Caucus for Art. In 1974, after returning from Los Angeles, Frank was inspired to create a women's arts center in Washington, D.C., and in 1975 organized Womansphere, a women's inter-arts festival held at the Glen Echo National Park in Maryland. A small group then formed to organize the Washington Women's Arts Center, which opened in 1975/1976. Frank served as director and president of the board, as well as director of the arts programs. An artist and a non-profit organization director, Frank holds a B.A. and M.F.A. from the University of Maryland, College Park. Archives: Washingtoniana Archives of the Martin Luther King Public Library and the National Women's Museum, Washington, D.C.   (ABS)

Frank, Marion Rudin (1942 –) (also known as Marion Husik) is a clinical and consulting psychologist. In 1971, while working on her doctorate, she became part of a newly formed women's weekly peer support group at Temple University, Philadelphia. In 1975, she joined the faculty of The Institute of Awareness in Philadelphia, an innovative school for women under the leadership of Dr. Mattie Gershenfeld. Frank marched in Washington in support of the ERA and abortion rights, and conducted seminars about the women's movement for the Bicentennial Celebration in Philadelphia in 1976. In 1979, as a member of the board of directors of the Philadelphia Women's Network, she helped found one of the first coalitions of corporate women in that city. She established and chaired the psychology of women committee for the Philadelphia Society of Clinical Psychologists, and served on the founding boards of the Women's Health Alliance and the Widow/Widower Referral Service. She

F

has led breast cancer support groups and assertiveness training groups for many years, and is (2004) Philadelphia chapter president of the Gold Star Wives of America, a national political action nonprofit organization for military widows. Frank is the author of "Feminism as a Therapy Modality," published in *The PA Psychologist* (1985); "Group Design & Intervention for Women with Breast Cancer," published in *Breast Cancer: A Psychological Treatment Manual* (1995); and "Women Crying in the Workplace," published in *EAP Digest* (1987). Frank's husband died when she was just 23, when a woman's identity was closely tied to her husband's. The newly emerging women's movement helped her see new possibilities. Frank, who has an M.A. from Columbia University and an Ed.D. from Temple University, Philadelphia, has one child. (ABS)

Frank, Phyllis B. (1942 –) An activist, community organizer, psychotherapist, consultant, speaker and trainer in domestic violence, anti-racism and heterosexism, Frank was a co-founding board member, New York State Coalition Against Domestic Violence (1978). She was also a founding board member of the grass roots feminist women's organization, Women's Way (Rockland, NY, 1972), and the Rockland, NY, Family Shelter (1976), and has been a member of NOW (including national NOW and the NYS and Rockland County chapters) since 1975. She served as a member of NOW's committee on pornography, and also was chair of NYS NOW's task force on pornography and of Rockland NOW's battered women's task force, among other activities. Frank became a member of the National Organization for Men Against Sexism in 1984 and the Rockland County Commission of Women's Issues in 1985. She is also an officer on the national board of directors of The Black Church and Domestic Violence Institute (2001 – 2003), and was a member, appointed by governor Mario Cuomo, of the Governor's Commission on Domestic Violence (1983 – 1988). The author of *Confronting the Batterer: A Guide to Creating the Spouse Abuse Educational Workshop*, Frank developed and directed a batterers intervention program in a NYS maximum-security prison. She has received numerous awards, including Woman of the Year from the Tappan Zee Business & Professional Women's Club (1987) and the Rockland County District Attorney's Recognition Award (1992). Frank has a B.S. from Boston University (1962) and an M.A. from Fairleigh Dickinson University (1976). She has two children. (ABS)

Frankfort, Ellen (1936 – 1987) was a visionary and crusader who exposed the horrors of male-dominated medicine, including botched abortions and denial of abortions. She is best remembered for her groundbreaking work *Vaginal Politics* (1972). Her particular bent for investigative feminism culminated in *Rosie: The Investigation of a Wrongful Death* (1979), written with Francis Kissling about Rose Jimenez, the first fatality of the Medicaid abortion-funding cutoff in 1977. This book earned Frankfort the Columbia DuPont Journalism Award for investigative reporting. Frankfort was also a contributor to several progressive publications, including *Ms.* magazine, *Sojourner*, and the *Village Voice*, for which she wrote a weekly feminist health column. She described her experiences in *The Voice: Life at the Village Voice* (1976). In 1984 she published *Kathy Boudin and the Dance of Death*. A graduate of Barnard College, Frankfort was an assistant professor of journalism at Brooklyn College. In later years she lived in Sag Harbor, NY. The medical profession's hostility to Frankfort's exposés affected the major publishing houses, a phenomenon that eventually made it difficult to get her work published. This factor is believed to have contributed to her periodic depressions and eventual suicide. She died from an overdose of prescription drugs.

Franklin, Barbara Hackman (1940 –) graduated from Harvard Business School in 1964, one of the first women to do so. In 1971, she was appointed staff assistant to President Nixon for the recruitment of women to high-level positions in the federal government. Within a year the number of women in these positions had nearly trebled, and some 1,000 women had moved into middle management positions. Franklin was a founder of Executive Women in Government (1974); more than 30 years later, the group still serves as a network for women and a source for learning about opportunities for career advancement. In 1981, Franklin was a founding member of the Washington Women's Forum, which later banded with the Chicago Network and the New York Women's Forum to form the National Women's Forum. In 1982, the NWF joined forces with Forum UK and the Canadian Women's Forum to create the International Women's Forum. Since 1980, Franklin has served on the boards of a number of public and private companies, often as the first and frequently as the only woman director. She was the first woman to chair the Economic Club of New York (2003), and the second woman U.S. Secretary of Commerce. In 1997, Franklin launched a project to document some of the achievements of the 1970s, A Few Good Women, a collection of oral histories now housed at the Pennsylvania State University Libraries. In addition to her M.B.A. from Harvard, Franklin has a B.S. from Penn State (1962). Archives: Paterno Libraries, Pennsylvania State University, University Park, PA. (ABS)

Franklin, Nurk (1949 –) has helped women in the areas of sexual assault, rape, AIDs and education since 1975, beginning as a staff member on the first federally funded rape crisis center, Sacramento Women Against Rape. Outcomes include the formation of Women's Stress Alternatives (NIMH funded), a drug-treatment program for prescription-drug addicted women; the first Take Back The Night conference and march in San Francisco, CA (1978); rape prevention workshops for the State of

California workforce located in Sacramento; and one of the first grant proposals requesting federal rape prevention education. From 1980 – 1985 Franklin was the fiscal director of Women's Stress Alternatives, where she helped create Womenstrength Unlimited, a for-profit arm to bring in non-governmental funds. From 1985 – 1991, she was the fiscal director, Sacramento AIDS Foundation. During that time, the agency grew from seven to 33 employees and developed a $2.8 million budget. She created groups for women with AIDS, street outreach and a large volunteer pool. In 1991, Franklin stepped into the Governor's Office of Emergency Services, which oversees funding to statewide rape crisis centers and the California Coalition Against Sexual Assault. In addition, she has served on the board of directors of the LAMBDA Center in Sacramento. Franklin is working in the California Governor's Office of Emergency Services as a senior program specialist in the Sexual Assault Section/Criminal Justice Programs Division. (ABS)

Franklin-Shutan, Georgia (1934 –) entered law school in 1957 at Southwestern University School of Law and was usually the only woman in the class. She was admitted to practice in California in 1962. "I actually felt like a misfit because my peers were nesting and raising children, decorating houses, etc. I thought something was wrong with me because I wanted a career," she recalls. "It wasn't until I read Betty Friedan's *Feminine Mystique* that I realized those women without careers—or at least the option of pursuing careers—were hurting just as much as I was. I wasn't really a misfit after all." She became active in Women Lawyers Association of Los Angeles "at the time when it was transformed from a tea party into an activist feminist organization," she says. That experience led her to become a founding member of California Women Lawyers under the leadership of Roberta Ralph. In the early to mid 1970s, Franklin-Shutan also served as a volunteer counsel for NOW in Los Angeles and headed a legal program at the Feminist Women's Health Center that helped women process their own divorces. She developed programs for both WLALA and CWL to monitor legislation and advocate for or against pending bills. As a part of that program, she created the first Summary Dissolution of Marriage bill, and traveled regularly to Sacramento for five years advocating for its passage. It was the first in the nation to be enacted. She also practiced family law and was a staff attorney for the Legal Aid Foundation. She was resident counsel of the Writers Guild of America, West (1964 – 1968). In addition, she was executive director of the Los Angeles County Bar Association (1979 – 1984) and the Dallas Bar Association (1990 – 1995). For the past 10 years (beginning in 1995), she has been active in the National Alliance for the Mentally Ill, and as a volunteer teaching about mental illness and helping persons with mental illness obtain and maintain jobs. Retired from the law since 2000, she received her master's degree in counseling psychology from Ryokan

College in 2005 and went to work as a marriage and family therapist intern at the Women's Clinic and Family Counseling Center in Los Angeles. Franklin-Shutan has two children. (ABS)

Franzosa, Susan Douglas (1946 –) As a graduate student at SUNY Buffalo with a two-year-old daughter, Franzosa joined the movement to establish a cooperative day care center on campus. When the American studies group at SUNY began offering women's studies courses in 1970, Franzosa, an anti-war activist, attended as an auditor and, with other activist women, formed a caucus to develop a community slide presentation on violence against women in Vietnam. At the University of New Hampshire, where she is a professor and coordinator of the women's studies program, Franzosa was a member of the Women's Commission that, in the early 1980s, wrote and advocated for the adoption of the first university anti-sexist language policy in the country. The group also succeeded in winning university adoption of a sexual harassment policy and establishing the Sexual Harassment and Rape Prevention Program. As co-chair of the UNH diversity committee in the 1980s, Franzosa obtained funding to sponsor feminist and multicultural curriculum reform projects, and lobbied successfully for the establishment of an Office of Multicultural Affairs. Within that context, she co-authored *Integrating Women's Studies into the Curriculum* in 1984, and served as a core faculty member in two National Endowment for the Humanities summer institutes for teachers on women in the 19th Century. She was a member of special-interest groups on women in the profession in the American Educational Studies Association and American Educational Research Association, and joined NWSA in the early 1980s. She became an associate editor of *NWSA Journal* in the 1990s, and has been a core faculty member in the women's studies program at UNH since 1979. Franzosa, who has two children, earned her B.A. from the University of Connecticut and her M.Ed. and Ph.D. from SUNY Buffalo. (ABS)

Fraser, Arvonne Skelton (1925 –) organized the Nameless Sisterhood, a group of women associated with government either as wives or workers in Washington, D.C., in the 1960s. With Bunny Sandler and others, she then organized WEAL's legislative office, serving as legislative chair (1970 – 1971) and president (1972 – 1974). Fraser was also a co-founder of WEAL Education and Legal Defense Fund, among other activities. She assisted in the production of the "WEAL Washington Report," a newsletter begun in the early 1970s that reported on legislation affecting women, and assisted in the formation of the WEAL Fellowship Project (1971) that helped open Nieman, Rhodes and other prestigious fellowships to women. Fraser was one of the initiators of—and lobbied and testified before the House and Senate on—the Women's Educational Equity Act. In the 1970s, Fraser chaired the constitution committee, National Women's

Political Caucus Convention; helped organize the National Women's Education Fund to train women for political participation; was co-founder of the Women's Campaign Fund (1974); and was first chair of the women's subcommittee of the Leadership Council on Civil Rights. She was also a delegate to the first two U.N. world women's conferences. From 1983–1985, Fraser served on the board of the National Women's Law Center. From 1976–1981, she was coordinator, Office of Women in Development, a U.S. Agency for International Development, and became a leader in the field of women in international development. While in the Carter administration, she was a co-founder of the Washington Women's Network. From 1985–1993, Fraser first organized and then directed the International Women's Rights Action Watch to publicize and encourage implementation of the U.N. Convention on the Elimination of All Forms of Discrimination Against Women. Fraser, who has written widely on issues affecting women, is co-editor, with Irene Tinker, of *Developing Power: How Women Trans-formed International Development* (The Feminist Press, 2004), and is author of *U.N. Decade for Women: Documents and Dialog* (Westview Press, 1987). She was awarded the Prominent Women in International Law of the American Society of International Law, the first non-lawyer to receive that distinction. Fraser has a B.A. from the University of Minnesota (1948) and six children. Archives: Minnesota Historical Society, St. Paul, MN. (ABS)

Fraser, Clara (1923 – 1998) A feminist in the 1950s and 1960s before women's liberation took root, Fraser put forward a vision of the revolutionary leadership of the most oppressed. She powerfully welded the issues of race, class, sex and lesbian/gay rights into the framework of the Freedom Socialist Party. The FSP itself, marked by its commitment to women's liberation, was created in 1965 when Fraser and the entire Seattle branch of the Socialist Workers Party left the national organization and formed a new party. Earlier, in 1948, Fraser, then an electrician on the Boeing Aircraft assembly line, helped lead an innovative picket line of mothers and babies that defied an anti-picketing injunction during a strike against the company. In 1967, Fraser was a co-founder (with Gloria Martin) of Radical Women, a socialist feminist organization that combined activism with teaching women the leadership skills they had been denied in the male-dominated anti-war, anti-poverty and civil rights movements. With Martin and Nina Harding, Fraser led WA State's first abortion rights demonstration. "She had the roots in the African American community, and was one of the few white revolutionaries that had the guts to argue with the Black Panther Party when she thought they were wrong," says Barbara Winslow. Overall, Radical Women supported the Panthers and mobilized the community to defend their Seattle headquarters when police threatened an assault. Fraser fought and won a seven-year sex and political ideology discrimination case against Seattle City Light,

which had fired her in retaliation for her leadership of an 11-day wildcat strike and her defense of a program Fraser designed to bring women into the electrical trades. After four years back on the job, Fraser retired from City Light in 1986 and became a full-time adviser to the Freedom Socialist Party and Radican Women. She launched and guided the first International Feminist Brigade to Cuba, undertaken jointly in 1997 by RW and the Federation of Cuban Women, and at the time of her death was national chair of FSP. Fraser, who had two children, earned her B.A. from UCLA in 1944. She is author of *Revolution, She Wrote* (Red Letter Press, 1998). Archives: Freedom Socialist Party, Seattle, WA.

Fraser, Karen Riese (1944 –) In 2004, Washington State senator Fraser finished her third term working for equal rights and equal opportunity. She was elected to a fourth four-year term in November 2004. An ardent supporter of the ERA, she began her political life in 1969 in NOW, first as the local chapter treasurer and legislative liaison in Thurston County, WA, and in 1973 as the state legislative coordinator for the WA State chapter. Active in the Washington State WPC in the 1970s, she was a member of the original group that established the practice of jointly interviewing, with other women's organizations, state-wide candidates on their stands on women's issues. She was a delegate to the State Labor Convention AFL-CIO several times (1970s), and worked to create a women's committee to focus on women's workplace issues. She was also a member of the Washington State interagency committee for women, representing the Department of Employment Security. In 1973, Fraser was elected the first woman member of the Lacey City Council and, in 1976, became the first woman mayor of the City of Lacey to eventually serve three terms. Fraser served on the evaluation committee of the Washington State Comparable Worth Study, and was a founding member of Elected Washington Women (late 1970s). From 1976–1977, she was a member of the Washington State planning committee for the IWY Conference in WA State, held in 1977. In the 1980s, Fraser became the second woman elected to the Thurston County Board of Commissioners, becoming chair on her first day in office and serving two terms. She also served as co-chair of the host committee for the first U.S. Women's Olympic Marathon Trials, and was a board member of Women Can Do, a committee that conceived of and sponsored a number of educational programs about the history of women in sports. In 1989, Fraser was elected to the Washington State Legislature and served two terms (four years) as a member of the Washington State House of Representatives. Since 1990, she has been a member of Women's Olympic Trials Legacy. In 2002, she completed her work at the Foreign Affairs Institute for women state legislators sponsored by The Women's Policy Center in Washington, D.C. Fraser, who has one adopted child, earned a B.A. (1966) and an M.P.A. (1969) from the University of Washington. (ABS)

Frazer, Heather Turner (1940 –) has been a member of South Palm Beach NOW since 1972. A history professor, she was involved in developing and teaching a women's studies program at Florida Atlantic University, and teaches courses about women and history. She has published widely on women and history, including "Female Power in Changing India: Myth or Reality?" (*Review Journal of Philosophy and Social Science*, 1977), and "The Self-Employed Women's Association: One Solution to Women's Continued Economic Inequality in India," (*Journal of Third World Studies*, 1993). Frazer, who has three children, holds a B.A. from Connecticut College, and an M.A. and Ph.D. from Duke University.   (ABS)

Frazier, Elizabeth (1915 –) In the fall of 1970, Margaret Shannon, executive director of Church Women United, appointed Frazier to represent the loosely gathered group of 50 million church women on the religious advisory committee of Planned Parenthood World Population. "Upon entrance to my first meeting," says Frazier, "I faced the priest, the rabbi and 20 assorted Protestant clergy, all male, all agonizing over the female body." The two-hour discussion ended with Frazier "compelled to dust off my 1940 Yale University Divinity School degree and seek ordination (1972) in the United Church of Christ (then Congregational)." Ordination to accept a call to church as pastor fit the rules, but "ordination to raise serious issues of women's health and institutional religion was then and continues to be highly controversial," she says. Three items of importance emerged: Planned Parenthood and Yale Divinity School held a one-day conference on Issues of Planned Parenthood and Theology; a 10-week seminar series, Search for Livable Life Styles, including population trends and human sexuality; and Frazier became by decree of the conference minister the "token woman preacher in many Connecticut Congregational Churches."   (ABS)

Frechette, Joy Ann – See Alwan, Joy Ann

Frederich, Sue Ellen – See Errington, Sue Ellen

Freedman, Estelle (1947 –) As a historian and college professor, Freedman helped create Princeton University's women's studies committee, which led to the founding of the women's studies program. A member of the women's faculty group, Stanford University (1976 –), she co-founded, co-chaired and chaired the program in feminist studies, served on the women's faculty caucus steering committee, and was co-author of the "Report on the Status of Women Faculty to Stanford Faculty Senate" (1997). Concurrently, Freedman worked on the San Francisco Lesbian and Gay History Project as both a study group member and co-producer of "She Even Chewed Tobacco: Passing Women in Nineteenth Century America," a slide-tape and later a video distributed by Women Make Movies. Freedman also presented the Women's History Through Folk Songs workshop at San Francisco Free Folk

Festival (1990 – 2001), and at Herstory, Stanford Women's Center. Freedman's consulting as a historian includes television ("A Century of Women," 1994) and documentary films: "The Celluloid Closet," "Common Threads: Stories from the Quilt," and "Isadora Duncan: Movement From the Soul." Freedman also offered expert testimony for the Federation of Women Teachers of Ontario (1986 – 1987). In addition to dozens of articles on feminism, women's prison reform and sexuality, Freedman has written a number of books, including *Their Sisters' Keepers: Women's Prison Reform in America* (University of Michigan Press, 1981); *Intimate Matters: A History of Sexuality in America* (with John D'Emilio, University of Chicago Press, 1988); *Maternal Justice: Miriam Van Waters and the Female Reform Tradition* (University of Chicago Press, 1996); and *No Turning Back: The History of Feminism and the Future of Women* (Ballantine Books, 2002). She earned a B.A. (1969) from Barnard College and an M.A. (1972) and a Ph.D. (1976) from Columbia University.   (ABS)

Freedwoman, Nancy M. – See Friedman, Nancy

Freeman, Jo (1945 –) Activist, political scientist, writer and lawyer, Freeman became one of the earliest radical feminists of the women's liberation movement in 1967. Freeman grew up in California and graduated from U.C. Berkeley in 1965. She credits her extensive involvement in the civil rights movement (1963 – 1967), including 17 months in the SCLC, with developing her understanding of feminism. After the *Jackson (MS) Daily News* "exposed" Freeman as a "professional agitator," the SCLC sent her to Chicago. She soon shifted to working for the *West Side TORCH*, a community newspaper, where she honed her skills as a photographer and journalist. When seeking a position at a daily newspaper in Chicago, Freeman was told that they hired few women as journalists (and none as photographers) because "women couldn't cover riots." In September 1967, Freeman met Shulamith Firestone at the women's caucus of the National Conference of New Politics. They soon started the Westside Group in Chicago. She founded the "Voice of the Women's Liberation Movement," the movement's first newsletter, early in 1968 and edited three of its seven issues. While a graduate student in Political Science at the University of Chicago (1968 – 1973), Freeman helped start a women's center (1968); chaired the student subcommittee of the committee on university women (1969); taught an unpaid, noncredit course on the legal and economic position of women (winter quarter, 1969); organized a major conference on women (October 1969); founded the University Women's Association (fall quarter, 1969); and began speaking and organizing at other campuses (1970 on) and in Europe (1970 – 1971). She published her dissertation as *The Politics of Women's Liberation* (1975), and later wrote *A Room at a Time: How Women Entered Party Politics* (Rowman and Littlefield,

F

2000). Both books won prizes for scholarship at the Political Science Association. Her book *At Berkeley in the Sixties: Education of an Activist 1961–1965* was published in 2004. Freeman edited five editions of *Women: A Feminist Perspective* (1975–1995). It became a leading text for women's studies courses, which multiplied in the 1970s. She also served as editor of *Social Movements of the Sixties and Seventies* (1983) and co-editor of *Waves of Protest: Social Movements Since the Sixties* (1999). In addition, Freeman is the author of several important early feminist articles, including three written under her movement name, Joreen: "The BITCH Manifesto" (1969); "The Tyranny of Structurelessness" (1970); and "Trashing: The Dark Side of Sisterhood" (1975). Freeman joined with Catherine Conroy and Nan Wood to found the Chicago chapter of NOW in 1969, joined NYC NOW in 1974 after moving to NY, and was treasurer of the Washington, D.C., chapter from 1977–1979. Freeman chaired the NYC NOW IWY committee, and was a delegate to the National Women's Conference in Houston in 1977. From 1974–1977, Freeman was active in the Women's Martial Arts Union. She is a charter member of VFA, and was its first official photographer. Freeman holds a Ph.D. from the University of Chicago (1973) and a J.D. from NYU School of Law (1982). Archives: Extensive archives of the early women's liberation movement are in her home.   (ABS)

Freespirit, Judy (1936 –) (also known as Judith Ackerman) In 1970, Judith Ackerman walked into the Los Angeles Women's Center and opened the door to a life of feminism and (later) the name change to Freespirit. She worked on the center's hotline; organized and led meetings; taught the class Radical Therapy; and attended lesbian feminist meetings. By 1972, she was a member of the board of the Feminist Women's Health Center in Los Angeles. Over the next decade, she was a guest lecturer at numerous universities, including Cal State Long Beach and the University of California, Irvine, speaking on feminism, lesbianism and fat liberation. In Los Angeles, she was a founding member of the Radical Feminist Therapy Collective, The Fat Underground, The Westside Women's Center and The Alternative Institute Women's Liberation School. She was also a founding member and performer, Fat Lip Reader's Theatre and the Fat Chance Dance Troupe. Freespirit has served on the board of the Westside Women's Clinic and the Westside Women's Center, Santa Monica. She was also a member of an advisory group for a research project on ovarian cancer in large women funded by the California State Health Department Cancer Research Center. A few of her many contributions in the Fat Liberation Movement are working on a 2002 research project on barriers to emergency medical care for fat people, and organizing the 5th and 11th Annual Fat Feminist Gathering. On behalf of gay rights, Freespirit served on the 1978 statewide committee to defeat the Briggs Initiative, which would have denied the rights of gay teachers. For the last 25 years, she has been working in the disability movement, serving at the Berkeley Center for Independent Living, the World Institute on Disability and the Women's Braille Press. Her published works include "On Ward G," published in *The Strange Life of Suzanne LaFleshe*, edited by Susan Koppelman (The Feminist Press, 2003); *A Slim Volume of Fat Poems* (Bound and Determined Books, 1996); *Whole Lotta Quakin' Goin' On* (Bound and Determined Books, 1996); and *Keeping It in The Family* (Bound and Determined Books, 1996). In 2003, Freespirit wrote, directed and produced a play, "Polly's Phat Phollies," as a fundraiser for the First Unitarian Church of Oakland, CA. She was an editor of *New Attitude*, the quarterly journal of the NAAFA Feminist Caucus. Her many awards include Pat Bond Memorial Old Dyke Award, 2004; the Service Award from the National Association to Advance Fat Acceptance, for leadership of Feminist Caucus 1999; Community Awareness Award from the NAAFA, 1998; and the Gold Award for fat activism in London, 1996. Freespirit, who has one child, earned her B.A. from California State University at Los Angeles (1966) and her M.A. from Pepperdine University (1970). Archives: Some papers are with the June Mazer Lesbian Archives, Los Angeles. (ABS)

Freifrau von Gleichen, Tobe Levin (1948 –) Studying for an M.A. at NYU in Paris, France, Freifrau von Gleichen applied feminist literary criticism to her classes. She later received a maitrise for her memoir, "La Conception de la Femme chez Rousseau et Diderot" at l'Universite de la Sorbonne Nouvelle (1974). As a graduate student at Cornell, she continued her feminist criticism in both her course work and teaching, and was a member of NARAL. Returning to Europe in 1979, she was a founder of Women's International Studies Europe, and has edited its newsletter since 1990. She was also a founder of *Feminist Europa Review of Books*, a journal written in English that reviews feminist scholarship and creative and popular works by women published in all European languages other than English. As chair of Forward-Germany, she campaigns against female genital mutilation. Freifrau von Gleichen, who has one child, earned her undergraduate degree from Ithaca College; her M.A. from NYU in Paris; a Maitrise from the University of Paris III; and her Ph.D. from Cornell University.   (ABS)

French, Marilyn (1929 –) A teacher, writer and "a feminist from age five," French is the author of two studies of feminist theory, five feminist novels and a book on violence against women. Her non-fiction history book, *From Eve to Dawn*, deals with women in pre-history and the rise of patriarchy in most major cultures to the present. From 1965–1975, French was working on what became *The Women's Room*. The book, which brought her into prominence as a feminist writer, was translated into 20 languages and made into a TV movie in 1980. Her second novel, *The Bleeding Heart*, was published in 1980. A non-fiction book, *Shakespeare's Division of Experience* (1981), analyzed the polarity of masculine and feminine principles. *Beyond Power: On Women, Men and Morals*, essays on the effect of patriarchy on both women and men, was published in 1986, and the novel *Her Mother's Daughter* was published in 1987. Subsequent books include *Our Father* (1995), *My Summer with George* (1996), and *A Season in Hell* (1998), an account of French's treatment for cancer. French, who has two children, holds a B.A. from Hofstra College (1951), an M.A., and a Ph.D. from Harvard (1972). (ABS)

Friedan, Betty (1921 – 2006) was the author of *The Feminine Mystique* (1963), a major impetus for the second wave of feminism. After reading Friedan's book, millions of women saw themselves for the first time as victimized by a patriarchal society that stereotyped all women as housewives deriving their identity solely from their husbands and children. In 1966, Friedan was a founder and first president of NOW, which activated the second-wave feminist movement. Friedan created the name and acronym for NOW, as well as its first slogan, "Full equality for women in truly equal partnership with men." She personally recruited dozens of women and men throughout the U.S. who became major leaders in the feminist movement. Friedan led successful campaigns that forced government officials and lawmakers to implement Title VII of the Civil Rights Act of 1964 by outlawing sex-based help-wanted ads, as well as discrimination in jobs, credit, education, public accommodations and other aspects of society. She and other feminist leaders persuaded President Lyndon Johnson to sign Executive Order 11246, creating affirmative action programs that later opened up the job pipeline for many millions of women. In November 1967, Friedan enlisted NOW in the fight for abortion rights and the ERA. When her NOW presidency ended in March 1970, Friedan proposed the August 26, 1970, Women's Strike for Equality, which proved a turning point in the consciousness of American women. Although her interpersonal behavior was sometimes hostile and controversial, Friedan is credited by friends and foes alike as the foremost mobilizer of the modern feminist movement. In addition to NOW, she also helped found the NWPC and the predecessor organization to NARAL. Friedan's books include *The Second Stage; It Changed My Life; Beyond Gender, the New Politics of Work and Family;* and a memoir, *Life So Far.* Her *Fountain of Age* (1993) was the first major book to point out the potential for people in their seventies, eighties and beyond to pursue alert and active lives rather than lapsing into dependence and senility. Friedan was criticized in the early 1970s for opposing the lesbian influence in the women's movement. However, Friedan later apologized publicly for this stance and supported the resolution for lesbian rights that was overwhelmingly passed at the National Women's Conference in Houston in 1977. Friedan has been awarded numerous honorary degrees from various universities and colleges, including Smith College and SUNY Stony Brook. She has also received numerous awards from organizations including VFA, American Public Health Association, ASJA, NYS NOW, University of Nebraska at Omaha, Pen Center USA (Lifetime Achievement Award), St. Mary's College of Maryland, Columbia University School of Nursing, *Ladies' Home Journal*, National Council of Jewish Women, and the National Arts Club. Born Betty Goldstein in Peoria, IL, she was a summa cum laude graduate of Smith College (1942) and a University of California Fellow in Psychology (1943). She taught and lectured at the New School for Social Research, Temple University, Yale University, Queens College, Columbia University and the Kennedy School of Government at Harvard University, among others. She was also co-director of the Women, Men and Media Think Tank at the University of Southern California, Distinguished Visiting Professor at the Cornell University School of Industrial and Labor Relations, and director of the New Paradigm Program at the Institute for Women and Work, with the help of a special grant from the Ford Foundation. She had three children. Archives: Schlesinger Library, Radcliffe Institute, Cambridge, MA. (ABS before death)

Friedland, Claire (1915 – 2005) began a 25-year career in the male-dominated field of book production in the 1970s, re-entering the job market after a 30-year stint as a housewife and mother of two. She fought for and eventually won the title of production manager at Meredith Corporation. Friedland joined NOW in 1971 to work on the marriage and divorce committee. She was instrumental in organizing the groundbreaking NOW New York State Conference on Marriage and Divorce. In 1988 she was named Woman of the Year by the Women's National Book Association for her influence as one of the first women in management in the book production field; for her efforts as WNBA's representative to the Non-Governmental Organizations of the UN; and for her participation in the UN International Conferences on Women in Mexico and Copenhagen. She was also representative to the UN from the National Council of Women of the U.S., and served as president of the Council in 1990. Friedland was also honored by the VFA in 1998, where her efforts in organizing the "70 Book Women Who Have Made a Difference" program for the 70th anniversary of WNBA were noted. Friedland attended Hunter College and Queens College.

Friedlander, Spring (1943 –) (also known as Ruth Friedlander) entered the women's movement in 1969 after attending a NOW hearing in NYC. She participated in a feminist teach-in at the University of Chicago that year, and in 1970 moved to San Francisco, where her mother's family settled after escaping Hitler's Germany. She helped start CR groups in Berkeley (1970–1976), and helped coordinate a conference on Women's Theory in November 1971. She has since helped set up many

F

discussions and presentations on women's theory. Friedlander came out as a bisexual in 1970 "before we had the word 'bi,'" she says. In 1972, Tish Summers and Friedlander purchased a large house for their feminist collective household, named Prudence Crandall House. From 1972–1973, she was a volunteer at the San Francisco Sex information switchboard. She also led drop-in bisexual discussion groups at the East Bay Women's Center (1974–1976). From 1971–1980, she was in a collective that coordinated Breakaway, A Women's Free School in San Francisco and Berkeley. She was the coordinator of Bay Area Women Planners (1972–1976), and has been a member of OWL, national and Ohlone East Bay Chapter, since 1974, and did a successful capital fundraiser to purchase the Berkeley-Oakland Women's Shelter in 1978. She served on the board of the NWPC (2002–2003), and has been active in her local NOW chapter since 2001. She co-organized the first national conference of tradeswomen in 1983. She participated in the leadership of Self Employed Trades-women from 1980 till its dispersal in 1990, the Skilled Workers Network (1980–1987), and the Organization of Women Architects (1978, and 2002 forward). Friedlander holds a B.S. from the University of Wisconsin, Madison (1965), a master's from Hunter College CUNY (1969), and a Certificate in Carpentry/Residential Construction (1982). (ABS)

Friedler, Maya (1928 –) became an activist in the women's peace movement as an organizer for Women for Peace. Friedler, an actress, began her feminist work in Chicago in the 1960s when she served as legislative aide for the first woman state senator, Esther Saperstein. In that capacity, Friedler wrote speeches supporting the ERA and participated in legislative analysis and presentations. She also helped organize the NWPC caucus in IL and ran as a Eugene McCarthy peace delegate for the 1968 convention. Later, as board president of the YWCA, Friedler worked on flexible careers for women, violence against women, and other feminist issues. She also produced, wrote and moderated, with Diann Smith, "Talk In," a program that ran for several years on Chicago Public Radio and featured interviews with prominent feminists. After "Talk In" went off the air, Friedler teamed up with Eileen Mackevitch to air "Public Report." Both radio shows were from a feminist perspective. Friedler served as an organizing and active member of the Jane Addams Conference, an international women's leadership organization that became a United Nations NGO. Their work focused on women's leadership exchange groups, encouraging collaboration between women from the U.S. and women leaders from all over the world. Friedler has remained active in promoting women's issues and candidates in Chicago-area campaigns, in addition to her work with Women's Media Group, which produced "Isa: The People's Diva." Friedler has two children and earned her undergraduate degree from the University of Illinois. Archives: University of Illinois, Chicago, IL. (ABS)

Friedman, Nancy Marjorie (1948 –) (also known as Nancy M. Freedwoman) was active in the West Philadelphia Women's Center (1971–1973), where she lectured on feminism and the women's movement. She also offered basic survival skills to divorced women as part of the Women in Transition program in Philadelphia (1972), and was an active member of Union Women's Alliance to Gain Equality in California (1975–1982). A psychotherapist, Friedman was chair and then executive director of Vote Health (2001–2004), a group that believes that healthcare is a basic human right, and whose mission is to win accessible, high-quality healthcare for everyone, regardless of legal status or ability to pay. Friedman earned her B.A. from Chatham College and her M.A. from Sonoma State University. (ABS)

Friedman, Paula – See Kassell, Paula Sally

Friedrich, Rena Bakeberg – See Rae, Erena

Friedrich, Su (1954 –) A filmmaker (Downstream Productions, Inc.) and film teacher (professor of visual arts in the Council of the Humanities, Princeton University), Friedrich was a member of the Women's Graphics Collective in Chicago (1974–1975), which produced hand silk-screened feminist posters. She also did photographs for *Lavender Woman*, a feminist press in Chicago, and her own feminist photographic work. In 1976 she moved to NY and became involved in various feminist groups. As a member of Women Against Violence Against Women (1976–1977), she made numerous presentations in local high schools about violence in media images, especially album covers and ads. She was a member of the Heresies Collective (1977–1981), and was an editorial member of several of its quarterly issues, including the sex issue, the Third World women's issue, and the lesbian issue. She also did production work on most of the issues. From 1978 forward/2004, Friedrich has been a filmmaker focusing on the issues of women/feminism/ lesbian identity. Her work is distributed by Women Make Movies. From 1991–1994, Friedrich was a member of The Lesbian Avengers. Friedrich participated in actions, did the bookkeeping, and co-directed a video, "The Lesbian Avengers Eat Fire." A member of the WAC for several years in the early 1990s, she holds a B.A. from Oberlin College (1975). Archives: Museum of Modern Art, New York, NY. (ABS)

Frieze, Irene Hanson (1944 –) In 1969, Frieze helped set up the women's studies program at UCLA and co-taught the first psychology of women course there. The University of Pittsburgh hired Frieze in 1972 to help establish its women's studies program, where she is (2004) a professor of psychology, business administration and women's studies. Earlier, while at UCLA earning her B.S., M.S. and Ph.D. degrees, Frieze worked on the planning committee for the Women's Center for Los Angeles. In the 1960s, she taught an informal course on the psychology of women and helped organize CR groups throughout Los Angeles. Frieze, who was a member of several peace and civil rights groups in the 1960s, has two children. (ABS)

Froines, Ann (1942 –) (also known as Ann Rubio) Beginning in 1971, Froines taught for two years at the Cambridge Goddard Feminist Studies Program. She was a member of an East Coast Marxist-feminist discussion group. In 1974, Froines began a 28-year career at the University of Massachusetts, Boston, as instructor and program director of its women's studies program, the first such program in Eastern MA. As program director, she worked to link the university program and its resources to feminist activism in the community by supervising student internships with women's organizations. Froines organized with others two important women's conferences in the Boston area, one on women and racism in New England (1980), and the other on women and poverty in New England (1984). In addition, Froines was a founder and longtime steering committee member of New England Women's Studies Association. She served on the boards of several feminist groups, including *Sojourner: A Women's Journal*. Froines, who has one child, has published articles on women's activism and women's studies in scholarly journals, and has lectured in Havana, Cuba, about feminist theory. She holds a B.A. from Swarthmore College (1964), an M.A. from the University of London (1968) and an Ed.D. from the University of Massachusetts, Boston (2004). (ABS)

Fruchter, Rachel Gillett (1940 – 1997) was involved in many women's health groups and causes. She was a founding member of the Women's Abortion Project (circa 1968 – 1972), a NYC group that worked to repeal NY State abortion laws and help women get abortions from providers willing to perform them in the tri-state area (NY, NJ, CT). She was also a founding member of the Women's Health Collective (1968 – 1971), a group that grew out of Health PAC and worked on many issues relevant to women, including birth control and childcare. Fruchter was a member of the Women's Health Forum (1973 – 1980), which worked on women's health issues, national and international, including forced sterilization, breast feeding, breast cancer and ob/gyn care in general. She was also a frequent contributor to the Forum's newsletter, "HealthRight." From 1975 – 1997, Fruchter was a researcher, epidemiologist and associate professor in the dept. of obstetrics and gynecology at SUNY, Downstate Campus, where she worked on numerous women's issues, including extensive work around women and HIV/AIDS. She was a founding member of the Arthur Ashe Institute for Urban Health. Born in London, England, Fruchter graduated from Oxford University with a degree in biochemistry, and went on to receive a Ph.D. in biochemistry from Rockefeller University (1966) and an M.A. in Public Health from Columbia University (1973). She was killed by a van while bicycling in her local park.

Frueh, Joanna (1948 –) Art critic, art historian and performance artist, Frueh became director of Artemisia Gallery, a woman-run artists space in Chicago, in 1973. She is author of *Erotic Faculties* (1996) and *Monster/Beauty: Building the Body of Love* (2001). Frueh co-organized the exhibition Picturing the Modern Amazon (New Museum of Contemporary Art) and was principal co-editor of the book of the same title that accompanied the exhibit (2000). She has published extensively on contemporary art and women artists in *Art in America, Art Journal, Afterimage, High Performance* and *New Art Examiner*. She was co-editor and contributor to *New Feminist Criticism: Art, Identity, Action* (1994) and *Feminist Art Criticism: An Anthology* (1991), and author of *Hannah Wilke: A Retrospective* (University of Missouri, 1989). She has also contributed chapters to books on contemporary women's art such as *The Power of Feminist Art: The American Movement of the 1970s; History and Impact* (1994) and *Women Artists and Modernism* (1998). Her writings are included in *Art and Feminism* (2001) and *Feminism-Art-Theory* (2001). She is professor of art history at the University of Nevada, Reno. (ABS)

Frye, Marilyn (1941 –) Philosopher, educator and activist, Frye taught a course on feminist philosophy at the University of Pittsburgh, where she was an assistant professor, in January 1974. She then began teaching ever-evolving versions of that course at Michigan State University in the fall of 1974. Much of the material for Frye's book *The Politics of Reality* (The Crossing Press, 1983) came from that class. Says Frye, "Philosophy as a discipline was conceived as an entirely rational enterprise, and rationality was strongly marked 'male.' So a woman philosopher was a contradiction in terms. A woman philosopher was bizarre, you had to pretend not to have a gender or sex. Starting around 1970, we changed all that." Frye gave a paper on rape at a 1975 APA meeting in Chicago. From the early 1970s, Frye was also involved in the Society for Women in Philosophy. In 1992, she published a book of essays, *Willful Virgin* (The Crossing Press). Frye holds a B.A. from Stanford University (1963) and a Ph.D. from Cornell University (1969). (ABS)

Fuchs, Jo-Ann - See Pilardi, Jo-Ann Theresa

Fuentes, Sonia Pressman (1928 –) In 1966, Fuentes was a co-founder, with Betty Friedan and other women and men, of NOW. After working for more than six years for the National Labor Relations Board in Washington, D.C., Fuentes served as the first woman attorney in the Office of the General Counsel for the EEOC (1965 – 1973), where she drafted many of the EEOC's landmark guidelines and decisions. She was most noted for the articulation of the sex discrimination prohibitions of Title VII of the Civil Rights Act of 1964. In the early 1970s, she was a co-founder of WEAL and FEW. Describing her life and work, Fuentes says, "The fact that my life was saved from the

Holocaust left me with the feeling that I had to use that life to make the world a better place." Fuentes published her memoirs *Eat First—You Don't Know What They'll Give You, The Adventures of an Immigrant Family and Their Feminist Daughter* (XLIBRIS) in 1999. She retired as an attorney in 1993, becoming a writer and public speaker. She has served on the board of NWP and on the advisory committee of VFA, and is a lifetime member of the NAACP. Fuentes graduated from Cornell University (1950) and the University of Miami (FL) School of Law (1957), and has one child. Archives: Schlesinger Library, Radcliffe Institute, Cambridge, MA. (ABS)

Fulcher, Claire (1925 –) As dean of women, associate dean of students, and professor of education at the University of Bridgeport in CT (1954 – 1973), Fulcher worked with students, faculty and administrators using her feminist approach. She began her private practice as a psychotherapist and organizational consultant in New York in 1975. Fulcher has served as director of the National YWCA Women's Resource Center, and has been an activist in the AAUW, International Federation of University Women, and the United Nations on behalf of women worldwide. Permanent NGO representative to the United Nations for the International Federation of Business and Professional Women since 1981, Fulcher was awarded its Badge of Honor in 2005. Fulcher was also the founding convener of the NGO committee on UNIFEM; was on the planning committee and served as a delegate to the U.N. conference on women and forum; and was a member of the planning committee for Beijing in 1995. Fulcher also represented the IFUW on the executive committee of the NY NGO committee on the status of women, was VP of the IFUW, and was a delegate to the UN Conference in Copenhagen (1980). She has been involved in branch, state, regional and national sectors of AAUW, serving as president of CT state, and as first VP of AAUW (1969 – 1977) and the National AAUW Educational Foundation Board. In honor of her service, the Dr. Claire Fulcher AAUW International Fellowship Endowment was created. Fulcher, who received the VFA Medal of Honor in 1998, received her B.A. from Pomona College, her M.A. from Stanford University, and her Ed.D. from Columbia University Teachers College. (ABS)

Fulcher, Patsy Gayle (1940 – 1994) A civil rights activist and feminist, Fulcher was one of the few women skilled in first-generation computers when she began her working life as an information systems specialist. She served as Western Regional Director of NOW, co-chaired NOW's national task force on minority women and women's rights, and served as chair of the CA delegation to the 1977 IWY conference in Houston. Fulcher was a founding member of Black Women Organized for Action and the Bay Area (CA) Women's Coalition. She became deputy assistant secretary of the California Health and Welfare Agency in 1975, and in 1977 joined Aileen C. Hernandez

Associates, a San Francisco urban consulting firm, where she remained until her death from Lou Gehrig's disease. Fulcher also served as vice chair of the Bay Area Black United Fund, as a trustee of the United Way of the Bay Area, and as a board member of the Northern California ACLU and Public Advocates.

Fuller, Barbara Ann – See Cook, Barbara Ann

Funk, Cynthia Ellen (1941 –) joined Women's Liberation Group Number 3 in NYC in the late 1960s. The group, which later became WITCH, organized the Miss America demonstration of September 1968. As part of the demonstration, the group rented a sheep from a farm in New Jersey; Funk took responsibility for returning it. Funk also participated in picketing a men-only bar; was part of a protest at a bridal fair to highlight the patriarchal laws of ownership and dominance implicit in marriage; and picketed porno shops in Times Square and women's magazines that portrayed unrealistic, demeaning standards for women's beauty and behavior. "After NOW began to be concerned that too many lesbians were infiltrating that organization and Betty Friedan dubbed the lesbians the Lavender Menace," Funk says, she became part of a short-lived collective in NW Washington called Amazing Grace (1971). Funk was later a co-founder of a second collective house on Capitol Hill in NE Washington, the Easter Day Collective. (The remaining members of Amazing Grace then regrouped and formed The Furies.) In 1972, Funk and Edith Rosenthal started The Women's Painting Crew, which lasted for 15 years. Funk left in 1974 to open Moon Works, a women's craft shop on Chincoteague Island, VA. Funk was later hired as social work supervisor in the Accomack County (VA) Dept. of Social Services (1978). While in that job, Funk obtained funding for and helped found the Eastern Shore Coalition Against Domestic Violence. She also helped found the Eastern Shore Hospice. Funk, who obtained her M.S.W. in the mid 1980s, continues to foster feminism in public agencies, community organizations and, in 2005, in a private practice setting. Funk has one child. (ABS)

Fure, Tret (1951 –) An out lesbian performer and independent woman artist since 1971, Fure was one of the first female recording engineers in Los Angeles (1974). She was staff producer and engineer of Olivia Records from 1982 – 1990. Her contributions to women's music include Postcards From Paradise, Between the Covers and Radio Quiet with Cris Williamson (Olivia Records, 1993, and Wolfmoon/Goldenrod Records, 1997 and 1999); and Back Home and My Shoes (Tomboy Girl, 2001 and 2003). A co-owner of Tomboy Girl Clothing line, she was co-producer of the 2003 Tomboy Girl Fest, an all-women artists festival. Fure is (2004) VP of the first non-geographical-based musicians union in North America, as well as chair of the diversity committee for local 1000. She attended University of California, Berkeley. (ABS)

Furie, Noel (1944 –) served as VP and then president of the Westport and Weston, CT, chapters of NOW in the early 1970s, focusing on pornography, sexuality, motherhood, lesbian rights, and the politics of marriage. In 1977, she joined a feminist collective that founded Bloodroot Restaurant, a vegetarian restaurant and feminist bookstore serving as a political and informational gathering site for 28 years. Furie, co-owner of Bloodroot Restaurant with Selma Miriam, co-produced three cookbooks: *The Political Palate, The Second Seasonal Political Palate* and *The Perennial Political Palate*, each enriched with quotations from feminist authors. Also a photographer, Furie has two children and is a cook at the restaurant.   (ABS)

Gabel-Brett, Carolyn (1941 –) (also known as Carolyn Gabel Allen) became active in reproductive rights in the late 1960s when she helped found the Central FL chapter of Planned Parenthood. Moving to Connecticut in 1972, Gabel-Brett immediately joined the Greater Hartford chapter of Planned Parenthood, where she served on the board as chair of public affairs. Later she served on the board and as chair of public affairs for Planned Parenthood League of Connecticut. Gabel-Brett was also a primary organizer, with Nancy Lister and others, in establishing a CT affiliate of NARAL. She served on NARAL's national board, and fought for the ERA in CT. She was chair of reproductive rights and issues chair for the CT WPC. She worked with senator Betty Hudson, the leader for women's issues during the 1970s at the Connecticut General Assembly, to pass laws providing protections for women. And she worked with Martha Stone, then legal director of the CCLU, successfully challenging the state policy on Medicaid reimbursement for abortions for low-income women. As part of their organizing, they formed an advocacy group in the name of Rosie Jimenez, who had died from an illegal abortion. In 1979, Gabel-Brett became an assistant professor at the University of Connecticut School of Social Work. The administrator for a project on domestic violence, she established a course on violence against women. In the 1980s and 1990s, Gabel-Brett, with Tollie Miller, organized a feminist/progressive bookstore-café, The Reader's Feast, in the Greater Hartford area. She continues to work for full marriage equality and LBGT civil rights. She is the recipient of the Maria Miller Stewart Award, Connecticut Women's Education and Legal Fund (2003); the Public Citizen of the Year Award for the Promotion of Social Justice from the CT chapter of the National Association of Social Workers (2002); and the Eleanor Roosevelt Feminist Leadership Award from CT NOW (1998). Gabel-Brett, who has three children, holds a B.A. from Sweet Briar College (1963) and an M.S.W. from the University of Connecticut (1976). Archives: The Elihu Burritt Library, Equity and Diversity Issues Collections, Central Connecticut State University, New Britain, CT.   (ABS)

Gabree, Judy - See Thibeau, Judith Henrietta

Gabriel, Andrea - See Andreas, Carol

Gabriner, Vicki Levins (1942 –) began her feminist training early watching her mother, who was president of the PTA at Gabriner's Brooklyn, NY, elementary school. From 1964 – 1968, Gabriner was a civil rights activist in NYC and West Tennessee, and involved in the anti-Vietnam War effort at the University of Wisconsin. Returning to NYC, she joined an early CR group (1968 – 1969), became involved with the Weathermen and Venceremos Brigade, and marched in the first gay pride march, 1970. Moving to Atlanta, she came out as a lesbian; helped found the Atlanta Lesbian/Feminist Alliance (1971); a founder of Georgians for the ERA (1973); and wrote for *Quest, Feminary, Great Speckled Bird*, and a lesbian version of *Sleeping Beauty*. In 1973, she was arrested for participating in a Weathermen action several years earlier. She was convicted in a 1977 trial, won her appeal in 1978, moved to Boston in 1978 and wrote for *Gay Community News* and *Sojourner*. Gabriner was the executive director of Sojourner Feminist Institute, publisher of *Sojourner: The Women's Forum*, (1999 – 2002). She earned her B.A. at Cornell University (1963), her M.A. at the University of Wisconsin, Madison (1966). Archives: Schlesinger Library, Radcliffe Institute, Cambridge, MA.   (ABS)

Gage, Suzann (1952 –) joined NOW in 1971, working for abortion rights. After attending the first National Feminist Self-Help Conference, she helped organize the first Midwest regional Self-Help Clinic Conference in Normal, IL. Moving to Los Angeles in 1973, she became active full time in the Feminist Women's Health Center, ultimately becoming a director and clinic administrator providing woman-controlled abortion services and complete well-woman health services. Gage co-authored and illustrated several books on women's health, including *A New View of a Woman's Body, How To Stay Out of the Gynecologists Office, Woman Centered Pregnancy and Birth*, and *When Birth Control Fails*. She also illustrated *The Hite Report on Male Sexuality*, by Shere Hite. Active in the lesbian and gay rights movement, Gage served on the committee of the Los Angeles Coalition for Human Rights, co-founded the Union of Lesbian and Gay Men in Los Angeles, co-founded Los Angeles Women Against Violence Against Women, founded the Lesbian Well-Woman Clinic of the Feminist Women's Health Center, and was founder and facilitator of Women on the Sexual Fringe, a support group for women of any sexual orientation or identity. Gage was also the founder of Wholistic Health for Women and the Lesbian Health Clinic in West Hollywood (now Progressive Health Services). She co-founded Feminist Health Press, which published *A New View of a Woman's Body, Menopause Myths and Facts* (for which she was the illustrator), and *Lesbian Health Activism-The First Wave*. She also illustrated *Garden of Fertility*, by Katie Singer. Gage coordinated the National Lesbian and Bi-Women's Health Survey of over 6,000 women in 1994, and co-presented women's health workshops at the UN International Women's Conference in Beijing, China (1995). She was a member of the West Hollywood women's advisory board, and founded the CARES program for lesbian/LBT women with cancer and other life-challenging illnesses in San Diego, 2003. Gage is the executive director for Progressive Health Services, Wholistic Health for Women, and the Lesbian Health Clinic in West Hollywood and San Diego. Archives: June Mazer Collective in West Hollywood, CA. (ABS)

Gaines, Martha Wren (1939 – 1987) was a co-founder of the Atlanta chapter of NOW, serving as president, state coordinator and Southern regional director. Gaines also served as president of the Georgia chapter of the Abortion Rights Action League, and lectured on equal employment opportunities for clients such as the U.S. Civil Service Commission, U.S. Forestry Commission, U.S. Department of Education, and the University of Georgia Center for Continuing Education. In addition, she was actively involved in the Girl Scouts Northwest Georgia Council, the YWCA of Greater Atlanta, ERA Georgia, and the DeKalb County NAACP. She served as president of the Colony Square Business and Professional Women's Club, and president of the Georgia affiliation of the ACLU. She was honored for her civil rights activities with a memorial service held by the Martin Luther King Center. Gaines, who traveled tirelessly on behalf of feminist causes, often accompanied by her daughter Kelly, was a graduate of the University of Georgia. Archives: Georgia State University Library, Atlanta, GA.

Gale, Sandra McCorkle – See de Helen, Sandra

Galen, Elaine (1928 –) was a prominent painter in the 1960s – 1970s when she began lecturing and teaching other women artists about the importance of self-sufficiency. She served as a board member and then president of the feminist gallery SOHO20 in New York City. Her early works embodied the woman as the object of sacrifice, goddess figures, and the concept of the victim including the Holocaust. Her multimedia art has been shown extensively throughout the U.S. Galen received her B.A. from the University of Pennsylvania (1951) and her M.A. from New York University. (ABS)

Galland, Holley – See Haymaker, Holley Galland

Galloway, Barb (1952 –) A musician and teacher, Galloway joined Babayaga, the first women's Latin/jazz band, in 1974. The women—Latino, Native American and Caucasian—toured the U.S. and often performed in women's prisons. Babayaga also performed for women's functions, fundraisers and for lesbian/women's issues, as well as at major colleges including Harvard, Oberlin and the University of Oregon. Galloway and her partner, Donna Luckett, are the duo Galloway & Luckett; they have

released two CDs, When I'm With You and Simple Kind of Life. Together, they work as advocates for women/LGBT and the disabled. Galloway holds an A.A. in music. (ABS)

Galvin-Lewis, Jane (1940 –) first became active in civil rights, participating in the Freedom Ride and the Woolworth picket line and sit-in. She entered the women's movement in 1971. Encouraged by attorney Flo Kennedy, she and Margaret Sloan founded the National Black Feminist Organization in NYC in 1973. The organization became national quickly and was not prepared to handle the overwhelming response. For this and other reasons, NBFO lasted only two years, but sparked the formation of other groups. After her work with NBFO, Galvin-Lewis and her partner started Social Change Advocates, a business that consulted on issues of workplace diversity for businesses. She was also a founder of the NWPC, deputy director of the Women's Action Alliance, chair of the Radical Women's Program, co-author of a non-racist, non-sexist K-12 curriculum, and a speaking partner with Gloria Steinem. A Baptist with a career as an administrator, she received a B.A. from Boston University and an M.A. from New York University. Archives: The Sophia Smith Collection, Smith College, Northampton, MA. (ABS)

Gandy, Kim Allison (1954 –) An attorney, Gandy was elected president of NOW in 2001 after serving as NOW's national secretary (1987–1991) and executive VP (1991 – 2001). Gandy also chaired (2004) the NOW Foundation and the NOW Political Action Committees, and has held offices in the Association of Democratic Women, Louisiana Lesbian and Gay Political Action Caucus, the Association for Women Attorneys, BPW and Woman Focus (1970 – 1980). In 1981, Gandy founded the Louisiana Women's Lobby Network and was founding director of the Metropolitan Battered Women's Program. The LA Child Support Enforcement Act and LA's first Domestic Abuse Assistance Act were based on Gandy's model. In 1991, Gandy directed the WomenElect 2000 Project. This grassroots recruiting effort in LA tripled the number of women in the legislature, and turned out the women's vote to elect the first woman lieutenant governor and to defeat former Klan leader David Duke for governor. Gandy also served on drafting committees of the Civil Rights Act of 1991, which entitled women to a jury trial and monetary damages in cases of sex discrimination and sexual harassment, and the FACE Act, which decreased the violence at abortion clinic entrances. Gandy, who has two daughters, received her B.S. from Louisiana Tech University (1973) and her law degree from Loyola University School of Law (1978). (ABS)

Ganucheau, Anita Hamann (1943 –) An ERA advocate, Ganucheau lobbied the Louisiana Legislature for its passage, and in the 1970s traveled throughout South LA appearing on TV debates and radio talk-shows in its support. She also worked to eliminate LA's Head and Master community property system in favor of joint management of community property. Ganucheau attended the Louisiana Governor's Conference on Women twice and addressed numerous civic and political organizations in various areas of the law. She has been a judge since 1980, serving the Orleans Parish Juvenile Court. Ganucheau also served on the children's code committee and helped draft the Louisiana Children's Code. Ganucheau earned her B.S. from Loyola University (1965) and her law degree from Tulane University School of Law (1971). Archives: Newcomb College Center for Research on women, New Orleans, LA. (ABS)

Garcia-Dobles, Barbara Price
– See Price, Barbara ("Boo") Easter

Gardiner, Judith Kegan (1941 –) arrived at the University of Illinois, Chicago, as assistant professor of English in 1969. Almost immediately she advocated for a childcare center. She helped establish undergraduate, interdisciplinary and graduate certificate programs in gender and women's studies (1970–present/2005). Gardiner and her UIC colleagues also formed the Circle Women's Liberation Union, which implemented women's studies programs, healthcare, research and resource centers for women on campus. She also organized the Circle Children's Center at UIC (1970–1973), and served as an advisory board member (1973–1976 and 1979). As an advocate of women's issues, Gardiner is a founder and member of the NWSA (1977– present/2005); co-founded the Newberry Library Feminist Literary Criticism Group (1976–1995) and the Chicago-Area Women's Studies Association (1977–present/2005); and was editor at *Health Rights News* (1971–1974). Gardiner is the editor of *Masculinity Studies and Feminist Theory: New Directions* (Columbia University Press, 2002), and her article "Forum on Sex, Gender, and Sexuality" was published in *Transformations: The Journal of Inclusive Scholarship and Pedagogy* (Spring 2002). Since 1989 she has been a member of the editorial collective of the journal *Feminist Studies*. She is (2005) a professor of English, gender and women's studies, and director of the Gender and Women's Studies Program at UIC. Gardiner earned her A.B. from Radcliffe (1962) and both her M.A. (1964) and a Ph.D. (1968) from Columbia University. (ABS)

Gardner, Gerald H.F. (1926 –) joined NOW with his wife, JoAnn Evansgardner, in 1968. Gerald Gardner served on the national board for two years, as treasurer of PA NOW, and as president and treasurer of First Pittsburgh NOW. He also volunteered as an offset-press operator for KNOW Inc., the first feminist publishing house that was founded and run for several years by his wife and others. Gardner, who was born in Ireland, "prudently became a U.S. citizen and an upfront feminist" when his wife was arrested for defending the artist who put a papier-mâché statue of Susan B. Anthony over the

head of the statue of Father Duffy in NYC (1970). As an officer of First Pittsburgh NOW, he filed the complaint against the *Pittsburgh Press* that ultimately led to the Supreme Court decision in 1973 that ended sex-segregated help wanted ads in newspapers. Gardner earned his Ph.D. from Princeton. Archives: Included with his wife's at the University of Pittsburgh, Pittsburgh, PA. (ABS)

Gardner, Jennifer – was a member of NYRW, then Bay Area Women's Liberation in California. She worked on the Bay Area newspaper, *The Woman's Page*, which began publication in 1970.

Gardner, Kay (1939 – 2002) Musician, composer, spiritual leader and pioneer in the healing properties of music, Gardner was co-founder (with Alix Dobkin and Patches Attom) of the band Lavender Jane, which produced the groundbreaking album Lavender Jane Loves Women (1972). In the late 1970s, in pursuit of her dream of conducting a symphony orchestra, Gardner worked with the New England Symphony, where women musicians performed women's compositions. In 1975, she produced her first solo recording, Mooncircles. As her focus began shifting during the 1980s to the healing properties of music, she wrote *Sounding the Inner Landscape—Music as Medicine* (Caduceus Publications, 1990). In 1993, she co-founded (with Colleen Fitzgerald and Pamela Gross) Women With Wings, a women's sacred singing circle that met at the Unitarian Universalist Church in Bangor, ME, where Gardner was musical director. An ordained priestess in the fellowship of Isis, she founded the Temple of the Feminine Divine, also in Bangor. Just before her death, she produced Women With Wings' first CD, Hand in Hand & Heart to Heart. Gardner studied music at the University of Michigan, then earned her B.A. and a Master of Music (1972) from SUNY Stony Brook. The recipient of numerous awards, including the Maryanne Hartman Award from the University of Maine-Orono, Gardner had two children from an early marriage.

Gardner, Mary Penelope ("Penny") (1941 –) co-chaired Howard County, MD's successful campaign for the ERA, and in 1975 helped organize the Aspen Women's Caucus, which became the Pitkin County (CO) chapter of NOW. In Aspen, she worked to remove sexist language from the training materials given to police officers. In FL, Gardner was an activist and leader in Dade NOW, serving in various leadership positions, and was active in ERA Florida. She was also executive director of The Women's Emergency Network, Miami, which then, as now, provides funding to give poor women access to legal abortions. Gardner also "spoke out on the courthouse steps about my own illegal abortions," she says. Gardner met with reproductive rights activists across the country in their hometowns, and participated in their local actions. A Ph.D., Gardner is a member of the NWPC, NOW and NARAL. She has five children, and is (2005) program director with Michigan Equality, a statewide LGBT political organization. (ABS)

Garfield, Laeh Maggie (1942 –) Writer, lecturer, teacher and shaman, Garfield began her activism in 1967 when she sat in the cafeteria at Queens College, NY, and fasted with a group of nearly 100 other women who were protesting restrictive dress codes. They won. Also in 1969, she organized and participated in women's poetry readings, and founded, helped run and taught at alternative schools for children. In the process, she became a liaison person for people across the U.S. who wanted alternative schools. From 1970–1972, Garfield was a member of Women of the Free Future. Among other activities, this group forced the *San Francisco Chronicle* to stop running gender-based help-wanted ads, and in a demonstration at the University of California, Berkeley, burned their diplomas to protest their worthlessness in the job market. In addition to starting CR groups (1970), Garfield helped arrange for women to get abortions with doctors. She negotiated with physicians and clinics for teenagers to get abortions, and did abortion counseling through the Berkeley Free Clinic (1970–1973). In 1972, Garfield taught women's studies at California State University, Hayward, and from 1973–1974 was editor of *Woman-Spirit* magazine. In Wolf Creek, OR, Garfield and other women ran a kindergarten and a private school for children. She was then arrested for failure to send her minor child to school (1974). Taking the case to court, Garfield won the right to home school her child. Garfield, who holds a B.A. degree, owns an organic farm in Oregon. (ABS)

Garrard, Mary DuBose (1937 –) Professor emerita of art history at American University, Garrard was an early activist in the women's art movement and the second national president of WCA (1974–1976). She produced and edited *Slides of Works by Women Artists: A Source Book* (1974) for the WCA, and as president facilitated WCA's incorporation as an independent organization. She also served as WCA's first liaison to the College Art Association board of directors after the CAA board expelled the WCA from its membership. From 1978–1979, as a member of the CAA board of directors, Garrard served as chair of the CAA committee on the status of women and produced a detailed survey of the status of women in art and the art history professions. Her feminist scholarship began in the 1970s with the publication of articles such as "Feminism: Has It Changed Art History?" (*Heresies*, Spring 1978) and "Of Men, Women and Art: Some Historical Reflections" (*Art Journal*, Summer 1976). She is the author of *Artemisia Gentileschi: The Image of the Female Hero in Italian Baroque Art* (Princeton University Press, 1989) and *Artemisia Gentileschi Around 1622: The Shaping and Reshaping of an Artistic Identity* (University of California Press, 2001). Garrard is co-editor, with her partner, Norma Broude, and contributor to the anthology *Feminism and Art History: Questioning the Litany* (1982) and its sequel *The Expanding Discourse: Feminism and Art History* (1992); *The Power of Feminist Art: The American Movement of the 1970s, History and Impact* (1994); and *Reclaiming Female Agency: Feminist Art History After Postmodernism* (University of California Press, 2005). With Broude, Garrard was the recipient of the Art History Recognition Award for the year 2000, for a body of work representing Pioneering Feminist Scholarship, conferred by the committee on women in the arts of the College Art Association of America. Garrard has lectured extensively on feminist art and feminist issues in universities, colleges and museums across the country. With Broude, Garrard received the Mississippi Institute of Arts and Letters Award for *The Power of Feminist Art: The American Movement of the 1970s, History and Impact* (Abrams, 1994). In 2005, Garrard received a WCA Lifetime Achievement Award for Outstanding Achievement in the Visual Arts. She holds a B.A. from Newcomb College (1958), an M.A. from Harvard University (1960) and a Ph.D. from Johns Hopkins University (1970). (ABS)

Garrigues, Carol – See Henden, Carol Mae

Garry, Ann (1943 –) (also known as Ann Garry Winslade) A philosophy professor, department chair and currently (2004) director of the Center for the Study of Genders and Sexualities at California State University, Los Angeles, Garry was an early contributor to feminism in the academic world. She introduced feminist writings into her "regular" philosophy courses in 1970, and taught the first feminist philosophy course at California State University, Los Angeles, 1974–1975. She was co-founder of the Pacific division of the Society for Women in Philosophy, and organized and hosted its first regional conference in 1975. In the mid 1970s, Garry was a member of the founding collective of the Women's Resource Center at CSU. She was also a member of the American Philosophical Association's committee on the status of women (1975–1980), and served a subsequent term as well. Post-1975, she has continued to work on behalf of women in the academy and to teach, write and edit feminist philosophy. She was a principal organizer of *Hypatia: A Journal of Feminist Philosophers*, which has flourished for decades. Garry, who has three children, earned her B.A. from Monmouth (IL) College (1965), her M.A. from the University of Chicago (1966), and her Ph.D. from the University of Maryland (1970). (ABS)

Garskof, Michele Hoffnung – See Hoffnung, Michele

Gartner, Diana (1934–2005) A market researcher, Gartner was a member of NY NOW and at the same time a VP of BBDO Advertising in New York City in the mid 1960s. Working within that agency to change the image of women in advertisements, Gartner challenged—to no avail—the Wisk commercial that "attempted to shame women because their husbands' shirts had 'ring around the collar,' a socially unacceptable condition." Gartner was also part of the sit-in challenging the all-male policy at the Oak Room at the Plaza Hotel (1969). After having her secretary make a reservation for "Dr. Gartner," Gartner, with Betty Friedan and several other NOW members, appeared at the Oak Room asking to be seated. Refused, they sat down anyway, only to have the waiters physically remove the table, leaving them exposed and subject to the ridicule of other diners present. They then left and joined the prearranged picket line outside. Gartner took part in the demonstration against Colgate-Palmolive, which was discriminating against women. At that time a market research manager at Lever Brothers, Gartner was nonetheless spat upon and pushed into the gutter "by the same type of men, dressed in three-piece business suits, that I worked with—who now saw us as legitimate targets for hostility." Gartner, who had one child, earned her B.A. from Radcliffe College, Harvard University (1956); and her M.A. (1964) and A.B.D. from The New School for Social Research.

Gaulden, Mary Esther (1921 –) A medical scientist, educator and writer, Gaulden was one of a very few women undergraduate science majors at the University of Virginia in the early 1940s. Deeply aware of the disadvantages women faced, Gaulden became a founding member of NOW. Moving to Texas in the 1960s, she joined Dallas NOW and worked to improve women's lives. She also used her position at Southwestern Medical School to foster the hiring of women. In addition to her work at Southwestern, Gaulden served as a consultant to Oak Ridge National Laboratory (1960–1979); was a member of the radiation bio-effects and epidemiology advisory committee, FDA (1972–1975); and adviser to the U.S. Army NAS-NRC (1973–1976), among other positions. She was a founding member of the American Society for Cell Biology, the American Society of Photobiology, the Radiation Research Society, and the American Society of Preventive Oncology. Gaulden, who has two children, holds a B.S. from Winthrop College (1942) and an M.A. (1944) and Ph.D. (1948) from the University of Virginia.

Gayle, Marilyn - See Hoff, Marilyn Gayle

Gearhart, Sally Miller (1931 –) has taken to the streets for feminism, civil rights, disability dignity, LGBT pride, AIDS education, Central American solidarity, peace, jobs, justice, animals, clean air, the redwoods, the Constitution, and the Union. Her activism began in 1970 when she participated in a strike that closed down the University of Kansas at Lawrence in the wake of the Kent State killings. After moving to San Francisco, she joined Marxist-Maoist study groups and focused on the lesbian-feminist agenda, becoming the first open lesbian to be on the boards of the SF Family Service Agency and the SF Mental Health Association. In 1971 she convened the first women's course to be taught at Berkeley's Graduate

Theological Union. Her 1972 article, "The Lesbian And God-The-Father—Or, All The Church Needs Is a Good Lay, On Its Side," was one of the earliest lesbian challenges to established religion. In 1974 she became the country's first open lesbian to be awarded a tenure-track position (by San Francisco State University). She was one of the architects of that university's radical Women Studies Program. Her 1979 article, "The Womanization of Rhetoric," indicting persuasion as violence, roused her feminist colleagues to a continuing search for nonviolent paradigms of communication. Gearhart's 1978 utopian novel, *The Wanderground: Stories of the Hill Women* became an underground feminist classic. She is also the author (with Susan Rennie) of *A Feminist Tarot* (1975) and (with William R. Johnson) of *Loving Women/Loving Men: Gay Liberation and the Church* (1974). Gearhart has a B.A. from Sweet Briar College (1952), an M.A. from Bowling Green State University (1953), and a Ph.D. from the University of Illinois (1956). Archives: The Knight Library, Special Collections, University of Oregon, Eugene, OR. (ABS)

Geary, Caroling Constance (1934 –) An artist, Geary dropped out from the mainstream pursuit of job and family in 1966, having developed an awareness of the need for a women's movement. In 1967, she conceived the idea of a "stained glass lib, entwined with women's lib." She completed the dream artwork "Wholeo Dome," a 14-foot stained glass dome, in 1974. Her article "Liberating the Handmaiden," which explains the rationale behind the piece and links it to feminist thought, was published in *Glass Magazine* in 1977. "Wholeo Dome" was also written about in an article by Phyllis Birkby, "Herspace," published in *Heresies II: Making Room, Women and Architecture* (1981), and is installed at The Farm School in Summertown, TN. Geary, who has two children, was also active in the peace movement. She holds a B.A. (1956) and M.F.A. (1960) from the University of Minnesota. (ABS)

Gehman, Mary Elizabeth (1943 –) Born into a small Mennonite community in Pennsylvania, Gehman was living in NYC in 1968 when she participated in the Miss America Pageant protest in Atlantic City, NJ, as well as the 1969 protest. In New Orleans in 1972, she joined the Women's Center and the local chapter of NOW, and in the fall of that year helped found the feminist newspaper *Distaff*. The only radical women's press at the time in the Deep South, *Distaff* took on issues like abortion rights and lesbian rights, and challenged the head-and-master law of community property in marriage in Louisiana. She and other women kept the publication going until 1982. In 1981, Gehman had founded Margaret Media Inc., which she used to research and publish the book *Women and New Orleans* (1988). She also began researching free women of color in New Orleans in the late 1700s and early 1800s, and in 1994 published *The Free People of*

Color of New Orleans, also by Margaret Media Inc. Among other books and articles, Gehman is author of the chapter "Toward an Understanding of the Quadroon Society of New Orleans, 1789–1860," published in *Southern Women*, edited by Caroline Dillman (Hemisphere Publishing Corp., 1988). Gehman holds a B.S. (1966), a B.A. (1972) and an M.A. (1986). Her "greatest pride is to have two kind, progressive and non-chauvinistic sons." Archives: Newcomb College Center for Research on Women, New Orleans, LA. (ABS)

Geisser, Mary Lee – See Antiga

Gelb, Joyce (1940 –) (also known as Joyce Klein) Professor of political science, City College and the Graduate Center of CUNY (2004), Gelb was an organizer and founder of the women's studies department at CCNY and helped develop its curriculum (1969–1970). She is (2005) director of the CCNY women's studies program. Gelb is co-author (with Marian Lief Palley) of *Women and Public Policies: Reassessing Gender Politics* (Princeton, 1982); author of *Feminism and Politics: A Comparative Perspective* (University of California Press, 1989); and editor, with Marian Lief Palley, of *Women of Japan and Korea: Continuity and Change* (Temple University Press, 1994). Her most recent book is *Gender Policies in Japan and the United States* (Palgrave Macmillan). Gelb, who has two children, earned her B.A. from CCNY, her M.A. from the University of Chicago, and her Ph.D. from New York University (1969). (ABS)

Gelbard, Esther K. (1931 –) joined Middlesex, NJ NOW in 1974. Elected state treasurer of NJ NOW in 1980 and re-elected in 1985, she created a voucher system to pay bills that remains in use today (2004), and set up their NJ NOW PAC system. In 1981, Gelbard was elected treasurer of Princeton Area NOW, a position she retains. She also participated in campaigns to elect feminists to political office, and was active in the pro-choice movement. She was a co-founder of the ERA Campaign Network in 2000, and serves as treasurer of that organization. Currently active in AARP, she has been the women's issues specialist since 1996 and the speakers bureau chair. Gelbard, a retired administrative analyst, has two children. (ABS)

Gelobter, Barbara Lamont – See Lamont, Barbara

George, Kathi (1946 –) was founding editor and publisher of *Frontiers: A Journal of Women's Studies* (1974–1987). She was also a founder of the women's studies program at the University of Colorado (1974) and attended the first NWSA convention at the University of San Francisco (1977). She was honored by the VFA for her work as a feminist educator. Archives: Personal papers at Schlesinger Library, Radcliffe Institute, Cambridge, MA; *Frontiers*' complete archive is at the Bancroft Library, University of California, Berkeley. (ABS)

Gerber, Barbara W. (1934 –) was a founder of a women's center at SUNY Oswego (1971) and a member of the president's task force to study women's issues on campus. She used this appointment to incorporate more about women into the curriculum, to initiate a speaker's series about women, and to pressure various offices on campus to recognize the unequal treatment of women and men. As a result of this work, she became, in 1975, the first female dean of graduate studies and research on her SUNY campus. She was also one of the founders of NWSA (1977), and served as president (1997–1998). She remained active in NWSA through 1999, and was a board member for most of the 1980s. She is the author of numerous articles about women and women's studies, including "What is Feminism? Who is She?" published in *Lake Effect*, Spring 1987; "Sexual Harassment: A Matter of the Exertion of Power," published in *Oswego County Business Magazine*, June/July 1995; and "The Future of NWSA: Through the Looking Glass," published in *NWSA Journal*, 1999. A college professor and administrator, Gerber earned her A.B. (1955), M.S. (1959) and Ed.D. (1963) from Syracuse University. She has one child. Archives: Penfield Library, SUNY-Oswego, Oswego, NY. (ABS)

Gerber, Ellen W. (1936 –) is a life-long pioneer of women's rights in sports and the law. At the 1970 National Association of Physical Education for College Women Conference, Gerber presented several controversial resolutions in support of women's equality. The debates she sparked helped make support of the ERA at the next conference, held two years later, pass easily. From 1970 to 1977, Gerber spoke at conferences and on campuses around the country on issues including support for Title IX, requiring equity for women athletes in sports competitions and scholarships in colleges and universities. As a sports historian, Gerber, along with Jan Felshin, Pearl Berlin and Waneen Wyrick, published the first academic book on women in sport (*The American Woman in Sport*, Addison-Wesley, 1974). In 1977, Gerber graduated from the University of North Carolina Law School. Her law career included working for Legal Services and founding the local battered women's shelter. She was a founder of the North Carolina Association of Women Attorneys, which works for the advancement of women attorneys and for the rights of women in the law. Gerber retired from full-time legal work in 1991. In 1994, she co-founded the North Carolina Gay and Lesbian Attorneys Association. She practices law at home on behalf of lesbians and gays, sits on the North Carolina ACLU state board, and works with the legal committee on abortion rights and lesbian/gay issues. (ABS)

Gereau, Mary Condon (1916–2006) joined the American Red Cross in 1943 and served as a program director for the ARC Services to the Armed Forces in the China-Burma-India Theater. In 1945, she became dean of men for Eastern Montana College in Billings, and subsequently served two terms as superintendent of public education (1948–1956). In 1957, she became secretary of the Penn State Board of Education of the National Education Association, and in 1960 transferred to the Legislative Dept. as a lobbyist. While at NEA, she served as president of the ERA Ratification Council. In 1974, she was appointed legislative director for the National Treasury Employees Union. She served as a consultant to the U.S. Senate Interior Committee, subcommittee on Indian affairs, and was executive director of the White House Conference on Education. The recipient of many awards and honors, she was given the 1999 President's Medal of Freedom Award, and in 2000 was awarded the Medal of Honor by VFA. Her husband, Gerald Robert Gereau, was the first male member of the National Woman's Party. Gereau earned her B.A. (1939) and M.A. (1941) from the University of Iowa.   (ABS before death)

Gereighty, Andrea Saunders (1938 –) In 1970, Gereighty established New Orleans Field Services and Public Opinion Poll, a business that trains women who are displaced homemakers, parolees, Welfare recipients and others for entry-level positions as research field interviewers. Because of the hands-on training from Gereighty and the skills and confidence the women gained, many went on to responsible positions in the New Orleans community. Gereighty managed the business from 1970 – 1998, at which time her daughter took over. Also active in the arts, Gereighty is (2005) director of the New Orleans Poetry Forum, which includes all ethnic groups in its workshops, readings and educational performances in schools and prisons. From 1968–1972, Gereighty established an experimental community where members instructed children ages one to 18 in the changes in the Catholic Church of Vatican II. Gereighty, who has three children, holds a B.A. in English Education and a Reading Certificate from Exeter College, Oxford University, England, as well as a master's degree from the University of New Orleans. Archives: Earl K. Long Library, University of New Orleans, New Orleans, LA; Howard Tilton Memorial Library, Tulane University, New Orleans; Xavier University Library, Lester Sullivan, archivist, New Orleans. (ABS)

Gerlach, Jeanne Marcum (1946 –) As a graduate student in 1974, Gerlach was introduced to feminism and its concepts by Judith Stitzel, professor of English and later director of the Center for Women's Studies at West Virginia University. She joined NOW in the early 1970s and began working for women's rights. She also began research on sexism in the language of books, which led her to co-edit the National Council of Teachers of English's Guidelines for Nonsexist Language. At the same time (1967–1977), Gerlach began establishing women's studies. In 1994 she directed the women's studies program at West Virginia University. She is the representative for Feminist Majority Leadership Alliance at the University of Texas at Arlington and serves on the women's studies

board. She is also working with the women of Texas Instruments, the Dallas Women's Foundation, and Jo Sanders from Seattle to start a Gender Studies Institute at the University of Texas, Arlington. Her awards include the National Council Teachers of English recognition as Outstanding Woman in English Education and Great Women of Texas Most Influential Woman Award.   (ABS)

Gershenfeld, Matti Kibrick (1925 –) A psychologist, Gershenfeld directed three major projects that helped women increase their understanding of themselves and advance in the world. In 1968, she founded, with Mary Gaynor, The Institution of Awareness. Based in Philadelphia, it had three main branches: self-knowledge, knowledge of the world from a scholarly standpoint, and career development. The school started with one class of 12 women; in 1975, when Gershenfeld left, there were 1,800 enrolled and the school continued until 1980. From 1972–1982, Gershenfeld was the consultant hired by the U.S. Civil Service Middle Atlantic Region to design and lead one-week programs for women being considered for management positions, which included a component on sexual harassment. Each program included two men against whom a sexual harassment or sexual discrimination complaint had been filed, allowing men to hear the issues that concerned the women. Another project involved consultation with women's religious orders after Vatican II, which required that nuns change from a role of passive obedience to active decision-makers. Previously protected by long habits, they now had to learn how to dress, and that meant learning about clothes, hairstyles and make-up. They also had to learn the answers to a Sex Knowledge and Attitude Test, all of which dramatically changed the way they interacted with themselves as women, with men and with children. Gershenfeld, who has four children, earned her A.B. from the University of Pennsylvania; her M.G.A. from the Wharton School; and her Ed.D. from Temple University.   (ABS)

Gesmundo, Lydia Mali (1936 –) (also known as Lydia Gomez) In 1972, Gesmundo was a co-founder (with Margo St. James) of COYOTE, an organization that works to prevent violence against women, in particular against prostitutes. She has been active in this area ever since. She produced workshops on women's sexuality and self-defense (1972), and also studied and interned for a year in Los Angeles to be an abortionist. She then included this topic, with graphic accounts of the mental, emotional and physical impact of this action, in her workshops. In 1972, Gesmundo was one of the founders of the Institute for Advanced Study of Human Sexuality, and became a sex therapist in order to understand women's sexuality for outreach in lecturing in the U.S. and abroad. In 1974, she traveled to her ancestral home in the Philippines to lecture on public health for prostitutes, fighting the subjugation of women, child slavery, and mail-order brides. With attorney Florynce Kennedy, Gesmundo participated

G

in hundreds of public demonstrations (1973 – 2000) from San Francisco and Los Angeles to New York City and Washington, D.C. She is (2004) focusing her attention on Asian and Filipino women. "Known for their non-complaining sweetness and beauty," says Gesmundo, "they have been abused since early childhood. It is an enormous challenge." Gesmundo, who has one child, was a Ph.D. candidate in Psychology. (ABS)

Giardina, Carol (1946 –) In 1968, Giardina was co-founder (with Judith Brown) of Gainesville (FL) Women's Liberation, the first women's liberation organization in the South. The group was active until 1973, was reactivated in 1985, and remains active as of 2006. Giardina attended the 1968 Miss America Protest in Atlantic City, NJ, and was present at two founding movement conferences, both in 1968: Sandy Springs, MD, and Lake Villa, IL. There, she collaborated with Judith Brown, Carol Hanisch and Kathie Sarachild in the development of CR, and in the concepts "Personal Is Political," "Sisterhood Is Powerful" and the "Pro-Woman Line." In 1988, Giardina and Brown developed Stop Child Sexual Abuse in Gainesville, FL, and Gulfport, MS, to defend mothers jailed for hiding sexually abused children. A coordinating committee member of Gainesville Women's Liberation (1995 – present), Giardina also developed and conducted a community education class, Women's Liberation: Where Do I Fit In? that has been given continuously since 1991. Following the death of Judith Brown in1991, Giardina created The Judith Brown Women's Liberation Leadership Scholarship to support radical feminist scholarship. That same year, she assisted in the development of a catalog and distribution center for Redstockings Women's Liberation Archives for Action, and became a member of the Redstockings board. She is (2006) the lead organizer of Redstockings Allies and Veterans and its social wage committee in NYC. Also active in NOW, Giardina was state coordinator for the ERA in FL (1969). Active in Gainesville NOW (1986 – 1996) and NY NOW (1997 – present), Giardina led the successful FL organizing against the first state attempt to roll back abortion rights after the Supreme Court Webster ruling in 1989. Earlier, from 1963 – 1970, Giardina had developed a referral network at the University of Florida, Gainesville, for then-illegal abortions. She raised money, assisted with transportation, screened abortion providers and counseled pregnant women. Also active in the labor movement, civil rights and the black power movement, Giardina has worked aggressively for the rights of mental patients (1979 – 1991) and in support of the people of Latin America. Archives: Redstockings Women's Liberation Archives for Action, Gainesville, FL. (ABS)

Gibbs, Beth (1943 –) (also known as Beth Rawles) A charter member of the Connecticut Permanent Commission on the Status of Women, Gibbs also served a term as commission chair. During the 1970s and 1980s, she was an active member of Women in Communications and the Connecticut Caucus of Black Women for Political Action. Her focus was on sex equity and the history, cultural and media images of women. She lectured widely and wrote and published several papers on these issues. Gibbs helped create the Connecticut Historical Society's exhibition spotlighting influential Connecticut African American women. She also produced a documentary on women in history that won a New England Regional Emmy Award, and created and produced "What About Women," a long-running locally produced public-affairs programs on women's issues. Gibbs is executive director of Hartford's Camp Courant, the largest free day camp for city children in this country. (ABS)

Gibson, Mary Cordelia Atkeson (1945 –) (also known as Mary Atkeson Trawick) Gibson joined the Baton Rouge (LA) chapter of NOW in 1971. In 1972 she became co-coordinator/co-founder (with Sue Bailey Dunn) of Athens, GA. NOW, and later served two terms (1974 – 1978) as the first elected state coordinator of GA NOW. In 1971, she was a delegate to the first NWPC gathering in Houston. Gibson was also a co-founder of the Athens Rape Crisis Line in the mid 1970s, one of the earliest rape crisis lines in the country. In 1979, she co-founded the Alabama Women's Agenda. Gibson, who has two children, earned her B.A. from Brenau College and her M.A. from the University of Alabama, Birmingham. (ABS)

Giese, Elizabeth Ann – See Homer, Elizabeth Ann

Gilbert, Ilsa (1933 –) A writer, poet, playwright and author of opera and musical theater librettos and songs, Gilbert joined early CR groups in NYC. In the late 1970s, she joined the Dramatists Guild, where she became active in the women's committee working to improve the life, recognition, status and opportunities of women playwrights. In 1992, she was asked to form and develop the PEN Women's Literary Workshop. She is the author of *Survivors and Other New York Poems* (Bard Press, 1985) and is (2004) working on an opera set in the Holocaust period. Gilbert earned her B.A. from Brooklyn College (1955). Archives: Plays and opera librettos are in The Library of Performing Arts, Lincoln Center, NY, NY. (ABS)

Gillespie, Andrea (1944 –) joined the Daughters of Bilitis in Boston (1972 – 1973), and worked with them on numerous issues of concern to feminist lesbians—from lobbying *Ms.* magazine to use of the word "lesbian," to organizing the East Coast Lesbian Conference. Gillespie began promoting women's music in 1973, producing concerts as Calliope Productions. She later joined with other women to form Artemis Productions, which produced a number of concerts and the Boston Women's Music Festivals through 1979. Artemis Productions also created the Boston Women's Fund to distribute back to the women's community profits from the concerts. Since that time, Gillespie, who is a certified Registered Nurse Anesthetist, has concentrated on promoting lesbian philanthropy. She is a graduate of the Quincy City Hospital School of Nursing and the Tufts-New England Medical Center's School for Nurse Anesthetists. (ABS)

Gillespie, Dorothy (1920 –) An artist and painter, Gillespie joined the feminist movement in the 1970s. She was a member of various women artists groups; picketed the Whitney Museum (NYC) to protest its emphasis on male artists; and helped found the Women Artists Historical Archives at the Women's Interart Center (1972 –1977). She also developed (with Alice Baber) a course for the New School of Social Research. Called Functioning in the Art World, it emphasized working as a community to attain personal fulfillment as an artist, and was taught by Gillespie until 1982. In 2001, Gillespie was honored by the WCA for outstanding achievement in the visual arts. Gillespie, who has three children, is a graduate of the Maryland Institute College of Art, Baltimore (1941). She holds two Honorary Doctorates, from Caldwell College and Niagara University, and for 10 years was a Visiting Fellow for the Woodrow Wilson Foundation. Distinguished Professor of Art at Radford University, Radford, Virginia, She has had over 150 one-person shows, and in 2003 became the first artist to have an installation in Rockefeller Center. (ABS)

Gillespie, Marcia Ann (1944 –) Editor, writer, lecturer and fighter for gender and racial justice, Gillespie became editor of *Essence* at the age of 26, a position she held from 1971–1980. During that time, she was named One of the Fifty Faces for America's Future by *Time*. From 1980 – 1996 she was an adviser to editors and publishers, and from 1987–1990 and again in 1992, she served as executive editor of *Ms.* magazine. In 1993, Gillespie became editor in chief, a post she held until the magazine was purchased by the Feminist Majority Foundation in 2001. Gillespie has also served as president of Liberty Media for Women, Inc., which at one time owned *Ms.* A frequent speaker on the rights of women, civil rights and racial justice, Gillespie is the recipient of numerous awards. These include the Matrix Award from New York Women in Communications, the Mary MacLeod Bethune Award from the National Council of Negro Women, and the Missouri Honor Medal for Distinguished Service in Journalism from the University of Missouri School of Journalism. She holds an Honorary Doctorate from Lake Forest College, her alma mater. Gillespie has served as a member of the board of the Planned Parenthood Federation of America, the Arthur Ashe Institute for Urban Health, the Violence Policy Center and the Global Fund for Women. Archives: The Sophia Smith Collection, Smith College, Northampton, MA. (ABS)

Gillespie, Patti Peete (1938 –) As a faculty member and chair of the human rights committee at the University of

Iowa (1970), Gillespie became involved in women's issues and was active there "in early stabs at affirmative action." At that time she also chaired the women's program of the American Theatre Association and spearheaded its boycott of conventions in states that had failed to ratify the ERA. She also instigated a move for a similar boycott in the Speech Communication Association. Gillespie, who has published numerous articles on women's historical role in the theater, published her first article on that topic—on the development of feminist theaters in the U.S. and their role in advancing the goals of the movement—in the early 1970s. In 1974, she moved into academic administration and added articles about women in theater administration to her continuing work. Gillespie earned her B.S. from the University of Kentucky, her M.A. from West Kentucky University, and her Ph.D. from Indiana University. (ABS)

Gilligan, Carol (1936 –) is a pioneer in gender studies and, in particular, the psychological and moral development of women and girls. Her interest in this topic grew when, teaching at Harvard in the late 1960s and early 1970s, she interviewed young men thinking about resisting the Vietnam draft and then, when the draft ended, women contemplating abortions. Her book, *In a Different Voice: Psychological Theory and Women's Development* (1982) expounded her discoveries. After the book was published, Gilligan became known as the founder of "difference feminism." Gilligan was the first holder of the Patricia Albjerg Graham Professorship in Gender Studies at Harvard (1997). The Harvard Center for Gender and Education was created in 2001 to continue her research on how culture shapes psychological development. Gilligan is the author or co-author of numerous books, including *Women, Girls and Psychotherapy: Reframing Resistance* (1991), *Meeting at the Crossroads: Women's Psychology and Girls' Development* (1992), *Between Voice and Silence: Women and Girls, Race and Relationship* (1995) and *The Birth of Pleasure* (2002). She earned her undergraduate degree from Swarthmore College (1958) and holds an M.A. from Radcliffe College (1960) and a Ph.D. from Harvard University (1964). (ABS)

Gilmor, Jane Ellen (1947 –) An artist whose work both embraces and questions the Great Goddess archetype, Gilmor has spent a lifetime investigating the ways in which culture constructs the definitions of gender. She was a leader in the women's art movement of the 1970s in the Midwest and nationally. As a graduate student at The University of Iowa (1970s), she traveled to Los Angeles to exhibit video work at the Women's Building, and to NYC to attempt to organize a traveling exhibition of Images of The Goddess in Contemporary Women's Art. In 1973, she began a 30+-year teaching career at Mount Mercy College, where she introduced women's studies courses such as Women's Art History and Art, Gender and Politics. Gilmor was also a founding member of the IA

WCA and the Rapid Peters Feminists. In the 1980s, her work became more community-based. For 15 years, she worked on a series of public installations in storefronts, shelters and alternative spaces with women and children living in homeless shelters. In 2002, she co-produced a site activation/performance work in the Midwest that dealt with a local history of women and labor and the shift from an industrial to an information-based society. Gilmor's work has been exhibited nationwide, included in numerous publications and anthologies, and reviewed by scholarly journals. She has lectured widely on women and art, and her work is in numerous permanent collections, including the Des Moines Art Center; Tokyo University Museum, Tokyo, Japan; First National Bank, Chicago; and the Museum of Contemporary Crafts, NYC. She holds a B.S. from Iowa State University, Ames (1969); and an M.A.T. (1973), an M.A. (1976) and M.F.A. (1977) from the University of Iowa, Iowa City. (ABS)

Gilpatrick, MaryAnn (1948 –) A teller of women's stories, a singer of women's songs, and a member of the Blue Mountain chapter of NOW, Gilpatrick was active in CWLU from June 1970 until its dissolution (around 1976). She was also an activist in the American Federation of State, County and Municipal Employees Union before, during and after the City of Chicago white-collar organizing campaign, 1976–1985. In addition to her feminist work, Gilpatrick has participated in the peace, labor and anti-imperialist movements. (ABS)

Ginger, Ann Fagan (1925 –) Born in Lansing, MI, attorney Ginger followed her parents into the progressive movement. At the first integrated meeting of lawyers in Georgia called by the National Lawyers Guild and the Southern Christian Leadership Conference, she noticed that she was the only woman in the room. Later she was glad to help young SNCC women stop the practice of militant SNCC males assigning women to coffee service ("and sometimes bed duty," she says). After 1974, Ginger taught courses in sex discrimination, labor and constitutional law at five law schools. In 1974 she joined the Women's Alliance to Gain Equality and began working on the case of homemakers suing the California Industrial Welfare Commission to continue time-and-a-half for overtime for women workers. In 1965, she founded Meiklejohn Civil Liberties Institute, and serves as its executive director. MCLI has trained 160 women college and law students in Peace Law, which Ginger defined and taught until 2003 at San Francisco State University. In 1993 her biography *Carol Weiss King: Human Rights Lawyer* was published. Ginger earned her LL.M. at the University of California, Berkeley, in 1960. She has two children. Archives: The Bancroft Archives, University of California, Berkeley. (ABS)

Ginn, Elizabeth J.
– See Tessner, Elizabeth (Libby) Jeanne

Ginsburg, Charlotte S. – See Arnold, Charlotte S.

Ginsburg, Ruth Bader (1933 –) Even if she had not become the second woman Justice of the U.S. Supreme Court, Ginsburg would be honored as a distinguished American feminist because of her historic contributions to gender equality as a scholar, activist and trailblazing litigator. As a student at Cornell University, she met and married fellow Cornellian Martin D. Ginsburg. Both attended Harvard Law School, where Ruth Ginsburg became an editor of the *Harvard Law Review*. She transferred to Columbia Law School, where she served on the *Columbia Law Review* and tied for first in her 1959 graduating class. Despite this achievement, she failed to receive a single job offer from a law firm. Ginsburg finally became clerk to a federal district judge and spent two years working on a Columbia Law School project on international procedure. She then taught at Rutgers University Law School, one of the first 20 women to teach in an American law school. In the 1960s and 1970s, Ginsburg began to take on sex discrimination cases for the ACLU, becoming its general counsel and director of its Women's Rights Project. She taught a course on women and the law for Harvard, and then became the first tenured female professor for Columbia Law School. Ginsburg argued six gender equality cases before the U.S. Supreme Court for ACLU, and won five of them. She was the principal author of the winning brief Reed v. Reed (1971), a unanimous Supreme Court judgment holding unconstitutional an ID law that gave preference to men over women in selecting the administrator of an estate. In Frontiero v. Richardson (1973), the Court agreed with Ginsburg that military housing allowances and medical care should be granted equally for the spouses of servicemen and servicewomen. Ginsburg triumphed with another unanimous judgment in Weinberger v. Wiesenfeld, where a widower had been denied the childcare Social Security benefits that widows received. Ginsburg's fifth Supreme Court victory, Duren v. Missouri (1978), struck down a state law that made jury duty optional for women but not for men, supporting her contention that states should not place a lower value on the citizenship of women as compared to men. In 1980, President Jimmy Carter appointed her a judge of the U.S. Court of Appeals for the District of Columbia Circuit, where she served until President Bill Clinton appointed her to the U.S. Supreme Court in 1993. Ginsburg's reputation for fairness and moderation won overwhelming Senate approval for her appointment. Her majority opinion in the Supreme Court's 1996 decision in the case of the United States v. Virginia is often quoted. In overturning Virginia Military Institute's 157-year refusal to accept female students, she wrote that while Virginia "serves the state's sons, it makes no provision whatever for her daughters. That is not equal protection." Ginsburg, who has two children, has frequently spoken out in favor of men and women sharing childcare, and offers flexible work schedules to her own male and female court clerks alike so they can share childcare with their spouses. In her Supreme Court acceptance speech, Ginsburg paid tribute to her deceased mother, Celia Amster Bader, saying "I pray that I may be all that she would have been had she lived in an age when women could aspire and achieve, and daughters are cherished as much as sons." Archives: Library of Congress, Washington, D.C.   (ABS)

Giordano, Noel – See Furie, Noel

Gioseffi, Daniela (1941 –) A retired professor, feminist lecturer and poet, Gioseffi is the author of 13 books of prose and poetry. Her feminist awakening began in 1961 in Selma, AL, where she was a civil rights journalist and activist. After appearing on an all black Gospel TV show announcing freedom rides and sit-ins, Gioseffi says, she was "arrested in the middle of the night and then raped as a virgin of 20 at the station house by a deputy sheriff who was a member of the Ku Klux Klan." Her feminist awakening continued in 1966, she says, when she "almost died in childbirth due to doctor's errors." In the mid 1960s, Gioseffi began to give feminist readings and talks for WBAI-Radio in NYC. In the late 1960s, Gioseffi's work began appearing in feminist poetry anthologies. At the same time, she joined New Feminist Talent and lectured on college campuses on The Birth Dance of Earth: A Celebration of Women and the Earth in Poetry, Music and Dance. She published *Eggs in the Lake*, a book of poetry that celebrated women's freedom and erotic power and won a grant from the New York State Council for the Arts. Her drama "The Sea Hag in the Cave of Sleep" was produced at The Cubiculo Theatre in Manhattan and also won a multimedia grant award from The New York State Council for the Arts. Gioseffi wrote *Earth Dancing: Mother Nature's Oldest Rite*; published *The Great American Belly*, a comic feminist novel about surviving divorce and raising a child alone; and toured England speaking on her feminist theories. She later joined a group of feminists in Brooklyn Heights who formed a chapter of the Coalition of Unitarian Universalist Pagan Societies. She served as editor of *Women on War* (Touchstone/Simon & Schuster, 1988). The book became a women's studies classic, won an American Book Award (1990), and was reissued in 2003 by The Feminist Press. In 1993, she edited *On Prejudice: A Global Perspective* (Anchor/Doubleday), which won a World Peace Award from the Ploughshares Fund and was presented at the United Nations. Gioseffi, who has one child, holds a B.A. from Montclair University and an M.F.A. from the Graduate School of Arts and Sciences, Washington, D.C. Archives: Beinecke Library, Harvard; and SUNY Buffalo Library: Special Collections.   (ABS)

Gladden, Nyla — joined early CR groups in the San Francisco area, and participated in establishing the newspaper *Mother Lode*. A Welfare mother, Gladden was involved in the abortion movement, writing articles, pick-

eting and leading CR groups. She helped mimeograph copies of *Edward the Dyke* (printed by Judy Grahn and the Women's Press Collective); was published in Diana Press; and was involved in the beginnings of the West Coast women's music festivals. She was also involved in the San Francisco Women's Health Collective, where women were taught how to do menstrual extraction, a procedure developed by Carol Downer of Los Angeles. Gladden also taught women how to use speculums in order to empower their gynecological experience.

Gladstein, Mimi Reisel (1936 –) Nonplussed when told in the mid 1960s that the University of Texas at El Paso did not "hire housewives" to teach American Literature, Gladstein settled for part-time employment in the freshman English program. But she did not give up her goal, and eventually added Ph.D. to her credentials. Believing that a woman need not achieve her identity from her husband and family, Gladstein electrified her community when she made the bold decision to stop focusing on keeping her floors clean and moved with her three children to pursue her studies. After chairing the UTEP English and philosophy departments twice, Gladstein became associate dean for the humanities. From 2002 – 2005, she chaired the department of theatre, dance and film. Gladstein was the first female faculty to teach women's studies courses at UTEP, in the early 1970s, and was the first director of the women's studies program there (1981–1983). Awards include El Paso WPC Woman of the Year in Education (1975); the Burlington Northern Award for Teaching Excellence (1988); Bukhardt Award for Outstanding Steinbeck Scholar, an international award, (1996); and College Liberal Arts Outstanding Achievement Award (2003). She was also named the John J. and Angeline Priuis Outstanding Steinbeck Teacher for the 1978–1987 decade. Her books include *The Ayn Rand Companion* (1984) and *The Indestructible Woman in Faulkner, Hemingway and Steinbeck* (1986). Gladstein coedited, with Chris M. Sciabarra, *Feminist Interpretations of Ayn Rand* (1999), and published *The New Ayn Rand Companion* in 1999. *Atlas Shrugged: Manifesto of the Mind*, was published in 2000.   (ABS)

Glaesemann, Frances E. – See Burton, Frances E.

Glaser, Vera (1916 –) was a writer, journalist and Washington correspondent. At a White House news conference, Glaser asked President Nixon, shortly after he took office, if he intended to appoint more women. Nixon did, in fact, appoint a task force on women, with Barbara Hackman Franklin in charge and Glaser a member. The task force report recommended legislation to equalize the status of women, and 19 of the 20 recommendations are now law. Glaser then wrote a five-part series on American women, with considerable material drawn from Catherine East. East credited Glaser with giving the early movement fair and generous coverage, and always noted that there was more advancement for women during the Nixon administration than later because of the number of women in important positions. Glaser has been president of the Washington Press Club; was on the board of the International Women's Media Foundation; was a member of the IWMF delegation meeting with African journalists in Zimbabwe; co-chaired, with Maureen Bunyan, IWMF's Latin American conference in Santiago; was a judge of the Robert Kennedy Journalism Awards in 1981; and has served on many boards, including the Public Members Association of the U.S. Department of State. She has one child.   (ABS)

Glass, Carole – See Raimondi, Carole

Glass, Ruth Minka – See Minka, Ruth

Glazer, Nona Y. (1932 –) (also known as Nona Glazer-Malbin) A professor of sociology and women's studies, emerita, Glazer is the author of *Women's Unpaid and Paid Labor* (Temple University Press, 1993). She was a co-founder of the women's studies certificate program at Portland (OR) State University (1971), and served as president of national SWS (1976 – 1978) and as a member of its steering committee (1974 – 1976). From 1977 – 1978, Glazer was a chair of the sex and gender section and the family section of the ASA. She also co-organized regional feminist theory conferences, women's caucus meetings at regional and national associations, and many sessions at sociology and women's meetings (1972 – 1990). Since 1982 she has advocated for the integration of feminist studies into their relevant disciplines, as distinct from remaining within courses on women. Since 1972, she has consulted for grants with local women's groups. Glazer has also served as an advocate for women with the university and profession; and has researched, published and presented on women's unwaged work in the U.S., as well as the decommodification of women's paid labor. Glazer holds a B.A. and M.A. from the University of Oregon, and a Ph.D. from Cornell (1965). Archives: Schlesinger Library, Radcliffe Institute, Cambridge, MA.   (ABS)

Glazer, Penina Migdal (1939 –) taught women's studies classes, beginning in 1970, and helped organize feminist curriculum at Hampshire College, Amherst, MA. She is co-author, with Miriam Slater, of *Unequal Colleagues, The Entrance of Women into the Professions* (Rutgers University Press, 1987). A Ph. D., she has two children.   (ABS)

Glazer-Raymo, Judith (1933 –) In 1970, Glazer-Raymo helped form Women for Honor and Integrity in Government in Westchester County, NY. The group worked for passage of women's rights legislation, including Title IX, ratification of the ERA in NY State, and passage of a statewide equal pay act. Glazer-Raymo also helped form the NY State Women's Political Caucus in Albany (1971), and served as a delegate to the NWPC

convention in Houston (1971). From 1963 – 1972, she served as an elected trustee of the Blind Brook Board of Education (Rye, NY), and also as its first woman president. Since 1970, as a university administrator and professor, Glazer-Raymo has organized and participated in symposia, lectured both in the U.S. and abroad, and published widely on feminist policy analysis, gender equity, and women in academe and the professions. She is the author of *Shattering the Myths: Women in Academe* (The Johns Hopkins University Press, 1999). She is also lead editor of *Women in Higher Education: A Feminist Perspective* (2000), in its second edition in 2003. She is (2004) involved in an international project comparing gender equality in higher education in the European Union and the U.S., and is conducting research on women and the sciences. Glazer-Raymo, who has two children, earned her B.A. from Smith College, and her M.A. and Ph.D. from New York University.   (ABS)

Gleason, Janice Monica (1932 –) served as national president of Catholics for Free Choice for four years. As a member of NOW and state chair of the human reproduction committee, Gleason drafted the abortion resolution that was adopted at NOW's national meeting in Houston in 1974. She also called for the removal of the tax-exempt status of the Roman Catholic Church, based on the church's lobbying for a Constitutional amendment to make a fetus a person under law and abortion a homicide punishable by death. "By tackling these two big issues, we drew attention to ourselves and our chapter, San Diego NOW. Then in 1975, I and all my fellow San Diego NOW members were excommunicated by Bishop Leo Maher. Needless to say," says Gleason, "this doubled our membership in San Diego NOW." At the International Women's Year Conference in Mexico City, Gleason drafted a resolution calling for Social Security for housewives in their own names. Gleason, who also served on the national board of NOW, has three children and is a Registered Nurse and a lawyer. She holds a B.S., an M.A., and a J.D.   (ABS)

Glenn, Wanda Graham
– See Sobieski, Wanda Graham Glenn

Glick, Phyllis Mandel – See Mandel, Phyllis

Gluck, Sherna Berger (1935 –) A feminist scholar and researcher, Gluck is a pioneer in women's oral history. Her feminist activities began in Los Angeles in 1971, where she was one of the founding members and activists at the Venice Women's Center. That led to the founding of the Westside Women's Clinic. During this time, Gluck had several articles in *Sister*, often together with Joan Robins, assessing the state of the women's movement in Los Angeles. Gluck, who co-founded (with Ann Forfreedom) the Feminist History Research Project (1972), conducted oral histories with women involved in the suffrage and labor movements. Her book of interviews with five suffragists, *From Parlor to Prison*, was first published in 1976 and subsequently reissued by Monthly Review Press. Her oral history article that appeared in the special Women's Oral History issue of *Frontiers: A Journal of Women's Studies* is still widely used. From 1971–1976, she was a member of anarcha-feminist collective. From 1976 on, she worked to revive the women's liberation movement in Los Angeles, forming various groups and holding events—for example, Feminist Revival, 1977 (put on by Feminist Revival Collective) and Women's History Day, 1981 (put on by Women Rising Collective). She was a member of Feminist Revival Collective (1976–1978); Women Rising Collective (1980–1983); founding member, Feminists in Support of Palestinian women, later named Feminist Focus on Middle East and Africa (1989–2000); Feminists for Justice (where she organized protests against the 2000 Democratic Convention in Los Angeles); member of women's studies faculty, California State University, Long Beach (1977–2000); and founding director, Virtual Oral/Aural History Archive. Other published works include *Rosie the Riveter Revisited: Women, the War and Social Change, Women's Words: The Feminist Practice of Oral History* (anthology, co-edited with Daphne Patai), and *An American Feminist in Palestine: The Intifada (first) Years.* Gluck has supported the anti-war and labor movements, the Palestine Solidarity movement and GREENS. She received a B.A. from Berkeley and an M.A. from UCLA. Archives: Los Angeles Women's Liberation Movement papers: California State University Long Beach. Anti-war papers: Southern California Library for Social Research, Los Angeles. (ABS)

Glutting, Sandra Smith - See Smith, Sandra L.

Godlin, Irma (1940 –) A founding member of the NY NOW textbook committee in the early 1970s, Godlin helped develop the slide show, "Non-sexist Career Choices for Women" and gave numerous presentations with Alma Graham and Freda Leinwand. Godlin served as secretary of the NYC chapter of NOW (1974–1975) and was a delegate from that chapter to NY State NOW (1973–1975). From 1973–1984, Godlin was Title IX coordinator and coordinator of a career resource center, Bureau of Education and Vocational Guidance, Board of Education. She served as liaison to the NOW education committee from the Board of Education (1973–1975) and worked on a joint project between the board and the federal government, the Role Model Project. Godlin also trained school aides to become supervising school aides, a significant increase in responsibility and salary: 85 percent of the participants were women. Godlin also developed the training program. In addition, Godlin campaigned heavily for passage of the ERA. She holds a B.S. from Syracuse University (1962) and three M.A. degrees—one from Rutgers (1965), one from Brooklyn College (1979) and one from Pace (1982). (ABS)

Gold, Joyce Sheila (1942 –) was an active member of NOW during the 1970s, and served as treasurer of NY NOW from 1971–1973. She also served on the image of women committee, and was part of the challenge to ABC TV's right to be on the air because of its sexist programming, commercials and employment practices. She supported numerous demonstrations for the ERA, and lobbied for the ERA and other issues in Albany, NY, and Washington, D.C. Gold later established the Joyce Gold History Tours of New York. She earned her B.A. from Queens College and her M.A. from NYU. Archives: The Lesbian Herstory Archives, Brooklyn, NY. (ABS)

Goldberg, Merle (1936 – 1999) was the founder and president of the National Women's Health Coalition, which became the International Women's Health Coalition, and is credited as being the woman who started the first legal outpatient abortion clinic in the country (in NY). A graduate of Brooklyn College and the Columbia School of Journalism, she wrote for *Newsweek, Newsday* and the *Herald Tribune*, and was one of 20 contributors to the best-selling sex and mystery spoof, *Naked Came the Stranger*. Goldberg died in Washington.

Goldblatt, Arlene Bobroff (1939 –) was a plaintiff in Women v. Connecticut, a suit that struck down CT's anti-abortion statutes and contributed to the success of Roe v. Wade in 1973. Goldblatt also participated in the civil rights, labor and peace movements. She organized picketing during a lunch-counter sit-in when she was president of Temple University's Students for Democratic Action; organized the AFL chapter of the teachers union in Philadelphia; and participated in the anti-Vietnam War movement as a faculty member at Quinnipiac (CT) College. A math specialist, Goldblatt holds an M.A. from Wesleyan University. (ABS)

Goldenberg, Judith - See Plaskow, Judith

Goldenberg, Naomi R. (1947 –) While studying for a Ph.D. in religious studies at Yale (1972–1976), Goldenberg wrote one of the first feminist dissertations at the university, published in 1979 as part of *Changing of the Gods: Feminism and the End of Traditional Religions* (Beacon Press). From 1969–1977, she was active in feminist groups inside and outside of academia. A feminist theorist who writes about religion, gender, psychoanalysis and popular culture, Goldenberg is a professor of religious studies at the University of Ottawa in Ontario, where she has also taught classes in women's studies. Her other books include *The End of God* (1982) and *Resurrecting the Body: Feminism, Religion and Psychoanalysis* (1993). She holds a B.A. from Rutgers University, and an M.A., M.Phil. and Ph.D. from Yale University. (ABS)

Goldfield, Evelyn ("Evi") (1942 –) A member of SDS long before it became *de rigueur* on college campuses,

G

and an initial member of the West Side Group in Chicago, Goldfield was co-author, with Heather Booth and Sue Munaker, of the seminal 1968 article "Toward A Radical Movement," which investigated the mythology of the liberated woman as defined by the popular media of that day. Earlier, she was co-author of "Trade Your Pedestal for Power," which was written for the CR group at the University of Chicago. Goldfield took women's groups to task for concentrating on CR instead of action. She also argued that the idea of a separate women's movement was divisive, that there could be no liberation for women outside the general movement for liberation. But, an article she co-wrote in 1969 warned male radicals that radical women might withdraw from the movement unless treated with dignity, respect and justice. Goldfield, who teaches and does research in chemistry at Wayne State (2006), says she would "no longer call myself a radical as we defined it then, and am mainly interested in environmental and animal welfare issues." (ABS)

Goldfine, Judith Gisser – See Stacey, Judith

Goldmacher, Sheila Lee (1934 –) (also known as Sheila Lee Israel) Attending a state NOW conference in the early 1970s held at Rutgers University (NJ), Goldmacher was "blown away" and began fighting for equal opportunities for women. From 1970 – 1972, she helped make her school district (West Windsor, NJ) aware of sexist literature, tried to register her daughter in the local PAL basketball league (succeeding on the second try), and worked for the election of women candidates. By 1974, she had left her marriage, moved to Philadelphia, and helped to start a feminist bookstore, Alexandria Books. From that store came a newspaper, *Hera*. The bookstore became a women's support center, and in 1975 was the starting point for the first International Women's Day march into downtown Philadelphia. Goldmacher also participated in the women's center at the YWCA in Germantown, in socialist feminist study groups, and in groups exploring women's health. The bookstore women spoke on radio about children's literature and provided feminist materials for classes in local colleges and universities. In 1975, Goldmacher moved to San Francisco and "plunged into the women's community with full force." She volunteered at the women's center and at a political bookstore, Modern Times, and participated in women's political CR groups. In addition to this work, Goldmacher was part of the anti-Vietnam War movement in NJ, worked for the election of George McGovern in 1972, and was a member of the NJ LWV. A retired librarian, she holds a B.A. from Brooklyn College, an M.L.S. from Rutgers University, and a J.D. from Golden Gate University, San Francisco. (ABS)

Goldsmith, Judy (1938 –) is a Midwesterner who rose through the NOW ranks to become president of NOW in 1982. She was a founding member of the Two Rivers/ Manitowoc, WI, chapter of NOW (1974 – 1985) and served as WI NOW state coordinator (1975 – 1977). In 1977, she was elected a member of the NOW national board, and served until 1985. She was elected national executive VP in 1977 and 1979, and served as national president, 1982 – 1985. Among her accomplishments, Goldsmith was a delegate to the 1976 national NOW Constitutional Convention, which rewrote the bylaws. As president of NOW, she spearheaded the drive to have the 1984 Democratic presidential candidate select a woman VP running mate, resulting in Walter Mondale's tapping Geraldine Ferraro. Goldsmith also led NOW's increased commitment to civil rights and the inclusion of women of color, and co-chaired (with Coretta Scott King and other civil rights leaders) the 1983 March on Washington commemorating the historic "I Have a Dream" speech by Martin Luther King Jr. In 1984, she was arrested at the South African Embassy for protesting that nation's policy of apartheid. Goldsmith also led NOW's challenge to an increasingly militant anti-abortion movement in 1985 with nationwide abortion clinic protection actions, and articulated NOW's position on reproductive rights in a nationally broadcast debate before the National Press Club (1985). Goldsmith, who is retired, serves (2004) on the Fond du Lac County (WI) Board of Supervisors. She has one child. (ABS)

Goldsmith, Silvianna (1929 –) A multimedia artist and eco-feminist, Goldsmith was part of the first feminist art show, the X-12 (NYC, 1970), writing the press releases as a call to arms. She was also a founding member of WAR, Women Artists in Revolution (1969 – 1971). The group took part in many protest marches, and also met with the curators of the Museum of Modern Art to demand more shows for women artists. Goldsmith founded a group called X that created protest street theater actions. The first, "Mother Earth Is Poisoned," was a feminist protest against the polluting of the environment and the dangers of birth control pills. A member of the Guerrilla Art Action Group of the Artworkers Coalition, Goldsmith participated in the "bloodbath" action against the Museum of Modern Art. In 1973, she showed a film, "The Transformation of Persephone," at the Women Choose Women show held at the Cultural Center, NYC. She also made "Lil Picard," a biographical portrait of the artist, 1975. Goldsmith was a founding member of Women Artists Filmmakers Inc. The group showed its films internationally and still (2004) meets. From 1974 – 1981, Goldsmith taught a film workshop at the Women's Interart Center. Goldsmith has studied at the Chicago Institute of Design, Brooklyn College, at New York University, and in Paris and Havana. Archives: The Smithsonian Archives of American Art, Washington, D.C. (ABS)

Goldstein, Joan (1932 –) organized and served as first coordinator of national NOW's task force on women's health (1970 – 1975). In that capacity, she spoke at national meetings of psychiatrists and ob/gyn's on the needs of women, and debated Stephen Goldberg, author of *The Inevitability of Patriarchy*, on national TV. In addition, she was interviewed for a *New York Times Magazine* article on unnecessary surgery on women and spoke at national meetings about unnecessary hysterectomies. Goldstein was also a founding member of the NJ branch of the NWPC and served as NJ coordinator of the older women's task force. She was a co-founder of the August 26th Traveling Theater in NJ, and performed plays by feminist writers. A college professor and sociologist, Goldstein has written three books on the environment, including *Demanding Clean Food and Water: The Fight for a Basic Human Right* (Plenum Publishing, 1990). She earned her B.A. in 1954, her M.S. in 1968 and her Ph.D. in 1978. (ABS)

Goldstein, Marilyn (1937 –) A retired journalist, Goldstein was a feature writer for *Newsday* in 1969 working on the women's pages when she was assigned to write about what was described to her as "this ridiculous, but surely passing phenomenon, women's lib." After some weeks of reading, researching and interviewing, she realized that this was a huge and continuing story. She wrote the article and then continued to cover the women's movement for more than a decade—"probably the first reporter for a large mainstream newspaper to have the women's movement as a regular beat," she says. In 1973, Goldstein was one of four named plaintiffs in a Title VII suit against *Newsday*. The suit was settled in 1982, giving the women some "meager cash and a written policy from *Newsday* of promoting, paying and assigning stories to women comparable to men." But "by the mid 1980s, progress slowed." Goldstein continued to cover women's issues—from the mid 1980s to the mid 1990s—as part of her work as a reporter and feature writer, and for the last 10 years of her career as a columnist. Goldstein, who has two children, holds a B.S. from Syracuse University. She continues (2005) to work as a publicist for not-for-profit organizations. (ABS)

Gologorsky, Beverly (1943 –) (also known as Beverly Leman) A founder of the Women's Union in NYC (1970), Gologorsky set up several childcare centers in NYC (1971 – 1972). She was editor of *Leviathan* magazine (1969 – 1971), and wrote articles for it and other magazines and newspapers on women's oppression and liberation. In 1969, she was a founder of a committee to free Black Panther women, and in 1971 served as an organizer of the women's march on the Pentagon. Gologorsky is author of the novel *The Things We Do to Make It Home* (Random House, 1999), about women who live with Vietnam veterans. She has one child. (ABS)

Gomez, Lydia – See Gesmundo, Lydia Mali

Gonzales, Sylvia Alicia (1943 –) A Chicana activist, Gonzales was working in the director's office of the U.S.

Civil Service Commission in Washington, D.C., in 1969 when she was assigned to edit a newsletter, "Women in Action," for the federal government. Gonzales notes that because of her activism in civil rights and the Chicano movements, the idea of the women's movement did not excite her. However, one of her assignments was to interview women at the Department of Health, Education and Welfare, including Holly Knox (who was later instrumental in promoting Title IX). "This was a turning point in my life," she says. "I suddenly realized I was always a feminist." In 1970, as a Robert Kennedy Fellow, Gonzales traveled to New York with other Chicanas to meet with Puerto Rican women. There it was decided that there should be a national Puerto Rican women's organization (NACOPRW) and a national Chicana organization (MANA). Says Gonzales, "My most important contributions were the publication of *La Chicana Piensa*, a collection of prose and poetry (1974) that provided a textbook for the emerging classes on Chicanas; and the National Hispanic Feminist Conference (1980), which captured the Zeitgeist of Latina feminism." In 1976, Gonzales was coordinator of the InterAmerican Women Writers Conference, which for the first time included a Chicana section. She served as director, National Hispanic Feminist Scholarship Conference 1980, San Jose, CA; as first executive director, NWSA, San Jose State University 1977; and was national committee chair, minority women's committee, NOW 1979—1980. A member of the NWPC, she was also a consultant on sex discrimination in schools in San Francisco, Los Angeles and Fresno (1976); a member of the Hispanic women's advisory committee, Women's Research Program, U.S. Department of Education (1976); a grant evaluator for Women's Educational Equity Program (1977); a delegate at large to the Houston IWY conference (1977); and a keynote speaker at several conferences, including the First Statewide Conference on the Mexican American Woman, Women's Council, Albuquerque, NM (1977); and the Mexican American Women's National Association, Washington, D.C. (1980). Gonzales has spoken widely and published broadly on issues important to Latina women and Latina feminists. Her articles include "The Latina Feminist: Where We've Been, Where We're Going," published in *Chicana Feminist Thought: The Basic Historical Writings* (Routledge Press, 1997), and "The White Feminist Movement: The Chicana Perspective," published in *Women's Studies: An Interdisciplinary Collection*. Gonzales has received numerous awards, including Outstanding Young Woman of America (1978) and Santa Clara County Woman of Achievement Award (1980). She holds a B.A. from the University of Arizona and an Ed.D. from the University of Massachusetts. Archives: University of Arizona Library, Tucson, AZ. (ABS)

Good, Barbara J. (1927–2004) As a student at the University of California, Berkeley, Good hoped to be a painter and professor of art history. To get to Rome, she took a job with the Foreign Service, then began to grow in its ranks. In 1970 she was the only woman on the American Foreign Service Association board. At that time, women's issues were being ignored by the 13 task forces convened by the State Department and AFSA. After Jean Joyce, a journalist, contacted Good about how Foreign Service regulations negatively affected women, the two brought together a group of nine women to form the ad hoc committee to improve the status of women in foreign affairs agencies. In November 1970, the committee became the Women's Action Organization, which monitors the status of career women and provides programs for advancement. By working with management, WAO increased recruitment of women to the career service, revised regulations adversely affecting single officers (chiefly women) at overseas posts (Good couldn't marry for 20 years in the Foreign Service), and eliminated references to sex or marital status in performance evaluations, and provisions for appointing tandem couples to the same post. Good was appointed director of International Women's Programs and alternate delegate to the United Nations Commission on the Status of Women (1979–1980), and was nominated president of WAO. Archives: 1992 interview resides with the Association of Diplomatic Studies Foreign Affairs Oral History Program, Lauinger Library, Georgetown University, Washington, D.C.

Gooding, Barbara (1933 –) has spent a lifetime in public service in Washington State. She worked with the LWV studying women's rights and lobbying for the ERA, then worked for the state House of Representatives while earning a degree in public policy at the Evergreen State College. In 1983, her paper "Women in the Washington State Legislature 1913–1983" was published and distributed nationwide at the request of the state House of Representatives. She worked for governor Booth Gardner and as director of the State Department of Community Development, where she retired in 1993.   (ABS)

Goodman, Emily Jane (1940 –) Elected a Justice of the Supreme Court of the State of New York in 1990, after seven years as a NYC civil court judge, Goodman was a founder of New York Women's Law Center. In the 1960s and 1970s, she worked with Flo Kennedy on civil rights and feminist cases. In 1974, she taught a course on women and the law at Staten Island Community College, CUNY. Goodman has published numerous articles on issues such as custody, divorce, healthcare and battered women; was co-author of *Women, Money and Power* (William Morrow & Co., 1976); and editor of *A Women's Guide to Marriage and Divorce* (Women's Law Center, 1972 and 1981). She served on the committee on women and courts, Association of the Bar of the City of New York; the committee on judiciary, Women's Bar Association; was a member of the board, Abused Women's Aid in Crisis; and a member of the advisory board, Organization of Women for Legal Awareness. She was also co-chair,

Children in Prison, Association of Women Judges. Goodman also served as an adviser on housing policy for the National Council of Negro Women. She has been honored by the YWCA for outstanding service to women of New York; Black Women United for Political Action; the National Lawyers Guild; and New York Asian Women's Center. Goodman, who has one child—Justine, named for Justice—earned her B.A. from Brooklyn College (1961); her J.D. from Brooklyn Law School (1968); and an M.S. from the Columbia University Graduate School of Journalism (1980).   (ABS)

Goodman, Janice (1935 –) joined NYRF in the mid 1960s. With Susan Deller Ross, Goodman founded the first women and the law committee at NYU Law School (1968). In 1969, the two led the fight to open the Root Tilden Scholarship to women, and in 1970 founded the National Women and the Law Conference. In 1972, Goodman and her partners formed the first feminist law firm, Bellamy, Blank, Goodman, Kelly, Ross & Stanley. Goodman was the lead attorney in a number of class actions claiming sex discrimination in employment, including NOW v. WABC (1972); Women's Committee v. NBC (1974–1978); Wire Service Guild v. Associated Press (1985); and Scotti v. NYC Police Dept. She was appointed by NY governor Mario Cuomo to his task force on sexual harassment, and has also taught courses on women and the law and employment discrimination at the Rutgers School of Law and the New York School of Law, among others. She also co-chaired the NY conference, Women Tell the Truth, featuring Anita Hill (1991). A member of Goodman & Zuchlewski, Goodman continues to represent women and minorities in employment discrimination matters. She earned her B.A. from the University of Pennsylvania (1958) and her J.D. from New York University School of Law (1971).   (ABS)

Goodridge, Francea ("Francie") Kraker (1947 –) A role model for young women athletes, Goodridge was the first girl to train for track and field in Ann Arbor, MI, and as a competitive athlete set a number of track records for women. She was also a member of the 1968 and 1972 U.S. Olympic teams. When she stopped competing, Goodridge founded one of the first girls' and women's track programs in schools across MI, and held athletic administrative positions that were firsts for females at that time. In 1975, at the University of Wisconsin, Milwaukee, Goodridge held one of the first administrative athletic post in a Division I university after passage of Title IX. In 2001, Goodridge was inducted into The Michigan Women's Hall of Fame.   (ABS)

Gordon, Elaine (1931 – 2000) was a trailblazing legislator for women, children and the elderly. She became an advocate of equal rights in 1964 when, as the divorced mother of three young children, she was denied opportunities solely because she was a woman, and could not even establish credit. Gordon was a founding member of the Miami/Dade County chapter of NOW (1968) and served as its chair of the committee on economic discrimination (1971). Gordon was elected to the FL House of Representatives in 1972 and served for 22 years. In 1984–1985, she became the first woman elected as Speaker Pro Tempore, and in 1993 became Dean of the House (the longest serving member). Gordon was a lead sponsor of ratification of the ERA amendment to the U.S. Constitution, and headed the House health and rehabilitative services committee, the first woman to do so. She was a member of the Metropolitan Dade County Commission on the Status of Women, and helped initiate the county's first childcare center. She was a founding member of the NWPC and the FL WPC (1971). During the 1970s, Gordon fought sexual harassment in the workplace and demanded that the leadership in state government create sexual harassment workshops with mandated attendance by employees. She helped create the first rape treatment center in FL, and was responsible for legislation providing women with the right to receive compensation for sexual assault from the state's Victim's Compensation Fund. Throughout her political career, Gordon worked to attain pay equity for women. She also fought to have women athletes receive sports scholarships and equal time using sports fields. She was responsible for funding the Gender Bias Study Commission of the Florida Supreme Court. Gordon received numerous awards and accolades during her lifetime. She was once complimented by one of her male colleagues as being "slicker than owl spit" after Gordon defeated him with a particularly stealthy strategy. Gordon was one of the first women inducted into the Florida Women's Hall of Fame (Tallahassee, 1982); was honored with Impact Awards by the Community Coalition for Women's History; was the first person to receive the State of Florida United Way Award; and in 1994 received the Anne Ackerman Distinguished Floridian Award. She also received the *Miami Herald*'s Spirit of Excellence of Award. Gordon attended CUNY, Miami-Dade Junior College and Florida International University. She also received an Honorary Doctor of Laws from Barry University. Archives: Florida International University, South Campus, Miami, FL., and Florida State Archives, Tallahassee FL.

Gordon, H. Rusty (1942 –) In the mainstream music industry producing concerts, benefits and fundraisers since 1960, Gordon started her work in women's music and culture in 1972 when she produced a multi-act concert at Yale University for lesbians, using only women for all aspects of production. She has produced concerts for mainstream artists and lesbian singer/songwriters and national women's festivals. Earlier, in 1967, she founded The Whimsy Political Clearinghouse in Coconut Grove, FL, housing academic archives (non-fiction), with a heavy focus on women's studies and LGBT issues, and also including music archives featuring folk and women's music.

Gordon became active in NOW in 1970 and joined the lesbian task force in New Haven, CT. She has been directly involved with FL NOW and the LGBT Equal Rights movement since 1985. Gordon was a founding mother (1995) and is (2005) VP of the Florida LGBT Democratic caucus. She holds a B.Ed. and an M.S. Archives: The Lesbian Herstory Archives, Brooklyn, NY.   (ABS)

Gordon, Laura Suzanne (1946 –) has been active in feminist organizing, radio broadcasting, poetry and spirituality. From 1969–1971, Gordon was a member of a women's liberation study and activism collective at Washington, D.C.'s Institute for Policy Studies. Her task force was charged with starting CR groups in women's homes in the Maryland suburbs; the first such group convened in Takoma Park in 1969. From 1971–1975, Gordon worked for the National Park Service in Glen Echo, MD, at the Clara Barton Home/Glen Echo Park. There she helped set up the Washington Writers Center as well as the Women's Automotive Workshop and Garage, which offered a series of courses by and for women on auto mechanics. Gordon also created and produced Womansphere '74 and Womansphere '75, among the first large-scale women's arts and music festivals, designated an IWY event by the United Nations. From 1975–1977, Gordon was one of the first three women to have on-air radio news/public affairs director positions in the Washington market at WHFS-FM. The radio station was a major source of news about women's movement activities and issues. In 1973, Gordon became a founding grandmother of the contemporary, grassroots women's spirituality movement. Since then, she has organized women's ritual and study groups and events, and participated in and helped organize festivals including Womengathering and In Gaia's Lap. In 1995, she became a founding member of the National Women's Studies Association's international task force on women's spiritualities. Gordon's poetry has been published in journals and anthologies including *Arts in Society*, *Feminist Studies*, *Rolling Stone* and *Women: A Journal of Liberation*. A college instructor, writer and near-death studies ethnographic researcher, Gordon holds a B.A. from the University of Maryland, College Park (1968), an M.A. from Johns Hopkins University (1969) and an M.A. from the University of Maryland, College Park (1996), where she is (2005) a doctoral candidate. (1996).   (ABS)

Gordon, Linda (1940 –) was a member of Bread and Roses in Cambridge (1968). In those early days she wrote several socialist-feminist position papers and leaflets while also teaching history at University of Massachusetts/Boston, where she was part of a successful movement to start a women's studies program (1969–1972). Gordon also taught the first women's history course at the Cambridge branch of Goddard College (1971–1972). She remained at the University of Massachusetts until 1984, then began to teach history and women's studies at the

University of Wisconsin. In 1999 she moved to the history department at New York University. Now an internationally renowned historian of women, Gordon has specialized in the historical roots of contemporary social policy as they concern gender and family issues. Her first book, edited with Rosalyn Fraad Baxandall, was *America's Working Women* (1976). Her other books include *Woman's Body, Woman's Right: A Social History of Birth Control in America* (Viking, 1976), which was nominated for the National Book Award in History; *Heroes of Their Own Lives: The Politics and History of Family Violence* (Viking, 1988), winner of the AHA's Joan Kelly Prize; *Pitied but Not Entitled: Single Mothers and the Origins of Welfare* (The Free Press, 1994), winner of the Berkshire Prize; *The Great Arizona Orphan Abduction* (Harvard University Press, 1999), winner of the Bancroft and Beveridge Prize; and *The Moral Property of Women: The History of Birth Control Politics in America* (University of Illinois Press, 2002). Gordon has also written many articles on these topics. She holds a B.A. from Swarthmore College (1961) and an M.A. (1963) and Ph.D. (1970) from Yale University. Gordon, who has one child, remains active in reproductive-rights work, and has done numerous amicus briefs in cases involving reproductive rights, domestic violence and gay rights. Archives: Tamiment Library, New York University, New York, NY. (ABS)

Gornick, Vivian (1935 –) From 1970 on, Gornick wrote as a feminist and an advocate for women's rights in newspapers and magazines across the country. She was a staff writer at the *Village Voice* (1969 – 1977), and has been published in *The Nation, The New York Times Book Review, The New York Times Magazine*, the *Washington Post, Los Angeles Times, The New Yorker* and *Threepenny Review*. Her books include *Woman in Sexist Society: Studies in Power & Powerlessness* (edited by Barbara K. Moran, 1971); *Essays in Feminism* (Harper & Row, 1979); *Women in Science* (Simon & Schuster, 1983); *Fierce Attachments: A Memoir* (Farrar, Straus & Giroux, 1987); *Approaching Eye Level: Personal Essays* (Beacon Press, 1996); and *The End of the Novel of Love: Critical Essays* (Beacon Press, 1997). In 1998, Gornick founded—with a group of New York artists and activists—THEA, The House of Elder Artists. The project plan is to build a senior residence for women and men in the arts in NYC. Gornick has taught creative writing at Pennsylvania State University, the University of Colorado and the University of Houston, and was a tenured professor (1991 – 1998) at the University of Arizona. She earned her B.A. from CCNY (1957) and her M.A. from New York University (1960). (ABS)

Gould, Carol C. (1946 –) was co-editor (with Marx Wartofsky) of the first published collection of feminist philosophy, *Women and Philosophy: Toward a Theory of Liberation* (G.P. Putnam, 1976). The book first appeared as a special issue of *The Philosophical Forum* (Fall/Winter, 1973 – 1974). Gould's article in that collection proposed that concrete differences among people, including gender, race and class, are important subjects for philosophical inquiry and critique. Gould's other early work in socialist-feminist theory concerned the conception of freedom and its implications for understanding gender roles in the family. This theme, along with reconceptions of the private and the public domain, was the subject of her article in her second collection of feminist theory, *Beyond Domination: New Perspectives on Women and Philosophy* (1984), in which Gould also introduced the idea of political androgyny. In 1999, she published her third collection on feminist theory, *Gender* (Humanities Press). In addition, Gould served as president of the National Conference on Women's Liberation (1981) and as a member of the committee on the status of women of the APA. In 1981, she was honored with the Medal of the Institute of Women Today. Gould, a professor in the department of philosophy at George Mason University, holds a B.A. from the University of Chicago (1966) and an M.Phil. (1969) and Ph.D. (1971) from Yale University. (ABS)

Gould, Jane S. (1918 –) (also known as Jane Schwartz) spent her professional life helping women expand their options. She is the author of *Juggling: A Memoir of Work, Family and Feminism* (The Feminist Press, 1997) and was the first permanent director of the Barnard Women's Center (1972 – 1983). As assistant director of the Alumnae Advisory Center in New York City (1954 – 1965), Gould was a leader in the pioneer movement to help adult women return to school and work. From 1965 – 1973, she was director of the Office of Placement and Career Planning at Barnard College. She played a leading role in two landmark projects funded by the Carnegie Corporation: The Seven College Vocational Workshops, a pilot series for mature women (1962 – 1966); and Part-Time Employment: Employer Attitudes on Opportunities for the College-Trained Woman, published in 1964. As director of the Barnard Women's Center, Gould prepared the first of several annual interdisciplinary bibliographies, *Women's Work and Women's Studies* (1972). Under Gould's direction, the Center hosted a 1973 conference, Women Learn From Women, a joint effort of women's groups from eight metro-area colleges, which led to the creation of the annual Scholar and the Feminist, a flagship in women's movement conferences. In 1975, Gould was a member of the Women's Counseling Project advisory board, which provided early abortion counseling and referrals. She also served as a member of a Russell Sage Foundation task force for a project on women in higher education; served as co-chair of the Columbia University seminar Women and Society (1983 – 1985); gave a paper on women's centers at the United Nations NGO Forum on the Decade of Women (Nairobi, 1985); and was a board member, Center for Constitutional Rights (1984 – 1992), writing a history of women's rights at CCR. Gould earned her B.A. from Barnard College (1941) and her M.A. from Teachers College, Columbia

University (1970). She has two children. Archives: Barnard College, New York, NY. (ABS)

Gould, Roberta (1942 –) was a co-organizer of a 1970s research project to reveal the sexism of the influential St. Mark's Poetry Project. The results, written up and sent to the *Village Voice,* showed that of 243 poetry readings, only 23 had been given by women and that of these, four had been given by the director, Ann Waldman. Subsequent to the investigation and publication of the reading tallies, more women were given readings at the St. Mark's Poetry Project. Gould's poems have been published in magazines, newspapers and literary reviews, and she has eight published books, including *In Houses with Ladders* (Waterside Press, 2001). Gould holds a B.A. from Brooklyn College, studied at the National University of Mexico under a grant by the Mexican government, and earned an M.A. from the University of California at Berkeley. (ABS)

Gozemba, Patricia Andrea (1940 –) (also known as Patricia Andrea Curran) A professor and writer, Gozemba was a founding member of the women's studies program at Salem (MA) State College (1972). She also successfully organized colleagues to push for salary equity for women (1973), first at the college and eventually in all the MA state colleges. A founder of the Florence Luscomb Women's Center at Salem State (1973), Gozemba also organized a lesbian support group for the Salem area at the center, facilitating film festivals and book discussions. In 1970, she founded a student-faculty CR group that worked together until 1974. Earlier, as a high-school teacher, Gozemba had organized women in teachers unions (1963). She also brought anti-Vietnam War feminists together to protests in Boston (1968 – 1970), and in 1972 created a 30-minute slide show exposing how advertising demeans women, which she showed at local schools, colleges and community gatherings. In addition to working for peace and labor issues, Gozemba has been active in the civil rights and environmental movements. She holds a B.A. from Emmanuel College, an M.A. from the University of Iowa, and an Ed.D. from Boston University. Archives: The Lesbian Herstory Archives, Brooklyn, NY.(ABS)

Grady, Kathleen ("Kathy") (1942 –) Inspired by Betty Friedan's book *The Feminine Mystique,* Grady marched down Fifth Avenue in NYC in the Women's Strike for Equality, August 26, 1970. She then joined NYC NOW and its education committee, where one of the struggles was the acceptance of girls into the city's prestigious science high schools. Grady taught the first in-service training course for teachers on sexism in the schools, called Consciousness-Raising: Women's Liberation. Wanting to organize young mothers like herself, Grady became a founder of Brooklyn (NY) NOW (1971). She was also a co-founder of the Brooklyn Self-Help Health Clinic, which gave demonstrations of breast and vaginal self-exams to small groups of women and encouraged as-

sertiveness with their physicians. Upon admission to graduate school, Grady became an activist for equality for women within the psychology profession and for non-sexist research. Her dissertation was titled "The Illusion of Sex Differences," and was supported by a grant in Women Studies from the Woodrow Wilson Foundation. With a post-doc at the University of Connecticut Health Center, she began a 20-year career researching women's health issues, particularly ways to encourage the practice of breast self-examination and mammography by women and physicians. During that time, she wrote articles and books, lectured and taught, and managed her own research firm, which employed predominantly women. Now retired, Grady indulges her other passions, politics and music. She is an elected official in her hometown in Massachusetts and sings songs of the 1940s and 1950s throughout the region. Grady holds a B.A. from Brown University (1964) and a Ph.D. from the City University of New York Graduate Center (1977). (ABS)

Graham, Alma (1936 –) While a dictionary editor for Funk & Wagnalls (1963 – 1970), Graham became conscious of the sex bias embedded in the English language. In 1970, she joined American Heritage to help create a new school dictionary, to be based on a computer study of elementary textbooks. In this study, editor Peter Davies discovered a pattern of discrimination against girls and women in overall coverage and in words and images. Graham reported on this discrimination—first in a "Fact Sheet on Sex Bias in School Reading Materials" and later in an article for *Ms.* magazine, "The Making of a Non-sexist Dictionary" (December 1973). Graham was also the first lexicographer to put the courtesy title "Ms." into a dictionary: *The American Heritage School Dictionary,* 1972. Because of her concerns about the state of children's textbooks, Graham joined the NYC chapter of NOW and became a member of the education committee, "from which we spun off a textbook committee." In 1973, Graham joined a committee set up by the McGraw-Hill Book Company to write a set of guidelines to eliminate sex bias from its textbooks. She, Sally Pacheco and Tim Yohn became major writers of the guidelines. Graham was also the final writer and became the corporate spokesperson for the guidelines after they were issued to the media. In 1976, she became senior manager for editing and styling at McGraw-Hill, and from 1978 – 1980 was managing editor for science and practical arts. In 1978, Graham was honored for her work to remove bias from textbooks and reference books as one of "50 Extraordinary Women of Achievement" by the National Conference of Christians and Jews, New York Region. In the 1980s, she became both editor and co-author of McGraw-Hill's new elementary social studies program, *Our Nation, Our World.* From 1991 – 2001, she was editor of *New World Outlook,* the mission magazine of The United Methodist Church. Now retired, she does freelance writing and editing. (ABS)

G

Graham, Patricia Albjerg (1935 –) A professor, Graham worked aggressively to obtain fairness for women in education. At Barnard College (1965 – 1974) she was involved in the early discussions making women's experiences part of the legitimate curriculum, and from 1969 – 1970, she advised Princeton University on how to become as good a place for women students as for men. In 1972, Graham organized an annual meeting on women in higher education for the American Council on Education. Also in the early 1970s, she chaired the first American Historical Association standing committee on Women in the Historical Profession. As dean of the Radcliffe Institute (1974 – 1977), she fostered a supportive environment for women to do excellent scholarly and artistic work. As the first woman dean at Harvard (School of Education, 1982 – 1991), Graham oversaw the growth in women professors in her faculty so that the School of Education led the university in the percent of tenured and non-tenured women faculty. Graham has published numerous articles on women in higher education. She has one child and holds a B.S. (1955) and M.S. (1957) from Purdue University, and a Ph.D. from Columbia University. (ABS)

Graham, Richard (1920 –) As commissioner of the EEOC (1966 – 1967) appointed by President Lyndon B. Johnson, Graham fought strenuously for women's equality. Some say his feminist activism was the reason he wasn't reappointed, but Graham says he promised the Hispanics that if they didn't get an appointment, he would give up his position so they would have representation. "This was not well received by the White House because they did not know any Republican Hispanics," he says. When Graham left, an Hispanic commissioner was appointed. Graham's first EEOC case involved flight attendants who complained "because they were sex objects and the airlines thought they couldn't be hostesses after age 26; they were grounded with reduced wages." However, notes Graham, "We found that was discriminatory, and I would not even let the airlines pay for my lunch." Graham was also involved in the decision to desegregate help-wanted ads nationally. "I was convinced of the sexism when, as a commissioner, I took want ads at *The Providence* (Rhode Island) *Journal* and heard what people said." Women at mills and plants in the South complained of being unfairly laid off, so Graham visited the work sites, found the layoffs to be discriminatory and ended the practice. Graham urged Betty Friedan to form an organization to pressure government to force compliance with Title VII in handling cases covering women. At the founding meeting of NOW in 1966, Graham was elected VP, one of five men on the 20-member board of directors. In 1967, shortly after not reappointing Graham to the EEOC, President Johnson appointed Graham director of the National Teacher Corps. Graham was also a founding commissioner on the District of Columbia Status of Women Commission, a member of the federal interagency committee, and executive director of the

Center for Moral Development at Harvard, which Graham helped create. While president of Goddard, Graham helped found the Goddard-Cambridge Center for Social Change, one of the earliest centers of women's studies. Graham received a B.S. (1942), and an M.A. from The Catholic University of America (1970), and a Ph.D. from Union Graduate School (1972), connected to Antioch College. (ABS)

Grambs, Marya Dresden (1946 –) was co-founder and co-director of La Casa de las Madres (1975 – 1978), the third battered women's shelter in the U.S., which became a model for domestic violence programs in the San Francisco Bay Area. During that period, she made public the story of her mother, a university professor, being battered, resulting in Grambs spending a year in a mental hospital when she was 17. From 1977 – 1979, Grambs taught women's studies classes at San Francisco State University and Foothill College. She was the core organizer of the San Francisco Women's Building, a women-owned-and-operated community center located in San Francisco's Mission District. In addition, she was the co-founder and co-director (1979 – 1989) and board member (1979 – 1993) of the San Francisco's Women's Foundation, one of the first and largest women's philanthropic organizations in the U.S. Grambs was a core organizer of the Women's Funding Network. She was also the founder, planner and resource developer of the Girls After School Academy, San Francisco (1991 – 1998), a program for low-income African American girls that teaches prevention of violence, pregnancy and substance abuse, and promotes academic achievement, gender and ethnic self-esteem, and economic empowerment. She co-founded and served as executive director of the Fatigue Clinic, U.C. San Francisco, and Chronic Fatigue Immune Dysfunction Syndrome Foundation, 1988 – 1997. Working with the U.S. State Department, Grambs was an international consultant (1999 – 2002) assisting domestic-violence organizations throughout Turkey and Botswana. Grambs also worked in the Bay Area as an advocate of anti-violence, and from 1993 – 1996 was co-founder and director of the Women Against Gun Violence California Campaign. From 1989 – 2001, she was the senior program developer for the Family Violence Prevention Fund. Grambs is (2004) a project consultant for the International Center to End Violence, Family Violence Prevention Fund, San Francisco. She has received the San Francisco Foundation 50th Anniversary Community Leadership Award, 1998; the Ms. Foundation's Gloria Steinem Award for National Leadership, 1995; and The Women's Foundation Founder Award, 1999. Grambs holds an M.A. and has one child. (ABS)

Grant, Bev (1942 –) joined a NYC CR group in 1967 that included Pam Allen, Robin Morgan, Peggy Dobbins, Shulamith Firestone, Kathy Sarachild and Cathy Barrett, among others. Grant attended NYRW meetings and became a member of WITCH. She also joined a radical film-making group, Newsreel, and helped produce a short documentary film called "Up Against the Wall, Miss America," about the historic 1968 protest against the Miss American Beauty Pageant in Atlantic City. With Laura Lieben and Loraine Shapiro, Grant formed a band called Goldflower that performed original feminist songs each of them wrote, including Bev Grant's song "I'm Tired of Bastards Fuckin' Over Me," which became something of an anthem in the women's movement. In 1972, Grant formed The Human Condition, a mixed-gender band with a strong feminist message. She wrote a song about Inez Garcia (who was raped and killed one of her rapists) that was later included on a Grammy-nominated compilation put out by the Smithsonian Institute called The Best of Broadside. Grant's band was together for 19 years and released two albums: The Working People Gonna Rise and Kulonyaka. Grant has been cultural director of the UALE Northeast Union Women's Summer School since 1991, and director of the Brooklyn Women's Chorus since 1998. She has two children. (ABS)

Grant, Polly Walker (1945 –) (also known as Polly Riley) was a board member of Boston NOW (1972 – 1973), and helped start CR groups in the area. In 1975, she was co-founder, with Nona Ferdon, of the Boston Psychological Center for Women, which she ran until 1990. Grant did her doctoral dissertation on the influence of running on women's self-esteem. Grant holds a B.A. from the University of Georgia (1967), an M.S.W. from Boston University (1975) and a Ph.D. from Boston College School of Social Work in 1987. (ABS)

Grant, Terry Lynn (1951 –) has spent her life bringing music to women's and lesbian communities. From producing events, to marketing records, sponsoring artists, and record sales, Grant has worked in every area of the music industry. While attending graduate school at Michigan State University, East Lansing, she volunteered at the Women's Center. She was involved with the Lansing Area Lesbian Feminist Collective, formed in 1973 (initially part of the Women's Center). In 1974, the LALF Collective produced the Midwest Lesbian Conference. In 1975, the Lesbian Connection and the Lansing Area Lesbians (formerly LALF) sponsored another national conference: Expanding Lesbian Culture, a Spring Surge of Sapphic Spirit. Olivia Records was looking for distributors, so Grant signed on and formed Goldenrod Music, the only remaining distribution company (in 2003) of about 80 at the time. Grant was co-founder, with her partner, Sue Emmert, of Mellow Muse Productions, Act Two Productions, The Greater Lansing Women's Coop (which became the Lesbian Alliance), and Sharing Our Assorted Resources. Grant and Susan Frazier, her business associate, formed Goldenrod Records in 1997 and produced albums by Cris Williamson, Tret Fure and Nedra Johnson. Grant was awarded the 1992 Hot Wire Readers Choice Award for outstanding contributions to women's music and culture, and the 1993 Prism Award for outstanding contributions to the lesbian/gay community. She also has received the Jane Schliessman Music Award, presented by Women in the Arts at the National Women's Music Festival (1999). Grant holds a B.S. from Clark University, and an M.S. from Michigan State University. (ABS)

Grasso, Ella (1919 – 1981) With decades of public service behind her, Grasso was elected to the U.S. Congress from Connecticut in 1970, and was re-elected in 1972. In 1974 she became the first woman governor in the U.S. elected in her own right—not as a widow, not as a place holder—defeating her opponent by 200,000 votes. Grasso was re-elected in 1978, but ill health forced her to resign in 1980. As governor, she embraced women's issues. She endorsed a state travel ban by government personnel to unratified ERA states. She also declared August 26, 1977, "Alice Paul Day in Connecticut." (Alice Paul, who lived in Connecticut for 40 years before her death, was the author of the original ERA introduced in Congress in 1923.) According to Grasso's daughter, Suzanne Grasso, Grasso did lots of work with mothers and children, and helped single mothers get state funding. Grasso was a member of the Democratic National Committee from 1956 – 1958, and served as Connecticut's secretary of state for three terms, working in the areas of mental hospital reform, day care and civil rights. Grasso graduated from Mount Holyoke College in 1940, received a M.A. in 1942, and joined the LWV in 1943. She had two children.

Graves, Helen M. (1925 –) An emeritus political science professor (2005), Graves was the first woman to run for the Grosse Pointe Park City Council (1961). Although she won the primary, she was defeated in the general election. In 1976, Graves organized the first women's commission at the University of Michigan, Dearborn, which continues to represent women's interests on campus today. Graves also organized the first course on Women, Politics and the Law at UM (1976), which she taught seven times (1976 – 1994), and originated the first women's studies minor at UM (1977 – 1978). Graves served as the first woman president of the Michigan Conference of Political Scientists (1979 – 1980); was president of the Women's Caucus of the Midwest Political Science Association (1983 – 1985); and was a member of the Michigan Women's Commission, twice appointed by governor James Blanchard (1984 – 1986 and 1986 – 1988). In 1989, Graves received the Sarah Goddard Power Award from the University of Michigan. From 1992 – 1995 Graves served on the Fulbright Program for Canadian Awards, International Institute, Screening Committee. Graves, who has three children, earned her Ph.D. from Wayne State University (1975) at age 50. (ABS)

Gray, Fredrica (1946 –) joined the staff of the Permanent Commission on the Status of Women as public informa-

G

tion and program manager in 1975. In an effort to improve women's economic status, Gray, working with Glenda Boyd, developed the commission's focus on non-traditional jobs for women. She worked with the Connecticut State Police, State Department of Administrative Services, and the Hartford Fire Department to effect the hiring (late 1970s) of the first women state troopers on CT roads and the first women in New England to hold paid jobs as firefighters. Gray also helped produce educational materials on non-traditional jobs for women and women's job rights. Gray conceived of and helped produce the PCSW publication *Great Women in Connecticut History*. Gray also produced the first edition of "Facts About the Status of Connecticut Women," a statistical overview on earnings, income, poverty status, education, and wage disparities between women and men, and job segregation by gender. The data also helped to show the economic impact of the "double jeopardy" imposed by combined race and sex discrimination. Gray helped create the PCSW task force on women of color, and in a move aimed at increasing the representation of women on state boards, councils and commissions, conceived and developed the PCSW talent bank. As executive director of the PCSW (1985–1994), she played a key role in developing CT's family and workplace agenda, which furthered legislation to support working families. The cornerstone of this effort was Connecticut's Family and Medical Leave law, passed in 1987 for state employees, and in 1989 for all employees in CT. (ABS)

Gray, Geri – See Ariel

Gray, Susan – See McGreivy, Susan Douglas

Green, Adrienne – See Momi, Adrienne

Green, Edith (1910 – 1987) was a schoolteacher and later a 10-term member of Congress (D-OR) (1954–1974). The principal author of Title 1X federal legislation banning sex discrimination in federally funded educational programs, Green was also a sponsor of the 1963 Equal Pay Act, which passed in 1964 over the opposition of the Chamber of Commerce and many corporations. She did oppose the ERA, but not without a feminist awareness.

Greenberg, Elinor Miller (1932 –) was a founding member and chair of the Littleton (CO) Council for Human Relations (1963–1969), and was responsible for bringing Dr. Martin Luther King Jr. to Littleton in 1954. These civil rights activities led her into the women's movement. Greenberg was founding executive director of the Arapahoe Institute for Community Development (1969–1971), and was appointed founding director of the University Without Walls at Loretto Heights College in CO in 1971. With Sheila Tobias, Greenberg organized the first CO symposium on women and math anxiety. During her tenure, she developed individualized baccalaureate

education programs in the Colorado Corrections System, including the women's prison, on the Navajo Reservation for mental health workers, for competency-based teacher education, and for students at a distance. Says Greenberg, "All these efforts focused attention on women's career and education needs, so sorely neglected in prior years." Greenberg subsequently designed, co-founded and implemented many education and community programs, including Pathways to the Future for US West and the Communications Workers of America, which served 40,000 workers, most of whom were women, in 14 states; and the Mountain and Plains Partnership at the University of Colorado Health Sciences Center with 16 institutional and agency partners, which created online master's degree programs for nurse practitioners, nurse midwives and physician assistants in CO, WY and NM. She co-founded the state-level Colorado Women's Economic Development Council and the Women's Business Office; and chaired the Colorado Math, Science and Technology Commission under governor Roy Romer. She has been a member of the Colorado Women's Forum since 1981 and served as president in 1986. Among her numerous awards, Greenberg received the Dolls for Democracy Award from the B'nai B'rith and the Anti-Defamation League, the Distinguished Service Award from the Littleton Education Association, Citizen of the Year from the black fraternity Omega Psi Phi, and the Sesquicentennial Award from the Mount Holyoke College Alumnae Association. She was also named Woman of the Decade by the Littleton Newspapers (1970). A 1953 graduate of Mount Holyoke, Greenberg is a certified speech pathologist, earning her master's degree from the University of Wisconsin (1954). She earned her doctorate from the University of Northern Colorado (1981), and has been awarded two Honorary Doctorates for her work in adult and women's education. She has three children. Archives: Littleton Historical Museum, Littleton, CO. (ABS)

Greenberg, Mary Lou (1940 –) A revolutionary Communist who organized some of the first CR groups in the San Francisco Bay Area, Greenberg helped form the Liberation Women's Union (1969) to connect women's liberation with working class women (and men). She met weekly with 25 or 30 women in the San Francisco Bay Area with whom she developed a 10-point program that called for equal pay for equal work; free 24-hour childcare centers for all children; free complete healthcare, including birth control, abortions, maternity care and an end to forced sterilization; self-determination for Third World peoples; an end to U.S. imperialist wars of aggression; control over social institutions, and more. The group helped initiate a major International Women's Day rally on March 8, 1970, in Delores Park, San Francisco, the first mass re-introduction to the U.S. of that international event. That effort to make the struggle for women's liberation an integral and essential part of the struggle for total revolutionary change was, in Greenberg's view, an important contribution to both the women's movement and the anti-imperialist/revolutionary movement generally. In 1971, Greenberg went to China during the Cultural Revolution and saw the beginnings of a new world, including women "holding up half the sky." She was a founding member of the Revolutionary Communist Party, USA, in 1975 and is a spokesperson for the party in NYC. From the late 1980s through the 1990s, she was active in the pro-choice and clinic defense movement with Refuse and Resist and other groups, and worked with the NY Pro-Choice Coalition to develop the first national response to Operation Rescue. Her writings include "Women Are Not Incubators! The Assault on Abortion Rights: Where It's Coming From, What Has to be Done About It, and Why All Who Hate Oppression Must Fight for Women's Liberation" (RCP Publications, 1989). In recognition of her long-time work for women's rights, Greenberg received the 2001 Susan B. Anthony Award for grassroots activism by the NYC Chapter of NOW.   (ABS)

Greenberger, Marcia Devins (1946 –) was the first full-time women's rights lawyer in Washington, D.C., in the early 1970s. It was the secretaries at the Center for Law and Social Policy who insisted that a female lawyer be hired to initiate a women's rights project at the Center, and it was the male lawyers who gave in to their demands and hired Greenberger. Greenberger's first case, which dealt with the policy at G.E. to exclude pregnancy from disability coverage, ultimately resulted in the Pregnancy Discrimination Act as well as the EEOC's 2000 decision that prescription contraceptives be covered with other preventive care medicines. A 1970 graduate of the University of Pennsylvania Law School, Greenberger became co-president of the National Women's Law Center in the early 1980s, and remains in that position. She was given the Woman of Distinction Award from Soroptomist International of the Americas in 2000, and was named Woman Lawyer of the Year by the D.C. Women's Bar Association in 1996.   (ABS)

Greene, Gayle Jacoba (1943 –) came to the women's movement through books, and makes her contribution through books as an educator and writer. A teacher at Scripps College starting in 1974, Greene has taught courses such as Contemporary Women's Writing and The Second Wave. Author of *Changing the Story: Feminist Fiction and the Tradition* (Indiana, 1991), and co-editor of *Changing Subjects: The Making of Feminist Criticism* (Routledge, 1993), Greene also wrote a book about Doris Lessing, *Poetics of Change* (Michigan, 1994) and a biography of a British woman scientist, *The Woman Who Knew Too Much: Alice Stewart and the Secrets of Radiation* (Michigan, 1999), about the woman who discovered in the 1950s that if you x-ray pregnant women, you give children cancer. Greene holds both a B.A. and M.A. from the University of California, and a Ph.D. from Columbia University.   (ABS)

Greenwald, Maurine W. (1944 –) (also known as Maurine Weiner) "The Rhode Island Women's Liberation Union was founded in my apartment living room in Providence, RI, in 1969," says Greenwald. A graduate student at Brown University at the time, Greenwald was also a member of a CR group that met weekly for about two years. Greenwald taught what she believes was the first women's studies course at Brown, an undergraduate seminar in American civilization in women's history. That course launched a career-long focus on research and teaching about women and gender. Greenwald also belonged to a collective of women graduate students and activists who met in Boston to promote women's liberation. At the University of Pittsburgh in 1972, Greenwald was hired with two other faculty members from different disciplines to design and coordinate the women's studies program; Greenwald taught the first history courses. She eventually shifted to gender history in the 1990s. Says Greenwald, "In the first decade of the women's studies program, the work was highly political and it was very challenging to convince administrators that women's studies involved legitimate intellectual pursuits with staying power. Male administrators expected women's studies to fade away." However, she adds, "As is the trend in the history profession, women's history has become increasingly transnational and global in its concerns." Greenwald's dissertation became her first book—*Women, War, and Work: The Impact of World War I on Women Workers in the United States* (1980). Over the years, her professional work has extended to museums and art centers where she regularly trains docents in the history of women and provides historical guidance for public exhibits. Greenwald, who has one child, holds a B.A. from the University of Illinois, Urbana (1966), and a Ph.D. from Brown University (1977).   (ABS)

Greep, Nancy Carde (1944 –) was a member of New Haven (CT) Women's Liberation and worked on the class action suit to overturn anti-abortion laws in that state. She also led classes based on *Our Bodies, Ourselves* in New Haven. In part because of these experiences, Greep changed her major and later earned her M.D. Currently (2004) and over the last decade, she has been working to establish healthcare for all nationally, and especially in California. She has two children.   (ABS)

Greer, Germaine (1939 –) An Australian feminist and writer, Greer moved to England in 1964 and became active in the counterculture movement there, helping to write and found underground newspapers in London. At one point, she edited the European pornographic journal *Suck*. Greer received international media attention with the publication of *The Female Eunuch* (1969). In the book, she presented sexual liberation as the path to fulfillment, arguing that women's passive sexual role prevented them from playing an active role in society. Despite criticism from American feminists, *The Female*

Eunuch was widely read by everyday women. The book had enormous impact in England, where Greer became known as the "high priestess of women's liberation." Greer's aura of aggressive sexuality and sexual liberation drew praise from such unlikely supporters as Henry Miller and Norman Mailer. Her other books include *The Obstacle Race: The Fortunes of Women Painters and Their Work* (1979), *Sex and Destiny: The Politics of Human Fertility* (1984), and *The Madwoman's Underclothes: Essays and Occasional Writings, 1964 – 1985* (1986). Since 1988, Greer has been director and financier of Stump Cross Books, a publishing house specializing in lesser-known works by early women writers. Greer obtained an M.A. from Sydney University and a Ph.D. from Newnham College, Cambridge (1967).

Greer, Holly Stair (1931 –) served as director of the Women's Center, Northern Michigan University-Marquette. Under her direction, the center created a spouse abuse shelter, rape/crisis line, role model teams, and women's awareness meetings. From 1976 – 1978, Greer served as secretary and historian for the Lansing, MI, coordinating committee, Michigan International Women's Year. From 1972 – 1978, she was a member of the Marquette, MI, City Commission—the first woman elected to serve on that body. From 1975 – 1978, she served as the first woman mayor of Marquette. Greer, who has four children, earned her B.A. from Smith College and her M.A. from Northern Michigan University. (ABS)

Grefe, Mary A. (1922 –) joined the NWPC in 1971, and later served as Iowa president of the AAUW. In both capacities, she worked aggressively for ratification of the ERA. When Grefe became national president of the AAUW, she authorized $250,000 in 1980 to promote ratification, met with President Carter and met monthly with other national leaders to strategize on unratified states. She followed Jerry Falwell wherever he spoke and countered his Biblical quotes and arguments with logic and facts. In the late 1980s, Grefe became the first VP of Planned Parenthood, and in the early 1990s worked on reproductive rights. In addition, Grefe served as chair of the board of the Iowa Peace Institute for six years, and in 1982 chaired a conference of women leaders in Washington, D.C., that dealt with peace strategies. She earned her B.A. from Morningside College. Archives: Iowa Women's Archives, 100 Main Library, Iowa City, IA. (ABS)

Grier, Barbara (1933 –) A writer, publisher, reviewer and editor, Grier was co-founder, with her partner Donna J. McBride, of Naiad Press (1974). At its founding, Naiad was the largest publisher of lesbiana in the country. Grier began her career in lesbian publishing as a contributor (under the pseudonym Gene Damon) to the first national lesbian magazine, the *Ladder*. She also published articles and reviews in *ONE Magazine*, the *Mattachine Review* and *Tangents*. In 1968, Grier became editor in chief of the

Ladder, but was increasingly at odds with its founders, San Francisco-based Daughters of Bilitis. In 1970, Grier and Rita Laporte took over the magazine, but could not support it on subscriptions only; it ceased publication after the October 1972 issue. Many of the essays from the magazine were published in book form in 1976 with Grier serving as an editor. After co-founding Naiad Press, Grier and McBride began a 30-year stint of publishing a wide variety lesbian authors. When the two retired in 2003, Naiad Press ceased to operate, but gave its working authors and all of its workers to Bella Books. Archives: The James C. Hormel Collections, San Francisco Public Library, CA. (ABS)

Griesinger, Jan (1942 –) In 1969, Griesinger was one of the founders of Dayton (OH) Women's Liberation, and was active there until the group's demise in 1975. In 1974, she was a co-founder of the Dayton Women's Health Center (abortion clinic). Ordained in the United Church of Christ (UCC) in 1970, Griesinger was the chief national organizer for Women in Campus Ministry from 1971 – 1975, and traveled the country searching for and giving support to women doing campus ministry in Protestant-based organizations. The group challenged male-dominated organizations such as the National Campus Ministry Association. Griesinger came out in 1977 and has worked as an out lesbian pastor since that time. In 1977, she participated in the UCC Gay Caucus at the UCC General Synod and has continued her leadership in that organization, now the UCC Coalition for LGBT Concerns. She served on the first Coalition Council in the late 1970s and early 1980s, and as national coordinator from 1984 to 1997. In 1990, she was a co-founder of Christian Lesbians OUT, a national ecumenical organization. She served as its treasurer and became national coordinator in 1998. Griesinger served on the first steering committee for the National Religious Leadership Roundtable organized by the National Gay & Lesbian Task Force. A co-director for Old Lesbians Organizing for Change, Griesinger was also a co-founder of the Susan B. Anthony Memorial UnRest Home Women's Land Trust near Athens, OH (1979). Griesinger holds a B.A. from DePauw University and an M.Div. from United Theological Seminary. Archives: Some papers are with Campus Ministry Women, Yale University Divinity School, New Haven, CT; others are at the Congregational Church Library in Boston, MA. (ABS)

Griffin, Susan Emily (1943 –) In 1972, Griffin "wrote the first article analyzing rape as an act of oppression and domination against women for *Ramparts Magazine*." Part of a women's health counseling network with the Berkeley Women's Building (1970 – 1971), she also published a series of conversations on abortion in 1971. She has published 17 books, many of which articulated groundbreaking feminist theory. These include *Rape, the Politics of Consciousness* (Harper Collins, 1979); *Pornography and*

Silence (Harper Collins, 1981); *A Chorus of Stones* (New York, 1992); *What Her Body Thought, A Journey into the Shadows* (San Francisco, 1999); *The Book of the Courtesans* (New York, 2001); and *Woman and Nature, The Roaring Inside Her* (Harper and Row, 1976). An original member of Unreasonable Women of the Earth and Code Pink, Griffin has worked to connect issues such as ecology and peace with feminism, and has been active in the civil rights, pro-Democracy and anti-war movements. A teacher, she earned her B.A. (1965) and M.A. (1973) from San Francisco State University, and received an Honorary Doctorate from Graduate Theological Union (1985). Griffin has received numerous awards and grants, including the Ina Coolbrith Prize for Poetry (1963); the Women's Foundation Award for Women in the Arts (1988); and the Bay Area Book Reviewers Award for non-fiction. The local TV production of her play "Voices" won an Emmy Award; *A Chorus of Stones* was a finalist for a Pulitzer Prize in 1992. She has one child.   (ABS)

Griffiths, Martha Wright (1912 – 2003) A legend in Michigan Democratic politics, Griffiths served in Congress 1955 – 1974. The first woman to serve on the House Ways and Means Committee, she also sat on the Joint Economic Committee of Congress, and was chair of the House Subcommittee on Fiscal Policy. She achieved two major wins for women during her tenure: She successfully led the debate in the House of Representatives to include sex discrimination in the employment portion (Title VII) of the Civil Rights Act of 1964; and her arguments in front of a male-dominated House were pivotal in securing House approval of the ERA in 1970. "There will be a day when the Supreme Court says, 'Yes, the Constitution really does apply to women,'" she said. Although the other nine women in the House urged her to be considered for an appointment to the High Court, she considered such an event "out of the range of possibility" and privately called the Justices "idiots" for failing to apply the Civil Rights Act to women as well as blacks. Born in Pierce City, MO, she met her husband, Hicks G. Griffiths, at the University of Missouri. The two studied law, and in 1940 became the first couple to graduate together from the University of Michigan Law School. The two formed law firm Griffiths & Griffiths in Detroit (1946). From 1949 – 1952, Griffiths was one of two women serving in the state House. After leaving Congress in 1974, she served on various corporate boards, then in 1982 became MI's first woman lieutenant governor (serving with Democratic governor James J. Blanchard). She was re-elected in 1986. Griffiths, who received 29 Honorary Ph.D.s, was inducted into the National Women's Hall of Fame.

Griffo, Michela (1947 –) An artist and activist, Griffo was an outspoken critic of NY NOW for being "homophobic, racist and classist." She, along with Rita Mae Brown and Susan Vinucci, resigned from NOW in 1970, with a scathing critique in the chapter's newsletter. At the time,

Brown was the editor. "Lesbians were the backbone of NOW, and most were closeted. We were willing to put our bodies on the line," Griffo says. Griffo was also on the leading edge of the radical lesbian movement in NYC. Still an art student at Pratt Institute when the now-famous sit-in at the *Ladies' Home Journal* was planned, Griffo designed the cover of the *Women's Liberated Journal*, a protest publication to be used in the action. But she declined to attend because she felt betrayed by Susan Brownmiller, then a member of Media Women, who responded to Betty Friedan's comment that lesbians were the "Lavender Menace" by saying in an article she wrote for *The New York Times* that lesbians were a "Lavender Herring." Griffo then created a T-shirt with "Lavender Herring" on it and wore it to a GLF dance, where other lesbians decided Lavender Menace was better suited for a "coming out" of lesbians in the women's movement at the takeover of the Second Congress to Unite Women on May 1, 1970. Brown and Griffo had come into GLF with the intent to politicize lesbians and get them to leave the male-dominated organization, which led to Lesbian Liberation, later renamed Radicalesbians. Griffo also did paste-ups and graphics for the *liberated Rat*, an underground revolutionary newspaper. Griffo changed her life after 1976 when the women's movement was in decline. She began to support mainstream gay and lesbian PAC organizations. Later she took a position as manager of Web-based communications for Colgate-Palmolive, a position she held for 14 years. Griffo, a convent-educated doctor's daughter originally from Rochester, NY, remains an artist and lives in New York City, Connecticut and Italy.   (ABS)

Grigoriadis, Mary (1942 –) was a founding member of AIR Gallery, the first cooperative gallery of women artists in the U.S. Barbara Zucker, Dotty Attie, Susan Williams and Grigoriadis reviewed hundreds of slides, visited over 60 studios, and organized a core group of 20 members. Remodeling a machine shop in SOHO, NY, they established the gallery based on parity for women artists at a time when exhibition opportunities for them were extremely limited. The gallery developed a supportive art-world audience, shows were reviewed in the major art journals, and the gallery received grants from the NEA and NYSCA for public programs and workshops. The gallery, which became a model for other women's cooperatives both nationally and internationally, celebrated its 30th Anniversary in 2002. Grigoriadis exhibited at AIR from 1972 to 1989, while also serving on various committees. She has a B.A. from Barnard College and an M.A. from Columbia University.   (ABS)

Grimstad, Kirsten J. (1944 –) was a member of New York Radical Feminists (1972–1975), and part of the Circle of Support for Jane Alpert (1975). In 1971, she edited *Women's Work and Women's Studies*, a bibliography published by the Barnard Women's Center. She was co-author (with Susan Rennie) of *The New Woman's Survival Cata-*

log (Coward, McCann & Geoghegan, 1973) and *The New Woman's Survival Sourcebook* (Knopf, 1975). In 1976, Grimstad moved to Venice, CA, and joined forces with the founders of the Woman's Building and the Feminist Studio Workshop, where she served as co-founder, executive editor and publisher of *Chrysalis: A Magazine of Women's Culture* (1977–1981). Grimstad earned her B.A. from Barnard College, her M.A. from Columbia University, and her Ph.D. from The Union Institute.　　(ABS)

Groneman, Carol (1943 –) In 1969, Groneman was a faculty wife at Columbia University and attended a tea given by the wife of the dean of Columbia College. There she was encouraged to participate in the Columbia community by, for example, volunteering at the Thrift Shop or pouring tea at the freshman orientation (all boys). "Egad! I thought. There must be more than this," Groneman recalls. She joined the then-fledgling Columbia Women's Liberation group and for the next five years met weekly with them or an affiliated CR group. Among other activities during that time, CWL prepared one of the first studies of discrimination against women faculty at Columbia and Barnard. They also organized the Columbia maids, who were doing similar work for less pay than the janitors. When some of the maids were fired, while the university was hiring janitors, CWL filed a lawsuit and won. "We were up against some very white-shoe Columbia lawyers who suggested to the Puerto Rican judge handling the case that the maids could always go on Welfare," says Groneman. CWL also helped to organize a regional conference, Women Learn from Women, attended by hundreds of women in 1973. A feminist historian and member of the Berkshire Conference of Women Historians, Groneman has taught women's history and written about 19th century immigrant women. Her book *Nymphomania: A History* (W.W. Norton, 2000) examines the myths surrounding sexualized women. Groneman, who has one stepchild, holds a Ph.D.　　(ABS)

Gross, Eva – See Magill, Rosalind M.

Gross, Rita (1943 –) In 1967, Gross began to research the value of women in aboriginal Australian religions. This eventually became the subject of her Ph.D. dissertation for the University of Chicago, which was the first dissertation on women's studies in religion. The author of several early articles on women's studies in religion, Gross published one of the first anthologies in the field, *Beyond Androcentrism: New Essays on Women & Religion* (1977). Gross began teaching courses on women and religion in 1972, and in 1974 was named head of Women and Religion, a new section of the American Academy of Religion. She is also the author of *Buddhism After Patriarchy* (State University of New York Press, 1993).　　(ABS)

Grossholtz, Jean (1929 –) (also known as Thelma Jean Grossholtz) In the early 1970s, Grossholtz was active in the Northampton (MA) Valley Women's Union, Mount Holyoke's women's studies program, the battered women's movement and the emergent lesbian movement. She has fought to end violence against women and worked for cultural and biological diversity, peace and justice. Now retired, Grossholtz was professor of politics and chair of the women's studies dept. at Mount Holyoke. She taught classes such as The Politics of Patriarchy, Global Feminism, Violence Against Women, and Women Organizing Women. She is a founding member of Diverse Women for Diversity, a group working at the international level on such issues as the Biodiversity Convention and the Kyoto Treaty; helped organize the Women's Pentagon Action (1980 – 1982); and is the author of a series of books and films that show how local, national and global struggles combine to affect the lives of women. She seeks to mobilize people against unfair global trade policies. Her books include *Dolls and Dust: Voices of Asian Women Resisting Globalization* (2000) and its video; *Marketisation of Governance: Critical Feminist Perspectives from the South,* and its video (Cape Town, South Africa, 2000); and the three-part video "New Directions," which describes women-centered projects intended to improve women's lives in Zimbabwe, Thailand and Guatemala (1997). She is also author of *Forging Capitalist Patriarchy: The Economics & Social Transformation of Feudal Sri Lanka & Its Impact on Women.* Grossholtz earned her B.A. from Penn State, holds an M.A., and earned her Ph.D. from MIT. Archives: Mount Holyoke College, South Hadley, MA.　　(ABS)

Groves, Susan Stevens (1938 –) A public school teacher of history and women's studies in Berkeley, CA, Groves was one of the earliest to develop and teach courses in black studies, feminist studies, community service and environmental studies. In 1972, she was appointed coordinator of the Women's Studies Program, created by the Berkeley School Board. The first women's studies program in the U.S., its goal was to create a pioneer feminist and multicultural educational program for Berkeley's students that could also be made available to the national educational community. Over the next 10 years, an extensive library of lessons, units, activities and resources was created by the WSP, including *Black Women Poets*; a Susan B. Anthony folder with biographies of important women activists; instructions for an International Women's Day festival; and *The Story of Mei-Ling.* The group also produced the two-volume *We Were There! Integrating Women into U.S. History.* By the 1990s, Groves was teaching the Women's Studies Seminar at Berkeley High School. In 1995, she attended, with a group of Berkeley high-school students, the Fourth United Nations Conference on Women, held in Beijing. When they returned to Berkeley, the group again rewrote the curriculum for the Women's Studies Seminar. Groves, who has one child, retired from teaching in 1998. She earned her B.A. from the University of Wisconsin, and her

M.A. and Teaching Credentials from the University of California, Berkeley. (ABS)

Growe, Joan Anderson (1935 –) Active in the Democratic party in Minnesota for most of her adult life, Growe was elected to the MN House of Representatives in 1972 —a time when there was only one woman out of 201 legislators. In 1974 she became the first woman elected secretary of state and served in that capacity for 24 years (winning six elections to do so). She was co-author of the MN ERA and an early member of the NWPC. Growe also served as board member of the Women's Campaign Fund and was a founding member of the Minnesota Women's Economic Roundtable. In addition to her work in government and for women, Growe was active in the peace movement, particularly in regards to America's role in Central America, and the civil rights movement. She implemented progressive voter registration methods that resulted in MN leading the nation in voter turnout, and observed elections in many foreign countries. Her numerous awards and citations include Breaking the Glass Ceiling Award (1998) from Women Executives in State Government, and the Woman Who Makes a Difference Award (1991) from the International Women's Forum. Growe, who has four children, earned her B.S. from St. Cloud University and a degree in special education from the University of Minnesota. She also attended the Kennedy School of Government-Executive Management Program, Harvard University. Archives: Minnesota History Center, St. Paul, MN. (ABS)

Grusse, Ellen (1946 –) A student at the University of Connecticut in the early 1970s, Grusse joined a community of women in Hartford, CT. She marched for equal rights, abortion rights, equal pay and equal credit. In 1974, she was subpoenaed to a grand jury investigation regarding the whereabouts of anti-war activists Susan Saxe and Kathy Power. Grusse refused to testify or give information about the communities in which she lived, and as a result spent several months in Niantic State Prison. Grusse later traveled around the country speaking to women's groups about the danger of infiltration by the government and the FBI. In addition, Grusse served as a member of the board of New Haven Women's Liberation Center for many years, and was a founding member of the Feminist Union in New Haven (CT). She went to work for the Connecticut Women's Education and Legal Fund in 1977 and is (2005) financial director of that group. She holds a B.A. from the University of Connecticut. (ABS)

Guerra, Petra (1949 –) (also known as Petra Guerra Lopez) Born in the city of Cadereyta Jimenez in the state of Nuevo Leon, Mexico, Guerra went from being a migrant in the fields to operating a statewide program of child development centers for the migrant children of Chicano and Native American families in Utah. She was also one of several people responsible for the develop-ment of migrant child development centers throughout Idaho, many of which are still operating today. She fought for healthcare and safe housing for migrants in UT, where 90 percent of the migrant housing was condemned, and was a member of the Chicana/o movement for self-determination. A fighter for reproductive rights, she is a member of United Farm Workers Union, Utah Migrant Council, Idaho Migrant Council, MEChA, Venceremos Brigade, and the National Organization for Status of Women. She was also a member of Teatro Los Malqueri-dos & Teatro El Trompo. She has organized against the wars in Nicaragua, El Salvador and Panama, and is an activist for Palestine, peace, environmental issues, gay rights and labor. A Ph.D., Guerra teaches at the communication department of the University of Texas Pan American. She has two children. (ABS)

Guggenheimer, Elinor C. (1912 –) An ardent feminist, urban planner and consumer affairs advocate, Guggenheimer has spent her life working to improve working conditions, especially for women, children and the elderly. She was a co-founder of the NWPC, and the primary founder of the New York Women's Forum (1973), the National Women's Forum (1981), the International Women's Forum (1983), and the New York Women's Agenda (1992). These forums transformed the "Old Boys Club" into the women's verb "networking." In addition, Guggenheimer founded and directed the Day Care Council of New York (1948–1964) and the Day Care and Child Development Council of America (1958–1965). She served as commissioner of the NYC Dept. of Consumer Affairs and was the first woman member of the NYC Planning Commission. In 1979, she founded the Council for Senior Citizens and Centers, which changed the image of seniors to reflect their productivity and value to society. She has received many honors, including the Eleanor Roosevelt Leadership Award. She holds honorary degrees from Marymount Manhattan College and the Graduate Center of the City University of New York, among others. Educated at Vassar and Barnard, Guggenheimer earned an A.B. in 1934. (ABS)

Gullick, Johanna Marie (1950 –) (also known as Johanna Handywoman) A member of Los Angeles NOW in 1969, Gullick organized a women's liberation group at El Camino College in Torrance, CA, and in 1971 helped organize the first West Coast Lesbian Conference in Los Angeles at the Metropolitan Church. In 1970, she became involved in the Lesbian Feminists group at the Crenshaw Women's Center in Los Angeles, organized a rape hotline there, and helped found the Gay Women's Coalition in Los Angeles (including Lesbian Feminists, Daughters of Bilitis and the UCLA Lesbian Feminist Group). In 1972, *Lesbian Tide* was "born on the floor of my apartment." In the mid 1970s, she worked crew on the Four Women's Music Tour (Holly Near, Meg Christian, Margie Adams and Cris Williamson) as a lighting and sound tech. Also

G

in the mid 1970s, working as Johanna Handywoman, she successfully broke the gender barrier and became the first woman in two unions, the Painters Local in Santa Monica, CA, and the Operating Engineers Local 506 in Los Angeles. She also ran her own general and painting contracting company for many years and was actively involved in the Humanist Construction Co-Op in Venice, CA. In 1974, she worked with strikers protesting unfair practices at the Gay Services Center in Los Angeles, and worked off and on at Sisterhood Bookstore in both Westwood, CA, and the Women's Building in Los Angeles. In the mid-1970s, she worked against the Briggs Initiative and helped organize the first Take Back the Night March with the women's group that met at the Unitarian Church on West 8th St. in Los Angeles. From 1975–1979, Gullick was involved in the Women's Building at the old Chanard Art Institute in the McArthur Park neighborhood in Los Angeles and the new location in downtown Los Angeles on Spring St. Gullick has a bachelor's degree from Southern California Institute of Architecture. (ABS)

Gunn Allen, Paula (1939 –) Descendent of Laguna Pueblo and mixed-blood Blackfoot as well as Lebanese and Scots, Gunn Allen is a poet, novelist and scholar. Her exposition of Native American themes is grounded in a multi-cultural, multi-awareness, feminist framework, which signifies her specific contribution to U.S. feminism. In her work, Gunn Allen seeks to achieve two goals. The first is to show that every lifestyle and a multitude of languages, beliefs and opinions have been present and respected in Indian Country; the second is to remind the community of the powerful role of women in Native American society, the template for American feminism. Gunn Allen published her first book of poems, *The Blind Lion*, in 1974 (Thorp Springs Press). She received a postdoctoral fellowship at UCLA to study Native American women's writings (1980–1981), and in 1983 edited *Studies in American Indian Literature: Critical Essays and Course Designs* (Modern Language Association of America). That year, her novel, *The Woman Who Owned the Shadows*, was published by Spinsters Ink. Other books include *The Sacred Hoop: Recovering the Feminine in American Indian Traditions* (Beacon Press, 1986) and *Grandmothers of the Light: A Medicine Woman's Sourcebook* (Beacon Press, 1991). *Pocahontas: Medicine Woman, Spy, Entrepreneur, Diplomat* (Harper San Francisco, 2003) was nominated for a Pulitzer Prize. Gunn Allen holds a B.A. (1966) and M.F.A. (1968) from the University of Oregon, and a Ph.D. from the University of New Mexico (1975). She retired from UCLA, English/American Indian Studies, in 1999. Archives: University of Oregon, Eugene, OR. (ABS)

Gunnell, Kathleen D. – See Saadat, Kathleen D.

Guracar, Genevieve Leland (1936 –) (known professionally as Bulbul) A freelance cartoonist and technical illustrator, Guracar took the penname Bulbul (which means "bird of protest" in Middle Eastern poetry). She began cartooning during the 1970s. Her work, which shows the hypocrisy of patriarchy, has appeared in feminist, labor, peace, environmental, children's and senior rights publications. She is the author of *Drawing My Times: Cartoons by Bulbul* (Arachne Publishing, 2003), a retrospective of 30 years of her feminist cartoons. Her work also appears in numerous books, including *Crème de la Femme* (Random House, 1997); *Justice Denied* (Women's International League for Peace & Freedom, & International Institute for Human Rights, 1994); *Women's Glibber* (Roz Warren, The Crossing Press, 1992); and *Readings for Older Women* (Bowman & Haywood, editors, Hot Flash Press, 1992). Bulbul earned a B.S. from the University of Michigan, College of Architecture and Design, Ann Arbor (1959). Archives: Love Library, San Diego State University, San Diego, CA. (ABS)

Gurko, Jane (1941 –) With a B.A. from Smith College, and an M.A. and Ph.D. from Univerity of California, Berkeley, Gurko became a professor of English at San Francisco State University in 1971. Working with several other women teachers and students who were interested in developing courses on women, she created a six-unit course, Woman as Hero, and three-unit courses in Contemporary Women's Novel, Women's Short Story and Lesbian Literature. In 1973, she joined with Sally Gearhart, Nancy McDermid and Gretchen Milne (now known as Forest) to create and offer a women's studies course, The Block, which was four courses taken as a group. The idea for The Full Moon Coffeehouse, the first of its kind, began to percolate there. And courses for the future women's studies major also were developed there, such as the disability course called Women and Appearance ("arguably the most radical of all our courses, ever"). Gurko was one of the chief architects and drafters of the Women's Studies Major (and Minor), one of the first in the country. (ABS)

Guthrie, Linda B. (1951 –) A teacher and union leader, Guthrie has participated in every march to Washington, D.C., for abortion rights. In the Northeast, she helped escort women into health clinics (1971–1973) once full access to birth control was obtained, and prior to that offered abortion counseling. From 1974–1976, she was a member of the Durham (NC) Women's Radio Collective, which aired on WDBS until the station decided "to de-ghettoize women's news, which meant to ignore it completely," she says. During this same period, Guthrie wrote her Master's thesis on women in Utopian societies in the 19th century. Her premise was that, despite the differences in their views of sexuality, celibacy, group marriage and free love, each was a form of liberation for women from the confines of 19th century America. As an oral historian, she recorded the experiences of black female tobacco workers in Durham. A black American, Guthrie was involved with Solidarity groups in the newly liberated countries of Africa, and as part of the New

American Movement tried to instill feminist values. With her young daughters, she attended women-only functions, such as the West Coast Women's Music Festival, to broaden their understanding of women's roles in society. Guthrie, who has three children, holds a B.A. from Adelphi University and an M.A. from Duke University. (ABS)

Gutierrez, Irene Blea – See Blea, Irene Isabel

Gutierrez, Theresa — launched "Feminine Franchise," Chicago's first weekly feminist television program dealing with topics of concern to women, in the early 1970s. She interviewed "all the national feminists of the time," she says. From 1973 – 1978, Gutierrez, the first Hispanic woman to break into television journalism, was first the producer and then the host of the series. Later she was the host of "Sunday in Chicago with Theresa Gutierrez." At the same time she was the moderator of the WLS Radio's "Ms. Understood," a talk show that addressed women's issues, and of "Hispano," which focused on social and economic issues in Chicago's Hispanic community. She is (2005) a general assignment reporter and host of "Tapestry," a series featuring Hispanic community leaders. She was a reporter for ABC for 20 years. Guitierrez was the recipient of the Anti-Defamation League's Women of Achievement Award (2005). In 2004, an educational book by Lou Ann Walker, *Women Who Broke Barriers: The New Face of TV News*, was published showing Gutierrez, Barbara Walters, Connie Chung, Christine Amanpour and Jane Pauly on the cover. Gutierrez has been recognized for her achievements in broadcast journalism by the Latina Coalition on the Media, *Latina Glamour* magazine, the Mexican Fine Arts Museum, *Today's Chicago Woman* (as one of 100 Woman Making a Difference) and *Hispanic USA Magazine* (as one of six outstanding broadcasters in the country). (ABS)

Guttmacher, Sally Jeanne (1941 –) joined Columbia Women's Liberation in 1968. From 1969 – 1971, the group had a number of victories. They instigated a report on the ratio of tenured women faculty compared to men, worked with the Columbia maids to get their salaries on a par with male janitors, and integrated the Columbia swimming pool (formerly for men only). The women also insisted that the university health service address women's reproductive health. Additionally, they set up soap boxes around NYC and the shopping malls to explain how being against the Vietnam War was a feminist issue, reviewed children's books and wrote to editors about the books' sexist aspects, and tried to show how perfume manufacturers were ripping off women. To that end, the women developed a perfume that, says Guttmacher, "smelled exactly like Joy, according to experts, and we sold it for $1." In addition to this work, Guttmacher was a member of MF2, a Marxist-feminist group, and from 1969 – 1971 represented all Columbia graduate students on the executive committee of the University Senate, where she brought a feminist perspective to the issues being discussed. Guttmacher, whose father was a physician who worked hard for women's rights to birth control and abortion, is also active in the reproductive rights movement; as of this writing she is a member of the board of the National Abortion Federation. A professor of public health and director of the public health program at New York University, Guttmacher has traveled to Cuba (first trip in 1971) and El Salvador (1980). When the coup occurred in Chile in 1973, Guttmacher, with Barbara Ehrenreich and Helen Marieskind, formed Action for Women in Chile as a means to send money and supplies to Chilean women. Guttmacher was also a member of an anti-apartheid support group focused on health workers. She continues to work part of the year in South Africa. She has one child. Guttmacher holds a B.S. from the University of Wisconsin and a Ph.D. from Columbia University. (ABS)

Guy-Sheftall, Beverly (1946 –) is widely recognized as an authority on black feminist scholarship. She was co-editor (with Roseann P. Bell and Bettye J. Parker) of *Sturdy Black Bridges: Visions of Black Women in Literature* (Anchor Books, 1979), the first anthology of African American women's literature published in America. Her doctoral dissertation was published in 1991 as *Daughters of Sorrow: Attitudes Toward Black Women, 1890 – 1920*, appearing as a volume in the series *Black Women in United States History*. She was also co-editor of *Double Stitch: Black Women Write About Mothers & Daughters* (Beacon Press, 1992), and *Words of Fire: An Anthology of African American Feminist Thought* (The New Press, 1995). A professor of English and women's studies at Spelman College (beginning in 1971), Guy-Sheftall was founder of the Women's Research and Resource Center (1981) and founding co-editor (with Patricia Bell Scott) of *SAGE: A Scholarly Journal of Black Women*, two pioneering resources for black women. She was also co-author, with Johnnetta Betsch Cole, of *Gender Talk: The Struggle for Women's Equality in African American Communities* (Ballantine, 2003). As a professor at Spelman, Guy-Sheftall was a founder of the women's studies program, designing it to include issues pertinent to African Americans. Her awards include the Spelman's Presidential Faculty Award for outstanding scholarship. She was also named to the Anna Julia Cooper Professorship, an endowed chair in the women's studies dept. that honors the daughter of a slave who earned a doctorate degree from the Sorbonne. Guy-Sheftall earned her B.A. from Spelman College (1966), her M.A. from Atlanta University (1970), and her Ph.D. from Emory. (ABS)

Gwynn, Bethroot (1941 –) (also known as Betsy Gwynn) While a staff member of the National YWCA, College and University Division, in Chicago, Gwynn attended the First National Women's Liberation Conference, held outside Chicago in 1968. She also attended meetings of the

G

CWLU, but was primarily involved in bringing feminism into the Student YWCA. Gwynn raised women's liberation as an issue on college campuses. In the summer of 1969 she facilitated a women's liberation caucus at the National Student YWCA Convention. That group successfully lobbied for a full-time staff position devoted to women's liberation organizing on college campuses; Gwynn became that person. She was also coordinator for the National Student YWCA's January 1970 project on women's liberation, which brought 10 college women to live in Chicago for a month-long intensive study program. In the fall of 1970, Gwynn moved to Portland, OR, where she was active in Portland's gay women's liberation movement. She helped redefine the Gay Women's Coffeehouse as a woman-only space and helped found a gay women's center (1971) and newsletter. She was also part of the takeover of the local counter-culture newspaper for a women's issue. Gwynn worked at bridge-building between radical-movement women and lesbians, and also helped organize Portland's delegation of women to a conference in Vancouver, British Columbia, bringing together women from the U.S. and the National Liberation Front of South Vietnam (Viet Cong) in 1971. In the mid 1970s, Gwynn became part of the women's spirituality and lesbian land movement. An early contributor to *Woman-Spirit* magazine, she was by 1976 one of many women creating a goddess-focused ritual and land-based alternative culture, and had co-founded Fly Away Home, a women-only piece of land in Southern OR. Gwynn has since performed and taught personal theater workshops for women, helped organize a conference for lesbians about end-of-life issues, and helped to found a midwifery clinic in OR. In 2003, she created and performed in "Women: The Longest Revolution. A Performance Documentary." Gwynn holds a B.A. from Duke University (1963) and an M.A. from Union Theological Seminary (1965). Archives: Special Collections (Southern Oregon Lesbians), University of Oregon Library, Eugene, OR. (ABS)

Haber, Barbara (1934 –) From 1968–2002, Haber served as a curator of books at the Arthur and Elizabeth Schlesinger Library on the History of Women in America, now part of the Radcliffe Institute for Advanced Studies at Harvard University. Recognizing a shift in the culture as well as in the intellectual movement that was to become women's studies, Haber developed a collection that reflected the impact of the women's movement on both academic research and popular writing. As of 2006, the library's holdings include over 80,000 volumes and over 500 current periodicals, as well as 2,500 unique manuscript collections. Haber also collected relevant fiction and culinary literature showing the connection between women's history and the history of food. In addition, she wrote and edited bibliographies and anthologies for the emerging field of women's studies. These include *Women in America: A Guide to Books, 1963–1975, With an Appendix on Books 1975–1979; American Women in the Twentieth Century Series, 1900–2000; The Woman's Annual: The Year in Review, 1980–1984;* and *The Women's Study Index.* She is also author of *From Hardtack to Home Fries: An Uncommon History of American Cooks and Meals* (2002) and co-editor of *From Betty Crocker to Feminist Food Studies* (2006). Haber administered regional and national grant programs, including the Boston Edison Project (late 1980s), which allowed Boston area schoolteachers to bring women's studies into school curricula, and Radcliffe College's Women in the Community Project (1981–1983), a $250,000 NEH grant that publicized women's history and women's studies scholarship in 10 U.S. locations. (ABS)

Hacker, Sally (1936–1988) realized her feminism in the 1960s while doing graduate work under Alice Rossi of the University of Chicago. With Rossi's encouragement, Hacker and her husband convened a NOW chapter in Houston, TX, after Hacker moved there in 1966. In the early 1970s, Hacker served as national coordinator for NOW's AT&T task force. Her research on AT&T, which she began in Houston and continued in Des Moines, IA, shaped NOW's key role in AT&T's $54 million landmark settlement of the EEOC's sex and race discrimination case (1973). Hacker went on to research why the settlement resulted in declining numbers of women employed at AT&T. She also conducted groundbreaking research in engineering, technology, the military and gender, and researched gender relations in Mondragon, the famous Basque cooperative community in Spain. Hacker also convened the NOW chapter in Ames, IA, and served on NOW's national board. Born in Litchfield, IL, Hacker had one child. She received her Ph.D. from the University of Chicago (1969), and was professor of sociology at Oregon State University at the time of her death. Archives: Schlesinger Library, Radcliffe Institute, Cambridge, MA.

Hackett, Amy (1941 –) A member of Columbia Women's Liberation (1969–1973) with Kate Millett and Ann Harris, Hackett worked on early efforts to achieve affirmative action at Columbia University. She attended an early women's studies conference organized by Sheila Tobias at Cornell, and was involved in the early years of feminist studies with Ann Calderwood. She took part in CR groups in the 1970s, and marched for the ERA and abortion rights. Hackett is director of institutional relations at Legal Momentum (formerly NOW Legal Defense and Education Fund) and serves as treasurer of VFA. (ABS)

Hackman, Barbara Ann
– See Franklin, Barbara Hackman

Haddad, Margaret P. – See Hogan, Margaret P.

Hadditt, Marylou (1928 –) (also known as Mary Louise Stauffer) Hadditt's contributions to the movement focused on menopause. Her involvement in the women's movement began in 1972, when, after reading the biography of Zelda Fitzgerald, she decided to move to Berkeley "where the women's action was" and got involved with the women's center there. In 1977, she was a re-entry student at Sonoma State, where she took courses in women's studies. Her performance piece "Garden in Second Bloom" sparked discussion throughout the San Francisco Bay Area from 1979–1984. In addition to starting and facilitating mid-life and menopausal groups at the Commonwoman's Health Project, Santa Rosa, CA, she co-facilitated a mid-life task force of the Sonoma County Commission on the Status of Women, which held the first mid-life women's conference in Northern California. As a co-editor of *Women's Voices* (established in 1980), she instituted a series of special issues on child abuse, ageism and mental health, a series the paper continues today. In 1981, she was one of the founding mothers of The Sitting Room, a woman's reading room and library, in Cotati, CA. She has been active in the Lesbian Voters Action Caucus since 1993, and is a member of Raging Grannies, Santa Rosa, CA. Haddit, who is a retired social worker and mental health counselor, has four children. She earned a B.A. from Sonoma State University (1980) and an M.A. from the University of San Francisco (1989). Archives: The Sitting Room, Cotati, CA. (ABS)

Haegele, Dorothy (1922 –) Married in 1952, Haegele discovered the women's movement two decades later. While typing papers for her daughter's women's studies class, Haegele became a committed fighter for women's rights. After attending the Houston National Women's Conference in 1977, she opened an ERA office across the street from Phyllis Schlafly's husband's office. Haegele was one of President Carter's appointees to the IWY Continuing Committee. She chaired the National Women's Conference Committee peace caucus, and worked for children's rights, women's rights, world peace, racial equality and the preservation of the environment. For the State Department, she attended the United Nations Mid-Decade Conference and the Copenhagen Conference. At the same time, Haegele was bi-state coordinator for the ERA MO and IL coalitions. In 1992, she was director of Program Delivery and Training for the NWCC board, and was director of Clearinghouse Media Monitoring Project, Women's International New Service, and the U.N. Women's Conference in Nairobi. She also represented the NWCC at the World Congress of Women in Moscow. After the election of President Reagan, Haegele moved to Costa Rica to work with U.S. Citizens for Peace in Latin America and the Costa Rican section of WILPF. The new ERA initiative brought her back to the U.S., where she resumed the fight. Haegele has three children. (ABS)

Haener, Dorothy (1917 – 2001) was one of about a dozen women who met in Betty Friedan's hotel room in Washington, D.C., in June 1966 during the Conference of State Commissions on the Status of Women. The following day NOW was organized, with Haener as one of its founders. Haener brought 20 years of experience as a labor movement activist to NOW. During WWII, she had worked as an inspector at Ford Willow Run, a large bomber plant. As an officer in UAW Local 143, she fought for the union to protect the jobs of the "Rosie the Riveters"—women who had worked during the war. On the staff of the women's dept. of the United Auto Workers, Haener participated in the work of the President's Commission on the Status of Women and the 1965 White House Conference on Equal Employment Opportunity. With her boss, Caroline Davis, who was NOW's first secretary/treasurer, Haener implemented most of NOW's member services, mailings and finances in its first year of operation. In 1967, however, Haener opposed a NOW resolution for passage of the ERA because her union saw the ERA as a threat to protective labor laws. This position prompted Haener and Davis to resign from the secretary/treasurer duties for NOW. Haener ultimately became a supporter of the ERA. Years later, she joined the NOW LDEF board. Haener was appointed to the Commission on International Women's Year, 1975, and was a delegate to the 1976 Democratic National Convention, where she pressured for a provision in the party platform protecting a woman's right to determine her own reproductive life. After her retirement from the UAW in 1982, Haener was appointed to the Michigan Civil Rights Commission. In 1983, she was one of the first women inducted into the Michigan Women's Hall of Fame.

Haggard, Mitzi (1933 –) was part of the first wave of CR groups in NYC. She delivered a protest to the Indian ambassador following the invasion of Bangladesh by Pakistan and the politically motivated raping of Bangladeshi women. Haggard helped organize day care groups in Greenwich Village, and was a contributor to the *New York Woman's Directory* (Workman Publishing Co., 1973). She is a graduate of the Goodman Theater Conservatory (Chicago, 1955), and has one child. (ABS)

Hahn, Hannelore (1926 –) Hahn is a writer and the founder and executive director of the International Women's Writing Guild. After attending a planning meeting for the United Nations IWY (1975), she was selected to head its literature committee. In that capacity, she organized an event to celebrate the official declaration of IWY. Called Women/Voices 1975, it featured readings by writers both famous and obscure. Hahn read a brief excerpt of her then not-yet-published memoir, *On the Way to Feed the Swans* (Tenth House Enterprises, 1982). She then planned a writing conference for 1976 at the Harrison House Conference Center in Glen Cove, NY, and, that same year, founded the International Women's Writing Guild. Hahn, who has one child, earned her B.A. from the University of Southern California, and holds an Honorary Doctorate in Literature from Skidmore College. Archives: Private Manuscript Archives of the North Carolina State Archives, Raleigh, NC; and The Sophia Smith Collection, Smith College, Northampton, MA. (ABS)

Hale, Kendall (1950 –) An anti-war and feminist activist at the University of Wisconsin (1968 – 1973), Hale went on to Boston to join the New Harmony Sisterhood Band (1973 – 1980). This well-known feminist string band raised money for and awareness of women's causes for eight years. At this time, she also worked in union drives with unorganized women in the electronics industry. From 1976 – 1978, Hale was a labor organizer and welder at the General Dynamics shipyard in Quincy, MA, one of 50 women welders trained and hired in a shipyard of 5,000 men, following a federal affirmative action mandate. In 1985 during the Contra war in Nicaragua, Hale went with her husband and three-year-old daughter to work on the construction of a health clinic, organized and led by local women in Esteli. From 1986 – 1992, Hale advocated for low-income women at Greater Boston Legal Services on the Medicaid and disability unit. She is one of six authors of *Written Out of History*, a book on the Internet, and the author of a memoir. (ABS)

Hale, Sue Sally (1938 – 2003) As a teenager, Hale played on the men's polo team at the Riviera Country Club (CA) disguised as a man, because polo was off limits for women. Competing under the name A. Jones, she tried repeatedly to gain admission to the United States Polo Association, but was rebuffed. Finally, in 1972—after pressure was applied by friends and a lawsuit was threatened—Hale became the first woman admitted to the association. She became a leading player, and in 1990 she and her two daughters, and France's Caroline Anier won the first U.S. Women's Open. Hale coached teams at the Marine Corps Air Station El Toro in Santa Ana, CA, and gave polo lessons to handicapped people. She had three children.

HaLevy, Libbe S. – See Lotman, Loretta

Hall, Peggy W. (1930 –) (also known as Margaret Hall Mazeika) was a charter member of Houston NOW, helped develop other NOW chapters in TX, and also helped organize CR groups. Hall worked on the 1977 National Women's Conference in Houston, the NWPC and NOW national conferences, and was active in the Harris County WPC on issues such as the ERA. She also lobbied the TX State Legislature and testified in the 1970s for and against state textbook selection "a particularly important action because TX set the textbook selection standard for all the other states." In the 1980s, she formed a woman-owned business "that took me out of many activities, but I would always show up to picket or give a talk." The owner and business manager of a private gymnastics club, Hall has three children. She earned a B.A. from Rice University (1952) and an M.P.H. from the University of Texas (1974). Archives: Women's Studies Dept., University of Houston, Houston, TX. (ABS)

Hall, Yolanda ("Bobby") (1922 –) Active in women's liberation in the late 1960s and 1970s, Hall founded the Women and Labor History Project in Chicago, now the Working Women's History Project. Earlier, she had been a true "Rosie the Riveter," working as a skilled tool grinder at Bendix Aviation during WWII. The daughter of union workers, she swiftly joined the UAW when it arrived at the plant, and became the first union steward. That led to her rapid rise into UAW leadership—VP and then president of Local 330 in 1944, then a very rare achievement for a woman in the machine shop industry. She was the first woman on the IL CIO Industrial Union Council. She worked for women at the UAW, first for jobs training, then for leadership training. After demands of family kept Hall home for a while, she started a new career in preventive medicine and community health, achieving faculty status in the medical college at Rush University in Chicago. There she worked for women's equal access to promotions and equal pay, becoming president of the Rush University Faculty Women's Association. (ABS)

Halprin, Sara (1943 –) (also known as Barbara Halpern Martineau) was a faculty adviser to the first women's studies course offered at the University of Toronto (1971). She began researching and writing about women's films and writings, and in 1972 was part of the first wave of feminist/women's film festivals in NYC. She wrote articles on the topic for several publications, including *Take One* and *Cinema Canada*, and in 1972 – 1973 wrote a book, *Women Imagine Women*, interviews with women directors and writers such as Agnes Varda, Jill Johnston, Anais Nin and Alice Munro. Despite this impressive lineup, the book was never published. "Publishers said they wouldn't know how to market it," she says. During this time, Halprin continued to teach at universities in Canada, focusing on literature and films by women. In 1976, she programmed a week of women's films for the first Toronto International Film Festival. From 1975 – 1985, she produced and directed independent feminist documentary films, first in Canada (including "Good Daycare: One Out of Ten" and "Keltie's Beard: A Woman's Story") and then in the U.S. (including "Namechange: A California Film" and "For a Woman in El Salvador, Speaking"). During the late 1970s and early 1980s, Halprin wrote a feminist film column for *Broadside*, a feminist paper published in Toronto. Halprin's books include *Look at My Ugly Face: Myths and Musings on Beauty and Other Perilous Obsessions with Women's Appearance* (Viking, 1995) and *Seema's Show: A Life on the Left* (University of New Mexico Press). Halprin, who has one child, earned her M.A. from the University of Edinburgh and her Ph.D. from Columbia University and a Diploma in Process Work from the Process Work Center of Portland, OR. (ABS)

Halsted, Anna Roosevelt (1906 – 1975) One of the 28 founding members of NOW, Halsted was the daughter of

Franklin D. Roosevelt and Eleanor Roosevelt. During her life, she was never very far from her parents' spotlight. As well as helping with social affairs at the White House, she worked on the *Seattle Post-Intelligencer* newspaper with her second husband. A few years later, her mother, Eleanor, joined her on a short-lived ABC radio program. Continuing her interests in writing, she edited a 1949 magazine, *The Woman*, and contributed a series of columns called "My Life with FDR." In 1963, President Kennedy appointed her to the Citizen's Advisory Council on the Status of Women. There, she became acquainted with others who saw the need for an organization to advance women's rights. Her role as a founder of NOW provided interest and credibility to the new organization. She was also active in organizations such as Americans for Democratic Action and the United Nations Association of the United States. Archives: Franklin D. Roosevelt Library & Museum, Hyde Park, NY.

Halushka, Delina Anibarro (1926 –) Born in Bolivia, Halushka came to the U.S. under a State Department fellowship program in 1951 and became a citizen in 1958. While teaching at Santa Monica College (1972), she became involved in the Association of Women for Active Return to Education, serving as coordinator of community services for the group. She served as VP of educational affairs (1973 – 1974), and as president in 1975. The organization's goal was to help mature and underprivileged student women through scholarships. While doing postgraduate work at UCLA in 1973, Halushka took a seminar that inspired her to look for the reasons why capable women were behind in work-related areas in higher education. In 1976, Halushka founded the Association for the Full Employment of Doctorates, to help women Ph.Ds who could not find work because of age or other discriminatory biases. Halushka, who has two children, holds an M.A. from Ohio State University, another M.A. from Northwestern University at Evanston, IL, and a Ph.D. from UCLA. She has taught at UCLA and Loyola Marymount University, as well as Santa Monica College, and is a co-founder of the Language Communication Institute, which trained bilingual teachers in CA.   (ABS)

Hamburg, Iris – See Krieg, Iris J.

Hamer, Fannie Lou Townsend (1917 – 1977) A major player in changing the face of politics in the South, Hamer helped make voting and political-party participation a reality for African Americans. As a result of her efforts, she suffered searing racism: beatings, job loss, harassment and threats to her life. Yet her spirit was undaunted. Hamer also gave support to the second wave women's movement, helping, in 1971, to found the NWPC. She was also active with the National Council of Negro Women, working on childcare issues and Pig Bank, a livestock cooperative. She realized early the connection between lack of political power and extreme poverty, and

also saw that white women "on their pedestals" were shackled by the same chains as black people. She believed that white women could not be free until black women were free, and she urged white women to work for civil rights as a common cause for all who faced discrimination. A granddaughter of slaves and the last of 20 children born into a family of sharecroppers, Hamer began picking cotton at age six and left school after the sixth grade. At age 45, she began working with the SNCC to implement the Constitutional right of African Americans to vote in Mississippi. Her efforts extended to reform of the Democratic Party in MS when, in 1964, she co-founded the Mississippi Freedom Democratic Party, which challenged the all-white delegations at the Democratic National Convention. As a result, in 1968, the convention seated an integrated challenge delegation from MS. At the same time that Hamer was achieving those reforms, she was developing anti-poverty programs. In addition to an award from the National Association of Business and Professional Women's Clubs, she received honorary degrees from many colleges and universities. In 1965, *Mississippi* magazine named her one of six Women of Influence in the state, and in 1967, she published *To Praise Our Bridges: An Autobiography* (KIPCO). Archives: Papers (1966 – 1978) are at the Newcomb College Center for Research on Women, New Orleans, LA.

Hammer, Barbara Jean (1939 –) is a pioneer in lesbian feminist cinema. Since 1968, when she started working in film and video, she has created more than 80 films and videos, including "Dyke Tactics" (1974), the first sexually-explicit lesbian film made by a lesbian. "I wanted to put a lesbian on the screen in the 21st century because when I began filmmaking I could find reference to none," she says. Three classic lesbian/gay films recuperate a lost and marginalized history and are her proudest achievements: "Nitrate Kisses" (1992); "Tender Fictions" (1998); and "History Lessons" (2000). Other films include "Resisting Paradise" (2003), a documentary about how war forces people to make choices, and "Lover Other" (2006), the story of two women artists and war resisters in Paris. Hammer's work has been shown nationally and internationally and is in major collections, such as The Museum of Modern Art (NYC) and the Centre Pompidou (Paris). Hammer has a B.A. from UCLA, and two M.A. degrees from San Francisco State University, one in English literature and one in film.   (ABS)

Hammer, Signe (1940 –) (also known as Signe Clutz) A feminist writer and editor, Hammer joined Media Women, an organization of NYC Women in Communications, in 1969. In 1970, she was part of the sit-in at *Ladies' Home Journal*, which was originated by Media Women and planned with a coalition of feminist groups. In 1970, she joined NYRF, becoming a member of its Mary Wollstonecraft Brigade. This group helped train a number of new CR groups, initiated a "Directory of

Working Women in NYC," and helped liberate a number of men-only bars, including McSorley's Ale House. From 1980–1983, Hammer was part of a networking and support group of NYC-area women writers, and in the early 1990s helped defend New York City abortion clinics against Operation Rescue. Hammer has published three non-fiction books that examine women's issues from a feminist standpoint. Hammer was editor of *Women: Body and Culture: Essays on the Sexuality of Women in a Changing Society* (Harper & Row, 1975); author of *Daughters and Mothers: Mothers and Daughters* (Quadrangle, 1975); and author of *Passionate Attachments: Fathers and Daughters in America Today* (Rawson Associates, 1982). Her memoir looks at, among other things, her mother's plight as a 1940s wife and mother: *By Her Own Hand: Memoirs of a Suicide's Daughter* (Soho, 1991). Since the 1970s, she has written many feminist articles for national publications, including *Ms.*, the *Village Voice, Parade* and *Harper's Bazaar*. From 1976–1978, she taught at Womanschool, a feminist continuing-education institution. Hammer earned her B.A. from Wellesley College. (ABS)

Hammond, Harmony (1944 –) A feminist artist, Hammond was part of the Women's Conscious Raising Art Work Group (NYC) from 1970–1974. In addition to using CR techniques to discuss their art, the women participated in various feminist political actions and in 1974 exhibited as A Woman's Group at the Nancy Hoffman Gallery. Hammond was a founding member of the AIR Gallery (1972), the first women's cooperative art gallery in NYC, where she had her first solo exhibition (1973). In 1975, she taught at Sagaris (Session I), an educational institute and think-tank for radical feminist political thought, and in 1976 began meeting with a group of women in the arts who founded *Heresies: A Feminist Publication on Art and Politics*. Hammond was co-editor of the first issue (1977) and co-editor of Issue #3, *Lesbian Art and Artists* (1977). In 1978, she curated A Lesbian Show at the 112 Green Street Gallery (NYC). Her work was included in The Great American Lesbian Art Show at the Women's Building (Los Angeles, 1980), and Extended Sensibilities at the New Museum (NYC, 1982). Her anthology *Wrappings: Essays on Feminism, Art and the Martial Arts* was published by TSL Press in 1984. Her book *Lesbian Art in America: A Contemporary History* (Rizzoli, 2000) received a Lambda Literary Award in 2001. Since 1973, Hammond has lectured extensively about feminist and lesbian art in the U.S. She is a tenured professor of art at the University of Arizona in Tucson, studies and teaches Aikido (5th degree black belt), and is a volunteer firefighter in Galisteo, NM, where she lives. (ABS)

Hammond, Max – See Dashu, Max

Hammond, Nancy (1937 –) helped to found the Michigan WPC in 1971. In 1972, she co-authored the *Michigan Legislative Report, 1971–1972*, which ranked legislators'

votes affecting the status of women. She was also vice chair of the Michigan Co-ordinating Committee for abortion law reform before Roe v. Wade, and from 1974 – 1977 was assistant director of the Michigan Women's Commission. During this period, she developed the first statewide network of women's organizations focusing on legislative activity, prepared a monthly newsletter on the status of bills affecting women before the Legislature, and testified at legislative hearings. She is credited with crafting vital segments of MI statutes affecting the status of women: the 1972 Public Accommodations Act, the 1974 Fair Credit Reporting Act, and the 1975 Michigan Fair Housing Act. These bills were not only new to the Michigan Code, but were also models for statutes being introduced elsewhere in the country. (ABS)

Handywoman, Johanna – See Gullick, Johanna Marie

Haney, Eleanor Humes (1931 – 1999) A feminist theologian and community activist, Haney is the author and/or editor of six books on feminist theology, ecological ethics, economic justice, anti-racism and alliance building. These include *Vision and Struggle: Meditations on Feminist Spirituality and Politics, A Feminist Legacy* and *The Great Commandment: A Theology of Resistance and Transformation* (1998). An active member of the Fargo-Moorehead Indian Association, she founded the first Native American childcare center in Fargo, ND, in the late 1960s. After moving to Maine in 1979, Haney became the founder and/or initiator of several groups, including the Feminist Spiritual Community in Portland, Astarte Shell Press, the Center for Vision and Policy, MaineShare, the Maine Community Loan Fund, Communiversity and the United Voice Community Land Trust. She often served as a Humanities Scholar for grants, and was central to the vote by the Bath United Church of Christ to become an open and affirming congregation for gay and lesbian people. She consistently engaged in anti-racist work across economic and gender lines, building alliances with a vision of a sustainable, justice-working, environmentally sound way of life. She was the recipient of the Mary Ann Hartman Award of the University of Maine, The Just Peace Award of the United Church of Christ, and the Social Landscape Artist Award of Maine Initiatives. She earned a B.A. from William and Mary College, an M.A. from Wellesley College, an M.R.E. from the Presbyterian School of Christian Education, and a Ph.D. from Yale University. She taught at Virginia Union, Concordia College, the University of New England, Westbrook College, Maine College of the Arts, Bangor Theological Seminary and the University of Southern Maine.

Hanisch, Carol (1942 –) Radicalized by nine months in the Mississippi civil rights movement in the mid 1960s and learning about racism, poverty and how to fight for one's rights, Hanisch went to NYC in 1966. In 1968 she was a founding member of NYRW, and conceived the group's protest of the Miss America Pageant as a means to raise public consciousness and spread the idea of women's liberation nationally. Her early writings helped launch such concepts as The Personal Is Political, The Pro-Woman Line, and Women of the World Unite! into the movement. Also in 1968, Hanisch participated in the Sandy Springs Conference of radical women and the first National Women's Liberation Conference in Chicago. From 1969 – 1973, she helped organize Gainesville (FL) Women's Liberation. In 1973, she became managing editor of the Redstockings book *Feminist Revolution*, and in 1977 was a founding editor of the feminist journal *Meeting Ground* and published a songbook, *Fight on Sister & Other Songs for Liberation*. From 1991 – 1995 she wrote the "Frankly Feminist" column for the *Hudson Valley Woman*, and in 1995 was a co-founder of Hudson Valley Women's Liberation. A graduate of the journalism department of Drake University (1964), Hanisch worked for United Press International; She was the first woman reporter in the Des Moines Bureau. Hanisch has also been active in environmental issues, organized farm workers in the Mid-Hudson Valley (NY), and supported the anti-apartheid movement in South Africa. (ABS)

Hansen, Christine (1947 –) has been a nurse, educator, filmmaker, writer, editor, translator and teacher. Working at the *LA Free Press* (1968) and with the UCLA anti-war movement, Hansen began to believe that isolating feminism was a mistake, and began integrating women's issues with her daily life. Radical men encouraged her earliest feminist understanding, which grew in the radical film group LA Newsreel. Quoting Roz Payne's archival Newsreel Web site, Hansen says: "We had many struggles in Newsreel around class, women, political education, cultural and worker politics, the haves and have-nots. Little by little the groups changed from filmmaker control to worker control, to women control, to third world control." With other Newsreel veterans, Hansen joined a post-SDS leftist collective (1969 – 1970). A nurse who jumped early into the 1980s San Francisco AIDS epidemic, Hansen says the first HIV-afflicted females were somewhat lost in the system created by/for gay men. In 2003 she began protesting persistent inferior care of women patients in general, and non-white and poor women in particular. Hansen, who has one child, attended UCLA (1967) and San Diego City College (1977) and the University of the State of New York (1983). (ABS)

Hansen, Judy – See Pehrson, Judy L.

Hansen, L.C. (1952 –) (also known as Linda Hansen) attended the 1970 GAY IN in Los Angeles, "radicalized by the oppression of gay people that I witnessed in my life." She campaigned for George McGovern for President while living in Turkey, then moved to Portland, OR, where she joined a CR group at the new Women's Bookstore. Hansen played ball for Lavender Menace and coached Sappho's Sluggers softball. She also helped produce women's music concerts and became a DJ at a local community radio station. "For paid work, I'm president of the local branch of my blue collar labor unionand I still go to peace demos." Hansen has one child. (ABS)

Hanson, Anne Coffin (1921 – 2004) Hanson was the first woman to be hired as a full tenured professor at Yale University (1970). From 1974 – 1978, she served as chair of the art history department, the first woman to be named a department chair at Yale. In the early 1970s, Hanson was the plaintiff in a suit demanding that Mory's, a New Haven eating club for men only, admit women. The club complied in 1974. During her years of teaching at Yale, Hanson was both mentor and role model, inspiring many women to become art historians and curators. Hanson, who had three children, earned a B.F.A. from the University of Southern California (1943), an M.A. from the University of North Carolina (1951), and a Ph.D. from Bryn Mawr (1962).

Hanson, Jo has worked to develop opportunities and recognition for women artists by museums, galleries, publications, the San Francisco Arts Commission and the art world in general. In the mid 1970s, Hanson "single-handedly introduced the first awareness of Mexican women artists and Frida Kahlo in the broader San Francisco Bay Area and California Universities" with her slides and lectures. In the early 1970s, she moderated a WCA delegation that addressed the staff of the U.C. Berkeley Art Museum in a successful bid to increase attention to women artists, and in 1977 curated an outdoor exhibit by women artists, H'errata (meaning Corrections), that ran parallel to the San Francisco Museum of Modern Art outdoor exhibit that featured only men. Hanson also initiated two projects by the WCA for honoring women artists of both regional and international standing. As an arts commissioner in the 1980s, Hanson initiated the practice of equal presentation for all artists in all projects, and was significantly responsible for the restoration and long-term preservation of important New Deal period murals in the Beach Chalet and in Coit Tower, where there are several women muralists. In 1987, she wrote *Artists Taxes, The Hands-On Guide*, which showed artists how to document themselves as artists, not hobbyists, for IRS purposes. Since 1996, she has co-produced, with Susan Leibovitz Steinman and an advisory board, the *Women Environmental Artists Directory*. In 1990, she initiated and designed an artist-in-residence program in San Francisco, which has been a significant resource for artists, especially women. Named Distinguished Woman Artist of the Year 1998 by the Fresno Art Museum, Hanson has also been recognized by regional chapters of the WCA, and in 1997 by the national WCA. (ABS)

Harden, Patricia — was one of the founders, with Rita Van Lew, Sue Rudolf, Jocye Hoyt and Catherine Hoyt, of a

Mount Vernon (NY) group that called for reproductive choice for black women. It was created in reaction to the Black Unity Party's decision that "none of the sisters should take the pill." Although Harden was a Welfare recipient, the group was multi-class and multi-generational, and was often called "The Damned." In addition to her work as a founder of the group, Harden was one of the authors of "A Historical and Critical Essay for Black Women" (1969–1970) was generated by the Mount Vernon Group.

Harder, Sarah Snell (1937 –) In 1971, Harder helped organize Wisconsin's first local chapter of NOW. Denied sick leave from the University of Wisconsin, Eau Claire, for the birth of her fourth child, Harder challenged the Board of Regents, which led to the overturn of that policy by the entire UW system. She joined AAUW in 1975, and in 1979 was appointed to its national board and elected co-chair of the continuing committee of the National Women's Conference. That year she also helped found the Wisconsin Women's Network. She was appointed chair of the Wisconsin Women's Council (1983 – 1987), and served as president of AAUW and chair of its foundation board (1985–1989). It was under her leadership that AAUW's research/action focus on girls and equity took shape. Harder was an organizer of the President's Council of National Women's Organizations in Washington in 1985, a creator of its annual Women's Agendas of policy priorities, and a key organizer of the 1988 Women's Agenda Conference, which brought presidential candidates to address a national feminist constituency in Iowa. She also participated in the United Nations World Conferences on Women in 1980, 1985 and 1995. In 1988, she helped form Women for Meaningful Summits, a coalition of U.S. groups committed to expanding nuclear disarmament talks through connections with women in the former Soviet Union. After 33 years as an administrator at the University of Wisconsin-Eau Claire, Harder finished her university career in 2000 as head of the women's studies program, which she had founded. She is president of the National Peace Foundation and an emeritus professor in Eau Claire. Harder, who has four children, earned both a B.A. and B.S. from La Crosse State College and her M.A. from Bowling Green State University. Archives: Wisconsin Historical Society, Madison, WI. (ABS)

Hardesty, Nancy (1941 –) A Christian feminist and co-author (with Letha Dawson Scanzoni) of *All We're Meant to Be: Biblical Feminism for Today* (Word Books, 1974), Hardesty argues that the Bible can be interpreted to support the equality of women. Her doctoral dissertation, *Your Daughters Shall Prophesy: Revivalism and Feminism in the Age of Finney* (Carlson, 1991), revised and published as *Women Called to Witness* (Abingdon Press, 1984), explores the Biblical feminism of the 19th century women's movement. Hardesty is also author of *Great Women of Faith* (Baker Books, 1980); *Inclusive Language in the Church* (John Knox Press, 1987); *The Memory Book*

(Presbyterian Publishing House, 1989); and *Faith Cure: Divine Healing and the Holiness and Pentecostal Movements* (Hendrickson, 2003). In addition, she has contributed numerous chapters to other books and reference book entries on women's issues. Hardesty was a founder of the Evangelical and Ecumenical Women's Caucus and "Daughters of Sarah," a Christian feminist newsletter published from 1974–1995. From 1976–1980 she taught church history at Candler School of Theology, Emory University. In 1988, she began teaching religion at Clemson University. Hardesty earned her Ph.D. in the history of Christianity from the University of Chicago Divinity School. (ABS)

Harkins, Mary Ellen – See McNish, Mary Ellen

Harms, Valerie (1940 –) A writer and workshop leader, Harms was part of a 10-woman CR group in Ridgefield, CT (1969–1972). All artists, the women formed a statewide network, Feminists in the Arts. Harms edited tapes of their meetings for a book, *Unmasking: Ten Women in Metamorphosis* (Swallow Press, 1972). She then formed Magic Circle Press with Adele Aldridge (1972) to publish works by women. In 1973, she edited *Celebration with Anais Nin*, her friend and mentor, and in 1974 organized a Women's Writers Conference in Bridgeport, CT, for NOW. In 1975, she began teaching poetry sessions, with Ann McGovern, to women imprisoned in the Bedford Hills, NY, correctional center, and later produced a small book of their poetry. She is the author of a book of essays on mentors, *Stars in My Sky/Nin, Montessori, Steloff* (1976). After her divorce in 1982, Harms helped form Parents for the Enforcement of Court-Ordered Child Support. Also active in environmental issues, she is the author of *The Ecology of Everyday Life* (Putnam, 1994). Always interested in depth psychology, she is also author of *The Inner Lover* (Shambhala, 1992). Harms has taught writing for 25 years and is a graduate of Smith College (1962). She has two children. Archives: The Sophia Smith Collection, Smith College, Northampton, MA. (ABS)

Harragan, Betty (1921 – 1998) A writer, activist, and consultant, Harragan was a true champion of women's equality in the workplace. In the 1970s, she was a widow with a young daughter and employed at ad agency J. Walter Thompson when she tired of training men for positions she herself would never get. She decided to file a sex discrimination case against the company, but was fired from her job after launching her fight for equal pay. The case wore on for years and, needing to support herself and her young daughter, Harragan wrote *Games Your Mother Never Taught You: Corporate Gamesmanship for Women* (Rawson Associates, 1977), which sold more than one million copies as a Warner Books paperback. Used as a textbook in college undergraduate courses and business schools, it was also the basis for a TV film of the same name (1982). Her second book, *Knowing the Score: Play-*

by-Play Directions for Women on the Job, was published in 1983 by St. Martin's Press. Although Harragan's lawsuit eventually won an EEOC decision, that decision won her nothing and she was blackballed from the advertising industry. Harragan's lawsuit is credited with breaking up the logjam of sex discrimination in the advertising business; many of the largest firms (including JWT) began naming women VPs soon after Harragan's suit became public. In 1972, she formed a consulting company that specialized in women's issues in the workplace, Betty Harragan & Affiliates. A 27-year member of NOW, for which she frequently handled publicity and PR, Harragan was also a columnist for *Savvy* and *Working Woman* in the 1980s. She graduated from Marquette University (1944) and earned an M.A. from Columbia University (1947).

Harrington, Charlene Ann (1941 –) As a graduate student at the University of California Berkeley in the 1960s, Harrington supported the faculty, staff and student class action suit against the university by collecting and analyzing data. For example, she obtained personnel material and salaries for men and women faculty to illustrate discrepancies. She also conducted a study (later publicized by the Graduate Student Association) of women's athletics at UC Berkeley that showed the university's violations of Title IX. Also active in the anti-Vietnam War movement, Harrington earned her Ph.D. at UC Berkeley. (ABS)

Harris, Ann Sutherland (1937 –) Currently a professor of the history of art and architecture at the University of Pittsburgh, Harris was an assistant professor at Columbia in 1968 during the student riots. Shortly afterwards, she met Kate Millett and read her book, *Sexual Politics*, which, with Betty Friedan's *The Feminine Mystique*, finally made Harris conscious that women were assumed to be capable of success in a narrower range of human endeavors than men, and so had been excluded from many professions, especially at the upper levels. Harris attended an early meeting of Columbia Women's Liberation in 1970. The group decided to count the number of women faculty in all departments by rank and to research the percent of women with Ph.D.s in all fields for the past 30 years. Concluding that there were plenty of qualified women available in all fields, and thus that there was no excuse for having only three women at the rank of full professor at Columbia, the group wrote a report and distributed it to all the members of the newly formed Columbia University Senate. They also sent a copy to *The New York Times*. After *The New York Times* published a story about the report in a Sunday issue, CWL was contacted by women at other campuses working along similar lines, and by Bernice Sandler, who was collecting data to use to sue colleges and universities for discriminating against women. These lawsuits forced many of the colleges and universities to institute affirmative action programs. Harris continued to collect data and testified before the House Subcommittee on Higher Education about sex dis-

crimination. The lengthy report she compiled was printed in the *Congressional Record* and edited as an article in the *Bulletin of the American Association of University Professors* in 1970. From 1970–1971, Harris served as chair of the Columbia University Senate committee on the status of women. She became the first president of the WCA (1972–1974), and from 1975–1979 was a director of the College Art Association, serving on its committee on the status of women from 1972–1976 and as committee chair from 1974–1976. She has also served as a consultant at three planning workshops for the National Museum of Women in the Arts, Washington, D.C. (1983–1984), and was co-curator (with Linda Nochlin) of the exhibition Women Artists, 1550–1950 (Los Angeles County Museum, et al, 1976–1977). In 1977, she and Nochlin were named *Mademoiselle* magazine's Women of the Year for the exhibition. In 1986, Harris was named Woman of the Year in the Arts by the Pittsburgh YWCA. She holds honorary degrees from Eastern Michigan University and the Atlanta College of Art. Harris earned her B.A. (1961) and Ph.D. (1964) from the University of London. (ABS)

Harris, Bertha (1937–2005) Novelist, editor, teacher and literary feminist, Harris coordinated and taught in the women's studies program at Richmond College, CUNY (Staten Island) in the 1970s. She also created a theory of lesbian literature, "The Purification of Monstrosity: The Lesbian as Literature," which she presented at the first symposium on homosexual literature at the Modern Languages Convention in NYC. Harris did editorial work at Daughters Publishing Co. Inc., and wrote three novels: *Catching Saradove* (Harcourt Brace and World, 1969), *The Confessions of Cherubino* (Harcourt Brace Jovanovich, 1972) and *Lover* (Daughters Inc., 1976, reprinted by New York University Press in 1993). At the time of her death, Harris was working on a fourth novel, *Mi Contra Fa*. Harris, who had one child, earned her A.B. from The Woman's College, University of North Carolina, and her M.F.A. from the University of North Carolina at Greensboro. Archives: The Sophia Smith Collection, Smith College, Northampton, MA. (ABS before death)

Harris, Fran (1909 – 1998) was a pioneer for women in broadcasting. She was the first woman radio newscaster in Michigan, on WWJ (1943); the first woman on television, WWJ-TV (1946); and the first woman to serve in broadcasting at the corporate level (WWJ, 1964). In 1986, Harris was the first woman and only broadcaster installed in Michigan's Journalism Hall of Fame; in 1987, she was the only woman to win the Governor's Award from the National Academy of TV Arts and Sciences in Detroit. From 1971–1973, she served as national president of Women in Communications, and in 1973 was selected by the secretary of defense to chair the Defense Advisory Committee on Women in Service. She was appointed to the Status of Women Commission by Michigan Governor Swainson in 1963, then served through 1976 with appointments by MI Governors Romney and Milliken. In 1977, Harris wrote *Focus Michigan Women, 1701 – 1977* under the auspices of the Michigan Women's Commission in honor of the International Year of the Woman. She was inducted into The Michigan Women's Hall of Fame in 1988. Archives: Radio and TV tapes of her broadcast scripts and her autobiographical tape are in the Archives of Broadcast Pioneers, Washington, D.C.

Harris, Helaine (1953 –) was a co-founder, with Nancy Adair, of Southwestern Female Rights Union and an original member of the Lesbian Come Out CR Group in Washington, D.C. In 1971, she was a member of the group first known as Those Women, and later as The Furies. Harris wrote several articles for *The Furies* newspaper, published between January 1972 and mid 1973. These include "Queen Christina: Lesbian Ruler of Sweden," published in the first issue, "Out of the O Zone," "All I Want," and "Fantasies of a Wheat Lady." She was co-author, with Coletta Reid, of "Away With Your Man-Visions," and with Lee Schwing of "I Was a Teenage Lesbian." Harris was also co-author with Schwing of "Building Feminist Institutions," published in the final issue. The article, considered controversial at the time, called for women to be entrepreneurs and start and own their own businesses as a means of gaining financial independence and supporting women who traditionally had difficulty finding employment. When The Furies experience ended, Harris, other ex-Furies members, and other women started Olivia Records, an attempt to put into practice the theories found in "Building Feminist Institutions." When the company moved to California, Harris stayed in Washington, D.C. With Cynthia Gair she began another feminist business, Women in Distribution, created to distribute (across the U.S. and internationally) the books and periodicals coming from the burgeoning women's presses of the period. In 1980, Harris co-founded (with Robin Moody) Daedalus Books, which specialized in remainder (bargain) books. She remains (2005) part owner of and is executive VP at Daedalus Books. (ABS)

Harris, Janice Hubbard (1943 –) began her teaching career at Tougaloo College, Mississippi, in 1969. She earned her Ph.D. at Brown University in 1973 and became a professor of literature at the University of Wyoming, where she taught the course Images of Women. In October 1975, Harris spoke at a Denver conference on the organization of women's studies programs. In 1976, she joined a team of six to teach Sex Roles and Society. Her books are *Edwardian Stories of Divorce* (Rutgers University Press, 1996) and *The Short Fiction of D. H. Lawrence* (Rutgers University Press, 1984). Articles include "Wifely Speech and Silence: Three Marriage Novels by H. G. Wells," (*Studies in the Novel*, 1994); "D. H. Lawrence and the Edwardian Feminists," (*The Challenge of D. H. Lawrence*, University of Wisconsin Press, Spring 1990); and "Our Mute Inglorious Mothers" (*The Midwest Quarterly*).

Harris, who has two children, earned her B.A. from Stanford University (1965). (ABS)

Harris, LaDonna (1931 –) A Comanche, Harris is a long-time national leader of various progressive issues. In 1967, she was invited by Lyndon Johnson to chair the National Women's Advisory Council of the War on Poverty. She was also asked to join the National Council of Indian Opportunity, but once the Nixon administration was in place, her work seemed blocked by Washington bureaucracy. She resigned in 1970. Harris was an original convener of the first NWPC meeting in 1971, and helped organize the Global Tomorrow Coalition and Women for Meaningful Summits. She has served on the national boards of NOW, Girl Scouts USA, Save the Children and the Independent Sector. She has founded several influential Native American organizations. She also served on Presidential commissions, including Carter's Commission on Mental Health, Ford's Commission on Observance of International Women's Year, and Johnson and Nixon's National Council of Indian Opportunity, and Clinton's Commission on the Celebration of Women in American History. (ABS)

Harrison, Evelyn Barstow (1910 – 2000) A native of the District of Columbia, Harrison was the first woman to graduate from the College of Engineering of the University of Maryland. In her government career, she was concerned with the legislation and policies governing federal employees and the job standards and tests covering their occupations at all levels. A cohort of Eleanor Roosevelt and a champion of equality for women and minorities, Harrison served on numerous boards, commissions and committees in and out of the government, including the President's Commission on the Status of Women, the District of Columbia Commission on the Status of Women, and the Women's Advisory Council on Poverty. She initiated and was the first director of the Federal Women's Program, concerned with providing equal opportunity for women in the federal government in hiring, promotion and training (1964–1969). The author of numerous articles about the employment of women in the U.S., Harrison received the Federal Woman's Award from President Kennedy. After retiring in 1971, she became a consultant to the general council of HUD, the Bicentennial Commission and the National Council of Negro Women. Archives: Papers will be offered to the Schlesinger Library, Radcliffe Institute, Cambridge, MA.

Harrison, Pat (1935 –) was co-founder (with Robin Tyler) of the first feminist comedy team, Harrison & Tyler, in the 1970s. They appeared in numerous demonstrations, including at a Raider/Rams football game where they ran out into the middle of the field and cheered for more athletic scholarships for women. Harrison was dragged off the field, which made headlines all over the world. The duo is credited with "changing women from being the object of humor to the subject of humor." Harrison & Tyler recorded two feminist comedy albums as well as the first lesbian record (single), "Angry Athis." Harrison is currently writing an autobiography on her life, as an orphan, later becoming a top model, a feminist performer and activist. She remains as radical as ever.   (ABS)

Hart, Deborah — was coordinator of NOW's first Take Back the Night action in 1975. NOW called all members to protest violence against women and "to claim the night and the streets as ours." Hart also called for vigils in memory of "our sisters who have died in the streets."

Hart, Lois (1933 – 1987) A former nun, Hart was a charismatic radical with a soft demeanor and clear vision who said "no" to many aspects of society. She spent time at the Millbrook, NY, estate of Timothy Leary and Richard Alpert before turning her attention to Indian mysticism (as a follower of Meher Baba), anarchism at Alternate University in NYC, gay liberation, feminism and lesbian feminism. She was part of the New Left and tried—with little success—to put the concerns of homosexuals on the New Left agenda. For Hart, the quest for sexual liberation was inextricable from sex-role liberation. She joined a Redstockings CR group in 1969 and was active with the GLF and its newspaper, *Come Out!* Hart wanted the GLF to support all movements, including the Black Panthers. She abandoned the GLF in 1970 to work with lesbian liberation. Hart was a key member of Radicalesbians, a separatist group of feminists in NYC committed to consensus and structurelessness. Hart re-emerged in the late 1970s to help organize a local group, the committee of lesbian and gay male socialists, one of many groups working to synthesize the revolutionary gay and lesbian feminist positions. Hart died of breast cancer in the 1980s. Hart lived in NYC for 22 years.

Hart, Virginia (1914 –) was a labor educator and the first woman appointed to a Wisconsin governor's cabinet. Exposed to the labor movement while working with the YWCA in Rochester, NY, in 1937, Hart became an education director of the Ladies Garment Workers Union in 1942 at a textile mill in Knoxville, TN. After receiving an M.A. in labor economics in 1945 from the University of Wisconsin, Hart became a full-time staff member of the UW School for Workers. As a teacher, she traveled the state giving classes for labor unions breaking barriers for women in the movement. From 1963 – 1973, Hart worked with labor activist Helen Hensler developing programs for women in labor and education. She was also part of the first AFL-CIO Coalition of Labor Union Women. In the early 1970s, Hart served on the Judicial Commission, which dealt with complaints against state judges. In 1973, she was appointed by Governor Patrick Lucey to the Department of Regulation and Licensing, making her the first female cabinet officer in Wisconsin. In 1975, Governor Lucey appointed Hart chair of the

Department of Industry, Labor and Human Relations. Hart retired in 1983, but continued her commitment to women's rights and social justice. In addition to her M.A., Hart holds a B.A. from the University of Rochester. She has two children. Archives: Tapes of interviews given for Documenting the Midwestern Origins of the 20th Century Women's Movement, an oral history project directed by Gerda Lerner, are at the University of Wisconsin System Women's Studies Library. Other tapes of interviews are at the Wisconsin Historical Society.   (ABS)

Hartman, Sylvia – See Cary, Sylvia

Hartmann, Heidi Irmgard (1945 –) An economist, researcher and activist, Hartmann was a graduate student in economics at Yale University in 1969 when she joined New Haven (CT) Women's Liberation. Hartmann demonstrated outside Mory's, a social club for Yale undergraduates that refused to admit women students, when they first arrived in 1969. Also in 1969, Hartmann was part of the Graduate Student Alliance, a group that met across departments and tried to pressure the university to help women students and hire women faculty. She taught a senior seminar on women and economics in the economics department and wrote much of the essay "The Unhappy Marriage of Marxism and Feminism." With Laurie Nisonoff, Hartmann helped organize a large conference on women and economics that was held at Yale Law School. She also helped found a women's caucus within the Union for Radical Political Economics. During this same time, Hartmann was a member of the Socialist Feminist Group I. She wrote her Ph.D. dissertation (1974) on the economic history of housework in the U.S. from 1900 to 1930, and went on to teach gender and political economy at the New School for Social Research in NYC for two years. There she wrote (and later published in 1976) an article on the origins of sex segregation in the labor market. Hartmann moved to Washington, D.C., in 1976. She was the founder, with Terry Odendahl, of the Institute for Women's Policy Research (1987). In the mid 1990s, she became active in the National Council of Women's Organizations and has served as vice chair since 2000. She is the recipient of a MacArthur Fellowship (1994) for her work in women and economics, and was awarded the Wilbur Cross Medal from Yale University. Hartmann, who has three children, holds a B.A. from Swarthmore College (1967) and an M.Phil. from Yale University (1972), as well as her Ph.D. from Yale.   (ABS)

Haskell, Jean Ruth (1932 –) A psychologist, Haskell helped organize marches on Washington for the ERA and reproductive rights. In the 1960s, she was involved in Women's Strike for Peace, WILPF and NOW. As a researcher, program developer and trainer in building women's confidence, she began training women to be effective in a man's business world in the late 1970s. Her publications include articles on women and corporate politics, the glass ceiling and career development. They have been published in *Management World, Executive Excellence* and *Training and Development Journal*. A human resources consultant, Haskell earned her doctorate from Temple University in 1976.   (ABS)

Hasper, Dido (1949 – 2004) A pioneer in women's health, Hasper helped women travel to Mexico for abortions in the mid 1960s when she was in high school. In the early 1970s she moved to Chico, CA, where local doctors would neither prescribe birth control to unmarried women nor provide abortions. She joined with a group of non-medical women who held women's health nights at the local free clinic, where they provided pregnancy tests and helped women go to the Oakland Feminist Women's Health Center for abortions. After her group learned medical self-help and menstrual extraction from the Oakland women, Hasper became an ardent advocate of self-help. In 1974, her group incorporated as Chico Feminist Women's Health Center, and in 1975 they founded their first clinic in Chico, providing self-help, reproductive health screening, birth control and abortion. Hasper headed the Chico Feminist Women's Health Center (later named Women's Health Specialists) as executive director from its founding in 1975 until 1992, and was active as founding director until her death. A great success with women in northern California and southern Oregon, the Chico clinic was boycotted by the local medical community. This and many other early problems were overcome and clinics were established in Redding, Sacramento, Santa Rosa and Petaluma. In the 1980s, there were three evictions prompted by anti-abortion pressure on landlords, as well as picketing and fire bombings. Hasper rallied the community and staff to combat these attacks and rebuild the burned-down facilities. Hasper was active with the Federation of Feminist Women's Health Centers, a nationwide group of women-controlled clinics, and is co-author of the manuscript, "Women's Health in Women's Hands," which became the basis of three books published by the Federation. Archives: Women's Health Specialists, Chico, CA.

Hathaway, Susan – moved to Washington, D.C., in 1968, and began working at *Off Our Backs*. She joined a group known as the "anti-imperialist women's house," and in 1971 the Lesbian Come-Out CR Group. After leaving *Off Our Backs*, Hathaway became an original member of The Furies, originally known as Those Women (1971). She went on to publish several articles in *The Furies* newspaper, including "The Price Is Wrong," which appeared in the first issue, January 1972, "That's Capitalism for You," "The Power and the Glory," and "It's Now or Never, Baby." She was co-author, with Lee Schwing, of "Corporate Capitalism: Survival of the Richest."

Havens, Catherine (1947 –) (also known as Catherine Havens-Brown and Catherine Havens-McColgan) was the first director of the Women's Center at the University of Connecticut (1974). Accomplishments under her tenure include hiring directors for the women's studies dept; advocating for the needs of all levels of women workers within the university and for the needs of women athletes; establishing a rape crisis service and other counseling services; advocating for the establishment of day care services and the enhancement of women's health services; and developing a full range of programs offered by the Women's Center. As director, Havens worked not only within the university but also with other women's organizations to advocate for women's issues and programs statewide. Earlier (1969 – 1972), Havens was a social worker at Associated Catholic Charities in Baltimore, MD, and a senior probation officer at the Connecticut Juvenile Court in Hartford, CT. In both positions, she worked with girls and young women and advocated for programs and support services to overcome the oppression they experienced because of their sex. On entering graduate school in 1974, Havens began her master's thesis, "A Feminist Perspective on Women in Prison" (Beers, Susan and Havens-Brown, Catherine, 1974). She also helped develop and team-taught the first women's studies course offered at the School of Social Work. Havens, who has published widely on women's issues in scholarly journals, is associate dean for academic affairs, School of Social Work, University of Connecticut. She holds a B.A. from St. Joseph College (1969), an M.S.W. from the University of Connecticut School of Social Work (1974) and a J.D. from the University of Connecticut Law School (1984). She has one child. (ABS)

Hawkins, Helen (1930 – 1989) Scholar and activist, Hawkins was fired up after reading Betty Friedan's *The Feminine Mystique* and set out to join a local NOW chapter, only to find there was none. She remedied that by becoming a co-founder and first president of San Diego (CA) NOW (1970). She was involved in the picketing of Pacific Bell in 1970, and in 1971 participated in the action that integrated the men-only U.S. Grant Grill. Hawkins also worked to educate the public about the ERA. A local Emmy-award winning TV producer at KPBS and a lecturer in women's studies at San Diego State University, she also served on several city commissions dealing with affirmative action and women's rights. In 1999, the Helen Hawkins Feminist Activist Awards and Lecture was created by the women's studies department at SDSU, with the support of Bill Hawkins, to honor the memory of Hawkins and her work. Hawkins was inducted into the San Diego Women's History Hall of Fame in 2005. Archives: Tapes of Hawkins' television interviews are at the UCSD Special Collections Library, CA.

Hawley, Nancy Miriam (1942 –) As a founder of the Boston Women's Health Book Collective, Hawley has helped empower women to take charge of their health and sexuality. Born into a family of social activists involved in progressive causes, Hawley sought other like-minded activists after entering the University of Michigan in 1960. She joined a group that was a precursor to the SDS and participated in the civil rights movement. Married by her sophomore year, she graduated in 1964 and then studied community organizing in the School of Social Work, where she organized graduate students to give them a voice with the faculty. She and her husband moved to Cambridge (MA) in 1966, where Hawley's consciousness about her own issues as a woman and a mother were raised by her friend Kathie Amatniek Sarachild, and by Hawley's reading of Simone de Beauvoir's *The Second Sex*. In May 1969, Hawley helped organize the first women's liberation conference in Boston. At that conference she presented the original workshops on women and their bodies. Out of that, weekly meetings took place, followed by research, mimeographed papers, and the book *Our Bodies, Ourselves*. The original book was self-published, in 1971, and 250,000 copies were sold through networking in less than two years. Major publishers became interested, and Simon & Schuster published the first edition in 1973. As of 2006, there are about two dozen translations and/or adaptations of *Our Bodies, Ourselves*-inspired books. "We didn't set out to write a book," says Hawley. "And we didn't set out to change the global conversation on women's health and sexuality. But that's what happened." Since 1976, Hawley has been in private practice as a psychotherapist, and, with her husband, Jeffrey Mc-Intyre, has a business coaching and consulting company specializing in leadership development and organizational change. (ABS)

Hayden, Casey (1937 –) (maiden and legal name, Sandra Cason) The daughter of a divorced, self-supporting woman in a small South Texas town, Hayden was active in Campus YWCA at the University of Texas, and through the Y, joined and became a leader in the sit-in movement at the University of Texas at Austin (1960). She was a founding member of SDS and SNCC. As a staff member of SNCC, reading *The Second Sex* and Doris Lessing's *The Golden Notebook*, Hayden began defining women politically in the context of the civil rights movement. A document reflecting this thinking was co-authored with several other women at an SNCC conference in 1964. *The Position of Women in the Movement*, a comparison of women's roles in the movement to African American roles in the larger society, is widely noted as the first writing about women from inside the young left. Following a summer organizing women Welfare recipients in Chicago, Hayden drafted a three-page document, finalized and co-authored with Mary King in November 1965, called "Sex and Caste: A Kind of Memo," based on their insights and experiences within the civil rights movement. It was sent to 40 women in SDS, the National Student Association, the Northern Student Movement, the Student Peace Union, and SNCC. A call to action, the paper incorporated the philosophy that personal relation-

ships have political components. It discussed gender as similar to the Hindu caste system, women and the problems of work, and women and personal relations with men, among other topics. Published in *Liberation* magazine of the War Resisters League (1966), the paper is seen as one of the salient documents of the second-wave women's movement. Hayden has published autobiographically in *Deep In Our Hearts, Nine White Women in the Freedom Movement* (Connie Curry et al, University of Georgia Press, 2000) and *Being Bodies, Buddhist Women on the Paradox of Embodiment* (Lenore Friedman and Susan Moon, Shambhala). (ABS)

Haymaker, Holley Galland (1944 –) (also known as Dr. Holley Galland) joined NYRF in 1969. After moving to Louisiana in 1971, she lobbied for the ERA and, since 1977, has been a volunteer with the Baton Rouge Rape Crisis Center as both a speaker and physician examiner. In 1989 she began the effort to open a Planned Parenthood Clinic in Baton Rouge. She also lobbied against the anti-abortion bills in the LA Legislature in 1990 and 1991, including committee testimony and local and national TV appearances, and worked at the Battered Women's Shelter as a physician and speaker, primarily in the late 1980s and into the 1990s. The medical director of the Baton Rouge school-based clinics, Haymaker is active with Planned Parenthood of Louisiana/Mississippi Delta region. In 1992, she and her husband were the host parents for Yoshi Hattori, a Japanese exchange student who was shot and killed in Louisiana. Following that tragedy, they became active gun-control advocates and founded Louisiana Ceasefire and Yoshi's Gift, a fund to support advocates. Haymaker, who has two children, earned her B.A. from Smith College (1967); her M.A. from Columbia Teachers College (1969); her M.D. from Tulane University (1976); and her M.P.H. from Johns Hopkin's Bloomberg School of Public Health. (ABS)

Haywoode, Terry Levey (1938 –) discovered feminism in the early 1970s when she joined an older women-sponsored CR group. She then became part of the National Congress of Neighborhood Women (Brooklyn, NY), a group focused on supporting activism, on helping working class and poor women to define their own feminism, and on meeting local women's needs for education and employment. Haywoode was one of a small group of feminist scholar/activists who helped develop a neighborhood-based college program for local women. Says Haywoode, "Our conference presentations influenced the curriculum of some women's studies departments to be more inclusive of the perspective of working class women." Haywoode's related publications include *Neighborhood Women Putting It Together* (Office of Self Help and Neighborhood Development, HUD/NCNW, 1983); "Working Class Feminism and Higher Education: The NCNW College Program," published in *Learning Our Way: Essays on Feminist Education*, edited by Charlotte

Bunch and Sandra Pollack (Crossing Press, 1983); "World of Our Mothers: College for Neighborhood Women" (with L. Scanlon), published in *Women's Studies Quarterly* (Spring 1987); "Working Class Women and Neighborhood Politics," published in *Readings in Contemporary Sociology*, edited by J. DeSena (Kendall and Hunt, 1989); and "Working Class Women and Local Politics: Styles of Neighborhood Organizing," published in *Research in Politics and Society*, Vol. VI, edited by Nancy Klenowski and Gordana Rabrenovic (JAI Press, 1999). Haywoode, who has also been active in the civil rights and peace movements, has two children. She holds a B.A. from Brooklyn College, an M.Phil. from the CUNY Graduate Center, and a Ph.D. from CUNY. (ABS)

Hazlewood-Brady, Anne (1925 –) A poet and writer starting a new life after raising five sons, Hazlewood-Brady moved to NYC in 1969 and became an active independent in the women's movement. In 1970 she worked with June Arnold and Sheila Delaney to found the Women's Center (it was Hazlewood-Brady who came up with the $1,000 for an office), and worked in the office of Women Strike for Equality. She is the author of the poem "We Took to the Streets Like a River," which commemorates the 1970 Women's Strike for Equality march, and took photographs of the Statue of Liberty action. She moved to Maine in 1971 and became a registered lobbyist for the ERA, which passed in ME in 1973. She attended the International Women's Year Conference in Mexico City (1975), and was a delegate from ME to the National Women's Conference in Houston (1977). Hazlewood is a founder of Maine Women in the Arts (1977); was poetry editor of *Maine Life* (1979 – 1985); and is the author of six books of poetry. She also wrote "Matriot/Patriot" for Catherine East. Hazlewood-Brady is a graduate of Vassar College (1946). (ABS)

Healy, Anne Laura (1939 –) An artist and retired professor at the University of California, Berkeley, Healy was a founding member of AIR Gallery (1970 – 1972), where she served as panel moderator and curator of various exhibits. She was an editor of *Heresies #5: The Great Goddess* in the 1970s, and from 1981 – 2003 served as a teacher, professor and mentor of women at U.C. Berkeley. President and member of the San Francisco Arts Commission (1989 – 1996), Healy sponsored public art by women artists. In 1995 she served as a delegate to the United Nations 4th World Conference on Women (Beijing, China), representing the Women's Caucus for Art, and in 1997 was curator of an exhibition of five Chinese women artists at U.C. Berkeley, Worth Ryder Art Gallery. Healy earned a B.A from Queens College, City University of New York (1962). Her art has been exhibited internationally, and is in permanent collections of the Museum of Contemporary Crafts (NYC); Allen Art Museum (Oberlin, OH); and the Art Museum of South Texas (Corpus Christi), among others. (ABS)

Healy, Regina (1937 –) Beginning in 1969, Healy and Diane Lund worked on drafting, getting filed, lobbying for and ultimately defending from repeal a bill that forbade discrimination in Massachusetts public schools on account of gender. Signed into law in 1971, the bill was, at least in part, a model for the Federal Title IX. It ended the practice of separate classes for boys and girls and allowed girls to enroll at Boston Latin. In 1976, Healy and Lund founded a law firm taking cases primarily in the area of family law. The two also taught Women and the Law at Northeastern Law School and Harvard. Healy has been on the boards of legal services organizations serving primarily poor women for 20 years. From 1965 – 1968 she was a community organizer in Baltimore working with African Americans, American Indians and very low-income people of all races. From 1973 – 1977 she was a commissioner at the MA Commission Against Discrimination. In 1977, she served as a delegate to the IWY Convention in Houston. Healy, who has two children, earned an undergraduate degree from Boston University (1958) and a J.D. from Suffolk Law (1971). (ABS)

Heath, Mariwyn (1935 –) Founder of ERAmerica and an authority on the ERA, Heath established ERA offices with BPW/USA and the International Women's Year Commission, and was consulted on the ERA by both the Ford and Carter administrations. She was chair of the Ohio Women's Policy and Research Commission and chair of its women and law committee, and was chair of BPW's PAC, covering congressional races in the U.S. Heath served on the National Council on the Future of Women in the Workplace and was a charter member of Ohio Women, Inc. She has worked on credit for women and women's employment, and was the first woman elected president of the Presidents Club of Dayton (OH). (ABS)

Hedgeman, Anna Arnold (1899 – 1990) Raised by parents and grandparents who were former slaves, Hedgeman became the first black woman to graduate from Hamline University (St. Paul, MN, 1922). In 1948, Hamline awarded her an Honorary Doctorate degree. Hedgeman attended the NOW organizing conference in 1966 and served on NOW's first board. She was the first African American to serve in a New York City mayor's cabinet (1954 – 1958). A civil rights activist, she was the only woman on the executive committee of the 1963 March on Washington, and is credited with recruiting over 40,000 churchwomen to participate. She was also part of the leadership that fought for the successful passage of the Civil Rights Bill (1964). Hedgeman is the author of *The Trumpet Sounds* (Holt, Rinehart, 1964) and *The Gift of Chaos* (Oxford University Press, 1977). Her portrait hangs in the National Gallery in Washington, D.C.

Hedges, Elaine (1927 – 1997) was an educator and professor of women's studies at Towson University. An activist in women's studies in the early 1970s, Hedges was a charter member of NWSA and a founder, with Sara Coulter, of the Towson University women's studies program. Active in the Feminist Press, Hedges was a scholar of women's art, crafts and, especially, quilt-making.

Heide, Wilma Scott (1921 – 1985) A Registered Nurse, sociologist and teacher, Heide was the third national president of NOW (1971 – 1974), and served as chair of the board and national secretary prior to that. She was also the founder of the Pittsburgh chapter of NOW. In 1973, she helped form the Women's Coalition for the Third Century and served as the organization's VP. Heide was a force behind the *Pittsburgh Press* case that ended sex-segregated help-wanted ads, and led the action that eventually won a hearing for the ERA in the Senate. Heidi held visiting professorships at the University of Massachusetts (1974 – 1976), Wellesley College (1974 – 1975) and Goddard College (1978 – 1980), and was a professor of women's studies and innovative and experimental studies, and director of the women's studies department at Sangamon State University (1980 – 1982). A civil rights activist who marched in Selma, AL, with Martin Luther King Jr., she earned her R.N. from Brooklyn State Hospital (1945), her B.A. (1950) and Litt. M. (1955) from the University of Pittsburgh, and her Ph.D. from the Union of Experimenting Colleges and Universities (1978). She had two children. Archives: Schlesinger Library, Radcliffe Institute, Cambridge, MA.

Height, Dorothy (1912 –) A caseworker for NYC's Welfare Department, Height began her civil rights career in 1937 when she joined the National Council of Negro Women. In 1957, she was elected president of NCNW, a post she held for 40 years. During her tenure, she fought aggressively for equal opportunity for all women. In 1944, Height joined the staff of the YWCA, where she remained active until 1977. She is credited with ensuring the success of the YWCA's mission to provide equal opportunity and facilities for women of all cultures and nationalities. During the peak of the 1960s civil rights movement, Height organized Wednesdays in Mississippi, which brought together black and white women from the North and South to create a dialogue. Height encouraged President Eisenhower to desegregate schools and President Johnson to appoint African American women to positions in government. Inducted into the National Women's Hall of Fame, Height received the Citizen's Medal from President Reagan, the Medal of Freedom from President Clinton and the Congressional Gold Medal from President George W. Bush. Height holds an M.A. from New York University. (ABS)

Heilbrun, Carolyn G. (1926 – 2003) Author, professor and administrator, Heilbrun was the first director of the Institute on Women and Gender at Columbia University (1986 – 1988) and she served as director of the women's studies program from 1988 – 1989. She was the founding president of the Virginia Woolfe Society (1976 – 1978), and wrote nine scholarly books, including *Toward a Recognition of Androgyny: Aspects of Male and Female in Literature* (1973); *Reinventing Womanhood* (1979); and *Writing a Woman's Life* (1988). She also wrote a biography of Gloria Steinem, *Education of a Woman* (1995), and numerous articles that looked at women's writings from a feminist standpoint. In addition, Heilbrun published more than a dozen mystery novels, some under the pseudonym Amanda Cross. The mysteries offered social commentary on the changing roles of women in society. In a 1997 book, *The Last Gift of Time: Life Beyond Sixty*, Heilbrun wrote of taking her own life, and in fact did commit suicide, according to her son. She had a B.A. from Wellesley (1947); an M.A. from Columbia (1951); a Ph.D. from Columbia (1959); and an Honorary Degree from Smith (1989). In addition to her son, she had two daughters. Archives: The Sophia Smith Collection, Smith College, Northampton, MA.

Heins, Marilyn (1930 –) A pediatrician, Heins started her medical training when fewer than 400 women were accepted to medical school in the entire country. In 1965 she became the first woman to head a department at Detroit Receiving Hospital. In 1971 she became the first woman to serve first as assistant, then as associate dean at Wayne State University School of Medicine, where she established the Office of Student Affairs. She served on many medical school and university committees, including the University Council and its policy committee, the Faculty Senate, and the Commission on the Status of Women, of which she was chair (1973 – 1975). She sat on a joint coordinating council on a medical education committee to consider opportunities for women in medicine, the Advisory Council to the Radcliffe Programs in Health Care, and a committee to write child-abuse legislation for the state of Michigan. She was the first woman to chair the Group on Student Affairs of the Association of American Medical Colleges, and the first woman to chair the medical education committee of the American Hospital Association. She also served on the editorial board of the *Journal of the American Medical Association*, and the National Board of Medical Examiners. With several other women, she met with the officers of the Association of American Medical Colleges and persuaded them to establish the Office of Women. Heins is the author of *ParenTips* (Developmental Publications, 1999), and writes a parenting column for the *Arizona Daily Star*. (ABS)

Heinz, Maria T. – See Mangual, Maria T.

Held, Virginia (1929 –) At a convention of the American Philosophical Association in the 1970s, Held and a number of women formed a caucus to discuss the status of women in philosophy and as philosophers. "This provoked much snickering and disdain among the male philosophers at the meetings," Held says. But the women soon "came to see how exciting it was to take up philosophical topics from a feminist point of view, and how valuable to do so with an interested and sympathetic audience instead of a hostile and defensive one." The caucus grew into the Society for Women in Philosophy. Held also helped organize the Society for Philosophy and Public Affairs and was active in the Democratic Socialists of America, where she constantly brought women's issues to the male-dominated table. As a professor at Hunter College, Held fought for classes in feminist philosophy and for the inclusion of feminist scholarship in other courses. Her writings have included dozens of feminist articles, the book *Feminist Morality: Transforming Culture, Society, and Politics* (University of Chicago Press, 1993), and the edited collection *Justice and Care: Essential Readings in Feminist Ethics* (Westview Press, 1995). She is a member of the Hunter College Women's Studies Collective, which produced the textbook *Women's Realities, Women's Choices* (Oxford University Press, 1983), and is a contributor to *Singing in the Fire*, edited by Linda Alcoff, which recounts the early experiences of women philosophers. Held, who has two children, earned her Ph.D. from Columbia University in 1968.   (ABS)

Heldman, Gladys (1922–2003) is credited with being the inspiration and power behind women's professional tennis. Heldman began playing tennis at age 25, competing in the U.S. National Championships and at Wimbledon. In 1953, she started *World Tennis* magazine and used it not only as a forum for the sport's news and views, but also as a platform to build her own authority and credibility in women's professional tennis. In 1970, Heldman gathered nine of the top women players, including Billie Jean King and Rosie Casals, and formed their own pro tour, which later became the Virginia Slims tour. A graduate of Stanford University, she had two children and was inducted into the Tennis Hall of Fame in 1979.

Helly, Dorothy O. (1931 –) In the mid 1970s, Helly helped establish the women's studies program at Hunter College, City University of New York, and from 1977 – 1983 served as an associate dean. She taught both introductory and senior seminar courses for the program, chaired a faculty interdisciplinary seminar on the study of women, and became part of the collective that wrote the textbook *Women's Realities, Women's Choices: An Introduction to Women Studies* (1983). While an ACE fellow (American Council on Education), she served as a special assistant to Marguerite Ross Bennett (the first black woman vice chancellor for academic affairs at CUNY), and was a founder, with Barbara Omolade, of Friends of Women's Studies. In 1987, the group called for a faculty-development seminar on balancing the curriculum for gender, race, ethnicity and class. Helly and Omolade were two of its three co-facilitators (1987 – 1988). Helly remained with the seminar, which was awarded a national AAUW Award for progress in equity,

until 1998. She introduced a monthly seminar at CUNY for all faculty interested in these curriculum issues, and in 1994 – 1996, with a Ford Foundation grant, organized national panels on changes in the disciplines brought about by women's studies and ethnic and area studies. She also became an adviser to the National Center for Curriculum Change (Towson College, MD). Helly is co-editor of *Gendered Domains: Rethinking Public and Private in Women's History* (1992). Helly retired as a professor of history and women's studies at Hunter and the CUNY Graduate School in 1999. Since that time she has been a member of the board of directors of the Feminist Press at CUNY and of the steering committee of a seminar titled Women Writing Women's Lives. Helly earned an A.B. from Smith College (1952), an A.M. from Radcliffe College (1953) and a Ph.D. from Harvard (1961). Helly has one child.   (ABS)

Hemingway, Beverly L. (1926 –) was one of the first members of the Palo Alto, CA, chapter of NOW (1973), and served as membership chair. The chapter successfully proposed a policy change to the local school board that the sex-segregated shop and home economics classes be changed to open enrollment. The chapter also participated in the nationwide Alice Doesn't …. Day (1975), and picketed Sears to protest hiring discrimination. Says Hemingway, "A few other women and I cut up our Sears credit cards and were photographed handing them to the store manager." During the mid 1970s, Hemingway worked in a women's bookstore and helped organize a women's credit union. She was also a volunteer at a newly-organized Women's Resource Center, which helped women with employment needs. During the 1950s and 1960s, she was active in local and state political campaigns as a member of the LWV. Hemingway, who has two children, is a retired medical librarian.   (ABS)

Henden, Carol Mae (1939 –) (also known as Carol Garrigues) Director of the Los Angeles NOW Center (1972 – 1982), Henden was also chair of its affirmative action committee. Although she is not a lawyer, many lawsuits were filed by NOW under her direction, including Hughes Aircraft and Southern California Edison. Henden also helped women locate feminist attorneys. She holds a B.A. and teaching credentials from UCLA, and has three children. Archives: Her affirmative action files will be donated either to National NOW or the Schlesinger Library, Radcliffe Institute, Cambridge, MA. (ABS)

Henderson, Hazel (1933 –) An author and activist, Henderson founded Citizens for Clean Air, a largely women-based organization of mothers fighting for their children's health, for which she earned the Citizen of the Year Award (1965) from the New York County Medical Society. She is the author of several books on overhauling economics to account for women's unpaid work. These include *Creating Alternative Futures: The End of Econom-*

ics (1978); *The Politics of the Solar Age* (1981), which theorized a feminist economics; *Paradigms in Progress: Life Beyond Economics* (1991); *Building a Win-Win World: Life Beyond Global Economic Warfare* (1996); and *Beyond Globalization: Shaping a Sustainable Economy* (1999). Henderson, who coined the term "love economy," was educated in private schools in Britain. She holds Honorary Doctorates from Worcester Polytechnic University (1975), Soka University (Japan, 1999) and the University of San Francisco. She has one child. Archives: Florida Community College, Jacksonville, FL. (ABS)

Henes, Donna (1945 –) (also known as Donna Trugman) was a member of one of the first CR groups in NYC (1968 –1972), and of the editorial collective of the Goddess issue of *Heresies* magazine (1975–1977). She was also a member of a feminist performance group, and with other women toured the U.S., Canada and Italy (1979–1982). From 1975 forward, Henes has been a producer of public rituals dedicated to the female divine. She has written three books on the subject, the newest being *The Queen of Myself: Women Stepping into Sovereignty in Midlife* (2004). She is also author of and performer on a CD: *Mythology, The Matriarch & Me* (1988). A fighter for civil rights, Henes spent the summers of 1963–1964 doing voter registration in the South for Student Nonviolent Coordinating Committee, and continues to be active in both the civil rights and peace movements. She holds a B.S. (1970) and M.S. (1972) from CCNY. (ABS)

Henneman, Nadine Edith (1936 –) was the founder of the Hammond, LA, chapter of NOW in the late 1960s and served as it president. In addition, she founded the Hammond area ERA coalition (1973–1974); served on the funding task force for LA ERA United (1973); and was a LWV representative to the Louisiana Legislature (1974). Describing herself as somewhat reserved and shy, Henneman says she was surprised and proud to find herself in Washington, D.C., in the late 1970s carrying a poster and marching for the ERA. Also a supporter of reproductive freedom, she met with a group of Unitarian ministers "and other like-minded people" in New Orleans in the late 1960s to locate places where women could get safe abortions. Later, Henneman escorted women through picket lines at a New Orleans abortion clinic. A member of the ACLU, Henneman worked to support women's issues within that group. A social worker and therapist, she was also a member of Feminist Therapists from 1975–1978. Henneman, who has three children, holds an R.N. degree from St. Luke's Episcopal Hospital in Davenport, IA (1957). She also earned a B.S. from Southern University in 1975, then an all-black school where she was the only white person, and an M.S.W. from Louisiana State University, Baton Rouge, in 1977. (ABS)

Hennessee, Judith (1932 –) VP of NY NOW under Dorothy Crouch and Judy Wenning, Hennessee worked on a license challenge to WABC-TV that focused on sexism in the media and forced the station to make changes. The FCC ordered that the station post jobs previously reserved for men, many of which women had never heard about before. And the station took a serious look at how women were portrayed "as secretaries, maids and never as intelligent movers and shakers." Hennessee is author of the first biography of Betty Friedan, *Betty Friedan: Her Life* (Random House, 1999). During the McCarthy period, she was secretary to Fred Friendly, producer of "See It Now." Hennessee, who has a B.A. from Barnard (1953), lost her eyesight in 2000, but is still communicating using a computer that tells her the letters she types. Archives: Duke University, Durham, NC. (ABS)

Hensler, Helen (1919 – 2001) helped organize a Wisconsin conference for union women (1970), the first AFL-CIO conference about women in the labor movement. A participant in the founding convention for the National Coalition of Labor Union Women (1974), Hensler later founded the Milwaukee chapter. She also served on the Wisconsin Governor's Commission on the Status of Women. In 1977, she became the first woman president of the Office and Professional Employees International Union, Local 9, breaking long-standing barriers for women within the labor movement. In addition to her work with OPEIU, Hensler worked for the Smith Steel Workers Local 19806 and the Iron Workers Local 471 before retiring in 1993. Hensler's commitment to the labor movement continued after her retirement when, she served as a business representative for OPEIU Local 9.

Herman, Alexis (1947 –) Named the 23rd U.S. Secretary of Labor by President Clinton (May, 1997), Herman was the first African American ever to be nominated for the position. Herman began her career as an advocate for minority women's employment at Catholic Charities immediately upon graduating from Xavier University in 1969. In 1977, President Carter tapped Herman to be director of the Labor Department's Women's Bureau, the youngest person ever to serve in that position. While at the Women's Bureau, Herman pressured Delta Airlines and Coca-Cola to hire female professionals. In 1981 she formed A.M. Herman & Associates, advising state and local governments on labor markets until 1989. Herman has also served as chief of staff and vice chair of the Democratic National Convention (1992) and national director of the Minority Women Employment Program of R-T-P, Inc., where she established programs to place minority women in white collar and nontraditional jobs. After President Clinton's election in 1992, Herman was appointed assistant to the President and director of the White House Public Liaison Office.

Herman, Debra (1950 –) transferred to Yale University from Vassar College as a sophomore in 1969. Choosing to study women's history, Herman arranged for Gerda

Lerner to speak to a graduate student history group at Yale. Later, Herman formally asked the Yale history dept. to add women's history to its course offerings, but was rebuffed. Herman joined New Haven (CT) Women's Liberation and worked to support the Women v. Connecticut lawsuit that sought to legalize abortion. She was a key mover behind a petition calling for an end to sex discrimination at Yale, and was a co-creator (1971) of a booklet, titled "She," that was designed to orient incoming Yale women. Under her picture in the class of 1972 yearbook, Herman listed as her future occupation "feminist," rather than historian, because she "relished the idea of the word appearing in a Yale publication!" As a graduate student at Stanford, she became involved in the struggle to bring a woman to the history faculty. She also advocated for more women students as a member of the dept. admissions committee. With other graduate students, Herman helped found the Women's Research Network, which later evolved into the Center for Research on Women. As an instructor at the University of Georgia (1979), she sued under the Equal Pay Act to end employment discrimination. The case went to court, but Herman did not prevail. Herman is the author of "Does Equality Mean Sameness? A Historical Perspective on the College Curriculum for Women with Reflections on the Current Situation," published in *Feminist Visions: Toward a Transformation of the Liberal Arts Curriculum* (University of Alabama Press, 1984). She earned her B.A. from Yale University (1972), and her M.A. (1973) and Ph.D. (1979) from Stanford University. (ABS)

Herman, Irene Sofian (1934 –) A broadcaster and print journalist (now retired), Herman was the first president of Raleigh, NC, NOW (1971), where her first project was to desegregate help-wanted ads. From 1973 – 1974 she was assistant state coordinator of CT NOW and worked for the passage of the ERA. She also participated in Eastern Region NOW's "No Myth America" action as Wonder Woman from Connecticut. From 1974 – 1976, Herman was CT NOW's state coordinator. As a member of the YWCA board, Herman helped create the safe homes project and later served at the Rape Crisis Center in Stamford, CT. She represented the Stamford mayor on the Tri-State Metropolitan Regional Council on Domestic Violence, and created a confidence-building and public-speaking course for women. President of the Midday Club in Stamford, Herman was awarded the club's first Lillian Moran Award for Community Service (1982). Herman holds a B.A. and has two children. Archives: University of Connecticut, Stamford, CT. (ABS)

Herman, Sondra (1932 –) was asked to teach women's history at the University of California, Santa Cruz, in 1972. Because no one had ever taught the class before, Herman had few materials, and no easily available anthologies. She nonetheless put together a successful curriculum, and later moved to De Anza College, where she introduced

and then taught women's history for 24 years. She also taught women's history to high-school teachers at San Jose State for one quarter. In the early 1970s, Herman became curious about the relationship between Swedish Social Democracy and women's equality. With the support of the Fulbright Commission, she was first a visiting and then an affiliated scholar at the Institute for Research on Women and Gender at Stanford, where she pursued this interest. Out of this work came Herman's article, "Dialogue: Children, Feminism and Power: Alva Myrdal and Swedish Reform, 1929 – 1955," published in the *Journal of Women's History 4* (Fall 1992).

Hernandez, Aileen Clarke (1926 –) The only woman appointed by President Lyndon Johnson in 1965 to the first EEOC, Hernandez has spent a lifetime working to improve the political and economic status of minority groups and women. A native of Brooklyn, NY, she moved to California in 1951 to become an organizer and later education and public relations director for the Pacific Coast Region of the International Ladies Garment Workers Union, where she worked for 11 years. Before accepting the EEOC post, Hernandez was assistant chief of the California Division of Fair Employment Practices. Elected as executive VP at the founding conference of NOW in 1966, Hernandez declined that position but later agreed to serve as VP West, soon after resigning from the EEOC and launching her urban consulting business, Aileen C. Hernandez Associates, in San Francisco in 1967. She has chaired the national advisory committee of NOW, served on the board of NOW LDEF, and co-chaired a NOW task force on minority women and women's rights. She facilitated sessions at the founding meeting of the NWPC in 1971 and at the 1973 NOW-sponsored International Feminist Conference held in the Boston area. She also founded and was active in Black Women Organized for Action, Bay Area Black Women United, The National Hook-Up of Black Women and Black Women Stirring the Waters. She has served on numerous boards and commissions at national and local levels, including The Urban Institute, National Urban Coalition, Citizens Commission on Civil Rights, Ms. Foundation for Women, Bay Area Urban League, National Advisory Board of the American Civil Liberties Union, African American Agenda Council, and Center for Governmental Studies. She chaired the California Council for the Humanities, the Center for the Common Good, the Coalition for Economic Equity, and the board of the Working Assets Money Market Fund. In 1996, Hernandez helped create and became chair of the California Women's Agenda, a virtual network of over 600 women's groups organized to implement the Platform for Action adopted by 189 nations at the Fourth International Conference on Women held in China. Hernandez holds a B.A. from Howard University, an M.A. from California State University at Los Angeles, and an Honorary Doctorate in Humane Letters from Southern Vermont College. Archives: Her papers will be donated to the Howard University archives in Washington, D.C. (ABS)

Herr, Lois Kathryn (1941 –) (also known as Lois Kerkeslager) Author, educator and executive, Herr was a founder of the women's rights committee at Bell Telephone Laboratories in Naperville, IL (1970), and a founding member of the AT&T Women's Alliance (1971). She was also a member of NOW's AT&T task force (1971 – 1973) and played a major role as a link between the task force and women within the company. In her book *Women, Power and AT&T: Winning Rights in the Workplace* (Northeastern University Press, 2003), Herr documents how the EEOC-AT&T case revolutionized corporate affirmative action. During the EEOC-AT&T case, she published "The Private Line," a newsletter circulated within AT&T covering feminist news and information (1970 – 1973). She made radio, television and other public appearances on behalf of NOW from 1968 – 1971, and was a moderator of The Impact of Women's Liberation on Technical Communications at the International Technical Communications Conference (1973). She has been a member of The Women's Alliance in Lancaster, PA, from 1990 forward (2004), and served as president from 1994 – 1996. Herr has a B.A. from Elizabethtown College (1962), an M.A. from the University of Pennsylvania (1963), and an M.B.A. from Fordham University (1974). (ABS)

Herron, Kathleen M. (1947 –) was one of the first two women law clerks for the Multnomah County (OR) Court (1974), and worked for one of the first woman judges in OR, Jean Lewis. Herron was a founder (1976) of the first all-women law collective in Portland, OR, the Community Law Project. The project, which lasted for 10 years, did legal work for people with low incomes, lesbians fighting for child custody, and protesters of all kinds. The office filed the first suit in OR on sexual harassment in the workplace, and acted as attorney advocates for many women harmed by domestic violence. Herron was also a member of the National Lawyers Guild for many years, working on issues such as violence against women, poverty and minority rights, and concerns of particular interest to lesbians. Herron, who has one child and is a teacher, consultant, mediator and writer, holds a J.D. (ABS)

Herschberger, Ruth M. (1917 –) Poet and playwright, Herschberger is the author of *Adam's Rib*, a book of feminist essays published in the U.S. in 1948. Says Herschberger, "The publishers soon withdrew the U.S. edition from print. Subjects of birth control and abortion could not be included due to religious opposition. It was the first book to extol the clitoris as empowerment." *Adam's Rib* was also published in England and Scandinavia in 1954 under the pseudonym Josephine Langstaff, and chapters have appeared in several anthologies. The author of two books of poetry, *Nature & Love Poems* (Eakins Press, 1969) and *A Way of Happening* (1948),

Herschberger has had poems published in several literary magazines and anthologies, including the feminist *We Become New: Poems by Contemporary American Women*, edited by Lucille Iverson and Kathryn Ruby (Bantam Books, 1975). She has received several awards, including a Hopwood Award for Poetry, the Midland Authors Award for Poetry, and the Harriet Monroe Memorial Prize, as well as a Rockefeller grant for verse writing and a Bollingen Grant for translations of Vladimir Mayakovsky, with Marina Prychodko. Born in Philipse Manor, NY, she attended the University of Chicago (1935 – 1938) and Black Mountain College in North Carolina (1938 – 1939). She studied theater at the University of Michigan (1941) and playwriting at the Dramatic Workshop of the New School for Social Research, NYC (1942 – 1943). (ABS)

Herschfang, Ann – See Forfreedom, Ann

Hersh, Blanche Glassman (1928 – 1995) is the author of *The Slavery of Sex: Feminist Abolitionists in America* (University of Illinois, 1978), which analyzes the antebellum women's movement of the 1840s and 1850s. Hersh received an M.S. in chemistry at age 19, then married and raised three children. Active in the LWV, Hersh returned to school in 1964 to earn an M.S. in urban history and a Ph.D. in women's history from the University of Illinois, Chicago. She then founded the women's studies dept. at Northeastern Illinois University. She was a founder of the Great Lakes Women's Studies Association, and a member of several organizations for professional women.

Hershman, Lynn L. (1941 –) An emeritus professor at the University of California, Davis, A.D. White Professor at Cornell, as well as a filmmaker and artist, Hershman was part of the Women's Building in Los Angeles (1974), and part of the first group of women exhibiting in museums. As a young artist, she (like many women artists of that time) had difficulty finding galleries that would show her work. To overcome this, she created three fictitious by-lined critics, "each of whom had her own particular style." Often they would disagree with each other in print, but they would almost always mention the work of Lynn Hershman in their columns. Soon Hershman had enough printed reviews to show the galleries, which then accepted her work. Says Hershman, "Was it ethical? The work remained the same and the dialogue engendered community interest. Without critical support, even fictional support, my work would not have had the opportunity to be seen." Hershman, who has one child, earned a B.S. from Case Western Reserve and an M.A. from San Francisco State University. Archives: Stanford University, Palo Alto, CA. (ABS)

Hewat-Stone, Janet – See Stone, Janet

Hickey-Reiff, Maureen Anne (1939 –) (also known as Maureen Reiff) was a co-founder of Chicago Catholic

Women in the mid 1970s and served on its board for 10 years. Describing herself as a "recovering Catholic," Hickey-Reiff was also a 10-year board member of the National Assembly of Religious Women, and served on the regional board of American Friends Service Committee, Midwest Region, for two years. Hickey-Reiff coordinated the first Women Church Conference (Chicago, 1983), and co-founded the Women Church Convergence, a coalition of national and local Catholic women's organizations. In addition, Hickey-Reiff served as program chair and co-chair for two major Women Church conferences (Cincinnati and Albuquerque, 1987 and 1993, respectively), which thousands of women attended. She is (2005) working on a project, Women Against Violence Everywhere, involving the radical voices of women of faith. Hickey-Reiff, who has two children, holds a B.A. and an M.A.   (ABS)

Hickox, Peg – See Rapp, Peg

Hicks, Frances Marie (1942 –) has worked with NOW, for the ERA, to take sexism out of textbooks, and to implement Title IX. From 1974 – 1976, she served as president of the Bay Area NOW chapter in Clear Lake City, TX. In 1977, she was administrative assistant to Helen Cassidy, the co-chair of the IWY conference. From 1974 – 1980, Hicks participated in a statewide NOW textbook task force reviewing public school books for sexist content; lobbied for the ERA; and worked to start a women's studies department and women's center at the University of Houston at Clear Lake City. From 1973 – 1975, she organized a campaign to implement Title IX in Friendswood, TX, schools by filing a complaint on behalf of her daughter Jeanne, who was in grammar school. As a result of the pressure of the pending complaint with HEW, several qualified teachers were appointed as principals, and several girls' teams were added to the high-school roster. Hicks continued her Title IX work as NOW state coordinator for Title IX, leading CR groups in small towns in Southern TX (1975 – 1980). In the early 1980s, Hicks started a NOW chapter in Mt. Vernon, VA, and worked to promote women's issues on Democratic Party platforms. From 1985 – 1990, Hicks held a political appointment on the Fairfax County Childcare Council. Since 2000 she has served on the Fairfax County Commission for Women, primarily in the area of domestic violence. She teaches (2005) courses on women and public policy and sociology at northern VA colleges. Hicks, who has three children, holds an A.A., a B.A., an M.A. and an A.B.D.   (ABS)

Hilder, Allie Jane – See Light, Allie

Hill, Cindy Judd (1926 –) One of the six founders of Pittsburgh area NOW (1967), Hill attended NOW's first national conference in Washington and was a delegate to each succeeding conference through 1991. As PR director of the Pittsburgh chapter in 1968, Hill changed its name to Greater Pittsburgh Area Chapter. In 1969 she and several other members picketed the newspapers to desegregate the help-wanted ads, and she became VP of GPA NOW. In 1970, as PR director, she programmed 12 hours of talk show for WJAS featuring feminists. She became a charter member of South Hills NOW (1971), and has since served in many capacities, including three terms as co-president. Hill lobbied the weather bureau to include men's names for hurricanes (1972); published an article in the *Christian Science Monitor* on the ERA (1980); and served as an ERA missionary to the Mormons in Salt Lake City (1981). In 1982, she left her family to spend six months in Chicago during the countdown for the ERA. She participated in countless marches and pickets, and for 25 years had numerous letters to the editor published supporting the feminist movement.   (ABS)

Hill, Mary Lou (1916 –) joined the LWV in 1951, serving on the Minneapolis LWV board from 1952 – 1961 and as executive director from 1961 – 1964. She was executive assistant to Governor Rolvaag from 1964 – 1967, during which time she served as vice chairman of the Governor's Commission on the Status of Women. For three years (1964, 1965, 1966), members of the Commission represented MN at the citizens advisory committee on the status of women in Washington, D.C. At the 1966 meeting, NOW was organized. As a member of the Governor's Commission, Hill assisted in the editing and managed the printing of its materials, including "A Woman's Guide to Minnesota Laws" and "A Working Code for Household Employment." Hill became a member of WEAL in the 1970s and served on its board for several years. Since 1996, she has been a member of the MN LWV action committee, serving as the long-term healthcare member and representing the LWV on issues related to older people and long-term care. Hill, who has three children, holds a B.A. from the University of Minnesota.   (ABS)

Hill, Myrna (1944 –) became active to a minor degree in the student and civil rights movements as a college student tutoring ghetto kids in 1963. By 1967, as a new teacher, she began learning about black nationalism at the Brooklyn African Teachers Association, which took part in the struggle for community control of black schools in New York. In the women's group of the Black Anti-Draft Union, Hill began learning about the anti-colonial struggles in other countries. "By 1969," she says, "I had concluded that African Americans' best bet for transforming our lives was to make common cause with others for revolution, so I joined the Young Socialist Alliance, the youth group of the SWP." After attending a Redstockings meeting at the invitation of Maxine Williams, Hill was "instantly hooked." Also in 1970, Hill, with SNCC's Fran Beale, Eleanor Holmes Norton and Maxine Williams, formed the short-lived Third World Women's Alliance, an African American feminist group. After a period of writing news briefs for *Majority Report* and contributing poetry to *Azalea*, Hill moved to Los Angeles, where she first joined the 9to5 clericals group, and briefly contributed to its local newsletter. Then Hill discovered a large clerical workers local led by an African American female president and a 100 percent African American female executive board. She became involved with issues of concern to the union's mostly female membership, and remained a union activist until her retirement. (ABS)

Hillinger, Edith Gabrielle (1933 –) Born in Berlin, Hillinger fled with her family from Germany in 1937 and lived in exile in Istanbul and Ankara, Turkey, until 1948. That year, they emigrated to NYC. In 1971, Hillinger, a painter, joined Women in the Arts, working at all levels in the organization making fliers, sending out invitations and press releases, hanging shows. In 1975, she participated in the exhibition Works on Paper/Women Artists at the Brooklyn Museum, and in 1976 was awarded the International Women's Year Award by the Women Artists Historical Archives, New York. In 1976, Hillinger was Artist in Residence at the MacDowell Colony (Peterborough, NH) and Montalvo Center for the Arts (Saratoga, CA). Her work, which has been exhibited nationwide, is in private collections throughout the United States and Europe. Hillinger holds a four-year certificate in painting from the Cooper Union School of Art (1964) and earned a B.A. from New York University (1976). (ABS)

Hillyer, Barbara Davis (1934 –) A professor of women's studies and human relations, Hillyer is a feminist activist, women's studies scholar, writer and theorist in feminist disability studies. In 1971 and 1972, she organized an Assembly for Equal Rights, the first in Oklahoma, and spent the years from 1970 to 1976 lobbying and working toward the ratification of the ERA and toward exposing of its enemies. A founding member and officer of the OK WPC and the Norman WPC, she spoke in schools, churches and universities on the history, literature, and roles of women, and was presented with the Women of the Eighties award of the OK WPC. Working with women faculty members from the University of Oklahoma in 1974, she wrote a proposal that started the University's women's studies program, and became the first director in 1976. A founding member of the NWSA, Hillyer founded the Oklahoma Women's Studies Association and worked with others to found the South Central Women's Studies Association (1977 – 1980). She served on the coordinating councils of all three for several years. From 1972 – 1985, she organized and coordinated five statewide conferences on women's issues and published books of essays from three of them. She was a member of the Governor's Commission on the Status of Women and several statewide women's organizations. Her book, *Feminism and Disability* was nominated for a Pulitzer Prize and received the Emily Toth award for Best Women's Studies book in 1993. In addition to serving on the boards of a number of women's and disability organizations, she facilitated a support group for parents of child-

ren with disabilities from 1985 – 1989. Her teaching focused on cultural values from feminist perspectives. She holds a B.A. from Rockford College, (1956), an M.A. from Claremont College (1957), and a Ph.D. from the University of Wisconsin, Madison (1962). (ABS)

Hilton, Sue (1950 –) was a member of New Haven (CT) Women's Liberation from 1972 – 1974. In New Haven, she was involved in SheWoman Theatre, a gay/straight discussion group, organizing new women's classes, and staffing the women's center. She also lived in a women's collective household. From 1976 – 1978, in Santa Cruz, CA, Hilton organized presentations on body image and women of color, and helped organize a conference by/for women in prison. Fired for being a lesbian, Hilton was backed by groups that organized a public response and eventually won an apology, another job and back pay from her employer. Hilton was also involved in "civil disobedience that was environmental and anti-war, but done in an explicitly feminist manner" at Diablo Canyon Nuclear Plant and Lawrence Livermore Labs, among others. Archives: June L. Mazer Lesbian Archives, West Hollywood, CA. (ABS)

Hinderer, Eve (1947 –) was a founding member of NYRW in 1967, where she helped formulate the principles of CR (*e.g.*, The Personal Is Political). While she was involved in early women's liberation, Hinderer was active in the anarchist community as it existed at that time on NYC's Lower East Side. In 1968, she organized a second CR group with Judith Ann Duffett. When meetings at the Southern Christian Leadership Conference office on East 11th St. in NYC grew too large, Hinderer dropped out, feeling strongly about the importance of small-group interaction as an organizing tool. In 1971 she joined the lesbian separatist community in lower Manhattan; three years later she withdrew, acknowledging her bisexuality. Hinderer holds a B.A. from Brooklyn College (1985). Archives: The Sophia Smith Collection, Smith College, Northampton, MA. (ABS)

Hirchert, Mary Jane Elizabeth (1946 –) joined the AAUW in Micbigan in the 1970s and worked as a fundraiser for the association and an interviewer for girls in alternative education. She also served as treasurer of the Livingston County, MI, chapter of NOW for five years in the 1980s. A social worker with a B.A. from Marygrove College (1968), Hirchert worked for George McGovern's presidential campaign. She has two children. (ABS)

Hirsch, Gilah Yelin (1944 –) Artist, professor, writer, facilitator and theorist, Hirsch joined a group of feminist artists brought together by June Wayne in Los Angeles in 1970. That group grew to become the Los Angeles Council of Women Artists, which in turn was the mother organization of Womanspace and later Womanhouse. Hirsch's works were in the first exhibitions. She also created a compendium of adjectives and adverbs that males used to critique female work. One of the council's first actions was to protest the lack of women artists exhibited at the Los Angeles County Museum of Art. Hirsch and other members met with many museum directors and curators, which "definitely made an enormous difference." In 1971, Hirsch took a seminar on the business aspects of being an artist, conducted by June Wayne. Hirsch named the seminar "Joan of Art" and took over the teaching the following year with two other women. Hirsch then took a tenured position in the art dept. of California State University, Dominguez Hills, where she implemented a semester course based on the seminar. This was, to her knowledge, the first university course dealing with the business aspects of being an artist. In 1974, Hirsch presented the work of (then unknown) Canadian artist Emily Carr to the College Art Association in Washington, D.C. She also published several articles on Carr (*Feminist Art Journal*, Summer issue, 1976; and *Women's Studies: An International Journal*, Vol. 6, 1978). Born in Montreal, Quebec, Hirsch holds a B.A. from UC Berkeley (1967) and an M.F.A. from UCLA (1970).   (ABS)

Hirsch, Jeanne Louise - See Ingress, Jeanne Hirsch

Hirsch, Lolly (1922 – 1987) (also known as Lura Grace Hirsch) was a homemaker, mother of five, activist, speaker, author and publisher. A member of the DAR, the Federation of Feminist Women's Health Centers, NOW and NARAL, she had knowledge and expertise in women's health, including gynecological self-help for women, feminist perspectives on childbirth, and issues of population. She served as an organizer and coordinator at the First International Childbirth Conference, Cloonan Middle School, Stamford CT, in 1973. She attended the United Nation's World Population Conference in Bucharest, Romania, as a press representative of New Moon Communications, Inc., and was a delegate from the Global Gynecological Self-Help Clinics to the Population Tribunal, August 1974. With her daughters, Hirsch founded New Moon Publications, Inc., later to become New Moon Communications, Inc., which published: *Women: To, By, Of, For and About; The Monthly Extract: An Irregular Periodical; The Witch's OS;* and *Proceedings from the First International Childbirth Conference.* Her writings include "Practicing Health Without a License," published in *New Women's Survival Sourcebook* (Knopf, 1975), "Directions for a Non-Traumatic Abortion" and "The Breeders: Technology's Effect on our Mothers and Babies from the Woman on the Delivery Table's Perspective." Hirsch was the only white person picketing against social discrimination with the NAACP in Stamford, CT, in the 1960s, and was a member of Fair Play for Cuba, SANE Nuclear and other peace and disarmament groups. The film "No Going Back – A Pro-Choice Perspective" was dedicated (posthumously) to her. Born in Chicago, Hirsch had two years at Antioch College.

Hirschberg, Vera Hinde (1929 –) A journalist, press secretary, speechwriter and public affairs officer, Hirschberg was the only woman on the White House speechwriting staff from 1972 – 1974. From 1974 – 1976, she was director of the White House Office of Women's Programs, which helped bring into being legislative initiatives important to women, including Title IX in education and the ERA. Later, as a speechwriter and public affairs officer for NASA, she managed the first flight of a woman (Sally Ride) aboard the space shuttle as a crew-member. Says Hirschberg, "As a speechwriter for the NASA administrator, I wrote whenever possible and appropriate praise for women in science and technology, and of the importance of women entering those fields." She has two children and holds a B.A. from Hunter College (1949).   (ABS)

Hirschstein, Susan (1946 –) A member of the Queens, NY, NOW chapter, Hirschstein lobbied for the ERA, and in 1972 became a member of Nassau (NY) NOW, running the legislative committee. She also formed the Nassau NOW PAC, and interviewed candidates on issues pertinent to women's rights to determine if the group would endorse them or not. Hirschstein helped start the WPC on Long Island, NY., serving as head of the Caucus for several years, and became a pro-choice activist and speaker. This led to a position with Family Planning Advocates, which in turn led to a job as the director of public affairs at Planned Parenthood of Nassau for six years. Hirschstein then spent 12 years as the director of residential services of the Nassau County Coalition Against Domestic Violence. "I worked and lobbied for fairer treatment of women in violent relationships, ran the Safe Home, and started three federally funded transitional housing projects for women fleeing violent situations," says Hirschstein. She also worked as a consultant to a childcare agency, and was a co-founder of her Nassau school district's Title IX committee. Hirschstein holds an M.S. degree and has two children.   (ABS)

Hirshman, Rhea (1947 –) came into the women's movement in the early 1970s through participating in Women v. Connecticut, which challenged the state's anti-abortion laws, and through writing for *Sister*, the New Haven, CT, feminist journal. An educator with Women's Health Education, which brought women's health issues to schools and community groups, Hirshman became a founding board member of Women's Health Services in 1974. Focusing on education and public speaking, she coordinated the speakers bureau of the New Haven Women's Center, taught courses there, hosted the weekly feminist radio show "Sound Sisters," and worked with the Theatre of Light and Shadow. Hirshman also brought the first women's studies courses to Choate Rosemary Hall, where she taught from 1969 – 1977. From 1978 – 1980, Hirshman was the first full-time coordinator for the Connecticut Coalition Against Domestic Violence. She later co-founded Golden Thread Booksellers, New Haven's feminist bookstore. Hirshman is (2005) a freelance writer and editor, teaches women's studies at the University of Connecticut, Stamford, and writes a women's issues column for the *New Haven Register*. She holds a B.A. from Wells College (1968), as well as a master's degree from Wesleyan (1975). (ABS)

Hite, Shere (1942 –) A cultural historian now living in Paris, Hite is internationally recognized for her work on psychosexual behavior and gender relations. Her research, which revealed the truth about women's sexuality and their attitude toward family, was often attacked by the press and traditionalists, who looked for ways to discredit the author and her findings. Hite is best known as the author/researcher of *The Hite Reports*. The first is *The Hite Report: A Nationwide Study of Female Sexuality* (Macmillan, 1976). From 1978 – 1988, she was a lecturer in female sexuality at New York University. Other books include *The Hite Report on Male Sexuality* (Knopf, 1981); *Women and Love: A Cultural Revolution in Progress* (Knopf, 1987); *The Hite Report on the Family: Growing Up Under Patriarchy* (Bloomsbury, 1994); and *The Hite Report on Hite: Voice of a Daughter in Exile* (Arcadia Books, 2000). She is also author of *Sex and Business: Ethics at Work* (Financial Times – Pearson, 2000). Hite says she decided to leave the United States after some of the conservative media frightened publishers off publishing her reports in the U.S. in the late 1980s. A group of famous feminist writers defended her with a press conference, but much of the media did not report on the conference, preferring instead to call Hite a charlatan. Other works include *Women as Revolutionary Agents of Change* (1994); *Women With Women* (1997); *Oedipus Revisited* (2004); and *The Shere Hite Reader* (Seven Stories Press, 2005). Hite has two degrees in history, a Ph.D. in Clinical Sexology and a Ph.D. in Gender and Politics. Archives: Library of Congress, Washington, D.C. (ABS)

Hively, Janet McNeil (1932 –) was a member of the Twin Cities Women's Liberation Group (1968 – 1969). In 1970, she left a leadership position in the LWV to help establish the first chapter of NOW in MN, chairing the convening group through the process of developing bylaws and setting up a nominating committee. Early actions included picketing Sears Roebuck for gender discrimination in pay and promotions, and the Rochester, MN, newspaper where women were still identified only as "Mrs. John Smith" as late as 1972. The group also organized for the first Women's Strike for Equality day (1970), and joined with members of WEAL to desegregate the Oak Grill in MN's largest department store, Dayton's, which had been reserved for men only at lunch. In 2000, Hively initiated the Vital Aging Network, a grassroots liberation movement to combat ageism and create a new vision of what it means to grow old. She has also been active in the peace movement, particularly in the design and development of the Peace Garden in Minneapolis. Hively, who has two chil-

dren, earned a B.A. from Harvard/Radcliffe and an M.A. and Ph.D. from the University of Minnesota. (ABS)

Hixson, Allie Corbin (1924 –) is the founding chair of the ERA summit (1992). In 1969, Hixson became the first woman to earn a Ph.D. in English from the University of Louisville, but was denied a full-time teaching position. The dean of the college said he had full-time salaries only for men, and that Hixson already had a job as a wife and mother. After researching the second-class Constitutional status of women, and hearing congresswoman Martha Griffiths speak at a 1975 national AAUW conference in Seattle, WA, Hixson became a feminist and full-time volunteer for the ERA. She co-organized the Kentucky ProERA Alliance to help Indiana ratify the ERA, and later traveled the country lecturing and organizing for the ERA. She was chair of Kentucky's International Women's Year coordinating committee; led KY's delegation to the National Women's Conference in Houston in 1977, and served as one of five vice chairs with Bella Abzug. She was appointed to the National Women's Conference continuing committee, to the AAUW ERA ad hoc committee, and was delegated speaker for the AAUW at the national ERA rally in Washington. Says Hixson of her work for the ERA, "I am most proud of initiating the three-state strategy." A founding member of KY OWL, she helped pass displaced homemakers legislation in her state, and helped poor farm women in danger of losing their farms through death or divorce. She has also been active in civil rights. Hixson, who has three children, has a B.A. from Oklahoma A&M and an M.A. from the University of Louisville, in addition to her Ph.D. (ABS)

Hixson, Mary Emma (1950 –) was a founder of the Women's Law Caucus at the University of Louisville School of Law (1972), and was also active with the National Conference on Women and the Law (1972 – 1974). President of Louisville NOW from 1974 – 1975, Hixson started its lesbian task force, and was also active in the Kentucky Women's Political Caucus. In 1976 she moved to Washington, D.C., and joined the Feminist Radio Network, serving as a radio producer and VP in 1977 and 1978. While there, she covered the NWPC and the Houston National Women's Conference, and also produced one of the first media reports on the Karen Silkwood case. After moving to Missouri in 1978, she became active with the Missouri Women's Network. Relocating to MN in 1984, she was a YWCA volunteer and member of the board from 1996 – 200), and served as president of the board from 2001 – 2002. Also active in civil rights, she has been executive director of the Coalition to End Grand Jury Abuse (1976 – 1978); director of the Campaign for Human Development, Prisoner Advocacy and Education Project (1978 – 1980); deputy director, Missouri Commission on Human Rights (1980 – 1984); and Civil Rights Director, City of Minneapolis (1984 – 1994). Hixson earned her B.A. from Transylvania

University, and her J.D. from the University of Louisville School of Law. Archives: Heartland Lesbian Archives, Spring Valley, WI. (ABS)

Hlass, Cynthia Welch (1944–2003) worked for six years to get the ERA ratified in Georgia. She served as president of Atlanta NOW (1973–1974) and board member (1974–1975). She was also legislative coordinator for GA NOW (1974–1975) and a member of the international feminist committee (1974–1975). Hlass, who had two children, graduated from Mercer University in 1977. She worked as a real estate broker in Georgia for 30 years. Archives: Georgia State University Library, Atlanta, GA.

Hoagland, Sarah Lucia (1945–) A professor of philosophy and women's studies, Hoagland successfully lobbied for the first feminist philosophy class at Vassar College (1973). While teaching the class, she developed her arguments about masculinity and femininity, "that they are not empirical concepts but conceptual frames normalizing male domination and obscuring female resistance." Hoagland also served as adviser to the Women's Liberation Union, a student organization at the college (1973–1974). At the same time, she began attending the newly formed Society for Women in Philosophy. Moving to the University of Nebraska (1974–1977), she was a panelist on "Women and Mental Health" (1975), a segment of the Nebraska Educational Television series "Nebraska Women and the Law." As chair of the Lincoln Coalition Against Rape (1976–1977), Hoagland lobbied every congressman and thus helped pass the law that included acknowledging that wives could be raped. In 1975, she became part of the committee that founded the women's studies program at the University of Nebraska and served as the first chair of the ad hoc committee for women's studies. She was a member of the women's studies board from 1976–1977, a member of the AAUP's committee W(omen) (1976–1977), and served as NWSA regional coordinator that year. As part of the Lincoln Legion of Lesbians (1976), Hoagland worked with Julia Penelope to prepare for IWY in New England, and was regional editor of "Matrices," a lesbian research newsletter that Penelope founded. At the same time, she served as regional coordinator for the NWSA, was a member of the committee on women for the AAUP, and served as program chair, Midwest Feminism Conference on Political Thought and Action (1977). Also in 1977, Hoagland went to Northeastern Illinois University to teach feminist philosophy. Says Hoagland, "I became part of the women's studies faculty, joined the women's studies and women's services boards, and came out publicly, immediately. I believe I was the second out gay academic in the Midwest." Her books include *For Lesbians Only: A Separatist Anthology*, co-edited with Julia Penelope (Onlywomen Press, 1988); *Lesbian Ethics: Toward New Value* (Institute of Lesbian Studies, 1988); and *Re-Reading the Canon: Feminist Interpretations of Mary Daly* (co-edited with Marilyn Frye,

Penn State Press, 2000). Hoagland, who holds a Ph.D., teaches and lectures on issues affecting the lesbian community. Archives: The Lesbian Herstory, Brooklyn, NY, and the Ohio Lesbian Archives, Cincinnati. (ABS)

Hobson, Tina Clapp (1929–) was an early activist with Federally Employed Women. A graduate of Stanford University, Hobson was told when she first applied for a government job that they were saved for male heads of households—which, in the late 1940s, she did not find odd. She then married in 1951, had two children, and divorced in 1969. After taking a civil service exam, Hobson went to Washington, D.C., where she worked as the first director of the Federal Women's Program, established by President Johnson. Appointed executive director, she began collecting data on the status of women in government, which was used in the formation of FEW. In 1977, she was named director of the first Office of Consumer Affairs of the U.S. Dept. of Energy. There she developed a nationwide education program credited with generating federal support for Sun Day in 1978 and Earth Day in 1980. When Hobson retired after 20 years of government service, she was the first government senior executive to become executive director of the Solar Lobby and Center for Renewable Resources. (ABS)

Hoch, Helen (1941–) (also known as Helen Hoch Kotsonis) A faculty member at Jersey City State College in 1970, Hoch joined the women's collective that was designing a women's studies program and women's center. She and a colleague from the psychology department designed two courses on female sexuality and psychology that they team-taught for almost 10 years. Hoch also taught other women's studies classes, and from 1976–1986 was director of the women's center. In 1976, Hoch helped organize a contingent of marchers for the Washington, D.C., demonstration in support of the ERA. In 1978, she was invited by the Jersey City police dept. to become a member of its faculty, giving lectures on police and their attitudes toward women. In following years, Hoch served as a member of NJ governor Kean's Commission to Integrate Race, Class and Gender into the Curriculum, and as chair of the New Jersey College and University Coalition on Women's Education. She has run many large conferences for high-school students featuring non-traditional careers for women, and continues to teach women's studies. Hoch, who has one child, holds an Ed.D. (ABS)

Hochman, Sandra — A poet and revolutionary, Hochman has written 22 books. She is author of the novel *Walking Papers* (1971), a humorous account of the difficulties of fulfilling all the roles of a woman in a world that assigns different roles to men and women. In 1972 she was one of the first literary voices for feminism. Her poems earned her a Yale Younger Poets Award, and she produced a weekly poetry program on local public radio. In 1972, Hochman wrote, directed and produced a biting and humorous film on the women's movement "Year of the Woman," which was shown at the Fifth Avenue Cinema in NYC. Hochman later made it into a musical. The film disappeared for 30 years, as film companies who viewed it considered it too hot to handle. In 1985 the film was shown again at Lincoln Center, raising $1 million for the Schlesinger Library. Hochman was a co-founder of Women in the Arts and Women in the Cinema, and founder of a feminist program for children called "You're an Artist Too." Hochman was arrested many times for demonstrations with Flo Kennedy. She has written her memoir, *The Brick King's Daughter*, which she expects to publish. "Everything I've done was done as a poet," she says. "I see poetry and humor as political tools." (ABS)

Hoddersen, Guerry (1945 –) (also known as Anne Guerry Durham) A socialist feminist, Hoddersen attended the founding meeting of Women's Liberation-Berkeley (1969), the first feminist organization in the San Francisco Bay Area. In Seattle in the summer of 1970, she joined Radical Women, and was elected president in 1973. As an organizer of RW, Hoddersen was directly involved in its wide-ranging issues, including its successful fight for passage of the state ERA. The group also formed an historic alliance of organized labor and feminists, the Coalition for Protective Legislation, which drafted and lobbied for non-discriminatory health and safety work rules. In addition, Hoddersen helped draft and lobby for a feminist divorce reform bill that was used in Washington State's no-fault divorce act (mid 1970s). In 1973, Hoddersen co-founded Action Childcare Coalition, which mobilized the community to provide high-quality, free childcare for poor women. That same year, she entered the non-traditional trades, becoming one of the first women in Seattle to drive a truck for UPS. In the late 1970s, she urged the membership of Teamsters Local 174 to oppose City Initiative 13, which would have destroyed legal protections for Seattle's lesbians and gay men. Subsequently, her union became the first in the Northwest to publicly support sexual minorities. Hoddersen later became the first woman to run for office in the 7,000-member local, running on a platform calling for an end to sex, race and age discrimination in the trucking industry and the union. Hoddersen has also been an active supporter of the Native American movement, and in 1979 took part in the founding meeting of the Northwest Indian Women's Circle. In 1983, she became the national secretary for RW's sister organization, the Freedom Socialist Party (FSP), and ran for state representative as a party candidate in 1998. In the 1980s and 1990s, she was very involved in anti-Nazi organization through the United Front Against Fascism. She continues (2004) to be an active socialist-feminist organizer and writer on international issues, economics and popular culture, and is (2004) international secretary of the Freedom Socialist Party. Hoddersen earned her B.A. from the University of California, Berkeley. (ABS)

Hoekje, Marjory Nelson – See Nelson, Marjory

Hoff, Marilyn Gayle (1942 –) (also known as Marilyn Gayle was co-editor and co-publisher (with Barbary Katherine) of *What Lesbians Do* (1975). Her other books include *Free Ride*, a novel about lesbians. (These books were written under Hoff's nom de plume, Marilyn Gayle.) Hoff also taught women's studies and women's literature at Portland State University (1973–1974), and from 1972 –1978 wrote and sang lesbian/feminist songs for various gigs. In 1977, she wrote, illustrated and published a collection of her songs, *Dyke Music*. Hoff has also been active in the civil rights, anti-Vietnam War, environmental, peace and anti-nuclear movements. She holds a B.A. from Macalester College (1964) and an M.A. from Syracuse University (1968). (ABS)

Hoffberg, Judith A. (1934 –) A librarian, archivist, lecturer, curator, art writer, editor and publisher, Hoffberg helped form the Art Libraries Society of North America. A critical issue for women librarians in the 1960s and 1970s was that they were being paid "thousands of dollars less than men," says Hoffberg. Through the association "we fought that issue and helped to change things." Hoffberg also worked with Judy Brodsky to formulate the best way to create the WCA, and helped establish the first chapter in Los Angeles. Hoffberg holds a B.A., M.A. and M.L.S. from UCLA. Archives: UCLA Arts Library Special Collections, University of California, Los Angeles. (ABS)

Hoffert, Iris E. (1941 –) In 1969, Hoffert co-founded, with Naomi Penner, the first NOW chapter on Long Island (NY) (called Nassau NOW in 2003). She served as treasurer and wrote its newsletter until the mid 1970s. As a social-studies teacher, Hoffert taught about women's rights and the women's movement "as much as I could within the curriculum," and for a few years taught a course called The American Woman to 12th graders. She retired in 1996 after teaching for 34 years. (ABS)

Hoffman, Dorothy Tennov – See Tennov, Dorothy

Hoffman, Joan – See Robins, Joan Ellen

Hoffman, March – See March, Artemis

Hoffman, Merle (1946 –) A social psychologist, author, speaker, publisher, political organizer and pioneer in the delivery of women's health services, Hoffman founded one of the first abortion clinics in the country, Choices Women's Medical Center, in 1971 (formerly, Flushing Women's Medical Center). She later added Choices Mental Health Center to address the psychological impact of rape, incest and domestic violence, and to meet women's general psychiatric and psychological needs. In 1975, she founded STOP (Second Treatment Option Program), the first ambulatory breast cancer program specializing in an interdisciplinary model of patient care. A lifelong pro-choice activist, Hoffman organized the first pro-choice civil disobedience action at St. Patrick's Cathedral in New York City (1989), and was a co-founder of the National Abortion Federation and founder of the New York Pro-Choice Coalition. She produced, wrote and directed the documentary film, "Abortion: A Different Light" (1982), and in 1986 produced and hosted a 30-minute news and talk show, the first feminist cable talk show, "MH: On the Issues." She also spearheaded attacks against the Hyde Amendment, banning Federal funding for abortions, and "convinced Congress to pass legislation requiring the accurate labeling of over-the-counter birth control." In 1992, Hoffman began work on Choices East, the first outpatient feminist medical center in Russia, and led Russian feminists in delivering an open letter to Boris Yeltsin demanding better, safer choices for birth control. She was the publisher and editor of *On the Issues: The Progressive Women's Quarterly* (1982 – 1989). Hoffman is the recipient of numerous awards, including recognition by the Department of Corrections of NYC NOW; the Women's Health Care Services, Ecovisions; the Community Action Network, the National Victim's Center, and the Congress of Racial Equality. She has a B.A. from Queens College (1972) and did her doctoral work at CUNY Graduate Center. Archives: Salle Bingham Center, Duke University, Durham, NC. (ABS)

Hoffman, Nancy (1942 –) Active in the civil rights movement of the early 1960s, as well as the anti-war movement, Hoffman found the women's studies classroom "the place where politics and intellectual interests could come together." She was a founder of the women's studies programs at the University of California, Santa Barbara (1969 – 1970) and Portland State University (1970 – 1972); and in 1974 held a Gilman Fellowship, Carnegie Foundation, Women and Career Options. She is the author of *Women's "True" Profession: Voices from the History of Teaching* (the Feminist Press, 1981) and was co-editor, with Florence Howe, of *Women Working: Stories and Poems* (the Feminist Press, 1979). She also edited two volumes of *Women's Studies Quarterly: Women, Girls and the Culture of Education,* and *Women, Race and Culture.* From 2002 – 2005, Hoffman chaired the board of directors of the Feminist Press, the oldest women's press in the U.S. She writes on education policy and women's studies and has been particularly engaged in improving access to and success in college for inner-city high-school students. For many summers, she co-convened the academic environment unit of HERS Summer Institute for Women in Higher Education Administration. She is (2005) VP, Youth Transitions Cluster, Jobs for the Future. Hoffman holds a B.A. (1964) and a Ph.D. (1971) from the University of California, Berkeley. (ABS)

Hoffnung, Michele (1944 –) (also known as Michele Hoffnung Garskof) A professor of psychology with an emphasis on the psychology of women, Hoffnung has been director of women's studies at Quinnipiac University, Hamden, CT, since 1982. She began her work for women in the late 1960s as a member of CR groups in Ann Arbor, MI. From 1969 – 1970, she was a member of Washington, D.C., Women's Liberation, working primarily on issues surrounding childcare. She started The Children's House, a parent cooperative day care center. She also organized a cooperative childcare service at Center Church Parish House, New Haven, CT, in 1970, and from 1972 – 1976 was an organizer of the State Street Cooperative Child Care Center in New Haven. During the 1970s, Hoffnung was a member of the New Haven Socialist Group and New Haven Women's Liberation. From 1983 – 1984, Hoffnung was a Mellon Scholar, Wellesley College Center for Research on Women, and from 1984 – 1985 participated in the Mellon Social Science Seminar, Wellesley College Center for Research on Women. From 1985 – 1986, Hoffnung was at Yale on a Mellon Visiting Faculty Fellowship, and from 1985 – 1999 took part in the Anna Wilder Phelps Social Science Seminar, Wellesley College Center for Research on Women. She has been a Visiting Fellow in women's studies at Yale University since 2000, and in 2003 received the Ruth Steinkraus-Cohen Memorial Outstanding Woman of Connecticut Award. Hoffnung is the editor of *Roles Women Play: Readings in Women's Liberation* (Brooks/Cole, 1971), and author of *What's a Mother To Do: Conversations on Work and Family* (Trilogy Books, 1992). Hoffnung, who has three children, earned her B.A. from Douglass College and her Ph.D. from the University of Michigan. (ABS)

Hogan, Elisabeth Woodbridge (1932 – 1985) was the first Massachusetts director of NOW and served as co-chair of NOW's ERA lobby for passage through the state legislature. Hogan was a consultant to the Governor's Commission on the Status of Women during Governor Dukakis' first term in office in MA. In addition, she was a member of WEAL and American Women in Radio and Television. Through the Eastern MA chapter of NOW, she provided one-on-one consultations with women considering sex discrimination complaints. From 1971 – 1982, Hogan served as editor and publisher of *The Equal Employment News* (originally called *WomanPower*), a monthly publication for Affirmative Action executives. From 1972 – 1974 she wrote, produced and broadcast a daily news feature, "Women at Work," for WEEI-CBS Boston, and in 1974 a "History of Women" series for the CBS Radio Network. Hogan was also president of Betsy Hogan Associates, one of the first management consulting groups in the U.S. focused on the cultural, legal and organizational issues of working women. She conducted equal employment opportunity seminars for large public and private-sector organizations and lectured on the subject at the Sloan School of Advanced Management at MIT. Hogan, who had two children, graduated from Vassar College in 1953.

Hogan, Margaret P. (1940 –) (also known as Margaret P. Haddad) was a founding member of the faculty of El Paso Community College (1971 – 1976) and worked to make the curriculum and faculty more sensitive to women and Hispanics. In 1973, Hogan served as an officer in the American Association of Women in Community/Junior Colleges, now referred to as AAWCC, and started a chapter in El Paso, TX. A member of the El Paso WPC, she served as president (1975 – 1976), and was an advocate for the ERA, civil rights and abortion rights. Hogan was on the board that designed the first community college leadership program for women, the National Institute for Leadership Development Instruction at Chandler-Gilbert Community College. Retired, Hogan, who has three children, continues (2005) to mentor young women about the challenges of their work environments. She holds a B.A., M.A. and Ed.D.   (ABS)

Holcomb, Coletta Reid – See Reid, Coletta

Holder, Anne H. (1937 –) began working to establish a rape crisis center in El Paso, TX, in 1973. She was the chief fundraiser for three years; mediated a "rather painful fight" between the group that felt such a center was needed and the police chief and his officers, who were opposed; and interfaced with doctors, judges and a variety of city officials to make the center a reality. She also spoke about rape and the larger feminist questions to a number of civic organizations, college classes and church groups. She worked with the WPC for several years, winning Woman of the Year in Public Welfare in 1975 and Woman of the Year in 1976. From 1977 – 1979, Holder helped establish a women's center at the YWCA. Holder, who has two children, holds two B.A. degrees, two M.A. degrees and an A.B.D. She also published a paper on the reason for women's almost universal disadvantaged status in the *Berkeley Journal of Sociology*.   (ABS)

Hole, Judith (1939 –) (also known as Judith Hole Suratt) A researcher at CBS News in 1970, Hole was assigned to write an internal research report for producers and correspondents on the women's movement as a background report for the August 26, 1970, Women's Strike for Equality—a sort of "who's who" of both individuals and organizations in the women's movement. At the time, CBS had a department that re-purposed works such as this—for example, the research report "who's who" of civil rights had been turned into a book. Thus, Hole's work on the women's movement (co-written with Ellen Levine) became the *Rebirth of Feminism* (Quadrangle Books, 1971), a standard text for women's studies programs for many years. In addition to her work on the book, Hole was one of a group of activist CBS women who worked with management to make significant changes in the company's employment practices regarding women. Hole attended Middlebury College and holds a B.A. from S.M.U. (1961).   (ABS)

Holladay, Wilhelmina Cole (1922 –) A student of art history at Elmira College (NY) and then in Paris, Holladay developed an interest in art by women that was intensified when she and her husband, Wallace, visited the Prado in the 1960s and saw the works of 17th century Flemish painter Clara Peters. Wanting to learn more about Peters, Holladay discovered that the principal art history texts of that time did not include women. Determined to bring the works of women artists into fuller recognition and to change the prevailing climate of exclusion, Holladay and her husband began a 30-year term of collecting and documenting art by women from the Renaissance to the present. That collection became the cornerstone of the National Museum of Women in the Arts, which Holladay incorporated in 1981. The museum opened in 1987. Holladay is the recipient of more than 25 Honorary Degrees and awards, including induction into the National Women's Hall of Fame in 1996, and the Award for Outstanding Achievement in the Visual Arts from the WCA in 2001. Holladay has one child.   (ABS)

Holland, Eunice ("Tootsie") (1931 –) was a founding member of Columbia, SC, NOW in 1972. The chapter worked to change the rape law; sued the local radio and television stations for not employing women and blacks; stopped the local newspaper from running segregated employment ads; and stopped the local school district from paying men teachers $500 more per year than women. The group also started the first rape crisis center and battered women's shelter. Holland traveled the state and helped other cities set up rape crisis centers. She served on the national board of NOW, and organized and served as executive director of a coalition of groups and individuals, ERA SC, to fight for passage of the ERA. Because she was a member of NOW, Holland was asked to resign as manager of Dictaphone Office Temporaries Girls in Columbia. Holland, who has an M.S. degree, has supported civil rights and gay rights by marching and donating money. Archives: Winthrop College, Winthrop, SC. (ABS)

Hollander, Nicole (1939 –) grew up surrounded by women who valued wit and taught her everything she knows about irony and, more important, the value of female friends. "Feminism," she says, "has been my source and a lifelong commitment." Hollander has published 15 cartoon collections, many of them featuring her main character, Sylvia. Hollander says that she created Sylvia so that she could have a feisty role model, a decade older than herself, to show her the way. Hollander's first book was *I'm in Training to be Tall and Blonde* (1979); her first cartoon was done for the feminist publication *The Spokeswoman*. Hollander began her syndication of Sylvia, which she writes and draws, after the publication of her first book. The strip appears in major newspapers across the country. She has also written, "along with wonderful collaborators," two musicals: "Sylvia's Real Good Advice" and "Female Problems."   (ABS)

Hollinshead, Ariel Cahill (1929 –) Coming from a family that always considered women equal, Hollinshead says she was "born to feminism." A research oncologist and educator and now professor emerita, Department of Medicine, George Washington Medical Center, Hollinshead began writing about the inequities women scientists experienced in the workplace when she was a graduate student (1950s). She has spoken at schools, workshops and on radio and TV to encourage women to enter scientific careers. Since 1961, she has worked to establish monitoring and networking for women in science through Sigma Delta Epsilon/Graduate Women in Science. Through the Women's Bureau, she did networking and research reports about the concerns working women had about childcare and wage inequities, and later testified on Capitol Hill, along with the AAUW and other groups, for childcare laws and regulations. She has served on the boards of the National Women's Economic Alliance and The Women's Institute, and in 1971 persuaded the president of her university to establish an advisory committee to form a summer Educational Opportunity Program of tutorials to prepare underprivileged blacks and women to be on an equal footing for college entry. Hollinshead is on the advisory board of or is a reviewer for several scientific journals, and has received numerous awards, including Distinguished Scientist AAAS, Alumna Merit Awards and Honorary Doctor of Science degree (1977) from Ohio University. In 1988 Hollinshead received the Outstanding Woman of America Award, and in 1975 – 1976 was named Medical Woman of the Year by the Joint Board of American Medical Colleges. Archives: Drexel/Medical College of Pennsylvania; Ohio University, Athens, GA; and George Washington Medical Library, Washington, D.C. (ABS)

Holm, Jeanne M. (1921 –) spent 33 years in the Armed Forces, from 1942 until her retirement in 1975, rising from truck driver to two-star general. She was the first woman in the Armed Forces promoted to the rank of Major General (1973), and the first woman in the Air Force to become a Brigadier General. While progressing rapidly through the ranks, Holm was appointed director, Women in the Air Force (1965), which carried the temporary rank of full Colonel, the highest rank then allowed by law for military women. During the seven years she served in that position, she was a leader in challenging all gender-based laws and policies that limited career opportunities or affected the quality of life of women in the Armed Forces. She advocated the removal of arbitrary recruiting ceilings designed to limit women's access to the military, opening all commissioning programs and service academies to women, as well as assignments including flying and duty aboard Naval vessels. Congress removed the military promotion ceilings on women in 1967. Holm says, "I worked to open doors for women in the Armed Forces and to keep the system honest. A lot of studies were done to prove that women could not do cer-

tain things. I worked to make sure research asked the right questions and, when necessary, used the press. My basic philosophy at the time was, the progress of women is inevitable." Among Holm's military awards are two Distinguished Service Medals and the Legion of Merit. After retiring from the military, Holm was appointed special assistant for women to President Gerald Ford, a position she held until the end of his administration. During the Carter and Reagan years, Holm served on numerous boards and committees and in advisory positions focusing on personnel, including women. She is the author of *Women in the Military: An Unfinished Revolution* (Presidio Press, 1982) and editor and co-author of *In Defense of a Nation: Servicewomen in World War II* (Military Women's Press, 1997). Archives: Papers will be going to the Air Force Academy Library in Colorado for a special collection. (ABS)

Holmes, Doloris (1929 – 2001) In 1969, Holmes was an original member of Women Artists in Revolution, a group that lobbied for free days at museums and more shows by women artists. She originated a series of programs on art at WBAI (1968 – 1969), and was in the first feminist art show, X-12, in February 1970. She founded the White Mask Theater later and produced many plays. In 1973 she produced a film, "Room of the White Mask," about "transformation through newly created rituals, including rebirth of an individual woman through identification with all women." This was based on a trip to the caves in the South of Spain in the early 1970s. Nude against the ancient cave drawings, her feminist consciousness was aroused. Her plays and taped performances include "Fish Joy" and "Women of the Left Bank." She wrote an autobiography, *Our Lady of the Grape Arbor*, which she self-published and distributed in places like the Gotham Book Mart. Until the end of her life, she did theater works in New York City. She was also a poet and the mother of two.

Holmes, Tiffany – An editor and writer of mystery stories, Holmes became a member of NOW just before the 1970 strike, and helped produce the parody of *The New York Times*, *The NOW York Times*. "Some of us went out at night to sneak copies of it into newsstand copies of the real thing, giving unsuspecting buyers a bonus with their morning coffee." Holmes continued to write satirical articles for the paper in 1971 and 1972. She is also author of *Woman's Astrology: Your Astrological Guide to a Future Worth Having* (1977), which "debunks the sexist programming that so many horoscope articles, and individual readings, provided." Holmes has a B.A. from Queens College (NYC), and is a graduate of Lynne Palmer's School of Astrology (1969 – 1972). (ABS)

Holmstrom, Nancy (1943 –) In 1969, Holmstrom (with assistance from fellow-graduate student Irvene Brawer) sent a letter to all women listed in the *Directory of Philosophers* asking for help in organizing a women's caucus at

(ABS) indicates Approved By Subject

the American Philosophical Association. With Alison Jaggar, who responded, Holmstrom drew up a list of resolutions based on those introduced at the Modern Language Association. Mary Mothersill introduced the resolutions at the Eastern Division meeting of the APA in 1970, and thus was born both the APA committee on the status of women and the Society for Women in Philosophy. In the mid 1970s, Holmstrom introduced a course on the philosophical issues of feminism at the University of Wisconsin, and did the same in the late 1970s at Rutgers University, where, as of this writing, she is chair of the philosophy department. Holmstrom was also active in CARASA in NYC and Los Angeles in the late 1970s. Editor of *The Socialist Feminist Project* (2002), her articles on feminist theory include "Women's Work," "Do Women Have a Distinct Nature?" and, with Johanna Brenner, "Autonomy vs. Community in Feminist Politics." Holmstrom holds a B.A. from City College of New York (1964) and a Ph.D. from the University of Michigan (1970).   (ABS)

Holt, Sibal (1945 –) Holt was a founding member of the Baton Rouge commission on the needs of women, a member of the LA WPC, the governor's commission for women, and former president of the Baton Rouge Women's Resource Center. Holt has been chalking up "firsts" in her professional career since 1965. She was one of the first African Americans hired by the Bell System in Louisiana, the first African American hired by the LA AFL-CIO, the first African American to be registered as a professional lobbyist in the LA Legislature, and the first African American to be elected as a statewide officer for the state AFL-CIO. In November 2004, Holt added another first when she was honored by Governor Blanco and the Louisiana Women's Commission as the first black and the first black woman to take the helm of the state AFL-CIO. Holt, who has three children, received her B.A. from Louisiana State University after going to school for 10 years part time.   (ABS)

Holtzman, Elizabeth (1941 –) worked for and won an extension of the deadline for ratification of the ERA in New York, and in the early 1970s submitted an amicus brief against NY's law making abortion illegal. In 1976 – 1977, she helped form the Congresswoman's Caucus and was elected (and later re-elected) first Democratic chair. She was also a co-founder of the Brooklyn Women's Political Caucus. She authored and won passage of the Federal Rape Privacy Act, and added the right to counsel fees to Title IX. Holtzman led a Congressional women's delegation to Cambodia, which resulted in food being allowed in to feed Cambodian children. As of 2003, she was the youngest woman elected to the House of Representatives; and was the first woman elected district attorney in NYC history, and the second in NY State (1982). She was also the first woman elected comptroller of NYC. She instituted screening mammograms in NYC hospitals, and called for Medicare to pay for them. Holtzman also issued

a report on sexual harassment in NYC government. As district attorney, Holtzman did important work on violence against women. For example, she filed an amicus brief in People v. Liberta, challenging the constitutionality of the marital rape law. The Court of Appeals adopted their argument and declared the law unconstitutional. She also worked to reform NY's rape law to eliminate the requirement that a woman suffer permanent bodily injury, increased the use of the rape evidence kit, and reformed procedures on domestic violence. Holtzman is the author of *Who Said It Would Be Easy?* (Arcade Press, 1996). She has an A.B. from Radcliffe College (1962) and a J.D. from Harvard Law School (1965). Archives: Radcliffe College and the Schlesinger Library, Radcliffe Institute, Cambridge, MA.   (ABS)

Homer, Elizabeth Ann (1943 –) (also known as Elizabeth Ann Giese) joined Michigan NOW in 1968 and immediately served on the childcare task force. As director of NOW LDEF MI project on equal education rights (1978 – 1984), the first statewide grassroots effort to ensure compliance with Title IX, Homer created a 1980 report on sex equity in MI schools. It was the first state study in the nation to show how sexism functions in schools, and included statistical data showing sex bias and discrimination. As chair of MI NOW's education task force, Homer initiated a lawsuit (by NOW LDEF and the MI ACLU) in 1991 against the Detroit Public Schools that stopped a nationwide movement to establish all-male academies, in violation of Title IX. Homer is (2005) chair of the MI NOW education task force. Also active in the political advancement of women, Homer served as spokesperson for the Democratic Women's Caucus (1976 – 1978). Earlier, she persuaded a gubernatorial candidate to ask a question about women in a statewide polling, "a huge breakthrough at that time," she says, and counseled candidates on women's issues. She also developed the first presidential campaign literature aimed at women's issues for Jimmy Carter's presidential campaign in MI. In other areas, Homer pioneered the development of women's history in MI, and served as education director and historian curator of the Michigan Women's Historical Center (1987 – 1997). Homer's writing includes *Michigan Women's Suffrage: A Political History* (1995). She also served as editor of *How the Suffragists Changed Michigan* (1989). She was a convening member of MI ERAmerica (1976) and was a Michigan Women's Hall of Fame honoree in 1999. Homer, who has one child, holds a B.A. from the University of Michigan (1964) and an M.A. from Ferris State College (1986). Archives: Bentley Archives, University of Michigan, Ann Arbor, MI.   (ABS)

Homer, Nancy Jane (1946 –) co-founded a women's history seminar at Monteith College. Homer was a founding member of one of the first CR women's liberation groups in Detroit, along with Dolores Bargowski and Barbara Burris. She traveled with the group to Atlantic City to protest the Miss America Pageant, and marched in New York City, Chicago and Washington. In 1981, she joined a group that assisted battered women in Wyoming, and helped pass legislation in Wyoming to benefit women who were victims of violence. Homer also worked in a women's shelter in Albuquerque. She is a graduate of Monteith College, Wayne State University, Detroit. (ABS)

Hood, Alix – See Dobkin, Alix

Hooke, Helen Booth (1948 –) Musician, composer and performer, Hooke organized the first all-woman band, Maggies Farm, at Smith College in 1967. She went from that to an all-woman band with women from Mount Holyoke's The Moppets, called Ariel. Ariel played at the Fillmore East in NYC, and came close to a major deal before breaking up in 1970. Later, Hooke and three members of Ariel formed The Deadly Nightshade, which became closely involved with the Valley Women's Center and played hundreds of gigs at women's marches. The Deadly Nightshade was featured in *Ms.* magazine before finally getting a major record deal with RCA Records in 1975. Hooke became a music producer and technician, areas many women were barred from, and was one of the first women to use synthesizers in the 1970s. In addition to touring extensively, Hooke made many television appearances, including several "Sesame Street" segments (she wrote several popular songs for the Muppets). Hooke, who has a B.A. from Smith, continues (2004) writing and performing, and is active in the North Fork Women for Women Fund, a North Fork of Long Island (NY) group that benefits lesbians with healthcare needs. She has played several Smith reunions with The Femmes, her all-woman dance-party band, since 1998. (ABS)

Hope, Leslie Hoag (1944 –) In 1969, her first year as a college teacher, Hope was fired for using a poem in class that her superiors considered "dirty." The case eventually was settled in her favor, and it was around that time that Hope joined the women's movement. In the late 1970s and early 1980s, as a single parent, she adopted three black infants and moved to Leimert Park, a black neighborhood in Los Angeles, to raise them. She devoted time and energy to the Feminist Women's Legal Center in Los Angeles, and was active in CR groups and in feminist women's health empowerment. She also participated in Women Against Violence Against Women, and in 1975 won the academic freedom award from her union, the AFT College Guild. She took part in the early organizing meetings of the Coalition of Labor Union Women and studied Kenpo Karate. She also volunteered at the June Mazer Collection Lesbian Archives in West Hollywood. Although she is not a lesbian, she did this out of respect for and appreciation of trailblazing lesbian women. Hope earned her B.A. and her M.A. at UCLA. She is (2004) a professor of English at Los Angeles Valley College and volunteers in matters of sexuality, violence against women,

health, and marriage and divorce. She has also become active in an organization of women peace activists, Code Pink, and in 2004 was a member of an 11-woman Code Pink delegation to Baghdad, where she met with women representing a wide spectrum of Iraqi society. (ABS)

Hopponen, Mary Helen (1931 –) A counselor in Brookings, SD, specializing in sexual abuse, satanic ritual abuse, mind control and gender issues, Hopponen has been active in NOW and the Brookings Women's Center. As a member of NOW, she worked to have women's names listed in phone books; to include girls' books in schools; and to get women counselors in local service groups and on city boards. When her chapter of NOW joined with the LWV to support a lawsuit against the Brookings School Board to obtain equal funding for girls' sports and athletics, Hopponen was one of three mothers who filed. Associated with the Brookings Women's Center from 1973 – 1987, Hopponen was first education coordinator (1973 – 1977) and then coordinator of women in crisis (1978 – 1987). She served as counselor/coordinator for domestic violence and rape crisis services to the community and the area, and facilitated similar organizations in other SD cities. In 1978, she began teaching gender-issues classes at South Dakota State University, and in 1980 began counseling adult survivors of child sexual abuse, prostitution and pornography. She was a founding mother/ member of the SD Coalition Against Domestic Violence and Sexual Assault (1980 forward). As a member of the First United Methodist Church, Hopponen served a chair of the state committee on the status and role of women; equalized representation of men/women on all committees; helped reorganize United Methodist Women in SD; and planned and delivered recruitment programs for young women for seminary and full clergy professions. Also a member of the Brookings Public Library board, she fought for and obtained expanded resources on women and children. Hopponen, who has three children (one deceased), holds a B.A. from the University of Kansas (1953); an M.A. from the University of Kansas Medical School (1955); an M.Ed. from SDSU (1978); and an A.B.D. for Ed.D. from the University of South Dakota (1996). (ABS)

Horn, Helen Steere (1932 –) (also known as Helen Weaver Horn) was part of the first feminist CR group in Athens, OH, in the early 1970s. The meetings evolved into a monthly Feminism & Faith group of 20 women who met for over 25 years. Horn was also active in the LWV education committee, and helped develop a community learning resources project for the public schools. Later, Horn received a grant from the United Mine Workers, the Ohio Humanities Council, the Ohio University Women's Studies Program and others to interview older women in local mining towns about their experiences. This resulted in a video called "The Other Half Speaks: Reminiscences of Athens County Coal Town Women, 1900 – 1950," which won a prize from the Humanities Council. Live readings have been performed six times. Horn has also written for a Quaker feminist magazine, *Friendly Woman*, since the 1980s. In addition to this work, Horn has been active in the civil rights and peace movements. Her spiritual autobiography, *There Is a Fountain: A Quaker Life in Process*, was published by the Friends center for study and contemplation, Pendle Hill (1996). Horn, who has one child, holds a B.A. from Oberlin College, an M.A. from Radcliffe College, and an M.Ed. from Ohio University. (ABS)

Hornstein, Francie (1947 –) A medical social worker (2005), Hornstein was part of the women's liberation front in Iowa City, IA, from 1969 – 1972. A contributing writer to the feminist newspaper *Ain't I A Woman*, she co-founded several community/campus daycare centers, and helped open the first day care center in IA that provided care for infants as well as young children. As a member of a health collective, Hornstein ran car pools from Iowa City to Des Moines Planned Parenthood (1969 – 1971) to enable students to get birth control. She also worked with the local clergy consultation service to refer women to underground abortionists in the Midwest. After traveling with friends to Los Angeles (1971) to learn how to do self-help clinics and menstrual extraction, Hornstein began offering the clinics in and around Iowa City. In 1972, she and Debi Law, Shelley Farber and Boach Hanson moved to Los Angeles to join Carol Downer and Lorraine Rothman at the Feminist Women's Health Center, where they opened the Women's Choice Clinic and started a pregnancy testing and abortion referral service. These services then developed into a full-service women's reproductive health clinic. Hornstein is co-author of *How to Stay Out of the Gynecologists Office, A New View of a Woman's Body*, and *Woman-Centered Pregnancy and Birth*. She has also written on donor insemination, and with her partner, Ellen Peskin, has two sons conceived by donor insemination, "which we were able to do ourselves with the help of the donor/father and our knowledge from working at the clinic." Hornstein also worked on the legal team for two court cases involving the Tallahassee Feminist Women's Health Clinic, one of which ultimately resulted in a change in regulations allowing parents unrestricted visits to their newborns. Hornstein holds a B.A. from John F. Kennedy University and a M.S.W. from the University of California, Berkeley. (ABS)

Horowitz, Arlene (1946 –) In 1971, before Title IX had passed, Horowitz was a secretary on the Hill doing clerical work despite her college education. She went to Bunny Sandler about the idea of a Congressional bill that would commit the government to funding materials for teachers and others about women and girls to counter the effects of sex-role stereotyping. During a tribute to Patsy Mink (November 19, 2002), Juanita Millender-McDonald said she thought Horowitz "was crazy, and no one in Congress in their right mind would ever support such a bill. Arlene, fortunately, did not listen to me, but went to other

women who were also skeptical, and then to Patsy Mink. Patsy Mink did not think Arlene was crazy. She gave us the go-ahead." Sandler, too, was eventually won over. And so the Women's Educa-tional Equity Act was born. Horowitz produced the first rough draft, reportedly lifting whole sections from similar legislation to make sure she had the right language. Mink held hearings on it in 1973, and in 1974 the bill passed. Just like Title IX, WEEA was hidden away in another bill, the Elementary and Secondary Education Act. The program developed hundreds of resources for educators and others concerned about the education of women and girls. In addition to developing materials to get women into the sciences, math and computers, materials were developed to address immigrant girls, Native American girls, Chicanas, Cuban American women and single mothers. (ABS)

Horowitz, Ida – See Applebroog, Ida

Horowitz, JoAnn (1931 –) helped found ERA Illinois immediately after the passage of the amendment by Congress in 1972. The first head of Chicago NOW's ERA committee, Horowitz also served in ERA Illinois as a representative of the AAUW, the LWV in IL, and Business and Professional Women. Horowitz continues (2005) working for the ERA. In recognition of her work, she received the Pathfinders Award from ERA Illinois. As a union woman, Horowitz brought her feminist agenda to her own profession, heading the women's rights committee of the Illinois Federation of Teachers for 15 years (in the 1970s and 1980s) and co-founding the national CLUW in Chicago in 1974. As a teacher, she spearheaded the effort to amend the Illinois School Code to make February 15, the birthday of Susan B. Anthony, a commemorative day in Illinois schools. (ABS)

Horton, Geralyn (1940 –) (also known as Geralyn Williams) was a member of the Women's Caucus, a group centered around the Arlington St. Church in Boston, MA, during the 1960s and early 1970s. A playwright, director and actor, Horton did chancel dramas, street theater and demonstrations, and stage-managed for Bobbi Ausubel's Caravan Theatre. Two songbooks, a record and a book, *Honor Thy Womanself* (Audrey Drummond, Skinner House, 1982) emerged from the 1970s folk group, which was led by composer Carolyn MacDade. In addition, Horton and her daughter, Robin Williams, were part of a Bread and Roses CR group loosely connected to Redstockings. By 1971, Horton had completed a one-act about her grandmother, "What Kind of a Life Is That?" which after its 1972 workshop was put on by community theaters in the mid to late 1970s and was part of the Women In Theater Festival in NYC in 1983. The script was honored by the Eileen Heckart Senior Theatre play contest in 2004. In 1973, Horton entered Goddard's off-campus M.A. program in feminist spirituality. Her 1976 thesis project was a play about Victoria Woodhull, "Spirit and Flesh."

H

Feminist essays, theater criticism and Horton's more than 70 play scripts—including one about Goddard's Separatist witches titled "Amazons"—are published under the pen name G.L. Horton. Plays include "The T Show," based on her experience as a bus driver in a ghetto area. Her 1987 play about Boston abortion counselors, "Under Siege" by pro-life fanatics, aka "Choices," was developed at the Sundance Lab in 1990 and has been staged in South Africa and translated into Russian. Horton has one child. Archives: Lawrence and Lee Institute's Theatre Research Collection, Ohio State University, Columbus, OH. (ABS)

Horwitz, Channa Davis (1932 –) In 1972, Horwitz, a California artist, attended a meeting of women artists including, among others, Joyce Kosloff, June Wayne and Miriam Schapiro. Realizing how little women were represented in the art world, the women agreed to learn some business basics to help them compete with men professionally. At a gathering of 20 Los Angeles women artists in June Wayne's studio, Horwitz revealed that she had been the only woman in the 1973 Los Angeles County Museum of Art and Technology catalog. This became a rallying point for the feminist movement to fight the Museum. "We filled the Bing Auditorium of the County Museum with a symposium of women challenging Maurice Tuckman and the museum on its lack of inclusion of any one-women shows," she relates. "The result was the show Women Artists: 1550 – 1950." Horwitz, who has three children, holds a B.F.A from Cal Arts. (ABS)

Horwitz, Diane S. (1938 –) was a member of a CR group in NYC in the late 1960s, and from 1969 – 1970 was a member of the NY Women's Union. In 1970, Horwitz moved to Chicago and became active in CWLU (1970 – 1975), where she helped organize young women in community colleges, did speaking engagements through the speakers bureau, served on the steering committee, and was active in a local chapter. Horwitz also served on the national steering committee of the Socialist-Feminist Conference (Yellow Springs, OH, 1975). In 1970, Horwitz began a 30-year career at Moraine Valley Community College, just outside Chicago. While there, she organized women's groups, Our Bodies, Ourselves classes, and an educational program for adult women coming to college for the first time, the Moraine Valley Returning Women's Program. The program enabled over 1,000 women over a 25-year period to enter a college program and served as a model for other programs; it was written up in the *Chicago Tribune* on its 25th anniversary. Horwitz was also a member of her union's women's committees (1971 – 1980) and the Coalition of Labor Union Women. After retiring in 2000, Horwitz published an essay in the book *Women Confronting Retirement, A Non-Traditional Guide*. Archives: Chicago Historical Society, Chicago, IL. (ABS)

Hosken, Fran P. (1919 –) is a journalist, architect and photographer. She is founder and coordinator of *Women's International Network News* (1975), a quarterly reporting worldwide on women's issues. She has done extensive research into the epidemiology of female genital mutilation and its consequences, and is author of *Stop FGM: Women Speak – Facts and Actions* (WIN NEWS, 1995) and a research work, *The Hosken Report: Genital and Sexual Mutilation of Females* (1994). Hosken, who reads and understands four languages, served as an accredited journalist for the United Nations International Women's Year Conference on Women in Mexico, 1975; the U.N. Mid-Decade Conference on Women in Copenhagen, 1980; the U.N. Decade for Women Conference in Nairobi, 1985; and the Fourth World Conference on Women in Beijing, 1995. Hosken was named Woman Leader 1980 by *Marie Claire* magazine, France; Humanist Heroine 1987 by the American Humanist Association for promoting women's welfare worldwide; and cited by the Inter-African Committee for Excellent Work Accomplished to End FGM, 1994. She was also cited by the Feminist Majority Foundation for her contributions for women's equality and human rights, and was the first recipient of the Donna Allen Award for Advocacy. Hosken earned her B.A. from Smith College (1940). From 1944 – 1945 she served as an Ensign with the U.S. Coast Guard Women's Reserve (Communications Intelligence); and in 1942 earned her Master of Architecture degree from the Harvard Graduate School of Design. In 1971, she says, "I filed the first ever discrimination suit against Harvard with the federal government and the state government. Harvard was investigated and has had to file annual Affirmative Action reports ever since." She has also testified with the international relations committee on discrimination by U.S. AID, "specifically their health programs in Africa and their failure to address female genital mutilation." Her books include *The Language of Cities* (1969); *The Functions of Cities* (1972); and *The Kathmandu Valley Towns* (1974). She has three children. Archives: Library of Northwestern University Women's Collection, Evanston, IL; documentation of the Harvard complaint at the Radcliffe Library, Cambridge, MA. (ABS)

Hounsell, Cindy (1945 –) A pension attorney and former flight attendant, Hounsell became active with Stewardesses for Women's Rights in 1972, the year it was founded, and worked as its Northeast regional coordinator to build its membership. The organization, although short-lived, improved working conditions and employment rules for flight attendants and for all women. In order to combat airline advertising that was demeaning to flight attendants and to women in general, Hounsell and her group produced a counter-commercial in which the seriousness and responsibility of the job was emphasized. They also picketed films—both porno and mainstream— where flight attendants were shown as sexually available. Working with the FAA, they were able to stop the practice of shipping hazardous cargo on passenger flights without notifying the passengers. SFWR served as a legal liaison, linking flight attendants who had been discriminated against to lawyers who defended them. Their cases succeeded in striking down marital and age restrictions enforced against flight attendants and later winning the right to remain employed while pregnant. After 17 years with Pan Am, Hounsell retired and earned a J.D. from CUNY Law School. With a fellowship to Georgetown Law School she began doing policy work on women's retirement issues. In 1996, she founded the Women's Institute for a Secure Retirement in Washington, D.C., where she serves as president. Archives: The Tamiment Library & Robert F. Wagner Labor Archives, New York, NY. (ABS)

Householder, Ruth (1924 –) tried for two years to gain admittance to Ohio State University College of Veterinary Medicine, finally succeeding in 1945. After such a long struggle, she was amazed to hear the doctor in charge of admissions tell her that he wanted women in the classes "because the language of the classes would change with women present; it would be more scientific." Householder joined NOW in 1968 in North Western PA. When she later moved to Miami, she became part of the first NOW chapter in that area, where she was involved in upgrading the status of the Eastern Airline stewardesses and in improving the treatment of rape victims, among other actions. She also organized the ERA march in downtown Miami just before the vote in Congress. While the speakers were talking, she says, "two large garbage trucks pulled up to the bottom of the Court House steps, stopped and revved their motors until the program ended." (ABS)

Howard, Bonnie Newman (1935 –) In the 1970s, Howard began attending meetings of the North Shore Feminists and the Eastern MA chapter of NOW. At the 1973 national NOW conference, she was elected national treasurer, and worked to create financial systems to handle the work of the three newly opened national NOW offices in Chicago, NYC and Washington, D.C. In 1975, she was elected to a second term. On the board of NOW LDEF from 1979 – 1995, she served as treasurer, and later (1989 – 1990) as president. Several times, Howard has served as either president or treasurer of her local Cape Ann/North Shore (MA) chapter of NOW. In 2002, she became a founding member of the North Shore Coalition to Protect Choice, and in 2003 joined the board of the VFA. Active (2004) in the peace movement, she is a convener of Women's Action for New Directions (North Shore, MA chapter), which works to empower women to act politically to reduce violence and militarism and redirect resources going to the military to meet human and environmental needs. Howard, who has one child, holds an A.B. from Radcliffe College (1956) and an M.B.A. from the University of Michigan (1965). Archives: Schlesinger Library, Radcliffe Institute, Cambridge, MA. (ABS)

Howe, Florence (1929 –) Author, editor, publisher and teacher, Howe has been described by colleagues as "the

Elizabeth Cady Stanton of women's studies." She spent 11 years at Goucher College, "where, for me, women's studies began," Howe says. "I then moved to a non-traditional college—SUNY Old Westbury—where I rediscovered women's studies for older multicultural women." Believing that "a different curriculum would help to change consciousness, perhaps more effectively than laws forbidding sexism," she began teaching women's studies courses even before they had that name. Unable to find fiction or biography to use in the classroom, she helped found the Feminist Press (1970). She served as its president until 2000, and from 1985 – 2000 was also publisher/director. She is founder of "Women's Studies Newsletter," which became *Women's Studies Quarterly,* the first national journal to focus on feminist teaching. Howe served as editor from 1972 – 1982. Howe also edited *The Politics of Women's Studies: Testimony from Thirty Founding Mothers* (2000). She was an originator (1993) and is (2004) co-director of Women Writing Africa, a major project of cultural reclamation still in progress. In 1969, Howe became the first chairperson of the Modern Language Association's Commission on the Status and Education of Women, and in 1971 was elected to a three-year term as an officer of the Modern Language Association, where she served as president in 1973. In 1975, she was appointed to the executive committee of MLA's Division of Women's Studies in Language and Literature, and served in that office for five years, chairing the division from 1978 – 1979. She has published many essays and 12 books on women's studies, women and literature, women writers and women and politics. These include *Myths of Coeducation: Selected Essays 1965 – 1984; Tradition* and *Talents of Women;* and *No More Masks! An Anthology of Twentieth Century American Women Poets.* Howe was educated at Hunter College, Smith College and the University of Wisconsin, where she began her teaching career in 1951. She is (2004) emerita professor of English at the Graduate Center, CUNY. Archives: Brown University, Providence, RI. (ABS)

Howell, Mary Catherine Raugust (1932 – 1998) A physician, psychologist, lawyer and musician, Howell championed medical careers and better healthcare for women. She was the first woman dean at Harvard Medical School (1972 – 1975) and led the fight to end quotas and to open medical schools to women. As dean of student affairs, Howell sent out a questionnaire asking for students' perceptions of their medical education. The responses encouraged her to send the questionnaire to women students at every medical school in the country, and the result was Howell's book, *Why Would a Girl Go into Medicine? Medical Education in the United States* (1973). A documentation of the discrimination women faced, the book was instrumental in increasing the percentage of women medical students. In 1975, Howell helped organize a national women's health conference at Harvard. From that conference came the idea for the National

Women's Health Network, of which Howell was one of five co-founders. Although Howell moved to Maine in 1975, where she opened a pediatric practice, she was a contributor to *Our Bodies, Ourselves*, a book from the Boston Women's Book Collective, and also to *Working Mother* magazine. Her book *Healing at Home: A Guide to Health Care for Children*, was published by Beacon Press in 1978. Howell returned to the Boston area to practice geriatrics and psychotherapy, and from 1992–1994 was a member of the Division of Medical Ethics at Harvard Medical School. Howell, who had seven children, earned her undergraduate degree from Radcliffe College in 1954. She received her M.D. and Ph.D. in psychology from the University of Minnesota in 1962, and her J.D. from Harvard Law School in 1991. She used her law degree to help women and families adopt children.

Howes, Carollee (1947 –) A university professor and, since 1972, a feminist researcher on childcare, Howes was a member of CR groups that grew out of the American Friends Service Committee in San Francisco (1970 – 1972). She was also a member and part of the leadership of the New American Movement (1972) and of Solidarity until 1982. She joined the Boston Women's Union in the mid 1970s, and was part of the group that formed the Somerville (MA) Women's Center. In addition, Howes was a founding mother of Child Care Employee Project, to become Child Care Workers (1978). Howes, who was active in the peace and civil rights movements in high school and college (1962–1969), has one child.   (ABS)

Hudson, Betty (1931 –) An active supporter of the ERA and pro-choice in Connecticut, Hudson was also a co-founder of the East Shore WPC in 1972. Believing that gender titles should match the gender of the office holder, Hudson contacted Bruce Morris, a legislator from the 111th House district, and persuaded him to introduce a bill to that effect. Hudson organized supporters and spoke at public hearings, and the Gender Title Bill was passed in 1972. As a state senator (1975–1979), Hudson co-chaired the human rights and opportunities committee and the human services committee, which addressed all the feminist issues of the day. In the General Assembly, Hudson led the fight for legislation redefining rape as sexual assault, a landmark first-of-its kind law that became a model for other states. Under her guidance, the state passed laws strengthening court-ordered child support with automatic wage attachment, a law requiring police intervention in domestic violence to protect women from retribution, and the establishment of a statewide program of shelters for battered women. She also initiated laws for affirmative action, child day care and Medicaid funding for abortion. When the Senate passed the Gay Rights Bill (1975) that Hudson had introduced, CT became the first state in the nation to have gotten such a bill through even one chamber of its Legislature. (The bill did not become law until 1991.) Hudson, who has two children, remains active in NOW, NWPC and the gay and lesbian task force. Archives: Connecticut Women's Hall of Fame, University of Hartford, Hartford, CT.   (ABS)

Hudson, Carolyn Ann – See Steele, Carolyn Ann

Hughes, Dorothy Pitman (1938 –) A childcare activist and community organizer, Hughes founded and ran the New York City Agency for Child Development. She was a founder (1971), with Gloria Steinem, Brenda Feigen and Catherine Samuels, of the Women's Action Alliance. The organization's original mission was "to stimulate and assist women at the local level to organize around specific action projects aimed at eliminating concrete manifestations of economic and social discrimination." The alliance folded in 1997 but its offshoot, Women Initiating Self Empowerment, continues. During the years surrounding the birth of *Ms.* magazine, Hughes and Steinem traveled and spoke as a team, appearing at hundreds of public meetings. Hughes is the author of *Wake Up and Smell the Dollars! Whose Inner City Is It Anyway! One Woman's Struggle Against Sexism, Classism, Racism, Gentrification and The Empowerment Zone* (Amber Books, 2000). Hughes has been a member of several organizations that support the economic and social development of inner cities and of poor rural communities in the U.S., including the National Black Woman's Caucus, Black Women Enterprise and The Harlem Business Alliance, Inc. She was also an organizer of the first battered women's shelter in NYC, was a founding member of the governor's task force on human services, served at the Black Economic Summit in Washington, D.C., and was a member of the committee of the Harlem empowerment zone. Born in Georgia, Hughes is founder, president and CEO of Harlem Office Supply Inc.

Hull, Joan (1927 –) joined NOW in 1967, serving as treasurer of the New York chapter (1968); a member of the national board (1969); VP of NY NOW (1971); and member of the NY NOW advisory committee (1972). In her roles, she worked on Title VII and contract compliance projects, helped organize a NY State legislative conference for women, and organized NOW's participation in public hearings in NYC before the state joint legislative committee on industry and labor problems. She also helped stage Women's Role in Contemporary Society by the New York City Commission on Human Rights in September 1970. Hull gave testimony on behalf of NOW before the FCC, NYS Public Service Commission, EEOC and the NY State legislative committee. She secured the support of District 65 of the National Council of Distributive Workers to pressure the NY State legislative committee on labor to amend the law to include pregnancy as a temporary disability. On the AT&T task force and a coordinator of the national task force on compliance and enforcement, she was successful in getting the attorney general of NY to intervene in the EEOC suit against AT&T. In Hull's view, however, her major contributions to the women's movement were the shareholder actions of 1974, 1975 and 1976, when she submitted the NOW shareholder proposals at the annual stockholder meetings of Celanese Corporation. As a result, the corporation added two women to its board; The National Council of Churches Interfaith Center on Corporate Responsibility began to submit its own feminist proposals to corporations; and other NOW members were inspired to file their feminist proposals with corporations. Archives: Schlesinger Library, Radcliffe Institute, Cambridge, MA. (ABS)

Hulme, Marylin Ann (1939 –) has worked steadily to assure gender equity in education. Chair and legislative chair (1999 – 2001) of the steering committee of the National Coalition for Sex Equity in Education, she also served on the Gender Equity Expert Panel of the U.S. Department of Education, Office of Educational Research and Improvement (1996 forward). In 2001, she was national adviser, Gender and Science Digital Library Project at the Education Development Center and the Eisenhower National Clearinghouse. Hulme has served on numerous other committees, given several presentations, and written widely on gender equity in education. In 1973, she became a member of Somerset County NOW, and served as newsletter editor, chair of the education task force, president, and board member of both the Somerset County chapter and the NJ state chapter. Hulme, who has two children, holds a B.A. from the University of Southampton (United Kingdom), and an M.A. from the University of London. Archives: Rutgers The State University of New Jersey, Archives and Special Collections, New Brunswick, NJ. (ABS)

Hultin, Jill Foreman (1943 –) In 1968 – 1969, as a graduate student at UCLA, Hultin made a film, "Sisters," which explores how three different generations of women responded to society's expectations of them. In New Haven, CT, from 1969 – 1972, Hultin joined New Haven Women's Liberation, and was one of the plaintiffs in a lawsuit challenging the constitutionality of Connecticut's anti-abortion laws. From 1969 – 1971, she taught film and TV production at the University of Connecticut, where she and several others formed a Women's Film Cooperative that promoted and rented films featuring non-traditional roles for women. After moving to Columbus (OH) in 1972, she worked as director of the Ohio ERA implementation task force, which was responsible for reviewing all OH statutes and recommending changes necessary to assure that OH law was sex neutral. Ultimately, all of its recommendations were enacted by the Ohio General Assembly. Hultin is the author of a chapter in a memoir, *Journeys that Opened Up the World: Women, the Student Christian Movement and Social Justice Activism, 1955 – 1975* (Rutgers University Press, 2003), and served as editor of "Report of the Ohio Task Force for the Implementation of the Equal Rights Amendment"

(1975). She earned a B.A. from Ohio University (1965); was a Coro Fellow in Public Affairs, Coro Foundation (1966); and has an M.A. from University of California,, Los Angeles (1969). Hultin has two children. (ABS)

Hunt, Gloria – See Bowles, Gloria Lee

Hunt, Jean (1945 –) was a member of the Philadelphia Women's Center Staff Collective (1971 – 1972). Hunt explains that this was full-time work and meant living and working at the center, and being involved with CR groups as well as health, education, divorce and self-defense groups. Since 1971, she has been a member of the Philadelphia Women's Health Collective, created to read *Our Bodies, Ourselves* and then go out and teach it to community groups. The women organized a women's health conference in Philadelphia in 1971. The health collective also worked on abortion, sterilization abuse, birth control, inequities in healthcare provision, support for women's health workers and support for strikes in local hospitals. Hunt was a member of Women Against Sterilization Abuse (1975 – 1976), and as a result of her work in women's health, went to nursing school and earned an R.N. degree. During the 1980s she worked in healthcare administration, and from 1988 – 1992 was executive director of the Elizabeth Blackwell Health Center for Women. In addition to this work, Hunt created a girls sports effort in North Philadelphia that allowed young girls to play sports year round with coaching, equipment and parental support (1990s). She has been active in campaigns to elect women, and runs (2005) Campaign for Working Families, which seeks to help low-wage working families, most headed by women, to secure more income for their households. Hunt has also been active in the civil rights and anti-war movements. She earned her R.N. from Community College of Philadelphia and has two children. Archives: Papers from the Women's Health Center and the Women's Health Collective are in the Walter Lear Collection, Philadelphia, PA. (ABS)

Hunt, Jean S. (1931 –) A retired professor of history, Hunt was a faculty sponsor of the CWLU, Loop College, and a member of a CR group and the Roslyn Group, a women's reading group. In 1971, she organized the Chicago Area Women's History Conference (now Council), which provided over 300 free programs on topics in women's history, sponsored *Women Building Chicago 1790 – 1990: A Biographical Dictionary*, organized the first women's history tours of Chicago, and held conferences and workshops for high-school/grammar-school teachers to help them bring women's history into their plans. Co-author of *Walking With Women in Chicago History* and author of *WWWII – Three Women's History: Walking Tours of The Loop*, Hunt also chaired the women's studies committee at Harold Washington College (1986 – 1993) and coordinated the exhibition of Judy Chicago's Dinner Party in Chicago (1982 – 1983). Hunt also helped sponsor the first

H

women musicians concert in Chicago, was a committee member of Women's Park Chicago, and helped develop Chicago Tribute Markers that celebrate many Chicago women. In addition, Hunt did educational programs on civil rights for the ILGWU in the late 1950s, and led a committee to integrate Spanish-speaking and other new workers into the union committees. From 1953 – 1955, she worked with young workers in San Francisco to help them become politically active and achieve equal rights. Hunt, who has two children, holds a B.A. (1952) and two graduate degrees from the University of Chicago. Archives: Special Collections, University of Illinois at Chicago, Chicago, IL. (ABS)

Hunt, Linda – See Beckman, Linda Hunt

Hunt, Mary Elizabeth (1951 –) became committed to feminist work as a graduate student in theology at Harvard Divinity School and then as a doctoral student at the Graduate Theological Union in Berkeley, CA. Seeing many churches and the religious use claims of divine favor to justify many forms of discrimination, she became involved in several efforts to develop feminist work in theological education at Harvard and Berkeley. In 1975, she participated in the first Women's Ordination Conference (Cleveland, OH), the first time Roman Catholic women came together to strategize around that issue. In Buenos Aires in the early 1980s, she taught theology and worked with women and in the women's movement. In 1983, she co-founded (with her partner Diann Neu) the Women's Alliance for Theology, Ethics and Ritual. Based in Silver Spring, MD, it offers programs, projects and publications on feminist issues in religion. Through that organization, Hunt continues to write and lecture, and works on feminist ethical issues including lesbian/ gay rights, reproductive health, and transformation of patriarchal religious institutions. Hunt, who has one child, earned her B.A. from Marquette University (1972); her Master of Theological Studies from Harvard Divinity School (1974); her Master of Divinity from the Jesuit School of Theology at Berkeley (1979); and her Ph.D. from the Graduate Theological Union (1980). (ABS)

Hurley, Katie (1921 –) As president of the Alaska Board of Education, Hurley put her efforts into implementation of Title IX in AK as soon as it passed Congress in 1972. From 1971 –1978, she used her position to work on affirmative action and advocated that women receive higher positions within the Alaska Dept. of Education. Hurley was the first woman to win a statewide election in AK when she was the Democratic nominee for lieutenant governor in 1978. She has served as the executive director of the Alaska Commission on the Status of Women (1980 – 1983) and chair of the Alaska State Commission on Human Rights. She served in the AK State House in 1985 – 1986. In 1995, the University of Alaska Southeast granted her an Honorary Doctorate of Laws in recognition of her service

to AK. On a personal level, Hurley found that the 5:00 a.m. practice time for her daughter's basketball team was unfair and worked out a compromise with the school.

Hurn, Karen Nelson – See Nelson, Karen Benveniste

Hurt, Paula B. (1945 –) joined NOW in 1967, and in the late 1960s and early 1970s was a co-founder of a rape crisis center in Emporia, KS. In 1974, as part of the requirements for her master's degree, Hurt was writing a research paper on domestic violence in a rural setting when she interviewed the local chief of police—who laughed at her and told her there was no domestic violence in Emporia. Her further research in the hospital emergency room proved otherwise. Once her paper was completed, Hurt presented it to the rape victims organization, Save Our Sisters. As a result, the group decided to add domestic violence services; now has a house for victims of domestic violence and their children; has added a child advocacy center; and has a child visitation exchange center and a supervised visitation center in addition to the rape crisis services. Hurt's work with SOS gave her "the confidence to go on to law school, and I am now a child protection attorney for the state of Kansas." Hurt, who has five children, was also active in the civil rights movement in Birmingham, AL, participated in ERA marches in Oklahoma City, and was part of the anti-Vietnam War movement. She earned her M.S. from Emporia State University and her J.D. from Washburn University, Topeka, KS. (ABS)

Husik, Marion – See Frank, Marion Rudin

Hynes, H. Patricia (1943 –) Now known as a member of the environmental justice movement, Hynes was a founder of Bread and Roses, a feminist restaurant and cultural center in Cambridge, MA (1974 – 1978). A professor of environmental health, Hynes is the author of *The Recurring Silent Spring* (Pergamon Press, 1989), a study of Rachel Carson's book 25 years post-publication, and "Taking Population out of the Equation," an essay written to influence the United Nations Conference on Population and Development, held in Cairo in 1992, that argues that patriarchy, not population growth, is the root cause of environmental degradation. Hynes is also author of *A Patch of Eden: America's Inner City Gardens* (Chelsea Green Publishing Company, 1996), which documents the role of women of color in the community garden movement in inner cities—a movement that revives neighborhoods and restores urban ecology. She holds a B.A. and M.S. (ABS)

Ian, Janis (1951 –) An acclaimed artist, musician, writer and Grammy Award winner, Ian began fighting for her rights as a woman at age eight, when she persuaded a nine-year-old boy to let her have half of his boys-only paper route in New Brunswick, NJ. She also forced the boys-only baseball team to let her play. Her mother began taking her to CR groups when she was 12. Beginning in 1965, when she was 14, Ian was one of two women in New York leading recording sessions and arranging the music. At a time when all women wore skirts, Ian wore pants on "The Tonight Show," and was refused admittance to Sardi's for wearing pants in 1966. Ian was the first solo woman artist ever to receive five Grammy nominations (1975). She was also one of the first women to write, produce, arrange and play on their own records. Ian came out in 1977 and again in 1992. Her song, "At 17" deals with being a young woman who doesn't feel pretty or popular. And "His Hands," which deals with spousal abuse, is used in women's shelters and by therapists around the world. Discussing her music, Ian says, "I get told a lot, 'You play like a guy.' I'm not sure what that means. I guess it's meant to be a compliment. I do know that back when I started, women just didn't play." (ABS)

Ikeler, Ruth – See Mountaingrove, Ruth Elizabeth

Ince, Helene (1947 –) (also known as Helene Fishbein) In 1968, Ince and other members of the Bronx Coalition formed a women's caucus. The intent was not just to continue the coalition's work of community, abortion and contraception counseling and referral, draft counseling, and tenant organizing, but also to help change the attitudes and actions of the males in the organization. The caucus met with other women's groups to talk about and demonstrate self-exams, and in 1970 met with the CEO of Montefiore Hospital and Medical Center to learn about its plans for performing now-legal abortions. Ince was involved in the planning and opening of the Bronx Community Abortion Center, and became one of its two co-coordinators. She has continued to do abortion counseling, family planning, prenatal care administration and genetic counseling. At age 50, she returned to school, becoming a nurse and then a nurse practitioner. Ince has two children. (ABS)

Indritz, Phineas (1916 – 1997) An attorney and fighter for equal rights for all people, Indritz was a staff member on Capitol Hill for 20 years. He helped congresswoman Martha Griffiths research and write major pro-feminist speeches and worked behind the scenes with Catherine East, Mary Eastwood, Marguerite Rawalt and Betty Friedan to motivate the founding of NOW. Through the NOW legal committee, he and Rawalt obtained the overthrow of Pennsylvania's Muncy Act (1968), which had mandated longer sentences for convicted women prisoners than for men. He wrote briefs for the four most important school desegregation cases, and is the author of the Pregnancy Disability Act of 1978, as well as additional legislation in Maryland in the late 1970s and the 1980s prohibiting discrimination against women. In 1996, he persuaded the American Veterans Committee to join the amicus curiae brief in the New York Supreme Court case of Long Island Gynecological Services v. 1103 Stewart Ave. Association,

which later ruled that a landlord may not evict a reproductive health clinic. Indritz earned a B.A. (1936) and his law degree (1938) from the University of Chicago. He had three children.

Ingress, Jeanne Louise Hirsch (1945 –) and her mother, Lolly Hirsch, became radical feminists in 1968 after meeting Alice Paul and visiting the National Women's Party headquarters in Washington, D.C. In 1971, they met Carol Downer and Lorraine Rothman, founding mothers of the gynecological self-help clinic movement and the later Federation of Feminist Women's Health Centers. Ingress spoke across the U.S. on the self-help philosophy, and funded the newsletter, "Global Gynecological Self-Help Clinic Network." Ingress and her mother also founded New Moon Communications, Inc., a feminist mother-daughter publishing company that was entirely to, by, of, for and about women. Together, they worked as speakers, writers and organizers on the issues of gynecological self-help and home-birth for women, and on feminism and the arts. She also organized lunchtime discussion groups at the American Museum of Natural History and initiated the election of the museum's first woman union leader. Ingress demonstrated with NOW and NARAL as a pro-choice and ERA advocate, and demonstrated against the Gulf War and the war in Iraq. She has two children. Archives: The Federation of Feminist Women's Health Centers and The Alice Paul Foundation, or The Sophia Smith Collection, Smith College, Northampton, MA. (ABS)

Ireland, Patricia (1945 –) President of NOW from 1991 – 2001, Ireland has also been active in the civil rights, antipoverty and gay and lesbian movements. She became an active feminist around 1970, when, as a flight attendant for Pan American Airlines, she learned that the company's health policy covered the families of male employees, but not the families of female employees. She contacted the Labor Dept. Office of Federal Contract Compliance, fought for change, and won. At law school in 1972, Ireland helped start a feminist law student group at Florida State University, and began work supporting the ERA. In 1981, NOW opened an ERA Countdown Campaign office in Miami Dade County, which Ireland ran with Janet Canterbury (then president of Dade County NOW). Ireland also chaired the audit committee of the Florida Feminist Credit Union; helped revitalize the Florida Association for Women Lawyers; and chaired FL NOW's lesbian rights committee and Dade County NOW's PAC. In 1987, Ireland moved to Washington, D.C., to become executive VP of NOW. In 1991, she began her 10-year tenure as president, where she developed NOW's Project Stand Up for Women; helped originate the class-action suit NOW v. Scheidler, which in 1998 found Operation Rescue and others guilty of racketeering; in 1992 helped organize NOW's March for Women's Lives and initiated the Elect Women for a Change campaign; and built stronger NOW links with Welfare and poor women's rights activists, civil rights leaders, and LGBT groups. In addition, she was the architect of NOW's Global Feminist Conference. Ireland has served as an equal opportunity consultant, and in May 2003 was hired as CEO of the YWCA. She was dismissed in October 2003, reportedly because of concerns about her relationship with NOW, which supports gay and lesbian rights and is pro-choice. Ireland is the author of *What Women Want* (Dutton, 1996). She earned her J.D. from the University of Miami Law School (1975). Archives: The Schlesinger Library, Radcliffe Institute, Cambridge, MA. (ABS)

Ireton, Barbara – See Blackmon, Antonia

Irwin, Joan J. – See Brumberg, Joan Jacobs

Isasi-Diaz, Ada Maria (1943 –) A professor and Roman Catholic, Isasi-Diaz has worked at the intersection of church and society since 1975. She helped organize and develop the membership base of the Women's Ordination Conference, and also worked on models of leadership that responded to feminist understandings of power and enablement. After her work with that group, Isasi-Diaz started developing a theology from the Latina perspective, Mujerista Theology, and has published widely in that field. She has worked internationally with the women's committee of the Ecumenical Association of Third-World Theologians, and with the World Council of Churches Decade of the Churches in Solidarity with Women. Born in Cuba, Isasi-Diaz has also worked for Latina/Hispanic rights with Las Hermanas, a Roman Catholic women's group, and supported the ERA—in particular the work of Sonia Johnson, a Mormon woman who pressured state legislatures to approve the amendment. Isasi-Diaz holds an M.A and a Ph.D. Archives: Union Theological Seminary, New York, NY. (ABS)

Israel, Joan (1930 –) was a founding member of Detroit NOW (1969) and served as VP and chair of the childcare committee. She was instrumental in the founding of the Wayne County childcare committee, which for the first time involved county and city in childcare planning. She prepared and successfully presented legislation to improve the childcare situation in Michigan; prepared and distributed a childcare brochure; and organized four childcare conferences. She also surveyed four large firms to determine childcare needs and visited childcare centers in Europe. As the second president of MI NOW, Israel challenged the licenses of local television stations, influenced programming, and helped get women into technical and managerial positions. In 1974, when MI NOW celebrated Women's Equality Day, Israel received the Feminist of the Year Award. In 1975, Israel was a co-founder of Now Options, a firm whose goal was to find non-traditional jobs for women. Also concerned about women and aging, Israel developed a three-day confer-

ence on the topic in 1973, put together a slide presentation, What's Wrong With Wrinkles, and with others held workshops about menopause for two years. "No one was talking about menopause in the 1970s!" says Israel. She is the co-author of *Looking Ahead: Problems & Joys of Growing Older* (Prentice Hall, 1977); is the creator of two films, "Woman Alone," about a single mother on Welfare, and "To Life," about three aging people; and co-wrote *Surviving the Change: A Practical Guide to Menopause* (Cinnibar Publications, 1980). Israel, who has two children, holds a B.A. from the University of Rochester and an M.S.W. from Smith College. Archives: Walter Reuther Library, Wayne State University, Detroit, MI. (ABS)

Israel, Sheila Lee – See Goldmacher, Sheila Lee

Iverson, Lucille Karin (1925 –) organized women's poetry readings at New York University (1971–1973), and used the readings as a political forum for women's rights. With Kathy Rubin she published an anthology, *We Become New: Poems by 44 Contemporary Women* (1975), as well as her own book of poems, *Outrage* (1975). A member of NYRF and a CR group, Iverson also wrote film reviews from a feminist perspective for the *Manhattan Tribune*. A member of the civil rights and peace movements, Iverson is a graduate of New York University, and holds an M.A. She has one child. (ABS)

Jackson, Dauris Gwendolyn (1933–1979) was the first African American woman elected to the Wayne State University board of governors (1976), and the first ever elected to any Michigan university. In 1977, she was one of 10 authors selected to create multiracial textbooks focusing on non-stereotypical depictions of African American children. During the 1970s, she was active in MI's Democratic Women's Caucus. Jackson, who earned a B.A. (1955) and M.A. (1958) from Wayne State University, had two children.

Jacobs, Carol P. (1936 –) was one of six women from NOW who in 1969 formed the group Women on Words & Images. The group conducted a landmark study on sexism in children's books and published *Dick & Jane as Victims: Sex Role Stereotyping in Children's Readers*. The group also created a slide show for a presentation Jacobs made at the Authors & Publishers Guild in NYC (1970). Copies of the book and the slide show were subsequently purchased by many universities in the U.S. and worldwide. The group then consulted with the editorial staff at Scott Foresman and McGraw-Hill so that language in textbooks would be sex fair. Jacobs' other publications include *Channeling Children: Sex Role Stereotyping in Prime Time TV; Sex Role Stereotyping in Foreign Language Texts*; and *Sex-Role Stereotyping in Vocational Educational Materials*. In addition to her work in making children's books sex fair, Jacobs was active in the peace movement protesting the Vietnam War. She holds a B.S. from CCNY and an M.Ed. and M.S.W. from Rutgers University. A learning consultant for the Princeton Regional Schools in NJ, Jacobs has two children. Archives: Rutgers University Libraries, New Brunswick, NJ. (ABS)

Jacobs, Jo (1933 –) led a large group of women and men in Kalamazoo, MI, in investigating and preparing one of the early studies of sex discrimination in the schools. The group filed a suit against the Kalamazoo Public Schools for the purchase of the Houghton-Mifflin's elementary reading series, citing stereotyping and lack of inclusion of girls and women in the company's books. In response, the school district and Houghton-Mifflin worked with the committee to improve the contents of its textbooks for children. In 1976, Jacobs was appointed first coordinator of the Michigan Office for Sex Equity in Education, a post she held for 18 years. In the early 1990s, Jacobs was inducted into the Michigan Women's Hall of Fame. (ABS)

Jacobs, Joan – See Brumberg, Joan Jacobs

Jacobs, Karen Folger (1940 –) was a co-founder of the San Francisco Women's Center, which became the Women's Building. She graduated from Antioch College and earned a master's at Boston University, where she co-chaired a teach-in on the war in Vietnam. Her Ph.D. thesis at the University of California, Berkeley, comparing how women and men make moral decisions, won the Chancellor's Dissertation Award. In the early 1970s she designed and taught a course, Sexism in Schools, at UC Berkeley. She has published three books: *Girlsports*, about 15 female athletes, ages nine to 17; *Ward 81*, about eight women in a locked ward; and *The Story of a Young Gymnast: Tracee Talavera*, about an Olympic athlete, age 13. She has worked on films in Italy, Mexico and the U.S. Trained as a script consultant, she consults to writers and has taught screenwriting workshops in New York, Texas and California. Her film "Breathtaking Women," about the national champion underwater hockey team, won a prize in France and sold to European television. Her new film, "Surviving Breast Cancer," about eight uninsured women coping with cancer, will premiere in 2006. (ABS)

Jacobs, Rhona Beth (1949 –) A Registered Nurse, Jacobs worked in a free healthcare clinic in the 1970s, and through the people she met there became involved in women's healthcare and reproductive rights. Around 1973, she worked with others to help keep the Chicago Maternity Center, run by Dr. Beatrice Tucker, open. Staffed by RNs and LPNs as well as medical students and residents who had done their OB rotation, the center saw women through their pregnancies and delivered them at home. Jacobs and others helped organize women from all over the city who had had their babies through the center, but ultimately the center was closed and a new women's hospital built. Jacobs has since been involved in abortion rights and reproductive rights issues. (ABS)

Jacobs, Sue-Ellen (1936 –) A teacher in the anthropology department at Sacramento State College in 1968 and a member of the Sacramento Women's Liberation Front, Jacobs was working on tenure and kept her status as an instructor at SSC from other SWLF members. At one meeting, however, community women challenged the "closet faculty members" to develop courses that would show women's contributions to the history of the world. Jacobs was inspired to seek permission from her department chair to create a course called Women Cross-Culturally. Jacobs' bibliography for that course was eventually published in her first book, *Women in Perspective: A Guide for Cross-Cultural Studies*. In 1974, Jacobs became the first tenure-line director of women's studies at the University of Washington, a post she held until 1982. She served as acting director from 1987 – 1988 and became director of the women's studies undergraduate program in 1997. Her research has included women in commercial fishing and in international human rights conventions, among other topics, as well as Native American women's health. In 1972, she began work in San Juan Pueblo, Mexico, and has looked at topics including ethno-historical studies of women's and men's changing roles and lives. She is particularly interested in women's oral and documentary history, and issues in feminist spirituality. Jacobs holds a B.A. from Adams State College (1963), and an M.A. (1966) and a Ph.D. (1970) from the University of Colorado. She retired from the University of Washington in 2004 and is (2005) professor emerita of women's studies there. (ABS)

Jacobskind, Barbara Rachael (1945 –) has been teaching women's studies courses since 1974. She founded the women's studies program at the University of Massachusetts, Dartmouth, in 1978 (known then as Southeastern Massachusetts University) and directed the program from 1978 – 1981. Jacobskind was a founding member of the board of trustees committee on the status of women, founded in the mid 1970s, and represented the Southeastern Massachusetts region at the Houston National Women's Conference in 1977. She was also the New England region representative on the NWSA coordinating council from 1978 – 1980. Jacobskind holds a B.A. from Pennsylvania State University (1966), and an A.M. (1967) and Ph.D. (1970) from Brown University. (ABS)

Jacobson-Wenzel, Dorothea (1942 –) (also known as Dori Jacobson) began her involvement in the women's movement in 1971 when she was an English teacher and artist doing printmaking and photographic etching. As a member of Chicago NOW fighting for reproductive rights and equal pay in the early 1970s, Jacobson-Wenzel was angered when she saw photojournalists (mostly male) laughing at women, and decided to photograph women's events herself. She has been doing this ever since and plans to publish the photos in a book titled *The Women's Movement: Faces of Protest*. Jacobson-Wenzel has one child. She earned her B.A. (1963) and her M.Ed. (1967)

from the University of Illinois, Urbana; her M.S. (1974) from the Illinois Institute of Technology; and her Psy.D. (1996) from the Illinois School of Professional Psychology. Archives: The Sophia Smith Collection, Smith College, Northampton, MA; Schlesinger Library, Radcliffe Institute, Cambridge, MA; and Yale University's Peter Palmquist collection of women photographers and their work, New Haven, CT. (ABS)

Jacquette, Yvonne (1934 –) (also known as Yvonne Burckhardt) Painter, printmaker and teacher, Jacquette and Sylvia Mangold organized a group of artist mothers in NYC (1968), asking them to bring examples of their children's artwork to a meeting. The objective was to see if there were any gender differences in their work. Continued informal discussions explored how mothering related to the women's creativity, and where husbands fit into the mix. With three other women artists, Jacquette looked in vain for a NYC gallery that would put on a women's show (1970). "A few years later, it became hip for galleries to have women's shows—once statistics were published proving what an imbalance existed." Today (2004), Jacquette is part of a two-woman committee that chooses prints for the Library of Congress to buy. They were the first two in approximately 80 years to serve on the Pennell committee. Jacquette, who has one child and one stepchild, attended the Rhode Island School of Design and studied with Herman Cherry. (ABS)

Jaffe, Jacqueline Anne (1942 –) (also known as Jacqueline Anne Marshall) was among the first feminists who joined Columbia Women's Liberation in 1969. She participated in the move to unionize the maids at Columbia, who were not paid on the same scale as male workers doing essentially the same work. Eventually, a case was brought against the university (CWL helped raise the money for court costs) and the maids won a significant victory. Jaffe also attended a CR group for two years and helped NY high-school women start their own CR groups. CWL also wrote pamphlets to help high-school students deal with class and racial diversity within the context of gender inequality. Jaffe also participated in successful CWL gay pride, anti-war and pro-abortion initiatives. After 1972, Jaffe went to graduate school where she wrote on gender issues for her M.A. and Ph.D. Born in Yorkshire, England, Jaffe has one child. She is a professor of humanities at New York University. (ABS)

Jaffe, Nancy Linda (1942 –) (also known as Nancy Cornet) A teacher at Riverside City College (1969–1981), Jaffe created and taught a course on the history of women in America. She was a member of the Western Association of Women Historians (1969–1990), as well as WILPF. While in Berkeley, CA, she participated in demonstrations against the war in Vietnam. Jaffe, who has two children, earned a B.A. at the University of California, Berkeley (1963), and an M.A. from Yale University (1964). (ABS)

Jaggar, Alison M. (1942 –) taught a course on the philosophy of women's rights at Miami University of Ohio in 1971, which she believes was the first anywhere on feminist philosophy. It became a model for other, similar courses after Jaggar distributed her syllabi through the Society for Women in Philosophy, an organization that she co-founded in 1971. Jaggar's paper "Philosophies of Women's Liberation," presented in April 1971, was the first on feminist philosophy ever read to the American Philosophical Association (APA). Jaggar also worked aggressively within the APA on behalf of women. She was co-editor, with Paula Rothenberg, of *Feminist Frameworks* (McGraw-Hill, 1978), one of the earliest women's studies readers, and in 1983 published *Feminist Politics and Human Nature*. Outside academia, she was a co-founder of Women Helping Women in Cincinnati and worked with many other women's organizations. Since the late 1990s, she has been writing on topics of global gender justice in a context of neo-liberal globalization. Jaggar holds a B.A. from the University of London, Bedford College (1964); an M. Litt. from the University of Edinburgh (1967); and a Ph.D. from the State University of New York at Buffalo (1970). Jaggar is a professor of philosophy and women's studies at the University of Colorado, Boulder. (ABS)

Jagucki, Stephanie – See Clohesy, Stephanie June

Jaimes-Guerrero, Marie Anne (1946 –) has studied and written about Native and Indigenous women and women of color, addressing issues of cultural and ethnic identity in pre-patriarchal and pre-colonialist times and the present since the 1970s. She has been an active supporter of the American Indian Movement and the Indigenous Women's Network, on issues of racism, colonization and gender inequities in AIM. She has also done research on Native women's cancer control, linking it to environmental as well as genetic concerns. A tenured faculty member in the WOMS (Women's Studies) Dept. at San Francisco State University, Jaimes-Guerrero earned her doctorate in education and public policy, with an emphasis on American Indian education and identity issues. Her current (2005) research is on genetic engineering targeting Indigenous peoples worldwide, called biocolonialism. She has two children. (ABS)

James, Laurie (1930 –) An actor and author, James developed the "New Day" books for Camp Fire Girls Inc. (1970 – 1973). An expert on the life of Margaret Fuller, James began her solo drama on Fuller, titled "Men, Women, and Margaret Fuller," in 1971. She then went on to produce a three-volume series on Fuller, and in 1989 received a fellowship from The New York Foundation for the Arts for Volume III, also titled *Men, Women and Margaret Fuller*. Volumes I and II are *The Wit and Wisdom of Margaret Fuller Ossoli* and *Why Margaret Fuller Ossoli Is Forgotten*. In addition, James has lectured and published various articles on Fuller, and under a grant from The National Endowment on the Humanities toured as Fuller in the 1991, 1992 and 1993 American Renaissance Program sponsored by the Great Plains Chautauqua Society. James was co-founder, with Ramona Barth, of The Margaret Fuller Ossoli Network. In 1981, they dedicated the Margaret Fuller Ossoli Square in front of Radcliffe, and in 1987 unveiled a plaque in Cambridge City Hall. On the demise of the ERA, James represented the Network when she spoke Fullers' words on the equality of women on national TV. James, who has five children, has attended the New York University Writing Center, Lewis & Clark College, and the American Academy of Dramatic Arts.   (ABS)

James, Nancy Ann (1933 –) (also known as Nancy Pirsig) became aware of the inequities between men and women, in both the civil service and the faculty, while working in a civil service position at the University of Minnesota (1964 – 1975). In the late 1960s, she was part of a small group of women (faculty and civil service) who formed the Council for University Women's Progress. Welcomed by the administration as an official part of the university's Minneapolis-St. Paul Campus, CUWP improved the lives of women on many fronts. James also helped rewrite the large civil service manual to make it gender neutral. CUWP encouraged the administration to recognize the problem of sexual harassment and provide training in sexist behavior to supervisors; persuaded the administration to request that all committees include women; encouraged fearful or intimidated women with grievances to confront their supervisors (and provided an escort, if requested); and mediated disputes between individual women and their bosses. Unfortunately, says James, "It was because of some of these activities that, after several years, the university's attorney persuaded the administration that CUWP was behaving like a house union, which was prohibited by law, and the organization was ordered to disband." In other work, James wrote the article "From Nothing to Everything Just As It Is," published in *The Divine Mosaic: Women's Images of the Sacred Other* (Yes International Publishers, 1994). She has also been active in the peace, civil rights, alternative education and environmental movements in MN and FL, and, in 2004, helped start a women's group to discuss political issues and actions that the women might take. James, who holds a B.A. from the University of Minnesota, has two children, one deceased.   (ABS)

James, Paula (1943 –) helped initiate and was elected secretary of the Texas chapter of WEAL (1971) and president (1972). She also served on the national board during that period. The chapter filed sex discrimination complaints with the EEOC and OFCC (1971 – 1972) against 100 employers in Dallas and other TX cities, including Sears, the Dallas city and county governments, 40 Dallas banks, and several colleges and universities, as well as a number of private employers. The suits brought public attention to the practice of firing women for being pregnant, and the failure to promote or pay women according to their experience and merits. In 1982, James co-founded the Women's Advocacy Project, which provides free legal services and advice to indigent women and women in violent situations. In 1992, she founded the Match Program, which matches low-income clients with attorneys who will charge no more than $50 an hour. Most clients are women. In 2002, James co-founded the Texas Women's Coalition, pulling all the progressive women's groups in the state into a coalition that can speak on behalf of hundreds of thousands of TX women on feminist issues, modeled on the National Council of Women's Organizations. James, who holds a Ph.D. and a J.D., has one child.   (ABS)

James, Selma (1930 –) Born in Brooklyn, NY, James became organizing secretary of the Campaign Against Racial Discrimination (1965), the first major organization of the anti-racist movement in Britain. By 1969 she was a founding member of the Black Regional Action Movement. She entered a London feminist group in 1970 and in 1972 founded the International Feminist Collective. This grew into the International Wages for Housework campaign. Working toward an international redefinition of work, WFH has campaigned for recognition and compensation for all unwaged labor in the home, on the land and in the community, for pay equity, and for reduction of women's tremendous workload. "Putting a price tag on women's unwaged contributions establishes our entitlement to economic independence and all the civil, economic and human rights which have long been denied women everywhere," says James. In 1972, James co-authored *The Power of Women and the Subversion of the Community*. James' work set off a firestorm by some feminists who argued that women could find liberation only in jobs outside the home, and that wages for their work would institutionalize women in the home. Many later changed their minds, since women who go out to work have not been relieved of the work they have traditionally done at home. In 1975, WFH became active in the United Nations Decade for Women, ultimately pulling together support from 2,000 NGOs to win the 1995 UN decision of the World Conference on Women in Beijing that governments measure, value and include unwaged work in national statistics. In 2000, WFH gave birth to the Global Women's Strike, which brings together actions and initiatives in over 70 countries under the banner "Invest in Caring, Not Killing." James coordinates the Strike's global network. James resides in London where, since the bombings of Afghanistan and Iraq, she has participated in the weekly anti-war pickets outside the House of Parliament. She has one child.   (ABS)

Janeway, Elizabeth (1913 – 2005) began her career as a novelist in the 1940s, and began to write non-fiction books about feminist issues in the 1970s. These include

J

Man's World, Woman's Place: A Study of Social Mythology (Morrow, 1971), *Between Myth and Morning: Women's Awakening* (Morrow, 1974), *Powers of the Weak* (Knopf, 1980), and *Improper Behavior* (Morrow, 1987), among others. Janeway believed that "women need to read books to have their thoughts and experiences confirmed and thus be reinforced for action." Janeway, who was born in Brooklyn, graduated from the Shore Road Academy and then spent a year at Swarthmore. After the Depression wiped out her family's savings, she went to work writing advertising copy for a department store. She received her B.A. from Barnard College in 1935. Janeway was also active on behalf of writers, serving as president of the Authors Guild from 1965–1969. She was a trustee at Barnard, a fellow at Berkeley College at Yale University, and director of the NOW LDEF.

Jardine, Lauren Lovett (1946–) While in graduate school at Arizona State University in the early 1970s, Jardine became involved with NOW and local university feminist organizations, and worked on Title IX compliance for the state of AZ. She was the first Ph.D. candidate/graduate from ASU with a specialization in women's studies, and taught women's studies/feminist theory classes at ASU through 1979. Having come out as a lesbian in 1978, she later moved to California and became a director of Lesbian Central at Los Angeles' Gay & Lesbian Community Services Center. After working there for three years, she co-founded and served as executive director of Connexxus Women's Centers, West Hollywood and East Los Angeles (1983–1989). She also taught feminist/lesbian classes at Cal State Northridge and UCLA, and in 1995 taught the first lesbian film class at UCLA. In 1996, she moved to Hawaii and has "remained a feminist lesbian activist, working now with young queer kids on Maui." Jardine, who has two daughters, earned her B.A. from Barnard College (1967), and her M.A. (1974) and Ph.D. (1978) from Arizona State University. Archives: The Mazer Collection, Los Angeles, CA.   (ABS)

Jarrell, Sandra (1949–2005) was a flight attendant with Eastern Airlines for three years, where she was constantly weight-checked and harassed about her weight, which the airline said could not be above 132 pounds. At 5 ft. 9 in. tall, 132 pounds was below what was medically approved for her height. She quit the airline and, with Jan Fulsom, took Eastern Air Lines to court on discrimination charges. Then, in 1972, she co-founded and became executive director of Stewardesses for Women's Rights, the first all-women national organization for flight attendants, which was dedicated to fighting the airlines' unfair employment and promotion rules, unsafe cargo practices, and policies that stripped flight attendants of their dignity. SFWR served as a legal liaison, linking flight attendants who had been discriminated against to lawyers who represented them. The stewardesses filed lawsuits against Continental Airlines and National Airlines, alleg-

ing that a hostile work environment was created by the airlines' sexist advertising: "I'm Carol, Fly me," "We really move our tail for you." To combat airline advertising that portrayed flight attendants as sexually available airborne bunnies, SFWR launched a media campaign showing a flight attendant as a responsible professional woman with a serious job to do. They also picketed sexist films that denigrated flight attendants, as well as bookstores displaying books in the "Coffee, Tea or Me" genre. Many of those cases succeeded in striking down marital and age restrictions enforced against flight attendants and helped gain the right to remain employed while pregnant. Archives: Stewardesses for Women's Rights papers at Tamiment Library, New York University, New York, NY.

Jawin, Ann Juliano (1922–) A career guidance specialist, Jawin began working on the problem of sex bias in education in the late 1960s. As chair of NYC NOW's task force on education and employment, she edited the 1977 edition of "The Report on Sex Bias in the New York City Public Schools." With others, she testified before the board of ed. and won the establishment of the chancellor's task force to eliminate sex bias in the NYC public schools. Jawin served on that commission for several years. In 1970, she developed the first Inservice Course for teachers on women's rights. The board of ed. later included units from this course on eliminating sex bias and discrimination in its policies, practices and curriculum in a course mandated for all new teachers. In 1980, with another guidance counselor (Mary Selzer), Jawin initiated a class action against the board of ed. for discriminating against women in appointments to supervisory positions in high schools. It was settled successfully in 1990. Jawin also developed workshops at NOW headquarters for women seeking to re-enter the workforce and wrote *A Woman's Guide to Career Development* (Anchor Press, 1979). In 1987, Jawin founded the Queens Women's Center (later renamed the Center for the Women of New York). Jawin has also been active in the Democratic Party, and in 1972 was the first woman in her area of northeastern Queens to run for NY assemblywoman. She is the recipient the New York State Advisory Council on Vocational Education Award, the Susan B. Anthony Award, and the Ralph Bunch Award for Human Rights. The mother of two children, she holds a B.A. from Hunter College (1943); an M.S. from C.W. Post (1972); and a P.D. (1976) from St. John's University.   (ABS)

Jay, Karla (1947–) An author and activist, Jay was a member of Redstockings (1969–1970); was on the editorial staff and was a contributor to *Rat* (1970); and participated in the Lavender Menace action at the Second Congress to Unite Women, where lesbians came out of the closet to the women's movement (1970). A professor, editor and reviewer, she is the author of *Tales of the Lavender Menace: A Memoir of Liberation* (Basic Books, 1999). She was series editor of *The Cutting Edge: Lesbian Life and*

Literature, and editor of *Dyke Life: From Growing Up to Growing Old – A Celebration of the Lesbian Experience* (Basic Books, 1995), and *Lesbian Erotics* (New York University Press, 1995). *Dyke Life* was Best Lesbian Studies Book, Lambda Literary Foundation (1996). Jay holds an A.B. from Barnard College, and an M.Phil. (1978) and Ph.D. (1984) from New York University. Archives: New York Public Library, New York, NY. (ABS)

Jeannet, Angela M. (1931 –) was co-founder of the Lancaster Women's Liberation Group in Lancaster (Lancaster Co.), PA in 1970. One of the earliest local women's liberation groups, it began with political action and CR; its purpose was to help create a community in which all women are able to make their own choices in all the areas of their private and public lives. Jeannet has also written *Under the Radiant Sun and the Crescent Moon: Italo Calvino's Storytelling* (2000) and edited *New World Journeys: Contemporary Italian Writers and the Experience of America* (1977) and *Natalia Ginzburg: A Voice of the Twentieth Century* (2000). Archives: Sallie Bingham Center, Duke University, Durham, NC. (ABS)

JEB – See Biren, Joan Elisabeth

Jeffrey, Mildred (1911–2004) was an influential, behind-the-scenes activist in the women's rights, labor and civil rights movements. The eldest of seven children, she was born into an Iowa farm family of hard working, independent women. (Her mother became Iowa's first female registered pharmacist in 1908.) While a student at the University of Minnesota (1928), she joined the Women's International League for Peace and Freedom and the YWCA. After graduating, she organized women in the cotton garment factories around Allentown, PA; became the first woman UAW official (1940s); organized UAW's women's department; and served as special assistant to Walter Reuther from 1944 – 1976. At the end of WWII, when women production workers were subject to massive layoffs as the men returned, Jeffrey organized the first UAW women's conference. She began campaigning for the ERA as early as 1948; was an early NOW member; and was a founding member of the NWPC (1971), which she chaired for several years. She became a leader in the Democratic Party committee that ensured that half the delegates to the 1980 convention were women, and was influential in persuading Walter Mondale to name Geraldine Ferraro as his running mate in the 1984 presidential election. The founding mother of the Michigan Women's Foundation, Jeffrey served on the boards of NARAL and the National Council of Churches. In 1985, she organized Women for a Meaningful Summit to ensure that women's viewpoints were heard when President Reagan and Mikhail Gorbachev met. A civil rights activist as well, she was awarded the Presidential Medal of Freedom from President Clinton (2000). Jeffrey graduated from the University of Minnesota (1932) with a B.A.

and earned an M.A. from the Department of Social Economy and Social Research, Bryn Mawr College (1934). Archives: Walter P. Reuther Library of Labor & Urban Affairs and the UAW Community Relations Department, Detroit, MI.

Jeffrey, Sharon – See Lehrer, Sharon Jeffrey

Jenness, Linda Jane (1941 –) An outspoken supporter of feminism and socialism in the South in the 1970s, Jenness ran for president of the U.S. on the Socialist Workers Party Ticket in 1971 – 1972. Speaking at Oshkosh State University in 1971 on "Why Feminism Is Revolutionary," Jenness explained that the basic demands being made by women include free, legal abortions, no forced sterilizations, equal work for equal pay, and free 24-hour childcare centers. She served as both chair and national committee member of the Socialist Workers Party. Jenness is a co-author of *Women and the Cuban Revolution* (1970); author of *Socialism and Democracy* (1972); and editor of *Feminism and Socialism* (Pathfinder Press, 1972). Jenness is a graduate of Antioch College (1962).

Jensen, Katherine Ruth (1946 –) During 1969 – 1972, when she was in Arizona in the middle of a Navajo Reservation, Jensen got together with other women for what others would call a CR group. In 1976, Jensen was able to convince the provost that the University of Wyoming ought to have a women's center and women's studies courses. The sociology department harbored the incipient program for several years before Joan Wadlow, a new woman dean of arts & sciences, brought it full-fledged into the college in 1981. Jensen served as director of the program for its first 10 years, when "everything we did was tediously precedent-breaking in institutional terms" and met with resistance. Jensen, who did her Ph.D. dissertation at the University of Wisconsin, Madison, on women Ph.D.'s, also holds an M.A. from the University of Wisconsin and a B.A. from Carleton College. She has four children. Archives: The American Heritage Center, University of Wyoming, Laramie, WY. (ABS)

Jervis, Jane Lise (1938 –) (also known as Jane Pruett) In the late 1960s and early 1970s, Jervis attended CR meetings in New Haven, CT, and participated in Women v. the State of Connecticut, an abortion-rights lawsuit. In the early to mid 1970s, she was a participant in and then a facilitator of a Sunday-afternoon group for divorced and separated women. With the support of her women's group, she entered graduate school at Yale in her mid thirties, graduating with a Ph.D. in 1978. Her career in academic administration, which started at Yale, took her to Hamilton College as dean of students (1982 – 1987), Bowdoin College as dean of the college (1988 – 1992), and Evergreen University as president (1992 – 2000). At Hamilton and Bowdoin, she was the first woman to be in the senior administration, and at Evergreen she was the first woman to

J

be president of a public university in Washington State. She made a point of hiring, developing and promoting women. "One of my male presidential colleagues in Washington once took me to task because two-thirds of my VPs were women. 'What's going on over there?' he asked, and he was serious. All of his VPs were men!" In addition to her Ph.D., Jervis, who has two children, holds an A.B. from Radcliffe College (1959). (ABS)

Jetter, Elizabeth Susan (1932 –) joined the San Fernando Valley (CA) chapter of NOW in 1972, and is still (2004) a member. As president of the chapter, she organized pickets at the Oscar Awards for Hollywood's unflattering presentation of women. She also organized pickets at the local courthouse because "judges were just giving a slap on the wrist to rapists." She served as a representative to CA NOW and, at one time, as membership coordinator. She also served as a delegate to the national NOW conferences. SFV NOW organized a marching band (Jetter played clarinet and later trumpet) that led the march for the ERA in Chicago. A retired senior engineer's assistant at the Jet Propulsion Laboratory, Jetter has five children. Archives: NOW, Washington, D.C. (ABS)

Jimenez, Cherie Colette (1950 –) experienced domestic violence at a young age, had her first child when she was a teenager, and by 1973 was determined to fight abuse against women even though at that time it was a topic rarely discussed by society in general. That year, Jimenez moved to Cambridge, MA. Intent on creating real solutions to the problems of violence in the lives of women and children, she participated in the first battered women's shelter on the East Coast. Called Transition House, the shelter opened in 1976. As of this writing (2005), Transition House is still sheltering women and children, and Jimenez continues her activism for this cause. Jimenez, who has three children, was able to educate herself later in life, earning a B.A. from the University of Massachusetts in 1995.

Jo, Bev (1950 –) (also known as Bev Jo Von Dohre) is a working-class, lifelong lesbian of European descent. Turned away from the Daughters of Bilitis in 1969 because she was underage (21 or older was required for legal reasons), Jo nonetheless became active in the lesbian community in California in 1970, supporting various events. In 1972, she helped develop the Lesbian Feminist Conference in Berkeley, CA, one of the first in the country. She also worked at Woman's Place Bookstore and participated in lesbian feminist demonstrations. In 1972 Jo became a lesbian separatist, and put out *Dykes & Gorgons* in 1973, a lesbian separatist newspaper and one of the first that printed articles against classism and racism. She was also part of the Lesbian Coffeehouse Collective and a dyke separatist group that, among other actions, protested the harm that the male psychiatric profession was doing to females. She began teaching

self-defense classes for Bay Area Women Against Rape (1975 –1985) and did workshops about equal love relationships at lesbian events. She has written many lesbian-focused articles published internationally, and much of *Dykes & Gorgons* has been reprinted in the anthology *For Lesbians Only*. In 1990, Jo co-published *Dykes Loving Dykes: Dyke Separatist Politics for Lesbians Only*. (ABS)

Joans, Barbara (1935 –) (also known as Barbara Joans-Schwartz) As a sociology and anthropology instructor at the New School for Social Research (1965 – 1975), Joans created a women's studies course. From 1965 – 1970, she ran an underground railway for women needing abortions; co-organized a women's caucus conference in NYC; and co-founded (1968 – 1969) Local 55 (Cell 55), a women's liberation small group. Joans co-organized the first and co-organized the second Congress to Unite Women (1969, 1970). She was arrested at the second Congress, but not jailed, for refusing to hand over tapes of the event. She was part of the sit-in at the *Ladies' Home Journal*, and with June Arnold staffed the first Women's Center with money from that magazine. Joans marched (and was arrested for marching) for abortion rights. In 1970, she was a co-founder of Older Women's Liberation and anonymously wrote its material on childrearing, divorce and economic survival, among other topics. In 1974, she received her Ph.D. from CUNY, writing her dissertation on women's liberation small groups. From 1975 – 1977, she was a member of the core faculty, women's studies, San Jose State University. Assistant professor of anthropology at Idaho State University (1978 – 1979), she served as director of Women's Re-Entry. Joans, who earned her B.A. from Brooklyn College and her M.A. from New York University, is co-author of *Identity; Female*, a women's studies multimedia book (Dun Donnelley Publishing Corporation, 1975). Joans has been published in *Off Our Backs*, *On the Issues* and numerous academic journals. Director (2004) of the Merritt Museum of Anthropology and chair of the anthropology department, Merritt College, Joans has two children. (ABS)

Johnson, Clara Elizabeth (1924 –) As a member of Peoria NOW, Johnson served as VP (1974) and president (1976 – 1977). She chaired a project that attempted to force Sears Roebuck to end its discriminatory practices against women. The group also worked for the ERA. From 1978 – 1979, Johnson was VP and board member of Women Strength (Peoria). From 1982 – 1984, Johnson was office manager for IL NOW. In 1983, she served as secretary of Des Plaines/Parkridge NOW, and was director (1990 – 1995) of its Feminist Writers Contest, which successfully raised money to support the chapter. A chemist, Johnson has one child. (ABS)

Johnson, Dixie (1933 –) founded a NOW chapter in Grand Coulee, WA, during the ERA campaign; she was later elected VP and then president of Washington State

NOW. Johnson was part of the state leadership group of all the major women's organizations that created Washington Women United, which in turn led to WA being the national leader in women's rights in the 1980s. She served as national chair of NOW's feminist CR committee and traveled nationally leading CR groups. She joined Sonia Johnson's Women's Fast for Justice, in Springfield, IL, and later arranged a book tour so that Sonia Johnson could promote her book *From Housewife to Heretic*, which chronicles her dismissal from the Mormon Church. Dixie Johnson has served in various positions through three NOW administrations, including office manager, national conference manager and celebrity coordinator. She also brought desktop publishing to the NOW office. Having served as a member of the Air Force in the WAF Band in the 1950s, Johnson became president and organizer of the Women of the Air Force Band in the late 1990s. Because "the Air Force had forgotten there had even been such a band," she created the band archives, housed at the Schlesinger Library of American Women's History in Cambridge, MA. Johnson is also the author of the *U.S. WAF Band Story*, published in 2004. Archives: Schlesinger Library, Radcliffe Institute, Cambridge, MA. (ABS)

Johnson, Gloria (1937 –) was a founder of the San Diego County chapter of NOW in the early 1970s. She served as chapter president and chair of the lesbian rights task force, was a member of the national lesbian rights committee, and was director of the NOW Lesbian Conference in 1988. A member of Local Service Employees International Union (SEIU) since 1970, Johnson has served as committee chair, employment rights for lesbians and gay men. As a member of the San Diego Democratic Club (1972 –), she has held various offices and worked to elect supporters of lesbian and gay rights. A political consultant, she was formerly a social worker. (ABS)

Johnson, Kathryn Kenley (1944 –) was a member of the sociology department's women's caucus, University of California, Berkeley (1968), and participated in the university's first women's liberation conference, Breaking the Shackles. Involved in educational reform efforts for a relevant education at the university, Johnson taught the first class on women's health (1972–1976). She was a founding member of the women's caucus in the New American Movement and was co-author, with Peggy Somers, of a position paper on socialist feminism titled "Behind Every Sexist Stands the Boss: The Political Economy of Sexism." The paper was adopted by the New American Movement as its platform on socialist feminism. As an original member of the Berkeley/Oakland Women's Union (1972 – 1976), Johnson gave the keynote address, Beyond Anger, at the Union's convening conference and was a member of the Union's political theory group. Concerned with issues regarding women's health and women in the public health professions, Johnson was a member of the Women's Collective, Berkeley Radical Psychiatry (1972)

and a board member of the Coalition for the Medical Rights of Women, San Francisco (1984). As a policy analyst in the California Department of Health Services, Sacramento, CA, she chaired the women's advisory committee (1982 – 1984) and served as vice chair of the department's EEO (1984). As a research associate at the Women's Resources and Research Center, University of California, Davis, she designed and implemented a research support program to promote women's studies and feminist scholarship and improve the status of women in higher education (1985–1992). As a senior policy analyst and program officer, she directed the Program on Gender and Social Policy at the San Francisco Urban Institute, San Francisco State University, and established the Stay in School Family Resource Center, a program to encourage the college option for women on Welfare (1998 – 2002). Johnson is (2005) a policy analyst at the Marian Wright Edelman Institute at San Francisco State University, and is the organizer of an annual public lecture series in honor of Women's History Month and International Women's Day. She serves on the task force for the working poor of the National Economic Development and Law Center (2002 –). She is the author of several articles, including "Why Do Women Kill Themselves: Durkheim Revisited," published in the *Journal of Suicide and Life-Threatening Behavior* (Fall 1978) and "Sexual Harassment: No Longer an Individual Problem on College Campuses," published in *California Women, III* (1986). She is co-editor of *Catalog of Research on Women and Gender* (Women's Resources and Research Center, UC Davis, 1992) and *Academic Women at UC Davis: Barriers to Retention and Promotion and Recommendations for Action* (Women's Resources and Research Center, UC Davis, 1989). Johnson, who has one child and a stepchild, earned her B.A. from Barnard College, and her M.A. and M.P.H. from UC Berkeley. Archives: Social Protest Archives, Bancroft Library, University of California, Berkeley. (ABS)

Johnson, Linnea (1946 –) (also known as Linnea Sallach and Linnea Becker) became a feminist during college (University of Nebraska-Lincoln, 1966). When, in anger, her husband called her a feminist, she looked up the word, found deBeauvoir, and decided that was indeed who she was, strong and glad. From 1970 – 1972, Johnson was part of CWLU's Abortion Counseling Service and performed abortions. She then worked alongside the Lincoln Legion of Lesbians (1977 – 1987) agitating for human rights. She was also elected delegate to a White House Conference on the Family in 1980. Johnson developed and taught the first women's poetry course at the University of Nebraska (1979–1980), and in 1981 organized a women's literature course taught at the Lincoln YWCA ("because the university English department just couldn't manage to schedule it, even though a full class of women petitioned to take it"). She co-founded *The Women's Journal-Advocate* in Lincoln (1981 – 1982), and developed and co-hosted a public radio show featuring women in the arts in Normal, IL (1987). Johnson, who lobbied for the ERA nationally and in Nebraska, sued Muhlenberg College for tenure and promotion on the grounds of sex discrimination and won a monetary settlement as well as a paper tenure and promotion. A widely published fiction, poetry and essay writer, Johnson's books include *The Chicago Home* (alice james books, 1986), which was First Winner of the Beatrice Hawley Prize; and *Making Sense: Nine Love Poems* (Polemic Number One Press, 1988). She is also the creator of the CD Swedish Christmas (BummerTent Records, 2000). Her fiction and poetry have been published in several anthologies. She is the recipient of the Vreeland Award in Fiction and Poetry, 1977, and Pushcart Prize nominations in 1985, 1986, 1991 and 1992. Johnson, who has two children, received her B.A. and Ph.D. from the University of Nebraska-Lincoln, and her M.A. from Goddard College.   (ABS)

Johnson, Margaret Katherine (1940 –) (also known as Flowing) In 1971, Johnson and three other women sponsored a conference at Washington University that ultimately became a network of professional lesbians in St. Louis. She attended the first Midwest Women's Festival in 1972, then helped organize the next four. In 1979, she was an organizer of the first Take Back the Night March in St. Louis. Also in 1979, Johnson joined the workers community at the Michigan Women's Music Festival and eventually became land coordinator. She remains (2004) on the staff. In 1983, Johnson facilitated a citywide forum on battering in the lesbian community. She organized a Women Gathering in St. Louis (1984), and began traveling in Missouri and Arizona doing gatherings for local communities. From 1980–1985, she served as an escort at the Reproductive Health Center, St. Louis. In 1985, Johnson organized Women Rising in Resistance to publicize and protest against judges who handed down weak or ineffectual sentences against rapists or others abusing women. In 1986, Johnson and others conceptualized and organized the first national Women Rising in Resistance Action, held at the Statue of Liberty in NYC. In 1987, Johnson was a member of the steering committee of the action held at the Supreme Court to object to the Hardwick decision that upheld laws against sodomy. Called "Out and Outraged," the action was "the biggest action in D.C. since the Vietnam War, resulted in over 600 arrests, and catapulted the LGBT movement into national view." From 1991–1993, Johnson organized a St. Louis chapter of Queer Nation. She was also on the statewide steering committee that stopped an anti-gay, Colorado-style amendment from passing. Johnson continues to serve as an escort at a local abortion/reproductive health clinic. Johnson is (2005) a teacher and holds an M.A. Archives: Missouri Historical Society, St. Louis, MO. (ABS)

Johnson, Marlene Marie (1946 –) was a founder of the Ramsey County chapter of the MN WPC and served as chair for two years. She was also founding president of the

MN chapter of the National Association of Women Business Owners. She holds a B.A. from Macalester College. Archives: Minnesota Historical Society, St. Paul, MN. (ABS)

Johnson, Mary Beth – See Edelson, Mary Beth

Johnson, Nan Heffelfinger (1930 –) As trustee of the State University of New York (1976–1990), Johnson developed and taught three women's studies classes in 1983: Women in Politics; Women and the Law; and Women, Politics and Science Fiction. In 1995, she served as chair of the celebrations for the 75th anniversary of suffrage, and became founding director of the Susan B. Anthony Center at the University of Rochester. In 1998, she served as chair of Forum 98, a national celebration of the 150th anniversary of the Seneca Falls Convention. Politically active, Johnson was the first woman elected to represent the 21 District of the Monroe County (NY) Legislature (1975); was the first woman majority leader of the Legislature (1978 and 1979); and was the first woman to chair the human services committee. In that capacity, she founded the maternal, infants and children task force to focus on concerns in those areas, particularly infant mortality. (This task force was later institutionalized into the County Board of Health.) Johnson also worked to create the first library for information on AIDS, and to develop services for women in prison. She was also a founding member of the Rochester Coalition of Labor Women. Johnson, who has two children, earned her A.B. from Barnard College (1952); attended Cornell Law School (1952–1953); and was the first woman to earn an M.A. in political science from the University of Rochester. She is the founding president (2003) of Friends of Women's Rights National Park. Archives: University of Rochester, Rochester, NY.   (ABS)

Johnson, Nancy Rae (1936 – 2005) was best known as a healer. She was also a champion of the lesbian/feminist movement, gay rights, women's rights and civil rights beginning in 1963. After participating in the march from Selma to Montgomery with her partner, Dinah Utah, the two moved to NYC, where Johnson was a member of CR Group Four and spoke on radio and TV as an activist. In 1970, she started her own business, Aenjai Graphics, and designed and printed thousands of posters, fliers, ads and personal papers for NOW, Kent State, civil rights and lesbian/gay rights, among others. She participated in The Firehouse on Wooster Street (a lesbian and gay meeting place), spoke on panels, and fought to have "lesbian" be a separate name in gay rights politics. "I believed that lesbians would be invisible in a movement that used the title 'Gay Rights.'" Johnson grew up in Utah when nuclear bombs were being tested. Because authorities insisted the bombs were perfectly safe, she would go outside to observe the colors in the sky when the dust passed. Later she developed thyroid cancer, cured by white light treatments. That experience prompted her to devote herself to white light healing. Johnson attended Brigham Young University. She raised two adopted black sisters, and later, when they were grown, she raised two other children.

Johnston, Jill (1929 –) Author and critic, Johnston began her writing career in 1955 as a contributor to the *Dance Observer*. In 1959 she joined the *Village Voice* as its dance critic and was soon covering art happenings and events as well; at the same time, she was a reviewer for *Art News*. Her specialty was everything new and shocking, the avant-garde in every medium. By the late 1960s Johnston had abandoned criticism to write an intimate column recording her adventures from week to week. Her writing style changed radically, abjuring normal syntax, punctuation and paragraphing, and creating neologisms and non sequiturs in tying anecdotal material together. In 1970 Johnston was overtaken by the feminist movement. Her stylistic extremism continued unabated as she grappled with feminist and lesbian feminist issues, putting her column at the service of the women's movement. During the early 1970s she had three books published: *Marmalade Me* and *Gullibles Travels*, collections of columns and criticism from the 1960s and 1970s, respectively, and *Lesbian Nation: The Feminist Solution*. In the mid to late 1970s Johnston adjusted to the new national conservatism, straightening out her prose for more accessible writing. In 1983 and 1985 she had two autobiographical books published by Alfred A. Knopf: *Mother Bound* and *Paper Daughter*. In 1985 she began writing for two establishment publications: *Art in America* and *The New York Times Book Review*. Critical essays from these publications were collected in 1994 in a volume titled *Secret Lives in Art*. In 1996 her scholarly work on Jasper Johns was published: *Jasper Johns—Privileged Information*. In 1998 *Admission Accomplished: The Lesbian Nation Years 1970-75*, an expanded edition of *Gullibles Travels*, was published. Johnston graduated from Tufts University in 1951 and received an M.F.A. from the University of North Carolina in 1953. She has two children. Johnston married Ingrid Nyeboe in Denmark in 1993. (ABS)

Jones, Ann (1937 –) began her feminist activity in the mid 1960s tutoring Welfare mothers preparing for high-school equivalency exams. As an English professor at a developing black college in the South in 1969 – 1970, she brought feminism and race issues into the classroom. Teaching from 1970 – 1973 in the Open Admissions program of the City College of New York, Jones taught courses on feminist theory and gay culture in an experimental studies program, and with other faculty members developed a formal women's studies program. From 1973 – 1975 she served as academic coordinator of women's studies at the University of Massachusetts at Amherst, organizing feminist courses into a formal degree-granting women's studies program. By 1975, she was writing about women and violence. Jones left academic life and moved back to NYC to work on *Women Who Kill* (Holt, Rinehart & Winston, 1980). Since 1980 she has been speaking, lecturing, lobbying, writing books and articles, and performing as a talking head in documentaries in the U.S., Canada and the United Kingdom on behalf of battered women. Her other books include *Uncle Tom's Campus* (1973), about her teaching at a black college; *Everyday Death: The Case of Bernadette Powell* (1985), the story of an African American battered woman who killed her husband; *When Love Goes Wrong: What To Do When You Can't Do Anything Right* (with Susan Schechter, 1992), a self-help guide for women in relationships with controlling partners; and *Next Time She'll Be Dead: Battering & How To Stop It* (1994, updated edition 2000). For an exposé of abuse of women prisoners published in *The Nation* (1982), Jones was named Journalist of the Year by the National Prisoners Rights Union. From 1986 – 1996, she taught writing and women's studies at Mount Holyoke College, while maintaining a career as a writer and international journalist/photojournalist. During 1996 – 1998 she traveled throughout Africa to produce *Looking for Lovedu* (2001). During 2003 – 2005, she worked in Afghanistan on women's rights and education. Jones earned her M.A. at the University of Michigan and her B.S. and Ph.D. at the University of Wisconsin. (ABS)

Jones, Beverly R. (1927 –) With Judith Brown, Jones was co-author of *Toward a Female Liberation Movement* (New England Free Press, 1968). Credited as one of the most influential pamphlets of the reawakening feminist movement, it has been extensively republished in books such as *Sisterhood Is Powerful* (1970), *Voices From Women's Liberation* (1971), *Women Together* (1976) and *Radical Feminism: Theory and Practice* (2000). Prior to its publication, Jones served as president of the Pensacola (FL) LWV (1958 – 1960), as VP of Democratic Women of Florida (1962 – 1963), and as founder and president of Gainesville Women for Equal Rights (1963 – 1964), a civil rights organization. She also served as co-founder and VP of PA NOW (1973 – 1975), and was a board member of national NOW (1976 – 1979). Her other publications include *Toward a Strong and Effective Women's Movement* (PA NOW, 1972), *Control Over Our Own Organization: Control Over Our Own Movement* (PA NOW, 1972), and *Out of the Mainstream, Into the Revolution* (Majority Caucus platform, 1975). Jones, a psychologist who has two children, holds a B.A. (1952) and M.A. (1954) from the University of California, Los Angeles (ABS)

Jones, Davlyn (1934 –) As a member of the Sunnyvale-South Bay (CA) chapter of NOW (1971 – 1976), Jones served as media chair, speakers bureau chair and editor of its newsletter. Among its extensive activities, the chapter supported female political candidates; protested pay inequities in county and city jobs; protested the preference for male veterans over higher qualified females in social service jobs, and worked for fair credit laws and fair representation in the media. The chapter, working with lawyer Joan Bradford, was responsible for the Amicus Right to Privacy Brief that was accepted by the Supreme Court in Roe v. Wade. The chapter also started the policy of addressing its news only to women in the media; initiated radio and TV channel blacklisting to the FCC citing incidences/examples of prejudice in the programming; was prominent in obtaining a California State recognition of equal rights for credit; and supported Title IX equality in sports and reproductive rights. As president of the Sunnyvale-South Bay chapter of NOW from 1972–1973, Jones increased membership tenfold, and was a founder of the first Status of Women Commission for Santa Clara County. She was also general manager for the 1973 Annual NOW Conference held in San Jose. Jones also served as third state coordinator for CA NOW (1974–1975), was a member of NOW's national board, and was a NOW CR leader and trainer. She was coordinator for Alice Doesn't! Strike Day, an international NOW-sponsored strike (1975). Jones, who has three children, holds a B.A. from the University of California, Santa Barbara.   (ABS)

Jones, Del (1926 –) A community organizer in the civil rights movement, Jones says, "It came to me that the reason I worked so hard against racism was that I had experienced sexism!" She was VP of NOW, Cleveland chapter, in the early 1970s; helped form the Cleveland Rape Crisis Center, where she served on the board for several years in the mid 1970s; and was one of the founders of Woman-Space, a Cleveland resource center for women. Also active in the ERA and abortion rights movements, Jones marched on Washington in 1976 and participated in the televised response to the Roman Catholic Bishop of Cleveland on abortion rights. Jones was also involved in the Women's News show on the NBC station in Cleveland, and worked one year for the Office of Civil Rights. Jones holds a B.S. and an M.S. She has three children, and is (2004) involved in peace building and domestic violence education.   (ABS)

Jones, Donna Marie (1950 –) As a senior at the University of Wisconsin, Madison, in 1971, Jones worked as a residence hall house fellow. Of the 60 co-eds on her floor, 20 were African Americans—a concentration that was viewed as terrible, and in need of rectifying. Jones held her ground, however, and all of the women were able to stay together "without succumbing to ignorance, prejudice and fear." After graduation, Jones served on a municipal task force that reviewed and revised the fire-fighter hiring standards, opening the door for the first women fire fighters to join the Madison fire department. As a student at the University of Wisconsin Law School, Jones joined the Women's Law Student Association and Black Law Student Association. She worked on the 8th National Conference on Women and the Law and later served on the conference's national steering committee. In 1977, she was a WI delegate to the National Women's Conference in Houston. During this time, she was also an active

supporter of the ERA. After becoming an attorney, Jones served on the State Bar of the Wisconsin Board of Governors, and was a longstanding member of the committee for the participation of women in the law. In addition, Jones was appointed by the Chief Justice of the Supreme Court of WI to the WI equal justice task force, which examined the state court system and recommended changes to ensure fair and equal treatment of all, especially women. Jones also served as co-chair of the Wisconsin governor's task force on single mothers/single women; testified before the Legislature in favor of pro-choice abortion rights, against early punitive Welfare reform proposals, and in favor of changing the law to allow parents of "illegitimate" children easier access to their child's long-form birth certificate. She was also a member of the Minority Women's Network. Jones has also been active in the civil rights and anti-Vietnam War movements, and in the Black Student Movement. She marched with Dr. Martin Luther King in Chicago in the late 1960s, and served as a county disadvantaged business development director, as municipal contract compliance officer, and as a Big 10 Affirmative Action officer for the University of Wisconsin-Madison. Jones, who has two children, earned her B.A. (1972) from the University of Wisconsin-Madison; her J.D. (1978) from the University of Wisconsin School of Law; and her M.P.A. (1984) from the City University of New York.   (ABS)

Jones, Mary Alice – See Dan, Alice Jones

Jones, Mary Gardiner (1920 –) was one of only two women in her class at Yale Law School to graduate (1948), and was the only woman member of the *Yale Law Journal.* Despite graduating with honors, she had to interview with over 50 law firms before getting a job offer, and once hired was the only woman at the firm. She was appointed to the Federal Trade Commission in 1964 and served until 1973, the first woman FTC appointment by President Johnson. Hired by Western Union (1975–1982), Jones was again the company's first venture in working with a woman executive. "In my day, glass ceilings took second place to just getting one's foot in the door. Someone had to break down doors and get the male world to recognize that people are people despite their gender!" Jones earned her undergraduate degree at Wellesley (1943) and was awarded an Honorary LLD from New York Law School in 1975. Archives: Syracuse University, Syracuse, NY.   (ABS)

Jones, Wanda Lane (1923 – 2002) studied journalism at Ohio State, then moved to NYC in the early 1960s, where she was a social worker for the Workmen's Compensation Board. Hired by *The New York Times* in 1964, she was unable to break through the doors to the news department, and worked for 30 years selling classified ads. An African American, Jones was a leader in the black caucus during her tenure at *The Times,* and was a constant source of energy for the women's caucus. She was a plaintiff in the class action Title VII employment suit that was brought by the black caucus and settled in the 1970s, and that led to promotions for women and minorities. She also served as a Newspaper Guild shop steward and grievance chair.

Jong, Erica (1942 –) is the author of eight novels and a half dozen volumes of poetry. Her best known work is *Fear of Flying*, first published in 1973 and later re-released in a 30th anniversary edition by New American Library. When it was published, *Fear of Flying* created a sensation because of its graphic depiction of sexuality from the woman's viewpoint and for its slap at the bastion of psychiatry. Her other books include *Fanny, Being the True History of the Adventures of Fanny Hackabout Jones* and *Sappho's Leap*, a historical fantasy about the bisexual Greek poet. Jong grew up on Manhattan's Upper West Side, the second daughter in a "New York Jewish intellectual family." She is the recipient of numerous awards, including the United Nations Award for Excellence in Literature (1998). She has one child. Jong holds a B.A. from Barnard College (1963) and an M.A. from Columbia University (1965). She left Columbia before completing her Ph.D. to write *Fear of Flying*.

Joost-Gaugier, Christiane L. (1934 –) In her first teaching position in the late 1960s, Joost-Gaugier began the process of bringing the first class action for sex discrimination, against Tufts University. After observing "the extremely negative way the system operated for women faculty and female students," she contacted the AAUP and the ACLU, which both declined to assist her. However, a team from the then-newly established EEOC in Boston did investigate over a period of about three years, and the case was ultimately decided favorably by the EEOC in Washington, becoming the precedent-setting case for a class action on the basis of sex discrimination in an American university. During this time, Joost-Gaugier says, she was harassed and ostracized by her university and was widely blackballed despite her Ph.D. and international publications. "These were horrible and difficult years," she says. Joost-Gaugier, who was born in France, holds an A.B., A.M. and Ph.D. from Radcliffe and Harvard, as well as an Honorary Phi Beta Kappa from Harvard. Archives: Schlesinger Library, Radcliffe Institute, Cambridge, MA.   (ABS)

Jordan, Rosan Augusta (1939 –) (also known as Rosan Jordan deCaro) A professor and folklorist, Jordan joined the Baton Rouge chapter of NOW in the early 1970s and was active in its prison program, visiting women in the Louisiana State Correctional Facility in St. Gabriel. At the same time, she was active in Women in Politics, an affiliate of the NWPC. Jordan was the founder and editor of "Women's Information Bulletin," a newsletter that "given the climate of the times, was published and distributed anonymously through a network of women in various offices" at Louisiana State University. She was among the

organizers (1973 – 1974) of a women's caucus in the American Folklore Society. During the same period, she was a co-founder, with Susan Kalcik and Claire Farrer, of the *Folklore Feminists Communication*, and began working on a book with co-editor Susan Kalcik, *Women's Folklore, Women's Culture*, published by the University of Pennsylvania Press, 1985. She was also co-author of a review essay on folklore scholarship relating to women for *Signs* (1986). Jordan earned her B.A. and M.A. from the University of North Texas, and her Ph.D. from Indiana University (1975). Archives: Louisiana State University, Special Collections, Baton Rouge; and the American Folklore Society, Columbus, OH.   (ABS)

Jordan, Rose (1935 –) joined NYC NOW and NYRF in 1970. As a member of NYRF, she helped create the first rape conference as well as the first CR groups, of which she became a facilitator. She also participated in the takeover by women of the Fifth Street building. Jordan also helped initiate and participated in the sit-in at the *Daily News* after the newspaper insulted lesbians and gays in an editorial. As a reporter for WBAI, she attended the National Women's Conference in Houston (1977). She created the Justice for Jennifer (Levin) task force in 1986 and recruited feminists and others to join her in demonstrations in front of the court during the trial. In 2006, she runs meetings for women at the LGBT Center in NYC.   (ABS)

Jupiter, Linda (1944 –) began volunteering at the Women's Center in Los Angeles in 1969. There she organized gay/straight dialogs and a conference that brought together diverse feminist organizations in the Los Angeles area. In 1974 she was a founder of the Bay Area Feminist Federal Credit Union, the first feminist credit union in the U.S. Participating organizations were Black Women Organized for Action, the Golden Gate Chapter of NOW, Daughters of Bilitis and San Francisco Women's Centers. The credit union operated for five years, then folded "mostly because we had a hard time calling women who were late in their loan payments, until our losses were too great to stay in business. Learning that women had ripped us off was a hard lesson," Jupiter says. "Many other feminist federal credit unions learned from our mistakes." Jupiter, who has two children, continues (2005) to do political work. Her activism is now more global in nature and includes fighting for the rights of all peoples. Archives: Gay, Lesbian, Bisexual and Transgender Historical Society, San Francisco, CA.   (ABS)

Justesen, Jim (1937 –) joined Twin Cities NOW in 1972 and was soon appointed to the board. Involved in fundraising and public-speaker training, Justesen also recruited a number of co-workers to NOW. He and his wife, Jackie, frequently served as hosts to board and committee meetings. Justesen, who is blind, went on to create the volunteer, nonprofit Eye-Link Foundation with his wife. Its mission is to provide assistive technology to blind or visually impaired Minnesotans who do not qualify for public assistance, or who lack funds. (ABS)

Kabler, Beatrice Ann Parks (1928 –) In the mid 1960s, Kabler, a nurse, helped form a group to support Planned Parenthood in Wisconsin, and for 10 years was leader of Wisconsin Citizens for Family Planning. This resulted in "my most important accomplishment," a law that legalized birth control in WI (1976). Once the law was passed, Kabler established the Wisconsin State Family Planning Coordinating Council to bring in federal money and develop statewide services for parents. She served as Great Lakes Regional Chair for Public Affairs, Planned Parenthood, and was on its national board in the late 1970s and early 1980s. She served three terms as an elected County Board supervisor (1976, 1978 and 1980), a highlight of which was the opening of the first battered women's shelter in WI. Kabler, who has five children, has also been very active in the civil rights and conservation movements. She worked to pass the Madison Equal Opportunity Ordinance, one of the first in the nation; was a member of Wisconsin Citizens for Fair Housing; was a delegate to a five-state Conference on Religion and Race; and in 1965 marched from Selma to Montgomery. Active in the Republican Party, she was appointed to the Governor's Commission on Prevention and Wellness (1978) and later served on the Governor's Initiative for Women. In 2003, she received the Manfred E. Swarsensky Humanitarian Service Award for outstanding volunteer contributions on behalf of race relations, women's health, conservation and public service. Kabler is a graduate of the University of Kansas. Archives: Wisconsin State Historical Society Archives, Madison, WI. (ABS)

Kady (1927 – 2003) Born Kady VanDeurs, a name she used only under duress, insisting it was her father's name, not hers, Kady was an activist, craftswoman, artist and writer who used her talents to express the need for social justice, women's liberation and peace. For 20 years, Kady, a silversmith, could be seen at women's studies conferences, music festivals, activist events, and crafts and art fairs, often with her handmade display cart. She called herself "Axe-Maker to the Queen." She became a union organizer in the 1980s when she helped start the Craftswimmins Mutual Aid Society, a national organization. She was distressed by the treatment of craftswomen-artists by the producers of women's music festivals and women's studies conferences, even though these same craftswomen helped construct the festival sites. Shocked that women's writings were not available in Braille, in large print and on recordings, she co-founded the Womyn's Braille Press and became a reader for sound recordings of women's words. With others, she compiled a massive library-use catalog of all available women's writings in recorded format, with updated supplements. Kady also published two books: *The Notebooks that Emma Gave Me* (1978) and *Panhandling Papers* (1989). Even though she was committed

to non-violent civil disobedience, Kady was arrested many times and spent time in jail and in prison for protests against the Gulf War, for civil rights, and for women's rights. Born in Pensacola, FL, Kady spent the latter years of her life in Greenfield, MA, where she was a painter and graphic artist. In 1970, she graduated from Hunter College. Archives: Artwork and papers at The Sophia Smith Collection, Smith College, Northampton, MA.

Kahn, Felicia S. (1926 –) served as VP and then president of the LWV in New Orleans (1963 – 1969). In 1972, Kahn helped form a NWPC chapter in New Orleans, and in 1975, after campaigning for Jimmy Carter, was appointed to the rules committee of the Democratic Convention. At a rules meeting preceding the convention, Kahn joined with women working on a resolution to have half the delegates at the next convention be women. They won and Kahn became a delegate at the next convention. In 1972, Kahn ran for the Democratic State Central Committee and was one of five women elected. Also in the early 1970s, Kahn was part of a group "making what turned out to be a hopeless effort" for the ERA in Louisiana. She was more successful in getting women to be one of the categories of people with rights under the law in the new Louisiana State Constitution, which was rewritten in 1973. After 1973, Kahn continued to focus on community property and displaced homemakers. She helped organize IWY Louisiana, and served as a delegate. Also active in the civil rights movement (1963 – 1970), Kahn worked on voter registration and voter education, and on keeping public schools open. Active in a community relations council, she headed a study on police and was appointed as a white person to integrate the black board of a black YWCA. Kahn, who has three children, is a graduate of Newcomb College of Tulane University. Archives: Newcomb College Center for Research on Women, Tulane University, New Orleans, LA. (ABS)

Kahn, Lana Clark (1920 –) (also known as Lana Clark Phelan) With Rowena Gurner and Patricia McGinnis, Kahn was a pioneer in the abortion rights movement in CA. In 1963, they co-founded the Society for Humane Abortion in San Francisco. In the late 1960s, Kahn became an active member of NARAL. In 1969 she wrote "The Abortion Handbook"; more than 50,000 copies were distributed. As VP of Los Angeles NOW in 1971, Kahn was the first speaker on feminism to students, faculty and staff within the Los Angeles school district. Archives: Schlesinger Library, Radcliffe Institute, Cambridge, MA. (ABS)

Kahn, Phyllis Lorberblatt (1937 –) was a founding member of a MN NOW chapter and helped found the MN WPC (1971). She lobbied the State Legislature for women's issues in 1972, and that year ran for and was elected to the Legislature with five other women (up from one the year before). Kahn was elected to her 17th term in 2004, and served as speaker pro tempore in 1994, 1995 and 1996. During her terms, Kahn has obtained funding for battered women's shelters and a displaced homemakers program; established a commission on the economic status of women; was responsible for a rape victims assistance program and laws to facilitate prosecution of sex offenders and protect the rights of victims; and was the author of many women's equality laws, including the right of a woman to keep her own name after marriage. Kahn also worked to establish the Women's Suffrage Memorial Garden, and is "particularly proud of the work done for women's athletics, especially ice hockey." She has also done work on science and public policy issues as one of the few elected officials with a science background. Kahn holds a B.A. from Cornell University (1957), a Ph.D. from Yale (1962) and an M.P.A. from the J.F.K. School of Government, Harvard University (1986). Early in her career, as a research associate at the University of Minnesota, Kahn sued the school for discrimination. She has two children. Archives: Minnesota Historical Society, St. Paul, MN. (ABS)

Kahn-Hut, **Rachel** (1938 –) was involved in the early development of Sociologists for Women in Society, serving as the original executive VP (1969). Kahn-Hut also participated in the creation and development of the women's studies major at San Francisco State University (1974). Born in Moscow, Russia, Kahn-Hut is a professor of sociology, emerita. She holds a B.A. from Pomona College, an M.A. from Harvard University and a Ph.D. from Brandeis University. Archives: Sociologists for Women in Society materials will go to the Radcliffe Institute, Cambridge, MA; San Francisco State materials will go to San Francisco State University Library, San Francisco, CA. (ABS)

Kaiser, **Nina Irene** (1953 –) was a member of Jacksonville, FL NOW (1974) and worked for the ERA. Also active in the civil rights movement, Kaiser taught race relations in the U.S. Navy (1972 – 1974). In 1975, she moved to San Francisco and joined Daughters of Bilitis, where she worked for lesbian education and rights. Kaiser eventually became president of, then closed, the San Francisco chapter (1978). She also worked with Planned Parenthood providing women's healthcare and education, and was a founder (1986 – 1990) of Buena Vista lesbian and gay parents association, working in the San Francisco School District for the rights of children with lesbian and gay parents. Kaiser, who has two children, earned her B.A. and a B.S. in nursing from SFSU, and her M.B.A. from the University of Phoenix. Archives: The Lesbian Herstory Archives, Brooklyn, NY. (ABS)

Kamarck, **Elizabeth** – See Minnich, Elizabeth Kamarck

Kantor, **Karen Frances** (1952 –) was "radicalized the day I was turned away from Little League Baseball tryouts, a huge slap in the face." Shortly after entering Barnard College (1970), Kantor joined Columbia Women's Libe-

ration, whose membership, she says, was open to self-defined feminists of every age, race and viewpoint. Kantor's contributions to the movement were more action-oriented than philosophical, she adds. "I hung the first women's conference banner on the Barnard gate, ran the mimeograph machine, bottled faux perfume in defiance of the cosmetics industry, and demonstrated on behalf of pay parity for the maids at Columbia University." She also demonstrated for abortion rights in Albany, NY, and stood in sub-zero conditions outside the Women's House of Detention when Angela Davis was incarcerated there. Also active in the civil rights, gay rights and peace movements, Kantor, a lyricist and music producer, has supported reproductive rights and sought to improve childcare options for women. (ABS)

Kantrowitz, **Joanne Spencer** (1931 –) is the author of the essay "Paying Your Dues Part-Time" (*Rocking the Boat: Academic Women & Academic Processes*, Modern Languages, 1981), which describes her experience fighting for her rights (under Title IX and Title VII) when a young man less qualified than she was appointed at Kent State University in 1974. "That act began a terrible eight years during which my husband and I were harassed by the University, and received little help or sympathy from our colleagues in the academic world." Subsequently returning to NYC, Kantrowitz was able to find "only part-time teaching courses, despite a stellar resume." She became VP of Westchester NOW during the 1980s and spent two years as a speaker for a women's group in the Reformed Church locally. She also served on the Westchester County Women's Board, testified on local political issues, and organized the first celebration of NOW's 25th anniversary in a formal benefit honoring the founding women of the Westchester chapter. She also wrote the chapter's history and, with Charlotte Moslander, organized and stored its archives. Beginning in 1987, Kantrowitz began working for Professional Women in Construction, and "invented their first newsletter in NYC." Kantrowitz's husband, Nathan, was a founding member of the women's caucus in the American Sociological Association. They have two children. Kantrowitz earned her B.A. (1953) from Michigan, and her M.A. (1957) and Ph.D. (1967) from the University of Chicago. Archives: Schlesinger Library, Radcliffe Institute, Cambridge, MA. (ABS)

Kaplan, **Clair** (1953 –) (also known as Clara Kaplan) was expelled from high school in the early 1970s for distributing birth control information in the underground student newspaper she edited, *The Gadfly*. She was active in the anti-Vietnam War and youth movements of the 1960s in Chicago, and was (and remains) a member of Circle Pines Center (a progressive cooperative) in MI. In the early 1970s in Denver, she was in the collectives that ran Woman to Woman Bookstore and *Big Mama Rag*, a radical feminist newspaper. She helped organize events for International Women's Day and worked to produce various feminist concerts and benefits, and organized on behalf of the Coors boycott in Denver and San Francisco. Much of Kaplan's work involved building bridges between the women's movement and other social justice movements. She has one child. Kaplan, who is a nurse practitioner, holds master's degrees in nursing and in health policy and medical ethics. She "finds it delightful" that having been harassed for distributing birth control information, she now practices and teaches in women's health. Archives: Her issues of *Big Mama Rag* are in the Western History Collection, Denver Public Library. (ABS)

Kaplan, Felicia Hebert (1946 –) From 1971–1978, Kaplan was a volunteer lobbyist for the LWV, working on legislation for battered women's shelters, the ERA, and for the removal of "Head and Master" wording from Louisiana divorce law. She was also a member of the board of directors and president of the Lafayette LWV State Committees, Louisiana LWV, and was a founding member and first director of Acadiana Women's Political Caucus, a branch of the NWPC. Kaplan, who has three children, is a graduate of Louisiana State University, Baton Rouge. (ABS)

Kaplan, Judith Helene (1938 –) has worked in the fields of women and finance and women and history. At various times in the 1960s and 1970s she was a life insurance agent specializing in women's insurance. She lectured on women and finance at the Lexington Ave. (NYC) YWCA, and on women and Social Security at NY NOW meetings. Recognizing the inequities of Social Security for women, she recommended at one NOW meeting "that women do housework for their friends and pay each other, thus becoming part of the paid workforce and getting Social Security and unemployment and other economic, cultural and political benefits." In 1977, she founded a toy company, which she took public in 1984, one of the first women to do so. Believing that the self-esteem and self-image of young girls would be bolstered by their knowing about women of achievement, Kaplan created a women's history collectible series (1976–1980), "The Women's History Series of First Day Covers by NOW NY." Beginning in the 1960s, she started collecting women's history memorabilia, and letters from suffragists. She wrote *Woman Suffrage on U.S. First Day Covers* (Tipex Inc. 1977), about the suffrage portion of her philatelic collection. In 1991 Kaplan donated her entire collection to create the Kaplan Women's History Collection, to Central Florida Community College, Ocala, FL. Kaplan has been an active member of NY NOW, Ocala, FL, NOW, and Boca Raton, FL NOW. She was especially active in the Ocala ERA campaign, and served as director (1985) at the women's center there. She is (2005) a director and secretary of the National Women's History Museum, Washington, D.C., and a director of the Feminist Scholarship Fund, Boca Raton. In 1995, she bought a professional women's baseball team, the Orlando Orange, which was the number-one team in the two years the Women's

Baseball Association survived. A graduate of Hunter College (1960), Kaplan has two children. Archives: Kaplan Women's History Collection of Central Florida Community College, Ocala, FL. (ABS)

Kaplan, Warren (1937 –) With his wife, Judith, Warren Kaplan collected (1964–1991) women's history and founded the Kaplan Women's History Collection of the Central Florida Community College in Ocala, FL. From 1972–1980, he championed women in politics by selecting and funding them while in Queens, NYC. During that same period, he marched for the ERA, and helped create and implement fundraising ideas for NY NOW. From 1981–1983, he donated the facilities and telephone for the ERA campaign in Ocala, FL. From 1976–1980, he helped fund and market the Women's History Series of First Day Covers by NY NOW, and from 1980–1990 helped fund the spouse abuse center in Ocala. From 1995–1996, he helped run, publicize and fund a professional women's baseball team. Archives: Judith and Warren Kaplan Women's History Collection, Central Florida Community College, Ocala, FL. (ABS)

Kaprow, Vaughan – See Rachel, Vaughan

Karant, Roberta K. (1940 –) A member of NOW for 20 years, Karant was co-chair of Mid-Suffolk (NY) NOW's lesbian task force and founder of the Long Island Lesbian Initiative. Karant, who has two children and holds a Ph.D., has also taught women's studies at Stony Brook University. She has two children. She came out as a lesbian in 1985. (ABS)

Karasov, Doris – See Unger, Doris

Karlin, Ginger – See Whittington, Ginger

Karp, Barrie (1945 –) Artist, philosopher and educator, Karp attended her first CR meeting in 1970, the same year she began teaching philosophy at City College as a graduate student. "I was especially concerned about pedagogy, the intersections of race, sex, gender, class and sexuality," she says. In 1975 she lost her teaching job after telling "the School Affirmative Action officer about the current and historical lack of female philosophy department faculty members at CCNY." Karp filed a discrimination case, but lost. In 1978, Karp taught the first feminist theory course offered in the philosophy dept. of Hunter College. In the 1980s, Karp became a pioneer in teaching "experimental design and pedagogy of interdisciplinary, anti-racist feminist theory courses," and continues (2005) to design and teach such courses at New School University and School of Visual Arts. Her paintings "embody a feminist subjectivity yet are not didactic." She has a B.S. (1967), Columbia University; M.A. (1977); M.Phil. (1979); Ph.D. (1980), The Graduate Center, CUNY. Her work has been published or discussed in *Feminist Studies*:

Gender/ Body/Knowledge—Feminist Reconstructions of Being & Knowing; Ikon Magazine; Art & Observance—School of Visual Arts Commemorates 9/11 catalog. (ABS)

Karp, Lila (1933 –) Writer, educator and feminist psychotherapist, Karp is author of the novel *The Queen is in the Garbage* (1969) and of the essay "Genderless Sexuality: A Male-Female Psychological Exploration of the Future of Sexual Relationships," published in *Woman in the Year 2000* (1974). In NYC in 1968 (after 10 years in Europe), Karp joined The Feminists, and throughout the 1970s was a guest lecturer around the country. In 1971, she became a visiting professor at Bryn Mawr College, teaching its first women's literature course and a course in creative writing for women. She then moved to the University of the New World, in Valais, Switzerland, and directed the Feminist Studio and Writing Workshop. From 1971–1977, she was a visiting lecturer at SUNY, New Paltz (NY), teaching a course on the sociology of women's literature. As faculty adviser to the Women's Alliance, she worked with students to press for a women's studies program. She continued that same push as director of the Princeton University Women's Center (1978–1986) and as Faculty Lecturer for the Council of Humanities at Princeton. In 1979, she was on a NWSA panel, "Women's Studies: Fear and Loathing in the Ivy League." During 1987 and 1988, she taught women's studies at the University of Southern California, Los Angeles, and at California State University in Northridge. In 1991, she became co-director of The Institute for the Study of Women and Men at the University of Southern California. In 1996, she received an M.A. in clinical psychology, Antioch University, Los Angeles, and in 2001 received her M.F.T. (Marriage & Family Therapist), California State Board of Behavioral Sciences. She is (2005) a feminist psychotherapist in private practice and teaches at Antioch University, Los Angeles. (ABS)

Karp, Sandra R. (1945 –) Active in the New Orleans, LA, women's movement (1970–1981), Karp was one of six members of the Amazon Tribe CR group (1970); was an organizer/participant of the Women's Liberation Coalition (1970–1971); and a participant in the early publication (1971) of *In Her Own Right*. She was also an organizer/participant in the International Women's Day Conference (1971); was a co-founder/counselor at Sisters Helping Sisters (1972–1979), a problem pregnancy counseling and referral service; and a co-founder of the Jackson Avenue Women's Center (1971–1972), where she participated in governance, the socialist study group, and the lesbian CR group, among others. She was a co-founder of Tulane Women for Change (1971–1972), and served as a court-appointed temporary parent for runaway girls at Greenhouse, a city shelter (1972–1973). At the Women's Work Collective, Karp was a coordinating member of the Welfare advocacy program (1972–1974), which was conducted jointly with the New Orleans legal community and the National Welfare Rights Organization. In the mid

1970s, she was a co-founder of Felicity Street Women's Center and Willow Street Women's Center; was director of operations for Clothes-Line, a clothing exchange (1975–1977); and participated in the Gertrude Stein Democratic Club (1977–1979). In 1980, she was a steering board member of Take Back the Night March, and was editor of the March report, "Victims No More." Karp is working on *A History of Sentience*, a six-volume feminist theoretical work. The first volume, *Origins*, is projected for publication by Graeae Press, 2006. Karp earned her B.A. (1967) from Case-Western Reserve University, Cleveland; her M.A. (1969) from Brown University; and her Ph.D. from Tulane University (1978). (ABS)

Kaschak, Ellyn (1943 –) A professor of psychology, Kaschak was one of the developers of feminist psychology and psychotherapy. With three other women, she organized the Women's Counseling Service of San Francisco (1972), at which feminist psychotherapy was offered. She has done extensive cross-cultural research on gender, and was the originator, with Sara Sharratt, Ph.D., of the Latin American Sex Role Inventory. She also served as adviser on gender issues to the VP of Costa Rica (1998 – 2002). She is (2003) editor of *Women and Therapy*. Kaschak has written extensively on issues of theory and epistemology. These include *Endangered Lives: A New Psychology of Women's Experience* (Basic Books, 1992); *Assault on the Soul: Women in the Former Yugoslavia* (Haworth Press, 2002); *The Invisible Alliance: Psyche and Spirit in Feminist Therapy* (Haworth Press, 2001); and *Intimate Betrayal: Domestic Violence in Lesbian Relationships* (Haworth Press, 2001). She received her B.A. from Harpur College of the State University of New York at Binghamton (1965); her M.A. from George Washington University (1968); and her Ph.D. from Ohio State University (1974). (ABS)

Kasper, Anne Sharnoff (1942 –) was founding co-chair of the National Women's Health Network (1976–1977), and was founding co-director of the Women's Health Clearinghouse (1976–1978), the first national resource file on women's health. A member of the National Commission on the Observance of IWY (1976–1977), she was responsible for all research, analysis and writing on women's health issues for IWY. From 1981–1986, she served as chair, federal policy committee of the NWHN, and in 1982 received the Health Advocate of the Year Award. Kasper was a founding board member of the Women's Studies Endowment Fund (1985–1989), Washington, D.C., and was director of The Campaign for Women's Health, a coalition of 100 organizations for national healthcare reform (1991–1994). From 1994–2001, she was senior research scientist and adjunct assistant professor, Center for Research on Women and Gender, University of Illinois at Chicago. She was the senior editor and author, with Susan J. Ferguson, of *Breast Cancer: Society Shapes an Epidemic* (St. Martin's Press, 2000); served as editor, *Women and Health* (1978 – 1984);

K

and as health editor, *New Directions for Women* (1979 – 1984). She was also associate editor, *Textbook of Women's Health* (1996 – 1997) and editor, *Women's Health: Research and Gender, Behavior and Policy* (1998 – 1999). She was also principal, Finding My Way, a coaching service for women with breast cancer. Kasper, who has two children, earned her B.A. (1964) from Douglass College, Rutgers University; her M.A.(1982) and her Ph.D. (1988) from George Washington University. Archives: The Sophia Smith Collection, Smith College, Northampton, MA. (ABS)

Kassell, Paula Sally (1917 –) (also known as Paula Friedman) Journalist and editor, Kassell was the founder and editor of the first national feminist newspaper, *New Directions for Women* (1971 – 1993), and wrote a regular column on employment discrimination (1974 – 1986). To broaden the newspaper's influence, she created a series of 11 conferences relevant to the women's movement, and established the Positive Image of Women Award. She was instrumental in getting *The New York Times* to use the title Ms. when referring to women. She was the co-founder (1970) of the Lakeland Area chapter of NOW; was a member of WEAL (1971); and worked to integrate the help-wanted ads in *The New York Times* and the *Daily Record*, Morris County, NJ. A graduate of Barnard College (1939), Kassell has two children. Archives: National Women and Media Collection, University of Missouri School of Journalism, Columbia, MO. (ABS)

Katz, Marilyn (1945 –) A civil rights and anti-war activist, organizer and founder of women's rights groups, Katz began her work in the Uptown neighborhood of Chicago. In the mid 1960s, she helped organize working-class black, Appalachian, and southern white women on Welfare, and in 1967, with Heather Booth and others, founded a city-wide women's group. Also in 1967, Katz was a co-founder of WITCH. In 1968, she was a co-founder of the CWLU, and in 1979 was a co-founder of the Los Angeles Women's Union. Active in the pro-choice movement, she was a co-founder (1977) of the Reproductive Rights National Network and Women Organized for Reproductive Choice (1978 – 1983), in Chicago. Active in international feminism, Katz has written feminist theory. She has two children. Archives: Some papers donated to Northwestern University, Evanston, IL. (ABS)

Kaufman, Gloria (1929 – 2004) was a supporter of peace, environmental and feminist causes, a music lover and a dolphin fan. She was founder and first director of the women's studies program and Women's Resource Center, University of Indiana, South Bend. During her long tenure at IUSB, she served as professor of English, affirmative action officer and adviser to numerous South Bend and ISUB committees. She published two collections of feminist humor and 14 video documentaries. She was also active in the NWPC and South Bend YWCA and did extensive research on Wiccan spirituality and paganism.

Kaufman, Jane A. (1938 –) A painter and sculptor of feminist themes, Kaufman was teaching in the art department at Bard College in the early 1970s, "the first female faculty member to join an academic institution that could easily be described as a boys club," says her former student Elizabeth Hess. As a teacher, her artwork "demonstrated the then-radical notion that women could not only be artists, but make whatever kind of art they desired." Women's work has been an underlying theme of her art, in particular with references to the historical quilt. She created posters for pro-choice marches, raising money for Iris House (whose mission is to offer services for women and their families infected and affected by HIV/AIDS) with an art auction. She holds a B.A. from New York University and an M.A. from Hunter College. (ABS)

Kaufman, Robin (1943 –) A grassroots community organizer and leader in Chicago, Kaufman taught auto repair to women in the early 1970s, the early days of CWLU's Liberation School for Women. Kaufman also staffed an "underground" childcare center in Chicago started by Heather Booth and others from CWLU, and, she says, "made a major contribution by helping care for Booth's two children so that Booth could do her work in the movement." Kaufman was co-chair of the abortion task force that was a joint effort of NOW and CWLU. After Roe v. Wade, the task force pushed for public availability of abortions, and evolved into a referral service, visiting and evaluating abortion clinics and pushing for improvements. Working for lesbian rights within NOW, she struggled to have the straight and gay factions understand the commonality of their issues, so they could unite and build on the strengths of each. In the early 1970s, she helped draft the first municipal gay rights ordinance in Chicago and brought it to national NOW as a model for other cities. Kaufman was an Illinois state officer for national NOW, and worked in political campaigns to elect pro-ERA candidates in that state. With her partner, Lyda Carter, a founder of the Chicago Coalition of Labor Union Women, Kaufman adopted two children (1984 and 1986), and has long advocated parental and partnership/marital rights for gay people. (ABS)

Kavars, Linda Boyd (1941 –) began producing rock concerts in 1965 on the West Coast. Because she produced and managed only women artists, "which was unheard of at the time," she broke down barriers for women in music. She signed the first female rock band to a major label (Fanny to Warner Bros. in 1969), and spent 20 years promoting women musicians and moving them into mainstream music. She began videotaping mainstream feminists and documenting their lives in the 1980s, starting with Kate Millett and her Farm and Women's Art Colony, which she managed for three years. Kavars was the founder of the Lorena Hickok Memorial and Scholarship Fund and Great Dames Productions, which has produced women's concerts since 2000 in the Hudson

Valley area of NY. She is (2006) a founder and editor/publisher of *InsideOut*, a magazine launched in 2004 for the LGBT community in the Hudson Valley. Born in Mason City, IA, Kavars has two children. Archives: The Sophia Smith Collection, Smith College, Northampton, MA. (ABS)

Kaye, Sandy – See Polishuk, Sandy

Kazickas, Jurate Catherine (1943 –) Kazickas was a young reporter at the Associated Press in New York in 1969 when she was assigned to cover the women's movement. She quickly realized that "this story was *huge*, and though I had never thought about it, I was *one of them*." With her AP colleague Lynn Sherr, Kazickas developed the idea of a calendar commemorating what a woman had done for each day of the year. Although it took Kazickas and Sherr a long time to find a publisher ("This movement is not going to last," publishers said), when it was published for the year 1971, *The Liberated Woman's Appointment Calendar and Survival Handbook* got a lot of attention, including from *Time, Newsweek* and the "Today Show." It later morphed into *The Woman's Calendar* and was published for 10 years. With Sherr, Kazickas also wrote *The American Woman's Gazetteer* (1976), which listed all the places in America where women had made history. An updated version, *Susan B. Anthony Slept Here*, came out in 1994. Says Kazickas: "Because of the calendar's light-hearted tone (though serious content), we were known as feminists with a sense of humor." Born in Vilnius, Lithuania, Kazickas has three children. She holds a B.A. from Trinity College, Washington, D.C. (ABS)

Kearon, Pam (1943 –) An Irish Catholic from a working-class background, Kearon was a member of NYRW. She took part in the Miss America Pageant protest in Atlantic City, NJ, in 1968, and monitored rape trials. Later she joined The Feminists, the Class Workshop and the Circle of Support for Jane Alpert. "Pam was a theorist, a powerhouse of ideas," recalls Mary Lutz, a friend and member of The Feminists. "She had well-articulated, well-thought-out revolutionary ideas and separated the political from the emotional in her work. Her ideas were very controversial at the time. Her 'Man-Hating' pamphlet (1969) was really important. The paper implies that vigorous fighting back is politically appropriate." Kearon is also co-author of "Prostitution" and "Rape: An Act of Terror" with Barbara Mehrhof. Kearon and Dolores Bargowski read a statement about women's oppression in front of a NYC pornography store—a media action filmed by Marlene Sanders and aired on ABC-TV network news. Kearon is a graduate of St. John's Law School in Queens, NY (J.D., 1978).

Keating, Jean – See Conger, Jean Tastrom

Keck, Donna Poggi (1941 –) In 1968, Keck joined the first feminist CR group in Baltimore, MD. The group, which met for several years, organized conferences, performed guerrilla theater on various feminist issues, and did public speaking. Keck was also a co-founder of one of the first publications of the second wave feminist movement, *Women: A Journal of Liberation*, which published from 1969 through the 1980s with a distribution of 20,000 at its height. Keck, who served on the editorial board until 1974, did writing, editing, layout, marketing and distribution. At the same time, she participated in the anti-Vietnam War movement as a member of the Baltimore Defense Committee, which was organized initially as a support group for the Catonsville Nine, a group of Catholic religious activists who were tried in Baltimore for burning draft files in Catonsville, MD. Keck is (2004) a team leader in the Office of Public Housing Investments, U.S. Department of Housing & Urban Development, Washington, D.C. She has one child, and earned her M.A. from Johns Hopkins University. (ABS)

Keesling, Karen Ruth (1946 –) helped open over 50,000 jobs, including pilot, missile specialist, security police and more, to women in the United States Air Force from 1981 – 1989. Keesling served in several positions in the Air Force, finally as assistant secretary of the Air Force for manpower and reserve affairs (1988 – 1989). An attorney, Keesling also served as legal adviser, U.S. committee for the U.N. Fund for Women (1977 – 1997). Among her other positions, Keesling was legal aide to Senator Nancy Kassebaum (1979 – 1981); women's rights analyst, Civil Rights Division, Library of Congress (1977 – 1979); director, Office of Women, The White House (1975 – 1977); and executive secretary, Secretary's Advisory Commission on Rights and Responsibilities of Women, Department of Health, Education and Welfare (1972 – 1975). Keesling earned her B.A. and M.A. from Arizona State University, and her J.D. from Georgetown University Law Center. Archives: Arizona State University, Phoenix, AZ. (ABS)

Kefauver, Lee (1934 –) (also known as Lee Lavalli) As a member of the Dearborn chapter of the LVW (1968 – 1975), Kefauver served as publicity chair, board member, and chair of the ERA, among other roles. In 1970 she joined the Michigan Organization for the Repeal of Abortion Laws and, after joining the Detroit chapter of NOW in 1971, was elected chair of its reproductive rights task force. As part of the MI abortion referendum committee, she testified before the senate committee on health and social services (1971). In June 1972, she was appointed MI NOW coordinator for reproductive rights. She also testified and lobbied for MI's ratification of the ERA. In 1973, Kefauver developed a methodology for inspecting and rating abortion facilities in the Detroit Metro area, and led an inspection team of Detroit NOW members to do so. In 1973, she was elected MI NOW state coordinator, and lobbied and testified on many bills affecting women. In 1975 – 1976, she created a compilation of the voting records of MI State legislators, which was distributed by the MI WPC. Remaining active in areas affecting women's right to choose, and marriage and divorce laws, Kefauver won the WEAL Lobbying Award for best efforts in the nation on lobbying for women's issues in 1978. In 1979–1980, she helped fight against and defeat bills on divorce and property settlements that would have harmed women who made homemaking a career. At the same time, she was elected president of the MI division, WEAL. A graduate of Boston University, Kefauver has two children. Archives: Bentley Historical Library, University of Michigan, Ann Arbor, MI. (ABS)

Keiser, Susan (1947 –) (also known as Susan Loren) Attorney, mediator, teacher and activist, Keiser worked with other women in Livingston Manor, Liberty and Sullivan County, NY, to bring Head Start, Planned Parenthood (1969), mental health programs, the first private nursery school and a PTA into the area. Active beginning in the late 1960s, she helped develop a NOW chapter and anti-domestic violence programs, and ran as a candidate for school boards. She was later a major party candidate for family court judge. Keiser was also active in the civil rights and peace movements, and "raised a feminist son and an activist daughter" and "civilized her husband," says her husband, Michael. Keiser, who supported herself through college by opening and running a dance studio, earned her B.S. at the University of Chicago, an M.A. at New York University, and a second M.A. and Ph.D. at the Fielding Institute. (ABS)

Kelber, Miriam ("Mim") (1922 – 2004) A writer and journalist, Kelber was a close associate, speechwriter and adviser to Bella Abzug. Kelber and Abzug were friends and colleagues for 60 years, beginning at Walton High School in The Bronx, NY, and continuing at Hunter College, where Kelber was editor of the Hunter College newspaper and Abzug was president of the student body. From 1943 – 1955, Kelber was national news editor and Washington bureau chief of Federated Press, a nationally syndicated labor news service; in 1945, she covered the founding meeting of the United Nations in San Francisco. Editor/writer for *Science and Medicine* (1958–1970), she left to become executive assistant and chief speechwriter for congresswoman Abzug (1971–1976). Kelber was a founder, with others, of Women Strike for Peace (1961). She was also a co-founder/writer/organizer, with Abzug, of Women USA (1980), Women USA Fund, Women's Foreign Policy Council (1987) and Women's Environment and Development Organization (1990). From 1970 – 1998, she served as speech writer/policy adviser for Abzug. A co-founder of the NWPC, Kelber chaired NWPC's media committee (1974) as well as Campaign '74 to elect more women to Congress. Following the Houston IWY conference in 1977, Kelber was the chief editor/writer, with Caroline Bird, of "The Spirit of Houston" report; was a policy adviser/writer for Carter's national advisory committee for women; and participated in most of the big ERA demonstrations, peace demonstra-

tions, and the 1970 march down Fifth Avenue. She is the author, with Abzug, of *Gender Gap: Bella Abzug's Guide to Political Power for American Women* (Houghton Mifflin, 1984), and *Women and Government, New Ways to Political Power*, a Women USA Fund Study (Praeger, 1994). She also contributed a chapter on nuclear war for the book *Women in the Year 2000* (Arbor House, 1974), and wrote hundreds of articles for magazines and newspapers, including *The Nation, Ms., Redbook, Columbia Law Review*, U.N. publications, and *The New York Times* Op-Ed page. She was the initiator of the "News & Views" newsletter, published by Women's Foreign Policy Council (1988) and WEDO (1990 –), and served as editor/writer, 1988–2000. Among her many awards: Wonder Woman Award for peace work; Clarion Award, Women in Communications; Hunter College Hall of Fame (1996); Feminist Majority Foundation (2000); and VFA Award (2001). Kelber had two children. Archives: Butler Library, Rare Books and Manuscripts Library, Columbia University, New York, NY.

Keller, Suzanne (1929 –) The first woman to receive tenure at Princeton University, Keller joined the sociology dept. in 1968. She was involved in the women's movement in the 1960s in national and local events. At Princeton "I became aware of the difficulty of integrating women into such a distinguished, historic, male-defined institution and concentrated my efforts on gown and town," Keller says. This included devising new cirrucla, teaching the first courses on Gender and Society; on Human Sexuality; and on the History of the Family. Keller's books include *Building for Women* (Lexington Books, 1975), *Beyond the Ruling Class* (Random House, 1964), and *The Urban Neighborhood* (Random House, 1968). She was co-author of *Sociology* (Random House, 1970), a national best seller in sociology containing the first chapter on gender in the modern conception. She holds a Ph.D. from Columbia University (1953). (ABS)

Kelly, Casey (1941 –) is the creator of The Feminist Follies, a madcap fundraising evening emceed by Studs Terkel in 1974 and Mike Royko in 1975. Noting friction among feminist organizations, Kelly created a faction-free annual marching group, The Chicago Irish Feminists for the ERA, winning Mayor Daley's plaque for Best Political Marching Group (1976). Marchers included NOW, the WPC, CWLU, Girl Scouts, Moms for ERA, and ad hoc groups of office workers, nuns, nurses and rugby dads. Countless parade watchers joined in—and would for years to come. Kelly also spearheaded actions on employment agency discrimination and worked with major media for coverage of the 1976 National Rally for Equal Rights in Springfield. Now 65, Kelly calls herself "The World's Oldest Living New Filmmaker," winning awards for her 1999 American Film Institute directing debut short "The Other Woman" and, recently, directing "The Bracelet of Bordeaux," a girl-power kids feature. (ABS)

Kelly, Joan (1928 – 1982) (also known as Joan Kelly-Gadol) Historian and Renaissance scholar, Kelly was a pioneer in rethinking history from a female perspective. She participated in the Scholar & Feminist Conference, speaking on "History and the Social Relations of the Sexes" (1975). Her essay, "Did Women Have a Renaissance?" (Renate Bridenthal, Claudia Koonz, eds., *Becoming Visible: Women in European History*, Boston, 1977), has been called "a seminal work" that changed the field of Renaissance and women's history in the 1970s. The author of *Women, History, and Theory* (Chicago University Press, 1984), Kelly was a founder of the Coordinating Committee on Women in the Historical Profession and an active member of CARASA. She took the initiative in the collaborative creation of a pamphlet on sterilization abuse that was used as an organizing tool in the academic community. Kelly said in 1987, "Women's history has a dual goal: to restore women to history and to restore our history to women." The Joan Kelly Memorial Prize was established in 1984 and is awarded annually for the book in women's history and/or feminist theory that best reflects the high intellectual and scholarly ideals exemplified by the life and work of Joan Kelly. The award was established by CCWHP and the Conference Group on Women's History, and is administered by the American Historical Association. Archives: Schlesinger Library, Radcliffe Institute, Cambridge, MA.

Kelly, Marion Hursey (1923 –) was a ship builder during WW II, and worked as a secretary for Pan American Airways "until I was fired for being pregnant!" She was a charter member of Miami NOW in the late 1960s and participated in marches and actions. She protested against Jordan Marsh Department Stores for not serving women in its restaurant, and marched to the county courthouse in Dade County to bring attention to the need for childcare. Kelly, who has four children, also worked for 23 years selling guns, and completed four years of college.

Kelly, Nancy (1946 – 2002) fought for lesbian and women's rights beginning in 1970, when she rallied in San Francisco's People's Park to celebrate the 50th anniversary of woman suffrage and engaged in feminist dialogues with those who had come to jeer. Also in 1970, Kelly joined the lesbian feminist group at the Crenshaw Women's Center in Los Angeles, where she was active in outreach, organizing and participating in workshops on lesbian/feminist issues for groups as diverse as a Unitarian Church and a group of businessmen who met for lunch. In 1971, Kelly and Johanna Gullick (as representatives of the Crenshaw Women's Center) formed, with Del Whan of the Gay Women's Service Center and Jeanne Cordova of the DOB, the Intergroup Council of Gay Women. That year, the Intergroup Council hosted the First West Coast Lesbian Conference at the Los Angeles Metropolitan Community Church. During the early 1970s, Kelly networked for abortion rights and demonstrated in protest of "snuff" movies. She remained active in lesbian and feminist issues into the 1980s, when ill health forced her to curtail her activities.

Kelly, Nancy Lorene (1950 –) (also known as Nancy Carson Neff) In 1974, Kelly was hired as the first woman police officer in Roanoke, VA. Although she had graduated at the top of her class, she met with widespread resentment, and "the chief of police made it very clear that I was hired in order to comply with new legislation that prohibited sex discrimination." She survived a humiliating job interview; was forced to share a locker room with male counterparts; and struggled with a uniform (a skirt) that hampered movement while working in the field. However, a change in attitude came when Kelly skillfully handled a rape case, and she was eventually elected to serve as an officer on the board of the Police Patrolman's Association. In 1968, as an undergraduate at Radford College, Kelly co-founded a women's campus group that worked for equal opportunity for women and repeal of laws criminalizing abortion. In Roanoke in 1970, she organized a group of women to work as lobbyists promoting women's equality. The women concentrated on enforcement of civil rights legislation and securing scholarships and funding for women's athletic programs. In August of that year, Kelly invited 50 women to attend a strike for women's equality commemorating the 50th anniversary of suffrage. "Over 200 women showed up. We didn't have enough room on the bus, so we piled in cars and drove to NYC to join thousands of other women marching down 5th Avenue." Kelly, who has two children, earned her B.S. from Tempe University (1980) and her M.B.A. from the University of Phoenix (2002). (ABS)

Kempton, Sally (1943 –) (also known as Swami Durgananda) Writer, teacher and spiritual guide, Kempton was a feminist activist when she participated in the sit-in against *Ladies' Home Journal*. She also challenged Hugh Hefner, publisher of *Playboy*, on national television, and published the influential article "Cutting Loose," in which she wrote about rage, dependence and seductiveness, in *Esquire*. She was a member of West Village-1, with Alix Kates Shulman, and Media Women, which included Susan Brownmiller. Kempton's writing has appeared in numerous magazines, newspapers and journals, including *The New York Times*, the *Village Voice*, *Rolling Stone, Yoga Journal* and *Harpers*. The author of *The Heart of Meditation*, she is (2005) a columnist for *Yoga Journal*, and a workshop leader who has been a guest speaker at Naropa University, Boulder. She has also been a participant in many conferences. (ABS)

Kendall, Kathryn (1945 –) (also known as Kathy McQueen, Kathy Kendall, K. Limakatso Kendall or, simply, Kendall) A college teacher both in the U.S. and Southern Africa, Kendall is also a performer and author. Her focus is women, lesbians and people of color in letters and in theater. Kendall's theater career included writing and performing feminist one-woman shows (1970 – 1992). She was part of a grassroots movement in New Orleans (1970 – 1981) providing support for rape and domestic violence survivors, and was both a telephone volunteer and editor of grant proposals and publications for the New Orleans Rape Crisis Center. She was a member of the Feminist Writers Guild steering committee in 1979, 1980 and 1981. She toured the United States. in 1980 with Andrea Canaan, performing "Characters," poetry and drama by and about women, sponsored by the Feminist Writers Guild, and from 1982 – 1986 worked with a feminist theater group in Austin, TX, Word of Mouth. She taught at Smith College (1986 – 1992), the National University of Lesotho, and the University of Natal in South Africa. She is the editor of *Singing Away the Hunger: The Autobiography of an African Woman*, by Mpho Nthunya (Indiana University Press, 1997); *Basali! Stories by and About Women in Lesotho* (University of Natal Press, 1995); and *Love and Thunder! Plays by Women in the Age of Queen Anne* (Methuen, 1988). Kendall is also the author of *A Passionate Guest: Two Years in Southern Africa* (Graeae Press, 2005). The Press and all books were destroyed in Hurricane Katrina in 2005. Kendall holds a B.A., M.A. and Ph.D.   (ABS)

Kennedy, Elizabeth Lapovsky (1939 –) was a founder of and participant in women's studies at SUNY Buffalo. In 1969 she was faculty sponsor for an experimental course, Women in Contemporary Society, being designed by graduate students. Kennedy and the graduate students then created Women's Studies College and the women's caucus in American studies. Despite an initially unwelcoming attitude from the university administration, women's studies had a substantial undergraduate program by 1972. And by 1974 American studies offered an M.A. in women's studies. After 29 years at SUNY Buffalo, Kennedy became head of the women's studies dept. at the University of Arizona, where she remains. She is co-author, with Ellen Carol DuBois, Gail Paradise Kelly, Carolyn W. Korsmeyer and Lillian S. Robinson, of *Feminist Scholarship: Kindling the Groves of Academe* (University of Illinois Press, 1985) and co-editor, with Agatha Beins, of *Women's Studies for Future Foundations, Interrogations, Politics* (Rutgers University Press, 2005). Also a pioneer in lesbian history, Kennedy is co-author, with Madeline Davis, of *Boots of Leather, Slippers of Gold: The History of a Lesbian Community* (Routledge, Chapman and Hall, 1993). With Davis, Kennedy was a founder of the Buffalo Women's Oral History Project (1978). Kennedy received her training in social anthropology from the University of Cambridge, England.   (ABS)

Kennedy, Florynce Rae (1916 – 2000) In 1976, *People* magazine called Kennedy "the biggest, loudest and, indisputably, the rudest mouth on the battleground where feminist activists and radical politics join in mostly common cause." Kennedy's outrageous comments and attire, often cowboy boots and hat, drew attention to her work in civil rights and feminism, and gained her a reputation for being flamboyant and effective. She earned a B.A. in pre-law from Columbia University in 1948, but was then refused admission to Columbia Law School because she was a woman. After threatening to sue for racial discrimination, she was admitted and completed her degree in 1951, becoming one of the first black women to graduate from Columbia Law School. After representing the estates of Billie Holiday and Charlie Parker to recover money owed them by record companies, Kennedy began to question the profession of law, feeling that true justice could not be found in what she saw as a bigoted and racist legal system. By the early 1960s, her legal cases were almost always political and she began a move towards activism. In 1968, Kennedy represented civil rights leader H. Rap Brown and sued the Catholic Church for interference with abortion. In 1969, she represented the Black Panthers (on trial for conspiracy to commit bombings), and organized a group of feminist lawyers to challenge the constitutionality of New York State's abortion law. Gloria Steinem, who often lectured with Kennedy, coined the phrase "verbal karate" to describe Kennedy's style, and referred to herself and Kennedy as "the Thelma and Louise of the seventies." In 1966, Kennedy created the Media Workshop, an organization that fought discrimination in the media. She was a founding member of the NWPC; and helped organize Shirley Chisholm's campaign for the Presidential nomination in 1972. She also founded the Coalition Against Racism and Sexism and the NBFO. She participated in all four Black Panther conferences and began the "Flo Kennedy Show" on Manhattan Cable in 1972. Kennedy helped organize many highly visible demonstrations, including the Miss America demonstration, a pee-in at Harvard to protest the lack of toilet facilities for women, and a demonstration against gender-segregated help-wanted ads in *The New York Times*. She is the author of *Abortion Rap* (1976), one of the first books on abortion, and *Color Me Flo: My Life and Good Times* (1976). Her numerous awards include the Ms. Foundation Lifetime Courageous Activist Award (1997); Columbia University's OWL Award for Outstanding Graduate (1998); and the Women of the Century Award. Archives: Schlesinger Library, Radcliffe Institute, Cambridge, MA.

Kennedy, Kathleen Rose (1942 –) joined PA NOW in the mid 1970s. She picketed a Little League World Series (Williamsport, PA, 1973) to protest the exclusion of girls, and in Virginia worked successfully to unseat Jim Thompson, a powerful member of the legislature who was holding up ratification of the ERA. Kennedy also stood vigil during the excommunication hearings of Sonia Johnson, a Mormon who supported the ERA. From 1973 – 2003, Kennedy was employed by the Commonwealth of Pennsylvania, where, from 1974 – 1996, she was a Title IX technical assistance resource person for grades K

–12. In that capacity she worked aggressively on issues related to discrimination against girls in sports, sexism in textbooks, disparate classroom treatment, and women's history. Prior to 1974, Kennedy was a civil rights complaint investigator, including employment complaints from women. From 1996–2003 she was one of the state coordinators for Act 101, a tutoring, counseling and cultural program for low-income college students that is available at 76 Pennsylvania campuses. Kennedy serves (2004) on two boards that oppose the death penalty. She holds a bachelor's degree. (ABS)

Kenny, Kay (1945 –) An artist, photographer and painter, Kenny began working with a CR group in Syracuse, NY, that had grown out of the anti-war movement (1969). She marched for women's rights and freedom of choice, and as an artist began to explore the kind of imagery "that best reflected my sense of being a woman in this society." Attending M.F.A. programs at both Rutgers and Syracuse University in the 1970s, Kenny realized that her class was the beginning of a major shift for the arts. "Up to that point, few women were accepted into the M.F.A. programs, despite the predominance of undergraduate women. There were no women teaching graduate students in either school, and just a handful in the undergraduate programs. Making art that was both personal and intensely feminine was therefore a challenge to the status quo." In 1977, Kenny began working for an organization called The Grail, whose purpose was to survey the employment problems of women in Orange County, NY. Kenny and others went to small towns around the county, talked to women about their job problems, held resume and job interview seminars, and spoke to employers about what they looked for in female job applicants. Kenny also created a directory for women that included health-related resources as well as education and childcare. At the same time, Kenny taught photography at the Women's Studio Workshop in Rosendale, NY. Later, she began to work closely with *Heresies*, and was a member of the collective until 1989. Kenny holds a B.F.A. and M.F.A. from Syracuse University, and an M.A. from Rutgers. (ABS)

Kenworthy, Roz (1935 –) worked for 20 years at Planned Parenthood and was the first sex counselor at Gannett, Cornell University Health Services (1970 – 2000). She is a recipient of the Constance E. Cook Community Service Award, 2001. Archives: Human Sexuality Collection, Cornell University Library. (ABS)

Kenyon, Geri Mona (1929 –) served as president of the Syracuse, NY, chapter of NOW (1972). She was a member of the NOW board of directors, and from 1974 – 1976 was legal VP of national NOW and a member of the NOW LDEF. She was also chair of the national NOW task force for women in prison. As a candidate for sheriff in Onondaga County (NY), she received more votes (6,000) than any other Liberal Party candidate ever had. Moving to California in 1976, she worked at the Feminist Women's Health Clinic, then was hired as a school psychologist by the Los Angeles Unified School District. Kenyon has also taught at Michigan Technological University and conducted research on women in academia and on developing leadership in women. Kenyon holds both a B.S. and M.S. She has four children. (ABS)

Kepler, Patricia Budd (1934 –) worked for women's rights primarily in the area of religion. From there, in cooperation with women in the secular women's movement, she became involved in childcare, education, employment and labor, health, international affairs, lesbian issues, marriage/divorce, minority rights, reproductive rights, sexuality, violence against women, and the formation of feminist theory. In 1968, Kepler became director of women's programs for the Board of Christian Education of the Presbyterian Church, USA, and staff for the task force on women. Their advocacy led to the exploration of the issue of language for people and God in worship, and theology from a worldview beyond traditional patriarchy. It also led to amendments to the *Presbyterian Book of Order*, and ultimately to the establishment of a Council on Women, Church Employed Women, which advocated for women employed by the church, and Women in Leadership, which explored women's leadership in local communities. Out of that came the Third World Women's Task Group. Kepler co-chaired (with Wilma Scott Heide), and then chaired The Women's Coalition for the Third Century, a bicentennial organization that promoted women's contributions to the nation in history, media, religion and art, and that wrote the "Declaration of Interdependence of 1976" and the accompanying "Declaration of Women's Imperatives." Kepler wrote a musical for that occasion titled "Eve and Adam and the Curse." Kepler subsequently became director of ministerial studies at Harvard Divinity School, and "was able to bring my feminist perspective to that adventure as I gave leadership to the shaping of theological education for ministry." Kepler then began working on a book-in-progress, *Gender and Work*, and consulted for the Vocation Agency of the Presbyterian Church. She served as pastor of the Clarendon Hill Presbyterian Church for 17 years. As interim university chaplain at Tufts University, she continued her commitment to a feminist perspective on life and religion, connecting with the interfaith community and students wrestling with issues of faith and values. She has three children. Archives: Schlesinger Library, Radcliffe Institute, Cambridge, MA. (ABS)

Kerber, Linda K. (1940 –) A historian of women, Kerber was one of the younger generation who in the 1960s joined the Berkshire Conference of Women, founded in the 1920s to oppose discrimination against women. She was a member of the first permanent Committee on Women Historians, established by the American Historical Association in 1971, and served as its chair in 1972.

K

The Committee had a broad-ranging agenda that pressed the AHA, the largest learned society devoted to the practice of history in the U.S., to play a role in making professional practice more equitable. As of 2006, Kerber is president of the AHA. She is the May Brodbeck Professor in the Liberal Arts & Sciences, as well as professor of history at the University of Iowa and a lecturer in the College of Law, where she teaches courses in gender and legal history. In both her teaching and writing, Kerber has emphasized the history of citizenship, gender and authority. She is the author of *No Constitutional Right to be Ladies: Women and the Obligations of Citizenship* (Hill and Wang, 1998), for which she was awarded the Littleton-Griswold Prize for best book in U.S. legal history and the Joan Kelley Prize for the best book in women's history (both awarded by the American Historical Association). Her other books include *Toward an Intellectual History of Women* (University of North Carolina Press, 1997), *Women of the Republic: Intellect and Ideology in Revolutionary America* (The University of North Carolina Press, 1980), and *Federalists in Dissent: Imagery and Ideology in Jeffersonian America* (Cornell University Press, 1970). She is co-editor (with Alice Kessler-Harris and Kathryn Kish Sklar) of *U.S. History as Women's History*, essays in honor of Gerda Lerner (University of North Carolina Press, 1995), and (with Jane Sherron De Hart) of the widely used anthology *Women's America: Refocusing the Past* (6th edition, 2004), which has been translated into Japanese. Kerber has also served on many editorial boards and as historical adviser to several museum exhibitions. The recipient of numerous awards and distinctions, Kerber received her A.B. from Barnard College in 1960 and her Ph.D. from Columbia University in 1968. (ABS)

Kerkeslager, Lois – See Herr, Lois Kathryn

Kerry, Peggy (1941 –) After graduating from Smith College (1969), Kerry worked for Elinor Guggenheimer, the first woman to run for president of the New York City Council. In 1970, at the inaugural meeting of the National Women's Political Caucus, Kerry and Brenda Feigen started a youth caucus to ensure that young women had a voice. Kerry was also a member of the first Manhattan WPC. In the early 1970s, Kerry persuaded Gloria Steinem and others to dramatize the pitiful inadequacy of New York State's Welfare allowance by living for a week on that sum of money. Kerry also worked with Dorothy Pitman Hughes on affordable day care; on a Vietnam Moratorium to end the war; and on legalizing abortion in NYS. In the 1990s, she served on the board of Women's Action for New Directions (WAND) and worked as a consultant for Planned Parenthood of New York City for the United Nations Population Conference (1994) and the Women's 1995 Conferences. From 1991 to 1997, she served as a Democratic state committee women from the Lower West Side of Manhattan. Kerry campaigned around the country to many women's

groups on behalf of Senator John Kerry, her brother, who ran for President of the United States in 2004. (ABS)

Keskinen, Kay ("Sharl") (1948 –) became a charter member of Moscow, ID, NOW in 1975. Involved on both state and regional levels, Keskinen served as conference coordinator for ID NOW and the Northwest Regional NOW conference. In 1979 she was elected to NOW's national board and served for two years. She also chaired the credentials committee for NOW's 1980 national conference. In addition to her work with NOW, Keskinen coordinated two North Idaho conferences on Practical Politics for Women, and helped organize many ERA marches and walkathons and pro-choice rallies. As a member of the board of the University of Idaho women's caucus, she worked to have the university comply with the conciliation agreement that the administration signed with the women's caucus in 1974. She also served two three-year terms (1979 – 1985) on the Idaho Commission on Women's Programs. A professional in information technology, Keskinen retired in 2003. Archives: University of Idaho Library, Special Collections, Moscow, ID. (ABS)

Kesselman, Amy V. (1944 –) Historian and women's studies teacher, Kesselman participated in the caucus at the National Conference for New Politics that generated the West Side Group (Chicago), an early women's liberation group. Kesselman was also a founding member of CWLU and taught a high-school class in women's studies in Chicago in 1968. As a West Coast organizer for New University Congress (1970), she organized women's studies conferences in California. She also taught in the women's studies program at Portland State University and Mt. Hood Community College. Kesselman, who has a Ph.D. in history from Cornell, has written widely on feminist issues. She wrote "Our Gang of Four: Friendship and Women's Liberation" with Heather Booth, Vivian Rothstein and Naomi Weisstein, published in *The Feminist Memoir Project* (1998). Other articles include "Women's Liberation and the New Left in New Haven, Connecticut," published in *Radical History Review* (Fall, 2001); "Feminism 1965 to the Present," published in the *Encyclopedia of New England Culture* (Yale University Press); and "Outrageous/Liberating Acts: Putting Feminism Into Practice," with Ann Mussey, published in *Teaching Introduction to Women's Studies: Student Resistance and Classroom Strategies* (Greenwood, 1999). Kesselman is the author of *Fleeting Opportunities: Women Shipyard Workers in Portland and Vancouver During World War II and Reconversion* (SUNY Press, 1990), and co-editor of *Women: Images and Reality*, a multicultural anthology (2002). (ABS)

Kessler, Sheila – See Michaels, Sheila Shikiy

Kessler-Harris, Alice (1941 –) Thought to be one of the most important women's historians in the United States,

Kessler-Harris has been a leading advocate for university-level women's studies and a feminist labor history for more than 30 years. A professor of history and women's studies at Columbia University and chair of the history department (2004), she was one of three women historians who spoke at a White House symposium on Women as Citizens (1999), and served as director of the women's studies program at Rutgers University (1990–1995). She has also taught at Sarah Lawrence College, Temple University and Hofstra University. Born in England, Kessler-Harris earned her B.A. from Goucher College (1961), and her M.A. (1963) and Ph.D. (1968) from Rutgers. She is the author of *In Pursuit of Equity: Women, Men, and the Quest for Economic Citizenship in Twentieth-Century America* (New York: Oxford University Press, 2001); *Out to Work: A History of Wage Earning Women in the United States* (Oxford University Press, 1982); *A Woman's Wage: Historical Meanings and Social Consequences* (Kentucky, 1990); and *Women Have Always Worked: A Historical Overview* (Feminist Press, 1981). She is also the author of numerous articles focusing on the history of wage-earning women in the United States. (ABS)

Kettler, Ernestine Hara (1896–1978) came to the U.S. from Rumania in 1907, and at age 13 began associating with the Young People's Socialist League and attending political meetings in Union Square, New York City. A member of the NWP, Kettler was one of about 16 suffragists—some of whom chained themselves to the White House gates—who were arrested in 1917 and served time in Virginia's Occoquan Workhouse for "obstructing traffic." The women said they were "political prisoners" and refused to work. As punishment, they were beaten by trustees and fed weevil-infested food. Kettler was still fighting for women's rights in 1970 as an active member of the Los Angeles chapter of NOW. She and nine other suffragists were honored by NOW at an evening rally celebrating the 50th anniversary of the 19th amendment on August 26, 1970.

Kettley, Dorothy Kirby (1931–) (also known as Dorothy Kirby) As a member of the technical staff at Bell Telephone Laboratories (Holmdel, NJ), Kettley was appointed to the company's affirmative action committee in 1971, where she served for five years. Although the initial emphasis was on minorities ("statistics we compiled for women employees were presented in parentheses"), Kettley and another committee member, Olga Mitchell, pointed out the unfair treatment of technical women, who were often passed over for promotion, while men were generally put on the fast track. They also pointed out the need for maternity benefits. Kettley earned her B.A. from the University of Vermont (1952) and her M.A. from New York University (1961). (ABS)

Keyserling, Mary (1910–1997) Beginning in the 1930s, Keyserling worked with women experts and activists to improve the lives of women, and working women in particular. She served as director of the Women's Bureau, Dept. of Labor, and was the author of "Windows on Day Care," a 1972 report published by the National Council of Jewish Women that was subsequently used as a blueprint for implementing changes in day care programs. Archives: Schlesinger Library, Radcliffe Institute, Cambridge, MA.

Khosrovi, Carol M. – See Marshall, Carol Mayer

Kilander, Ellie – See Chaffee, Ellen Earle

Kilbourne, Jean (1943–) is probably the first person to study the image of women in advertising in depth. She began collecting advertisements and lecturing on the topic in 1969, and turned her lectures into a film, "Killing us Softly: Advertising's Image of Women," in 1979. Remade twice (1987 and 2000), the film is used worldwide. She is also the author of *Deadly Persuasion: Why Women and Girls Must Fight the Addictive Power of Advertising* (Simon & Schuster, 1999), which won the Distinguished Publication Award from the Association for Women in Psychology. Among other topics, Kilbourne has addressed are the tyranny of the beauty ideal, the obsession with thinness, and the link between objectification and violence. Kilbourne is the recipient of numerous awards, including awards from the Academy for Eating Disorders, the National Council on Alcoholism, the WAA, and NOW. In 1995, she received the Women's Image Now Award from the American Federation of Television and Radio Artists. Kilbourne, who has one child and three stepchildren, received her B.A. from Wellesley and her Ed.D. from Boston University. Archives: National Women and Media Collection, University of Missouri, Columbia, MO. (ABS)

Kimber, Lucia ("Kim") B. (1932–) Now a retired speech pathologist, Kimber became hooked on women's music after attending the First Boston Women's Music Festival in 1975, which she recorded with a small tape recorder held in her lap. In 1977, Kimber began attending and recording the National Women's Music Festivals. In 1979, she, Ruth Dworin of Womynly Way Productions, and others established the Women's Music Archives. They subsequently attended and recorded every NWMF through 2003. In 1981, Kimber was one of 13 women gathered in Connecticut by Christine Pattee to organize and produce a regional music festival, the Northeast Women's Music Retreat. Kimber was a member of the planning committee every year until the organization was dissolved in 2002. Says Kimber, "My role was primarily to serve as producer—first for the Day Stage and later for the Night Stage." Kimber holds a B.S. (1954) from Danbury Teachers College and an M.S. (1972) from Southern Connecticut State University. Archives: The Sophia Smith Collection, Smith College, Northampton, MA. (ABS)

King, Billie Jean (1943 –) A tennis legend and a fighter for equality for women in athletics, King broke the gender barrier for good in 1973 when, as defending champion, she demanded and succeeded in getting equal prize money from the U.S. Tennis Association for women competing at the U.S. Open at Forest Hills, NY. That same year, she founded the Women's Tennis Association, served as its first president, and beat Bobby Riggs in a media-hyped tennis match, dubbed the "Battle of the Sexes." She founded *WomenSports* magazine in the 1970s, which, unfortunately, lost money. When King stopped playing competitively in 1984, she had won 71 singles championships and been ranked #1 in the world five times. King has been an ongoing supporter of Title IX, which mandates that programs receiving federal money do not discriminate on the basis of gender. In 1974, King founded and is chair of the Women's Sports Foundation, a non-profit initiative that supports girls and women in sports. King has written six books, including (with Cynthia Starr) *We Have Come a Long Way, The Story of Women's Tennis* (1988). In 2004, King received the Alice Award (in memory of Alice Paul) for her contribution to breaking barriers and setting new precedents for women. (ABS)

King, Carol Louise (1948 –) has been an abortion-rights, freedom-of-choice activist since the early 1970s. After joining the Macomb County (MI) chapter of NOW in 1974, King became abortion task force chair, and from 1975 – 1977 served as president. In 1977, she became chair of national NOW's first abortion rights task force and helped put together one of the first packets on the question of abortion for NOW chapters. From 1978 – 1980, King served as president, Michigan Conference of NOW. She has served on many boards, including the national NOW board from 1980 – 1986. In 1988 she served as chair of the executive committee, People's Campaign for Choice, a statewide effort to preserve Medicaid funding for abortion. ("We lost," she says.) From 1989 – 1996, King was a convener/board member, Citizens for Personal Freedom, a bipartisan, statewide pro-choice organization; from 1989 – 1995, she was executive director, Michigan Abortion Rights Action League; and from 1993 – 1995 was a national board member, NARAL. A documentary filmmaker, King holds a B.A. from Western Michigan University (1971). She was an Inaugural Fellow, Michigan Political Leadership Program at Michigan State University (1992) and part of Michigan Women's Leadership Program at the University of Michigan (1994). (ABS)

King, Dorothy (1943 –) Part of a CR group in 1970 and founder of a women's group at Suffolk Law School (Boston) in 1974, King began working as a legal intern at Cambridge and Somerville Legal Services (Cambridge) in the matrimonial unit in 1973. Representing women who were divorcing, she did key work in spousal abuse, attempting both to give the women courage and to educate the courts. She also kept the women informed about

Welfare and housing options, thus making an independent life possible for them. King, who holds a J.D., has continued with matrimonial law throughout her career, empowering women to leave unsuccessful or abusive marriages, understand their options, and dare to start out on their own. In 1976, King helped found a battered women's home in Boston/Cambridge, and assisted in writing a handbook about battered women's rights. From 1975 – 1978, she worked with the disabled and elderly (mostly women), informing them of their rights under the then-new SSI system. (ABS)

King, Jean Ledwith (1924 –) Beginning in the late 1960s, King, an attorney, has fought for women's rights in the political, legal, educational and athletics areas, and has worked aggressively to assure women's right to choose. She was co-chair of the Michigan Abortion Referendum Campaign in 1972, and convened the meeting in April 1973 at Methodist headquarters in Washington, D.C. from which sprang the organization whose original name was Religious Coalition for Abortion Rights. In January 1970, with the support of five other women, King founded the women's caucus of the MI Democratic Party, which she chaired for three years. The caucus voted to challenge the composition of the MI delegation to the 1972 Democratic National Convention as a violation of the McGovern-Fraser rules. King argued the challenge at a party hearing in Detroit and again with Jacqui Hoop in Washington, D.C. The challenge was upheld in Miami with the help of women delegates from other states, and 11 women were added to the MI delegation. "This was the only women's challenge under the 1972 Rules that succeeded," says King. In 1970, King founded Focus on Equal Employment for Women with a dozen faculty members and graduates of the University of Michigan. In May 1970, this group filed a detailed administrative complaint drafted by King and Mary Yourd against the University of Michigan with the U.S. Department of Health, Education and Welfare with regard to sex discrimination in faculty hiring, promotion, salary, nepotism and benefits, and the treatment of women students and staff. By January 1971, the salaries of 100 women faculty were doubled and the University was forced by the federal government to address the other issues. In 1974, at the request of a group of Kalamazoo, MI, citizens, King drafted an administrative complaint relating to sex discrimination in the Houghton-Mifflin textbooks used in the elementary schools. In response, the publisher almost immediately issued a 100-page supplement and began to revise its books. Later, King expanded the Kalamazoo complaint into an illustrated book, *Sex Discrimination in Elementary Textbooks*. In 1980, King served as attorney for two students who had brought complaints of sexual harassment at the University of Michigan. The result was the resignation of one tenured faculty member; the banning of another from having graduate students for five years; and a substantial increase in the clout of the UM sexual harassment policy. King served as co-chair of the research and fund report committee of the federal Glass Ceiling Commission; was a member of the steering committee of the National Women and the Law Conference (1974, 1976 and 1982); and served as president of the Women's Law Fund from 1981–1983. In 1989, she was inducted into the Michigan Women's Hall of Fame. King, who has three children, earned her B.A. (1948), M.A. (1953), and J.D. (1968) from the University of Michigan. Archives: Bentley Historical Library, University of Michigan, Ann Arbor, MI. (ABS)

King, **Maora Jane** (1924 –) (also known as Skippy King) A retired LPN and midwife, King worked with other women and in her own home to help battered women in St. Petersburg, FL, in the late 1960s and early 1970s. In 1972, she helped open a women's center in Tampa. Designed to serve all the various needs of women, the center branched out to offer home births as well as women's group meetings in the 1970s and 1980s. King has four children. (ABS)

King, **Mary** (1940 –) was co-author, with Casey Hayden, of "Sex and Caste," first circulated in 1965 to women in the New Left and published in *Liberation* magazine (April 1966). King worked alongside of the Reverend Dr. Martin Luther King Jr. in the civil rights movement. King's book on that experience, *Freedom Song: A Personal Story of the 1960s Civil Rights Movement*, won a Robert F. Kennedy Memorial Book Award in 1988. Her book *Mahatma Gandhi and Martin Luther King, Jr.: The Power of Nonviolent Action* was published by UNESCO in 1999. As an appointee of President Jimmy Carter, King oversaw the Peace Corps as well as VISTA and other national volunteer service corps programs. Since 1984, she has served as special adviser to Carter, acting as his personal emissary to political and business leaders in the Middle East. King is Senior Fellow at the Rothermere American Institute of the University of Oxford (2004). As professor of peace and conflict studies, University for Peace, affiliated with the United Nations (UPEACE), Costa Rica, she teaches graduate students and also serves as academic adviser to its Africa Programme. King is also Distinguished Scholar with The American University Center for Global Peace in Washington, D.C. In November 2003, in Mumbai (Bombay), she was awarded the Jamnalal Bajaj Foundation International Award for the promotion of Gandhian values outside India. King holds a B.A. from Ohio Wesleyan University and a Ph.D. from the University of Wales at Aberystwyth, U.K. Archives: Her civil rights papers from the SNCC are at the Wisconsin State Historical Society, Madison, WI; Carter administration papers are in the Carter Library, Atlanta, GA; civil rights books and memorabilia are in the Hefner Civil Rights Collection, Vere Harmsworthy Library, Rothmere American Institute, University of Oxford, United Kingdom. (ABS)

King, **Nancy Elizabeth** – See Reame, Nancy Elizabeth

King, **Susan Elizabeth** (1947 –) developed and taught Women in Art with graduate student and artist Christina Kruse as part of graduate work at New Mexico State University in 1973. After completing her master's degree, King moved to Los Angeles and became part of an experimental feminist art program, the Feminist Studio Workshop, in 1973. In 1974 she did much of the rehabilitation work on the old Chouinard Art School, converting it into the Woman's Building, a women's cultural center. There she organized many exhibits and was coordinator with Michele Kort in 1974. She also started Women and Film Society screenings with Kort. In 1975, King founded Paradise Press, giving herself and other women the opportunity to publish their writings. In more recent years she became studio director at the Women's Graphics Art Center. She lives in Mt. Vernon, NY. (ABS)

Kingsley, **April** (1941 –) A museum curator, Kingsley joined a group of women artists in Los Angeles in 1971, and later that year started a group in NYC with Michelle Stuart and other New York artists and writers. She published an article in *Artforum* about Women Choose Women, the first major feminist exhibition in NYC, and has included women "in every exhibition I organized and every art history class I taught at the School of Visual Arts." As an independent critic, she has written catalogs, articles and reviews of work by major women artists. She is the author of "Six Women at Work in the Landscape," published in a 1978 issue of *Arts*, which, she says, "was pivotal for women's future success in public art." In 1981, she organized Women Artists: Indiana-New York Connection, for Notre Dame, and in 2002 published a monograph, "The Paintings of Alice Dalton Brown." Kingsley, who has one child, holds a Ph.D. (ABS)

Kirby, **Dorothy** – See Kettley, Dorothy Kirby

Kirsch, **Ruth Gabriele** (1928 –) (Also known as Ruth G. Andersen and Ruth G. Walsh) Living in Maryland in the late 1960s, Kirsch read about a tax reform act in progress that would give tax breaks to widows, but not to divorced women. She called the *Washington Post* and argued the case for divorced women with an editor, who then wrote a strong article on the topic. Result: The tax benefit for divorced women was included in the act. After moving to Boston in 1970, Kirsch became active in the ERA effort. She had speaking engagements, held small coffee hours, and lectured to women's groups, "notably the Boston Irish community, who were very opposed—until they heard me," she says. Kirsch also did a weekly hour-long radio show from the MIT radio station and was a guest on a couple of television shows. A member of NOW, Kirsch was on the task force on the image of women in the media. Born in West Berlin, Kirsch has one child. She holds a B.A., M.S.W. and J.D. (ABS)

K

Kjos, Edi – See Falk, Edith Sharon

Klaich, Dolores (1936 –) is the author of an early attempt at the social history of lesbianism, *Woman Plus Woman: Attitudes Toward Lesbianism* (1974). The book led to a number of speeches, including A Movement in Transition, given at the Gay Academic Union Conference, Columbia University (1975). It also aired live on WBAI and was printed in *Body Politic/25* (1976). A delegate from New York to the National Women's Conference in 1977, Klaich was a member of the caucus formed to ensure passage of the sexual preference resolution, which in fact passed. "After passage of the resolution, hundreds of helium balloons saying, 'We Are Everywhere,' were released." Klaich has continued to speak on gay and lesbian issues, and in the early 1980s served three terms as co-chair of EEGO in Southampton, NY. Klaich was also a judge of the Ferro-Grumley Foundation Literary Awards (for lesbian literature) from 1989–1991. From 1989–1999 she was an HIV/AIDS educator/trainer and sexuality lecturer at the State University of New York at Stony Brook, on women with AIDS and lesbian healthcare. (ABS)

Kleckner, Susan (1941 –) Film/video photographer, performance artist and curator, Kleckner joined her first CR group in the late 1960s with Kristin Booth Glen, Alice Harris, Louise Bernikow and Joyce Aarons, among others. In 1969, she began to seek funding for WAR from the New York State Council. To do so, she worked on and succeeded in bringing together the members of WAR and those in Feminists in the Arts (who were primarily writers, actors and dancers). They rewrote the original manifest, made new budgets, and then resubmitted the grant application, eventually receiving around $5,000—a substantial sum in those days. Kleckner was the first woman to teach photography at the Pratt Institute in NYC (1969). She founded the women's Interart Center (1970), and was co-director of the first all women's feature film released internationally: "Three Lives," produced by Kate Millett (1971). Kleckner's "Birth Film" (1973), with Kris and Jeffrey Glen, premiered at the Whitney Museum (1973). Several years later, Kleckner spent considerable time photographing and videotaping at Greenham Common, a feminist peace camp near London, England. And she initiated an activist/installation, a one-year performance on West Broadway (NYC), called WindowPeace, in which 40 women artists agreed to spend seven days each in voluntary incarceration behind the bulletproof glass. Outside, many street activities occurred, including a portable garden of organic greens, while other women set up tables for people to sign petitions and write postcards to promote peace. Kleckner continues to teach at the International Center of Photography, where she initiated and designed important curriculum. (ABS)

Kleiman, Carol — became a columnist at the *Chicago Tribune* in the early 1960s. As the newspaper's "Jobs" columnist, Kleiman introduced the first column in the country on women's issues, "Women at Work," which has run for over 30 years and evolved into a column titled "Work/Life." Kleiman, whose writing helped launch many feminist organizations, projects, ideas and dreams, was a contributor to *Ms.* magazine from its inception. She has marched for both women's rights and civil rights, has spoken nationwide on women's equality, and has been a strong voice for feminists in Chicago and across the country. The most recent of her nine books is *Winning the Job Game: The new rules for finding and keeping the job you want.* She does commentary on WBBM radio and has a television show on CLTV called "The Career Coach." In all, she writes three nationally syndicated columns: "Work/Life," "Jobs" and "Letters," all from a feminist viewpoint. Archives: University of Missouri, Columbia, MO. (ABS)

Klein, Charlotte Conrad (1923 –) A PR executive, adjunct professor at New York University and consultant (2004) to the Center for the Advancement of Women, Klein created the Women's Hall of Fame at the New York World's Fair (1965). With a nominating committee headed by Margaret Truman Daniel, the 10 living and 10 deceased most important women of the 20th century were voted on by women broadcasters and newspaper editors. In 1969, the Hall moved to the Seneca Falls historical preserve, and subsequently became the National Women's Hall of Fame. At the 1976 Democratic Convention in NYC, Klein created and ran (through the National Women's Political Caucus) the Women's Political News Service, which provided information to the media on women delegates and women's issues. Says Klein, "This gave Bella Abzug and others ammunition to demand 50/50 female/male delegates to future conventions." Klein also did PR for the First Women's Bank in NYC, and taught pioneering courses on women's issues at the New School. She also created a survey on sexual harassment for women executives in PR; developed a seminar on sexual harassment for the Women's Forum; and created the task force on sexual harassment for the Public Relations Society of America. In 1994, she developed a pilot program on domestic violence for the International Women's Forum, which led to the development of the IWF task force on violence against women globally, of which Klein was chair. She was also co-chair of the issues committee of the Women's Forum of New York, and created a hospital brigade to make heads of private NYC hospitals aware of the urgent need to make identifying and treating battered women a priority. Eleven hospitals subsequently did this, establishing training and treatment programs and appointing a domestic violence advocate for victims. Klein earned a B.A. from University of California, LA (1944), and took graduate courses at the New School for Social Research. Archives: The Sophia Smith Collection, Smith College, Northampton, MA. (ABS)

Klein, Joyce - See Gelb, Joyce

Photo Essay

The "takeover" of The Statue of Liberty on August 10, 1970 required careful planning and bravery on the part of Pat Lawrence and a small group of feminists. They studied the wind velocity and measured the width of the base, then snuck the 40-foot banner up to the base and secured it as women cheered below.

World Wide Photo

WOMEN OF THE WORLD UNITE!

Founding conference of the National Organization for Women, October 29 and 30, 1966, gathered in the basement of the *Washington Post,* Washington, D.C.

Photo by Vince Graas

In San Francisco, sewing workers strike a subsidiary of Esprit de Corp (1974) over lowered piece rates and laid off workers. Thirty-eight women were arrested for blocking trucks. The National Labor Relations Board awarded them a favorable settlement—almost ten years later.

Photo by Cathy Cade

Attorney Flo Kennedy reads proclamation at Sexism in the Media event May 1975.

Photo by Bettye Lane

Attendees huddle at the Forum on the Future, held by the Foundation for Matriarchy, New York City, September 16, 1978.

Photo by Bettye Lane

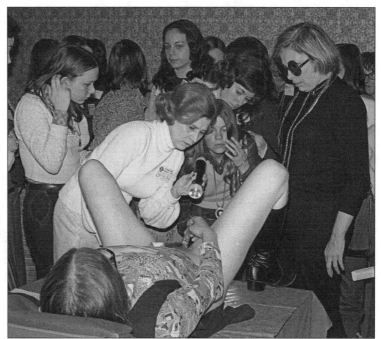

Carol Downer, Feminist Women's Health Clinic, conducts "self-help" demonstration at NOW, Washington, D.C., 1973.

Photo by Dori Jacobson-Wenzel

Feminist architect and filmmaker Phyllis Birkby in the Wholeo Dome created by Caroling Geary, late 1970s.

Photo from Sophia Smith Collection. Copyright unknown

Booth for the Feminist Radio Network at feminist fair, circa 1975, Washington, D.C. Shirl Smith standing at left.

Photo by JEB (Joan E. Biren)

Dobie Dolphin of Dobie Housebuilding at work in Albion, CA, 1972 or 1973. Women learned new skills, including how to build a house. San Francisco.

Photo by Lynda Koolish

Columbia University maids demonstrate for higher wages, May 1972.

Photo by Bettye Lane

Betty Friedan at Humanist-Feminist meeting, March 1974.

Photo by Bettye Lane

December 14, 1967 NOW chapters nation-wide barraged EEOC offices with baskets of red tape to protest the agency's failure to desexigrate Help Wanted ads. San Franciso protesters included NOW's secretary-treasurer Inka O'Hanrahan (third from left), second president Aileen Hernandez (holding tape) and lesbian activists Del Martin and Phyllis Lyon (far right).

Photo by Morton-Waters Co.

Feminists Who Changed America, 1963 – 1975

Wrenchwoman, a women-owned and operated auto repair shop, Washington, D.C., 1978. Valerie Mullin, owner, at right.
Photo by JEB (Joan E. Biren)

Muriel Fox leading the 1978 parade for extension of the ERA deadline, holding the hand of an eight-year-old Brooke Schafran, Washington, D.C.

Photo by Judith Meuli

Washington, D.C., Area Feminist Alliance meeting in 1977. At far end, head of table are Mary Spottswood Pou and Alexa Freeman.

Photo by JEB (Joan E. Biren)

Womanpower speaks at Second Women's March for Equality, August 26, 1971.

Photo by Bettye Lane

Little League baseball tryouts in Hoboken, NJ, April 1974, two years after NOW won lawsuit forcing the team to permit girls to try out.

Photo by Bettye Lane

Los Angeles NOW members picket the *Los Angeles Times* (1969) over Want Ads that had all the good jobs under Help Wanted, Male.

Photo by Judith Meuli

Rita Mae Brown at home in Washington, D.C., 1973, the year that *Rubyfruit Jungle* was published.

Photo by JEB (Joan E. Biren)

Irish feminists in Chicago march for the ERA during St. Patrick's Day, 1975. *Photo by Dori Jacobson-Wenzel*

Feminists Who Changed America, 1963 – 1975

Jenny Ingalls arrested at women's takeover of abandoned city-owned building on Fifth Street to be used for health and drop-in center for poor women in the area. Women refused to vacate the building. The women arrested paid fines and were released. New York City, January 1971.
Photo by Bettye Lane

Policeman confronts protester at Playboy Club demonstration, New York City, 1969.

Photo by Bettye Lane

Women listen to speeches at rally following August 26, 1970 Women's Strike for Equality march that attracted thousands.

Photo by Bettye Lane

Mujeres Latinas and the Coalition of Labor Union women join in the march in International Women's Day, Chicago, March 1974.

Photo by Dori Jacobson-Wenzel

Miss America Beauty Pageant protest initiated by New York Radical Women, Atlantic City, NJ, September 7, 1968.

World Wide Photo

"But Can She Type?" is the question asked about Israeli Prime Minister Golda Meir in poster, created by Linda Blair Miller, on sale at NOW conference display, Washington, D.C., 1973.

Photo by Bettye Lane

Feminists line up to speak at resolutions session of NOW conference in Washington, D.C., 1975. Toni Carabillo is in the center. Lucy Komisar is at the microphone. Dolores Alexander is seated in front.

Photo by Judith Meuli

Ti-Grace Atkinson speaking with bullhorn at daycare demonstration, August 1973.

Photo by Bettye Lane

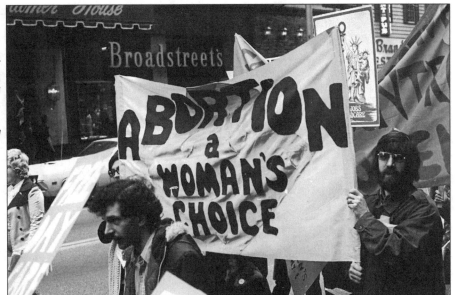

Women and men picket for women's right to abortion during International Women's Day march down State Street, Chicago, March 1974.

Photo by Dori Jacobson-Wenzel

Jayne West (left) and Abby Rockefeller (right) practice martial arts in Boston (1972). With Dana Densmore they began serious martial arts training and teaching other women martial arts for their self-protection.

Photo by Joe Demusz

Sister Joel Read, a member of NOW's first board who later became president of Alverno College, with Betty Friedan at NOW's first press conference, in Friedan's New York City apartment, November 1966.

Photographer unknown

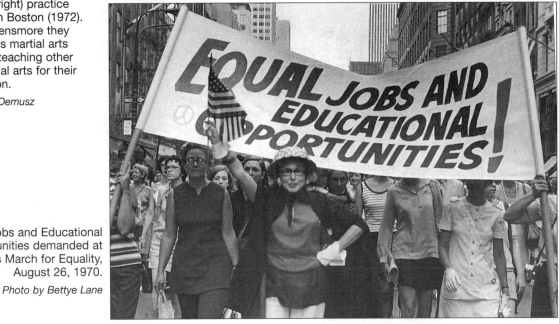

Equal Jobs and Educational Opportunities demanded at Women's March for Equality, August 26, 1970.

Photo by Bettye Lane

Thousands of women join first Women's March for Equality, Fifth Avenue, New York City, August 26, 1970.

Photo by Diana Davies. Copyright Sophia Smith Collection

Domestic violence attacked by "Battered Housewives" demonstration, 1977.

Photo by Bettye Lane

Dolores Huerta, Bella Abzug and Gloria Steinem at the United Farm Workers Rally, New York City, May 1975.

Photo by Bettye Lane

Feminists Who Changed America, 1963 – 1975

When California passed the ERA (1972), Bank of America eliminated taxi service for women clerical workers going home in the early morning. Union Women's Alliance to Gain Equality and other groups demonstrated in San Francisco to have the service reinstated and extended to men.

Photo by Cathy Cade

Three-term NOW president Eleanor Smeal addresses convention during ERA evening at NOW conference 1977. NOW logo at right was created by Ivy Bottini.

Photo by Judith Meuli

Members of Wages for Housework, an international organization, demand that women's labor be counted as paid labor. International Women's Day, New York City, March 1974.

Photo by Bettye Lane

Economic justice is demanded at International Women's Day march in Chicago, March 1974.

Photo by Dori Jacsobson-Wenzel

As part of an early international action, New York Radical Feminists picket (July 1973) to protest arrest of Portuguese women writers, The Three Marias, jailed for writing a feminist book. The women were acquitted in 1974.

Photo by Bettye Lane

Women United for Action demonstrate against high utility rates at Con Edison in New York City, April 1974.

Photo by Bettye Lane

Los Angeles NOW members at mailing party for an early issue of NOW Acts newsletter, January 1970.

Photo by Toni Carabillo

Pioneers of women's music. Front row left to right: Meg Christian on stool with guitar, Cris Williamson on floor with Joan Lowe, engineer. Margie Adam is on stool at right. Second row directly behind Meg Christian are Judy Dlugacz and Ginny Berson. Washington, D.C., 1974.

Photo by JEB (Joan E. Biren)

Third World Women's Caucus members march for social and economic rights, New York City, circa 1971. P.O.W. stands for Power of Women.

Sophia Smith Collection. Photo by Diana Davies

Sarah Kovner, chair of First Women's Bank, proclaim bank's debut at ERA demonstration, November 1975.

Photo by Bettye Lane

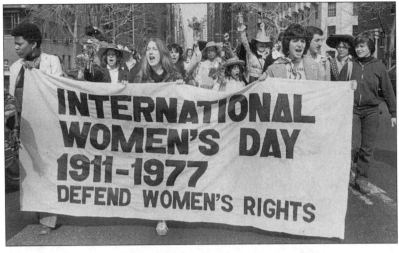

Feminists in International Women's Day march in New York City (1977) chant for women's rights.
Photo by Bettye Lane

Homemakers rights were a key demand of the feminist movement. Mothers demonstrate at Union Square, New York City, 1977.
Photo by Bettye Lane

Jacqui Ceballos at action renaming Madison Avenue "Dolly Madison Avenue" in New York City, August 1971.

Photo by Bettye Lane

Boardwalk demonstration at NOW Regional Conference in Atlantic City, NJ, September 1972.

Photo by Bettye Lane

Feminists Who Changed America, 1963 – 1975

NOW leaders don Supreme Court robes (1973) to make the point that there were no women on the highest court of the land. "Justices" are (l-r) Roberta Benjamin, Muriel Fox, Jacqui Ceballos, Wilma Scott Heide, Karen DeCrow, Nola Claire, Dorothy Haener and Toni Carabillo. Washington insiders provided the robes. Washington, D.C.

Photo by Judith Meuli

Sidney Abbott, Barbara Love and Kate Millett at NOW New York panel on lesbianism and feminism, 1969. *Photographer unknown.*

Women across America protested the war in Vietnam. Here women join in Strike for Peace and Equality in 1970.

Photo by Bettye Lane

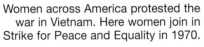

Students at the Women's School of Planning and Architecture first session in 1975 forming a woman symbol, Biddeford, ME, 1975.

Sophia Smith Collection. Copyright unknown

Feminists Who Changed America, 1963 – 1975

Klein, Pauline M. (1953 –) became active in the Women's Center of Lexington (KY) in 1972. The group was responsible for the founding and continuing services of the Rape Crisis Center, Spousal Abuse Center, and a substance abuse program for women who abuse prescription drugs and other substances. Klein remained with the group until 1978 and continued her financial support until 1990. From 1975–1990, she was active in several women's newsletters and a feminist paper, *Emergence*. From 1974–1976 she was "a minor player" in a Grand Jury abuse case. "The FBI were looking for fugitives from the Weather Underground and used strong-arm tactics to try to destroy the burgeoning women's movement in Lexington. They tried to force me (as treasurer and historian of the Women's Center) to turn over membership records for our group. I refused. Others who refused to help them ended up in jail for up to 18 months. I did not. I believe it was because at the time I had not come out and was considered straight." Over the years, Klein has traveled to numerous ERA, pro-choice and lesbian rights marches. "I have been harassed by police for my bumper stickers and nearly run out of South Carolina for my radical feminist beliefs. I remain and always will be a radical, lesbian feminist and very proud to call myself that." Klein is (2006) a librarian and incorporates her feminist principles into her collection-development selections and reference work on a daily basis. Archives: University of Kentucky Special Collections and Archives, Louisville, KY. (ABS)

Klement, Vera (1929 –) An artist born in the Free City of Danzig, Klement was a founding member of Artemisia Gallery, Chicago, in the early 1970s. According to the ArtWorld Chicago Web site, "The goals of gallery founders were to emphasize the role of women in the arts, to encourage the creation of innovative and experimental art which would not otherwise be seen in commercial galleries, and to provide a forum for the exchange of aesthetic ideas." Klement's work has been exhibited in the U.S. and abroad, and is in major collections in NYC and Chicago. Klement, who attended Cooper Union, was a professor at the University of Chicago, beginning in 1969, until her retirement. She has one child. Archives: Smithsonian Museum, Washington, D.C. (ABS)

Klemesrud, Judy Lee (1939 – 1985) became one of the first female reporters and a top reporter at *The New York Times*. She covered many women's movement events and wrote the first *Times* article about NOW's founding (an interview with Betty Friedan published in November 1966 and printed under an article headed "How to Prepare Your Thanksgiving Turkey" on the Women's Page). About one-fifth of her articles from 1970–1985 were about the women's movement and its issues. She won two Page One Awards from the Newspaper Guild of New York—one for a 1973 story titled "In a Small Town U.S.A. Women's Lib is Either a Joke or a Rarity." In 1969 she won a Front Page Award from the Newspaper Women's Club

of New York for a story about adoption by single women. Klemensrud was a feminist herself, beckoning the NY NOW women to enter a back door to the building (there were guards out front) to distribute *The NOW York Times*, "all the news that would give *The New York Times* fits." A few weeks later, *The Times* women successfully sued *The Times* for sex discrimination. Archives: Iowa Women's Archives, University of Iowa Libraries, Iowa City, IA.

Klevs, Mardi (1952 –) As a graduate student in labor history at the University of Minnesota at Minneapolis, Klevs did research on women in the labor movement. By 1975, she was working in factories and doing rank-and-file organizing at a number of them, including a laundry and sewing factory. Working at Litton Microwave Industries, she represented her union, the United Electrical Workers, as the health and safety representative. Most of the workforce at this plant was female and under the age of 25. Because the workers had children and major childcare issues, Klevs helped organize several walkouts that dealt with overtime. She later moved to Chicago, again doing labor organizing at a major machine shop. She was one of the first 12 women hired in a plant of 1,200 workers, and was very active in a rank-and-file caucus of Steelworkers Union Local 15271, which represented the interests of people of color and women. In the economic downturn of the early 1980s, she left factory work and started teaching history and political science, including feminist lectures. An environmental engineer and manager, Klevs has worked for the United States Environmental Protection Agency since 1986. Klevs earned her B.A. from the University of California at Berkley, her M.A. from the University of Minnesota at Minneapolis, and her M.S. from the Illinois Institute of Technology. She has two children. (ABS)

Klindt, Jenifor Leigh Thompson (1946 – 1994) joined the Moscow, ID, chapter of NOW in 1975. A vocal feminist, Klindt often spoke to groups about NOW and feminism. With Kay Keskinen, she helped organize two conferences on practical politics for women (North Idaho). Klindt also served for one term on NOW's national board representing the Northwest Region (1977 – 1979). When Illinois' ratification of the ERA became essential to the passage of the amendment, Klindt moved back to Illinois to build momentum for the vote. During that time she also traveled to other states as part of NOW's national ratification campaign. Klindt remained politically active, managing political operations for Mike Madigan, IL house speaker, toward the end of her life. In 1993 she helped establish the foundations for the Democratic legislative campaign committee, then served as its first executive director.

Knaak, Nancy (1928 – 1996) In June 1966, Knaak, a psychology professor at the University of Wisconsin, River Falls, attended the Conference of State Commissions on the Status of Women (Washington, D.C.). There she was invited by Kay Clarenbach to attend a late night meeting in Betty Friedan's hotel room. It was the meeting that led to the founding of NOW, and Knaak's role was the same as the other women's: to strategize, raise questions, brainstorm. However, Friedan became annoyed when Knaak questioned the need for another organization, and demanded that Knaak leave; when Knaak refused, Friedan locked herself in the bathroom for 15 minutes. She later returned to the room, and the meeting continued, with Knaak present. Knaak discussed the event for the *Feminist Chronicles, 1953–1993*: "Among the limited legends of NOW, 'the woman thrown out who never returned' has been a sort of symbol of constancy of those who remained. That I am still among the membership does make me feel a bit subversive sometimes. I have regret that I am still that legendary woman." Knaak had been a dean of women at the University of Wisconsin, River Falls. She began teaching psychology in 1957 and taught until 1968, when she was named associate dean of students and dean of women. During her teaching career she participated in the Wisconsin Association of Women Deans and Counselors as president and VP. She was also active with the River Falls branch of the AAUW. At the time of her death she was a member of NOW.

Knapp, Kristan B. (1948 –) (also known as Kristan Aspen) joined the Red Emma Collective in Portland, OR, in 1971. Together, the women helped start the Feminist Women's Health Clinic (which closed in 2003) and Prescott House, a halfway house for women coming out of prison, which evolved into Bradley-Angle House (1974 –1975). In 1972, Knapp became a certified auto mechanic, one of the first women in Portland to do so, and taught and served the community in that capacity until 1984. A performing musician since 1974, Knapp and Naomi Littlebear Morena formed the Ursa Minor Choir, Portland's first lesbian choir, and the Izquierda Ensemble, a quartet that recorded and toured nationally from 1977–1980. Knapp also worked with Women's Energy, a production company in Portland that produced concerts and two years of the Northwest Women's Music Festival (1977–1978). Since 1984, Knapp has performed with her partner of 24 years, Janna MacAuslan, as the flutist in the Musica Femina Flute Guitar Duo. The duo has two CD recordings, and toured nationally for 12 years, breaking ground with a program of classical and original music by women composers. Both Knapp and MacAuslan were regular contributors to *HotWire Magazine*, writing a column about women in classical music. Throughout this time, Knapp worked consistently for lesbian rights. In the 1990s, she helped facilitate logistics for the Walk for Love and Justice; from 1995–1999, she served on the board of Pride Northwest; and in 1999 became interim program director at the Lesbian Community Project, where she helped create a Deaf Culture Night that was picked up by Deaf and Hearing People. This in turn created a separate organization to bring deaf and hearing queers together.

Earlier, in 1970, Knapp traveled to Cuba as part of the Venceremos Brigade and worked in the lime and other citrus fields on La Isla de la Juventud. Knapp holds a B.S. from Oberlin College (1970). She is (2006) development director of Bradley-Angle House. Archives: The Lesbian Herstory Archives, Brooklyn, NY; West Coast Lesbian Archives, Los Angeles, CA; and the Oregon Historical Society, Portland, OR. (ABS)

Knauss, Jennifer L.M. (1937 –) (also known as Jennifer L.M. Dobbin) has dedicated her life to gender equality and better healthcare for women. She joined CWLU in 1969, at its beginning, and remained a member until it dissolved. She served on the steering committee several times, and was a founding member of the Chicago Women's Liberation School. Particularly interested in healthcare issues, Knauss worked with two other CWLU members in a program at the University of Illinois that brought medical students, nursing students and community women together to discuss ways of fighting for a more satisfactory healthcare system. The program led to the development of new projects at CWLU, including some Liberation School courses, such as Hers. Knauss represented CWLU at the Women's Conference at Antioch College in 1973, which led to CWLU becoming more involved in sterilization issues, and working more closely with Latinas. Knauss has been a supporter of civil rights, marching with Dr. King in Chicago, and for 21 years was executive director of the Illinois Caucus for Adolescent Health. She attended the Fourth World Conference on Women in Beijing, and taught for four years in Ghana and Nigeria. She has Alzheimer's disease and is now a leader of Alzheimer's Spoken Here, Inc., an Illinois not-for-profit corporation. Knauss, who has two children, attended Somerville College, Oxford, England, and Northwestern University, Evanston, IL. Archives: Jenny Knauss Archive, Northwestern University Library, Evanston, IL. (ABS)

Knee, Judith (1946 –) joined Essex County (NJ) NOW in 1973, and served two terms as president of NJ NOW (1974–1976). She was a NOW national board member and MidAtlantic regional director (1977–1983); worked at the NOW National Action Center (1980–1981); and was NOW bylaws chair for over 15 years in the 1980s and 1990s. She continues (2004) as a consultant to NOW on parliamentary issues. Her primary responsibilities at the Action Center (Washington, D.C.) were to maintain the vote count in Congress for the ERA extension; serve as liaison to NOW's attorneys for court cases involving ERA issues; and write ERA campaign materials. In addition to her work for the ERA, Knee has been active in reproductive rights, lesbian rights and economic issues. A supporter of the Feminist Majority, Knee received her B.A. from the University of Pennsylvania (1967). (ABS)

Knox, Holly (1946 –) In 1972, while serving as a legislative specialist in HEW, Knox chaired a U.S. Office of

Education task force examining the impact of federal education programs and funding on opportunities for women and girls in education. With Mary Ann Millsap, she wrote the task force report, which documented extensive inequities facing women and girls, both as students and employees, at all levels of U.S. education. The report guided federal policy on Title IX, passed that year, and provided feminists with ammunition to press for enactment of the Women's Education Equity Act (which Congress passed in 1974). Earlier, Knox had drafted the administration testimony on the bill that became Title IX. From 1972–1974, Knox served on internal HEW working groups developing regulations for Title IX, as one of a handful of feminists working inside HEW. In 1974, she left the government to found and direct the Project on Equal Education Rights as part of the NOW LDEF. Knox served as director of PEER until 1983. Also in 1974, she was instrumental in the creation of the National Coalition for Women and Girls in Education, and served as its first chair. In 1981, working with WEAL's Pat Reuss, Knox spearheaded a coalition lobbying campaign that saved the Women's Education Equity Act from elimination. Knox was born in Princeton, NJ, and holds a B.A. from Wellesley College (1968). (ABS)

Koedt, Anne (1939 –) Born in Denmark to parents involved in the resistance during WWII, Koedt—a writer, artist, radical feminist and socialist—was active in the formation of the women's liberation movement that emerged from the New Left in NYC. Koedt was a founding member of NYRW (1967) and a founder of The Feminists (1968) and NYRF (1969). Her article "The Myth of the Vaginal Orgasm" first appeared in *Notes from the First Year* (1968), a journal written and distributed by NYRW. Koedt denounced the Freudian notion that clitoral orgasm alone was immature and a sign of frigidity. Koedt also denounced the vaginal orgasm as a myth and a conspiracy against women, examined the connection between female oppression and male sexual exploitation, and negated the authority of male sexual "experts." The essay became part of the CR culture of the 1970s and introduced some of the main terms of the movement for sexual freedom. Koedt also served as co-editor of *Notes from the Second Year* (1970), *Notes from the Third Year* (1971), and the anthology *Radical Feminism* (1973), a collection of radical feminist writings gathered largely from *Notes*. She is the author of several other influential articles and speeches, including "Politics of the Ego" (1969) and "Lesbianism and Feminism" (1971). (ABS)

Koetler, Deborah – See Silvermoon, Flash

Kolasinski, Ginger – See Whittington, Ginger

Kolb, Frances Arick (1937–1991) was a national authority on gender and women's issues, as well as an early and longtime activist with NOW. Kolb was curriculum coordi-

nator, Training Institute for Sex Desegregation, Douglass College, Rutgers University (1975–1979). From 1981–1982, she was coordinator, New England Center for Equity Assistance, a program funded by Title IX, U.S. Department of Education, to help school districts in New England promote Title IX compliance and sex equity. She was a founder of the South Hills (PA) chapter of NOW, an activist in NJ NOW, a national board member, and the director of the Eastern Region from 1971–1974. In the late 1970s, she was the first chair, a volunteer, of NOW's economic boycott campaign to put pressure on unratified states to pass the ERA. As a Bunting Fellow at Radcliffe College's Schlesinger Library in 1979, Kolb began writing a history of the first 10 years of NOW. She was also a member of the Pittsburgh WPC; the National Council of Jewish Women (NJ); Pittsburgh Association for the Advancement of Women; the Women's Liberation Group, East Lansing, MI; and the ad hoc committee on family planning in East Lansing, of which she was chair. Kolb earned her B.A. from Washington University (1958); her M.A. from the University of Pennsylvania (1959); and her Ph.D. from Washington University (1972). Archives: Schlesinger Library, Radcliffe Institute, Cambridge, MA.

K

Kolodny, Annette (1941 –) An assistant professor in the English dept. at the University of British Columbia in 1970, Kolodny was a co-founder of the women's studies dept. (1971–1974). It was an arduous, multi-year process that repeatedly met opposition from faculty and administration. After classes began, the dept. received little if any institutional support. Nonetheless, by the end of the 1980s, the university "was one of the very few Canadian campuses with either a major or minor in the field." And the program in 2000 is robust. A course originated by Kolodny, Women in Literature, continues to be taught there. Kolodny, who began publishing a series of articles on feminist literary criticism in 1975, is author of *The Lay of the Land: Metaphor as Experience and History in American Life and Letters* (1975), a study of the male-centered cultural mythology of the U.S. frontiers. When the University of New Hampshire voted against Kolodny's promotion and tenure in 1975, she sued the university for sex discrimination and anti-Semitism. She used part of the settlement money (1980) to establish the legal fund of the task force on academic discrimination within the NWSA. Kolodny is also author of *The Land Before Her: Fantasy and Experience of the American Frontiers, 1630 – 1860*, an analysis of women's responses to frontier landscapes (1984), and *Failing the Future: A Dean Looks at Higher Education in the Twenty-First Century* (1998). In 1997, Kolodny became the first woman named an Honored Scholar by the Modern Language Association Division on Early American Literature. Archives: University of Arizona, Tucson, AZ. (ABS)

Komer, Odessa (1925 – 2004) became a member of United Auto Workers Local 228 in 1953, as an assembler at the Ford Sterling Plant, and began a lifetime of working for the rights of women in labor. During 14 years as a member of that 7,000-member local, Komer was elected to numerous leadership positions, each time being the first woman to hold that post. In 1967, she was appointed to the staff of the international union as education director of Region I in Michigan. The UAW elected her an international VP in 1974 and returned her to that office at each convention until her retirement in 1992. During that time, she led the UAW drive to create women's councils and conferences across the United States. The intensive training provided resulted in women being elected to top local union posts in roughly the same proportion as their membership. Komer also led the challenge to corporate policies that kept women of childbearing age from dangerous areas, insisting that those areas be made safe for all workers. She took her views to the U.S. Supreme Court, where they were upheld. Komer served as a member of NOW's advisory board, as national VP of CLUW, and a member of the advisory boards of Women's Occupational Health Resource Center and the NWPC. Komer was also appointed to the President's Advisory Committee for Women, by President Carter. In 1995, she was inducted into The Michigan Women's Hall of Fame.

Komisar, Lucy (1942 –) A journalist in NYC, Komisar joined NOW in 1969, and served as national VP and member of the board, NY NOW (1970 – 1971). Working with NOW VP Ann Scott, Komisar was able to get the Labor Dept.'s contract compliance office to apply to women the regulations requiring affirmative action by government contractors and common carriers, including radio and TV stations. Following the ruling, affected companies had to file plans with goals and timetables for hiring women as well as minorities. Komisar was also a member of Media Women, NYC, and participated in the *Ladies' Home Journal* action. She is the author of *The New Feminism* (Franklin Watts, 1972), as well as numerous magazine and newspaper articles on women's issues. These include "Feminism as National Politics" (*The Nation*, December 10, 1977); "Sellout on Abortion" (*Newsweek*, June 9, 1975); "Right-wingers v. the ERA" (*Philadelphia Inquirer*, June 27, 1977); and "A Feminist Manifesto" (*Reader's Digest*, August 1971). Active in the civil rights movement in the early 1960s, Komisar took part in a 36-hour sit-in at the NYC offices of ABC Paramount to protest the segregation of its movie theaters in Texas, and was arrested on a freedom ride to protest the segregation of restaurants in Maryland. She also served as editor of *Mississippi Free Press*, a weekly newspaper, 1962 – 1963. Komisar has a B.A. from Queens College, CUNY. Archives: Women's rights papers: Schlesinger Library, Radcliffe Institute, Cambridge, MA; civil rights papers: University of Southern Mississippi, Hattiesburg, MS.   (ABS)

Koolish, Lynda (1946 –) saw women's culture beginning to flourish in the early 1970s and wanted to be part of it.

She took her camera to the first Country Women's Festival, in Albion, California, in 1972. From the early 1970s forward, her photographic work has centered on writers of color, and her scholarly work has centered on black writers. Koolish, who is (2006) professor of English and comparative literature at San Diego State University, teaches primarily African American literature, poetry of witness, and contemporary feminist poetry. During the 1970s her photographs, poems, essays and drawings appeared in numerous publications, including *Plexus, Moving Out, Libera, Small Press Review, Sinister Wisdom, Women: A Journal of Liberation, Country Women, San Francisco Bay Guardian, Motive* and *Gallery Works*. In 1973 she self-published *Journeys on the Living: Poems, Photographs and Drawings*. She has had numerous one-woman photographic exhibits. Her book *African American Writers: Portraits and Visions* (University Press of Mississippi, 2001) won a 2001 American Library Association Award. Koolish holds a B.A. from the University of California, Berkeley, an M.A. from San Francisco State University, and a Ph.D. from Stanford. Archives: Some papers are at the San Francisco Public Library; some feminist poetry broadsides are at the University of California, San Diego, and San Diego State University.   (ABS)

Koontz, Elizabeth Duncan (1919 – 1989) Koontz was the first African American to be appointed president of the National Education Association (1967). Following her appointment to the U.S. Department of Labor in 1969, Koontz became the first African American to serve as the director of the Women's Bureau in the Nixon administration. Subsequently, Koontz became deputy assistant secretary for Labor Employment Standards. While in that position, she became the United States delegate to the United Nations Commission on the Status of Women. After leaving Washington, Koontz returned to her home state of North Carolina to coordinate the nutrition programs of the Department of Human Resources. Later, from 1975 until her retirement in 1982, she served as assistant state schools superintendent. Koontz received her bachelor's degree from Livingstone College and her M.A. from Atlanta University.

Kopelov, Connie (1926 –) A feminist labor activist and women's labor scholar, Kopelov worked to fight McCarthyism, advance civil liberties, and stop the Vietnam War before she took up feminism. She traveled widely for the education dept. of the Amalgamated Clothing Workers, and as head of the education department of the National Union of Hospital and Health Care Workers. In 1972, she was a member of the New York Trade Union Women's Seminar, whose goal was to get women active so that they could achieve their rightful places in their unions and in society. Kopelov was a founding member of CLUW in 1974 and was elected VP of its NYC chapter in 1975. Kopelov also tried to gain a greater voice for workers within the women's movement, which she felt lacked understanding of the underlying economic issues faced by union workers. After 1975, Kopelov was engaged in feminist labor activism and scholarship on women's labor history. She wrote extensively on that subject and taught at Cornell University's women's studies program in NYC. Her contribution to women's history has been honored by the New York State Labor History Association and by the NYC chapter of CLUW. She was given the Susan B. Anthony Award by NYC NOW for her contributions to the women's movement. Kopelov holds a B.A. from Northwestern University and an M.A. from Goddard College. She also studied as a Fulbright Scholar at the University of Sheffield in Great Britton. Archives: Tamiment/Wagner Archives, New York University, New York, NY.   (ABS)

Koppelman, Susan Huddis (1940 –) (also known as Susan Cornillon) An activist for women's liberation, disability rights, fat acceptance, and social justice, as well as a writer, editor, literary historian, and networker, Koppelman believes that women's literature helps us understand and change our lives. "I have made it the mission of my life to seek out and restore to women our stories." Koppelman organized CR groups with Cell 16 in Boston, where she began teaching women's studies in 1967. She organized Women's Liberation Conferences at Bradford Jr. College (1969); Bowling Green State University (1972); and the Tri-State Feminist Conference (MI, OH and IN) in 1973; and the very first national gathering of feminist scholars: the Popular Culture Association, Indianapolis (1973). She is a founder of NWSA (1977), its Jewish and disability caucuses, and the Popular Culture Association Women's Caucus. After her first book, which was also the first collection of feminist literary criticism, *Images of Women in Fiction: Feminist Perspectives* (Popular Press, 1972), she began making U.S. women's short stories available. Her 10 books include *The Other Woman: Stories of Two Women and a Man* (the Feminist Press, 1984); *Between Mothers and Daughters: Stories Across a Generation* (the Feminist Press, 1985); *Two Friends and Other Nineteenth-Century Lesbian Stories* (Penguin/Meridian, 1994); *Women in the Trees: U.S. Women Writer's Short Stories of Battering and Resistance, 1839–1994* (Beacon Press, 1996); *The Strange History of Suzanne LaFleshe and Other Stories of Women and Fatness* (the Feminist Press, 2003); and *The Stories of Fannie Hurst* (the Feminist Press, 2005). Since 1985, the Susan Koppelman Award is given annually to outstanding edited feminist books. She has one son, one foster son, and holds a B.A. (1962), M.A. (1969) and Ph.D. (1975). Archives: Brown Popular Culture Library, Bowling Green State University, Bowling Green, OH; and The Schlesinger Library, Radcliffe Institute, Cambridge, MA.   (ABS)

Kornbluh, Joyce Lewis (1928 –) has spent more than 50 years improving workplace conditions and the economic status of working-class people, especially low-paid women and minorities. In 1974, Kornbluh initiated the Program on Women and Work at the University of Michigan's Labor Studies Center, and later started the contemporary movement of regional, state and national Summer Schools for Working Women. With Hilda Patricia Curran, Kornbluh initiated and co-chaired the Michigan task force on sexual harassment in the workplace. This resulted in the first state-level sexual harassment law in Michigan and served as a model for other states and national legislation. Kornbluh also developed and taught the first credit course at the University of Michigan on women and work. In 1985, she was asked to advise the first major effort to assess workplace sexual harassment in Sweden. Kornbluh, who has three children, was inducted into The Michigan Women's Hall of Fame in 2003.   (ABS)

Kort, Michele Faye (1950 –) became an administrator of Womanspace, a women's art gallery in The Woman's Building in Los Angeles, in 1974. When it closed in the spring of that year, Kort and Susan King became co-administrators of The Woman's Building, a position Kort held until the fall of 1975. As co-administrator, she curated many art exhibits, "most memorably, a retrospective of photographer Imogen Cunningham's work. She was 92 at the time, and hadn't shown in LA in years," says Kort. In subsequent years, Kort served on various advisory boards at the Building, taught a class on Grantsmanship, and produced one of the first "artists books" at the Women's Graphics Center titled *Some of My Friends*. In the 1980s, she began writing for women's publications, including *Ms.* and *Women's Sports and Fitness*. In 2002, she published a biography of singer/songwriter Laura Nyro. Kurt is (2004) senior editor of *Ms.* She earned her B.A. (1971) and M.B.A. (1975) from the University of California, Los Angeles.   (ABS)

Kosokoff, Sandy – See Polishuk, Sandy

Kosower, Trudy Margaret (1931 –) Kosower, who writes under the name Trudy Riley, joined the women's movement in 1969 and has been working to support the rights of women and lesbians since then. She served as co-chair of the federal women's program at the VA hospital in West Los Angeles in 1972, consulted with the Crenshaw Clinic on the lack of services for addicted and alcoholic women in Los Angeles, and demonstrated for reproductive rights. In addition, Kosower was a member of the lesbian radical therapy collective in Ocean Park, CA, and helped create a lesbian mother's group. After 1975, she became active in OLOC and also began working to prevent violence against women. Kosower, who has two children, holds an M.S.W. from the University of California, Los Angeles. She is retired and is living in "a mostly lesbian and for sure women's community." She says, "It takes a bit of courage for 600 of us to live in the middle of a redneck town in Arizona, but we are doing it." (ABS)

Kotsonis, Helen Hoch – See Hoch, Helen

Kovacs, Midge (1926 – 2004) An advertising executive in the early 1970s, Kovacs used her skills to force media to treat women more honestly and fairly, and later, to empower the disabled. She was inspired by the Strike for Equality (1970) to join NY NOW, and served as coordinator for a committee on the image of women in the media (1972 – 1976). The committee challenged the broadcast license of NYC television station WABC, on the grounds of programming that discriminated against women. In addition, it launched a public service ad campaign through the Advertising Council, based on women's rights, "Womanpower: It's Much Too Good to Waste." A famous print ad created for this campaign was of a man showing his legs, with the caption, "Hire him, he's got great legs." Fed up with the suffocating corporate world and weary of having men younger and less experienced as bosses, she started her own ad agency, ran it for about 20 years, then sold it to a larger agency. In later life, after suffering a stroke that left her unable to use her left side, Kovacs directed her passion to disability rights. In the early 1980s, she developed Spasmodic Dysphonia, which greatly impaired her ability to speak, and became an activist for that cause and the disabled. Kovacs earned a B.S. degree in marketing and journalism from New York University (1947). Archives: The Sophia Smith Collection, Smith College, Northampton, MA.   (ABS before death)

Kozak, Lillian (1923 –) Exposed to the legal system through her divorce in the 1970s, Kozak became obsessed with seeking justice for women in similar circumstances. Referred to NOW, she eventually established a Long Island (NY) NOW committee, and became chair of the NYS NOW domestic relations law task force. In that capacity, she fought for revisions to the Equitable Distribution Divorce Bill and the Preferential Joint Custody Bill; had pre-divorce standards of living considered in the establishment of settlements; educated delegates to the NYS NOW Council on Domestic Relations Issues; co-founded the Coalition on Women's Legal Issues (COWLI); and started a career as an investigative accountant in divorce cases. (Earlier in her life, as a college major in business and accounting, Kozak had been told by her professor, "Women don't belong in accounting.") She also frequently counseled women caught in the throes of divorce litigation. In 1940, when she was admitted to City College of New York, "women were admitted by quota," she says. "My class had 75 women chosen from the top applicants from all the NYC high schools."   (ABS)

Kozloff, Joyce (1942 –) (also known as Joyce Blumberg) An artist, Kozloff called the first meeting of the Los Angeles Council of Women Artists in her apartment in Santa Monica (CA) in 1971. Among other actions, the group protested the all-male Art in Technology show at the Los Angeles County Museum of Art, and succeeded in getting the museum to sponsor an exhibition of women artists, curated by Ann Sutherland Harris and Linda Nochlin, in 1976. Kozloff, who moved to NYC in 1971, had her first solo show at the Tibor de Nagy Gallery in New York in 1970, and continued exhibiting there throughout the 1970s. During that time, she published several articles in arts and feminist publications. In 1972, she began attending meetings of the ad hoc committee of women artists, an activist/support group, and in 1973 taught the first course about women artists at the School of Visual Arts in NYC. In 1975, Kozloff chaired a panel at the College Art Association's annual conference, Women Artists Talk on Women Artists; and curated a show, with Joan Semmel, Women Artists Here and Now, at Ashawagh Hall in Springs, NY, the first all-women show in the Hamptons ("historically a bastion of male abstract expressionism"). In November 1975, Kozloff was part of the group that initiated Heresies, a publishing collective that produced *Heresies* magazine for almost two decades. Kozloff has a B.F.A. from Carnegie Institute of Technology (1964) and an M.F.A. from Columbia University (1967). Archives: Heresies papers are at the Rutgers Feminist Archive, New Brunswick, NJ.   (ABS)

Krall, Ruth Elizabeth (1940 –) A nurse, Krall was a member of the women's health movement in Tucson in the 1970s. She provided speculums to women so that they could do their own internal exams, and became involved in feminist therapy and theory networks. Krall was one of the first women in several organizations to speak out about sexism inside the professions of medicine and nursing, "including the medical school and college at Arizona, where I was working at the time," she says. As a teacher of human sexuality at the University of Arizona, Krall introduced battering and sexual violence as part of the medical team's responsibility. Prior to Roe v. Wade, Krall was part of an AZ women's network that supported Planned Parenthood and provided airfare to California for women who needed abortions. She also supported and marched for the ERA. As director of Peace, Justice and Conflict Studies at Goshen College (1986 – 2004), Krall became the "teaching backbone" of the women's studies program and taught the first radical student-requested feminist course on the campus. Called Contemporary Women's Issues, it became the core course around which the women's studies curriculum was developed (1984 – 1985). Krall earned a B.S.N. from Goshen College (1962), an M.S.N. from the University of Cincinnati (Psychiatric/ Mental Health Nursing) and a Ph.D. from Southern California School of Theology at Claremont (1989). Archives: Goshen College peace and women's studies papers will go to the Archives of the Mennonite Church, Goshen, IN; personal and professional papers will go to the Graduate Theological Union, Berkeley, CA.   (ABS)

Kramarae, Cheris (1938 –) (also known as Cheris Rae Kramer) In the late 1960s and early 1970s, Kramarae was teaching full-time at university level and working on her Ph.D. when she decided to bring her growing interest in sexist language into the classroom. She was working with feminist colleagues to win approval for a women's studies program and, in 1973, introduced the course Sex-Related Differences in Language, which, under various titles, has been offered ever since by the University of Illinois. Her dissertation, defended in 1975, was on the stereotypes of women's language. She has since published widely on this topic. Her authored and edited books include *Women and Men Speaking* (Newbury House, 1981); *Language and Power*, co-edited with Muriel Schulz and William O'Barr (Sage, 1984); *Technology and Women's Voices*, of which she was editor (Routledge, 1988); and *The Knowledge Explosion: Generations of Feminist Scholarship*, of which she was co-editor with Dale Spender (Teachers College Press, 1992). She is the author, with Paula Treichler, of *A Feminist Dictionary* (Pandora Press/Unwin & Harper Collins, 1986), and the new edition titled *Amazons, Bluestockings and Crones* (Harper San Francisco, 1992). In addition, Kramarae has published works on women in education, and gender and the new information technologies, as well as studies of the feminist press in the 1850s and 1860s. In 2000, she served as a dean at the International Women's University, held in Germany. Kramarae, who has two children, earned her Ph.D. from the University of Illinois, Urbana-Champaign. Archives: Feminist Language and Communication Collection, Knight University Library, University of Oregon, Eugene, OR. (ABS)

Kramer, Cheris Rae – See Kramarae, Cheris

Kramer, Marjorie Anne (1943 –) A painter, Kramer organized shows of women artists from 1968 – 1973. A highlight was the First Open Show of Feminist Art, held in 1970 at Museum on Broadway in NYC. She was part of two other very early women's shows: Soho Women Artists, at a loft on Canal Street, with WAR; and another held at International House at Columbia University, co-organized with Pat Mainardi. In 1970, Kramer had the idea of petitioning the Whitney Museum to include Alice Neel in its exhibit, and circulated a petition among artists, art writers and feminists. Says Kramer, "It worked. Alice was 70 and had never been in the annual show!" Kramer was also a member of Redstocking Artists (1968 – 1971). She was a founding editor, with Irene Peslikis and others, of *Women and Art Quarterly* (1969 – 1971), the first women artists publication. Kramer's work has been in numerous group shows and seven one-artist shows. In the late 1980s, she worked to pass the ERA in a Vermont referendum, serving as coordinator for the town of Lowell. Kramer, who has one child, holds a B.F.A. from Cooper Union (1966). She was a founding student of the New York Studio School (1964 – 1968). (ABS)

Kreloff, Bea (1925 –) As an artist, Kreloff connected to the burgeoning feminist art movement in the early 1970s and was also involved with *Heresies*, the feminist art maga-

zine. She was a member of the organizing committee for a large conference in support of Anita Hill at Hunter College, and worked as a volunteer for Bella Abzug and her organization, WEDO, on and off for many years, organizing conferences, meetings and demonstrations. Kreloff was also active in the women's Pentagon group until it disbanded. When Act-Up began, mostly as a gay male organization, she became involved with the small women's group attached to it. Kreloff was involved from the beginning with the Women's Action Coalition, which started as a women artists coalition. Kreloff, who has two children, has worked in support of lesbian issues, reproductive rights and the rights of older women. (ABS)

Kreutz, Eileen M. (1947 –) In 1972, Kreutz traveled as a representative of a Chicago women's affinity group to meet with Vietnamese women in Paris, where they discussed local work against the war. In 1974, Kreutz was a founding member of WICCA, Women in Crisis Can Act, Chicago's feminist hotline/crisis service, and in 1975 was one of five founders of Mountain Moving Coffeehouse, which featured women performers and artists. Kreutz served as advisory board member and then as lead teacher for the Chicago Women in Trades pre-apprenticeship training program for women (1986 – 1997), and ran special programs for middle-school-age girls to acquaint them with tools (1995 – 1997), doing woodworking projects in the Girls at Work program for the Chicago Public Schools. She is the author of *In For a Change: A Curriculum Guide for Pre-Apprenticeship Training* (1992), and had her poems published in *Half a Winter to Go, Poems by Sheila Collins, Renny Golden and Eileen Kreutz* (Sunburst Press, 1976). Also active in the civil rights, anti-war and environmental movements, Kreutz stands in a weekly vigil of Women in Black, begun in Israel-Palestine in 1988. She lives (2005) in Maine. (ABS)

Krieg, Iris J. (1948 –) (also known as Iris Hamburg) As a university student in Florida in the late 1960s, Krieg realized that rules for women students were more stringent than those for male students, so "I got myself on the rules enforcement committee and proceeded to play havoc with discriminatory enforcement." After returning from the Peace Corps in 1970, she helped start a small women's center in Tampa and was part of a CR group. In the early 1970s, as a caseworker for the State of Florida, she "saw the abominable practices of public welfare and how they harmed women and children," and resolved to learn how to change public policy. She enrolled in the School of Social Service Administration at the University of Chicago in 1973 and majored in public policy. Upon graduation in 1975, she entered the foundation field. Recognizing the relative paucity of private funds available to women's concerns, she started Chicago Women in Philanthropy in the early 1980s, which supports women in the field of philanthropy and promotes grant-making to meet women's needs. In the mid-1980s, she co-

K

founded the Chicago Foundation for Women, the largest regional women's foundation in the country. Krieg, who received her M.B.A. from Northwestern University Kellogg School of Management, has one child. (ABS)

Kriesberg, Lois Ablin (1928 –) An attorney and college teacher of social science, Kriesberg joined Central NY NOW in 1967 and remains active today (2004). She served as a member of the steering committee and was active during the organization's first years "recruiting and spreading the word." She was an early participant in the women's caucus of the American Sociological Association (now known as Sociologists for Women in Society), advocating the inclusion of childcare at national conventions through the 1970s and early 1980s. She was also an early member of the women's caucus of the American Anthropological Association, and of the WPC in Syracuse (NY). Kriesberg was a founding member and first VP of the Women's Bar Association of Central NY in the early 1980s. She participated in several actions to support women in the 1970s and 1980s, including a sit-in at a hotel in Syracuse where bars and lounges were closed to women unless they were escorted by a man, and a protest of Syracuse Bar Association meetings held in private clubs closed to women. With five other women, she petitioned the board of directors of the Bar Association for election in the early 1980s. Although they lost, the nominating committee began listing women candidates thereafter. Kriesberg taught the first women's studies courses at Kirkland College, Clinton, NY (1973 – 1974). She is the co-author (with Louis Kriesberg) of "On Educating Children," which appeared in *Children of Separation & Divorce* (Viking Press, 1972); and "On Supporting Women's Successful Efforts Against Violence," written testimony before the House of Representatives Subcommittee on Domestic Planning (1978). Kriesberg, who has two children, earned her B.A. from Roosevelt University, Chicago; her M.A. from the University of Chicago; and her J.D. from Syracuse University. (ABS)

Kriesberg, Louis (1926 –) Professor emeritus of sociology at Syracuse University, Kriesberg has been a supporter of and participant in the Syracuse, NY, chapter of NOW since 1972. He was a member of Sociologists for Women in Society (1973 – 1983), and supported and voted and campaigned for childcare provisions at the American Sociological Association and the Eastern Sociological Association (1968 – 1973). As chair of the sociology department at Syracuse (1974 – 1977), he helped advance affirmative action and equal academic opportunities for minorities and women, and strengthened the position of women in the university by championing equal rights in employment. He supported various actions to open bars and lounges to women, and to desegregate want ads in the newspaper. A prolific writer, he is the author of *Mothers in Poverty* (Greenwood Press, 1970) and *The Sociology of Social Conflicts* (Prentice Hall, 1973). In 1967, he pub-

lished the article "Rearing Children for Educational Achievement in Fatherless Families" in the *Journal of Marriage and Family* (May issue). Kriesberg earned his Ph.B. from the University of Chicago College (1947); and his M.A. (1950) and Ph.D. (1953) from the University of Chicago. He has two children. Archives: Syracuse University Library, Syracuse, NY. (ABS)

Kritzler, Helen (1942 –) Attending an anti-Vietnam War rally in early 1968, Kritzler was impressed by a group of U.S. women wearing Vietnamese clothing and yelling "Get out of Vietnam." She soon joined the group, later named New York Radical Women. An organizer of the first international women's conference in Chicago (1968), Kritzler also helped organize the 1968 Miss America protest (she went to Atlantic City to scope out a route for the protest), and was one of the first women to speak at the Redstockings abortion speak-out (1968). Moving to California in 1970, Kritzler was a founder of the newspaper *Tooth and Nail* (1971). Her motto for the newspaper, "Free Love is the Last Nail in the Coffin," was designed to counter men pressuring women into sex they did not want. *Tooth and Nail* brought the NYC point of view to Berkeley women, who, Kritzler says, at that time were still involved with the radical Left. Kritzler returned to NYC in 1972 and joined Women Rite Theater. Kritzler notes that the feminist work she and others were doing was very much a collective effort. A grade school teacher during the movement, Kritzler later worked in a drug program as a special education teacher, then created games for Atari. Kritzler's mother, Gertrude Wellikof, was a member of the Lucy Stone League. Like her mother, Kritzler is a palm reader as well as a feminist. She believes politics and spirituality go together: "If you are looking for the truth, you have to look behind all doors." (ABS)

Kross, Barbara Marcia (1932 –) Born in Brooklyn, NY, and a graduate of Brooklyn College, Kross joined the Nassau chapter of NOW (1971) and served as legislative VP (1973) and president (1974 – 1975), working diligently to repeal the state anti-abortion laws, to gain passage of the ERA, to reform rape and divorce laws, and for childcare and women-in-prison programs. Kross spoke publicly for women's issues, attended demonstrations, lobbied on women's issues, worked for feminist candidates, and ran for office locally. In addition, she marched, contributed money, wrote letters, worked with Women Strike for Peace and belonged to Another Mother for Peace. She has two children. (ABS)

Kross, Robert David (1931 –) served as treasurer of the Long Island, NY, chapter of NOW, co-chair of the women's health committee, and co-editor of the newsletter "Nassau NOW Times." He also organized and ran a series of male, and then mixed, CR groups in Nassau City, Long Island. Kross participated in demonstrations in NY and Washington, D.C., for the ERA, and spoke during this period throughout Long Island on the Human Liberation movement. A scientist, Kross was an intervener in the siting of the nuclear power plant at Shoreham Long Island, which resulted in a protracted and successful effort for prevention of the construction of the plant. In addition, he has worked to inform the public about contaminants in food and the environment. Kross has two children.   (ABS)

Krouse, Agate Nesaule – See Nesaule, Agate

Kruger, Sylvia – See Morgan, Sylvia Arlene

Krupsak, Mary Anne (1932 –) Elected to the New York State Assembly from an Upstate NY district in 1968, Krupsak later became the first woman in the country elected lieutenant governor (1974). She served two terms in the assembly, where she sponsored or co-sponsored every piece of legislation that advanced women's interests. She was also one of the critical 74 "Yes" votes needed to legalize abortion in NY (prior to Roe v. Wade). Elected to the NY State Senate in 1972, Krupsak sponsored the ERA, a displaced homemakers law, equal pay for equal work legislation, divorce reform, rape victim reforms, criminal law changes on domestic violence, and numerous other bills affecting women's rights and supporting women's interests. She also strongly supported healthcare reform, recognizing how women suffer most from low incomes and poor health coverage. As Lieutenant Governor, Krupsak succeeded in getting the state budget to allocate money for the first shelter for victims of domestic violence, and many others followed. Krupsak's concern for women's needs reached into some unexpected areas: Says Krupsak, "I led the fight to save Radio City Music Hall from the wrecking ball. Not only was it a serious effort to save a historic landmark, it also saved the jobs of generations of women known to the world as the Rockettes!" A member of NOW and the NWPC, Krupsak owns several restaurants in the Rochester, NY area. She holds a B.A. from the University of Rochester, an M.S. from Boston University and a J.D. from the University of Chicago. Archives: Rush Rhees Library, University of Rochester, River Campus, Rochester, NY.   (ABS)

Kuehl, Sheila James (1941 –) Elected to the California State Senate in 2000, Kuehl's work for women began in 1969 when she was an assistant dean of students in the campus programs and activities office of UCLA. In 1972, she was a co-founder of the UCLA Women's Resource Center, and also became adviser to all the women's groups on campus. She served as adviser to the Women's Liberation Front, and was on-campus adviser for the West Coast Lesbian Conference held at UCLA (1973). In 1973, Kuehl helped organize the first Women's Week at UCLA. In 1975, at age 34, Kuehl entered Harvard Law School, and in 1976 organized and chaired a student-driven committee to plan celebrations in 1978 for the 25th anniversary of the graduation of the first women from

Harvard Law. It was the first event bringing women alums together in the history of the school, and has been repeated every five years since then. As an attorney in Los Angeles, Kuehl helped found the Sojourn Shelter for Battered Women (1979), and chaired its advisory board from 1979–1994. She joined the board of the National Woman Abuse Prevention Project in 1981, and that year taught the first women and law course in any law school in Southern California, at the University of Southern California. In 1983, Kuehl served as chair of the Women Lawyers of Los Angeles delegation to the California Bar Convention, and from 1984–1989 taught Gender and Law, as well as other courses, as a full-time professor at the Loyola Law School in Los Angeles. In 1989, Kuehl was a co-founder of the California Women's Law Center, was part of the domestic violence model code-drafting project (sponsored by the National Council of Juvenile and Family Court Judges), and helped craft the custody and family law section. In 1990, she was part of the California Judicial Council's committee on gender bias in the courts, and chaired the subcommittee drafting the section on domestic violence. From 1991–1993, Kuehl was managing attorney at the California Women's Law Center and helped various California legislators draft more than 40 pieces of legislation related to domestic violence and family law. She was elected to the California State Assembly in 1994, and from 1997–1998 was the first woman in CA to serve as speaker pro temps in the Assembly. She was elected to the California State Senate in 2000. During her 11 years in the State Legislature, she has written many bills on domestic violence, including one establishing a rebuttable presumption against custody to a batterer, as well as many bills improving women's rights in divorce and women's healthcare. Kuehl began working with gay and lesbian organizations in Los Angeles in 1982, and was the first openly gay/lesbian person elected to the California State Legislature. She holds a B.A. from UCLA (1962) and a J.D. from Harvard (1978).   (ABS)

Kuhn, Margaret ("Maggie") Eliza (1905 – 1995) Attended the White House Conference on Aging (1961). In 1970, working as a program executive for the Presbyterian Church's Council on Church and Race, Kuhn was distressed and depressed to think that she might have to stop working just because she had become 65. She met with five of her friends to discuss the problems of retirees, and with them formed the Consultation of Older and Younger Adults for Social Change. In 1972, that group became the Gray Panthers; by 1973 there were 11 chapters; and in 1975 the Gray Panthers held its first national convention, in Chicago. By 1990, the Gray Panthers public policy office had opened in Washington, D.C. Kuhn remained active with the Gray Panthers until her death at age 89. Kuhn, who never married, published her autobiography, *No Stone Unturned*, in 1991. An outspoken, lifelong feminist, Kuhn exalted in having lived to see the Year of the Woman. She graduated with honors from Western Reserve University in 1926, and in 1995 was inducted into the National Women's Hall of Fame.

Kupinsky, Esther – See Gelbard, Esther K.

Kurtz, Linda Farris (1939 –) (also known as Linda J. Farris) served as president of Atlanta NOW (1970 – 1971) and as a member of the national board (1972 – 1973). As president, Kurtz worked to provide women with safe abortions, and spoke widely about women's issues. During Kurtz's tenure, Atlanta NOW produced a speakers manual to help NOW members across the country prepare for public speaking. Earlier (1961 – 1970), Kurtz had been active in the civil rights movement in Topeka, Pittsburgh and Chicago. A professor of social work (retired), Kurtz holds a B.A. from Washburn University (1961), an M.S.W. from the University of Pittsburgh (1965) and a D.P.A. from the University of Georgia (1983). (ABS)

Kurz, Diana (1936 –) An artist, Kurz has taught for many years at the university level and—in reaction to her own experience as a student with no women teachers, no women mentors, and no encouragement to apply for a teaching job on graduation—has always encouraged her women students and young artists and worked to help them professionally. In the 1970s and 1980s, Kurz (who was born in Vienna, Austria) met with other women artists to discuss their work and the sex discrimination in exhibiting and teaching. She also took part in feminist demonstrations for equality in museums and galleries, and throughout the 1970s, 1980s and 1990s exhibited her work in numerous feminist and all-women exhibits. A "highlight of my career," she says, "was participating in the Sister Chapel, a 12-artist collaborative feminist work in 1977 that celebrated a variety of female heroes." Kurz earned her B.A. from Brandeis University and her M.F.A. from Columbia University. (ABS)

Kushner, Rose (1929 – 1990) A journalist, author and advocate for women with breast cancer, Kushner is credited as the single most important person to influence the elimination of "one-step" radical mastectomy as the only treatment option for breast cancer. Kushner originally took pre-med courses in college, thinking she might become a doctor, but changed her major to journalism. As a journalist she wrote for the *Baltimore Sun* and *Washingtonian Magazine*. In 1974 she was diagnosed with breast cancer, which changed her life and ultimately the lives of other women with cancer. In 1975, Kushner founded the Breast Cancer Advisory Center to provide information and support to patients. She frequently testified in Congress on breast cancer issues, was a founder of the National Alliance of Breast Cancer Organizations, and served on its board from 1986 to 1989. As a result of this work, she was responsible for changing laws and medical practices, giving women alternatives. Before Kushner advocated a "two-step" procedure, women would learn that they had

lost a breast only after they awoke from anesthesia. With the new "two-step" procedure, which Kushner is credited with promoting, women have a biopsy before any decisions about treatment are made. Kushner wrote seven books on breast cancer and received awards from the American Medical Writers Association in 1980 and 1985. She had three children.

Lader, Lawrence (1919 – 2006) Author of a biography of Margaret Sanger (published in 1955), Lader became convinced during its writing that "only through controlling her procreation could a woman have the independence to make her own life." He fought continuously for women's right to choose after that. In 1965, he published an article on abortion in *The New York Times Magazine*, and in 1966 published the book *Abortion*. Lader helped organize the Chicago conference on abortion (1969), which led to the founding of NARAL, of which he served as chair from 1969 – 1975. In 1970, he helped organize a campaign for the landmark NY State abortion law, and also helped organize legal challenges, including Roe v. Wade. Lader became president of Abortion Rights Mobilization in 1975 and developed many strategies, including a federal lawsuit against the Catholic Church for illegal political action. In addition to *The Margaret Sanger Story and the Fight for Birth Control*, Lader published *A Private Matter: RU 486 and the Abortion Crisis*; *RU 486: The Pill that Could End the Abortion Wars and Why American Women Don't Have It*; and *Abortion II: Making the Revolution*, among others. In 1998, Lader wrote that his main project since writing *RU 486 and the Abortion Crisis* was "to bring the pill to U.S. women." In 2003, he published a challenge to George W. Bush in *The New York Times* and the *Los Angeles Times*, among others, via an ad campaign "The Future of America," addressing questions about federal judges and women's rights. Lader, who earned an A.B. from Harvard in 1941, had one child. Archives: New York Public Library; the Widener Library of Harvard University; and the Schlesinger Library, Radcliffe Institute, Cambridge, MA. (ABS before death)

Ladewig, Anita C. ("Nita") (1929 –) joined Northern California NOW shortly after it was founded. She served as president in 1968 when NOW protested the exclusion of women as astronauts in the space program. Ladewig initiated a six-month correspondence with NASA, and also protested using the names of masculine gods for space ships. In 1969, Ladewig and others successfully integrated the Squire Room, the men's restaurant at the Fairmont Hotel in San Francisco. Ladewig also introduced the ERA to the San Francisco area in 1968, where she gave speeches, organized demonstrations and picketed two San Francisco newspapers. When a NOW chapter was to be founded in Marin County, Ladewig provided all the documents needed to start the group. Ladewig holds a B.S. from the University of Texas, and taught in the San Francisco School District for 30 years. Retired since 1994, she continues to follow feminist issues and calls legislators to promote women's rights, animal rights and the environment. (ABS)

Ladky, Anne (1948 –) entered a segregated workforce in 1971, where women were relegated predominately to secretarial and clerical jobs. As a graduate of Northwestern University with a degree in English literature, she found a job at Scott Foresman, a textbook publishing firm, where she worked as a writer. She also worked with women employees to address mistreatment. Ladky co-founded (with Janet Kanter) Women at Scott Foresman, an early in-company women's caucus, and published *Guidelines for Eliminating Sexism in Textbooks*. In 1972, she co-founded Chicago Women in Publishing and joined Chicago NOW. From 1973–1975, Ladky served as president of the chapter, and co-chaired (with Mary Jean Collins) national NOW's task force on Sears. In 1973, she was a founding member of Women Employed, formed to address employment discrimination and unfair conditions for women workers. She served as staff organizer (1977–1979); associate director (1979–1985); and executive director (1985 –). In 1976, Ladky was on the steering committee for the ERA rally and march in Springfield, IL, and from 1975–1977 was associate editor, *The Spokeswoman*, a national news monthly about women's rights. Archives: University of Illinois, Chicago. (ABS)

LaDuke, Betty (1933 –) Professor of art emeritus, Southern Oregon University, LaDuke has traveled and researched women artists in Latin America, Asia and Africa for 35 years. She has published *Africa: Women's Art, Women's Lives* (Africa World Press, 1997); *Women Against Hunger, A Sketchbook Journey* (Africa World Press, 1997); *Women Artists: Multi-Cultural Visions* (Red Sea Press, 1992); *Africa Through the Eyes of Women Artists* (Africa World Press, 1991); and *Companeras, Women, Art, and Social Change in Latin America* (City Lights, 1985). She has also published four videos on these topics, and is herself the subject of a book by Gloria Orenstein, *Multicultural Celebrations, The Paintings of Betty LaDuke, 1972 – 1992* (Pomegrante Publications, 1993). Her work has been exhibited internationally, and is in private collections in Mexico, Africa and the U.S. She has put on more than 300 one-person exhibits on multicultural themes, and organized three circulating exhibits of her research on women artists. LaDuke attended the University of Denver (1950 –1951); the Cleveland Institute of Art (1951 – 1952); Instituto Allende, San Miguel, Mexico (1953 – 1954); and California State University (1959 – 1962). She has two children. Archives: University of Oregon, Special Collections Library, Eugene, OR. (ABS)

Lagarde, Pamela – See Astarte, Pamela Ann

Lahey, Maureen Elizabeth (1945 –) served as president of Hawaii Women's Political Caucus (1971–1973), and

as Western Regional Representative to the NWPC in 1973. In the early 1970s, she was asked by the CBS affiliate in Honolulu to host a radio call-in program, called "Viewpoint," which she did from 1972–1974. Lahey stipulated, however, that she would have no male guests on the program, although men were welcome to call in with their opinions. Lahey attended Columbia University (1984–1986), and has four children. (ABS)

Laiken, Amy Frances (1949 –) joined a CWLU workgroup, the Health Evaluation and Referral Service, in 1974. Initially, she served as a telephone counselor, providing callers with detailed information about abortion clinics. She also visited the clinics to evaluate them for inclusion on HERS's referral list. She eventually was a board member at HERS, concentrating on raising funds and building membership. Laiken also became involved in CWLU itself, serving on its steering committee in 1975. After leaving the HERS board in 1984, Laiken met with various women's health groups to aid indigent women who wished to terminate their pregnancies. Laiken helped form the Chicago Abortion Fund, which raises money specifically for that purpose, and served on its board until 1993, working on fundraising and board development. In addition to her work in support of reproductive rights, Laiken was deeply involved in anti-nuclear and anti-war efforts in the 1970s and 1980s. In 1984, she visited Nicaragua to witness that country's election, then became involved in the Chicago committee in support of the Nicaraguan people (later the Nicaragua solidarity committee), serving on its steering committee from approximately 1987 to 1990. Laiken, who worked for state and county governments for 30 years, is a retired hearing officer for the Illinois Dept. of Human Services. She serves on the board of directors of the Web site that documents CWLU's contributions to the women's movement from the late 1960s to 1977. She holds a B.A. and M.A. (ABS)

Lamb, Myrna Lila (1930 –) is a playwright, lyricist, producer and director. Author Vivian Gornick described Lamb as "the first true artist of the feminist consciousness." Among Lamb's works is "Scyklon Z: A Group of Pieces with a Point" (1969), a collection of six one-scene, one-act plays designed to be performed together. Produced by Jacqui Ceballos and Anselma Dell'Olio of The New Feminist Theatre (1969), they include "But What Have You Done for Me Lately," "Monologia," "Pas de Deux, "The Butcher Shop," "The Serving-Girl and the Lady," and "In the Shadow of the Crematoria." Other short plays include "I Lost a Pair of Gloves Yesterday" (1972) and "Two-Party System." She wrote full-length works beginning in 1969. "The Mod Donna," an indictment of modern marriage first produced in 1970 by the New York Shakespeare Public Theatre, was directed by Joseph Papp. Another play, "Apple Pie," was a music-drama of Holocaust victims who "escape" to America, only to find sexism, racism and anti-Semitism as Amer-

L

ican as apple pie. Margot Lewitin of Interart Theatre produced "Crab Quadrille" in 1976, "Olympic Park" in 1978, followed by a play with music titled "Yesterday is Over" (1980). Lamb gave speeches about feminism, sex roles and the oppression of women in and out of conventionally assigned lifestyles. She also wrote for numerous anthologies and magazines. In addition, she was active in the peace and civil rights movements, and was responsible for bringing Martin Luther King and Dr. Spock to the Manhattan chapter of the committee for a sane nuclear policy, and participated in a landmark legal case for fair housing in New Jersey. Lamb grew up in Newark, NJ, and took theater classes at Rutgers University. She has two children. Archives: The Lincoln Center Library of the Performing Arts, New York, NY. (ABS)

Lamb, Patricia Anne Frazer (1931 –) (also known as Patricia Anne Latham) Professor emeritus of English at Westminster College in Pennsylvania (2004), Lamb was a founder (1969) of the first Upstate NY chapter of NOW, and of the women's studies program at Cornell University. She also led a group of part-time female instructors at Cornell in an effort to improve their status, and succeeded in getting salary increases, inclusion in TIAA-CREF, and admittance into faculty clubs. In 1970, Lamb began organizing a course about women in literature that drew 400 students instead of the expected 60. Lamb, who is the author of *Touchstones: Letters Between Two Women, 1953 – 1964* (Harper and Row), also researched and wrote legislation that expanded the hours that women could work in NY State. It passed in 1974. Lamb, who has two children, earned her B.A. from Boston University (1966), her M.A. from Brandeis (1968), and her Ph.D. from Cornell (1977). Archives: Schlesinger Library, Radcliffe Institute, Cambridge, MA. (ABS)

Lamont, Barbara (1939 –) (also known as Barbara Lamont Gelobter) was a founding member of NARAL, and helped write and pass the NY State Abortion Repeal Act of 1970. A board member of NYC Planned Parenthood, she was Democratic district leader, West Side of Manhattan. Also active in the peace and civil rights movements, Lamont, an African American born in Bermuda, organized peace rallies in the 1960s and 1970s, and led anti-war coalitions to pressure big banks into withdrawing financial support from pro-Vietnam War companies. A Telecom CEO (2004), Lamont has three children. She earned her B.A. from Sarah Lawrence and her M.P.A from Harvard University. Archives: Sarah Lawrence College, Bronxville, NY. (ABS)

Lanai, Delores Darlene (1943 –) (also known as Delores Darlene Cole) joined the Washington, D.C., Rape Crisis Center, the first city center in the nation, in 1972. To spread the message that rape is violence, not sex, she spoke on many TV shows, including bringing this concept to national TV on the "Today" show. She also helped or-

ganize task forces to change rape laws in the United States; joined several feminist groups in Washington, D.C.; and served on the Gay Education Fund board. In 1985, she began her journey in women's spirituality. Lanai is an astrologer, witch and Crone, and in 1986 founded Venus Adventures, which offers goddess tours to Great Britain. She is a board member and president of the Rape Crisis Center, Sexual Assault Center of Southern Maine. Lanai earned her M.Ed. from Antioch Graduate School of New England (2001). (ABS)

Landau, Brooksley Elizabeth
– See Born, Brooksley Elizabeth

Landerman, Diane – See Crothers, Diane

Lane, Ann J. (1931 –) A historian and professor of women's studies, Lane taught her first class in women's history in 1970 at Douglass College, Rutgers University. She also ran the women's studies program at Colgate, and then at the University of Virginia. Lane has published several books on the writer Charlotte Perkins Gilman, including *To Herland and Beyond: The Life and Work of Charlotte Perkins Gilman* (Pantheon, 1990). Lane is also co-editor of *Making Women's History: The Essential Mary Ritter Beard*. Lane holds a B.A. from Brooklyn College (1952), an M.A. from New York University (1959), and a Ph.D. from Columbia University. (ABS)

Lane, Bettye (1930 –) is well known for her extensive photo-documentation of the second wave women's movement. A professional photographer, Lane entered the women's movement in 1970 and began photographing women who had achieved "firsts" in their fields —women bus drivers, astronauts and women at West Point, for example. Her photos have been widely used by television stations and in major magazines in the U.S. and abroad. Lane was also involved in the anti-war, black civil rights, gay and lesbian civil rights, Native American, and anti-nuclear movements. Her photos are in numerous archives, including the Schlesinger Library on the History of Women in America, the Smithsonian Institute, the Women's Museum of the Arts, the New York City Public Library, and the Library of Congress. (ABS)

Lanfear, Marilyn Terry (1930 –) An artist, Lanfear joined the Women's Caucus for Art (Houston chapter) in the late 1970s, then the San Antonio chapter, which was formed shortly thereafter. In 1980, the group ramped up to support The Artist & The Quilt Exhibition at San Antonio's McNay Art Museum. Lanfear, whose quilt was exhibited at the show, organized and directed a six-week, citywide series of activities related to the opening of the exhibition, securing funding, including an NEA grant. After moving to Manhattan, Lanfear joined the NYC chapter of Women's Caucus for Art, and attended its annual conferences for 20 years. Lanfear, who has a B.F.A. and M.F.A., taught at the University of Texas, the University of Oregon and Lewis & Clark College. She has four children.   (ABS)

Lange, Geraldine ("Jerri") Bernice (1925 –) A broadcast journalist, Lange was the first African American woman in the editorial department at *Newsweek*, 1952; at the *San Francisco Chronicle* (editorial secretary), 1963; and on the San Francisco mayor's staff (personal secretary), 1967. In 1975, Lange served as host of "Womantime," a KQED (PBS) program about the changing roles of women, which became a national television show. Also in 1975, she served as San Francisco host for the International Year of the Woman. Lange, who has three children, attended Merritt College and San Francisco State University. Archives: African American Historical Museum & Library, Oakland, CA.   (ABS)

Langer, Cassandra ("Sandra") L. (1941 –) A writer, arts critic, appraiser and art historian, Langer conceived the idea of creating an anthology of feminist art criticism, and is the co-author of three such works. She is the author of *What's Right With Feminism* (HarperCollins, 1996), hundreds of reviews of women artists, and numerous articles in magazines such as *Women's Art Journal, Art Journal, New Directions for Women, Victoria* and *Ms.* She helped organize the Miami chapter of Women's Caucus for Art in 1974, and initiated the first Woman and Art course in the state of Florida at Florida International University; she also helped establish the Southeastern Regional Women's Caucus for Art of the College Art Association during the mid 1970s. Langer continues (2004) as a community activist fighting for women's rights and lesbian rights, and is (2004) working on a critical study of the lesbian expatriate painter Romaine Brooks, as well as a book on Femine Noir. Langer has a B.A. and M.A. from the University of Miami, and a Ph.D. from New York University. Her partner, Irene Fay Javors, is also a pioneering feminist and psychotherapist. Archives: The Lesbian Herstory Archives, Brooklyn, NY.   (ABS)

Lansing, Marjorie J. (1916 – 1998) is co-author (with statistician Barbara Baxter) of *Women in Politics: The Invisible Majority*. The book, which coined the term "gender gap," was based on Lansing's dissertation on women in politics for her Ph.D. from the University of Michigan political science dept. (1971). Lansing's work demonstrated that women constitute a distinct voting bloc and don't simply mimic their husbands' voting choices or the choices of men in·general. Active in the Democratic Party, Lansing was a political science faculty member at Eastern Michigan University, 1966 – 1986. She was inducted into The Michigan Women's Hall of Fame in 2000.

Lanyon, Ellen (1926 –) An artist, Lanyon participated (with co-founders Lucy Lippard and Miriam Schapiro) in the creation of West East Bag in 1971. In 1972, a newsletter "W.E.B." was established to link NYC (Lippard), Los

Angeles (Schapiro) and Chicago (Lanyon), and the three women took turns producing the monthly publication. As a board member of OXBOW, a summer school of art in Saugatuck, MI, Lanyon facilitated the first Midwest Women Artist's Conference, held there in 1973. In 1975, she began to travel out from Chicago to lecture and teach, introducing many women to the power of feminism and helping them with their careers. In NYC, she attended meetings of Heresies and served on the board of the women's caucus. In 1980, she joined the Heresies Collective and worked on two issues, *Environment* and *Satire*; and was commissioned to create a mural, "Nine Notable Women of Boston," for the Workingman's Bank of Boston (now hanging in the Boston Public Library). Lanyon, whose work has been exhibited widely, received the Lifetime Achievement Award, Women's Caucus, 2001. Grants won early on for women include a Fulbright (1950), Cassandra (1971) and National Endowment for the Arts (1974). She earned her B.F.A. from the School of the Art Institute of Chicago, and her M.F.A. from the University of Iowa. She has two children. Archives: Archive of American Art, Washington, D.C.   (ABS)

LaRouche, Janice (1924 –) A pioneer in career development and assertiveness training for women, LaRouche joined NY NOW and served on the board (1968 – 1969). She founded Career Workshops for Women in 1968, and was featured in an article in *The New York Times*, "A Women's Liberation Approach to Solving Career Problems" (April 11, 1970). She wrote a column in *McCalls* in the 1970s, and a column in *Family Circle* in the 1980s. Her work on career planning developed out of CR groups that she held in her apartment for NYC NOW. This led LaRouche to create the first assertiveness training programs for women. She is the author, with Regina Ryan, of *Janice LaRouche's Strategies for Women at Work* (Avon Books, 1985), which was published in 10 countries.(ABS)

Larson, Zelle – See Andrews, Zelle

Lashine, Carol – See Ellis, Carol Lashine

Lassnig, Maria (1919 –) Born in Austria, Lassnig was part of a women's film group in NYC (1970 – 1980), then returned to Vienna to become the first woman professor in the German language at the University of Applied Art. She taught painting and animation filmmaking, and made a short film, "Kantate," which was "a big success for women and men in Europe." Lassnig has won three international art prizes, had a single exhibition in London; and many international exhibitions of her artwork, especially her painting. She continues to work as an artist.   (ABS)

Latham, Patricia Anne – See Lamb, Patricia Anne Frazer

Latimer, Allie B. — An attorney, Latimer was a founder and first president of Federally Employed Women in

1968. "We founded FEW because we saw that no one was really focusing on what the world's largest employer was doing about sex discrimination in the government following the 1967 presidential amendment to an existing executive order that prohibited sex discrimination in the federal workplace as well as in the public workplace," says Latimer. Latimer also served as president of the National Bar Foundation, as a member of the steering committee of the Washington, D.C., NAACP Legal Defense Fund, as a director of Black Women's Agenda, and as president of the District of Columbia Mental Health Association. She worked for civil rights for African Americans and women, was on the governing board of The National Council of Churches, and served as president of the Washington, D.C. chapter of Black Presbyterians United and of the Interracial Council. She has been honored by VFA, and received Presidential Rank Awards from Presidents Reagan and Clinton. Latimer earned her B.S. from Hampton University, and her J.D. from Howard University. She also earned an L.L.M. from Catholic University, and an M.Div. and D.Min. from Howard University. (ABS)

Latimer, F. Clayton ("Clay") (1944 –) An attorney working in child protection since 1983, Latimer served as a member of the board on New Orleans NOW from 1972 – 1977 and from 1985 – 1986. She was LA representative to the National Bylaws Commission; was a member of NOW's women in politics task force; and from 1976 – 1977 was state coordinator of LA NOW. Latimer was named Woman of the Year, Jefferson Chapter, of NOW in 1978. In 1985 she was a delegate to the NOW national convention and secretary to the board of New Orleans NOW. From 1977 – 1980, Latimer was director for parish programs and administrative assistant, YWCA, in New Orleans. In this capacity, she was able to help secure funding for programs and services for women and their families in areas such as adult classes, day camps and family violence protection. In 1974, Latimer wrote and directed a forum on WGNO-TV on the legal status of women in LA. That year she also wrote "How Marriage Can Change your Life," a pamphlet for New Orleans NOW. As a member of the attorney general's task force in 1975, she helped create a similar pamphlet. A member of the NWPC, Latimer worked on the National Women's Education Fund, which she describes as "a sort of fellowship to study politics, political actions and the role of women in politics. The year I participated, the NWPC theme was Win With Women '74." In 1977, Latimer was a delegate to the IWY conference in Houston and was a member of the LA women's conference coordinating committee and the women and law task force. From 1977 – 1978, she served as director of ERA United of Louisiana. Latimer has also been active in the civil rights and peace movements, and has worked for lesbian/gay rights. She holds a J.D. from Loyola University School of Law (1976). Archives: Newcomb College Center for Research on Women, Tulane University, New Orleans, LA. (ABS)

LaTourelle, Elaine Day (1938 –) A charter member of the Seattle (WA) chapter of NOW (1970 – 1980), LaTourelle served two terms on the NOW national board (1973 – 1975), and was elected NOW national legislative VP (1975 – 1977). In Seattle NOW, she was a member of the speakers bureau, legislative task force, and board of directors, and served as chair of the program committee (1971), and of the childcare task force (1971 – 1972). In 1972, LaTourelle served as president of the chapter, initiating a task force on women in poverty and a study on prostitution, and organizing support for the Seattle Office of Women's Rights, among other actions. She worked aggressively for the ERA, and was president when the state ERA, credit, property management, housing and employment discrimination laws were passed in Washington State. In 1971, she was a charter member of Washington State WPC, and in 1972 was a charter member of the Seattle Feminist Coalition. In 1973, when she was first elected to NOW's national board, LaTourelle coordinated a Seattle NOW justice for women task force, which focused on the problems of women as offenders and victims, and initiated model rape legislation. In 1974, she initiated and chaired a violence against women task force for Seattle NOW. In 1975, as NOW national legislative VP, she was responsible for all actions taken by the organization with congress, states' legislation for women's rights, and the ERA. In this capacity she was on the boards of the National Leadership Conference on Civil Rights, ERAmerica, and the ERA joint ratification project. Also in 1975, she was program chair of the WA State IWY conference and elected as a WA delegate to the national Houston conference. She was a convener of Washington Women United (1978 – 1979), which lobbied the legislature on issues of importance to women and children; and was the first president and convening board member, Northwest Women's Law Center (1978 – 1981). An associate professor of architecture at the University of Washington, she was instrumental in getting more women into the department. LaTourelle earned her Bachelor of Architecture (1961) from the University of Washington and her Master of Architecture (1964) from Yale University. She was a convening member of Seattle Women in Construction and Seattle Association of Women in Architecture. In 1983 she received the Woman of Achievement in the Field of Architecture Award, and was named the Mentor of the Year by the Seattle Women's Professional & Managerial Network. Archives: University of Washington, Seattle, WA. (ABS)

Laurence, Margaret Muth (1916 – 1996) A self-taught attorney, Laurence founded Women United, a lobbying group that helped secure passage of the ERA. In addition, she was a co-founder of the NWPC, served as president of the Women's Bar Association for the District of Columbia, and was regional director for the National Association of Women Lawyers. Laurence was also the first woman member of the Canadian Patent Bar Association.

Laurence was inducted into the Michigan Women's Hall of Fame in 1996.

Laurenti, Luellen (1939 – 2000) A legislative consultant, Laurenti was an early fighter for the passage of the ERA in Illinois. Serving as the lobbyist for IL NOW and the AAUW, first as a volunteer and then full-time, Laurenti continued her work for women after the ERA failed to ratify. Laurenti lobbied the IL Legislature for childcare, equity for girls in education and sports, reproductive rights and gay rights, and the prevention of sexual assault and domestic violence. In 1977 she was executive director of the IL IWY Commission. Her last efforts were on behalf of The Gender Violence Act. She received her B.A. from Marietta College (1961), and her M.A. from University of Illinois (1963).

Laurila, J. Kathleen (1940 –) has been active in women's education, reproductive rights, women in sports and several feminist organizations. She joined AAUW (Des Moines) in 1968 and served as a state officer and president, and national officer. From 1989 – 2004, she served as delegate to and program presenter at triennial conferences of International Federation of University Women, and from 1995 – 2001 was a member of IFUW's status of women committee, serving as VP from 2001 – 2007. She was also a member of Planned Parenthood (1980 – 1994), including service on the national board. From 1971 – 1972, Laurila was an advocate for the establishment of the IA WPC, and in the early 1970s was a lobbyist and marcher in IL and Washington, D.C., for the ERA. From 1978 – 1982, she was an organizer and first president of Metro Women's Network, and developed a "Women's Resource Directory" that was placed in the office of the State of Iowa Commission on the Status of Women. From 1982 – 1983, she was a member of the advisory committee, women's prison at Mitchellville, and in 1983 was a member of the steering committee, Small Business Administration's Midwest Women Business Owner's Conference. In 1982 Laurila was inducted into the first group for Women of Achievement, Des Moines. From 1984 – 1985, she served as chair, Women of Achievement Council, Des Moines, and in 1985 was state committee member, Title XIX study of indigent care and prenatal services in IA. From 1986 – 1988, she was on the advisory committee, Charter Hospital Women's Center. Laurila has also worked with the United Nations on women's issues, and from 2001 – 2002 was coordinator for women's issues, University of Wisconsin-Stout. She has also been active in peace and environmental issues. Laurila, who has three children, earned her B.A. from the University of Minnesota, and her M.A. from Drake University. Archives: Iowa Women's Archives, University Libraries, University of Iowa, Iowa City, IA. (ABS)

Lavalli, Kari L. (1960 –) A teenager in 1974, Lavalli helped integrate drafting, shop and homemaking classes at William B. Stout Jr. High School, Dearborn, MI, as a claimant in a Title IX complaint against the school. In 1976, Lavalli was a founding member of the Northwest Wayne County NOW, and served as a delegate to NOW's bylaws conference in October. Lavalli also worked with NARAL to foster pro-choice legislation in MI. In 1977, Lavalli was elected as a MI representative to the IWY's National Women's Conference in Houston, and organized the youth caucuses of women under age 20. From 1978 – 1982 Lavalli was a President Carter appointee to the continuing committee of the 1977 National Women's Conference. From 1979 – 1982, Lavalli was a member of the women's studies committee at Wells College and participated in the creation of a women's studies interdisciplinary major and the planning of special lectures on issues relevant to women. In addition to her B.A. from Wells College (1982), Lavalli earned a Ph.D. from the Boston University Marine Program (1992). A biologist teaching natural science at Boston University, and VP The Lobster Conservancy, Lavalli is (2004) active in civil rights and is "fighting the discriminatory and retaliatory actions as well as reduction in free speech rights at universities." Archives: Seneca Falls Women's Museum, Seneca Falls, NY. (ABS)

Lavalli, Lee – See Kefauver, Lee

Law, Sylvia A. (1942 –) An attorney, Law has been a leading scholar in the fields of health law, women's rights, poverty and constitutional law. When Roe v. Wade was decided in 1973, Law (an expert on Medicaid programs) realized that Medicaid coverage for abortion would be a major area of conflict. Believing that federal law clearly mandated coverage, Law helped file the first federal case challenging a Pennsylvania rule that required doctors seeking Medicaid reimbursement for abortion to provide a special certification that the abortion was medically necessary. At the same time, Rhonda Copelon filed a similar suit in New York. From 1973 until 1980, Law, Copelon and eventually others litigated Medicaid abortion in every state and fought the issues in Congress and state legislatures. In 1976, Law, with Harriet Pilpel, helped persuade the ACLU to create a Reproductive Freedom Project. Law served on its advisory committee until 1992 when, with Janet Benshoof, she helped create the Center for Reproductive Rights. Law continues (2004) to serve on its board. From 1977 – 1981, Law served on the board of NOW LDEF, and has continued to work with NOW on its projects relating to poor women. From 1985 – 1989, Law was chair of Non-Traditional Employment for Women. In 1980 she served, with Nan Hunter, as counsel to the feminist anti-censorship task force and did political and legal work on the debate about pornography. She has written articles about the intersection of sexism and heterosexism, and feminist perspectives on commercial sex. Law earned her B.A. from Antioch College (1964) and her J.D. from New York University School of Law (1968). (ABS)

L

Lawrence, Eleanor — was a founding mother of Richmond, VA, NOW. Chartered in 1973, the chapter initially met in Lawrence's home. Concerned about the archaic rape laws, Lawrence headed a task force that was instrumental in developing a crisis intervention team for rape victims. She also designed a brochure that explained how women could protect themselves against rape, which was used by law enforcement agencies. Since retiring from her job as a buyer for a women's clothing store, Lawrence has devoted her time to her artwork, which has been in exhibits and one-woman shows in several galleries.

Lawrence, Marlene – See Crosby, Marlene Suzanne

Lawrence, Patricia — In 1970, coordinators of the Women's Strike for Equality march down 5th Ave. in NYC knew they needed a dramatic action to attract the thousands they had boasted would march. Lawrence suggested taking over the Statue of Liberty. She and a friend, Marian, planned the takeover; they measured the balconies' length and width, as well as the wind factor, bought the material, and created the banners. They also secretly got the banners in position on the day of the march, then secured them to the cheers of the women below. Lawrence and the Ms Liberty battalion later led the march, banner held high, to 42nd St. and into Bryant Park. In other work, Lawrence urged Congress to pass the ERA. She also tried (unsuccessfully) to replace a statue on the grounds of Queens Borough Hall; the statue is of a nude male (named Civic Virtue) who has his feet planted on the necks of two nude women (called Vice and Corruption) and is threatening them with a sword.

Lawton, Esther Christian (1910 – 1998) had a distinguished career in the federal government. After moving through the ranks at the U.S. Dept. of the Treasury, she was appointed deputy director of personnel—then the highest-ranking woman at the Treasury. She founded the Training Officers Conference, the Classification and Compensation Society, and the International Association for Personnel Women. She was part of a Nixon administration push to get more women into policy-making positions in the 1970s, and was the first woman elected president of the American Society for Public Administration. In addition, Lawton was among the founders of Federally Employed Women. She received numerous awards, including the Federal Woman's Award, and was named Professional Woman of the Year twice by Washington's Business and Professional Women's Clubs.

Leader, Shelah Gilbert (1943 –) served as president of the Buffalo, NY, NOW chapter from 1967–1969. She was treasurer of the American Political Science Association's women's caucus (1971–1973), and a founder and member of Cornell University's women's studies program advisory board. In 1975, Leader was chair of the insurance discrimination task force of the Montgomery, MD, NOW chapter, and from 1975–1978 was a senior staff analyst of the IWY commission. Leader, who has one child, is (2004) a health researcher. She earned her B.A. from Hofstra University, her Ph.D. from SUNY, Buffalo, and was a post-doctoral fellow at Cornell University. Archives: Schlesinger Library, Radcliffe Institute, Cambridge, MA. (ABS)

Leaming, Marjorie Newlin (1915 –) Believing that the best way to promote feminism was as an ordained Unitarian Universalist minister, Leaming went back to school in 1965 and earned her B.D. degree from Meadville Theological School in 1967. Her second sermon while there was a public declaration of her feminism. In 1973, the Universalist Unitarian Church of Santa Paula (CA) published a book of her sermons, *Feminism from the Pulpit: Thirteen Sermons on Sex Etc.* In 1974, Leaming became coordinator of the Ministerial Sisterhood Unitarian Universalist group, and continued as its coordinator and editor of its triannual newsletter through the Spring 1994 issue. Leaming did her undergraduate work at the University of Tulsa, and earned an M.A. from the University of Chicago Divinity School (1956). Leaming received an Honorary D.Div. from the Meadville Lombard Theological School (University of Chicago) in 1985. Archives: Meadville Lombard Theological School Library, in a room to be built and named after Leaming, the Leaming Special Collection Library, Chicago, IL. (ABS)

Lear, Frances (1923 – 1996) was a businesswoman, publisher, philanthropist, writer and activist feminist. During the early 1970s, she co-founded an executive search firm on the West Coast that specialized in placing women and minorities in compliance with Title VII of the Civil Rights Act. In those days, companies with federal contracts were required to have numbers of women and minorities in their work forces commensurate with their numbers in the community. Companies routinely ignored that requirement, saying that they could not find qualified people. Lear would find good women and minorities with suitable qualifications and present their resumes to these companies. She was not a NOW member, but did help raise money for the Los Angeles chapter and worked with NOW on the ERA and other feminist causes. Her articles on feminist issues appeared in a number of national publications. Lear was married for 28 years to Norman Lear, the highly successful television producer of series such as "All in the Family" and "Maude." Frances Lear is considered to have been the inspiration for Maude, the feisty and opinionated title character. In the mid 1970s, in an effort to counter her frustration with her role as Hollywood wife, she inaugurated St. Patrick's Day women's dinners at her home to introduce Los Angeles women leaders to prominent feminist thinkers from around the country. She became unhappy in her marriage when she realized that "we had become he" and was divorced in 1985. She moved to New York City, where she created *Lear's*, a magazine for "the woman who wasn't born yesterday." *Lear's* began publication in 1988. It had more than 500,000 subscribers when it ceased publication in 1994, when Lear became ill. In 1989 Lear was named Editor of the Year by *Advertising Age*. She wrote an autobiography, *The Second Seduction* (Alfred A. Knopf, 1992) in which she detailed her difficult journey through life, including being sexually abused as a child and struggling with manic-depressive illness as an adult.

Lease, Carol Teresa (1948 –) worked on *Big Mama Rag*, a feminist newspaper published in Denver, CO, from 1971 – 1977. Lease was a delegate to the National Women's Conference in Houston in 1977, representing lesbian feminists in Colorado, and from 1978 – 1980 helped develop statewide lesbian/feminist conferences, Lesbians-Colorado. She served as executive director of the Gay and Lesbian Community Center of Colorado from 1980 – 1984, and was a member of the board of the Denver chapter of the ACLU, founding the lesbian and gay issues task force. From 1976 – 1980, Lease worked with CO NOW on issues of women involved in prostitution. She was a founder of the Empowerment Program in Denver, which works with women involved in the criminal justice system, women living with HIV/AIDS, homeless women, and women living with severe mental illness or who are drug users involved in prostitution. Lease is (2006) executive director of the program. From 1992 – 2005, Lease worked with Coloradans Working Together in HIV prevention planning throughout the state, and served as the urban co-chair for four terms. Lease holds a B.S. from the University of Colorado. (ABS)

Leck, Glorianne Mae (1941 –) was one of 14 people who organized the Moxie Collective in rural Pennsylvania (1970). Anti-war activists, they did political mentoring and feminist consciousness raising with other anti-war, alternative lifestyle, and organic gardening and farming groups in the area. In October 1972, women from the collective met to plan a women's liberation meeting. The Moxie Collective women wrote position papers and presented objections to patriarchal leadership within other organizations. In 1972 – 1973, Leck and other faculty and student feminists constructed the first women's studies courses at Penn State. In 1972, the women of the Moxie Collective created Woman-Safe, a crisis line for women abused by men. In 1974, having moved to a teaching position at Youngstown State University in Youngstown, OH, Leck advocated the implementation of Title IX. In March 1974, she attended the Coalition of Labor Union Women Conference in Chicago. From 1978 – 1986, she served on the Youngstown Human Rights Commission. In 1984, the Youngstown YWCA named Leck Outstanding Woman of the Year. In the early 1990s, she worked to create, then served as president of, Ohio's Outvoice, which fought legislative attacks on gay rights. In 1994, the

Youngstown State University Office of Student Affairs acknowledged her wide-ranging work on behalf of women's rights and lesbian and gay students. In 1994, she received the O.E.A. Holloway/Human and Civil Rights Commission Award. Subsequently, the Moxie Collective, working with the YWCA, developed a Battered Persons Crisis Center and opened a women-run print shop. Elected president of the American Educational Studies Association and currently (2004) professor emeritus, Leck was named Distinguished Professor for Community Service in 1997. Leck holds a B.S. (1963); M.S. (1966); and a Ph.D. (1968) from the University of Wisconsin, Madison. Archives: Western Reserve Historical Society, Cleveland, OH. (ABS)

LeCocq, Karen Elizabeth (1949 –) Artist and college instructor, LeCocq was a founding member of the original feminist art program created by Judy Chicago at CSU Fresno (1970), and continued in the program at the California Institute of the Arts, Valencia, under the direction of Chicago and Miriam Schapiro (1972 – 1973). LeCocq was part of Womanhouse, a collaborative project in which women transformed an abandoned mansion into an environment reflecting their dreams, ideas and emotions. Her work has been pictured in numerous books, including *The Power of Feminist Art* and *Sexual Politics*, and in her autobiography, *The Easiest Thing to Remember, My Life as an Artist, a Feminist and a Manic Depressive* (1st Books Library, 2001). Her work was included in two major feminist shows on the West Coast: Sexual Politics, at the Armand Hammer; and Division of Labor, at the Los Angeles Museum of Contemporary Art. LeCocq earned her B.A. and M.A. from California State University, Fresno. (ABS)

Lee, Nancy (1941 –) (also known as Nancy L. Van Beek) was coordinator (1972 – 1975) of the Austin (TX) Women's Center, an umbrella agency that made possible the formation of the Rape Crisis Center, housed NOW meetings, hosted consciousness raising groups, and held workshops. During this period, Lee was an active member of NOW, helping to host the regional meeting held in Austin in the early 1970s. Lee has also been a supporter of women's health and reproductive rights, women-positive legislation, and the arts. (ABS)

Lee, Pelican (1947 –) (also known as Ellen Ackerman and Ellen Leo) In 1970 in Berkeley, CA, Lee found feminism, came out as a lesbian, and worked on the feminist newspaper *It Ain't Me Babe*. She was active in the Berkeley Women's Health Collective (1970 – 1972), where she helped organize a successful demand for the Wednesday Women's Night at the Berkeley Free Clinic. Lee left Berkeley in 1972 and began a journey living in several emerging feminist communities, including Elana Mikels' farm in New Mexico, chronicled in Mikels' book *Just Lucky I Guess* (Desert Crone Press, 1995); and Cabbage Lane Women's Land in Wolf Creek, OR. She helped or-

L

ganize the Oregon Women's Land Trust, which bought 160 acres of land in 1976 and became Owl Farm in Days Creek, OR. She related her experiences there in *The Owl Farm Stories*. Lee moved to Arf Women's Land near Santa Fe, NM, in 1978 and helped organize Women for Survival, a lesbian feminist antinuclear activist group based in Santa Fe. In 1985, she moved to Flagstaff, AZ, where she worked at the Big Mountain Legal Defense/Offense Committee, coordinated support groups, and published a newsletter in efforts to support the rights of traditional Navajo and Hopi People. In 1989–1992, she helped organize the New Mexico Women's Land Trust, which raised $100,000 to save Arf Women's Land from being sold. In 1993 she was one of five lesbians who organized a new women's land community, West Wind; in 1995 they collectively bought land in Ribera, NM, where she lives today (2004). Most recently, Lee has been working to organize the Association of Lesbian Intentional Communities, and is working on a songbook of lesbian land circle songs and a slide show of lesbian lands. Archives: June L. Mazer Lesbian History Archives, West Hollywood, CA; and Oregon Lesbian Collection at Knight Library, University of Oregon, Eugene, OR.　　(ABS)

Leeder, Elaine (1944 –) (also known as Elaine Sneierson) joined a Redstockings CR group in NYC in 1969, and participated in actions including the women's liberation march down Fifth Avenue. After moving to Ithaca, NY, Leeder founded an anarcha-feminist group called Tiamat. She moved to Berkeley, CA, and worked with the Berkeley Radical Psychiatry Collective, then co-founded a feminist crisis training team dealing with mental health issues. Back in Ithaca, she wrote on anarchist/feminist theory and history for the journal *Social Anarchism*. Also active in the civil rights and peace movements, Leeder marched with Martin Luther King in the early 1960s in Boston, was involved in anti-Vietnam War demonstrations in the 1970s, and in the 1980s became involved in the gay rights movement and wrote on lesbian battering. Her books include *The Gentle General: Rose Pesotta, Anarchist and Labor Organizer* (SUNY, 1993); *Treating Abuse in Families: A Feminist and Community Approach* (Springer, 1994); and *The Family in Global Perspective: A Gendered Journey* (Sage, 2003). Leeder, who has one child, earned an M.S.W. from Wurzweiler School of Social Work, Yeshiva University; an M.P.H. from the University of California, Berkeley; and a Ph.D. from Cornell University. Archives: Anarchist Archives, Boston, MA.　　(ABS)

Leet, Mildred Robbins (1922 –) was the first chair of the United Cerebral Palsy women's division (1948 – 1952). In 1958 she became a member of the National Council of Women, USA, and was their U.N. representative from 1958 – 1964. In 1964, she was elected president NCW/USA and served for four years, running conferences on civil rights and women's rights. In 1974, with her husband, Glen Leet, she founded Hotline International,

which used computer technology to cover several U.N. conferences. In 1975, she participated in the U.N. Women's Conference using computer technology. She and her husband founded the Trickle Up program in 1979, an international NGO designed to alleviate poverty worldwide by encouraging women and men to start their own businesses. Leet was also VP of the U.S. committee for the United Nations Development Fund for Women, which she helped found in 1984. In 1995, she was honored by InterAction, an umbrella organization of 168 U.S.-based non-profit international development organizations, with the creation of the Mildred Robbins Leet Award, established in recognition of her contributions to raising awareness on gender issues. In 1989, WomenAid honored her in England, along with Mother Theresa, with the Women of the World Award presented by Princess Diana. In 1992, she was honored in the National Women's Hall of Fame Book of Lives and Legacies. Leet holds a B.A. from New York University. Archives: Schlesinger Library, Radcliffe Institute, Cambridge, MA.　　(ABS)

Lefferts, Sybil (1930 –) As a graduate student in Boston in the late 1960s, Lefferts became involved in women's groups at both Brandeis and Harvard. When she moved to Long Island (NY) in 1971, she brought all the materials on women's issues and women's health with her, and then helped start a women's center on the campus of SUNY Stony Brook. She participated in actions to persuade the administration to fund day care on campus and stop the exploitation of low-wage maintenance staff, most of whom were women. Lefferts also participated in the work of Health House, a counseling, information and referral service for women, and created a course in the Interdisciplinary Social Sciences Dept. called Healthcare and Society. One result of that course was the publication of three editions of *Suffolk County People's Guide to Healthcare*. A member of NOW, Lefferts has been marching on Washington "since the early days of the civil rights movement." A retired social work psychotherapist, she still lectures on women's issues. Lefferts, who has one child and two stepchildren, earned her Ed. M. from the Harvard Graduate School of Education, and her M.S.W. from SUNY Stony Brook. Archives: Women's Program, Old Westbury College, Long Island, NY.　　(ABS)

Leghorn, Lisa (1951 –) (also known as Lama Shenpen Drolma) was a member of Cell 16 (1968), which published its radical feminist analysis in the nationally distributed journal *No More Fun and Games*. In 1971, Leghorn went to West Africa for two years and lived in Togo, where she researched women's roles in traditional Ewe society. When she returned in 1973, Leghorn continued working with Betsy Warrior, also a member of Cell 16 and a pioneer in fighting domestic abuse, who linked women's unpaid housework to domestic violence. Together they wrote *The Houseworker's Handbook*, which went into libraries around the country. In 1974, Leghorn and Warrior teamed up with two ex-battered women to found Transition House in Cambridge, MA, the first battered women's shelter in New England. They maintained a 24-hour hotline and also helped people around the country who were interested in starting shelters. In addition, they and others in the National Coalition Against Domestic Violence joined with anti-rape and sexual harassment activists to found the National Coalition Against Violence Against Women. Leghorn also did extensive public education, including work with court clerks, social workers and police. After earning an M.A. from Goddard-Cambridge Graduate Program in Social Change, Leghorn expanded on her master's thesis and co-authored (with Katherine Parker) *Woman's Worth: Sexual Economics and the World of Women*. She also testified at the White House and at the Civil Rights Commission and was a delegate to the Houston conference celebrating IWY (1977). Leghorn later came to believe that the self/other, us/them duality of the mind was the root of suffering and had to be overcome spiritually. She was ordained a Buddhist lama in 1996 and lives (2005) and works in a Buddhist retreat center and offers training for activists. (ABS)

Lehrer, Sharon Jeffrey (1940 –) While a student at the University of Michigan in the early 1960s, Lehrer was one of the original three founders of Students for a Democratic Society, the largest and most influential New Left organization of the 1960s, concerned with equality, economic justice, peace and participatory democracy. Daughter of Mildred Jeffrey and so a born feminist, she refused to assume subservient roles—getting coffee and taking notes, for example—in SDS meetings. Although the organization fought for egalitarianism, the gender relationships within it reflected the culture as a whole. Prior to the December 1965 SDS convention in Champaign-Urbana, Casey Hayden and Mary King circulated a memo on sex and caste, arguing that women, like blacks, were an oppressed caste in society and in the movement. At the convention, Lehrer and other veteran Students for a Democatic Society members attended a workshop to discuss the problems of women in the movement. After discovering that these difficult matters could not be discussed in the presence of men, the women moved to another room, where they talked about the humiliations they experienced in SDS, sexual exploitation and the roots of their subjugation in marriages and movement offices. After the convention, Lehrer returned to Students for a Democratic Society's Cleveland organizing project, where there were strong women and receptive men, and was successful in organizing Welfare mothers. In 1968, Lehrer moved to Chicago and became executive director of the Hyde Park-Kenwood Community Conference, whose goal was to create and maintain a stable, racially integrated community. In 1973, Lehrer made a radical turn to the human potential movement and spent a year at the Esalon Institute in Big Sur, CA. She holds a B.A. from the University of Michigan. (ABS)

Leight, Claudia Robin (1950 –) served as a representative, International Women's Conference, Toronto (1971). She was a staff collective member, *Women: A Journal of Liberation* (1971 – 1974); a founding member, Women's Union of Baltimore (1975); and a member of the Socialist Feminist Commission, New American Movement (1977 – 1982). Leight was "on the fringes" of the civil rights movement, joined SDS while in college, and was active in the anti-Vietnam War movement in the late 1960s and early 1970s. She also helped start a free clinic, food co-op and political coffee house in Baltimore, MD. Leight, who holds a master's degree in counseling, is (2005) a counselor at Morgan State University in Baltimore. She has one child. (ABS)

Leinwand, Freda (1932 –) A New York City-based photographer, Leinwand has had her pictures of working women, people with disabilities and the women's rights movement of the 1970s and 1980s widely published. They have appeared in *The New York Times* and the *Village Voice*, and in magazines including *Forbes*, *Ms.* and *Popular Photography*, and in numerous books by major publishers including McGraw-Hill, Simon & Schuster and The Encyclopedia Brittanica. She was a founding member of the NY-NOW textbook committee, and worked with Alma Graham, Irma Godlin, Lucy Simpson, Ruth Ullman and others on guidelines for bias-free images in textbooks and books for children. Leinwand served on the board of the Organization for Equal Education of the Sexes, and was a frequent contributor to its newsletter, posters and other educational materials. She attended Columbia University, The New School, and Art Students League. Archives: Women's Rights National Historical Park, Seneca Falls, NY, and the Schlesinger Library, Radcliffe Institute, Cambridge, MA. (ABS)

Leith, Priscilla Marie (1935 –) joined Oshkosh, WI, NOW (1970) and was a member of Newton, MA, NOW (1971 – 1977). She served as state treasurer of MA NOW (1974 – 1977); state conference coordinator (1977); and in ERA boycott coordination, Newton, MA (1979 – 1980). Leith was office manager, ERA Ratification Office, in Chicago (1979), and was involved in fundraising projects for IL NOW (1979) and national NOW (1982). From 1977 – 1979, she was MA NOW state coordinator. She was NOW representative to Massachusetts Citizens for Choice (1977 – 1978), and a member of the legislative committee, Governor's Commission on the Status of Women (1977 – 1978). She also worked with the Lexington (MA) area NOW chapter as a member of the ERA Action Team (1979 – 1981); board member (1977 – 1979 and 1983 – 1985); and president (1981). She was a member of the bylaws committee and the budget committee, and served as a delegate to national NOW conferences (1977 – 1985). Leith was also active in the civil rights movement, and in Madison, WI, helped pass the second Fair Housing Ordinance in the U.S. (1962 – 1964). Active in the Democratic Party and the MA WPC, she worked to elect numerous women to public office. Leith, who has two children, is a graduate of Vassar College (1956) and earned her M.B.A. from Babson College (1982). Archives: Vassar College Library, Poughkeepsie, NY. (ABS)

Leman, Beverly – See Gologorsky, Beverly

Lemay, Marie Jeanne (1936 –) (also known as Marie Jeanne Laberge) A civil rights activist in the 1960s and a lifelong peace activist, Lemay also worked for poverty abatement and against violence against women. She became affiliated with Planned Parenthood in the 1970s, and began working on rape crisis intervention as a member of NOW in the 1980s. As a member of the Burlington (VT) Women's Council and NOW, she worked against Workfare for Welfare mothers, for gay and lesbian rights, and reproductive freedom. A retired office manager, she is a high-school graduate and has nine children. (ABS)

Lemisch, Jesse (1936 –) A professor of history who has written and lectured widely on American history, Lemisch taught one of the first courses in women's studies, Women in America, at Northwestern University in 1968. He also published "A College Course on Women's Liberation" in two newsletters: "American Institute for Marxist Studies" (March/April and May/June, 1969); and "New University Conference Newsletter" (May 1968). Lemisch married feminist Naomi Weisstein in 1965. With her he published *The Godfathers: Freudians, Marxists, and the Scientific and Political Protection Societies* (Belladonna Publishing, 1976) and "Boogeyman's Background," in *Harper's* magazine (January 1975). In 1975 – 1976, Lemisch led the successful struggle to keep committees of the American Historical Association from meeting at NYC's Century Club, which at the time banned women as members. Lemisch earned his B.A. from Yale University (1957); his A.M. from Columbia University (1958) and his Ph.D. in from Yale University (1963). (ABS)

Leo, Ellen – See Lee, Pelican

Leon, Barbara Linda (1944 –) joined Redstockings in the late 1960s and helped run orientation meetings and write literature. She was also an editor/contributor to Redstockings' newspaper *Woman's World* (1971 – 1972) and the book *Feminist Revolution* (1975). Leon wrote an article on Gloria Steinem and the CIA for *Feminist Revolution*, and "Women and Brainwashing" for the book *The Radical Therapist*. Leon also contributed articles to *Meeting Ground*. As a student, Leon was a founding member and officer of the Columbia University committee to end the war in Vietnam and Columbia Students for a Democratic Society. Later, living in Upstate New York, she helped organize the Mid-Hudson Coalition Against Apartheid and the Nicaragua Support Project, was an area organizer for the national Harvest Brigades to Nicaragua, and a participant in the Venceremos Brigades to Cuba. Leon, who has one child, earned her B.A. from Barnard College and her M.S.W. from Hunter College School of Social Work. (ABS)

Leone, Vivien (1929 –) A New York City journalist, Leone joined OWL in 1969. At the same time, she received the premier issue of *Aphra*, whose coverline "Free Women, Thinking, Doing, Being" enticed her to its offices, where she worked as *Aphra's* poetry editor for the next five years. Archives: Her reporting on Media Women's invasion of the *Ladies' Home Journal* is in the Women in Journalism Archives, University of Missouri, Columbia, MO (ABS)

Leopold, Ellen (1944 –) An economic planner and writer, Leopold was a co-founder of a conscious raising group in New York City in the early 1970s, and collaborated with members of the group on a feminist soap opera, "Through the Looking Glass." In 1974, she traveled with one of the first groups of Western women to China, under the auspices of the Society for Anglo-Chinese Understanding, and wrote about the experience of women in China for SACU's journal, *China Now*. While working for the Greater London Council (England), Leopold revised the pay structure and conditions of employment for part-time, non-union workers on municipal contracts (primarily women and recently arrived ethnic minorities); the policy was subsequently incorporated into the National Labour Party Programme. She also organized an exhibition of women's employment in the London County Council, 1889 – 1964, using material from a book she wrote for the Greater London Council on public-sector employment, *In the Service of London* (1985). Since 1990, she has been a member of the Women's Community Cancer Project in Cambridge, MA, and in 1999 published the first cultural history of breast cancer in the United States, *A Darker Ribbon: Breast Cancer, Women and Their Doctors in the Twentieth Century* (Beacon Press). Leopold, who has two children, has also been active in nuclear disarmament campaigns and the campaign against Trident missiles in England. She earned her B.A. from Radcliffe College (1966), and holds an M.Sc. from Birkbeck College, University of London. (ABS)

Leppke, Gretchen Buenger (1927 –) In 1971, Leppke joined a group of Lutheran women in the Chicago area who were learning about the struggles of Lutheran women teachers. In 1973, she and other members formed the Lutheran Women's Caucus to work for equal opportunities for women in all phases of church life. They published "Sistersources," a resource packet covering issues such as inclusive language, ordination and violence against women, as well as a quarterly paper, *WellWoman*. The group also held several convocations. It was from a 1986 convocation that Leppke founded Women of Faith Resource Center in Chicago. From 1978 – 1982, Leppke was in a Master of Theology program at the Lutheran School of Theology. Her thesis, "Women in the Image of

God," allowed her to claim that, "I took a degree in women's studies in a place that didn't give that degree, as all my work and papers were on women." Leppke has continued to work to advance understanding among women from different parts of the world, to further women's rights, and to enhance the presence of women in the church. A recent project is videos of women's daily lives. Women around the world do many of the same things, but in different ways, Leppke says, and by recording their daily lives, understanding will grow and fear and distrust decrease. Leppke, who has been married to her husband, Delbert, for 50 years, has two children. She holds a B.A. from the University of Minnesota, an M.A. from Loyola Chicago, and an M.T.S. from the Lutheran School of Theology, Chicago. Archives: Gannon Center, Loyola University, Chicago, IL.   (ABS)

Lerner, Gerda (1920 –) is one of the founding scholars of women's history, and is a feminist writer and activist. Lerner has written 12 feminist-oriented books on women's history, edited 20 books on the subject, and helped numerous colleges establish women's studies departments. Founder of the graduate program in women's history at the University of Wisconsin in 1980 (where in 2005 she is a professor emerita), Lerner was one of four historians who initiated the creation of the Women's History Sources Survey, a finders guide to archival resources on women that changed the way archives classified their holdings on women. Born in Austria, Lerner was imprisoned at age 18 by the Nazis, but escaped to the U.S. in 1938. She married film editor Carl Lerner and raised two children, then launched her academic life at the age of 38. She received an M.A. and Ph.D. from Columbia University and taught a course on the history of women in 1963 at the New School for Social Research. In 1972, she established America's first graduate women's history program at Sarah Lawrence. A founding member of NY NOW, Lerner organized and became the first co-president of the caucus of women historians, CCWHP. She was a co-founder of the Columbia Seminar on Women, and in 1982 became the first woman in 50 years elected president of the Organization of American Historians. She directed a Summer Institute in Women's History for leaders of women's organizations in 1979, which as its class project undertook to make Women's History Week a national event in the U.S., proclaimed by every President since Jimmy Carter. She directed an oral history project, the Midwestern Origins of the 20th Century Women's Movement, that preserves the stories of leading Midwestern feminists. Lerner's writings and lectures frequently focused on the history of African American women because she saw an analogy between how she was treated as a Jew in Austria and how black people were treated in America. In her book *Why History Matters*, she stressed that race, class and gender oppression construct, support and reinforce one another. Lerner is the author of *Fireweed: A Political Autobiography* (2002).

She has delivered more than 145 lectures and keynote addresses and holds 17 Honorary Degrees. Her honors include the Berkshire Conference of Women Historians Special Book Award, the Lucretia Mott Award, the Kathe Leichter Prize, and the Gerda Lerner-Anne Firor Scott Prize for best dissertation in U.S. Women's History, established by the Organization of American Historians in 1991. Archives: Schlesinger Library, Radcliffe Institute, Cambridge, MA; and Special Collections, Memorial Library, University of Wisconsin, Madison, WI.   (ABS)

Lerner, Judy (1922 –) was a founding member (1961) of Women Strike for Peace, and was active in Westchester County, NY, for women's rights, as well as for peace and human rights. She was a delegate-at-large to the National Women's Conference in Houston (1977), and was appointed by President Carter to the continuing committee of the National Women's Conference (1978) and chaired the NY region for that group. Also in 1978, Lerner founded and co-chaired Women of Westchester (WOW). As a member of NWPC (1975), she was a member of the original committee to help promote women for political office. She also ran the Westchester campaign office for Bella Abzug's senate race, and attended all of the United Nations Conferences for Women. A teacher and reading specialist, Lerner began writing for *Women's News* in 1999. Lerner, who received her B.A. from Hunter College and her M.A. from Teachers' College, Columbia University, has three children.   (ABS)

Leuchten, Joyce McKenzie (1935 –) As a member of AAUW (1963), Leuchten helped raise money for college scholarships for women. In 1968, she organized women's teams to compete in the formerly men-only track meets in her New Jersey area, and in 1969 brought Wilma Scott Heidi to her AAUW chapter to speak on women's liberation. She was the first woman elected to serve on the Borough Council of her town (1971), and continued working through the 1970s to further girls athletics in the local schools. In 1979, she did a study of police dept. policies and procedures regarding domestic violence, alerting her community officials to the problems faced by battered women. She began marching for abortion rights in 1985, and was active in reproductive rights issues through the Morris County, NJ, chapter of NOW (1980 – 1990). She was a founding member (2002) of the first NJ chapter of Girls Inc., Girls Inc. of Northern New Jersey. Leuchten, who has five children, holds a B.A.   (ABS)

Levin, Beatrice Schwartz (1920 –) is the author of 16 books and over 1,000 articles, most of which "represent a passionate concern for the rights of women." Her book *Women and Medicine* (Scarecrow Press, 1979) explores issues such as abortion, child abuse, hysterectomies and breast cancer, and includes biographical chapters on women such as Elizabeth Blackwell and Marie Curie. Levin has been a member of NARAL for 37 years, and has

L

published many articles on abortion rights and freedom of choice. She was also very active in a liberal Zionist organization (1938–1942) teaching and raising funds for concentration camp victims, with special programs to provide care to women survivors and children. Levin, who has three children, served in the WAC from 1944–1946. She attended Rhode Island College and the University of Wisconsin. In May 2004, Rhode Island College honored her with a Doctor of Letters degree. (ABS)

Levin, Marj Jackson (1925 –) was a co-founder, with Patricia Burnett, of MI NOW (1970). Decades later, Levin and Burnett joined VFA, MI chapter, "troubled and upset by the setbacks in abortion rights," says Levin. She had a feminist television show on PBS, "A Woman's Place," and served as president of Detroit Women Writers and chair of the Oakland Writers Conference. As a reporter for the *Detroit Free Press* (1980–1993), Levin published many articles supporting feminist issues, particularly safe houses for abused women. In 1994, she co-founded and was president of Michigan Citizens for Handgun Control. Levin, who has three children, holds a B.A. from the University of Michigan. (ABS)

Levine, Barbara Hoberman (1938 –) was an early feminist organizer and activist expanding choices for women and men. She was the second president of Western Connecticut NOW (1970). When she left in 1973, there were five chapters, where originally there had been only one. She helped found the CT WPC and the first women's center in Norwalk, CT. Before Roe v. Wade, she and others brought Carol Downer and members of the women's clinic to the Fairfield, CT, library to teach menstrual extractions. Levine organized and gave the keynote address at the first women's sexuality conference on the East Coast (Fairfield, CT, 1972). In 1970, at age 32, Levine was diagnosed with a brain tumor. It became life threatening and was surgically removed in 1985. During those years, she did extensive research on the Language of the Body-mind Connection and in 1991 *Your Body Believes Every Word You Say* was published. Levine and her husband own Aslan Publishing. They have three children. Levine holds a B.A. and an M.A. Archives: Tapes from the 1972 sexuality conference are at The Lesbian Herstory Archives, Brooklyn, NY. (ABS)

Levine, Ellen (1939 –) A feminist, writer and cartoonist, Levine was co-editor (with Anne Koedt and Anita Rapone) of *Radical Feminism* (Quadrangle Books, 1973), an anthology of radical feminist writing. She was also co-author (with Judith Hole) of *Rebirth of Feminism* (Quadrangle Books, 1971). Again with Rapone and Koedt, Levine worked on *Notes From the Third Year.*. Levine's book of cartoons, *All She Needs*, was also published by Quadrangle Books in 1973. Some of Levine's cartoons appeared in "Notes 3" and *Radical Feminism* as "feminist graffiti." Levine has written 23 books, many of

which deal with the struggle for equality (for example, of women, African Americans and immigrants). Her books range from picture book to adult level. In addition to writing, Levine's career experiences include sculpting, law, filmmaking, illustrating and photography. She holds a B.A. from Brandeis University (1960), an M.A. from the University of Chicago (1962) and a J.D. from New York University (1979). (ABS)

Levine, Faye – A writer, Levine was consulting editor for *Feminist Revolution* (Random House, 1978). She has written several articles about feminism and its history, including "The British Suffragettes," published in *Feminist Revolution*, and "Simone de Beauvoir: Prophet of the New Feminism," written for the Harvard Dept. of History & Literature (1965). She is also author of *Solomon & Sheba* (Putnam's, 1980), and a novel, *Splendor & Misery* (St. Martin's Press, 1983) about Harvard in the 1960s in which a feminist action plays a large part. In 1965, Levine was a candidate for Class Marshal of Harvard College, an event that garnered a lot of press coverage, including the Associated Press and *The New York Times*. (ABS)

Levine, Suzanne Braun (1941 –) was editor of *Ms.* magazine from 1972–1988, and "had the honor of participating in the conversation that was the women's movement in the company of some of the most inspiring and challenging voices of the time." Levine produced the HBO documentary "She's Nobody's Baby: A History of American Women in the 20th Century," which won a Peabody Award (1981), and in 1982 edited a book of the same name. Levine was editor of *The Columbia Journalism Review* (1989–1996); writes essays for *More* magazine; and is a contributor to *Sisterhood is Forever*, edited by Robin Morgan (2003). She is the author of *Father Courage: What Happens When Men Put Family First* (Harcourt, 2000) and *Inventing the Rest of Our Lives: Women in Second Adulthood* (Viking, 2005). Levine, who has two children, graduated from Harvard in 1963. Archives: Western Historical Manuscript Collection, 23 Ellis Library, University of Missouri, Columbia, MO. (ABS)

Levison, Cathryn A. – See Adamsky, Cathryn Ann

Leviten, Sara Bess (1947 –) was the youngest woman member of Dade County (FL) National Women's Political Caucus. Leviten joined Dade NOW in the early 1970s, worked aggressively to foster women political candidates, and served as corresponding secretary and/or board member in the 1970s, 1980s and 1990s. She was a member of the Dade County Commission on the Status of Women (1985–1990) and of the Young Democratic Club of Dade County (1969–1976). A member of the Miami-Dade Women's Association (1986–1999), Leviten was a winner of its Caring & Sharing Award (1992) and Special Recognition Award (1995–1996). Leviten, who was also a member of the League of Women Voters (1970s and

1980s) and Business and Professional Women (1980s), has been a volunteer tutor for the functionally illiterate. Leviten earned her B.A. (1972) from Florida Atlantic University.   (ABS)

Levrant, Sheila – See de Bretteville, Sheila

Levy, Judy (1935 – 1987) A child psychologist and ardent activist for women's right to choose, Levy was a leader in the women's medical self help and health movements. As chief child psychologist for the Children's Mental Health Unit of Shands Teaching Hospital, Gainesville, FL, Levy opened minds with her defiance of the patriarchal and academic orientation of the medical/psychology profession. She was a co-founder (1974), with Byllye Avery, Margaret Parrish and Joan Edelson, of the Gainesville Women's Health Center. The center offered abortions, treatment for sexually transmitted diseases, and gynecological and primary care services in an environment that encouraged information exchange and respect between patient and caregiver. The center was controversial in Florida's conservative climate, and as a result of her involvement with it Levy was denied tenure in the University of Florida's Department of Psychiatry. She spent the rest of her professional career as a consultant and in private practice. Levy wrote and gave speeches analyzing everyday sexism, racism and classism in a concise but powerful way, becoming a well-known feminist in her region. In 1978, Levy was a co-founder, with Avery and Parrish, of Birthplace, the seventh freestanding birth center in the United States. Levy, who earned her Ph.D. from the University of Florida, was also co-editor of Sage-Femme and co-organizer of the Mother's Day March for Equal Rights from Key West to Tallahassee. She was a board member of the Battered Women's Shelter, and a member of the human rights ad hoc committee and the Counsel on Rape and Sexual Abuse. The NOW chapter in her area is now named the Gainesville, Central Area/Judy Levy Chapter. She had three children.

Levy, Marilyn Ruth (1937 –) In 1964, Levy attended a seminar at the University of Chicago about women's reproductive rights and heard the story of one woman's illegal abortion."It was shocking at the time, and the entire audience was silent as she softly told of her humiliation and sorrow and the difficulty she had finding a doctor who would help her. That seminar woke me up," says Levy. Since then she has tried to make her mark helping women. The second female faculty member hired by Roosevelt University in Chicago, Levy encouraged her female. students to speak up, and let her own voice be heard at faculty meetings. Levy has published 17 young adult novels about strong young women and women who had no idea of their strengths until they were tested. Her film about Alma Mahler (a composer and the wife of Gustav Mahler, Walter Gropius and Franz Werfel) was released in the U.S. in 2001. Through One Voice, Levy has

worked with many young women of color, encouraging them to apply for college and reach for the unreachable. Also active in the peace and civil rights movements, Levy was a founding member of the Peace and Freedom Party in Evanston, IL, and marched with others of like mind. Levy, who has two children, holds an M.A.   (ABS)

Lewine, Frances L. (1921 –) A journalist, Lewine was a leader in the battle to get women reporters out of the balcony of the National Press Club in Washington, D.C., and into the thick of things as they happened. She served as member and president of the Women's National Press Club in Washington, and was named a plaintiff in a sex discrimination suit against the Associated Press. The case was won, with a $1 million settlement, in 1977. Lewine was also a leader in the struggle to allow women into the prestigious, all-male Gridiron Club in Washington, D.C.. That involved launching "Counter Gridiron" carnivals on the same nights the Gridiron Club held its white tie dinners. Lewine was the second woman admitted in 1975. Lewine holds a B.S. from Hunter College. Archives: Lyndon Bains Johnson Library, Austin, TX.   (ABS)

Lewis, Jane Galvin – See Jane Galvin-Lewis

Lewis, Patricia Lee (1937 –) (also known as Pat Lewis Sackrey) While married with three small children, Lewis entered college at age 27. She attended the University of Texas, Ithaca College and Cornell, and graduated Phi Beta Kappa in 1970 from Smith College with a degree in anthropology. In the spring of her senior year, Lewis helped organize workshops on Women & War, and began speaking publicly on women's issues. In the fall, as a member of Amherst (MA) Women's Liberation, she initiated the idea of a community-based women's center, which became The Valley Women's Center in Northampton (MA). She was hired as the first director of continuing education for women at the University of Massachusetts (1972) and founded Everywoman's Center. Among the many improvements for women that Lewis initiated in that role was a health center policy of providing birth control for unmarried women. In 1974, she was appointed to the Governor's Commissionon the Status of Women (under Governor Dukakis), and initiated a working group called Women in Agriculture, Food Policy and Land Use Reform, which created the New England Small Farm Institute (MA). As a member of the national women's delegation to visit China in 1977, she focused on the role of women in agriculture and food supply. Lewis then became rural specialist for the State Cooperative Extension Service, and organized and ran a conference for rural women in the 12 northeastern states. At the same time, she served as chair of the board of Rural American Women, a Washington, D.C., advocacy group. Lewis later served as the first elected female county commissioner in Hampshire County (MA), 1984 – 1988. Archives: The Sophia Smith Collection, Smith College, Northampton, MA.   (ABS)

L

Leys, Andrea – See Rankin, Andrea Evelyn

Lichenstein, Sandra – See Emmachild, Sandra

Lichtman, Judith (1940 –) began her legal career as a civil rights attorney for the Office of the General Counsel of the U. S. Department of Health, Education and Welfare. In 1971, a group of women lawyers from all fields of practice, interested in working on women's legal rights, formed the Women's Legal Defense Fund, now known as the National Partnership for Women and Families. Lichtman became the first staff member in 1974. Early work of the organization included the Pregnancy Discrimination Act. Throughout the years, access to healthcare and civil rights have been major issues under Lichtman's leadership. She paved the way within the Washington, D.C., lobbying community for women to be powerbrokers equal to men. For this she was recognized by *Washingtonian* and *Ladies' Home Journal* magazines. She has also worked effectively to have women appointed to important positions and policymaking boards. A founder of Emily's List, Lichtman has served on boards and received awards and recognition concerning numerous human rights issues. (ABS)

Lieberman, Marcia R. (1936 –) taught English at the University of Connecticut (1967 – 1974), and proposed the first women's studies course there, Women in Literature, which she taught. She was a key organizer of Faculty and Professional Women at the university, serving as co-chair from 1970 – 1972, and was one of the women who demanded that the university provide a Women's Center. At the same time, she and another woman gained women's access to the university gym, which had been closed to women, and demanded that women's sports teams be eligible for funding and athletic scholarships. Denied tenure (1972 – 1973), Lieberman brought a federal lawsuit charging sex discrimination and violation of her First Amendment rights. She lost both the case and a subsequent appeal, and was forced to declare bankruptcy when the university sought restitution of its costs. "This essentially ended my academic career," she says, "as I was unable to get another full-time teaching position." Lieberman became a freelance writer, and is the author of several works relevant to women. These include "Sexism and the Double Standard in Literature," published in *Images of Women in Fiction: Feminist Perspectives* (Bowling Green University Press, 1972); and "The Most Important Thing For You to Know," published in *Rocking the Boat: Academic Women and Academic Processes* (Modern Language Association of America, 1981). Since 1978, Lieberman has been a member of Amnesty International, serving as coordinator of the Providence (RI) chapter for more than 10 years. She is (2005) president of the board of Hands In Outreach, which provides educational opportunities for disadvantaged children in Nepal, mainly girls. Lieberman has a B.A. from Barnard

College; an M.A. from Columbia University and an M.A. from Brown University; and a Ph.D. from Brandeis University. She has two children. (ABS)

Lieberman, Sharon Ann (1943 –) was the health editor and columnist (1975 – 1977) for *Majority Report*, NYC's first feminist newspaper. In that role, Lieberman says, she "exposed the cynical marketing strategy of Ayerst drug company and their PR consultants, Hill & Knowlton, to promote estrogen replacement therapy." She was a founding member of Mass Transit Guerilla Street Theater (1970); founding member of CARASA in NYC (1977); a member of HealthRight (1975 – 1981) and a contributor to its quarterly publication on women's health issues; a board member of Alternative Birth Crisis Coalition, NYC (1979 – 1983); and of Health Evaluation and Referral Service, Chicago (1989 – 1992); and a member of the NY steering committee of R2N2. She was also a contributing editor of *Lilith*, a Jewish feminist magazine (1983 – 1990). Lieberman, who has two children, earned her B.S. from Ohio State University (1966) and her M.S. from Hunter College (1975). Archives: Social Action Archives, State Historical Society of Wisconsin, Madison, WI. (ABS)

Lifton, Barbara G. (1934 –) Following 10 years of activism in the peace and civil rights movements (where Lifton had noted with frustration that women did most of the work, while men dominated and took credit in the news), Lifton became a staffer for the newly established New Haven (CT) Women's Liberation Center (1970). She was also a co-founder, with Lee Novick, of the New Haven WPC (1971) and the CT WPC (1972). As issues chair of CT WPC (1972 – 1976), Lifton lobbied the state legislature and helped draft the bill in 1973 that created the Connecticut Permanent Commission on the Status of Women, of which she was a founding commissioner and later VP. CT WPC joined other organizations to form the ConnERA coalition to lobby for both the federal and state ERAs. Working closely with Helen Pearl of the AAUW for passage of the state ERA, Lifton also co-authored (with professor Thomas Emerson of Yale Law School) an article published in the *Connecticut Law Journal* on the need for such legislation. The coalition's efforts resulted in passage of Connecticut's ERA and ratification of the federal ERA, affirmed by a statewide referendum in 1974. Lifton became co-chair of CT WPC in 1975, and her testimony on legislative proposals helped bring about fair credit for CT women, repeal of the corroboration requirement for conviction of defendants accused of sexual assault on women, and reform of the state's civil service laws, among many other bills passed in the 1970s. Lifton, who holds a J.D. from the University of Connecticut Law School (1976), was appointed a hearing officer by Governor Grasso to try cases brought to the state's Commission on Human Rights, a post she held for 19 years. The recipient of Distinguished Service Awards from both the Connecticut General Assembly and the Connecticut Bar

Association, Lifton retired after more than 30 years of legal advocacy for women. (ABS)

Light, Allie (1935 –) A filmmaker and writer, Light made her first film, "Self Health," in 1972 with the San Francisco Women's Health Collective. Widely distributed to women's clinics and health groups, the film was the first of its kind and showed how to do one's own cervical exam. In the same year, Light began teaching women's art at Laney College in Oakland, CA. In the following two years, she published a book of poetry, *The Glittering Cave*, and co-edited *Poetry From Violence*, a collection that included work by known and unknown women poets. With her friend Lynn Lonidier, Light organized and presented a film festival about women writers. (The two latter projects were fundraisers to help purchase the Women's Building of the Bay Area.) Realizing that there were no films about Asian American writers to show at this festival, Light created (1980) the film "Mitsuye and Nellie," about Mitsuye Yamada and Nellie Wong, with her partner, Irving Saraf. In 1974, Light began teaching in the women studies program at San Francisco State University. She stopped teaching in 1985 to pursue her own work, including the film "Dialogues With Madwomen," directed by Light and produced by Saraf. In 1994, when her daughter was diagnosed with breast cancer, she made the film Rachel's Daughters, Searching for the Causes of Breast Cancer (HBO, 1997). In 2005 her song "Iraqi Lullaby for Children Who Are About to Die," was in a soundtrack for a short film about the war in Iraq. Light, who has three children, holds an M.A. She is the recipient of both an Academy Award and an Emmy Award. (ABS)

Lightfoot, Judith – See Cormack, Judith Lightfoot

Lightman, Marjorie (1940 –) In 1969, Lightman organized the first CR group outside of NYC, in Teaneck, NJ. The group created a textbook committee that reviewed the local schools' books for race and gender bias, and also formed a Feminist Action Coalition that ran candidates for town council and board of education seats (1972 – 1975). Lightman was part of the first NJ NOW meetings in the 1970s, and at Rutgers organized the women graduate history students for the first lunchtime seminars on women's history (1971). As a young historian, Lightman joined AHA in 1973 and became active in the Coordinating Committee of Women in the Historical Profession. This latter group was the center for developing new feminist curricula in the early to mid 1970s when women's studies and women's history were emerging. Lightman co-founded the Institute for Research in History out of CCHWP and became its executive director in 1974. Lightman, who has published four books, was co-editor (with Joan Hoff-Wilson) of *Without Precedent: The Life and Career of Eleanor Roosevelt* (Indiana University Press, 1984). She earned her B.A. and M.A. from Hunter College and her Ph.D. from Rutgers. She is (2003) senior scholar

at the Women's Research & Education Institute in Washington, D.C. She has three children. Archives: Papers for the Institute for Research in History are at Cornell University Library, Ithaca, NY. (ABS)

Lind, Nancy Engbretsen (1939 –) was founder of the women's studies department at Manhattanville College (1969) and lobbied successfully for paid maternity leave there. She was a member of the Englewood, NJ, chapter of NOW (1971 – 1996) and worked for abortion rights and the ERA. She contributed articles to the *Encyclopedia of British Women Writers*, edited by Paul Schlueter, and to *Victorian Encyclopedia* (Garland Press) and *The 1890s* (Garland Press). Lind, who has three children, holds a Ph.D. and earned a certificate in psychoanalysis. (ABS)

Lindemann, Kate (1935 –) Lindemann, a philosopher, first engaged in feminist work within the Catholic Church while a Dominican Sister. The Second Vatican Council (1963) said religious communities should "update and renew," and Lindemann reports this sent a "wave of reflection, action and change through Sisters communities." Most communities held Special Chapters (legislative working bodies) and these "did for religious women what consciousness raising groups were doing for women in the wider U.S. society. Sisters came into their own, established new directions and made radical changes in their personal, communal and work lives." Lindemann's other feminist work was philosophical. She was present at the initial meeting at Michigan State University for establishing Mid-West Society for Women in Philosophy (SWIP); she also presented papers, gave workshops and hosted an Eastern SWIP conference at Mt. St. Mary College. For several years Lindemann co-chaired feminist teaching workshops at the American Association of Philosophy Teachers. Later she joined Mary Christine Morkovsky in initiating dialogue between Latin American Philosophy of Liberation and North American Feminism. After recovering from an auto accident in 1997, Lindemann published a work on traumatic brain injury and feminist philosophy. Lindemann's work after 2000 has focused on creating a history of women philosophers Web site. Lindemann holds a B.A. from Seton Hall University, an M.A. from Fordham University, and a Ph.D. from Michigan State University. (ABS)

Lindh, Patricia Sullivan (1928 – 2004) began working in the federal government in 1974 as special assistant to Anne M. Armstrong, counselor to Richard Nixon. During the Ford administration, Lindh was special assistant to the President for women. In both administrations, she served as liaison with women's organizations and oversaw the Office of Women's Programs. She helped formulate anti-discrimination legislation and regulations, encouraged qualified women to seek top-level jobs in the federal government, and helped develop administration policies and programs for IWY. She once noted that the

L

Watergate scandal wouldn't have happened if the Nixon administration had put more women in top staff positions, because "women have more moral sensitivity than men." Archives: Gerald R. Ford Library, Ann Arbor, MI.

Lindsey, Karen (1944 –) has written extensively about women and women's issues. She began by writing articles, first for the feminist magazine *Women: A Journal of Liberation*, published in 1969. In 1972, Lindsey moved to Boston and joined Female Liberation, becoming an early member of its magazine, *Second Wave*. She wrote extensively for that publication, and eventually began writing freelance for the *Phoenix*. Soon thereafter, she began an every-other-week column for the *Phoenix* titled "For and About Women," in which she analyzed much of what was happening in the Boston-area women's movement. Says Lindsey, "I saw myself as a propagandist for the movement." Lindsey has written about the Jo Ann Little trial, and published one of the earliest articles on sexual harassment in *Ms*. She also published an article on battered women who kill their husbands in the magazine *Foxy Lady*. Also a poet, Lindsey gave numerous readings of feminist poems, often at rallies. She began teaching women in the media in the early 1980s at the University of Massachusetts, Boston, and has done so ever since. She is author of the book *Divorced, Beheaded, Survived: A Feminist Perspective on Henry VIII's Wives* (1995), and worked as co-author of all editions of *Dr. Susan Love's Breast Book* and *Dr. Susan Love's Hormone Book*. Lindsey has also co-authored other doctors' books, helping bring feminist perspectives to their works. Lindsey, who describes herself as "a spinster with no children," holds an undergraduate degree from Queens College and a Master of Arts from Vermont College (1981). (ABS)

Link, Theodora D'Amico (1925 –) joined Twin Cities (MN) NOW in 1975 and continues (2005) as a member. She served as 2nd VP for two terms and was elected a delegate for a regional convention. In 1976, she redesigned the chapter newsletter and began typesetting it. At the Detroit National Convention, she conducted a workshop on newsletters for the novice editor with a small budget. In 1980, Link started a NOW chapter in northeast Minneapolis, but "it only lasted about a year, as this part of Minneapolis is very ethnic and conventional." Link actively supported the ERA, and has worked for freedom of choice and financial equality for women. Link, who has three children, earned a B.A. in journalism. She worked as a catalog editor, copywriter and keyliner (making page layouts camera-ready for reproduction or printing). (ABS)

Lipke, Ann – See Jones, Ann

Lipow, Anne Grodzins (1935 – 2004) was a founder, in the late 1960s, of Women's Alliance to Gain Equality. A librarian, Lipow wrote a 1971 report for the Library of the University of California, Berkeley, detailing how, as a "women's profession," librarians (with many degree and technical requirements) were paid less than "men's profession" jobs, such as parking lot attendant. The result was an upward adjustment of librarians' salaries. Lipow, who had three children, earned her undergraduate degree from American International University and her master's in librarianship from the University of California, Berkeley.

Lippard, Lucy R. (1937 –) is a feminist art writer and activist, author of 20 books of cultural criticism on art, politics and place, and a co-founder of the feminist art movement in New York. Books include *From the Center: Feminist Essays on Women's Art* (1976), *Eva Hesse* (1976), *Overlay: Contemporary Art and the Art of Prehistory* (1983), *Get the Message? A Decade of Art for Social Change* (1984), *The Pink Glass Swan: Selected Essays on Feminist Art* (1995), *Mixed Blessings: New Art in a Multicultural America* (1990) and *The Lure of the Local: Senses of Place in a Multicentered Society* (1997). She has been a columnist for the *Village Voice*, *In These Times* and *Z Magazine*, and has curated over 50 exhibitions. Lippard was also a co-founder of many artists' organizations, including Ad Hoc Women Artists, the Heresies Collective and its journal, Printed Matter, Political Art Documentation/Distribution, and Artists Call Against U.S. Intervention in Central America. Lippard received a B.A. from Smith College and an M.A. from New York University of Fine Arts at New York University, and has received five Honorary Doctorates in Fine Arts. She has made political comics, written a feminist novel, performed guerrilla street theater, and for nine years has edited her community's newsletter in Galisteo, NM. "My work has apparently zigzagged all over the place," says Lippard, "but there is a hidden logic. Feminism and feminists changed my life. Everything I do is informed by my lived experience as a woman and by the movement that taught me to be a critical thinker." (ABS)

Lister, Nancy (1940 –) A long-time advocate of women's reproductive rights, Lister was a member of Greenwich, CT, NOW in the early 1970s and Southeastern CT NOW from 1973 – 1980. She also served as coordinator for reproduction and population issues on the NOW state board during the 1970s. In 1973, she and Carolyn Gabel-Brett co-founded the CT chapter of NARAL. That same year, Lister moved to New London where, as chair of Southeastern CT NOW, she coordinated efforts to get abortion services provided by Lawrence & Memorial Hospital. The campaign involved meeting with hospital administrators, creating a coalition of pro-choice religious groups to pressure the hospital, and organizing sidewalk demonstrations at the hospital each year on January 22, anniversary of the Roe v. Wade decision. In 1979, when CT-NARAL opened an office in Hartford, Lister became the organization's first executive director. She worked closely with pro-choice groups and Planned Parenthood, the Religious Coalition for Abortion Rights and the CT WPC on legislative and legal issues related to women's reproductive health until 1982. (ABS)

Livingston, Elaine (1918 –) (also known as Elaine Redfield) As a member of NOW, Livingston worked with Betty Berry and others to change NY State's divorce law, which in 1969 allowed only adultery as grounds. After testifying in Albany and "crashing ABA meetings," Livingston saw the divorce law changed in 1974 to include irreconcilable differences. Livingston, who wrote for the newsletter "Marriage and Divorce," was an NGO observer at the United Nations for several years and attended the first International Women's Year Conference in Mexico in 1975. She was assigned by Theodore H. White to cover the women at both presidential conventions in 1972, and although "he gave me credit in the forward of his book, *The Making of the President 1972*, he paid me half of what he paid the male researcher," says Livingston. Livingston, who has two children (one deceased), graduated from Vassar College in 1940. (ABS)

Lockhart, Bonnie (1947 –) attended her first CR group with other women from the San Francisco incarnation of the NYC-based Sixth Street Theater. With the support of the women's movement, Lockhart became a musician and songwriter, and performed and recorded with the anti-war folk-rock quartet, The Red Star Singers. In 1973 she joined the Berkeley/Oakland Women's Union, and in the early 1970s led the Berkeley/Oakland Women's Chorus with help from Elaine Magree, Laurie Olsen and Janet Rachel. Lockhart also taught a singing class for women at Breakaway University, an experimental school for women that offered a wide variety of classes. In 1974, with the help of singer and activist Barbara Dane, the Red Star Singers recorded The Force of Life, still available in the Paragon Catalogue, now distributed by the Smithsonian Institution. For that recording, she wrote and performed "Still Ain't Satisfied," for which new words have been written throughout the years to support hundreds of feminist and other progressive actions and campaigns. In 1975, Lockhart began working as songwriter, arranger, vocalist and pianist with the Berkeley Women's Music Collective, a band including Debbie Lempke, Susann Shanbaum, Nancy Vogl and Nancy Henderson. In the late 1970s, Lockhart worked with the Union's Cultural Workers, some of whom later formed The Whole Works Theater. In 1983 she worked in the anti-intervention movement in support of the Nicaraguan revolution and toured Nicaragua with the women's jazz band Swingshift. In 1984, Lockhart was arrested with a thousand other anti-war, anti-nuclear activists at the Livermore Labs. Active in the gay and lesbian movement, she marched on Washington in 1987 with the 40-piece percussion ensemble, Sistah Boom. Her current work (2005) is primarily with children, affirming values of peace, justice and inclusion through participatory music in schools and a variety of children's programs. (ABS)

Lockpez, Inverna (1941 –) An artist born in Havana, Cuba, Lockpez entered the women's movement in January 1970 in NYC when she and 12 other women showed their work in an exhibit that art critic Emily Genauer called the first feminist exhibit in the United States. Having left Cuba during the revolution, Lockpez became part of NYC Women Artists in Revolution and worked to organize demonstrations against museums and galleries that did not exhibit the work of women artists. In 1973, Lockpez exhibited a 15-foot sculpture, titled Ms., in NYC. It was the first time the word had been used as a title for a woman in a public exhibition. In 1978, she became the director of INTAR Gallery, NYC, which focused on exhibiting the work of artists with multiracial heritages. From 1982 to 1993, Lockpez curated or produced a series of feminist art exhibits in NYC. In 1993, she and others curated a portfolio for *Heresies*, issue #27. In 1994, Lockpez moved to the Catskill Mountains to concentrate on her own art. She has been the director of The Catskill Center Erpf Gallery and the Platte Clove Residency for Artists and Writers. (ABS)

Loercher, Donna – See Ferrante, Donna

Lojek, Elsie – See Feathersong, Elsie

Lombard, Linda Marcella (1940 –) A member of Washington State NOW (1968 –), Lombard lobbied to get women's issues (as well as civil rights and gay rights issues) into party platforms. She also worked for passage of the state ERA and ratification of the federal ERA. A prochoice activist and NARAL member, she was also a childbirth educator, helping women get what they needed/ wanted in the delivery room (1971 – 1975). A founding member (1973 – 1976) of Thurston County Rape Relief, the third such group in the country, Lombard helped create a training manual and worked with local medical staff and law enforcement to foster better treatment and understanding of rape victims. Lombard helped change the state rape law, which when passed in 1975 became the model for other states. She also helped develop and teach a self-defense class for women. From 1969 – 1975, she worked to get a women's center started at Evergreen State College, as well as a funded childcare center. From 1983 until her retirement in 2002, Lombard was active in AFSCME, Local 443, serving as chair of the women's committee for most of that time. In the mid 1990s, she worked on the Hands Off Washington campaign, a coalition to keep anti-gay rights people out of Washington State. Since her retirement, she has remained active in the Democratic Party. She also helped plan a local Feminist Summit in 2005. Lombard, who has two children, earned a B.A. from The Evergreen State College (1978). (ABS)

Long, Judy (1940 –) joined activism with her research, which focuses on sex roles, marital happiness, female sexuality, and how research paradigms in the social sciences distort women's lives. She became the first woman faculty member in the Graduate School of Business, University of Chicago, in 1967. There she taught (with Marlene Dixon) the first graduate course on women in an American university. In 1971, she moved to Cornell (a joint sociology and psychology appointment). She also testified on the ERA before the House/Senate joint committee of the Judiciary. In 1972, she wrote and presented "the first (or second)" proposal in the country for a women's studies program; and published articles and prepared expert testimony on sex discrimination for the AT&T case. Long was subsequently denied tenure at Cornell, despite two book manu- scripts under contract and strong recommendations. She joined with four other named plaintiffs in the Cornell Eleven lawsuit, which resulted in improved conditions for women faculty. In 1977, Long published (with Pepper Schwartz) *Sexual Scripts: The Social Construction of Female Sexuality*. In 1978, she moved to Syracuse Univer-sity as an associate professor. In 1979, *The Second X* was published. Long attained tenure in 1980, and became a full professor in 1990. She published *Telling Women's Lives* in 1999. (ABS)

Long, Priscilla (1943 –) A writer and political activist "who lived on the margins of society by choice in the 1960s," Long helped found a CR collective in Boston (1969), one of the collectives that started Bread and Roses. "As part of Bread and Roses, we served as the outreach committee—giving talks on how women are paid less than men, etc." A writer, Long is the editor of *The New Left: A Collection of Essays* (Porter Sargent Publisher, 1969), and the author of *Where the Sun Never Shines: A History of America's Bloody Coal Industry* (Paragon House, 1989). She is also the author of numerous stories, poems, reviews and essays, including the essay, "We Called Ourselves Sisters," for *The Feminist Memoir Project*, edited by Ann Snitow and Rachael Duplessis (Three Rivers Press, 1998). Long participated in the Gwynn Oak Amusement Park sit-in, July 4, 1963, Baltimore, MD, where she was arrested, and for years was part of the anti-war movement, primarily in Boston. She earned her B.A. from Antioch College and her M.F.A. from the University of Washington. Archives: University Archives and Special Collections, Manuscripts, University of Washington, Seattle, WA. (ABS)

Lonidier, Lynn (1937 – 1993) A poet, Lonidier was a founding mother of the San Francisco Women's Building. She published five books of poetry including *A Lesbian Estate*, *Woman Explorer* and *Clitoris Lost*. Lonidier was co-editor, with Allie Light, of *Poetry from Violence* (1972).

Lonnquist, Judith Alice (1940 –) A plaintiff's employment and labor attorney since 1966, Lonnquist served as legal counsel and employment committee chair of Chicago NOW (1968 – 1969). A member of NOW's national board from 1969 – 1974, Lonnquist was also national NOW legal vice president and board member of NOW LDEF (1971 – 1974). From 1974 – 1978, she was co-president of the Seattle (WA) chapter of NOW, and in 1977 served as chair of the WA State delegation to the IWY conference in Houston and co-chair of the national Pro Plan caucus. In 1978, Lonnquist became co-founder of the Northwest Women's Law Center. Earlier, as NOW legal VP, Lonnquist established and maintained a national registry of lawyers willing to volunteer on NOW-generated causes. This was the first time NOW had a nationally coordinated legal program to assist women at the local level to pursue discrimination lawsuits. Lonnquist developed an amicus curiae program for NOW to file briefs on legal cases of significance to women. She also brought litigation on NOW's behalf challenging inadequate EEOC class settlements, such as the steel industry settlement. In addition, Lonnquist lobbied on NOW's behalf for the Fair Credit Act, amendments to the Equal Pay Act and Title VII, and for Title IX. Lonnquist, who has one child, earned her A.B. from Mount Holyoke College (1962) and her J.D. from the University of Chicago Law School (1965). (ABS)

Looby, Marvelene M. (1939 –) A leader in business development, property management and real estate development in Sioux Falls, SD, Looby has been as a mentor, role model and advocate for women who want to enter the business world. In the 1970s, she was president of the Sioux Falls LWV, has served on many boards, and has been an active member of several civic organizations. She received the YWCA Leadership Award for Business in 1989, and was nominated for the Women in Business Advocate award in the 1990s. Looby, who has three children, holds a B.A. from Yankton College (1961) and an M.A. from the University of South Dakota (1964). (ABS)

Lopez, Lilia Garcia (1928 –) In 1963, Lopez founded a small group of Latinas to address the needs of children and families at Lowell School in San Diego. Called Grupo de Madres Hispanas, the group grew and with that expansion came the realization that it was not just the children who needed help; many of the women on Welfare desperately wanted to work, but lacked the necessary education and job skills. By 1970, Lopez had incorporated the group as Organizacion de San Diego, Inc. She met with representatives from San Diego County who helped the group connect with the California Dept. of HEW, the San Diego Community College District, and REXY (a funding organization). The group then initiated a program that paid the female students as they studied. In addition, the group was able to assure the successful job placement of 82 percent of the students in the program. Lopez continued as director of Organizacion de San Diego until 1986, when she began focusing on leadership development among women and youth, and on helping people to become legal residents of the United States. She continues to work to unite Latinas and to help them "break the cultural chains of machismo that endures in the Latino culture and the United States culture in general." Lopez, who has five children, has also worked to bring Hispanics and minorities into political, educational and work arenas in both the public and private sectors. (ABS)

Lopez, Petra Guerra – See Guerra, Petra

Lorber, Judith (1931 –) Writer and professor of sociology, Lorber developed and taught women's studies courses in sociology and in the women's studies program at Brooklyn College (CUNY) from 1971–1995, and at the Graduate Center from 1981–1995. She was one of the first members of Sociologists for Women in Society (organized in 1972), and served as president (1981–1982) and founding editor (1987–1991) of its journal, *Gender & Society*. Lorber was also the first coordinator of the CUNY Graduate School Women's Studies Certificate Program (1988–1991). She is the author of *Breaking the Bowls: Degendering and Feminist Change* (W.W. Norton, 2005); *Paradoxes of Gender* (Yale University Press, 1994); *Gender Inequality: Feminist Theories and Politics* (Roxbury, 1998); *Gender and the Social Construction of Illness* (Sage, 1997); and *Women Physicians: Careers, Status and Power* (Tavistock, 1984). The author of numerous articles on gender, women as healthcare workers and patients, and the social aspects of the new procreative technologies, Lorber was also co-editor (with Myra Marx Ferree and Beth B. Hess) of *Revisioning Gender* (Sage, 1999) and co-editor (with Susan A. Farrell) of *The Social Construction of Gender* (Sage, 1991). In 1996, she received the American Sociological Association Jessie Bernard Career Award for her contributions to feminist scholarship. Lorber, who has one child, earned her B.A. from Queens College, CUNY (1952); and her M.A. (1966) and Ph.D. (1971) from New York University. (ABS)

Lord, Jane Sorensen (1942 –) An occupational therapist, small business consultant and writer, Lord was asked in 1971 to work with Betty Friedan to form a national women's political caucus. Elected chair of the organizing committee of what became the National Women's Political Caucus, she subsequently became involved with the WPC in New York State, which trained women to run for office, led lobbying efforts and planned legislative action. In 1970, she served as chair, rap group committee of NY NOW, which trained leaders for the monthly meetings. In 1976, she was chair of the ad hoc special project committee, United Nations Decade for Women, troubleshooting and consulting on projects in Portugal and Egypt. She is the author of *The New Way to Become the Person You'd Like to Be: The Complete Guide to Consciousness Raising* (David MacKay Co., 1973). Also active in the civil rights and environmental movements, Lord has one child. She earned her B.S. from Tufts University (1965); her N.D. from Clayton University (1971); and her Ph.D. from Indiana Northern University (1974). (ABS)

Lorde, Audre (1934–1992) Self-described as "a black feminist lesbian mother poet," Lorde was a prolific writer —poet, essayist, novelist and critic—as well as a teacher and fighter for the rights of women, especially black women. Her first book of poetry, *The First Cities*, was published by Poet's Press in 1968. Her seventh, *The Black Unicorn* (W.W. Norton, 1978) is widely considered her masterpiece. In it, African mythology underpins themes about women, and in it Lorde affirms her lesbianism and political concerns. As a feminist, Lorde believed that both her strength and her oppressions came from her being a woman and being black. Because she believed the two were inseparable, the battle had to be waged on both fronts. She did just that with women of color in many different countries. She was a co-founder of Kitchen Table Press; of Women of Color Press, and of Sisters in Support of Sisters in South Africa. Among her numerous awards, Lorde received the Walt Whitman Citation of Merit, which made her New York State Poet for 1991–1993. She earned a B.A. from Hunter College (1969) and an M.A. from Columbia University (1961).

Loren, Susan – See Keiser, Susan

LosCalzo, Susan (1947 –) was a volunteer with Mary Gehman, founder of *Distaff*, a feminist newspaper in New Orleans, LA. LosCalzo sold advertising and distributed the newspaper to various retail outlets. She belonged to several lesbian feminist groups, raising awareness and promoting political issues. (ABS)

Losowski, Dorothy (1931 –) joined the National Women's Party in 1957, and served on the board of advisers for at least two years. In 1969, she was co-founder of the Central New Jersey chapter of NOW. As legislative chair, Losowski wrote to her government legislators asking for their support for women's rights, abortion rights and the ERA. She also helped produce the chapter's monthly newsletter with other groups from the local area. The group was later renamed Princeton Area NOW. Losowski served as president for several terms. In addition, she was part of a group of women who picketed the Mormon Church because of its opposition to the ERA. Losowski also petitioned women in her area to support the ERA, using tables that she set up to provide information. In the early 1970s, Losowski went to Washington, D.C., to picket the Senate Office Building to demand passage of the ERA. Also active in abortion rights issues, Losowski provided a security escort to women entering an abortion clinic in Bordentown, NJ, during the 1970s and 1980s. Losowski was a travel agent for over 30 years and is now retired. Losowski is a member of the ERA Education Fund. (ABS)

Lotman, Loretta (1949 –) (also known as Libbe S. HaLevy) was active on the campus of the University of Illinois, writing and reading poetry at coffeehouses with a campus women's group. She was the first woman editor of *The Illini Tumor*, a satirical newspaper raising funds for Sigma Delta Chi, the professional journalism society. Her work in gay liberation included being founder and director of Gay Media Action; a columnist for *Gay Community News*; and producer of "Closet Space" on WCAS Radio. She led many media protests in Boston and became the media director of the National Gay Task Force, 1974–1975, and co-host (with Vito Russo) of the Gay Pride Rally in Central Park New York City in 1976. In 1975 Lotman turned to freelance writing, becoming a columnist for *Michael's Thing* and a contributor to the *Village Voice*, a Greenwich Village (NYC) newspaper. Lotman has a B.A. from the University of Illinois, and an M.A. from the University of Santa Monica (CA). Archives: Video work at the One Archives, Los Angeles, CA.   (ABS)

Loubet, Susan Thom (1942 –) (also known as Susan Maria Thom) After working for *Ms.* magazine (1973) and serving as executive assistant to Gloria Steinem (1975), Loubet moved to New Mexico and became involved with NWPC-NM. She served initially as chair of finances, and from 1979–1985, as chair of the caucus. In 1981, she organized state activities for the NWPC national convention. She served as executive director of the New Mexico Commission on the Status of Women (June 1994 – January 1995, and September 1995 – December 1995), and was "twice fired by Governor Gary Johnson, the first time illegally and the second time legally." Loubet was also a founder of the New Mexico Women's Foundation and first chair of its projects committee. In 1991, she was a founder of the New Mexico Women's Agenda and has served as executive director continuously (to 2003). She has supported pro-choice candidates; was on the YWCA board for six years; and was chair of the first Women on the Move planning committee. Since 1990, Loubet has been co-host of a radio program, "Women's Focus," and has produced several documentaries, including "Women in Prison," "Voices of Domestic Violence" and "Women and Smoking—Taking Control." She is the recipient of the Governor's Award for Outstanding Women in New Mexico, 1986 and 1995, and the Woman on the Move Award from the YWCA, 1994. In 2001, she was awarded the Clarion Award for Radio Concerning Women's Issues from the National Association of Women in Communications. Loubet, who has one child, earned her B.A. from Bryn Mawr (1964) and her M.A.T. from Yale (1965). Archives: Zimmerman Library, University of New Mexico, Albuquerque, NM.   (ABS)

Love, Barbara Joan (1937 –) joined NOW in 1967 and was immediately asked by Betty Friedan to chair the Colgate-Palmolive action to expose discrimination and harassment of women on the assembly line. An editor, Love published *Foremost Women in Communications* (1970) to bring attention to women in her male-dominated field. Love was a member of Gay Liberation Front and Radicalesbians, and took part in the Lavender Menace action at the Second Congress to Unite Women (1970). From 1969–1971, Love and Sidney Abbott worked within NOW for recognition of lesbianism as a feminist issue, which happened formally in a 1971 resolution. Love founded CR Supergroup One, which led to 28 lesbian groups. She and Abbott are co-authors of *Sappho Was a Right-on Woman: A Liberated View of Lesbianism* (Stein & Day, 1972). Love was also one of the founders (with Morty Manford and his mother, Jean Manford) of Parents of Gays (later called Parents and Friends of Lesbians and Gays), and a founder and on the steering committee of Identity House, a counseling center for gays and their families. For eight years, she was a board member of the National Gay (and now Lesbian) Task Force, where she was active in the women's caucus. Love was co-founder, with Elizabeth Shanklin, of The Foundation for Matriarchy and *The Matriarchist*, and co-producer of The Forum on the Future (1978). She was a White House-appointed New York delegate to the National Women's Conference in Houston (1977). Love is founder of the Pioneer Feminists Project and editor of *Feminists Who Changed America, 1963 – 1975* (University of Illinois Press, 2006), working in partnership with VFA and in collaboration with feminists around the country. Archives: The Sophia Smith Collection, Smith College, Northampton, MA.   (ABS)

Lowen, Marilyn Norma (1944 –) (also known as Maryam and Marilyn Lowen Fletcher) A dancer, poet and teacher for 40 years, Lowen was a co-founder with Joan Lester of The New Woman (1969), whose purpose was to develop theory and organize for the early radical women's movement. Lowen brought to the women's movement experiences as a 1960s civil rights worker in Mississippi. She had been active in Student Nonviolent Coordinating Committee and other civil rights and black power groups there. She also worked with black women to create more options than agricultural work, domestic work and caring for white women's children. Moving to NYC's Lower East Side, she connected with other Southern civil rights veterans. She wanted "to perpetuate the anti-racist (human rights) struggle which provided the inspiration and strength for the early women's movement, following the precedent of the suffrage movement evolving from the abolitionists' struggle." Carol Hanisch and Kathie Sarachild invited Lowen to their forming group. An active participant of Redstockings and other NYC groups (1969–1972), Lowen supported a telephone help line for women seeking abortions, and participated in the cooperative childcare movement on the Lower East Side. Lowen served as a tutor and tutorial supervisor and trainer (1963–1964) of college students who went to Harlem to tutor public-school students. Lowen, who has two children, earned her B.A. from Goddard College Adult Degree Program (1973) and her M.A. from CUNY (1976). Her poetry and writings have been anthologized in *Sisterhood is Powerful* and *Reflections*, and published in various alternative and underground newspapers and publications of the late 1960s and early 1970s. Archives: Papers from SNCC women in the 1960s at the University of Wisconsin, Madison, WI. (ABS)

Lowther, Carolyn Adele (1945 –) A longtime member of NOW, Lowther served as treasurer of Philadelphia NOW in the late 1970s; more recently, she was on the television crew for Morris County (NJ) NOW. She also marched down Fifth Ave. in New York City for pay equity. As part of her job as a financial adviser (2004), Lowther helps women with financial issues. Lowther earned her B.A. from the University of Pennsylvania and her M.B.A. from the Wharton Graduate School. (ABS)

Lubensky, Margot Truman Patterson (1918 –) An educator and legislator, Lubensky began working for women's recognition in 1946 when she taught at the women's college, Stephen's College, in Columbia, MO. She was co-founder of the Continuing Education for Women program at the University of Missouri (1966), retiring from the university as assistant professor emeritus in 1982. In 1963, she lobbied the MO Legislature for equal pay for equal work, and as a member of the Missouri House of Representatives (1965 – 1966), sponsored funding for the Status of Women Commission. Lubensky was also VP, Democratic Women's Club (1959 – 1963) and on the board of Community Day Care, Columbia (1965 – 1973). Lubensky, who has two children, holds a B.A. (1941) and an M.A. (1947). Archives: Western Historical Manuscripts Section, University of Missouri, Columbia, MO. (ABS)

Lubetkin, Rebecca L. (1938 –) A professor at Rutgers University (1975 – 2000) and now (2005) professor emerita, Lubetkin was the founder and director of the Consortium for Educational Equity (1975) and associate director for equity of the Rutgers Center for Mathematics, Science and Computer Education (1993 – 2000). In 1995, she served as a delegate from the YWCA to the Fourth World Conference on Women in Beijing, China. In addition to making many presentations on methods to foster equity of educational opportunity for women, she served as a member of the advisory board for the Douglass Project for Rutgers Women in Math, Science and Engineering (1977 – 2000). She also was part of the chancellor's task force on sex equity, New York City Board of Education (1983 – 1997). Lubetkin also served as special policy adviser to Madeleine M. Kunin, deputy secretary, U.S. Dept. of Education, regarding policies for enhancing the full participation and achievement of females in math, science and technology (1996). Lubetkin was also founder and director (1997 – 2000) of the New Jersey Center for the Advancement of School Excellence. Lubetkin, who has two children, earned her B.A. from Barnard College and her M.A. from Rutgers University. (ABS)

Lucas, Roy (1941 – 2003) As a third-year law student at New York University, Lucas wrote a research paper that showed how the Bill of Rights, 14th Amendment and the Supreme Court's 1965 decision that allowed married couples to use birth control could be expanded into Constitutional protection for a woman's right to an abortion. The paper, published in the June 1968 issue of the *North Carolina Law Review*, helped shape the battle for abortion rights. After the paper's publication, Lucas established the James Madison Constitutional Law Institute (NYC) to advance abortion rights. In 1969, he filed the first abortion rights lawsuit in New York, and was closely associated with almost all abortion rights suits filed in the U.S. over the next several years. Although he had hoped to argue Roe v. Wade before the Supreme Court in 1970, the assignment was instead given to Sarah Weddington. Lucas argued Baird v. Bellotti (1976), the United States Supreme Court victory that gave minors the right to abortion without parental veto.

Lund, Diane Theis (1938 – 1995) An attorney and law professor, Lund helped draft several pieces of legislation that dramatically changed the lives of women in Massachusetts. In 1971, she and her colleagues, in particular Regina Healy, were responsible for new laws that gave women in MA equal access to public education opportunities in the state. For several years after passage of the legislation (which pre-dated Title IX), Lund and Healy traveled to schools in MA to explain the changes to parents and teachers. Also in 1971, Lund and her colleagues were responsible for the passage of the first maternity leave legislation in MA that gave women the right to return to their jobs after childbirth with no loss of seniority or benefits. In addition, from 1969 – 1971, Lund and her colleagues changed MA Welfare rules to eliminate discrimination against women who were single heads of households, and helped reform the bail system so that Welfare mothers would not be held in "preventive detention" until they revealed the names of their children's fathers. Lund has several "firsts" to her credit. She was the first woman law school professor at Northeastern Law School (1971); the first woman hired on a tenure-track professor's position at Harvard Law School (1972); and after being appointed to the state's Board of Bar Overseers (1978), became its first woman chair (1983). In 1972, Lund became the only woman member of the board of the Massachusetts Advisory Council on Vocational-Technical Education. In 1975, she was appointed to the state's first Judicial Nomination Commission. Lund graduated from Stanford University (1958), Harvard Law School (1961) and the Harvard Graduate School of Education (1989). She has three children.

Lunden, Blue (1936 – 1999) was among the women who resisted stifling mores before the organized women's liberation movement began. Only seven when her mother died, Lunden was brought up by her grandmother in New

Orleans. She was arrested many times in the 1950s for "wearing clothing of the opposite sex." When the lesbian bars were raided, a woman who did not have at least two articles of "feminine" clothing would be arrested and her name and address published in the newspaper. When the women's movement took hold, Lunden got sober, started to accept herself as a woman, and went to every demonstration that she could for 10 years—anti-nuclear, the Women's Pentagon Action, Seneca Falls, Welfare mothers, Feminists Against Censorship Taskforce, and Older Lesbians Organizing for Change. After she and other women learned civil disobedience, Lunden was arrested many times. She was a matriarch and co-founder, with Barbara Deming, of Sugar Loaf Women's Village, outside Key West, FL, where women could live "gently on this earth." A film on Lunden's life, "Some Ground to Stand On," produced by Joyce Warshower and distributed by Women Make Movies, won numerous awards, including the National Education Media Bronze Apple Award.

Lunt, Laurel – See Prussing, Laurel Lunt

Lunt, Sally Herman (1929 –) The daughter of a suffragist who volunteered at a Margaret Sanger clinic, Lunt was told by her mother that she was a feminist "genetically." In 1974, Lunt established a feminist psychotherapy practice for adult women. At that time, she was also an associate clinical professor at Boston University School of Social Work, where she taught social policy using a feminist consciousness. From the mid 1960s through the 1970s, Lunt was invited to lead seminars on feminist therapy throughout the country. She was the founding consultant for Womanspace, a feminist therapy collective in Boston, and served as its supervisor from 1974 – 1977. She was also a consultant to many government and private organizations and was an adviser for the feminist newspaper *Sojourner*. In 1971, Lunt was a charter member of the Massachusetts Women's Political Caucus, served as its chair for many years, and represented it at NWPC meetings, where she served the board in many key roles. In the 1970s, her group worked successfully for Massachusetts ratification of the national ERA. A state ERA was passed as well. From 1974 – 1978, Lunt served on the Massachusetts Governor's Commission on the Status of Women as chair of its health task force. She was on the committee that organized the 1975 Conference on Women's Health held at Harvard Medical School, and was a delegate to the United Nations IWY Conference in Mexico City. Lunt was also part of a group that defeated an effort by right-to-life forces to pack the state's delegation to the 1977 IWY Conference in Houston, and was chair of the MA delegation. In a speech at a State Department reception for women, she introduced the concept "seduction of access," arguing that proximity to the powerful should not be confused with having power. She also wrote on women gaining power in "Understanding Paradox and Power," which was published in the *Hood College Alumnae Bulletin*. Her later career segued into mediation, and she worked with consumer assistance programs. Lunt graduated from Hood College (A.B.), Simmons College School of Social Work (M.S.), Harvard University (Ed.D) and Massachusetts School of Law (J.D.) In 1984 she received the Distinguished Alumni Award from Hood College. Now retired, Lunt crews on Tall Ships. She has two children. Archives: Schlesinger Library, Radcliffe Institute, Cambridge, MA.   (ABS)

Luomala, Nancy Ann Bepko Puumala (1940 –) A professor of art and art history, Luomala helped establish the women's studies degree programs at Mankato State University, where she taught a course on women in art from 1972 until her retirement in 1984. She has lectured widely in the upper Midwest and abroad on feminist topics in art and art history, and in 1975 served as Southern Minnesota coordinator of the Smithsonian Institution's Bicentennial Inventory of American Painting. She has been an active member of Minnesota state women's faculty organizations, including the Women's Art Registry of Minnesota and the WCA, as well as a member of WEAL and the LWV. Her paintings and sculpture (1957 – 1970) focus on women as subject and symbol. Luomala, who has two children, earned her B.A. from the University of Minnesota (1961) and her M.F.A. from Arizona State University (1964).   (ABS)

Lupa, Mary-Ann (1944 –) was a graphic designer recruited by Mary Jean Collins to attend a small organizing meeting at the Sherman House, Chicago, in 1966. The meeting, directed by Catherine Conroy and Kay Clarenbach, was the start of the Chicago NOW chapter. Lupa then formed an artistic collaboration with legislative coordinator Ann L. Scott to develop a national Women Strike for Women button. The Lupa-designed button was published in *Time* magazine as a symbol of August 26th Strike Day in 1970. In 1971, Lupa became Chicago NOW chapter president, serving two terms (1971 – 1973). Her administration established the first staffed chapter office and collaborated with Day Piercy to develop and provide leadership from the chapter for a new single-issue organization, Women Employed. In 1976, as IL ERA coordinator, Lupa rallied chapters to attend the National Rally for Equal Rights in Springfield, IL—her first direct action with buses and walkie-talkies. Lupa, who has one child, holds a B.A. from Alverno College (1964). Archives: Midwest Women's Archives, University of Chicago, IL.   (ABS)

Lutz, Alma (1890 – 1973) was author of *Emma Willard, Daughter of Democracy* (1929); *Created Equal; A Biography of Elizabeth Cady Stanton, 1815 – 1902; Susan B. Anthony: Rebel Crusader, Humanitarian*; and *Emma Willard*. She also helped Harriet Eaton Stanton Blatch, an early suffragist in England and feminist in the United States, write her biography, *Challenging Years* (1940). As a feminist, Lutz opposed so-called protective legislation and specifically legislation designed to keep women out of the workplace. A 1932 American anti-nepotism law for government workers, for example, stated that only one spouse could work. Passed at a time when wages were sinking and jobs were scarce, the law did not state that it was the husband who could work, but the meaning was clear. Lutz, arguing that women were capable, competent workers, demanded instead that laws be passed guaranteeing them equal pay for equal work. In 1934, she published the article "Women and Wages" in *The Nation*. As a member of the NWP, Lutz supported the ERA and urged Betty Friedan and NOW to do the same. According to Mary Eastwood, it was at the urging of Lutz that Friedan decided to establish a NOW committee to write a position paper on the ERA and come up with "new" language for the amendment so that it would not be associated with the ERA that had failed to pass for so many years. Says Eastwood, "I did come up with new language, but when Caruthers Berger and I went to Miss Paul with it, she said it should not be changed because of all the Congressional sponsors and the organizations with whom they had worked so hard using the traditional language. So we dropped the idea." Archives: Schlesinger Library, Radcliffe Institute, Cambridge, MA; The Sophia Smith Collection, Smith College, Northampton, MA.

Lutz, Mary E. (1949 –) became a member of The Feminists (1972) in NYC, a group that wrote and published tracts against marriage, for man-hating, and for re-establishing matriarchy. Members also conducted actions and gave speeches advocating political education and direct action. "Once I gave a talk at Dartmouth College in which I shocked students by proclaiming women should consider aborting male fetuses, a remark for which I paid dearly," she says. In 1973, TF targeted Manhattan rapists by identifying their workplaces and homes, and stenciling "A Rapist Lives Here" in red paint on buildings and sidewalks. Lutz was also a member of Daughters of Great Promise, taking a vow never to marry, agreeing that marriage was the patriarchal institution creating the most legitimized havoc in women's lives. In 1974, she joined a Woman's Martial Arts Union, which helped intervene in domestic violence, and set up self-defense and anti-rape groups, demonstrations, conferences and workshops. Lutz, who has two children, continues (2005) to be involved in progressive movements. She has marched for GLBT rights, housed homeless activists, worked for peace, and fought against gutting Welfare. Lutz, who works in social and health research and administration, holds a B.A. from Columbia (1973), an M.S. from CUNY-Hunter (1975), and a D.S.W. (1987) and M.P.H. (1992) from Columbia University. (ABS)

Lydon, Susan Gordon (1943 – 2005) was a founding editor of *Rolling Stone* magazine and the author of a widely distributed benchmark feminist essay, "The Politics of Orgasm," written in 1970. Her essay, published in *Sisterhood is Powerful*, challenged men's view of women's sexuality. At the time of publication, Lydon was a freelance writer active in Berkeley (CA) Women's Liberation. In 1971 she quit the magazine to raise her daughter, and she and her husband were divorced. Later in life she returned to the Bay Area, where she worked on the *Oakland Tribune* and wrote several books, including her memoir, *Take the Long Road Home*, about her struggle with drug addiction in the 1980s, published in 1993. Lydon was also a passionate knitter and wrote two books on knitting. During her lifetime she wrote for *Ramparts*, *The New York Times*, *Village Voice*, the *Daily News*, *London Life* and the *Times of London*. Lydon received a full scholarship to Vassar, where she studied history, in 1961.

Lynden, Patricia (1937 –) A writer and editor, Lynden was a reporter at *Newsweek* in the 1970s when a group of women filed suit for pay and status equity. Today (2005), women work at all editorial levels, including top jobs, although, says Lynden, "so far the editor's job has never gone to a woman." Lynden was "one of the most active in the groups' organization," she says, and was later elected to the negotiating committee that met with the male editors. Eleanor Holmes Norton, then of the ACLU, was the attorney. Lynden, who has a B.A. from the University of California, Berkeley, was also active in the civil rights and peace movements. She has one child. (ABS)

Lyon, Phyllis Ann (1924 –) was a co-founder of Daughters of Bilitis in San Francisco (1955), the first national lesbian organization. In 1967, Lyon and her partner, Del Martin, applied for membership as a lesbian couple in the Northern CA chapter of NOW. Says Lyon, "We were warmly welcomed by Inka O'Hanrahan, the national treasurer. But couples membership was initiated by national to get husbands involved. Couples membership was soon canceled." Lyon was a founder of the National Sex Forum (1968), which offered human sexuality courses for adults and pioneered the use of sexually explicit films as teaching tools. In 1971, she and Martin chaired a workshop on the lesbian issue at NOW's national conference, held in Los Angeles. Says Lyon, "Although we expected a lot of anti-lesbian rhetoric during the workshop, we were dead wrong. There was little said against the idea and much said in favor of a resolution introduced and passed that stated, in essence, 'The oppression of lesbians is a legitimate concern of feminism.'" In 1972, Glide Publications published *Lesbian/Woman*, written by Lyon and Martin. In 1973, Lyon was a founder of the Golden Gate chapter of NOW (San Francisco), and in 1976 was a co-founding faculty member of the Institute for Advanced Study of Human Sexuality. Lyon was also appointed by Mayor George Moscone to be a commissioner on the San Francisco Human Rights Commission (1976). Lyon served for 12 years, two as chair. An elected delegate to the IWY conference in Houston (1977), Lyon helped pass the plank

L

upholding the rights of lesbians and the parental rights of lesbian mothers. Lyon has been a member of Old Lesbians Organizing for Change since its inception in 1989, and in 1995 was appointed by congresswoman Nancy Pelosi as her delegate to the White House Conference on Aging. With Martin and another lesbian, Lyon was able to get the words "sexual orientation" included in a resolution on discrimination and to get their resolution on homosexuality included in the list of resolutions the 2,000 delegates would vote on. On February 14, 2004, Lyon and Martin were married at San Francisco's City Hall, becoming the first same-sex couple legally married in the United States. Lyon has received numerous awards and honors, including the award for work in the lesbian and women's movements from the Alice B. Toklas Memorial Democratic Club (1979) and the Woman of Courage Award from NOW at Lesbian Summit in Washington, D.C. (1999). In 1972, Lyon was a founder of the Alice B. Toklas Democratic Club. She was also a founder of the Susan B. Anthony Democratic Club, and in 1978 served as chair of San Franciscans Against Proposition 6, the statewide initiative that would have kept lesbians and gays from being teachers. Lyon holds a B.A. from the University of California, Berkeley, and an Ed.D. from the Institute for Advanced Study of Human Sexuality. Archives: The Museum and Archives of the LBGT, San Francisco, CA. (ABS)

Lyons, Harriet (1939 –) An original editor of and writer at *Ms.* magazine (1972 – 1980), Lyons oversaw visual arts coverage of the emerging women's art movement, and covered childcare issues. As a member of the 80th St. Day Care Center (NYC), she helped organize affordable childcare services, petitioning government agencies to change policies. She also served as an adviser and organizer (1978 – 1989) of the New York Feminist Art Institute and was involved in fundraising and publicity. As an adviser to the Coalition of Women's Art Organization, Washington, D.C. (1979), she lobbied for priority for women artists. In 1970, Lyons took part in protests and picketing at the Whitney Museum and MOMA (NYC), demanding more exhibits by women. Lyons was co-producer and editor of *The Decade of Women* (Putnam, 1980), which won the Women in Communications 1980 Clarion Award. She served as press secretary to the Brooklyn Borough president (1982 – 1986), was an editor of *Redbook* (1994 – 1997), and is (2005) Special Sections editor of the *Daily News*. Lyons, who has one child, earned her B.A. from Brooklyn College (1961). (ABS)

Lytel, Elaine (1923 – 2000) was a founding member of Syracuse, NY, NOW. In 1981, she wrote a play about Margaret Sanger, "Woman Rebel," that was produced in Lytel's memory by NOW and the Syracuse Community Theatre a la Carte. A Democrat in a largely Republican area, Lytel was elected to the Onondaga County (NY) Legislature in 1973, 1975 and 1977, representing the Ninth District. She was the first woman to represent that area in county government. During her tenure, she initiated the rewriting of the Onondaga County Administrative Code to reflect gender-neutral language; developed a federally funded program for part-time employment of women, minorities, middle-aged and senior citizens; and was an advocate for alternatives to incarceration. She participated in the IWY conference in Houston (1977). In 1982, she was chosen as the Syracuse, NY, *Post-Standard* Woman of Achievement in Politics, and in 1983 became the first woman and first Democrat elected to the office of county clerk. In 1986 she received the Jeannette Rankin Day Award from the Onondaga County WPC for being the first woman elected county-wide and the highest ranking woman in the executive branch of the Onondaga County Government. Lytel was a member of the LWV, AAUW, NWPC and the National Council of Jewish Women. In addition, she served on the board of the Public Broadcasting Council of Central New York. Lytel attended the Fifth Berkshire Conference on the History of Women at Vassar College (1981). In a subsequent article she wrote for the *Syracuse Herald-American* she commented, "I used to say if my consciousness were raised any higher, I would fall off it. Not so. My mind will never be the same. I am a permanent and persistent feminist and will remain so for the rest of my life." Lytel, widowed in 1966, raised her two children as a single parent. She earned a B.A. from Antioch College, a master's degree from the Maxwell School at Syracuse University, and her teacher's certification from Bank Street College.

MacAdams, Monica (1949 –) attended the 1970s charter meeting of the NWPC in Washington, D.C. In 1971, as a staff member to congressman Thomas Ludlow Ashley (D-OH), MacAdams was part of a team, organized by congressman Don Edwards (D-CA) that lobbied members of Congress for passage of the ERA. MacAdams wrote the Congressional Record Statement delivered by congressman Ashley in support of the amendment. During her tenure on Ashley's staff (1971 – 1974), MacAdams also researched legislation to create shield laws to protect rape victims from having their sexual lives subjected to exploration while they testified as complaining witnesses at the trials of their alleged assailants. While in law school (1972 – 1974), MacAdams worked as a volunteer on a lawsuit demanding that women be considered for admission to the U.S. military academies. From 1991 – 1992, MacAdams served as an officer of Bella Abzug's National Parity Campaign; from 1996 – 1999, she represented, pro bono, poor women seeking child support in Family Court; and from 1997 – 1999, she served as chair of the Brooklyn WPC. MacAdams, who has one child, earned her B.A. from Brown University and her J.D. from Georgetown University Law Center. (ABS)

MacGregor, Molly Murphy (1946 –) was a co-founder of the National Women's History Project and became its executive director in 1980. Earlier, in 1972, MacGregor taught one of the first classes on women's history at the high-school level in California. After completing graduate studies in history at Sonoma State University, she became active on the women's studies board there (1974). She went on to teach classes in women's studies at Sonoma State and Santa Rosa Junior College (1975 – 1980). During that time, MacGregor joined the education task force of the Sonoma County Commission on the Status of Women, where she developed the plan for the first Women's History Week in Sonoma County (1978). In 1979, she became director of the Sonoma County Commission on the Status of Women. In that capacity, she traveled to Sarah Lawrence College for the meeting of the Women's History Institute, where she presented her plan for a Women's History Week. There she met Pam Elam, who became a prime mover in getting Congress to declare a National Women's History Week. MacGregor is the recipient of numerous honors and awards, including the Women Educators' Curriculum Award from the American Education Research Association. She was honored by the Giraffe Foundation for "sticking her neck out," by the Sonoma County NAACP as a Woman of the Year, by the California Commission on the Status of Women as one of California's 12 Outstanding Women of 1987, and by congresswoman Lynn Woolsey for helping shape women's political and social landscapes. (ABS)

MacIntyre, Barbara Ann (1945 –) MacIntyre's ire was raised for the first time when she was job-hunting in 1962. It suddenly hit her: All the interesting jobs were listed under "Help Wanted: Male"! So she and six friends decided to answer those ads in person. But in an astonishing turn of events, the women were taken seriously. Three took those jobs. From then on it was politics all the way for MacIntyre. She has devoted herself since 1966 to civil rights, anti-war marches, NOW and local protests. MacIntyre worked with unions on legislation, education about local strikes, and on Democratic political organizing. She was a Kennedy delegate to the 1980 Democratic National Convention, and served as Bennington County (VT) Democratic chair from1985 – 1993. She was also a Bennington County Regional Commission board member involved in local environmental concerns from 1997 –2002, and Bennington School District clerk from 1986 – 1996. MacIntyre continues her work at the Peace Resource Center and a local homeless shelter. For anti-war civil disobedience for blocking four-way traffic on Main Street dressed as an Iraqi woman holding a baby, MacIntyre negotiated a $125 fine after a court refused to take $150 in $1 checks from supporters as half of the $300 "donation." She is active in older women's issues, peace and justice organizations, minority rights, violence against women, and reproductive rights. (ABS)

MacKay, Anne (1928 –) A teacher, writer and poet, MacKay is the author of three books, including *Wolf Girls*

at Vassar: Lesbian and Gay Experiences 1930 – 1990 (St. Martin's Press, 1993) and *Sailing the Edge* (Bay View Books Orient, 1993). Her letter to the Vassar's alumnae magazine, "Being Gay at Vassar" (1970), later led to the founding of the Lesbian & Gay Alumnae of Vassar College. Mackay, who has worked to preserve lesbian voices and experience, created and directed three lesbian musical reviews, including "Taking Liberties," a fundraiser for The Lesbian Herstory Archives and Astraea, at Symphony Space in NYC (1984). In 1993, she was awarded the Uncommon Woman Award for outstanding contributions to the women's community by the Legacy Foundation, and in 1996 the Dalton School (where she taught from 1953 – 1971) awarded her with Honored Teacher status. MacKay earned her B.A. from Vassar College in 1949. Archives: The Sophia Smith Collection, Smith College, Northampton, MA. (ABS)

Mackey, Mary (1945 –) A feminist poet, novelist, screenplay writer and critic, Mackey has written under the name Kate Clemens. Mackey's works have explored women's lives in past and present eras. Her novel *Immersion* (Shameless Hussy Press, 1972) "may have been the first feminist novel published on a second-wave feminist press." Four of her novels—*The Last Warrior Queen* (Putnam, 1983); *The Year the Horses Came* (Harper, 1993); *The Horses at the Gate* (Harper, 1996); and *The Fires of Spring* (Penguin, 1998)—recreated Goddess-worshipping, earth-centered cultures in Sumeria and Old Europe. Involved in various CR groups and demonstrations in Chicago and Berkeley in the late 1960s and early 1970s, Mackey was a founder of the women's studies program at California State University, Sacramento, where she taught and was on the board. She was a member of the CSUS English department's women's studies committee (1972 – 1982), and in 1978 was a founder of the Feminist Writers Guild, serving on its board from 1978 – 1980. As chair of PEN West, Mackey helped form and then supervise the PEN women's committee (1986 – 1991). She also worked with feminist groups in the areas of women's health and psychiatric and reproductive issues (1969 – 1978). In 1996, Mackey received the award for "enrichment of our literary and political lives" from the NWPC, California. Mackey holds a B.A. from Harvard (1966), and an M.A. (1967) and Ph.D. (1970) from the University of Michigan. (ABS)

MacKinnon, Catharine Alice (1946 –) Law professor, writer and activist, MacKinnon conceived of and was instrumental in establishing the legal claim for sexual harassment as a form of sex discrimination, beginning in 1972. Prior to 1975, she took part in New Haven Women's Liberation, wrote a feminist theory of sexuality as a social construct, and designed and taught seminars on feminist theory and the first women's studies course at Yale University. From 1983 forward, she worked with Andrea Dworkin domestically and internationally to se-

M

cure legal and political recognition of pornography as a violation of women's civil and human rights. In the late 1980s and early 1990s, the Supreme Court of Canada, in litigation in which MacKinnon participated, largely adopted her theories of equality, hate speech and pornography. The U.S. Supreme Court accepted her theory of sexual harassment in 1986 in a case in which she was co-counsel with Patricia Barry. Beginning in 1993, she represented Bosnian Muslim and Croat women and children who had been victimized by Serbian genocidal sexual atrocities, establishing rape as an act of genocide in law. She also consulted for international tribunals, and with Equality Now, an international NGO, engaged in international activism for women's rights. MacKinnon is the author of numerous articles and many books on women's rights. Her books include *Sexual Harassment of Working Women: A Case of Sex Discrimination* (Yale University Press, 1979); *Feminism Unmodified: Discourses on Life and Law* (Harvard University Press, 1987); *Pornography and Civil Rights: A New Day for Women's Equality*, with Andrea Dworkin (Organizing Against Pornography, 1988); *Toward a Feminist Theory of the State* (Harvard University Press, 1989); *Only Words* (Harvard University Press, 1993); *In Harm's Way: The Pornography Civil Rights Hearings* (edited and introduced with Andrea Dworkin) (Harvard University Press, 1997); *Sex Equality* (Foundation Press, 2001); *Directions in Sexual Harassment Law*, edited and introduced with Reva Siegel (Yale University Press, 2003); and *Women's Lives, Men's Laws* (Harvard University Press, 2005). Among many awards and recognitions, MacKinnon was named one of the Fifty Most Influential Women Lawyers in America by *The National Law Journal* (1998). She earned her B.A. from Smith College in 1969; her J.D. from Yale Law School in 1977; and her Ph.D. from Yale University in 1987. (ABS)

Macleod, Jennifer Selfridge (1929 –) was co-founder and first president of Central NJ NOW (1969), the first NOW chapter in that state. At the 1970 national NOW conference, Macleod, with Ellen Morgan Steingarten, broke the tie at the end of a roll-call vote so that the resolution urging feminists to use the honorific Ms. was adopted. Also in 1970, Macleod served as an expert witness in one of the early lawsuits that, case by case, opened athletic opportunities for girls and women in high schools and colleges. She served as board chair of the first non-sexist, non-racist day care center in Central New Jersey (1971), and was part of the initial organizing meeting for the NWPC, held in 1971 in Washington, D.C. Macleod was also first director of the Center for the American Woman and Politics, Eagleton Institute, Rutgers University (1971). At the 2000 national NOW conference, she led the group that succeeded in obtaining approval for the "three-state strategy" to get the Equal Right Amendment added to the Constitution, and co-founded the ERA Campaign Network to achieve that purpose. In 2001, she designed and directed a major national survey

on the ERA, which is widely used in ERA ratification campaigns around the country and in the U.S. Congress. She is (2005) national coordinator of the ERA Campaign Network, editor of its e-mail newsletter, and manager of its Web site. Macleod is author of *"You Won't Do": What High School Textbooks on U.S. Government Teach High School Girls* (Know Inc., 1973). She contributed the chapter "Women in Management: What It Will Take to Attain Truly Equal Opportunity" to *Our Vision and Values: Women Shaping the 21st Century*, Frances C. Hutner, editor (Praeger, 1994). Macleod, who was born in London, England, has two children. She earned her B.A. from Radcliffe College and her Ph.D. from Columbia University. Archives: Schlesinger Library, Radcliffe Institute, Cambridge, MA. (ABS)

Madar, Olga M. (1915 – 1996) Hired to work at the Willow Run (MI) bomber plant during WWII, Madar served as director of UAW Local 50's recreation department and coordinator of women's activities. After the war, she was appointed director of recreation for the UAW by Walter Reuther. Because of Madar's leadership in eliminating racial bias in organized bowling, the American Bowling Congress and the Women's International Bowling Congress dropped their "white only" membership policies in 1952. In 1966, Madar became the first woman elected to the executive board of the UAW, and in 1970 became the UAW's first woman vice president. Also, Madar helped found CLUW (1973) and became its first national president (1974). She was also a convener of the Michigan Pay Equity Network (1985) and after her retirement from the UAW was a continuing advocate for the rights of senior citizens. A graduate of Michigan Normal College (now Eastern Michigan University), Madar was inducted into The Michigan Women's Hall of Fame in 1989.

Madden, Roberta Margaret (1936 –) Director (2005) of public policy and women's health, YWCA of Greater Baton Rouge (LA), Madden organized a NOW chapter in that city in 1968 and served as VP. From 1972–1975, the group lobbied in the Louisiana Legislature for the ERA. Although they failed to secure ratification of the ERA, later they did win repeal of the state Head and Master law (effective in 1980), which gave men control over all properties of the marriage. During the 1970s, Madden was a board member of ERA United of Louisiana, and in 1977 was a founding member, Capital Area Women's Network. In 1979, she ran for the Louisiana Senate and received 32 percent of the vote. From 1980–1983, she was executive director of the YWCA of Greater Baton Rouge and started Connections, a networking group. In 1995, she started a breast and cervical health screening program at the YWCA, which she continues (2005) to direct, and was founder of the NWPC of Louisiana. She also served as the first female president of Early Risers Kiwanis Club of Baton Rouge (1997–1998). In 1972, Madden opened the Consumer Protection Center in LA and served as director for three years. She also served on the board of the Louisiana Consumers League during the 1970s and 1980s, and was a member of the Advisory Council, U.S. Consumer Product Safety Commission (1973 – 1975). From 1981 forward (2005), she has been a member of the state advisory committee, U.S. Commission on Civil Rights, serving as chair since 1999. From 1983 – 1990, she served as field director of Common Cause in Louisiana, Mississippi and Arkansas; in 2003, she served as vice president in LA. Madden, who has one child, earned her B.A. from Ohio University. Archives: Newcomb College Center for Research on Women, New Orleans, LA. (ABS)

Magan, Lee Ann – See Bourcier, Lee Ann MacDonald

Magenta, Muriel (1932 –) Professor of art at Arizona State University (2005), Magenta organized Woman Image Now at Arizona State in 1975 to encourage the hiring of women faculty members in the School of Art. The group became the largest feminist university art organization in the United States (1975 – 1988). Magenta was responsible for many key affirmative action projects within the university, and formed liaisons with national feminist organizations in art and feminist politics. Active in the WCA, Magenta served as president from 1982 – 1984. During her administration, the WCA established national headquarters for the first time (at Moore College of Art, Philadelphia). Magenta also presented art projects at three United Nations World Conferences on Women (Copenhagen, 1980; Nairobi, 1985; and Beijing, 1995). She was appointed press photographer for KAET, the PBS Arizona affiliate, at the Beijing conference, and was press photographer for the New York feminist publication *Women Artist News* at the Copenhagen and Nairobi conferences. In 1995, Magenta designed and began hosting an international Web site, The World's Women On-Line!, which exhibits over 1,000 women artists from 64 countries. In 2002 – 2005 she produced and directed Shelter Against Violence: A Case for Empowerment, a digital-art-community outreach project in Phoenix. Magenta holds a B.A. from Queens College, an M.A. from Arizona State and Johns Hopkins University, and an M.F.A. and Ph.D. from Arizona State University. (ABS)

Magill, Rosalind M. (1944 –) (also known as Christine McGuire, and has published under the name Eva Gross) Magill began her activism as a high-school student when she became the first girl to take drafting as an elective course (1959). She joined the NYC chapter of DOB in the 1960s, and was one of its last presidents. Under her presidency, the group held one of the first public dances at the Hotel McAlpin. During this time, she was also a member of the national governing boards of DOB and the Mattichine Society. As a delegate to the first gay congress (NYC), she attended several back-room discussions with the Archdioceses of New York and NOW, where several major policies were decided. She was also a speaker at the

American Psychiatric Association meeting that helped take homosexuality out of its *Diagnostic and Statistical Manual*. In 1974 Magill moved to Massachusetts; she began to work with women in recovery from addiction in 1978. She continues (2005) to work in the field of mental health, primarily with the homeless and gay populations in MA, and also with victims of rape, incest and abuse. She is a member of the Massachusetts Freedom to Marry Coalition, and Salon, an elder gay group on Cape Cod. Magill earned her M.Ed. in 1993. (ABS)

Maginnis, Patricia T. (1928 –) worked diligently and in close unity with Rowena Gurner and Lana Phelan to provide women with safe abortions, even though she lived under felony indictment for doing so for the six years leading to the 1973 Roe v. Wade Supreme Court decision. In 1961, Maginnis started the Citizen's Committee for Humane Abortion Laws in California, a time when the word "abortion" was so taboo that the media used "miscarriage" or "illegal operation" instead. (The organization's name later became the Society for Humane Abortion.) In 1966, she set up the Association to Repeal Abortion Law in California, putting together curriculum and workshops on the history of abortions, and "how to" methods women had used as well as some new approaches. In 1967, Maginnis was arrested for publishing methods of inducing abortion. Her book, *The Abortion Handbook*, prepared with Phelan, was published in 1968. By 1969, Maginnis reported that she and her co-workers had sent 12,000 women outside the country for abortions. In later years she published political and anti-war cartoons. Archives: Schlesinger Library, Radcliffe Institute, Cambridge, MA. (ABS)

Mahaffey, Maryann (1925 –) During a long career in social work and politics, Mahaffey has been a leader in the elimination of sexism, racism and classism. She was elected to the Detroit City Council in 1973, serving as president pro-tem (1978 – 1982 and 1998 – 2002) and as president (1990 – 1998 and 2002 – 2006). She was also professor at Wayne State University (1965 – 1990). From 1972 – 1974, Mahaffey served as spokeswoman for the Democratic Party women's caucus. She won a landmark legal case in 1972 that allowed women to run for office using their maiden names. Mahaffey was the first woman elected president of NASW, and appointed the first committee on gay and lesbian affairs. She was delegate to the 1975 IWY conference in Mexico, and the 1977 National Women's Conference in Houston. She was also a delegate to the founding convention for the NWPC. She chaired the 1995 Michigan delegation to the Beijing United Nations' Women's Conference. Mahaffey has served in Women in Municipal Government in many capacities including president in 1995. On the city council she wrote legislation outlawing sexual harassment in city government and changed zoning laws to permit in-home day care. She also designed and established the rape crisis center, paid for with police dept. funds, the first in the country. She founded the local task force on hunger and malnutrition in l969 and chaired the statewide Nutrition Commission in the 1970s. Her numerous awards include the Michigan Federation of Teachers Outstanding Leadership and Service Award, an Honorary Doctor of Humanity (Cornell College, Iowa), Women's Justice Center 2nd Annual Image Award, and the Sapphire Award for service to the Asian community and Japanese Americans. She is a life member of National Council of Negro Women, NAACP, JACL, NWPC, and WILPF, among numerous others. She was inducted into the Michigan Women's Hall of Fame in 1997. Mahaffey earned a B.A. from Cornell College of Iowa in 1946 and a M.S.W. in 1951 from the University of Southern California.   (ABS)

Mahoney, Caroline Bird – See Bird, Caroline

Maicki, Carol (1936 – 2004) In the 1970s, Maicki and her family moved from Detroit to Rock Springs, WY, to a house across from a trailer court. Because theirs was the only phone in the area, women running from abusive men came to use it. Maicki accompanied rape victims to the ER, sat with them through five-hour exams, and then went with them for police polygraph tests. Herself a survivor of rape, she joined the Sweetwater County task force on sexual assault, and with other women organized a state coalition to lobby for funding. In 1979, she attended the organizing meeting for the National Coalition Against Sexual Assault (NCASA) in Geneva, WI. "On that day, my friend, Toasty Bunning, one of our board members, was murdered as she was going to teach a class on women's history at the local college in Rock Springs," Maicki said. A man visited Maicki saying that she and the women with whom she worked were being watched and their groups infiltrated, and that they were all subjects of FBI files. "It was a terrifying time," Maicki said, "but none of us quit what we were doing." Later, Maicki was the first state program manager to disburse state funds and develop a statewide system of services for battered and raped women. In 1985, she moved to South Dakota and served as state senator. She was appointed to the Defense Dept.'s advisory committee on women in the Services, and worked as a consultant to women's organizations, governments and attorneys. An expert witness in federal, state, tribal and military courts in cases that involve battered women or survivors of rape, Maicki wrote manuals for first responders to rape and, allied with Native American women, developed curriculum for cultural competency for non-Native advocates. Maicki, who had five children, earned her B.A. from the University of Michigan.

Mainardi, Patricia (1936 –) A founding member of Redstockings, Mainardi is author of the article "The Politics of Housework," originally published by Redstockings in 1970. Though housework seemed a trivial topic to many at the time, Mainardi used women's work as a tool for ar-

guing that traditional gender roles limit women. Mainardi has done extensive work to bring quilts and quilting into the public awareness. She describes quilts as a universal female art form and part of women's cultural heritage, providing community, cooperation and communication. Mainardi wrote an essay "Quilts: The Great American Art," published in *Ms.* (1973) and *The Feminist Art Journal* (1973), later expanded and published in book form under the same title in 1978. She is also author of *Art and Politics of the Second Empire: The Universal Expositions of 1855 and 1867* (1987), *End of the Salon: Art and the State in the Early Third Republic* (1994), and *Husbands, Wives, and Lovers: Marriage and its Discontents in Nineteenth-Century France* (2003). Mainardi has taught at Williams College, Harvard University and Princeton University and received numerous fellowships.   (ABS)

Mainker, Marlene Crosby
– See Crosby, Marlene Suzanne

Mairs, Nancy (1943 –) A writer, Mairs has published numerous books out of a feminist consciousness, and three that deal explicitly with women's issues: *Plain Text: Deciphering A Woman's Life* (University of Arizona Press, 1986), which explores what it means to be a woman in a patriarchal world; *Ordinary Time* (Beacon Press, 1993), which was a *New York Times* "Notable Book"; and *Voice Lessons* (Beacon Press, 1994), a tribute to the liberating power of feminist ideas and literature. Her first formal activity on behalf of women was a personal letter-writing campaign to various legislators demanding tax deductions for childcare, began in 1971. Shortly thereafter, she began to attend graduate school and to establish herself as a feminist writer. Mairs earned an A.B. from Wheaton College (1964), and an M.F.A. (1975) and Ph.D. (1984) from the University of Arizona. Mairs, who has two children, has taught writing and literature at Salpointe Catholic High School, the University of Arizona, and the University of California at Los Angeles. In addition to her feminist writings, Mairs has been involved in a wide variety of pacifist activities, including the Catholic Worker and Sanctuary movements. Archives: University of Arizona Special Collections, Tucson, AZ.   (ABS)

Malamud, Phyllis C. (1938 –) In 1966, Malamud was one of the first women reporters at *Newsweek*, and in 1977 became one of the first women bureau chiefs. When a group of women employees brought suit against The Washington Post Company in 1970, charging it with discrimination, Malamud was one of their elected negotiators. This lawsuit was the first to invoke the Equal Opportunity Commission law to protect professional women. Two years later, Malamud was again a negotiator, this time working to break the lock on such upper masthead positions as bureau chief and senior editor. From 1977 – 1983, she was *Newsweek*'s New England bureau chief, and from 1983 – 1988 was editor of the "My Turn" column. Malamud, who has also worked as a freelance writer and adjunct assistant professor of social science at New York University School of Continuing Education (1995 – 1997), has three step-children. She earned her B.A. from City College of New York (1960).   (ABS)

Malanchuk-Finnan, Linda Marie (1947 –) (also known as Linda M. Malanchuk) began working for the rights of women, children and organized labor in the late 1960s. In Boston, she joined Female Liberation, participated in the self-help movement, and supported the Cambridge Child Care referendum. She worked with NOW in marches and demonstrations, and was involved with the Women's National Abortion Action Coalition. She also worked with the Boston Women's Abortion Action Coalition, and in 1971 spoke in the Massachusetts State-house against the existing abortion law. In addition, she attended the founding conference (1974) of the Coalition of Labor Union Women in Chicago, and helped organize a Boston chapter of CLUW later that year. Her work for the ERA began in Boston and in 1976 moved to Tacoma/Seattle. An anti-war activist, Malanchuk-Finnan also supported the civil rights movement. She was a member of the Massachusetts Teachers Association, where she helped organize the developmental center teachers in the Massachusetts Dept. of Mental Health. She has one child. (ABS)

Mallin, Kathy (1951 –) An epidemiologist, Mallin helped form the women's liberation group at the University of Illinois, Chicago, and served as its president (1970 – 1973). During the 1970s and 1980s, she worked in Chicago's abortion movement and helped form the Chicago branch of the committee to end sterilization abuse. Mallin was a co-founder of the Abortion Loan Service at the University of Illinois, Chicago, and belonged to CWLU (1970 – 1976). There, she worked primarily on reproductive rights issues. Mallin wrote her master's thesis on sterilization abuse (1976). For her Ph.D. (1984) she did a study of occupational exposures and mortality. Mallin, who has one child and was also active in anti-war and anti-imperialist work, earned her B.A. in 1973. Archives: University of Illinois, Chicago.   (ABS)

Malone, Glenda M. Bailey
– See Bailey-Mershon, Glenda Mariah

Mandel, Phyllis (1939 –) joined the original Berkeley Women's Liberation Group in California in 1966. Particularly interested in job equality and equal access to jobs for women, as well as the childcare necessary to enable women to work outside their homes, Mandel headed a research project that ultimately showed that in the city of Berkeley, there were provisions for only 600 children out of the 14,000 who needed day care at that time. Because of the report, the group was able to facilitate many more spaces and more after-school programs. The group also worked successfully to improve family leave and maternity leave, and in 1966 decided to "reinvent the celebration of International Women's Day, a day commemorating a strike of female American workers in 1908." Eventually, the group persuaded the city of Berkeley to recognize International Women's Day as an official local holiday (1976) with schools and public buildings closed. As members of the group became more vocal, women who were also students were being physically attacked on campus. In response, the women demanded that the University of California at Berkeley open its martial arts program to women. The request was initially denied ("We don't have a dressing room for women"); however, after negotiation, newspaper publicity and a speech by Mandel, the program was opened to women. In 1973, Mandel embarked on a five-year study of Tae Kwon Do at a local institute. She also spoke to local junior-high and high-school women about the importance of learning self defense. Mandel has been active in labor unions, and the civil rights, anti-war and environmental movements. She has two children (one deceased).   (ABS)

Mandel, Tanya Millstein (1917 – 2001) is described by her son David as having "spent a lifetime committed to and active in causes that were and are relevant to the women's movement—childcare, quality education, affordable housing for working families, peace, justice, freedom." She met her husband-to-be, Bill Mandel, while picketing in support of chiefly African American and female laundry workers seeking union recognition. In 1937, she organized the movement that won the construction of the first public housing project in Akron, OH, a major step forward in replacing slum tenements as homes for the working poor. In New York after WWII, Mandel was instrumental in obtaining a government-funded childcare center—an institution essentially unknown in the United States at that time. Moving with her family to Berkeley, CA, in 1957, she participated in activities that won racial integration of the Berkeley schools and was a member of the Boatrockers Democratic Club. In the early 1960s she joined Women for Peace and helped organize protests of atmospheric testing of nuclear weapons when strontium 90 began showing up in mothers' milk. In 1966, Mandel traveled to the Soviet Union to assess the status of women in that country. Although she was impressed by the advanced level of education for women and the social services provided for mothers and children, she was struck by what she called the male domination of every facet of life. In 1974, Mandel and Laura X edited Mandel's husband's book *Soviet Women* (Anchor-Doubleday, 1975), bringing him around from a purely Marxist to a feminist-influenced interpretation of the subject. Mandel had three children. Archives: William Mandel papers: Social Action Collection, Wisconsin State Historical Society, Madison, WI.

Mandell, Betty Reid (1924 –) While teaching at the University of Iowa, Mandell formed a Welfare rights

M

group of mothers who were recipients of Aid to Families of Dependent Children. They successfully raised the Welfare grant from 67 percent to 93 percent of "need," and were also part of the Welfare rights movement of the 1960s and early 1970s, which increased benefits and led to an increase of African American families in AFDC. In 1983, Mandell helped found a Welfare rights organization, Survivors Inc., in Boston. The group publishes a newspaper, *Survival News*, and does outreach at Welfare offices to inform people of their rights. In 2004, Mandell worked with a coalition of women's groups in the Boston area to send low-income women to the Women's March on Washington (April 25). Mandell, who has two children, has also been active in anti-war movements and union and labor organizing, and is a board member of *New Politics*, an independent democratic socialist journal. A professor of social work (emerita), Mandell earned her B.S. from Colorado State University, her M.A. from Union Theological Seminary, and her M.S.W. from Columbia University. (ABS)

Mangual, Maria T. (1944 –) (also known as Maria T. Towns and Maria T. Heinz) has been a voice and role model for Latinas in the greater Chicago area. In 1972, Mangual organized La Mujer Despierta, a Latina woman's conference and educational and leadership development effort, in Chicago. This led to forming Mujeres Latinas en Accion (Latina Women in Action), incorporated in 1973. The group started out providing services from a storefront. From 1978 – 1980, Mangual served as executive director of Mujeres Latinas en Accion. (In 2004 the group was a $1.7 million agency serving 6,000 clients annually.) From 1992 – 1996, Mangual was director of development for the Chicago office of Mexican American Legal Defense and Education Fund. She also served on the board of directors of the Chicago Foundation for Women, where she was board chair from 1995 – 1997. Mangual has worked for the ERA, reproductive rights, economic justice for women, and an end to violence against women. She is (2005) on the board of the Women's Funding Network, where she also serves as a consultant. Mangual grew up in El Paso, TX, lives (2005) in Chicago, and earned her B.S. from Kenn College in NJ. (ABS)

Mann, Jacinta (1925 –) A Catholic nun from 1950 – 1980, Mann was director of admissions at Seton Hill College from 1958 – 1968, where she saw firsthand families' overwhelming preference to educate their boys, rather than their girls. As dean of the college from 1969 – 1972, she tried to understand the favoritism toward males, and taught a course called Women in Society to try to explain it. Mann began speaking to women's organizations in churches, at NOW, and at local women's clubs. In 1975, the Sisters of Charity sponsored her attendance at the First International Conference for Women, in Mexico City. In 1977, she was a delegate to the National Women's Conference in Houston. Until her retirement in 2000, she

taught women's studies, conducted gender research, and gave papers at local and regional conferences. (ABS)

Mannes, Marya (1904 – 1990) A columnist and essayist, Mannes was a voice for feminism at a time when few voices were being heard. She wrote about the importance of women having the right to control their reproductive life, the damage the media does to the image of women, and the effects of divorce on women. From 1933 – 1936, she was a feature writer for *Vogue*. During WWII, she worked at the Office of War Information and later as an analyst for the Office of Strategic Services. Her 1958 book *More in Anger*, a collection of essays criticizing American mores and concerns, drew widespread comment. In 1961 she published *The New York I Know* and in 1964 *But Will It Sell*. Other books include *They* (1968); *Out of My Time*, an autobiography (1971); *Uncoupling*, co-written with Norman Sheresky (1972); and *Last Rites*, a plea for legalizing euthanasia. She also wrote for *The New Yorker*, *Glamour* and *Harper's*, among other magazines.

Manning, Diane – See Destiny, Diane

Mansbridge, Jane (1939 –) (also known as Jane de Long) As a member of Our Bodies, Ourselves, the Boston health collective (1967 – 1968), Mansbridge created and taught the first sexuality course, and then wrote the first draft of the chapter of the same name that appeared in the published version of *Our Bodies, Ourselves*. At the same time, Mansbridge was a member of Bread and Roses, and was one of a group of women who took over 888 Memorial Drive for several days. She later helped find and fund the Cambridge Women's Center, and helped set up its governance structure. She was also part of the group that put out the short-lived "New England Women's Liberation Newsletter." In addition, Mansbridge worked on getting the ERA passed in Illinois, and later wrote *Why We Lost the ERA* (University of Chicago Press, 1986), which was co-recipient of the American Political Science Association's Kammerer Award in 1987 and the Schuck Award in 1988. As a professor at Northwestern University, she co-founded the Organization of Women Faculty. She served as president of the Women's Caucus of Political Science (1996 – 1997), and helped create the *Directory of Women of Color in Political Science*. As a professor of public policy at the John F. Kennedy School of Government at Harvard, Mansbridge was the first faculty chair of the Women and Public Policy program. Mansbridge, who has one child, was active in the anti-war and anti-nuclear movements. She earned her B.A. from Wellesley, and her M.A. and Ph.D. from Harvard. Archives: Early second wave papers at women's Women's Collection, Northwestern University, Evanston, IL. (ABS)

Mantak, Ruth (1931 –) was the first woman to run for and be elected to the town council in Bloomfield, CT (1969). After failing to be re-elected in 1971, Mantak ran for the State Legislature (1972), winning the primary but losing the general. Mantak then joined the newly formed CT WPC and the NWPC, remaining active in the state organization for several years. Her last office was as co-state chair with Barbara Lifton in 1975–1976. Both as a caucus member and individually, Mantak was active in the statewide effort to pass the ERA. She was also an early and continuing member of the board of Connecticut Women's Educational and Legal Fund. An attorney, she opened her law office in West Hartford, CT, in 1974. (ABS)

Marano, Cindy (1947 - 2005) The executive director of Wider Opportunities for Women (1985–1987), Marano was a "tireless and strong advocate for the rights of women who put her beliefs into practice in her life and work," says Vivian Staples, who was hired by Marano in the mid 1980s. Marano was a founder, leader or board member of numerous national groups and coalitions, including Equal Rights Advocates, the National Displaced Homemakers Network, OWL, the National Coalition on Women, Work and Welfare Reform, and the National Women's Vote Project. At Wider Opportunities for Women, she developed legislative proposals on job training, Welfare to work, and vocational education, which became law. She also developed WOW's groundbreaking work on women's literacy and was a leader in getting women into nontraditional jobs. As a result, she was named to national advisory commissions of three secretaries of labor, and was awarded the Gloria Steinem Award for Women's Economic Justice.

March, Artemis (1941 -) had a lightbulb moment with Ti-Grace Atkinson in February 1968 when Atkinson observed, "When people try to discredit me, they call me a lesbian, so lesbianism is political." Two years later, March drew on that insight, her deep interest in social theory and social systems, and six weeks of discussions with five other women (Ellen Shumsky, Cynthia Funk, Rita Mae Brown, Lois Hart and Barbara Gladstone) to become the synthesizer and lead author of the article "Woman-Identified Woman." Presented at the Second Congress to Unite Women (NYC, 1970), the paper argued sexuality, femininity, and the lesbian taboo are co-constructed and operate as a social-political system of male control over women. A social theorist, March soon questioned its historical limits, and her work at the Radcliffe Institute (1973 - 1975) asked "under what conditions the lesbian taboo had become politically strategic to male control of women in Western societies." It led to her creating a social-historical framework of changes in control of female sexuality, which she developed further in her dissertation at the University of California (1976 - 1982). In the early 1990s, she "had a monumental breakthrough" to an entirely new paradigm of thought she calls Quantum Social Theory, which is to be published in five volumes. "QST makes transparent the mystified and heretofore invisible constituitive processes of creating any social world," says

March. In addition to her Ph.D., March holds a B.A. from Vassar College and an M.B.A. from Simmons College. Archives: The Sophia Smith Collection, Smith College, Northampton, MA. (ABS)

Marciano, Andrea – See Rankin, Andrea Evelyn

Marcus, Stephanie Lynne (1940 -) was co-founder, with Rose Fontanella, of Liberation Enterprises (1972). The women designed and produced "beautiful and useful things to wear and use that would raise consciousness, express the goals of the movement, and reach out to like-minded people." Customers for the items, sold by mail-order catalog, came from across the U.S. and included many women in the military. Although the company grew rapidly, it closed in 1975, "a casualty of the Arab Oil Embargo and deep economic recession that strangled small businesses." In addition to her work with Liberation Enterprises, Marcus helped plan for and marched in the August 26, 1970, march down 5th Ave. in NYC, demonstrated against sexist advertising by the Katherine Gibbs School and National Airlines, and picketed Brooklyn Family Court with Brooklyn NOW to protest a misogynistic judge. In addition, she demonstrated against the Miss America pageant, participated in and helped keep score for a survey of sexism and lack of women on ABC-TV, and marched in Washington, D.C., for abortion rights. A member of OWL and Brooklyn (NY) NOW and national NOW, Marcus attended several NOW conferences in New York City, Washington, D.C., and Atlantic City. In 1973, she was awarded the Brooklyn NOW Women's Achievement Award. (ABS)

Margaret, Joan (1942 -) (also known as Joan Margaret Medlin) In 1972, Margaret began recording and broadcasting women composers and musicians on KPFA-FM radio's Women's News Collective in Berkeley, CA. Throughout the early 1970s, Margaret worked in collectives writing for *Ms.* and *Ramparts*, and was an inside agitator for staff and journalistic feminists at *Mother Jones* magazine. In 1977, Margaret came out as a lesbian and a Dianic witch. (In the early 1970s, Margaret had witnessed her mother being stalked and shot, and later joined the Yellow Springs Dead Bolt Gang, a group of six lesbians who installed dead bolts for free for women.) In Yellow Springs, OH, from 1979–1985, Margaret wrote and edited a syndicated weekly newspaper column, "Women's Voices." As a member of the Feminist Writers Guild board, she wrote and won a grant for Women's Voices Out Loud, a continuing, annual showcase of women's art, music and writing in Yellow Springs. Diagnosed with cervical cancer in 1980, Margaret raised funds through Women, Inc., for expenses. When cured by homeopathy, she used the money to establish the Feminist Health Fund, which continues (2005) to fundraise and help women in Ohio. Inspired by having taken her healthcare into her own hands, Margaret studied to become a chiropractor, and in

1991 opened her own practice in Oakland, CA. It grew into the Labrys Healthcare Circle and the nonprofit Lesbian Fund and Labrys School of Self-Healing for Women and Girls. Margaret earned her B.A. from the University of California, Berkeley, and is a graduate of the Los Angeles College of Chiropractic. (ABS)

Margolin, Bessie (1909 – 1996) A Labor Dept. lawyer, Margolin attended NOW's organizing conference in Washington, D.C., in 1966. Named associate solicitor with the U.S. Dept. of Labor for the Division of Fair Labor Standards in 1963, Margolin administered the Equal Pay Act and the Age Discrimination in Employment Act by supervising litigation that interpreted these laws, thus furthering equality in the workplace. During her career, she argued 27 cases before the U.S. Supreme Court, winning 25. Chief Justice Earl Warren credits Margolin with making the federal wage and hour law "meaningful and responsible." Born in New York to Russian Jewish parents who had just immigrated to the United States, Margolin lost her mother when she was a small child and was sent to a Jewish Children's Home in New Orleans. She graduated from Newcomb College and received a law degree from Tulane University, and then a doctorate in law from Yale. She began her career in the midst of the Depression, working first for the Tennessee Valley Authority, and then (1939 – 1972) for the Labor Department.

Margulies, Leah (1944 –) (also known as Leah Shultz) was an organizer and member of New Haven Women's Liberation (1969 – 1974), as well as a founder and member of New Haven Women's Liberation Rock Band (1970 – 1974), for which she played flute and bass. As co-director (with Dusty Miller) of the Women's Research Project (1972 – 1974), Margulies wrote articles and did slide shows, seminars and presentations on the role of women in the media, and women as workers and consumers in the global economy. She was founder and chair of the Infant Formula Action Coalition, the international advocacy campaign known as the Nestle Boycott (1976 – 1984), and was a founding member of the International Baby Foods Network, dedicated to the enforcement of the International Code of Marketing of Breastmilk Substitutes (1979). In 2000, she was a member of the organizing committee of New Haven Women's Liberation Reunion in New Haven, CT. Margulies is the author of "The International Code of Marketing of Breastmilk Substitutes: A Model for Assuring Children's Nutrition Rights Under the Law," published in *The International Journal of Children's Rights* (1997). Other published works include "Codes of Conduct for Transnational Corporations: Strategies Toward Democratic Global Governance," published in *WEDO Primer No. 1: Understanding the Impact of the Global Economy on Women and the Environment* (1995) with Riva Krut, and "Bottle Babies: Death and Business Get Their Market," published in *Business and Society Review* (Spring 1978). Margulies, who has one child,

earned her B.A. from Boston University (1966) and her J.D. from Brooklyn Law School (1985). Since 2001, she is international adviser for Corporate Accountability International and rejoined its board in 2005. (ABS)

Marion, Jennifer – See Belcher, Jennifer Marion

Marrow, Joanne (1945 –) became aware of sexism as a child and decided at the age of eight to refuse marriage and childbirth. She entered the women's movement in 1968. In 1972, Marrow started the women's center at Florida State University and taught the first course at FSU on women's studies. When the Florida Legislature held hearings on the ERA in 1972, Marrow and eight others marched in front of the State Capitol. The ERA failed in Florida. In 1974 Marrow introduced the first psychology of women course at California State University, Sacramento. She was active in the women's studies program there for 30 years. In 1977, Marrow founded a pagan coven, and in 1978 she started Women Escaping a Violent Environment in Sacramento, CA, a shelter for battered women. In 1995 a fundamentalist student who attended her lecture, The Anatomy and Function of the Clitoris, sued her for sexual harassment because he became sexually aroused during the lecture. The story was carried on the front page of *The Wall Street Journal* and became an international sensation, partly because it appeared to be a rare case of a female perpetrator. Afterwards, Marrow was completely exonerated. In 1997 her book, *Changing Positions: Women speak out on sex and desire*, was published. In 2003, after a diagnosis of kidney cancer, Marrow retired from her position as professor of psychology and women's studies at California State University, Sacramento. In 2004 Marrow founded the Center of Love and Light, a rural retreat for women in Northern California. Marrow holds an M.S. and Ph.D. from Florida State University. (ABS)

Marshall, Carol Mayer (1935 –) (also known as Carol M. Khosrovi) The first woman to serve as a congressional intern (1955), Marshall went on to serve as a legislative assistant to several congressmen and senators and then into important federal government posts. In these positions she was able to help introduce the ERA and help draft Title VII of the Civil Rights Act of 1964. She was also the only Republican woman invited to attend the organizational meeting of the NWPC. In 1969, she became the first woman appointed to a Congressional Relations post in any administration when Donald Rumsfeld, then director of the Office of Economic Opportunity in the Nixon administration, asked her to represent the poverty program on Capitol Hill. In 1970, she became the first woman appointed by the President (with Senate confirmation) as director of VISTA. From 1972 – 1983, Marshall was the first and only woman on the board of the Opportunity Funding Corporation. She served as the director of the OEO for three departments: Congressional and Intergovernmental Relations, VISTA and Program Development; assisted with the Poor People's March, and helped draft the Homeownership for the Poor program of 1967. As congressional relations director, Marshall was the speaker for the poverty program on Capitol Hill; and as director of the Office of Program Development, ran the OEO demonstration programs on health, economic development and communications. In 1989, President Bush appointed Marshall, with Senate confirmation, to be the first woman superintendent of the San Francisco Mint. Marshall, who has one child, holds a B.A. from George Washington University and a J.D. from the University of California at Berkeley. Archives: Papers will be donated to the program A Few Good Women at Penn State.   (ABS)

Marshall, Jacqueline Anne – See Jaffe, Jacqueline Anne

Martin, Barbara – See Duke, Barbara Martin

Martin, Barbara A. (1930 –) joined NOW in 1970. She was a founder and served as president of Greenwich (CT) NOW in 1971, and assistant state coordinator in 1975. Martin worked to repeal sexist legislation and to pass the ERA in CT. A librarian, she wrote a book list on women's history that was distributed nationwide. She also lectured, did general CR, especially among suburban women, and was active in community affairs. With Joyce Rooker, Martin created an oral history of the early women's movement in Greenwich that is part of the Greenwich Library's Oral History Project.   (ABS)

Martin, Del (1921 –) has been a leader in the lesbian community before and after lesbian liberation, and a feminist active on the local and national level. In 1955, Martin was co-founder, with Phyllis Lyon, of Daughters of Bilitis, a secret lesbian society in San Francisco and the first national lesbian organization to bring about an awareness of the discrimination and sexism that women, not just lesbians, faced. Martin served as DOB's first president (1957 – 1960) and second editor of its publication, *The Ladder* (1960 – 1962). In 1964, Martin and Lyon worked on the founding of The Council on Religion and the Homosexual in San Francisco. Martin helped found many other organizations, including the Lesbian Mothers Union (1971), the Alice B. Toklas Memorial Democratic Club (1972), and the Coalition for Justice for Battered Women (1975). A member of NOW since 1967, Martin was asked to co-chair, with Lyon, a session on lesbianism at NOW's 1971 national convention, held in Los Angeles, out of which developed the resolution that passed "that women have the right to control over her own sexuality and to choose her own life-style," says Martin. In 1973, Martin was elected to NOW's national board, the first out lesbian to hold that post. In that position, Martin was able to enact significant changes in the organization, including the establishment of a grievance committee to deal with complaints of discrimination within NOW, and

a rule change allowing NOW committees and task forces to choose their own leaders and members. Martin served on the board from 1973 – 1974, and co-chaired the national task force on battered women and household violence from 1975 – 1977. Martin is co-author, with Lyon, of *Lesbian/Woman* (Glide Publications, 1972), and author of *Battered Wives* (Glide Publications, 1976). She spent over 10 years speaking, writing and advocating for more and better organizational help and understanding for battered women. In 1976, Martin was appointed to the Commission on the Status of Women by Mayor George Moscone, a position she held for three years (also serving as chair). In 1977, she was a delegate from California to the International Women's Year Houston Conference. She was particularly involved in the passage of the sexual preference and violence against women planks of the National Women's Plan of Action recommendations, later presented to President Carter for implementation by congresswoman Bella Abzug. In 1989, Martin joined Old Lesbians Organizing for Change, and in 1995 was appointed as Senator Dianne Feinstein's delegate to the White House Conference on Aging. In February 2004, Martin and her partner of 51 years, Phyllis Lyon, were the first lesbian couple to be legally married in the United States, in a service that took place in San Francisco. Martin has received numerous awards and honors, including the Alice B. Toklas Memorial Democratic Club award, in recognition of her work for human rights (1981). Martin has one child. Archives: The Museum and Archives of the GLBT Historical Society, San Francisco, CA.   (ABS)

Martin, Diana S. – See Read, Diana Sue

Martin, Gloria Hermena (1916 – 1995) was an author, pioneer feminist and revolutionary. In Seattle in the 1960s, she joined forces with militant black women, including Mary Louise Williams, to organize Welfare recipients into the Aid to Dependent Children Motivated Mothers project. She helped unionize anti-poverty workers, was an early advocate of lesbian and gay rights, and served as executive director of the South King County Multi-Service Center. In 1966, she created a series of workshops, Women in Society, taught at Seattle's alternative Free University. In 1967, she joined Clara Fraser, Susan Stern and others to found Radical Women, the country's first socialist feminist women's organization. From 1968 – 1970, Martin was instrumental in the mobilization of low-income women that resulted in the legalization of abortion in Washington State three years before Roe v. Wade. Her book *Socialist Feminism: The First Decade 1966 – 76* (Freedom Socialist Publications, 1978) describes this and other efforts to unite the Old and New Left, and feminist and socialist values. From 1973 – 1978, Martin served as Freedom Socialist Party organizer—a time when the group morphed from a local to a national entity with a quarterly newspaper, the *Freedom*

Socialist. A tireless archivist of civil rights and collector of feminist memorabilia, Martin opened Shakespeare & Martin Booksellers with family members in 1980. In 1990, she was elected organizer of Radical Women's Seattle branch. Martin had eight children.

Martin, Jane Roland (1929 –) A professor of philosophy, Martin was an unemployed scholar at the Radcliffe Institute in 1971 – 1972 when she and three other women students formed Philosophy and Education Research Association. The group, which still (2005) exists, was created as a support forum to discuss the problems women were having in a male dominated field. In the mid 1970s, as a teacher in the philosophy department at the University of Massachusetts, Boston, Martin helped design a course on philosophy and feminism, which she then taught from 1979 until 1992, when she retired. Beginning in the mid 1980s, she also taught a course in feminist theory for the UMB women's studies concentration. In the mid 1970s, as a member of the Eastern Division of the APA, Martin was part of a series of informal discussions that led to the formation of the Society for Women in Philosophy. In the late 1970s, Martin called an informal meeting of the women members of the Philosophy of Education Society, which ultimately became the women's caucus of that group. In 1981, Martin served as president of the society. In 1980, having received a fellowship from the Bunting Institute of Radcliffe College, Martin began work on the place of women in the philosophy of education. In 1985, Yale University Press published *Reclaiming a Conversation: The Ideal of the Educated Woman*, which grew out of that work. Martin is the author of other works that look at the ways in which the field of educational thought changes when women are brought into it. These include *The Schoolhome: Rethinking Schools for Changing Families* (Harvard University Press); *Changing the Educational Landscape: Philosophy, Women, and Curriculum* (Routledge); *Coming of Age in Academe: Rekindling Women's Hopes and Reforming the Academy* (Routledge); and *Cultural Miseducation: Toward a Democratic Solution* (Teachers College Press). She is (2005) working on two books that, although not explicitly feminist, are both informed by her ongoing research on women and education and her continuing commitment to feminism. Martin holds an A.B. and a Ph.D. from Radcliffe College, and an Ed.M. from Harvard. She has two children. (ABS)

Martin, Linda J. (1940 –) An emeritus professor of finance (2005) and a yoga instructor, Martin became active in NOW in 1972 when she served as secretary of the Baton Rouge, LA, chapter. She was a convener of the Shreveport/Bossier chapter of NOW (1972) and served as its president from 1972 – 1973. In 1973, Martin became the first president of LA State NOW. In addition, Martin has been a member of the NWPC and the LA State ERA coalition. She was an active lobbyist and public speaker for the ERA and the women's movement throughout the state, especially in the northern areas. A lifelong environmentalist, Martin is a member of the Sierra Club and the Nature Conservancy. Martin holds a B.A., an M.S., and an M.B.A. and D.B.A. (ABS)

Martin, Lois Ann – See Bronfman, Lois Ann Martin

Martin, Marcelina (1950 –) From 1969 to 1978, Martin contributed photographic images of women and lesbians living in Atlanta, Austin, Boulder, Washington, D.C., and New York to publications such as *Women of Power, Sage Women, Frontiers, Heresies, Southern Exposure, The Advocate, Calyx* and *Off Our Backs*. Martin's photography was featured in *The Great Speckled Bird*'s women's issue of October 1970 for the first Women's Festival in Atlanta. During the summer of 1972, she lived with the Furies Collective in Washington, D.C., while working as art director for the lesbian issue of *Motive* magazine. From 1991 – 1994, Martin produced *Lesbian Sacred Sexuality*, opening the door for photography books on lesbian sexuality. Her prints have been exhibited in Australia, Germany, Denmark and throughout the U.S. Martin's works are included in the Women's History Archives Collection at Harvard University and Brown University and are being used in online courses at the University of New Mexico, Columbia University and Purdue. One of the original founders in 1971 of the Atlanta Lesbian Feminist Alliance, Martin helped form the ALFA Omegas, the city's first out-lesbian softball team. Martin received her B.F.A. from Georgia State University in 1974. Archives: James C. Hormel Gay and Lesbian Center, San Francisco Public Library, CA. (ABS)

Martin, Nancy Skreko (1939 –) An artist, Martin was a founder (1974) of WomanKraft. Still in existence (2005), WomanKraft's mission is "to claim, empower and validate women artists." The members worked with other women artists groups, including the Arizona WCA, to facilitate a statewide show of women artists in 1975 at the Tucson Museum of Art, in conjunction with International Women's Year. More recently, they have been involved in an international exchange show of Polish women photographers. Martin, whose work has been exhibited nationally and internationally, has had several specifically feminist shows. These include Women/Arizona, at the Tucson Museum of Art (1975); WomanKraft (a group show) at the University of Arizona (1975); Craftswoman as Artist, at the Woman's Art Center, San Francisco (1975); and Woman*Woman*Works, at the Woman's Building in Los Angeles (1980). In addition to her work as a feminist artist, Martin has been an ERA marcher and activist, a speaker and activist for the right to choose, a peace marcher, and a campaign worker for George McGovern as part of the United Farm Workers team. Martin holds a B.A. (1960) and M.A. (1968) from Bradley University, and was a scholarship student at the Art Institute of Chicago from 1950 – 1955. (ABS)

Martin, Wendy (1940 –) A professor of American literature and American studies and chair of the department of English at Claremont Graduate University (2005), Martin describes herself as being "part of the generation that pioneered the field of feminist criticism and history and made it possible for the work and accomplishments of women to be studied with the same seriousness and intensity as the work of men." Martin became an active feminist in 1968 as a graduate student at the University of California, Davis. After moving to New York City to be an assistant professor at Queens College, she published "Seduced and Abandoned: The American Heroine in American Fiction," which appeared in Gornick and Moran's *Woman in Sexist Society*. In the early 1970s, she taught a course called The Feminist Movement in America from the Colonial Times to the Present. In 1972–1973, she was hired "to bring feminism to Stanford University," where she taught the first course on women writers. Also in 1972, Martin founded *Women's Studies: An Interdisciplinary Journal*, which she continues (2005) to edit. Among Martin's published works are *An American Sisterhood: Feminist Writing from the Colonial Times to the Present* (1972); *An American Triptych: Anne Bradstreet, Emily Dickinson and Adrienne Rich* (1984); *New Essays on the Awakening* (1988); *We Are the Stories We Tell: The Best Short Stories by North American Women Since 1945* (1990); *The Beacon Book of Essays by Contemporary American Women* (1997); *The Cambridge Companion to Emily Dickinson* (2003); *More Stories We Tell: The Best Contemporary Short Stories by North American Women* (Pantheon, 2004); and *The Art of the Short Story* (Houghton Mifflin, 2005). Martin, who has one child, is also author of numerous articles and reviews of women writers. She holds a B.A. (1962) and Ph.D. (1968) from the University of California, Davis.   (ABS)

Martineau, Barbara Halpern – See Halprin, Sara

Martinez, Elizabeth ("Betita") (1925 –) (also known as Elizabeth Sutherland) An activist since 1960, Martinez has spent 10 years in each of three movements: the black civil rights struggle, where she was on the staff of the Student Nonviolent Coordinating Committee; the Chicano *movimiento*, when she lived in New Mexico for eight years; and the Left's efforts to build a revolutionary party in San Francisco, where she lives now (2005). Says Martinez, "The two causes, racism and feminism, cannot honestly be divided—although some would have it otherwise." Martinez "looked hard at the sexism in the *movimiento* and knew a Chicana feminism needed to be born." Martinez has published six books on these struggles, including *500 Years of Chicano History and De Colores Means All of Us: Latina Views for a Multi-Colored Century*. Her most recent work is *500 Years of Chicana Women's History* (2006). She is co-founder, with Phil Hutchings, of the Institute for MultiRacial Justice in San Francisco, a resource center to help build alliances among

people of color and combat divisions. She has also taught women's studies in the California State University system. Martinez has one child.   (ABS)

Martinez, Inez (1939 –) was a co-founder of Half of Brooklyn (1970), a community organization in Park Slope, NY. She developed a course on women and literature in the early 1970s at Kingsborough Community College, and in 1974 was a co-organizer of a three-day conference on women's liberation at KCC. She was co-director of women's studies at KCC from 1995–2003. In the late 1990s, she twice served as co-instructor of a women's studies pro-seminar at CUNY. Martinez was an organizer against the Vietnam War and chaired the environmental education committee at KCC. She served on the executive committee of the University Faculty Senate of CUNY and was one of the founders and the first chair of the Community College Caucus of the UFS. She also served on the KCC College Council and represented those attempting to reinstate faculty responsibility for educational decisions at the college. Martinez is the author of "So You Want Sisters to Unite?" published in *Women: A Journal of Liberation* (1972). A professor of English literature, Martinez earned her B.S. and M.A. from St. Louis University, and her Ph.D. from the University of Wisconsin, Madison.   (ABS)

Martinez, Virginia (1949 –) As a member of the women's law caucus of DePaul University College of Law, Martinez lobbied the school to be more sympathetic to the needs of women students. She asked for more stalls in the women's room, the elimination of sexist language from classrooms, and more classes of interest to women. A co-founder of the Latino Law Student Association, Martinez was one of the first two Latina attorneys in Illinois when she began to practice in 1975. In 1976, Martinez entered an internship program with the Mexican American Legal Defense & Educational Fund. She litigated the first re-districting cases on behalf of Latino voters in Chicago wards and IL legislative districts. She fought for and won victories that led to Latinos being elected to the City Council and State Legislature. Martinez, who was born in Chicago, has two children. She earned her J.D. from DePaul University College of Law, and today (2005) is director of a university-based collaborative leadership-training program.   (ABS)

Marting, Diane Elaine (1952 –) While at Ohio State University, Marting was the only undergraduate in a group that filed sex discrimination papers against the university (1974) for its support of men's sports and male employees unequally to women's sports and female employees. The group was eventually given start-up funds for a gender studies research center that continues today (2005). Now a professor at the University of Mississippi, Oxford, Marting has published a series of books on women writers in Spanish and is active in women's studies programs.

Her books include *Spanish-American Women Writers: A Bio-Bibliographical Source Book* (Greenwood Press, 1990) and *The Sexual Woman in Latin American Literature: Dangerous Desires* (University Press of Florida, 2001). Marting holds a B.A., M.A. and a Ph.D. (ABS)

Marvin, Shirley Green (1922 –) Attending an early organizing meeting of the NWPC in Washington, D.C., Marvin was encouraged to establish a chapter in her home state, Louisiana. She subsequently helped found the Baton Rouge chapter and served in numerous leadership capacities, including VP of the local and state caucus and national secretary. "Although I received hate calls about mixing races at meetings in my home, a memorable moment occurred there when two women realized that their grandmothers had both lived on the same plantation in White Castle—one as a slave and one as its mistress." Marvin, who co-chaired the IWY conference committee for LA, was also involved in early CR in NOW and worked on the ERA, lobbying a highly resistant LA Legislature. In 2000, she was national secretary of the WPC and an active state and local board member. Marvin, who has three children, holds a B.A. from Wellesley and an M.A. from Louisiana State University. Archives: Radcliffe Women's Center, Cambridge, MA. (ABS)

Maryam – See Lowen, Marilyn

Mason, Marcia L. (1932 –) Mason was at a Friends General Conference Quaker Gathering in Beria, KY, in 1976 where she was part of a group "demonstrating with a hastily painted ERA bedsheet at the main intersection. After a short time, the police made us move back onto the college grounds. Through that activism, I met many women involved with the LWV, and returned home to become totally involved with the League." Mason joined the LWV in the late 1970s and served as president of the Methuen (MA) chapter. In 1987, Mason traveled with the Women's Peace Caravan to raise consciousness about the United Nations Convention for the Elimination of all Forms of Discrimination Against Women. She also organized an ad hoc committee to get the cities of Burlington and Montpelier, as well as the state of Vermont, to pass resolutions supporting the Senate foreign relations committee to approve and release CEDAW so that the Senate might ratify it. This started a movement throughout the U.S. for other cities and states to do the same. From 1989 – 1993, Mason worked to establish OVUM PACIS: The Women's International Peace University, including obtaining NGO status at the United Nations for the school. In the early 1990s she was a member of Women for Meaningful Summits in Washington, D.C., and was one of 35 women who met with Soviet women in NYC and Washington to create a paper for the summit between Reagan and Gorbachev at Reykjavik, Iceland. At the same time, Mason was involved in Peace Watch near Austin, TX. Mason is (2005) an active supporter of numerous women's organizations, including AAUW, LWV, NOW, WILPF and the OWL. Mason, who has one child, holds a B.S. and an M.A. (ABS)

Mason, Trudy L. (1942 –) As an undergraduate at Wheaton College, Mason campaigned for President John F. Kennedy, formed the Wheaton College Young Democrats, and in that role escorted Eleanor Roosevelt for her last college speaking engagement in 1962. After graduating cum laude in 1963, Mason was a founding member of the New York Women's Caucus, a press secretary for Geraldine Ferraro's vice presidential campaign (1984), and was appointed to the NYC Commission on the Status of Women (1978). She also served on the American Jewish Congress Commission on Women's Equality, which she represented at the United Nations Women's Conference in Beijing (1995) and at the first International Jewish Feminist Conference in Jerusalem (1987). She worked with her "political godmother," Bella Abzug, on the Anita Hill—Women Tell the Truth Conference. Mason was cited by the U.S. House of Representatives with special Congressional recognition for "70 Women Who Made a Difference"..."for outstanding contribution and commitment to the struggle for equality and women's rights (1999)." A communications consultant, Mason is on the executive council of the Democratic National Committee's Women's Leadership Forum and has been the New York Democratic State Committee woman, representing Manhattan's Upper East side since 1990. Archives: Wheaton College, Norton, MA. (ABS)

Massenburg, Katherine B.
  – See Rinehart, Katherine Black

Matson, Jana – See Everett, Jana G.

Matson, Rosemary (1917 –) A humanist and global feminist, Matson began fighting for civil rights in the 1960s and then, after reading *The Feminine Mystique*, began to see the world through the eyes of a feminist. In 1980, she co-founded Continuing the Peace Dialogue, a grassroots global network that conducted seminars to promote gender equality. Realizing that Russian women and American women shared the same joys, sorrows and concerns, she also created "friendship trips," ferrying groups of Americans interested in peace to Russia for more than two decades. She has also worked for the rights of women in the U.S.; to end the violations of women's human rights "in the name of tradition"; and to achieve parity in wages and responsibilities for men and women. The recipient of many awards, she was honored by the United Nations Association as a champion of women's and human rights, receiving the 6th annual Pearl Ross Feminist Activist Award in 2000. She was also commended as an outstanding woman in Monterey County (CA) by the Commission on the Status of Women, and as a humanist heroine by the American Humanist Association. (ABS)

Matthews, Patricia Ann (1948 –) (also known as Pat Miller and Pat Solo) A member of the Chicago Women's Liberation Rock Band, Matthews performed throughout the Midwest and on several East Coast campuses, and participated in making the album Mountain Moving Day with the New Haven Women's Liberation Rock Band in 1973. Matthews helped formulate many position papers written by various focus groups of the CWLU, spoke at Chicago high schools on gay rights, gave car maintenance clinics, and participated in Witch actions against the Vietnam War. From 1981 – 2003, Matthews worked as a ranger naturalist at a major water company in the East San Francisco Bay area. As a union steward, she participated in contract negotiations and, in the mid 1980s, succeeded in having the district include in its definition of "immediate family" anyone listed as primary beneficiary on the employee's life insurance. Says Matthews, "After years of work, this initial definition ultimately resulted in successful inclusion of domestic partners into the benefit and retirement systems." (ABS)

Mauer, Joelle (1931 –) A Roman Catholic nun, Sister Joelle was a charter member of NOW in Baton Rouge, LA, in 1969. Because she was a nun in the women's movement, she was asked to speak at Louisiana State University. She also lobbied for the ERA with the Louisiana Legislature, "unfortunately, to no avail." A pastoral musician, Sister Joelle holds an M.A. degree. (ABS)

Maurer, Susan Hazel (1940 –) A retired social worker, Maurer planned the NY NOW sexuality conference in 1973. She also started NY NOW's task force on battered wives, made it safer to talk about sex; raised issues around decriminalizing prostitution; campaigned for reproductive rights; and helped women poets get published. In 1974, Maurer served as chair of NOW's task force on reproduction and its control. She was also chair of the psychology committee (1980), and served as assistant women's adviser, special services to children for the Beame administration, NYC. Maurer is the author of *By the Blue Light of the Morning Glory* (Linear Arts, 1996). She earned her A.B. from Barnard College (1962) and her M.S.W. from St. Louis University (1973). (ABS)

Mazeika, Margaret Hall – See Hall, Peggy W.

Mazzello, Carolyn (1941 – 2004) was a co-creator of X12, the pioneer feminist art exhibition for living artists in NYC. Planning for the exhibition began in 1969; the opening was in 1970. Mazzello, who had one son, attended the Parsons School of Design and the Academie Di Bella Arte in Rome.

Mazzone-Clementi, Vivien – See Leone, Vivien

McAlister, Linda Lopez (1939 –) A retired professor of philosophy and women's studies, McAlister was an ac-

tivist in the U.S. and Germany. She was a Sr. Fulbright Researcher at the University of Wurzburg, Germany, from 1973 – 1974. There she and Dr. Wiebke Schrader called the first meeting ever of German women philosophers. From that meeting, the Assoziation von Philosophinnen in Deutschland was created, which later became the International Association of Women Philosophers. In 1982, McAlister became dean of the University of South Florida's Fort Myers Campus, but "was removed from my position by the USF administration and kicked upstairs to Tallahassee when it was rumored (accurately) that I am a lesbian." She was special assistant to the vice chancellor for academic programs of the State University System of Florida from 1985 – 1987. In 1987, McAlister joined the faculty in the department of women's studies at USF, and from 1990 – 1995 was general editor of *Hypatia: A Journal of Feminist Philosophy*. She served as co-editor from 1995 – 1998. In 1990, she began doing movie reviews on Tampa's weekly feminist radio magazine, "The Women's Show." In 1998, McAlister organized the 8th Symposium of the International Association of Women Philosophers. Held in Boston, it was the first to take place outside of Europe. In 2000, McAlister moved to New Mexico and became active in various groups, including working to educate people about domestic violence. She served as editor of *Hypatia's Daughters: 1,500 Years of Women Philosophers* (Indiana University Press, 1996), and is the author of "Feminist Cinematic Depictions of Violence Against Women: Three Representational Strategies," published in *Krieg/War* (1997); and "Feminism Meets History of Philosophy," published in *APA Newsletter on Feminism and Philosophy* (Spring 1996). She earned her A.B. from Barnard (1961) and her Ph.D. from Cornell (1969). (ABS)

McAllister, Ada Clare (1945 –) An actress and director, McAllister joined the Women's Center on Manhattan's West Side in 1970, and participated in the takeover of the 5th Street Women's Building. As a graduate student at Goddard College she taught in the women's studies program and lived in the feminist dorm. After graduation, McAllister spent four years with the Rhode Island Feminist Theater, where she did productions on women's health issues and violence against women. In 1977, she left RIFT and moved to Washington, where she spoke publicly about the ERA. Archives: Wellesley College, Wellesley, MA. (ABS)

McAnaney, Margaret Mary ("Maggie") (1933 –) served as president of the Sacramento, CA, chapter of NOW in the 1980s, and a founder of NOW chapters in Salinas, San Louis Obispo and Moonpark. She also served as president of the San Luis Obispo Women's Resource Center, and as administrative assistant to the director of the CSUS Women's Center. In 1984, she bought a house in Sacramento and transformed it into a boarding house for women—an affordable "stopping place while they are on their way to greater things." At the same time, she ran the Women's Information Referral Service, and later formed Rowdy Old Women to bring attention to the plight of older women, especially their financial troubles. McAnaney, who has four children, was also a supporter of the ERA and the Farmworkers in Salinas. (ABS)

McAulay, Mary Henry (1930 –) As a young school-teacher, McAulay challenged her principal, who had put into writing "Hire only male teachers." Her case was taken by the Commission on Human Rights in the early and mid 1970s, and, she says, "I won big time. It made *The New York Times*." She continued to bring cases to court, counseling over 20 teachers "who were also causing 'trouble.' I won every case. Our union never won any!" In 1979, she left teaching and founded Urban Ventures, a Bed & Breakfast agency in NYC that she ran for 12 years. The agency, which had 800 B&Bs in NYC, also encouraged other women in the U.S. and in Canada to set up B&Bs. McAulay, who has four children, earned her M.A. from Columbia University. She is the author of *Prudence's Progress*, a 1920s tale of a woman's success in business in the wake of blackmail, murder and skullduggery. (ABS)

McCarthy, Beverly Fitch (1933 –) (also known as Beverly Bosque) founded the San Jaoquin County Commission on the Status of Women in 1974, and served as chair for 14 years. In 1975, she founded the Susan B. Anthony Award for San Jaoquin County Women of Achievement. In addition, McCarthy served as president of her California chapter of NOW for a year, and was a CA delegate to the National Women's Conference in Houston (1977). She was a member of the board of the National Association of Commissions for Women (NACW) from 1977 – 1978, and was state president of California Women in Higher Education from 1977 – 1979. While a member of the Stockton (CA) city council, she introduced a resolution on decriminalizing prostitution (which failed 1-6). She was active in Planned Parenthood and served as an escort at abortion clinics. A retired community college teacher and counselor, McCarthy has two children. She earned her B.A. from the University of California at Berkeley, and her M.A. from Stanford University, Palo Alto. Archives: Holt-Atherton Library, University of the Pacific, Stockton, CA. (ABS)

McCarthy, Eugene Joseph (1916 – 2005) Senator McCarthy introduced the ERA in the U.S. Senate in 1967. He had 37 co-sponsors for S.3567. That year, when McCarthy announced his intention to run in the Democratic primary against President Johnson, thousands of young people who believed in his ideals and intellectualism and supported his opposition to the Vietnam War rallied behind him. McCarthy stunned the nation by upending the re-election campaign of President Lyndon Johnson. Nonetheless, he lost the nomination to Hubert Humphrey. McCarthy served five terms in the U.S. House of Representatives (1949 – 1959) and two terms in the U.S. Senate. He graduated from St. John's University (1935) and the University of Minnesota (1939). He had four children. Archives: Minnesota Historical Society, St. Paul, MN.

McClanahan, Mabel (1918 –) In the mid 1960s, McClanahan served as national president of BPW. A native of Appleton, WI, McClanahan stressed the importance of women having goals other than getting married, at a time when marriage was typically the main objective of most young women.

McClish, Vernita Ellen – See Nemec, Vernita Ellen

McClure, Kit (1951 –) (also known as Kathleen McClure) Bandleader, saxophonist and originator of the Kit McClure Band, McClure was accepted at Yale (1969) as part of the university's first undergraduate class of women. While at Yale, she joined The New Haven Women's Liberation Rock Band. In 1982, her vision of a band of women jazz musicians became a reality as the Kit McClure Band, which made its debut at the Ritz in NYC. The band was soon noticed by the recording industry and put on the payroll of Island Records to prepare a show with the late rock star Robert Palmer. This show toured two years later, playing sold-out houses at Radio City Music Hall, Garden State Arts Center and similar venues across the Northeast. Eight tours of Japan quickly ensued, with time out to produce the CD Some Like It Hot (Redhot Records). The Band's second CD release, Burning, also on Redhot Records, was produced in 1996 by jazz legend Teo Macero. In recognition and celebration of the achievements of women in jazz, the band transcribed historical arrangements and compositions from the International Sweethearts of Rhythm, a popular all-women big band of the 1940s. The resulting recordings are The Sweethearts Project, on Redhot records, released in 2004, and The Sweethearts Revisited (2005). McClure graduated from Yale in 1975, then moved to NYC to attend Manhattan School of Music. (ABS)

McConahay, Shirley Frey (1940 –) Living in New Haven (CT) in the early 1970s, McConahay was a member of the New Haven and Western Connecticut feminists. In 1971, she coordinated a statewide, four-day women's arts festival, Metamorphosis I, held at a church on the New Haven Green. She also taught human sexuality at the University of Bridgeport (CT), and was the keynote speaker at NYC NOW's first conference on sexuality. After moving to North Carolina, she researched women's history for the NC Dept. of Education, which resulted in a book about a Revolutionary War woman soldier, Deborah Sampson. An artist, McConahay runs (2005) a nonprofit program teaching soft sculpture to indigenous women, including Lakota, Chippewa and Navajo. McConahay, who has three children, was also active in the peace and environmental movements. She marched frequently against the

Vietnam War and did draft counseling at Santa Monica City College. McConahay earned her B.A. from Transylvania University and her M.A. from Southern Connecticut State University. (ABS)

McCorvey, Norma (1947 –) was the anonymous "Roe" in Roe v. Wade, the 1973 Supreme Court decision that made it legal for women to have abortions. McCorvey does not consider herself a feminist, and in 1995 became an advocate against Roe v. Wade. Historically, however, she was part of a case supported by feminists. In March 1970, two lawyers first argued a case in a Federal District Court in Dallas, which sought to overturn a Texas statute making it illegal for any woman to have an abortion except for the purpose of saving a woman's life. McCorvey, then 25 years old and pregnant, wanted an abortion that was illegal under the laws of Texas, where McCorvey lived. Contacted by former classmate Linda Coffee, Sarah Weddington successfully argued the case. A Federal Court in Texas declared the Texas law unconstitutional, but refused to grant an injunction against its enforcement, so McCorvey carried her baby to term. Weddington argued the case in the Supreme Court in October 1972. Three months later, seven of the nine Supreme Court Justices affirmed the right of women to a legal abortion.

McDaniel, Judith Adair (1943 –) taught the first woman-focused courses at Tufts University (1971); at Middlebury College; and at Skidmore College (1974 – 1983) as assistant professor and rotating head of the women's studies program. She attended the Feminist Institute (Sagaris) at Lyndon State College in Vermont. Her political career includes serving as chair of the gay caucus of the Modern Language Association, 1975 – 1977; as part of the Women's Encampment for a Future of Peace With Justice, Seneca Army Depot, NY, 1983; member of the Witness for Peace group on Rio San Juan in Nicaragua, 1985; and as director of the Peace Unit, American Friends Service Committee, 2000 – 2002. In 1978, McDaniel co-founded, with Maureen Brady, the lesbian feminist press Spinsters Ink. Its publications include Audre Lorde's *Cancer Journals* (1979). McDaniel's writings include *November Woman, Poems* (Loft Press); *Sanctuary: A Journey* (Firebrand, 1987); *Metamorphosis: Reflections on Recovery* (Firebrand, 1989); *Just Say Yes* (Firebrand, 1991); *The Lesbian Couples Guide* (HarperCollins, 1995); *Yes I Said Yes I Will*, a novel (Naiad Press, 1996); and *Taking Risks*, poems (Rising Tides Press, 2001). McDaniel earned a Ph.D. from Tufts University. (ABS)

McDaniel, Mary (1946 –) In September 1970, McDaniel was a kindergarten teacher at the McDonough School in Middletown, CT. In mid-October, she learned that a new teachers' contract contained a clause mandating that pregnant teachers vacate their jobs in their fifth month. McDaniel, who was pregnant at the time, decided to protest on the grounds that when she'd become pregnant, the old contract (which did not require resignation) had been in effect. When the school superintendent responded that, "Rules are rules," McDaniel appealed to the Middletown board of education. Her ob/gyn, Virginia Stuermer, wrote a letter of support calling such policies "arbitrary and artificial." *The Middletown Press* derided the board. But still, McDaniel's request was denied and she hired a lawyer and appealed again. At the second hearing, two dozen parents presented a petition of support from 57 of the 61 children in McDaniel's class. Shirley Byciewicz, working for the Connecticut Civil Liberties Union, added her efforts to take the case to arbitration. On April 2, arbitrator John Hogan heard the two sides and on April 26 found the contract clause "contravenes public policy as embodied in Title VII of the Civil Rights Act," thereupon saving not only McDaniel's job, but all other teachers' right to work. (ABS)

McDonald, Eva (1917 – 1997) was a lifelong campaigner for women's rights, a leader in the fight to pass the ERA, and one of the founders of NOW in Alton, IL. In the late 1970s, she helped organize the silent vigil outside the IL General Assembly in Springfield as lawmakers considered the ERA. When it failed, McDonald continued to work tirelessly for women's rights, despite ill health. She helped establish the Oasis Women's Center in Alton (1976), a haven for battered women, and later organized the shelter's Caravan resale shop. McDonald also led the teacher's union in Alton for many years and was active in the Women's History Coalition. In 1976, she ran unsuccessfully as a Republican candidate for the IL House, campaigning for the ERA and reduced taxes for seniors, among other issues. She was the recipient of numerous awards, including the Alice Paul Award from the Alton/Edwardsville Chapter of NOW. She was also named Woman of Distinction by the Alton YMCA (1995) and the AAUW (1984). McDonald retired from Alton School District 11 in 1976 after teaching for 39 years.

McDonald, Noreen Forde (1941 –) A member of CR groups in Long Island (NY) in the early 1970s, McDonald served as co-chair of South Shore NOW's childcare committee (1973 – 1974) and took part in a sit-in at Suffolk Community College to establish day care for children. She also advocated for a mall tot-lot. She was a member of the Women's Center in Islip from the mid 1970s forward. A published poet, McDonald served as emcee and editor of Islip Town Poetry Festivals (1975 – 1978 and 1982 – 1983), and editor of *Women's Work: Poems by GG Murray et al* (1975). McDonald, who has two children, earned her M.A. from SUNY Stony Brook (1992). (ABS)

McDonald, Pamela – See Astarte, Pamela Ann

McEldowney, Carol (1943 – 1973) A student at the University of Michigan in the early 1960s, McEldowney joined SDS and became part of its leadership. She also worked in the SDS Economic Research and Action Project in Cleveland organizing Welfare mothers. In 1967, she was one of a group of 10 activists on a month-long visit to North Vietnam, during which she wrote *Hanoi Journal*. She moved to the Boston area in 1969, became immersed in the women's movement, and joined Bread and Roses. Also that year, she co-authored, with Rosemary Poole, "A Working Paper on the Media." Published in *Women, A Journal of Liberation*, the paper criticized the mass media and stressed the importance of strengthening the emerging women's communication network. McEldowney was also co-editor of the chapter on self-defense for *Our Bodies, Ourselves*. Believing that women should do things for themselves, she worked with a group to develop a series of classes taught by women to women, creating a catalog of teachers and classes, and herself teaching self-defense and auto mechanics. She participated in the occupation of a Harvard building in the spring of 1971, demanding a women's center, and helped the center to become a reality. During this time she came out as a lesbian and became active in the gay liberation movement, going to lesbian bars and encouraging the women in them to become politically involved. McEldowney also participated in one of the first women's martial arts exhibitions in the country in Boston during the 1973 International Women's Day. McEldowney was killed in a car crash at the age of 30. Archives: Healey Library, University of Massachusetts, Boston, MA.

McGreivy, Susan Douglas (1939 –) was a founding member of the Los Angeles Lesbian Feminists, and was one of four lesbians who, in 1970, went public on TV, WETA Los Angeles. She was the first member of the Susan B. Anthony coven number one, founded by Z Budapest; and was a founder of the first West Coast lesbian conference, the first lesbian feminist speakers bureau, and the first West Coast female sexuality conference. In addition, she was a founder of the Laguna Beach chapter of NOW and the Orange County Lesbian Feminists, and served as chair of the State of California abortion rights task force. She was staff attorney, Lesbian and Gay Community Services Center (1978–1979) and staff attorney, ACLU of Southern California (1979 – 1988). She served on the legal committee of Los Angeles NOW; as chair of the Los Angeles Anti-Briggs Initiative committee; and as founder, Harvey Milk Lesbian and Gay Democratic Club. She was also a founder of Lawyers for Human Rights and Lambda Lawyers. In 1987, she was co-chair of the Los Angeles committee for the 1987 lesbian and gay march on Washington, and was a member of the national steering committee. In 1956, McGreivy was a member of the United States Olympic Swimming Team, and from 1962 –1965, was a coach of the Thailand Olympic Swimming Team, U.S Peace Corps volunteer. McGreivy, who has two children, is a member of the California Bar Association, the Women Lawyers Association, and Lawyers for Human Rights. She earned her B.A. from Northwestern University

(1961) and her J.D. from Western State University College of Law (1977). (ABS)

McGrew, Clara Elizabeth – See Johnson, Clara Elizabeth

McGuire, Christine – Magill, Rosalind M.

McIntyre, Mary Adelaide (1919 – 2003) A noted artist who sculptured massive stone monuments, McIntyre founded the Lafayette, LA, chapter of NOW in the early 1970s. The chapter's work centered on the ERA, the establishment of day care centers, and a national campaign for universal childcare supported by government. She was a resource specialist in art for the Louisiana State Dept. of Education (1974 – 1977). McIntyre pursued her art in many different media, including sculpture, stained glass, tapestries and murals. Her work can be found in churches and public institutions in the U.S., and especially throughout Louisiana. It has been exhibited widely in the U.S., and is in private collections here and in South America. A native of Michigan and a graduate of Marygrove College in Detroit, she also studied church architecture and liturgy at the University of Notre Dame.

McKinney-Drake, Paula – See Hurt, Paula

McMenemy, Jack W. (1944 –) A retired routeman for a milk company, McMenemy was involved in CR groups for men and women in New York, and was a member of the masculine mystique committee. He attended the weekend-long Masculine Mystique Conference at New York University organized by Warren Farrell, and also worked on the divorce hotline giving information and referrals. He has two children. (ABS)

McMenemy, Teri M. (1946 –) As chair of her NOW chapter's marriage and divorce committee (1970s), McMenemy created the first divorce information center for women in Suffolk County, NY. Located in the Women's Center, Oakdale, NY, it provided women with referrals to feminist lawyers and counselors. It also had a speakers program to inform women about their legal rights; a hotline (which was in McMenemy's home); and a directory of professionals to help women in the transition from married to single. The group running the center also picketed Family Court to enforce child-support rulings, and accompanied women who were going through the various stages of divorce proceedings to court, offering information and emotional support. The group also held CR groups for men and women together. McMenemy, who has two children, earned her B.A. from St. Joseph's College, and her certificate in Interior Design from the New York Institute of Technology. (ABS)

McNaron, Toni Ann (1937 –) helped design and then chaired the women's studies program at the University of Minnesota, where she was a professor from 1973 – 1976.

(ABS) indicates Approved By Subject

From 1980–1982, she served as director of the Center for Feminist Studies at the university. In addition, McNaron designed the LGBT program at the university and served as its first director (1997–1999). A lecture series sponsored by that center was formed after McNaron's retirement (2001) and named in her honor, The McNaron Lecture on LGBT Culture and the Arts. Earlier in her career, McNaron was part of a collective in Wisconsin that established a school for women and children. Housed in a converted barn, the school, Maiden Rock Institute, lasted from 1970–1975. From 1972–1976, McNaron was co-editor of a lesbian-feminist journal, *So's Your Old Lady*. McNaron is the author of *I Dwell in Possibility: A Memoir* (the Feminist Press, 1992), and *Poisoned Ivy: Lesbian and Gay Academics Confront Homophobia* (Temple University Press, 1996). She was co-editor, with Bonnie Zimmerman, of *New Lesbian Studies—Into the 21st Century* (the Feminist Press, 1996). McNaron holds a B.A. from the University of Alabama, an M.A. from Vanderbilt University, and a Ph.D. from the University of Wisconsin. (ABS)

McNeely, Juanita (1936 –) McNeely, a painter, made important contributions to the feminist movement by addressing taboo subjects—the myths surrounding monthly bleeding, the horror of pre-abortion days, birth and the violence of bringing life into the world, the close alliance with death and women's sexuality, women as the active agent. McNeely moderated a panel of women at the Friday night meeting of NYC's Figurative Alliance at the Educational Alliance, which until the late 1960s had been an all-male affair. At that meeting, only women hung their works, and although "it was an explosive and hostile evening, the all-male tradition was forever broken," she says. In the early 1970s, McNeely met with a group of women (Anita Steckel, Hannah Wilke, Louise Bourgeois, Joan Semmel, Martha Edelheit and Anne Sharp) whose art was considered erotic, sexual or "vaginal iconography." They decided to exhibit and speak collectively. "Sexual imagery had been created by men for men. The history of modern art was being challenged and changed by women. Sensuousness and sexuality, as depicted by women, were being used by women to make their own sexual and political statements. We were no longer alone." McNeely, whose work has been exhibited internationally, studied at Washington University, St. Louis School of Fine Arts, and Southern Illinois University. She received grants for painting from the New York Council for the Arts, the Adolph and Esther Gottlieb Foundation, and the Jackson Pollack-Lee Krasner Foundation, among others. Her work is in numerous private collections, including Women Artists, Bryn Mawr College; Art Collection, National Museum of Art History, China; and Palacio de las Bella Artes, Mexico City. (ABS)

McNiel, Maura Anderson (1921 –) was a founding director of the Women's Center (Dallas, TX) in 1973. She helped organize its Rape Crisis Center (1973), the Women's Coalition, and a shelter for battered women (Family Place, 1979). Because the group could not start a bank, they formed the Southwest Credit Union. In 1972, McNiel made 72 speeches "to every imaginable group in macho Dallas." She also worked and lobbied for the ERA, and in 1975 was an NGO delegate from the Dallas United Nations group to the IWY in Mexico City. She also became Texas co-convener of the National Women's Agenda that year, and helped persuade the mayor to establish a Commission on the Status of Women, to which she was appointed. McNiel, who helped start the TX WPC, was also active in many political campaigns, including Ann Richards for Governor and Annette Strauss, who became the first woman mayor of Dallas. In 1978 a dinner honoring women who helped women was established and in 1986 its prestigious award was renamed "The Maura." In 1985 McNiel was a founding member of the Dallas Women's Foundation, one of the first in the country. Also a member of NOW and WEAL, McNiel has four children (one deceased). She earned her B.A. from the University of Minnesota. Archives: Archives of Women of the Southwest, Southern Methodist University, Dallas, TX. (ABS)

McNish, Mary Ellen (1946 –) (also known as Mary Ellen Harkins) General secretary/CEO of the American Friends Service Committee in Philadelphia (2005), McNish has worked consistently for women's equal rights and reproductive rights, and at age 37 began concentrating on women and leadership. She initiated an award for women in business at the YWCA in Camdem, NJ, called Success by Design, that honored not only women, but also companies that have women/family-friendly policies. Earlier, she was a co-founder of the Northeast Philadelphia chapter of NOW; president of the Bucks County, PA, Chapter of NOW; a member of NOW's PA state council; and a member of the coordinating committee of the PA NOW state conference. She also served on the women's committee of Philadelphia's Yearly Quaker Meeting, and was a coordinator of the Friends General Conference women's center. McNish participated in all national and local marches for the ERA and freedom of choice, and served as VP of Planned Parenthood in Maryland. She was a member of the coordinating committee of Maryland for Choice, a coalition of organizations that passed a referendum codifying Roe v. Wade into MD law. In addition, she was a founding member of the Overground Railroad, a network of 3,000 Quakers and other people of faith organized to transport women across state lines should Roe v. Wade be overturned. McNish, who has one child, was also active in the peace and ecology movements. She earned her B.S. from East Stroudsburg University (1968) and her M.S. from Johns Hopkins University (1993). Archives: American Friends Service Committee, Philadelphia, PA. (ABS)

McQueen, Kathy – See Kendall, Kathryn

McQuillan, Patricia Fogerty (1925 – 1974) An ex-Marine and founder and director of Catholics for a Free Choice (1972), McQuillan received a great deal of press when she had herself crowned Pope on the steps of St. Patrick's Cathedral (1974) in NYC on the anniversary of the U.S. Supreme Court decision on abortion. The action countered publicity by Right to Life demonstrators in Washington the same day. McQuillan, who spoke around the country as a Catholic feminist, described Catholic women as being among the most oppressed and ghettoized in the world. Unflagging in the face of terminal cancer, McQuillan, with the help of Joan Michel, organized the first New York Conference on Marriage and Divorce (1974), which drew 1,000 women, plus attorneys, judges and legislators. On McQuillan's death, friends sought a service at a Catholic Church in Manhattan. "One East Side Catholic Church finally allowed us to have a service if we promised not to mention abortion or women in the priesthood," says Jacqui Ceballos.

Mead, Joy Ann – See Alwan, Joy Ann

Medlin, Joan Margaret – See Margaret, Joan

Mednick, Martha T. (1929 –) A professor at Howard University (1968 – 1994) when she retired, Mednick was an early teacher of the psychology of women and the psychology of gender, and developed some of the first courses on these topics. She focused her research on the issues of women and achievement, and in 1972 was a co-author (with Sandra Schwartz Tangri) of a special issue of the *Journal of Social Issues*, called *New Perspectives on the Psychology of Women*. This special issue later became a book by Mednick and Tangri called *Women and Achievement* (Hemisphere Press, 1975). In 1973, Mednick became first chair of the committee on women in psychology of the APA, and was an organizer and later president of the Division of the Psychology of Women of the APA. She was a co-founder of the *Psychology of Women Quarterly* (1975) and served for several years on its editorial board. A longtime member of NOW, Mednick became president of the Psychological Study of Social Issues division of the APA in 1980. Mednick earned a B.S. from City College of New York in 1950 and a Ph.D. from Northwestern University in 1955. (ABS)

Meek, Carrie (1926 –) was instrumental in helping women in the black community join the woman's movement for equality. Meek, whose grandfather was a slave, was born in Tallahassee, FL. Starting as a maid, she sought education at a local community college and then graduated from Florida A&M University (1946). Because African Americans could not attend graduate school in Florida at that time, she went to the University of Michigan, graduating with an M.S. in 1948. Meek helped found the NWPC in 1971 and worked aggressively to help women get elected both locally and at the state level. She

was elected to the FL House of Representatives. In 1992, she was elected to the U.S. House of Representatives from Florida's 17th Congressional District. In 1992, Meek and Corrine Brown of Jacksonville were the first two female black lawmakers elected to represent Florida in Congress since Reconstruction. She worked closely with Nikki Beare (lobbyist for the AAUW) to get the Florida Commission on the Status of Women and the Florida Women's Hall of Fame established statutorily. Meek retired from Congress in 2003. Archives: Black Archives, Florida A&M University, Tallahassee, FL. (ABS)

Mehrhof, Barbara Viola (1942 –) was a member of NYRW, Redstockings and The Feminists, all in New York City. Mehrhof and Sheila Cronan were both social workers with the Bureau of Child Welfare when they went to the NOW demonstration against Colgate-Palmolive in the spring of 1968. They attended their first women's liberation meeting the next week. Also in 1968, Mehrhof attended the first Women's Liberation Conference, held outside Chicago; driving back to NY she and others talked about the anti-inaugural demonstrations planned for January 1969 and thought about the idea of giving back the vote, even calling Alice Paul for support. "She quite rightly declined," says Mehrhof. With Redstockings, Mehrhof participated in the Speak Out on Abortion in February 1969 and helped sew a large banner to drape on the Statue of Liberty proclaiming "Free Abortions for All Women." Unfortunately, the group never carried out the action. She contributed articles on equality in the women's movement, rape and prostitution to *Notes from the Second Year* and *Notes from the Third Year*. In 1976, Mehrhof was co-coordinator, with Florence Rush, of an ad hoc group known as the Circle of Support for Jane Alpert. At the end of that decade, Mehrhof was one of four coordinators of Women Against Pornography. The group conducted tours of the Times Square pornography district, held a conference and march in NYC, and spoke out on the issue at colleges and universities throughout the country. Mehrhof, a teacher with two stepchildren, holds a Ph.D. from New York University. (ABS)

Meier, Diane (1950 –) (also known as Diane Meier Spiegel) wanted to take mechanical drawing in high school (1963), but was refused; wanted to swim on the boys' team (1967), but wasn't allowed; and wanted a men's college to grant matriculating credits to those women who attended classes, but found "we weren't even on the books." Then along came the women's movement. In 1971, married to Martin Spiegel, one of the first men to claim (and win before the Illinois Supreme Court) conscientious-objector status on non-religious grounds against conscription to fight in Vietnam, Meier began teaching in Project Learn, the elementary offshoot of the Parkway School Without Walls in Philadelphia. She also helped to form one of the first CR groups in that city. That group in turn founded the city's first women's center (1971), which soon became a refuge for battered women. At the same time, Meier worked on the PA state committee for abortion reform with Mary Lou Tennyson. In New York City in 1973, Meier became PR director of NYC NOW. She worked intensively for a year on developing and presenting a program about the condition of rape, from definition to law enforcement, and left NOW after its completion. A marketing executive and writer, Meier's education includes courses at Princeton, University of Pennsylvania, New York University and the Negotiation Program at Harvard. (ABS)

Meisner, Myra Terry – See Terry, Myra

Melich, Tanya Marie (1936 –) is a political writer, consultant and analyst who has worked in coalition-building in both political parties and the women's movement. Her main areas of service have been the chronicling of the Reagan-Bush political backlash strategy against the women's movement; forcing a floor debate on abortion on national television at the 1976 GOP convention, and preserving GOP platform support for the Equal Rights Amendment; and providing a bipartisan framework for women's issues. Melich helped found the NWPC in New York City and New York State, and in 1972 worked to increase the number of women represented at the GOP national convention. There, Melich was successful on the inclusion of a women's plank that supported the ERA, women's pay equity and childcare. In 1973, she co-founded Republicans for Women's Issues, whose goal was passage of the feminist public policy issues advocacy, especially pro-choice positions, ERA and childcare. Her group lobbied in Albany and New York City. In 1974, Melich joined the National Women's Education Fund Board, the first national feminist organization with the specific goal of increasing the number of women elected and appointed to public office, serving on its board until 1983 and as president from 1980 – 1983. Melich worked on the executive committee of the NY State ERA campaign in 1975, and was the alternate delegate to the 1976 National GOP Convention, where she led the effort to protect the pro-choice position within the GOP platform. She worked throughout 1978 – 1980 to build a pro-choice Republican movement in NY and the nation; lobbied for the ERA extension and for pro-choice positions; and recruited and trained woman to run for office. Melich co-founded the Republican women's task force, which organized advocacy and training efforts for GOP women and the Republican family committee, a pro-choice organization of Republicans protecting Roe v. Wade and reproductive health legislation. Melich is author of *The Republican War Against Women, an Insider's Report from Behind the Lines*, 1996, which won the Gustavus Myers Center award as a an outstanding book on human rights in North America. Archives: M.E. Grenander Department of Special Collections and Archives, State University at Albany, NY. (ABS)

Melnick, Gisele (1935 – 2006) was an early member of Westchester, NY, NOW in the early 1970s. In 1975 she was a founder of the Yonkers Women's Task Force, which founded My Sister's Place, the Yonkers shelter for domestic violence. On the front lines protecting women's right to abortions, Melnick started "abortion coffees" in the 1970s to help erase the stigma facing those who had abortions. Most notably, she was among the leadership group that protected and defended the right of women to gain entry to the Dobbs Ferry Women's Health Pavilion when Operation Rescue repeatedly blocked their passage. She advocated changing penalties at the federal level for those who blocked passage; these penalties were later upgraded from misdemeanor to felony. She was a founder of the women's issues committee of the National Association of Social Workers.

Mendelson, Martha A. – See Ackelsberg, Martha A.

Mendenhall, Janice (1946 – 2001) worked to advance the rights of women in the public sphere throughout her career in the federal government. Mendenhall was national president of FEW, an organization established to prevent discrimination based on sex within the federal government (1974 – 1976), and in 1976 became the Civil Service Commission's director of the Federal Women's Program. During the Carter administration, Mendenhall served as the national comptroller. Later, Mendenhall worked with the EEOC, where she helped change the rules so that an equal number of women and men served as Capitol guards. At the time of her death, Mendenhall was assistant regional administrator for the GSA's Federal Technology Services in Atlanta. Mendenhall received the Presidential Rank Meritorious Award, the GSA Distinguished and Meritorious Service Award, and induction into the Women's Hall of Fame at the University of Kansas, from which she obtained her B.A. and M.A.

Mendez, Chris – See Womendez, Chris

Mendez Banales, Irene (1935 –) In 1972, Mendez Banales was working in the East Los Angeles area when she joined with other Latinas to form the Comision Femenil Mexicana de Los Angeles, a feminist group for Latinas. In the group's second year, she was president. The organization provided scholarships, a day care center and a women's shelter, and became Mendez Banales' training ground for leadership. In 1974 she co-founded (with Connie Destito) America's first bilingual, bicultural rape crisis hotline. Raising money through cake sales, they trained volunteers and did community outreach. Mendez Banales says the rape crisis center is her proudest contribution to the movement. She holds a B.A. and is retired from a career in social services. (ABS)

Meredith, Ann P. (1948 –) A writer/director/producer, filmmaker, fine art photographer, performance/installation artist, curator and adjunct professor, Meredith began documenting women's and LGBT culture in 1970. Her work chronicles such subjects as women and aging, women in non-traditional jobs, lesbians, cowgirls, women in prison and women with AIDS. She documented United Nations International Conferences on Women in Nairobi and Beijing, and the Gay Games in San Francisco and Sydney, Australia. Meredith was also an original member of the first women's art gallery in Berkeley, CA, A Room of Our Own Gallery Collective (1973). She was president and conference chair of the Northern California Women's Caucus for Art; served for three years on the women's board of the College Art Association; and was a member of the International Women in Leadership League for Nairobi in 1987. Meredith earned a B.A. from the University of California, Berkeley (1970), and received a Lila Wallace Reader's Digest International Artist fellowship in 1992 collaborating with the Brooklyn Museum & Arts International in New York. Her work is in permanent collections of the Smithsonian Institution, the Library of Congress, SONY Theatre, and New York and San Francisco Public Library Collections, among others. Archives: Swordfish Productions, Berkeley, CA. (ABS)

Meredith, Susan Rebecca (1944 –) (also known as Susan M. Watson) raised sex discrimination issues in pay and promotion at the Boston Redevelopment Authority in 1969. In 1970, she and other women filed a complaint with the Massachusetts Commission Against Discrimination. As a result, they asked for and received a Whitney Foundation grant to study Boston's employment of women. And that prompted Meredith to enter law school. She graduated from Northeastern University School of Law in 1974. Her first job was associate director, Connecticut Women's Educational and Legal Fund, a public interest law firm litigating sex discrimination cases. She became executive director in 1976 and legal director in 1978. A labor arbitrator in 2005, Meredith stayed with CWEALF until 1980. She also holds a B.A. from Vanderbilt University. She has two children. (ABS)

Merklin, Elaine Margaret (1945 –) joined NYC NOW in the early 1970s and served on its rape subcommittee. She participated in many actions, including picketing outside a NY TV station in protest of sexist remarks by Tex Antoine ("Uncle Weatherbee"). In addition, Merklin, who holds a B.A. from Rutgers State University, has been active in various human rights campaigns, the NGLTF and The Lesbian Herstory Archives. (ABS)

Merriam, Eve (1916 – 1992) Born of Russian parents, Merriam is one of the most anthologized poets in the U.S. and author of over 50 books for adults and children. She won the Yale Younger Poets prize for her book *Family Circle* in 1946. Three of Merriam's noted feminist books are *Mommies at Work* (1955), *After Nora Slammed the*

Door: American Women in the 1960's; the Unfinished Revolution (1964) and *Growing Up Female in America: 10 Lives* (1971). In 1969, Merriam wrote *The Inner City Mother Goose*, which she called "just about the most banned book in the country." *Inner City* became a Broadway musical in 1971. Merriam's next musical play, The Club, opened in 1976, winning many awards and securing her reputation as a dramatist. Merriam was one of the rare feminists who spoke up during the years between the first and second waves. Archives: Kerlan Collection, University of Minnesota, Minneapolis, and the Schlesinger Library, Radcliffe Institute, Cambridge, MA.

Mertic, Elizabeth Frances (1934 –) A Quaker, Mertic was one of a group of women who created a women's magazine for Quakers, *The Friendly Woman*, in the 1970s. Through her association with the 57th St. Meeting of Friends, in Hyde Park, Mertic served as an abortion counselor until the year that abortions were made legal. In addition to her work in support of women's rights, Mertic has been an activist for civil rights and peace, beginning in 1958 when she moved to Chicago. She took part in the 1960 demonstration in Washington, D.C., where a group of Quaker men and women ringed the Pentagon. In 1959, she participated in a three-day, 25-mile walk from Fort Sheridan to downtown Chicago to protest war, and was also part of the Chicago civil rights protest with Dr. Martin Luther King. And, she "continues [2005] to join with other like-minded people to further the cause of peace and justice, as often as I am able." Mertic, who has three children, earned her B.S. in 1957 from the University of Wisconsin. (ABS)

Messing, Sue – See Sznajderman, Suzanne Messing

Messinger, Ruth (1940 –) In the mid 1970s, Messinger decided that politics was the way to make a difference for women. She served a two-year term (1975 – 1977) on the school board for the West Side of Manhattan (NYC), then ran for the State Assembly in 1976, but lost. From 1977 – 1989, she held an elected seat on the City Council, and from 1989 – 1997 served as Manhattan Borough president. In 1997, Messinger was the first woman selected to be the Democratic Party candidate for mayor of NYC. Although she lost, she lost with a respectable 42 percent of the vote. During her time in office, Messinger worked extensively on women's issues. She exposed inequities in the foster care system, fought for equitable salaries and pensions for women city employees, and helped expand and improve childcare options. She also did extensive work to promote awareness of domestic violence and to require hospital staff to be trained to deal with victims of rape and abuse. As Borough president, Messinger convened a major task force on domestic violence, which published the report "Behind Closed Doors." She was also responsible for the report "Work to be Done," on Welfare-to-work issues. She worked with the City Council's women's issues committee on all aspects of women's status in city government, and was also a founding member of a group that created Iris House, a service and treatment center in East Harlem for women and children living with HIV/AIDS. Messinger, who has three children, earned her B.A. from Radcliffe College (1962) and her M.S.W. from the University of Oklahoma (1964). She is (2005) executive director of American Jewish World Service, an international development organization. (ABS)

Metrailer, Rosemary (1944 –) joined the Fort Wayne (IN) Feminists in 1970. The group brought feminist speakers to the city, held large meetings to educate the public about the women's movement, and was instrumental in founding the Fort Wayne Women's Bureau. The group also worked for the ERA, lobbying the state legislature in Indianapolis. Moving to California in 1974 to attend law school at the University of California, Davis, Metrailer was part of the women's caucus, which worked to recruit women students to the school and to recruit women and feminist-sensitive men to the faculty. In 1982, Metrailer founded an all-women law firm in Sacramento, which advocated for women in cases of sexual harassment and employment discrimination, as well as advocating for gays and lesbians. In a landmark case, Dees v. U. S. Air Force, Metrailer and others represented a group of blue-collar women in a class action against the U. S. Air Force, charging sex discrimination in promotion and pay that had gone on for decades. They won a judgment in federal court that granted back pay and retirement benefits for the women and mandated that the Air Force's future promotion policy be changed to eliminate discrimination against women. Metrailer also founded the Sacramento Area Career Women's Network, a lesbian social and business networking group. In addition to her J.D. from the University of California at Davis, Metrailer holds a B.A. from Wellesley College. (ABS)

Metzger, Sue (1933 – 1986) A member of San Diego NOW (1970), Metzger became its second president in 1971. She participated in the chapter's action to integrate the men-only U.S. Grant Grill and worked on the women's credit alert to help make credit equally available to women and men. Under Metzger's leadership, the chapter was also active in the Equal Rights Amendment, Title IX and sexism in the media. From 1972 – 1975, Metzger was workshop coordinator for Project Repair, which trained women in carpentry, plumbing and electrical work. An attorney, Metzger was also active in lesbian organizations and activities.

Meuli, Judith (1938 –) has been an activist and organizer in the women's movement since joining NOW in 1967. In 1968, she began a two-year term as secretary of the Los Angeles chapter of NOW. From 1971 – 1977 she served almost continuously as a member of NOW's national board, and from 1971 – 1974 was chair of the national

membership committee. Also in 1974, Meuli chaired NOW's national nominating committee, and in 1976 was elected coordinator of NOW's Hollywood chapter. Meuli was co-editor of NOW's national newsletter, "NOW Acts," from 1970 – 1973; editor of "Financing the Revolution," a catalog of fundraising tips, in 1973; and co-editor of NOW's national newspaper, the *National NOW Times*, from 1977 – 1985. From 1998 – 2000, Meuli served as president of Los Angeles NOW. She was co-founder (with Eleanor Smeal, Toni Carabillo, Peg Yorkin and Katherine Spillar) of the Feminist Majority Foundation (1987) and a member of the board (1987 –). In 1993, she co-wrote (with Carabillo, her partner, and June Csida) *The Feminist Chronicles: 1953 – 1993*. The two also wrote *The Feminization of Power* in 1988. In 1990, Meuli designed and constructed a building to house the media center and archives of the Feminist Majority. A university research scientist for 10 years, Meuli has worked primarily as a writer, graphic designer and jewelry designer, as well as a real estate broker and developer. In 1969 she co-founded the Women's Heritage Corporation, and in 1970 formed a graphic arts firm with Carabillo. Meuli designed many of the symbols and logos of the women's movement, including the designs for Woman's Equality, Human Liberation, Sisterhood, Matriarchy Lives, Woman's Peace, Older Women's League and NOW's Commemorative medallion. She also designed the VFA pin and medal of honor. Meuli holds a B.A. from the University of Minnesota. Archives: Schlesinger Library, Radcliffe Institute, Cambridge, MA. (ABS)

M

Meyer, Elaine — was a member of the founding board of the Palo Alto (CA) chapter of NOW (1972), and served in almost every capacity from treasurer to president. For several years, Meyer published the chapter's newsletter. She also distributed questionnaires to members asking for recommendations for doctors and attorneys, and then maintained and answered the chapter's phone, giving referrals to callers. In addition, Meyer organized self-help health workshops and, as part of CA NOW, wrote the first draft of the bylaws for the State board. Meyer was also active in getting the city of Palo Alto to adopt an affirmative action plan and to establish a childcare program. During time spent in Washington, D.C., Meyer attended Congressional hearings on the ERA and meetings of the National Women's Health Network. Meyer, who has one child and is a technical writer and editor, holds an M.A. from Columbia University. Archives: California NOW, Sacramento, CA. (ABS)

Meyners, Hazel Vivian Staats
– See Staats-Westover, Hazel Vivian

Michaels, Sheila Shikiy (1939 –) (also known as Sheila Kessler) While being interviewed on WBAI radio in 1969, Michaels used a term she had been promoting since 1961, "Ms." Its meaning was relayed to Gloria Steinem, who adopted it as the title for her feminist magazine. At early meetings after the Miss America action, Michaels urged usage of "feminist," rather than "women's liberation," in tribute to the pioneers of the 1920s. She was a member of several feminist groups: New Women, The Feminists and NYRF. She also did publicity for the Rape Speak-Out, the Rape Conference and the Prostitution Conference. Working with Madeleine Smith, Michaels co-founded The Bastard's Caucus, which promoted rights for children of unwed parents. In India from 1974 – 1975, Michaels interviewed women who had been active in the Independence Movement and in politics and social work. In Laos, she worked with an orphanage of Vietnamese paraplegics; in Singapore, she wrote about American feminism; and in Japan, she worked with Hokie Boshie, a feminist clubhouse, teaching English conversation and participating in political discussion. Since 1999, she has been collecting oral histories of civil rights/nonviolent activists, many of whom are founders of the feminist movement. Michaels was a member of Congress of Racial Equality. She was one of only six women field secretaries of the SNCC's paid staff of 90 in 1963, and was manager in Hattiesburg, the largest project, during Mississippi Freedom Summer 1964. Archives: Columbia University's Oral History Dept. and Washington University in St Louis.   (ABS)

Michel, Joan (1930 –) has been, and continues to be, a force behind the scenes in the women's movement. She helped the late Pat McQuillan organize the first-ever Marriage and Divorce conference (1974). Her activist journey began in 1971, when she borrowed $1 from Irma Diamond Newmark to get from Riverdale, NY, to the New York City NOW office to help Jacqui Ceballos, then the president, who was swamped with paperwork. Michel later helped with the Women's Forum and the National Women's Political Caucus, and wrote press releases out of Jacqui's apartment. One of the founders of VFA in 1992, she has been vice president of public relations. Michel, a writer and former editor for *Hadassah Magazine* and a freelance food writer and editor, has written and published her own cookbook, *The Hadassah Jewish Holiday Cookbook*. A single mother of three, Michel holds a B.A. from Adelphi (1952) and an M.S. from Columbia in speech pathology and audiology, but never worked in that field because President Nixon cut the funding to hospitals at the time of her graduation. She worked with Geraldo Rivera on the One to One project for the mentally retarded, for Dave Garroway and for Stewart Mott, founder of Women for Congress.   (ABS)

Middleton, Dana (1945 –) was involved in consciousness raising groups in San Francisco in the 1970s. From 1973 – 1978, as part of her Latin American studies, she traveled and photographed women and children in Latin America. Following a rape (in the fourth month of her second pregnancy) in 1985, Middleton discovered and then worked with the Rape Crisis Center in Taos, NM,

later called the Commission Against Violence. Middleton served as its coordinator from 1986 – 1990. In 1999, Middleton co-founded a NOW chapter in Taos, then served as its president from 2001 – 2003. Middleton, who has two children, is (2005) involved with the NOW chapter in Santa Fe, NM, where she lives and works for a Bed & Breakfast Inn.   (ABS)

Milam, Mindy (1956 –) joined NOW in 1975 and was involved in the struggle for ratification of the ERA in Louisiana, which was introduced in 1972 and never passed. She was president of the Jefferson Parish chapter of LA NOW (1977 – 1979); picketed the Catholic Church for trying to fire an unmarried pregnant woman who was an employee; and worked with the violence against women task force to improve services to rape victims. For three years in the late 1970s, Milam and her group held the Mr. ERA beauty and talent contest as a fundraiser and consciousness raiser. When the chapter dissolved in 1980, members marked the dissolution with a wake and memorial service for the death of the Head and Master provision of Louisiana law, which gave men control over all the properties of the marriage; the repeal became effective in 1980. "That was a direct result of the intensive ERA campaign in Louisiana," says Milam. "During the wake we buried 'the body of law' (the contents of the law) in a coffin." Milam holds a B.A. from the University of New Orleans and an M.S.W. from Tulane University (1983). She is (2006) in full-time private practice as a clinical social worker. Archives: Newcomb College Center for Research on Women, New Orleans, LA.   (ABS)

Miles, Julia Hinson (1930 –) As an actress in the 1950s, Miles realized that the real power in the theater is wielded by producers, and so became one. In 1961, she was a co-founder, with two other women, of Theater Current in Brooklyn Heights, one of the first theaters founded and run by women. In 1964, she became associate artistic director of the nonprofit American Place Theater at St. Clement's Church in Manhattan. Realizing that women playwrights were largely being ignored, Miles founded the Women's Project and Productions (1978) to give them a forum for their work at the American Place Theater. As the artistic director of the Women's Project for 25 years, Miles produced more than 100 productions and workshops of plays by women, more than 400 readings and nine anthologies of those plays. The theater was later renamed the Julia Miles Theater in her honor. In addition to this work, Miles joined NY NOW in the early 1970s and was a founder of the League of Professional Theatre Women. She is the recipient of numerous awards, including the Susan B. Anthony Award. But, she says, "My proudest achievement is giving voice to the many women artists for whom I have provided a stage and an audience." Miles, who has three children, holds a B.A. from Northwestern University. Archives: The Sophia Smith Collection, Smith College, Northampton, MA.   (ABS)

Milio, Nancy Rosalie (1938 –) A retired nurse and policy analyst, and a professor emeritus of health policy, Milio was the organizer, in 1963, of a health and childcare Mom & Tots Neighborhood Center in a Detroit ghetto. Among its many services, the center offered teen sex education, family planning, prenatal care, child clinics, midwife support and transportation. The story of the center is chronicled in Milio's book, *9226 Kercheval: The Storefront That Did Not Burn* (University of Michigan Press, 1970). Milio has lectured and written extensively on women's health, maternal and child health, occupational and safety issues for women at work, and policy issues affecting women, children and their health. The head (2005) of a low-income housing group, Milio was a member of the advisory board, women's studies, at the University of North Carolina, Chapel Hill (1983 – 1985). In 1994, she was inducted into the Archives of Oral History Project at the University of Michigan Leaders in Community Health Nursing. In 1968, she was awarded the Women of Wayne State University Award. Milio holds degrees from Wayne State University (1960 and 1965) and Yale University (1970). Archives: Oral History Project, University of Michigan, Ann Arbor, MI. (ABS)

Miller, Anita Mae (1928 –) began her lifetime advocacy for women's rights when she worked to have "sex" added to the 1964 Civil Rights Act. Her various leadership roles in established women's organizations, such as the AAUW, LWV, the California Medical Auxiliary and civic and cultural groups, were the base from which she promoted understanding and acceptance of the changing roles of women in society. Her focus was to influence public policy related to equal rights for women. In 1972, Governor Ronald Reagan appointed Miller chair of the California Commission on the Status of Women, a post she held for eight years. In 1976, she secured and directed a major grant from the Rockefeller Foundation to assess the impact of the ERA on state laws and institutions. This two-year ERA project organized interstate conferences to provide information on issues and training for lobbyists, and also published four books: *The Equal Rights Amendment: A Bibliographic Study* (Greenwood Press, 1976); *ERA Limitations and Possibilities* (Les Femmes Publishing, 1975); *ERA Conformance: An Analysis of California State Codes* (1975); and *A Commentary on the Effect of the ERA on State Law and Institutions* (1975). Miller served two terms as president of the National Association of Commissions on the Status of Women, and 12 years as executive director and lobbyist for California Women Lawyers, where her major focus was the appointment of women judges. Miller earned her B.A. from San Francisco State University and her M.A. from Stanford University. (ABS)

Miller, Casey (1919 – 1997) was a pioneer advocate of nonsexist language, and co-author (with Kate Swift) of *Words and Women* (Doubleday, 1976) and *Handbook of Nonsexist Writing* (Lippincott & Crowell, 1980). She was also author, with Swift, of numerous articles on language and women. These include "Desexing the Language," published in *New York* magazine (1971); and "One Small Step for Genkind," published in *The New York Times Magazine* (1972). Miller, who graduated from Smith College in 1940, served in the Navy for three years during World War II, working in Washington, D.C., in naval intelligence. She served as curriculum editor of the Seabury Press for 10 years, and had been an editor at Appleton-Century. In 1970, Miller and Swift formed a freelance editorial partnership, out of which arose their work on women and language. She was a member of national NOW (1970s) and also joined area chapters in Connecticut. In the 1980s, she helped Terry Ferguson edit the CT NOW newsletter, "The Waterfall." Miller was also a member of the Women's Institute for Freedom of the Press, and as an associate participated in conferences and was a coordinator at a workshop on sexist language in media, held at the National Press Club. A supporter of reproductive rights, Miller joined as a litigant in a class action suit, Women v. Connecticut (1972). Archives: Knight Library, University of Oregon, Eugene, OR.

Miller, Dusty (1944 –) (also known as Judy Miller) A psychologist and writer, Miller is the author of *Your Surviving Spirit: A Spiritual Workbook for Coping with Trauma; Women Who Hurt Themselves*; and *Addictions and Trauma Recovery: Healing the Body, Mind and Spirit*. She was one of the original members of New Haven Women's Liberation (1968 – 1973), and was the drummer in the New Haven Women's Liberation Rock Band (1969 – 1971). At the same time, she was part of a political action that involved spray-painting symbols of the patriarchy and then claiming in court that it was a legitimate form of public communication. Miller helped organize day care and women's support groups in Fair Haven, CT, and as part of a research project worked with Leah Margulies at Yale University to produce a slide show and a variety of mixed media on the exploitation of women by multinationals. Miller moved to Boston in 1973, where she taught in the Goddard College women's studies master's program for several years. A member of the civil rights movement (1963 – 1966), Miller was student director of the Cornell University Fayette County project, working in voter registration projects in West Tennessee. She was, and remains, active in the peace movement, and is (2005) a member of the Raging Grannies, singing songs of peace and justice. Miller earned her B.A. from Cornell University, her M.A. from Goddard College, and her Ed.D. from the University of Massachusetts. (ABS)

Miller, Geraldine (1920 – 2005) was a catalyst in Brooklyn (NY) for securing equal rights and protection for women who work in service jobs such as waitress, nanny or cook. From her teenage years in the 1930s, Miller herself worked in hotels, restaurants and kitchens, but primarily in private homes as a domestic. She was not aware that she could be putting money away for her retirement until 1970, when she started looking into Social Security for herself. There was a great difference between the benefit amount due to her and what she would have received had her employers enrolled her in Social Security all along. That difference propelled her to found the Household Technicians Union in 1971, which spread to states in the South, Ohio and Kansas. The union pressures employers to comply with the Federal Minimum Wage Act; and works to enforce Social Security laws for all employees. Miller also served as president of the National Congress of Neighborhood Women, whose goal is to support poor and working class women rebuilding their communities. A workshop that Miller ran for NCNW's Project Open Doors brought to light the similarities and shared concerns of homemakers and household workers, thus breaking down the barriers of class and race. Miller was also a founder and president of Bronx, NY, NOW, a board member of national NOW, the first chair of NOW's women of color task force, a governing board member for NOW Foundation, and chair of NOW's national committee on eliminating racism. She was awarded NOW's Presidential Award and its Lifetime Feminist Award.

Miller, Gretchen L. (1950 –) In 1976, Miller opened the first women's law office in Eugene, OR, with Jill Heiman. Miller was also a founder of Women Space, a domestic violence shelter, and served on the Eugene City Council (1979 – 1984). Miller, who taught at the University of Oregon for six years, continues to teach law to undergraduates and has been an administrative law judge since 1995. Active in the peace movement since 1970, Miller continues to fight for human rights. She helped draft and lobby for changes in the Eugene Human Rights Code, including gay rights and domestic partner benefits, and did similar work as a member of the school district equity committee. Miller, who has three children, is a graduate of the University of Kansas (1971) and the University of Oregon Law School (1976). (ABS)

Miller, Isabel – See Routsong, Alma

Miller, Jean Baker (1927 –) A psychiatrist who grew up in the Bronx (NY) in a poor family during the Great Depression, Miller observed, as a child, that the only people who managed to keep their jobs were doctors. With the encouragement of two nurses who helped her overcome polio, Miller eventually graduated from Sarah Lawrence College (1948) and earned an M.D. from Columbia University (1952). After reading *The Feminine Mystique* in the early 1960s, Miller began attending, then leading, consciousness raising groups. As a doctor, her goal became to "depathologize" women's behaviors. Miller believed that women were struggling to be more like men—and in the process losing sight of their unique strengths: providing the kind of psychological connec-

tions that are the basis of growth. In developing a more realistic psychology of women, Miller worked to erase the perception that women were somehow "men that had gone wrong." Miller is the author of *Toward a New Psychology of Women* (1976) and co-author, with Irene Striver, of *The Healing Connection*. In 1981, Miller became director of the Stone Center for Developmental Services and Studies (a part of Wellesley College). In 1995, she became director of The Jean Baker Miller Training Institute, which advances the study and practice of relational-cultural theory. The recipient of numerous awards and honors, Miller has been a professor of psychiatry at Boston University School of Medicine and a lecturer at Harvard Medical School. She has two children. (ABS)

Miller, Joyce D. (1928 –) worked for decades to improve conditions for working women. She was an organizer/co-founder of Coalition of Labor Union Women (1972 – 1974). At the founding convention (1974) Miller was elected East Coast VP (1974 – 1978). She was later elected national president, a post she held for 15 years (1978 – 1993). Miller was also director of social services for the Amalgamated Clothing Workers Union (1972 – 1993), and served as head of women's activities. In addition, she was elected to the AFL-CIO executive council, where she served from 1980 – 1993. A member of numerous feminist groups, Miller joined NOW and NARAL in the early 1970s. She lobbied, marched and wrote letters in support of the ERA while living in Illinois (1962 – 1972) and later in New York. Miller, who has three children, holds an undergraduate degree (1949) and an M.F.A. (1951) from the University of Chicago. (ABS)

Miller, Linda Blair (1944 –) A member of Seattle NOW, Miller wrote its newsletter and served as secretary (1972) and co-president with Dorothy Sale (1973). The chapter worked to change the state's archaic property and credit laws, and on passage of the ERA. Concerned about the demeaning stereotypes of women portrayed in the media, Miller headed the chapter's image of women committee. She also wrote an audiovisual show titled "If I've Come Such a Long Way, Why Do You Call Me Baby?" which she presented many times, including to the Seattle Advertising Club. Miller's work also included feminist posters that were sold at street fairs and meetings, and nationally in the classified ads section of *Ms.* magazine. Among them is a picture of Israeli prime minister Golda Meir, captioned *But Can She Type?* The poster is at the Smithsonian Museum and in several major library collections. Earlier, Miller helped to found a chapter of the NAACP and persuade local factories to follow the new federal equal employment laws. She has two children. (ABS)

Miller, Midge Leeper (1922 –) was elected state representative to the Wisconsin Assembly in 1970 and served for 14 years. She was a co-founder of the NWPC in 1971 and, as a member of its first national steering committee, helped found the WI WPC. Miller, who served as a delegate to the IWY conference, was also author of the bill that Wisconsin ratified for the ERA, and served as chair of the committee that brought WI statutes into conformity with the ERA. Miller, who had nine children, was founder of the National Council for Alternative Work Patterns to promote part-time and flextime employment, thus helping women to more easily meet family needs. She earned her B.A. from the University of Michigan and her M.A. from the University of Wisconsin. (ABS)

Miller, Pamela Gundersen (1938 –) was a member of a CR group in East Palo Alto (CA) in 1969, and in 1972 joined NOW. She later joined the Kentucky WPC, the ERA Alliance, and a pro-choice lobby group. In 1973, she became the first woman elected to public office in Lexington, KY (as a member of the City Council), and in 1993 became the first woman elected mayor of the combined city-county government. She has been a speaker at Take Back the Night Rallies (1991–1998) and a supporter of civil rights. A 1960 graduate of Smith College, Miller has three children. Archives: Library Archives, University of Kentucky, Lexington, KY. (ABS)

Miller, Pat – See Matthews, Patricia Ann

Miller, Rosalie J. (1944 –) After marching for the ERA in Tallahassee (1974), Miller became "a very active and enthusiastic" participant in a seven-member CR group. That year, she also played first base on the lesbian team in the local women's softball league and joined a Take Back the Night march. In 1975, Miller co-founded and became director of Women Unlimited, a community center for women in Gainesville, FL, that included a center for information, education, meetings, referrals and events; a feminist bookstore (originally WomanBooks and then Amelia's); and a feminist newspaper, *WomaNews*. Women Unlimited also acted as an essential, central contact point for the many women's groups in the area. In 1976, Miller was a core organizer of the Southeastern Women's Health Conference, held at the University of Florida. When UF realized "how radical the conference was," it tried to retract permission, Miller says, but Dr. Jackie Resnick confronted the administration and the conference was held. Also Miller helped organize marches in Tallahassee for the ERA and participated in various political campaigns. A professor of occupational therapy, Miller holds a B.A. from Earlham College (1966) and a Ph.D. from the University of Florida (1978). (ABS)

Millett, Kate (1934 –) is a sculptor, a lecturer, a militant activist and prolific writer, best known for her first book, *Sexual Politics*. A stinging indictment of patriarchal literary icons, the book was a bestseller in 1970. Millett joined NYC NOW in 1966 and served as chair of the education committee from 1966–1970. In that capacity, Millett wrote *Token Learning*, which showed that women's colleges were vastly inferior in terms of the number and quality of courses offered in major fields of study, the credentials of their professors and other criteria. Millett's doctoral thesis, which turned into *Sexual Politics* (Doubleday, 1970), landed her on the cover of *Time* magazine and brought her instant notoriety as "the principal theoretician of the Women's Liberation Movement," according to *The New York Times*. Shortly thereafter *Time* magazine wrote an article implying that Millett's announcement of her bisexuality damaged her credibility in the women's movement, but many leaders in the movement spoke out publicly in her defense. Millett was a founder of Columbia Women's Liberation and an early member of Downtown Radical Women. She participated in all actions, protests and marches of the time, and led a weeklong demonstration to force integration of the help-wanted ads in *The New York Times*. Other books include, *The Prostitution Papers* (Basic Books, 1971), *Flying* (Knopf, 1974), *Sita* (Farrar Straus, 1976), *The Basement* (Simon & Schuster, 1979), *Going to Iran* (Coward & McCann, 1982), *Looney-Bin Trip* (Simon & Schuster, 1990), *The Politics of Cruelty* (WW Norton, 1994), *A.D. A Memoir* (WW Norton, 1995) and *Mother Millett* (Verso Books, 2001). An artist as well as a writer, Millett has exhibited her paintings, photography, sculpture and drawings in New York, Provincetown, Amsterdam, Berlin and Tokyo. Millett founded the Women's Art Colony at Millett Tree Farm in Poughkeepsie, NY (1979), where several hundred artists and writers in summer residence learned new skills, worked the tree farm, and shared feminist thoughts. Millett has been an active supporter of civil rights, gay rights and the rights of mental patients, was a volunteer for CORE, and involved with the Disabilities Rights Movement. In 1998, she was honored by the VFA. Millett graduated from the University of Minnesota (1956), studied at Oxford University (England), and earned her Ph.D. from Columbia University in 1970. Archives: Sallie Bingham Center, Duke University, Durham, NC. (ABS)

Milliken, Christine (1949 –) (also known as Christine Topping) was on the founding staff of the NWPC as the 1972 Republican Convention coordinator. Their activities at the 1980 convention led to the commitment by candidate Ronald Reagan to nominate a woman for the U.S. Supreme Court if elected president, with the selection of Sandra Day O'Connor a direct result. During this time period, Milliken served as a member of the D.C. Republican committee and as an alternate delegate to the 1976 Republican Convention. She was a volunteer in the ERA extension battles and in various political and policy issues that affected women in the 1970s and 1980s. She was also involved in bridge-building between Republican and Democratic women. In 1986, Milliken was selected as executive director and general counsel of the National Association of Attorneys General, the first woman to hold that post, and for several years one of the few women at that level in law enforcement. NAAG's unqualified support for the Violence Against Women Act tipped the balance in the U.S. Senate. The organization also became involved in other areas relevant to women, including juvenile justice reform and sexual predator laws. After serving as director of the NAAG for 15 years, Milliken retired. Milliken earned degrees from George Washington University and Catholic University Law School. (ABS)

Milliken, Helen Wallbank (1922 –) In 1974, Milliken was co-founder, with Elly Peterson, of Michigan ERAmerica. A speaker for pro-choice and Planned Parenthood issues, she was also Michigan delegate to the 1977 National Women's Conference in Houston. From 1976 – 1981, Milliken served as national chair of ERAmerica, campaigning, lobbying and speaking across the country for ratification. She also worked to ensure reproductive freedom for women, and to end violence against women. Milliken, who has two children, earned her B.A. from Smith College in 1945. Archives: Bentley Library, Ann Arbor, MI. (ABS)

Millington, June Elizabeth (1948 –) Musician and pioneer record producer, Millington found her entrée to women's music when she played on Cris Williamson's Changer and the Changed in 1975. In 1976, she played with Cris Williamson on her first national tour, and in 1977 played on Live Dream, Williamson's second album. In 1978, Millington, who had extensive experience in studio recording, produced Williamson's third album, Flying Colors. Among other work, in 1986 Millington co-founded (with Ann Hackler, Roma Baran, Vicki Randle and Angela Davis) the Institute for Musical Arts, a place for women to create music, attend concerts and learn about the recording process. In 2002 they began Summer Rock and Roll Girl's Camps at IMAEast in Goshen, MA. Just outside Northampton, it will be expanded to include a performance and workshop center, as well as a full-time recording studio. Millington has also been active in the peace movement through her Buddhist studies and practices. Archives: Papers will be at The Institute for the Musical Arts, Goshen, MA. (ABS)

Millsap, Mary Ann (1943 –) A policy analyst, Millsap was working in the Office of Planning and Evaluation in Washington, D.C., in 1972. At that time, in response to criticism that HEW was doing little to end sex stereotyping or sex segregation in federal educational programs, the commissioner of education established a task force to assess federal education law and make recommendations. Millsap was a member of that task force, which was chaired by Holly Knox. She was also a major author of its report. Although few of the report's recommendations were implemented, "the report was later cited to justify passage of the Women's Educational Equity Act (1974) and the inclusion of Sex Equity Coordinators in the revisions to the Vocational Education Act (1976)," says

Millsap. With Knox, Millsap later wrote up the activities of the task force and published them as "Sex Discrimination and Bureaucratic Politics: The U.S. Office of Education Task Force on Women's Education" in *National Politics and Sex Discrimination in Education* (Lexington Books, 1977). From 1972 – 1981, Millsap—working as a senior associate in the federal government's National Institute of Education—served as a consultant on sex equity in vocational education to interdepartmental task forces. She also assisted staff in the Women's Research Program and was co-author, with Naida Tushnet Bagenstos, of an evaluation handbook for the directors of women's studies programs. When Millsap returned to graduate school in 1981, she interviewed extensively the women who had organized and been active in the National Coalition for Women and Girls in Education and turned their stories into her doctoral dissertation. From that dissertation, she wrote and published three articles on women and sex equity in education (1983, 1985 and 1988). From 1987 – 1989, Millsap directed a national study of the implementation of the Vocational Education Act, including the sex equity provisions. Millsap holds an Ed.D. from Harvard University. (ABS)

Milstein, Jeanne (1955 –) As an undergraduate at Cornell (1973 – 1977), Milstein was a member of various groups focusing on reproductive rights, domestic violence and the economic status of women. She also worked at a rape crisis center and was a volunteer at Planned Parenthood. A VISTA volunteer with the 9to5 movement in Connecticut (1977), she also organized women in low-paying jobs and publicized their concerns with innovative actions such as a "Raises, Not Roses" demonstration by women at the Capitol steps on National Secretaries Day (1978). A member of Connecticut's Permanent Commission on the Status of Women (1978 – 1986), she was named legislative director in 1978. In that capacity she lobbied for bills ranging from pay equity and health services for women to legal restraint of domestic violence and sexual harassment. In the early 1980s, she helped feminist legislators draft the country's first law giving tax credits to companies providing child day care for working mothers. Milstein has also directed the Women's Center of Southeastern CT (1991 – 1993), was legislative director of the state's Commission on Children (1993 – 1998), and director of government relations in the Department of Children and Families (1998 – 2000). Milstein is (2006) Child Advocate, state of Connecticut. She holds a B.S. from Cornell (1977). (ABS)

Mink, Patsy T. (1927 – 2002) A lawyer and legislator, Mink was an advocate for women, the poor and the disenfranchised. She was the first Asian American to practice law in Hawaii and the first woman of Asian descent to serve in the U.S. Congress when, in 1965, she was elected to the U.S. House of Representatives. She served six consecutive terms. Mink introduced the first comprehensive Early

Childhood Education Act and was author of the Women's Educational Equity Act (1974), which established a Presidentially appointed National Advisory Council on Women's Educational Program. She was one of the founders of the NWPC in 1971. She also played a key role in the enactment of Title IX in 1972. In 1977, she made an unsuccessful run for U.S. Senate, then in 1990 was re-elected to the House. Mink, who had one child, earned her B.A. from the University of Hawaii (1948) and her L.L.D. from the University of Chicago (1951). Although she had originally planned to be a doctor, none of the 20 medical schools to which she applied in 1948 would accept women. Mink was honored posthumously by the VFA. Archives: The Sophia Smith Collection, Smith College, Northampton, MA.

Minka, Ruth (1937 –) (also known as Ruth Minka Glass) Born in Gdansk, Poland, Minka attended women's liberation classes at Columbia University Free School in the late 1960s and participated in the bridal fair demonstration with WITCH in 1967. After moving to California in 1969, she joined a CR group. In 1971 – 1972, she worked on the journal *Tooth and Nail* with Margie Stamberg, Helen Kritzler and Pat Fineran, and from 1972 – 1974 was part of a women's theater group, She Who Plays With Words. Minka says, "I took my energy from the women's movement to go into an alternative health profession, become a chiropractor and practice for 19 years, treating and teaching people ways to optimize heath and wellness." A long-time supporter of the National Women's Health Network, and long-time practitioner of Tai Chi, she has two children. (ABS)

Minnich, Elizabeth Kamarck (1943 –) (also known as Elizabeth Kamarck) A senior fellow (2005) with the Office of Diversity, Equity and Global Initiatives at the Association of American Colleges & Universities, Minnich has worked throughout her life to make the case for feminist scholarship—"to open doors, change minds, and protect the insurgent scholarship and ways of teaching from sometimes fierce opposition." She has spoken, written and consulted on changing the curriculum to include women at more than 100 campuses, as well as at many conferences, professional associations and community groups, and later put all that she learned from that crusade into her book *Transforming Knowledge* (Temple University Press, 1990). At graduate school at the University of California, Berkeley, in the late 1960s, she was one of very few women in the political science dept. Moving to NYC, she became assistant to the dean at The New School College and returned to graduate work, this time in philosophy, at the New School's Graduate Faculty. There she worked primarily with, and was teaching assistant for, Hannah Arendt. In 1972, Minnich became director of continuing education at Sarah Lawrence College. With others, she helped get a grant that brought women activists to campus for a year to study, write and participate in classes. In 1973, Minnich became director of studies at Hollins College. There, she was deeply involved in making the case for women's education and women's schools, working with the women's college coalition. She also founded a continuing education program for women, worked with activist feminist student groups, and began speaking about feminist issues, "including abortion—at first, because no one else would do it." As assistant to the president and then associate dean of faculty at Barnard College (1976), Minnich helped plan several of the early The Scholar & The Feminist conferences. From Barnard, Minnich became a dean of the graduate school of The Union Institute & University, which gave its first Ph.D. in women's studies in 1972. She remained there until 2004. Minnich, who has three children, earned her B.A. from Sarah Lawrence College (1965) and her M.A. (1971) and Ph.D. (1977) from the Graduate Faculty of Political and Social Science, The New School for Social Research. (ABS)

Mintz, Lorna – See Peterson, Lorna

Miracle, Billie (1944 –) In 1973, Miracle and a group of other women moved to Southern Oregon, where they bought land and founded WomanShare. As a summer camp for women, WomanShare held workshops on numerous topics relevant to women. The group was instrumental in forming the Oregon Women's Land Trust, as well as many local events and political actions. Miracle's part in WomanShare, she says, "has been vision holder, teacher, caretaker and leader for 30 years." WomanShare continues (2005) as a resource center/ retreat/community for women. Miracle left the U.S. during the Vietnam War to live in Canada, where she attended graduate school in art education at Sir George Williams University. She came out as a lesbian, then lived with a group of women who formed a collective and founded The Flaming Apron, Women's Craft Store. The store sold women's art on consignment, some of which was so successful that the group decided to present an exhibition, called Powerhouse. This, in turn, was so successful that the group created the first women's art gallery in Montreal, also called Powerhouse. Miracle holds a B.A. and M.A. Archives: Library Special Collections, University of Oregon, Eugene, OR. (ABS)

Miriam, Selma (1935 –) (also known as Selma Bunks) served as a president of NOW in CT in the early 1970s. Under her direction, the members started numerous CR groups, had the first anti-pornography rally day (1973), protested when men were exonerated of rape, and did a study of sex stereotyping in children's readers and math books. In 1975, Miriam was a co-founder of Bloodroot, a women-only dinner club that was originally held in her house. Eighteen months later, the women opened Bloodroot Restaurant, a vegetarian restaurant based on feminist principles, and feminist bookstore in Bridgeport,

M

CT, still operating (2006). Miriam, who holds a B.S. from Tufts, has two children. (ABS)

Mitchel, Claire Furman (1921 –) A journalist, public relations expert and administrator, Mitchel was the senior staff member (1965 – 1970) of the Ohio, Kentucky, Indiana (OKI) Office of Economic Opportunity, funded by the U.S. Congress as part of the War on Poverty. She was with the Broward County (FL) Human Relations Agency from 1972 – 1982, first as communications person and then (1975) as director. She caused to be created an Office for Women's Concerns, through which she conducted a survey showing the skewed pay scale—with women receiving less pay than men—in the school system, the third largest in the U.S. Once the Office of Women's Concerns was in place, Mitchel moved to head it and brought in and became staff support for the Commission on the Status of Women. The Commission held forums; persuaded the board of commissioners to hold training sessions for heads of departments regarding sexual harassment; dedicated Secretary's Day to seminars on legal rights and benefits; persuaded the county commissioners to endorse a WoMen's theater that highlighted women's original works; brought the Older Women's League into Broward County; started Women's Advocacy for the Majority Minority; and visited the women's state prison with people who could fill needs there, and followed up with schooling and skills training. The commission also put pressure on the county to set up a rape crisis center. Mitchel also helped start Women in Distress, which serves thousands of women yearly. In 1982 Mitchel retired to run (unsuccessfully) for the FL State Legislature and to practice public relations for social service agencies. In 1985, when the *Miami Herald* called to invite her to do a weekly column, the editor asked, "Do you remember the five 'Ws' of journalism?" Mitchel replied that she would write about her own five "Ws", which are What's Wrong With Women's Wrinkles? After 20 years, she is still writing her Sunday column, "The Third Third," which is about women as they age, from a feminist viewpoint. Mitchel was included in the first Women's History Coalition Hall of Fame and received the Lifetime Feminist award from NOW. (ABS)

Mitchell, Joyce M. (1930 – 1996) Professor of political science at the University of Oregon at her death, Mitchell was active in the anti-Vietnam War movement of the 1960s. Shortly after, she became an early feminist leader at the university, where she was one of a very few women on the faculty. Mitchell was a prime force in a 1969 study of the status of women at the university, and then led a group of women in a campaign for affirmative action. She also organized the first women's political caucus in the American Political Science Association, and established a Center for the Study of Women on the university campus. Mitchell earned a B.A. from Pomona (1952), and an M.A. (1954) and Ph.D. (1964) from Berkeley.

Mitchell, Joyce Slayton (1933 –) founded Vermont NOW after meeting Wilma Scott Heide, and served as national coordinator of women and religion for NOW in the 1970s. She also wrote a newsletter, "The Sisterhood for Personhood," and was elected from VT to attend the IWY in both Texas and Mexico City. Mitchell ran workshops for VT legislators on women and body language. She was also elected from Vermont to train in Washington, D.C., to give workshops to teachers on sex equality. Mitchell, who is (2005) a college adviser in high school, is the author of *I Can Be Anything: Careers for Young Women* (The College Board, 1976); *Other Choices for Becoming a Woman*, the first high-school feminist book (Delacorte, Dell, 1975), and *Winning the Heart of the College Admissions Dean* (2005). Mitchell, who has two children, earned her A.B. from Denison University (1956), her M.S. from the University of Bridgeport (1958), and her M.A. from Columbia University (1996). (ABS)

Mitchell, Olga Mary Mracek (1933 –) In 1971, Mitchell was appointed to the first affirmative action committee at Bell Telephone Laboratories in Holmdel, NJ. She served for five years, and was chair for the last two. The committee's goal was to provide support and reduce stereotyping of minorities and women by holding awareness programs for employees. Initially, discrimination against women was largely ignored by management until statistics showing its existance were compiled. Stereotyping of women was widespread in the 1970s and extended to members of the committee, as determined in an informal survey compiled by Lois Herr, whom she had invited to participate. Mitchell, working with committee member Dot Kirby, pointed out to management that technical women in an entry program were routinely passed over for promotion, while the men were generally steered into the fast track. The two also pointed out the need for maternity benefits. In addition to her work at Bell Labs, Mitchell was a charter member of the Summit (NJ) chapter of NOW. Mitchell, who has two children, earned her B.A. (1955), her M.A. (1958) and her Ph.D. in nuclear physics (1962) from the University of Toronto. She also holds an M.S. from Pace University (1982). (ABS)

Moberg, Verne (1938 –) In 1970, Moberg wrote the leaflet "Consciousness Razors," which presented 12 situations and questions that encouraged new thinking about gender. The leaflet was commissioned by the National Education Association and widely distributed. It was reprinted in *Dear Sisters* (Basic Books, 2000). Moberg was VP of the Feminist Press from 1972 – 1974. She earned her Ph.D. from the University of Wisconsin-Madison and has taught Swedish and Scandinavian literature at seven U.S. universities and colleges. Since 1988 she has been teaching at Columbia University. (ABS)

Mohlman, Carol (1930 –) was a member of Los Angeles NOW from 1971 – 1981, and served as chair of its education committee. The committee's goals were to assess the extent of gender stereotyping and to offer models for alternative adult/child interactions. Projects included making feminist recommendations on textbooks being considered by the California Department of Education, sensitizing librarians and booksellers to the importance of providing children with more books showing girls in active rather than passive roles, and (their "most ambitions effort") creating and presenting a slide show for junior high and senior high school classes that illustrated gender stereotyping. The group also demonstrated against sexist toys at a stockholders meeting of a large Southern California toy company, and provided testimony at hearings regarding Title IX. Mohlman, who has two children, was also a volunteer in the California Abortion Rights Action League and managed its monthly pledge program (1981–1986). (ABS)

Mojica-Hammer, Ruth (1926 –) (formerly Rhea Mojica-Hammer) As a Chicana, says Mojica-Hammer, "I carried a double load in the women's movement—my constituency was Chicanos/Hispanics. In the Chicano movement, my constituency was my Hispanic and Caucasian sisters." Mojica-Hammer was a role model and catalyst for Hispanics, both women and men, to enter the political arena. In 1972, she was one of the first, if not the first, Mexican-American woman to run in the Democratic primaries for the U.S. Congress (in IL). Although that bid failed, she was elected VP of the NWPC in 1973 and re-elected in 1975 at the second national convention in Boston. In 1977, Mojica-Hammer became chapter president of the Mexican-American BPW of Chicago. She was also appointed to President Carter's IWY Commission in 1977. Mojica-Hammer is (2005) executive director of the El Paso (TX) Council for International Visitors. She has one child. Archives: Pan American Library, University of Texas, Austin, TX. (ABS)

Mokcsay, Zsuzanna Emese
– See Budapest, Zsuzanna Emese

Mokotoff, Susan – See Reverby, Susan Mokotoff

Molina de Pick, Gracia (1930 –) An activist for women, Chicanos, laborers and the poor, Molina de Pick was part of the second wave of American feminism from the beginning of the movement. Born in Mexico, where the role of women in society was strictly defined and confined, Molina de Pick's pro-choice stance resulted in early hostility from the Mexican community, which was Catholic. Women in Mexico were not allowed to vote, so at age 17 Molina de Pick became the leader of the youth brigade of a party that promised the vote for women. "I used to go to the popular open markets, get on top of a crate and use a horn to invite everyone to join the party to get women the vote," she says. It took 10 years, until 1957, for women to be able to vote for president. That year she married

Richard Pick and moved permanently to San Diego, CA. In 1959 she joined efforts of the minority communities in California to integrate the Democratic Party. She started organizing Mexican students and parents to end the practice of segregating Spanish-speaking-only students in classes for the mentally retarded. She joined and helped the Farm Workers Union. She developed Chicano studies programs in higher education and the Movimiento Estudiantil Chicano de Aztlan student action group. In the early 1970s, Molina de Pick formed the first Latino Women's Liberation group and helped launch the NWPC nationwide. She worked in Africa as part of the first AIDS Human Resources Team to include women, has participated in all United Nations International Women's Conferences, and organized the Southwest contingent that took part in the 1977 IWY Conference in Houston. Along with Francisca Flores, Reies Lopez Tijeriena, Corky Gonzalez and Cesar Chavez, she founded the Chicano civil rights movement. For years she has helped new citizens register to vote. Always, she has worked arduously to promote coalitions between white women and women of color. Molina de Pick, who has three children, holds a B.A. from the Feminist University of Mexico City, an M.A. from San Diego State University, and has done doctoral studies in comparative literature. She served on the faculty of the University of California, San Diego, and Mesa College faculty. (ABS)

Mollenkott, Virginia Ramey (1932 –) A professor emeritus, Mollenkott is the author or co-author of 13 books, including several on women and religion. Books include *Women, Men and the Bible* (1977); *The Divine Feminine: Biblical Imagery of God as Female* (1983); *Sensuous Spirituality: Out from Fundamentalism* (1992); and *Omnigender: A Transreligious Approach* (2001, and winner of the Lambda Literary Award in 2002). In the mid 1960s, as her feminist awareness grew, Mollenkott began including women's literary achievements in her classes and guest lectures. In 1973 she spoke at the first conference of evangelical feminists at the conservative Baptist Theological Seminary (Denver), and also wrote the introduction to Paul King Jewett's theological book *Man as Male and Female*. In 1974, she gave the first women's liberation speech at Malone College (OH), but was picketed by the students there "who brought newspapers to the chapel, opened them, and loudly rattled the pages while I was speaking." In 1975, she spoke at the first national gathering of the Evangelical Women's Caucus in Washington, D.C., and has delivered plenary speeches at almost every gathering of this organization since then. She is a member of NOW, the Women's Institute for Freedom of the Press, and the Religious Coalition for Reproductive Freedom. She also serves as a manuscript evaluator for the *Journal of Feminist Studies in Religion*; and was a member of the translation committee for the *New International Version of the Bible* (1970–1978); and of *An Inclusive Language Lectionary* (National Council of

M

Churches, 1980 – 1988). She is also a member of the Fellowship of Reconciliation and the Baptist Peace Movement, and has been an active supporter of gay rights. In 1978, she co-authored *Is the Homosexual My Neighbor? A Positive Christian View*. She has lectured widely on lesbian rights, and has also been active in the transgender cause, serving as co-author of *Transgender Journeys* (2003). Mollenkott, who has one child, earned her B.A. from Bob Jones University, her M.A. from Temple University, and her Ph.D. from New York University. Archives: Union Theological Seminary Library, NYC; the Center for Gay and Lesbian Studies, Pacific School of Religion, Berkeley, CA; and the LGBTrans Religious Archives Network, Chicago Theological Seminary, Chicago, IL. (ABS)

Moment, Joan Velma (1938 –) An artist and educator, Moment noted how few women artists were invited by the art dept. at California State University, Sacramento, to be guest lecturers. She also noted that there were very few full-time women faculty in the art department—and thus, few role models for women art students. Consequently, in the early 1970s, she introduced a course for women graduate students on contemporary women artists and issues that confront women who pursue careers in art. Moment, now professor emeritus, continued to teach this class every two years until her retirement in 2005. She continues to teach painting as a visiting artist/lecturer for Winter 2006 at California State University, Stanislaus. In addition to teaching, Moment was one of very few women to have a solo show at the Whitney Museum of American Art (1974), and was included in the Whitney Biennial (1973). Her paintings were also included in the Fresno Museum of Art's Survey of California Women Artists: The Years 1969 – 1975. Moment, who has one child, earned her B.S. from the University of Connecticut (1960) and her M.F.A. from the University of Colorado (1970). (ABS)

Momi, Adrienne (1943 –) As an artist, Momi has focused on issues of motherhood, sexuality and the divinity in everyone. In 1962, as a student at the University of Miami, she was outraged to learn that the university planned to close its School of Interior Design—almost exclusively female. Because of Momi's efforts, the administration agreed to phase out the program, thus allowing enrolled women to complete their degree work. Since then, she has worked for women's recognition in the arts as a member of the WCA, and has taught women's studies at the University of Missouri, St. Louis. As a member of the board of the St. Louis section of the National Council of Jewish Women, Momi advocated for better childcare, reproductive rights and elder care. When Roe v. Wade was challenged in Missouri, she went to Jefferson City on many occasions to support not only the pro-choice members of the legislature, but the attorney who successfully argued the Missouri challenge in the Supreme Court. In addition, Momi served on the board of the only county-wide shelter in St. Louis for homeless families, 90 percent of which were headed by single mothers, and served on the board of a shelter for abused women in St. Louis. She also helped produce the first information video for use by the St. Louis police and healthcare workers to assist them in identifying and helping battered women, and was instrumental in raising over $1 million to build a Section 8 apartment building for elderly women. Momi, who has one child, earned her B.S. and M.S. from Washington University, St. Louis, and her M.A. and Ph.D. from Pacifica Graduate Institute. (ABS)

Monson, Shirley (1924 –) Active in NOW, Monson was a member of the Detroit and Oakland, MI, chapters. In 1973, she served as VP and political action chair of the Oakland County chapter, and from 1974 – 1977 was state chair of MI NOW and chair of its selection committee for the Houston conference. In the early 1970s, she participated in a demonstration against Sears in which members destroyed their charge cards. In addition, she was part of a public demonstration and signed a petition in support of Roe v. Wade. To raise funds for more actions, Monson created feminist jewelry and sold it at meetings. An attorney, Monson was also active in the NWPC in California. Monson, who has three children, holds a B.A., M.A. and J.D. Archives: Bentley Historical Library, University of Michigan, Ann Arbor, MI. (ABS)

Montoni, Hope Haley (1931 –) was a founding member of the Sojourner Truth Chapter of NOW on the campus of Kent State University in 1970. She produced the first Women Artist Festival for the Kent State Summer Series (1973), which included exhibits of jewelry, crafts and paintings by nationally known women artists, opera scenes with a feminist perspective, dances by women choreographers, and films about great women artists. During her time at Kent State, Montoni lectured the honors classes on feminism and spoke to women's clubs and community groups on the ERA and feminism. After moving to Richmond, VA, in 1973, Montoni joined Richmond NOW, and in 1974 produced the August 26th Equality Day festival at A.P. Hill Park. As an associate of the Richmond Community Orchestra, Montoni researched and presented music by women and black composers in Virginia and the U.S. She is the recipient of a Woman of Achievement Award from Richmond NOW for her "unique blending of art and feminism." (ABS)

Moore, Frances Campbell (1926 –) Living in Indiana in the early 1970s, Moore was a member of the LWV, served on the ERA committee, and lobbied for the ERA on behalf of Hoosiers for the Equal Rights Amendment. She also served as precinct committeeman of the Democratic Party of Monroe County, IN. Moore, who has three children, earned her B.A. from the University of Illinois. (ABS)

Moore, Grace Jones (1926 –) Ordained by the United Church of Christ in 1973 and a foremother of women clergy, Moore has "felt called since 1970 to enable women to become equals with men in all facets of life." She served as president of the San Bernardino Association Women's Fellowship and of the Conference Women's Fellowship, and was an original member of the women's task force. She also organized Women Organizing Women and facilitated the Long Beach Women-Church for 20 years. In addition, she served as president of the International Association of Women Ministers for three terms. Her current project (2005) is Feminist Education Action Support Spirituality Theology, whose goal is to bring together women of all spiritualities for support and ritual. As a member of the women's task force, Moore worked aggressively to facilitate inclusive language in the church. She wrote an inclusive "Doxology" and "Gloria Patri," and rewrote the entire *Pilgrim Hymnal*. The group also went through the church school materials, church bulletins, the calendar, etc. to eliminate sexist language. In the mid 1970s, when the ordination of women was a divisive topic among denominations, Moore spoke for women on television in Los Angeles and on talk shows, and wrote articles for the newspapers. Moore also spoke against the advertising industry's treatment of women, and from 1974–1975 was coordinator of the Southern California Religious Coalition for Abortion Rights. Moore, who has three children, earned her B.M. from the University of Redlands (1948), her M.R.E. from Eastern Baptist Theological Seminary (1950), and her M.F.S. from Immaculate Heart College Center (2000). (ABS)

Moore, Laura Ann (1945 –) was a co-founder in St. Louis of the Lesbian Alliance in the late 1960s. With others, Moore helped found a rape crisis center and the St. Louis Abused Women's Support Project (which as of 2005 receives government funding and has a professional staff and apartment building to serve battered women). The group protested the Miss Universe contest when it came to St. Louis and organized a state lobbying day to protest when Anita Bryant came to town. In the early 1970s, Moore and her group successfully challenged the sexually biased admittance policies of Ranken Tech. The school initially let in two women, including Moore, who went on to open a garage and form The Women's Garage. Joining NOW in the mid 1970s, Moore became chair of the legal committee. The committee lobbied the mayor's office for women's rights, to get funding for women's initiatives, and to get women appointed to city government. It also wrote a booklet that told women what to do in cases of sexual-orientation harassment, held protests, and lobbied for abortion rights. She was also an elected delegate to IWY in Houston (1977). The first woman in St. Louis to be a housing inspector, a building inspector and a multi-discipline inspector for commercial and residential property, Moore was fired from her job as building commissioner of Vinita Park when the fact that she was a lesbian made the front page of the *St. Louis Post Dispatch*. She sued, received a settlement, and became the first avowed lesbian appointed St. Louis Civil Rights Commissioner (1990s). Moore holds a B.A. from the University of Missouri, St. Louis. (ABS)

Moore, Laurie Jo (1947 –) was deeply influenced by several generations of doctors on both sides of her family who were humanitarian, compassionate and devoted to public service. She was shocked to find instructors at medical school were not humanitarian. Moore was a second year medical student when a group of women, The Red Emma Collective, came to Portland, OR, to start a women's health clinic. Moore took part in the early planning and helped the group establish the Women's Health Clinic in Portland. The clinic provided women with pregnancy testing, counseling and Pap smears, but its major contribution was to help empower women to be in control of their own bodies and health. In 1975, Moore was general physician for the Virginia Garcia Memorial Health Clinic in Cornelius, OR. The clinic, named in memory of a little girl who died of dehydration in a major hospital waiting room because her family had no money, was a center for migrant field workers. From 1976–1983, Moore was the physician for a free clinic in an African American and Hispanic community. (ABS)

Moore, Ollie Butler (1919 – 1973) An African American who came through the public schools in Georgia, Moore was dean of women for 20 years at Southern University in Baton Rouge, LA. Established in 1880, the university was one of the five campuses comprising the only historically black Land Grant university systems in the U. S. Involved in anything having to do with the advancement of women, Moore was on the first board of directors of national NOW, serving from 1966–1969. She was a member of NOW's image committee and NOW's committee on continuing education for women in 1970. She worked with many organizations, including the YWCA, the Southwest Regional Association of Guidance Workers, the National Association of Women Deans, the Family Relations Council of LA and the National Association of Deans of Women and Advisors to Girls in Negro Schools. After she died in 1973, a new building at Southern University was named Ollie Butler Moore Hall, honoring her initiatives and leadership for women. Moore held a B. A. from Dillard University in New Orleans (1939) and an M.A. from Fisk University (1942). She did further study at Duke University and the University of Chicago before establishing a career in guidance. Archives: John B. Cade Library, Southern University, Baton Rouge, LA.

More, Rebecca Sherrill (1947 –) was the first woman to receive a B.A. degree from the University of Virginia at Charlottesville, in 1970, but not without overcoming university-imposed obstacles to that achievement. Reason prevailed and More ultimately was awarded a degree in history with honors. More was also involved in the University of Virginia WITCH grouping in 1969–1970. In

M

1994, she was invited back to speak at the 20th anniversary of the graduation of the first fully matriculated class of women at U.VA. In 1995, she spoke on hidden values and historical changes in assumptions about gender equity in education at Concord Academy from 1961–1995. More holds an M.A. and Ph.D. in history from Brown University. She has directed Brown's professional development center in pedagogy for faculty and graduate students since 1992. She is also an adjunct professor of History, Division of Liberal Arts: HPSS, at the Rhode Island School of Design, where she has taught courses in women's history since 1995. (ABS)

Morehouse, Betty Parrish (1934 –) was a founder of West Chester, PA, chapter of NOW in the mid 1970s and served as president in 1977. Morehouse was active in establishing the Rape Crisis Council and in establishing two domestic violence shelters, and also marched and lobbied for reproductive rights and the ERA. Morehouse, who has three children and served as primary caretaker for her two siblings, earned her A.B. from Radford College for Women (1960). (ABS)

Morena, Naomi Littlebear (1950 –) A musician and "homeless hippie crashing at the Women's Center in Santa Ana" in 1972, Morena met Robin Sauers (also known as Robin Flowers) and with her formed an acoustic guitar duo called Sisterhood. The two soon met Maxine Feldman, an out lesbian folksinger whose single, "Angry Atthis" and "Bar Song" was, "as far as we know, the first lesbian recording ever made on the West Coast." Morena moved to Portland (1973), where she met Kristan Knapp, an auto mechanic. After taking an auto mechanic course at the local community college, Morena joined Knapp in her auto shop, and continued writing songs. After writing "Why Did You Come to America," Morena co-founded the Ursa Minor Choir, a women-only group that later broke into a smaller group, the Izquierda Ensemble (1975–1980). In 1981, Morena wrote a rock opera called "Survivors" that was produced in Portland and addressed the impact of abuse in lesbian relationships. From 1983–1984, Morena worked as a dishwasher for a feminist-run restaurant called Old Wives Tales. While working there one evening, she heard her song "You Can't Kill the Spirit" being sung by a group of 30,000 women at the Greenham Common Women's Camp in England. Morena then traveled in England for five months and there learned how her song was sung at protests around the world, as a prayer, as a means of gathering courage. "It was a humbling experience," she says. In 1990, Morena co-organized an event called The Way Back, whose purpose was to gather singers, musicians, poets, dancers and artists who were survivors of abuse and put their creative works on display. Morena is (2005) a probation officer for Washington County, OR, where she supervises the Hispanic Offender Team and works with domestic violence offenders. (ABS)

Moreno, Dorinda (1939 –) is a San Francisco-raised "Chicana/Mescalero Apache" whose grandfather fought in the Mexican Revolution in 1910. Her feminist consciousness grew from her involvement with other movements, particularly her work as a civil rights activist in 1964–1965. In 1969, Moreno was at the center of a group of Spanish-speaking women at San Francisco College who formed Conclio Mujeres. A single mother of three, she returned to school after being in the workforce for a number of years. She saw CM as a place for Raza women with higher education to gain support. In 1973, CM opened an office in the Mission District, where Latinos live. In 1974 Moreno was the director of CM's Library Collection. The Chicana Collection Project was a key focus of CM for a number of years. Moreno protested the Vietnam War, boycotted grapes with the United Farm Workers, and helped develop ethnic and women's studies programs. She published the anthology, *la mujer – en pie de lucha*, directed a women's theater, "Las Cucarachas," and introduced Frida Kahlo to U.S. and world audiences. Moreno, who graduated from San Francisco State in 1973, was honored by the UFW with a Lifetime Achievement Award in 2003. Archives: Stanford University, Palo Alto, CA; and University of California, Berkeley, CA. (ABS)

Moreno, Irene Blea – See Blea, Irene Isabel

Moresky, Lana (1946 –) In 1970 Moresky met Eleanor Smeal and Jo Ann Evansgardner, who were starting suburban NOW chapters in the Pittsburgh area. Moresky, who became VP of the South Hills chapter, did a study showing the sexist influences in primary education, which she took to school boards and superintendents. She and others also started the first feminist day care center where all the books and toys stood up to feminist scrutiny. She participated in challenging discriminatory state labor laws and eliminating the gender segregation of employment advertising. When the ERA was passed by Congress in 1972, Moresky began 10 years of work for its ratification. She also participated in challenging the FCC license renewals of Pittsburgh TV stations, demanding that they have more women on the air and in advertising. That project forced three television stations to develop goals and timetables for hiring women, while teaching broadcasters how to use non-sexist language. When Moresky moved to Ohio in 1973, she led the effort to establish five NOW chapters in the Cleveland area, becoming president of the Cleveland East chapter. Moresky built on her Pittsburgh experience and led a successful license-renewal action with local broadcasters that affected three TV and six radio stations. She also continued her work in education, teaching feminist ideas at Inservice days for teachers, working to establish school lunch programs so that mothers could work, and helping to implement Title IX. She became president of OH NOW in 1975, growing it from three to 19 chapters in one year, and later served on NOW's national board. She was responsible for the law requiring the City of Cleveland and the County of Cuyahoga to give contracts to women business owners. Active in Democratic politics, Moresky chaired the coalition to get the first woman Federal District Judge of the Northern District of Ohio appointed by President Jimmy Carter; was a delegate to the National Democratic Convention several times; was on the Democratic Platform Committee in 1980; ran for the OH State Senate in 1990; and was the largest OH fundraiser for John Kerry for President campaign in 2004. She was on the national steering committees of Americans for Democratic Action and the NWPC, and in OH for Hope Chest, which raised money to elect OH women to public office, and for Women Elected Democratic Officials. She has been honored by the Ohio Women's Hall of Fame. Archives: Western Reserve Historical Society, Cleveland, OH. (ABS)

Morgan, Ellen Elizabeth – See Raintree, Elizabeth

Morgan, Mary Lou (1938 –) has worked to obtain social reforms for women and civil rights for everyone since 1968. With the women's liberation front at Wichita State University, she formed a Wichita NOW chapter, serving as the group's first president, as well as VP and program chair. Morgan also fought to make newspaper help-wanted ads gender neutral, and served on the Wichita Commission on the Status of Women. She helped obtain funding for the Wichita Women's Crisis Center; was NOW assistant state coordinator in Kansas; and served as NOW ERA lobbyist on the state board in Missouri. She has served as president of the Grover Beach Branch of the AAUW, 2002 –2004; and on the League of Women Voters board of directors, 2003 – 2004. Morgan holds a B.A. (1971) and M.Ed.(1974) from Wichita State University. Archives: Wichita State University Library, Wichita, KS. (ABS)

Morgan, Penelope G. – See Colman, Penny Morgan

Morgan, Robin (1941 –) Compiler/editor of the now classic anthologies *Sisterhood Is Powerful* (Random House, 1970), *Sisterhood Is Global* (the Feminist Press at CUNY, 1984) and *Sisterhood Is Forever* (Washington Square Press, 2003), Morgan is also an award-winning poet, novelist, political theorist, journalist and author of 20 books. A significant force in the feminist movement in the U.S. and abroad, Morgan was a founder of WITCH and member of many women's groups, including NYRW, the Feminist Women's Health Center, National Alliance Against Rape, Battered Women's Refuges, Women for the Abolition of Pornography, and the NWPC. She organized the first Miss America protest (1968); founded the first feminist grant-giving organization (The Sisterhood Is Powerful Fund); co-founded (with Simone de Beauvoir) the Sisterhood Is Global Institute, the first international feminist think-tank; and was editor in chief of *Ms.* magazine from 1989 to late 1993. She is a recipient of the National Endowment for the Arts Prize (Poetry), Front

Page Award for Distinguished Journalism, Feminist Majority Foundation Woman of the Year Award (1990) and many other honors. Morgan, who has one child, lives in New York, where she co-founded the first Women's Media Center. Archives: The Sallie Bingham Center, Duke University, Durham, NC. (ABS)

Morgan, Ruth Prouse (1934 –) became a feminist in 1961 when she applied to law school and was told that women would not be accepted. Morgan's role as a professor and feminist academic includes many "firsts." She was the first woman Ph.D. in political science at Louisiana State University, Baton Rouge (1966); the first woman elected president of the Southern Methodist University Faculty Senate (1972 – 1973); and the first woman to serve as provost and VP for academic affairs at SMU, Dallas (1986 – 1993). Morgan devised strategies to assure equity in faculty salaries and equitable treatment of women in promotion and tenure processes; drafted and established university policies fair to women, such as the first university maternity leave policy with pay at SMU; pioneered the implementation of sexual harassment policies at SMU; and lectured and counseled on strategies for overcoming discriminatory treatment. Morgan initiated the establishment of the Archives of Women of the Southwest in the DeGolyer Library, SMU, in 1994. She has been a member of SMU's annual Women's Symposium on the Education of Women for Social and Political Leadership since its inception in 1967. She also served as a member of the board (1989 – 1994) and president (1992 – 1993) of the Dallas Summit, founded in 1989 so that women could become full participants in all decision-making processes in the city, and was a founding member of the Dallas Forum, an affiliate of the International Women's Forum. She served as a member of its board (1990 – 1999) and as president (1996 – 1997). Morgan earned her B.A. from the University of Texas at Austin (1956); and her M.A. (1962) and Ph.D. (1966) from Louisiana State University, Baton Rouge. Archives: Archives of Women of the Southwest, DeGolyer Library, Southern Methodist University, Dallas, TX. (ABS)

Morgan, Sylvia Arlene (1930 –) (also known as Sylvia Kruger) In 1970, Morgan developed the first women's studies class at Moorhead State University (now Minnesota State University, Moorhead, MN). She encouraged other faculty members to develop women's studies classes in their specialties, and in 1974 was named coordinator of the women's studies program. She developed applications for MSU and for Minnesota curriculum committees, and chaired the women's studies campus committee through 1986. Morgan also taught a women's studies class yearly until her retirement in 1994. In 1973, Morgan was a member of the Tri-College University Women's Speakers Bureau. In 1974, she was a member of the coordinating committee for ERA ND, and took students to an ERA debate in the Bismarck, ND, Legislature. As a mem-

M

ber of the advisory committee for a Tri-College University outreach program, Declaration of Interdependence, Morgan developed names of appropriate people to invite, such as Karen DeCrow and Elizabeth Janeway. During the 1970s and 1980s, Morgan was constantly in the field conducting workshops and women's programs. In 1977, she attended the founding conference of the National Women's Studies Association, and served as an interrogator for the employment workshop of Bismarck's International Women's Year. In 1985 she was a panelist on the Minnesota Municipal Commission for "A Photo-History of American Finnish Women," and also worked with the Women's Union of Greece to organize craftswomen of Crete to raise their wages. Morgan has held memberships in NOW, NARAL, the WPC, the Women's Network of the Red River Valley, AAUW, LWV and the YWCA. She served on the board of the YWCA in 1982. Morgan, who has two children, earned her B.S. and M.A. from Northwestern University. Archives: Moorhead State University, Moorhead, MN; and Institute for Regional Studies, North Dakota State University, Fargo, ND. (ABS)

Morley, Evan (1934 –) With the arrival of the women's movement, Morley, who had been involved in the peace and civil rights movements, finally found a movement that spoke to her. In 1969, Morley joined the CR group that founded the Stanton-Anthony Brigade of NYRF (1969). Between 1970 and 1975, NYRF held speakouts on prostitution, marriage, motherhood, illegitimacy, rape and abortion. Morley, who was treasurer of NYRF and editor of its newsletter, was involved in all NYRF events until the group wound down in 1977. Morley was also one of the founders of the Women's Coffee House, a gathering place for feminists from October 1973 to July 1978. Born in Lake Placid, NY, Morley is an editor of children's school books. (ABS)

Morris, Muriel (1917 –) is a peace, human rights and feminist activist. In 1975 Morris joined NOW as well as the NYC, national and international segments of Women's International League for Peace and Freedom. She was also a member of the North Shore Community Arts Center in Roslyn and Great Neck, NY (1952 – 1980). In 1964, she demonstrated with Women Strike for Peace in protest against the draft and the war in Vietnam, and in 1965 participated in demonstrations and human rights actions to have people of color come to live in Great Neck. Morris, who has two children, earned her B.A. from Cornell University.

Morrison, Kathryn Mae (1942 –) was active in the Wisconsin WPC, 1972 – 1974, serving as state coordinator and also on the national board. She was also appointed to a governor's commission responsible for developing a public-school funding system that provided each school with an equitable share of state resources. In 1974, Morrison became the first woman elected to the WI State Senate. During her tenure, she authored divorce and inheritance laws that created equity for women, and served on the joint finance committee, the most powerful committee in the WI Legislature. Morrison holds an M.B.A. from the University of Wisconsin, Madison. (ABS)

Morrison, Lonnie Leotus (1926 –) As a graduate student at Indiana University in the 1950s, Morrison chafed at not being allowed to take some courses on athletic training and coaching because they were reserved for men; she nonetheless went on to make significant changes for women in athletics. At James Madison University, she helped create the faculty women's caucus and was responsible for developing the women's athletic program. In the 1960s and early 1970s she was a member of the executive committee of the Virginia Association for Girls and Women in Sport, and was a founding member and first president of the Virginia Association for Intercollegiate Athletics for Women (1970 – 1973). In addition, Morrison served as chair of the intercollegiate committee of the Southern Association of Physical Education for College Women. Morrison began a long association with the Association for Intercollegiate Athletics for Women in 1970 when she became a founding board member representing 13 Southern states. She held numerous positions, including newsletter editor and president, and from 1976 – 1982 was chair of its international commission. Morrison has served on numerous committees at state, regional and national levels of the National Association for Girls and Women in Sport, including president; was a member of the U.S. Olympic Executive Board (1975 – 1983); and in the 1980s represented women in athletics as a member of the Virginia identification program of the American Council on Education. In addition, Morrison was one of five U.S. women invited by the Federal Republic of Germany for a three-week tour of West Germany's sports facilities (1977); was a member of the U.S. delegation to the UNESCO conference on physical education and sport, held in Paris in 1978; and presented a paper on women's athletics in the U.S. at the First International Congress on Women and Sport in the Americas (1981). She was also a speaker and participant in the First Pan American Congress on Women and Sport, held in conjunction with Pan American Games in Venezuela (1983). Morrison is author of "From the Playing Fields and Courts," published in *Educating the Majority: Women Challenge Tradition in Higher Education* (ACE/MacMillan Series in Higher Education, 1989). She holds a B.S. from Georgia State College and University, an M.A. from George Peabody College, and a P.E.D. from Indiana University. In addition, she holds a Doctor of Humanities, honoris causa, from James Madison University. Archives: AIAW Region 2 Archives, Eastern Kentucky University and AIAW Archives, University of Maryland; personal papers are at The Sophia Smith Collection, Smith College, Northampton, MA. (ABS)

Morrison, Toni (1931 –) A Pulitzer Prize winning novelist, short-story writer, playwright, essayist and editor, Morrison was the first black woman to receive the Nobel Prize in Literature (1993). Concerned with the elaborately socialized world of black people and the female quest for selfhood, Morrison's writings have contributed to the ideology of black feminism by creating a framework for self-identity. Describing the black woman, Morrison said, she "had nothing to fall back on: not maleness, not whiteness, not ladyhood, not anything. And out of the profound desolation of her reality she may very well have invented herself." Morrison, the second of four children, was born Chloe Anthony Wofford in 1931, in the small Midwestern town of Lorain, OH. In 1949, she entered Howard University, and in 1953 she began graduate work in English at Cornell University. After receiving her M.A. in 1955, Morrison taught briefly in the English department at Texas Southern University (1955 – 1957), then returned to Howard to teach English. In 1966, with two children to support, Morrison left teaching and accepted a job as a textbook editor at Random House; in 1968, Morrison became a trade book editor there. In 1970, Holt published her first novel, *The Bluest Eye*. Morrison rose through the ranks at Random House to become a senior editor, the first black woman ever to hold that position. At Random House, she edited books by such black authors as Toni Cade Bambara and Gayl Jones. She also continued to teach at two branches of the State University of New York. In 1984 she was appointed to an Albert Schweitzer chair at the University of New York at Albany, where she nurtured young writers through two-year fellowships. Working as an editor by day and a writer by night, Morrison published her second novel, *Sula* (Knopf, 1973). Morrison's third novel, *Song of Solomon* (Knopf, 1977), won the National Book Critic's Circle award, and *Tar Baby* (Knopf, 1981) helped propel her to the upper echelon of American writers. Her Pulitzer Prize winning novel, *Beloved* (Knopf, 1987), explores the themes of motherhood and infanticide within the context of slavery. In 1989, Morrison was named the Robert F. Goheen Professor in the Council of the Humanities at Princeton University.

Morrissey, Claudia Susan (1947 –) has worked consistently for women's rights and women's health. She is (2005) deputy director, Center for Research on Women and Gender, University of Illinois, Chicago. She has served as director, Women in Science and Engineering; and assistant clinical professor, Northwestern University School of Medicine, Department of Preventive Medicine. As a member of the feminist/socialist community in Des Moines, IA (1973 – 1978), she developed and taught women's awareness workshops that included self-help/health empowerment issues, and demonstrated and gave presentations for reproductive and sexual rights. She also participated in the first Socialist/Feminist Conference at Antioch, OH. Active in NOW, Morrissey campaigned against United Way's inequitable use of funds in favoring boy's/men's programs. She also helped to develop a directory of women's opinions about doctors in the community. Morrissey was one of the first female construction workers in the Des Moines area. She spent 1976 in Mexico City where she taught self-help classes, demonstrated for abortion rights, helped translate *Our Bodies, Ourselves*, and helped establish the first women's center in Mexico. In medical school from 1978 – 1982, Morrissey earned an M.D. in internal medicine, became a member of the American Medical Women's Association, and continued as a cultural worker (singer) for feminist/socialist events in Chicago. She served as the AMWA delegate to the International Conference on Population and Development, held in Cairo in 1994, and to the United Nations Fourth World Conference on Women, held in Beijing in 1995. She continued her work on international women's health issues after receiving her M.P.H. from Johns Hopkins University. Morrissey, who has three children, is a member of the steering committee of the International Consortium for Emergency Contraception. Morrissey holds an undergraduate degree from the University of N. Iowa, Cedar Falls. Archives: Women's Archives, University of Iowa, Iowa City, IA. (ABS)

Morrow, Ann (1939 –) began graduate work at the University of Colorado in 1968, worked with local feminists in CR training, and led feminist workshops on reproductive rights, feminist theory and lesbian issues in Boulder. In 1970, she began working for the Boulder Public Schools as a counselor, but became discouraged by the schools' political climate and the restrictions about coming out to gay and lesbian students who were in need of positive role models. After three years, Morrow left high-school counseling to go into private practice, and began working with other women who were trying to start a feminist institute in Boulder for graduate studies in feminist therapy. She co-founded a small feminist newspaper, the *Some Times*, and in 1977 was a co-founder of the Feminist Counseling Collective in the Boulder area, the first therapy group in Denver to openly advertise as lesbians. As a result, the women were asked to teach classes at the University of Denver School of Social Work, Metro State College and Arapahoe State College on treatment issues for lesbians. They also facilitated workshops at Planned Parenthood on lesbian/feminist issues and reproduction. In 1981 Morrow and a partner purchased 160 acres of mountain property in Colorado to create Womanventure, a women's retreat. Morrow remained involved with Womanventure until 1991. In 1995, Morrow was hired as the clinical supervisor for the Domestic Violence Initiative for Women With Disabilities, a non-profit serving the greater Denver area. Morrow, who continues to do workshops and retreats, has completed a book, *Applecrate Stories*, that grew out of 13 years of leading a feminist therapy group in Denver. Morrow holds a B.A. and M.A. (ABS)

M

Morton, Carole Joyce (1945 –) has worked aggressively in support of women's rights, and in particular for the rights of lesbian mothers. She was a co-founder of Dykes & Tykes and The East Coast Lesbian Mothers Defense Fund (NYC, 1971); helped establish the NJ chapter of Daughters of Bilitis (1974); and co-founded the Downtown Welfare Advocate Center (NYC) on behalf of Welfare mothers and poor women, providing legal representation, social action and CR to individual women and through the media (1973). In addition, she produced and hosted "Women Loving," a one-hour lesbian feminist entertainment weekly television show in San Francisco (1981). Morton has been a grassroots organizer of and participant in numerous organizations, including Jane Adams House for Battered Women, the first such shelter in NYC (1970); La Casa De Las Madres, a battered women's shelter in San Francisco (1976); the Artificial Insemination Clinic at the Lesbian Clinic in NYC (1972); Radicalesbians (1970); and Lesbian-Feminist Liberation in NYC (1971). She also served as publicity co-chair in San Francisco for the first national march on Washington for lesbian and gay rights (1978). In 1973, Morton taught Welfare law and advocacy, as well as lesbian herstory, at the Brooklyn Women's School. She has spoken widely on lesbian-feminist issues, including a speech on unity among lesbians and straight feminists, which took place at the Sheep Meadow in Central Park (NYC), at the first women's march, despite protests by Betty Friedan. At the request of Florence Kennedy, Morton spoke at United Nations Plaza in support of legalizing prostitution and providing support, education and opportunity for other work (1974). Morton was also a member of the speakers committee of National Gay Task Force (1970–1974). The book *A Long Way Home*, by Jeanne Jullian (1981), chronicles Morton's trip to Italy where she successfully "kidnapped" the son of a lesbian mother who had been taken by the father. Morton, who has one son, helped write the first *Lesbian Mothers Legal Custody Manual* (1976), and was a contributor to the anthology *Lesbians Raising Sons* (1992). She holds a B.A. from SUNY Old Westbury, as well as an M.A. in clinical psychology and an M.A. in speech communication. Archives: The Lesbian Herstory Archives, Brooklyn, NY. (ABS)

Moseley-Braun, Carol (1947 –) has been a voice for women in the U.S. Senate and the Illinois House of Representatives, and throughout her career in public service has been committed to preventing discrimination on the basis of gender, race or sexual orientation. An attorney, Mosely-Braun worked as an assistant U.S. attorney in the early 1970s, primarily in the area of civil litigation. She served in the Illinois State Legislature from 1979 to 1987, and was the Cook County recorder of deeds from 1988 to 1992. She was elected to the U.S. Senate in 1992, the first African American woman to achieve that honor. From 1999 to 2001, she was the U.S. ambassador to New Zealand. A candidate for U.S. President in the 2004 primary, she worked on the "Every Open Seat, a Woman's Seat" campaign to increase female representation. (ABS)

Moses, Claire Goldberg (1941 –) A professor (2005) in the women's studies department at the University of Maryland at College Park, Moses serves as editorial director of *Feminist Studies* and is the author of several books on the history of feminist movements. These include *French Feminism in the 19th Century* (SUNY Press, 1977), which received the Joan Kelly Memorial Prize for the Best Book in Women's History (1985), and *U.S. Women in Struggle: A Feminist Studies Anthology* (University of Illinois Press, 1995), of which Moses was co-editor with Heidi Hartmann. In 1970, Moses organized Reston (VA) Women's Liberation, the first women's group in Northern VA. She created an information resource center for the group, and organized and presented discussions on women's issues to the community during the summers of 1970 and 1971. In addition, Moses wrote articles for the local paper, organized protests of local establishments with discriminatory policies, and organized a local contingency for participation in the August 1970 demonstration in Washington, D.C. Moses has two children. (ABS)

Moses, Yolanda T. (1946 –) An educator, anthropologist and administrator, Moses has worked to connect women's studies and ethnic studies and to show that race, ethnicity, gender and class are all legitimate parts of a women's studies knowledge base. She began graduate studies in anthropology at the University of California, Riverside, in 1970, helped form a feminist group within that department, and in 1971 was a co-organizer of a seminar called Women in Cross-Cultural Perspective. Moses is a former president of CUNY, president of the American Anthropological Association, member of the board of the Ford Foundation, and member of The Women's Forum. As a consultant for the Association of American Colleges and Universities, she produced the seminal monograph "Black Women in Academe." She holds a Ph.D. from the University of California, Riverside (1976). (ABS)

Moskowitz, Marcia – See Suttenberg, Marcia Lee

Mosley, Mary A. Krehbiel (1943 –) A freelance writer/editor, lobbyist and adjunct professor at William Woods University in Fulton, Missouri (2005), Mosley began fighting for women's rights in 1974 when she joined the WPC and NOW in Columbia, MO. She taught the first women's studies classes at Shimer College in Illinois (1977), then moved to Columbus to teach at Ohio State University. President of the Columbus chapter of NOW from 1978–1979, she and four other NOW members created a stir when they began writing feminist slogans on a sound barrier wall next to the Interstate—a move that made the more conservative members of the chapter unhappy. In 1981, Mosley moved to Evanston, where she served as VP (1983–1984) and president (1986–1987) of the Evanston/North Shore chapter of NOW. In 1986, when treasury secretary Donald Regan said women didn't want sanctions against South Africa because they would have to give up their jewelry, the group held a Rhinestones for Regan action, gathering letters of protest which they mailed daily until Regan lost his job. The group held numerous other actions, including a shoe burning, a signature gathering to protest the appointment of Robert Bork to the Supreme Court, and a Turkey of the Year Award to people who had disparaged women. In 1988, Mosley moved to Fulton, MO, where she served as NOW state coordinator (1991 – 1994) and regional director (1996 – 1998). Mosley also served on NOW's national board (1994 – 1998). She is (2005) legislative director of the Missouri Women's Network and was a founding member of the Missouri Alliance for Choice (serving as president from 1997 – 1998, and treasurer, beginning in 1998). She was also a founder and board member of the Missouri Women's Leadership Coalition, created in 2001 to identify and train women to run for office. Mosley, who has one child, earned her B.A. from the University of Puget Sound (1964), and her M.A. (1969) and Ph.D. (1976) from the University of Missouri. Archives: Western Historical Manuscripts, 23 Ellis Library, University of Missouri, Columbia, MO. (ABS)

Moss, Lauree Ellen (1946 –) was a member of the Berkeley Feminist Counseling Collective (1972), one of just a few collectives in the country at that time that provided feminist therapy. In the late 1970s, she was a founding member of the Feminist Therapy Institute (which still functions today/2005). In 1975, she was co-author, with Nikki Sachs, of one of the first papers on feminist therapy to be presented at the American Orthopsychiatric Association annual meeting. Says Moss, "We were the only radical feminist therapists on the panel. I was also the only out lesbian, and this was my first professional presentation." Earlier (1967 – 1969), Moss had been part of anti-Vietnam War demonstrations at Wayne State University. She was also part of the Free Clinic Movement, working by day as a clinical social worker and by night at Open City, Detroit's first free clinic. After moving to Berkeley in 1970, Moss joined the radical psychiatry movement and the women's health (self-help) movement, teaching women to give themselves vaginal exams and running CR groups on health and sexuality. Moss is (2005) a psychotherapist in private practice in Santa Monica, CA, a certified life coach, and a teacher at the Institute of Integrative Body Psychotherapy in Venice, CA. Moss holds a B.A. from the University of Michigan (1967), an M.S.W. from Wayne State, and a Ph.D. from the Union Institute (1981). Archives: June Mazer Collection, Los Angeles, CA. (ABS)

Moss, Vicki (1936 –) began running CR sessions in her home in Englewood, NJ, in 1969. In 1972, as a graduate student at the CUNY Graduate Center, Moss was selected to represent the philosophy dept. at the founding meeting of the Society of Women in Philosophy. She has been a member of SWIP since that time. In 1974, forced to leave graduate school to support her family, Moss began working for Central State Bank (NYC), where she created and headed a women's department for women business owners. She later became the first loan officer there specifically to serve women. In 1975, Moss was one of 10 founding members of the New York Association of Women Business Owners. In 1976, she served as director of the Women's Rights Information Center, Teaneck, NJ. In 1977, she ran workshops and developed a job-hunting program for Women Working, a Dept. of Labor-funded program to train women for non-traditional jobs. She also campaigned for the ERA in NY State, and in 1978 worked for two domestic violence shelters in NJ, again running workshops to help women enter training programs and/or find jobs. She has spoken widely on issues regarding women and money, and is the author of "Financial Problems of Women," published in *Women In Industry* (1977). Moss, who has two children, earned her B.A. from CUNY (1969), and holds an M.A. in English from Colorado State University (1984) and an M.A. from the Graduate Center, CUNY (1987). (ABS)

Mountaingrove, Jean Janette (1925 –) (also known as Jean Janette Tangeman) In 1970, then the mother of two teenagers, Mountaingrove came to the realization that she was a lesbian, and began searching for a commune where she and her children could live. In the process, she discovered *Country Women* magazine, and wrote for it and for the *Women's Press* newspaper in Eugene, OR. When she and her partner were evicted from their Mountain Grove home for being lesbians, they began traveling the West Coast looking for a place to live. *Country Women* invited them to help with an issue on spirituality, and from there came the inspiration to launch their own magazine, *WomanSpirit*, which published from 1974 – 1984. It was distributed by women's bookstores in the U.S., Canada, England and France. In 1980, Mountaingrove co-founded a magazine of feminist photography, *The Blatant Image*. Workshops on menstruation began in 1972 and, as menopause became a reality, Mountaingrove began offering workshops on that experience at women's gatherings and conferences. During this time, she also wrote regular columns in *MAIZE*, a country lesbian magazine, and for *Crone Chronicles*, a magazine of conscious aging. She has had articles published in several anthologies, including *OFF The Rag: Lesbians and Menopause*. Mountaingrove holds a B.A. from the University of Iowa (1947) and an M.S.W. from the University of California, Los Angeles (1967). Archives: Special Collections Library, University of Oregon, Eugene, OR. (ABS)

Mountaingrove, Ruth Elizabeth (1923 –) (also known as Ruth Ikeler) joined Philadelphia NOW in 1966, worked on changing abortion laws, and wrote the song,

"Who Killed This Woman?" which was copyrighted by Philadelphia NOW and used at rallies and meetings. A full-time worker in the Philadelphia women's liberation movement from 1968 – 1971, she wrote for the newspaper *Awake and Move*, helped found Women in Transition for battered women, managed the speakers bureau, and helped facilitate the first lesbian group in Philadelphia. She moved to Mountain Grove, a commune in Oregon, in 1971 – 1973, and then to Golden, where she wrote more songs, published a book, *Turned On Woman*, and a book of poetry, *For Those Who Cannot Sleep*. She also co-founded *WomanSpirit*, a quarterly, with Jean Mountaingrove, in 1974. The feminist spirituality magazine published for 10 years with the help of many women. In 1980, 1981 and 1982, the two Mountaingroves also published *The Blatant Image*, a magazine of feminist photography, and hosted Photography Ovulars, weeklong workshops. In 1985, Mountaingrove enrolled in Humboldt State University, where, she says, she was known "as a flaming feminist as well as an out lesbian." She graduated with an M.A. in Art and Photography in 1990, and in 2002 with an M.A. in Theater Production and Dramatic Writing. Her play "The Cat" (about two lesbians dealing with the problem of a cat) was produced by the World Premiere Theatre. Her short stories, poetry and photographs have appeared in *Country Woman, New Women's Press, Sinister Wisdom, Manzanita Quarterly, Women's Liberation, Aphra, Lesbian Lives, Common Lives* and *Communities*, among other publications. Since 1985, she has been a producer of a feminist radio program on KHSU-FM. She also writes book reviews for "L-Word," a lesbian newsletter. Mountaingrove, who earned her B.S. from Kutztown University, has three children. Archives: Ruth Mountaingrove Collection, University of Oregon, Eugene, OR. (ABS)

Mulhauser, Karen (1942 –) (also known as Karen Webber) began working for reproductive freedom in 1969 as a counselor at Pregnancy Counseling Services in Boston. She also joined MORAL, the NARAL affiliate in MA, and lobbied for contraceptive and abortion services. From 1971 – 1973, Mulhauser worked at Seattle Planned Parenthood and lobbied the Washington State Legislature for continued abortion and contraception services. In 1973, Mulhauser became director of the Washington, D.C., office of national NARAL, where she organized the first annual celebration of the Roe v. Wade decision. In 1975, Mulhauser became executive director of NARAL, a position she held until 1981, when she became executive director of Citizens Against Nuclear War. She also founded and chaired an ad hoc effort in the 1980s to bring women leaders to the first Reagan/Gorbachev summit in Geneva and to the following summits. In 1988, Mulhauser began her own consulting firm and continues to provide services to both domestic and global women's movements (and others). She has served on over 30 boards, including Planned Parenthood of Metropolitan Washington, Women's EDGE, Voters for Choice, Choice USA, Women's Information Network, and Women's Foreign Policy Campaign. Mulhauser, who has one child, earned her B.A. from Antioch College. (ABS)

Mullins, Sandy — In the early 1970s, Mullins was a member of Northwest Women for Peace and served on the national field staff for George McGovern. In 1973, she became political action chair of Detroit NOW and worked to have feminist candidates elected to office. Mullins was a founder of the Michigan Democratic Party women's caucus and served as its first treasurer. She was also a participant and panel member of the first Campaign Techniques Workshop, conducted by the National Women's Education Fund at Alverno College in Milwaukee. From 1976 – 1982, she worked full time on ratification of the ERA. She organized in Florida and, after the 1977 defeat, was sent by Gloria Steinem to California where she directed two programs: The California ERA Campaign Fund and the committee to ratify ERA. The former was the first successful effort to raise political-candidate money to be used in the unratified states. The latter, of which Mullins was a founder and executive director (1979 – 1982), boasted Governor Jerry Brown and Barbara Streisand as honorary chairs. After ERA, Valerie Harper and Mullins used the committee to ratify to create a poverty program in Los Angeles that provided supplemental food to women and children. Called LIFE, the program operated for about 15 years, at one point supplying food to 187,000 people a week. Since 1998 Mullins has been living in Eastern Tennessee and studying political science at Carson-Newman College.

Munaker, Susan Phyllis (1939 –) was an activist organizer supporting full equality for women and women's right to choose (1964 – 1979). She also supported, through demonstrations and forums, the work for gay rights. Munaker was part of the 1966 meeting in the Lincoln Park area of Chicago, perhaps the first gathering of women in that city, to discuss the emerging women's consciousness. After the Conference for New Politics (1967), the first Chicago women's groups were formed, including the West Side Group, of which Munaker was a part. Within that group, a network was created to help women obtain abortions, and "often, we took the women to the abortion, and afterwards fed them and cared for them for a day and a night," says Munaker. She helped in the planning for the Jeannette Rankin Brigade in 1968, and chaired many of the planning sessions for the August activities at the 1968 Democratic National Convention. She moved to New Orleans in 1969 and joined a Movement for a Democratic Society chapter. There, with Dottie Zellner, she organized a women's group and established a women's Marxist study group. From 1972 – 1979, Munaker was a member of the Spartacist League, which "lived the Marxist principle of supporting women's rights within the context of the general struggle," says

Munaker. In 1973, she helped form a contingent from Buffalo (NY) to travel to Toronto for a large demonstration for women's right to choose. Also active in the anti-war and civil rights movements in the mid 1960s, Munaker "had my car turned over and destroyed at one of the large marches led by Dr. King." Munaker, who has one child and two children by marriage, earned an undergraduate degree from Towson State Teachers College (1961), an M.S. from DePaul University (1989) and a Ph.D. from The Union Institute (1996). (ABS)

Munts, Mary Lou (1924 –) was elected to the Wisconsin State Assembly in 1972, where she was one of seven women out of 99 members. Because of the negative campaign against the ERA and failed attempts to secure equal rights in the Wisconsin constitution, Munts became more involved in women's rights issues. In 1975, she was a co-sponsor of an omnibus equal rights bill that eliminated sex-based references from the state statutes. However, divorce, marital property and sexual assault were left for separate legislation. Munts was asked by Kay Clarenbach, chair of the Governor's Commission on the Status of Women, to lead efforts to draft divorce reform legislation that included economic protections for women. This bill became law in 1978. Subsequently, Munts was the major author of marital property legislation. In 1984, Wisconsin became the first separate property state to become a community property state. Munts chaired the committee on environmental quality for eight years. In 1983 she became the first woman to co-chair the joint committee on finance. Munts also authored legislation recodifying the mental health act and the state's anti-trust laws. She took special interest in measures affecting persons with disabilities. After retiring from the WI Assembly (1984), Munts was appointed by Governor Anthony Earl as the first woman to serve on the Wisconsin Public Service Commission, where she served until 1991. Munts was a member of the board of the Energy Foundation and the national board of Common Cause. She also served for 10 years as co-chair of WI Common Cause. Munts, who has three children, attended Swarthmore College and received an M.A. from the University of Chicago and a J.D. from the University of Wisconsin Law School. Archives: Papers from her legislative career are with the Wisconsin Historical Society, as are taped interviews for an oral history project, "Documenting the Midwestern Origins of the 20th Century Women's Movement." (ABS)

Murphy, Betty Southard — An attorney, adjunct professor of law, and partner, Baker & Hostetler LLP, Murphy was the first woman to chair the National Labor Relations Board and the only woman to do so in its first 65 years. She was also the first woman Wage & Hour Administrator, responsible for 72 labor statutes including the Fair Labor Standards Act and child labor laws. She also successfully handled cases of discrimination against women at the U.S. Dept. of State and other government departments.

Murphy, who has had seven presidential appointments and U.S. Senate confirmations, was a Republican founder of the NWPC and serves as co-chair of the Republican National Lawyers Association. She did pro bono legal work in establishing Stewardesses for Women's Rights and other women's organizations, and is the first and only lawyer solely in private practice elected to the prestigious National Academy of Human Resources. Murphy, who has held numerous positions on various committees, served as chair of the committee on the status of women, Women's Bar Association (1973 – 1974), and from 1973 – 1975 was chair of the committee on Equal Opportunity and Collective Bargaining of the Federal Bar Association, and is chair of the ABA's dispute resolution section international committee. She has received a number of Woman of the Year awards and was selected by the D.C. Bar Association, which has over 70,000 members, as a "Legend in the Law." She earned her B.A. from Ohio State University and her J.D. from American University Washington College of Law. In addition, Murphy, who has two children, holds Honorary Degrees from Eastern Michigan University, Capital University, University of Puget Sound Law School and Tusculum College. Archives: The Ford Foundation and Schlesinger Library, Radcliffe Institute, Cambridge, MA. (ABS)

Murphy, Brianne (1933 – 2003) Born in London, Murphy was a founder of Women in Film (1973), organized to "empower, promote, nurture and mentor women in the industry"; and a founding member of Behind the Lens, an organization of female film technicians. The winner of the Women in Film Lucy Award for Innovation in Television in 1995, Murphy was admitted to the Cinematographers Guild in 1973, the first female director of photography in the Hollywood area. Seven years later, she became the first female director of photography to work on a major studio film—"Fatso," written and directed by Anne Bancroft. In 1980, Murphy was invited to join the American Society of Cinematographers, and was its only female member for 15 years. Murphy attended Pembroke College (which later merged with Brown University) and studied acting at the Neighborhood Playhouse in New York City.

Murphy, Judy Ann (1933 –) was a member of Northern NJ NOW (1970 – 1991), of the NJ WPC (1970 – 1975), of national NOW (1970 – 1982), and of VT NOW (1991 – 2005). Active at all levels in NJ NOW, she served on the state board, edited the newsletter and co-chaired the statewide ERA task force. She was also coordinator of the Northeast Region NOW conference in Atlantic City known as Wonder Woman: It's No Myth, America. Earlier, Murphy had been instrumental in organizing a demonstration against the New Jersey Commission on Women, which had tried to hold closed meetings and then held a state conference that excluded NOW. Murphy was the second state coordinator and one of the organizers of the

WPC in New Jersey. As a member of national NOW, Murphy served as press secretary to president Ellie Smeal during the ERA Countdown Campaign, "a whirlwind two years working day and night." Now retired and living in Vermont, Murphy has served as state coordinator for Vermont NOW and serves on the board of directors of Vermont's Freedom to Marry Task Force. She was one of three coordinators of the Northeast Region NOW Les/Bi/Trans/ Allies Strategy Summit and Celebration in 2001. Murphy, who has three children, serves as president of the AAUW Bennington chapter 2003 – 2007. She earned her Bachelor of Journalism degree from Carleton University, Ottawa, Canada.   (ABS)

Murra, Laura – See X, Laura

Murray, Anita Jean (1943 –) was active in the early 1970s as a committee head on reproduction and its control and later VP of NY NOW. As such, she worked to get disability benefits for pregnant women and insurance benefits for maternity costs in NY State. In the late 1970s, Murray was a founder of Married Americans for Tax Equality, which lobbied against the marriage tax because it penalized working women who were married. Murray, who had a long career in computer systems management, earned her B.S. from the University of Pittsburgh and her M.S. from Stanford University.   (ABS)

Murray, Anna Pauline ("Pauli") (1910 – 1985) was a lawyer and poet from Baltimore whose experience as a woman of color in the early 20th century impelled her to a life of activism. She organized lunch counter sit-ins in Washington, D.C., in the 1940s, and was arrested in 1940 for not sitting in the back of a bus during a demonstration with the Fellowship of Reconciliation in Virginia. She was a founder of the Congress of Racial Equality in 1942. Murray was denied admission to Harvard Law School for graduate study—not on racial grounds, but because she was a woman. Murray declared that "Jane Crow," or gender discrimination, was just as pernicious as Jim Crow. By the time she entered Howard University Law School, Murray was a seasoned labor and civil rights activist. When she graduated, the only woman and first in her class, she was an "unabashed feminist as well." After earning a law degree at Howard University (1944) and an L.L.M. at the University of California, Berkeley (1945), she became the first woman and African American to earn a Doctorate of Juridical Science from Yale Law School. She later became the first African American to be deputy attorney general of California, where she wrote the state's *Laws on Race in Color* (1951), a massive reference work. Recognizing the need for a NAACP-like organization for women, she was a founding member of NOW in 1966. She worked as a civil rights lawyer in New York, and taught law at Ghana School of Law (1969 – 1971) and African American studies at Brandeis University. She was named Woman of the Year in 1946 by the National

Council of Colored Women, and in 1947 by *Mademoiselle* magazine. In 1971, she received the Eleanor Roosevelt Award from the Professional Woman's Caucus. Murray left public life in the mid 1970s to study at the General Theological Seminary in New York. She became a deacon in 1976 and, before her death, added one more "first" to her list: In 1977, she became the first African American woman Episcopal priest. Murray is the author of *Dark Testament and Other Poems* (1970) and *Proud Shoes: The Story of an American Family* (1956). *Song in a Weary Throat: An American Pilgrimage*, her autobiography, was published posthumously (1987). Archives: Schlesinger Library, Radcliffe Institute, Cambridge, MA.

Murray, Ruth M. (1909 – 1975) was an early organizer in the ILGWU, which she joined in 1936. Particularly interested in women's political action, she served as the women's activity director for the AFL-CIO committee on political education in Baltimore in the 1960s. She was also appointed to the Governor's Commission on the Status of Women, and worked to establish childcare programs. At her retirement in 1972, Murray was director of the union label sector of ILGWU, Upper South Dept. She had three children.

Myers, Lonny (1922 –) (also known as Lonny Myers Wang) A medical doctor and ardent supporter of women's right to choose, Myers actively opposed the Colorado law that said women could have abortions "under special circumstances." Although some said it was at least a step in the right direction, Myers saw it as allowing someone else to have control over the decision—a step in the wrong direction. In response, in 1969, she met with Don Shaw and Ruth Smith in the basement of her home and founded NARAL. Earlier, she had been a founder of Citizens for the Extension of Birth Control Services (1961), which won the fight for tax-supported birth control in Illinois in 1965, and of Illinois Citizens for the Medical Control of Abortion (1966), the first state organization to advocate the repeal of all abortion laws. In 1970, she was an instigator and sponsor of the First National Conference on Optimum Population and Environment, and in 1973 was instigator and sponsor of the Chicago Conference on Bisexual Behavior. From 1975 – 1979, Myers was director of Sexual Health Services, Midwest Population Center, Chicago. In 1985, she was a counselor in the management of menopause, and in 1987 worked in AIDS testing and counseling. Myers has also worked to end genital mutilation and to implement physician-assisted suicide. Myers, who has five children, earned her B.A. from Vassar College (1944) and her M.D. from the University of Michigan, Ann Arbor (1948). Archives: Special Collections, University of Illinois, Chicago, IL.   (ABS)

Myers, Mary Lynn (1945 –) (also known as Mary Lynn Crandall) The first female management intern hired by the General Services Administration in Chicago, Myers immediately began experiencing blatant sex discrimination in the Federal Civil Service. In response, she founded and served as the first president of the Chicago chapter of FEW (1969), and from 1969–1971 was a member of its national board. As a member of the Chicago chapter of NOW (1969–1972), she served as compliance task force coordinator and worked aggressively for women who had discrimination cases. Myers moved to South Dakota and was a founding member of the Pierre, SD, chapter of NOW (1972) and served as SD state coordinator (1972–1974). From 1971–1977, she was a member of NOW's national board, serving as national compliance task force coordinator and national finance VP, and was a candidate for national president in 1975. She also served as chair of the SD committee preparing for the 1977 National Women's Conference, and was a delegate from SD to that meeting. In addition, Myers was a member of the board and treasurer of NOW LDEF (1977–1981), and a member of the NWPC and NARAL in the late 1970s into the 1980s. From 1972–1976, Myers was director, SD Division of Human Rights. During her tenure, the group issued one of the first orders in the country directing that girls be permitted to join Little League teams (1974). An active supporter of the ERA, Myers spoke often on the topic before civic and legislative groups and debated Phyllis Schlafly at a 1977 SD Humanities Council event. Myers was the winner of the Sioux Falls YWCA Leader in Business Award (1981) and of the Minnehaha County, SD, WPC Foremother Award (1982). In 1983 and 1996, she was named SD Small Business Administration Advocate for Women in Business. Myers earned her B.A. from the University of South Dakota, Vermillion (1967) and her M.S. from DePaul University (1974). She also holds a diploma from the Colorado Graduate School of Banking (1982). Archives: NOW papers are at the Schlesinger Library, Radcliffe Institute, Cambridge, MA. (ABS)

Myerson, Marilyn (1945–) (also known as Marilyn Ferrandino) As a graduate student in philosophy at SUNY Buffalo in 1967, Myerson was deep into studying and reading about the women's movement and its goals and premises when she had an epiphany during one CR group: "Let's teach this!" At that time, SUNY Buffalo had "bulletin board classes," meaning that if a person got 20 students to sign up, the class would become a class for credit. Myerson and a number of other graduate students set up sections under the rubric Women in Contemporary Society, which they team-taught. This was the original women's studies program at SUNY, the first college, along with San Diego, to offer for-credit classes in that field. When Myerson later moved to Sarasota, FL, she taught feminist classes at New College, helped start the Women's Resource Center, and helped start community as well as university CR groups. In 1973, Myerson was the first outside hire at the University of South Florida's fledgling women's studies program. She helped start the B.A. pro-

gram in 1987 and the M.A. program in 1997. Myerson is (2005) graduate director for the department of women's studies. She is also a board member and past president of Planned Parenthood of Southwest and Central Florida. Myerson, who was born in Quebec and has one child, holds a Ph.D. (ABS)

Mylen-Kelly, Beverly Anne (1953–) became involved with the women's movement at the age of 19, when she went to the Connecticut Feminist Federal Credit Union to see about getting a loan. She saw the energy and commitment there and quickly went from credit applicant to volunteer, to staff member and emergency loan officer. She worked there from 1972–1974. CFFCU was a feminist financial institution, with both men and women members, many of whom could not access credit at traditional banks and credit unions. Overwhelmed by requests for money for abortions, CFFCU established the policy that no woman needing money for an abortion would be turned down. A member of the New Haven Women's Liberation Center and NOW, Mylen-Kelly participated in the New Haven marches of Women Unite to Take Back the Night from 1973–1976, dramatizing the need to keep the streets safe for women at night. She has worked in human resources for over 30 years and remembers the women's movement as inspiring and enabling. (ABS)

Myron, Nancy (1943–) A member of the Washington, D.C.-based feminist collective The Furies, Myron, in partnership with Charlotte Bunch, edited *Class and Feminism* (Diana Press, 1974), *Women Remembered* (Diana Press, 1974) and *Lesbianism and the Women's Movement* (Diana Press, 1975). A writer and artist, Myron was a frequent contributor to publications produced by The Furies, including the magazine *Motive* and the collective's own *Lesbian/Feminist Monthly*, which was produced and distributed nationally from January 1972 until mid 1973. Myron's writings are particularly concerned with class issues. In the essay "Class Beginnings," Myron writes, "Class keeps women down and divided through middle class women's oppressive behavior toward lower class women." Before moving to Washington, D.C., and joining The Furies collective, Myron had been active in the civil rights movement. (ABS)

Nachman, Elana – See Dykewomon, Elana

Nagler, Iris (1940–) A founding member of Essex County (NJ) NOW (1970), Nagler served as secretary, then as VP. In 1973, she shared the position of president/coordinator with Toni Spiotta and Merle Breitenfeld. In 1975 and 1976, Nagler was as finance coordinator of NJ NOW. She fought to end credit discrimination and sex-segregated help-wanted ads. She lobbied for the right to choose, for the ERA and for women in the workplace, and fought to integrate girls into the softball league. Nagler, who has two children, holds a B.A. and M.S. in education. (ABS)

M

Nailor, Vicki – See Noble, Vicki Jo

Nappi, Maureen Antoinette Jacqueline (1951 –) A member of Philadelphia Women's Liberation in 1970, Nappi was an artist and writer for the feminist newspaper *Through the Looking Glass*. After moving to New Haven, CT, in 1971, she became a member of New Haven Women's Liberation and a full-time coordinator of the Women's Center (1972 – 1973). In addition, she started an all-women house painting company, She Who Paints, in 1972. In 1974, she moved to NYC to continue her studies at New York University's Tisch School of the Arts, during which time she directed such film classics as "What Is an Early Abortion?" "Women's Basketball – 1975," and "The Clit Tapes." A theorist as well as an artist, Nappi's work is particularly concerned with humanistic issues including spiritualism, feminism and civil rights, as well as the relationship between humanity and technology. Her work has been exhibited and awarded internationally, including at the Museum of Modern Art, The New York Digital Salon, Art Futura (Barcelona), and the Hiroshima City Museum of Contemporary Art. She holds three degrees from New York University: a B.F.A. Films & Televison (1976); an M.A. Cinema Studies (1978); and a Ph.D. Art & Art Profession (2002).   (ABS)

Nastali, Patricia – See Alea, Patricia Veith

Navaretta, Cynthia (1925 –) was a founding member of the Women's Caucus for Art, the Coalition of Women's Arts Organizations, and Women in the Arts in 1972. She founded *Women Artists News* in the early 1970s, and is the author of *Guide to Women's Art Organizations and Directory for the Arts* (Midmarch Arts Press, 1979). In addition, she has edited dozens of books on women in the arts. Navaretta served on the Permanent Commission to International Women's Year in 1975, 1980, 1985 and 1990, and has maintained one of the four major archives of women artists in the U.S. since the late 1960s.   (ABS)

N'Cognita, Vernita Ellen – See Nemec, Vernita Ellen

Near, Holly (1949 –) Singer, songwriter, actor and teacher, Near is one of the founding mothers of women's music. She has been an inspirational performer at women's music festivals and national demonstrations for progressive causes over several decades. Near was active in the peace movement in the early 1970s, and worked with the United Farm Workers and organizations that were confronting the role of the U.S. and the CIA in Central and Latin America. She was also involved in ERA work and women's choice organizations, among others. With her sister, who was a hearing actor in the National Theater of the Deaf, she introduced sign language to the women's movement "and it seems that, as a result, use of American Sign Language interpreters at political and cultural events expanded." In 1972 she founded Redwood Records,

releasing her first album the following year. When Near came out in 1976, an article in *People* magazine covered it. She was part of an early women's music tour produced by Marianne Schneller that went to seven cities in California in 1975 – 1976, presenting—for the first time on that scale—outspoken feminist and lesbian music. Near, Meg Christian, Margie Adam and Cris Williamson also did a concert in a women's prison, as well as a half-hour television special called "Come Out Singing," directed by Lynn Lipman, that won a local Grammy in Los Angeles. Near also worked with The Wall Flower Order Dance Collective, a radical feminist dance company from Oregon founded by Krissy Keefer (which included her younger sister, Laurel Near), and toured and recorded with Ronnie Gilbert, bringing her out of retirement from music. A tour with Inti Illimani, presented by a national coalition of political groups in the United States, was one of the first opportunities allowing the exile community, the solidarity community, the feminist community and the lesbian community to work together. Near is the author of *Fire in the Rain, Singer in the Storm*, an autobiography. She has written many articles, appeared in several films and television programs, and has over 20 recordings. With her sister Near wrote a one-woman play that was presented in Los Angeles at the Mark Taper Forum for an extended run, as well as in San Jose, San Francisco and off Broadway, New York City. Near, who does workshops for peace and feminist groups, works with Dr. Amy Horowitz at the Merchon Center at Ohio State University on projects focused on social-change music and how it affects domestic and foreign policy and critical thinking. Near's portrait was unveiled at The Freedom Center in Ohio, along with other social-change artists (including Harry Belafonte, Marian Anderson and Joan Baez) whose work has been dedicated to freedom. Archives: Schlesinger Library, Radcliffe Institute, Cambridge, MA.   (ABS)

Necol, Jane B. (1944 –) was part of a CR group with her co-workers from the Museum of Modern Art (NYC) and others, and part of the 1970 Women Strike for Equality August 26th march. Once abortion became legal in NYC, before Roe v. Wade was passed, Necol made her apartment available to two young college women from Boston to rest in after they terminated their unwanted pregnancies at a Park Avenue South clinic. "On a lighter note," she says, "whenever construction workers or other unenlightened men whistled at me or made sexual comments, often in Spanish, I would grab the nearest cop and, with him in tow, give the sexist you-know-what a piece of my mind." Necol, who is a college professor, also took part in anti-war and civil rights demonstrations in New York City and Washington, D.C.   (ABS)

Neel, Marilynn – See zana

Neff, Nancy Carson – See Kelly, Nancy Lorene

Neglia, Zoe – See Nicholson, Zoe

Neiberg, Vicki Barbara Evans (1940 –) In 1971, Neiberg and Mary Craypo formed the Alliance to End Sex Discrimination at Michigan State University. Under the aegis of the Alliance, Neiberg also helped form the first clerical/technical union at any university (1972). Documented gender discrimination at MSU led to the Connecticut Union, elimination of gender-specific courses and majors, all salaries of university faculty and staff being made public, a full complement of women's varsity sports, and an office, procedure and ombudsman to track the progress of stated goals and programming for women and minorities. She was also part of a group that lobbied to include birth control information in sex education in Mississippi. As the first woman union representative at the Michigan Nurses Association, Neiberg negotiated, renegotiated and/or organized 17 hospitals, including the University of Michigan Hospital. Among the issues she introduced into contract negotiations were paid medical leave for childbirth with the right to return to the job; gender unspecified disability leaves; on-site childcare; and sick leave to cover children, spouses and parental care. From 1971 – 1974, Neiberg served as the first chair of the WPC in MI, and from 1972 – 1974 sat on the WPC national board. Neiberg has two children and holds a B.A. from the University of Cincinnati and an M.Ed. from Xavier University. (ABS)

Neiditz, Minerva (1932 –) was the first chair of the Connecticut Permanent Commission on the Status of Women. Under her leadership, the commission was able to set up its office, change most of the sex discriminatory laws still extant in Connecticut, and set up task forces on rape, discrimination in state employment and discrimination in insurance, among other issues. Before her appointment, Neiditz was campaign manager for representative David Neiditz and helped write his speeches, most particularly the one in which he supported the ERA. Neiditz was an assistant professor of managerial communications at the University of Connecticut for 10 years and president of The Writing Consultants for 15 years. She is still active as a writer and a philanthropist. She conducts workshops on How to Find the Right Man and teaches Mind, Body, Spirit Poetry. She is the author of four books. Her poetry books are *On the Way* and *Angel Tongues and Lobster Tails*. Other books: *Business Writing at Its Best* and *Romance After 60: What Men Think They Want*. Neiditz, who has two children, holds a B.A. from Smith College, an M.A. from Radcliffe College and a Ph.D. from the University of Connecticut. (ABS)

Nelsen, Vivian Jenkins (1945 –) An African American always concerned about human rights, Nelsen was interested in the feminist movement from its inception. She joined WEAL when it was organized in Minnesota in the early 1970s, and became Minnesota state president in 1975. Nelsen worked within WEAL on a number of legal cases, most concerning women in education and, to some extent, minorities in education. Some of the cases resulted in women receiving positions as principals and coaches, as well as substantial improvements in girls athletics. Nelsen was director of administration for the Hubert H. Humphrey Institute of Public Affairs at the University of Minnesota for several years. She also co-founded and served as president and CEO of the Inter-Race International Institute for Interracial Interaction. Born in Selma, AL, Nelsen graduated from Dana College in 1965 and later received its Distinguished Alumni Award. Archives: Minnesota History Center, St. Paul, MN. (ABS)

Nelson, Karen Benveniste (1933 –) (also known as Karen Nelson Hurn) wrote the proposal for the Center for Continuing Education for Women at the University of California, Berkeley. She was a co-founder and coordinator (1974 – 2005) of the Organization for the Advancement of Women and a coordinator (1969 – 1973) of the League of Academic Women. Active in WILPF and the LWV, Nelson was also a signer of a class action lawsuit against the University of California, Berkeley, regarding enforcement of the executive order of Lyndon B. Johnson requiring that universities receiving federal funds implement equality of gender in employment. A researcher in early childhood socialization, Nelson holds a Ph.D. from the University of California, Berkeley. She has two children. Archives: University of California, Berkeley. (ABS)

Nelson, Marjory ("Marge") (1928 –) (also known as Marjory Nelson Hoekje) As a member of the Ecumenical Movement at her church in Akron, OH, in 1963, Nelson began bringing feminist ideas into the youth group and women's circle. In the late 1960s, she circulated a petition to give girls equal access to the basketball gym at the local schools. In 1970, Nelson wrote a prospectus for and co-taught a course on women's studies at SUNY Buffalo. She also went to Washington, D.C., to meet Alice Paul, and accepted an invitation to spend the next year working with the National Women's Party as a lobbyist for the ERA. Nelson was in the gallery of the House when the ERA passed there. From 1971 – 1973, she taught women's studies and sociology at Antioch College. During that time, while attending an AFT state conference, Nelson successfully lobbied the group to support the ERA. In 1973, Nelson returned to SUNY Buffalo to teach a course in general sociology to nursing students, and used the opportunity to teach health issues from a feminist perspective. In 1975, she came out, and that spring went to Antioch to attend the Socialist Feminist Conference. Later that year, Nelson went to Raleigh, NC, to work on the Joann Little trial, and arranged through the legal team for local black feminists to see and help Little. In 1976, Nelson joined the National Women's Health Network. She also created a feminist living collective with her partner and taught women's studies at SUNY and the Cornell

N

Labor School. Nelson organized the Crones Caucus for feminists over 50 in San Francisco (1978), then co-founded a center for older women at the San Francisco Women's Center. By 1979, Nelson was organizing a conference on ageism. She joined the fat liberation movement, and taught a course on racism and feminism. Nelson has three children, holds a Ph.D., and is a certified hypnotherapist. Archives: The Sophia Smith Collection, Smith College, Northampton, MA.   (ABS)

Nemec, Vernita Ellen (1942 –) An artist, curator, writer and photographer, Nemec was a member of Women Artists in Revolution with Lucy Lippard, Nancy Spero, Silvianna Goldsmith and others, protesting the exclusion of women artists in museums (1969 – 1970). At that time, she was also co-curator of X12, the first all-female artists exhibit since the 1930s, and was a member of Political Art Documentation Distribution, whose meetings and events combined art and politics. Nemec was an active member of Soho20, a feminist artists collective, and served as the last VP of the Heresies Collective. She was also executive director (1989 – 1999) and interviewer conducting weekly panel discussions with art world personalities for Artists Talk On Art. Since 1994, she has been deeply involved with the environmental movement, specifically recycling, and has organized and curated over a dozen art exhibits across the U.S. of art made from trash. Performance artworks that Nemec wrote and performed include Humorette, presented at Soho 20, NYC in 1978; Private Places, which received a Jerome Foundation grant through Franklin Furnace and was presented at Franklin Furnace and the Los Angeles Women's Building in 1986; How to be the Perfect Woman, a collaboration with Kazuko Miyamoto, presented at Gallery 128 in NYC and abroad in 2000; and It all Goes so Quickly, presented at Gallery 128, NYC, 2002. Nemec holds a B.F.A. from Ohio University and an M.A. from New York University. (ABS)

Nemser, Cindy (1937 –) was a founding member of Women in the Arts (1971), and served as publisher and editor in chief of the *Feminist Art Journal* (1972 – 1977). She published feminist articles in *Arts Magazine*, where she served as contributing editor from 1972 – 1975, as well as in *Art in America, ArtForum, Journal of Esthetic Education* and other publications (1970 – 1975). Nemser organized three sessions on women artists for the College Art Association in 1973; was a co-organizer of Philadelphia Focuses on Women in the Arts (1974); and curated In Her Own Image for the Philadelphia Museum of Art (1974). From 1975 – 1978, Nemser served as an advisory board member of the WCA. She is the author of *Art Talk: Conversations With 12 Women Artists* (Charles Scribner & Sons, 1975), and has been a guest lecturer on women artists and women's issues at many universities and museums (1971 – 1977), as well as a panelist and host, WBAI Radio, NYC (1975). "Stereotypes and Women Artists" was reprinted in *Feminist Collage*, edited by Judy Loeb

(Teachers College Press, 1979). Nemser is also the author of *Eve's Delight* (Pinnacle Books, 1982), an exploration of women's sexuality, and *Art Talk: Conversations with 15 Women Artists* (Harper Collins, 1995). Nemser, who has one child, earned a B.A. and an M.A. in English Literature from Brooklyn College, and an M.A. in Art History from the Institute of Fine Arts, New York University. Archives: Brooklyn Museum, Brooklyn, NY.   (ABS)

Nemzoff, Ruth (1940 –) (also known as Ruth Nemzoff Berman) Living in Nashua, NH, in the early 1970s, Nemzoff joined and formed CR groups, and worked with Claire Helfman and Sarah Dickman to increase the participation of women in their Temple. By 1973, the members of various CR and church groups had established a counseling service for women in Southern NH, called WISE. Nemzoff received the regional award for her leadership in that organization. Unable to found a NOW chapter in that conservative region of NH, Nemzoff and others founded Women United. The group raised issues at schools and meetings, spoke widely about injustice, and created and marched in a Susan B. Anthony Day parade. In 1974, Nemzoff was elected to the NH Legislature, the first pregnant woman to serve in the NH House of Representatives. There, she "managed to have the problem of rape in marriage recognized and even limited some anti-abortion legislation." In 1977, during her second term, she sponsored legislation to grant pro-rated benefits to part-time workers. "I knew it would fail, but I wanted the conversation to begin." She successfully sponsored a bill that granted scholarship money to displaced homemakers, and—working with various groups representing members of the adoption triangle—wrote one of the first successful laws in the nation opening adoption records. In the mid 1970s, Nemzoff was hired by the American Personnel and Guidance Association to develop teams to implement Title IX of the 1972 Education Amendments. In 1980, she was hired to start the sex equity section of the Equal Opportunity Office in the New Hampshire Dept. of Education. In 1982, she became the first female deputy commissioner of health and welfare in NH. She organized prominent women in the state to run a conference at the state house on the feminization of poverty, worked for abortion rights, and fostered a women's political caucus. In 1988, as national field director of WAND, Nemzoff co-founded the National Women's Legislators Lobby. From 1996 – 2000, she was the gender issues co-coordinator at Bentley College. She also ran programs to encourage junior-high and high-school girls to become entrepreneurs. Since the early 1990s, Nemzoff has taught gender courses to business students, and is (2005) a resident scholar at Brandeis University. She is chair of the advisory committee of the Center for Women and Politics at the University of Massachusetts, on the advisory committee of the MA WPC, and involved in the political action committee of MA Planned Parenthood. Nemzoff, who has four children, holds a B.A. from Barnard College (1962), an M.A. from Columbia University (1964), and an Ed.D. from Harvard University, School of Education (1979).   (ABS)

Nesaule, Agate (1938 –) (formerly known as Agate Nesaule Krouse) A professor of English and women's studies from 1963 – 1996, Nesaule started the women's studies program at the University of Wisconsin, Whitewater, in 1972. From 1969, when she developed the first course, Women in American Culture, to 1994, she taught and created numerous other courses about women. She also spoke to community groups and wrote about feminist pedagogy, feminist criticism and women writers. She is the author of *A Woman in Amber: Healing the Trauma of War and Exile* (Soho Press, 1995), which won an American Book Award. Born in Riga, Latvia, Nesaule has one child. She earned her B.A. and M.A. from Indiana University, and her Ph.D. from the University of Wisconsin, Madison.   (ABS)

Nestle, Joan (1940 –) was born in the Bronx and raised by her widowed working mother, Regina, who sometimes turned tricks to support herself and her daughter. Never having known her father, who died in 1939, Nestle started work at 13. In the 1960s, she was involved in the anti-HUAC, anti-war and civil rights movements, including voter registration work in Alabama and participation in the march from Selma to Montgomery. Concurrently, she was part of the working class butch-fem lesbian bar community in Greenwich Village. This community of women resisting the policing powers of the state became the major influence in her version of lesbian feminism. In 1970, she joined the Gay Activist Alliance. From 1966 – 1995 she taught writing in the SEEK Program at Queens College, a program brought into being by the black and Puerto Rican caucus under the leadership of Shirley Chisholm to ensure that working class students of color had a chance to succeed in the city's university system. In 1970, she and others organized lesbian Sunday events at the Firehouse on Wooster Street where GAA met. Those meetings gave birth to Lesbian Feminist Liberation. In 1972, she was one of the CUNY graduates who helped organize the Gay Academic Union of NYC. In 1973, Nestle, Deborah Edel and other women in GAU formed a CR group, out of which grew the Lesbian Herstory Archives, a grassroots lesbian project that embodied Nestle's vision of creating an historical memory of women who had "the courage to touch another woman." After 18 years in Nestle's Upper West Side apartment, the Archives moved to its own four-story building in Park Slope, Brooklyn. In the early 1970s and for much of the next 20 years, Nestle wrote and performed sexually explicit lesbian texts. Sometimes wearing a black slip at her readings, Nestle says, "I was never more political than when I was putting my fat, old-time fem Jewish woman's body into the story of liberation." She is the author of two memoirs, *A Restricted Country* and *A Fragile Union*, and edited the anthology *A Persistent Desire: A Fem-Butch Reader*. Nestle lives (2005) in Melbourne, Australia, with Dianne Otto, a feminist who helped create the first shelters for battered women in Australia. Archives: The Lesbian Herstory Archives, Brooklyn, NY.   (ABS)

Neuwirth, Joan Carol Steinberg (1930 –) helped establish the Middlesex, NJ, chapter of NOW (1969), and served as board member, treasurer, PAC treasurer, assistant coordinator for administration, and chair of the economic security task force. In 1974, she was state coordinator of the WPC, and went on to form WPC chapters in Middlesex County and East Brunswick, NJ. In 1977, Neuwirth was a delegate to International Women's Year Conference, focusing on childcare issues. From 1976 – 1978, she served as editor of the Majority News Service, and in 1980 was the interim chair of the Central Jersey OWL. In addition to her feminist work, Neuwirth was elected to the East Brunswick board of education and chaired the Middlesex Coalition for Better Education (1969 – 1972), and was a founding member of the East Brunswick Human Relations Council (1961 – 1969). Also active in labor issues, she was a member, branch representative and VP of the Professional Bargaining Unit of Local 1039-CWA 1983-1987. She is (2005) a member of an active adult community and continues to lead groups studying women's history. She earned her B.A. from Hunter College and her M.Ed. from Rutgers University, and has two daughters (one deceased).   (ABS)

Newcomb, Betty Harman (1926 –) Newcomb was a board member of the LWV of Indiana and the Muncie mayor's Human Rights Commission, when she and Virginia Jackson Adams founded IN NOW (1970). As NOW state coordinator, Newcomb helped found 13 chapters in other parts of the state. As a member of NOW's national board she chaired the NOW national bylaws committee and was on the national conference planning committees in 1973 and 1974. As a member of the international committee, Newcomb also helped found NOW chapters abroad. From 1970 – 1972, Newcomb organized and led a successful national caucus within the LWV to gain endorsement of the ERA from LWV US. Also in the early 1970s, Newcomb organized and taught with others the first women's studies course at Ball State University, and helped form the IN WPC. In 1972, she initiated the formation of Hoosiers for ERA with the LWV and IN WPC, and spoke around the state for the ERA. During the same time, Newcomb served as Alice Paul's NWP representative in Indiana. In 1973, Newcomb founded the American Association for Affirmative Action, an organization of directors of equal opportunity affirmative action programs. Says Newcomb, "This was my effort to provide equal opportunity to women and minorities peacefully. Minorities were then fighting women's efforts for equal access." Newcomb served on the AAAA board for several years, and as presi-

N

dent from 1978–1979. In addition, she wrote most of the articles for, edited and published the association's newsletter from 1973–1978. Newcomb, who has three children, holds a B.A. from the University of Maryland (1948) and an M.A. from Ball State University (1965). Archives: Ball State University Library, Muncie, IN. (ABS)

Newlin, Marjorie Stevens
– See Leaming, Marjorie Newlin

Newmark, Irma Diamond (1927 –) joined NY NOW in 1967 and served as spokesperson for the committee on the image of women. Newmark was also a founder and first president of the Bronx chapter of NOW, and a member/speaker for the Association of Feminist Consultants. As such, she testified before Congress at a hearing on women and employment. In 1975, her article "Women and the Full Employment Society" was published in *The Annals of Political and Social Science*. Newmark taught the first women's studies course at Brooklyn College CUNY and was a co-founder of the Women's Center there. She was also a co-founder, with Jacqueline Ceballos and others, of VFA. As a member of the status of women committee of NY (1989–1996), Newmark raised issues pertinent to women's needs at the United Nations. She also chaired the caucus on the rights of the child at UNICEF. In 2004–2006, she was president of South Palm Beach Chapter of NOW. Newmark, who has two children, earned her B.A. from Queens College, CUNY (1970), and her M.A. (1975) and Ph.D. (1983) from the Graduate Center, CUNY. (ABS)

Newton, Esther (1940 –) A professor of anthropology, Newton is known primarily as an authority on gay and lesbian culture. A founder of Purchase College, she became a faculty member in 1971 and helped establish the anthropology, women's studies and lesbian/gay studies programs. Newton was an editor (with Bertha Harris, Jill Johnston and Jane O'Wyatt) of the 1973 collection *Amazon Expedition* (Times Change Press). She and her collaborator, Shirley Walton, also contributed an essay to the collection that examined feminist CR groups from an anthropological perspective in terms of William James's model of religious conversion. Newton also collaborated with Walton on the 1976 work *Womenfriends* (Friends Press), a dialog between two feminist friends, one gay and one straight. Newton's other works include *Mother Camp: Female Impersonators in America* (Prentice-Hall, 1972), *Cherry Grove, Fire Island: Sixty Years in America's First Gay and Lesbian Town* (Beacon Press, 1993), and *Margaret Mead Made Me Gay: Personal Essay, Public Ideas* (Duke University Press, 2000). Newton, who identifies herself as a butch lesbian, has given a series of lectures/slide shows about her life as a writer and intellectual who is also butch. Originally the Kessler Lecture for the Center for Lesbian and Gay Studies at the Graduate Center at CUNY, the lecture, called "My Butch Career: A Memoir,"

deals with issues of race, class, sexuality, professionalism and middle age as lived by a gender dissident. Newton holds a B.A. from the University of Michigan (1962) and an M.A. (1964) and Ph.D. (1968) from the University of Chicago. She served as an associate, then full professor at SUNY at Purchase, NY, from 1971–2005. (ABS)

Niccolini, Dianora (1936 –) As a recent graduate of the Germain School of Photography in 1961, Niccolini struggled against the unwritten rule that no one hired a woman for photographic work. It wasn't until her involvement with the women's movement in the early 1970s that Niccolini realized she could do something to help other women photographers who were being excluded as she was. In 1974, she placed an ad in the *Village Voice* inviting women photographers to join together and, under her direction, 18 women formed Women Photographers of New York. The group survived for two years. In 1975, Niccolini's work was exhibited in Breadth of Vision, a U.N.-sponsored International women's Year exhibit at the Fashion Institute of Technology. She and other exhibitors from that show formed The Professional Women Photographers under the direction of Dannielle Hayes. Niccolini served as chair and president from 1980–1984. Under her direction, PWP grew to include a newspaper, a gallery and monthly meetings that continue today (2005). During this period, Niccolini began working on an anthology of women photographers, *Women of Vision* (Unicorn, 1982). Niccolini, who was born in Florence, Italy, has also been active in the peace movement. She holds a B.A. from Marymount Manhattan College. Archives: The Professional Women Photographers, New York, NY. (ABS)

Nicholson, Catherine (1922 –) A college professor and lesbian feminist, Nicholson organized to get pay equity for women when she was teaching at the University of North Carolina, Charlotte. She joined the Charlotte Women's Center in the early 1970s, did consciousness raising there and met Harriet Ellenberger, a founding member of the center. The two women founded *Sinister Wisdom*, a lesbian feminist literary and art journal, in 1976. After five years, they handed it over to Adrienne Rich and Michelle Cliff, who changed the emphasis somewhat into a purely lesbian journal. It continues to be published today (2006), making it the longest-running lesbian journal in the country. Nicholson holds a B. A. from Flora McDonald College, an M.A. from the University of North Carolina at Chapel Hill, and a Ph.D. from Northwestern University. Archives: Sallie Bingham Center, Duke University, Durham, NC. (ABS)

Nicholson, Zoe Ann (1948 –) (also known as Zoe Neglia, Zoe Ann Ananda) Nicholson's life-long focus has been religion and spirituality. Beginning with Catholic Church reform and teaching, she has worked consistently for women's equality. In 1975, she opened and operated

The Magic Speller Bookstore, a women's and metaphysical bookstore in Newport Beach, CA. She served as the assistant director of the local chapter of NOW for four years. In 1982, she joined six women in Springfield, IL, in a public and political fast for 37 days in support of the ERA. She is (2005) the owner of Lune Soleil Press and her books are *Matri, Letters from the Mother, The Passionate Heart*, and *The Hungry Heart*, a memoir of the 1982 fast. Nicholson holds an M.A. from the University of Southern California Archives: Schlesinger Library, Radcliffe Institute, Cambridge, MA.   (ABS)

Nies, Judith E. (1941 –) In her first job out of graduate school, Nies worked as a peace lobbyist for Women's International League for Peace and Freedom, where she met and was inspired by numerous international feminists. In 1968, she became a speechwriter and staff person for an ad hoc committee of anti-war congressmen. Nies succeeded in persuading the congressional leadership to do away with the Ladies Gallery, the only location where women could sit if they wanted to view the proceedings of the House. Aware of how discriminatory the institution was to congresswomen, Nies published "Women's Lib on Capital Hill" in *Progressive magazine* (1970), in which she described the men's club rules of Congress and what it would take to make it a truly representative institution. In 1970, Nies founded WEAL's Women and Fellowship Project, whose goal was to open up every prestigious fellowship program, such as White House Fellows and Nieman Fellows, to women. In response, all the programs took steps to change their selection boards and actively encouraged women to apply. In 1973, she published "The Bella Abzug Campaign: A Lesson in Politics" in *Ms.* magazine. In 1977, she published *Seven Women* (Viking and Penguin), a book on women leaders in American radical social and political movements. In 2002, the book was republished as *Nine Women: Portraits from the American Radical Tradition* (University of California Press). Nies continues to write about women, politics and culture, and has published in *Sojourner, The New York Times* and the *Christian Science Monitor*, among others. Nies, who has one child, earned her B.A. from Tufts University (1962) and her M.A. from John Hopkins (1965).   (ABS)

NietoGomez, Anna (1946 –) is professor, writer, social worker and activist on behalf of Chicano and Chicana rights. She was the first woman elected president of her college's MECha chapter and was burned in effigy in an unsuccessful attempt to get her out of office. She was a founding member of the group and newspaper *Hijas de Cuauhtemoc* (1971); an editor of the first Chicana scholarly journal, *Encuentro Femenil* (1973); and wrote an early critique of sexism in the Chicano movement (1976). She also worked with *Comision Femenil*, the Chicana Service Action Center and the East Los Angeles Welfare Rights Organization. Her research and slide show on the history of Chicanas was the basis for the script of the

ground-breaking film, "Chicana" (1979). In the 1970s, she was hired by California State University Northridge Chicano Studies to teach Chicana studies. "I was denied tenure because I reported child abuse to the authorities," she says. Undeterred, she earned an M.S.W. from the University of Southern California. She is a licensed clinical social worker, treats victims of domestic violence at the Centro de Desarrollo Familiar and is a section chief at the Department of Health Services. Born in San Bernardino, CA, NietoGomez now lives in Long Beach, CA.   (ABS)

Nixon, Joan E. (1941 –) Activist, writer and financial supporter of women's projects, Nixon attended and wrote about the West Coast Lesbian Conference. (Los Angeles, April, 1973). She accompanied the Family of Woman Band in April 1973 and attended the first feminist music festival, produced by Kate Millett in Sacramento, CA (May 1973). She was also a member of and wrote columns for the *Lavender Woman* newspaper collective (1973 – 1976). Nixon loaned the money to record the first Olivia Records album, Cris Williamson's "The Changer and the Changed." Over the years, Nixon has quietly lent and given money to various projects and individuals in the women's and lesbian movements. She is best known for being Bella Abzug's driver from 1978 until the time of Abzug's death on March 31, 1998. Following Abzug's death, Nixon organized Abzug's papers for *The Bella Abzug Reader*, edited by Mim Kelber and Libby Basset. 150 copies were printed by Harry Kelber in 2003. Born in Peru, IN, Nixon is a member of the family that owned Nixon Newspapers, a chain of 11 Indiana papers sold in May 1998. Nixon holds a B.A. from Wellesley College (1963) and an M.A. from Indiana University (1969). She worked as a news photographer (1969 – 1972) for *The Frankfort Times*.   (ABS)

Noble, Elaine (1944 –) Noble was elected to the Massachusetts House of Representatives in November 1974, the first openly lesbian state representative in U.S. history. At every turn, being a lesbian was used against her. Her headlights were smashed, people purposely bumped into her car, and a local Catholic priest said anyone who voted for her would be excommunicated. Re-elected in 1976, Noble declined to run in 1978, citing the effects of a massive redistricting that reduced the Massachusetts House from 240 to 160 members. Noble and her friends wanted to "belong and be counted" in the women's movement, so they joined a local chapter of NOW in 1970. However, she says, "as lesbians we were told to get out—in no uncertain terms." Noble and her friends then attended the first meeting of the WPC, where Noble was elected one of three chairs. Also active in Minnesota, Noble helped raise money for Karen Clark, an elected Minnesota state representative, and was founder of the Pride Institute in Minneapolis (an alcohol and drug treatment center for gays and lesbians). Noble holds a B.S.A. from Boston University (1966) and two graduate

N

degrees, one in Speech from Emerson College and another in Education from Harvard University.

Noble, Vicki Jo (1947 –) (also known as Vicki Nailor and Vicki Ziegler) In 1971, Noble moved to Colorado Springs with her husband, and was divorced by 1972. After discovering a women's self-help group in Irvine, CA, she returned to Colorado Springs with 12 speculums and introduced women's health to her feminist group. They then became a women's health group advocating for women in the areas of problem pregnancy, birth control and abortion. Group members spoke on panels around the state, marched in Denver for abortion rights, and published a women's health handbook, *Circle One: A Woman's Guide to Self Health and Sexuality*, which was used in clinics around the country. In 1975, they borrowed enough money to start a feminist gynecological clinic in Colorado Springs that served women in the community for the next 10 years. While working as a feminist in women's health, Noble decided to return to college, but was not happy with the "normal" curricula. When an adviser at Colorado College suggested that Noble create an interdisciplinary women's studies major, she did. It was the first women's studies major at the college, and Noble was the first to graduate from the college with a B.A. in women's studies (1975). In 1978, Noble—a writer, healer and feminist spiritual teacher—and Karen Vogel created the Motherpeace Tarot deck. Noble, who has three children, has since published eight books on women's history, healing and women's spirituality, including *Shakti Women: Feeling Our Fire, Healing Our World* (Harper, 1991). (ABS)

Nochlin, Linda (1931 –) Currently (2005) Lila Acheson Wallace Professor of Modern Art at New York University's Institute of Fine Arts, Nochlin taught the first college course on women and art at Vassar College in 1969. She is author of *Women, Art and Power* (Harper & Row, 1988) and "Why Have There Been No Great Women Artists?" an article published in 1970. A pioneer in feminist art history, Nochlin structured her seminar at Vassar to provide a total cultural conception of women in the society of their age. Nochlin, who has two children, holds a B.A. from Vassar (1951), an M.A. from Columbia (1952), and a Ph.D. from the Institute of Fine Arts of NYU (1963). Archives: New York University, New York, NY. (ABS)

Norby, Marian (1917 – 2002) was an activist for the ERA and a founding member of the Washington, D.C., chapter of NOW (1967). After the chapter folded, Norby organized another in 1968. Says Mary Eastwood, "Norby functioned as a one-woman action center, writing many letters and making many phone calls to government officials, editors of newspapers, and the media protesting inequitable treatment of women." Norby was a charter member of both WEAL and OWL. As a young woman in Washington during WWII, Norby worked for the govern-

ment. After the war, she worked at the Truman White House for the head of personnel, and accompanied the President on his whistle-stop tours typing and retyping his speeches. Archives: Schlesinger Library, Radcliffe Institute, Cambridge, MA.

Nordby, Virginia Cecile Blomer (1929 –) A 1954 honors graduate of Stanford University Law School, Nordby joined the University of Michigan law school where she developed and taught a course on women and the law. In 1973 – 1974, Nordby was a consultant to the Michigan women's task force on rape, and was the principal drafter of the Michigan Criminal Sexual Conduct Act, which labeled rape a violent crime and also protected the rights of the victim. The law has been widely copied by various states in the U.S. As a member of the Women's Commission in Michigan, Nordby instigated an analysis of gender-based differences in application language, and used this knowledge to eliminate discrimination in the many positions she held at the University of Michigan, where she worked for 19 years until her retirement in 1993. A mentor to numerous women entering law school, Nordby is the recipient of several awards, including the 1987 Harriet Myer Service Award from the Michigan Association of Women Deans, Administrators and Counselors, and the Susan B. Anthony Award from the University of Michigan. In 1991, Nordby was inducted into The Michigan Women's Hall of Fame. Archives: Bentley Historical Library, The University of Michigan, Ann Arbor, MI. (ABS)

Nordlinger, Zelda K. (1932 –) organized and worked with Women's Rights of Richmond, VA (1969 – 1973), which later became a chapter of NOW. She served on NOW's legislative task force (1973 – 1975), and lobbied the General Assembly for rape reform laws (1975 – 1976) and for ratification of the ERA (1975 – 1978). Earlier (1969 – 1970), she testified before the General Assembly for abortion reform. In 1970, Nordlinger and five other women successfully challenged the male-only policy of the soup bar at Thalhimer's department store. She also picketed Richmond Newspapers to protest sex-segregated help-wanted ads; gave a speech on women's liberation to the Richmond First Club; participated in a reproductive rights pro-choice panel for the Jaycees; and submitted numerous cases to the EEOC on sex discrimination. She also delivered The Gospel of Women's Liberation to numerous groups and organizations and was present at the founding of the Virginia Foundation for Women. In addition, Nordlinger served as assistant state coordinator for NOW, was an adviser to the board of WILPF, and was a founding member of the NWPC (Houston). Nordlinger, who has four children, graduated from Marjorie Webster Jr. College (1952) and the Sally Tompkins School of Practical Nursing (1963). She holds a B.A. from Virginia Commonwealth University. Archives: The Library of Virginia, Richmond, VA; The Wrenn Library, William &

Mary College, Williamsburg, VA; and The Cabell Library, Virginia Commonwealth University, Richmond, VA. (ABS)

Nordstrom, Kristina (1938 –) was founder and director, with assistance from several women in her NYC CR group, of two International Festivals of Women's Films (1972 and 1976). The first-ever women's film festival was held in June 1972 in NYC at the Fifth Avenue Cinema. The two-week event broke the house record at that theater, says Nordstrom, attracting a lot of press attention to the work of women directors. In addition, program notes from that festival were circulated by the Association of American Colleges to campuses around the country and led to local women's film events. The second two-week Festival was held in September 1976 at the Cinema Studio near Lincoln Center. Nordstrom's co-director was Leah Laiman. Nordstrom also coordinated the Festival's five-day Women's Film Conference at the Barbizon Hotel. This conference and the subsequent six-city National Tour of Festival Films were supported by grants from the National Endowment for the Arts. For their work, the two directors received Outstanding Achievement Awards from *Mademoiselle* magazine. In 1979, Nordstrom founded the Women Filmmakers Symposium to encourage a dialogue among women directors, screenwriters, producers and production executives. She is (2006) working on Women Filmmakers Program to spur more women's films into production. Nordstrom holds a B.A. and M.A. from New York University. Archives: Documentation on the 1972 and 1976 Festivals of Women's Films and the 1979, 1981, 1999 and 2000 Women Filmmakers Symposiums is at the Lincoln Center Library, New York, NY, and the Library of the Academy of Motion Picture Arts and Sciences, Los Angeles, CA. (ABS)

Norman, Eve (1935 –) In the 1970s, Norman was associated with both Los Angeles NOW and the Los Angeles Women's Center, the only two feminist organizations in the area at the time. As VP of the Los Angeles chapter of NOW, she developed and conducted NOW orientation and speakers bureau programs (1971). She was a co-founder of the Los Angeles Commission on Assaults Against Women (1971). Norman was one of a diverse committee of five Los Angeles feminists who developed the position paper and resolution (#128), introduced at the national NOW conference, that stated that lesbian oppression was a legitimate concern of feminism (1971). Communication between Norman and Aileen Hernandez evolved into NOW's resolution (#109) opposing war/violence as an extension of the masculine mystique at the same 1971 national NOW conference. Norman served as first state coordinator of CA NOW (1972 – 1974). Norman and other California NOW members, helped by Geri Sherwood, CA NOW lobbyist, and Charlene Suneson, CA NOW legislative coordinator, worked to pass precedent-setting women's rights legislation in California. The legislation was often drafted by the feminists

themselves. This alliance was deeply involved in CA's ratification of the ERA—encouraging community coalitions and local actions, facilitating statewide communication, and successfully pressuring CA state senators to get the amendment out of committee and to the floor for a vote. As a result, CA became one of the first states to ratify the ERA. As a member of the CA attorney general's task force on women's rights (1975), Norman chaired the committee investigating the conditions of women in prison. Upon hearing horror stories from inmates about forced sterilizations, botched and unnecessary medical procedures and unsanitary conditions, the committee ultimately recommended the "radical" proposal that inmates receive quality medical care and civil rights identical to those given citizens outside of prison. From 1975 – 1977, Norman was NOW's western regional director, and from 1975 – 1976 spoke at numerous college campuses on the issue of rape; focusing attention on local crisis centers and women's programs. From 1977 – 1979, Norman was NOW national treasurer. In 1977, she proposed that all-white garments, reminiscent of the 19th century women's suffrage marches, be worn at the memorial march to honor Alice Paul. A massive 1978 march on Washington for Congressional extension of the ERA followed the same pattern, including the purple/gold/white banners identifying organizations and NOW chapters. Norman, who raised two children, served on many boards addressing women's concerns, and has worked, spoken and written for decades for the rights of women. Archives: Schlesinger Library, Radcliffe Institute, Cambridge, MA. (ABS)

N

Norris, Judy (1939 –) was a founding member of the Cambridge, MA, Women's Center (1971), the longest continuously running women's center in the country, and one of the first organizations to deal with incest. It also created The Women's School, faced rape and battering head-on, and provided a safe place for women to meet, talk about their concerns, and take action. Volunteering there for over 33 years, Norris played a significant role in sustaining the Center. (ABS)

Norsigian, Judy L. (1948 –) A women's health activist and administrator for over three decades, Norsigian was a member of the Boston Women's Health Book Collective and contributed to all Simon & Schuster editions of *Our Bodies, Ourselves*, starting with the 1973 edition. She served on the board of the National Women's Health Network for 14 years, focusing on reproductive health, the media and women's health, genetics, tobacco and women, women and healthcare reform, and midwifery advocacy. She has been a member of numerous boards, including Public Responsibility in Medicine, and Research and Community Works (Boston's alternative fund for social-change organizations). She was also a member of the editorial advisory boards of *The Journal of Midwifery and Women's Health*, *Reproductive Health Matters and Birth: Issues in Perinatal Care*; was a member of the technical advisory committee of Contraceptive Research and Development Program; and served on the strategic advisory board of Consortium for Industrial Collaboration in Contraceptive Research. In addition, she was a member of the steering committee of the committee on women, population and the environment. Norsigian has received numerous awards, including the Public Service Award from the Massachusetts Public Health Association (1989); a Doctor of Humane Letters, Honoris Causa, from Worcester State College (1994); and the Radcliffe College Alumnae Association Annual Recognition Award (1995). In 1996, she was inducted into the Boston YWCA's Academy of Women Achievers, and in 2002 received the Massachusetts Health Council Award. Norsigian, who has one child and two stepchildren, earned her B.A. from Radcliffe College in 1970. Archives: Schlesinger Library, Radcliffe Institute, Cambridge, MA. (ABS)

Norton, Eleanor Holmes (1937 –) An African American lawyer and government official, Norton has spent a lifetime fighting for justice and fairness. As an attorney with the American Civil Liberties Union (1965 – 1970), she specialized in First Amendment cases. The first woman to chair the New York City Commission on Human Rights (1970–1977), she pursued the private business clubs that didn't admit women and pressured them to do so or lose their tax-exempt status. She later became the first woman to head the federal Equal Employment Opportunity Commission (1977 – 1983), appointed by President Carter. Norton was also a co-founder of the South Africa Divestment Movement, the NWPC, and the National Congress of Black Women. She remains a tenured professor of law at Georgetown University Law School, served on the Rockefeller Foundation board and the boards of three Fortune 500 companies, the Board of Governors of the D.C. Bar Association, and the boards of several civil rights and other national organizations. Since 1991, Norton has been the District of Columbia's elected, nonvoting delegate to the U.S. Congress. She has also been a senior fellow at the Urban Institute and assistant legal director of the ACLU. As congresswoman for the District of Columbia, Norton served as Democratic chair of the women's caucus and, among other achievements, fought for statehood, congressional voting representation and full democracy for the people of the District of Columbia. She holds a B.A. from Antioch College, and both a master's and a law degree from Yale University. The recipient of over 50 Honorary Degrees, Norton was named one of the most powerful women in Washington by *Washingtonian* Magazine and one of the most distinguished women in America by surveys in national magazines. She has two children. (ABS)

Norvell, Patsy (1942 –) During the late 1960s and early 1970s, Norvell was a member of the women's art movement in NYC. She helped start and was a member of an art-based women's group (1969 – 1974) dedicated to "merging consciousness-raising, art production, and changing the politics and conditions of art exhibition for women," says Norvell. In 1972, she was a founding member of the AIR Gallery and over the years served on almost all of its committees. Also in 1972, she exhibited in 13 Women Artists, the first women's group show in NYC. As an educator, Norvell taught at various colleges and universities. At Montclaire State College (1970–1974) and at Hunter College, Graduate Program (1982–1983), she introduced courses on women in the arts. Norvell served on numerous panels, including Women in Contemporary Art at Mount Holyoke College (1971), and the AIR Gallery's Monday Night Program in 1973, 1974 and 1979. She is the author of *Recording Conceptual Art: Early Interviews with Barry, Huebler, Kaltenbach, LeWitt, Morris, Oppenheim, Siegelaub, Smithson, and Weiner* (University of California Press, 2002). Norvell, who was also active in civil rights and anti-Vietnam War efforts, has one child. She earned her B.A. from Bennington College and her M.A. from Hunter College. (ABS)

Noun, Louise Rosenfield (1908 – 2002) Author, historian of Iowa women, and collector of women's art, Noun came of age during the struggle for suffrage. She joined NOW in 1971 after Pauli Murray and Dorothy Kenyon failed to get the national ACLU, of which Noun was a member, to support women's issues. She was one of the 10 founding members of the Des Moines chapter of NOW (1971) and later served as its president. In 1978, she was a founder of the Chrysalis Foundation, A Young Woman's Resource Center, where she served as president and continued as an active member until her death. She is the author of *Iowa Women in the WPA* (Blackwell Publishing, 1999). Earlier works include *Strong-Minded Women: The Emergence of the Woman-Suffrage Movement in Iowa* (1969), *More Strong-Minded Women: Iowa Feminists Tell Their Stories* (1992), and *Journey to Autonomy: A Memoir*, all published by the Iowa State University Press. Noun was honored by the State Historical Society of Iowa for her contributions to Iowa history, and also by the University of Iowa, Drake University, and Grinnell and Cornell Colleges. Noun, who had one child, earned her B.A. from Grinnell College and her M.A. from Radcliffe/ Harvard. She co-founded the Iowa Women's Archives at the University of Iowa. Archives: Women's Archives, University of Iowa Library, Iowa City, IA.

Novas, Himilce (1944 –) Born in Havana and raised in NYC, Novas was a founding member of NOW, and a founder and leader of CR groups as early as 1968. She helped organize and participated in the August 26, 1970 march down Fifth Avenue, and picketed, wrote letters, lobbied and met with publishers of women's magazines (including John Mack Carter of *Ladies' Home Journal*) to help raise awareness of the need for equal rights and respect for women. She participated in the first women's convention in Seneca Falls, NY, and wrote the first feminist play published by Joseph Papp in *Scripts*, a publication of the New York Shakespeare Theater. The play, "Free This Day: A Play in Seven Exhibits," was also produced there and elsewhere. Novas is the author of *Everything You Need to Know about Latino History* (Plume/Penguin, 1994), which traces the history of Latinos in North America, and several other books on Latino history and culture, and is the author of several novels. A college professor of literature and writing, Novas earned her B.A. from Hunter College. (ABS)

Novick, Leah (1932 –) A rabbi since 1987, Novick writes about and teaches feminism in Judaism. Through her work, she has inspired and influenced many women of diverse ages and backgrounds to become involved in the women's movement and political action. She was a founder and served as president of the CT WPC in the early 1970s, helping to organize in support of the ERA, childcare and abortion rights, and was instrumental in the election of Governor Ella Grasso. She served as vice chair of the NWPC in the mid 1970s. In California, she was executive director of the California Commission on the Status of Women under Governor Jerry Brown. From 1975 – 1976, Novick was chief aid to representative Bella Abzug, helping to develop and obtain passage of major women's rights legislation. In the late 1970s, Novick was director of the Justice Fund, Planned Parenthood of America, overseeing grants and loans to poor women for abortions. She was coordinator for the IWY commission, 1977 Houston conference, where she helped develop a national women's rights agenda. During the 1980s, she was a lecturer in women's studies in public policy, University of California, Berkeley, where she organized comparable worth seminars. Novick, who has three children, was also active in the civil rights, peace and environmental movements. In addition to her rabbinical ordination, she holds a B.A. from City University of New York and an M.A. from Southern Connecticut State College. (ABS)

Nower, Joyce (1932 –) was a founding member of San Diego Women's Liberation (1969), a founding member of the ad hoc committee for women's studies at SDSU (1969), and thus co-founder of the first women's studies program in the U.S. She was also a co-founder of the community-based Center for Women's Studies and Services. She then lectured in the program on women in literature (1970); convened all-women poetry readings and arts festivals; and compiled and edited *Selected Bibliography of International Women Writers* (1971). Nower also developed CR groups in California women's detention facilities and prisons; organized and became director (1972 – 1974) of Project Repair, a home-repair skills training program for women; and co-published *The Greater Golden Hill Poetry Express*, a poetry journal by and for women (beginning in 1975). From 1976 – 1983, Nower was a columnist for *The Longest Revolution*, a progressive

feminist newspaper. She also wrote and distributed a polemic titled "Theses on Art and the Movement" (1977), and throughout the 1970s wrote poetry and criticism while teaching in what became the women's studies department at SDSU. As an advanced Black Belt in Tae Kwon Do, Nower has also taught self-defense classes for women. Her article "Martial Arts and Feminist Consciousness – Prevention of Violence" was published in *Fighting Woman News* (1994). Nower is author of *Year of the Fires* (Center for Women's Studies & Service, 1983); *Column of Silence* (Avranches Press, 2001); and *The Sister Chronicles: A History of the Origins of the Women's Studies Program at San Diego State University in Prose and Poetry* (Avranches Press, 2005). Nower, who has three children, earned her B.A. from Middlebury College, her M.A. from Harvard University, and her Ph.D. from The Union Institute and University, Cincinnati. She retired from SDSU's department of rhetoric and writing studies in 1996. In addition to her work in establishing women's studies at the university, she also initiated the first black American literature course at SDSU in 1966. Archives: San Diego State University Archives, San Diego, CA. (ABS)

Nussbaum, Karen Beth (1950 –) A labor activist, Nussbaum was co-founder of 9to5, Boston's organization for women office workers (1973). In 1975, she founded Local 925, Service Employees International Union, primarily for women office workers, and in 1978 was a founder of Working Women, National Association of Officers Workers. She became the first president, SEIU District 925 (national jurisdiction for office workers) in 1981. From 1993 – 1996, Nussbaum was director, Women's Bureau, U.S. Department. of Labor, and in 1996 became the first director of the Working Women's Department, AFL-CIO. Nussbaum is the co-author of *9to5, The Working Woman's Guide to Office Survival* (Penguin Books, 1983) and co-author of *Solutions for the New Workforce* (Seven Locks Press, 1989). Nussbaum, who has three children, earned her B.A. from Goddard College. Archives: Schlesinger Library, Radcliffe Institute, Cambridge, MA; and Walter P. Reuther Library, Wayne State University, Detroit, MI. (ABS)

Nussbaum, Rhoda Ivy (1947 –) (also known as Rhoda Ivy Schnitzer) While attending an early CR group, Nussbaum had the sudden realization that she had become a physical therapist rather than a physician because the culture she lived in had convinced her that she did not have the choice of being a doctor. Making a huge effort to overcome her own lack of self-esteem, she says, she began her medical studies in Belgium because she was rejected by American medical schools. After learning medicine in French, she was successful and therefore able to transfer to medical school in the U.S., the University of Miami. She moved to California to do her residency in obstetrics and gynecology at Kaiser Permanente. After completing her training, she stayed at Kaiser, where she eventually be-

N

came assistant physician in chief of her medical center. "In all the many hospitals and Kaiser medical centers in California, there were only four women in that position and none serving as physician in chief or executive director," she says. Feeling lonely and vulnerable, the four women invited other women physicians in the medical group to come together and formed Women Physicians in Leadership to increase the number of women in leadership positions. In the late 1990s, Nussbaum was asked to lead a task force on women's health, and then to lead organizational efforts to implement improved healthcare services and outcomes for women members and their families. In her medical practice, Nussbaum championed lesbian, bisexual and transgender health issues, as well as the unique needs of women of color. She also supported humanitarian organizations and national and international women's and human rights groups. Nussbaum has two children. (ABS)

Nute, Jean S. – See Pauline, Jean

Nystuen, Arlene M. (1934 –) was on the campaign committee to elect Joan Grove to the Minnesota House in 1972—a landmark year, with six women being elected. In 1973, Nystuen was a co-founder of Women Helping Offenders, and volunteered to teach self-esteem at the Women's Workhouse. Also in the 1970s, she lobbied for a new women's prison in Shakopee, MN, participated in the first Minnesota Women's Issues meeting in St. Cloud, and lobbied with the Minnetonka Hopkins Eden Prairie LWV at the capitol to put into law equal gender pay, then monitored the city to enforce it. She lobbied legislators to pass Title IX (1974), and helped enforce the bill at Hopkins, MN, schools. In 1975, Nystuen was a co-founder of Genesis II, a women-offender program that was an alternative to prison. Also in 1975, Nystuen was part of a group to obtain a city permit for a battered women's shelter in Minnetonka. In addition to this work, Nystuen—who has three children and an elementary teaching degree—was part of groups protesting Dow Chemical for spraying chemicals on Chavez' migrant farmers growing grapes (1960s). She has been active in environmental and anti-war groups, was co-founder of St. Luke's Church homeless shelter, and served as chair of a committee to obtain low-income housing in several areas in Minnetonka. She was a consultant for battered women programs for 20 years. (ABS)

Oak, Fabi Romero – See Romero, Fabi

O'Barr, Jean Fox (1942 –) Writer and teacher, O'Barr came to Duke University in 1969 and was the first director of continuing education, a re-entry program for women. While there, she established the Duke Institute for Learning in Retirement, now (2005) a 1,200-member community where she teaches. In 1983 she established the women's studies program at Duke. As director, she

raised $4 million in endowment to support the program. She was also the first woman to be named a Distinguished University Service Professor. O'Barr has published extensively, and served as editor of *SIGNS: Women in Culture and Society* (1985 – 1990). She was co-editor, with Elizabeth Minnich and Rachel Rosenfeld, of *Reconstructing the Academy: Women's Education and Women's Studies* (University of Chicago Press, 1988); with Mary Wyer and Deborah Pope of *Ties That Bind: Essays on Mothering and Patriarchy* (University of Chicago Press, 1990); with Micheline Malson and Mary Wyer of *Feminist Theory in Practice and Process* (University of Chicago Press, 1989); and with Eugenia DeLamotte and Natania Meecker of *Women Imagine Change: A Global Anthology of Women's Resistance from 600 BC to Present* (John Wiley & Sons, 1997). In addition, she is author of *Perspectives on Power: Women in Africa, Asia and Latin America* (Duke University Press, 1991) and *Feminism in Action: Building Institutions and Community Through Women's Studies* (University of North Carolina Press, 1994). She served as editor of *Women and a New Academy: Gender and Cultural Contexts* (University of Wisconsin Press, 1989). O'Barr has also published numerous articles on these and other topics in scholarly journals. O'Barr holds a B.A. from Indiana University (1964), an M.A. from Northwestern University (1965), a Ph.D. from Northwestern University (1970), and an Honorary Degree from Indiana University (2001). An endowed professorship in her name, as well as an annual symposium bearing her name, exists at Duke University. Archives: Duke University, Durham, NC. (ABS)

O'Brien, Dorothy A. (1948 –) For many years, O'Brien was part of Chicago NOW's efforts to change Marshall Field's credit-card policy and Sears' discriminating job placement practices. She also worked with Kathy Rand on Chicago NOW's public relations committee (1971 – 1972), effectively increasing public knowledge of women's issues. In 1973, O'Brien helped establish the first chapter office in the country for Chicago NOW and served as its first director. Earlier, O'Brien had supported women's issues on the campus of the University of Wisconsin, Madison. O'Brien holds a B.S. (ABS)

O'Brien, Kate (1940 –) (also known as Kaye Pender) In 1970, as a member of Gay Liberation Front, O'Brien participated in the takeover of the American Psychiatric Association's Convention in Los Angeles to protest a program on "curing" homosexuals by shock therapy. (The following year, the APA removed homosexuality from its list of disorders.) O'Brien also helped form and put on workshops on feminist issues for the men of the GLF; helped form and work with the Gay Women's Speakers Bureau of the GLF; and was an active participant in many of the GLF agit-prop events. In 1970 she became involved with the lesbian feminists group at the Crenshaw Women's Center in Los Angeles, and was active, she says, "in its outreach and hell-raising throughout the Los Angeles area." Also in 1970, she compiled and illustrated *Lesbia Now: The Voice of Sappho's Children*. In 1974, O'Brien marched with strikers protesting unfair and sexist/racist labor practices, and accusations of fiscal mismanagement at the Gay Services Center in Los Angeles. She was also in charge of renovation and beautification of the Victorian houses purchased by the Alcoholism Center for Women, on Alvarado Street, and later joined the staff as a peer counselor. In the late 1980s, O'Brien moved to North Carolina to work with the state's alcoholism program, "displeasing many for bringing up issues of feminism in places where they had been tucked out of sight." (ABS)

O'Connor, Lynn E. (1941 –) After working on the "new left" O'Connor joined Jennifer Gardner in 1968, founding a small CR group in San Francisco. In 1969, she wrote "Redstockings West Manifesto," distributed as a pamphlet and reprinted in *Masculine-Feminine* (Harper and Row, 1969). O'Connor's "The Small Group," and "Niceness" appeared in I*t Ain't Me Babe*, 1969. An evolutionary psychologist, O'Connor then wrote her classic theoretical article "Male Supremacy" (1970), reprinted by Jo Ann Evansgardner. Other publications include "Alternative Life-Styles," published in "In The Women's Page," a newsletter founded by O'Connor, dedicated to radical feminist theory and first person accounts of women's conditions in the clerical workforce. This analysis of the counter-culture was reprinted in *Radical Therapist*, 1972, and "Office Politics." First published in 1971, "In the Women's Page" was reprinted in *The Women Say, The Men Say*, 1979. In 1970 O'Connor led the disruption of the American Psychiatric Association Convention, during which the idea of shocking homosexuals' genitalia was presented as a "new cure for homosexuality." This led to homosexuality being removed from *Diagnostic and Statistical Manual of Mental Disorders*. O'Connor received a B.A. from San Francisco State University (1969), and a Ph.D. from The Wright Institute, Berkeley (1991). She is (2005) a professor at the Wright Institute, director of the Emotion, Personality and Altruism Research Group, and adjunct clinical associate professor at The University of California, Berkeley. (ABS)

Oestreich, Sandy (1934 –) joined NOW in 1972, focused on women's healthcare, and "marched anywhere NOW told me to in New York and North Carolina." A nurse practitioner, she served as Pinellas (FL) NOW co-president (1989 – 1990) and president/VP (1999 – 2001). Oestreich also created the Coalition for Religious Freedom in our Secular Hospitals. The goal was to remove Catholic hierarchy from public hospitals so that "women and elders could get healthcare again. St. Petersburg is one of only two cities in America to have done that." An ERA campaign coordinator and founder/president of Florida's Equal Rights Alliance, Inc., Oestreich has spoken widely, makes numerous speeches, presentations, and TV appearances for the ERA in Florida and elsewhere, and has enabled two ERA bills to be introduced since 2002 in the Florida Legislature. Oestreich, who has two children, is (2005) a Ph.D. candidate in educational research. She is professor emerita, Adelphi University, NY, and advisory board member, University of South Florida. (ABS)

Oglesby, Carole (1938 –) Deeply involved in promoting women's sports, exercise and recreation, Oglesby was appointed commissioner of championships of the Commission on Intercollegiate Athletics for Women, then became the first president of the Association for Intercollegiate Athletics for Women. Both organizations, created by the Division of Girls and Women's Sports (a professional organization for women physical educators) were very active with the National Coalition for Girls and Women in Education throughout the creation—and battles for maintenance of—Title IX. In addition to extensive speaking, writing and volunteer work for women's sports, Oglesby gave testimony in Congressional hearings on behalf of Title IX and the 1978 Amateur Sport Act (which brought new equity to the Olympic Movement). In addition, Oglesby was coordinator of the Torch Relay that moved a torch from Seneca Falls, NY, to Houston, TX, during the weeks leading up to the 1977 Houston conference. Oglesby herself ran with the torch on the opening day in Seneca Falls, in Philadelphia and as it went through her home town, in Washington, D.C., and then as the torch was run into Houston for the conference itself. By its end, the relay had garnered extensive favorable press for both the conference and the movement. In addition, Oglesby worked with Katherine Switzer to get a women's marathon event into the Olympic Games. The two succeeded in time for the 1984 games in Los Angeles. She is the author of *Women and Sport: From Myth to Reality* (Lea & Febiger, 1978). The book contains a chapter by Wilma Scott Heide. Oglesby holds a Ph.D. in Physical Education from Purdue University (1969) and a Ph.D. in Counseling from Temple University (1999). Archives: The Sophia Smith Collection, Smith College, Northampton, MA. (ABS)

O'Hanrahan, Inka (1911 – 1970) was an early organizer of national NOW. Born in Warsaw, Poland, and educated in Berlin and Switzerland, she came to the U.S. in 1932 to marry an Irish attorney. A clinical biochemist, she owned and directed her own laboratory in San Francisco until its sale in 1969. O'Hanrahan served as vice chair of the California Commission on the Status of Women (1965 – 1967) and was active in numerous national women's organizations, including BPW and AAUW. A member of the small steering committee set up in June 1966 to recruit more members for NOW and to plan the October conference, O'Hanrahan was named chair of the national membership committee, and herself organized the Northern and Southern CA chapters of NOW. She later became national treasurer of NOW. O'Hanrahan, who contributed to professional journals and lectured here and in Europe on the status of women, also served as president of the San Francisco Soroptimist Club and public affairs chair of the 13-county Soroptimist Federation of America. She also assisted Mothers Alone Working, a local organization for women who were the sole support of their children, had low-paying jobs and little or no money, and no childcare. In addition, O'Hanrahan, who had three children, helped organize a pilot childcare center in her office building.

Okazawa-Rey, Margo (1949 –) A feminist scholar of gender, race, class, nation equality and anti-militarism, Okazawa-Rey became involved in community and feminist activism and theorizing while a social worker in Boston. She joined the Combahee River Collective in 1975 just as it was reforming itself as a study group. Over a period of about three years, the group came up with "A Black Feminist Statement." In a 1999 interview for Benita Roth's book *Separate Roads to Feminism*, Okazawa-Rey described the discussion that went into the statement as not just about race or gender, but also about class and imperialism. She also observed that the document "pretty much holds up currently." As a black lesbian identified group, the Combahee River Collective rejected black liberationist politics that did not admit to the existence of lesbian relationships. At the same time, the members rejected lesbian separatism, arguing that it left out far too many people. CRC members were also activists, supporting, for example, Dr. Kenneth Edelin, an African American physician who had been arrested for performing a legal abortion, and challenging the media and the city of Boston for minimal coverage of the murders of a dozen black women in the late 1970s. Okazawa-Rey also worked successfully with other organizations, predominantly white feminist groups. Okazawa-Rey is (2005) research consultant at the Women's Centre for Legal Aid and Counselling in East Jerusalem, Occupied Palestinian Territories, and professor at Fielding University. She is also professor emerita at San Francisco State University. A prolific writer, she is co-editor of the textbook *Women's Lives: Multicultural Perspectives* (McGraw Hill, 1998); *Beyond Heroes and Holidays* (1998); and *Encyclopedia of African American Education* (1996). She has published articles, book chapters and book reviews on women, and economic, social and racial justice. Okazawa-Rey holds a B.A. from Capital University, an M.S.W. from Boston University and a Ed.D. from Harvard. (ABS)

Olds, Sally Wendkos (1933 –) is a feminist writer, author of more than 200 magazine articles and several books that deal with women's lives, child development, family life, human relations and mental health and medicine. Her books include *The Complete Book of Breastfeeding* (Workman, Bantam, 1972), *The Working Parents Survival Guide* (Bantam, 1983) and *The Eternal Garden: Seasons of our Sexuality* (Times Books, 1985). Her articles have been published in *Ms., McCall's, Woman's Day, Redbook, The New York Times Magazine, Reader's Digest* and numerous other magazines. From 1968 – 1972, Olds participated in two CR groups and demonstrated many times in NYC and Washington, D.C., for reproductive rights. She spearheaded a committee to eliminate sexism in the Port Washington, NY, public schools, and spoke about female sexuality, childcare and women's health to numerous audiences. She was a charter member of Nassau, NY, NOW and a member of NARAL. Olds, who has three children, worked for the national committee against discrimination in housing and volunteered on fair housing projects for the Urban League and the American Friends Service Committee. She also demonstrated against the Vietnam War and both Gulf wars. Olds earned her B.A. from the University of Pennsylvania. Archives: Kinsey Institute, Bloomington, IN, and the University of Wyoming, Laramie, WY. (ABS)

O'Leary, Jean (1948 – 2005) An ex-nun and a charismatic leader, O'Leary had a long career as a lesbian feminist and Democratic Party activist. Angered that her complaints about lesbian invisibility were dismissed at the male-dominated Gay Activists Alliance in New York City in 1971, she founded Lesbian Feminist Liberation. A lesbian separatist early on, O'Leary broadened her perspective and served as co-executive director of the National Gay Task Force with Bruce Voeller in 1975 – 1976. Active in the Democratic Party beginning in 1976, O'Leary was appointed by Massachusetts Governor Michael Dukakis as an at-large member of the Democratic National Committee and served as a Dukakis whip at the Democratic National Convention in Atlanta in 1988. In 1977 she was appointed by President Jimmy Carter to serve on the National Commission on the Observance of International Women's Year, which made her the first openly gay person to be appointed to a presidential commission. She also organized the first meeting of gay rights leaders at the White House, which took place during the Carter administration. O'Leary's work changed policy regarding lesbians and gay men in key federal agencies, including the State Department, the U.S. Department of Justice, and the U.S. Civil Rights Commission. In the 1980s she moved to California. With Rob Eichberg, she founded Coming Out Day October 11, 1988. In 2003, she was chair of the Democratic National Committee's gay and lesbian caucus, and a member of the executive committee, the governing body of the DNC. She received a medal from the city of West Hollywood, CA, in 2003 for her contributions to the community. O'Leary was born in Kingston, NY, and joined the Sisters of the Holy Humility of Mary Convent in OH in 1966, and while there graduated from Cleveland State University. Her experiences as a nun are in a much-discussed chapter in *Lesbian Nuns: Breaking the Silence*. Her career in CA consisted of real estate sales and the development of a large telemarketing operation. (ABS before death)

Olivarez, Graciela (1928 – 1987) In the 1950s, Olivarez, a high-school dropout, became the first woman disc jockey in Arizona. Concerned about women workers, Olivarez was able to use her popularity as a radio host to promote rights for Chicanos in general and for Chicanas specifically. During the 1964 Civil Rights Commission Hearings, she was directed by the owners of the radio station she worked for to not testify, or she would be fired. Olivarez did, in fact, testify, which brought her to the attention of the president of the University of Notre Dame, Father Theodore Hesburgh. From 1965 – 1966 she worked for a local independent television station producing a Spanish-only show every Sunday. But Olivarez had so impressed Father Hesburgh that, just 18 months after his initial meeting with her, he had admission requirements waived to allow Olivarez to enter law school. She thus became the first Hispanic woman to graduate from Notre Dame School of Law. From 1970 – 1972 she was appointed director of the Arizona branch of the federal Office of Economic Equal Opportunity. Later, while living in New Mexico, she served as head of the State Planning Agency and taught Constitutional Law at the University of New Mexico School of Law. After learning about the formation of National Organization for Women, Olivarez served on its first board of directors. She also served as director of the Community Services Administration during the Carter presidency. At that time, she was the highest-ranking Hispanic woman in the federal government. In 1984, Olivarez returned to broadcasting by forming Olivarez Television Company, Inc., an affiliate of the only Spanish-language television network in the country. She continued her work in broadcasting and philanthropy until her death from cancer. An award in Olivarez' name is now presented annually by the Notre Dame Hispanic Law Association. Archives: Arizona State University, Tempe, Arizona.

Oliver, Lee Bleda (1931 – 2005) Active in the civil rights movement in the 1960s, Oliver joined NOW and became a national board member in 1971. Oliver was co-chair, with Nancy Gordon, of the political affairs committee and produced the booklet "Women and the City: How to Use the Machinery." Oliver was a founding member of the women's advocacy committee in 1971, and with other women formed a resume bank. The group also issued the report "A Study of the Women in New York City Government: Clerical Workers." The report showed that women received lower pay, needed more education, received fewer promotions and had fewer options than men in similar job categories. In subsequent years, Oliver picketed, made lobbying trips to Washington, D.C., for the Equal Rights Amendment, and "tried to make life uncomfortable for politicians and firms that discriminated against women." With Pat Korbet and Mary Vasiliades, Oliver formed Women's Interprises, a mailorder catalog of women's products. A special librarian, Oliver held an A.A. degree. (ABS before death)

Olsen, Tillie (1913 – 2007) was best known in feminist circles as the author of *Silences* (1978), a nonfiction book that describes the literary void created by the absences of women's voices and the voices of the poor and disenfranchised, but her activist years go back before the second wave. Born to political refugees from the Russian Czarist repression that followed the 1905 revolution, Olsen was forced to leave high school without graduating to help support her family during the Great Depression. Olsen herself became an activist, joining the Young Communist League at age 17. She was jailed in 1930 after trying to organize workers in a meat-packing house in Kansas City, and was arrested in 1934 for participating in the San Francisco Maritime strike. After marrying in 1936, Olsen remained politically active. She served as president of the California CIO's Women's Auxiliary and the Parent-Teachers Association. In 1946 she wrote a women's column in *People's World*. In 1953, when her youngest child entered school, Olsen joined a class in fiction writing at San Francisco State College. She was later awarded a Stegner Fellowship in creative writing at Stanford Uni-versity (1955 and 1956). Acknowledged as a champion of the re-emerging feminist movement, Olsen wrote "I Stand Here Ironing," published in *The Best American Short Stories of 1957*. It was also the central story in Olsen's short story collection, *Tell Me A Riddle* (Lippincott, 1961). Olsen, who received many Honorary Degrees, was also a feminist educator, teaching at Amherst, Stanford Univer-sity and the University of California at San Diego and at Berkeley, among others. The reading list Olsen developed was published in the "Women's Studies Newsletter" and used in numerous women's studies courses. (ABS before death)

O

Olshan, Arleen (1945 –) was a founding member of Radicalesbians in Philadelphia (1971 – 1975), and fought for abortion rights in the early 1970s in Pennsylvania. At the same time, she was involved in The Lesbian Hotline, Women Organized Against Rape and Women in Transition, and was an art instructor at the Free Women's School. She served as treasurer and a member of the steering committee for Philadelphia Focuses on Women in the Visual Arts (1973 – 1974), and was co-coordinator of the Philadelphia Gay and Lesbian Community Center (1974 – 1976). She was also a founder of A Rose By Any Other Name: Women's Art Collective (1976 – 1980), and from 1976 – 1986 was co-owner of Giovanni's Room – Feminist, Lesbian and Gay Bookstore. Olshan, who holds a B.F.A., displays and sells custom leather accessories at various women's festivals, and shows (2005) her drawings and paintings in a variety of venues. She is (2005) a counselor at a residential D&A treatment center for women and children. Archives: The Lesbian Herstory Archive Brooklyn, NY; Radcliffe Lesbian Arts Archive, New York, NY; and Gay & Lesbian Artists, Philadelphia, PA. (ABS)

Olson, Kathleen A. (1942 –) was a co-organizer, with Ann Crisp and Sandra Lee Byrd, of the Kansas City, MO, chapter of NOW (1969 – 1970). She served variously as VP, president and secretary of MN NOW (1970 – 1975), and headed several committees and actions. She was also active in the Twin Cities NOW chapter (1970 – 1979), holding various positions including president. For the celebration of Women's Suffrage in the Twin Cities (August 26, 1971), Olson promoted, produced, directed and moderated an all-day radio call-in show that coincided with the organizing rally to launch the MN WPC. In addition, Olson has testified in support of the ERA, and served as co-coordinator of the Midwest Regional NOW conference (1972). Olson, who has one child, holds a B.A. from St. Olaf College (1964). Archives: Primarily Minnesota NOW, but also The Women's History Project, Minnesota History Center; and the Radcliffe Center, managed by Cheri Register, Ph.D., and under the Emma Willard Task Force on Education (circa 1969 – 1978). (ABS)

Omolade, Barbara (1942 –) An early feminist and civil rights activist, Omolade was a member of the NAACP (Queens College Chapter) and the Student Non-Violent Coordinating Committee helping to organize students (including civil rights martyr Andrew Goodman) for the Mississippi Summer Project. She graduated from college in 1964, spent a few more years in the civil rights movement, married and had a child. While caring for that baby, Omolade began to wonder how slave women cared for their children, and her scholarly passion was born. After the publication of the novel *Roots* by Alex Haley (1976), Omolade envisioned a similar work focusing on African American women's history. In 1994, her book *The Rising Song of African American Women* was published by Routledge. First, however, Omolade worked for a feminist-run domestic violence shelter (early 1970s) and then for Women's Action Alliance. In 1977 she taught one of the first social science courses on African American women at the College of New Rochelle, Co-Op City Evening Program. In 1981, she started working at the CCNY Center for Worker Education, joining the faculty in 1981. By 1983 she had helped found Friends of Women's Studies at CUNY, which was instrumental in establishing the CUNY faculty development seminar on balancing the curriculum for gender, race, ethnicity and class. Omolade was one of three facilitators for this seminar in 1987 – 1988, and continued in that capacity for some time afterward. Omolade, who has two graduate degrees and four children, is both a feminist and a Christian scholar. In 2004, she became dean of multicultural affairs at Calvin College in Grand Rapids, MI. (ABS)

O'Neil, Beth (1952 –) was a founding member of WICCA (Women in Crisis Can Act), a women's hotline. Established in Chicago in 1973, the crisis line started getting calls from battered women, which influenced the 1979 creation of a battered women's shelter. O'Neil was part of the original staff of that shelter. In 1975, O'Neil worked with several women to open Mountain Moving

Coffeehouse. Earlier, as a student at a junior college on the southwest side of Chicago, O'Neil joined the Women's Liberation Union, which was also involved in anti-war activities. At the same time, O'Neil attended one of the first lesbian organizations, Chicago Lesbian Liberation, on the north side of Chicago. She has participated in gay rights, anti-war, women's rights and peace marches and demonstrations. (ABS)

Orear, Jill – See Richmond-Covey, Jill

O'Reilly, Jane (1936 –) contributed to the feminist movement as a journalist who focused on political, social, and personal issues affecting women, such as equal pay, equal rights, equal parenting, the redistribution of wealth and the reallocation of power. While working at *New York Magazine* in the late 1960s, O'Reilly was encouraged to get involved in the women's movement by her friend and colleague Gloria Steinem. Asked by Steinem to become one of the founders of *Ms.*, O'Reilly wrote the cover story for the magazine's first issue, January 1972. In the article, titled "The Housewife's Moment of Truth," O'Reilly coined the term "Click!" to describe an epiphany or moment of truth for feminists. During the Carter administration, O'Reilly wrote a six-week column for *The Washington Star*. That resulted in a three-year syndicated column that appeared in several papers and eventually became O'Reilly's first book, *The Girl I left Behind* (1980). O'Reilly notes that her column was sometimes rejected by papers on the grounds that they already had "a woman columnist." In 1978, O'Reilly went to work for *Time* magazine, where her journalism focused on women's issues such as domestic abuse and abortion and the Kenya U.N. conference on women. O'Reilly's second book, *No Turning Back: Two Nuns Battle with the Vatican over Women's Right to Choose* (1987), written with Patricia Hussey and Barbara Ferraro, describes two nuns who publicly disagreed with the Vatican over abortion. O'Reilly lives (2005) in Vermont and teaches a writing workshop on Memoir. She holds several elected positions locally and works with the committee for the equality of women at Harvard, an independent group once described by the Harvard administration as "very dangerous women." O'Reilly, who has two children, holds a B.A. from Radcliffe College (1958). Archives: The Schlesinger Library, Radcliffe Institute, Cambridge, MA. (ABS)

Orenstein, Gloria Feman (1938 –) is an ecofeminist and professor of comparative literature and the Program for the Study of Women and Men in Society at the University of Southern California. She has spoken and published widely on literature, art, ecofeminism and religion, and is the author of *Multicultural Celebrations: The Paintings of Betty La Duke 1970 – 1990* (Pomegranate Art Press, 1993), *The Reflowering of the Goddess* (Pergamon Press; Athene Series, 1990), and *The Theater of the Marvelous: Surrealism and the Contemporary Stage* (New

York University Press, 1975). She was also co-editor, with Irene Diamond, of *Reweaving the World: The Emergence of Ecofeminism* (Sierra Club Books, 1990). Orenstein was the first to write about the women of Surrealism and the first to write about Frida Kahlo in *The Feminist Art Journal*. She co-created (with Erika Duncan) The Woman's Salon for Literature in NYC (1975–1985), and with Susan Schwalb co-created the first International Festival of Women Artists at the Ny Carlsberg Glyptotek in Copenhagen for the International Women's Year Mid-Decade Conference on Women (1980). She also co-created (with Irene Diamond) the conference Ecofeminism: Culture, Nature, Theory at USC (1987). Orenstein taught and directed women's studies at Douglass College in the 1970s; was the first hire in the Program for the Study of Women and Men in Society at USC; and was the student of the Shaman of Samiland, from 1987–1990. She has published in feminist journals, and was active in Jewish feminist circles in Los Angeles in the 1990s. Orenstein earned her B.A. from Brandeis University (1959), her M.A. from Radcliffe Graduate School of Harvard University; and her Ph.D. from New York University (1971). Archives: The Woman's Salon photo archives are at Schlesinger Library, Radcliffe Institute, Cambridge, MA. (ABS)

Orovan, Mary (1937 –) Prior to 1968 Orovan was active in the abortion movement. After attending the first Congress to Unite Women (NYC, 1969), she began speaking and writing on other feminist topics, attending demonstrations, helping to organize conferences and consciousness raising groups, and planning actions. She was a member of NOW, New York Radical Feminists and Feminists in the Arts. Working on her M.A. at New York University, Orovan wrote "Humanizing English," which she believes was the first tract to deal with the impact of using "he" in gender-neutral situations. In the 1970s, she was involved in many art, photography and image projects. One was at the former Huntington Hartford Museum in New York City, where Orovan, Jacqui Ceballos and Pat Lawrence were able to negotiate a change in tenor of a large international photo exhibit titled "Women" by having several photos removed and a plaque put up at the entrance that decried the stereotyped, demeaning images of the show. Later, Orovan and Mina Bikman formed Media Women to film conferences and feminist concerts. Orovan lobbied for more statues of women by women, tried to have input into changing street names to reflect women's contributions in art and politics, and worked with ad agencies to obtain more positive images of women on television. In addition, Orovan participated in the sit-in at *The Ladies' Home Journal* and worked to make classified ads at *The New York Times* gender neutral. Orovan was also part of the group that desegregated the male-only bars at McSorley's and PJ Clarke, and was part of the sit-in at the Plaza Hotel (NYC). Archives: Schlesinger Library, Radcliffe Institute, Cambridge, MA. (ABS)

Orthwein, Laura Rand – See X, Laura

Osborn, Torie (1950 –) Writer, music producer and lesbian activist, Osborn participated in the first CR group at Barnard College (1970). In 1971, she and Peg Strobel founded the Middlebury College Women's Union, where Osborn participated in the anti-war movement, co-founding the Middlebury College Radical Education and Action Project. After graduating, Osborn organized two Socialist Feminist Conferences: North Carolina (1972) and Ohio (1973). She was also a member of a lesbian community in Burlington, VT (1972–1976). From 1976–1977, she was a member of Blazing Star, a lesbian workgroup, and CWLU. She was also part of the founding staff (1976) of *In These Times*, a Chicago leftist newspaper. During this time, she became a producer and promoter of women's music, working with musician Holly Near. In 1980 she co-founded (with Robin Tyler) the West Coast Women's Music and Cultural Festival, which brought together leaders in women's music, art and politics. She was the promoter for artists such as Sweet Honey in the Rock, Ferron and Kate Clinton from 1984–1987. From 1981–1982, she was the Northern CA coordinator for NOW's San Francisco office. Around 1984, Osborn began to shift her activism toward issues in the gay community, including lesbian awareness in the gay community and AIDS. She was the first woman executive director of the Los Angeles Gay and Lesbian Center, 1987–1992, and in 1993 was executive director of NGLTF. Since 1997, she has been the executive director of the Liberty Hill Foundation. Born in Denmark (a U.S. citizen), Osborn has a B.A. from Middlebury College (1972) and an M.B.A, UCLA Anderson School of Management (1984). (ABS)

O

Osborne, Ollie Tucker (1911 – 1993) A leading advocate of women's rights in Louisiana during the 1970s, Osborne worked to get the LA Legislature to ratify the ERA; and fought a long-running battle to strike down LA's antiquated and discriminatory Head and Master law through her association with the court case *Hansen v. C.I.R.* A member of the LWV in Lafayette (1959–1994), Osborne was the official observer for the Louisiana LWV at the State Constitutional Convention of 1973. She was chair of the Louisiana Women's Conference in 1975 and area coordinator for the Governor's Conference for Women in 1976. In her work for the ERA, Osborne served as public information officer for, and was a member of, the steering committee of ERA United of Louisiana. She was also co-director and chair of the Evangeline ERA Coalition and a member of the Louisiana WPC. Osborne was fearless in her ERA lobbying efforts, particularly in her attempts to persuade Governor Edwin Edwards to speak out favorably about the ERA to the state legislature. In 1971, Osborne met Barbara Hansen and vowed to help her with a tax problem. Though divorced and nearly impoverished, Hansen was being asked to pay back taxes owed by her ex-husband. Although Osborne had no legal experience, she researched the tax law, learned how to prepare a legal brief, and accompanied Hansen to the federal tax court in New Orleans to argue her case. While Osborne was not able to get help from legal or women's groups, she lobbied the state legislature. Help did come from Sylvia Roberts, an attorney in Baton Rouge, and Janet Mary Riley, a law professor at Loyola Law School in New Orleans. In 1978 the LA Legislature repealed the Head and Master law, effective in 1980. Osborne, who had three children, earned a B.A. from New York University in 1932. She worked in publishing and advertising in New York and real estate and journalism in Lafayette, LA. Archives: Edith Garland Dupré Library, University of Louisiana, Lafayette.

O'Shea, Ann Elizabeth (1949 –) An attorney, O'Shea is the author of "Women's Washington Watch," published in *Working Woman* magazine from 1976 to 1978. She has also published various legal briefs in employment discrimination. A supporter of the ERA, she has been active in areas of childcare and women's health, as well as the peace and labor movements. O'Shea developed the first Women's Equal Rights workshop for the National Student Association's 1970 Student Congress. In 1971, she became the underground distributor of the tract "Why Would a Girl Go into Medicine?" Written by Mary Howell (under the pseudonym Margaret Campbell) while Howell was a dean of Harvard Medical School, the piece exposed the maltreatment of women medical students in U.S. medical schools. Also during the early 1970s, O'Shea twice worked as an assistant for Betty Friedan, "editing her writings, keeping her life glued together, patching up relationships she seemed hell-bent on destroying, and organizing a feminist think-tank conference at Columbia," says O'Shea. She also worked with Jacqui Ceballos to set up a feminist PR firm in the early 1970s. "It didn't last," she says, "but it was great fun while it did!" O'Shea, who has two children, earned her B.A. from Dunbarton College and her J.D. from the Benjamin Cardozo School of Law. (ABS)

Osmer, Judith Ann (1940 –) A scientist and entrepreneur, Osmer joined Los Angeles NOW in 1969, served as its membership chair and treasurer, and counseled women on labor laws and helped them file sex discrimination claims with various government agencies. In 1971, working as a scientist for the Aerospace Corporation, Osmer filed her own sex discrimination case with the CA FEPC, the EEOC and the Contract Compliance Office of the Department of Defense. Sexism was overt and especially blatant in engineering and the physical sciences at that time. Osmer's was the first class-action lawsuit alleging sex discrimination against technical women. The Aerospace Corporation was found guilty by all agencies and given a 30-day cease and desist order to comply with the law. It was also ordered to establish an affirmative action office at the company. In federal court for 12 years,

the case was finally settled out of court. Although little money went to the underpaid women, the lawsuit changed the employment practices of all the large defense contractors. Osmer donated all of her settlement money to NOW LDEF and held a press conference encouraging other women involved in the suit to do the same. Osmer also helped start a very successful women's committee at the Aerospace Corporation, which raised feminist consciousness by holding monthly meetings and putting on programs. In 1983, Osmer started her own company growing the laboratory gemstone ruby known as the Ramaura Cultured Ruby. It is the only laboratory-grown gemstone shown in the Gem Hall of the Smithsonian Natural History Museum, where both the crystal forms and faceted gems are displayed. (ABS)

Ostema, Claire – See Cummings, Claire

Osterhoudt, Donna – See Schaper, Donna E.

Osterud, Grey (1948 –) (formerly known as Nancy Grey Osterud) A founding member of Bread and Roses in Boston, MA, Osterud began working as an historian of American women in the early 1970s. She is the author of *Bonds of Community: The Lives of Farm Women in Nineteenth-Century New York* (Cornell University Press, 1991), and from 1991 to 1997 was American co-editor of *Gender & History*, an international feminist journal published by Blackwell. She earned a Ph.D. from Brown University, taught at Lewis & Clark College, San Jose State University and Regis College, and worked for museums and historical societies on exibitions and public programs in women's history. Osterud now works as a freelance book development editor for authors and publishers in American women's history, African American studies, and international human rights. Archives: Schlesinger Library, Radcliffe Institute, Cambridge, MA. (ABS)

O'Toole, Virginia Anne (1932 –) (also known as Virginia Brautigam) In 1972, O'Toole established the Muskegon – Ottawa chapter of NOW, after having been a member of Grand Rapids NOW. She served as education chair for MI NOW and was later state president of Women's Equity Action League. O'Toole is (2004) secretary of the Muskegon chapter of NOW. A pioneer fighter for equality of education, O'Toole went to the Civil Rights Commission in 1970 to stop the tradition of putting girls into home economics classes and boys into shop classes. She has three children. Archives: University of Michigan, Ann Arbor, MI. (ABS)

Ouellette, P. Savanna (1945 –) A Native American, Ouellette was a member of New Haven (CT) Women's Liberation Rock Band (1970 – 1973), where she played bass. Ouellette, who holds a B.S., M.A. and J.D., is a mediator. Also active in the civil rights movement, Ouellette has two children. (ABS)

Packer, Sara (1949 –) During her senior year at Oberlin (1970), Packer and her friends founded a campus feminist group and successfully agitated for a women's history class. Caught up in the sense of rebellion that permeated those years, Packer left Oberlin without graduating and moved to Portland, OR, where she joined several feminist groups and a consciousness raising group. She also helped start a Women's Liberation School, where the women taught each other everything from automechanics to drawing, and film-making. Packer came out as a lesbian in 1973, a time when lesbian feminists and straight feminists were at odds, and when the Portland feminist/lesbian community began to reflect the growing discontent of women of color with the white, middleclass feminist movement. In 1976 Packer began her first job as a childcare worker and remains in the field of early education today (2004). Throughout those years she worked to promote diversity awareness within the early childhood community. Packer, who has one child, holds an M.A. from Pacific Oaks College. (ABS)

Pagan, Dylcia Noemi (1946 –) ran as a Democratic candidate in Shirley Chisholm's campaign for president in 1968. In 1975, she promoted the first Latino national TV series "Realidades," and in 1976 organized Latina social workers in Boston regarding public housing for homeless families. In 1977 she did programs on WCBS concerning the exploitation of women in media, the fashion industry and music. A political activist, she was captured April 4, 1980, along with other comrades, for participating in the underground wing of the Puerto Rican Independence Movement and spent 20 years in prison. In 1999 she was granted clemency by President Clinton and returned to Puerto Rico, where she was named Woman of the Year. In 2002, she received the Lifetime Achievement Award at the Latino Legislative Somos el Futuro conference. She is (2004) writing her life story and a documentary about five Puerto Rican nationalist heroines. Her poetry has appeared in *Have You Seen La Nueva Mujer Puertorriqueña?* Pagan, who has a B.A. from Brooklyn College, has one child. Her biography has been published in *Puerto Rican Women: A History of Oppression and Resistance*. Part of her life story was included in a book by anthropologist John Langston Gwaltney: *The Dissenters: Voices from Contemporary America*. Archives: Centro Hunter College, New York, NY, and the University of Puerto Rico, Rio, Piedras branch.

Paint, Donelle – See Estey, Donelle

Palley, Marian Lief (1939 –) professor of political science and international relations, and director of women's studies at the University of Delaware, Palley has served as president of the Women's Caucus (2005) for Political Science, chair of the committee on the status of women in the profession of the American Political Science Association, and chair of the Delaware state advisory committee for the Institute for Women's Policy Research study on the status of women in Delaware. She has been a member of the policy committee of the New Castle County, DE, YWCA, and has written numerous articles and books on the women's movement. She was co-author of *Women and Public Policies: Reassessing Gender Politics* (University Press of Virginia, 1996), and co-editor of *Women of Korea and Japan: Continuity and Change* (Temple University Press, 1994) and *Race, Sex and Policy Problems* (D.C. Heath, 1979). Palley, who has two children, earned her B.A. from Syracuse University, her M.A. from the Maxwell School, Syracuse University, and her Ph.D. from New York University. (ABS)

Pam, Eleanor (1936 –) joined NY NOW with her friend Kate Millett in 1966/1967. She was a founding member of the chapter's first education committee in 1967. In 1968, she founded and directed the first Women's Center at the City University of New York. This was such a novel idea that politicians, academics and the media gave it much attention. Becoming a professor (with two master's degrees and a doctoral degree from New York University), Pam remained at CUNY for 34 years. Her last job was as professor and director of the Domestic Violence Research and Resource Center at John Jay College of Criminal Justice, CUNY. While at CUNY, she says that she continued "to raise and change institutional consciousness and behaviors with respect to gender inequity." She assisted in drafting and litigating a major sex discrimination class action lawsuit against CUNY. The case, which ran from the mid 1970s to the mid 1980s, was settled favorably on behalf of the female plaintiffs. Pam also negotiated and implemented CUNY's first sexual harassment policy, and founded and directed its first Domestic Violence Research and Resource Center. During Rudolph Giuliani's tenure as mayor of New York City, Pam served as a member of the Mayor's Commission to Combat Family Violence. She is also known for ongoing work with incarcerated women at Bedford Hills Correctional Facility and Albion (NY) Correctional Facility, serving as an academic mentor and assisting in legal and quality of life issues. She has received awards for her feminist activities from VFA, City University of New York (2001), and Florida Atlantic University (2002). Pam has three children. (ABS)

Panzarino, Concetta Jean ("Connie") (1947 – 2004) A psychotherapist, writer, public speaker and disabilities rights activist, Panzarino helped improve the lives of disabled women. Born with a rare spinal disease, Panzarino recounted the challenges of growing up handicapped and the dawning of her political activism in *The Me in the Mirror* (Seal Press, 1994). She was founder of the Disabled Lesbian Alliance (1972); organized women with disabilities at Hofstra University; wrote articles for women about genetic screening; worked at Seneca Peace Camp; and used her therapy practice to enhance women's understanding of feminism. She also bought a farm and

P

created and ran a shelter/independent living home for women with disabilities. An activist for the elimination of architectural, attitudinal and economic barriers, she showed women that it was wonderful to celebrate differences in color, size, shape and strength. Panzarino sat on the boards of the Disability Law Center, the Project on Women and Disability, and the Boston Center for Independent Living. Archives: The Lesbian Herstory Archives, Brooklyn, NY.

Pariser, Abby Joan (1945 –) attended the founding conference of Chicago's Women's Liberation Women (1969), and worked at the Emma Goldman Pregnancy Testing Center, a project of Chicago Women's Liberation Union, from 1969 – 1970. A member of Jane, the abortion counseling service (1970 – 1972), Pariser was arrested with six other abortion providers on May 2, 1972. She helped found a Planned Parenthood clinic in DuPage County, IL (1972), which she worked in for six years. A member of NOW, Pariser worked on the DuPage County, IL, newsletter committee and the ERA campaign (1975). She was also a delegate to the Illinois Conference on the Status of Women (1975), held in Bloomington. After moving to New York, Pariser served on the Huntington, NY, NOW board (1980 – 1997), and was president in 1984, 1985 and 1986. Pariser was also a founder of the Long Island NOW Alliance (1985); was a Long Island NOW PAC board member (1994 – 1997); and a member of NY State NOW, serving as VP for membership (1985 – 1987). In addition, Pariser was a NOW State Council Representative (1984 – 1988) from the Huntington chapter. From 1980 – 1994, Pariser served on the board of the Suffolk Abortion Rights Coalition. In addition, Pariser has worked since the early 1980s to facilitate after-school childcare and to bring awareness of AIDS to junior high and high school students. A founder, board member (1985 – 1991) and president (1990 – 1991) of Huntington After School Care, Pariser was also part of the anti-Vietnam War effort, was active in the Democratic Party, and served on the board and as board president of the YWCA, West Suburbs, DuPage County, IL, from 1977 – 1979. Pariser has two children and holds a B.A. from Barnard College (1967) and an M.A. from Roosevelt University (1975). (ABS)

Parish, Pauline (1920 –) A university dean, Parish was one of the very early members of NOW in 1966. Nancy Knaak noted in 1986 that she had recruited Parish the day after the decision to found NOW was made at a national meeting of State Commissions on the Status of Women convened in Washington by the Women's Bureau in June 1966. Parish was dean of women at the University of Colorado, Boulder from 1960 – 1970. She also served as director of the women's center for a number of years, starting in 1964, and state implementation chair for the American Association of University Women. She holds a B.A. from Ohio Wesleyan University (1942) and a M.A. from Stanford University (1954). (ABS)

Parisky, Flora Bowles (1937 –) A feminist organizer, Parisky co-founded the Hartford, CT, chapter of the CT WPC in 1972. She founded the Women's Issues Network-Political Action Committee to raise funds for and endorse candidates that support women's issues, in 1974. Two years later, Parisky was appointed to the CT Permanent Commission on the Status of Women, and in 1982 was elected chair. She helped pass landmark legislation during the 1970s, including the elimination of marriage as a defense against rape, increased funding for domestic violence shelters, and equal pay legislation. She is the author of three reports that led to better services for women and girls. "Out of Poverty," published in 1982, led to the creation of employment and education entitlements for Connecticut women receiving Welfare. A 1983 report led to the creation of Hartford's Infant Mortality and Teen Pregnancy Prevention Initiatives. A third report helped change laws affecting domestic violence and led to the creation of Connecticut's innovative partnership between courts and domestic violence centers. Parisky, who has four children, holds a B.S. from New York University (1970) and an M.P.H. from Barney School of Public Administration (1976). She created The Parisky Group, a public policy firm, in 1983. (ABS)

Parker, Laura Lee (1947 –) Artist and designer, Parker was part of a group of women photographers in California, including Corrine Tee, who in the early 1970s were involved in self-portraiture and the depiction or objectification of the female body. Parker later became involved with lesbian rights groups and women's music groups as a designer, and in the 1980s designed album covers for Olivia Records and ads for Olivia Cruises. She studied at the San Francisco Academy of Art and the San Francisco Art Institute, University of California Extension. (ABS)

Parker, Pam – See Allen, Chude Pamela

Parker, Pat (1944 – 1989) A black revolutionary, feminist and lesbian poet, Parker's life and work were greatly influenced by the murder of her sister by her sister's husband, who was convicted not of murder, but of "womanslaughter," and sentenced to one year in a work-release program. A member of the Black Panther Party in the 1960s and the Black Women's Revolutionary Council, Parker was a founder of the Women's Press Collective. She gave the first public reading of her poetry in 1963 while still the wife of a writer. Her first collection of poetry, *Child of Myself*, includes the poem "Goat Child," which decries the confinement and conformity of marriage. There are also several love poems to women in which she comes out as a lesbian. Parker gained notice when she began reading to women's groups in the late 1960s. Her five collections of poetry include *Movement in Black*, her classic that remains consistently in print, and *Womanslaughter* and *Jonestown and Other Madness*, which reveal a black lesbian-feminist perspective. Her poetry dealt with contemporary political issues as well as domestic and sexual violence against women; it also challenged classism and honored unsung African American heroines. Parker moved to Oakland, California, in the early 1970s. There she was active in gay and lesbian organizations and was a leader in women's health issues. From 1978 to 1987, Parker was medical coordinator of the Oakland Feminist Women's Health Center, which grew from one clinic to six during her tenure. Parker had two children.

Parker, Sharon (1948 –) Transformed by a 1975 WPC presentation in Phoenix, AZ, Parker became active with Albuquerque, NM, NOW and took the lead in New Mexico for the displaced homemakers awareness initiative. Learning about other issues affecting women at the NOW state convention, Parker returned to Albuquerque where she established CR groups and became involved in issues such as the right to choose, economic needs of women in poverty, and women in the trades. She also worked to build alliances with women across all racial/ethnic boundaries. In this regard, she put forth the concept of "women of color" rather than "minority women" as a means to overcome the negative connotations of the term "minority." Attending NOW's national board meeting in Denver, she wrote and lobbied for a national NOW minority women's committee, eventually becoming chair of that committee. In that capacity, she organized the first minority women's conference for NOW at Howard University and produced the first NOW brochures and ERA materials targeting women of color. Parker also worked on national NOW conferences in Washington, D.C.; organized the first childcare program for NOW national events; and helped ensure that women of color would be a major part of NOW programs and agendas. Parker says she eventually left NOW after loosing her campaign for national NOW secretary in 1978. She continued her feminist and racial/ethnic bridging work serving numerous other organizations, and spread the "women of color" nomenclature through a large number of organizations, including the WPC, Women's Defense Fund, Women's Economic Justice Task Force, Women for a Meaningful Summit, Women's Economic Development Roundtable, Girls Clubs of America, OWL, gender free insurance advisory committee, National Coalition Against Domestic Violence, National Commission on Working Women, and National Institute for Women of Color. She has two children. (ABS)

Parks, Joanie Marie (1946 –) (also known as Joanie Marie Parks-Hughes) In 1972, Parks began helping the chair of the education task force of NJ NOW, Jean L. Ambrose, by typing reports. In 1973, Parks became co-convener (with nine other women) of the Westfield Area (NJ) chapter of NOW. The many offices she held include president, secretary, newsletter editor, education task force chair, lesbian rights task force chair and membership chair. Parks also served as secretary to NJ NOW for two consecutive terms, was a member of the NJ NOW lesbian rights committee, and was active in both the ERA campaign and the ERA extension campaign. The Westfield Area chapter of NOW merged with the Union County chapter several years ago, and is now known as Union County NOW. Parks served as VP/secretary, and attends most state and national demonstrations, as well as national NOW conferences and NJ NOW state conferences. Also active in environmental and animal rights groups, Parks has four children. (ABS)

Parlett, June Marie (1947 –) (also known as June Smith) From 1972 – 1976, Parlett traveled and lectured with her first slide show, The Image of the Lesbian. From 1973 – 1976, she traveled with her sound filmstrip "A 700 Year Review of Women Artists: 1200 – 1900," which she compiled and wrote for the Dun Donnelley Publishing Corporation. From 1971 – 1975, Parlett traveled with a slide show of superimposed transparencies, Sandwiched Slides, accompanied by the songs of Margie Adam (and flute playing by Parlett). The feminist show was shown at women's music festivals, including the Michigan Women's Music Festival (1980,1982) and the Pan Pagan Festival (1980). In addition to her work as an artist/photographer, Parlett served as editor, illustrator, artist/photo illustrator, typist, writer and paste-up and layout person for *Tres Femmes, A Literary Quarterly* (San Diego, 1970 – 1972); did typesetting and layout for *Good-Bye to All That!*, a monthly newspaper in San Diego (1969 – 1971); and was a photo contributor to early lesbian and lesbian/feminist newspapers and monthly magazines such as *The Ladder* (1969 – 1971), *The Lesbian Tide* (1974) and *Sister* (1975 – 1976). She was contributing writer to *Lesbians Speak Out*, published by The Women's Press Collective (1974) and *Dyke, A Quarterly* (1977). Parlett, who has one child, holds a B.A. and M.A. from San Diego State University. Archives: James C. Hormel Gay & Lesbian Center, San Francisco Public Library, CA. (ABS)

Parlin, Nancy Catherine (1934 –) participated in a major equal pay lawsuit brought against the Minnesota State University system in the early 1970s. As an academic dean, and later as a vice chancellor at the University of Wisconsin, Parlin was able to further the hiring and promotion of women and the growth of women's studies programs. Says Parlin, "There was tremendous progress made in higher education from 1970 – 1990, including greatly improved hiring practices, establishment of sexual harassment policies, and in the curriculum. Textbooks in sociology improved greatly, and the culture of the university really changed." Earlier, in 1964, Parlin was one of the first women appointed to an overseas staff position in the Peace Corps. She has also been active in the civil rights, anti-war and environmental movements. Parlin holds a B.S. from the College of St. Catherine, an M.A. from St. Louis University, and a Ph.D. from the University of Minnesota. (ABS)

Parrent, Joanne Elizabeth (1948 –) was an organizer of the Women's Liberation Coalition of Michigan in 1971, where she was involved in abortion counseling and referral. The Detroit group also did Stop Rape workshops and published *The Stop Rape Handbook*, which was sent to women across the U.S. Also in 1971, Parrent's CR group wrote "The Fourth World Manifesto," later published in *Radical Feminism* (Quadrangle, 1973), which argued that women everywhere—not just in the Third World—were a colonized people. In 1974, Parrent co-founded The Feminist Federal Credit Union, the first women's credit union, which quickly grew to over 4,000 members and inspired women to start credit unions in many other states. In 1975, the Detroit NOW awarded Parrent its Feminist of the Year award for this work. Also in 1975, Parrent helped found the Feminist Economic Network, "for which I was immediately trashed in papers like *Off Our Backs* and *Big Mama Rag* for being a capitalist." Parrent moved to Los Angeles in 1977 to be editor of *Chrysalis*, a magazine of women's culture. She also served as a member of the board of the Los Angeles Women's Building at that time. In the late 1970s, Parrent worked with the ERA campaign fund of the NWPC, raising money and training celebrities to lobby legislators and speak on TV and radio for the ERA. In 1980, she wrote a documentary film about sexual harassment, "The Workplace Hustle." She also wrote, produced and directed a film for elementary to junior-high students, "The Childhood of Susan B. Anthony." In 1993, she began work on a women's movement mini-series for television. At the same time, Parrent chaired the reproductive rights committee of the Creative Coalition. Parrent is co-author of three "as told to" books about women: *Life After Johnnie Cochran* (Basic Books, 1995), *You'll Never Make Love in This Town Again* (Dove, 1996), and its sequel, *Once More With Feeling* (Dove, 1997). She holds a B.A. from University of California, Los Angeles. (ABS)

Parrish, Margaret (1943 –) was a co-founder, with Byllye Avery, Joan Edelson and Judy Levy, of the Gainesville (FL) Women's Health Center (1974). Established shortly after the Roe v. Wade decision, the center offered abortions, annual exams, treatment for sexually transmitted diseases, and other gynecological and primary care services. It broke ground in taking a pro-woman, pro-patient, partnership approach to medical care. Knowing education to be the key to success, four women established the Birth Center where births could take place in the warmth of the mothers' family and friends. All four were at the forefront of breaking the male dominance of the University of Florida by staging a demonstration that eventually won women the right to admission. (ABS)

Parsons, Barbara (1933 –) Despite being told by a Catholic priest in 1954 that women could not be philosophers because their minds were not suited to deal with philosophy's abstract ideas, Parsons ultimately earned a Ph.D. in philosophy from Tulane University. She then taught philosophy at the University of Wisconsin-Platteville (1969–2003), where she introduced "thousands of students to philosophy in a feminist mode." Parsons was co-founder of the women's studies program at UWP (1975), and taught the class Philosophy's Feminist Future: From Powerism to Personalism. In 1976, Parsons was co-founder of the Egg Brigade, which pelted eggs at a sexist sign, "Keep 'Em Pregnant, Barefoot and out of the Mine," a slogan from the mining engineering students that had a traditional place in UWP's homecoming parade. Parsons served on more than 40 university governance bodies, and spoke and wrote widely on feminist topics. Her papers include "The Woman Educator in a Heraclitean World" (1974); "Feminism and Christianity: Are They Compatible?" (1975); and "Ideas Have Consequences: The 'Woman' Created by Male Thinkers" (1975). Other papers include "Why the Mothers of Feminist Theory Should Divorce the Fathers of Modern Thought," "Does Feminism Have a Moral Imperative?" and "Backlash Is Inevitable; Post-Feminism Is Not." In 2003, Parsons was one of the first four people inducted into the university's Arts & Letters Hall of Fame. In addition to her Ph.D., Parsons holds an A.B. from Rosary College and an M.A. from St. Louis University. Archives: Sinsinawa Dominicans, Sinsinawa, WI. (ABS)

Partnow, Elaine T. (1941 –) In 1973, Partnow decided to create a collection of quotations from the works of women in order to cheer herself up. The resulting book, *The Quotable Woman, The First 5,000 Years*, became a standard in the field of women's studies and continues to be reissued. It contains over 19,000 quotations from the works of 3,750 women from all over the world, from earliest times to the present day, and four indexes: biographical, subjects, occupation and nationality/ethnicity. She is the co-author with her niece Lesley Hyatt of *The Female Dramatist* (Facts On File, 1998); co-author with her sister Susan Partnow of *Everyday Speaking on All Occasions for Women* (Doubleday, 1998); and author of *The Quotable Jewish Woman, Inspiration & Humor from the Mind & Heart* (Jewish Lights Publishing, 2004). She writes a column, "Women of Wisdom," for the Web site Feminist.Com. As a performer, Partnow created a series of living-history portraits of 35 notable women, and has given over 400 presentations to more than 50,000 people internationally. Partnow was a Theatre Arts major at UCLA and studied acting at the HB Studio in NYC. She has also marched in civil rights and peace demonstrations in Los Angeles, San Francisco and Seattle. (ABS)

Parun, Phyllis Belle (1941 –) A philosopher, poet, sculptor and health teacher, Parun was a staff member of New Orleans' first abortion counseling center (1965). She was a co-organizer of New Orleans Gay Liberation (1970), an artist and illustrator for gay papers, and a theorist and organizer of the Women's Liberation Coalition. In 1970, she founded the New Orleans Women's Center, a Marxist study group, and co-organized one of the first all-women art exhibits, Ten Women Artists, exhibited at St. Mark's Community Center, New Orleans. She was a founder and president of the Louisiana chapter of the Association of Humanistic Psychology (1970–1971), founder-coordinator of the Artist Information Bureau (1976–1977), and a founder-president of the Louisiana chapter of the Artists Equity Association (1976–1980). As a healing arts pioneer and teacher, she was the organizer of two Healing Arts Festivals (1994–1995), and founder-executive director of The Foundation for the Macrobiotic Way (1984). Parun holds a B.A. and M.A., and is a certified practitioner in American Oriental Bodywork Therapy of Asia and the International Macrobiotic Shiatsu Society, and is a health and Qigong instructor at People Program (1984 –). Archives: Newcomb College Center for Research on Women, New Orleans, LA. (ABS)

Pascal, Erica (1950 –) An attorney and developer of affordable housing, Pascal coordinated the legal clinic for Chicago Women's Liberation Union (1976–1982), counseling women on their rights regarding housing, divorce, domestic violence and benefits, and worked on campaigns to change rape and domestic violence laws. Pascal has been active in the affordable housing movement for more than two decades, serving as the executive director of the Lawyer Committee for Better Housing, the staff attorney for the Chicago Rehab Network, and currently (2006) as vice president of the Hispanic Housing Development Corporation. Pascal, who has three children, earned her J.D. from Northwestern University Law School (1976). (ABS)

Paschall, Eliza K. (1917 – 1990) In the early 1950s, Paschall led the Georgia LWV, of which she was then president, to racially integrate its membership—a move that led to national publicity and her picture on the front page of *The New York Times*. For eight years, as executive chair of the Greater Atlanta Council on Human Relations, she worked closely with Martin Luther King Jr. to integrate Atlanta. After King's death, however, when the Black Power movement replaced King's integrationist policies, Paschall became disillusioned. Paschall was an early member of NOW, serving as secretary of its national board until 1970, and on its national bylaws committee (1971 – 1974) while working in the Atlanta office of the EEOC. An early and strong supporter of the ERA, Paschall told a friend in the mid 1970s that "the ERA would not do the things that the ERA supporters said it would do." She sent a letter opposing the ERA to *Time* magazine, signing herself as a former national secretary of NOW—a move that angered former NOW colleagues. Soon, she began arguing just as strongly against the ERA as she had earlier argued for it. When the Reagan administration approached her to be its liaison with black organizations and asked what her politics were, she is reported to have replied, "I have been a Democrat all my life, but no

Democratic president ever asked me to serve in the White House." Working with Betty Newcomb, founder of the American Association for Affirmative Action, Paschall successfully brought the heads of the Office of Federal Contract Compliance Programs and the U.S. Civil Rights Commission together with leaders of several affirmative action organizations for meaningful discussions, on the condition that it not be publicized in the press. At the end of her life, Paschall lived with one of her two daughters in England. Archives: Emory University, Atlanta, GA.

Passlof, Pat (1928 –) A painter and professor of art at the College of Staten Island, CUNY, Passlof was active in founding and running Women in the Arts (1971). She and others met with directors of NYC museums, which resulted in the parade and demonstration down 53rd Street in front of the Museum of Modern Art (1972), protesting the unfair treatment of women artists. Passlof was also co-author of the grant application and coordinated the work for Women Choose Women (1973), the first exhibition of women artists in a museum (the NYC Cultural Center). Passlof also contributed panel and lecture reviews to "Women Artists News," the WIA newsletter. Archives: Smithsonian Museum, Washington, D.C. (ABS)

Pasternak, Judith Mahoney (1939 –) In August 1970, Pasternak invited some women from her southeast Queens, New York, neighborhood to get together to talk about women's liberation. Two days later, Pasternak says, some of them were marching in the August 26th march. Within a week they had a CR group, and within months she had spearheaded the creation of a Queens Women's Center and was writing a column on women's issues for a local paper. Two years later, she and her husband separated, and Pasternak herself became news, in a small way, when she gave primary custody of her children to her husband. Says Pasternak, "The media called us 'runaway wives,' although in my case I hadn't run away at all and, like many non-custodial mothers, was far more present in my children's lives than 90 percent of non-custodial fathers." Pasternak moved to Manhattan and joined NYRF. She was an organizer and speaker at the NYRF marriage conference in 1973, a primary organizer of the group's lesbian conference in 1974, and an editor of its newsletter (1973–1975). Pasternak also wrote for *Majority Report* and had some poems published in *So's Your Old Lady*. In 1976, Pasternak succeeded Irene Yarrow as host of NYC's only regularly scheduled, specifically lesbian radio program on WBAI, the local Pacifica station. She helped organize a department of women's programming in 1977 and did lesbian and feminist programming there for almost 10 years, including talk shows and interviews, documentaries and radio drama. The latter included the all-woman, lesbian-themed comedy soap opera "Oakdale, Indiana." From 1981–1984, Pasternak worked for the reproductive rights project of the ACLU. From the early 1980s forward, she wrote for many feminist publications

P

including *WomanNews, New Directions for Women* and *Hotwire*. In 1984 she began writing regularly, primarily on women's issues, for *The Guardian*. She has published eight books, all with a feminist perspective and most with substantial feminist content. Pasternak, who has three children, has also been active in the wider Left and the peace movement.   (ABS)

Patel, Marilyn Hall (1938 –) was the first woman to serve as the Chief Judge of the Northern District of California (1997 – 2004). In 2003 she received the Rose Bird Memorial Award from California Women Lawyers for her "groundbreaking public service and inspiration to women lawyers of California." Patel created and taught the first class on gender bias for judges and presided over a class action suit brought by women and minority workers against San Francisco firefighters. Prior to becoming a judge, Patel was counsel to NOW. She was attorney for the U.S. Department of Justice, Immigration and Naturalization Service, San Francisco (1967 – 1971) and in 1970 became a founding member of NOW LDEF. From 1974 – 1976 Patel served as adjunct professor of law at the University of California, San Francisco, Hastings Law College, moving on to become Municipal Court Judge for California's Oakland-Piedmont Judicial District (1976 – 1980). Patel is a graduate of Wheaton College (1959) and Fordham University School of Law (1963).

Pattee, Christine (1941 –) A retired health planner, Pattee was active in New Haven (CT) Women's Liberation (1970 – 1976), and helped organize a reunion in 2000. From 1973 – 1978, she was active in Connecticut's sexual orientation committee, the first statewide gay rights lobby. In the early 1970s, she gave several public lectures, as part of New Haven's Women and Our Bodies courses, on female sexuality. She also helped start New England Women's Musical Retreat and Women's Music Series in Hartford. Pattee earned her undergraduate degree from Douglass College (1963), and holds an M.P.H. (1971) and Dr.P.H. (1979) from the Yale University School of Medicine. Archives: Gender Equity Archives, Connecticut State University, New Britain, CT.   (ABS)

Patterson, Margot
– See Lubensky, Margot Truman Patterson

Paul, Alice Stokes (1885 – 1977) A legend for leading the final campaign for women's right to vote in 1920, Paul did not stop trying to improve the lives of women with that stunning victory. Believing that suffrage was not enough and what was needed was "equality of rights under the law," Paul introduced the ERA at the Seneca Falls Convention in 1923 and fought for it for five decades. Making another epic contribution to women, Paul organized and ran the campaign to include sex discrimination in the Civil Rights Act of 1964. Working from the headquarters of the National Women's Party in

Washington, D.C., Paul and her associates convinced congressman Howard W. Smith to introduce the amendment to include sex discrimination in Title VII. Once the bill was under consideration, the NWP and Paul played a critical role in its passage. When the ERA passed Congress in 1972, "Alice knew the ERA would never gain ratification by the states within the seven-year time restriction," according to Elizabeth Chittick, then chair of the National Women's Party and living with Paul at the time. "She was also depressed because her cause was over. She wasn't going to lobby state by state. What was she going to give her life to now?" Paul refused to celebrate the passage of the ERA by Congress, but Chittick organized a celebration, which Paul did not attend. Born to a Quaker family in Moorestown, NJ, Paul had academic credits that were almost unheard of in her day, and enviable by the standards of today. She earned her B.A. from Swarthmore in 1905 and later graduated from the Columbia University School of Social Work. After earning an M.A. from the University of Pennsylvania, Paul studied in England at the Woodbrooke Settlement for Religious and Social Study, at the University of Birmingham, and at the School of Economics. Paul then earned a Ph.D. from the University of Pennsylvania, an L.L.B. from the Washington College of Law (1922), an L.L.M. from American University (1927), and a Doctor of Civil Law degree from American University in 1928. Archives: Alice Paul Centennial Foundation, Mount Laurel, NJ; Records of the National American Woman Suffrage Association, Cornell University; NWP papers, 1913 – 1974, Library of Congress; Alice Paul papers, Schlesinger Library, Radcliffe Institute, Cambridge, MA.

Paule, Chay – See Chay

Pauline, Jean (1921 –) (also known as Jean Nute) Working at the Modern Times Bookstore in San Francisco in 1971, Pauline attended an eight-week class in women's liberation at the Bay Area School. After completing the class, she and 10 other women formed the Women's Teaching Collective to share the marvels of the movement with other women. "It was an incredible experience to watch the hundreds of women in the classes find that they didn't have to expect to remain voiceless and powerless in the world," says Pauline. The collective functioned for three years. As a 24-year member of the Modern Times Bookstore collective, Pauline helped bring in women writers to make presentations. Modern Times was the only San Francisco bookstore to carry women's liberation and gay liberation books from 1972 until the mid 1970s. Pauline has also been a member of Women for Peace, Neighbor to Neighbor (healthcare in California), Project Inform (AIDS information), Amnesty International and the Living Wage Coalition. She has marched in Washington, D.C., for civil rights, peace and gay rights. Pauline, who has two children, earned her B.B.A. from City University of New York in 1942.   (ABS)

Payne, Roslyn Berkman Cristiano (1940 –) was a founding member of New York Newsreel (1967), which made the first women's documentary films, including "Up Against the Wall Miss America," "She Is Beautiful When Angry," and "Make Out." A history teacher at Burlington (VT) College (2003), Payne was a founding member of WITCH (1968); a founding member and first patient at Vermont Women's Health Center; founding member of various women's centers in Vermont, including Everywoman's Place; and a founding member of an older women's group. In addition to teaching women's history at Burlington College, she teaches history of racism, history of the sixties, history of the civil rights movement, and wild mushrooming. A graduate of University of California, Los Angeles, she has a master's degree from City College of New York. She has two children.   (ABS)

Pearl, Helen Zalkan (1938 –) Pearl was "founding mother" of the Connecticut Permanent Commission on the Status of Women (1972 – 1973). From 1975 – 1981, Pearl was appointed and reappointed by Governor Ella Grasso to serve as a member of the Commission, serving as vice chair (1981) and treasurer (1979 – 1981). In 1974, Pearl served as state chair of "People for Question #1," which successfully campaigned for passage of a Connecticut state constitutional amendment prohibiting discrimination on account of sex. Earlier, in 1972 – 1973, she represented the American Assn. of University Women in ConnERA and helped to secure ratification of the federal ERA in Connecticut. In 1976, she helped to convene the ERA All the Way committee, which opposed two successive efforts to rescind Connecticut's ratification. During the 1970s and into the early 1980s, Pearl debated federal and state constitutional gender equality throughout Connecticut. She served on the editorial board of *Alert, Women's Legislative Review* (1972 – 1975); was an active member of the CT WPC in the mid 1970s; and from 1974 – 1982 was feminist representative on the Minority Advisory Board to WFSB-TV in Hartford, CT, a CBS affiliate, and its first woman chair (1980 – 1981). From 1972 – 1974, Pearl served as Status of Women chair on the board of directors of the Connecticut division of the AAUW, a position created in response to Connecticut's 1972 defeat of the ERA. Pearl was president of the New Britain, CT, branch of the AAUW from 1970 – 1982. Pearl is co-author of the first study of the percentage of women in the Connecticut State Executive Branch. She was instrumental in a wide range of issues, including a prohibition against discrimination on account of pregnancy, a prohibition against sexual harassment in e ployment (the first in the nation), and eliminating the quaint statute prohibiting women from standing or loitering in bars. Pearl's feminist activism led her to law school in the mid 1970s. Pearl, who has three children, earned a B.A. from Vassar College and a J.D from the University of Connecticut School of Law. Archives: "People for Question #1" materials are at the Connecticut State Library.   (ABS)

Peek, Mary (1922 – 2004) Author, teacher and civic leader, Peek was a pioneer in the Minnesota women's movement, a longtime Democratic Farmer Labor Party activist and a "founding mother" in 1972 of the DFL feminist caucus. She was also a salary negotiator and educational consultant working to strengthen academic freedom and eliminate sexism in schools. In 1982, Governor Albert Quie and the Minnesota Council on Education honored her "outstanding contribution to education." Peek also worked as a newspaper editor and reporter and wrote political commentaries. She is the author of *The Awful Lightning* (1980), a book about her experience as a victim of a 1970 terrorist bombing in the St. Paul Dayton's department store. Born in Albert Lea, MN, Peek is survived by three children.

Peelen, Jean P. (1941 –) In 1972, while living in Mobile, AL, Peelen and friends started The Association of New Women. They invited speakers, especially women who, with no support, independently entered fields such as medicine, law and politics. As part of their promotion of feminism, the group created a TV show, "New Women." Working for ratification of the ERA, Peelen debated Phyllis Schlafly on radio and TV. In 1974, Peelen began to study for a combined law/master's in political science at the University of Alabama in Tuscaloosa. While there, she helped form AL NOW; produced a radio news spot that played one minute of women's news, along with the regular news, three times a day; and produced a radio show called "Feminist Forum." In 1978, having graduated from law school and moved to Washington, D.C., she worked within the Office for Civil Rights and the U.S. Department of Education, writing (with others) the key policy on Title IX and intercollegiate athletics. (She directed the investigations and negotiations for the first university athletics cases.) She also created policy regarding girls' pregnancy and sexual harassment in public schools. Retired from the federal government in 1999, she presented workshops, called Women of a Certain Age, that asked women over 50, "What shall you do with the rest of your life?" Since her retirement, she is working as a model and an actress. With two friends, she wrote the book *The Secret Lives of Women Over Fifty*.   (ABS)

Peery, Harriet ("Sue Ying") (1927 – 2002) An artist and revolutionary, Peery created sculptures of the Goddess, representing societies where women were the dominant social force and all people lived cooperatively. Moving to Los Angeles in the 1960s, she became a founding member of the California Communist League, the Communist League, the Communist Labor Party, the National Organizing Committee and the League of Revolutionaries for a New America. In these organizations, she served as a role model for women comrades, helping them to overcome the obstacles women then faced as emerging leaders. The daughter of a Norwegian mother and a Chinese father, Peery used her art to "put a moral searchlight on culture and class struggle." She had two children.

Pehrson, Judy L. (1945 –) (also known as Judy Hansen) As a graduate student at the University of Michigan in the early 1970s, Pehrson took a class on the history of women in the media, then taught the course at Michigan and a variety of colleges. After receiving her M.A. in 1972, she became a staff writer for *The Pittsburgh Press* and covered the women's movement, especially the activities of NOW and the Women's Political Caucus. She also wrote an award-winning series on women in prison and girls in the juvenile justice system, and featured many of the issues affecting women. As a result, she was named "a reporter you can trust" in a NOW publication. After leaving the paper to accompany her husband to Japan for a year, Pehrson freelanced articles in the U.S. on the status and plight of Japanese women. When she returned to the U.S. in 1974, Pehrson took a job helping to set up the Pennsylvania Program for Women and Girl Offenders. She was director of communications and also ran the program's volunteer services and helped match women in the community (many of them feminists) as buddies to the program's clients. In 1975, Pehrson served as press secretary for The Pennsylvania Commission for Women in Harrisburg, which was charged with implementing Pennsylvania's ERA. She wrote an award-winning weekly, column, "The Women's Report," which ran in newspapers across the state, and published a bimonthly tabloid newspaper, *Womenews*. In New Zealand in 1981, Pehrson became very active in Women Against Pornography and Media Women, and spearheaded a project that studied women's portrayal in television commercials. In 1988, Pehrson took a job as associate editor at a small daily newspaper in York, PA. She received an Exceptional Merit Media Award from the National Political Women's Caucus for a special supplement, "Women in Politics: An Uphill Battle," that she had edited and helped write. Pehrson is (2005) director of The Women's Center at Franklin & Marshall College. She also spent a year as a Fulbright Scholar in China teaching journalism and writing at Nanjing University, "where I created a furor by insisting that my women students have equal opportunity to interviews when companies came to recruit." In addition to her M.A., Pehrson holds a B.A. from the University of Michigan (1968). She has one child. (ABS)

Pender, Kaye – See O'Brien, Kate

Penelope, Julia (1941 –) (also known as Julia P. Stanley) A writer and scholar, Penelope was teaching at the University of Georgia in 1971 when she agreed to be faculty sponsor of a newly formed women's liberation group. In 1973, she attended the first Gay Academic Union, and joined its women's caucus, a controversial move at the time. Soon after, Penelope became a lesbian separatist. In 1974, when the group held a women-only panel at the second conference at Columbia University, it was attacked and disrupted by gay men. With five other women from GAU, she formed a consciousness raising group that went on to found The Lesbian Herstory Archives. In 1972, she wrote "Semantic Features of the Machismo Ethic," in which she collected 220 words meaning "prostitute" or "loose woman." In her book *Speaking Freely: Unlearning Lies of the Fathers' Tongue* (Pergamon Press, 1990), Penelope shows how sexism and misogyny are embedded in the English language. In addition to language theory, Penelope has contributed important scholarship in lesbian studies, especially lesbian theory and literary criticism. Penelope also collaborated with Susan Wolfe on many books and anthologies, including *The Coming Out Stories* (Persephone Press, 1980) and *Sexual Practice, Textual Theory* (Blackwell, 1993). Penelope holds a B.A. from CUNY and a Ph.D. from the University of Texas. Archives: Duke University Special Collections, Durham, NC. (ABS)

Penner, Naomi Joy — In 1969, Penner was a co-founder, with Iris Hoffert, of NOW's third chapter, Long Island NOW, which later became one of the largest chapters in the country. Penner served in many capacities, including membership, newsletter and media chair. She spoke extensively to other groups, facilitated consciousness raising groups, and made radio and televison appearances. As an educator, she worked to integrate gym, home economics and industrial arts classes, and taught feminism in an alternative school. In addition, in 1980, Penner was a co-founder and first VP of the National Coalition of Free Men, a men's liberation organization. A language instructor and counselor, Penner holds an M.A. and is a NY State certified counselor. (ABS)

Perl, Harriet Marna (1920---) Perl served as secretary of California NOW, and as NOW's national consciousness raising coordinator. As the primary organizer of the consciousness raising committee in Los Angeles NOW, Perl developed and led many consciousness raising conferences, first in Fresno and then throughout California. In 1975, she drove across the country to do CR conferences with NOW chapters from Colorado to Maine. She also led CRs for NOW chapters in Alaska and many other states. With help from Gay Abarbanell, Perl wrote *Guidelines to Feminist Consciousness Raising*, which was sold to individuals, organizations and university libraries from 1975 – 1982, when NOW bought the copyright. Perl was also responsible for making gender neutral the liturgy of Beth Chayim Chadashim, "the world's first gay/lesbian synagogue. To my knowledge, our gender-neutral policy was the very first in any congregation of any denomination," she says. A retired teacher, Perl holds a B.A. from the University of Cincinnati. (ABS)

Perman, Florence (1922 –) A founder and former VP of FEW, Perman was in the government from 1965 – 1984. She was a member of the Atomic Energy Commission; coordinator of the Federal Women's Program for the Food and Drug Administration (where she developed a plan for women employees that was chosen by the Civil Service Commission as a model for the federal government); and was director of the division of personnel policy of Health and Human Services. She was actively involved in advancing the status of women in her various departments, and wrote one of the first sexual harassment policies for Health and Human Services (before the EEOC created one). She is also author of *Career Paths for New Delegates to the United Nations Secretariat; Handbook of Major Career Paths in HHS; The International Women's Decade: Three Plans of Action, 1975–1985;* and *Career Development Handbook for General Service Staff Headquarters.* She served as a U.S. delegate to the United Nations Commission on the Status of Women (1976–1980). Perman earned her undergraduate degree from New York University and her M.A. from Yale University.

Perreault, Geraldine ("Gerri") (1940 –) has worked consistently to raise awareness of sexism in education. She was a founding member of Twin Cities NOW (1970), and served as chair of its speakers committee (1970 – 1972) and high school committee (1970 –1971). In 1971, she co-founded (with Cheri Register) the Emma Willard Task Force on Education to fight sexism in education. The group (with which Perreault was associated until 1974) published *Sexism in Education,* conducted more than 200 workshops, and pressured the Minnesota State Department of Education and the Minneapolis school board to include coverage of sexism in their human relations requirements for teachers. Perreault served on the Minnesota State Department of Education task force on sex bias (1971–1974), and in 1974 was awarded a Certificate of Recognition for Leadership in Development of Minnesota Human Relations Programs. In 1971, Perreault went to court to get back her maiden name, then wrote an article for *Pro/Con* magazine about the experience. Perreault also participated in demonstrations against men-only lunchrooms in downtown restaurants, and worked to desegregate the employment ads in newspapers. Perreault is the author of "Futuristic World Views: Modern Physics and Feminism—Implications for Teaching and Learning in Colleges and Universities," published in *Education: A Time for Decisions* (World Future Society, 1980), as well as several articles on women and education published in various scholarly journals. She is also one of the co-authors of *Born Free Training Packet to Reduce Sex-Role Stereotyping in Career Development: Post Secondary/Higher Education* (Education Development Center, 1979). Perreault's current (2005) scholarship includes work on redefining leadership, using friendship as a metaphor to develop a feminist and relational model of leadership. Archives: Social Welfare History Archives, Minneapolis, MN. (ABS)

Perry, Elizabeth (1933 –) A Broadway, film and television actress and playwright, Perry was a co-founder (with the late Robert Elston) of the American Renaissance Theatre Company in NYC (1976). She was playwright and performer in "Sun Flower, The Life and Loves of Elizabeth Cady Stanton," which made its debut in Mrs. Stanton's birthplace, Johnstown, NY, and played in the Capitol Rotunda, the Senate Building, at Governor Pataki's Summit for Young Women, at the Celebration of Women's Rights in Seneca Falls, and at the invitation of the White House for the Millennium Celebration in Washington, D.C. Perry was also writer, producer and performer for "A Difficult Borning," a compilation of the works of Sylvia Plath (1972 – 1983), which won the Villager Award for its revival in 1983. She has been a producer of women's concert series, and a two-act play that explores single motherhood. Perry has been a member of the advisory board and a speaker for The National Museum of Women's History and was active in NOW. She participated in the early days of the civil rights movement, and worked with CORE and the ACLU. She is author/director of The African American Portrait Gallery. (ABS)

Perry, Patricia — An early feminist activist, Perry worked with Muriel Fox in the Washington, D.C., office of Carl Byoir, a public relations specialist. There Perry helped Fox create and produce PR for the October 1966 founding conference of NOW.

Peskin, Ellen Raff (1955 –) had just turned 19 when she began working at the Feminist Women's Health Center in Los Angeles. The FWHC's goal was to give women information to help them control their own healthcare, de-mystifying women's medical care and childbirth. After Roe v. Wade, the FWHC opened its own abortion clinic, offering doctor-performed early abortions. It also had an advocacy program for women seeking late-term abortions in hospital settings. Peskin worked 60-to-80 hours per week going to schools, churches and community organizations to speak about the work of the health center, and to Sacramento to lobby state lawmakers on family-planning legislation. As part of a program to inform women's conferences globally, Peskin attended the first IWY Conference in Mexico City (1975). After working for the FWHC for five years, Peskin attended People's College of Law and Mills College, where she received a B.A. She subsequently worked in legal affairs for several business and law offices and was involved in children's education in the Waldorf Schools. In 1999 – 2000, Peskin was operations manager for the Three Guineas Fund's Women's Technology Cluster, which offers financial support for women-owned high-tech start-up companies in return for their developing philanthropic programs to be funded by the companies' future profits. (ABS)

Peslikis, Irene (1943 – 2002) Artist and teacher, Peslikis was a principal founder and organizer of the women's art movement on the East Coast. She organized the first show of second wave women artists, taught the first Women & Art course on a college campus (SUNY, Old Westbury,

NY), and was a founder of the Feminist Art Institute, which ran a full-time radical feminist art education program for women for years. Peslikis was also a founder of the New York Studio School for Drawing, Painting and Sculpture, and was a founder of Women & Art. In addition, Peslikis was a founder of the NoHo Gallery, one of the first cooperative feminist art galleries. Her political cartoons were widely circulated and published in the early women's liberation movement. Peslikis was a member of NYRW and a founding member of Redstockings (1968). She wrote "Resistance to Consciousness," a paper printed in *Notes from the Second Year*, which helped further the understanding of CR. She was also a key organizer and participant in the Redstockings Speak-out on Abortion held at the Washington Square Methodist Church, and served as a representative to the National Association for Repeal of Abortion Laws and New Yorkers for Abortion Law Repeal. Her work has been exhibited across the country and is in numerous private collections. Peslikis earned her B.A. from Queens College, CUNY (1973) and her M.F.A. from City College, CUNY (1983). Archives: Sallie Bingham Center, Duke University, Durham, NC.

Petchesky, Rosalind Pollack (1942 –) A distinguished professor of political science at Hunter College and the Graduate Center, City University of New York, Petchesky has been writing and speaking about human rights since she wrote *The Individual's Rights and International Organization* (Smith, 1966). During the 1970s and thereafter, she wrote extensively on reproductive rights. Petchesky founded the International Reproductive Rights Research Action Group, which she directed from 1992 – 1999. IRRRAG's research teams conducted comparative, cross-cultural research in seven countries to assess women's sense of entitlement in making reproductive and sexual decisions. The findings of that project were published in *Negotiating Reproductive Rights: Women's Perspectives Across Countries and Cultures*, published by Zed Books/St. Martin's Press in 1998 and edited by Petchesky (with Karen Judd). Earlier, she published *Abortion and Woman's Choice: The State, Sexuality, and Reproductive Freedom* (2d edition, 1990, Northeastern University Press), which won the Joan Kelly Memorial Prize of the American Historical Association and was cited by the U.S. Supreme Court in its landmark decision, *Planned Parenthood of Eastern Pennsylvania v. Casey* (1992). Her numerous published articles, including the widely cited "Fetal Images: The Power of Visual Culture in the Politics of Reproduction" and, more recently, "Phantom Towers: Feminist Reflections on the Battle Between Global Capitalism and Fundamentalist Terrorism," have been translated into many languages and reprinted in numerous anthologies. Petchesky's latest research interests have entailed a revisioning of reproductive and sexual rights in the context of globalization, militarism and transnational feminist activism. In August 2003 her book on this topic, *Global Prescriptions: Gendering Health and Human Rights*, was published by Zed Books in London (in collaboration with the United Nations Research Institute for Social Development in Geneva and Palgrave-MacMillan in the United States). She received her B.A. from Smith College and her M.A. and Ph.D. from Columbia University (1974). Petchesky received a MacArthur "genius" award in 1995. She is a board member of WEDO and chair of the board of *Reproductive Health Matters*, a peer-reviewed journal published in London. Archives: The Sophia Smith Collection, Smith College, Northampton, MA. (ABS)

Peterman, Jean Paulson (1942 –) A retired professor of sociology, Peterman was active in NOW in both Ohio and Illinois. She was president of Bowling Green (OH) NOW from 1975 – 1979, and worked aggressively for the ERA and abortion rights. She has been a member of the West Suburban (Chicago) chapter of NOW since 1980, serving as president, reproductive rights chair and treasurer. In 1986, her chapter was the first in the state to provide escorts at abortion clinics. From 1980 – 1997, Peterman was a member of Illinois Pro-Choice Alliance, serving as chair, co-chair, on-call escort and head escort. She has been a board member since 2002 of the Chicago Abortion Fund, which provides referrals and cash assistance to low-income women. Peterman is the author of *Telling Their Stories: Puerto Rican Women and Abortion* (Westview Press, 1996). She published "Marisol's Story: Culture, Family, Self and the Decision to Get an Abortion" in *Applied Behavioral Science Review* (1998). It was later reprinted in *Dialogo*, Center for Latino Research, DePaul University (2002). Peterman is also the author of "Puerto Rican Women Deciding to Get an Abortion: Beginning a Collective Story," published in *Latino Studies Journal, Special Issue on Latina Women* (1993). Peterman, who has two children, earned her A.B. from the University of Chicago (1964), and her M.A. and Ph.D. (1994) from the University of Illinois at Chicago. Archives: Special Collections, University of Illinois at Chicago, Chicago, IL. (ABS)

Peters, Ellen Ash (1930 –) The first tenured woman on the Yale Law School faculty (1964), Peters was an early pioneer in academia who straddled a fine line between succeeding in a male environment while advocating for the advancement of women. She mentored scores of women law students and chaired a Yale University committee for the recruitment of women faculty members. She served on the first Mory's board of directors in the early 1970s after it opened its membership to women. In 1978, Governor Ella Grasso appointed Peters the first woman Justice on the Connecticut Supreme Court. She became Chief Justice in 1984 and later was president of the National Conference of Chief Justices and the National Center for State Courts. Throughout her judicial career, she has served as a mentor to women law clerks. She currently participates in the work of the Connecticut

Appellate Court. She is the recipient of numerous awards and Honorary Degrees. (ABS)

Peters, Joan K. (1945 –) In 1973, Peters was part of the collective that organized Sagaris, a feminist think tank that opened in the summer of 1975 and again 1976. Over 200 women attended from all over the United States for a one- or two-month session, held at Lyndon State College in Lyndonville, VT. In the second session, the group joined with the National Black Feminist Organization. The purpose was to synthesize the efforts of feminists in different areas (theory, lesbian issues, minority rights, older women, childcare, etc.) and to train grassroots organizers. "The first session was filled with a tremendous sense of the possibility of unifying the movement, but in the second session infighting began," Peters says. "The dream of Sagaris was ambitious, but it was short-lived, destroyed by political and cultural differences and paranoia resulting from suspicions of FBI infiltration." A professor of English at California State University, Peters has published two books on motherhood, work and equality: *When Mothers Work: Loving Our Children Without Sacrificing Ourselves* (Addison Wesley, 1997) and *Not Your Mother's Life: Changing the Rules of Work, Love, and Family* (Perseus Books, 2001). She has one child. (ABS)

Peterson, Carol Libbie (1949 –) worked for Ohio Bell in the early 1970s as one of the first outside telecommunications technicians. She started a women's committee for Communications Workers of America, focusing on women's labor/union issues. She also began and participated in several CR groups, one of which initiated guerilla actions in both education and civil disobedience. Prior to joining the women's movement, Peterson marched in Chicago for the anti-war movement (1968) and participated in sit-ins supporting the black students at the University of Wisconsin, Oshkosh. (ABS)

Peterson, Claudia Susan – See Morrissey, Claudia Susan

Peterson, Elly (1914 –) An overseas Red Cross volunteer in WWII, Peterson was the first woman in the nation to be elected state chairman of a political party, the Michigan Republican Party (1960s), and was the first MI woman to run for U.S. Senate. In 1972, she was a member of the Delegation for Friendship Among Women, and traveled to China and many countries in the Middle East to promote international friendship among women. In 1974 she was organizational director of the National Center for Voluntary Action, and in 1975 worked with American Women for International Understanding and the observance of IWY. She became co-chair, with Liz Carpenter, of ERAmerica in 1976. She resigned that position in 1978, but has continued working aggressively for the ERA. (ABS)

Peterson, Esther (1906 – 1997) Long before the second wave of feminism began, Peterson had a husband, four children and a fulfilling career. Following some highly visible successes in the 1930s in education and labor organizing, she received a series of presidential appointments—the best known being special assistant for consumer affairs in both the Johnson and Carter administrations. But it was as head of the newly formed Women's Bureau in the Kennedy Administration that she saw her most profound achievement: Peterson oversaw the development of a report by the Commission on Sexism in the Workplace, and on October 11, 1963, presented Kennedy with that report, titled "American Women." It was widely read and proved useful to those who began the revival of the feminist movement in 1966. Like many other women who had worked within the labor movement, Peterson supported protective laws for women and therefore did not support the ERA at first. She eventually changed her mind. Peterson worked for many women's rights issues, including prohibiting sex discrimination in the executive order regulating government contractors. In 1993, when Peterson was 87, President Clinton named her as a delegate to the United Nations' General Assembly, where she continued to be a representative to UNESCO and a visionary advocate for the needs of working Americans. Archives: Papers and additions, 1910 – 1984, are at the Schlesinger Library, Radcliffe Institute, Cambridge, MA.

Peterson, Jan M. (1941 –) joined NYRF, West Village Brigade # 1, in 1969, helping to organize CR groups across the city. She also organized conferences and speakouts, and spoke on rape, battering and the need for a new form of mental health focusing on women's empowerment. She worked steadily to build a diverse multicultural women's movement, and has worked aggressively to empower poor and working-class women of diverse racial and ethnic backgrounds. Peterson has also been a groundbreaking leader in producing innovative community structures led by grassroots women. In Williamsburg, Brooklyn, NY, she founded numerous community-based organizations and developed a leadership support process to help grassroots women build leadership while working across ethnic and racial lines. Supporting the knowledge and contributions of grassroots women, Peterson also ran the National Institute for Women and Community Development, the Neighborhood Women College Program and, more recently, supported the development of Local to Local Dialogues. In 1975, she developed a national network of grassroots women leaders, called the National Congress of Neighborhood Women, to exchange information, experiences and resources. Also in 1975, she founded the first battered women's shelter in New York State, the Center for Elimination of Violence in the Family. In 1976, Peterson created Project Open Doors at Neighborhood Women. The project obtained over $1 million a year in federal CETA money (until Reagan was elected), which allowed "almost every feminist project in New York City, from NOW to COYOTE, to obtain funds,

P

most for the first time, to hire women, moving them from volunteer to paid work," and to build formal organizations that could receive funds and staff. Peterson also worked with NY NOW, the NWPC and other women's groups to improve the financial and political status of women, and has worked to build organizations that are run by and focus on the priorities of poor and working class women. In 1975, she made an international link between Neighborhood Women and women in other countries by participating in the first United Nations program focused on women in Mexico City. In 1976, Peterson worked in the White House under President Carter. There she was instrumental in enabling the development of legislation that funded battered women shelters. Peterson's activism began with the civil rights movement and the march on Washington in 1963. She then joined CORE, and in 1968 joined the October 17th Movement and became involved in demonstrations and organizing. Archives: The Sophia Smith Collection, Smith College, Northampton, MA.   (ABS)

Peterson, Lorna M. (1939 –) was a member (1969) of the original group that constituted Amherst (MA) Women's Liberation, which became the Valley Women's Center in the early 1970s. Peterson belonged to the VWC speakers bureau and the abortion and birth control counseling committee (1970 – 1973), helping women with information about birth control and in obtaining abortions pre-Roe v. Wade. During the 1970s and 1980s, as an adjunct at several of the Five College campuses, Peterson taught courses on women in literature, among them one of the first in the area on women in Russian literature. She also taught the works of Doris Lessing, and published a chapter on Lessing's reception in the Soviet Union in the book *In Pursuit of Doris Lessing* (edited by Clare Sprague). Peterson is (2006) executive director of Five Colleges Inc., and a founding and continuing (2006) member of the steering committee for the Five College Women's Studies Research Center. Peterson holds a B.A. from the University of Buffalo (1961) and a Ph.D. from Yale University (1973).   (ABS)

Peterson, Susan – See Wiseheart, Susan Elizabeth

Peterson, Tasha — began working at *Off Our Backs* in Washington, D.C., in 1970. She was a founder, with Betty Garmon, Susan Hathaway and Susan Gregory, of an anti-imperialist women's house in the city and the Lesbian Come-Out CR Group (1971). After resigning from *Off Our Backs*, Peterson became an original member (1971) of a group first known as Those Women and later as The Furies. Peterson was the author of the article "Gimme Shelter," which appeared in the second issue of *The Furies* newspaper (February 1972).

Petrus, Janice Corene (1930 –) After attending a NOW board meeting in Madison, WI, in the late 1960s, Petrus attended a national NOW conference in Chicago, where she became a national NOW board member under Aileen Hernandez. Petrus then founded Milwaukee NOW (1970), serving two terms as president. The chapter forced the *Milwaukee Journal* to abandon its sex-segregated help-wanted ads, but only after a fight. The paper was so hostile that it refused to allow NOW to advertise its name and address in the classifieds, hoping to thwart its growth. The chapter got around that when a woman reporter published an article about Petrus, giving NOW's location in the article. The chapter also integrated the men-only dining room in Heinemann's restaurant in downtown Milwaukee, worked on getting equal pay for men and women at large companies like AT&T, and supported the Equal Rights Amendment. Petrus helped organize for the ERA in Illinois and Washington, D.C., where she met Alice Paul. Petrus holds a B.S. from the University of Wisconsin at Milwaukee, and a graduate degree in guidance and counseling from Marquette University. Before her retirement, Petrus worked on rehabilitating psychiatric patients as they left mental institutions.   (ABS)

Petty, Kay Cole – See Cole, Kay Walter

Phelan, Lana Clark – See Kahn, Lana Clark Phelan

Phillips, Lynn (1945 –) In the late 1960s, Phillips attended Redstockings, WITCH and NOW meetings, and coined the slogan, "Free Our Sisters, Free Ourselves" for incarcerated Panther women. The formulation, she says, was later used for the title of the book *Our Bodies, Ourselves*. During the same period, Phillips organized the first female film crew in New York Newsreel, organized the women's caucus within New York Newsreel, and was the first woman to edit a Newsreel film, "The Columbia Revolt." She also wrote a paper widely circulated within the New York women's health movement urging a multi-cultural perspective on abortion, and was denounced as being "male defined" for suggesting that the women's movement needed an economically grounded strategy. Phillips' feminist activities continued into the 1970s. She wrote and illustrated a children's book for the daughters of feminists, *Exactly Like Me* (Lollipop Press). With Gay Falk in St. Louis, Phillips generated a pro-Shirley Chisholm campaign, and wrote and directed "Winds of Change," a feminist, antiwar soap opera for KDNA in St. Louis. Phillips was also active in the San Francisco and Los Angeles women's art movements, and in Los Angeles was a staff writer for the "Mary Hartman, Mary Hartman" show. In the 1990s, Phillips was co-founder, writer and co-editor of "Getting It Gazette," the women's newsletter for Republican and Democratic delegates in 1992 and 1996. She also originated the banner slogan, "Women can laugh and think at the same time," and created the "Measure of Man" bar chart rating a congressperson's support or lack of support for women's issues "with rather phallic arrows." Phillips has also been op-ed and editorial editor for *HER NY*, and a writer on women issues for *Glamour* and *The Nation*. (ABS)

Piccard, Jeannette (1895 – 1981) A trailblazer for women in religion, Piccard became an ordained deacon of the Episcopal Church in 1971, and in 1974 was one of the first 11 women ordained as an Episcopal priest. That controversial ordination occurred in Philadelphia and received much national publicity. Piccard, who held degrees in theology, philosophy, chemistry and psychology, was a member of Twin Cities NOW during the 1970s, and lived much of her life in Minneapolis. She distinguished herself in aeronautics as the first woman to enter space by way of a balloon ascent. On May 27, 1931, Piccard and Paul Kipfer climbed into the stratosphere in a spherical, airtight, metal cabin suspended from a specially constructed, hydrogen-filled balloon, reaching an altitude of 51,783 feet. Archives: Papers and a video recording done a year before her death are at the Minnesota Historical Society, St. Paul, MN.

Pick, Gracia Molina – See Molina de Pick, Gracia

Picker, Jane (1935 –) In 1973, Picker argued the La Fleur v. Cleveland Board of Education case before the Supreme Court. This case challenged mandatory maternity leave for teachers and set precedent for later pregnancy issues. Picker was a founder (1972) and served as president of the Women's Law Fund Incorporated, a critical organization in the days of precedent setting. She has argued major cases for female police and firefighters in employment law, directed the Cleveland Marshall Law School's Fair Employment Practices Clinic, and served on the executive committee of the NAACP (1991 – 1992). Professor of law emerita at Cleveland Marshall College of Law of Cleveland State University, Picker holds a B.A. from Swarthmore and an L.L.B. from Yale University. In addition to practicing law in a major U.S. law firm, she has practiced law internationally in Thailand, worked for the RAND Corporation and the Communications Satellite Corporation, and participated in many important fair employment practices cases. (ABS)

Pickering, Judith A. (1944 –) Known as the mother of the ERA in Connecticut, Pickering was founding president of New London (CT) NOW (1968 – 1971), founding president of CT NOW (1971 – 1973), founder and chair, ConnERA (1972 – 1974), a member of the national board of directors (1973 – 1975), and chair of the ERA task force (1973 – 1975). During Pickering's term as president of New London NOW, the chapter initiated the Brown v. Electric Boat division of General Dynamics suit, which led to gender integration of the Electric Boat shipyard. The chapter also initiated a number of FCC license challenges to area radio stations, which resulted in changes in the format and content of those stations' programs, and published the first pro se divorce instruction booklet in

Connecticut. During Pickering's term as president of CT NOW, the organization eliminated gender differentiated help-wanted ads in the state's newspapers and, among other actions, successfully lobbied on behalf of a state ERA. To facilitate this process, Pickering developed a computer-based support system for lobbyists that gave them current information on legislators' positions on the ratification of the ERA and provided projections on the expected vote. To celebrate the 1976 centennial, Pickering and Wilma Scott Heide created a traveling feminist road show that toured 25 cities and towns in unratified states from Hartford, CT, to Vail, CO. In addition to NOW, Pickering is a member of VFA. (ABS)

Pickett, Eugenia ("Jeannie") (1938 –) A social worker and psychotherapist, Pickett was a member of the first collective of women in Baltimore, MD (1967), was a founding editor of *Women: A Journal of Liberation*, and was one of the first wave of women who ran a center for women in Baltimore, The Women's Growth Center (1975 – 1985). She served as a day staff coordinator of The People's Free Medical Clinic (1972 – 1976), and was a liaison between the physical and mental health programs there (1974 – 1976). Pickett, who holds an M.A., has two biological children and one stepchild. (ABS)

Piercy, Marge (1936 –) Piercy's widely published poetry, fiction and nonfiction have had an impact in the U.S. and elsewhere in the world. Her books include *Woman on the Edge of Time; He, She and It; Three Women; Braided Lives*; and *The Longings of Women*. Piercy is also known for her poems, especially *The Moon Is Always Female, Circles on the Water, What Are Big Girls Made Of?* and *Colors Passing Through Us*. Piercy entered the feminist movement in 1967 when, operating out of the SDS regional office in NYC, she started a women's caucus. From 1969 – 1971, Piercy developed CR groups for the New York Women's Center, and in 1971 was a founder of Cape Cod Women's Liberation. In 1981, Piercy was a co-founder of a Cape Cod chapter of NOW, for which she ran the legislative project and put out a newsletter. In 1994, she was one of four women who founded Roots of Choice. The group organized pro-abortion demonstrations at the Cape Cod Hospital, and worked with the police department and the courts to improve the way battered women are treated. She has also given numerous benefits to raise money for women's causes. Piercy holds a B.A. from the University of Michigan and an M.A. from Northwestern. Archives: Department of Rare Books and Special Collections, University of Michigan, Ann Arbor, MI. (ABS)

Pilardi, Jo-Ann Theresa (1941 –) (also known as Jo-Ann Fuchs) joined a small CR group at Penn State (1968 – 1969), then moved to Baltimore where she joined the staff of *Women: A Journal of Liberation*. She worked there on the editorial collective for three years (1970 – 1972). She was active in Baltimore Women's Liberation from

P

1969 until it morphed into other organizations in the mid 1970s. During that time, she was also active in anti-Vietnam War organizations in Baltimore. In 1971, as a non-tenure-track, part-time faculty member at Towson University, Pilardi prepared a course in philosophy/women's studies, then taught it for the first time in 1972, presenting her work to the Society for Women in Philosophy. In 1972, she was a charter member of the women's studies committee at Towson University, which resulted in the women's studies program being set up in 1973. She eventually became a tenure-track faculty member, director and then chair of women's studies, serving until 2004, and developed courses on women for philosophy as well as women's studies. Pilardi was a member of the committee on the status of women at Towson, which founded the Women's Center in 1973. In 1972, many members of Baltimore Women's Liberation and *Women: A Journal of Liberation* formed a socialist-feminist political organization, The Women's Union of Baltimore, in which Pilardi was active until 1981. She also worked in the 1970s on speak-outs related to the Maryland Commission on Women, and in 1974 – 1978 founded, edited and wrote for "On Our Minds: A Women's Newsletter for Towson State College." In the mid and late 1970s, she taught a course in feminist theory for The Baltimore School, an alternative educational project. In 1977, she initiated the first International Women's Day event at Towson , which continued for years under her co-ordination. Pilardi, who has one child, earned a B.A. from Duquesne University, an M.A. from Penn State University, and a Ph.D. from John Hopkins University. (ABS)

Pildes, Judy - See Arcana, Judith

Pincus, Jane Abigail (1937 –) was a founder of the Boston Women's Health Book Collective, creators of *Our Bodies, Ourselves*, and has been a co-author and co-editor of each edition for 35 years. The founders began meeting in the fall of 1969, gave a course at the Massachusetts Institute of Technology in the early 1970s, and incorporated in the fall of 1971. "We had no idea that women's colleges would purchase the books and place them in every incoming freshman's mailbox," says Pincus. She traveled the country publicizing women's health issues and testified at government hearings regarding abortion and a woman's right to choose. An artist as well as a community activist, Pincus has two children. She holds a B.A. from Brown University (1959), an M.A.T. from Harvard Graduate School of Education (1964), and an M.F.A. from Vermont College (1993). Archives: Schlesinger Library, Radcliffe Institute, Cambridge, MA. (ABS)

Pindell, Howardena Doreen (1943 –) is an artist and professor at Stony Brook University, where she directs (2005) the M.F.A. program. Pindell came to New York City in 1967 and was a founding member of the AIR Gallery (1972), the first women's cooperative art gallery.

Pindell also named the gallery. (During the 1960s, A.I.R., standing for Artist In Residence, was stenciled on buildings used for another purpose to indicate that an artist was living and working there.) A painter whose autobiographical pieces integrate her own history with the collective African experience, Pindell has served on a number of panels on women's issues and the art world. These include Does Art Have a Gender (1972); How the Art World Evaluates Women (1973); Year of the Woman: The 1975 Art World/The Women in It (1975); and Women Evaluate the New York Art World (1978). She holds a B.F.A. from Boston University (1965) and an M.F.A. from Yale University School of Art and Architecture (1967). Archives: Schomberg Center for Research in Black Culture, New York, NY. (ABS)

Pinto, Jody (1942 –) founded Women Organized Against Rape in Philadelphia General Hospital (1972), and served as its director until 1974. WOAR was the first rape crisis center to organize institutions of a city to prosecute the crime of rape. With support from judge Lois Forer and judge Lisa Richette, as well as women DAs, WOAR developed an evidential form for hospitals to use to provide information on rapes to hospital staff, police and the DA's office. These efforts led to the establishment of a 24-hour hotline, an office with the DA, a Rape Crimes Unit, court monitoring, and the provision of company throughout a woman's or child's case. WOAR succeeded in changing laws, including allowing women to become detectives (only detectives were allowed to interview rape victims). The group also developed an extensive training and outreach program on rape. WOAR continues (2005) to be a community-driven force for change. Pinto, who is a public artist, earned her B.F.A. in 1973. (ABS)

Pintzuk, Theo (Martha) (1949 –) While in Madison, WI, (1971 – 1974), Pintzuk was a co-founder of the Madison Women's Center, the Women's Center Liberation School, and a lesbian coffeehouse. She was also a member of Madison Lesbian Sisters, the Bobby Seale Brigades and the Mother Jones Guerrilla Theater, and organized for Welfare rights. Moving to Chicago in 1974, she joined the CWLU and helped create a crisis line for women. She also co-founded the Chicago Women's Uprising, and was a member of Gay and Lesbian Socialists of Chicago. She has been a teaching assistant and co-chair of the board for IMPACT Self Defense for Women (in Chicago), and co-founder and core faculty of the Clinical Training Program: Clinical Practice with LBGT Individuals and Their Families. She is (2005) in private practice in Chicago as a clinical social worker. (ABS)

Pirsig, Nancy - See James, Nancy Ann

Plaskow, Judith (1947 –) (also known as Judith Goldenberg) A college professor (2005), Plaskow became a feminist when she joined the Yale Women's Alliance in

1969. The group did consciousness raising and organized around issues such as the law school interviewing in a men-only restaurant/club. Applying her feminist insights to her studies, Plaskow says, she wrote "the second feminist dissertation in religious studies in the U.S." In 1980, it was published by the University Press of America as *Sex, Sin, and Grace: Women's Experience and the Theologies of Reinhold Niebuhr and Paul Tillich*. As a graduate student, Plaskow co-chaired the Women and Religion group of the American Academy of Religion (1972–1973). She also helped the group become a section, and served on its steering committee for 15 years. In addition, Plaskow co-edited the papers from the group's first years, which were later published as one of the first collections on women and religion, *Women and Religion* (1973). Plaskow was co-editor of *Womanspirit Rising: A Feminist Reader in Religion* (1979) and *Weaving the Visions: New Patterns in Feminist Spirituality* (1989), and has published numerous articles in edited volumes and journals. Plaskow was a research associate in women's studies at Harvard Divinity School (1973–1974), the first year of the program, and served on its advisory board for many years. During the early 1970s, she began to raise questions about the role of women in Judaism. Speaking at the first Jewish feminist conference in 1973, she ended by reading her midrash on Lilith—which was widely reprinted and "started the feminist reclaiming of Lilith." In 1985, Plaskow co-founded the *Journal of Feminist Studies in Religion*, and served as its co-editor for 10 years. Co-founder of the women's studies program at Sir George Williams University (now Concordia), Plaskow also published, in 1990, the first Jewish feminist theology, *Standing Again at Sinai*. Plaskow, who has one child, earned her B.A. from Clark University, and her M.Phil. and Ph.D. from Yale University. (ABS)

Plitt, Jane (1948 –) A 1969 graduate of Cornell University's School of Industrial & Labor Relations, Plitt was directly hired as staff assistant in labor relations by Rochester Telephone as the company's first female management trainee. Promoted to several managerial positions, Plitt left in 1973 to become executive director of national NOW in Chicago, a post she held until 1975. Earlier (1971–1972), Plitt led a demand that the Rochester Jaycees allow women members, which they did. The chapter was then thrown out of the national/state organization, which ultimately led to a Supreme Court decision requiring the Jaycees, Rotary and Kiwanis to integrate. In 1978, Plitt co-founded the Rochester Women's Network, and in 1991 received its W award for her leadership of women. Plitt also started the Rochester chapter of National Association of Women Business Owners, and in the 1970s was involved in ending sex-segregated restaurants and help-wanted ads in New York State. In 1989, Plitt published "It's Harder for Women" as a chapter in the book *Startup*. In 1996, she was appointed a visiting scholar to the University of Rochester, where she researched the life of Martha Matilda Harper (a servant who in 1891 established the first business format franchising system). The result was the book *Martha Matilda Harper: How One Woman Changed the Face of Modern Business* (Syracuse University Press, 2000). As a result of that book, Harper is now in the National Women's Hall of Fame. Plitt is working on *Perilous Friendships*, documenting what happened to the friendships between German Jews and Christians under Hitler. Plitt, who has two children, has also been active in the civil rights and peace movements. Archives: Schlesinger Library, Radcliffe Institute, Cambridge, MA. (ABS)

Poeschl, Arlene R. – See Skorich, Arlene Rita Mae

Pogrebin, Letty Cottin (1939 –) is a writer, lecturer and activist. Born in NYC, Pogrebin graduated from Brandeis University in 1959 and began her career in book publishing as an editorial assistant and director of publicity and subsidiary rights at the publishing house of Bernard Geis Associates. Her journalistic career has included freelance writing for *The New York Times*, *The Nation*, *The Washington Post*, *The LA Times* and *Family Circle*. She contributed "The Working Woman" column to *Ladies' Home Journal* from 1971 to 1981. A co-founder of *Ms.*, she served as an editor for the magazine from the beginning through 1989, and has contributed many articles and two years' worth of columns to its pages. She was also a co-founder of the Ms. Foundation in 1972, the NWPC in 1971, the Ms. Foundation for Education and Communication, the women's task force of the UJA/Federation, and the directors council of the Women in Religion program at Harvard Divinity School. Pogrebin is author of *How to Make It in a Man's World* (Doubleday, 1970); *Getting Yours* (1975); *Growing Up Free* (1980); *Family Politics* (McGraw-Hill, 1983); *Among Friends* (1987); *Deborah, Golda and Me* (1991); *Getting Over Getting Older* (1996); and *Three Daughters* (2002). She is also editorial consultant for *Free to Be, You and Me*, with Marlo Thomas (McGraw-Hill, 1973), editor of *Stories for Free Children* (1982), contributor to numerous anthologies, and a lecturer on family life, feminism and Judaism. She has three children. Archives: The Sophia Smith Collection, Smith College, Northampton, MA. (ABS)

Pogue, Susan (1945 –) (also known as Susan Bucknell) was the second executive director for the Permanent Commission on the Status of Women in Connecticut (1975–1985). During this time, the PCSW was able to ward off legislative attempts to abolish it and efforts to reduce its budget. Instead, the budget grew substantially and grants allowed for program expansion. Pogue worked with a coalition of state officials, women's organizations, labor unions and legislators to secure pay equity for CT's clerical employees, largely women. In addition, she developed the PCSW's legislative program, which included expanding the pregnancy discrimination law to broaden

P

disability and provide some protection against occupational hazards, and enacting a sexual harassment statute. Expanding women's knowledge of discrimination laws and working to increase employer awareness, as well as opening non-traditional jobs for women, were all important accomplishments of the PCSW during the period to which Pogue contributed. Pogue is a licensed marriage and family therapist and continues to serve the needs of women and equality. (ABS)

Polan, Diane ("Cookie") (1951 –) was "catapulted" into the feminist movement when she entered Yale in 1969 as part of the first co-ed undergraduate class. That year she joined a group that disrupted a Yale Corporation meeting to demand full co-education. After graduating from Yale in 1973, Polan worked briefly in Washington, D.C., where she was involved in abortion counseling at the D.C. Women's Center. After returning to New Haven, Polan worked as a paralegal in the law office of Catherine Roraback. During that time, she was the unofficial legal liaison with the New Haven Women's Liberation Center, and her law office represented many women who were referred by the Center. With two co-authors, Polan wrote "The Pro Se Dissolution Kit" to help women get their own divorces, without lawyers. Polan was also active in setting up the New Haven Rape Crisis Center, and was part of the New Haven feminist-socialist organization in the mid 1970s. While at law school in the late 1970s, she contributed the chapter "Toward a Theory of Law and Patriarchy" to the anthology *The Politics of Law*. In 1980, after completing Yale Law School, Polan became a founding partner in New Haven's first all-women law firm, Levine, Kuriloff and Polan, where she practiced for 10 years. She currently (2006) practices law in New Haven, and is "the proud single parent of two 16-year-old feminists." (ABS)

Polishuk, Sandy (1940 –) (also known as Sandy Kaye and Sandy Kosokoff) is an oral historian specializing in radical women, and the author of *Sticking to the Union: An Oral History of the Life and Times of Julia Ruuttila*. Polishuk helped organize early CR groups in Portland, OR. She also participated in various demonstrations, including picketing a 1970 bridal fair; spoke about feminist issues on television and at local high schools; and was part of the Portland State University movement to establish women's studies and a day care center. Says Polishuk, "Our most outrageous event was crashing the university president's fall faculty party at his home. We brought our children. Some of us even nursed our babies around the swimming pool. We did eventually get a day care center, and the president never held that party at his home again." In the mid 1970s, Polishuk was part of a small group that offered workshops on vaginal infections and published a pamphlet with information on diagnosis and treatment. As a member of the Northwest Women's History Project, Polishuk helped produce a slide show/video, "Good Work Sister! Women Shipyard Workers of World War II, an Oral History" in 1981. In 1990, she was part of the first editorial collective of *Bridges: A Journal for Jewish Feminists and Our Friends*. Polishuk, who has two children, holds a B.A. from the University of Washington and an M.L.S. from the University of Oregon. (ABS)

Pollach, Donna Helen (1949 – 2002) (also known as Donna Suttles) As a student at Portland State University (1970), Pollach worked with Helen Clement and other PSU women to establish the women's studies department. She also facilitated the course Biology of Women, and spoke on a panel about being a lesbian at a class at Portland Community College in 1971. After studying for a year at Portland's Museum Art School, she began taking black-and-white pictures of lesbians, sisters and lesbian families in the Portland lesbian community. The photos were published in early feminist journals, in a publication featuring family diversity for Portland Public Schools, and on many community-event posters and fliers. From 1971 – 1976, Pollach lived in a house that was an experiment in collective living for lesbians and their children. The house (on Alder St. in Portland) became a center of political thought and a gathering space for alternative people, including gay adolescents and gay men. Pollach, who had one child, was educated at the University of California, Berkeley, as well as at PSU.

Pollack, Fanette (1952 –) worked at the Barnard College women's center as an assistant from 1971 – 1974. In 1972 and 1973, she was co-editor (with Kirsten Grimstad and others) of *Women's Work & Women's Studies*, the first interdisciplinary bibliography of feminist studies. It was published by Barnard in 1973. Pollack was also assistant editor (with Grimstad, Susan Rennie and Ruth Smith) of *The New Woman's Survival Catalog*. Pollack's thesis, written under Annette Baxter of the Barnard history department, was on images of women in 19th century feminist publications. Pollack, who became an attorney in 1978, practiced labor law for about 20 years, representing plaintiffs in civil rights cases as well as labor unions and their health and pension funds. Pollack, who has two children, earned her B.A. from Barnard College in 1974 and her J.D. from New York University in 1977. (ABS)

Pollard, Vicki Cohn (1943 –) A member of the Baltimore Defense Committee in 1967, Pollard quickly came to realize that she and the other women were as oppressed in society and in general as the people they were trying to free. After joining with women in Washington, D.C., Pollard—with Donna Kirk and Dee Ann Pappas—launched *Women: A Journal of Liberation*. The three women paid for and published the first copy, which had a 3,000 printrun, in February 1969. "My then-husband, our tiny daughter and I hawked the magazine in Harvard Square. We sold out, and by the third issue we printed 35,000 copies," says Pollard. The magazine remained in publication for 25 years. Two of Pollard's articles from the Journal have been included in anthologies, including "The Five of Us (With a Little Help from our Friends)," which appeared in *Dear Sisters: Dispatches from the Women's Liberation Movement.* Pollard eventually left the magazine to teach women's studies at the Baltimore Experimental High School. A licensed acupuncturist, Pollard has two children and holds a B.A. from Brandeis University (1965). (ABS)

Pollock, Clarice Barbara (1934 –) A retired insurance agent, Pollock joined Southern Westchester (NY) NOW in 1972. She served as task force chair for abortion and education, participated in ERA demonstrations, and lobbied congressmen. She is (2005) president of FL NOW, heads Broward Women's Emergency Fund Inc., which provides funding for abortions for women who are poor, and served on NOW's national board from 1992 – 1996. Pollock, who has four children, earned a B.S. from Columbia School of General Studies, an M.S. from Yeshiva University, and a C.L.U. from American University. (ABS)

Pollock, Mordeca Jane (1941 –) was a founder and president of Boston NOW (1969), and a member of NOW's national board from 1969 – 1978. Pollock served on NOW's national conference resolutions committee (1971 – 1973, and chair, 1971), and was a member of the Massachusetts Governor's Commission on the Status of Women (1971 – 1972). As a trustee of the Cambridge Family Y, Pollock and other feminist board members worked to promote equality and diversity in governance, facilities and programs for girls and young women. Pollock "left the movement in 1978 because of the malicious gossip I heard and heard of," she says. Pollock is the author of *Amazon Chronicles* (a historical novel) and *By the Tongue* (a mystery set in Provence), and is a consulting writer for high-tech companies. Pollock holds a B.A. and M.A. from City College of New York, and a Ph.D. from Harvard University. Archives: Schlesinger Library, Radcliffe Institute, Cambridge, MA. (ABS)

Polos, Patricia F. (1922 – 2003) was a staunch fighter for the Equal Rights Amendment. She served as president of ERA Illinois and worked aggressively for the amendment until it passed by a large margin in the Illinois House. Earlier, Polos had studied at Indiana University, then moved to Chicago with her family and studied acting. Polos was a consultant to the Governor's Commission on the Status of Women in Illinois (1965). In 1968, Polos received a degree in social science from Mundelein College and became legislative assistant to Senator Esther Saperstein. She was also president of the Loop chapter of OWL, which she left in 1994 to become a lobbyist for AARP. Polos had two children.

Pomerleau, Dolores ("Dolly") C. (1942 –) As a founding member of Catholics for the ERA, Pomerleau (with

several other women) chained herself to Republican headquarters in Washington, D.C., in 1974 to protest the removal of the ERA from the Republican platform. Pomerleau was also a founder of the Women's Ordination Conference (1975). As a founder/member of the Quixote Center, Pomerleau, with Maureen Fiedler, conducted a study on women in the church and published the results in "Are Catholics Ready?" which showed the positive impact of female role modeling in the church. During the early years of the Quixote Center, the group advocated for gay and lesbian rights in the Catholic Church. When Pope John Paul II first visited the U.S., Pomerleau helped organize national demonstrations with banners proclaiming in Polish, "Ordain Women, or Stop Baptizing Them" and "Sexism Is a Sin: Repent." She also coordinated a national conference on the ordination of women, attended by 2,000 women, and in 1975, at the U.N. International Women's Conference in Mexico City, sat next to Mother Theresa and talked to her about the urgent need for women priests in the church and that women who had abortions were not murderers. In 1991, Pomerleau and three other women traveled to Czechoslovakia to meet Ludmila Javorova, who had secretly been ordained in 1970 by a Catholic bishop to serve the underground church. The women subsequently sponsored a tour of the U.S. so that Javorova could meet with women's groups. Pomerleau holds an M.A. (ABS)

Pomerleau, Patricia ("Pat") Ann (1931 –) became a feminist in 1937, at the age of six, "when I first fell in love with another woman. I do not mean to be facetious," she says. "That early instinct had to do with a basic respect for women and a wish for their well being, and mine." Pomerleau served in the Women's Army Corps from 1953 – 1955, where she met numerous "unrealized feminists." In 1967, she participated in a nonviolent protest against the draft at the Oakland Army Induction Center, was arrested, and served 11 days in jail. Again, she met a great variety of women, "some sister war protesters, some prostitutes, some with drug addictions and others with legal problems. They were essentially independent women striving for equality, personal freedom and recognition as valuable human beings." In 1970, as part of a speakers bureau organized by Sally Miller Gearhart, Pomerleau participated in a series of informal talks at schools and organizational meetings in Marin County, CA, promoting lesbian and gay liberation. Pomerleau was an organizer and marcher representing lesbians for the first time in the Gay Pride Parade in San Francisco in 1972. As the parade progressed, the core of six women from a club called The Other Side were joined by two or three lesbians from the sidewalks. By the time the reviewing stand was reached, there were 10 women—a triumphant and proud moment for that small band. Pomerleau, who publishes short stories and essays under the name Pomerleau Chavez, holds a B.A. from the University of Denver and a Librarianship Certificate, General Secondary Level. Archives: James

Hormel Center, San Francisco Public Library, San Francisco, CA. (ABS)

Poole, Audrey G. (1928 –) has been a member of NOW since the early 1970s. She was a founding mother of Westchester (NY) NOW, and membership chair of its initial board. From the beginning, she has marched and attended meetings in New York, Philadelphia and Washington, D.C., planning, protesting and talking at abortion speakouts. She also organized ERA extension meetings and phone banks in her home, and attended domestic violence hearings at the World Trade Center and reported on them to groups. During the 1983 Women's Encampment for Peace and Justice at Seneca Falls, she was pepper-gassed. Since the early 1980s, Poole has been a member of a county-wide NOW book club reading works by women authors only. For more than 15 years, she has met with the inmates of the NOW chapter at Bedford Hills Correctional Facility, NYS's only maximum-security prison for women. More recently, Poole has spoken about Roe v. Wade at colleges and churches, under the combined auspices of NOW and Planned Parenthood. Poole has also traveled widely, often meeting the heads of women's delegations in Russia, Kazakstan, Uzbekistan, China, India and Cuba. In addition to this work, Poole has been very active in the anti-war movement, WILPF and the civil rights and anti-apartheid movements. She has also supported the United Farm Workers, the Southern Poverty Law Center, the Lakota Indian College Fund, the ACLU and the war against HIV/AIDS. Poole, who has two children, holds an A.A. from Fairleigh Dickinson University (1947) and a B.A. from Sarah Lawrence College (1978). (ABS)

Popkin, Annie (1945 –) Popkin's political activism began in 1959, when, at age 14, she picketed with her mother for fair housing in Freeport (Long Island, NY). She followed that by helping to organize northern picketing of Woolworth's in support of the 1960 sit-ins in the South. As a student at Radcliffe, she participated in the 1964 Freedom Summer in Vicksburg, MI, and was a member of the Harvard-Radcliffe Civil Rights Coordinating Committee and SDS. In 1967 – 1968, she worked for Noam Chomsky and Louis Kampf, analyzing U.S. press coverage of the Vietnam War, concentrating on uncovering contradictions between *The New York Times'* editorials and its news articles. In 1969, Popkin was a co-founder of Bread and Roses, the Boston-area socialist-feminist women's liberation organization. One B&R project resulted in the writing of *Women and Their Bodies*, which later became *Our Bodies, Ourselves*. Popkin took many of the photographs published in the book. She organized and led B&R study groups on the history of the American feminist movement and offered courses on the history of the new left and the women's liberation movement at the Women's School in Cambridge in the 1970s. She wrote about B&R in "The Personal is Political," published in

They Should have Served that Cup of Coffee: 7 Radicals Remember the 60s, and in "The Social Experience of Bread and Roses: Building a Community and Building a Culture," in *Women, Class, and the Feminist Imagination*. As a teaching assistant at Brandies University in 1970 – 1972, Popkin taught women's-studies-type courses. Since the 1980s, she has been facilitating unlearning racism and sexism workshops for college students and community members. She was the first director of the Difference, Power and Discrimination program, required of all undergraduates, at Oregon State University, Corvallis, where she teaches women's studies. Popkin is also a counselor with a private therapy practice in Portland, OR. Popkin holds a B. A. from Radcliffe College and a Ph.D. from Brandeis University. Archives: Schlesinger Library, Radcliffe Institute, Cambridge, MA. (ABS)

Porter, Nancy Maxwell (1936 –) A teacher, Porter was a co-founder of a women's studies program, one of the earliest in the country, at Portland State University (1970 – 1971). The program functioned as a collective of faculty, students and women from the community until 1976, when it acquired a full-time paid coordinator and began awarding Certificates. It later became a degree-awarding department of women's studies at Portland State. Porter, now retired, has published articles and books on women's studies and women's literature, and served as editor of *Women's Studies Quarterly*. (ABS)

Post, Dianne Lynn (1947 –) An attorney whose work on behalf of women's rights has taken her across the world, Post began her struggle for liberation in 1961 when she registered (unsuccessfully) for shop instead of home economics. It was a temporary setback. In 1977, Post was co-coordinator for the 8th National Conference on Women and the Law in Madison, WI. At the same time, she established the legal program for the Dane County Advocates for Battered Women. In 1979, Post served as state chair of the ERA movement to get the amendment on the ballot in Arizona, and also sued the state because it donated $10,000 to the Mountain States Defense Fund to kill the ERA. In 1980, Post was a founder of Phoenix Women Take Back the Night and served as chief fundraiser. She also did the legal work, negotiated with the police, and was part of several notable actions, including the hexing of a rapist (who was caught three weeks later) and the posting of an "ordinance" prohibiting men from being out after 6 p.m. unless accompanied by two women. The extreme radical nature of the group's work made shelters that were earlier considered "far out" now more moderate. Post secured funding for and founded the Domestic Violence Project at Community Legal Services (1985 – 1989), and then served as the first state director of Arizona Coalition Against Domestic Violence (1989 – 1991). Post, who has been active in the LGBT movement since 1992, was co-chair (1993) of Arizonans for Fairness, which was formed to stop an anti-gay state initiative from being passed. She served as attorney for Lesbian Resource Project (1993 – 1998), the first lesbian out and public organization in Phoenix, and was a member of the board of the Arizona Human Rights Fund (1994 – 1998). Post has traveled to South Africa, Russia and India on behalf of women's rights, and in 2003 was one of four original founders of the Freedom 400 and drafter of a petition against the stoning of women, which was submitted to the United Nations Special Rapporteur on Violence Against Women. Post, who has spoken widely on behalf of the rights of women, has also published numerous articles and booklets, including the *Domestic Violence Reference Manual for U.S. Marines* (Arizona Section). She has received numerous awards, including the Commitment to the Concerns of Women Award (1995) from the City of Phoenix Women's Commission. She was named Woman of the Year by *Echo Magazine* (1994), and also received its Distinguished Service by a Woman award (1994). Post earned her B.A. from the University of Wisconsin, her M.S. from California State University, San Jose, her J.D. from the University of Wisconsin, and a College of Trial Advocacy from the Hastings Law School, San Francisco. Archives: The Lesbian Herstory Archives, Brooklyn, NY. (ABS)

Powell, Betty (1945 –) (also known as Elizabeth Powell Rosenberg) In the late 1960s and early 1970s, Powell helped form the Episcopal Women's Caucus and advocated for women's ordination to the priesthood in the Episcopal Church. With the support of friends in the EWC and NOW, she presented herself for ordination to the priesthood, but the Church was still ordaining women only to be deacons. Nonetheless, when the first irregular ordinations occurred in Philadelphia in 1974, Powell stood with the 11 women being ordained, although there had been threats of violence. It was a day that changed their lives and the lives of many women forever. The Episcopal Church now had women priests, though irregular, with lots of ongoing controversy and church trials of male priests who allowed these women to celebrate Holy Communion in their parishes. As ecclesiastical consultant, Powell assisted one of the lawyers defending one of these men in his appeal in a church trial. Because the women realized they would need to continue their "ecclesiastical disobedience" to move things along, Powell helped organize the second irregular ordination (four women) in Washington, D.C., on September 7, 1975. At that time, she was ordained to the priesthood at St. Stephen and the Incarnation Episcopal Church with her three sisters, The Rev. Lee McGee, The Rev. Alison Palmer and The Rev. Diane Tickell. "Many times thereafter we were told that the two ordinations combined (1974 and 1975) had moved the church to finally vote in 1976 to allow women's ordination to the priesthood. One ordination could have been seen as a fluke, but two hinted that 'ecclesiastical disobedience' would continue until the church changed its ways." In 1977, women began being ordained "regularly" to the priesthood, and eventually all 15 of the original "irregular" women priests were recognized by the church. Powell holds a B.A. from the University of Delaware (1967), an M.S. from the University of North Carolina Medical School, Chapel Hill (1969), an M.Div. from Virginia Theological Seminary (1972), a D.Min. from Colgate Rochester/Bexley Hall/Crozer (1975), and an M.S.W. from Catholic University of America (1989). (ABS)

Powell, Peggy – See Dobbins, Peggy

Power, Sarah Goddard (1935 – 1987) As a regent of the University of Michigan for more than 12 years, Power worked aggressively to advance the position of women and minorities in faculty and administrative roles. She served as deputy assistant secretary in the State Department during the Carter administration, responsible for U.S. policy for WHO, ILO, UNESCO and other specialized U.N. agencies for international women's programs, human rights and communications. As a participant in the U.N. Decade for Women (1975 – 1985), Power was central to the drafting of the World Plan of Action for the economic, social and personal status of women worldwide. In 1983, the University of Michigan Academic Women's Caucus established the Sarah Goddard Power Award for members of the university community who had distinguished themselves through their leadership, scholarship, and sustained service on behalf of women. Active in the Michigan Democratic Women's Caucus, Power was inducted into The Michigan Women's Hall of Fame in 1988.

Pratt, Annis Vilas (1937 –) A writer and retired professor of English and creative writing at the University of Wisconsin-Madison, Pratt is the author of *Archetypal Patterns in Women's Fiction* (Indiana University Press, 1981) and *Dancing With Goddesses: Archetypes and Empowerment in Poetry* (Indiana University Press, 1994). She served as the first charter president and convener of Atlanta NOW (1967), as well as for the Georgia Citizens for Hospital Abortion (1970). In Detroit, she served as editor of "As We See It NOW" (1971 – 1973). She is (2005) editor of "The Strategist: Tips and Tactics for Women Faculty," a newsletter published by the Academic Discrimination Advisory Board of the NWSA. She has also served as coordinator of this board since 1981. Pratt, who has two children, holds a B.A., an M.A. and a Ph.D. Archives: Sophia Smith Collection, Smith College, Northampton, MA. (ABS)

Pratt, Minnie Bruce (1946 –) Poet, essayist and lecturer, Pratt is the author of *Crime Against Nature* (Firebrand Books, 1990), a book of poetry that explores her relationship to her two sons as a lesbian mother. The book was a Lamont Poetry Selection of the Academy of American Poets (1989), and received the Gay and Lesbian Book

Award in Literature from the American Library Association (1991). Other books include *The Sound of One Fork* (Night Heron Press, 1984); *We Say We love Each Other* (Spinsters/Aunt Lute, 1985); *Rebellion: Essays 1980 – 1991* (Firebrand Books, 1991); *S/HE*, a book of prose poetry (Firebrand Books, 1995); *Walking Back up Depot Street: Poems* (University of Pittsburgh Press, 1999); and *The Dirt She Ate: Selected and New Poems* (University of Pittsburgh Press, 2003), winner of a Lambda Literary Award for Poetry. From 1972 – 1973, Pratt worked on "The Feminist Newsletter," covering the women's liberation movement in Chapel Hill/Durham/Raleigh, NC. She was also editor of the Fayetteville, NC, NOW newsletter (1975 – 1976), and an organizer for the passage of the ERA in NC as well as coordinator of the Cumberland Country ERA speakers bureau (1975 – 1978). She served on the board of the Fayetteville Rape Crisis Line, and as coordinator, Fayetteville NOW (1976 – 1977), and was a member of the Cumberland County Council on the Status of Women (1976 – 1978). In 1976, Pratt was project director of a series of forums on women's issues in education, the military, spirituality, the arts, and on violence against women. In 1977, she was co-ordinator of a North Carolina Humanities Grant to Fayetteville NOW, "We See Women … Battered Women." At the same time, she was founder of WomanWrites: A Southeastern Lesbian Writers Conference, which continued into 1999. From 1978 – 1979, Pratt was a member of the board of Everywoman's Center in Fayetteville, and in 1980 served as editor of the SEWSA newsletter. From 1978 – 1983, she was a member of the editorial collective of *Feminary: A Feminist Journal for the South, Emphasizing Lesbian Visions*. From 1984 – 1987, she was a founder and member of LIPS, a lesbian multi-action political group in Washington, D.C. Pratt earned her B.A. from the University of Alabama, Tuscaloosa, and her Ph.D. from the University of North Carolina, Chapel Hill.　(ABS)

Prescod, Margaret (1948 –) has been a community activist against racism, environmental degradation and war, and for the rights of women, blacks, indigenous and other people of color for more than three decades. A black woman, Prescod was born in Barbados and immigrated to New York with her family as a teenager in the 1960s. She entered the women's movement in 1973, and in 1974 co-founded International Black Women for Wages for Housework in NYC. In 1977, Prescod was part of the NY State delegation to the National Women's Conference in Houston. At that conference, Prescod was part of the Wages for Housework Campaign delegation and helped form the "pro-money" coalition that rewrote the government's resolution, calling for "Welfare" to be called a "wage" to reflect the care-giving work done by mothers, and benefits to be increased. The resolution passed. In 1975 – 1985, Prescod was active in the U.N. Decade for Women. In 1995, at the United Nations Fourth World Conference on Women in Beijing, she led the lobby ef-

forts of the International Women Count Network, which won the United Nations' decision that governments should measure and value unwaged work and include that value in national statistics and their gross domestic products. More recently, Prescod co-founded and co-coordinates the Every Mother Is a Working Mother Network, which began in Los Angeles in the late 1990s. She is one of the founders of International Women of Color in the Global Women's Strike. Since 2000, she has been coordinating the GWS in the U.S., an ongoing network that, among other things, organizes International Women's Day March 8 under the anti-war theme "Invest in Caring Not Killing." She is the convener of the Women's Caucus of the People's Hurricane Relief Fund and Oversight Coalition and the Women's Reconstruction Network of Katrina survivors, evacuees and supporters. Prescod has one child.　(ABS)

Price, Barbara ("Boo") Easter (1943 –) (also known as Barbara Kay Price and Barbara Price Garcia-Dobles) As a student at the law school at the University of California, Davis, in 1973, Price created the lesbian caucus, which "was the first (and for some time only) lesbian caucus on campus for graduates or undergraduates." She did a great deal of research on lesbian custody and became a national speaker and expert witness for lesbian custody cases. Price was a panelist at the national American Psychiatric Association's annual conference at which the group declassified homosexuality as a disease. Price was later co-author, with Donna Hitchens, of one of the first law review articles on lesbian custody, and author of an article on litigation strategy for lesbian custody cases that became the basis of a chapter in Roberta Achtenberg's *Lesbian Manual*. In 1974, Price produced her first concert of women's music in Davis, CA, with Cris Williamson, Margie Adam and Vicki Randle. She has since produced hundreds of concerts, tours and festivals across the country. In 1975, she created Pleiades Records with Margie Adam, and was an active participant in the creation of the Women's Music Network as a recording company owner, producer and attorney. Since 1977, she has produced seven albums of women's music. Also in 1975, she began Women in Production, a production company to train other women producers and technicians; became a member of the executive committee of the Women & the Law Conference, which was the feminist law association of the 1970s and 1980s; and was the only student member of the state women's lawyer committee to create California Women Lawyers. She became national chair of the lesbian caucus of the NWPC at the same time, and was a member of the executive committee of the national board from 1977 – 1984. In 1981 she was elected a delegate at large to the national board. From 1976 – 1986, Price practiced law in San Francisco as a sole practitioner in family law and custody, entertainment law and small business for women. In 1977, she produced the entire cultural program of 40 performances for the IWY National Women's

Conference in Houston. She was a member of the board of directors of the Lesbian Rights Organization, which became the National Center for Lesbian Rights, and in 1978 was a delegate to the founding convention of the National Lesbian Feminist Organization in Los Angeles. Price was an initial adviser for the founding of the Michigan Women's Music Festival, where she produced the stage performances from 1976 – 1994, and was an owner/producer of the entire festival from 1983 – 1994. Since that time, Price has continued to produce musical events and tours celebrating women, women candidates and women's issues, often at the Montclair Women's Cultural Arts Club, which she opened for that purpose in Oakland, CA, in 1996. Politically progressive from a young age, Price was involved in the anti-Vietnam War, civil rights and consumer protection movements, and has supported cultural/ethnic rights and senior citizen advocacy. Price earned her B.A. from Mount Holyoke College (1965) and her J.D. from the University of California, Davis (1976).   (ABS)

Price, Colette – See Swietnicki, Colette A.

Pride, Anne (1942 – 1990) In 1974, Pride helped incorporate Pittsburgh Action Against Rape, a crisis center aiding victims of sexual assault. She served as executive director from 1979 – 1985, and in that capacity was held in contempt for refusing to turn over to the court the records of a woman who had come to her program for help. Ultimately, according to Pride's friend Lois Galgay Reckitt, this act of defiance resulted in a landmark Pennsylvania Supreme Court ruling protecting the confidentiality of rape victims. Says Reckitt, "No longer could the emotional reactions of a woman to her assault be forced into evidence by the court." Pride served on NOW's national board from 1975 – 1978 and as editor of *Do It NOW!*, NOW's national newspaper, from 1976 – 1978. Earlier, she had helped found one of the pioneer feminist publishing companies, Know, Inc. With Paulette Balogh, Pride also co-founded Motheroot in order to publish contemporary literature by women. From 1984 – 1986, Pride served as executive director of Women's Health Services, and from 1986 until her death from ovarian cancer, as director of Birthplace, a birthing center staffed by midwives. Archives: Schlesinger Library, Radcliffe Institute, Cambridge, MA.

Priesand, Sally J. (1946 –) Fortunately, Priesand's dream at 16 of becoming a rabbi was supported by her parents, even though there were no women rabbis in the world. In 1972, Priesand became the first ordained woman rabbi in the U.S., "no doubt aided by the unfolding of the modern feminist movement," she says. After her ordination by the Hebrew Union College-Jewish Institute of Religion (Cincinnati), a resolution reaffirming the equality of women in Reform Judaism and supporting the ERA was passed by the Central Conference of American Rabbis. From 1972 –

1975, Priesand served on the task force for equality of women in Judaism sponsored by the New York Federation of Reform Synagogues. In 1976, the executive board of the CCAR established a task force on women in the rabbinate, chaired by Priesand. The job of the task force was to oversee and facilitate the total integration of women as rabbis. In 1997, Priesand was honored for 25 years of service to the Jewish people during Founders Day Ceremonies at Hebrew Union College-Jewish Institute of Religion. During the ceremonies, an announcement was made about the establishment of the Rabbi Sally J. Priesand Visiting Professorship of Jewish Women's Studies. From 1981 – 2006, Priesand has served as Rabbi of Monmouth Reform Temple in Tinton Falls, NJ. In July 2006 she became Rabbi Emerita. Priesand is a graduate of the University of Cincinnati (1968). Archives: American Jewish Archives, Task Force on Women in The Rabbinate Collection, Cincinnati, OH.   (ABS)

Pruett, Jane – See Jervis, Jane Lise

Prussing, Laurel Lunt (1941 –) In 1963, Prussing was looking for work and asking potential employers during job interviews if the pay for women was equivalent to that of men. The answer from Harvard University, she says, was, "No, Harvard does not pay women the same as men." The answer from consulting firm Arthur D. Little: "No, our clients would not pay as much for a woman as for a man." Prussing was eventually hired by Arthur D. Little. In 1967, she became one of the first women to file a complaint with the EEOC. At the time, she says, Arthur D. Little was paying women 40 percent less than men for identical work. The Federal government found in her favor. Prussing received a retroactive increase, and the company had to adjust women's salaries as a result. In 1972, Prussing was one of the first women elected to the county board in Champaign County, IL. "Three of us were elected that year after the county had existed for nearly 150 years with no women ever serving as county board members," she says. "After that, it was okay for women to run." In 1976, she was elected county auditor and served four terms. In 1992, she was elected as a state representative, the only Democrat to win for 10 years in a district that, she says, had been drawn to be won by a Republican. In 2001, as a lobbyist for the AAUW in Illinois, Prussing initiated the effort to promote the ERA by recruiting legislators to co-sponsor the bill. In 2003, Prussing became legislative director for ERA Illinois, where she helped get the bill approved by the IL House, and continues working to get it approved by the Senate. In April 2005, Prussing was elected Mayor of Urbana, IL, the first woman mayor in Urbana's history. Prussing earned her B.A. from Wellesley and her M.A. from Boston University. She has three children.   (ABS)

Pulitzer, Roslyn K. (1930 –) A member and chair of the legislative committee of the Manhattan WPC and subse-

P

quently elected chair of the New York State WPC, Pulitzer played a major role in changing New York rape laws and the treatment of rape victims in an amazingly short period—10 months. In the spring of 1973, the Manhattan WPC went to Albany, NY, to lobby on a variety of women's issues and noted that legislators were most interested in the legislative program's call for the elimination of corroboration in rape cases. When research was released showing that the summer months had the highest incidence of rape, Pulitzer, with other members of the Manhattan WPC and New York Women Against Rape, declared August as Rape Prevention Month. They also drew up a list of 14 demands that they presented to NYC Mayor John Lindsay. Pulitzer worked to get press coverage for the issue and to hold rallies outside trials of rape suspects to call attention to the flaws in the rape law and the lenient sentences that resulted. Under public pressure, the mayor created a task force on rape. Pulitzer lobbied successfully to get feminist organizations appointed to the task force, and to have women representatives in the major city departments. All 14 demands were ultimately met. These included setting up special clinics in each borough to treat rape victims and to help victims establish corroborative evidence, training police to be more sensitive to rape victims, and designating one police unit to deal with rape crimes to enable a more aggressive investigation and a more compassionate approach to the victims. Within the Manhattan WPC, Pulitzer convened a panel of women attorneys to debate the changes that should take place in the law. The positions they formulated helped them prepare focused testimony before a hearing of the state legislature. At the beginning of the next legislative session in Albany, the rape law was changed and, among other things, the requirement of corroboration was eliminated. Pulitzer holds a B.S. from New York State University/ Empire College and an M.S.W. from Fordham University. She has worked as a medical technician and psychotherapist, and is now a photographer in Santa Fe, NM.   (ABS)

Quinn, Donna (1937 –) A nun, Quinn founded Chicago Catholic Women (1974) to foster women's rights in church and society. The group supported NOW on the passage of the ERA in Illinois, organized rallies, and held educational forums. Quinn attended the second meeting (called by Mary B. Lynch) on the ordination of women (1974); was a member of the coordinating committee of the first Women's Ordination Conference in Detroit (1975); and was voted onto the first core commission. She was also a coordinator of the Second Women's Ordination Conference, held in Baltimore (1978). In 1975, Quinn presented the results of Chicago Catholic Women's Testimony to the regional Bishops meeting in Minneapolis, and attended the Bicentennial Bishops Call to Action Conference in Detroit (1976), making sure that the women's testimony would be written into the conference's documents. In 1977, Quinn, with Dolores Brooks

and Rosalie Muschal Reinhardt, founded Women of the Church, which drew together 12 national and local Catholic feminist organizations. The group supported reproductive rights and Geraldine Ferraro, and sponsored the first Women Church Conference. In 1983, Quinn was one of 23 nuns told by the Vatican that they would be dismissed from their religious communities if they did not retract an advertisement placed in *The New York Times* ad asking the Bishops to discuss reproductive rights. Quinn did not retract. Quinn has been a member of the board of the National Coalition of American Nuns since 1975, serving as president from 1980 – 1983. From 1980 – 2000, she organized and worked in an employment program for shelter women, a project of Chicago Catholic Women. Quinn was one of six women who protested at the Vatican during the Bishops Synod on Religious Life (1995). The women were detained by the Italian police and had their identification confiscated. Quinn has spoken frequently on television and radio about women's rights, and has celebrated the Eucharist, advocated women priests, and spoken on behalf of the lesbian, gay, bisexual and transsexual community. Quinn holds a B.A. from Edgewood College, an M.A. in History from the University of Illinois-Champaign, and an M.A. in Administration from the University of Wisconsin-Milwaukee. Archives: The Gannon Center, Loyola University, Chicago, IL.   (ABS)

Quinn, Doris (1924 – 2003) was a founding member and served as president of both the Missouri State WPC and the Greater Kansas City WPC. Quinn was a state representative in the Missouri General Assembly (1975 – 1976) and served several times as Democratic committeewoman. A manager for H&R Block in her professional life, Quinn was also active in the Missouri ERA Coalition, Women in Communications, the Missouri Women's Campaign Fund, and the AAUW.

Quitman, Yolanda (1939 –) was the founder of POW! (Power of Women), which was the precursor to the NWPC. She served as founder and chair of the Nassau County (NY) WPC, as well as treasurer of the NY State WPC. She was a delegate to the first IWY conference in Houston (1977) and a member of the Nassau County committee for IWY. Quitman was a member of the Minority Women's Business Enterprise Program under Governors Mario Cuomo, David Dinkins and Rudolph Giuliani (who disbanded it). She designed campaign buttons for Bella Abzug, Marianne Krupsak and many others, and was a founder and VP of Women Business Owners –New York State. She was also a founding member of the Long Island (NY) chapter of the National Association of Women in Construction, a member of the board of Women's Economic Developers of Long Island, and a founder of Women's Forum, Inc. Quitman, who has two children, is president of an architectural corporation and executive director (2005) of the Women's Urban Renewal Development Corporation. She holds an M.F.A.   (ABS)

Rachel, Vaughan (1933 –) (also known as Vaughan Kaprow) An artist and photographer, Rachel was a founding member of the Pasadena Area Women's Political Action Group (1970). She was also a member of Double X, a women artists group that worked for greater exposure of women artists in Los Angeles, and was briefly on the board of the Women's Building in Los Angeles. Rachel became a volunteer at the Mazer Lesbian Archive in West Hollywood in the 1990s. She is a member of Coalition of Old Lesbians. Rachel, who has four children (one deceased), holds an M.F.A. from the California Institute of the Arts (1975). Archives: Smithsonian Institute, Washington, D.C. (ABS)

Radlow, Anne D. – See Ewing, Anne D.

Rae, Erena (1941 –) became editor of the Tippecanoe County (IN) NOW newsletter in 1972 and developed regular features. Later moving to Nebraska, Oklahoma and New Jersey, Rae remained an active supporter of the ERA. An artist and graphic designer, Rae realized that there was a huge need for good graphics in the feminist movement. From 1972 – 1994, she designed countless logotypes, newsletters and state conference materials—everything from the visual interpretation of conference themes to posters and name badges—for state and local chapters of NOW. She also waged a many-decades-long campaign to eliminate sexist language in society, writing to the editors of publications guilty of the practice. Her work as a visual artist also addressed the repercussions of sexist language in the home, at schools and in the workplace. Rae, also active in the peace and justice movement, has one child. She holds a B.F.A. from the University of Kansas. (ABS)

Raggio, Louise B. (1919 –) Until January 1, 1968, says Raggio, Texas had the most oppressive and discriminatory laws in the U.S. on property rights of married women, and many antiquated laws affecting all women. Raggio, who served as president of the LWV in Austin (1943) and successfully campaigned for Texas women to serve on juries (1955), formed a task force of legal experts (all male) who spent two years writing bills to remove these old statutes. She also lobbied for and promoted the changes before the Texas Legislature. All the bills were passed. Because the new statutes worked so well, TX adopted the ERA by a constitutional amendment in 1973. Raggio is also known as the Mother of the Texas Family Code, the first completed family code in the U.S., enacted 1965 – 1975. She served as chair of the family law section of the ABA (1975 – 1976); governor of the American Academy of Matrimonial Lawyers (1973 – 1981); and as a trustee of the National Conference of Bar Foundation (1986 – 1992). In 1995, she received the ABA's Margaret Brent Women Lawyers of Achievement Award. She graduated from the University of Texas at Austin in 1939, and became one of the first Washington, D.C., interns in 1939 – 1940. She later earned her J.D. from Southern Methodist University (1952). The only woman in her law school class, Raggio became the first woman criminal assistant district attorney in Dallas County, the first woman elected a director of the State Bar of Texas in its 100-year history, and the first woman trustee and chair of the board of the Texas Bar Foundation. The recipient of an Honorary Degree of Doctor of Laws from SMU, Raggio had an endowed lecture series named in her honor spotlighting women of distinction. She received the Jefferson Award from the ACLU, and has two awards named for her from Dallas Women Lawyers and NAWBO. She has three children. Archives: Archives of Women of the Southwest, Southern Methodist University, Dallas, TX. (ABS)

Rahmani, Aviva Alexandra (1945 –) An ecological artist whose work "was always based on making the connection between abuse in relationships and abusing the environment," Rahmani helped start the women's liberation movement at the University of California, San Diego, in the late 1960s and early 1970s. She spoke at anti-war rallies as a feminist and participated in and initiated many CR sessions. She also helped start the Women's Caucus in Los Angeles and the feminist newspaper *Goodbye to All That*. In the early 1970s, she worked on a series of short films on rape, and initiated "Ablutions" with Judy Chicago and other women artists, also about rape. With her work, Rahmani helped bring the topic of domestic violence and child abuse among feminist artists into active discussion. From 1990 – 2000, Rahmani worked on "Ghost Nets," a project on Vinalhaven Island, Maine, "that restored a salt marsh on a former town dump as I healed from abuse. It made the analogy that the salt marsh was the ultimate cunt for its vulnerability to degradation and fecundity." In 2000, Rahmani began working on restoring a variety of international sites, also feminist in their grounding. Rahmani holds a B.F.A. and M.F.A. from Cal Arts. (ABS)

Raimondi, Carole Glass (1943 –) helped organize and establish the women's studies program at Sonoma State University, Rohnert Park, CA (1972 – 1977). Raimondi also had a women's radio show aired Sunday evenings on KBBF, a public radio station in Santa Rosa, CA. In addition to feminism, Raimondi's work included the Peace & Freedom Party, minority rights, education, poverty issues and childcare. (ABS)

Rainone, Nanette (1942 –) was a member of The Feminists in 1969 when the group put together a pamphlet informing women of their rights in marriage. (At that time, women gave up rights when they became married—for example, the right to use their own names for credit; they also took on responsibility for the debts of their husbands.) The group demonstrated at the marriage license bureau at City Hall, handing out copies of their pamphlet. Later, working with NYRF, Rainone participated in the sit-in at the office of John Mack Carter, editor

R

of the *Ladies' Home Journal*, protesting the magazine's stereotypical and demeaning content. Carter agreed to and published a feminist insert for *Ladies' Home Journal* written by NYRF. Rainone was also the producer and interviewer for the first feminist radio program, which was broadcast from WBAI beginning in 1969 and through the early 1970s. She later conducted a weekly program, "Consciousness Raising on the Air," in which she used notes from her CR group as the format and took calls from the public. Rainone was president of Brooklyn Information and Culture (1980–2002). She has been working with the Women's Media Center since its founding in 2005. Rainone holds a B.A. from Queens College.   (ABS)

Raintree, Elizabeth (1942 –) (also known as Ellen M. Steingarten and Ellen Elizabeth Morgan) Raintree joined Central New Jersey NOW at its first meeting in 1969. In 1970, she coordinated a series of lectures, The New Feminism, held at the Princeton Adult School, and also served as chapter representative on the committees that planned the Congress to Unite Women (1969 and 1970). At the Congresses, held in New York City, Raintree served as convener and facilitator of the higher education workshops. Also in 1970, Raintree met with NOW members and friends in Washington, D.C., to begin a campaign in support of the ERA, and joined the NOW national board. She became coordinator of the Central NJ NOW higher education task force, and in that capacity signed the chapter's sex discrimination complaint against Princeton University. That led to her being appointed national coordinator of the NOW task force on university compliance (1972–1974). Raintree compiled and presented NOW's testimony in support of the Women's Educational Equity Act to the House of Representatives. Raintree also served as a consultant to the Modern Language Association Commission on the Status of Women in the Profession (1970), and as a member of the National Advisory Board of the Women's History Research Center from 1971 forward. She was a member of the national steering committee and coordinator of the curriculum committee of the Women's Caucus for the MLA (1971–1972). Raintree also served as a consulting member of the Minority Groups Advisory Council of the State Educational Assessment Program of the NJ Department of Education (1972), and as a consultant to the Project on the History of Women in the U.S. for the NJ Educational Media Consortium (1973–1974). In 1974, Raintree won the Florence Howe Award for Feminist Literary Criticism. From 1974–1975, she coordinated the women's studies program at the University of Delaware, and throughout her teaching career has taught women's studies courses. She was a member of the editorial board of the journal *Regionalism and the Female Imagination* (1975–1979), and in 1977 gave a National Endowment for the Humanities-funded guest lecture on women's studies for the curriculum development project at the University of Michigan. Raintree lived, worked and studied in England

from 1978–1993. Raintree is the author of numerous feminist articles and has published several short stories and poems. Raintree earned her Ph.D. from the University of Pennsylvania (1972), and in 1981 earned an M.A. from Antioch University International.   (ABS)

Ralph, Roberta (1926 –) A 1959 graduate of the UCLA School of Law, Ralph worked first for the Legal Aid Foundation, but quit after she realized that two male attorneys would be allowed to continue to "goof off," leaving more work for her and the other woman attorney in the office. By 1963, Ralph had opened her own law practice, taking civil cases in family law as well as bankruptcy, wills and personal injury. Working for herself gave Ralph the freedom to become involved in housing-rights organizations like the Hollywood Fair Housing Congress. Ralph saw evidence that discrimination extended beyond race to women, and joined NOW and the NWPC. In 1971 and 1972 she was elected president of the Women Lawyers Association of Los Angeles, turning the association from "a very genteel, tea-pouring organization to one more assertive for women's rights." In 1974, she served as co-chair of the organizing committee of California Women Lawyers. She chaired a committee dedicated to women's rights. With others she held a Constitutional Convention to organize women lawyers statewide to further the goal of equal rights for all women. Ralph also served as president of the Fair Housing Congress of Southern California for almost three years in the early 1970s. In 1976, fearing that Governor Jerry Brown was not going to appoint as many women judges as expected, Ralph and other women ran for election. Ralph challenged a sitting judge on the California Superior Court, the highest of three trial courts in California. Ralph, who successfully unseated the judge for the six-year term, believes she may have been the first woman candidate to unseat a male judge. She was re-elected to a second term without opposition.   (ABS)

Ramos, Sandra (1942 –) In 1970, Ramos took in a desperate woman fleeing an abuser, and before long was sheltering 25 women and children and her own three children in one house. Neighbors complained and Ramos was threatened with jail, but she persevered. Ramos also marched, staged sit-ins, threatened legal action and defied court orders in her efforts to protect women and children from abuse. She helped obtain funds to provide an official shelter in New Jersey, opened several safe houses, established the Family Transitional Institute, and regularly fought for legislation to protect victims of abuse. In 1987, Ramos helped organize and incorporate Strengthen Our Sisters. She has continued to establish shelters, provide day care to women in need, and speak out on abuse. In 1998, she developed and began teaching The Dynamics of Domestic Violence, at Ramapo College. The recipient of many awards, Ramos was a nominee for Woman of the Year by NOW (1981); and received Presidential Recognition for Outstanding Work in Domestic Violence (1985). In 1992, two of the cities where Ramos developed shelter programs declared October 4 Domestic Violence Awareness Day in honor of Ramos' 50th birthday. Ramos holds a B.A. from New York University. (ABS)

Rand, Kathy S. (1945 –) began her activism on August 26, 1970, when she went on strike from her job and attended the Women's Strike for Equality rally in Chicago. She was PR committee chair of Chicago NOW in 1971, served as NOW's Midwest regional director (1971 –1974), and in 1973 was the founding chair of Women Employed. She was also involved in actions against AT&T and Sears. A retired PR executive, Rand holds a B.A. from Michigan State University and an M.B.A. from the Kellogg Graduate School of Management, Northwestern University.   (ABS)

Randall, Margaret (1936 –) A writer, photographer and teacher, Randall has published over 100 books, largely about women and women's issues and experiences. These include *Cuban Women Now* (The Women's Press, 1974); *Sandino's Daughters* (New Star Books, 1981); *This is About Incest* (Firebrand Books, 1987); *The Price You Pay: The Hidden Cost of Women's Relationship to Money* (Routledge, 1996); *Hunger's Table: Women Food & Politics* (Papier-Mâché Press, 1997); and *Coming Up for Air* (Pennywhistle Press, 2001). She has published numerous poems and essays about women; five books of photography, including *Women Brave in the Face of Danger* (The Crossing Press, 1985); and read her poetry and lectured on women's issues and cultural and political topics at major universities and other institutions, including Yale, Harvard, MIT and Princeton. Randall has worked nationally and internationally at numerous events on behalf of women. For example, in 1973 she was invited by the International Labor Office of the United Nations to study Peruvian women. In 1974, she was invited by the Vietnamese Women's Union to visit the Socialist Republic of North Vietnam and the liberated zone of South Vietnam, and in 1975 was invited by the Women's Commission of the Presidency to the IWY Congress in Caracas, Venezuela. She attended the UNESCO meeting on Women and Communication in Mexico City in 1982, and was the keynote speaker at the Women and the Law Conference in Chicago in 1986. She was the recipient of a 1990 Lillian Hellman and Dashiell Hammett grant for writers who have been victimized by political repression; was a member of the board, Women for a Meaningful Summit; and in 1997 received the Barbara Deming Money for Women Award. She has taught women's studies the University of New Mexico, Trinity College, Oberlin College and the University of Delaware. In 1985, after returning to the United States after 23 years in Latin America, Randall was ordered deported by the U.S. Immigration and Naturalization Service under the ideological exclusion clause of the 1952 McCarran-Walter Act. "They judged my writing subversive, and pointed to opin-

ions in a number of my books as being contrary to opinions contained in U.S. foreign policy. My case was joined by PEN International and others, and in 1989, after a series of losses at lower judicial levels, I won my citizenship back." Randall attended the University of New Mexico for one year. Archives: Center for Southwest Research, University of New Mexico, Albuquerque, NM.   (ABS)

Rando, Flavia (1943 –) was a founding member of the Gay Liberation Front (1969) and Radicalesbians (1970), and a member of numerous other lesbian/feminist and queer organizations from 1969 forward. She wrote position papers, staged dances and cultural events, designed costumes and stage sets, and worked as a member of a food co-op, the Lesbian Food Conspiracy. As a founding member of the Lesbian Artists Collective (1970s), she participated in slide shows and art exhibits in the community, and art actions including posting lesbian art in public venues. In 1978, her painting was included in A Lesbian Show, 112 Greene Street Gallery, NYC, the first show by lesbian artists in an art-world context. Rando, who holds a Ph.D. from Rutgers University, has taught women's studies and art history at Rutgers, Purdue, the University of New Mexico and Brooklyn College, CUNY. As an academic activist, she has organized and served on numerous pro-diversity, pro-feminist/lesbian/queer committees, task forces and panels, including serving as co-chair of the gay/lesbian caucus of the College Art Association and as a founding member of the Astraea Lesbian Foundation for Social Justice visual arts committee. She has lectured and published widely on feminist, lesbian and Italian American issues, and is co-editor of the *Special Issue of the Art Journal: Gay and Lesbian Presence in Art and Art History* (1997). Rando is (2006) working on a history of the lesbian and feminist art movement in the 1970s in New York City.   (ABS)

Rankin, Andrea Evelyn (1942 –) (also known as Andrea Leys and Andrea Marciano) Active in the Cortland, NY, area, Rankin was director of a family planning clinic (1975 – 2000). She initiated women's gynecological self-help, as well as an award-winning teen pregnancy program that successfully met a goal set in 1990 to reduce teen pregnancy by 33 percent in 2000. In 1977, Rankin wrote the original grant to fund a director for Aid of Women Victims of Violence, a rape and domestic violence crisis hotline and shelter that became a program of the local YWCA. She initiated a pro-choice newsletter in 1989, and continues (2005) to serve as its editor. From 1984 forward, Rankin has maintained a coalition of women's groups, including LWV, AAUW, YWCA and others, to survey and publicize local, state and federal office seekers' positions on women's issues. From 1990 –1993, she was the only woman elected to serve on the Cortland City Council, and in 1990 organized a major demonstration at the school board meeting in support of the school's counseling rules regarding teen pregnancy privacy. ("The rules had been leaked to the local right-to-life group and they were quite vocal in opposition.") Rankin, who has two children, earned a B.S. from Nazareth College of Rochester and an M.S. from Cornell University. Archives: State University of New York at Cortland Library, Cortland, NY. (ABS)

Ranney, Mary Elizabeth (1928 –) In 1972, Ranney served as chair of the Florida Association for Repeal of Abortion Laws, Lee and Collier County, and was founder of the Abortion Referral Service of Southwest Florida. In 1975, she was a founder of Planned Parenthood in Naples, and in 1976 wrote a brochure on abortion. In addition to this work, Ranney was a charter member of NOW and served as chapter president from 1975–1977. She has two children. (ABS)

Ransohoff, Priscilla (1912 – 1992) From 1972 – 1974, Ransohoff served as president of Federally Employed Women, an organization dedicated to combating sex-based discrimination among federal employees, founded in 1968 during the Nixon administration. Under Ransohoff's leadership, FEW created 11 regions that paralleled those used by the Civil Service Commission. Ransohoff appointed the first five regional coordinators.

Rapone, Anita (1942 –) A professor at SUNY Plattsburgh, Rapone was co-editor of *Notes from the Third Year*. She was also co-editor, with Anne Koedt and Ellen Levine, of *Radical Feminism* (Quadrangle Press, 1973). Included in her teaching and research areas are women in the U.S. and women's history. Rapone holds a B.A. from Tufts University (1963), an M.A. from Boston University (1965) and a Ph.D. from New York University (1981). (ABS)

Rapp, Peg – (1943 –) (also known as Peg Hickox) contributed to the women's movement through radio shows and bookstores run by collectives. In Seattle, in 1973, Rapp, Shan Ottey, Vicki Piotter and Janine Carpenter started Women's Survival Kit, a three-hour cultural feminist weekly show that ran for several years on Pacifica Radio station KRAB. They also had a one-hour news program, Women Everywhere. Rapp and Piotter also started a lesbian feminist radio show in Denver in 1974. Back in Seattle, Rapp was also part of a bookstore, It's About Time, and took that knowledge with her to be a co-founder with Kay Young and Piotter of Woman to Woman bookstore and women's center in Denver in 1974. The women's center held classes, had a referral line and put on events. Rapp also contributed articles to *Big Mama Rag*, the Denver feminist newspaper, and *Northeast Passage*. Returning East in 1983, Rapp helped form a coalition to reinitiate the custom of celebrating IWY (March 8th) as a major event in NY, and has worked with women's groups in Nicaragua and El Salvador. She now works with solidarity groups including Women in Black, dealing with Palestinian Rights; and Code Pink. (ABS)

Rapp, Sandy (1946 –) A musician and writer, Rapp performed at Chez Pat (1968 – 1969) and Three (1970 –1971) in NYC. "My original work always had a feminist edge," she says, "and I wrote some early women-to-women songs." In 1985, she was influential in gaining passage of a gay civil rights bill in East Hampton, NY, and in 1988 did the same in Suffolk County, NY. Rapp's first feminist record, Hardweather Friends, was released in 1986, and in 1991 her book on lesbian gay civil rights, *God's Country: A Case Against Theocracy*, was published by The Haworth Press. That was followed by three CDs of feminist work: We The People (1995), Flag & The Rainbow (2003), and Still Marchin' (2005). Rapp holds an M.A. from the University of Aberdeen, Scotland. (ABS)

Rasmussen, Jeri Wharton (1934 –) was a lobbyist for the ERA and reproductive rights, public affairs coordinator for Planned Parenthood of Minnesota, and executive director of the Midwest Health Center for Women, providing abortion and reproductive health services. In 1973, Rasmussen, Koryne Horbal and four other women founded the Democratic Farmer Labor Party Feminist Caucus in Minnesota. The group was responsible for initiating equal division in the party, state and nationally; held workshops across the state to teach women how to own their rights in the political process; and supported candidates who supported its goals. In 1976, the group developed the Democratic Women's Agenda and achieved the Carter-Mondale ticket. Also in 1976, Rasmussen served on the National Party Platform and worked with others for the inclusion of reproductive rights. As the director of a women's health clinic that provided abortions, Rasmussen was subjected to picketing at her home, had a cement rock thrown through her dining room window, and was stalked on her walking path and on the freeway by a city fireman. She never backed down. Eventually, she was able to obtain restraining orders so that "my home and street were protected from the continuous assaults on me and my neighbors." Also involved in the legal aspects of reproductive rights, Rasmussen testified before Judge Dooling in New York regarding the McCrae vs. Califano case on the involvement of religion, most particularly the Catholic Church, in the political process, and the impact on the rights of women on public assistance to have access to abortion services. Rasmussen, who has two children, served on the board of the National Abortion Federation for six years. Archives: Minnesota Historical Society, Saint Paul, MN. (ABS)

Ratcliff, Mary Curtis (1942 –) A California artist (2005), Ratcliff was an early feminist contributor in the media and the arts. In 1969, a radical collective that used Sony portable recorders to provide unscripted documentaries was founded in Ratcliff's Manhattan loft. The group, called Videofreex, produced over 500 videotapes. In 1974, Ratcliff's work was part of the opening exhibition of the San Francisco Women's Art Center. Among her many art pieces are hoop and ribbon sculptures created from 1974 through 1976 and used in goddess ceremonies. A 10-foot-wide wind sculpture of a woman with wings, named "Amelia" after Amelia Earhart, was used in a ceremony by Harvard women's religion scholar, Carol Christ, at the University of California at Santa Cruz in 1975. In 1974, Ratcliff and Gail Waldron produced a feminist event, "Because," using video and slides at Sonoma State University. Ratcliff joined the WCA in 1976 when it came to California. She holds a B.F.A. from the Rhode Island School of Design (1967). Archives: San Francisco Museum of Modern Art, National Museum of Women in the Arts, Washington, D.C., and the Women's Caucus for Art, New York, NY. (ABS)

Ratner, Hedy M. (1941 –) Founding co-president of Chicago's Women's Business Development Center, Ratner has been an advocate and activist for women's issues for several decades. From 1970–1976, she was board member and president of the Metropolitan Chicago YWCA. From 1971–1976, she was founder and president of the IL WPC, and from 1975–1976 was a founding member of the Midwest Women's Center. Ratner was director and convener of Chicago Women in Broadcasting (1973), and founder and first president of Women in Film, Chicago. She worked for passage and implementation of Title IX and for the ERA, and co-chaired the women's health task force that resulted in an Urban Women's Health Agenda under Chicago's Mayor Richard M. Daly. Ratner was a founding member of the Illinois Governor's Commission on the Status of Women, appointed by two governors; and founder and member for a decade of the Illinois Women's Business Ownership Council. She has been working since 1995 on women's economic empowerment, and in particular affirmative action. Ratner has also worked for CEDAW and no-fault divorce. The recipient of numerous awards and honors, Ratner is a member of the International Women's Forum, The Chicago Network, the National Council of Women's Organizations and the Federation of Women Contractors. In addition, she was a founder of the Alliance of Minority and Female Contractors Association. She received her A.B. from the University of California (1968), her M.S. from the University of Chicago (1974), and an M.Ed. from DePaul University, Chicago (1974). Archives: Chicago Historical Society, Chicago, IL. (ABS)

Raven, Arlene (1944 – 2006) (also known as Arlene Rubin and Arlene Corkery) An art historian, Raven was a founder (in the early 1970s) of the Women's Caucus for Art, the Los Angeles Woman's Building and *Chrysalis* magazine. A pioneer in progressive education, she was also an architect of the educational programs of the Feminist Studio Work-shop. She attended the Conference for Women in the Visual Arts, Washington, D.C. (1972). In 1977, she was a leader in the Feminist Educators Workshop and an originator of the Lesbian Art Project.

The author of seven books on contemporary art, Raven had selected essays published as "Crossing Over: Feminism and Art of Social Concern" in UMI Research Press' *American Art Critics* series (1988). She is an author and editor of *Feminist Art Criticism: An Anthology* (UMI, 1988); *New Feminist Art* (Harper Collins, 1993); and *Art in the Public Interest* (UMI, 1989). In addition, she is an author of *Exposures: Women and Their Art* (New Sage, 1989). Her monographs are *Nancy Grossman* (Hillwood Art Museum, 1991) and *June Wayne: Tunnel of the Senses* (Neuberger Museum, 1997). She wrote for *Women's Review of Books* for 15 years. Raven, who holds an M.F.A., M.A. and Ph.D., received an Honorary Degree from Hood College (H.H.D.) in 1979, and the Lifetime Achievement Award, Women's Caucus for Art, College Art Assn. (1999).

(ABS before death)

Ravitz, Allyn Carol (1942 –) An attorney with many "firsts" to her credit, Ravitz has worked both inside and outside the courts to decrease violence against women, to increase their access to equal credit and housing, and to further their participation in the political process. A collaborator in the writing of Stop Rape, a booklet by Women Against Rape for Detroit's first conference on rape (1971), Ravitz was the first lawyer in Michigan "and quite possibly the entire U.S." to jury-try a sexual harassment case. Ravitz won the case, filed in 1976, and obtained an award of almost $190,000. In 1975, Ravitz was a founding member and steering committee member of the women's defense and education committee for Joanne Little and Inez Garcia—two women accused of killing their rapists. From 1976 – 1977, Ravitz served on the board of the Sexual Crisis Center, appointed by Detroit Mayor Coleman Young. In 1972, Ravitz was a law clerk for Michigan's first all-women law firm. In 1973, she became a founding member and board member of the first women's credit union, The Feminist Federal Credit Union, and helped draft Detroit's human rights ordinance to prohibit discrimination against any person because of sex or age. She also helped draft the Women and Credit Act of Michigan (1973 – 1974), and was a leader of the feminist lobbying effort for its passage, which occurred in 1974. A member of Detroit NOW's credit discrimination team, she met with department stores and banks to try to get them to change discriminatory practices (1973 – 1974). In 1975, she drafted legislation (passed in 1975), that extended the Fair Housing Act of Michigan to prohibit discrimination in housing on the basis of sex, age, marital status and handicap—which meant that women and women or men with children could not be denied housing. In 1977, she was a presenter at Focus: Michigan Women, appointed by the National Commission for the Observance of IWY, to plan and administer this meeting. A recipient of the 1978 Detroit City Council's Spirit of Detroit Award, Ravitz was a founding member and board member of Michigan Women's Campaign Fund (1986) and a founding member of the Mable Dingeman Dinner Committee for

R

Women, which raises money for that fund. Ravitz, who has three children, earned her B.A. from Smith College in 1964, and is a 1972 graduate of the University of Detroit School of Law. (ABS)

Rawalt, Marguerite (1895 –1989) A U.S. Government lawyer, Rawalt was appointed to the President's Commission on the Status of Women (1961), and was the lone voice on that commission in support of the ERA. Rawalt was a member of the Citizens Advisory Council on the Status of Women, established in 1963. A charter member of NOW (1966), she served as the first chair of NOW's legal committee and represented women in the first appellate test cases under Title VII. Rawalt was also an original incorporator of NOW LDEF, a charter member of WEAL, and served as president of WEAL Educational and Legal Defense Fund. She served as chair of its committee on civil and political rights. She was active in the National Federation of Business and Professional Women, the National Association of Women Lawyers and the NWP. Rawalt was the author of numerous articles for the organizations she worked with, graduated from Bayview College, the University of Texas and George Washington University Law School. Her biography, *Be Somebody, A Biography of Marguerite Rawalt,* was written by Judith Patterson (Eakin Press). Archives: Schlesinger Library, Radcliffe Institute, Cambridge, MA.

Rawles, Beth – See Gibbs, Beth

Raymond, Janice G. (1943 –) A professor, Raymond taught hundreds of students in the women's studies program at the University of Massachusetts, Amherst, from 1975 – 2002. She is the author of *A Passion for Friends* (Beacon Press, 1986), one of the first books on the political dimensions of women's friendships, and *Women as Wombs: Reproductive Technology and the Battle Over Women's Freedom* (Spinifex Press, 1998). In 1994, she became co-director of the Coalition Against Trafficking in Women, and helped expand its work against prostitution, sex trafficking and the global sex industry in the Philippines, Venezuela, Mexico, Bangladesh, Nigeria, Europe, the Republic of Georgia, Russia, Estonia, Canada, Australia and the U.S. Also active in the peace and civil rights movements, Raymond holds a B.A. from Salve Regina College, an M.A. from Andover Newton and a Ph.D. from Boston College. (ABS)

Read, Diana Sue (1944 –) (also known as Diana S. Martin) marched for the ERA in Richmond, VA, in 1973 and 1974. In 1973, she was one of four people to work with a union organizer to get a union started for secretaries and other nonexempt employees at The Mitre Corporation in McLean, VA. The author of *Layoffs, Revenge* and *Witchfire*, novels about women, Read has been active in the pro-choice movement and has worked to elect feminist candidates. She has three children. (ABS)

Read, Sister Joel (1925 –) A member of the School Sisters of St. Francis, Read served as president of Alverno College from 1968 to 2003, earning a reputation as one of the most notable educational reform advocates in the nation. Under her leadership, Alverno became a nationally recognized model of innovative curriculum and leadership training for women. It was the first college in the Milwaukee area to offer weekend courses for women not of traditional student age, and it offered a high level of interaction between students and faculty so that the women students sometimes complicated lives could be taken into account. During Read's tenure, the Alverno campus saw a lot of feminist activity and was the site for many feminist conferences and seminars. In 1966, Read attended the organizing conference of NOW and served on its first board. She chaired the Commission on the Status of Education of Women for the American Association of Colleges, and was president of the National Forum for Women. She was also a founding member of Wisconsin Women in Higher Education Leadership. Active in Milwaukee and WI civic affairs, she advocated for the hiring and promotion of women in area businesses. She was also a presidential appointee to the U.S. Commission for the Celebration of International Women's Year (1975 –1976). Read has served as president of the American Association for Higher Education as well as on the boards of the Foundation for Independent Higher Education, the American Council for Education, the Association of American Colleges and Universities, the National Catholic Education Association and other educational associations. The recipient of many honors and awards, Read was invited to the White House by two presidents to discuss education. A Fellow of the American Academy of Arts and Sciences and the Wisconsin Academy of Sciences, Arts and Letters, Read holds Honorary Degrees from Lakeland College (1972), Wittenberg University (1976), Marymount Manhattan College (1981), DePaul University (1985), Northland College (1986), State University of New York (1986), Lawrence University (1997), and Marquette University (2003). (ABS)

Reagon, Bernice Johnson (1942 –) Composer, singer, historian, music producer, author, and cultural activist, Reagon has been a major voice for freedom and justice for more than 40 years, addressing racism and organized inequities of all kinds. "It is crucial that the world knows what it looks like to African American women," she says, expressing the philosophical core of the work of Sweet Honey In The Rock, an internationally renowned a cappella ensemble of African American women singers she founded in 1973 in Washington, D.C. This ensemble, formed out of her vocal workshop at the DC Black Repertory Theatre Company, became a major African American music voice within the women's cultural network of the 1970s. Identifying herself as a radical black woman, Reagon consciously positioned this ensemble within the trajectory of the African American struggle for justice in

America. In the early years of Sweet Honey In The Rock, the group chose to be a part of the radical women cultural networks, performing in women-only spaces while at the same time maintaining their work and presence within the black cultural movement and other progressive struggles of that period. Reagon made it clear through her work and repertoire that homosexual partners and families would be welcomed within the group's community. For Sweet Honey In The Rock's inclusion of a Sign language interpreter as a member of the ensemble, Reagon was awarded an Honorary Doctorate from Gallaudet University, the major higher education institution for the Deaf. A child of Southwest Georgia, Reagon's career of activism began in the early 1960s with her participation in the in the civil rights movement while a college student at Albany State College in Albany, GA. (She was later expelled for taking part in a demonstration for which she and others were jailed). In 1964 she was a member of the original SNCC Freedom Singers formed in 1962 by SNCC field secretary Cordell H. Reagon. In 1966, she was a founding member of the Atlanta-based a capella ensemble Harambee Singers, a major voice in the expanding Black Consciousness Movement. Reagon has served as music consultant, composer, and performer for film and video projects, including the award-winning *Eyes on the Prize*, the Emmy-winning *We Shall Overcome*, and the feature film *Beloved*. Reagon's research and teaching career includes the 2002 – 2004 Cosby Chair Professor of Fine Arts at Spelman College. Reagon is also Professor Emeritus of History at American University and Curator Emeritus at the Smithsonian Institution National Museum of American History. Among Reagon's numerous awards are a MacArthur Fellowship, the Heinz Award for the Arts and Humanities, the Leeway National Award for Women in the Arts, and the 1995 Presidential Medal for contribution to public understanding of the Humanities. Reagon received her B.A. in History from Spelman College (1970), and her Ph.D. from Howard University (1975). (ABS)

Reame, Nancy Elizabeth (1947 –) (also known as Nancy Elizabeth King) A new RN in 1969 and working in a Catholic hospital in Michigan where abortion was illegal, Reame subsequently volunteered at Planned Parenthood of Detroit (1971). Since that time, she has worked consistently in the area of women's health and reproduction. She served on the advisory work group to the NIH Women's Health Initiative, as advisor to the Boston Women's Health Book Collective and as co-author of *Our Bodies, Ourselves*, and as scientific editor for the 2002 book by the National Women's Health Network, *The Truth About Hormone Replacement Therapy*. In the early 1980s, she served on the FDA task force that set the standards for tampon absorbency following the first outbreaks of menstruation-related toxic shock syndrome. Reame is the first holder of the Rhetaugh Graves Dumas Endowed Chair in Nursing and Health Care Systems at the University of Michigan Health System. She has been a faculty member of the School of Nursing since 1980 and a research scientist in the multidisciplinary Reproductive Sciences Program since 1990. From 1990 – 1995, she served as director of the National Center for Infertility Research at Michigan. Reame earned her B.S.N. from Michigan State University, her M.S.N. from Wayne State University, and her Ph.D. from Wayne State University's School of Medicine. She has been a visiting scholar at Stanford's Institute for Research on Women and Gender, and in 1997 was the Academy of Nursing Scholar in Residence at the Institute of Medicine. In 1998, she was inducted into the Institute of Medicine and elected as a Fellow of the American Association for the Advancement of Science in 2001. Reame has two children. (ABS)

Reckitt, Lois Galgay (1944 –) was co-founder of Southern Maine NOW (1971), NOW's first chapter in that state. She served as its second president, then in 1973 co-founded ME NOW. She instigated Maine's first gay/lesbian rights campaign (1975) and was a co-founder of the Maine Women's Lobby (1978). Although Reckitt worked extensively with NOW, serving, for example, as national board member (1976 – 1987) and executive VP (1984 –1987), it was her work with domestic abuse services that led to her induction into the Maine Women's Hall of Fame (1998). Since 1979, she has been a trainer/presenter on domestic violence issues throughout the state. She served as chair of the Maine Coalition for Family Crisis Services (1982 – 1983), and was the Maine representative to the National Steering Committee of the National Coalition on Domestic Violence (1983 – 1984). From 1986 –1987, she was coordinator of the National Resource Kit on Violence Against Women (through NOW), and from 1990 – 1992 was chair of NOW's pornography committee. From 1990 – 1991, Reckitt served as legislative chair of the Maine Coalition for Family Crisis Services, and from 1994 –1996 was chair of the Maine Commission on Domestic Abuse. She continues (2005) to work to end abuse against women. Reckitt is the recipient of numerous awards, including the Progress Award from the Maine Commission for Women (1991) and the F.E. Pentlage Award from the Maine Lesbian and Gay Political Alliance (2000). Reckitt holds a B.A. from Brandeis University (1966), an M.A. from Boston University (1968), and is a graduate of the Institute for Civic Leadership, Maine (1997). (ABS)

Reddy, Helen (1941 –) was the musical muse of the second-wave feminist movement. In 1972, "I Am Woman," which Reddy wrote (to music by Ray Burton) became the unofficial anthem of the movement. With Reddy's stirring opening lyrics, "I Am Woman, Hear Me Roar," and the chorus, "I Am Strong, I Am Invincible, I Am Woman," the song helped raise women's feminist consciousness around the world. The Capitol Record was a number-one best seller and won Reddy a Grammy for

R

Best Female Pop Vocal Performance. When she accepted the award, Reddy pointedly thanked God "because She makes everything possible." In 1975, the United Nations adopted "I Am Woman" as the theme for International Women's Year. Two decades later, Reddy performed the song at the opening ceremonies of Feminist Expo 96 for Women's Empowerment in Washington, D.C. Reddy was an early participant in the feminist movement during the 1970s, working to raise funds for NOW's ERA drive. She opened her house for a Rape Treatment Center fundraiser in Los Angeles, and made many appearances at NOW chapters across the country. Reddy says her own muse was Lillian Roxon, an expatriate Australian rock critic and pioneer feminist. Born in Melbourne, Australia, Reddy was on stage with her Vaudevillian parents at the age of four. A single mother at 24, she emigrated to the U.S. with her daughter, Traci, in 1966. Active in community affairs, Reddy served three years on the National Women's History Museum's board of directors and as commissioner of parks and recreation for the state of California. Reddy lives (2006) in Australia and serves on the board of directors of Sydney's Royal Hospital for Women. (ABS)

Redfield, Elaine – See Livingston, Elaine

Redman, Helen Barchilon (1940 –) Since 1962, Redman has been "creating, teaching and presenting female art that explores body image, personal identity and life cycle experience." This has included pregnancies, deaths, children, grandchildren, menopause and aging. Believing that the personal is political, she has worked to use art as a source for self-understanding and healing since the early 1970s. She has fought to gain support and recognition for women in the arts, for hiring women in universities, and for including women artists in art history. She has taught art at the University of Colorado, the University of Iowa and the Community College of Denver. She also helped curate and create exhibitions for women as the co-founder (1974) of Front Range Women in the Visual Arts in Boulder, CO. In 1992 she founded and served as the first president of the San Diego Women's Caucus for Art. She also trained with Betsy Damon to lead No Limits for Women Artists. Since 1994, she has been presenting workshops in her San Diego studio to "empower old women and women of all ages to secure the material and symbolic space necessary to compose the diverse narratives of their own creativity." Her ongoing series of art on menopause and female aging, Birthing the Crone, has been exhibited at universities across the country. Redman has two children and holds an M.F.A. from the University of Colorado (1963). (ABS)

Reece, Gene Kornfeld (1941 –) Born in Kansas City, MO, Reece graduated from Texas Christian University in 1963, and by the end of the decade had joined the women's movement. In September 1969 she moved to the Bronx and became involved in the Bronx Coalition, a group of left-leaning-to-radical men and women doing community service. Inevitably, the women in the group left to form Bronx Women's Liberation, which focused on community health issues; they offered free pelvic and breast exams and Pap smears, and solicited and donated the services of doctors and nurse/midwives. The group also offered free classes advocating self-help/self-exam concepts. When Montefiore Hospital (NYC) was hoping to build an abortion clinic, it invited BWL to be involved in the planning and running of what ultimately became the Bronx Community Center for Women's Health. Until 1980 Reece was also working with Bronx Women Against Rape as a rape crisis intervention counselor on call several nights a week. Subsequently, she was recruited into the Albert Einstein Hospital's Gynecological Teaching Associates program, and she and a few others pioneered a program that is now an integral part of nearly every medical school's curriculum in physical diagnosis. Since September 1976, Reece has been a client representative in the area of Equal Employment Opportunity and Affirmative Action. Most recently, she has been an instructor for breast exams in a number of workshops sponsored by the American Cancer Society in conjunction with the New York State Department of Health. (ABS)

Reese, Lyn Johnson (1938 –) has worked in education since the early 1970s to expand the availability of women's history in social studies courses. In 1972, she was an education developer for the women's studies program for the public schools of Berkeley, CA, the first of only two such public school efforts in the U.S. in the 1970s. Reese worked primarily with elementary school teachers until the program's demise. At the same time, she worked on a U.S. Department of Education Women's Educational Equity Act program to produce curriculum materials for women's history (published in 1976 – 1977), and a WEEA high school project called *Sources of Strength: Women and Culture, A Teachers Guide* (1978). In 1985, Reese received a WEEA grant to develop *Women in World History: An Annotated Bibliography for Teachers*. Following its publication, Reese served for two years as director of the Mathematics and Science Sex Desegregation Project for the public schools of Novato, CA. Reese is co-author of *I'm On My Way Running: Women Speak on Coming of Age* (Avon Press, 1983), and has assisted in creating school material for various projects such as the University of California, Berkeley, Emma Goldman papers, the Berkeley Repertory production of the life of Mother Jones, a CD on women scientists, and the film "Hearts and Hands: Quilts in the Lives of 19th Century Women." She has also contributed various articles about women's history to educational journals. Since 1986, Reese has directed the Women in World History Curriculum Project, for which she has created 16 units for middle to high school levels. She is (2005) developing content for San Francisco's International Museum of Women, scheduled to open in 2008. Reese, who has two children, earned her B.A. from Mt. Holyoke College and her M.A. from Stanford University. (ABS)

Register, Cheri L. (1945 –) (also known as Cheryl R. De Jong) A writer, teacher of creative writing and freelance editor, Register was a member of the graduate women's CR group at the University of Chicago (1968); of the Twin Cities Female Liberation Group (1969 – 1972), for which she did public speaking and worked on the newsletter; and Women Against Male Supremacy (1970 – 1972). She was co-founder (with Gerri Perreault) of the Emma Willard Task Force on Education (1970 – 1975), and served as co-ordinator of the University of Idaho's Women's Center (1973 – 1974). In addition, Register taught in the University of Minnesota's women's studies program (1974 – 1980) and was part of the Women's Literature Research Project in Uppsala, Sweden (1978 – 1982). Register was also a founder of the Anne Hutchinson Circle (1984 – 1988). In 1988, she became a member of the national pornography task force of the Presbyterian Church USA. Register, who participated in numerous actions to further women's rights, helped organize a sit-in at the Minnesota Human Rights Commission (1969) to persuade it to add sexism to the list of discriminatory practices, and also met with the Minnesota Dept. of Education to lobby for the inclusion of sexism in the department's sensitivity training workshops for teachers. Register has published numerous essays, articles and book reviews on women, and wrote the books *Mothers, Saviors, Peacemakers: Swedish Women Writers in the Twentieth Century* (University of Uppsala, Sweden, 1983) and *Women's Liberation and Literature in the United States and Sweden* (Raben & Sjogren, 1977). She was also co-author of the handbook *Sexism in Education* (1972). In addition, Register provided the conceptual organization and text for a traveling photo exhibit, "Courageous Enough: A Photohistory of Finnish Women in America" (1985). Register, who has two children, earned her B.A., M.A. and Ph.D. from the University of Chicago. Archives: Minnesota Historical Society, St. Paul, MN. (ABS)

Reichert, Carol Lynda (1941 –) An educator and organizer, Reichert joined Mid-Hudson NOW (Poughkeepsie, NY) in 1974, and from 1974 – 1978 organized participation in ERA activities such as national marches and local parades and debates. In 1978 she served as Mid-Hudson NOW reproductive rights chair, and co-founded the Mid-Hudson coalition for free choice. From 1978 – 1980, Reichert served as president of Mid-Hudson NOW; from 1979 – 1983 she was chair of NY NOW's reproductive rights task force; and from 1980 – 1983 was a member of national NOW's conference implementation committee on reproductive rights. Co-president of Albany, NY, NOW from 1982 – 1983, she was a founding member of the Eleanor Roosevelt Democratic Club of Albany (1983 – 1996) to advance lesbian and gay civil rights. From 1984 – 1993, Reichert served as organizer for the passage of the City of Albany Human Rights Ordinance, which prohibits discrimination of the basis of sexual orientation. The ordinance passed in 1993. From 1986 – 1994, Reichert was a member of the governor's task force on lesbian and gay issues in Albany, NY (appointed by Governor Mario Cuomo), and from 1986 – 1996 was director of the women's studies internship program at the State University of New York at Albany. She became a member of the board of the Family Planning Advocates of New York State in 1999. Reichert earned her B.S. from the State University of New York at New Paltz and her M.A. from Teachers College, Columbia University. (ABS)

Reichert, Julia Bell (1946 –) An award-winning, independent documentary film maker since 1970, Reichert was twice nominated for Academy Awards: for "Seeing Red" (1983), a documentary about the lives of American Communists; and for "Union Maids" (1976), a look at the early labor movement as related in the stories of three working-class women. The five films she created with former partner James Klein (including the above and "Growing Up Female," "Methadone: An American Way of Dealing," and "Men's Lives") have been screened at most international film festivals, including the New York, Telluride, Sundance and Berlin Festivals. Reichert began her feminist work at Antioch College as a member of a CR group (1968) and as host of feminist radio shows on WYSO-FM (1969). She was also a founder of the Antioch College Women's Center (1969). In addition, she attended the Miss America demonstration and the march on the Pentagon in the late 1960s. After making the film "Growing Up Female" (1970), Reichert traveled to many cities to set up screenings in living rooms, church basements, schools and universities, a process that was occurring as the women's movement was spreading across the U.S. Reichert was also a co-founder of New Day Films, a feminist co-op for the distribution of independent films (1971), and a founder of Dayton's Women's Center in the early 1970s, where she taught classes for women in photography. Chosen as one of *Ms.* magazine's significant women in the early 1970s, Reichert was part of the first International Women's Film Festival in NYC. In the late 1970s, she hosted many screenings for the film "Union Maids" in Europe and the U.S., including some on picket lines and for worker education. In 1976, She was a member of the steering committee, National Socialist-Feminist Conference. She has one child and graduated from Antioch College in 1970. She has won many awards, grants and fellowships for her work. (ABS)

Reid, Coletta (1943 –) (also known as Coletta Reid Holcomb) A publisher, editor and writer, Reid helped found two feminist newspapers and a publishing house. In late 1969, she co-founded feminist newspaper *Off Our Backs*, in Washington, D.C., and in late 1971 co-founded *The Furies*, also in D.C. Reid wrote for both these newspapers. She also served on the editorial committee for the feminist issue of *Motive* magazine. In 1972, Reid co-founded Diana Press, a lesbian-feminist publishing house and printing press in Baltimore, MD. She served as publisher and editor of the press for seven years. Reid also contributed to several books published by Diana Press, including *Women Remembered, Class and Feminism* and *Lesbianism and the Women's Movement*. In late 1975, Reid co-founded the Feminist Economic Network and the Women's Building, in Detroit, MI. (ABS)

Reif, Patricia (1929 – 2002) A nun, Reif founded the master's program in feminist spirituality at the Immaculate Heart College Center (1984). Her work as a scholar and her vision of how to implement feminist values was central to the religious community at Immaculate Heart—a group descended from an order that had pushed for reforms and strongly disagreed with the Los Angeles diocese in the 1960s. Active in many social justice issues, Reif was also a founding member of the Los Angeles Interfaith Hunger Coalition and the Interfaith task force on Central America, and worked against domestic abuse and poverty. Reif, who received a Ph.D. from St. Louis University, chaired the graduate department of religious studies at Immaculate Heart College in Hollywood for 10 years. She also taught at St. Bernardine's School in San Bernardino and at Immaculate Heart High School in Los Angeles. In addition, she was a member of the board of Uncommon Ground, a program that enables young lawyers to assist the poor. Following Reif's death, the Immaculate Heart Community and the CGU School of Religion created and funded the Patricia A. Reif Memorial Lecture Fund.

Reiff, Maureen – See Hickey-Reiff, Maureen Anne

Reitz, Rosetta (1924 –) joined NYRW in 1971, and later became a founding member of OWL. She facilitated menopause workshops, which led to her book *Menopause, A Positive Approach* (Penguin, 1977). A Book of the Month selection, published around the world, and in print for 20 years, the book showed menopause as a natural function not automatically requiring medication. A jazz buff, Reitz wondered why jazz was seen as a male domain; to preserve the work of the black women musicians who had recorded on the old 78-rpm records, she launched Rosetta Records in 1980, a company she ran for 17 years. In addition, she taught about women in jazz at the New School for five years. To build the image of women jazz musicians, Reitz produced all-women jazz concerts at Avery Fisher Hall (1980) and the Hollywood Bowl (1981). In 1982, she produced shows at Carnegie Hall and Avery Fisher Hall. Also in 1982, Reitz became one of the first recipients of The Wonder Woman Award, and in 1994 received a Grandmother Winifred grant. In 1986, Reitz was co-producer of a film about The International Sweethearts of Rhythm, a hot women's band during WWII, and was creative consultant for a Hollywood film about them. Reitz has three children. (ABS)

Remetier, Florika – See Florika

Rennie, Susan (1939 –) A member of NYRF (1971 – 1974), Rennie was a founding committee member of the Barnard College Women's Center (1971) and an organizer of the Columbia Conference on Straight/Gay Issues in the Women's Movement. She was also editor, with Kirsten Grimstad, of *New Women's Survival Catalog* (1972) and *New Women's Survival Sourcebook* (1974). Rennie and Grimstad traveled the country interviewing women in collectives, bookstores and rape crisis centers, and at women's newspapers, magazines and health groups. She talked to women writers, musicians, farmers, political activists, entrepreneurs and more, with the result that the two books essentially document the activities of the women's movement nationally during its foundation period. Earlier (1971 – 1972), Rennie served as assistant VP for academic affairs at Columbia University. During that time she was the administration representative on a committee with Ruth Bader Ginsburg, "whose staunch defense of women's rights was already evident," says Rennie. Rennie was able to use her office to help establish the Columbia Seminar on Women. A professor, Rennie holds a Ph.D. from Columbia University. (ABS)

Retter, Yolanda G. (1947 –) is a lesbian history and visibility activist, a librarian/archivist, bookseller and university lecturer. She manages the Lesbian History Project Web site and the UCLA Chicano Studies Research Center Library and Archive. She has managed a lesbian archive and is a diversity consultant for various archives and publishing projects. She describes herself as "an itinerant community worker, a lifelong Latina lesbian working for lesbians and women of all colors." Retter, who holds an M.L.S., M.S.W. and Ph.D., wrote her dissertation on lesbian feminist activism in Los Angeles, 1970–1990. She was a member of Lesbian Feminists (L.A.); manager of the Women's Liberation House (L.A. 1972); director of the Rape Hotline. (Pasadena, 1977–1978); co-founder of the Los Angeles Women's Yellow Pages (1977); and helped organize lesbian and feminist events and marches beginning in 1971. She was also a member of Latin American Lesbians (Los Angeles), one of the earliest lesbians of color groups in the U.S. (1974). Retter provided security for many events, including Alice Doesn't (Los Angeles, 1975), and was a Sergeant at Arms at the National Women's Conference, Houston (1977). As a member of Lesbians of Color (L.A.), she helped organize the first National Lesbians of Color conference (1983). She has co-edited two books on LGBT history and culture. (ABS)

Reubens, Claire – See Roerden, Chris

Reuss, Patricia Blau (1942 –) began her work for women's rights in Montana (1972 – 1977), where she helped start the Bozeman and Helena WPC, and was the chief lobbyist for passing the implementing legislation after Montana included the ERA in its state constitution. From 1977 – 1979, she reinvigorated the Boulder and Colorado WPC, and was coordinator for the volunteers at the 1977 National Women's Conference in Houston. After moving to Washington, D.C., in 1979, Reuss became the lobbyist for WEAL, leading the effort to pass COBRA, and save Title IX and pension reforms for women, among other achievements. In 1991, she opened the Washington, D.C., policy shop for NOW LDEF, and led the effort to pass the Violence Against Women Act, to soften the blows of the Welfare Act of 1996, and to pass FACE, the anti-clinic violence bill. Says Muriel Fox, "Pat was the guiding spirit of WEAL in the early days, then ran the D.C. office for NOW LDEF. Everyone gives Pat credit for getting the Violence Against Women Act passed. She created the coalition that pushed it through and personally persuaded both Joe Biden and Orrin Hatch to promote it." Reuss, who has three children, is (2006) working at NOW mobilizing and organizing the grassroots around feminist issues. A policy analyst, she holds a master's in public administration. (ABS)

Reverby, Susan Mokotoff (1946 –) A Wellesley College women's studies professor (2005), Reverby was sensitized to the women's movement in the late 1960s. With a background in the anti-war and civil rights movements, she supported the struggles of women of color in a multiracial Lower East Side, NYC community. Reverby became a champion of women's health. She worked at one of the first abortion clinics in NYC when the law changed in 1970, and then participated in critiques of the health system while working at the Health Policy Advisory Center, a New-Left think tank. Reverby wrote and spoke across the country on abortion, women's health and women health-care workers. She also testified on abortion issues; was involved with Helen Rodriguez-Trias and others in the beginning of the organizing around sterilization abuse; and worked with both the New York Women's Health and Abortion Project and HealthRight. In 1973, Reverby left for a year in West Virginia, where she was involved in issues affecting women workers. In 1974, she was a delegate to the founding convention of the Coalition of Labor Union Women (one of two from WV). Reverby, who has two children, earned her B.S. from Cornell University, NYS School of Industrial and Labor Relations (1967), her M.A. from New York University (1973), and her Ph.D. from Boston University (1982). (ABS)

Reyes, Barbara Carol – See Sandstrom, Boden

Ribner, Susan C. (1940 –) A writer, teacher and martial artist and instructor, Ribner has been writing on women's history, the martial arts and human rights since the late 1960s (initially under the pseudonym Rebecca Moon). During the 1970s she was a staff member of the Council on Interracial Books for Children, promoting children's books free of gender and racial stereotypes. From 1974 –

1988 she was the founder, director and chief instructor of the Women's Center Karate Club (NYC). She was also instrumental in forming the NY-based Women's Martial Arts Union and its outgrowth, the National Women's Martial Arts Federation. Because of her intense interest in fighting disciplines, Ribner "developed a passion for uncovering the women-warrior heroes of world history and legend, most of whom had been written out of the history books." Her third book for young adults is *In Search of Women Warriors*. She was awarded residencies at The Millay Colony for the Arts and Cummington Community of the Arts for work on this book. Ribner, who participated in the Fourth World Conference on Women in Beijing (1995), holds a B.A. and M.A. from Cornell University; an M.A. in Teaching English to Students of Other Languages from Hunter College; and an M.F.A. (ABS)

Rich, Adrienne (1929 –) is a poet with a passion for political issues including feminism, lesbianism, Jewish identity, racism, poverty and war. Since the selection in 1951 of Rich's first volume, *A Change of World* (Yale University Press, 1951) by W.H. Auden for the Yale Younger Poets Prize, her work evolved from closed forms to a poetics of change, rooted in a radical imagination and politics. Besides 16 volumes of poetry, her prose works include *Of Woman Born: Motherhood as Experience and Institution*; the essay collections *On Lies, Secrets and Silence* and *Blood, Bread and Poetry*; *What Is Found There: Notebooks on Poetry and Politics* (1993) and *Arts of the Possible: Essays and Conversations* (2001). Her work has been translated into many languages including Dutch, German, Japanese, Hebrew, Italian, French, Spanish, Hungarian, Croatian and Chinese. Rich was editor of *Best American Poetry 1996*, and of Muriel Rukeyser's *Selected Poems* (Library of America, 2004). Her work has received many awards including the Ruth Lilly Prize, the Wallace Stevens Award, the *Los Angeles Times* Book Award, the Lambda Literary Award, the Lenore Marshall/*Nation* Award, a MacArthur Fellowship, the Lannan Literary Foundation Lifetime Achievement Award, the Bollingen Prize and the National Book Critics Circle Award in poetry. She has lived in New England, New York City, and for over 20 years in California. She has three sons. Archives: Schlesinger Library, Radcliffe Institute, Cambridge, MA. (ABS)

Richmond-Covey, Jill (1944 –) (also known as Jill Orear and Jill O. Richmond) was a case aide in the social work department at St. Luke's/Women's Hospital in Manhattan in 1968. There she ran the birth control clinic and group for women who chose to have an abortion, and there she learned "from the inside out how important choice is, real choice." In 1969, Richmond-Covey was a social worker for the Newhallville office of New Haven, CT, Department of Urban Renewal, working primarily with women. After receiving her master's degree in social work from the University of Connecticut (1971), Richmond-Covey

R

worked for a crisis service in Provincetown, MA, and later volunteered at a crisis service in Cambridge, MA. Her focus was helping women get the mental health services they needed. A therapist in private practice in Cambridge from 1972–1977, she helped many women "claim their lives, deal with difficult issues and keep on keeping on." From 1978–1981 Richmond-Covey was a consultant with the Hartford Rape Crisis Service, and in 1978 became a private therapist, "working as a partner with individual women and men to help them become more of themselves, to accept themselves, to move beyond gender stereotypes, beyond childhood pain and limitations, and to interact with others in a truly respectful and compassionate way." Richmond-Covey has two children.   (ABS)

Rickey, Carrie (1952 –) A journalist, Rickey was an early supporter of the Woman's Building in Los Angeles in the mid 1970s, and hosted programs of films by women such as Yvonne Rainer. She was a member of the Heresies Collective from the mid 1970s into the 1980s, and was an art critic at The *Village Voice* from 1979–1980. There, she published the essay "Why Can't Women Express Themselves," which asked why the Expressionist art shows of that time excluded women artists. As a film critic at The *Village Voice* from 1980–1983, Rickey reviewed many films by emerging feminist filmmakers. In 1986, she was moderator and host for two panels for the Guerrilla Girls at Cooper Union. As a film critic at *The Philadelphia Inquirer* (1986 –) she has published many essays about movies by women, as well as the difficulties encountered by actresses and filmmakers in Hollywood—sexism, racism, typecasting of women as mothers and whores, etc. Rickey has served as a mentor to high school and college women interested in pursuing careers in journalism and film; taught courses that examined sexual and gender stereotyping at Rutgers University (Camden) and the University of Pennsylvania; and contributed a chapter to *The Trump of Feminist Art* (Abrams, 1994). Rickey, who has one child and one stepchild, has also supported NARAL and Planned Parenthood. She holds a B.A. and M.F.A. from the University of California, San Diego. (ABS)

Riddiough, Christine Ruth (1946 –) From 1970–1977, Riddiough was an activist and leader in the CWLU. She worked on the Liberation School for Women, founded the Blazing Star lesbian group, and was a staff person, steering committee member/planning committee member. At that time, she also wrote *Lesbianism and Socialist Feminism*. From 1974–1975, she was a member of the planning committee for the Yellow Springs Socialist Feminist Conference, where she spoke on lesbian feminism. From 1976–1978 Riddiough served as co-chair of the Gay and Lesbian Coalition of Metropolitan Chicago, and in 1980 was co-chair of the Illinois gay and lesbian task force. She served as lesbian action director for NOW from 1983–1985, and was chair of the Democratic Socialists of America Feminist Commission/DSA board

member, from 1985–1990. From 1992–1998, she served as VP for North America, Socialist International Women. In addition to this work, she served as staff and consultant/board member of the National Association of Gay and Lesbian Democratic Clubs (later Gay and Lesbian Democrats of America) from 1992–1998, and from 1986–1988 was chair of the Gertrude Stein Democratic Club, Washington, D.C. She also served as political director, Democratic Socialists of America, from 1996–1998, and from 2002–2005 as treasurer for Americans for Democratic Action. Riddiough, who is a technical trainer/instructor, holds a B.A. from Carleton College and an M.S. from Northwestern University, Evanston, IL.   (ABS)

Riddle, Dorothy I. (1944 –) A psychology professor and an advocate for women business owners, Riddle introduced feminist analysis at the College of William & Mary (1968) by creating and teaching a seminar titled Psychology of Social Issues. During this time, she traveled frequently to Washington, D.C., to lobby for the ERA and pressure the American Psychological Association to address women's issues fully. In the early 1970s, she spoke and wrote on women's health, sexuality and sex roles, and developed and taught courses on these topics. In 1971, Riddle founded the first B.A.-granting women's studies program at Richmond College (now the College of Staten Island, CUNY). She was appointed to the first CUNY affirmative action committee and "had the pleasure, as the only woman, to decline to take the minutes of committee meetings until all male colleagues had each had a turn." In 1973, in Tucson, AZ, she co-founded a feminist counseling service for women and their families, as well as a feminist astrology service. In 1974, Riddle was appointed to the APA task force on gays and lesbians, and subsequently developed the Riddle Homophobia Scale. She received an M.B.A. from the University of Arizona in 1980, and in 1996, three years after immigrating to Canada, became the first Canadian appointed by the prime minister to the Asia Pacific Economic Cooperation (APEC) Business Advisory Council. Riddle began a second career advocating for women business owners. Between 1997 and 1999, she helped organize the first trade missions between Canada and the U.S. for women business owners. In addition to her M.B.A., Riddle has a B.A. from the University of Colorado and a Ph.D. from Duke University.   (ABS)

Riegle, Rosalie (1937 –) (also known as Rosalie Riegle Troester) An early member of the Michigan Women's Studies Association, Riegle served as a board member and VP, and also edited for them *Historic Women of Michigan: A Sesquicentennial Celebration* (1987). A grant from the Michigan Council of the Humanities allowed the women to place the book in libraries throughout the state. As an adjunct professor at Saginaw Valley State College, beginning in 1969, Riegle taught several early women's studies courses and was active in the Chrysalis Center, for returning women students. As a resident of Saginaw, Riegle helped found a rape crisis center and the underground railroad for victims of domestic violence. She also led a bus tour to Chicago for Judy Chicago's exhibition The Dinner Party, and later coordinated local quilt-making to accompany that exhibit. Riegle also worked on "The Red Shawl," a short-lived newsletter of the Saginaw feminist movement. A retired professor of English and oral historian, Riegle holds a Doctor of Arts from the University of Michigan (1983). Archives: Saginaw Valley State University, University Center, MI. (ABS)

Ries, Jennie Lifrieri (1932 –) joined Southern Westchester (NY) NOW in 1972, where she served as chair of the CR task force and chair of the abortion rights task force. A practicing Roman Catholic at that time, she was in demand statewide as a pro-choice speaker. As president of her chapter from 1981 – 1983, she served as campaign manager for the ERA countdown. Ries became a member of Catholics for a Free Choice in 1975. She served as founder and president of the NY State chapter (1978 – 1981), was a lobbyist in Washington, D.C., and Albany, NY, and a principle speaker at many pro-choice functions. Ries was also "an eager Catholic plaintiff" in a suit brought against the Catholic Church in the 1980s to have it lose its tax-exempt status because it engaged in political activity (its anti-abortion, anti-free choice stance). She also organized community support for the Woman's Health Pavilion, Dobbs Ferry, NY, which performed abortions, when it came under attack from the late 1980s to 2000. She wrote weekly letters to the local papers and faced hostile crowds with her "Keep Abortion Legal" sign every Saturday morning for over 10 years. In addition to this work, Ries helped form the Yonkers (NY) women's task force as part of the 1975 IWY, which established a shelter for battered women in Yonkers that became My Sister's Place. She has also been active in the Democratic Party, organizing phone banks for pro-choice candidates on a local level, "especially in the 1970s, when it was political suicide to be pro-choice." Ries, who has three children, earned her B.A. from Emmanuel College (1954). She is a retired computer technology specialist. (ABS)

Riese, Beatrice (1918 – 2004) An abstract painter and textile designer, Riese was a member of the AIR Gallery—one of the first women's alternative galleries—in Manhattan, founded in 1972. Born in The Hague, the Netherlands, she studied art in Paris in the 1930s, then in 1940, just before the Germans invaded France, escaped with her parents to Africa. On a voyage to the U.S. she married a Spanish anarchist and lived in Richmond, VA, where Riese continued to study art. After a divorce, Riese moved to NYC, where she supported herself and her son as a textile designer. Her work is in the collections of the Museum of Modern Art, the Whitney Museum of American Art, and the National Museum of Women in the Arts in Washington, D.C.

Rila, Margo (1941 –) Since 1967, when she became coordinator of the Sexual Freedom League in San Francisco, Rila has served as sexual liberationist, sex educator and bi activist. She was one of the original volunteers with the San Francisco Sex Information Switchboard (1972), and served as training coordinator for 20 years. She was also one of the first women to promote safer sex education for women, bisexuals and heterosexuals (1982), and from 1985 to 1993 was with the Association for Women and AIDS Research and Education through the University of California, San Francisco. In 1990, Rila served on the coordinating committee for the First International Conference on Bisexuality. She earned a doctoral degree from the Institute for Advanced Study of Human Sexuality (1977), where she serves (2005) on the faculty. Rila has been a member of the board of directors of the LGBT Historical Society in San Francisco and continues (2006) as a volunteer. Archives: LBGT Historical Society, San Francisco, CA. (ABS)

Riley, Margaret Anne ("Peg") (1948 –) Riley was living in a third-floor tenement when she began attending meetings of a women's awareness CR group at the New Bedford (MA) YWCA (1975). The women created various action groups, including a Form in Fibers Workshop. By 1979, Riley had been hired, with another woman, in a shared full-time position as custodian at the YWCA, the first women custodians in the history of that organization. Reading about a woman who was gang-raped in the North End, she and others formed a candlelight vigil to protest violence against women, "but in retrospect, this incident signaled an awareness in me that this was a turning point in the women's movement in New Bedford; the violence against women was the backlash, and the backlash was breaking the back of the women getting together with women for women." When the YWCA moved to a new building, the YWCA Standish House, it became the location for the women's art activities, later known as Women in the Art Collective. Riley later worked at the New Bedford Free Public Library where she successfully expanded the women's studies section. By the late 1980s, Riley was working for Constructive Transformation Unlimited, a house and commercial fishing boat painting and construction business owned and operated by a woman. Riley also assisted this woman in her work for Healing Light Productions, a fundraising organization the woman had co-founded to help provide holistic alternatives to people with AIDS. (ABS)

Riley, Polly – See Grant, Polly Walker

Riley, Trudy – See Kosower, Trudy Margaret

Rinehart, Katherine Black (1921 –) (also known as Katherine B. Massenburg) A political activist, Rinehart was appointed chair of the Status of Women Commission by Maryland's Governor Agnew in 1966. In 1969, she was

R

appointed to the task force on women's rights and responsibilities by President Nixon. Also in 1969, she served on a special committee of two that visited every department in government to determine where women were working and where they could command jobs. Rinehart was also active in the civil rights battle, participating in marches and dealing with incidents of job discrimination. Rinehart, who has two children, earned an A.B. from Randolph-Macon Woman's College and did graduate work at Johns Hopkins University. (ABS)

Ringgold, Faith (1930 –) Artist, author and professor emeritus at the University of California, San Diego, Ringgold was one of the first visual artists of her generation to incorporate issues of social and racial justice into her work. In 1967, Flo Kennedy encouraged her to become active in the women's movement. At that time, however, "being black and a feminist was equivalent to being a traitor to the cause of black people," Ringgold writes in her book *We Flew Over the Bridge* (Little, Brown, 1995). In 1970, that view changed with the Liberated Venice Biennale and the Flag Show, which Ringgold describes as her first "out from behind the men exhibitions." Also in 1970, Ringgold was co-founder (with her daughter Michelle Wallace) of Women Students and Artists for Black Art Liberation, and participated in her first feminist art action, confronting Robert Morris and Poppy Johnson with demands for 50 percent women and blacks to be included in Liberated Venice Biennale. Ringgold was also part of the demonstration of the Ad Hoc Women's Art Group at the Whitney Museum Biennial Exhibition. Ringgold's recommendations resulted in Betye Saar and Barbara Chase-Riboud being included in the Biennale, the first black women ever to exhibit at the Whitney. In late 1970, Ringgold and others were arrested for organizing the People's Flag Show Exhibition at the Judson Church. In 1971, she was a co-founder (with Kay Brown and Dinga McCannon) of the black women's group Where We At, and won a CAPS grant to create a mural, For the Women's House, to be permanently installed at the Women's House of Detention on Rikers Island. As a consequence, Art Without Walls, an artists group that brings art to inmates, was formed in 1972. Ringgold acted as curator for Eleven, a black women's show at the Women's Interarts Center in NYC (1975), and in 1976 co-directed the Sojourner Truth Festival of the Arts, also at the Interarts Center. In 1986, Ringgold served as VP of minority affairs for the WCA. Ringgold is perhaps best known for her painted story quilts—art that combines painting, quilted fabric and storytelling. Her landmark works include the Feminist Political Landscape series, which portrays quotations of black women important to feminism. She has exhibited in major museums worldwide and is in numerous permanent collections, including those at the Studio Museum in Harlem, the Guggenheim, The Metropolitan Museum of Art, and the Museum of Modern Art. Ringgold has written and illustrated 14 children's books. Her first, *Tar Beach* (Random House, 1991) was a Caldecott Honor Book and winner of the Coretta Scott King Award for Illustration. Ringgold has received more than 75 awards, fellowships, citations and honors, including the Solomon R. Guggenheim Fellowship for Painting, two National Endowment for the Arts Awards, and 17 Honorary Doctorates. Ringgold, who has two children, earned a B.S. (1955) and M.A (1959) from City College of New York. Archives: Women Artists Archive, Rutgers University Libraries, New Brunswick, NJ. (ABS)

Ritchie, Rosemary Louise (1943 –) A leader in the Minnesota LWV (1974 – 1983) and an organizer of fundraisers for the ERA (1970s), Ritchie spent two decades working for sex equity in high-school sports and education. In the 1970s, she researched and testified on the disparity in boys and girls sports programs in high schools, and from 1978 – 1983 was a member of the Minnesota Coalition for Sex Equity in Education. From 1979 – 1981, Ritchie was an examiner for the Minnesota Department of Education to assure compliance with the sex equity laws at the state's vocational and technical schools. Ritchie, who has two children, earned an M.A. from the University of Minnesota, and holds a Master's certificate in organization development. (ABS)

Ritvo, Miriam M. (1916 –) started one of the first women's studies courses for credit at Lesley College in Cambridge, MA. Faculty resistance was heavy, and no department wanted the seminar "in their backyard" until the sociology department agreed to take it on. The seminar became the most popular course at the school, in spite of the rigorous requirements. Ritvo also sponsored Betty Friedan to come to Lesley College to coordinate the first International Feminist Conference (1971). Ritvo also self-financed a women's resource center that grew dramatically and was donated to Brown University's women's studies dept. (1999). As special deputy commissioner of education in Massachusetts, Ritvo was able to move 14 women into key positions after they had been passed over for years; they then did the same for other women. Ritvo, who has two children, earned an A.B. from Smith College (1937) and an M.S. from Boston University (1952). She is co-author (with Adelma Mooth) of *Developing the Supervisory Skills of the Nurse* (1974). (ABS)

River, Falcon (1952 –) was one of the "founding mothers" of the Lesbian Feminist Union in Louisville, KY (1975). The group formed a collective, opened a women's bar called Mother's Brew, and created a feminist library and safe room where battered women could shelter for a few days. The group also had an art gallery and brought early feminist women musicians to Louisville. Says River, "We did our part to subvert the dominant paradigm in a very hostile environment, in very hostile times." River was also among the first women to fight their way into the United Brotherhood of Carpenters and Joiners in KY. A

Dianic Priestess (2004), River has served as a guardian for women's circles since 1976. She is a co-founder (with Ruth Barrett) of the Temple of Diana, a national organization of Dianic Wicca, and is on the core faculty for The Spiral Door Women's Mystery School. (ABS)

Rivera, Sophie — Artist and activist, Rivera was an abortion counselor in New York City in the early 1970s and a member of the steering, abortion and library committees of the Women's Liberation Building. In 1973 and 1974, she was a gallery assistant at the Women's Interart Center in New York City and exhibited photographs in various exhibitions. Rivera joined NOW in 1973, and in 1974 worked at *Majority Report* as the arts editor and reviewer. In 1975, Rivera was a contributor to Women's Artists News, and also had several photographs in the International Art Festival held in Mexico City. Rivera's work appears in *Women Artists in America II* (University of Tennessee, 1975). (ABS)

Rivers, Caryl (1937 –) became aware of discrimination against women while covering the civil rights movement as a Washington correspondent in the late 1960s. In Boston by the early 1970s, Rivers began writing about women's issues for national publications such as *The New York Times, Ms., Washington Post, Saturday Review, Mother Jones* and others. She hosted a women's issues program on WGBH-TV, and helped to "liberate" the men's dining room at Locke-Obers, a Boston landmark. A prolific writer, she is the author of *Aphrodite at Midcentury* (Doubleday, 1973), a feminist look at growing up female and Catholic in the 1950s. In 1979 she co-authored *Beyond Sugar and Spice* (Putnam) with Drs. Grace Baruch and Rosalind Barnett, about the new psychology of women. Her volume of media criticism, *Slick Spins and Fractured Facts* (Columbia University Press, 1996) shows how the media systematically present women in a skewed light. Her writing on the women's movement is collected in *More Joy Than Rage: Crossing Generations with the New Feminism* (University Press of New England, 1991). She is author of the novels *Virgins* (St. Martin's Press, 1984); *Camelot* (Zoland Books, 1996); and *Girls Forever Brave and True* (St. Martin's Press, 1986). Rivers is working on *Monsters, Mommies and Madonnas: Women, News and Society* and, with Dr. Rosalind Barnett, *The Seduction of Difference*. Rivers has an A.B. from Trinity College and an M.S. from Columbia University. A professor of journalism at Boston University, she has two children. Archives: Special Collections, Boston University, MA. (ABS)

Rivlin, Lilly (1936 –) Activist, writer, director and producer, Rivlin grew up in the 1950s rebelling against the prevailing patriarchy. A graduate student in political science at the University of California (1959 – 1963), she co-founded the Graduate Student Association and became a female role model for younger undergraduates. Rivlin moved to Israel (1963), where, she says, her femi-

nist ideas "proved shocking." Rivlin later wrote about this experience in the feminist anthology *Which Lilith? Feminist Writers Re-Create the World's First Woman* (Jason Aronson, 1998). Rivlin returned to the U.S. in 1972, where she wrote an article for *Ms*. Titled "Lilith," the article "contributed to making Lilith an icon of the feminist movement." In 1973, Rivlin was a founder of the short-lived Jewish Feminist Organization. She was also one of the original "seder sisters," joining Esther Broner, Phyllis Chesler, Letty Cottin Pogrebin and Bea Kreloff in establishing the Feminist Seder, "which became the role model for the many feminist seders that take place today." Her many films include "Miriam's Daughters Now," about Jewish women transforming traditional rituals to feminist rituals (1986). She has also contributed to numerous anthologies, including *A Rising Public Voice*, edited by Alida Brill (the Feminist Press, 1995); *The Women's Passover Companion*, edited by Rabbi Sharon Cohen Anisfeld, Tara Mohr and Catherine Spector; *Women of the Wall* (Jewish Lights Publishing, 2003); and *Claiming Sacred Ground at Judaism's Holy Site*, edited by Phyllis Chesler and Rivka Haut (Jewish Lights Publishing, 2003). Rivlin has also demonstrated for civil rights and been an activist for co-existence between Israelis and Palestinians. She represented "the feminist religion" with Esther Broner at the Sinai Gathering in spring 1984. Rivlin earned her B.A. from George Washington University and her M.A. from the University of California, Berkeley. (ABS)

Roads, Barbara ("Dusty") (1928 –) Her childhood dream was to be a pilot, but in 1950 Roads had to settle for being a stewardess with American Airlines. She was unwilling, however, to quietly accept the discriminatory policies in effect at that time—mandatory retirement at age 32 and a requirement that stewardesses be unmarried, for example. As a legislative representative from 1958 – 1968 for the Airline Stewards and Stewardesses Association (ALSSA), Roads was a frequent lobbyist in Washington, where she met Ann Cooper Penning—who in turn introduced Roads to Michigan congresswoman Martha Griffiths. Roads and Griffiths formed a powerful friendship and attempted to pass a law against the restrictions. Dubbed "the old broad's bill," it languished and failed, so in 1965, Roads became the first to sue her bosses because of sex discrimination under the newly formed EEOC. It was a year before the EEOC held a hearing on the charges, and five years before the suit was won. However, when the EEOC finally released new guidelines in 1968, ALSSA established a new contract with American that invalidated the age and marriage restrictions. (ABS)

Robbins, Joan Hamerman (1932 –) A practicing psychotherapist for 40 years, Robbins counseled women and men of all sexual orientations, worked with couples with relationship problems, and with women who were the victims of sexual abuse. In the early 1970s, she worked with a local Calfornia group to address feminist issues in mental health. She served on the editorial board of *Women and Therapy* from its inception in 1982 through 1986, and was a founding member of the Association of Feminist Therapists (1980). She attended the group's yearly conferences, delivered papers and led workshops until 1990. As a member of the American Orthopsychiatric Association and the Association of Women in Psychology, Robbins delivered papers and led workshops on feminist topics across the U.S. from the 1980s through the 1990s. An adjunct faculty member of the New College, San Francisco (1989–1993), Robbins taught a course on human development in the graduate feminist psychology program, and from 1988–1994 developed a counseling program supervising interns from the graduate program at New College, at The Family School, in San Francisco. It was a comprehensive adult education program for women receiving public assistance. Robbins, who has two children, is the author of *Knowing Herself: Women Tell Their Stories in Psychotherapy* (Plenum, 1990) and co-editor (with Rachel Josefowitz Siegel) of *Women Changing Therapy: New Assessments, Values and Strategies in Feminist Therapy* (Haworth Press, 1983). Active in Women for Peace, 1963–2005, Robbins holds a B.A. from Brandeis University (1953) and an M.S.W. from the University of California, Berkeley (1957).   (ABS)

Robbins, Mildred – See Leet, Mildred R.

Robbins, Trina (1938 –) Writer, artist and historian, Robbins joined the staff of *It Ain't Me, Babe*, the first women's liberation paper on the West Coast, in 1970, working primarily as the publication's artist, cartoonist and layout-paste-up person. With the backing of the paper's staff, Robbins later produced the first all-women comic book, *It Ain't Me, Babe*. She later produced other feminist comic books, and in 1972 was a founding mother of *Wimmen's Comix*, the long running all-women comic book anthology (1972–1992). In 1990, she co-published and edited a pro-choice anthology comic book, *Choices*, as a benefit for NOW. Since the mid 1980s, Robbins has been a writer and herstorian of feminist pop culture. She has written histories of women cartoonists, women's and girls' comics, and superheroines, as well as books on goddesses and women who kill. In 1991, she wrote a Wonder Woman graphic novel on the theme of spousal abuse. She is (2005) writing an ongoing comic book (drawn by Anne Timmins) for girls, *GoGirl!* Robbins' numerous books include *A Century of Women Cartoonists* (Kitchen Sink, 1993); *The Great Women Superheroes* (Kitchen Sink, 1996); *From Girls to Grrrlz* (Chronicle Books, 1999); *Califia, the Queen of California* (1999); *Harriet Tubman* (Scholastic, 2001); *The Great Women Cartoonists* (Watson-Guptill, 2001); and *Tender Murderers* (Conari Press, 2003). Robbins, who has one child, attended Queens College and Cooper Union. Archives: Notes of her comic-related books will go to Ohio State University, Columbus, OH.   (ABS)

Roberts, Nancy May (1918–2005) joined Orange County, CA, NOW in 1970. She served as VP of that chapter before moving to Connecticut in 1974, where she joined New Haven NOW. In early 1975, Roberts co-founded South Central CT NOW and was membership chair of that chapter almost continuously until 1984. Roberts attended the NOW national convention in Los Angeles in 1970, and at the time of a big ERA march coordinated the buses going from New Haven. After retiring as a bookkeeper, Roberts and a younger friend, Judy Fettig, edited a book, *The End is the Beginning: Discussions with Friends About the End of This Physical Existence*. Roberts, a member of the Unitarian Church, held a B.A. from University of California, Los Angeles.   (ABS before death)

Roberts, Sylvia (1933 –) was the first woman from her parish of Lafayette, LA, to become a lawyer. After joining NOW in 1966, she was placed on its lawyers committee and given the opportunity to represent Lorena Weeks in her case against Southern Bell. When the United States Court of Appeal for the Fifth Circuit reversed the lower court in 1969, it established a rule that opened up to women jobs in all areas of work, since the court held that employers could not refuse to consider a woman for any kind of job unless "all or substantially all women" could be proved to be unable to do the job. Says Roberts, "That opened the floodgates, since that standard is well nigh impossible to meet, since women come in all shapes, sizes, strengths and intelligence." Roberts also served as NOW's first southern regional director (1968) and was general counsel and then president of NOW LDEF. During that time, she represented women in employment discrimination cases in Mississippi, Missouri, Maryland, Illinois and Pennsylvania, as well as Louisiana. Active in the ABA, Roberts says her group obtained the first resolutions from the ABA condemning discrimination against women under federal and state law and other contexts. Anxious to change institutions that controlled women's lives, Roberts, working with Marilyn Hall Patel, started the first judicial education project to present material to judges on discrimination as part of their training. "This spread across the country," says Roberts, "and raised the consciousness of judges as never before." Roberts also represented Dr. Sharon Johnson against the University of Pittsburgh Medical School, and obtained the first injunction preventing Johnson from being fired when she was denied tenure for reasons having nothing to do with her qualifications. Working to get the ERA passed in Louisiana, and to abolish the Head and Master community property laws in the state, Roberts gave a presentation of "witnesses" who had personally experienced sex discrimination under the law. She also gave a "hearing" of such witnesses on the subject of rape. A graduate of UCLA and Tulane College of Law, Roberts continues (2005) to practice law. She recently represented a woman in a domestic violence case that, for the first time in history, defined a history of family violence as one serious episode, or more than one of lesser severity. Says Roberts, "This ruling made it possible for a battered woman who could prove a history of family violence to obtain sole custody of her children, and to have some control over the conditions of visitation." Archives: Hill Memorial Library, Louisiana State University, Baton Rouge, LA. (ABS)

Robins, Joan Ellen (1947 –) (also known as Joan Hoffman) was a co-founder, with Dorothy Bricker and Marianne Yatrovsky, of the first CR group in Los Angeles at the radical Haymarket Center (1967). The group grew quickly and moved to a church closer to South Central Los Angeles. Members demonstrated often, including parading around the Santa Monica Mall in stereotyped costumes on Mother's Day, and protesting the image of women in the movie "Mash" in Westwood, where they were first harassed as lesbians. Robins also helped start the Women's Center "in half of a duplex between Los Angeles and South Central Los Angeles," and through the Center helped to start several more CR groups. Many other groups met at the Center, including labor union women and a group of lesbians who left the gay center and became the nucleus of Lesbian Feminist, of which Robins was an original member. This group sent representatives to an international anti-war meeting with North Vietnamese women; held the first gay-straight-bisexual dialogue; and invaded a NOW meeting to force members to address lesbians in their organization. Robins was also a founding member of the anti-rape squad. In 1968, with her then-husband Fred Hoffman (as ghostwriter), she co-wrote the *Handbook of Women's Liberation*, available only at the Women's Center. In 1973, she helped to organize the Los Angeles Commission on Assaults Against Women, and became its director of education in 1975. When LA-CAAW grew too fast (and collectivity intervened), Robins "quit in frustration," went on to the USC School of Social Work, and became a medical social worker. She also holds a B.A. from University of California, Los Angeles. Robins has been involved with many groups, actions and events since, including the founding of Women Rising. Archives: Social Research Library of Southern California, Lesbian and Gay Archives at USC. (ABS)

Robinson, Lillian S. (1941 –) Active in the Columbia University Women's Liberation (1969), Robinson co-wrote "I Am a Furious Female," with Ellen Cantarow et al, for the New University Conference. Also in 1969, Robinson introduced the first women's studies course at MIT. She later joined Bread and Roses, helping to recruit women into the movement and to form collectives to merge into the larger Bread and Roses group. As a professor at SUNY Buffalo in 1972, Robinson joined what was then the largest women's studies program in the U.S. Robinson is (2005) principal of the Simone de Beauvoir Institute at Concordia University in Montreal, the oldest women's studies department in Canada. A prolific writer, Robinson served as editor of *Modern Women Writers*

(Continuum International Publishing Group, 1996), co-wrote, with Ellen DuBois et al, *Feminist Scholarship: Kindling in the Groves of Academe* (University of Illinois Press, 1985). She is author of *Sex, Class and Culture* (Indiana University Press, 1978); *Monstrous Regiment: The Lady Knight in Sixteenth Century Epic* (Garland, 1985); *In the Canon's Mouth: Dispatches from the Culture Wars* (Indiana University Press, 1997); with Ryan Bishop, *Night Market: Sexual Cultures and the Thai Economic Miracle* (Routledge, 1998); and *Wonder Women: Feminisms and Superheroes* (Routledge, 2004), among others. Robinson holds an A.B. and M.A. (1962) from Brown University and a Ph.D. (1974) from Columbia University. (ABS)

Robinson, Mary Helen – See Hopponen, Mary Helen

Robinson, Pat — In 1960, Robinson, a progressive African American social worker who volunteered at Planned Parenthood in Mt. Vernon, NY, started a group around the issue of teenage pregnancy. The group opened a Freedom School for Children. In 1968, Robinson and other black feminists in the Mt. Vernon area challenged a statement of the Black Unity Party (Peekskill, NY) that insisted that black women not take the birth control pill because to do so would "contribute to our own genocide." The Mt. Vernon group, which also included Pat Haden, Rita Van Lew, Sue Rudolf, Catherine Hoyt and Joyce Hoyt, denounced the Party's demand in a September 11 response, stating that "poor black sisters decide for themselves whether to have a baby or not." In a separate statement written in 1968, Robinson and black sisters questioned the position of poor black women in society. In the early 1970s, the group agitated for Welfare rights and decent housing.

Robson, Jim (1942 –) attended NOW's 1968 national convention with his wife, Mary Jean Collins, and made an impassioned speech that NOW go on record as opposed to U.S. involvement in the Vietnam War. Robson withdrew his motion to oppose the war as it threatened to be divisive. At that convention, he was nominated and elected to the national board, but chose to step down on the same day, at the personal request of Betty Friedan. Robson went on to set up a national NOW office in Chicago (1969) that he and Collins ran until 1975. "We were not to be employees, but independent contractors. NOW was way ahead of modern management methods as it was probably the first organization to outsource support services," says Robson. From that office, Robson and Collins provided membership services such as a national newsletter, new member packets, and membership materials for chapters. At first, they did it all by hand with the help of a second-hand mimeograph machine. As NOW grew exponentially, they had as many as 14 people on their payroll, using three offset presses, an automated machine for the mailing list, and an industrial inserting

R

machine for mailings. Earlier, Robson had participated in various actions, including sit-ins, picketing and liberating men-only grilles, and lecturing and organizing more Illinois chapters. He also took part in attending Mass at a Catholic cathedral with women who went bareheaded to receive Communion, which was refused. The action got worldwide press and precipitated the Church's decision to abandon the centuries-old requirement that women cover their heads in church. Robson and Collins divorced in the mid 1970s. (ABS)

Roby, Pamela Ann (1942 –) A professor and chair of sociology at the University of California, Santa Cruz (2005), Roby was highly involved in the founding and development of Sociologists for Women in Society. She served as a member of its nominations committee (1971 – 1972); co-chair of its committee on social issues (1973 – 1974); and as its fifth president (1978 – 1980). In addition, she served as an elected representative to the ISA's research council (1976 – 1980); as chair of the section on sex and gender of the ASA (1974 – 1975); and as a member of the committee on the status of women of the ASA, founded in 1970 as an ad hoc committee and converted to a standing committee in 1972. She is the author of *Women in the Workplace* (Schenkman Publishing Company, 1981); served as editor of *Child Care – Who Cares? Foreign and Domestic Infant and Early Childhood Development Policies* (Basic Books, 1973); and is co-author (with Michelle Patterson) of *Women Today: Options and Opportunities* (Brandeis University Alumnae Committee, 1972). Roby co-taught (with Michelle Patterson) the first course on women in the sociology department at Brandeis University (1972); participated in the founding meetings of CLUW (1974) and the NWPC (1971); and participated in numerous actions, including sit-ins and demonstrations against NY State's prostitution laws. She was a member of the Commission on Women in Higher Education of the American Council on Education (1973 – 1976); an expert witness for the Massachusetts Commission Against Discrimination in a sex discrimination case against Smith College (1973); served as chair of the subcommittee on Women in Administration of Brandeis University's All-University Environmental Committee (1972 – 1973); was a member of the U.S. Office of Economic Opportunity, New England regional task force on childcare (1972); and served as a consultant for the White House Conference on Children (1970). Also active in the civil rights movement of the 1960s, Roby holds a Ph.D. from New York University (1971). (ABS)

Rockne, Sue Lorentzen (1934 – 2005) began fighting for women's rights in 1954 when she organized the first rally on the Vassar campus, for Governor Harriman. She was a charter member of NOW and the Democratic Farmer Labor Party Feminist Caucus, 1972. She held "every volunteer party office possible," including 12 years on the Democratic National Committee (1980 – 1992). She was also a candidate for the Minnesota State Senate in 1976, losing with 46 percent of the vote, and served as a consultant to many women's legislative campaigns in Minnesota. She received the Hubert H. Humphrey Award from the MN DFL Party. In addition to her political work, Rockne spent 23 years on the board of the women's shelter in Rochester, Minnesota, providing pro bono lobbying and moral support, and for eight years was the public member on the Goodhue County Welfare Board. She served as co-chair of the Minnesota delegation to the Houston IWY conference (1977), and was a member of the continuing committee for many years after that. A lifetime lobbyist for abortion rights, she was a member of all Minnesota and national NARAL predecessors. In her last years, she represented three abortion providers and the MN Civil Liberties Union. She was the recipient of the Jane Hodgson Reproductive Freedom Award. She was a Sunday School teacher for 15 years, a 4-H leader, a lobbyist for the handicapped, a member of the school board, and spent over 25 years on various employment and training councils that operate federal jobs programs. In addition, Rockne represented the victims in the successful lobbying effort for the 1993 Anti-Stalking legislation that was used as a national model, and in 1965 was the founder and original incorporator of the first citizens council in the nation, the Goodhue-Rice-Wabasha Citizens Action Council. She received the Excellence in Educational Equity Award from the MN Department of Education (1987), the MN NOW award for long-term action, the Faith and Freedom Award from the Religious Coalition for Reproductive Rights, and the first Eugenie Anderson Award. Rockne, who had one child, earned her B.A. from Vassar College (1955) and her M.A. from the University of Chicago (1956). Archives: Minnesota History Center, St. Paul, MN.

Rodriguez-Trias, Helen (1929 – 2001) As a physician, Rodriguez-Trias dedicated her life to support reproductive choice, to abolish the forced sterilization of women, and to provide medical care to poor women and their newborns. She graduated from medical school in 1960, at the age of 31, then completed her residency at University Hospital in San Juan, Puerto Rico. During the 1970s, she was a founding member of the committee to end sterilization abuse, the Women's Caucus of the American Public Health Association, and the Coalition for Abortion Rights and Against Sterilization Abuse. Because of her work, the fact that certain groups of women were at risk of being sterilized—poor women, women of color and women with physical disabilities—was brought into public awareness. In 1979, Rodriguez-Trias testified before HEW to foster passage of federal sterilization guidelines, which she helped write and which required that a woman give written consent, among other qualifications. In the 1980s, Rodriguez-Trias began working on behalf of women with HIV/AIDS, and in the 1990s began focusing on reproductive health as co-director of the Pacific

Institute for Women's Health. Rodriguez-Trias also spoke on women's health at both the Cairo and Beijing IWY conferences, and in 1991 received a Presidential Citizen's Medal for her work on behalf of women and children, the poor, and people with HIV/AIDS. Rodriguez-Trias had four children.

Roerden, Chris (1935 –) (also known as Claire Reubens) In 1970, Roerden began two decades of working for women's rights when she broke the invisible barrier to mothers getting a master's degree in English at the University of Maine-Portland/Gorham by organizing the UMPG Graduate Student Association and instituting receptions for national speakers. As a member of Syracuse NOW's education task force, she helped develop the original non-sexist life curriculum for the Syracuse, NY, public school system (1971–1972). She was also the first person certified as an instructor of non-sexist education by the Wisconsin Board of Vocational-Technical Adult Education (1974), and published a newsletter for three years, "The Waukesha Freewoman." In 1975, Roerden received a written apology from Shell Oil Co. headquarters for a sexist article in one of its publications, and began writing NOW's official 10th conference history, which is included, along with Roerden's companion poster, in the Smithsonian Institution's Special Collection on Women. Roerden organized walks in Wisconsin and traveled to Illinois, Indiana and South Carolina to help organize the fight for ratification of the ERA (1977–1979). She was twice elected WI NOW state president, and in 1978 was invited to be a founder, with Katherine Clarenbach and Gene Boyer, of the Wisconsin Women's Network. In 1980, Roerden was elected by a coalition of feminist organizations as WI delegate to the Regional White House Conference on Families. Roerden wrote and produced the feminist game Oops'n'Options as a fundraiser. (1980). Says Roerden, "Because of the military's million-dollar costs re sex-discrimination suits, this simulation game was used in officer training at Rickenbacker AFB in Ohio. The training instructor said male officers are so competitive that in order to participate, they really got into the discriminated-against roles of women!" Roerden was also author of the 1983 cover story for *Wisconsin Business Journal* that celebrated the 20th anniversary of the Equal Pay Act of 1963. In 1988, she founded and led for nine years Silver Space, a part of the women's program at The Counseling Center of Milwaukee, and in 1989 founded and led Wisconsin Feminist Business & Professional Women's Forum. In 1991, she received the Volunteer Service Award from The Counseling Center for these groups. Roerden, who has two children, holds a B.A. and M.A. from the University of Maine-Portland. (ABS)

Rogers, Barbara Joan (1937 –) An artist and professor at the University of Arizona, Tucson, Rogers became active in the San Francisco Art Institute in the early 1960s. There she was a student, faculty member, board member and ultimately director of the Master of Fine Arts program and chair of the painting, sculpture and ceramics areas. In the early 1970s she was voted to a three-person committee to name the recipient of the important Adeline Kent Award. Until Rogers' appointment to the committee, the award had always gone to a man. However, after several hours of negotiating with the other two members of the committee, both men, Rogers was able to swing the vote to a woman, Joan Brown. "I think my presentation of Joan Brown at that meeting was convincing enough that a precedent simply had to be broken, and talent, regardless of gender, had to be recognized and rewarded," Rogers says. Rogers, who has one child, earned her B.Sc. from Ohio State University (1959) and her M.A. from the University of California, Berkeley (1963). (ABS)

Rogers, Ferne M. (1936 –) began working in the late 1960s in Charleston, IL, to promote and support women. She was part of a group that encouraged women to return to school and women college students to seek their dreams in non-traditional career areas. In addition, Rogers helped organize a shelter for women and children (1980), worked for several years with a group to support aged women, worked for passage of the ERA in Illinois, and "fought tooth and nail to get opportunities for my four daughters to participate in sports." (ABS)

Rogers, Sherry (1946 –) joined a consciousness raising group in Schenectady, NY, after hearing Shirley Chisholm announce her candidacy for President. While helping to ferry women from the Schenectady area to NYC to get safe abortions, Rogers also worked to change the law to make abortion legally available to all women. Rogers moved to Brooklyn, NY and then to Forest Hills, NY. She joined Brooklyn NOW (renamed Brooklyn-Queens NOW) in 1974 and was elected president, VP, secretary and treasurer. She continues to work with the ERA Campaign Network to win passage of the ERA. (ABS)

Rogman, Maureen S. – See Slavin, Maureen M.

R

Rogne, Leah (1947 –) was a member of the Fargo, ND, chapter of NOW (1974), and in 1975 worked on the campaign to persuade the ND Legislature to ratify the ERA. She lobbied individual legislators and wrote personal thank-you letters to each person who voted to ratify. A member of NARAL (1975), Rogne helped organize local and state chapters and worked on the by-laws. A professor, Rogne earned her Ph.D. from the University of Minnesota. She has two children. (ABS)

Rogow, Deborah Beth (1951 –) Born in Los Angeles, Rogow has been a union organizer, environmental activist and antiwar activist. Strongly committed to reproductive rights and sex education, Rogow worked at the health center of the University of California, Santa Cruz, in the early 1970s to make contraception universally accessible. In 1974, she took graduate courses in public health/population studies at the University of Michigan, and earned her M.P.H. at the University of California, Berkeley. She then went to work for the San Francisco Dept. of Public Health, where she taught women methods of fertility awareness, improved abortion referrals, and helped establish a clinic for men. She was also active in the Coalition for the Medical Rights of Women, a San Francisco-based group concerned with DES issues, Pap smear quality, prenatal care access and other issues. When restrictions on publicly funded abortion began in 1977, Rogow co-founded the committee to defend reproductive rights, an organization that highlighted all aspects of reproductive freedom, including freedom from forced sterilization and the right to quality prenatal care. Since the early 1980s, Rogow has worked with feminist health organizations in developing countries and with feminist advocates in the international population and sexual/reproductive health field. Rogow considers her major contribution to the movement to be focusing attention on gender issues among policymakers and program leaders, which she has done through research, publishing, advocacy, and working with women's groups in developing countries.   (ABS)

Rohrlich, Ruby (1913 – 1999) (Also known as Ruby Leavitt) A pioneer scholar in the anthropology of women, Rohrlich was professor emerita at City University of New York and later research professor in the anthropology dept., George Washington University. Her course on the anthropology of women, which she instituted in 1971, was probably the first feminist anthropology course offered in the U.S. She lectured widely and organized and participated in numerous academic conferences and seminars on the topic. She is also the author of numerous articles on the anthropology of women and served as editor of and contributor to *Women in Search of Utopia: Mavericks and Myth-Makers* (1984). In the last few years of her life, she turned her attention to the Holocaust, and to Jewish issues, a subject she had knowledge of during WWII, when she worked as a propaganda analyst for the Office of War Information, and later as an editor of the Propaganda Analysis Department. There she analyzed German propaganda from Nazi-occupied Europe. In 1998, she served as editor of and contributor to *Resisting the Holocaust*. She co-organized a session on Jewish Resistance to Anti-Semitism for the 1966 American Anthropological Association meeting.

Rollin, Betty (1936 –) became a network correspondent for NBC News in 1970, one of the early women to do this, and reported on many serious topics of interest to women. Her work included creating and anchoring "Women Like Us," a series of NBC News special programs for and about women. She is the author of several books, including *First, You Cry* (1976). One of the first books to deal frankly with the subject of breast cancer, it was later made into a TV movie with Mary Tyler Moore. A native New Yorker, Rollin is a member of the board of Planned Parenthood of NYC and Death With Dignity. She holds a B.A. from Sarah Lawrence College. Archives: Madison Historical Society, Madison, WI.   (ABS)

Rollins, Ann — Women protesting a beauty pageant and their second-class status as anti-Vietnam War activists awakened Rollins' awareness that a women's movement was emerging. Around 1970, she made her first attempt to join the second wave of feminism by contacting Boston NOW, but declined to join when she learned that she had to pay dues to volunteer. Rollins went on to do volunteer work with three women's centers, a feminist bookstore and newspaper, and various women's groups. Independently, she honed her litigation skills by filing numerous discrimination complaints at human rights offices and in the courts. She was able to win changes on such issues as setting up grievance procedures in universities; gender pricing in the marketplace; equal pay; tenant rights; disability; and age and employment discrimination. Her greatest contribution to the women's movement, she says, is as founder (1979) of RIBE, which promotes women's history nationally and internationally by developing women's history tours, mounting plaques, donating women's history collections, providing speakers for conferences, and through publications. In conjunction with the women's liberation movement, Rollins also participated in causes promoting peace, environmentalism, consumer rights and women's art.   (ABS)

Rolnick, Charlotte – See Schwab, Charlotte Lois

Romero, Fabi (1940 –) joined NYRF in 1965, and was part of a CR group organized by Anne Koedt and Shulamith Firestone. With other members, Romero helped organize demonstrations to legalize abortion, and speakouts on rape, prostitution, motherhood, sexual abuse and violence against women. Romero also lobbied with NOW members in Albany, NY, to legalize abortion. In 1975, Romero was co-founder, with Karyn London and Eleanor Batcheldor, of Womanbooks, on the Upper Westside of NYC. Romero, who has one child, is a small-business owner in New Mexico.   (ABS)

Rominski, Zarod Frances (1943 –) (also known as Fran Rominski) was a founder, with several other women including Amy Kesselman, Betsy Vasquez and Judy Kissinger, of a women's group as part of the Citizens for Independent Political Action in Rodgers Park in Chicago in the late 1960s. She later attended the women's conference at Seneca Falls, and in 1969 moved to San Francisco to help found a feminist commune. During that time, Rominski had her first short story published in the first edition of *Aphra* magazine. In the early 1970s, Rominski moved to Oregon, and in 1973 helped found one of the first pieces of women-only land, called Cabbage Lane, near Wolf Creek, OR. On that land, she and the other members hosted gatherings focused on health and healing, sexuality, writing, building skills and spirituality. During that time, Rominski was an early contributor to *Woman Spirit* magazine. Rominski also helped found Oregon Women's Land Trust, which later established OWL Farm. She moved to Seattle, WA, in 1983 and worked with the Everywoman Delegation to the International Women's Conference to be held in Beijing. She also traveled to China with the delegation and, on her return, gave presentations and wrote articles for the local press on issues affecting women in Third World countries. Rominski, who holds an M.A., is the author of a book of short stories, *Seven Windows, Stories of Women* (Crones' Own Press, 1985). (ABS)

Roraback, Catherine G. (1920 –) has been one of Connecticut's most powerful advocates for women's equality. In 1965, with Fowler Harper and Thomas Emerson, she litigated Griswold v. Connecticut, which resulted in the U.S. Supreme Court landmark decision that secured the right to birth control and established for the first time a constitutional right to privacy. Roraback then headed the legal team for Women v. Connecticut, the Connecticut counterpart of Roe v. Wade, which struck down the state's 19th century law criminalizing abortion. She also participated in the litigation of the Connecticut Medicaid abortion cases. One of the founders of the Connecticut Civil Liberties Union, Roraback served as legal counsel to Planned Parenthood of Connecticut for more than 20 years, and for several years to New Haven Women's Health Services. Roraback defended many who were persecuted for their beliefs and associations during the McCarthy era; black activists in New Haven in the 1950s and 1960s, and blacks and civil rights workers in Mississippi in the summer of 1963; peace and anti-nuclear activists demonstrating against nuclear submarines in Groton, CT; young men asserting claims to conscientious-objector status during the Vietnam War; a woman in one of the Wounded Knee cases; and three of the women in the New Haven Black Panther case in 1969 – 1971. Long before the advent of public interest law, she was protecting the rights of individuals without status or funds. A former board member of Connecticut Women's Educational and Legal Fund, Roraback has served on the boards of a spousal abuse agency and a regional mental health organization, and is (2005) on the boards of a community health foundation and a community foundation. She received degrees from Mount Holyoke College and Yale Law School. (ABS)

Rose, Deborah A. (1947 – 2006) In NYC in 1970, Rose participated in many CR groups, initiated a teach-in on the Vietnam War, and was the first woman to wear pants at Harper & Row Publishing Company. Moving to Cambridge, MA, in 1971, Rose became an activist in Female Liberation: She agitated for abortion rights, taught gyne-

cological self-help, ran a CR group at Framingham State Prison for Women, organized a women's film series (the first ever in Cambridge), edited *Second Wave Magazine* (1971 – 1974), and became the office manager of the Central Square office of Female Liberation (1972). She was also co-founder of *Sister Courage* feminist newspaper. During the summers of 1972, 1973 and 1974, Rose lived in various Womanspirit land communities in California, learning drumming, meditation and the art of living without clothing. Back in Massachusetts, she became an organizer of women's spirituality festivals at Feathers Farm (1974, 1975 and 1976). Rose spent 12 years with Ananda, the women's massage collective of Harvard Square, Cambridge, before taking a degree in acupuncture with Taisophia Institute. She was also an activist, educator and workshop facilitator in the goddess movement of the 1980s and 1990s. (ABS before death)

Rosen, Ruth Eva (1945 –) Author of *The World Split Open: How the Women's Movement Changed America* (Viking, 2000), Rosen is a historian and journalist. She became professor of history at the University of California, Davis, in 1974. From 1968 – 1972 she was a member of Berkeley Women's Liberation, demonstrating against war, and demanding gym facilities for women, as well as courses in women's history and women's studies. As a graduate student, Rosen taught the first seminar in women's history at University of California, Berkeley, (1970 – 1972). A regular writer for *Dissent* magazine and the *Women's Review of Books*, Rosen has published numerous articles on women and women's issues in national newspapers such as *The New York Times, Los Angeles Times* and *San Francisco Chronicle*. Editor of *The Maimie Papers* (the Feminist Press, 1996), she is also author of *The Lost Sisterhood: Prostitution in America, 1900 – 1918* (Johns Hopkins University Press, 1983). A teacher of women's history for over 30 years, she has received numerous honors and awards, including two fellowships from the Rockefeller Foundation, the Distinguished Teacher Award from University of California, Davis, induction as an Honorary Member of Golden National Honor Society for contribution in women's history by the students at the University of California, Davis, and induction as an Honorary Member of Women at Cal, University of California, Berkeley (1995). From 2000 – 2004 she worked as an editorial writer and columnist at the *San Francisco Chronicle*. Rosen, who has two stepchildren, earned her B.A. from the University of Rochester (1967), her M.A. (1969) and her Ph.D. (1976) from the University of California, Berkeley. (ABS)

Rosenberg, Elizabeth Powell – See Betty Powell.

Rosenheck, Bara Susan (1940 –) has worked for educational equity and freedom of choice since the early 1970s. She joined Middlesex County (NJ) NOW in 1970, demonstrating and speaking for abortion rights and against offensive advertising, and from 1972–1982 was a member of Somerset County (NJ) NOW. During that time, she served as chair of the education task force, and in that capacity spoke to the faculty and administrations of many school districts about equity in education, sexism in the school environment, bias and stereotyping in textbooks and the curriculum, and inequity in sports and athletics. Rosenheck was also one of the women of her chapter who wrote articles on feminist philosophy for the local paper under the pseudonym Bea Freer. She also worked to desegregate help-wanted advertising in newspapers, and was a founding member of an early and long-lived CR group. In the mid 1990s, Rosenheck organized a group of activists, educators and healthcare professionals to educate others about female genital mutilation. Her committee played a major role in planning and presenting a conference on FGM and violence against women that was held at the U.N. She also established, developed and participated in the planning committee for the University of Medicine and Dentistry of New Jersey's annual national Conference on Culturally Competent Health Care, and was a founding member of the advisory board of the Women's Wellness and Health Care Connection at Robert Wood Johnson University Hospital in New Brunswick, NJ. Rosenheck, who has two children, holds an M.A. from Fairleigh Dickinson University. (ABS)

Rosenthal, Naomi Braun (1940 –) Professor emeritus of American Studies at State University of New York, Old Westbury (2005), Rosenthal was a political and civil rights activist in the late 1950s and the 1960s. Because of the negative publicity and commentary that followed the Women's Strike for Equality marches in 1970, she decided to study the women who had been involved in the basic organizing units of the movement—the CR groups. She became a participant/observer in the movement in both London and Long Island, "and not surprisingly, my studies led to activism." After that, she says, "there was no looking back." Rosenthal began teaching women's studies and gender courses at Stony Brook and SUNY Old Westbury in 1973. She has written about 19th century women's organizational networks, developed a directory of women's services for women on Long Island, and is the author of *Spinster Tales and Womanly Possibilities* (SUNY Press, 2002), a book about the conceptions of womanhood. Rosenthal, who has three children, earned her B.A. from the University of Chicago (1963), her Msc. Econ. from the London School of Economics (1966), and her Ph.D. from SUNY, Stony Brook (1976). Archives: State University of New York, College at Old Westbury, Old Westbury, NY. (ABS)

Rosenthal, Rachel (1926 –) Artist and activist, Rosenthal participated in numerous demonstrations in Los Angeles in the late 1960s and early 1970s against museums and galleries that showed no women. She was a founding member of Womanspace, Grandview Gallery and DoubleX, and also served as co-chair of Womanspace. She has lectured widely about art from a feminist viewpoint, and created and performed over 36 full-scale pieces, solo and group, with feminist perspectives and toured with those pieces nationally and internationally. In addition, Rosenthal (who was born in Paris) taught women artists about art marketing, sharing that task with two other women in California out of June Wayne's Joan of Art workshops. Rosenthal is also an animal rights activist, and includes animal issues in all of her artwork. (ABS)

Ross, Loretta June (1953 –) In 1976, Ross was one of the first African American women to sue the manufacturer of the Dalkon Shield, A.H. Robins, because the IUD had made her sterile at age 23. Her case, settled out of court, paved the way for the class-action suits that followed and nearly bankrupted the company. This event sparked Ross's activism in reproductive health issues. She has worked with NOW, the National Black Women's Health Project, and with the SisterSong Women of Color Reproductive Health Collective. Ross was also active in the anti-rape movement. "I was drawn to this movement," she explains, "because I had been kidnapped and raped when I was 11 years old." In 1979, Ross became the third executive director of the Washington, D.C., Rape Crisis Center, the first rape crisis center in the world and the only one at that time with a woman of color as its executive director. In 1980, Ross and others coordinated the First National Conference on Third World Women and Violence. From 1991 to 1996, she was the program director at the Center for Democratic Renewal (formerly the National Anti-Klan Network), which monitored hate groups and provided original research on the links between hate groups and anti-abortion violence. Founder and executive director of the National Center for Human Rights Education (1996 – 2004), Ross was co-director of the National March for Women's Lives (2004), which had over one million participants—the first woman of color to co-direct a major national pro-choice march. Ross received an Honorary Doctorate from Arcadia University, and has one child. Archives: The Sophia Smith Collection, Smith College, Northampton, MA. (ABS)

Ross, Mary Beth (1942 –) designed and promoted the first course in women's literature offered by the English department at Syracuse University, and also wrote a feminist dissertation there, "Tiresias Their Muse: Studies in Sexual Stereotype in the English Novel" (1973). Subsequently, she was the first successful litigant in a Human Rights complaint (salary discrimination) against the State University of New York (1973 – 1975). In 1975 she founded The Women's Writers' Center Inc. in Cazenovia, NY. Later she worked as a political speechwriter and on assorted campaigns of women-friendly politicians. Still (2005) writing, teaching and looking for ways to help women fight oppression, Ross lives near Charlotte. She has two children. (ABS)

Rosser, Phyllis Fewster (1934 –) A sculptor and journalist, Rosser has done extensive research into the SAT gender gap—the fact that girls get higher college grades, but lower average scores on the SAT, which is supposed to predict college performance. She published numerous articles on this topic, then in 1987 formed her own testing research company to investigate gender bias on the SAT. Also in 1987, she received a grant to study individual question bias, and in 1989 published a book about her research, *The SAT Gender Gap: Identifying the Causes*. She has testified before Congress on this issue (1988), and appeared on television news and talk shows. In addition, she received a grant to study sex differences on untimed SAT tests and included her findings in an extensive forward to *The Young Woman's Guide to Better SAT Scores* (Bantam Books, 1990). In addition to this work, Rosser was a contributing editor to *Ms.* magazine beginning in 1973, and worked in the Ms. office until 1982. She has published numerous articles on the arts in education, and over 20 reviews of feminist artists in *Women Artist News* and *New Directions for Women* (1986–1993), as well as in other venues. She served as president of Ceres Gallery, a feminist gallery founded in 1984 (2000 – 2004), and has had eight solo shows of her sculpture since 1986. Rosser, who has three children, earned her B.A. from Smith College (1956). Archives: The Sophia Smith Collection, Smith College, Northampton, MA. (ABS)

Rossi, Alice S. (1922 –) A retired professor of sociology, Rossi was a founding member of NARAL. She was also a founder of NOW (1966), and served as a board member from 1966 – 1970. Founder and first president of Sociologists for Women in Society (1971 – 1972), Rossi was also an organizer of the Women's Caucus, ASA, San Francisco (1969). In addition, she served as chair of the committee on women in academe, AAUP (1970–1973), where she worked on policy guidelines on nepotism, parental leave policy, and part-time appointments with full benefits in academe. From 1977 – 1978, Rossi served as commissioner, IWY, appointed by President Carter. Rossi is the author of *Feminists in Politics: A Panel Analysis of the First National Women's Conference* (Academic Press, 1982), and author and editor of *Essays on Sex Equality by John Stuart Mill and Harriet Taylor Mill* (University of Chicago Press, 1970). She is co-author (with Peter H. Rossi) of *Of Human Bonding: Parent-Child Relations Across the Life Course* (Aldine de Gruyter, 1990). She is also editor of *Caring and Doing for Others: Social Responsibility in the Domains of Family, Work, and Community* (University of Chicago Press, 2001); *Sexuality Across the Life Course* (University of Chicago Press, 1994); and *The Feminist Papers: From Adams to de Beauvoir* (Columbia University Press, 1973). The author of numerous articles on women's issues, her most important was "Equality Between the Sexes: An Immodest Proposal," published in *Daedalus*, Spring 1964, and reprinted in *Women in America* (W.W. Norton, 1965) and many an-

thologies over the next 30 years. Rossi made TV appearances in New York in 1964 in support of abortion, did research that was sent to state legislators in New York and Colorado when those legislatures were considering getting abortion out of the penal code, and was active in referrals from Baltimore to NYC for women seeking legal abortions prior to Roe v. Wade. Rossi, who has three children, earned her B.A. from Brooklyn College (1947) and her Ph.D. from Columbia University (1957). She holds Honorary Degrees from Rutgers University, Simmons College, Goucher College, Northwestern University and the University of Massachusetts. Archives: Schlesinger Library, Radcliffe Institute, Cambridge, MA. (ABS)

Rossi, Mary Ann (1931 –) (also known as Mary Ann Rossi Brackenridge) A college teacher of the classics and women's studies, Rossi says her greatest achievement is "my continuing research and activism for the revision of the history of women's roles in the early church, [where women were] fully ordained and acted as teacher, preacher and priest, as the documents fully attest." Catapulted into the women's movement in the 1970s by the shock of losing her position on the faculty of Lawrence (KS) University after 11 years, Rossi was a co-founder (with Agnes Van Eperen) of Appleton (WI) NOW (1973), and served as president from 1975–1978. She served as legislative coordinator of WI NOW (1973); was a member of the board, Lucy Stone Women's Center, University of Wisconsin, Green Bay (1977–1979); and was a member of the Governor's Commission on the Status of Women, appointed by Governor Patrick Lucey (1976), where she was elected legislative coordinator. She was then reappointed by Governor Martin Schreiber (1977) and re-elected legislative chair. During her tenure, she gave testimony for the following bills, all of which became Wisconsin laws: a bill to mandate equal credit (1973); a fair labor standards bill (1976); a bill to make domestic battering a felony (1977); and a displaced homemaker's bill (1978). In 1977, Rossi was elected to the board of the National Association of Commissions for Women. In 1980, she became a member of the founding board of the Wisconsin Women's Network, and was elected treasurer of the Women's Classical Caucus (1981 – 1985), a branch of the American Philological Association. From 1983–1986, she was a member of the women's studies committee and coordinator of the first women's week at Ball State University, Muncie, IN. Working internationally as well as nationally, Rossi attended the International Feminist Conference at Harvard Divinity School (1973); was invited by the U.S. Embassy in London and the Fawcett Society to address leaders of women's organizations in England (1975); and was a representative of the U.S. Commissions for Women and speaker on the women's movement in the U.S. at the U.S. Consulate in Florence and Rome, Italy (1978). In 1978, Rossi was also a keynote speaker for the Ohio State Conference on Battered Women. Rossi, who had four

R

children, three surviving, earned her undergraduate degree from Connecticut College for Women (now Connecticut College). She holds an M.A. from Brown University and a Ph.D. from the University of London. Archives: Wisconsin Historical Society, Madison, WI.   (ABS)

Roth, Joan (1942 –) A world famous photographer, Roth's photographs chronicle the second wave women's movement, bring insight to Jewish feminists, and change the way the world looks at homeless women. Although Roth was a self-supporting, single mother of two daughters, involved in starting CR groups throughout the U.S., she was at the beginning of her career as a photographer at the onset of the feminist movement, which forever changed her life and influenced her vision. She photographed such events as the National Women's Conference in Albany, NY the IWY conferences in Houston, Nairobi and Beijing, and many others. For her advocacy on behalf of homeless women she was awarded grants by the Fund for the City of New York and the Manhattan Bowery Project. Roth photographed Jewish women in Ethiopia, Yemen, and India, who were unknown to the rest of the world Jewish community. Roth is also an advocate on behalf of older women. Her books include *Shopping Bag Ladies of New York* (1980), *Jewish Women: A World of Tradition and Change* (1995) and *The Jews of Ethiopia* (2006). She is the recipient of many honors and awards and the founder and president of Jolen Press. She has also been photo-documenting VFA events.   (ABS)

Roth, Sandra ("Sandy") Ann Reeves (1946 –) entered the Philadelphia Police Dept. in 1970 as one of 50 female police officers among 8,000 men. Says Roth, "The men, and their wives, allegedly, did not want us there, and we were relegated to the Juvenile Aid Division, where we worked on stolen bikes, runaway girls and child neglect." Roth had been on the job less than a month when she apprehended four wanted men in a blind alley. She was "excited and proud" of her achievement—until being reprimanded the next morning "for actually doing police work" and being told that "this behavior would not be tolerated." When a fellow policewoman filed a class action suit against the City of Philadelphia later that year, Roth joined; the black police officers joined several years later. "It took 13 years to reach resolution, but in virtually every city and town, women police officers are eligible to serve in the same way men have served," she says. In 1973, after moving to West Virginia, Roth joined NOW and served as the Morgantown NOW chapter president. She worked on several state and regional projects, and was selected to serve as a delegate to the 1975 Constitutional Convention, which redrafted the NOW constitution. Roth was elected national NOW secretary, and served two terms, completed in 1981. During that time, Roth managed the day-to-day operations of membership and the national office, served as editor of the *National NOW Times*, worked on political actions and projects, and rep-

resented NOW in its successful defense of the ERA boycott of unratified states. When NOW was sued by various states, John Ashcroft, then attorney general, took the lead, alleging violations of the Sherman Anti-Trust Act. Their defense, led by John Vanderstar, was based on First Amendment protection. They won at every level. It was also Roth who came up with the idea of a march to honor Alice Paul after her death. The march was the formal style of the early suffragettes. Roth, a consultant, holds a B.A. from West Virginia University.   (ABS)

Rothchild, Alice (1948 –) entered Boston University School of Medicine in 1970 (although she had been advised not to do so by her alma mater, Bryn Mawr), joined a class of approximately 100 men and 10 women, and rapidly found feminism. It was an intensely sexist environment, she says: "Playboy Bunny slides in between microbiology slides, women called girls, a psychiatrist lecturing us on our unresolved penis envy, the head of ob-gyn giving an opening lecture titled 'What is a woman?' that defined a woman as a man's mother, a man's wife, a man's mistress, etc." Originally intending to be a psychiatrist, Rothchild, after much agonizing, decided to become an ob/gyn because she wanted to dramatically change the standards of care for women. "I started to see every interaction with a female patient as an opportunity to empower and educate her, to create a safe environment where we would work together to understand her issues and develop a strategy for health and treatment," she says. Rothchild graduated in 1974, did a medical internship at Lincoln Hospital in the South Bronx, NY, and then an ob/gyn residency at Beth Israel Hospital in Boston. She served as the medical director of Women's Community Health Center in Cambridge, opened the first all-woman ob/gyn practice in the Boston area, Urban Woman and Child Health, backed up home births that needed hospitalization, and tried to put her feminist ideology into practice. She also worked on the original *Our Bodies, Ourselves* book and subsequent editions, gave countless talks and radio and TV interviews, and wrote articles for and about women. Rothchild, who has two children, received the Best of Boston's Women Doctors Award from *Boston Magazine* in 2001, and in 2004 received the Community Service Award, Harvard Medical School Office for Diversity and Community Partnership.   (ABS)

Rothchild, Nina (1930 –) Now retired from state government, Rothchild was a member of the Mahtomedi (MN) school board (1970 – 1976), where she initiated a grant for a pilot program to develop nonsexist curriculum in public schools; lobbied for Minnesota's law requiring equal opportunity in athletics; and spoke at statewide workshops on women's issues. During this time, she was also board member and VP of Planned Parenthood of Minnesota and served as executive director of the Minnesota Legislative Advisory Council on the Economic Status of Women (1976 – 1982). She was commissioner,

Minnesota Dept. of Employee Relations (1983 – 1991). She was also founder and co-chair (1991 – 1994), Minnesota $$ Millions, an organization that raised money for a MN woman to run for the U.S. Senate in 1994. She is author of *Sexism in Schools: A Handbook for Action*. In addition, she was a member of the coordinating committee Minnesota Women's Meeting, and a delegate to IWY Houston (1977); was a founding member of the Minnesota Women's Consortium and the Center for Women in Government, Hamline University; and a charter member of the Women's Economics Roundtable. Rothchild was also a member of the LWV, the MN WPC, NOW, Women in State Employment, DFL Feminist Caucus and MN Working Women 9to5. In 1981, she received the St. Paul YWCA Leadership in Government Award. As commissioner, Minnesota Dept. of Employee Relations, Rothchild administered the state's Pay Equity Act. For this and other work, she received the Distinguished Service to State Government Award from the National Governor's Association (1984); the 1987 Pay Equity Award from the National Committee on Pay Equity; the Joan Fiss Bishop Award from the American Society for Public Administration (1988); and the Founding Feminist Award, St. Paul WPC. Rothchild is co-author, *In the Company of Women: Voices from the Women's Movement* (1996). She has three children, and graduated with an A.B. degree from Smith College. (ABS)

Rothman, Dorie Weiss (1923 –) A psychotherapist, Rothman served as president of Princeton (NJ) NOW (1988 – 1990) and attended most of NOW's national conventions and Washington, D.C., marches from 1970 – 1982. During 1971 – 1973, she held weekly CR groups. She served as Princeton NOW newsletter editor (1966 – 1968), and later as president of Princeton (NJ) NOW (1988 – 1990). In 2000, she was co-founder of the ERA Campaign Network and served as the NJ ERA campaign network state coordinator. She later served as women's and gender studies outreach coordinator, giving ERA talks in cities, colleges and universities on the East Coast, from FL to NY. Rothman is founder of the ERA Education Fund Inc., and is (2005) its president. She has two children, and holds an Ed.D. from Rutgers University. (ABS)

Rothman, (Evelyn) Lorraine (1937 –) A pioneer of the Self-Help Movement, Rothman has dedicated her life to women's rights of self-determination and control of their bodies. She was a founding member of Self-Help Clinic One (1971), and in the fall of that year traveled throughout the U.S. with Carol Downer, speaking to NOW chapters and other women's groups about self-examination and menstrual extraction. In 1972, Rothman applied for and received a U.S. patent for the Menstrual Extraction Kit, the Del'Em, and co-founded the first Feminist Women's Health Center (FWHC) in Los Angeles. Women were taught cervical and vaginal self-exams and how to perform their own pregnancy tests. They also set up a pa-

tient advocacy program with local hospitals, persuading hospital administrators and doctors to provide simple outpatient suction abortions, on demand, without the hospital board's approval or a medical necessity clause. Concurrently, Rothman co-founded the second FWHC in Santa Ana, CA. Following the Supreme Court's ruling on Roe v. Wade, both centers opened licensed out-patient well-women clinics providing a full range of well-women healthcare services, including abortion. Rothman served as an administrator and director of these facilities. From 1973 to 1974, feminist health activists from across the U.S. were introduced to the Self-Help Clinic's patient participatory and educational concepts and opened their own feminist women's health centers. In 1975 Rothman's self-help clinic concept was the subject of the books *A New View of A Woman's Body, How To Stay Out of the Gynecologist's Office* and *Woman-Centered Pregnancy and Birth*. She also co-wrote (with Marcia Wexler, Ph.D.) *Menopause Myths and Facts, What Every Woman Should Know About Hormone Replacement Therapy* (Feminist Health Press, 1999). Through 1986, Rothman worked in administration at the FWHCs in Los Angeles and Santa Ana, and with its umbrella organization, The Federation of Feminist Women's Health Centers, which included over a dozen sites. In 1999, she joined the FWHC's Web site as a consultant and self-help clinic advocate. (ABS)

Rothschild, Amalie R. (1945 –) Feminist filmmaker and photographer, Rothschild produced "Woo Who? May Wilson" in 1969 as her M.F.A. thesis project at New York University's Institute of Film and Television. She describes it as "possibly the first women's film from my generation of women filmmakers." It was shown at the 1970 New York Film Festival and excerpted in 1970 on an NBC TV special "The New Communicators," about young filmmakers. It was the only film by a woman included in the show. The film is a portrait of artist May Wilson, who, at age 60, discovered an independent life for the first time. Rothschild's second film, "It Happens to Us," grew out of her personal experiences with abortion. It was shot in 1971 with an all-woman crew and released in 1972. In the film, 12 women speak candidly and simply about their experiences, revealing the problems of illegal versus legal, medically safe procedures. "Nana, Mom and Me," shot over a two-year period (1972 – 1974), brought together Rothschild's two key themes: women and independence. Other films include "The Center" (1970), produced for the defense fund of a Black Panther, Robert Collier, and "It's All Right to be Woman" (1972). Rothschild was a founder (with Julia Reichert, James Klein and Liane Brandon) of New Day Films (1971), which grew out of Rothschild's awareness that women's films are important and deserve distribution and the chance to find their audience—this at a time when conventional distributors were turning down films about women and women's issues. New Day was the first distributor run entirely by and for independent filmmakers and is still (2006) an impor-

R

tant force in the distribution of progressive social issue films and videos. In 1972, Rothschild was an organizer (with founder Kristina Nordstrom) of the First International Festival of Women's Films. Active on other fronts as well, Rothschild was briefly a member of New York Radical Feminists. She was a founder of the Association of Independent Video and Filmmakers in 1974, served on its board of directors from 1974 – 1978, and edited "Doing It Yourself: A Handbook on Independent Film Distribution" (1977). She has been a member of New York Women in Film and Television since 1978. Her book monograph *Live at the Fillmore East: A Photographic Memoir* was published in 1999. (ABS)

Rothschild, Joan — was an active member of the women's caucus for political science, which was founded at the 1969 annual meeting of the American Political Science Association. In 1970, she co-founded Boston Area Women Social Scientists and became active in local feminist projects. These include the successful effort to pass the MA ERA (1972), the founding of the MA WPC, and a project to establish a women's data bank to promote women's volunteer and other nonpaid experience as valid criteria for paid employment. In 1971, Rothschild co-founded the Women's Research Center of Boston, which in 1972 published *Who Rules Massachusetts Women*, documenting the minuscule representation of women office holders in the three branches of Massachusetts government. In 1972, Rothschild joined the faculty of Lowell Technological Institute (later called University of Lowell, then UMass Lowell), where she taught until she retired in 1993. In 1975, she taught Lowell's first women's studies course, and in 1976 co-founded (with Mary Blewett) the women's studies program at the University of Lowell. Rothschild was an early and active member of New England Women's Studies Association (1976 – 1977), and served on its steering committee until the mid 1980s. In 1977, she was a delegate from Lowell's women's studies program to the founding conference of the National Women's Studies Association in San Francisco. Rothschild is an alumna of Cornell University and earned her Ph.D. from New York University (1970). She was instrumental in establishing the field that became known as gender and technology. Her publications include the following: author-editor, *Machina Ex Dea: Feminist Perspectives on Technology* (Pergamon 1983); author/editor, *Design and Feminism* (Rutgers University Press, 1999); and author, *The Dream of the Perfect Child* (Indiana University Press 2005). (ABS)

Rothstein, Vivian Emma (1946 –) An anti-war and civil rights activist in the late 1960s, Rothstein was part of a peace delegation that traveled to North Vietnam in 1967. There she learned about a Vietnamese women's union. In 1968, Rothstein helped found CWLU and served as its first staff director. She was active in CWLU from 1968 – 1973 in the Liberation School for Women, developing or-

ganizational structure, doing public speaking, and providing referrals for the Jane abortion service. In 1975, Rothstein staffed a statewide Coalition for Choice in North Carolina. From 1982 – 1987, she worked for the city of Santa Monica (CA), where she staffed the first women's commission in the city. From 1987 – 1997, Rothstein was executive director of Ocean Park Community Center, a network of shelters and services for battered women and their children, homeless mentally ill women, and homeless adults and families. In 1994, she returned to Vietnam in a women's delegation to work toward normalization of relations. In 1997, Rothstein became active in the local Living Wage movement. Rothstein, who has two children, earned her B.A. (1984) and an M.A. (1987) from Antioch University, Los Angeles. (ABS)

Rottmann, Betty Cook (1922 –) A 1958 re-entry journalism graduate of the University of Missouri, Columbia, and on its public information staff, Rottmann became an equality advocate with women faculty and staff as they called for salary fairness and family leave. Now (2005) a 45-year member of Missouri Press Women, she was 1966 president, and named in 1970 in *Foremost Women in Communications*. In the 1970s, she was one of the founders of the MO WPC, the Equal Rights Amendment Coalition, Women's Register for Leadership, and Missouri Women's Network. From 1973 – 1975 she was national media topic chairman for AAUW and from 1977 – 1979 its Southwest Central Region VP. While MO AAUW president (1975 – 1977), Rottmann coordinated the division's activities with the ERA Coalition, MO WPC, LWV, Business and Professional Women, and other organizations. She originated a "Rights of the Family" column, written by a woman attorney and carried in 40 state newspapers. She also initiated an AAUW survey of educational opportunities for women in Missouri colleges. A committee member for the 1977 Missouri Women's Meeting, she was an official observer and host for two international delegates to the Houston IWY conference. As VP of the National Women's Conference Center, she surveyed and helped develop a national directory of women's state networks with then-NWCC president Gene Boyer. In 1980, Rottmann was U.S. representative to a UNESCO seminar in Japan, presenting a paper on American re-entry women's education, training and employment. At University of Missouri, she served on status of women and women studies committees, receiving a 1985 Equal Opportunity Award for Enhancing the Status of Women. She was named 1998 University of Missouri Retiree of the Year for volunteer community service. She was also honored with a 2003 Governor's Humanities Excellence in Community Heritage Award, accompanied by a Supporting Resolution from the MO House of Representatives. In 2005 she received Missouri Women's Network Equity Award. Her collected poems, *Tyrant's Tears*, received the 1990 Missouri Writers Guild Best Book Award. Since 1994, Rottmann has performed in the role of Amelia Bloomer, nineteenth-century fighter for women's rights, for children and adults across the state. Rottmann has two children. Archives: The Women's Collection of Western Manuscripts, University of Missouri, Columbia. (ABS)

Rousso, Harilyn (1946 –) is a disabled feminist who advocates for the rights of women and girls with disabilities. Born in NYC with cerebral palsy, Rousso was fully mainstreamed in her neighborhood public schools before disability rights laws existed, thanks to the insistence of her parents. After graduating from Brandeis (1968), she then earned an M.Ed. from Boston University (1971) and an M.S.W. from New York University (1974). Her involvement in women's issues began in the early 1970s when she joined a women's CR group and discovered the commonalities (and differences) between the needs and concerns of disabled and nondisabled women, and the power of collective action. Her disability activism began in the late 1970s, after she was dropped from a psychotherapy institute because teachers there felt that clinic patients would not accept a disabled therapist. This led Rousso to organize an association of mental health practitioners with disabilities to fight discrimination and promote awareness. In 1979, she launched her own consulting business, Disabilities Unlimited. In 1984, Rousso combined her commitment to women's and disability issues by founding the Networking Project for Disabled Women and Girls, a mentoring program that brought adolescent girls with disabilities together with successful disabled women who served as role models. Originally sponsored by the YWCA of the City of New York, this project was later replicated around the country. More recently, Rousso has continued her work on gender and disability through advocacy, training, research and writing. Her publications include *Gender Matters: Training for Educators Working with Students with Disabilities*, co-authored with Michael Wehmeyer (WEEA Equity Resource Center, 2002); *Double Jeopardy: Addressing Gender Issues in Special Education*, co-edited with Wehmeyer (SUNY Press, 2001); and *Disabled, Female & Proud!*, co-authored with Susan G. O'Malley and Mary Severance (Exceptional Parent Press, 1989). Rousso is the co-producer, with Julie Harrison, of the award-winning videotape documentary "Positive Images, Portraits of Women with Disabilities" (distributed by Women Make Movies, 1989). Rousso has been a member of the New York City Commission on Human Rights, and has served on the boards of numerous women's and/or disability organizations including the National Women's Hall of Fame, the Center for Women Policy Studies, the Ms. Foundation for Women and the Sister Fund. (ABS)

Routsong, Alma (1924 – 1996) (also known as Isabel Miller) wrote about women, lesbians and feminism for three decades. In 1969, she wrote (under the pen name Isabel Miller) the classic lesbian novel *Patience and Sarah*, considered to be the first lesbian love story with a happy ending. The characters in the book were based on a real 19th century couple in Green County, NY. Routsong originally self-published the novel under the title *A Place for Us* and sold it at meetings of the New York chapter of the Daughters of Bilitis and on the street out of a shopping bag. McGraw-Hill re-issued the novel with the new title in 1972. The author later adapted the novel into a play of the same name, which had its debut in 1987. As an opera, Patience and Sarah was produced at a Lincoln Center Festival of the Arts after Routsong's death. Other writings include *The Love of Good Women* (1986), *A Dooryard Full of Flowers* (1993), a short-story collection that revisits Patience and Sarah living in their new farmstead, and also features "Strangers In Camelot," a story based on Routsong's experience of being interrogated about her lesbian lifestyle by the FBI in the 1960s. *Side by Side* (1990) is a 20th century version of *Patience and Sarah*, with a counterpart for every character in the original story. It also addresses the sexual revolution and the politics of the sixties and seventies. Her first novel, *A Gradual Joy*, was published in 1953; her second, *Round Shape*, was published in 1959; and her last, *Laurel*, was published in 1996 shortly after her death. Several of her novels have been translated for publication in Europe. Born in Traverse City, MI, Routsong graduated from Michigan State College in 1949. Her pen name is an anagram for lesbia, combined with her mother's original surname. Routsong had four daughters.

Rowell, Carol – See Council, Carol Diane

Rubin, Arlene – See Raven, Arlene

Rubin, Barbara (1937 –) co-founded the Women's Center at Jersey City State College (now New Jersey City University), leading it from an idea in 1971 to reality in 1973, and serving as both co-director and director until 1977. She also co-founded the women's studies program in 1974 and began teaching women's studies courses that year. Rubin, who holds a Ph.D. in women's studies, taught women's studies continuously until her retirement in 2000. An activist, administrator, teacher and scholar of women's studies, Rubin took a sabbatical year in 1975, traveling through Europe and Israel interviewing women activists and educators. On her return, she began publishing about international feminism in various magazines and scholarly journals. One of her projects, in the late 1970s and through the mid 1980s, was Generations of Women, a photo and oral history exhibition of women's studies students' work. It traveled all over the U.S., and in parts of Europe and Israel. Rubin was co-curator of the exhibition and co-editor of the book of the same name, with Doris Friedensohn. The book has been used by women's studies faculty at other universities. In 2001, the Women's Center was renamed in honor of Rubin and another activist, Kathryn Speicher. (ABS)

R

Rubin, Gayle S. (1949 –) was active in the Thursday Night Group (1968), a pioneering CR group in Ann Arbor, MI. The group disseminated feminist literature on the University of Michigan campus, protested the local Miss Ann Arbor contest, presented workshops, and held the first local women's liberation teach-in. Rubin wrote on women's liberation for the underground paper the *Ann Arbor Argus*, and also contributed to feminist papers such as *Herself* and *It Ain't Me Babe*. In 1970, Rubin helped found Ann Arbor Radicalesbians. She developed an independent major in women's studies, and in 1972 was the first person to graduate in women's studies from Michigan, where she later obtained a Ph.D. in anthropology. As a graduate student she helped found the University of Michigan Women's Studies Program, in which she taught feminist theory and lesbian literature and history. She contributed to the development of academic feminism through her writings, notably the 1975 essay "The traffic in Women." She did research on early 20th century lesbian writers and artists in Paris, and wrote the biographical introduction to the 1976 publication of Jeannette Foster's translation of Renee Vivien's *A Woman Appeared To Me*. In 1978, she began ethnographic research on gay male leather and S&M, and also helped found the lesbian S&M group Samois. She became embroiled in the early skirmishes of the feminist sex wars as a vocal opponent of the feminist anti-pornography movement and as a defender of the legitimacy of sexual variation. Rubin was active in the San Francisco Lesbian and Gay History Project, a support group for research on gay, lesbian, bisexual and transgender communities. Her scholarship has increasingly focused on sexualities, sexology and social geographies of urban sexual populations. She has taught at the University of California at Berkeley, the University of California at Santa Cruz, and at the University of Michigan. (ABS)

Rubin, Lillian B. (1924 –) A writer, teacher, sociologist and psychotherapist, Rubin began working for women's rights as a graduate student in 1968, when she was instrumental in developing the first women's caucus in the sociology department at the University of California, Berkeley. A year or so later, she helped organize the Faculty Women's Research Seminar, which drew women from several campuses around the San Francisco Bay Area. After earning her doctoral degree from UC Berkeley in 1972, Rubin continued to be active in feminist organizing and teaching. She has published 11 books, each focusing on some aspect of women's or family life while also advancing theory about class, race and gender: *Busing & Backlash: White Against White in an Urban School District* (University of California Press, 1972); *Worlds of Pain: Life in the Working-Class Family* (Basic Books, 1976); *Women of a Certain Age: The Midlife Search for Self* (Harper & Row, 1979); *Intimate Strangers: Men and Women Together* (Harper & Row, 1983); *Just Friends: The Role of Friendship in our Lives* (Harper &

Row, 1985); *Quiet Rage: Bernie Goetz in a Time of Madness* (Farrar, Straus & Giroux, 1986); *Erotic Wars: What Happened to the Sexual Revolution* (Farrar, Straus & Giroux, 1990); *Families on the Fault Line: America's Working Class Speaks about Family, the Economy, Race, and Ethnicity* (Harper Collins, 1994); *The Transcendent Child: Tales of Triumph Over the Past* (Basic Books, 1996); *Tangled Lives: Daughters, Mothers and the Crucible of Aging* (Beacon Press, 2000); and *The Man With the Beautiful Voice: And More Stories from the Other Side of the Couch* (Beacon Press, 2003). Rubin has also been active in various political movements since her coming-of-political age in 1948, when she was involved in the presidential campaign of Henry Wallace. Since then, she has been involved "in one way or another, in every struggle, from civil rights to gay rights and, of course, the present-day peace movement." Rubin has one child. (ABS)

Rubio, Ann – See Froines, Ann.

Ruckelshaus, Jill (1937 –) A feminist activist, community volunteer, corporate director and poet in Washington State, Ruckelshaus was the third head of the U.S. IWY Commission, and co-founder of the NWPC. In 1975, Congress passed legislation calling for a National Women's Conference to be preceded by 56 state and territorial meetings to elect delegates. Ruckelshaus (a Republican), along with Bella Abzug, put considerable pressure on Congress to approve $5 million in funding for the conference, held in Houston in 1977. As a co-founder of the NWPC (1971), Ruckelshaus wrote an often-quoted poem with the words, "We will never give up," which she read at the 1977 NWPC convention in California. Ruckelshaus, who has five children, was a commissioner on the U.S. Commission on Civil Rights (1980 – 1983) and delegate to United Nations Conference on Women, Mexico City (1976). She is (2006) on the board of Costco, Inc. and Lincoln Financial Group. (ABS)

Rucker, Zena Lee (1929 –) A member of the board of national NOW from 1987 – 1993, Rucker also helped start the North Dallas chapter (1980) and served as its first VP. Wanting to make the world a better place for women and to empower the disenfranchised, Rucker started a flight school and pilot training course to promote women in aviation, and ran it for 15 years. Rucker also worked for passage of the ERA in the 1970s, and has marched in Washington for women's rights on at least 100 occasions. A charter member of Emily's List, Rucker served as Democratic precinct chair for 20 years, and as an election judge as well. She was active in the civil rights movement in the 1950s and has been an anti-war activist since the Vietnam War. Born in Mexico, she has three children. (ABS)

Runte, Betty Joy (1933 –) A social worker, Runte supervised the first child protection unit in Calcasieu Parish, LA, from 1973 – 1975. As president of her area LWV and member of the state board, she worked for the ERA and for the protection of children and women. She was also a board member of the Calcasieu Women's Shelter and the Displaced Homemaker's Center, and was instrumental in forming the Women's Commission of the City of Lake Charles (LA). In 1980, she was selected to represent Louisiana at Partners of the Americas, speaking on women's issues. Also in 1980, Runte began working in the Office of Elderly Affairs, and became deeply involved in the various needs of elderly women in nursing homes. Runte, who has two children, earned her B.S. from Southwestern Louisiana College. (ABS)

Rush, Doris (1930 – 1991) An attorney, Rush assisted Betty Harragan in her 1970s sex discrimination suit against J. Walter Thompson. With Nancy Borman and Carole De Saram, Rush created the FBI (Feminist Bureau of Investigation) poster of men who represented banks and other businesses and were "wanted" for crimes against women. Rush also helped carry the banner "Women of the World Unite" down 5th Avenue on the first August 26th march (1970). For several years afterwards, Rush participated in August 26th actions such as closing CitiBank ("We want credit where credit is due"), shutting down the Stock Exchange, and taking over the Treasury Steps on Wall Street.

Rush, Florence (1918 –) A psychiatric social worker, Rush drew on her work with abused children and her own experiences of being sexually molested as a child to expose the extent of child abuse and the severity of its consequences. After speaking on the topic at a conference of New York Radical Feminists (1971), she published *The Best Kept Secret: Sexual Abuse of Children* (McGraw Hill, 1980). She also attacked the traditional Freudian approach that children who report sexual abuse are actually reporting wishful thinking or fantasies of being seduced by the father. In addition to this groundbreaking work, Rush was a member of the board of New York Women Against Rape, chaired NY NOW's media reform committee, was a member of the advisory committee on the treatment of sexual aggressors at the New York State Psychiatric Institute, and worked against the national and international child pornography industry. She was a founding member of Older Women's Liberation, served on its steering committee and organized a conference on older women's issues. When her son Matthew was diagnosed with AIDS in 1987, Rush became an AIDS activist and cared for both her son and his lover until their deaths (1990). She is also the author of the article "Women in the Middle" (published in *Radical Feminism*, 1973), which points out how adult women are often trapped between caring for older relatives and caring for their children. In addition to Matthew, Rush has two other children. She holds a B.A. from New York University and an M.S.W. from the University of Pennsylvania. Archives: Kalamazoo College, Kalamazoo, MI. (ABS)

Russ, Joanna (1937 –) A feminist since 1969, Russ also identifies herself as a lesbian and science fiction writer. She is the author of the science fiction novels *And Chaos Died* (1970) and *Picnic on Paradise* (1968), and the non-fiction books *The Female Man* (Beacon Press, 1975) and *How to Suppress Women's Writing* (University of Texas Press, 1983). She had more than 45 short stories in print by 1975. She has written numerous reviews for *The Magazine of Fantasy and Science Fiction*, and, in 1972 won the Nebula Award from Science Fiction Writers of America. Born in the Bronx, Russ attended Cornell University and the Yale Drama School. Archives: Correspondence at University of Oregon, Portland, OR. (ABS)

Russell, Diana E. H. (1938 –) Born in Cape Town, South Africa, Russell is an author, teacher, and activist who has vigorously fought sexual crimes against women and girls. In April 1971, she participated in a feminist protest against a sexist rape trial in San Francisco in which the victim, not the rapist, was treated as the accused. The protesters denounced the trial as "Rape in the Courtroom," and expressed our outrage with the "not guilty" verdict. In London (1974), she was arrested for protesting the 20-year sentence given to Inez Garcia for killing one of her rapists. In 1976, Russell launched "the most significant accomplishment of my life as a feminist," the first International Tribunal on Crimes Against Women, in Brussels, Belgium. That year she was also a founding member of Women Against Pornography and Media, the first feminist anti-pornography organization in the U.S. In 1990, she was arrested for tearing up pornography in a grocery store and a pornography shop in Washington State, with two other women. The store-owner, an incest perpetrator as well as a pornographer, "locked us in, then called the police. We spent a night in jail. The charges against us were eventually dropped." In 1993, she organized Women Against Incest, an activist organization whose goal was to support a deaf incest survivor whose case was to be heard in the Supreme Court in Cape Town. In 2000, she initiated a long-term boycott of a California restaurant owned by a man who trafficked in and enslaved underage girls from India over a period of 15 years to serve as his personal sex slaves and laborers. In doing so, Russell co-founded Women Against Sexual Slavery. In the end, the restaurant owner was sentenced to eight years. In 2002, Russell co-organized a protest against the opening of Larry Flynt's Hustler Club in Downtown San Francisco. In addition to her work against sexual abuse of women, Russell co-taught the first women's studies course at Mills College in 1969, continuing until 1990, and helped pioneer a women's studies major at Mills. A worldwide lecturer, Russell has authored, co-authored, edited or co-edited 17 books, mostly about males' sexual violence toward women and girls. (ABS)

Russell, H. Diane (1936 – 2004) An art historian and scholar of Baroque graphic art, Russell was co-chair (with

R

Mary Garrard) of a WCA-sponsored session at the 1979 NYC meeting of the CCA, Questioning the Litany. It was one of the earliest, if not the first such conference program to showcase feminist scholarship in art history. In 1980, Russell published a review essay in *Signs* that surveyed and assessed feminist directions in art history. Although she published widely, Russell's most important scholarly contribution, from a feminist perspective, was the exhibition and influential catalog *Eva/Ave: Woman in Renaissance Prints* (1990). Before retiring in 1998, Russell was curator and head of the Department of Old Master Prints at the National Gallery of Art in Washington, D.C. Russell earned an A.B. from Vassar College (1958) and a Ph.D. from Johns Hopkins University (1970).

Russo, Nancy (1943 –) started working on women's issues as soon as she graduated with a degree in psychology. In 1974 she co-authored a paper, "The History of Psychology Revisited or Up With Our Foremothers," was published in *American Psychologist*. The paper addressed the invisibility of women in psychology's history. Involved with women's issues in the American Psychological Association, Russo pushed for the use of non-sexist language in scientific reporting, which she calls "an important strategy for undermining stereotypes about women." She and others worked to establish the Division of the Psychology of Women, providing a vehicle for women scientists to conduct research on women's lives. The first conference on the psychology of women was held in 1974. In 1977, when the American Psychological Association became the first scientific society to establish an independent office solely devoted to women's issues, Russo was named head of the women's program office. At the same time, she headed the task force on the ERA for the Federation of Organizations for Professional Women and provided a hot-line counseling service to women's caucuses working to persuade scientific and professional societies to endorse the ERA.   (ABS)

Ruthchild, Rochelle Goldberg Ziegler (1940 –) was a member of Bread and Roses and Female Liberation in Cambridge, MA. She was also one of five women who wrote "Up from the Genitals," a critique of the sexism of U.S. historians presented at the 1970 American Historical Association convention in Boston. In 1971, Ruthchild was one of the women who occupied the Harvard building at 888 Memorial Drive and who later located and negotiated the purchase of the Pleasant St. building for a women's center, the oldest continuously operating community women's center in the U.S. A member of the center's core committee and its second president, Ruthchild became a member of the 888 Women's History Project in 2001, preparing a documentary film of the 888 building takeover, one of the few building occupations by women for women. Ruthchild, who came out as a lesbian in 1971, was appointed head of feminist studies at the Goddard-Cambridge Graduate Program in Social Change

in 1974. She finished her Ph.D. dissertation on the Russian Women's Movement 1859 – 1917 in 1976, and in 1978 received a Women's Educational Equity Act grant, with Deborah Pearlman, to produce curricula for women in rural and urban areas. One of the founders and first president of the Association for Women in Slavic Studies, she is author of *Women in Russia and the Soviet Union: An Annotated Bibliography* (1995). She is (2005) writing a book on feminism and suffrage in Russia, 1905 – 1917. In addition to her Ph.D., Ruthchild holds a B.A. from Hofstra University (1962) and an M.A. from the University of Rochester. She has one child. Archives: Schlesinger Library, Radcliffe Institute, Cambridge, MA.   (ABS)

Ruthsdotter, Mary Esther (1944 –) (also known as Mary Pegau Crawford) Part of a CR group in 1969, Ruthsdotter was an organizer at the University of California, Los Angeles, in married student housing. Prior to Roe v. Wade, she collected "many thousands of signatures" demanding abortion rights. In 1980, she was a co-founder of the National Women's History Project, which instituted March as Women's History Month on the national calendar of annual events and promoted March 8 celebrations of International Women's Day. Active in electoral politics, Ruthsdotter was a volunteer coordinator for Norma Bork for congress in Sonoma County, CA (1980), and field representative for assemblywoman Patricia Wiggins (2001 – 2005). Ruthsdotter, who has one child, holds a B.A. from the University of California, Los Angeles (1973).   (ABS)

Rutledge, Carol Brunner (1938 – 2004) Activist, advocate, writer and historian, Rutledge served the women's movement in Kansas on several fronts. She was an adviser to the Mothers Organized Movement, an advocacy group of mothers receiving public assistance (1970s). In the late 1970s, she twice challenged the status quo by running for the Sedgwick (KS) county commission. In her closest race she came to within 46 votes of unseating a 20-year veteran, thereby paving the way for women to later run successfully for the commission. In addition, Rutledge researched and performed several one-woman shows about women and Kansas history. The research was later used in books, such as *The Women of Hypatia* and *The Story of Wichita* (1979). The latter was written in non-sexist language for use in the public schools as a third-grade text, and included the history not only of women pioneers, but also of indigenous tribes, blacks and Hispanics. Rutledge is also the author of *Dying and Living on the Kansas Prairie* (University Press of Kansas). At her death, she was writing a book about the contributions of prairie women. Rutledge attended Manhattan Bible College (KS) and later graduated from Wichita State University (1977). She had four children. Says her husband, Donavan Roby Rutledge, "Everything Carol did had themes, and predominantly among them feminism. Whether running for office at a time when this simply was not done and should not be attempted, to marching for the ERA, to reading her liberation poems at gatherings of women, to giving one-woman plays about unsung women heroes, to supporting our daughter to become the first female member of her middle-school male track team because there was no program for girls, Carol lived as she believed women were intended to live."

Saadat, Kathleen D. (1940 –) (also known as Kathleen D. Gunnell) Saadat raised her voice consistently in the 1970s in support of a multicultural/multiethnic approach to justice. Active in the Portland, OR, area, she was an organizer of Black Lesbians and Gays United, Mujheres De Colores de Oregon, Black Women's Rap Group and Radical Activists for Sexual Minorities. She was also an organizer of the Portland chapter of Radical Women and the Freedom Socialist Party in the 1970s, and organized International Women's Day celebrations for many years. In addition, she was part of the defensive team and collective community effort to defend the Fred Hampton Clinic against the invasion of patients' privacy by the state attorney general, and in the 1970s was on the board of directors of Bradley Angel House, given credit for being the first women's shelter on the West Coast. An activist for the civil rights of people of color, women, lesbians and gays, Saadat says her point "was always to bring a unifying feminist perspective to all movements. I have no way to work on women's rights and not work on the rights of African Americans, lesbians, the poor. For me, as a woman, it is all the same struggle." Archives: Lesbian Archive Project, Portland, OR. (ABS)

Saario, Terry Tinson (1941 –) A foundation executive, Saario has served as program officer at the Ford Foundation, special assistant to President Carter's assistant for women's affairs in the White House, deputy assistant secretary in the education department during the Carter administration, director of corporate contributions and community affairs at The Standard Oil Company, VP of community affairs at The Pillsbury Company and president of the Northwest Area Foundation. In all these capacities, she worked to advance the rights of women and children. As program officer at the Ford Foundation (1972 – 1980), for example, her primary responsibility was funding women's rights activities in elementary and secondary education, especially implementation of Title IX. She has served on numerous nonprofit and corporate boards, and is currently (2005) a member of the Minnesota Women's Economic Roundtable and chair of the Abbott Northwestern Hospital Foundation board. She also serves on the board of Abbott's holding company, Allina Hospitals and Clinics. She served as chair and board member of the Minnesota Women's Campaign Fund. Saario earned her B.A. and M.A. from the University of California, Riverside, and her Ph.D. from Claremont Graduate University. (ABS)

Sabaroff, Nina – See Taylor, Katya Sabaroff

Sackman-Reed, Gloria (1938 – 2004) was the catalyst behind NOW's efforts that led to a change in Little League regulations allowing girls to play in that youth organization. A demonstration at the 1973 Little League World Series by Sackman-Reed, Carol Atkins, Martha Sykes and a handful of other NOW members drew several hundred activists. Sackman-Reed was also a co-founder of Williamsport, PA, NOW (1973) and president of Pennsylvania NOW (1974 – 1976). In 1975 she was a member of the Majority Caucus at the contentious NOW convention in Philadelphia and helped develop strategies that led to the expansion of the ERA campaign to unratified states. Sackman-Reed was also director of the NOW ERA campaign in Florida (1980 – 1982). According to her daughter, Celeste, she was born in rural Kansas and determined that the only way to escape was to marry. She never went to college, but did marry a Navy man, whom she later divorced. A beautiful woman, Sackman-Reed became a cocktail waitress in Las Vegas and "hung out" with Howard Hughes and friends. She moved to Pennsylvania with her third husband, a doctor. She was "too flashy for the Junior League," her daughter says, so she took up flying and earned a pilot's license. During her lifetime, she also owned a printing business and a bar, and was a successful realtor. She had three children.

Sackrey, Pat Lewis – See Lewis, Patricia Lee

Sacks, Karen Brodkin – See Brodkin, Karen

Saffy, Edna Louise (1935 –) was a convener of the Jacksonville, FL, NOW (1970). In 1972, as a doctoral candidate at the University of Florida, she posted notices across the campus announcing the organizational meeting of a UF chapter of NOW. Nearly 100 people showed up, and the women's movement was launched at the university. To those who formed UF NOW in 1972, the most open example of exclusion, discrimination and sexism was the all-male student group, funded through student activities fees, that boasted that their membership was closed to women. The group, Florida Blue Key, not only received funding from the activities fees of both men and women, but also received a large area for its offices in the Reitz Student Union. It had control over student government and held the majority of seats in the student senate. NOW brought the issue to Florida attorney general Robert Shevin, who in 1974 issued the opinion that FBK could not discriminate against women, and that if it continued to do so, FBK could not use student money or university facilities. Saffy, a professor who earned her B.A. (1966), M.A. (1968) and Ph.D. (1976) from the University of Florida, has also been active in various peace movements, including the Quaker Peace Movement Against War (Iraq) and Wage Peace. (ABS)

Sage, Sybil Adelman (1942 –) A writer who entered the women's movement in 1971, Sage used the media to fur-

S

ther the feminist message. After discovering that she was "not terribly effective" at raising money for the Equal Rights Amendment, she wrote an episode for the TV sitcom "Alice" in which three waitresses "discover that Mel, the owner of the diner and their employer, is hiring a waiter and paying him more because, well, 'he's a man.' The story," Sage says, "allowed me to make salient points about the economic disparities between the sexes." Sage, who has also supported pro-choice candidates, is a graduate of New York University and has one child. (ABS)

Salerno, Mary Beth (1945 –) A foundation executive, Salerno joined NOW in 1972 and was active at the local and state levels, first in Monmouth County (NJ) and then Northern New Jersey. Salerno worked with Ellie Smeal, Alice Cohan and others doing research that eventually led to the extension of the Equal Rights Amendment. In the mid 1970s, she traveled to Florida as a NOW volunteer to build support for the Equal Rights Amendment by speaking to groups throughout the state and later going door-to-door. Salerno has participated in dozens of marches and demonstrations for human rights, and was an at-large delegate to the National Women's Conference in Houston (1977). (ABS)

Sallach, Linnea – See Johnson, Linnea

Salper, Roberta Linda (1942 –) was the first director of the first women's studies program in the U.S., at San Diego State University (1970 – 1971). Says Salper, "That year was full of political debates (many not particularly constructive), petty jealousies and squabbles, but we never doubted the importance of what we were doing." Salper also co-taught women' studies courses at State University of New York, College of Old Westbury (1971 – 1974), and published articles on the San Diego women's studies program in *Ramparts* and *Edcentric* magazines. In addition, Salper published one of the first anthologies on the women's movement, *Female Liberation: Histories and Current Politics* (Vintage, 1972). Salper was an early activist in the women's caucus of the New University Conference (1968), was a member of the first committee on the status of women in the profession of the Modern Language Association (1969), and was a principal founder of Women's Liberation at the University of Pittsburgh (1968). As an assistant professor and assistant dean of the College of Arts and Sciences at the University of Pittsburgh (1969 – 1970), Salper both lobbied to create and taught the university's first women's studies courses. Salper, who has one child, holds a Ph.D. from Harvard University. Most recently, she has been dean of the School of Liberal Arts at Southern New Hampshire University and executive director of Political Research Associates, a progressive think tank. Salper teaches (2005) at Boston University. (ABS)

Salzman, Marilyn – See Webb, Marilyn Salzman

Samfield, Linda Catherine
– See Werden, Frieda Lindfield

Sanchez, Digna (1947 –) Born in Puerto Rico, Sanchez has worked for women's reproductive rights and against domestic violence. In 1971, she joined the Women's Commission of the organization promoting independence for Puerto Rico, the Movimiento Pro-Independencia (MPI). By 1975, she was the head of the Puerto Rican Socialist Party Women's Commission, which focused on machismo within the larger organization and in society. Major work involved the sterilization abuse of Puerto Rican women. At that time, Sanchez says, "35 percent of all Puerto Rican women of child-bearing age had been sterilized, because they had been misinformed that the procedure was reversible if a woman wanted to have children." The Women's Commission joined with other women activists and in the mid 1970s took over City Hall hearings on the Health and Hospitals Corporation regarding the sterilization abuse of Puerto Rican women in NYC municipal hospitals. The group won a major victory when they obtained a 30-day waiting period for a woman to give consent for sterilization. In 1974, they brought this issue before the United Nations decolonization committee hearings on Puerto Rico. From 1973 – 1976, Sanchez was a speaker on women's issues as part of Voices of the Third World. In 1975, she attended the Socialist Feminist Conference in Yellow Springs, OH, and spoke on a panel regarding the feminist movement and liberation struggles. She was a founding board member of Madre (1983) and in 1984 served as Madre's first program director. Sanchez also participated in the development of the first Spanish language film on domestic violence, "Dolores" (1986 – 1987), created to bring domestic violence to the forefront in Latino communities. In 1989, she was a founding board member of the Violence Intervention Program, the first Latina-organized battered women's program in the Northeast. Sanchez, who has one child, earned her B.A. (1968) and her M.S. (1981) from Hunter College. Archives: Center for Puerto Rican Studies, Hunter College, New York, NY. (ABS)

Sanders, Marlene (1931 –) was one of a handful of women network correspondents in the late 1960s. She joined ABC News in 1964, where she began reporting on the women's movement as not just the only woman in the newsroom, but the only person in the newsroom who understood the movement. Sanders produced and/or reported a series of documentaries on the movement, including "Women's Liberation" (1970); "Feminism in the Church" (1971); "Feminism in the Temple" (1972); and "Women & Catholicism" (1972). Her other feminist documentaries are "The Hand that Rocks the Ballot Box" (1972); "Population: Boom or Doom?" (1973); "Woman's Place" (1973); and "Women's Health: A Question of Survival" (1976). In the 1970s, Sanders was part of the women's group at ABC that pressured the company to admit and promote more women, an action that followed NOW's license challenge of ABC's local station, Channel 7. Sanders later co-authored (with Marcia Rock) *Waiting for Prime Time: The Women of Television News* (University of Illinois Press, 1988). Sanders also played a part in NOW's beginnings. In 1966, she was asked by Betty Friedan to help plan publicity strategy to get NOW launched. As a journalist, Sanders could not work up-front, but helped behind the scenes. She was also a founder of NOW's first chapter, NY NOW. A member of numerous professional journalism groups, as well as the Council on Foreign Relations, Sanders has served as chair of Retired & Senior Volunteer Program of the Community Service Society, co-chair of Women's e-News and board chair of the Web site womensnews.org. In 2002, she was appointed to the Mayor's Commission on Women's Issues. Sanders, who has one child and attended Ohio State University, says "I am proud of having been able to report accurately on the women's movement, and to have been a visible symbol of what a woman could do. I am proud of maintaining family life, along with my demanding work, and of raising a talented son who is also a feminist." Archives: University of Wisconsin Historical Society, Madison, WI.   (ABS)

Sandler, Bernice Resnick (1928 –) joined WEAL in 1969 and served as chair of its action committee for federal contract compliance. In 1969, she prepared the first complaint of sexual discrimination in colleges (signed by the president of WEAL), a class action against every college and university in the country, but specifically against the University of Maryland. Sanders subsequently filed charges against approximately 250 colleges and universities, including the entire state systems of Florida and California. At the time, there were no laws prohibiting sex discrimination in education, but Sandler learned that because many institutions had federal contracts, they were subject to a federal executive order covering several forms of discrimination, including that based on sex. The information Sandler gathered laid the groundwork for the amendment of Title VII to cover educational employment, the Equal Pay Act to cover executives, professionals and administrators, and the passage of Title IX. Sandler was associated with Title IX longer than anyone else, played a major role in its development and passage, and was referred to by *The New York Times* as "the god-mother of Title IX." Sandler was the first woman appointed to a Congressional committee to work specifically on women's rights (1970), and the first person to testify before a Congressional committee about discrimination against women in education (1970). After working for a short period as a consultant and deputy director for the Women's Action Program at the U.S. Dept. of HEW, putting together a report on sex discrimination in education and federal policy for the secretary of the department, Sandler was hired in 1971 by the Association of American Colleges to head the first project on women in higher education. There she wrote or supervised the writing of more than 100 papers on topics such as women of color in higher education, older women on campus, and the first nationally distributed report (1978) on sexual harassment in academe. Other reports included subjects such as women's studies, mentoring and evaluating course content for inclusion of women. During her years with this project, Sandler also edited its newsletter, "On Campus with Women." From 1991–1994, Sandler was a senior associate at the Center for Women's Policy Studies, and from 1994–2000 was senior scholar in residence, National Association for Women in Education. She is (2005) senior scholar, Women's Research and Education Institute, and has finished a report on student-to-student harassment K–12, published by Scarecrow Education in 2005. She has given over 2,500 presentations at campuses across the country. Sandler, who has two children, earned her B.A. from Brooklyn College (1948), her M.A. from CCNY (1950) and her Ed.D. from the University of Maryland (1969). Archives: Schlesinger Library, Radcliffe Institute, Cambridge, MA.   (ABS)

Sandstrom, Boden (1945 –) (also known as Barbara Carol Sandstrom and Barbara Carol Reyes) A founding member of Female Liberation in Boston, MA, Sandstrom helped create *The Second Wave*, a journal, in 1971. She was an office manager for the Boston Abortion Rights Coalition and, after moving to Washington, D.C., started Woman Sound Inc.—the first all woman-owned sound company—with Casse Culver (1975). Sandstrom has managed the sound and technical production for all-women's music events, and many political events, including major NOW and gay and lesbian rallies on the Mall since 1975. She also co-produced a documentary on women's music, "Radical Harmonies." Through Female Liberation, Sandstrom became politicized and worked on many causes, in particular the anti-war movement and gay liberation. She was office manager of Greater Boston Peace Action Coalition (1970); helped organize the largest anti-war rally in Washington, D.C. (1970); and was a member of the Young Socialist Alliance, Socialist Workers Party (1970–1973). She is (2005) a lecturer at the University of Maryland. Sandstrom holds a B.A. from St. Lawrence University; an L.M.S. from the University of Michigan, Ann Arbor; an M.S. from American University; and a Ph.D. from the University of Maryland. Archives: The Sophia Smith Collection, Smith College, Northampton, MA.   (ABS)

Sanford, Wendy Coppedge (1944 –) A new mother struggling with depression in the fall of 1969, Sanford attended a free women's health course given in a university lounge. When she entered she found 50 women discussing the clitoris, orgasm and masturbation, which was a new and shocking experience. She joined a discussion on post-partum depression. Learning that her experience happened to many women had the wonderful effect of re-

S

moving the blame she felt, and she decided to stay on and help other women. She joined what was to become the Boston Women's Health Book Collective, helped give courses, and assisted with chapters on post-partum depression and abortion for the group's 1970 course booklet, briefly called "Women and Their Bodies" and soon titled *Our Bodies, Ourselves*. That met with great success, and the 12-member group went on to publish with a commercial press, first with Simon and Schuster in 1973. Sanford continued to work on *Our Bodies, Ourselves* for over 30 years, co-writing the sexuality and lesbian chapters, creating the body image chapter and helping to expand the "we" of the book to include women with disabilities and transgendered women. She served as co-editor of the book's many editions until 1998, and edited *Ourselves and our Children*, a book for parents, and contributed to *Changing Bodies, Changing Lives: A Book for Teens on Sex and Relationships*. Sanford holds a B. A. from Radcliffe College, a Masters in Theological Studies from Harvard Divinity School and an M.F.A. from Vermont College. She is an active member of the Religious Society of Friends, writes creative non-fiction.   (ABS)

Santee, Barbara Ann (1937 –) has spent decades working for women's health and reproductive rights. She was a population intern from the University of Michigan doing abortion research at the Latin American headquarters of the United Nations in Santiago, Chile (1971–1973). The results of her doctoral dissertation on this topic were presented in the first book ever published by the WHO that used the word "abortion" in its title. She served as a research associate, Center for Population and Family Health, Columbia University (1974–1976); director of evaluation and research, Manhattan Regional Perinatal Network, Columbia Presbyterian Hospital, NYC, (1976–1979); and director of evaluation, International Planned Parenthood Federation, NYC (1979–1981). She was founding chair of Modern Oklahomans for the Repeal of Abortion Laws, the first pro-choice organization in Oklahoma (1970); founding chair of Women and AIDS Resource Network, the first women and AIDS group in the U.S. (1987); was instrumental in starting the Tulsa AIDS Coalition (1990); was a founding member of the Oklahoma Reproductive Health Coalition (1992); and was founding VP of the Incest Survivors' Network International, NYC, the first such group in NY State and the second incest survivors group in the U.S. (1985). From 1987–1989 she was a project director for the national board of the YWCA of the USA in NYC, where she worked on a post-mastectomy exercise training manual and feminist model mothers' center. As associate director of the Center for Health Policy Research at the University of Tulsa (1989–1991), she wrote the first policy paper ever written on abortion in Oklahoma. Santee was also co-founder of Oklahoma Women's Network (1992) and editor of its newsletter, and founder and chair of Oklahoma Women's Health Network (1995). In 1996,

she was a founding member of the Oklahoma Progressive Alliance and the Tulsa Interfaith Alliance. She has published numerous articles on women's health and women's issues, and has written two dramatic plays about the problem of incest, both produced. "Trespasses" was produced off-Broadway in 1987, and was the first theatrical work in the country to openly address incest as a serious social problem. Says Santee, "My story, added to the voices of hundreds of thousands of other survivors who found the courage to share their stories, opened the door for people to speak publicly about their abuse and led to the current environment where the victims of priests and other religious persons have the courage to tell what happened to them." Santee is (2005) the retired volunteer executive director, NARAL Prochoice Oklahoma. She also wrote and edited its newsletter. Santee, who has one child, is a member of numerous organizations including OWL, LWV, NOW and the Tulsa Women's Foundation. She earned her B.A.(1969) and M.S. (1970) from the University of Tulsa, her M.P.H. (1971) from the University of Michigan, and her M.Phil. (1977) and Ph.D. (1982) from Columbia University.   (ABS)

Saperstein, Esther (1902–1988) As an Illinois Senator, Saperstein was an unflagging supporter of the ERA, which she introduced into the Illinois General Assembly. The measure passed in the Senate in May 1972 (30-21). However, Illinois remained one of 15 non-ratifying states. A native of Chicago, she attended Chicago public schools and Northwestern University. She was active in many civic organizations, including the PTA, and served as president of the Chicago region. Saperstein first ran for public office in 1955 when, with the support of the Independent Voters of Illinois, she campaigned for alderwoman of Chicago's 49th Ward. She lost this race but impressed Mayor Richard J. Daley, who was first elected mayor in the same election. In 1956 she ran as the Democratic Party candidate for state representative. She served five terms in the Illinois House, representing the Rogers Park neighborhood, and was elected to the IL Senate in 1966. Altogether she served 19 years in the IL General Assembly. During this time Saperstein chaired the Illinois senate education committee, the Illinois Mental Health Commission, and the Illinois Status of Women Commission, which was created by legislation that she proposed. In 1975 Saperstein again ran for 49th Ward Alderwoman and won. She retired after one term. Throughout her career Saperstein was committed to mental health reform and the advancement of women. She started legislative workshops for women, founded the City of Hope, a medical center in California, and promoted women's right to informed choice. She realized that women still had to work harder than men to be as successful: "Women still have to work hard to prepare themselves for the role they want to play. You want to be a doctor, you've got to be the best doctor. If you're going to be a legislator, you'd better be a good one." Saperstein had one daughter and a son.

Sarachild, Kathie (1943 –) (also known as Kathie Amatniek) A founding member of NYRW in 1967 after participating in the Mississippi civil rights movement, Sarachild gave the keynote speech for the group's first public action at the convocation of the Jeanette Rankin Brigade in January 1968. The slogan "Sisterhood Is Powerful" was first used in a flier she wrote for this action. She was one of the four women who held the Women's Liberation banner inside the Atlantic City Convention Hall at the 1968 Miss America protest. An early Redstocking, Sarachild led off the group's disruption of the New York State Abortion Reform Hearing in February 1969, at which women first demanded to testify about their own abortions. She is the author of "A Program for Radical Feminist Consciousness-Raising," presented to the First National Women's Liberation Conference (1968), later published in *Notes from the Second Year* (1970). A theoretician of the feminist movement, Sarachild has published numerous articles and given many speeches, including "Consciousness-Raising, A Radical Weapon," presented to the First National Conference of Stewardesses for Women's Rights (NYC, 1973). Sarachild was founding co-editor of *Woman's World* newspaper (1971); chief editor of and contributing author to the Redstockings' anthology, *Feminist Revolution* (Redstockings, 1975; Random House, 1978); and is director of the Redstockings Women's Liberation Archives for Action (1989 –). She has four stepchildren. She took the matrilineal name "Sarachild" as a nomme de guerre in 1968. Archives: Redstockings Women's Liberation Archives for Action, New York, NY.   (ABS)

Sargent, Mary Lee (1940 –) (also known as Marilee Clore) With both her grandmother (a suffragist) and mother (one of the first women to serve on a jury in Texas and a co-founder of Black/White, a multicultural women's group dedicated to fighting racism by being seen publicly as friends) setting examples of the importance of fighting for women's rights, Sargent herself joined the fray in 1968 as a co-founder of a Champaign-Urbana, IL, chapter of WILPF. After coming out as a lesbian in 1970, she joined the group of women who had established a women's shelter, A Woman's Place, in Champaign-Urbana. She remained active there for the next 30 years as the shelter transitioned from an activist collective to an accountable social service agency receiving state and federal funding. Sargent served on its board until 1981 and participated in volunteer training until the late 1990s. As a college instructor/professor at Parkland College, Sargent initiated a women's history course (1973) and taught a gender-balanced multicultural U.S. history course from 1968 until she retired in 2003. In 1996 she became director of the Office of Women's Programs and Services at the college. As a lesbian, Sargent dedicated herself to creating a women's community. Her group created the newsletter "Lavender Prairie News," which ran from 1976 – 2001, making it one of the longest continuing lesbian publica-

tions in the U.S. Because of her interest in women's communities, Sargent produced a video documentary, "The Benedictine Sisters of Nauvoo," in 1976. An ardent supporter of the ERA, Sargent was one of six women who in 1981 formed Grassroots Group of Second Class Citizens, which carried out 17 direct actions for the ERA at the IL state capitol in Springfield. The women were arrested and served four days in jail. Sargent was a founder of Women Rising in Resistance, a part of the women's peace movement, which grew during 1983 – 1986 into a network of about 80 groups and over 500 individuals. Sargent also helped organize the Susan B. Anthony memorial committee; the Women for Habitat steering committee; and Women Against Racism. Sargent earned her M.A. from the University of Texas, Austin. Archives: Schlesinger Library, Radcliffe Institute, Cambridge, MA.   (ABS)

Sassower, Doris L. (1932 –) It was her "second-class citizen" experience at NYU Law School as one of six women in the 1955 class that turned Sassower into a future leader of the women's movement. By 1968, at age 35, Sassower was elected president of the New York Women's Bar Association. Her 1968 *Trial Magazine* article, "What's Wrong with Women Lawyers?" concluded that nothing whatever was wrong with women lawyers but the discrimination against them in the legal profession, reflecting the societal sexism of the time. In February 1969, Sassower presented these "radical" views to the National Conference of Bar Presidents, the first woman ever invited to do so. In that same year, four years prior to the U.S. Supreme Court ruling in Roe v. Wade, Sassower led the New York Women's Bar Association to become the first bar association to endorse repeal of New York's abortion law. In April 1970, Sassower co-convened a national conference on Breaking Down the Barriers in the Professions. More than 500 professional and academic women from across the country and abroad listened to documented reports on the unequal status of women in America. This, she says, led to the formation of the Professional Women's Caucus, the first respected professional support for what became known as the women's movement. In 1971, as head of PWC's legal arm, Sassower filed a class action complaint against every American law school receiving federal funds, based on their identified discrimination against women. Sassower brought a test case under NYC's human rights law and made new law for women by expanding city and state jurisdiction to include financial institutions and credit houses under the rubric "public accommodations." In 1972, she became the first woman practitioner nominated at a judicial convention for the New York Court of Appeals. She also became the first woman named to the New York State Bar Association's judiciary committee, serving for eight years. Sassower's advocacy skills transformed the world for women and men, particularly in family law. By the early 1970s, she had become known as "the mother of joint custody," also arguing—well before the U.S. Supreme Court so ruled—

S

that statutory denial of alimony to men was unconstitutional sex-stereotyping. In 1977, Harvard Law School hung her portrait as part of its 25th anniversary celebration of its admission of women. Her pioneering efforts have been recognized nationally. In 1981, NY State NOW honored her with a Special Award for "outstanding achievements on behalf of women and children in the area of family law." Since her retirement from law practice, Sassower has worked, *pro bono*, as co-founder and director of the Center for Judicial Accountability, Inc. In 1997, she won a national Giraffe Award, given to those who "stick their necks out for the Common Good." In addition to her J.D. from NYU Law School (1955), Sassower holds a B.A. from Brooklyn College (1954). She has three children. Archives: Schlesinger Library, Radcliffe Institute, Cambridge, MA. (ABS)

Saul, Shura ("Sulamith") Camenir (1920 –) During WWII, Saul organized an American Labor Party group in the East Bronx (NY). She also served as the director of the Bronx River Child Care Center, formed by women to care for children while their mothers worked. Once the war ended, NY State wanted to close the center, even though the women continued to work. Saul and Bronia Fink worked successfully to keep all the centers in NYC open. In the 1950s and 1960s, Saul was program chair for the PTA of PS 121 in the Bronx. She also helped start an after-school program for children whose mothers worked outside the home. In the 1950s, Saul began working with blind older people in the Jewish Guild for the Blind. Saul and her husband pioneered an effort to integrate a group of blind older women into their sighted neighborhood community centers. Saul was active in the civil rights movement of the 1960s, and participated in peace and civil rights in the 1970s. In 1983, Adelphi University Press published Saul's book *Sophia Moses Robison, Twentieth Century Woman*. She was co-author, with Dr. David Drucker and others, of a one-woman play about Bertha Reynolds, social worker and activist, titled "Somewhere a Door Blew Shut: Letters from Exile." It was performed at Smith College. After retiring, Saul continued to teach and began working in higher education for women in prison. In 2000, She was inducted into the Hunter College Hall of Fame. Saul, who has three children, holds an M.S.W. from Columbia School of Social Work and an Ed.D. from Teachers College. (ABS)

Sauvigne, Karen L. (1948 –) joined NYRF Lower East Side CR Group #2 and New York Radical Feminists in 1971. There she worked on various speakouts and wrote articles for the newsletter. In 1972, Sauvigne took a job as a clerk for the newly established women's rights project of the ACLU (directed by Ruth Bader Ginsburg) and later at the Law Student's Civil Rights Research Council (also associated with the ACLU), and, she says, "began learning that law could be a tool for social change." By 1973, Sauvigne was active in Lesbian Feminist Liberation. As po-

litical committee chair, she coordinated an overnight sit-in/occupation of NBC headquarters protesting NBC's depiction of lesbian violence in a weekly police drama. In accordance with her developing understanding of the law, Sauvigne also arranged for back-up attorneys to be available during the night if the sitters-in were arrested. In addition, Sauvigne also coordinated a day care rally with NYC NOW during this time. In 1975, while working at Cornell with Susan Meyer and Lin Farley, Sauvigne held the first speakout on sexual harassment on the job, and pioneered a national effort to bring the issue "out of the closet" and to public attention. Credited with coining the phrase "sexual harassment on the job," they founded Working Women's Institute to champion the cause. Sauvigne, who holds an M.A. from Rutgers University, is an educational administrator. Archives: Women's Center, Barnard College, New YorkY, NY. . (ABS)

Scanlan, Susan Patricia (1947 –) As the legislative director of rep. Charles H. Wilson (D-CA), Scanlan wrote legislation to allow the admission of women to West Point, Annapolis and the Air Force Academies (1975). In 1977, she co-founded (with Elizabeth Holtzman and Margaret M. Heckler) the Congressional Caucus for Women's Issues, and served as executive director from 1980 – 1983. Also in 1977, Scanlan co-founded the Women's Research and Education Institute, which for 25 years has provided nonpartisan data and policy analysis to the women and men of Congress. Its projects include Congressional Fellowships on Women & Public Policy, the only fellowships on Capitol Hill designed by, for and about women; the Center for Women in Uniform, the only feminist group working for the rights of women in the armed services, policing, firefighting and peacekeeping; *The American Woman*, a major resource on the demographic profiles of women today; Crossing Borders, showing the changing nature of citizenship caused by women immigrants; and a wide range of reports and seminars on women's health. Scanlan is (2005) president of WREI. She holds a B.A. from Sweet Briar College and an M.A. from Tulane University. (ABS)

Schaefer, Grace (1933 – 2000) A lesbian feminist activist, Schaefer became a Detroit policewoman in 1964. As a policewoman she handled rape cases, then in the early 1970s became involved with the Detroit Stop Rape movement. In that capacity, she spoke out on significant issues such as how women rape victims were treated by police, doctors and the courts. In 1973, Schaefer brought a class action lawsuit against the Detroit police department for sex discrimination in hiring, salary and promotion. The case went on for almost 23 years, was expanded to include new applicants, went up to Courts of Appeal and back on issues of seniority, and was eventually settled for millions of dollars. From 1973–1974, Schaefer helped start the first Feminist Federal Credit Union in Detroit. She then moved to San Diego with her partner, Mary

Forst, where the two started the California Feminist Federal Credit Union. They also started a home repair company, Ladybug Unlimited, while Schaefer started Womancar with Bobbie Bishop. Schaefer also worked on other projects, including Las Hermanas coffee house, and participated in political activities of the feminist and gay/lesbian movements in San Diego. Schaefer then moved to Portland, OR, in 1976 where she and Forst started the Portland Feminist Federal Credit Union, which lasted about 10 years. Although Schaefer lived in California from 1994–1999, she remained part of the Portland women's community, and returned to Portland in 1999.

Schaper, Donna E. (1947 –) (also known as Donna Osterhoudt) was one of the first women ministers in the United Church of Christ in the early 1970s. During her various appointments and as a member of Campus Ministry Women, she was a key player in the feminist movement within the church. She was the first woman to serve as associate chaplain of Yale University and as associate pastor of the Church of Christ in Yale (1976–1980), and was the first woman minister of the First Congregational Church of Amherst, MA (1980–1983). From 1983–1987, she was the first executive director of the Urban Academy in Chicago, then became the first woman minister of the First Congregational Church of Riverhead, NY, where she served until 1993. Schaper then served as the first woman Area Minister for the Massachusetts Conference of the United Church of Christ, and in 2000 became the first female Senior Minister of the Coral Gables Congregational Church, possibly the largest church headed by a woman in the denomination. One of the most widely published women ministers in the U.S., Schaper is the author of 18 books on topics ranging from becoming 40 to the differences between male and female ministerial styles to spiritual rock gardening. Schaper, who has three children, earned her B.A. from Gettysburg College (1969), her M.A. from the University of Chicago Divinity School (1971), her M. Div. from Lutheran Theological Seminary at Gettysburg (1973), and her Doctor of Ministry from Hartford Seminary (2000). Archives: Gettysburg College, Gettysburg, PA. (ABS)

Schapiro, Miriam (1923 –) A painter, "femmagist," sculptor and printmaker, Schapiro is known as a leader in the feminist art movement and for her pattern and decorations. She was co-founder, with Judy Chicago, of the Feminist Art Program at the California Institute of Arts. She developed her own style, which she called "femmage." This work often included buttons, scraps of lace and needlework, and represented an attempt to break the barrier between art and craft. Schapiro was active in the fight to have women artists' works exhibited in museums that, traditionally, had shown and showcased only work by men. A selected bibliography of her work includes *Miriam Schapiro: Works on Paper, a Thirty Year Retro-*

spective, an exhibition catalog published by the Tucson Museum; *The Power of Feminist Art: The American Movement of the 1970s* (Norma Broude and Mary Garrard, eds., Harry N. Abrams, 1994); Susan Grill, "From Femmage to Figuration," published in *Art News*, April 1986; and Norma Broude, "Miriam Schapiro and Femmage: Reflections on the Conflict Between Decoration and Abstraction in the Twentieth Century," published in *Feminism and Art History – Questioning the Litany* (Harper and Row, 1983). Schapiro is the recipient of six Honorary Doctorates and has been the subject of numerous doctoral dissertations and master's degree theses. Among her many honors are The National Endowment for the Arts Fellowship, a Ford Foundation Grant, The John Simon Guggenheim Memorial Foundation Fellowship and the Showhegen Medal for Collage, a Rockefeller Foundation Grant for Artists in Residency at the Bellagio Studio in Italy, and the National Women's Caucus for Art. Her work appears in many museums in the U.S., Germany, Australia and Israel, including the Metropolitan Museum of Art and the Museum of Modern Art, and the Whitney Museum of American Art, NYC. Schapiro, who has one child, was born in Toronto, raised in Brooklyn, NY, and lives in East Hampton, NY. She earned her B.A. (1945), her M.A. (1946) and her M.F.A. (1949) from the State University of Iowa, Iowa City. Archives: Miriam Schapiro Archives, Rutgers University, New Brunswick, NJ. (ABS)

Scharf, Laura (1942 –) joined NOW in 1970 and worked with Midge Kovacs and the image of women in the media committee on the public service ad campaign "Hire him; he's got great legs!" They also raised advertisers' awareness of sexism in their ad campaigns, such as "Fly me." A NY NOW board member, Scharf headed NOW's sexuality committee with Dell Williams, organizing two sexuality conferences that received national attention. (ABS)

Scharf, Yvette – See Altman, Yvette

Schattman, Ann Woleben (1923–2001) An early fighter for women's rights, Schattman helped women victims of domestic violence, supported and lobbied for the ERA, and fought child hunger. In the 1960s and 1970s, she used her home as a refuge for battered women and developed a network of supporters to whom she could send the overflow. This led directly to her establishing the first shelter for battered and abused women and their children in Fort Worth, Women's Haven, in the 1980s. Schattman also helped set up the Texas chapter of Women in Community Service in the late 1960s, which offered women job training so they could escape poverty. A Democratic Party leader who worked with Senator Hollings on child hunger issues, Schattman was also a Catholic lay leader who established the Christian Culture Series that brought international leaders to Fort Worth in the 1950s and 1960s to talk about Catholic social service.

Schattman, Mary Ellen (1947 –) says she was born to be a feminist—her mother was a Naval officer, both grandmothers were active in New York politics, and a great-grandmother sold real estate in NYC in the late 1880s—and her life has proved her right. Employed as a labor market analyst by the Texas Employment Commission in Austin, Schattman, who became pregnant in late 1969, was told that she would be fired at the seventh month. This was, she says, a policy that had been put in place after the Korean War to make job openings for men. Believing that, as a civil service employee, she couldn't be fired simply for being pregnant, Schattman went to the EEOC. Although EEOC did give her a "right to sue" letter and assigned a lawyer to her case, the lawyer was not allowed to prosecute it. This meant that Schattman had to hire and pay for her own attorney. Dave Richards (husband of Ann Richards) took on her case and Schattman v. Texas Employment Commission went to trial in Austin, "where the head of obstetrics for Seton Hospital testified that 'everyone knows that pregnancy turns women's brains to cottage cheese,' and that he, the gynecologist, would hire only 'neuters'—women who had had hysterectomies." This comment, says Schattman, had a profound effect on the populace of Austin and led to demonstrations. Although Schattman won her suit in District Court, the Texas Employment Commission appealed, the case went to the 5th Circuit Court in New Orleans, and Schattman lost. She then allowed the ACLU to place her case within its new women's division, headed by Ruth Bader Ginsburg and her assistant, Brenda Feigen Fastow. The case went to the Supreme Court, but, again, Schattman lost. In describing that time (1970 – 1972), Schattman says that "feminists were very concerned that the pregnant women fighting for the right to work would distract attention from women fighting for the right to abortion. They didn't want to change their focus." Active for many years in the NWPC, Schattman has also worked in the civil rights, peace and labor movements. In addition to fighting for improved healthcare opportunities, Schattman has been a hospital administrator, a HUD official under President Clinton, and has supported numerous candidates who understood the role of women in society. Schattman, who has three children, holds a B.A. from Dunbarton Holy Cross College.   (ABS)

Schechter, Susan (1947 – 2004) An author and social worker, Schechter helped organize Chicago's first shelter for abused women. She is author of *Women and Male Violence: The Visions and Struggles of the Battered Women's Movement* (South End Press, 1982) and co-author (with Ann Jones) of *When Love Goes Wrong: What To Do When You Can't Do Anything Right* (1992). Specializing in the intersection of domestic and child abuse, Schechter worked to educate others about the ways the public child welfare system fails battered women and their children. She wrote numerous publications for the National Council of Juvenile and Family Court Judges and other groups that offered guidance to the domestic violence and child abuse communities, and was co-author of *Effective Intervention in Domestic Violence & Child Maltreatment Cases: Guideline for Policy and Practice*, popularly known as the "greenbook." Schechter was appointed to the National Advisory Council on Violence Against Women by former attorney general Janet Reno and former U.S. secretary of health and human services Donna Shalala. The recipient of numerous awards and honors, Schechter received the National Association of Public Child Welfare Administrators Award for Leadership in Public Child Welfare in 2003. From 1986 to 1993, Schechter was program coordinator for and then a consultant to Advocacy for Women and Kids in Emergencies at Children's Hospital in Boston, the first program in the country to address child abuse in families that were also affected by intimate partner violence. Schechter, who had one child, earned her B.A. from Washington University and her M.S.W. from the University of Illinois. Archives: Schlesinger Library, Radcliffe Institute, Cambridge, MA.

Schein, Muriel – See Dimen, Muriel

Scher, Susan B. (1942 –) was a member of the New Haven Women's Liberation Center and the New Haven Feminist Therapist Collective in the 1970s. She was also an originator of the New Haven and Meriden Battered Women's Shelter in the late 1970s and early 1980s, and in the 1980s was a founder of the Southern Connecticut State University women's center. Scher says she was destined to be a feminist. Her mother was an organizer and member of OWL, and Scher herself was named for Susan B. Anthony. In addition to her feminist work, Scher was active in the civil rights, peace and environmental movements. A college professor and social worker, Scher holds a B.A. from Brooklyn College (1964) and an M.S.W. from Western Reserve University (1969).   (ABS)

Schetlin, Eleanor Margaret (1920 – 2007) Schetlin began teaching a short course on sex education and sexuality in the 1940s for nursing students "who had no background given to them before they went on wards where the male patients often made passes at them and the female patients on obstetric wards asked them questions they couldn't answer." In the early 1960s, as director of recreation and guidance at the Metropolitan Hospital School of Nursing, and then assistant dean of students for the Plattsburgh State College Nurse Teacher program, Schetlin initiated and conducted weekly discussion groups on feminist topics. After joining the National Association of Deans of Women, she continued to work on women's issues and began to write. "Fifty Years of Association – Ninety Years of Dreams," published in the *NADW Journal*, 1966, spoke of the women who became deans of women when coeducation began, many of whom were lone pioneers working toward the higher education of women. In "Disorders, Deans and Discipline:

A Record of Change," published in *NAWDAC*, 1976, she called attention to some of the outstanding women and men who changed American higher education to include women. In 1968, Schetlin began working to expand the role of women as nurses, serving as general editor of *The Teaching Function of the Nursing Practitioner* (written by Margaret L. Pohl, R.N., Ed.D.) The book introduced nonsexist language in a nursing textbook. Believing that the country would do well if led by a woman, Schetlin campaigned for Shirley Chisholm for President in 1972. Schetlin retired in 1985. "My purpose has been to break the myths and stereotypes that waste the talents, skills and brains of the competent in excluded or disrespected groups, and to keep the incompetent of any group from handling society's affairs." She earned her Ed.D. in 1967 from Teachers College of Columbia University. Archives: Roosevelt Island Historical Society, New York, NY. (ABS)

Schiess, Betty Bone (1923 –) was one of the first women ordained as a priest in the Episcopal Church, in a highly controversial service in 1974. "I do claim responsibility for challenging the church's sexism. This would not have happened without pressure and encouragement from the secular feminist movement. The issues we identified in 1974 have not yet been completely satisfied. In fact, most churches still suffer from confusion about sexuality—or 'gender gridlock,' as it has been called." Schiess is the author of *Why Me, Lord: One Woman's Ordination to the Priesthood* (Syracuse University Press, 2003). An adviser to Women in Mission and Ministry of the Episcopal Church in the United States since 1987, Schiess is the recipient of the Governor's Award for Women of Merit in Religion (1984) and the Ralph Kharas Award of the ACLU, among other awards. She also served as president of the International Association of Women Ministers. Schiess, who has two children (one deceased), earned her B.A. from the University of Cincinnati, her M.A. from Syracuse University, and her M.Div. from Colgate-Rochester Divinity School. Archives: Carl A. Kroch Library, Cornell University, Ithaca, NY. (ABS)

Schimmel, Nancy Reynolds (1935 –) was a member of the social concerns committee of the Northern California Association of Children's Librarians, which created and published a list of nonsexist children's books used by many public and school libraries in the area (1974). Active in the American Library Association/Social Responsibilities Round Table/Task Force on Women, Schimmel helped start the discussion group on sexism in library materials for children (1975), and spoke at the Library School at the University of Wisconsin, Madison, on role-freeing children's books and library programming. With Pat Finley, Schimmel started a childcare room as well as tours and programs for children of people attending ALA conferences (1976 – 1979). During the early 1970s, Schimmel wrote a children's services column for the radical librarians' magazine, *Booklegger*. In 1976, Schimmel

toured the U.S. for seven months with Carole Leita organizing Women Library Workers, a national feminist organization. She also gave storytelling workshops and performances including stories with feminist themes in libraries, women's bookstores and other venues. Later, Schimmel published *Just Enough to Make a Story: A Sourcebook for Storytelling* (Sisters' Choice Recordings and Books, 1978), which included an extensive annotated list of traditional stories with active heroines. From 1976 to 1980 Schimmel toured several months out of each year doing storytelling workshops and performances. Later, at a Women's Music Festival, Schimmel and Ann Hershey met Bonnie Lockhart, with whom they formed the Plum City Players, which presented nonsexist children's programs in the San Francisco Bay Area for 20 years. A participant in the peace and civil rights movements in the 1960s, Schimmel started a small peace center, The Olive Branch, in her San Francisco neighborhood. Since 1990 she has been active in Freedom Song Network, which provides singers for picket lines, rallies, marches and meetings. Schimmel holds a B.A. and M.L.S. from the University of California, Berkeley. (ABS)

Schlein, Betty (1931 –) became head of the political action committee of Long Island (NY) NOW in the late 1960s, and led a group to Washington, D.C., to lobby for the ERA. Elected president of the chapter in 1973 ("the turning point in my life," she says), Schlein led the chapter to become the third largest in the country. Elected as both a delegate to the Democratic National Convention and a member of the NY State Democratic Committee (1972), Schlein was able to help establish the Women's Caucus as an effective force within the party. In 1974, she nominated the first woman Lieutenant Governor of NY State, Mary Anne Krupsak. That year, Schlein became the first NOW president elected to be vice chair of the NY State Committee and head of its women's division. In 1976, when the Democratic National Convention was held in NYC, the joint roles helped her facilitate many feminist actions, including the important passage of equal division of delegates. "It was the basic foundation on which we built our power." In 1979, Schlein became an assistant to Governor Hugh Carey and brought many talented women into positions of leadership. She started a Long Island Women's Network, which worked as a feeder system for appointments in every area. Working with Emily's List nationally and with the Eleanor Roosevelt Legacy in NY State, which raises money and provides support for Democratic women candidates, Schlein is continuing the effort to bring women into power. Schlein is a founder and supporter of the Long Island Fund for Women and Girls, and serves on the board of the Long Island Community Foundation. Archives: Stony Brook University, Stony Brook, NY. (ABS)

Schleman, Helen (1902 – 1992) was one of six women from Indiana seated with Gene Boyer at the Washington,

S

D.C., meeting of the Commissions on the Status of Women (1966). Soon after, Schleman was among the women who met in Betty Friedan's Washington, D.C., hotel room to organize the details of the founding of NOW. As dean of women at Purdue and later as president of the National Association of Deans of Women, Schleman worked to advance the causes of feminism and feminist scholarship. She was elected to several national boards, including the AAUW and the Girl Scouts of America. Schleman was dean of women at Purdue from 1947 – 1968, where she ended the curfew for women students, who previously had to be in by 10:30 each night. "Having worked with enlisted women in the Coast Guard, she knew the women could take care of themselves and make the right decisions," says the former dean of women, Dorothy Stratton. Schleman also encouraged women to enter science programs and opened the doors of Purdue's veterinarian program to women.

Schmid, Margaret (1941 –) joined CWLU in 1969, working with Heather Booth. Schmid was one of the early office staff, was part of the speakers bureau (both giving speeches and training others to do so), and was an active member of one of its work groups, or CR groups. Schmid also served as an editor of *Womankind*, the CWLU's outreach newspaper. After becoming co-chair of CWLU, Schmid was deeply involved in discussions of policy, program, resource allocation, and relations with other organizations. In addition to this work, Schmid, as a faculty member at Northeastern Illinois University, was involved in the establishment of the women's studies program there (one of the earliest in the country) and taught several of the core courses. After many years in the labor movement, focusing in part on health issues, she is (2005) an independent health policy consultant. Schmid, who holds a Ph.D., has one child.   (ABS)

Schmidt, Carol (1942 –) Shortly after the 1968 protests at the Miss America pageant, Schmidt, a white reporter for the African American newspaper *The Michigan Chronicle*, attended her first CR meeting, then established several CR groups herself. After moving to Los Angeles, she worked on the "Women's Center on Crenshaw Newsletter" (1971), wrote feminist short stories, volunteered for the food cooperative and started more CR groups. Schmidt also worked at the Women's Center in Santa Monica and celebrated the emergence of the women's healthcare movement at the Crenshaw Center. Schmidt became involved with the Fat Underground. Nevertheless, she chose to go forward with weight loss surgery that almost killed her. After attending the March 1977 Women's Conference at Santa Monica, Schmidt joined NOW, signed up for the L.A. Women's Community Chorus, and began a life of radical lesbian feminist activism. She served on the CA NOW state board, helped run the ERA phone banks, demonstrated in hundreds of actions, wrote for the local *NOW Times*, and helped broaden the minority women's

task force to the task force on racism. Schmidt also helped form White Women Against Racism and wrote a column in the *Los Angeles Lesbian News* on the various aspects of unlearning and confronting racism. After meeting Norma Hair in 1979, Schmidt and Hair began founding, developing and directing many projects, such as leading the Women and Alternative Lifestyles Conference held by the Los Angeles NOW lesbian rights task force and the Sunset Junction Street Fair. In 1981, Schmidt and Hair moved to Michigan, where Schmidt wrote three lesbian mysteries published by Naiad Press: *Silverlake Heat*, *Sweet Cherry Wine* and *Cabin Fever*. Her writing has been included in an anthology, *Reporting Civil Rights*, published by the Library of the Americas, and honored by the National Gay and Lesbian Press Association, which named her Outstanding Lesbian Journalist of 1983 and awarded her first prize in Feature Writing and News Reporting.   (ABS)

Schneemann, Carolee (1939 –) Schneemann is credited, years before feminism hit the art world, with challenging the psychic territorial power lines by which women were admitted to the Art Stud Club. A multidisciplinary feminist artist, she is also credited with redefining art insofar as it is a discourse on the body, sexuality and gender. Her "Interior Scroll" performance, first performed in East Hampton, NY, in 1975, attempted the metaphoric transformation of the female body from passive object to speaking agent. Schneemann's painting, photography, performance art and installation works have been shown in museums and galleries such as the Los Angeles Museum of Contemporary Art, the Whitney Museum of American Art, the Museum of Modern Art, NYC, and the Centre Georges Pompidou, Paris. She has taught at New York University, California Institute of the Arts and Bard College, among others, and is the recipient of a National Endowment for the Arts Fellowship. Her books include *Cézanne, She Was a Great Painter* (Tresspass Press, 1976), *Vulva's Morphia* (Granary Books, 1997), *More Than Meat Joy* (McPherson & Co., 1997) and *Imaging Her Erotics – Essays, Interviews, Projects* (MIT Press, 2002). She holds a B.A. from Bard College and an M.F.A. from the University of Illinois, Urbana. Archives: The Getty Research Institute, Santa Monica, CA.   (ABS)

Schneider, Rosalind Edith (1932 –) An artist of mixed media and video installation, Schneider curated the exhibit Women Artists as Filmmakers, held at the New York Cultural Center, 1972 – 1973. She was a founding member of Women/Artists/Filmmakers (1974), and served as its project director responsible for grant development and proposal writing (1975 – 1976). Her works include "Les Femmes et Les Films," International Festival, Ontario, Canada (1973); "Women Artists as Filmmakers," Museum of Graz, Austria (1974); and "Year of the Woman Festival," Bleeker St. Theater, NYC (1975). In 1976, she was part of the International Women's Film Festival at the Kennedy Center, Washington, D.C., where she presented a lecture and a show. In 1977, she was a panelist on "Making Films on a Shoestring" at the Festival of Women's Films, and also lectured on women and art at Amherst College. In 2000, three of her films were included in The Color of Ritual, The Color of Thought, Women Avant Garde Filmmakers in America 1930–2000, held at the Whitney Museum of American Art. Schneider, who has two children, earned her B.A. from SUNY Empire State College (1974).   (ABS)

Schneider, Susan Weidman (1944 –) developed a social consciousness and was exposed to the burgeoning feminist movement while at Brandeis University in the 1960s. She is a founding mother and editor in chief of *Lilith*, a Jewish feminist journal named for the mythological creature Lilith, which Schneider acknowledges to be "gutsy." Founded in 1973, the magazine published its first issue in 1976. A speaker on contemporary women's issues, Schneider is also author of three books, including *Jewish and Female* (Simon and Schuster, 1984), the first book to take a broad-based look at the special concerns of Jewish women. Schneider attended Brandeis University and has three children.   (ABS)

Schneir, Miriam (1933 –) is the editor of two anthologies of feminist writings. The first, *Feminism: The Essential Historical Writings* (NY:Random House/Vintage, 1972), was reissued in a new edition 22 years later, along with *Feminism in Our Time: The Essential Writings, World War II to the Present*. Both books were also published in Great Britain. Schneir wrote frequently for *Ms.* magazine. During the U.S. bicentennial season (1975 – 1976), she was part of a team of women who mounted a traveling exhibition on Women in the Era of the American Revolution, which was shown at the New York Historical Society and other venues around the country. She was co-author of the catalog/book *Remember the Ladies* (Viking, 1976). Her book-length critique of the treatment of women in the *World Book Encyclopedia* resulted in extensive revisions. Schneir became involved in feminism during the early days of the women's movement. She joined a CR group in her town (Pleasantville, NY), and read everything she could find about present and past women's movements. With her husband, Walter Schneir, she co-wrote a book on the Rosenberg case, *Invitation to an Inquest* (Doubleday, 1965). Schneir and her husband together and individually have written on politics, education and the Rosenberg case for many national publications. She has a work-in-progress: a history of women in Western Europe and North America before 1848.   (ABS)

Schnitzer, Rhoda Ivy – See Nussbaum, Rhoda Ivy

Schoettler, Ellouise Diggle (1936 –) An artist, storyteller and administrator, Schoettler joined a Washington, D.C., chapter of NOW in 1970. This led her to join the Women's Caucus for Art, where she served as national

secretary, 1974 – 1976. She was also a founder of the Coalition of Women's Arts Organizations and served as director of the Washington office (1977 – 1982). In addition, Schoettler served as national ERA campaign director for the LWV (1979 – 1982) and coordinator, National Business Council for the ERA (1979 – 1982). In 1985, Schoettler conceived of and organized An American Album, a project with artwork from 325 women from 32 states, as an NGO project for the U.N. Conference on Women held in Nairobi, Kenya. The album is now part of the collection of the Museum of Women in the Arts, Washington, D.C. Schoettler, who has three children, holds a B.A. from Dunbarton College of the Holy Cross and an M.F.A. from American University.   (ABS)

Schonbachler, Joanne – See DePaola, Joanne

Schroeder, Melinda Lucy (1937 –) was an active member of NYRF. She helped form new CR groups and was a key organizer of its Marriage Conference. She also brought the play "Focus on Me" to New York City. In addition to this work, Schroeder was a member of the board of the Feminist Credit Union in NYC. She has been active in the civil rights and peace movements, and marched against the wars in Afghanistan and Iraq. A psychotherapist, Schroeder holds a B.S., M.L.S. and L.M.S.W.   (ABS)

Schroeder, Patricia (1940 –) was elected to Congress in 1972 and served there for 24 years. Among her many accomplishments, she served as Dean of Congressional Women, was co-chair of the Congressional Caucus on Women's Issues for 10 years, and served on the House Judiciary Committee. Schroeder was also the first woman to serve on the House Armed Services Committee. As chair of the House Select Committee on Children, Youth and Families (1991 – 1993), she saw the Family and Medical Leave Act and the National Institutes of Health Revitalization Act come into being in 1993. An early supporter of legal abortion, Schroeder sponsored legislation making it a federal crime to obstruct access to abortion clinics. She also expedited the National Security Committee's vote to allow women to fly combat missions (1991) and worked to help military families through passage of her Military Family Act (1985). Schroeder graduated from the University of Minnesota in 1961, and was one of 15 women in a class of more than 500 men at Harvard Law School, where she earned her J.D. She has two children. Archives: University of Colorado Library, Boulder, CO.   (ABS)

Schubert, Helen Celia — began organizing, marching, writing, speaking, teaching and lobbying for women's issues in 1969. As president of the Chicago chapter of Women in Communications (1969 – 1971), she organized an ad hoc committee to create public awareness among Illinois voters of the importance of having the ERA approved. In addition to organizing programs and rallies to generate publicity, she worked with editors and reporters on news and feature stories focusing on women's rights. Schubert also served as president of the Women in Advertising Club of Chicago (1988–1992) and spearheaded the donation of WACC's 65-year archive to the Center for Research on Women and Gender at the University of Illinois, Chicago. A public relations expert, she has helped hundreds of women find jobs and negotiate promotions in their professional lives. An adjunct professor in the School of Communication, Roosevelt University, Chicago, Schubert holds a B.S. from the University of Wisconsin, Madison. Archives: Women's Studies Archives, University of Illinois, Chicago. (ABS)

Schulherr, Anne – See Waters, Anne Schulherr

Schwab, Charlotte Lois (1933 –) (also known as Charlotte Rolnick) A psychotherapist, Schwab is the author of *Sex, Lies and Rabbis: Breaking a Sacred Trust* (1st Books, 2002), a combination memoir/nonfiction work and the first book to focus on rabbis as sexual offenders. In 1973, Schwab served as first co-chair of Manhattan NOW's psychology committee and spearheaded the creation of the booklet *How to Choose a Feminist Therapist*. She also served as founder and executive director of the Feminist Center for Human Growth and Development (NYC), the first organization to train feminist therapists. As professor of social psychology at Hunter College (1973–1978), Schwab was a co-founder of the first women's studies program in the CUNY system and designed and taught the first courses. During that time, she also wrote a column for *Majority Report* titled "Feminist Therapy." In 1982, she gave the keynote address, Sexist Language in the Liturgy and its Psychologically Damaging Effects, at the Hebrew Union College graduation. The Reform Movement's prayer book, Schwab notes, was subsequently changed to use nonsexist terms to refer to God. Schwab, who has two children, earned her B.A. from the University of Michigan, and her M.P.A. and Ph.D. from New York University. Archives: New York University, NY, NY. (ABS)

Schwab Rehorka, Rachel Ann (1959 –) was the only child delegate to the New York State Governor's Conference on Women, held in Albany in the early 1970s. There she and Carey Sassower, then a student at New Rochelle High School, spoke to over 500 delegates about the practical-arts requirements of public junior and senior high schools in New York State, and proposed that girls and boys be allowed to choose shop or home economics or both. She further proposed that funding be withheld from public schools that did not grant students a non-sexist choice of the practical-arts courses. The conference members voted yes, thus implementing gender-free practical arts requirements for New York State public junior and senior high schools. Schwab Rehorka's student politics continued in the establishment of the Students for Human Equality Club. As an adult, Schwab Rehorka

worked as a guidance counselor at the elementary-, middle- and high-school levels, always encouraging girls in math and science, respecting diversity, preventing harassment and seeking equality for all. She is the daughter of Charlotte Rolnick Schwab, a pioneer feminist psychotherapist and author. (ABS)

Schwalb, Susan Amelia (1944 –) An artist, Schwalb was part of the early 1970s actions demanding visibility for and protesting the exclusion of women artists at MOMA and the Whitney Museum in NYC. From 1973–1975 she was art director for the newsletter "Women in the Arts," and from 1974–1975 served as art director for *Aphra*, a feminist literary magazine. Active in WIA, Schwalb was art director for *Women Artist News* (1975–1977). In 1977, she was elected arts delegate from NY State for the IWY conference in Houston. She was a member of the founding executive committee, Coalition of Women's Art Organizations (1977–1978), and served on the advisory board of Women's Caucus for Art, New York chapter (1978–1979). In 1978, Schwalb was appointed by President Carter to the continuing committee of the National Women's Conference, and served as arts representative at a White House Conference. From 1979–1981, she was project director, U.S. committee for the First International Festival of Women Artists, Copenhagen, Denmark. From 1982–1983, she was co-coordinator, Women's Caucus for Art, Boston (MA) chapter, and from 1985–1987 served on the Caucus's steering committee and as VP, Coalition of Women's Art Organizations. From 1987–1991, Schwalb was a member of the Coalition's advisory board. From 1991–1994, she was a member of the committee on the status of women, College Art Association. The recipient of numerous art grants, Schwalb, who holds an M.F.A. from Carnegie-Mellon University, has seen her work exhibited nationally and internationally. Archives: National Museum of Women in the Arts, Washington, D.C.; and the Archives of American Art, Smithsonian Museum, Washington, D.C. (ABS)

Schwartz, Barbara Joan – See Joans, Barbara

Schwartz, Edna (1909 – 2002) In 1964, Schwartz was appointed by Governor Karl Rolvaag to Minnesota's first Commission on the Status of Women. She served for 13 years, being appointed by both Republican and Democratic governors. She was present at the founding of NOW in Washington, D.C. in 1966, served as president of the Minnesota BPW Federation, and testified before the Legislature ("with hat and white gloves") on equal pay for equal work, minimum wages and maternity leave. She also spoke around the state for the ERA. Schwartz was one of the women featured in the book *In the Company of Women: Voices from the Women's Movement*, published by the Minnesota Historical Society in 1996. Born in St. Paul, MN, Schwartz attended Valparaiso University, hoping to become a deaconess in her church. She started work at the height of the Great Depression. She spent 10 years working for the Electrical Workers Union, where they had never had a "girl" working in the front office before. She and a colleague left to form the St. Paul chapter of the Electrical Contractors Association, where she worked for 20 years.

Schwartz, Jane – See Gould, Jane S.

Schwing, Lee (1952 –) In her first semester at Goddard College (1971), Schwing took a class on feminism taught by Marilyn Salzman-Webb, a founding member of *Off Our Backs*. For her second semester, Schwing did an internship at *Off Our Backs*. Says Schwing, "I arrived in Washington, D.C., and moved into a room at Coletta Reid's home. As it turned out, I had moved into ground zero of the birth of what became known as The Furies—a group of lesbian women who were in the process of breaking away from *Off Our Backs* and figuring out what it meant to be a woman, to be a lesbian and to be a feminist. I dove into this cauldron of transformation and have never looked back." Schwing published several articles in *The Furies* newspaper, including "Women: Weak or Strong" in the first issue (January 1972), and "Building Feminist Institutions," co-written with Helaine Harris and published in the last issue (May/June 1973). Schwing moved to Berkeley, CA, in the mid 1970s, studied dancing, did bodywork, and got involved with theater arts and spirituality. She lived in India for a year, then moved to Los Angeles to work at UCLA. She developed her computer skills and continued studying spirituality. She has been chief technology officer at a major Hollywood entertainment law firm for the last 17 years. Schwing holds a B.A. from Antioch College, San Francisco.   (ABS)

Scott, Ann C. – See Crittenden, Ann

Scott, Ann London (1929 – 1975) Among her numerous achievements as VP legislation of NOW, Scott deserves major credit for pressuring the federal government into issuing Revised Order Number 4, which put teeth into affirmative action for women by assigning it to the Office of Federal Contract Compliance. This meant that non-complying contractors and subcontractors of the federal government would lose business if they failed to practice affirmative action. Gene Boyer recalled "watching Ann grab a government official by the lapels, sticking her face right into his and shouting. It looked like he withered under her grasp, and he did support our position." Scott was a founder of the Buffalo, NY, chapter of NOW. She was elected to NOW's national board in 1970, and served as VP legislation until her death in 1975. Scott was remembered by Jennifer MacLeod for her "superb work on affirmative action for women, equal employment opportunity for women, and the ERA." Scott, who held a Ph.D., was an English professor at the University of Buffalo prior to her work with NOW. Her husband, Tom, was an active partner in her NOW work. Archives: Schlesinger Library, Radcliffe Institute, Cambridge, MA.

Scott, Anne Firor (1921 –) As a college professor, Scott wrote about and taught the history of American women for more than 40 years. She served as editor of the report of the North Carolina Governor's Commission on the Status of Women (which she chaired in 1963 – 1964), "The Many Lives of North Carolina Women." She is also author of one of the first publications in the "new" Southern women's history, "The New Woman in the New South," published in *South Atlantic Quarterly*, 1962; of *The Southern Lady: From Pedestal to Politics* (University of Chicago Press, 1970); and of *Unheard Voices: The First Historians of Southern Women* (University Press of Virginia, 1993). W.K. Boyd Professor Emerita at Duke University, she served on President Johnson's Advisory Council on the Status of Women (1964 – 1966). Scott also taught the first course on women's history at the University of Washington in 1971, and at Duke University in the 1971 – 1972 school year. Scott, who has three children, joined the staff of the national LWV in 1944. Active in the civil rights, peace and environmental movements, Scott holds an A.B. from the University of Georgia, an M.A. from Northwestern University and a Ph.D. from Radcliffe. Archives: Rare Books and Manuscripts Division, Perkins Library, Duke Univer-sity, Durham, NC.   (ABS)

Scott, Arlie Costine — One year after joining Los Angeles NOW in 1970, Scott organized a successful effort at the NOW national conference to pass a national NOW resolution to include lesbian and gay issues as legitimate concerns of the organization's issues and agenda. She wrote the NOW position paper on lesbian rights, which was passed by more than 90 percent of the 1971 conference members. In 1971 – 1972, she was director of Los Angeles NOW Center for Women's Studies. She was NOW's first national VP-action (1977 – 1979), and executive director of the Women's Action Alliance (1980 – 1982). Scott was the California state coordinator and campaign director for the presidential campaign of congresswoman Shirley Chisholm, the first woman to head a statewide political campaign in the state's history. She was co-chair of the California Chisholm delegation at the 1972 Democratic National Convention, Miami, FL, and a member of the DNC credentials committee, 1972. Scott was also a member of the Southern California steering committee, NWPC, 1972, and on the NOW national board of directors, 1973 – 1979. She also initiated and organized the U.S. participation in the first international feminist action in support of the Three Marias, July 3, 1973. Scott was NOW coordinator for the national August 26th events (1973); she initiated and organized NOW's nationwide demonstrations supporting minority women factory workers in the Farah plant in New Mexico, and NOW national demonstrations in support of the 1973 minimum wage campaign. She was chair of NOW's inter-

S

national committee, 1974 – 1976. In 1976 Scott was NOW's National Democratic Convention coordinator, New York, and initiated and organized NOW's first formal organizing presence at a National Democratic Convention in which NOW lobbied delegates and candidates in support of women's issues, including the ERA. A board member of the NOW LDEF ERA committee, 1977 – 1979, she organized the first ERA march in Washington, D.C. (1977), and was a representative at the IWY National Women's Conference in Houston (1977). She was also director of Women's Action Alliance, 1981 – 1982. Scott was assistant attorney general, Commonwealth of Massachusetts, Public Protection Bureau, 1989 – 2002. She received her B.A. from the University of California, Los Angeles; her M.A. from the University of Southern California; and her J.D. from George Mason University. Scott was admitted to the Massachusetts Bar in 1988.   (ABS)

Scott, Elizabeth (1917 – 1988) A professor in the department of statistics, University of California, Berkeley, Scott worked behind the scenes to improve the status of women. In 1970, she was co-chair, with Elizabeth Colson, of a committee that looked at the position of women at the university in terms of salary, title and tenure. Scott's analysis showed that, in department after department, the number of women decreased as the job title went up. Scott also did two important national studies for the Carnegie Commission in the 1970s; one documenting the low number of women Ph.D.s hired into tenure track positions, and the other comparing salaries for male and female professors. No surprise that the report showed men earning more than equally qualified women. Scott also developed a model statistical method for identifying discrimination that led to class action settlements in universities across the country. Scott was personally involved in advising faculty women and students in the sciences, spoke at numerous meetings on improving the status of women, participated in AAUP and other meetings and workshops for women in science, and was a regular participant with other women faculty in delegations to the chancellor seeking remedies for wrongs for other women. Says Susan Ervin-Tripp, "Scott had always wanted to be an astronomer. In those days, however, women weren't allowed to use the great observatories."

Seaman, Barbara (1935 –) An author and women's health activist, Seaman has persistently challenged the medical establishment and pharmaceutical companies by exposing their drive for profit at the expense of women. Seaman, whose work has expanded the boundaries of full disclosure and informed consent in many aspects of healthcare, was cited by the Library of Congress in 1973 as the author who raised sexism in healthcare as a worldwide issue. In addition, the August 11, 1995, issue of *Science Magazine* cited Seaman as the founder of the women's health movement. In 1960, Seaman introduced a new style of health reporting that centered more on the patient and less on the medical fads of the day. She was first to reveal that women lack the information to make informed decisions on contraception, childbirth and breast-feeding. Seaman became a columnist or contributing editor at *Bride's*, *Ladies' Home Journal*, *Family Circle* and *Ms.* magazines. In 1967 – 1968, Seaman, a graduate of Oberlin, won a Sloan Rockefeller Advanced Science Writing Fellowship at the Columbia University School of Journalism. While there, she began her first book, *The Doctors' Case Against the Pill* (Wyden/Avon, 1969), which became the basis for a U.S. Senate hearing. Young feminists, led by Alice Wolfson, repeatedly disrupted the hearing demanding to know why patients were not testifying and why there was no pill for men. As a result of Seaman's book and the uproar that followed, a warning to patients was placed on oral contraceptives—the first on any prescription drug (July 1970). Her second book, *Free and Female* (Coward McCann/Fawcett, 1972), was followed by *Women and the Crisis In Sex Hormones* (with G. Seaman, Rawson/Bantam, 1977). That book precipitated a government task force on DES (diethylstilbestrol), an estrogen that had caused cancers in the daughters of women who were given the drug to prevent miscarriages. By the 1980s, Seaman had been blacklisted from most magazines and newspapers that took pharmaceutical advertising. She then turned her attention to biography. *Lovely Me: The Life of Jacqueline Susann* was published in 1987 (Morrow/Warner). *The Doctors' Case Against the Pill* was reissued in a 25th anniversary edition in 1995, and *Lovely Me* was reissued in 1996 and made into a movie starring Michele Lee. In 2000, Seaman was co-author (with Gary Null) of *For Women Only: Your Guide to Health Empowerment*, a collection of feminist classics on health and body issues. Seaman is also author of *The Greatest Experiment Ever Performed on Women: Exploding the Estrogen Myth* (Hyperion, 2003). From 2000 – 2003, Seaman's "Health Watch" column (edited by Joan Michel) appeared monthly in *Hadassah Magazine*. Seaman is a national judge for the annual Project Censored Awards and has served on the PEN Freedom to Write Committee. In April 2000, she was named by the U.S. Postal Service as an honoree of the 1970s Women's Rights Movement stamp. Earlier, in 1975, she was a co-founder (with Alice Wolfson, Belita Cowan, Dr. Mary Howell and Dr. Phyllis Chesler) of the National Women's Health Network. Seaman, who has three children, holds a B.A. and an Honorary Doctorate from Oberlin College. Archives: Schlesinger Library, Radcliffe Institute, Cambridge, MA.   (ABS)

Seaman, Judith (1940 –) served for many years as the voice for women's rights in the small town of Elkins, WV. In 1973, she helped organize the Elkins Women's Group. She also worked to support the ERA, and in 1978 went to Washington, D.C., to lobby Robert Byrd for the ERA extension. In 1979, she founded the Elkins chapter of NOW, serving as president from 1979 – 1986. Seaman lobbied legislators to defeat the pro-life amendment to the State Constitution, helped file discrimination complaints to the State Human Rights Commission (1980), and lobbied for equal distribution of property at divorce and child-support enforcement. Seaman also served on NOW-PAC and organized a walk-a-thon for PAC money. From 1984–1985, Seaman was West Virginia state secretary of NOW, and served as state NOW president from 1986–1988. Seaman has been a member of the board of Women's Aid in Crisis since 1991. In 1997, she chaired an Ecofeminism conference, and from 1997–2002 wrote a grant for and organized an after-school program through AmeriCorps. In addition, Seaman has been active in the peace movement. She has two children, and holds a B.A. from Wooster College, an M.A. from Stanford University, and an M.S. from Marshall University. Archives: Davis & Elkins College, Elkins, WV.   (ABS)

Sedey, Mary Anne (1947 –) A feminist lawyer specializing in employment litigation, Sedey was an early leader of NOW in Missouri. She served as first president of NOW's St. Louis chapter, as first state coordinator, as regional director, Midwest NOW (1974), and as a board member of national NOW. In addition, she was organizer and first chair, MO ERA coalition. A partner in the first women's law firm in St. Louis (Anderson, Everett, Sedey & Van Amburg), Sedey was also president of the National Employment Lawyers Association from 1995 to 1998, has served on its board for many years, and founded the St. Louis chapter of NELA. She and her partner, Jon Ray, were co-counsel for a nationwide class of women in the Rent-A-Center sex discrimination class action settled in 2002 for $47 million. Sedey, who has two children, earned her B.A. from Webster College (1970) and her J.D. from St. Louis University (1975). Archives: University of St. Louis, St. Louis, MO.   (ABS)

Segal, Phyllis Nichamoff (1945 –) was a law student at Georgetown University Law Center when she became involved in the creation of the NWPC. She analyzed the status of women in political parties, documenting the way women were relegated to limited roles. Over a two-year period, with the help of congresswoman Martha Griffiths (D-MI), this research was published in the *Congressional Record*. The analysis helped shape activities undertaken by the NWPC. At the 1972 Democratic National Convention, Segal was involved with the women's caucus and represented women in challenges to delegations from which they were excluded. As a member of the Mikulski Commission (1972 – 1976), Segal was active in educating women about the delegate-selection process. Segal was responsible for parliamentary rules at the 1977 International Women's Forum, where she worked closely with Bella Abzug. For the next five years, Segal was the founding legal director of NOW LDEF. Her achievements include building the fund's first legal department; litigating groundbreaking women's rights issues, including

defining sexual harassment as a legal wrong; standards for proving employment discrimination claims; and enforcing Title VII, Title IX, ERA extension and state ERAs. She was also instrumental in founding NOW LDEF's National Judicial Education Program, which increased awareness of the ways gender bias undermines fairness in decision-making and court interactions. In 1982, she became a Fellow at the Bunting Institute of Radcliffe College, where she wrote of subtle discrimination against women through laws and policies that were neutral on their face, but in reality adversely affected women. In 1988, Segal served as an elected trustee of NOW LDEF, and in 1990 she became president of the board. Segal's feminist activities continued throughout the 1990s as a trustee of the Planned Parenthood League of Massachusetts. She is (2006) a trustee of the Women's Education and Industrial Union, and chair of the Brady Campaign to Prevent Gun Violence, which includes the chapters of the Million Mom March. Segal has two children. Archives: Papers from her years at NOW LDEF are at the Schlesinger Library, Radcliffe Institute, Cambridge, MA.   (ABS)

Seghi, Laya – See Firestone, Laya

Seichter, Marilyn P. (1945 – 2002) was just out of law school and had been admitted to the bar when she joined the legal team for Women v. Connecticut, the case significantly cited by the U.S. Supreme Court in its decision on Roe v. Wade. Practicing family law until shortly before her death, Seichter pioneered several important advances for women and children, including work on CT NOW's 1974 suit to prevent newspapers from running separate help-wanted ads for women and men. She also served as president of Connecticut Women's Educational and Legal Fund, as the first chair of the State Ethics Commission, and as an adviser to Governor Ella Grasso on the selection of judicial appointees. In the 1980s Seichter became the first woman to head the Connecticut Bar Association, giving inspiration to the increasing numbers of young women then graduating from law schools.

S

Seidenberg, Faith A. (1923 –) is an attorney who made legal contributions to numerous cases affecting the well-being of women. The cases include Seidenberg v. McSorley's Old Ale House (1970), the first case in the U.S. that successfully attacked gender-based discrimination in places of public accommodation; Phillips v. Martin Marietta (1971), which dealt with the right of a mother of pre-school-age children to be employed under the same terms as a father; and U.S. v. Newak (1989), a case that stands for the proposition that, for the first time in the history of the U.S., a member of the Armed Forces cannot be provided with a lawyer who is also representing witnesses against her. Other cases include Kotcher v. Rosa and Sullivan (1992), a Title VII case that delineated sexual harassment in the workplace; Cook v. Colgate (1992), which held for the first time that a club team should be moved up to varsity status on the basis of gender discrimination (Title IX); and Schuck v. Cornell University (1993), which reinstated varsity gymnastics and fencing for women students. Seidenberg, who was active in the civil rights movement in the South in the 1960s and served as legal counsel for CORE (1963–1966), has published numerous articles relating to women and the law. These include "The Myth of the 'Evil' Female as Embodied in the Law," published in *Environmental Law Journal, Northwestern School of Law*, 1971; and "Family, Property and Domicile Law in the State of New York," published in *Women's Role in Contemporary Society*, the report of the NYC Commission on Human Rights (Avon, 1972). Seidenberg served as VP of NOW (1970–1971), belonged to the advisory board to the *Women's Rights Law Reporter*, and was a member of the board of Women's Action Alliance. She also served as a board member of the steering committee of the National Prison Project–ACLU, and as a member of the National Women's Rights Project. She has three children. Archives: Schlesinger Library, Radcliffe Institute, Cambridge, MA. (ABS)

Seidenberg, Robert (1920 –) A psychiatrist and psychoanalyst, Seidenberg is said by Betty Friedan to have been the first male member of NOW. He also served as president of NOW's Greater Syracuse (NY) chapter (1985–1987) and as a member of its steering committee. Seidenberg is credited in many history books about gay rights as being one of the first psychiatrists in the U.S. to insist that gay people are not sick. An expert on agoraphobia and anorexia, Seidenberg highlighted in his analysis that the overwhelming number of persons with these disorders are female. He was also an early critic of the manner in which women patients were given tranquilizers, in order that they not protest their discontent with the female role. This work evolved into Congressional testimony and a change in practices. Seidenberg was also a critic of the way corporations had traditionally dealt with families, and his work can be credited with a dramatic change in the way corporations move executive families from place to place. Seidenberg is co-author, with Hortence S. Cochrane, of *Mind and Destiny* (Syracuse University Press, 1964). He is also author of *Marriage in Life and Literature* (New York Philosophical Library, 1970); *Corporate Wives – Corporate Casualties?* (Amacon, 1973); and *Women Who Marry Houses: Panic and Protest in Agoraphobia* (McGraw-Hill, 1983). He earned his B.A. (1940) and M.D. (1943) from Syracuse University, and served as a Captain in the Armed Forces during WWII (1944–1947). (ABS)

Seligsohn, Joy (1926 –) An actress, Seligsohn served as co-editor, with Mary Jean Tully, of NOW's first national newsletter, "Do It NOW." In the 1970s, she hosted and produced live call-in shows on two Westchester County, NY, stations, WFAS and WVIP. The hour-long shows, which ran Monday through Friday, were a forum for feminist issues during the four years they ran. A freelance fiction writer in the 1950s and 1960s, Seligsohn published numerous stories in popular magazines featuring feminist issues and strong female characters. She also wrote romance novels showcasing heroines who were "strong, brave, and aggressive." Seligsohn, who has two children, holds a B.A. from New York University. (ABS)

Sellers, Georgiana ("Sue") (1913 – 1989) In 1970, at the Seneca Falls National Women's Rights Historical Park, Sellers said, "We do not want separate, little unequal, unfair laws and separate, little unequal, low-paid jobs. We want full equality." Putting her belief into practice, Sellers was a leader of a group of women at the Colgate-Palmolive plant in New Albany, IN, who filed a complaint with the EEOC under Title VII protesting sex-based seniority lists and old rules "protecting" women workers. A member of the League for American Working Women, Sellers also wrote numerous letters to her congressmen and senators about discrimination against women, and testified in support of the ERA in the early 1970s. Says Mary Eastwood, "There were a number of women who filed the first test cases under Title VII. Most were not active in the women's movement, although their cases certainly advanced the movement. One exception was Georgiana Sellers. I believe she also joined NOW, and remember that she spoke at one of the NOW conferences around 1967." Sellers had three children.

Sellery, J'nan Morse (1928 –) In 1970, Sellery joined Claremont Colleges' women's studies program, which originated under Gerda Lerner and was established by dean Jean B. Walton. Sellery was the program's fourth coordinator. She focused on the ERA through AAUW, where she served on both the national and California state board. In addition, she worked on issues regarding families and the workplace, such as childcare concerns. Sellery retired in 2005 as emer. Louisa and Robert Miller professor of humanities, Harvey Mudd College, and is (2005) an affiliate scholar, English, Stanford University. (ABS)

Sells, Lucy Watson (1932 –) Sells used every step of her formal academic education to uncover sexism and racism in the school system itself. While studying for her oral Ph.D. exams (1968 – 1971), she began collecting data on women earning Ph.D.s by field and institution ranking. She worked as a research assistant for the Academic Senate's committee on the status of women, gathered data on the under-representation of women on the Berkeley campus, and was active in Sociologists for Women in Society (1971–1975). Sells's investigations revealed that boys had five times more preparation than girls in pre-calculus mathematics when beginning college, which explained the low percentages of women in the calculus-based fields. While serving on several Academic Senate committees, including the long-range academic planning committee, Sells shared her findings with the people at the Lawrence Hall of Science. From that association, the Math Science Network was created, providing national conferences introducing thousands of junior and senior high-school girls to the importance of math and science for equal opportunity. Sells testified before California assemblyman John Vasconcellos' 1973 hearings on the Master Plan for Higher Education. She was an executive specialist for minorities and women with the American Sociological Association, and a founding mother of the NWPC in Alameda County, CA. She worked with the NWPC and the Democratic Party electing pro-choice candidates at local, state and Federal levels. She works (2005) with Democratic Clubs, five Assembly District committees and three County Central committees. Sells is (2005) immediate past director of Region 6 for the California Democratic Party. She has two children. (ABS)

Selwyn, Lillie (1919 –) At age 55, Selwyn received a B.A. in women's studies and went from teaching dress-making in adult education to introducing and teaching women's studies. Later, in the process of getting her master's degree (at age 65), Selwyn wrote her thesis on the importance of the professional community accurately regarding women and their issues and responding accordingly. Selwyn's work as a career counselor for the Nassau County (NY) Office of Women's Services gave her the opportunity to speak out about the needs of older women seeking job opportunities. She also lobbied state legislators for enactment of laws giving this particular group of women equal opportunities. "We have come a long way since the 1970s," says Selwyn. "We have a long road ahead—especially for the older woman." Selwyn, who has two children, was born in Toronto, Ontario. (ABS)

Semmel, Joan (1932 –) An artist whose work centered on issues of sexuality, body and self definition, Semmel picketed museums to demand that women artists' work be exhibited, did research on faculty hiring at universities, and spoke at numerous panels on issues concerning women in the art world. In 1977, she curated a show at the Brooklyn (NY) Museum titled Contemporary Women: Content & Consciousness, and in 1978 taught a course on women artists at Rutgers University. She was the first woman tenured in the studio art area at Rutgers, and worked toward expanding representation of women in the graduate school and on the faculty. Her work was featured in *Women's Art Journal* and *Womanart*, among other publications, and she was co-author, with April Kingsley, of an article on sexual imagery published in *Women's Art Journal* in 1980. Semmel's work was also represented in *The Power of Feminist Art*, edited by Norma Broude and Mary D. Garrard (Harry N. Abrams, 1994) and *The Nude in American Painting*, by David McCarthy (Cambridge University Press, 1998). Her work is in numerous public collections, including the Museum of Plastic Arts, Montevideo, Uruguay; Museum of Fine Art, Houston, TX; New Jersey State Museum of Art,

Trenton, NJ; Museum of Women in the Arts, Washington, D.C.; The Brooklyn Museum, NYC; and the Davidson Collection, Art Institute of Chicago. Semmel holds a B.A. and M.F.A. from the Pratt Institute. (ABS)

Senerchia, Dorothy Sylvia — Co-founder (with Jacqueline Ceballos) of VFA (1992), Senerchia was active in the women's movement from 1969 – 1974. She was a member of NY NOW, a supporter of the New Feminist Theatre, and marched for abortion rights and other feminist concerns. She was a member of the planning committee for the Women's Strike for Equality march in NYC in 1970, and participated in that march as well as a similar one that took place a few years later. As a member of VFA, Senerchia served as dining room coordinator for the first banquet, held in 1992 at the Seventh Regiment Armory Mess Hall in NYC, and numerous other VFA events held there. Senerchia also co-ran (with Ceballos) the Betty Friedan testimonial dinner and the VFA fundraising video screening of "Town Bloody Hall" (2004), both held at the National Arts Club in NYC. In addition, she served on the board and the finance committee of VFA. After an illness doctors couldn't diagnose, Senerchia wrote *Silent Menace: 20th Century Epidemic – Candidiasis* (1990). A retired city planner for the City of New York, Senerchia holds a B.A. from Brown University and a certificate from the University of Florence, Italy. (ABS)

Sergi, Janet (1945 – 1993) was a co-founder of the Denver-based feminist newspaper *Big Mama Rag*. She was "an early mover and shaker at the newspaper," says longtime friend Chocolate Waters. Sergi's contributions were primarily in the areas of political thought and theory. "We called her our very own Charlotte Bunch," adds Waters. "Janet was also famous for her quick, dark wit, which eased many tense moments during early organizational meetings at *Big Mama Rag*."

Shafer, Ann M. (1916 – 1991) Working at Battle Creek's Kellogg Company in 1946, Shafer joined Local 3, American Federation of Grainmillers, where she fought for women in a male-dominated union that represented workers in a female-dominated industry. In 1971, she was the first woman to run for president of Local 3. In 1974, Shafer was a co-founder of CLUW and was elected VP for the Great Lakes Region and Michigan. She also helped found the Kalamazoo and Battle Creek chapters of NOW (1974), and was appointed to many state and national family, women's and educational commissions. Active in the NAACP and Planned Parenthood, Shafer was inducted into the Michigan Women's Hall of Fame in 1992.

Shanbaum, Suzanne P. (1950 –) (also known as Susann Shanbaum) made early contributions writing, performing and helping to produce women's music and lesbian literature. She participated in collectives committed to finding a way to create, live and work in supportive, non-oppres-

S

sive and productive environments. She also broke out of stereotypical female roles, becoming one of the first female Xerox repair technicians in the San Francisco Bay Area. In 1971, Shanbaum joined the Berkeley/Oakland Women's Press Collective, whose mission was to publish lesbian works. Shanbaum raised $300 for the publication of *Edward the Dyke* and other poems by Judy Grahn, participated in its printing and distribution, and helped acquire and learned to use an offset printing press. In 1973, she moved to Eugene, OR, to join the Starflower Natural Fools Distribution Collective, where her job was to maintain the trucks. By 1974, Shanbaum was back in Berkeley. A founding member of the Berkeley Women's Music Collective, she wrote, recorded and performed lesbian classics such as "The Fury," "Thorazine" and "The San Francisco Bank Song," addressing subjects including coming out as a teen lesbian, surviving in the workforce and psychiatric assault. The group, which stayed together for six years, performed in the San Francisco Bay Area and toured nationally, put out two albums, and published a BWMC songbook. From 1974–1985, Shanbaum worked on many other lesbian and feminist-oriented recording projects producing, arranging or playing with Alix Dobkin, Deb Saunder, Nancy Vogel, Linda Hirschhorn, and Debbie Fier. Some of her colleagues meeting at the Twin Towers lost their lives in the 9/11 attack. Shanbaum was across the street at the time and escaped with a back injury. She holds a B.M. from the Berklee College of Music, Professional Music. (ABS)

Shanklin, Elizabeth Eve (1934 –) A matriarchist, Shanklin has made it her life's work to understand and contribute to the elimination of social structures that generate and perpetuate destructive human behavior. She concluded that these patterns "are caused by social institutions designed by men intentionally to alienate women's power to nurture the next generation into self-regulation." Her efforts to understand the structures of patriarchy led her "to uncover women's international struggle toward matriarchy, beginning at least in the Enlightenment with Mary Wollstonecraft." A theorist, scholar and activist, Shanklin joined the women's movement in 1972. She lived in two experimental lesbian communities (one in Alligerville, NY; the other a cross-class, cross-cultural community) in, she says, "an attempt to establish nurturant economic and social relations, despite being embedded in patriarchal competitive ones." She has been a member of NOW, The Feminists and was a co-founder, with Barbara Love, of The Foundation for Matriarchy, which held study groups and conferences and published *The Matriarchist*, a newspaper, in the 1970s. Her writings include "Toward Matriarchy: The Radical Struggle of 19th-Century Women to Reconstruct Mothering in the US, 1785–1925" (UMI 1991). She is co-author, with Love, of "Matriarchy is the Answer," published in *Our Right to Love* (Prentice-Hall, 1978), and later republished in *Mothering: Essays in Feminist Theory*,

edited by Joyce Trebilcot (Rowman & Allanheld, 1983). Actions include demand for a Susan B. Anthony holiday, City Hall, NYC, 1972; co-founder, Yvonne Wanrow defense committee; organizer, International Tribunal for Crimes Against Women, Columbia University, 1973; co-organizer, with Love, of Forum on the Future, 1978; keynote speaker, Matriarchal Awareness Week, University of Missouri, Kansas City, 1979; and committee in support of Bella Abzug and other members of the national advisory committee for women fired by President Carter. Shanklin's mother, concerned that her daughter be able to speak in public, provided her with elocution lessons at the age of seven and acting lessons at age 10. Shanklin continued to act, performing Inez in "No Exit" in Greenwich Village, and was one of the first people reviewed in the Off Broadway movement. The *Village Voice* reviewer, quoting poet William Blake, said "Her sigh is the sword of an angel king." Shanklin earned a B.S. from Columbia University (1956) and an M.A. from Sarah Lawrence College (1991), while teaching English in NYC high schools. Shanklin explored women's struggles toward matriarchy on the Ph.D. level at the Graduate Center, City University of New York. During that time, she presented papers on women's efforts to free themselves as mothers, and spoke on panels at the Canadian Historical Association, the Berkshire Conference of Women Historians, Lehman College and the Graduate Center, City University of New York. In 1998, Shanklin joined the Green Party and founded The Bronx Greens. In 2001, she was elected to represent the Green Party of New York State to the Green Party of the United States, and was re-elected in 2003. In 2002, she was the Green Party Candidate for U.S. Congress from the 17th District. (ABS)

Shanley, Mary Lyndon (1944 –) A college professor, Shanley has taught women's studies at Vassar College (1970s –), and served as acting chair of the women's studies program, 1982–1983. She also served as chair of the Northeast Political Science Association committee on the status of women, 1974–1976. A member of the American Political Science Association committee on the status of women, Shanley served as chair (1977–1980), and wrote *Women's Rights, Feminism, and Politics in the United States*, a text published by APSA in 1987. She was an active member of the APSA task force on women (1981–1983), was president-elect of the Women's Caucus for Political Science (1997–1998) and president (1998–1999). Shanley is the author of *Feminism, Marriage and the Law in Victorian England* (Princeton University Press, 1989); *Making Babies, Making Families: What Matters Most in an Age of Reproductive Technologies, Surrogacy, Adoption, and Same-Sex and Unwed Parents* (Beacon Press, 2001); and *Just Marriage* (Oxford University Press, 2004). She was co-editor, with Carole Pateman, of *Feminist Interpretations and Political Theory* (Pennsylvania State University Press, 1990); and co-editor, with Uma Narayan, of *Reconstructing Political Theory: Feminist*

Essays (Pennsylvania State University Press, 1997). She holds an M.A. from Wellesley College and a Ph.D. from Harvard University. She has two children.   (ABS)

Shapiro, Lynne Dianne (1947 –) A market and policy researcher in NYC, Shapiro describes herself as "one of the grassroots, entrepreneurial business-type women who wove the fabric of 1970s movement." A member of the New York Women's Liberation Center in the early 1970s, she served on a six-month steering committee after the Socialist Workers Party was expelled. She also worked on newsletter mailings, the coordination of structure meetings, staffing, and outreach at the NYRF 1971 rape conference. In 1972, she worked on a major fundraising committee for the Center. A member of NYRF (1971–1978), Shapiro was a CR group organizer, newsletter staff member, workshop leader, fundraiser, and speakout and conference organizer, as well as a writer of publicity material. In 1979, Shapiro was a member of Women Against Pornography, where she also served as a conference organizer and workshop leader. Shapiro participated in the 1970 Women's Strike for Equality march; was press manager for the Fifth Street Women's Shelter takeover; and served as seed funder and co-leader (with Rosemary Gaffney) of the August 26, 1980, Women's Equality Day march and rally (NYC). In 1977 and 1979, Shapiro was editor and researcher for the self-published book *Write on Woman! A Writer's Guide to Women's/Feminist/Lesbian Alternate Press Periodicals*. Archives: Alternate Press Collection, Thomas J. Dodd Research Center, University of Connecticut, Storrs, CT.   (ABS)

Shatter, Susan L. (1943 –) worked with Bread and Roses in Boston (1969–1972) and was part of the collective that eventually wrote and published *Our Bodies, Ourselves*. She helped run CR groups about health and sexuality issues, and was part of an early Cambridge co-op day care center in which parents participated. Shatter left the movement in 1973. "I had a child to raise and a career to pursue," she says, "and Bread and Roses became more concerned with lesbian issues." An artist, Shatter has taught art to many women and acted as a mentor helping them lead their own lives in the arts. Shatter holds a B.F.A. and an M.F.A.   (ABS)

Shavlik, Donna (1935 –) was associate dean of women, University of Kansas (1967–1971). She and her husband, who was working with the dean of the men's office, were advisers to groups concerned with equity and rights issues and to the emerging women's groups. From 1972–1973, Shavlik was associate dean of students at the University of Delaware, where she helped start racial awareness training for the campus, worked with faculty on a human sexuality course, assisted with the development of the first women's studies survey course, and began, with students, a women's studies residence hall. From 1973–1981, Shavlik served as assistant and then the associate director of the Office of Women in Higher Education of the American Council on Education. In 1982 she became director of the office, a position she held until she retired in 1997. During her tenure, Shavlik worked with Nancy Schlossberg and Emily Taylor on a number of initiatives to improve the lives of women. These include a change in retirement benefits for women in higher education in accordance with Title VII; the passage of the regulations on Title IX; and the founding of the National Coalition for Women and Girls in Education. Shavlik also served on the board for the Federation for Organizations for Professional Women. In 1977, Taylor, Shavlik and Judy Touchton founded the National Identification Program for the Advancement of Women in Higher Education Administration, later known as the ACE Network of Women Leaders. In 1989, Shavlik, Touchton and Carol Pearson produced the book *Educating the Majority: Women Challenge Tradition in Higher Education*. Shavlik has received numerous awards and honors, including Honorary Doctorate degrees from Marymount Manhattan College, Alverno, Wheaton, Olivet and Gettysburg College. The National Association for Women in Education honored Shavlik with several awards for distinguished service, culminating with the Lifetime Achievement Award in 1998 for Advancing Women in Higher Education. Also in 1998, the National Council for Research on Women awarded her the First Annual Award for Women Who Make a Difference. She earned a B.S. from Colorado State University (1957).   (ABS)

Shaw, Joyce – See Cutler-Shaw, Joyce Arlene

Shea, Gail (1940 –) In the early 1970s Shea was involved in various feminist activities, such as the Hartford (CT) chapter of NOW and serving on the minority affairs advisory board for WFSB-TV (Channel 3). However, her feminist activities were primarily focused on the University of Connecticut, where she was one of only a handful of feminist faculty members and later an administrator. As a faculty member, she initiated new courses in the sociology of gender, which meshed with changes being implemented in the English curriculum by Joan Hall and Marcia Lieberman. These new courses constituted the beginnings of the women's studies program at the university. As assistant provost, Shea was involved with developing the university's affirmative action plan, which included designing and implementing new faculty hiring procedures. These changes met much resistance. She also challenged long-held beliefs such as the one that capped the undergraduate enrollment of women on the grounds that there were only so many "female beds." Shea was also instrumental in launching a much-needed campus women's center. Although university president Homer Babbidge had created Shea's provost-level position to deal with women's issues, Shea was given an office not with the other provosts, but rather in the Home Economics building. When Shea was fired by the acting

S

president who succeeded Babbidge, she sued the university. For several years thereafter, her life centered on attorneys and the courts. Eventually, after losing in court, Shea found herself blackballed when she looked for other jobs. Undaunted, she went on to teach and do research at the University of Rhode Island, never giving up her CT home or her activism shaped by her feminist values. (ABS)

Shear, Linda (1948 –) performed (singing, piano, guitar) in what was, to the best of her knowledge, the first out lesbian concert (Chicago, 1972). Shear was accompanied by Ella Szekely on percussion. Shear and Szekely expanded the group to include Joan Capra (violinist) and various guitar/bass players including Sherry Jenkins, Judy Handler and Susan Abod. With Susan Kahn as sound technician, they became Family of Woman, the first out lesbian band in the country. The group played nationally for women and lesbian audiences, and was invited to play at the Los Angeles National Lesbian Conference (April 1973). After the band split up, Shear recorded her album, *Linda Shear, A Lesbian Portrait*. Shear was also a founding member of the Chicago lesbian newspaper *Lavender Woman* in the early 1970s. Shear holds an M.B.A. Archives: The Lesbian Herstory Archives, Brooklyn, NY. (ABS)

Shear, Marie (1940 –) A writer and editor, Shear attended early feminist meetings in the 1960s and participated in the annual Women's Equality Day marches in NYC in the 1970s, starting with the historic demonstration of 1970. The following year, she began writing about sexist language and the media, subjects to which she often returns. A member of NOW since the early 1970s, she founded and chaired the legislative and political committee of Brooklyn (NY) NOW and wrote regularly for the "Brooklyn NOW News," beginning in 1973. Shear researched and wrote a countywide voters guide, covering 200 Brooklyn candidates, and led a successful countywide campaign for the NYS ERA referendum in 1975. She began writing satiric columns titled "Shear Chauvinism," which she continued later during eight years as media-watch columnist for *New Directions for Women*. More than 40 popular and scholarly periodicals have published Shear's articles, columns and book reviews on street harassment, women and Nixon's Watergate scandal, racism, disability rights and homophobia. The first version of her article "Solving the Great Pronoun Problem" was published by the U.S. Commission on Civil Rights. Shear has received awards from VFA and International Association of Business Communications. (ABS)

Shedd, Patricia T. (1921 –) In 1942, as a junior at Keene Teachers College (now Keene State College), Shedd became one of the first—if not the first—women members of the Civil Air Patrol in New Hampshire. After successfully pleading with the college president for the chance to take the classes and flight training leading to a private pilot's license, Shedd was the only woman among the Naval cadets and college men in the program, and became certified in 1943. Working toward her M.A. in English at Queens College, CUNY, Shedd wrote her thesis on Kate Chopin and her work (1968). From 1970–1972, Shedd worked to promote and support the ERA in Cortland, NY, and in 1976 wrote her doctoral dissertation (Syracuse University) on the relationship between the attitude of the reader towards women's changing role and response to literature that illuminated women's role. In 1977, as professor of English and personnel committee chair, Shedd initiated and taught the first course on women in literature at New York State University, Cortland. Shedd is co-editor (1989 –) of "Choice," the newsletter of the Cortland Coalition of Women for Choice. Shedd has three children. (ABS)

Sheedy, Charlotte Nmi (1934 –) A literary agent, Sheedy began attending the women's liberation group meetings when she enrolled at Columbia University in 1970. She also began attending meetings of Columbia's Gay Liberation Front, continued an earlier association with Women Strike for Peace, and worked as a draft counselor. In addition, she was an organizer of and participant in the first Columbia Women's Liberation Conference (spring 1970). During her years at Columbia, Sheedy was a scout for a number of editors and publishers looking for books coming out of this embryonic movement. One of the first books she placed with a publisher (McGraw-Hill) was *Patience and Sarah* by Isabel Miller. Sheedy participated in many actions initiated by CWL, including a sex-discrimination suit against Columbia brought on behalf of the maids, and another brought on behalf of the women teaching at Columbia. They won each time. Sheedy has three children. (ABS)

Sheffield, Anne Helen (1941 –) (also known as Anne Sheffield Courtney) has been a feminist organizer devoted to the passage of the ERA and ending sexism in education. In 1972, Sheffield was a convening member of the Peoria (IL) NOW chapter and was legislative coordinator for five years as she worked on passage of the ERA. In 1973, she convened and co-chaired the Peoria ERA Coalition, and was a speaker and workshop presenter on the ERA. From 1975–1982 she chaired the coalition. In 1974, she co-wrote the booklet *Free to Dream*, which looked at sex-role stereotyping in elementary to intermediate educational settings. The study was used in Florida, Illinois and Oregon. At the same time, Sheffield was a member of the IL NOW education task force, served as its chair, and conducted workshops on sexism in education. She co-authored "Remember the Ladies," sketches of 15 women in American history. She also wrote *Portrait of American Women*, a booklet of biographical sketches of more than 250 women in American history. In 1977, Sheffield became secretary of IL NOW. She was a member of the IL IWY coordinating committee and served as a delegate from Illinois to the 1977 National Women's

Conference in Houston. In 1981 she became president of the Peoria NOW chapter. In 1982, she began a two-year term as president of IL NOW, became president of IL NOW PAC and a member of the board of Tri-County WomenStrength. From 1983–1984, Sheffield lobbied in Springfield to pass the Illinois Criminal Sexual Assault Act of 1983, and was awarded the Peoria Chapter ACLU Sam Belfer Libertarian Award. In 1985, she served as president of IL NOW LDEF. Sheffield, who has two children and holds an M.A., is a speech/language pathologist. (ABS)

Shelley, Martha Altman (1943 –) A radical lesbian feminist activist and writer, Shelley joined NY Daughters of Bilitis (1967) and served briefly as chapter treasurer and president, then as public speaker. She was a co-founder of both the New York Gay Liberation Front (1969) and Radicalesbians (1970), and played a major role in shaping the positions and strategies of both. She was on the collectives that published *Come Out!* and *RAT* newspapers. She also organized the first gay march (in NYC) after the Stonewall riots, as well as numerous demonstrations for gay and women's rights, and participated in the Lavender Menace action at the historic Second Congress to Unite Women, where lesbians "came out" to the women's movement. Shelley also worked with abortion rights groups in New York, as well as the anti-rape movement. She produced "Lesbian Nation," a weekly radio program for WBAI-FM in NYC, and "Women and Their Work," a series of interviews with women in different occupations (1972–1974). After moving to California, she worked in the Women's Press Collective (1975–1977). The co-parent of five children, Shelley is the author of many short stories and essays and three books of poetry: *Crossing the DMZ* (Women's Press Collective, 1974), *Lovers and Mothers* (Sefir Publishing, 1981), and *Haggadah: A Celebration of Freedom* (Aunt Lute Books, 1997). Shelley holds an M.A. (ABS)

Shepard, Elizabeth Louise (1918 –) Immediately after participating in the 1970 Women's Strike for Equality march down Fifth Ave. in NYC commemorating the 50th anniversary of passage of the 19th amendment, Shepard joined Nassau (NY) NOW and served on its image committee and speakers bureau. After completing the assignment to get a local radio station, WHLI, to promote the national campaign "She was born handicapped, she was born female," Shepard received an offer of a weekly broadcast as public service by NOW. She subsequently produced and presented "Speaking NOW," which focused on women's concerns, for five years. She also led workshops on women's issues, sexuality, religion, econo- mics, and sports, and lectured extensively to high-school classes and women's and community groups. A member of the WPC, AAUW and VFA, Shepard joined the Auxiliary to the Nassau County Medical Society and produced programs for them "breaking all attendance records." A lecture on female sexuality led to an invitation to repeat it for the

Medical Society. Now a retired therapeutic dietician, Shepard has two children. She holds a B.S. from the University of Wisconsin and an A.D.A. from New York Hospital, Cornell Medical Center. (ABS)

Sherfey, Mary Jane (1918 – 1983) A psychiatrist, Sherfey published an article in 1966 about female sexuality that challenged the Freudian beliefs about orgasms. Drawing on Albert Kinsey and the work of Masters and Johnson, she argued that it was the suppression of female sexuality that created civilization's "discontents." Sherfey was a psychiatrist in New York for many years and on the staff of Payne Whitney Clinic of the New York Hospital-Cornell Medical Center. She was a resident psychiatrist at Rusk State Hospital at the time of her death. She wrote many articles on female sexuality and was the author of *The Nature and Evolution of Female Sexuality* (1972). Sherfey, a native of Brazil, IN, received her B.A. and medical degree from Indiana University.

Sherif, Carolyn Wood (1922 – 1982) was a professor and social psychologist who did extensive and original research on gender and group studies. Sherif wrote several influential articles regarding the importance afforded gender in society and the role of gender in self-reference, and was an advocate for the responsible study of gender in the sciences. Although she was the co-author with her husband, Dr. Muzafer Sherif, of many early books and articles on gender, her name was often left off the work and she had to fight to receive recognition. With the advent of the feminist movement, however, things began to change. Before her death, Sherif said of this time, "To me, the atmosphere created by the women's movement was like breathing fresh air after years of gasping for breath. I know I did not become a significantly better social psychologist between 1969 and 1972, but I surely was treated as a better social psychologist." While a professor at Penn State, Sherif was a participant in the first graduate seminar on the psychology of women (1972). A member of the APA's Society for The Psychology of Women, Sherif served as its president from 1979 to 1980. Sherif received a B.A. from Purdue University in 1942, an M.A. from Iowa University, and a Ph.D. from the University of Texas (1961). She had three children.

Shields, Stephanie A. (1949 –) Shields's activism began when she was a graduate student and continued when she became a professor. In 1971, Shields entered graduate school in psychology at Penn State and organized its first women in psychology discussion group. This group initiated the first graduate seminar in the psychology of women in 1972, which was the basis for the psychology of women undergraduate courses and laid the foundation for the women's studies program. She published two groundbreaking articles in *American Psychologist* (1975), the flagship journal of the American Psychological Association: "Functionalism, Darwinism, and the Psychology of Women: A study in Social Myth," and "Ms. Pilgrim's Progress: The Contributions of Leta Stetter Hollingworth to the Psychology of Women." Shields remains involved in women's studies, directing programs at University of California, Davis, and Penn State.   (ABS)

Shinn, Ruth (1922 –) began fighting for civil rights and women's rights as a college student during WWII (1942), helping to free five Nisei (Japanese-American) women and men students from a California internment camp so they could come to her Ohio college campus. As a staff adviser in 1949, she helped the University of Nebraska YWCA students racially integrate university-segregated women's dorms. She continued working for racial equality in the 1970s, coaching local city YWCAs in performing self-audits and building diversity in all programs, board membership and staff. Shinn was a founding member of the NWPC and the Women's Vote Project. During nearly 25 years in the women's bureau of the U.S. Department of Labor, she helped transform public policies on equality in the workplace. She also helped rewrite administrative rules to eliminate bias and take into account the needs of women in such fields as affirmative action, safety and health, pensions, training and childcare. Shinn is a supporter of and advocate for Emily's List.   (ABS)

Shirley, Eleanor Freeman (1937 –) served as president and legislative liaison for the Baton Rouge (LA) LWV (1972 – 1975). As such, she helped develop position statements and adopt legislative agenda, and testified in various committees. Also president and lobbyist for the ERA coalition in LA (1972 – 1976), Shirley sought legislative sponsors, lobbied individual legislators, and prepared House hearings and individuals to testify. In 1977, she accepted a position with the Bureau for Women, the only state-funded agency for women within state government. There, she managed innovative, non-traditional training programs and helped create a teen parent center for pregnant and parenting teens. She administers (2005) contracts for family violence shelters (20) statewide. Shirley, who has one child, earned her B.A. from Wheaton College, Norton, MA, her M.A. from Hartford Seminary and her M.B.A. from Tulane Business School.   (ABS)

Shulman, Alix Kates (1932 –) An activist and writer, Shulman "rushed to NYC's Greenwich Village from Ohio" when she was only 20. In 1967 she became a member of NYRW. The next year she joined Redstockings and WITCH. After these groups folded, Shulman became a member of NYRF. Her activism ranged from helping plan the first national demonstration of women's liberation, the 1968 Miss America Pageant protest in Atlantic City, to teaching at the 1975 Sagaris Feminist Institute, to founding a Hawaiian branch of the abortion-rights guerrilla action group No More Nice Girls (1991 – 1992). Her early feminist stories and essays were published in *Aphra*, *Women: A Journal of Liberation* and *Up From Under*,

which also first published her much attacked "Marriage Agreement" proposing that men and women split housework and childcare equally. After three children's books, she wrote a biography of Emma Goldman, *To the Barricades* (T.Y. Crowell, 1971) and edited a collection of Goldman's works, *Red Emma Speaks* (Random House, 1972). Shulman's first novel, the feminist classic *Memoirs of an Ex-Prom Queen* (Alfred A. Knopf, 1972), was re-issued by Penguin in a 25th Anniversary Edition in 1997. Subsequent novels are *Burning Questions* (Alfred A. Knopf, 1978), about the rise of the women's liberation movement; *On the Stroll* (Alfred A. Knopf, 1981), about a shopping bag lady and a teen runaway; and *In Every Woman's Life* (Alfred A. Knopf, 1987), a feminist family comedy of ideas. Her 1995 memoir, *Drinking the Rain* (Farrar Straus & Giroux), was a finalist for the *Los Angeles Times* Book Prize and won a Body Mind Spirit Award. Her 1999 memoir, *A Good Enough Daughter* (Schocken Books) was listed as New and Notable by *The New York Times Book Review* in 2000. Shulman has taught writing and literature at New York University, Yale and the universities of Southern Maine, Colorado, Arizona and Hawaii, and has been Visiting Writer at the American Academy in Rome and Belagio. She has received awards from the National Endowments for the Arts and the Lila Wallace/Reader's Digest Foundation. Shulman, who has two children, earned her M.A. from New York University in 1978 and received an Honorary Doctorate from Case Western Reserve in 2001. Archives: Sallie Bingham Center, Duke University, Durham, NC.   (ABS)

Shultz, Leah – See Margulies, Leah

Shumsky, Ellen (1941 –) (also known as Ellen Bedoz) joined the newly-formed Gay Liberation Front in 1969, and in 1969 was a founding member of Radicalesbians. She was one of the authors of "Woman-Identified Woman," published in 1970, which articulated the Radicalesbian philosophy. A member of the first radical lesbian consciousness raising group, she was the coordinator of additional CR groups, and from 1960 – 1980 was a photojournalist documenting the gay, feminist and countercultural movements. She was the principal photographer for *Come Out*, the GLF newspaper, and published a radical lesbian comic strip, "Lesbiantics" (1970 – 1971), in that newspaper. She also published "Women's Songs from the Balkans," in *Traditions* magazine. Her article "Transforming the Ties that Bind: Lesbians, Lovers and Chosen Family" was published in *Sexualities Lost and Found: Lesbians, Psychoanalysis and Culture* (International Universities Press, 2001). Shumsky received a B.S. from Brooklyn College (1961); an M.L.S. from the Pratt Institute (1964); her M.S.W. from SUNY Stony Brook (1979); and certification as a psychoanalyst and psychotherapist, Psychoanalytic Psychotherapy Center (1996). Archives: The Sophia Smith Collection, Smith College, Northampton, MA.   (ABS)

Siebert, Muriel F. (1932 –) entered the securities business in 1954. In December 1967, she created a sensation by becoming the first woman member of the New York Stock Exchange. An article published in *The New York Times* (December 8, 1967) pointed out, however, that although "Miss Siebert could participate in floor trading, it is understood that she does not plan to do so." Tradition was broken, but with a nod to old-time decorum. A subsequent *Times* article (November 8, 2002) says of the membership, "she had to have it: no major firm would hire her, so she went into business for herself." In 1977, Governor Hugh L. Carey appointed Siebert as the state's first female superintendent of banking. In 1982, she ran in the Republican primary for U.S. Senate, coming in second in a three-way race. In 2001, Siebert was co-founder (with Barbara Stanbridge, president of NAWBO) of The Women's Financial Network. The author of *Changing the Rules: Adventures of a Wall Street Maverick* (The Free Press, 2002), Siebert attended Flora Stone Mather College, the women's division of Case Western Reserve. She was the only woman to take a financial course at the men's college. (ABS)

Siegel, Gonnie (1928 – 2005) was a founding member of Westchester NOW in 1970, having joined in the Armonk home of Mary Jean Tully, where she was part of an ongoing CR group. One of her favorite actions in 1972 was to integrate the all men's lunchroom at the Red Coach Grill in Yonkers. With a degree in journalism from West Virginia University, Siegel became a newspaper reporter in Ohio and helped edit the NOW national newsletter "Do It Now." She was a columnist for *The Feminist Bulletin* and established her own communications business. Siegel was the author of *Women's Workbook; Sales, The Fast Track for Women; How to Beat the High Cost of Learning;* and *How to Advertise and Promote Your Small Business.* Born Gonnie McClung, she was delivered by her mid-wife grandmother in the Appalachia Hamlet of Mount Lookout, WV. She was proud of her part Native American heritage and said she became a feminist during sixth grade, when she "discovered the right books in my village library." Along with her feminist activism, Siegel was an ardent civil rights activist throughout her life. She loved a good argument, a heated debate of the issues and humor. Her life-long credo was: "Change whatever you can and laugh at the rest."

Siegel, Marilynn – See zana

Siegel, Thyme S. (1944 –) was a pioneer in women's studies at the University of California, Berkeley. In 1969, wanting to get her B.A. degree under the then-nonexistent rubric of women's studies, and having been rejected by the only woman dean, she met Dr. Susan Ervin Tripp, who needed someone to do an analysis of roles played by girls and boys in textbooks adopted by California State. Dr. Tripp agreed to become Siegel's thesis adviser. Siegel's work, "A Continuing Analysis of the Number of Roles Little Boys Play, and Little Girls Play, in California Adopted Textbooks," was presented to the California State Textbook Committee. Thus, Siegel was allowed to graduate as she wished, and in the process helped engender a shift in academic consciousness. In 1970, Siegel taught a student-initiated class, Women and Anthropology, and her feminist analysis of the role of Desdemona in *Othello* was published in *Women: A Journal of Liberation*. In 1974, she moved to Eugene, OR, where she joined the lesbian feminist movement. For several years, she hosted a Eugene radio program, "As the Women Turn," and was a collective member of Mother Kali's Books. Siegel taught women's studies and Jewish women's history at various state universities and community colleges. In addition to her B.A., she holds an M.A. from San Francisco State University. Archives: The Lesbian Herstory Archives, Brooklyn, NY; the June Mazer Collection, West Hollywood, CA; and the Gay Archive, University of Southern California, Los Angeles. (ABS)

Sila, Mo (1953 –) (also known as Moe Zenko) At Warren Harding High School in Bridgeport, CT, in the late 1960s, Sila became involved in political actions demanding equal education for females and blacks. In New Haven (CT) in 1973, she participated in early rape crisis peer groups and political action, and in 1979 was one of the organizers of Connecticut's first Take Back the Night march. In 1982, Sila organized and facilitated the state's first incest survivor group, and in 1983 became co-founder of the newsletter "Incest Survivor Information Exchange." Organizer and instructor of a women's self-defense group in New Haven, Sila holds a B.S. in social work. While her primary area of work has been violence against women, Sila also continues to work for civil rights, gay rights, and the peace and labor movements through demonstrations, political action, financial support and education. (ABS)

Silvermoon, Flash (1950 –) (also known as Deborah Koetler) entered the women's movement from the Left, as a war protester, civil rights activist and one of the founders of Student Committee For Radical and Activist Politics. She ran for the Miss Trenton (NJ) State beauty pageant as a feminist in 1970. Moving to NYC, she volunteered at the Women's Liberation Center, performed widely in the burgeoning women's music scene, including performing at many of the NY Metro first women's dances, and formed her own bands, including Sister. Long before there was a public lesbian politic, she performed for NOW at their Gala at the Village Gate (1973) and broke their request to remain closeted. She went on to help form, and speak for, the Dyke Separatists, which articulated a lesbian politic and evolved in to LFL. Simultane- ously, her spirituality expanded including Tarot, Wicca and starting a coven, an outgrowth of a Cosmic Consci-ousness Group, after being initiated by Z

S

Budapest. Her books include *The Wise Woman's Tarot*, *Flash Silver-moon's Planetary Playbook*, *Lifetime Companions: Love Never Dies*, and *Temple of Isis*. Her recorded available music is Flash Silvermoon, Phases of the Silvermoon, Solstice and Inner Outer Space. She also works with crystals, animals and astrology. (ABS)

Silverstein, Helene (1938 – 1996) A member of Westchester (NY) Feminists (1970 – 1973), Silverstein was "the most radical and political of this very tight, but loosely organized, group of 20 to 25 suburban housewives," says Florence Rush. Among other actions, the group participated in the August 20, 1970, Women's Strike for Equality march and rally. Silverstein moved to Manhattan in 1973, where she was a member of NYRF (1972 – 1977). There Silverstein was a conference organizer, a representative of the collective, and a co-producer of the NYRF calendar. She was also a founding member of the 7th Avenue Women's Coffeehouse (1974 – 1978) and a founding member of the Women's Creativity Group Workspace (1974 – 1976). From 1973 – 1979, Silverstein was a feminist program producer at WBAI and weekly CR group moderator. In 1979, she served as a conference workshop leader for Women Against Pornography. An editorial freelancer (1973 – 1996), Silverstein was also a counselor at a Rockland County (NY) domestic violence shelter in the early 1980s. She was also active in lesbian cancer survivors groups.

Silverwoman – See Souder, Sandra Silverman

Simchak, Morag MacLeod (1914 – 1978) Born in London, England, Simchak came to the U.S. in 1941 and became a citizen in 1945. During WWII, which took the life of her first husband, a hero of the Polish Resistance, Simchak (who spoke several languages) worked for the U.N. She moved to Washington, D.C., in 1945, where she married her second husband, the Hon. M.S. Szymczak, a member of the board of governors of the Federal Reserve System. She later joined the staff of the office of the United Rubber Workers International Union. In 1961, she began a 15-year term of government service when she joined the Department of Labor as legislative assistant to assistant secretary Esther Peterson. In that capacity, Simchak helped draft and bring into law the Federal Equal Pay Act of 1963. Simchak was recognized as the Labor Department's leading expert on the Fair Labor Standards Act of 1938, the Equal Pay Act, Title VII of the Civil Rights Act of 1964, and the Age Discrimination in Employment Act of 1967. A founding member of NOW, Simchak was appointed by Betty Friedan to a committee of three to prepare a paper on the proposed ERA (1967). Simchak is also credited with being the person responsible for insisting in equal pay issues that men's salaries would never be lowered, but women's would be made higher to provide equal pay. Throughout her life, Simchak worked tirelessly to achieve equality for working women.

In 1975, she was a delegate to the IWY conference in Mexico City, and began work on programs for the advancement of women in Africa, Asia and Latin America under the auspices of the Agency for International Development. Educated in Britain and Europe, Simchak had three children. Archives: Archives of Labor and Urban Affairs, Wayne State University, Detroit, MI.

Simmons, Adele Smith (1941 –) entered the women's movement in 1968. As an assistant dean and later dean at Jackson College at Tufts University, Simmons worked with dean Antonia Chayes to launch a full-time early childhood center to meet the needs of faculty, employees and students at the university. Simmons also taught the first undergraduate course in women's history at Tufts, and co-founded the Higher Education Resource Service for Women, based at Brown University. She co-authored the 20th Century Task Force report on women and employment, "Exploitation from 9 – 5." After moving to Princeton University as the first woman senior officer (1972 – 1977), Simmons founded HERS mid-Atlantic, an early childcare center at Princeton. In 1977, she became president of Hampshire College and joined feminist colleagues in ensuring that the curriculum and experiences of both men and women were shaped by feminist values. She also helped start another early childhood center. During those years, Simmons wrote articles on women's history and her own feminist experiences. When she was appointed president of the MacArthur Foundation (1989), it was another first: the first woman president of one of the top-10 foundations in the country. In that capacity, Simmons helped develop and implement a program on women's reproductive health. Says Simmons, "As vice chair of Chicago Metropolis 2020, I am again in the trenches, working to ensure that all children in Illinois have access to quality and affordable early childhood education—which, for me, is a key issue if we are serious about opportunities for women in our country." She has three children and holds a B.A. from Radcliffe College and a D.Phil. from Oxford University. (ABS)

Simmons, Christina Clare (1948 –) A history professor, Simmons has contributed to the women's movement through teaching and writing on women's history and women's studies. She demanded and helped teach the first women's studies course at Brown University, 1974, with anthropologist Louise Lamphere. She was involved with Rhode Island's Women's Liberation Union, 1972 – 1978, working on the ERA and abortion rights. In the early 1970s, she was a member of several Marxist Feminist study groups. Moving with her husband to Nova Scotia, she was active in the women's action committee and the Canadian Abortion Rights Action League. She was a teaching assistant in a Canadian and women's history course at Dalhousie University, and later taught American history and women's studies at Raymond Walters College, University of Cincinnati. Simmons, who has two children, teaches (2005) in the history department at the University of Windsor, serves on the women's studies advisory committee, and works in the New Democratic Party. She holds a B.A. from Radcliffe College, 1970, and a Ph.D. from Brown University, 1982. (ABS)

Simmons, Katrina Wynkoop (1944 –) was a volunteer at the Emma Goldman Clinic, which offered safe abortions and women's health services, in Iowa City (1972–1974). She also worked informally with women's groups at Central Michigan University and Michigan State University (1974–1981). Simmons, who says she "stood up for myself and earned my way through college between 1963 and 1970," holds a B.A., M.A. and a Ph.D. A researcher, she has one child. (ABS)

Simmons, Lynda (1934 –) was a founding member of the Princeton University NOW chapter (1969), and from 1975–1992 spoke extensively on topics related to women's, children's and families' roles and needs in housing and the environment. A Registered Architect, State of New York, Simmons joined Phipps Houses in New York City in 1969, then built it to 500 staff members, developing 3,500 apartments in nine middle- and lower-income communities in Manhattan and the South Bronx. Many were occupied by single mothers and their children. Simmons describes her greatest contribution to the women's movement as "being a highly visible and successful CEO when there were very few of us, and when construction in NYC was totally a man's world." Under her guidance, Phipps Houses became the largest developer-owner-manager of social housing in the United States, doing business of $100,000,000 a year by 1993. When Simmons began, creating low-income housing in New York City was considered little more than providing minimal shelter. People could take no pride in their homes and eventually trashed and abandoned thousands of apartments. Simmons' vision of housing, "humane, enduring and beautiful communities," was based on her ideas that "community is, in and of itself, healing," and that "beauty is biologically important." She was editor/co-ordinator of the *Planning and Design Workbook for Community Participation.* Simmons is the recipient of many awards and honors, including the Women in Construction (NYC) Leadership Award and honors from the New York chapters of the American Institute of Architects and the American Planning Association. She led the Women's China Study Group in two architectural visits to China in 1977. The WCSG hosted leading Chinese architects in the U.S. in 1979. Simmons holds a B.A. from the University of North Carolina at Greensboro and a B.Arch. from The Cooper Union, NYC, as well as an Honorary Doctor of Laws degree from UNCG. (ABS)

Simone, Nina (1933 – 2003) Born Eunice Kathleen Waymon in North Carolina, Simone showed her prodigious talents as a musician and singer as a very young child when she played the piano and sang with her siblings at her church. At her first piano recital at age 10 at the town library, she loved the applause but was traumatized by her first encounter with racism: Her parents were removed from the first row to accommodate some white people. That incident is believed by some to be the origin of her commitment to the fight for freedom and civil rights. Her life's work had particular significance for African American women. It showed the black woman's point of view and spoke for the dispossessed. Many of her songs portrayed black women as beautiful, exotic objects of desire and admiration, and others, such as "Four Women," revealed the damning legacy of slavery. In an article published in the *Village Voice* (April/May 2003), Thulani Davis says that, "For African American women, [the song] became an anthem affirming our existence, our sanity, and our struggle to survive a culture which regards us as anti-feminine. It acknowledged the loss of childhoods among African American women, our invisibility, exploitation and defiance, and even subtly reminded that in slavery and patriarchy, your name is what *they* call you. It was an invitation to get over color and class difference" and to step boldly and with pride into the world.

Simonson, Joy R. (1919 – 2007) worked for the United Nations Relief and Rehabilitation Agency in Egypt and Yugoslavia during WWII, then for Army Headquarters in Frankfurt, Germany, from 1945–1948. She was the first woman to serve as chair of the Alcoholic Beverage Control Board in Washington, D.C. (1964–1972). In 1967, she initiated and organized the District of Columbia Commission for Women and served on it for almost 15 years. In 1970, Simonson helped organize the Interstate Association of Commissions on the Status of Women (later called the National Association of Commissions for Women), and subsequently served three terms as president. In 1975, she was a member of the staff in Washington, D.C., and Mexico City of the national commission on IWY and served as deputy director, Federal Women's Program. From 1975–1982 she served as executive director of the National Advisory Council on Women's Educational Programs. Although Simonson was later fired by Reagan Council appointees, she was commended in the House of Representatives for her work. A delegate from Washing-ton, D.C., to the 1977 National Women's Conference in Houston, Simonson also attended the 1980 and 1985 women's conferences in Copenhagen and Nairobi, respectively. As a staff member of the House committee on government operations, subcommittee on employment and housing (1983–1991), Simonson was responsible for hearings and reports on many issues vital to women, including EEOC, OSHA, Women's Bureau, child and elder care, and pay equity. In 1986, Simonson began her third term as president of the Clearinghouse on Women's Issues; in 2000, she began her second term on the national board of OWL; and in 2001 became a steering committee member of the National Council of Women's

S

Feminists Who Changed America, 1963 – 1975 | 425

Organizations. Simonson, who has three children, earned her B.A. from Bryn Mawr College and her M.A. from American University. (ABS)

Simpson, Lucy Picco (1940 – 2006) Simpson was a bored young mother of a five-year old girl when she started going to Brooklyn (NY) NOW meetings in the mid 1970s. She later went to Manhattan NOW meetings and worked on the education subcommittee, with a personal interest in gender bias in school textbooks. Simpson and others, including Freda Leinwand, Alma Graham, Ruth Ullman and Irma Gedlin, visited PTA groups and schools to talk with civics and history teachers from the lower grades through high school. To connect some teachers in each school who were really interested and were already devising and trying new techniques in their classrooms, Simpson started a newsletter, "TABS: Teaching Against Bias in Schools," which published quarterly from 1978 – 1984. It was run by a non-profit organization, and received early encouragement from a small Ms. Foundation grant for direct mail promotion. In her career as a freelance book editor and proofreader, Simpson said, "I did report on things abusive to women and offensive language and made suggestions, but they ignored me. I had no power." From 1974 until her death, Simpson was an active member and sometimes board member of the New York Pinewoods Folk Music Club. Simpson held a B.A. degree from Park College (1962), and an M.A.T. from Wesleyan University. (ABS before death)

Sive, Rebecca Anne (1950 –) (also known as Rebecca Sive-Tomashefsky) began her fight for women's rights as a student at Carleton College, where she was a lead organizer and spokesperson for a group of women who successfully worked to obtain gynecological services on campus (1971 – 1972). She was a founder of the collective Inforwomen (1973 – 1975), which published the *Chicago Women's Directory/Guia para las Mujeres de Chicago*, the first guide to women's services in Chicago. As part of the Illinois bicentennial year celebration (1976), Sive served as project director of the first statewide exhibit of the history of women in that state for the American Jewish Committee, Institute on Pluralism and Group Identity. As part of her work with that group, she was the first organizer of and the spokesperson for the National Women's Agenda in Illinois. The group later developed the Illinois Women's Agenda, a statewide coalition of dozens of major women's organizations. Also in 1976, Sive was appointed to the IWY IL committee, was PR director for it, and then a delegate to the Houston convention in 1977. During this time, Sive was also a fundraiser/PR consultant to the NWPC for its IL ERA ratification campaign. In 1977, Sive was a founder, with Heather Booth, Susan Stone, Karen Fishman and Carol Silverthorn, of the Midwest Women's Center, the first multiservice, citywide women's center in Chicago. After her election to the board of NARAL (1979), Sive became chair of the NARAL

Foundation (1980). In 1980, Sive was appointed by Governor James R. Thompson as a founding member of the Illinois Human Rights Commission, one of the first commissions of its kind in the U.S., and in 1982 she founded, with Rev. Addie Wyatt, Rev. Willie Barrow and Nancy Jefferson, Women for Washington, which supported Harold Washington's campaign for mayor of Chicago. Washington was the first African American mayor of Chicago and the first pro-choice mayoral candidate in Chicago history. In addition to her B.A. from Carleton College, Sive holds an M.A. from the University of Illinois. (ABS)

Sizemore, Iris Greer (1940 –) In 1974, Sizemore convened The Women's Group, a feminist group at the First Unitarian Church in Houston, TX. The group continues (2005) to meet every Sunday and is one of the oldest weekly, women-only organizations still meeting in the country. It serves as a forum for other organizations to announce their activities, and is networked with Rice University and the University of Houston. The group has received special recognition from national NOW and from Uncommon Legacy, and a proclamation from the City of Houston. Sizemore, who is a radiologic technologist and has two children, has supported Planned Parenthood and been a volunteer at the Houston Area Women's Center. (ABS)

Skeeters, Martha Clayton (1946 –) (also known as Martha Clayton Skeeters Behrens) In 1971, Skeeters rejected the suggestion of her mentor to write her M.A. thesis on Martin Luther's and Machiavelli's views on the state, and instead followed her feminist consciousness. Having read Luther's work on the *Old Testament*, which included much on how he perceived female figures, Skeeters decided to write on Luther's views of women. While her work remained unpublished, it was a pioneering effort and her mentor, William E. Painter, used it in his graduate seminar at the University of North Texas for the next two decades. Before Skeeters' work, scholars had confused Luther's positive view of marriage with a positive view of women. In fact, he showed the misogynist view of women that most people of the time (women as well as men) shared. A historian and university professor, Skeeters has one child. She earned her B.A. (1968) and M.A. (1973) from the University of North Texas, and her Ph.D. (1984) from the University of Texas at Austin. (ABS)

Skinner, Elin Malmquist (1936 –) entered the women's movement in 1972 when she joined the NWPC and worked on Shirley Chisholm's campaign for President of the United States. Skinner's home briefly served as Chisholm's Minnesota campaign headquarters. Skinner became secretary of the MN NWPC in 1972, and was a delegate to the first NWPC meeting in Houston in 1973. In 1973 she joined the Religious Coalition for Abortion Rights (later renamed Religious Coalition for Reproductive Choice). Skinner served on the NWPC board from

1997 – 2005; in 2003 she took on a two-year term as chair of the disability committee. Skinner has 27 plaques in her office recognizing her achievements. They are from women legislators, from both Republican and Democratic Minnesota governors, the University of Minnesota, and the Women's Consortium in Minnesota. A Swedish American, Skinner has two children. She holds a B.A. from Vassar and an M.A. from Syracuse University. (ABS)

Skjei, Jane Dushinske (1935 –) was a member of the co-ordinating council of the ERA staff in North Dakota (1974 – 1975), and from 1982 – 1983 spent three months in Oklahoma working on the ERA campaign. A member of the Tri-College women's speakers bureau (1974 – 1976), Skjei also served as VP of her local NOW chapter, Red River NOW (1975 – 1978) and then as president and ND State coordinator (1979 – 1980). In 1975, she helped establish a rape and abuse center in North Dakota that is still (2004) in existence. From 1981 – 1982, Skjei led a group to defeat anti-choice resolutions in the ND Legislature. Skjei, who has three children, was a member of the Agassiz Women's Political Caucus in North Dakota into the 1990s. She holds a B.A. from North Dakota State University and works at the North Dakota State University Institute for Regional Studies, Fargo, ND. (ABS)

Sklar, Kathryn Kish (1939 –) was a founder of the women's studies programs at the University of Michigan (1972 – 1973) and UCLA (1974 – 1975) and chaired committees that designed and instituted the programs. As a historian, Sklar has worked in various ways to develop women's history as a field of academic study. She was founder and for 10 years (1978 – 1988) coordinator of the Workshop on Teaching U.S. Women's History. With Gerda Lerner, Sklar co-coordinated the Conference of Graduate Teachers in U.S. Women's History (Racine, WI, 1988) and wrote its report. With Thomas Dublin she co-founded (1998) and co-directed (1998 – present) the Center for the Historical Study of Women and Gender, SUNY Binghamton. The two developed the online journal, Web site and database, "Women and Social Movements in the U.S., 1600 – 2000." Her books include *Catharine Beecher: A Study in American Domesticity* (Yale University Press, 1973); *The Autobiography of Florence Kelley: Notes of Sixty Years* (Charles Kerr, 1986), for which Sklar served as editor; *U.S. History as Women's History: New Feminist Essays* (University of North Carolina Press, 1995), for which she served as co-editor with Linda Kerber and Alice Kessler-Harris; *Florence Kelley and the Nation's Work: The Rise of Women's Political Culture, 1830 – 1900* (Yale University Press, 1995); *Social Justice Feminists in the United States and Germany: A Dialogue in Documents, 1885 – 1933* (Cornell University Press, 1998), for which Sklar served as co-editor with Anja Schuler and Susan Strasser; *Women's Rights Emerges Within the Anti-Slavery Movement: A Short History with Documents, 1830 – 1870* (St. Martin's Press, 2000);

Women and Power in American History: A Reader (Prentice-Hall, 1991), for which Sklar served as co-editor with Thomas Dublin; and *Women's Rights and Transatlantic Antislavery in the Era of Emancipation* (Yale University Press, 2006), for which Sklar served as co-editor with James Brewer Stewart. Sklar, who has two children, earned her B.A. from Radcliffe College (1965), and her M.A. (1967) and Ph.D. (1969) from the University of Michigan. Archives: The Sophia Smith Collection, Smith College, Northampton, MA. (ABS)

Skorich, Arlene Rita Mae (1936 –) (also known as Arlene R. Poeschl) was charter president of the Suburban Ramsey (MN) BPW (1961 – 1964). The chapter was sponsored by the St. Paul BPW, of which Skorich was an active member. In 1964, Skorich served as PR director for the State of Minnesota Federation of BPW Clubs, and from 1964 – 1965 was ad manager for the MN BPW magazine. In 1965, Skorich was named BPW Woman of the Year by the BPW of Suburban Ramsey. Also active in the LWV (1964 – 1966), Skorich served in various positions, including finance chair and member of the executive board. From 1968 – 1969, Skorich did volunteer work for the Advance Modeling School, an agency that trained non-white models and promoted them for work in the advertising and communication fields. The project was supported by all the major civil rights organizations in Minnesota, but "was difficult, as much prejudice was coming to the surface in the north areas." Skorich, who earned a Bachelor of Elected Studies Degree from the University of Minnesota (1975), served as a teaching assistant in the women's studies department at the university (1975). In 1989, Skorich joined Quota International of Minneapolis, which supports the hearing impaired and disadvantaged women, and served as director for several years. Skorich is a member of the DFL Feminist Caucus, a charter member of national NOW, and has remained a member ever since. Skorich has two children. (ABS)

Skorniak, Sandi (1943 –) joined Omaha NOW in 1972 after tracking down the founder (Jackie St. John) from an article in the local paper. She served in various capacities with Omaha NOW until about 1976, when she was elected state coordinator. Skorniak was elected as an at-large delegate to the 1977 National Women's Conference as a representative of Nebraska NOW. "The issues that took me down the path to NOW were childcare, job discrimination and, of course, reproductive rights," she says. "During those early years in the seventies, our Omaha chapter was very active doing outreach to other women's groups, picketing constantly on any number of issues, working with local schools and television stations regarding violence against women, etc. etc." Skorniak was also active in local Democratic politics, serving as county chair and vice chair, on local and state committees, and as the state party's liaison to women's groups. She continues (2006) to volunteer for various campaigns. (ABS)

S

Slaner, Barbara Joan – See Winslow, Barbara

Slavin, Maureen M. (1948 –) (also known as Maureen S. Rogman) In 1973, Slavin joined the McHenry County (IL) chapter of NOW, serving as a board member and co-chair until 1975. She then became the first IL NOW state president, serving until 1977. During those years, the ERA was the primary focus of attention in Illinois. Slavin helped coordinate the May 1976 National March for Equal Rights in Springfield, the first national march in the country. She also established the first Illinois state board of NOW and coordinated all the existing NOW chapters in the state for a statewide effort for passage of the ERA. In 1977, when Naomi Ross became IL NOW president, she and Slavin created 10 new NOW chapters with the purpose of lobbying for passage of the ERA. Slavin also traveled throughout the state with the ERA Caravan Campaign. In 1978, while serving as the logistics coordinator for the Washington July 9 national march to extend the ERA deadline, Slavin was appointed by the state presidents of the Great Lakes Region of NOW to NOW's national board. In September, at the request of Ellie Smeal, Slavin went to Alaska to develop a statewide lobbying campaign for Senator K. Hodges to secure his vote in favor of passage. This resulted in Hodges' impassioned speech in the Senate that was key to passage. Slavin served on NOW's national board for five years as a member and as Great Lakes regional coordinator. During that time, she directed the logistics for the 1980 Mother's Day March for the ERA in Chicago and appeared on numerous radio and TV spots in Illinois, including an NBC debate with Phyllis Schlafly. Slavin holds a B.A. (ABS)

Sleigh, Sylvia (1916 –) is the painter of the often-reproduced portrait of the members of the AIR Gallery (1978). Part of the feminist artists revolution that began in the late 1960s, Sleigh was a member of Women in the Arts (NY), the Women's Caucus for Art, the SoHo Gallery for Women Artists and the AIR Gallery. In 2003, she was honored at the VFA's Salute to Feminists in the Arts. Archives: The Getty Museum, Los Angeles, CA. (ABS)

Slepack, Donna Grund (1944 –) attended the first women's studies class offered at the University of Cincinnati (OH) given through the philosophy dept. in 1972. In studying the nature of oppression, says Slepack, she was inspired to combine her skill in German with her interest in socialist feminism. She pursued her doctoral research in the German Democratic Republic (East Germany), examining and comparing women's roles and sex-role stereotyping with their Western (Capitalist) counterparts. During her field study, she found that most women in East Germany worked outside the home in many non-traditional professions and enjoyed an excellent support system as well. After publishing her doctoral dissertation, "Women in the German Democratic Republic: A Field Study and Comparative Analysis of Sex-Role Stereotyping

in USA and GDR Children's Readers," Slepack published a number of articles and gave numerous multimedia presentations based on her dissertation research. "This was my contribution to the education of women regarding an alternative to the 'Competition, Fair and Square' model of feminism versus the socialist model, which provided many of the conditions that nurtured women's equality." Slepack also taught a number of women's studies classes in Portland, OR (1970s). She organized and coordinated a degree completion program that allowed women to get college credit for their experiences and contributions as mothers, activists, volunteers and workers. In addition, Slepack was a member of FeMail Art in Portland (1981 – 1990). The group developed and sold feminist post cards, and—believing that peace is a feminist issue—Slepack, as a socially concerned artist, published a number of Peace Post Cards. ("Silence is the Voice of Complicity" was commissioned by the Center for Constitutional Rights.) In 1986, she organized a street performance in Portland as a tribute to the courage of women of Latin America who protested the disappearance of their children and resisted "legal" injustice and institutional terrorism. Slepack is (2005) organizing support for women on death row in Uganda, while advocating and coordinating a support program for Oregon's death row inmates. A longtime member of WILPF, Slepack holds a B.A. from the University of Colorado and a Ph.D. from the University of Cincinnati. (ABS)

Slepian, Lorraine (1933 –) A member of the Hempstead (NY) Women's Liberation Center in the early 1970s, Slepian joined the group of Long Island women who designed the Hempstead women's liberation CR group structure and wrote the facilitating guidelines for the meetings. Slepian then used much of that feminist format in the design of the first Mothers' Center (1974). Adaptations of that model followed, and over the years hundreds of mothers' centers have been created worldwide. This effort in turn grew into the National Association of Mothers' Centers, an organization that today (2005) is in the forefront of the growing Mothers' movement. Slepian, who has four children, has served as founder, social work consultant, co-director, leadership adviser and board trustee. She also co-founded MOTHERS, a women's economic rights organization, in 2002. She holds an M.A. and is a graduate of the School for Psychoanalytic Psychotherapy. (ABS)

Slive, Zoya S. (1924 –) Active in the civil rights movement of the 1950s and 1960s, Slive was executive director of the Civic Unity Committee of the City of Cambridge (MA) from 1963 – 1971. In that capacity, she worked on fair housing and desegregation of schools, and was instrumental in establishing a citywide Women's Commission. A feminist therapist, Slive was affiliated with the Boston Psychological Center for Women, where she concentrated on women survivors of childhood sexual abuse, lesbian issues and older women. She also worked with couples, families and men from a feminist perspective, and published "The Feminist Therapist and the Male Client" in The Dynamics of Feminist Therapy (Haworth Press, 1986). In addition, Slive worked to legalize abortions. Slive, who has three children, holds an M.A. from the University of Chicago (1950) and an Ed.D. from Boston University (1986). (ABS)

Sloan-Hunter, Margaret (1947 – 2004) was an early editor of *Ms.*, a poet and an activist fighting for feminist, lesbian and African American causes. While based in NYC, Sloan-Hunter lectured in 48 states and three countries on racism and sexism, often with Gloria Steinem, and was awarded a key to the city of her birth, Chattanooga, TN. In 1973 she founded (with Florynce Kennedy and others) and was the first chairwoman of the National Black Feminist Organization (dismaying some who were uncomfortable with Sloan-Hunter having sung a love song to her lover on local television). In 1975 she moved to Oakland, CA, with her daughter, where she worked as an organizer for the Berkeley Women's Center, the Feminist School for Girls, and as a founder of the Women's Foundation. She also served on the board of the Women's Alcoholism Center in San Francisco. She was a popular and humorous master of ceremonies for many programs benefiting the women's community. Sloan-Hunter's writings appeared in *The New York Times*, *Chicago Tribune*, the *Civil Rights Digest* and the first and subsequent issues of *Ms.* Her essays and poems have been published in magazines such as *Lesbian Path*, *Intricate Passions* and *For Lesbians Only*. She also published *Black & Lavender: The Collected Poems of Margaret Sloan* in 1995. Sloan-Hunter was involved in the liberation of oppressed people from an early age. She joined Chicago CORE at age 14, organized tenant unions and rent strikes, and campaigned against lead poisoning on Chicago's West Side. At age 17 she founded the Junior Catholic Inter-Racial Council. Sloan-Hunter was involved in civil rights activities throughout the South and North working with Martin Luther King Jr. and Jesse Jackson. She attended Chicago College as a speech major, Malcolm X Community College and the graduate school in women's studies at Antioch University in San Francisco.

Slotnick, Linda – See Dittmar, Linda

Small, Jane (1930 – 1999) was a founding mother of the NWPC and a national officer for many years. Disabled with severe scoliosis, Small formed the disability caucus in the NWPC. She was an active campaigner for political candidates and causes. Nationally known as a civil rights/ disability rights advocate, Small was a longtime, active member of Californians for Disability Rights. Small was eulogized by Jane Crawford, assistant appointments secretary for former Governor Gray Davis, who read the governor's declaration that the day, October 15, 1999,

would become Jane Small Memorial Day. She received a law degree in 1961 and had four children. Archives: Shaloma Shawmut-Lessner, Miami, FL.

Smeal, Eleanor (1939 –) has been a leading force in determining the agenda of a major women's rights organization for more than three decades. She was a three-time president of national NOW (1977 – 1982), and again from 1985 – 1987. Smeal attended public schools in Erie, PA. At Duke University, from which she graduated in 1961, she was president of her dormitory and worked to racially integrate the school. After receiving her B.A., she considered pursuing a law degree, but chose not to when she learned of discrimination against women lawyers. She continued her studies in political science, receiving an M.A. from the University of Florida in 1963. The first daughter and the fourth child of Italian American immigrants, she married and had two children. In the late 1960s, she became increasingly aware of feminist issues, personally confronting the lack of day care facilities when she was working on her thesis, as well as the lack of disability insurance for wives and mothers. In 1968 she began a four-year term on the LWV and then joined NOW. In the 1970s, she rose through the ranks of NOW, serving from 1971 – 1973 as organizer and president of the South Hills, PA, chapter. In 1972 she became president of PA State NOW, a position she held until 1975. She was successful in having the state's equal rights statutes applied to physical education for girls. In 1973 she was elected to the NOW board of directors and was elected national chair in 1975. She was also a board member with NOW LDEF. Smeal led the NOW drive to ratify the ERA from 1977 to 1982. Also during that period, she led drives to pass the Pregnancy Discrimination Act, to stop the Human Life Amendment, and to build a women's political campaign to elect feminists to public office. In 1977, she organized a nationwide boycott of states that had not ratified the ERA by organizations that normally held conventions in those states. Attorney general John Ashcroft initiated a State of Missouri lawsuit against NOW to break the boycott. NOW went on to win the case in the Supreme Court, establishing the right to boycott under the First Amendment's protection of freedom of speech. She also worked for the extension of the ratification deadline. As part of this campaign, Smeal and NOW organized a march on Washington, D.C., in 1978, the first of the major national marches in the last half of the 20th century, attracting over 100,000 people. While the ratification deadline was extended from 1979 to 1982, the deadline passed without ratification, despite very close votes again and heavy lobbying efforts in key states. In 1985, Smeal successfully ran for president of NOW, this time focusing on abortion rights, a reintroduced ERA, and economic justice for women. In 1987 she became president of The Feminist Majority. Smeal has also focused on contemporary issues such as access to the Internet, which has helped build the organization. In 1979 she was named

S

one of The 25 Most Influential Women in the United States, World Almanac. Smeal is (2006) president of The Feminist Majority Foundation. (ABS)

Smeltzer, Martha – See West, Martha Smeltzer

Smith, Barbara (1946 –) Author, activist and independent scholar, Smith was a pioneer in black women's studies and black feminism. In a biography co-written by Maureen T. Reddy (a professor at Rhode Island College who nominated Smith for the Nobel Peace Prize), Smith is described as playing "a groundbreaking role in opening up a national, cultural and political dialogue about the intersections of race, class, sexuality and gender. Smith has been a political activist since her high-school years. She has worked to end sterilization abuse, for reproductive freedom and quality healthcare for all women, for an end to violence against women, and for an end to homophobia. She has also fought to end apartheid in South Africa and to end police brutality in the United States. In 1974, Smith was a co-founder of the Combahee River Collective, a Boston-based black feminist organization that included lesbian, heterosexual and bisexual women. Its purpose was to define black feminist issues and to do multi-issue black feminist organizing. The Combahee River Collective Statement continues to be cited as a work of groundbreaking black feminist analysis that served as a catalyst for the building of the black feminist movement in the U.S. She was co-founder of Kitchen Table: Women of Color Press, the first publisher for women of color in the U.S. She also served as editor of three collections about black women: *Conditions: Five, The Black Women's Issue* (Brooklyn, 1979) with Lorraine Bethel; *All the Women are White, All the Blacks are Men, But Some of Us Are Brave: Black Women's Studies* (the Feminist Press, 1982) with Akasha (Gloria) Hull and Patricia Bell-Scott; and *Home Girls: A Black Feminist Anthology* (1983). Her writing has been published in the *Village Voice, The Guardian, Gay Community News, Ms., The New York Times Book Review* and *The Black Scholar*. She is the author of an essay collection, *The Truth That Never Hurts: Writings on Race, Gender and Freedom* (Rutgers University Press, 1998), and served as editor for *The Reader's Companion to U.S. Women's History* (Houghton Mifflin, 1998). Smith is a recipient of the Stonewall Award (1994) and the Church Women United Human Rights Award (2000). *Essence* magazine named Smith a Black Woman Trailblazer (2000), and *The Advocate* listed her as one of the Best and Brightest Activists for Lesbian and Gay Rights (1999). Smith holds a B.A. from Mount Holyoke College (1969) and an M.A. from the University of Pittsburgh. In addition, Smith was a Scholar-in-Residence at the Schomburg Center for Research in Black Culture (1995–1996) and a Fellow at the Bunting Institute of Radcliff College (1996–1997), and a Rockefeller Fellow in the humanities at the Center for Lesbian and Gay Studies at the City University of New York. (ABS)

Smith, Barbara Turner (1931 –) One of the first performance artists, Smith worked primarily in California focusing on female empowerment, spirituality, the body, eros and community. At the University of California, Irvine (1969–1971), she helped start an early performance gallery called F-Space. She also protested the absence of women artists in art shows, participated and performed in and wrote reviews for WomanSpace, and was a founding member of Grandview 1 & 2 gallery in the Women's Building. She also taught feminist-oriented classes at many colleges and universities, including UCLA, UCSD, UC Irvine, the San Francisco Art Institute and Johnston College/University of the Redlands. After 1984, her work became overtly ecofeminist. Smith is a recipient of a Vesta Award from the Woman's Building (1983), a National Honor Award from the WCA (1999), and numerous NEA grants. She has three children (one deceased), and holds a B.F.A. from Pomona College and an M.F.A. from the University of California, Irvine. (ABS)

Smith, Betty Walker (1918 –) was a founding member of the NWPC (1971) and spoke at its inauguration in Washington, D.C., in July of that year. Earlier, in 1963, Smith and her husband worked through the Equal Opportunity Commission of the Madison (WI) City Council to pass the Equal Housing Opportunity bill in Madison, the first in the nation. In 1968, Smith helped found a day care center in South Madison, and served as its chair and a fundraiser for 15 years. From 1968–1980, Smith served on the Governor's Committee on the Status of Women in Wisconsin, and was its chair from 1969–1971. Smith joined Republican Women of Dane County, Madison, WI, in 1946 and served as vice chair (1961–1963). Smith, who has four children, was honored by the YWCA in 1989 as a Woman of Distinction, and in 1992 received the Ruth Gordon Service Award from the Madison Area Service Clubs Council. She earned her B.S. (1941) and M.A. (1975) from the University of Wisconsin, Madison. Archives: Wisconsin Historical Society, Madison, WI. (ABS)

Smith, Catherine Parsons (1933 –) A teacher and musician, Smith filed an affirmative action complaint against the University of Nevada, Reno, in 1972 for discrimination on the basis of sex in hiring, promotion and tenure. After Smith appealed a negative finding in 1973, a Right to Sue letter was granted by the EEOC (1975). However, an injunction to stay at UNR while the suit ran its course was denied. In 1976, Smith obtained an out-of-court settlement with outside tenure review. Tenure was granted, and Smith began feminist scholarship in musicology. In 1987, Smith appealed her application for promotion to full professor to the Nevada State EOB, with a settlement in her favor. Smith is the author of several feminist publications, including (with C.S. Richardson) *Mary Carr Moore, American Composer* (University of Michigan Press, 1987), and "A Distinguishing Virility: On Feminism and

Modernism in American Music," published in *Cecilia Reclaimed: Perspectives on Gender and Music*, edited by S. Cook and J. Tsou (University of Illinois Press, 1994). She is also author of "Athena at the Manuscript Club: John Cage and Mary Carr Moore," published in *Musical Quarterly 79* (1995). In 1986, Smith received the Alderman Award for Research on Women in Music from the International Congress of Women in Music. In 1998, she became a research associate, Five College Women's Studies Research Center. From 1979–1999, Smith played Principal Flute for the Reno Philharmonic Orchestra. In 1986, she became a full professor in the music department, University of Nevada, Reno. Smith earned her A.B. from Smith College (1954), her M.M. from Northwestern University (1957) and her Doctor of Musical Arts from Stanford University (1969). Archives: Special Collections, University of Nevada, Reno. (ABS)

Smith, Corinne – See Barnwell, Corinne

Smith, Diann DeWeese (1927 –) In 1968, Smith was one of the founders of the Loop Center, housed in the Chicago YWCA "just as the second wave of feminism hit Chicago," she says. Over the years Loop Center became a model for YWCAs in the United States and Canada. Smith served as executive director from 1969–1977. Under Smith's direction, the Loop Center's accomplishments include abortion referral, working with organizers such as Cindy Little; the founding of Chicago Women Against Rape, working with Pauline Bart and others; and the convening of The Chicago Abused Women Coalition, which in turn created the Women's Services Department. The need for women political candidates resulted in the Chicago WPC and then the Illinois Caucus. Loop Center volunteers trained themselves to assist women in prison and jails. Women attorneys provided free legal services. Eventually, 57 groups operated out of the Loop Center and 90 received some kind of technical assistance. In addition to her work at the Center, Smith was educational publisher at Scott Foresman (1967–1968), "where I was hired to dump Dick and Jane and provide non-racist material," she says. In 1968 Smith fought racism with the National Conference of Christians and Jews, running workshops that reached 13,000 participants in the Chicago area. She also produced guerrilla theater in the streets and helped compile *The Intelligent Women's Guide to Dirty Words* to combat racism and sexism. The many honors and awards that Smith has received include the Woman of Illinois Repute Award from the Illinois Women's Agenda; the Outstanding Achievement Award in the Field of Community Service, from the YWCA; and the Gladys Shute Award "To someone who has contributed significantly to women," from Oakton Community College. Smith, who has two children (one deceased) earned her B.A. from Beloit College. Archives: University of Illinois, Chicago; Chicago Public Library; and Northwestern University, Evanston, IL. (ABS)

Smith, Donna Marie (1941 –) As a girl, Smith witnessed her mother working in munitions and jet engines factories during and after WWII, a true "Rosie the Riveter." Her mother encouraged her to get a "man's job," because they paid more. Smith has been an active feminist in Connecticut, Massachusetts, Colorado and New York. She entered a CR group in Connecticut in 1969. After moving to Boulder, CO, she joined the Women's Center Collective, which started dozens of CR groups. The collective was the foundation of the Boulder Women's Center in 1973, and the Women's Health Education Group in 1974. Smith taught women's studies at the University of Colorado (1975–1977). She was a member of the founding editorial collective of *Frontiers: A Journal of Women's Studies* in 1975, and president and a member of the board, September School 1976–1979. She helped start the feminist psychotherapy study collective 1974–1977; was on the board of the Boulder Valley (abortion) Clinic 1974–1979; and the Women's Center 1974–1979. Smith was also involved in the peace and anti-poverty movements. In White Plains, NY, Smith joined The Loft, where she received awards for initiating new programs for gay youth and elderly gays. She was the founder of Loft Peer Support Services in 1985 and Lambda Peer Support Services in 2002, where she is (2006) counseling and training director. A psychotherapist in private practice, Smith received a B.A., Missouri Valley College (1963), an M.S.W. from the University of Kansas, and an Advanced Certificate, Columbia University (1983). (ABS)

Smith, Judith E. (1948 –) In the summer of 1970, Smith helped organize a women's health clinic in Somerville, MA. Staffed by volunteers, including women doctors and eventually women from the community, The Somerville Women's Health Project offered free medical care to approximately 2,500 low-income women and children in its seven years of operation (1971–1978). A related effort, the Women's Mental Health Collective, continues (2005) to operate. Smith remained on the Somerville Women's Health Project board until it closed. She was part of the mid 1970s International Women's Day demonstration that took over the building at 888 Memorial Drive and that resulted in the founding of the Cambridge Women's Center. In 1973–1974, she taught a women's history class for community activists as part of the Boston Community School, and was also part of a Marxist feminist conference group (1973–1976). In addition, she was part of the orientation committee of the Boston Women's Union (1974), which welcomed new members and continued to meet through 2001, even after the Boston Women's Union disbanded. Smith has taught U.S. social and cultural history at the college level full time since 1981, and has been associated with women's history and women's studies at Boston College (1981–1993) and University of Massachusetts, Boston, since 1993. Smith, who has three children, earned her B.A. from Radcliffe College (1970) and her Ph.D. from Brown University (1980). (ABS)

S

Smith, June – See Parlett, June Marie

Smith, Linda S. (1938 –) An instructor in philosophy at Michigan State University and an out lesbian in the late 1960s at the time of the lesbian feminist split within NOW, Smith was invited to speak on many NOW panels, but never became a member. Hired in 1972 to teach philosophy at a small experimental college in rural MI, Thomas Jefferson College, Smith helped develop a women's studies program, which remained in effect until the administration shut it down in 1978. In 1977, with other feminists from the college and the community, Smith helped form Aradia, whose organization's purpose was to help women and children, and especially to promote the economic independence and physical and psychological well being of women. When the college cancelled her women's studies program, Smith quit her tenured position and put her energy into Aradia, a community of like-minded women, while working as a house painter. In 1983, Smith moved to NY State and joined the Ithaca Women's Affinity Group. She participated in civil disobedience actions with the Women's Peace Camp at the Seneca Army Depot and was also active in the Ithaca women's spirituality movement. In 1989, she moved to the Ozarks Mountains of southern Missouri, where she joined other Michigan Aradians to found Hawk Hill Community Land Trust. The women built their own homes and "attempted to live in harmony with the land, its water, the air, the animals, the plants and each other." Smith holds a B.A., M.A., A.B.D. and M.Div.   (ABS)

Smith, Lucy (1933 –) Born in Cracow, Poland, Smith came to the U.S. in 1968 and, in 1971, joined a loosely organized group, Female Liberation. She then joined NOW. As a newly abandoned, struggling single mother, she was forced out of voluntary organizations by the need to support her son, and began writing. Articles from that time include one on the societal attitude toward children, and another on the difficulties single mothers face in obtaining a fair share of support from their deserting husbands. In 1982, a chance encounter resulted in her participation in the book *Every Woman Has a Story*, sponsored by Meridel Le Sueur and edited by Gayla Wadnizak Ellis (published by Ellis & Gayla Wadnizak, 1986). In 1990, Smith participated in the International Women's Right Watch at the Hubert Humphrey Institute. She also once again became active in NOW, in particular writing for the *Minnesota NOW Times*. Smith, who has one child, holds an M.F.A. from the Academy of Fine Arts, studying in Cracow, Warsaw and Paris.   (ABS)

Smith, Martha A. (1932 –) was a founder of the Ft. Myers, FL, chapter of NOW (1972 – 1977), where she organized CR groups, served as a delegate to FL State NOW, and helped start a WPC group and rape crisis hotline. A member of FL NOW from 1974 – 1982, Smith served as secretary, membership secretary and chair of the ERA boy-

cott committee. She edited and published the group's newsletter for three years, organized a state NOW conference, and picketed Disney World once a week for nine months. A member of the St. Petersburg chapter of NOW from 1977 – 1982, Smith served as treasurer and also as editor, for two years, of the "St. Petersburg NOW News." A book group founded at that time continues today (2005). Smith holds an M.S. and was a rehab counselor and supervisor for 30 years. She has two children.   (ABS)

Smith, Sandra L. (1945 –) (also known as Sandra Smith Glutting) In 1972, Smith was a co-founder of the Stark County Women's Political Caucus, Canton, OH. The women established CR groups, a NOW chapter, and a rape crisis center associated with the Red Cross. They also helped women run for office, worked for the ERA, and successfully challenged the Democratic Party in Ohio to follow its own rules requiring 50 percent women delegates to the convention. Says Smith, "My proudest achievement is the sense of shared purpose, empowerment and societal change I've witnessed. We came together without a model and shared our skills, fears and strengths. We've come so far in my lifetime and there is far to go. May younger women find a place to be themselves and a society which celebrates them—due in some part to our work."   (ABS)

Smith, Sondra Lou (1948 –) was a co-founder of the Iowa City Women's Liberation Front (1969), an outgrowth of the SDS. She was also a founding member of the group's childcare collective and helped establish five free cooperative childcare centers in Iowa City. Smith wrote the grants to secure funding, established hot lunch programs, and lobbied the university for housing. As of this writing, the five day care centers are still housed in university rent-subsidized buildings, the first of which was given to the day care group after a sit-in at which 17 people were arrested (1971). A caterer at the University of Iowa for 27 years, Smith has three children. Archives: The University of Iowa Library, Iowa City, IA.   (ABS)

Smith-Robinson, Ruby Doris (1942 – 1967) was a major force in African-American civil rights. She died at 25 of a mysterious cancer she believed was acquired by a transfusion given when she miscarried. A soccer captain and student leader at Spelman College, she was a member of SNCC from its founding days. Always at the forefront of danger, she was relegated to payroll supervision, administrative and secretarial duties as the movement became hierarchical—an exemplar of sidelined female leadership when power is achieved. Her dilemma was cited in "Sex & Caste," a paper Mary King and Casey Hayden circulated in 1966. Tragically, her tenure as one of the few women civil rights officials lasted only a few months, upon becoming SNCC's second executive secretary.

Smithson, Rosemary Leitz (1931 –) (also known as Rosemary Leitz Smithson Coker) joined the women's movement "inadvertently" in 1966 when she joined Planned Parenthood of Greater Kansas City, MO. "I went in as a conservationist, a supporter of Zero Population Growth, and came out a feminist," she says. She served as president of the board from 1970 – 1971. Realizing that the birth control movement had to get political, Smithson attended a meeting to launch the Missouri State NWPC in 1973. Soon thereafter, she attended the first meeting of the local Greater Kansas City WPC (GKC/WPC) and remains (2004) an active member. She served as president in 1973 and 1974. In 1972, after the ERA passed in the U.S. Senate, Smithson volunteered to be the caucus representative on the statewide ERA Coalition board, and in 1975, she served as president. "We worked day and night, even electing three Kansas City women to the state legislature in 1975. However," she says, "the Catholic Church in Missouri, under the leadership of Cardinal Carbury—a skilled strategist and politician in St. Louis—led the move to stop us four votes short in the Senate. While many of us quit working when the ERA failed in 1982, the good Cardinal and his lieutenants cleverly did not stop." In 1997, Smithson was called back into a leadership role as fundraising chair to help build the caucus and bolster its financial footing by co-founding the GKC/WPC Endowment and Education Fund. In 2001, she was a co-founder of the Missouri Women's Leadership Coalition, which takes political training workshops across the state, generally promoted by AAUW or BPW women. "I have become a crazy old feminist, recently attending the March for Women's Lives in Washington with my daughter. It's been a great ride. Wonderful friends, challenging problems, hilarious times, and perpetual fundraising." Smithson, who has two children, holds a B.A. from Missouri University. Archives: Western Historical Manuscripts Collection, University of Missouri at Kansas City, Kansas City, MO. (ABS)

Sneierson, Elaine – See Leeder, Elaine

Snider, Mary Beth – See Edelson, Mary Beth

Snitow, Ann Barr (1943 –) joined the Stanton-Anthony Brigade, the founding group of NYRF, in 1969. In 1970, Snitow began doing a series on women's diaries and letters on the first feminist radio show, "Womankind," on WBAI-FM in NYC. A founder (with Kate Ellis and others) of the women's studies program at Rutgers University (1972), Snitow was also a founder of the gender studies and feminist theory M.A. program at the Graduate Faculty of the New School for Social Research. With feminist interests that varied widely, Snitow was a founding member of many groups, including CARASA (1977), No More Nice Girls (a feminist street action group), the feminist anti-censorship task force (1984), and the Network of East-West Women (1990), which carried her interest in feminist organizing to East and Central Europe. She was co-editor, with Rachel Blau DuPlessis, of *The Feminist*

Memoir Project: Voices from Women's Liberation (Crown, 1998), and co-editor, with Christine Stansell and Sharon Thompson, of *Powers of Desire: The Politics of Sexuality* (Monthly Review Press, 1983). Snitow also wrote the introduction to the re-issued edition of *The Mermaid and the Minotaur*, by Dorothy Dinnerstein (Other Books, 1999). In addition, she has published numerous articles in scholarly journals and in contemporary publications on women's issues, and has lectured widely on these topics. Snitow, who holds a B.A. from Cornell (1965) and a Ph.D. from the University of London (1978), is a professor at The New School (Lang College and the Graduate Faculty) teaching gender studies and literature. (ABS)

Snortland, Ellen Barbara (1953 –) was co-founder of Theater of Process (1972 – 1984), a feminist theater company premiering works by and for women in Santa Barbara and Los Angeles, and also acted as executive producer, director, actress and playwright. In addition, Snortland writes a regular feminist column for *Pasadena Weekly* (1990 –), was a contributor to *On the Issues*, and served as a delegate/journalist to the U.N. Conference on Women in Beijing (1995). She is the author of *Beauty Bites Beast: Awakening the Warrior Within Women and Girls* (Trilogy Press, 1998) and was a contributor to *Ms.* magazine. She also wrote and performs a feminist one-woman show, "Now That She's Gone." Snortland holds a B.A. from the University of California, Irvine, and J.D. from Loyola Law School. (ABS)

Snyder, Elayne Phyllis (1931 –) joined NYC NOW in 1970 and served as president in 1974. She was also a member of the image, membership and fundraising committees. During her presidency, membership rolls for the NYC chapter topped 1,500. She helped promote both women in business and NOW issues with the creation of the NOW Christmas Fair, where women entrepreneurs sold their products and advertised their businesses; she also launched the NYC NOW Famous Women's Chair Project. This was the sale of chairs with the names of famous women stenciled on them as a method to raise money for NOW and honor women in history. Snyder also started the first monthly public speaking classes at NYC NOW to help women communicate the issues of the movement in a more effective manner. The success of this teaching experience led to Snyder's opening of her business, Elayne Snyder Speech Consultants, in 1978. Snyder also taught effective communication skills for women at the Woman School (1975), one of the first continuing education colleges addressing women's needs. A member of VFA, Snyder is the author of two articles and one book chapter on effective communication for women, and is the author of two books: *Speak for Yourself with Confidence* (New American Library, 1983), which used the pronoun "she" throughout and opened a whole new world to readers; and *Persuasive Business Speaking* (Amacon, 1990). Also a member of the WPC, she holds a

S

B.A. from the University of Miami (1952). Archives: Bobst Library, New York University, New York, NY.   (ABS)

Snyder, Joan (1940 –) A painter, Snyder was founder of the Mary H. Dana Women's Artist Series at Douglass College. Begun in 1971, the series celebrated its 35th anniversary in 2005. Snyder was also a founding member of *Heresies: A Feminist Magazine of Art & Politics*. Snyder, who has one child, holds an A.B. from Douglass College and an M.F.A. from Rutgers University.   (ABS)

Snyder, Mary-jane Ryan (1916 –) As a population communications specialist with Planned Parenthood and Mj Enterprises, Snyder has worked to bring birth control and family planning clinics to women around the world. She was a member of the Governor's Commission on the Status of Women (IL, 1964), was a founder of NOW (1966), and coordinated the PR battle for ratification of the ERA in Illinois, which was not ratified. From 1963 – 1985, she trained several thousand professionals from developing countries to set up family planning clinics and build awareness. In 1974, Snyder was part of the press-room for the first U.N. conference on population, held in Bucharest, and helped get women into the plan. In 1975, she was in the pressroom for the first U.N. conference on women, held in Mexico City, and was also part of population conferences held in Sri Lanka, Delhi, Rio de Janeiro and other areas. Snyder has served as executive director of Planned Parenthood Chicago (1974 – 1979), as chair of the Population Institute in Washington, D.C., and was a founding board member of the Population Communications Institute. Snyder, who has four children, earned a B.S. from the University of Illinois (1938). Archives: University of Illinois, Chicago; Population Reference Bureau, Washington, D.C.; and John Hopkins University Population Communications, Washington, D.C.   (ABS)

Sobieski, Wanda Graham Glenn (1947 –) (also known as Wanda Graham Glenn) was a member of Knoxville (TN) NOW from 1972 – 1982. She served as president, VP of action, ran phone banks, was involved in lobbying, demonstrations and freedom walks, and taught Nuns for Choice. She also lectured on religion ("Why Jesus Would Support the ERA"). In addition, she lectured on how feminine sex designators affect the credibility of women professionals. As a member of Women Against Violence Against Women and regional coordinator (1974 – 1980), Sobieski presented slide shows and gave lectures to civic clubs about the commercial use of violence against women as a marketing device. Because this was especially true in the recording industry, Sobieski and her co-workers successfully urged a boycott of Warner, Electra and Atlantic records. In addition to this work, Sobieski has served as a marshal for marches on Washington (1978 and 1976); marched in Nashville to support the ERA; and attended international women's conferences. An attorney, Sobieski has three children. She earned her B.A. from

Wichita State University (1969), and her M.A. (1974) and J.D. (1982) from the University of Tennessee.   (ABS)

Sogg, Joyce (1937 –) joined NOW in 1972 and immediately became active in the majority caucus. Sogg also became a NOW bylaws commissioner when the bylaws were rewritten in 1976, and was a member of the national board in 1977. Also in 1977, Sogg wrote the first PAC manual. Sogg, who has two children, holds a B.A. from Western Reserve University (1957) and a J.D. from the University of Santa Clara (1971).   (ABS)

Solo, Pat – See Matthews, Patricia Ann

Somer, Carol B. (1951 –) was a founding member and art director of *The Second Wave* and a member of Female Liberation in Boston and Cambridge, MA. She also helped organize Speakoutrage (1972), a public forum in Boston where women spoke out about abuses against their reproductive organs. After leaving Female Liberation, she studied environmental and graphic design at the New England School for Art and Design and worked as a Boston cabbie. She was the first female route driver for Frito-Lay in the U.S. After moving to Providence, R.I., Somer became involved with public relations, marketing and development for Sojourner House, a shelter and support network for battered women. She is working in PR and marketing in Costa Mesa, CA.

Sommers, Helen Elizabeth (1932 –) joined NOW in 1970 and was elected president of the Seattle-King County (WA) chapter in 1971. She serves (2005) as a representative in the Washington State House of Representatives, a position she has held since 1973, and as chair of the appropriations committee. Her numerous honors and awards include the 1978 Woman of Achievement Award from the Seattle Quota Club and the Seattle Women's Network Mentor Award, 1981. She was also named in Women of Achievement, 1995, Matrix Table, Women in Communications. Sommers holds a B.A. and M.A. from the University of Washington. Archives: NOW, University of Washington, Seattle, and Washington State Archives.   (ABS)

Sommers, Letitia ("Tish") (1914 – 1985) coined the phrase "displaced homemaker" to describe women who lose financial support through divorce or illness and do not have marketable skills. Sommers chaired NOW's task force on older women, formed in 1973, and, with Laurie Shields, introduced legislation to assist displaced homemakers in California in 1975. Sommers and Shields founded the Alliance of Displaced Homemakers in 1994 to address issues of divorced and widowed homemakers seeking employment. In 1980, Sommers and Shields co-founded OWL, which was originally headquartered at their home in Oakland, CA. Sommers was its first president. OWL grew from a local to a national organization rapidly and opened national headquarters in Washington, D.C., in 1983. It became a powerful voice for the concerns and needs of older women and has had political influence in many areas, including Social Security, pensions, healthcare and health insurance. The Tish Sommers Senior Scholar Program was established by the Institute for Health and Aging to honor Sommers and support the work of older postdoctoral and graduate students who are working to improve the lives of older women. Archives: Special Collections Library, San Diego State University, San Diego, CA.

Sorensen, Jane Forester – See Lord, Jane Sorensen

Souder, Sandra Silverman (1949 –) (also known as Silverwoman) created and coordinated The Woman's Place in Princeton, NJ (1969 – 1974). From 1970 – 1974, she served as founding coordinator for NJ NOW, and in 1974 for CT NOW task forces against rape; lobbied to create a $5 million center on sexual assault in the National Institute of Mental Health; ran the first conference against rape in NJ; helped begin several rape crisis centers; and worked to eliminate spousal immunity to sexual assault in NJ law. In 1975, Souder served as national co-coordinator of the NOW task force against rape, and helped reform sexual assault statutes in 35 states. She also served as co-author, with Jennifer Macleod, of *"You Won't Do": What Textbooks on U.S. Government Teach High School Girls* (Know Press, 1973) and as editor for the Association of Feminist Consultants. For several decades, Souder worked in various police departments, primarily focusing on assaults against women and children. As a uniformed patrol police officer in New Haven, CT (1976 – 1977), Souder lectured widely on topics such as women in policing, victim's rights, prevention of sexual assaults and criminal law reform. As an investigator in the sex crimes unit (1977 – 1978), she helped establish a sex offenders treatment program and a statewide computer bank of sexual assaults. From 1978 – 1984 Souder served as a felony investigator in New Haven Department of Police Services and was invited to be on the U.S. Law Enforcement Assistance Administration Advisory Board on Victim/ Witness Rights. Souder continued her work as senior investigator with the Onondaga County District Attorney's Office, Syracuse, NY; and then the Cayuga County Sheriff's Department as a grant writer/consultant, where she developed an Order of Protection Registry. Souder belongs to AAUW in Skaneateles, NY, Skaneateles Women's Investment Management Club. She also writes environmental grants, serves on the NYS Open Space Advisory Board for Region VII, and co-authored "Historic Erie Canal in Central New York," (2003). She went to Douglass College, Rutgers University, and graduated from the New Haven Police Academy (1976). (ABS)

Spalding, Elizabeth ("Betty") (1921 – 2001) joined CT NOW in 1968. Over the next three decades, Spalding be-

came involved in nearly every major undertaking of the organization, both in the state and nationally, and was president of Hartford (CT) NOW at the time of her death. A founder of Greenwich NOW in 1970, Spalding joined Judy Pickering and other feminist leaders working to ratify the ERA. After helping to establish the state's Permanent Commission on the Status of Women, Spalding became a charter member. At the national level, she served as coordinator of NOW's national task force on the family and helped organize marches in Washington, D.C., for reproductive rights and ratification of the ERA. Beginning in the early 1970s, Spalding lobbied the state legislature for Connecticut's committee on IWY and later the International Women's Decade. In 1977, she chaired the Connecticut delegation to the National Women's Conference in Houston. The following year, Spalding was named national secretary of the NWC committee, formed to ensure that the resolutions adopted at the Houston conference would be implemented state by state, as well as in federal legislation—a goal at least partly achieved in her lifetime. Spalding, who had six children, also worked on the problem of child support. In 1994, she was honored (with Betty Berry and others) for her work on marriage and divorce by the VFA, and again with the NOW pioneers in NYC at the Armory in 1997.

Spannaus, Olive Wise (1916 –) has worked to advance the basic ideas of the women's movement in the Lutheran church. In the late 1960s, she was a co-founder (with Carolyn Becker and Janet K. Larson) of the Lutheran Women's Caucus in Chicago. They demonstrated, leafleted and held meetings to influence the Lutheran Church-Missouri Synod (LCMS) at its 1971 and 1973 conventions, and in 1976 drew up bylaws and became a national pan-Lutheran organization with chapters across the U.S. Spannaus was elected secretary of the national board. In 1979 she co-founded the Puget Sound chapter of LWC. From 1964 – 1978, Spannaus served on the board of the LCMS English District women's organization, the Lutheran Women's Missionary League. As president (1970 – 1974), she successfully fostered understanding between the two organizations. In 1971 she spoke to the Northern Illinois District Pastoral Conference on the role of women in the church, and in 1972 became the first woman elected to the board of directors of the LCMS English District. Spannaus also worked within the church to develop a new marriage service that was less male-dominated (1969 – 1971); was a member of the LCMS task force on women (1973 – 1977); and in 1976 helped create the first English District committee on women in the church. In 1979 she served as chair of the Northwest District LCMS committee to draft a resolution creating the committee on women in the church, and from 1980 – 1995 chaired that committee. Spannaus has also written several hymns and original songs "to give the women's movement a good push." In addition to her work in the church, Spannaus has been an active member of the LWV

S

since 1959, holding offices including president of the Elmhurst and DuPage County (IL) Leagues, board member of IL State League and VP of Seattle (WA) League, which in 1995 named her recipient of the annual Carrie Chapman Catt Award. She marched in ERA parades, was part of the civil rights and environmental movements, and "in the interest of justice for homosexual people, protested when a church member was given permission to collect signatures on a petition denying protection to gays and lesbians." She has four children. (ABS)

Specktor, Peggy (1941 – 2001) A tireless advocate for the needs of women and children, Specktor spent more than 30 years in Minnesota politics. She was a founder of the DFL Party's feminist caucus in the early 1970s, and served for 15 years as the first director of the Minnesota Program for Victims of Sexual Assault. Credited with changing the term "rape" to "sexual assault," a move that puts more focus on the attacker, Specktor traveled throughout the state to help women set up sexual assault programs. She was also a lobbyist for the Minnesota chapter of the American Academy of Pediatrics, which honored her with its Child Advocate of the Year Award (1998). In 2000, she was honored at the DFL's Women's Summit with its Woman of Distinction Award. Specktor had two children.

Spencer, Lonabelle Ann ("Kappie") (1925 –) began a 30-year crusade to change the sexist language and laws of wills and trusts that discriminate against women when her mother died in 1965. While Spencer's brothers received their inheritances outright, Spencer's and her sisters' inheritances were put into trusts. Later, when Spencer asked the trust to release money for her children's education, she was refused, and her crusade began. She eventually prevailed and her trust was dissolved. She then lobbied and testified in Iowa and Washington to raise consciousness about the discriminatory practices and control of women's money, and published the pamphlet "Whose Money Is It Anyway?" In 1999, Spencer's friend, congresswoman Louise Slaughter (D-NY), introduced an amendment to the Financial Services Bill on Fair Treatment by Financial Advisors, and President Clinton signed it into law in November 1999. Spencer is the founder and director of the National Gender Balance Project (to have more women appointed to boards), was a pioneer member of Planned Parenthood, and took part in a number of U.N. international meetings on women, including the U.N. Conference on Women in Beijing (1995), where she gave a workshop. Spencer was a delegate to the National Women's Conference in Houston (1977), was state and national legislative chair of AAUW from 1978–1983 and director for women's issues from 1985–1989, and was involved in major ERA campaigns. She was also responsible for persuading the Iowa Telephone Company to list married women in its directory with their husbands' listings (1981), a practice that other states eventually adopted. After moving to Florida

(1985), Spencer initiated the formation of the Florida Women's Consortium, a result of the Gender Balance Project. In the 1990s, she waged independent battles against AT&T when they cut funding to Planned Parenthood for educational programs, and The Pioneer Hi-Bred International Corp. after they cut funding to 15 Planned Parenthood rural health clinics in Iowa. Spencer, who has four children, earned her B.A. from Grinnell College. Archives: Women's Archives, University of Iowa, Iowa City, IA. (ABS)

Spero, Nancy (1926 –) An artist, Spero was a founder of the AIR Gallery (NYC) in 1971. She was a member of the Art Workers Coalition (1968–1969), joined Women Artists in Revolution in 1969, and was a member of the ad hoc committee of women artists (1970). In 1974, Spero decided to concentrate on women in all her future works. She began work on "Torture of Women" that year, and had it exhibited at the AIR Gallery in 1976. She then began work on "Notes in Time on Women," which was exhibited at the AIR Gallery in 1979. Over the years, Spero has had numerous solo exhibitions at venues including the New Museum of Contemporary Art in New York City, the Renaissance Society at the University of Chicago, and the Museum of Contemporary Art in Los Angeles. She also had a traveling retrospective at the Institute of Contemporary Arts in London. Spero, who has three children, holds a B.F.A. from the School of the Art Institute of Chicago (1949). (ABS)

Spiegel, Diane – See Meier, Diane

Spikes, Eleanor Ruth (1936–1982) A civil rights and women's rights activist, Spikes was a coordinator of NOW's first minority women's task force in 1973. She was a staff member of the original (1965) EEOC, which enforced Title VII banning employment discrimination on the basis of sex. She was also a partner in the consulting firm, Aileen C. Hernandez Associates. In 1975, Spikes directed a project funded by the Mayor's Criminal Justice Planning Council, which assisted the first group of women to enter and successfully complete training as full-service police officers in San Francisco. In 1973 she was a co-founder and coordinator of Black Women Organized for Action, which, in coalition with other activist women's organizations, established the first women's credit union in the country. Spikes also served on boards of the local YMCA and Planned Parenthood.

Spindel, Karen S. (1947 –) In the mid 1960s, Spindel was a full-time female undergraduate mechanical engineering student at George Washington University. In 1969, her senior year, Spindel went with her Student Chapter of the Society of Mechanical Engineers on a tour to Bethlehem Steel in Sparrows Point, MD. When she arrived with her male classmates, Bethlehem Steel personnel prohibited Spindel from touring the plant because she was a woman. They positioned an armed guard in the seat next to her on the bus while the rest of the students toured. In 1968, Spindel earned a "women's badge" from Tau Beta Pi, the Engineering Honor Society, which at that time did not accept women as full members. A year later, when the rules changed, Spindel became the first woman member of Tau Beta Pi from GWU. After her graduation (1969), Spindel faced and fought rampant job discrimination against women, becoming an engineer for Robins Engineers & Constructors in Totowa, NJ. One of her first assignments was to design overland conveyors for Bethlehem Steel. Spindel joined Passaic County NOW in 1972 and remains active. She has served as membership coordinator for 20 years, lectured on the ERA "at any location that would invite us," and in the mid 1970s organized a protest at the Passaic Public Library, demanding that women be allowed to get library cards in their own names. "Prior to that protest, women had to declare their marital status and use Mrs. followed by their husband's name on their library cards!" Spindel adds, "During my 30 years-plus of activism, I have organized marched and rallied in New Jersey and D.C. and written enough letters on topics such as equal rights, sex discrimination and gender stereotyping to fill a book." Spindel has two children. (ABS)

Spitz, Lilly Therese (1947 –) An attorney and chief legal counsel to Planned Parenthood Affiliates of California (2004), Spitz began working for reproductive rights in the late 1960s. In 1968, she helped establish a family planning referral program in the Boston area, and in 1969 was a community organizer with the National Welfare Rights Organization in that city. Prior to Roe v. Wade (1971 – 1973), Spitz helped women from states that outlawed abortions to travel to Los Angeles for safe, legal abortions; after Roe v. Wade (1973 – 1974), she managed an outpatient abortion clinic in Los Angeles. Co-author of the first "Street Law" guide for battered women (San Francisco, 1976 – 1977), Spitz was also a member of Women In Politics (1977 – 1982), a network of women working in the California state capitol to push women's issues with legislators. Spitz was co-founder and first chair of the Sacramento Women's Campaign Fund (1982 – 1985), and founder and executive director of the Women's Legislative Institute (1982 – 1987). From 1987 – 1999, Spitz was a member of the legislative committee of Women Lawyers of Sacramento; a board member of California Women Lawyers and the Sacramento Birthing Project; and editor of the *Manual on California Domestic Violence Laws*, among other activities. Spitz has also been a member of the NAACP and active in local civil rights groups since 1978. Born in Vienna, Austria, Spitz has one child. She holds a B.S. from the University of California, Irvine, and a J.D. from Golden Gate University Law School. (ABS)

Sprague, Elizabeth ("Beth") Carole (1953 –) was a founder of the first feminist organization on the campus

of the University of Alaska, Fairbanks—the University Women's Center (1974 – 1975). Sprague was also founder of the Higher Ground Consciousness Raising Collective in Anchorage (1975 – 1980), which brought women into the city from all over the state, including bush communities and the Yukon Territories, for three-day training. The women then went back into their communities and set up CR groups that functioned as feeders of new volunteers into women's groups and feminist actions all over Alaska. In addition, Sprague was founder of Body Awareness Workshops in Anchorage (1976 – 1978), and served as director of the Alaska Women's Resource Center in that city (1978). As a founder of the Alaska Gay Coalition in Anchorage (1978 – 1980), Sprague organized Anchorage's first gay pride parade, and also brought suit against the city to force publication of AGC's information in a city resource book. Sprague was an original staff member of Abused Women's Aid in Crisis in Anchorage (1977 – 1981). From 1978 – 1984, she was a board member of the Alaska Women's Resource Center, and from 1978 – 1984 developed and hosted a once-weekly, one-hour live public affairs and women's music radio program on Alaska's first public radio station, KSKA. As the owner of Liberty Productions: Women's Music & Theater Productions (1982 – 1985), Sprague produced women's music concerts and theater events throughout the state. Since that time, Sprague has been active in various peace initiatives, has volunteered at Horizons Community Center's Anti-Violence Hotline, and edited and designed a Partner Violence Assessment Tool for the State of Illinois (2003). She is (2005) the field outreach coordinator at the Center on Conscience and War. Sprague holds an M.F.A. from Mills College (1986). (ABS)

Spretnak, Charlene (1946 –) A professor, Spretnak is the author of two pioneering books on the emergent women's spirituality movement: *Lost Goddesses of Early Greece* (Moon Books, 1978), and *The Politics of Women's Spirituality*, an anthology she edited (Doubleday, 1982). Earlier, Spretnak was associated with the Women's Center in Carbondale, IL (1973 – 1974), now one of the oldest women's shelters in the U.S. Spretnak founded he Mock Turtle Crafts Gallery, in which one-third of the purchase price of an item sold went to the Women's Center, and two-thirds to the artist/crafts person. A co-founder of the Green Party movement in the United States, Spretnak has also been active in the ecofeminist and women's spirituality movements. She holds a B.A. from St. Louis University (1968) and an M.A. from the University of California, Berkeley (1981). (ABS)

Springel, Nona – See Ferdon, Nona Marie

St. George, Katherine — In 1956, Congresswoman St. George (R-NY) became the first woman parliamentarian at the Republican National Convention. In her fight to have women included in the Civil Rights Act of 1964, she

S

argued in the House of Representatives that existing protective labor legislation did nothing for women but exclude them from higher paying jobs. It prevented them from serving in restaurants and cabarets late at night, when the tips are higher and the workload lighter, for example, and from running an elevator late at night—again, when the pay is higher. She introduced an amendment to the Equal Pay Bill in 1962 that asked that "equal" be substituted for "comparable." When the amendment passed, the Equal Pay Bill became law.

St. James, Margo (1937 –) was the founder (1973) of the sex worker's rights and education organization COYOTE. One of COYOTE's first acts was a successful 1974 protest against forced penicillin shots and quarantine of women arrested for prostitution in San Francisco. In 1976, St. James and Priscilla Alexander began to direct the National Task Force on Prostitution. Born on a dairy farm in Bellingham, WA, St. James married at 17 and gave birth to a son the same year. In 1958 she divorced her first husband and moved to San Francisco. Working in an after-hours club as a cocktail waitress in 1962, St. James was not a prostitute. Nevertheless, that year she was formally charged with "soliciting in prostitution" and "keeping or residing in a house of ill fame." When she told the judge that she had never "turned a trick in her life," the judge observed, "Anyone who speaks the language is obviously a professional" and found her guilty on both counts. After passing the California College Equivalency exam in 1963, St. James attended Lincoln University's Law school for two years. She then successfully appealed her conviction. This did not remove the stigma of being a "whore," however, and St. James found it difficult to find work. Working sporadically as a prostitute for about four years, St. James began attending CR meetings in Marin County, CA, in the late 1960s. In 1972, she organized WHO (Whores, Housewives and Others), the precursor to COYOTE. In 1985, St. James founded the Amsterdam-based International Committee for Prostitutes Rights with Gail Pheterson. The two are co-authors of *A Vindication of the Rights of Whores* (Seal Press, 1989).

Staats-Westover, Hazel Vivian (1923 –) (also known as Hazel Vivian Staats Meyners) After working for decades to foster women in religions and religious education, Staats-Westover became chaplain at Princeton University for the United Church of Christ and American Baptist denominations, with a job description that says "Ministry for Women," a position she retains (2005). Earlier, she co-taught the first class for women in any seminary in the U.S. at Chicago Theological Seminary, and with her students founded the Ecumenical Women's Center there. From 1972–1974, she studied at Boston Theological Institute's program for women in graduate religion, and in 1974 published a booklet, *Coming Out of Marriage*, with Emily Culpepper and Diane Miller. After helping construct the New Words Bookstore in Cambridge, MA,

Staats-Westover became the first director of the Women's Center at Princeton University when it became co-ed in 1974. From 1976–1977, she was outreach director of the Women's Resource and Survival Center, Keyport, NJ, and in 1978 taught the first class for women at New Brunswick Theological Seminary. In 1979, she helped the women in the Reformed Church in America become ordained. Her appointment as chaplain at Princeton University was part of "a complete revolution, as last year [2002] a woman president was elected, a woman provost and a woman of color VP to a formerly male Ivy League southern university!" In addition to this work, Staats-Westover held presidencies of NOW and Church Women United locally (1978–2003), and was a delegate to the U.N. Women's Conference in Beijing (1995) for the National Council of Churches and National Church Women United. Active in anti-war and civil rights movements, Staats-Westover worked with Jesse Jackson while she was on the staff of Chicago Theological Seminary (1966–1972). Jackson was organizing boycotts for Martin Luther King's Breadbasket program. Staats-Westover, who has two children and three stepchildren, holds a B.M. of Education from Northwestern University and an M.Div. from Chicago Theological Seminary.   (ABS)

Stacey, Judith (1943 –) was a founder of the women's studies program at Richmond College, City University of New York, in 1971. She then co-edited *And Jill Came Tumbling After: Sexism in American Education* (Dell, 1974), and from 1974–1976 taught in the free Women's School in Cambridge, MA. She was a member of the Boston Area Socialist-Feminist Organization (1974–1976) and of the first *Feminist Studies* editorial collective (1977–1983). In addition, Stacey was a member of Marxist-Feminist Group III in Boston (1975) and helped initiate a Bay Area socialist-feminist theory group in 1978. From 1979–1980, Stacey participated in a history of sexuality study group in the Bay Area. She also served as first director of the women's studies program at the University of California, Davis (1980), and worked extensively to build that program and system-wide women's studies at the University of California consortium. She has published extensively on feminism and family politics, including *Brave New Families* (1990), *Patriarchy and Socialist Revolution in China* (1983), and *In the Name of the Family* (Beacon Press, 1997) as well as scores of articles. She became Streisand Professor of Contemporary Gender Studies at the University of Southern California in 1997, and in 2003 became professor of sociology and professor of gender and sexuality at New York University. In addition to this work, Stacey has been active in civil rights and black history curriculum revision, anti-Vietnam War demonstrations, and gay/lesbian family rights. Stacey, who has one child, earned her B.A. from the University of Michigan (1964), her M.A. from the University of Illinois, Chicago (1966), and her Ph.D. from Brandeis University.   (ABS)

(ABS) indicates Approved By Subject

Stagg, Mary Ellen – See Capek, Mary Ellen S.

Stamberg, Susan Levitt (1938 –) A broadcast journalist, Stamberg was the first woman to anchor a nightly national network news broadcast. She joined National Public Radio in 1971, and was co-host of "All Things Considered" (1972–1987). In those years, as anchor and tacit managing editor of the program, she successfully lobbied to air women's issues, and put feminist leaders, causes and concerns on the air on a regular basis. She brought early, steady and deliberate attention to the women's movement, and put its issues on NPR's news agenda on a national level. She is (2005) a special correspondent with NPR. Stamberg, who has one child, earned her B.A. from Barnard College (1959), and holds numerous honorary degrees. Archives: University of Maryland Broadcast Archive, College Park, MD. (ABS)

Stambolian, Janet Beth (1948 –) worked for reproductive rights in support of Bill Baird on the Boston University campus in the late 1960s and participated in a number of local, state and national abortion-rights actions in advance of Roe v. Wade. By 1973, she was on her way "out," and became involved with a woman with whom she worked to start a women's restaurant/collective in Cambridge called Bread and Roses. In 1975, after teaching at Graham Junior College in Boston, Stambolian moved to Venice, CA. She later helped renovate a warehouse that became the Los Angeles Women's Building. Stambolian was also a founding member of Califia Community, which provided experiences for women and children in the late 1970s in California using a model that "the teachers are the taught." In 1976, she and other women from the Women's Building received a CETA grant to teach women the construction trades while providing services to low/moderate income families and social service agencies on the West Side of Los Angeles. The group of six women, which eventually grew to 12, was funded through the City of Santa Monica and the Ocean Park Community Center and worked from 1977–1980 as The Santa Monica Handywomen. The women then formed their own business, Building Women. "I love to blow men's minds with my love and knowledge of tools. But I find it so tiring it is still NOT the norm to see women using tools," she says. Stambolian, who is director of business development at the architectural firm Mackenzie Architects in Burlington, VT, earned her B.S. (1970) and her M.Ed. (1974) from Boston University. Archives: June Mazer Collection, Los Angeles; CA. (ABS)

Stanley, Julia – See Penelope, Julia

Stanley, M. Louise (1942 –) An artist active in the San Francisco Bay Area, Stanley joined an early artists CR group organized by Rita Yokoi and others. That group organized a number of other groups through monthly recruitment meetings, who organized the Bay Area Women's Slide Registry, housed at the Art Institute in San Francisco, CA. The women were invited to show their slide registry at the West Coast Women's Artist's Conference at Cal Arts, organized by Judy Chicago and Miriam Schapiro, in 1972. Also in 1972, Stanley's group and others put out a Bay Area issue of "West East Bag," a feminist newsletter started by Judy Chicago and Miriam Schapiro. Stanley's group met for more than five years, and in the late 1990s joined an "old guard" reunion at the U.C. Berkeley Museum for an oral history of the women artists movement as they remembered it. In 2004 Stanley completed a public art project, in collaboration with sculptor Vickie Jo Sowell, for the city of Emeryville, CA. Titled Neighborhood Convergence, it is a collection of 11 large steel figures designed and painted by Stanley and shown at the Powell Street Freeway underpass. Stanley holds a B.A. from LaVerne College, and a B.F.A. and M.F.A. from the California College of Arts and Crafts. (ABS)

Stanley, Mary T. (1927 –) joined the NWPC in 1976 and was a founding mother and organizer for the Fresno, CA, chapter. Stanley served as president of that chapter, Republican task force chair (CA and national), and as national representative from California. She was elected VP of the NWPC and member of the national advisory board. Stanley developed merchandise for the NWPC as a means of raising money, and successfully raised over $200,000 through special event auctions and fundraising for women candidates. From 1980 – 1984. Stanley produced and sold picture buttons of living women for VP. Stanley was appointed to the California Commission on the Status of Women in 1969 by Governor Ronald Reagan, spoke extensively in the state and elsewhere on the Equal Rights Amendment, and recruited businesswomen to join the struggle. In 1980, Stanley resigned from the California Republican delegation when the ERA was removed from the Republican Platform. In 1984, she chaired Republicans For Ferraro. In 1992, she registered as a Democrat, and in 2000 was named California Woman of the Year. Stanley has three children. (ABS)

Staples, Emily Anne – See Tuttle, Emily Anne

Stapleton, Jean (1942 –) joined Los Angeles NOW with her husband, John Clegg, in 1969. At that time a reporter for City News Service/Radio News West, Stapleton began recording the speakers and putting actualities from them on the wire service, which went to 22 radio stations. "We got a lot of coverage and my employer loved it because they didn't have to pay me to attend!" Stapleton says. Stapleton soon became PR chair, and in 1970 was appointed Los Angeles chapter chair for the August 26, 1970, Women's Strike for Equality. She also covered the event for her employer. Stapleton was then elected VP for communications, a post she held for two years. She also helped form a speakers bureau, and with her husband began speaking about equality in marriage. After serving

S

as co-president of the chapter, she was elected president for two terms (1973, 1974). Stapleton also served as newsletter editor for five years. Reading reports that religious people were opposed to the ERA, Stapleton founded Californians of Faith for the ERA, which was made up of United Methodists, United Church of Christ, Reform Jews, Mormons for the ERA, Catholics for Choice, Presbyterians, Lutherans and many other groups. Stapleton also started a Status of Women Commission in her church in the mid 1970s. Stapleton, who has two stepchildren, earned her B.A. from the University of New Mexico and her M.S. from Northwestern University. (ABS)

Star, Aura (1930 –) Professor emerita of biology at The College of New Jersey, Star began working in the late 1960s to organize women's caucuses statewide, locally and on campus. As part of a NOW initiative, she organized the first WPC in New Jersey, resulting in the formation of the (NJ) Office of Women. In 1971, she co-organized the women's caucus at Trenton State College (now The College of New Jersey) and organized the WPC in South Brunswick Township. As a result of Star's presentation to the mayor of South Brunswick of a manifesto demanding the appointment of women to political offices there have been women on all boards from 1971 forward. Star's work with the women's caucus of Trenton State College resulted in the establishment of a Women's Center (1970) and a women's studies program (1980s). Star, who has two children, holds a B.A. from Hunter College (1949), an M.A. from Mount Holyoke (1951), and a Ph.D. from Rutgers University (1967). (ABS)

Star, BJ (1949 –) A member of Detroit NOW, Star chartered the Western Wayne County (MI) chapter and served, variously, as president, VP and secretary. She also organized the ERA and CR task forces. A member of the Democratic Party, Catholics for Free Choice, NWP, Michigan ERAmerica, LWV, AFSCME and president of the Democratic Women's Club of Upper Pinellas, the oldest Democratic women's club in the U.S., Star has worked in support of the ERA for decades. For example, in 1974, she helped educate the public about ERA, the Educational Equity Act, the Equal Credit Opportunity Act and Roe v. Wade. In 1976, she organized the Michigan delegation and its transportation to the ERA march in Springfield, IL; in 1978, she participated in State of Emergency ERA actions and lobbied and marched for the ERA extension in Washington, D.C. She was also part of the movement to publicly censure Governor J. Thompson (IL), who had previously supported the ERA, but then backed down. In 1980, Star co-convened the Dearborn (MI) chapter of NOW, which sued its local shopping mall, in a case that went to the Michigan Supreme Court, for their right to gather petition signatures for the ERA. After moving to Florida in 1982, Star joined Pinellas County NOW and later became an at-large member of FL NOW. From 1989 – 1994, she lived in Hiroshima, Japan, where she taught English and (informally) feminism. An attorney who earned her J.D. from Michigan State University College of Law, Star has done pro bono work for needy women. She also holds a B.S. from Michigan State University and a Master of Public Administration from Wayne State University. Archives: Matilda Joslyn Gage Foundation, Fayetteville, NY. (ABS)

Stark, Mavra E. (1942 –) (also known as Mavra Steinberg and Mavra DeRise) In 1970, Stark was the founder and director of Play Groups Day Care Center in Brooklyn, NY, the first feminist day care center in the city. Also a member of the committee for community controlled day care, she served as its treasurer from 1973 – 1975. In 1985, Stark joined the Morris County (NJ) chapter of NOW, serving as treasurer (1986 – 1987), president (1990 – 1992), executive VP (1992 – 1994); television task force chair (1994 –), and president (2002 – 2004). She has been a member of NJ NARAL since 1986, served on its board from 1990 – 2000, and as VP from 1991 – 2000. Stark was also on the board of the New Jersey Religious Coalition for Reproductive Rights (1988 – 1990) and served as treasurer in 1989. In addition to this work, Stark has been a member of VFA since 1999 and a member of the board since 2002, has been a member of the ERA Campaign Network since 2000, and a member of the Redstockings of the Women's Liberation Movement Allies and Veterans. The many actions in which Stark participated include the takeover of the Statue of Liberty on Augutst 10, 1970 to publicize the Women's March of August 26, and testifying before the NYC Commission on Human Rights during its hearing on the role of women in contemporary society (1970). Since 1994, Stark has been executive producer and host of a feminist talk show on public access television, "New Directions for Women." She has also written many feminist columns for the Morris County newspaper *The Daily Record*. She has been involved in feminist spirituality since 1988 and has led many goddess rituals for women in large and small groups. Stark, who has two children, earned her B.A. from Brooklyn College. Archives: The Sophia Smith Collection, Smith College, Northampton, MA. (ABS)

Starr, Vicky (1915 –) helped organize 25,000 Chicago packinghouse workers into a union in the late 1930s, and was later featured in the 1970's Academy Award-nominated film "Union Maids." During a 1970 interview with Peg Strobel, Starr said, "I remember working in the stockyards and doing basically the same work that men did. I worked with a knife as a butcher, and we got less pay— 10 cents an hour." An early member of CWLU, Starr did extensive work with CR groups, focusing on childcare, education, minority rights, reproductive rights and the ERA. A high-school graduate, Starr has four children. (ABS)

Staudt, Kathleen (1946 –) A teacher of political science at the University of Texas, El Paso (2005), Staudt has served as a faculty adviser for women's/feminist organizations and was a co-founder of the women's studies program there. She is also involved in research and community work that addresses violence against women. Earlier, in the 1960s, Staudt was a member of the Women's Liberation Organization at the University of Wisconsin, Milwaukee. At the University of Wisconsin, Madison, where she earned her Ph.D. in political science (1976), Staudt worked with women's networks, especially those in male-dominated disciplines. Staudt's dissertation, "Women, Political Power, and Women Farmers in Western Kenya," was one of the few in political science to include attention to women and the services and benefits they received (and did not receive) as women farmers. Staudt has published 12 books, including *Policies, Politics and Gender: Women Gaining Ground* (Kumarian Press, 1998) and *Political Science and Feminisms: Integration or Transformation?*, co-authored with William Weaver (Twayne/MacMillan, 1997). She is also author of more than 60 academic articles/chapters that focus on women/gender or weave women/gender analysis into the writing, including work on gendered bureaucracies. Staudt has two children. (ABS)

Stauffer, Mary Louise – See Hadditt, Marylou

Steckel, Anita — has been a painter, collagist and visual pioneer of feminist sexual politics since the 1960s. Phyllis Rosser, in a cover story for *New Directions for Women*, said, "She may be the earliest creator of visual imagery that expresses the struggle against patriarchal oppression." In January 1973, *Ms.* magazine hailed her as a "Found Woman." Steckel started a Fight Censorship group of women artists in the early 1970s, which crusaded in many colleges and other venues. Steckel's art has been shown in over 20 museums nationally and internationally, including the Whitney, the Bronx, the Aldrich, and the Brooklyn museums (NYC). Steckel, who studied at Music and Art high school, Cooper Union and The Art Students League, where she now teaches, was also active in civil rights and the peace movement. Steckel has received a National Endowment of the Art grant for painting, the Pollock-Krasner award for painting and collage. Archives: The National Museum of Women in the Arts, Washington, D.C.; Rutgers, New Brunswick, NJ; and The Whitney Museum, New York, NY. (ABS)

Stecker, Vera (1926 –) convened and served as the first president of the Greater Bridgeport (CT) chapter of NOW. She also served as assistant state coordinator and as a member of the board of CT NOW. In 1972, Stecker lodged a complaint with the Human Rights Commission against the University of Bridgeport in an effort to force the university to stop allowing the Torch Club use of its campus facilities. She contended that all-male organizations such as the Torch Club limit women's ability to take part in decision-making aspects of their professions and

that, as the recipient of public funds, such clubs are in violation of the Code of Fair Practices of the State of Connecticut. In addition, Stecker organized and participated in CR groups and served on the advisory board of the Rape Crisis Service of the YWCA of Greater Bridgeport. She also wrote and produced the slide/lecture When God Was Our Mother, which was presented at women's centers, local colleges and in the community. Stecker also hosted two public-access radio interview programs on women's issues, one live on the University of Bridgeport station, WPKN, which she hosted for one year, and the second a taped show on WICC in Bridgeport. In addition, Stecker was a frequent guest speaker on feminist issues on local TV channels, and a guest lecturer on women's issues at the University of Bridgeport, Sacred Heart University, local high schools, the sisterhoods of several churches, synagogues and area YWCAs. She helped to organize and coordinate many all-day and multi-day conferences and workshops on women's issues. (ABS)

Steele, Carolyn Ann (1946 – 2004) An educator, Steele represented the AAUW in Peoria, IL, on the Peoria ERA Coalition. The group debated, lobbied, marched, picketed, held fundraisers and a torchlight parade, all to further passage of the ERA. In addition, Steele initiated a grade-school girls basketball program in 1970. Later in life she said, "Boys had had organized basketball for 50 years. It's a joy to see so many girls playing competitive sports today." Steele also organized a community resource pool of volunteers who shared their knowledge and hobbies with six area grade schools, emphasizing women role models in non-traditional occupations. Steele earned a B.S. and M.A. from Bradley University.

Steele, Clelia (1931 –) A member of the Washington, D.C., group advocating the ordination of women in the Episcopal Church (1971), Steele wrote press releases and also served as liaison with national women's groups. In addition, Steele worked with WEAL to promote passage of Title IX. After its passage, Steele joined NOW LDEF's Project Equal Education Rights (1972), whose mission was to monitor enforcement of Title IX at the elementary and secondary level. Steele was also a founding board member of the National Coalition for Women and Girls in Education, but believes her most significant contribution to the women's movement was "Cracking the Glass Slipper," PEER's monitoring tool for groups looking at enforcement efforts, or lack of them, in the government's regional offices. Steele designed the package, obtained funding and oversaw production. When the project was finished, she took it on the road for PEER, traveling across the country, training local groups, holding press conferences and appearing on local radio and television from Atlanta and Alabama to Iowa and San Francisco. *The New York Times* followed Steele on four of the stops, writing a series of articles on the project, which the paper called "the greatest citizen monitoring effort ever accom-

S

plished." Says Steele, "It was well worth doing for the education of little girls and for ensuring that hundreds of ordinary citizens would never again be flummoxed by their government." Before retiring, Steele's work covered senior administration and fundraising with Washington-based national public interest organizations. (ABS)

Steele, Joanne (1940 –) In 1964 Steele was introduced by her landlady to Ruth Herschberger. Subsequent discussions with her helped educate Steele to feminism. At a 1970 meeting of Women's Strike Coalition, the Socialist Workers' Party women's group, Steele and others decided to create a feminist newspaper. It was Steele who came up with the name *Majority Report*. After the apparent dissolution of the WSC, Steele wrote and helped produce the second and subsequent issues of *MR* and ran them off on a mimeograph machine at the 19th Street Women's Liberation Center in NYC. After a political struggle that Steele lost, *MR* was moved to an Upper West Side apartment. In 1974 it moved again to a cramped office in downtown Greenwich Village. Steele "wrote, edited, produced mechanicals, strategized, co-conspired and of course swept the floor." When the distribution company's driver quit, Steele took over, using her tiny Toyota and later a used USPS delivery van she had painted lavender pink to deliver *MR* to newsstand dealers who were less than anxious to display the publication. Steele was an organizer of Feminist Forums at P.S. 41. (The first one was titled Revolution or Reform?) In the first anti-rape demonstration in NYC, Steele carried a placard with the phrase she coined as a strategy to move male legislators: "Rape is Violence not Sex." She printed and distributed numbers of "Stop Rape" stickers in the now common stop-sign colors and design. Steele also participated in forming Gay Women's Liberation Front. When she moved to Upstate NY in 1987, Steele helped to revive Ulster County NOW. Steele holds a B.Sc. from Brown University and an M.A. from Yeshiva University. (ABS)

Steere, Helen Weaver – See Horn, Helen Steere

Stegall, Lael (1941 –) has spent her life helping women establish power and get the resources and learning tools they need to be effective in making positive democratic change. Following her work on the national staff of George McGovern's Presidential campaign, Stegall was asked by her Republican neighbor to join with others as founding staff of the NWPC, which was organized in 1973 by activists from many sectors who knew that women needed to develop political power to make change. Stegall raised millions of dollars for the NWPC, women candidates and causes, and then went on to spend 10 years full time in philanthropy working with women donors who were defining new ways to assert their leadership and financial resources. Stegall was also a co-founder of Emily's List, now a powerful financial resource for women in politics, and helped found the Communi-

cations Consortium Media Center in Washington, D.C. From 1994 – 2002, she took the tools for social change around money, power, politics and media and shared them with women in the war zones of the Yugoslav successor states. She has worked for UNIFEM and now (2005) the American University in Kosovo. Stegall, who has two children, holds a B.A. from Colby College and an M.S. from the University of Chicago. Archives: Schlesinger Library, Radcliffe Institute, Cambridge, MA. (ABS)

Stein, Beverly (1947 –) After graduating from the University of California, Berkeley, in 1970, Stein joined Female Liberation. With her friends, she then formed Berkeley Women Speakers, creating a show that the women took on the road and presented to over 1,000 people in California and beyond. The show included short skits that illustrated sexism, karate demonstrations, songs and personal testimonials. Berkeley Women Speakers also created dozens of CR groups. In 1972, Stein joined a collective of women who produced a radio show on KPFA, "Unlearning to Not Speak." Stein, who did a show on sexism in children's literature, was also active in the abortion movement at that time. In 1973, she moved to Madison, WI, to attend law school. While a student there, she became a socialist-feminist. She was a member of the National Lawyers Guild and organized a People's Law School. Moving to Portland, OR, in 1976, she became a Legal Aid lawyer. Stein was active in the New American Movement and later the Democratic Socialists of America, as well as many other activist and citizens groups she helped form. In 1993, she was elected chair of the Multnomah County (OR) Board of Commissioners and county executive. She holds a B.A. from the University of California, Berkeley, and an L.L.B. from the University of Wisconsin School of Law. (ABS)

Stein, Judith Ellen (1943 –) An art historian, curator and art critic who wrote her Ph.D. dissertation (1981) on the iconography of Sappho in Europe from 1777 – 1875, Stein has worked consistently to further the cause of women and the arts. She was a member of the core organizing group that put together Philadelphia Focuses on Women in the Visual Arts in May 1974. She served as editor of the WCA newsletter (1975 – 1977) and as a member of their national advisory board (1979 – 1981). Stein's first effort as a feminist scholar and writer was her essay accompanying the Sandak slide set documenting Women's Work: American Art 1974, a FOCUS exhibition. *Feminist Art Journal* (Winter 1975 – 1976) published her study of Cecilia Beaux, the first woman to teach at the Pennsylvania Academy of the Fine Arts; it was the first feminist discussion of the artist's work and career. Stein was a board member of the College Art Association, and reinvigorated their committee on women in the arts as its chair from 1992 – 1997. She served on the advisory board of Philadelphia's Leeway Foundation for women artists (1994 – 2002). Stein, who has one child, earned her B.A.

from Barnard College (1965) and her M.A. (1967) and Ph.D. (1981) from the University of Pennsylvania. (ABS)

Stein, Linda (1943 –) A sculptor, painter, curator, lecturer and writer, Stein's emphasis has been on feminist, androgynous and anti-war art. Her current series, Knights, scrambles expectations: the knights are not in the service of war and not male. While Stein's main focus is on her women-warrior sculpture, she also produced a print series on feminists including Flo Kennedy, Bella Abzug, Virginia Woolf, Margaret Sanger and Gloria Steinem. Since 1974, she has been the founder and president of Have Art: Will Travel (HAWT), a nonprofit corporation (since 1979) to help artists, particularly women, exhibit, teach and sell their art. After 1979, HAWT's ongoing cultural projects have included Breaking Up Gender Stereotypes (BUGS)—designed to help people examine and dissipate gender-based assumptions. Exhibits have included Fragile Fabrics: Not Female; Muscular Media, Not Male; and Men on Flowers, Women on Computers. Stein, who earned her bachelor's degree from Queens College and her master's from the Pratt Institute, was "reviewed as one of the BAD-GIRLS, addressing the issues of power and vulnerability with an emphasis on gender equality." She was awarded the outdoor sculpture for the entrance to the East Hampton (Long Island, NY) Airport, and has been curator of exhibitions and acquisitions for the Shirley Fitterman Gallery and the Triplex Gallery, both at the Borough of Manhattan Community College, as well as Art Acres, a 110-acre campus with sculpture garden in Boca Raton (FL). Since 1993, Stein was founder/president of The Art Club in Tribeca, offering free space for nonprofit organizations promoting feminism, diversity, peace and abortion rights. In 2004, she joined the board of VFA, as well as The House for Elder Artists and the Haworth Press HLF Quarterly Magazine. Archives: The Sophia Smith Collection, Smith College, Northampton, MA. (ABS)

Steinbacher, Roberta (1936 –) was one of three founding members of Womenspace (1974), a coalition of over 50 women's organizations in the Cleveland, OH, area. She has written extensively on the sexist bias in sex selection techniques. The articles, published in psychology journals and some popular magazines, include "Persuasability and Persuasiveness as a Function of Sex," published in *Journal of Social Psychology* (1976); "Firstborn Preference and Attitudes Toward Using Sex Selection Technology," published in *Journal of Genetic Psychology* (2002) and co-written with D. Swetkis and F. Gilroy; "The Hidden Agenda Is Fewer Female Babies," published in *USA Today*, August 15, 1986; and "Should Parents Be Prohibited from Choosing the Sex of Their Child?" published in *Health* (March 1994). Steinbacher, a professor who has lectured nationally and abroad on these topics, was a member of the women's task force, Cleveland Area Reserve Manpower Consortium (1974–1978). Among her many other affiliations, she served as a consultant and

lecturer, Institute of Women Today, Chicago (1974–1985); was a board member and state delegate, Cuyahoga WPC (1977–1980); served as a member of the Lieutenant Governor's Women's Issues Policy Development Committee, Columbus, OH (1978 – 1979); and served as president of Ohio Women Inc. (1978–1980) and board member (1980–1987). Steinbacher holds a B.A. from Creighton University, and an M.S. and Ph.D. from St. Louis University. Archives: Cleveland State University, Cleveland, OH. (ABS)

Steinberg, Mavra – See Stark, Mavra

Steinberg, Susan – See Danielson, Susan L.

Steinem, Gloria (1934 –) A journalist, feminist, political activist and lecturer, Steinem became a leader in the women's movement from her first address to feminists at the August 26, 1970, Women's Strike for Equality postmarch rally. She has been an independent thinker and a spokesperson on feminism worldwide. Co-founder in 1972 of *Ms.* magazine, the only women's magazine owned and controlled by women, Steinem was an editor there for 15 years. The staff stunned the advertising community when they refused to yield to advertiser pressures to compromise editorial (and in 1990, stopped taking advertising altogether). After the nonprofit foundation that owned *Ms.* sold it to the company of two Australian feminists, it fell into the hands of a traditional publisher. It continued to be editorially controlled by its staff, headed by Robin Morgan and then Marcia Gillespie, but eventually, Steinem secured a group of women investors to buy it back. After the magazine joined forces with The Feminist Majority Foundation, Steinem continued as a consulting editor. Steinem was also co-founder of the Ms. Foundation for Women, NWPC, the Women's Action Alliance, and Voters for Choice. In 1993, she was inducted into the National Women's Hall of Fame in Seneca Falls, NY. Her role in creating the annual Take Our Daughters to Work event for the Ms. Foundation won her the Lifetime Achievement Award for promoting girls' self-esteem. After growing up primarily in the Midwest, with no full year of schooling until she was 12, Steinem graduated Phi Beta Kappa from Smith College in 1956. She went to India for two years, where she absorbed grassroots organizing skills from followers of Gandhi. She moved to NYC in 1960 and wrote freelance for *Life*, *Esquire*, *Glamour* and *New York Magazine*, which she helped to found. In 1969, the young writer (who had gone undercover as a bunny to do an investigative article on the Playboy Club) was one of the few reporters covering an abortion-speakout held by Redstockings. Although her objective was to write up the meeting for her political column in *New York Magazine*, it was the "click" that brought her into the feminist movement. She has written the best-selling *Revolution from Within: A Book of Self Esteem* (Little, Brown and Company, 1992) and *Outrageous Acts and Everyday Rebellions*

S

(Holt, Rinehart and Winston, 1983), as well as *Moving Beyond Words* (Simon & Schuster, 1994) and *Marilyn: Norman Jean* (Holt, 1983), on the life of Marilyn Monroe. She also edited, with Wilma Mankiller, Gwendolyn Mink, Marysa Navarro and Barbara Smith, *The Reader's Companion to U.S. Women's History* (Houghton Mifflin Company, 1998). Archives: The Sophia Smith Collection, Smith College, Northampton, MA. (ABS)

Steingarten, Ellen M. – See Raintree, Elizabeth

Steingold, Jacqueline (1942 –) Much of Steingold's early work (1970s) focused on childcare issues in Detroit. After receiving a grant from New Detroit Inc., Steingold began a childcare center at Wayne County Community College (1971), where she was teaching. It was the first evening childcare center in Michigan. She became a member of the Michigan Women's Liberation Movement in the early 1970s, then joined Detroit NOW, where she is (2003) a member of the board. In 1985, Steingold received the Feminist of the Year Award from Detroit NOW, and from 1994–1998 served on NOW's national board. She was also named one of 25 Influential Detroit Women in 1990 at the annual Women's Equality Day event sponsored by the City of Detroit. Steingold was active with the Women's Conference of Concerns in the 1970s and 1980s; was on the Michigan women and AIDS committee (1989–2001); and has been a member of the board of the MI WPC since 1999. She was appointed by the mayor to the women's committee of the City of Detroit Human Rights Commission and served from 1990 –1996. In addition to being on the board of the Detroit Women's Forum for 25 years, Steingold was an escort at an abortion clinic for many years, and has participated in numerous roundtables and public discussions about reproductive choice and reproductive freedom. Steingold, who holds a master's degree in social work, has one child. (ABS)

Stellman, L. Mandy (1922 –) Once described as "probably the most active and outspoken legal advocate in Wisconsin for equal rights for women," Stellman has worked through NOW, the ABA, her own law firm and other groups to right the wrongs against women. She served as president and legal adviser to the Wisconsin Women's Coalition (1971), offering pro bono legal training; was a trainer for the Women's Crisis Line (1972), again offering pro bono legal advice; and in 1970 began acting as an attorney for Milwaukee NOW in many sex discrimination law suits. Stellman was an attorney for NOW during its 1970s action against Sears; successfully filed a Title VII complaint against the Milwaukee Board of Education; and in 1973 was the attorney of record in obtaining a court order forcing the Milwaukee fire and police departments to appoint women officers. From the 1970s through the 1990s, she participated in ERA marches and helped finance many trips for women who could not afford the costs. Says Stellman, "When I saw an

injustice, I was compelled to take action to fix it. Someone had to do it. So I just did it. I brought hope to people who were afraid to make the necessary change that would solve their problems." A member of the ABA, the State Bar of Wisconsin and the Milwaukee Bar, Stellman was the first woman in the nation to become a member of a legal fraternity, Tau Epsilon Rho (1970). Born in Canada and a graduate of the University of Toronto, Ohio State University and Marquette Law School (1970), Stellman has two children. Archives: Milwaukee Women's Center, Milwaukee, WI. (ABS)

Stender, Fay Abrahams (1932 – 1980) An attorney, Stender became active in the women's movement in 1973 when she joined the advisory board of the Women's History Research Center in Berkeley, CA. She also opened a small law firm in San Francisco with her husband, Marvin Stender. Her first case in this practice, Scherr v. Scherr (January 1974) sought enforcement of quasi-marital rights of an unmarried woman, foreshadowing income-sharing agreements between unmarried couples and helping pave the way for the concept of "palimony." Following this case, Stender was recruited for the advisory board of the *Women's Law Journal* at UCLA, and in 1975 became a member of the first elected board of governors of California Women Lawyers. After separating from her husband, Stender began an open lesbian relationship (1978). She served on the advisory committee for the Equal Rights Advocates Lesbian Rights project and chaired the San Francisco Bar Association's employment of women committee. In 1979, she was honored with the Loren Miller Legal Services Award from the California Bar Association for her long-term commitment to providing legal services to the disadvantaged. She continued to serve on the board of the Berkeley and Northern California ACLU, where she was instrumental in persuading the organization to hire its first female director, Dorothy Ehrlich, in 1974, and in increasing the number of women on the ACLU board. Early in the morning of Memorial Day 1979, Stender was shot by an intruder in her home in Berkeley and left to die. Confined to a wheelchair and in constant pain, she never recovered from the trauma of the shooting and took her own life the following May. In 1981 she was posthumously awarded the Earl Warren Civil Liberties Award by the Northern California ACLU. In 1982, California Women Lawyers established the Fay Stender Award in honor of the woman who showed commitment to women and had the courage and ability to effect change. Stender, who had two children, held a B.A. from Reed College (1952) and a J.D. from the University of Chicago Law School (1956). Archives: Materials from the Scherr case are at the Women's History Research Library and Center, Berkeley, CA.

Stephens, Wanda Brewer (1932 –) A member of the board of the Economic Opportunity Agency of Washington County, AR, Stephens helped write the bylaws and develop a countywide Head Start Program (1968–1969). The program, which continues today, provided a safe place for low-income women to leave their children while they worked or received job training. From 1971–1974, Stephens was chair of the board that founded the Infant Develop-ment Center, the first group day care center for infants in the state. Today, the center is part of the University of Arkansas at Fayetteville, serving as a labora-tory for child development classes and a place for UA student parents to leave their children. Active in the Central United Metho-dist Church in the mid 1970s, Stephens served on the administrative board and finance and nominating committees, where she tried to balance the men with women in leadership positions. During her tenure as chair of the education committee (1976–1978), she saw the launch of a childcare center that was open to the community. Today it is the premier childcare center in the community with a waiting list of about a year. Stephens has four children and holds an M.S. degree from the University of Arkansas. Archives: Special Collections, University of Arkansas, Fayetteville, AR. (ABS)

Stern, Beverly Bartko (1937 –) helped start three NOW chapters in Connecticut: Central CT NOW and New Haven NOW (early 1970s) and South Central NOW (1975). Stern held various offices in all three chapters, and was particularly involved in CR groups. Says Stern, "Probably my greatest contribution has been as a long-time, low-key continual worker for human rights, which —for me—includes equality, civil rights, peace and much, much more." Stern, who has two children, is (2005) chair of the Hamden (CT) Human Rights & Relations Commission and co-president of the United Nations Association of Greater New Haven. She holds a B.A. from the University of Connecticut and a master's equivalent from Southern Connecticut State University. (ABS)

Stern, Gwen (1946 –) In the early 1970s, Stern partici-pated in the Women's Health Network in Chicago, working on abortion rights and women's health issues. From 1971–1973, she demonstrated and lobbied in sup-port of the ERA, and in 1973 was a founder (and longtime board member) of Mujeres Latinas en Accion, a Latina women's organization based in the Pilsen community of Chicago. In 1977, Stern was project coordinator of The Latina Mother Infant Research Project, a community-based research effort to explore prenatal health and mental health issues. From 1978–1980, she served as director of Dar a Luz, a prenatal and community education project, based at Mujeres, that provided bilingual prenatal educa-tion classes and advocacy on women's health issues. From the late 1970s to the early 1980s, Stern was a board member of Planned Parenthood of Chicago. Stern, who started her own consulting company in 1998, has pub-lished and spoken widely on mental health, birth control and infant wellness for Latin Americans. She holds a Ph.D. from Northwestern University (1976). (ABS)

Stern, Mickey (1929 –) Born in Canada, Stern moved to Ohio and worked tirelessly there for abortion and repro-ductive rights for women. She was one of six women volunteers who ran a referral hotline in Cleveland (1972 – 1973). When abortion was legalized by the Supreme Court in 1973, the women hoped to carry on and expand their work, but were met with opposition from local reli-gious groups. Frustrated, they dreamed of forming a nonprofit abortion facility. "Dedication and selfless per-sistence, combined with the goodwill of the Cleveland community and the support of Preterm Institute, finally made the dream a reality," she says. The clinic opened its doors on March 15, 1974, with Stern serving as assistant director. In addition to this work, Stern, who has three children, was active in civil rights and antiwar groups, and was a member of WILPF. She served on the national board of Through the Flower, the arts group that supports Judy Chicago and her artworks, from 1991–1998. Stern is a re-tired social worker. Archives: Western Reserve Historical Society, Cleveland, OH. (ABS)

Stern, Susan (1943–1976) was a founder (1967) of Radical Women, the Seattle-oriented socialist-feminist or-ganization whose goals were to teach women leadership skills, social history and working-class consciousness. In 1968, at the first regional meeting of the Seattle SDS, Stern was chosen chair of a general assembly to discuss women's liberation. A member of the New Left and the Weather Underground, Stern gained national attention when she and six male defendants were tried on charges of conspiracy and violation of the Antiriot Act in 1970. The so-called Seattle Seven trial ended in a mistrial, but Stern's combative courtroom behavior led to a contempt citation and three months in jail. In 1975, Doubleday & Co. published her memoir, *With the Weathermen: The Personal Journal of a Revolutionary Woman*. Stern earned her undergraduate degree from Syracuse University and an M.S.W. from the School of Social Work in Seattle. She suffered a heart seizure at the age of 33 and died after sev-eral days without regaining consciousness.

Stevens, Wilma Theodora (1948 –) joined NOW after moving to Chicago in 1972 and focused on employment issues, including the task force looking into employment agency abuses. She was president of Chicago NOW from 1975 – 1976, and president of Illinois NOW in 1977. Stevens was a founding member of Women Employed, serving as spokesperson for several of its first public ac-tions. In the late 1970s, she joined the board of the Loop Center YWCA, becoming its first chair in 1978. In 1984, Stevens returned to Chicago NOW as chapter secretary. A graphic designer, Stevens used her skills to create buttons, posters and demo props for the women's movement, in-cluding a seven-foot model of the Sears Tower for a Sears shareholder action. In 2004, she was elected board presi-dent of Woman Made Gallery in Chicago, a nonprofit dedicated to exhibiting and encouraging women's art.

S

Stevens holds a B.F.A. from the Maryland Institute, College of Art. (ABS)

Stevenson, Florence Cozart Byrd (1922 –) As dean of women students at the University of Tulsa (1963), Stevenson became aware that many of the women students were older than the usual undergraduates. She started an organization for them, secured a lounge for their sole use, and persuaded influential town women to establish a loan fund for them, since these older students were part-time enrollees and not eligible for the usual financial aid. Stevenson also made sure additional women's housing was built, and encouraged all the women to go on for advanced degrees or train for more traditionally male jobs, such as doctor instead of nurse or attorney instead of elementary school teacher. Moving to Michigan State (1970), Stevenson also became involved in rectifying the poor situation of most women faculty members. Many of the proposals she put before the board of trustees—better pay, advancement and recognition of women all over the campus, from kitchen workers to administrators—were adopted within a few years. In Michigan, Stevenson was also part of an informal group that helped and protected abused women, and from 1980 – 1983 worked with a women's shelter in San Antonio. In 1970, Stevenson became deeply involved in the Association for Women Actively Returning to Education and eventually took it over. At Tulsa, Michigan and later in Los Angeles, Stevenson was always part of small women's groups. In Oklahoma, however, she was the first person in the state to belong to NOW, and in Michigan was asked to be a charter member. She also belonged to WEAL. In Washing-ton, D.C., she says, "I worked amid a hotbed of radical feminists at George Washington University's Center for Continuing Education for Women." Stevenson, who has two children, holds a B.A. from the University of Arkansas (1943), an M.A. from Ohio State University (1963) and a Ph.D. from Michigan State University (1973). Archives: The Sophia Smith Collection, Smith College, Northampton, MA. (ABS)

Stickles, Maureen – See Carrsyn, Maureen Doris

Stiehm, Judith Hicks (1935 –) As a teacher at the University of Wisconsin in the 1960s, Stiehm granted her students' request and brought Kathryn Clarenbach to speak after Clarenbach returned from the 1966 founding meeting of NOW. In 1969, Stiehm and four others founded the Women's Caucus: The American Political Science Association. After moving to the University of Southern California, Stiehm became a founder and first chair of the Women's Studies Program (1972), and then of the Program for the Study of Women and Men in Society (1975). The program included one junior male faculty, under the assumption that society would not change unless men changed also. The program grew quickly, and secured a chair in Women's Studies from

Barbara Streisand. She was a founder of the National Women's Studies Association (1977) and helped write its constitution. In 1975, Stiehm began working on her book *Bring Me Men and Women: Mandated Change at the U.S. Air Force Academy* (University of California Press, 1981). Since that time, she has worked on women in the military and women in peacekeeping. Stiehm's book on the 12 women with Nobel Peace Prizes has a projected 2006 publication date. Stiehm, who has three children, holds a Ph.D. from Columbia University. (ABS)

Stille, Darlene (1942 –) became a feminist activist after participating in a Women Employed-sponsored action against the Chicago Association of Commerce and Industry to force companies to publicize their affirmative action programs. Stille went on to become the first permanent chair of Women Employed, serving for over two years. Working with executive director Day Piercy and the membership, Stille helped create a series of campaigns to make equal opportunity a reality at many Chicago-based companies, including Sears, Kraft and the Harris Bank. Stille is also author of nonsexist science books for children and young adults, including *Extraordinary Women Scientists* and *Extraordinary Women of Medicine*.

Stimpson, Catharine Rosalind (1936 –) (also spelled Roslyn) was sharing an office with Kate Millett at Barnard College in the 1960s when Millett said, "Stimps, there's this civil rights movement for women. We should check it out." They did, and were among the first to meet in a church basement with the NY chapter of NOW. An early action was a visit to *The New York Times* with Betty Friedan to protest sex-segregated help-wanted ads. Stimpson was also one of the first chairs of the image committee, which was concerned about the negative representation of women in the media and in product advertising. By the late 1960s, Stimpson had refined her feminist focus to two primary areas—education and her own writing. In achieving the former, Stimpson taught the first women and literature course at Barnard College (also one of the first in the world), and with others helped create a women's studies program there. In the early 1970s, she became the founding director and chair of the executive committee of the Barnard Women's Center, one of the earliest centers devoted to women's issues within higher education. Stimpson later chaired its international body, the National Council for Research on Women (1985–1989). Also in the early 1970s, Stimpson began her pro bono work with the Modern Language Association, starting with membership in the division of women's studies, then serving as its chair in 1976 and president in 1990. Stimpson was also founding editor of *Signs: Journal of Women in Culture and Society*, a position she held from 1974–1980. That achievement was "perhaps my most salient contribution to the transformation of scholarship," says Stimpson. Stimpson published her first feminist piece, "Thy Neighbor's Wife, Thy Neighbor's

Manservant," in 1971. A study of historical and contemporary relations between black movements and women's movements, it appeared in *Women in Sexist Society*, edited by Vivian Gornick and B.K. Moran. In her writing, Stimpson focused on fiction, women's studies as a field, and feminist criticism, publishing in a variety of outlets. She was also a reviewer for *Ms.* magazine, which led to the establishment of the magazine's board of scholars (which Stimpson chaired). In conjunction with her work over the years to transform education and to write in a feminist mode, she has served on numerous committees and made many public appearances. Stimpson holds an A.B. from Bryn Mawr College; a B.A. and M.A. from Cambridge University; and a Ph.D. from Columbia University. Archives: Center for Pacific Northwest Studies, Western Washington University, Bellingham, WA.   (ABS)

Stoltenberg, Susan Irene (1953 –) led a sit-in at her junior high school over an inequitable dress code in 1967, and participated in several demonstrations during college (1971–1973). From 1976–1977, Stoltenberg headed the ERA-support chapter of NOW in Klamath Falls, OR, and in 1977 attended the IWY conference in Houston as a delegate from Klamath Falls. On her return, Stoltenberg founded the Coalition Against Violence, a network of shelter homes for domestic violence victims. The coalition involved police, the local DA, legal aid attorneys and social workers as well as community volunteers. Because of her visibility, Stoltenberg received bomb threats against her home, her children's childcare facility and on her windshield on several occasions. Stoltenberg then helped lead a series of public hearings in the OR Legislature (1978–1979) that resulted in proposed legislation that would allow police officers to use their own observations to prosecute domestic violence perpetrators, and not require the woman to file charges herself. "Today," says Stoltenberg, "it's standard." Stoltenberg joined the OR WPC in 1980, and over the years has held 10 appointed positions. She has also been an active advocate for gay rights, and in the mid 1980s was the director of the first adoption agency in Oregon that openly accepted same-sex couples into its prospective parent pool. The executive director of non-profit organizations, Stoltenberg has four children. She attended the University of Oregon, Oregon State, Portland State, and Willamette University's Atkinson Graduate School for Management.   (ABS)

Stonaker, Francesca – See Benson, Francesca

Stone, Janet (1945 –) (also known as Janet Hewat-Stone) A member of Eastern Massachusetts NOW (1972–1975), Stone served as chair of the employment task force and facilitated class action suits against Suffolk Law, Boston University athletic department and Harvard Business School to get more women enrolled and in faculty positions. She also led picketing of Boston's NBC affiliate to protest sexist programming and the scarcity of women anchors. Also chair of the membership committee, Stone cowrote *Sex Discrimination – What to Know About It, What to do About It*. Through her columns in the *Somerville Times* and articles in the NOW newsletter, she facilitated removal of coin entry to women's toilets at Logan Airport and elsewhere. She was coordinator of the state ERA campaign in MA, was a frequent speaker on women's issues and trained other women to speak, and served as chapter liaison to the Harvard Square waitresses union. She was an early producer and host of the radio show "The NOW Hour," and co-producer "Who Owns a Woman's Body," a prime time special on WBZ-TV, Boston. Prior to 1975, Stone was a member of the War Resisters League and worked to decriminalize prostitution.   (ABS)

Stone, Merlin (1931 –) An author, sculptor and art historian, Stone is also a prominent scholar of feminist theology. Extensive research, in particular of matrilineal societies, led to publication of her book *When God Was a Woman* (1976). Released the same year in England as *The Paradise Papers: The Suppression of Women's Rights*, it is an examination of the role of women in ancient religions and an exploration of goddess worship. The book was adapted into a radio series for Pacifica Radio (WBAI-FM New York) in 1978. She is also the author of *Ancient Mirrors of Womanhood: Our Goddess and Heroine Heritage* (1979), *Three Thousand Years of Racism – Recurring Patterns in Racism* (1981) and the play "The Voice of The Earth," which was produced at the Williamstown Theater Festival in 1990. Stone holds a B.S. from the State University of New York at Buffalo and an M.F.A. from the California College of Arts and Crafts.

Stoner, Lillian Mary (1940 –) A teacher and teacher union representative, now retired, Stoner lobbied for the creation of the Michigan Women's Commission (1967–1968). During the 1970s, she helped organize CLUW in Detroit, and in 1970 helped form MEAPAC, the political action arm of the Michigan Education Association. In 1972, Stoner became a founding member of MEA's women's caucus and the Michigan Democratic Party Educator Caucus, serving as first chair of the latter from 1972–1974. Also in 1972, both as a teacher (1972–1976) and as an MEA employee (1976–1985), Stoner began filing countless complaints with the EEOC demanding equal pay for coaches and sick day usage for disabilities related to pregnancy and delivery. In 1972, she sued the MEA for sex discrimination in employment, since 95 percent of the professional staffers were white males. Although she lost the case, as it dragged on Stoner was hired and MEA began to hire almost 40 minorities, blacks or women for the next openings. From 1976–1977, Stoner served as a delegate to the Women's Assembly, and in 1977 was a delegate to the IWY conference in Houston. In both 1976 and 1980, she was a delegate to the Democratic National Convention, working with MEA and women's caucuses to keep candidates

S

on track regarding women's issues. In Grand Rapids in 1980, Stoner bargained the first ("that I know of," she says) teacher collective bargaining agreement that required equal pay for coaches of women. From 1980–1985, she continued working to keep MEA a progressive voice for women, and to keep the Democratic Party "honest" regarding women's issues. Stoner has a B.A. and M.A. from the University of Michigan. (ABS)

Stonerock, Linda Sue (1953 –) Stonerock's first job after graduating from college in 1975 was with the Feminist Women's Health Center in Los Angeles. A licensed healthcare worker for the group, Stonerock provided abortion counseling and then stayed with the women one-on-one as they went through the procedure. She was also available to accompany women to local hospitals where their abortions were done by doctors. "These doctors who had often trained in our clinic in vacuum aspiration technique, performed saline and other forms of abortion," she explains. "These were the more typical long-standing techniques before the movement insisted that existing technology be put into practice to render early term abortion much less dangerous, painful, expensive and damaging to women." In addition to this work, Stonerock taught women how to do their own vaginal exams and participated in small satellite self-help groups that performed more radical procedures, such as artificial inseminations. Stonerock holds a B.A. (ABS)

Storch, Marcia L. (1933 – 1998) A medical doctor and innovator in women's healthcare, Storch moved to NYC in 1971. She became director of the Adolescent and Family Planning Clinic at St. Luke's-Roosevelt Hospital Center, where she insisted that her patients take an active role in all their healthcare decisions. This was a radical departure from the days when a male doctor would simply tell a woman—without discussion or information—what to use for birth control, for example, or whether to use pain medication during childbirth. After retiring from private practice in 1989, Storch became a television and radio producer, creating specialized programming for family physicians on the Lifetime medical network. She later became head of Ob/Gyn news for the Medical News Network. After her death, the Marcia L. Storch MD Scholarship Fund for Undergraduate Women was established to encourage undergraduate women to study the basic physiology and biochemistry of the ovary.

Straus, (Arlene) Susan (1950 –) In 1967, Straus and her high-school friends fought the system, went on strike to protest the skirt and blouse dress code for girls, and won. In 1968, she joined the Women's Liberation Club at her college, Northeastern Illinois University, Chicago, and worked on the official and alternative school newspapers reporting on women's issues (1969 – 1973). The alternative paper also published a special issue on abortion rights. In 1972, Straus was a member of the committee to form a women's studies program on the campus, and also worked on an anthology that the women's studies program published in 1973. After joining NOW (1972), Straus became active in the Chicago chapter on the speakers and newsletter committees, and also worked for passage of the ERA. She is (2004) on the board of the Chicago NOW chapter, a member of the Chicago NOW Education Fund, and a member of IL NOW and the anti-Patriot Act task force. Since 1974, she has been a speaker for women's issues on panels in the Chicago area, and has had letters to the editor published in local newspapers on abortion rights and other women's issues. Since 1999, Straus has been a member of Working Women's History Project, a Chicago-based organization that promotes bringing the history of working women to life for audiences in school and labor halls. She is (2004) president of Chicago NOW, and since 1999 has been its representative to the International Women's Day Chicago Coalition. Also active in the civil rights movement, Straus has been a member of the ACLU since 1973. She holds a B.A. from Northeastern Illinois University, Chicago. (ABS)

Straus, Sandy (1938 –) An artist, Straus was a member of the women's art movement in Chicago in the early 1970s, and a member of the Artemesia Gallery (1975). She served on the editorial committee of the "Women Working Together" issue of *Heresies* magazine and had a one-person exhibition at AIR Gallery in 1995. Currently a member of the National Arts Club exhibitions committee, she presents the feminist point of view when organizing lectures and also arranges feminist jurors for exhibitions. In 2003, she facilitated an event for Iraqi women visiting the U.S. Straus, who has two children, holds a B.F.A. from the Art Institute of Chicago (1976). (ABS)

Strauss, Mary Beth – See Edelson, Mary Beth

Streiker, Premrup (1943 –) (also known as Marci Streiker) is the author of the play "A Waltz for Women's Voices" (1975), which was produced worldwide. As a feminist psychotherapist, she has written many articles, including "The Little Deaths," published in a women's spirituality magazine. She also taught feminist courses at the college at Old Westbury and supervised many daycare workers in daycare centers in Chicago. She is a member of the New American Movement in feminist spirituality, and has trained in many methods of natural healing all over the world. She has three children. (ABS)

Striebel, Charlotte Thomas (1929 –) An associate professor of mathematics at the University of Minnesota (retired, June 1995), Striebel was a member of MN NOW and Twin Cities NOW, and worked to support the ERA. Believing that girls would never be able to achieve optimum health if they could not develop their natural athletic abilities, Striebel worked aggressively through legislation and task forces to help high-school girls in their efforts to join training and competition with boys—who were perceived as the "real" athletes. It was her litigation that set all of the Minnesota athletics and sexism processes in motion. In addition to her work with girls' sports, Striebel worked with the faculty advisory committee at the University of Minnesota focusing on the employment needs of existing faculty women and the efforts to hire women "where men were actively, although sometimes not hatefully, blocking the hiring of academic women," she says. In particular, the salary inequities between men and women academics were brought to light only through the statistical work done by Striebel. Striebel, who has two children, holds a B.A. and M.A. from Ohio State University, Columbus; her Ph.D. from the University of California, Berkeley (1960); and her J.D. from the University of Minnesota (1983).   (ABS)

Strobel, Margaret ("Peg") Ann (1946 –) was a member of the UCLA Women's Liberation Front from 1968 – 1971. As a graduate student in African history, Strobel helped form Graduate Women in History, with a small newsletter. She then helped start the women's liberation group at Middlebury College (VT), where she taught from 1971–1972. In 1973, she returned to Los Angeles and served as the first director of UCLA's women's studies program (1975–1978). Her Ph.D. dissertation, and later a book, *Muslim Women in Mombasa, 1890–1975* (Yale University Press, 1979) was the first English language historical monograph about a group of sub-Saharan African women. From 1974–1975 Strobel represented the New American Movement on Los Angeles' Coalition to Stop Sterilization Abuse. She was a member of NAM, a national socialist feminist organization, from 1973–1982. In 1979, she became the first interim director of women's studies at the University of Illinois, Chicago, a position she held until 1990. Strobel served on a three-person program committee for the NWSA, and as president of the of the American Historical Association women's caucus. She has one child and holds a B.A. from Michigan State University (1964), and an M.A. (1968) and Ph.D. (1975) from the University of California, Los Angeles.   (ABS)

Strober, Myra H. (1941 –) A professor at Stanford University, 1972–present, Strober has focused her teaching on the economics of education, gender and higher education, and feminist theories of work and family. She was co-editor of *Bringing Women into Management* (McGraw Hill, 1975), *Women and Poverty* (University of Chicago Press, 1986) and *Feminism, Children and the New Families* (Guilford Press, 1988), and co-author (with Agnes Chan) of *The Road Winds Uphill all the Way: Gender, Work, and Family in the United States and Japan* (MIT Press, 1999). She was founding director of the Stanford Center for Research on Women (1974); first chair of the board and a founder of the National Council for Research on Women (1982–1984); and founding member of the American Economics Association committee on the status of women in the economics profession (1972–1975). From 1993–1998, Strober was a member of the board of the NOW LDEF, and from 1996–1998 served as president of the International Association for Feminist Economics. Among her numerous service positions at Stanford, Strober has served as chair of the provost's committee on recruitment and retention of women faculty (1992–1993), and as faculty sexual harassment adviser (1993–1998 and 2001 – present). She has published extensively on women's employment, families, childcare and feminist economics in professional journals. Strober, who has two children and three stepchildren, earned her B.S. from Cornell (1962), her M.A. from Tufts (1965) and her Ph.D. from MIT (1969). (ABS)

Strom, Sharon Hartman (1941 –) A feminist scholar and author, Strom entered the women's movement in 1971, applying strategies of radical student politics to her life as a woman. She was teaching African American history and included a course on women's suffrage when the contradictions of her personal and professional life became apparent. She began teaching women's history in 1973 and team teaching women's studies. She joined a Marxist/feminist study group in Boston. "We were finding our way toward a theory of feminism that would engage gender, race and class," she says. She and other women formed the first women's studies course, Women and Society, at University of Rhode Island in 1972. In 1976, she participated in a women's history study group that met in Providence (RI). She did archival work at the Schlesinger Library and wrote an article on the women's suffrage movement in Boston, published in the *Journal of American History*, 1975. Strom was the only woman in the history department among 16 or 17 men. Strom and others—all untenured assistant professors—sued URI for sex discrimination (roughly 1978–1985) and eventually became full professors. Strom was co-author of *Moving the Mountain: Women Working for Social Change* (the Feminist Press, 1980), and author of *Beyond the Typewriter: Gender, Class and the Origins of Modern American Office Work, 1900–1930* (University of Illinois Press, 1992); *Political Woman: Florence Luscomb and the Legacy of Radical Reform* (Temple University Press, 2001); and *Women's Rights: Major Issues in American History Series* (Greenwood Press, 2001). Strom, who holds a Ph.D. from Cornell (1969), was also active in the civil rights and antiwar movements. Archives: Special Collections, University of Rhode Island Library, Kingston, RI.   (ABS)

Strothman, Linda Jean (1943 –) Strothman was an original member of Jane, the abortion counseling service, joining in 1969 and remaining active through 1972. From 1970–1971, she was the only woman in the Illinois Legislative Intern Program in Springfield. She later did significant work for the Equal Right Amendment in Illinois, particularly in preparing people to testify in committee. She also wrote packages of women's legislation

S

from 1971–1973. Says Strothman, "It was interesting that the bill making it an affirmative alternative for women to keep their birth names, something that would have cost nothing to implement, created the longest and most intense debate on the floor of the House of all the bills in the package." In addition to writing women's legislation and working for women legislators, Strothman also gave various talks and presentations and appeared on talk shows over the years discussing abortion, legislation and domestic violence. After starting the *Illinois Women's Legislative Bulletin*, Strothman joined NOW (1970) and became its first Illinois legislative coordinator (1971). During this time, Strothman also published feminist articles using the pen name Jean Lohrey. In the early 1970s, Strothman taught one of the first women's studies courses at Roosevelt University, and was also involved in establishing the Sojourner Truth Day Care Center in Chicago's Hyde Park community. From 1974–1976, she was director of a legislative intern program at Chicago State University that focused on involving more African American students in politics. She later became director of Constance Morris House, one of the early domestic violence shelters in Chicago. Strotman held this position from 1978–1988. A clinical social worker, Strothman earned a B.G.S. from Roosevelt University (1970) and an M.A. from the University of Chicago (1976). She is (2005) a Ph.D. candidate at the University of Chicago, writing her dissertation on violent couples. Archives: Some of Strotman's writing have been given to Roosevelt University, Chicago, IL. (ABS)

Stuermer, Virginia M. (1924 –) came to Connecticut as an instructor in obstetrics and gynecology, Yale School of Medicine in 1954, and rose to the rank of associate clinical professor. Early, she was associated with Planned Parenthood of Connecticut. In the run-up to Griswold v. Connecticut, she was serving as the clinician at the Planned Parenthood clinic in New Haven, CT, on the day that Dr. C. Lee Buxton and Estelle Griswold were arrested. When the case was won, Stuermer became director of Planned Parenthood League of Connecticut, serving for four years, and the chairman of the medical advisory committee for an additional seven years. The women of Yale Law School began a parallel action to what finally became Roe v. Wade. Stuermer was a medical adviser to Women v. Connecticut. A planning group comprising the law school students, organizations providing counseling services to pregnant women, and Planned Parenthood League of Connecticut represented by Stuermer opened the first free-standing abortion clinic in the state. Initially, the clinic functioned in Stuermer's private office. Stuermer remained attached to Women's Health Services as medical director (or co-director) and clinician into the 1990s. Stuermer earned her B.A. (1945) and M.D. (1948) from the University of Nebraska. She was an intern at Jersey City Medical Center in 1949 and a resident at the University of Iowa from 1949–1952. (ABS)

Stuhler, Barbara (1924 –) As assistant, and later associate director of the World Affairs Center, General Extension Division, University of Minnesota, Stuhler worked with a colleague in the 1950s and successfully obtained more equitable salaries for women. As a board member, Minnesota League of Women Voters (1952–1956) and vice president (1954–1956), she lobbied for passage of the Fair Employment Practices Act. From 1958–1964, Stuhler served as a member of the board of LWV US and as foreign policy chair from 1960–1964. In 1960, she received the Hope Washburn Award for Outstanding Service from the MN LWV. In 1968, Stuhler was head of an Overseas Education Fund delegation of four that went to the USSR on an exchange with the Soviet women's committee. From 1968–1970, she chaired a series of regional conferences on military spending and national security that ultimately led the LWV US to study and support programs enhancing arms control measures. She was a faculty member in Continuing Education of Women seminars (MN); was the first woman to be invited to join the American delegation attending a critical post-WWII conference in England (1961); and served on two governor-appointed commissions on discrimination (1960s). In 1970, Stuhler helped develop and moderated a local public television series on women's issues, and in 1969 began a 16-year series of weekly public affairs commentaries on KUOM, a university radio station. In 1972, she was one of the first two women invited to join the St. Paul, Minneapolis committee on foreign relations, and was a member of the United States delegation to UNESCO's third international conference on adult education in Tokyo. Stuhler is the author of *No Regrets: Minnesota Women and the Joan Growe Senatorial Campaign* (Braemar Press, 1986); *Women of Minnesota: Selected Biographical Essays*, co-edited with Gretchen Kreuter (Minnesota Historical Society Press, 1977); *For the Public Record: A Documentary History of the League of Women Voters* (Grennwood Press, 2000); and *Gentle Warriors: Clara Ueland and the Minnesota Struggle for Woman Suffrage* (Minnesota Historical Society Press, 1995). Stuhler holds a B.A. from MacMurray College and an M.A. from the University of Minnesota. Archives: Minnesota Historical Society, St. Paul, MN. (ABS)

Styers, Aleta Aslani (also known as Aleta Dionne Styers) — A founder and organizer of Chicago NOW, Styers served as president (1966–1969). A member of NOW's national board (1967–1970), she also served as NOW's national grievance coordinator (1969–1970). In 1969, Styers organized the first and possibly only major NOW job conference in Chicago; at the Chicago conference, Shirley Chisholm served as keynote speaker. Styers also initiated demonstrations and legal actions against the *Chicago Tribune* to end the practice of sex-segregated help-wanted ads. She also served as a fundraiser to prevent Senate ratification of judge Carswell's appointment to the Supreme Court (1969). Styers was the first woman in the management program of Paine Webber, a brokerage firm, and one of the early women members of the Yale Club of New York, where she served on the council and the house and finance committees. Says Styers, "These are the most powerful committees at those old male establishment clubs, and it was quite a success for women that I made them!" Styers wrote numerous articles for the business press, an almost totally male preserve at the time, that helped open minds about employment possibilities for women. In addition, Styers taught finance in universities and special schools and training programs for women, including the Women's School in New York City. Styers earned a B.A. from New York University, an M.A. in International Relations from Yale University, and an M.A. in Economics from Northwestern University. Archives: Northwestern University, Evanston, IL. (ABS)

Suelzle, Marijean (1940 –) was a founding member and first president of Berkeley, CA, chapter of NOW, and was elected to the NOW national board in 1971. She is the author of *The Female Sex Role* (University of Alberta, 1969), which was originally her M.A. thesis, and *What Every Woman Should Know About the Women's Liberation Movement* (Amazon Graphics, 1971). Her research projects at the University of California, Berkeley, include a study of changing sex roles and attitudes towards women's liberation, as well as a study of job discrimination against non-academic women on the campus. Suelzle earned a B.A. and M.A. from the University of Alberta, Edmonton, and studied for her Ph.D. at University of California, Berkeley.

Summers, Jane Frazer (1923 – 2002) served as president of the Grand Forks, ND, League of Women Voters from 1952 – 1953. She was also co-founder and first president of the North Dakota LWV in 1958, and first president of Democratic Women of Grand Forks in the 1960s. In addition, Summers was a member of the ND advisory commission for the U.S. Civil Rights Commission for 17 years; and was a lobbyist during the 1980s and 1990s at the state legislature for the ND ACLU, Planned Parenthood and on behalf of women's and children's groups from Grand Forks.

Suneson, Charlene Ida (1934 –) After receiving a B.A. from the University of Chicago (1954), Suneson says, she "joined the Navy to see the world, becoming the first woman line officer to be assigned to sea duty in 1961. As a result of the reactions to this assignment and other circumstances in the Navy, I dedicated my life to improving the status of women." She joined NY NOW (1967–1970), served as the chapter's first legislative and political affairs coordinator, and helped write "Token Learning: A Study of Women's Higher Education." She was later elected chair of the NY board. In 1971, Suneson became coordinator of the legislative action committee in Los Angeles, and later Southern California legislative coordinator. She published "Legislative Guidelines" and used a variety of strategies to help all women contribute to the ratification of the ERA in California, and initiated Marriage as Equal Partnership legislation, which was enacted into law in California. As a national board member (1971 – 1974), and national secretary (1974 – 1975), Suneson helped move NOW from a position of abstaining from political activity to that of using political action, by obtaining an IRS ruling enabling NOW to take political action without losing tax-exempt status. Suneson has participated in numerous actions and demonstrations, including a sit-in to open the Squire Room at the Fairmont Hotel in San Francisco to women (1969), and demonstrations to protest the omission of women from Labor Department affirmative action requirements in Los Angeles and other cities in 1970. In 1975, Suneson received the Everywoman Award from the ACLU for her efforts to have the EEOC give attention to sex discrimination. In addition to her B.A., Suneson holds an M.A. and Ph.D. (2005). (ABS)

Suratt, Judith Hole – See Hole, Judith

Surgal, Ruth (1937 – 2004) was a member of the Abortion Counseling Services of Women's Liberation, better known as Jane. From 1969 – 1972 Jane performed over 11,000 abortions before Rose v. Wade made abortion legal. Born in Chicago, Surgal began attending meetings in Hyde Park as the second wave of feminism was organized in that area. A member of a group of women for peace, Surgal was initially skeptical of the women's movement, but soon came to understand and believe in its premise and goals. The night before she died, Surgal said, "I was a social worker. I understood about emergencies and joined the abortion counseling service." Surgal taught ceramics at the Lille Street Studio and ran a boarding house for students at the University of Chicago. She was also an active member of the CWLU Herstory Project. Surgal, who had three children, held an M.A. Archives: Herstory Project, Chicago Women's Liberation Union, Chicago, IL.

Surrey, Paula (1947 –) has been a psychotherapist in private practice in Maine since 1989, specializing in women's issues. This work is the culmination of a lifetime of experiences that began in 1966 when she and a friend, both "18 but trying to look 21, stood in the rain on the Lower East Side of NYC at midnight with $600 in cash as we waited for the (hopefully) doctor who had agreed to perform an illegal abortion" on her friend. Surrey worked for a Boston pregnancy counseling service, then, after college, as a feature writer for a biweekly newspaper in Western Massachusetts. Surrey's articles quickly became known for their feminist viewpoints on subjects ranging from marriage customs and childbirth options to outmoded sexist laws to job and salary discrimination. Surrey moved to NYC in 1972, began graduate work, and was hired as a counselor at an abortion clinic, "a full-time job I continued throughout my two-year graduate pro-

S

gram." Before moving to Maine, Surrey worked as a feminist psychotherapist at several mental health agencies, and as a victim services counselor for a sexual assault crisis. Surrey holds a B.S. from Tufts University and an M.S.W. from New York University School of Social Work. (ABS)

Sutherland, Elizabeth – See Martinez, Elizabeth ("Betita")

Sutherland, Viv (1945 –) was catapulted into the women's movement when she overheard a passerby mock a solemn procession of women carrying coffins to honor other women who had died of back-alley abortions. She immediately joined Eastern Massachusetts NOW, and served variously as secretary, chair of the abortion rights committee, member of the speaker's committee and writer and editor for the chapter's newsletter. After moving back to NYC, Sutherland joined NYC NOW, serving as executive VP, chair of the reproductive rights committee and chair of the reproductive health committee. From 1972–1982, she was producer and host of the weekly radio program "Women's Studies" on WBAI, and from 1975–1982 was producer and host of the monthly radio program "Lesbian Studies," also on WBAI. In 1973, she was co-founder of the women's programming department at the station. In 1979, Sutherland became a founding member of the Lesbian & Gay Big Apple Corps. Marching Band. She left WBAI in 1982 to devote her activist efforts to improving the status and visibility of women in the band (which until that point had been known as the Gay Community Marching Band and was thought erroneously by the public at large to be an all male organization). During this time, Sutherland also produced a series of radio programs for the U.S. Department of Education on educational opportunities for rural women, in conjunction with a series of films on the same subject. A network administrator, Sutherland holds a bachelor's degree. (ABS)

Suttenberg, Marcia Lee (1947 –) (also known as Marcia Willems, Marcia Window and Marcia Moskowitz) As a member of the SDS in 1970, Suttenberg lived in various collective/communal households where the women began forming CR groups. Part of the collective that founded the Portland Women's Health Clinic, Suttenberg was also a writer of the original grant for the Portland State University women's studies program. She later taught women's studies classes, including courses on women in film, women's sexuality and women in their middle years. Suttenberg was part of the Women's Education Project, which published "High School Sexuality: A Handbook for Teachers," and was part of many women-led street actions. She later participated in Women in Black as part of Middle East peace work through New Jewish Agenda, and is (2005) executive director of the Portland Women's Crisis Line, which focuses on domestic and sexual violence. Suttenberg, who has two children, holds an M.S.W. (ABS)

Suttles, Donna – See Pollach, Donna Helen

Swanson, Edith Mays (1934 – 1989) As a member of the Ypsilanti (MI) teachers union, Swanson, an African American, raised staff awareness of race and sex bias in the curriculum. A powerful spokesperson in education labor negotiations, she successfully bargained for pay equity for female coaches in her district. After making affirmative action standard procedure in her school, Swanson helped the Michigan Education Association adopt the same policies. Swanson served as VP of the MEA from 1977–1983. As a member of the executive committee of the National Education Association, Swanson was part of NEA's Decade of Women planning group. Because of her efforts, both the MEA and the NEA established women's caucuses. Swanson was inducted into The Michigan Women's Hall of Fame in 1991.

Sweet, Ellen Barbara (1942 –) was a member of the Women's Action Alliance in NYC (1975–1980), where she created and edited a newsletter, "Women's Agenda," to connect the coalition of more than 100 women's organizations. A member of the editorial board of *Ms.* magazine (1980–1988), Sweet wrote numerous articles on such topics as national health insurance, the effect of the AT&T split-up on women and minorities, and date rape on college campuses. The date-rape article was the result of a three-year, federally funded (under President Reagan) grant to study acquaintance rape on college campuses that brought to public attention a hitherto neglected problem. The article was reprinted for more than 10 years in college textbooks and copied for use in many college courses. It also led to a trade book based on the study, for which Sweet served as consulting editor. At *Ms.* Magazine, Sweet also reported on cutting-edge developments in women's health long before they hit the mainstream press, such as alternatives to radical mastectomy and hysterectomy, cross-addiction, links between breast cancer and diet, and new advances in birth control. In 2000, Sweet returned to working in the movement and on health issues as vice president, public affairs, for the International Women's Health Coalition, where she supported women's work on reproductive health and rights on an international scale. She is director of communications at the Center for Reproductive Rights, which uses the law to advance reproductive freedom as a fundamental right that all governments are obligated to protect. Sweet, who holds a B.A. from Smith College and an M.A.T. from Yale University, has one child. (ABS)

Swenson, Norma Meras (1932 –) is the link between the childbirth reform movement of the 1960s, the second wave women's health movement and the global women's health movement. In 1962, she joined the Boston Association for Childbirth Education, which worked against surgically oriented childbirth then in ascension. Swenson became BACE president, and in 1966 became president of the International Childbirth Education Association. While still active in childbirth reform, Swenson saw *Women and Their Bodies* and met its writers. She explained that the childbirth chapter was poor and inadequately informed; the writers, in turn, told Swenson that she was not a feminist and would have to take a 17-week course on women's health given by and for women in a CR mode at the Women's School in Cambridge, MA. She completed the course and then she helped re-write the childbirth chapter for *Our Bodies, Ourselves* during the summer of 1971. Swenson became an incorporating member of the Boston Women's Health Collective in 1972, and for several years co-wrote the chapters on childbirth and the politics of women's health. She eventually became BWHBC's first director of international programs. As a Harvard School of Public Health student in 1972–1973, she helped organize the committee on the status of women in the Harvard medical area, and during that period met with federal government investigators about the treatment of the research and lab assistants in Harvard's institutions, who were mostly female. Swenson and Judy Norsigian were the main organizers of the 1975 Harvard Conference on Women's Health, attended by close to 2,000 women from the U.S. and Canada. Until 1998, Swenson acted as liaison for foreign editions of *Our Bodies, Ourselves*, and for many overseas groups with which the BWHBC collaborated. She traveled to most regions of the world and consulted for the WHO and major foundations. Swenson believes that the critical posture of the women's health movement—investigating and criticizing the science and technology of established women's health practices and challenging the power structure of medicine and the pharmaceutical industry—set it apart from the second wave women's movement. Swenson has taught at the Harvard School of Public Health for over 15 years. She holds a B. A. from Tufts University and an M.P.H. from the Harvard School of Public Health. (ABS)

Swerdlow, Amy (1923 –) is emerita professor of history and former director of the graduate program in women's history and the women's studies program, Sarah Lawrence College. From 1967–1972, Swerdlow was a full-time organizer of Women Strike for Peace and editor of its national publication, *Memo*. From 1972–1973, she was enrolled in the women's studies M.A. program at Sarah Lawrence, and from 1973–1977 served as a faculty member and associate director of the women's studies program at the college. In 1974 and 1975, she directed two institutes for high-school teachers on the integration of women's history into the high-school curriculum. Says Swerdlow, "My first feminist action was to persuade Women Strike for Peace to participate in the Women's Strike for Equality march (1970)." Swerdlow introduced the women's studies resolution at the National Women's Conference in Houston (1977), and also brought gender issues into the anti-Vietnam War movement. Her articles "Women Strike for Peace" and "Congress of American

Women" appear in the *Encyclopedia of the American Left*, 1990; and her article "Peace Movement" appears in *The Reader's Companion to U.S. Women's History*, 1998. She has published broadly on women in history and politics, and is author of *Women Strike for Peace: Traditional Motherhood and Radical Politics in the 1960s* (University of Chicago Press, 1994). She has four children and holds a Ph.D. Archives: Swarthmore College, Swathmore, PA. (ABS)

Swietnicki, Colette A. (1943 –) (also known as Colette Price) A certified nurse-midwife, Swietnicki attended the first National Women's Liberation Conference, held on November 27, 1968. From 1971–1972, she published *Woman's World*, and in 1975 served as associate editor of and contributor to *Feminist Revolution*. A member of Redstockings from 1973–1990s, she was involved in various consciousness raising groups. She helped organize, and was a speaker at Redstockings' Anniversary Abortion Speakout, held in the late 1980s. She also attended NYRW when it first met on the Lower East Side in New York City, and has supported the anti-war movement. Swietnicki, who has one child, holds an M.A. in Public Health in addition to her midwife certification. (ABS)

Swift, Earlyse (1940 –) In 1973, Swift was hired by Whatcom Community College in Bellingham, WA, to create its specialized women's program. Called FOCUS on Opportunity, the program was designed to reach out to women not enrolled at the community college. To launch FOCUS, Swift drove a restored bookmobile around the rural parts of the county, parking for several hours at each site so that women could learn about classes, pick up materials, and feel support as they explored their future. The male college administrators paid little attention to this effort until they learned that over 100 women came to the FOCUS mobile unit in that two-day period and 90-plus enrolled in classes. Swift directed and taught in the program from 1973–1977, when she and her family moved to Olympia. In 1983, Swift was appointed by the governor to be a member of the board at South Puget Sound Community College and Centralia Community College. In her nine years as a trustee, her primary goal was to see that a childcare center was established at South Puget Sound Community College. Her second goal was to inspire trustees across the state to consider female applicants when they were hiring community college presidents. Of the 26 community colleges, only one had a female president in 1983. She became VP of the state association because that role planned the trainings for trustees. Swift, who is executive director of TOGETHER! a youth violence, drug, alcohol, tobacco prevention program, has two children. She earned her B.A. (1962) from Washington State University and her M.A. (1978) from Antioch University. (ABS)

Swift, Kate (1923 –) is co-author, with Casey Miller, of *Words and Women* (Doubleday, 1976) and *Handbook of*

S

Nonsexist Writing (Lippincott & Crowell, 1980). The two began working together in 1970, when Miller/Swift was founded to eliminate sexism and adopt inclusive language in clients' publications. They were among the pioneers exploring and exposing the ways standard English reflects and reinforces oppression of women. Their articles include "Desexing the Language," published in *New York* magazine (December 20, 1971) and "One Small Step for Genkind," published in *The New York Times Magazine* (April 16, 1972). Their articles and book chapters or extended excerpts have been reprinted in more than 30 anthologies and textbooks from mainstream publishers. In addition to this work, Swift joined national NOW in the early 1970s, and area chapters in Connecticut in the 1970s and 1980s. She also assisted in editing the CT NOW newsletter, "The Waterfall," in the 1980s. During the 1970s and 1980s, she was a member of the Women's Institute for Freedom of the Press in Washington, D.C. She took part in marches for the ERA and reproductive freedom (1970s – 1990s). She also lobbied for repeal of abortion restrictions in Connecticut before Roe v. Wade, and joined litigants in the lawsuit Women v. Connecticut in 1972. Swift earned a B.A. from the University of North Carolina, Chapel Hill (1944). Archives: Women's History Special Archives, Knight Library, University of Oregon, Eugene, OR. (ABS)

Swigert-Gacheru, Margaretta (1949 –) helped establish the first women's history course at DePauw University in 1969. In 1970, Swigert-Gacheru co-created a slide-show critique of sexism in advertising, Women in the Media, that toured university campuses along the East Coast and through the South. In 1971, she joined CWLU and participated in the CWLU Liberation School. Swigert-Gacheru was among the first women to receive a Rotary International Ambassadorial Fellowship to study literature at the University of Nairobi in 1974. In 1976 she became the women's editor for *Target*, the weekly magazine of the National Christian Council of Kenya. She was also active in coordinating the NGO women's conference that took place in tandem with the 1985 United Nations women's decade conference in Nairobi. From 1986 – 1991, she was editor in chief of *Women's World Banking/Africa News*. In 1989 – 1990 she wrote an African women's position paper for the African Development Bank, Abidjan, Ivory Coast. She co-founded the National Commission on the Status of Kenyan Women in 1992, campaigning for women's entry into the political process. As a result of the Commission's efforts, the first National Political Convention for Women was held in Kenya, resulting in the election of many women to the Kenya Parliament, including professor Wangari Maathai, the 2005 Nobel Peace Prize winner. Throughout the 1980s and 1990s, Swigert-Gacheru wrote on women's issues, especially the areas of politics, economic development, law and the arts, for *The Nairobi Times*, *The Kenya Times*, *The Weekly Review*, *Trend*, *The East African Standard*, *The East African* and *The Daily Nation*. She holds a B.A. from DePauw, an M.A. from National Louis University, a B.A. and M.A. from the University of Nairobi, and an M.A. from Northwestern University's Medill School of Journalism. (ABS)

Syfers, Judith – See Brady, Judith Ellen

Symon, Mary Louise (1922 –) A member of the Madison, WI, LWV board of directors in 1955, Symon was present at the initial WPC in Washington, D.C., and helped start a caucus in Wisconsin, where she was a charter member (1973). In the 1960s, she served on the LWV minority housing (WI) study committee, and on the Dane County board of the ACLU. Symon helped form Friends of South Madison Neighborhood Center with Welfare mothers, as well as a women's caucus in the Wisconsin and National Associations of Counties. Appointed state Health and Welfare Commissioner by the legislature and to the state government organization committee, Symon was elected to the Dane County board in 1970 and became vice chair in 1972. She was elected chair of the board in 1974, the first woman chair in the state, and then first woman president of the Wisconsin Association of Counties (1980). She was also a member of the Dane County regional planning commission (1970 – 1980). She has been a member of the NAACP and the Urban League board of directors, and served as chair of Madison Citizens for Fair Housing. In the late 1960s, she was chair of the Madison Equal Opportunity Commission. Symon was later appointed by President Carter to the National Radioactive Waste Commission as a local government representative. Symon, who has four children, holds a B.A. from Wellesley College (1943). (ABS)

Sznajderman, Suzanne Messing (1932 –) Born in Warsaw, Poland, Sznajderman has contributed to the movement as both an activist and a writer. Following participation in a CR group, she joined Northern NJ NOW in the mid 1970s, and remains (2005) active as a member of the operating board. Over the years she headed various committees, chaired events and participated in marches in Washington, D.C. Sznajderman served as president of the chapter from 1982 – 1984, and was later active on the NJ NOW board and on the PAC. She attended the U.N. Conference on Women held in Nairobi (1985), and in 1992 formed her chapter's multicultural CR group, which lasted until 2001. In 1994, Sznajderman received the chapter's Award for Feminist Achievement. She is (2005) writer of the column "Sue's Views" for *Womanspace*, the publication of Northern NJ NOW. Under the name Suzanne Messing, she has served as associate editor of *New Directions for Women* (1985 – 1990) and published numerous articles, including "Unmasking Some Branches on a Family Tree" (*The New York Times*, September 14, 1980); "Boards Batter Shelter Founders" (*The Alternative Press Annual*, 1986); and "Northern New Jersey NOW Looks Back at 10" (*The Record of Bergen County*, 1980).

Sznajderman, who has three children, holds a B.A. from the University of Michigan and an M.A.T. from Fairleigh Dickinson University. (ABS)

Szymalak, Nola – See Claire, Nola

Tacha, Athena (1936 –) A public artist/sculptor, Tacha was a founding member of the WCA, participated in and organized shows of women artists, and compiled and self-published *Women's Studies in Art & Art History* (1974), the first compendium on that topic with descriptions of college-level courses. In her artwork and films, Tacha dealt with the female body and identity, particularly issues of aging. Two of her early essays were published in *Ms.* magazine and *Heresies.* Born in Greece, Tacha earned an M.A. in sculpture from the National Academy of Fine Arts in Athens, an M.A. in art history from Oberlin College, and a Ph.D. from the Sorbonne University, Paris. Archives: Archives of American Art, Washington, D.C.; Oberlin College Archives, Oberlin, OH; and the Historical Society of Pennsylvania, Philadelphia, PA. (ABS)

Talkington, Betty M. (1920 – 1998) was born into a labor family and began her life's work with women at a button factory in Muscatine, IA. There she championed working women's issues such as decision-making power, benefits, childcare, maternity leave and equal pay. She became the director of the Iowa Federation of Labor Women's Activities. In addition, she served on the Iowa Governor's Commission on the Status of Women, which was formed in 1963. Representing Iowa on the National Organization of States Commissions of Women, Talkington joined with others in promoting the ERA, worked to establish NOW, and served as a founding member of Des Moines NOW in 1971. She also attended the founding conference of the Coalition of Labor Union Women in 1974. Over the decades, she educated other labor leaders on women's issues. Talkington received the Christine Wilson Medal for Equality and Justice from the Iowa Commission on the Status of Women in 1995. Archives: Oral history at Iowa Women's Archives, University of Iowa Libraries, Iowa City, IA; AFL papers and oral history at Iowa Labor and State Historical Society, Iowa City, IA.

Tangeman, Jean Janette
– See Mountaingrove, Jean Janette

Tangri, Sandra Schwartz (1937 – 2003) Professor emeritus at Howard University, Tangri was a social psychologist who did pioneering research on the entry of college-educated women into jobs traditionally dominated by men. Her efforts helped map changes in the American workforce in the 1960s. In addition, she participated in what she described as "the raucous beginnings of the women's studies program at Richmond College" in Staten Island, NY, in the early 1970s, and taught one of the first psychology of women courses there. In 1974, Tangri moved from New Jersey to Washington, D.C., to become director of the Office of Research of the U.S. Commission on Civil Rights. She was the co-author, with Martha Mednick, of the groundbreaking book *Women and Achievement* (Hemisphere Press, 1975).

Tanner, Leslie B. (1926 –) compiled and edited the book *Voices from Women's Liberation* (Signet, 1970), a collection of contemporary essays as well as voices from the past. Tanner explains in the book's preface that she was inspired to create the book in 1969 after starting a women's liberation group in New York. The papers written by the women were being passed hand-to-hand, but "there were never enough to go around within our own growing group, and nowhere near enough to pass along to other women who expressed an interest in women's liberation." *Voices from Women's Liberation* contains over 90 essays and documents sorted under headings designed to promote discussion. (ABS)

Tatnall, Sally (1937 –) focused her activities on obtaining reproductive freedom for women, and on bringing more women into the movement through CR groups and conferences. In the early 1970s, Tatnall was instrumental in creating the Cleveland Women's Counseling Service, a referral service for women who needed abortions. From this, Tatnall created Pregnancy Information Referral Service, which she ran out of her bedroom. Later, Tatnall was one of a group of women who founded Preterm, an abortion and birth control clinic in Cleveland. In 1980, she was a member of the board of the Ohio/Chicago Art Project, which brought Judy Chicago's The Dinner Party to Cleveland in 1981. The exhibit raised $90,000, which was used to found the Cleveland Women's Foundation, still in existence (2005). In addition, Tatnall wrote feminist articles for a local women's newspaper, *What She Wants.* She was also active in the civil rights and peace movements. Tatnall, who has four children, holds a B.A. from Alfred University (1960). (ABS)

Tavenner, Patricia May (1950 –) (also known as Patricia Carson) Artist, teacher, lecturer and astrologer, Tavenner was a co-founder (with Terase Heyman and Suzanne Perkins) of the first Women's Caucus for Art group in California, Northern California WCA (1972). Tavenner was also a founding member of national WCA. She contributed to many exhibitions of women artists, curated a few all-women exhibitions, and taught women's art history at the University of California Extension and other California universities. Tavenner holds a B.A. from Michigan State University, East Lansing, and an M.F.A. from California College of the Arts, Oakland. (ABS)

Tax, Meredith (1942 –) has been a leader among women, a founder of women's organizations around the world, and a tireless worker for women's rights. In 1969, she co-founded Bread and Roses. Her work included helping to organize the first International Women's Day demonstration held in Boston since the 1920s, and supporting the committee for the General Electric strike of 1969, in which equal pay was an issue. She helped picket at two factories and a warehouse, brought union speakers to campuses and community organizations, and built an unofficial secondary boycott campaign. She worked on the groundbreaking 1971 conference for women office workers, linking women's liberation and union organizing. Tax also served on the steering committee for the CWLU (1972–1973), and was active in organizing a 1973 coalition for a March for Women's Equality and Economic Justice. Tax was on the editorial board of The New Feminist Library (1977–1986). She was co-chair (with Grace Paley) and chair of the women's committee of PEN American Center. Tax went on to found the International PEN Women Writers Committee. She is the founder of Women's WORLD, an Organization for Rights, Literature and Development, 1994. In partnership with local organizations, Tax worked on the first annual global women's writing contest, on Women's Voices in War Zones; on a global feminist anti-censorship Web site; an African women-writers network; a European team meeting in Bellagio, Italy, that initiated East-West programs in both the Balkans and Mediterranean; and an international structure and communications network linking local programs in Africa, Asia, Europe, Latin America and the U.S. She also worked on defense campaigns for journalists and writers around the world, and on the first world conference on gender-based censorship, held in Bellagio, 1996. She wrote a groundbreaking analysis of the relationship between gender and censorship, "The Power of the Word: Culture, Censorship, and Voice" (1995), and a follow-up pamphlet on Eastern Europe, "The Power of the Word II: Women's Voices and the New European Order" (2000). Tax was co-founder and co-chair of CARASA, 1977–1979, and the chair of the subcommittee for national work against sterilization abuse. She went on to co-found Reproductive Rights National Network, which coordinated the work of grassroots organizations similar to CARASA around the country. Archives: The Sophia Smith Collection, Smith College, Northampton, MA.　　(ABS)

Taylor, Katherine ("Kay") Wood (1927 –) A political activist, served as president of the Minnesota Council for the Legal Termination of Pregnancy in 1970, and from 1972–1980 was a lobbyist for abortion rights representing many different organizations. A member of the Minnesota Women's Consortium from the 1970s until 1991, Taylor became co-author/producer of its weekly feminist paper, *Legislative Reporter*. In 1976, Taylor filed a suit against Metro Airport to force it to remove coin boxes from the women's toilets. Pressured by Taylor, the Minnesota Legislature passed a bill requiring no fewer than three stalls, all free, and one-half of all others free. Because that was uneconomical, from a business perspective, all toilets in Minnesota are now free. In 1989, Taylor

and Grace Harkness met with the Minnesota commissioner of corrections to insist that pornographic magazines not be allowed in the prisons. After a two-year struggle, they succeeded in their demands. Taylor, who has one child, graduated from the University of Wisconsin, Madison. Archives: The Minnesota Historical Society, St. Paul, MN.　　(ABS)

Taylor, Katya Nina Sabaroff (1944 –) A radical journalist working for Liberation News Service in NYC in the late 1960s, Taylor (then Nina Sabaroff) joined with other women there to form a CR group, demanding a larger voice as writers and photographers, rather than as typists. Working briefly at the *Richmond Chronicle* (VA), she also published an essay on Margaret Sanger in *Women, A Journal of Liberation*. Returning to LNS, she published an essay about the IWD rally, later reprinted in the book *Women's Liberation, Blueprint for the Future*, by Sookie Stambler (1970). Her feminist essay on the film "Woodstock" was also published in that volume. Moving to Oregon in the early 1970s, Taylor helped found the Portland Free Women's Health Clinic. In 1972, she came out as a woman-loving women, moved into a house with other lesbians, and continued CR work, including forming a Radical Therapy group to look at issues of sanity and liberation for women. She was also part of the Women's Educational Project, which taught biology of women classes at the local high schools and offered the first women's studies class at Portland State. She had the task of creating the sexuality lecture. She soon began teaching human sexuality and female sexuality classes at Portland Community College. During this time (1973–1975), she began writing feminist songs and poetry, and had some of her photographs published in *Margins, A Review of Small Press Magazines*, in an issue devoted to lesbian work (1975). In 1976, having chosen the name Katya, she founded Creative Arts and Healing Seminars. At the age of 43 she married Thomas Taylor and later had a child. She holds a B.A. from Antioch College (1966) and a Master of Education from Columbia University.　　(ABS)

Taylor, Mary Emily (1915 – 2004) Dean of women at Kansas University from 1956 – 1975, Taylor later served as director of the Office of Women in Higher Education of the American Council on Education, Washington, D.C. During the 1970s, she helped Kansas University use Title IX to equalize women's athletics. Later in her life she became involved in health issues, serving on the Kansas State Board of Healing Arts, as well as helping to form the Caring Community Council, dedicated to death with dignity. Taylor earned a B.A. and M.A. from Ohio State University and a Ph.D. from Indiana University. She was the recipient of numerous honorary degrees and awards, including the Soroptomist Club award for service to women. She was inducted into the Kansas University Women's Hall of Fame, the Ohio Women's Hall of Fame, and Urbana University's Hall of Excellence.

Taylor, Sharon Elizabeth (1944 –) was part of the women's sports movement in the 1970s, serving in many capacities including VP of the Association for Intercollegiate Athletics for Women (1978 – 1981) and president of the Eastern AIAW (1982 – 1983). In addition to administrative and organizational activities, Taylor was a field hockey coach for 30 years and won six national championships. Working with the AIAW and the U.S. Field Hockey Association (1971 – 1975), she conceived of and created the first collegiate championship in field hockey, held at James Madison University in 1975. She also participated in the early organization of both national and local women's groups, including NOW; and marched for the ERA and maintenance of Title IX from 1972 forward. Says Taylor, "Without the AIAW, Title IX would have been lost in the 1970s!" She holds a B.S. from Lock Haven State College (1966) and an M.S.P.E. from the University of North Carolina, Greensboro (1971). (ABS)

Taylor, Sioux Nichols (1931 –) was introduced to NOW through the LWV of Westchester, NY, in the 1960s. "Freshly imbued with the message of feminism, I accepted the challenge and convened a meeting of women who lived in the southern tier of Westchester County." The group was soon chartered as Southern Westchester NOW (1972), with Taylor serving as its first president. Taylor is (2005) a member of the Westchester NOW chapter's planning committee. Taylor was also a founding member of the Westchester chapter of the NWPC and the Westchester Black Women Political Caucus (1973). She has served as district leader, Mount Vernon Democratic Party (1977 –); chair, Planned Parenthood's Hudson Peconic Westchester Council Steering Committee (1997 – 2000); and as a member of the board of the NYS chapter of National Association of Social Workers (2001 – 2004). She was executive director of the Mount Vernon Youth Bureau (1978 – 1992), and commissioner, Department of Recreation, City of Mt. Vernon, 1992 – 1997, when she retired. Taylor was named Social Worker of the Year, Westchester Division, in 1988, and of the NYS chapter in 1989. In 1993, she received the Second Annual Governor's Award for African Americans of Distinction. Taylor, who has one child, earned her B.S. from Fordham University and her M.S. from New York University. (ABS)

Taylor, Suzanne Saunders (1932 –) was the first woman to receive a Ph.D. in education administration from the University of Connecticut, in 1970. Although her dissertation, "Attitudes of Superintendents and School Board Members Toward Women in Administration," was controversial, it was published in various forms as articles and book chapters, and her study methodology was replicated in numerous states. Later, Taylor became the first woman hired on the professional staff of the Connecticut Education Association. In 1973 she became one of the first commissioners of the Connecticut Permanent Commission on the Status of Women, where she served as treasurer. She continued to fight for women's rights by sponsoring various conferences including The 51% Minority: A Connecticut Conference on the Status of Women (1972), and as a delegate to the National Women's Conference in Houston (1977). She says that her sweetest victory was her induction into the University of Connecticut chapter of Phi Delta Kappa, formerly an all-male honorary education fraternity. She was the first woman inducted by the chapter, no doubt a result, she says, of her articles on behalf of feminism in the fraternity's very own magazine, *The Kappan*. An indication of her "bravery and consistency of purpose," she says, is her suit in federal district court against her employer, the Connecticut Education Association, for sex discrimination. Although she did not prevail, she was able to continue working there for another 22 years. By 1982 Taylor began to focus on pension and healthcare issues as well as conflict resolution. In 1988 she was hired as an adjunct full professor to teach conflict resolution in the Labor Research Center of the University of Rhode Island. Four years later she accepted the position of executive director at the University of Rhode Island's chapter of the American Association of University Professors, where she remained until 2001. Before retiring, she was instrumental in resolving a major sex discrimination complaint against the URI College of Engineering. The settlement resulted in changed leadership, as well as improved working conditions and support for female faculty and students. In 2001 she retired as executive director. She continues to teach part time and do research on retirement issues. She has two children. Archives: Her thesis and research on women is at the Murray Research Center of Radcliffe College, Cambridge, MA. (ABS)

Taylor, Valerie (1913 – 1997) (also known as Velma Nacella Young, and published romance stories under the name Francine Davenport) A poet, short story writer and author of several lesbian-theme novels, Taylor was an activist involved in lesbian and gay rights, the rights of the poor and disabled, the rights of the elderly, and peace. In 1965, she was co-founder with Pearl Hart and others of Mattachine Midwest, and in 1974 was a co-founder of the first Lesbian Writers Conference, held annually for five years in Chicago's Hyde Park area. Her first novel, *Hired Girl*, was published by Universal in 1953; her first lesbian novel, *Whisper Their Love*, was published by Fawcett in 1957. She is also author of *The Girls in 3-B* (Fawcett, 1969), *Stranger on Lesbos* (Fawcett, 1960), *A World Without Men and Unlike Others* (Midwood-Tower, 1963) and *Journey to Fulfillment* (Midwood-Tower, 1964). In 1976, Womanpress published *Two Women Revisited*, presenting Taylor's poetry along with works by Jeannette H. Foster. Taylor continued to write poetry and novels into the 1990s. Her writing appears in numerous anthologies, including *Intricate Passions* and *The Poetry of Sex: Lesbians Write the Erotic*. In 1992, she was inducted into the City of Chicago's Gay and Lesbian Hall of Fame. Taylor had

T

three sons. Archives: Rare Manuscript Collections, Human Sexuality Collection, Cornell University Library, Ithaca, NY.

Teeling, Ursula – See Cano, Ursula Gerda

Tennov, Dorothy (1928 –) (also known as Dorothy Tennov Hoffman) Tennov says she had "feminist leanings" since childhood, and so was ready to join in 1965 when she met her first feminist, Lolly Hirsch. From 1965 – 1971, Tennov participated in NYC feminist meetings. Working on her doctorate in scientific psychology, Tennov spent her sabbatical in Europe in 1971 researching her first book, *Psychotherapy: The Hazardous Cure*, a critical examination of psychotherapies from a feminist viewpoint. During that trip she met feminists in Paris, Norway, Denmark and London; in particular, Simone de Beauvoir. That meeting led her to return to Paris to interview de Beauvoir for a PBS series on women, which aired in 1978. She is an active member of the Association for Women in Psychology. Her writings also appeared in *Prime Time* and *Women Speaking*, a London feminist periodical published by Esther Hodge. Her second book is *Super Self: A Woman's Guide to Self-Management*. Tennov is (2005) working on a book about human nature and the probable future of the human species. Tennov received a B.A. from Brooklyn College, and a master's and Ph.D. from the University of Connecticut. She was a professor of psychology at the University of Bridgeport (CT), where she introduced the first women's studies course. Tennov has three children. (ABS)

Terry, Myra (1944 –) (also known as Myra Terry-Meisner) Until Roe v. Wade, Terry was a member of the New Jersey Coalition for the Repeal of Abortion Laws (1971 – 1973). In 1971, she was a charter and organizing member of Union County (NJ) NOW, serving as chair of its abortion rights task force and as a member of the education task force. In 1977, Terry served as a state delegate (NJ) to the IWY Conference. From 1979 – 1981, she was executive director of the Center for Women in Crisis and chair of the homemakers' rights task force (NJ NOW). During that time, she also served as president of Essex County NJ NOW. In 1983, Terry was a founder and first VP of the Resource Center for Women. From 1979 – 1992, she was executive director of The Divorce Support Center, and from 1990 – 1992, chaired the New Jersey Coalition for Divorce Reform. Terry also served as director of the New Jersey Religious Coalition for Abortion Rights (1982 – 1992), and from 1992 – 1993 chaired Choice New Jersey. In 1994, she was appointed to the New Jersey Advisory Council on the Status of Women. She later served as chair of NJ NOW's PAC, working on campaigns of both Republican and Democratic women. She chaired national NOW's President's Caucus and founded the NJ NOW Foundation. From 1992 – 1995, she was president of NJ-NOW, and in 1995 founded the Women's Fund of New

Jersey. Terry, who has two children, is a graduate of the Laboratory Institute of Merchandising and holds a certificate from the New York School of Interior Design. (ABS)

Tessner, Elizabeth ("Libby") Jeanne (1945 –) (also known as Elizabeth J. Ginn) was a major complainant in Chicago NOW's 1974 investigation of sex discrimination in private employment agencies. Tessner researched the procedures and policies of the Illinois Labor Dept., Division of Private Employment, and tracked complaints to document the department's lack of compliance and legal assistance to female complainants. After recruiting other complainants, Tessner coordinated Chicago NOW testimony for—and testified in—the U.S. Commission on Civil Rights Hearings on Private Employment Agencies (November 1974). As treasurer of Chicago NOW (1975 – 1976), Tessner researched and filed its first tax return after NOW received 501.c3 status. She also coordinated a city-wide fundraising drive that netted over half the organization's annual income, and helped write and nationally market three training booklets: "Fundraising," "Recruitment" and "Developing Action Plans." Tessner was also organizer for NOW's ERA legislative committee, and initiated and coordinated a statewide "Moms for ERA" campaign, which included a 13-schoolbus convoy to a Springfield ERA rally. Since 1976, Tessner has focused on case and class advocacy for victims of violent crime, primarily women and children. In the early 1980s, she developed and implemented an advocacy program for child victims of sexual abuse and exploitation, a precursor of today's children's advocacy centers. Tessner, who has one child, is (2005) an advocate for victims of homicide families. She holds a B.A. from University Without Walls, Northeastern Illinois University (1993). Archives: Chicago NOW material is at the Dept. of Gender and Women's Studies, University of Illinois, Chicago, IL. (ABS)

Thibeau, Judith Henrietta (1943 –) (also known as Judy Gabree) was an activist in the student protest movement in Boston (1962 – 1965) and tenant organizing in NYC (1968 – 1970). A member of the NYRW from 1968 – 1972, Thibeau was a contributor to *Notes from The First Year*. In 1969, she testified at a NYC abortion speakout. Strongly influenced by her union-oriented, working class roots, she was an organizer of a group that "met to talk about the intersection of the hidden injuries of class and sex and to reach out to other women with similar experiences." Thibeau decided to raise feminist issues in a union where women were in the majority, but the leadership was male dominated. She sought employment with women's services at a time when NYS liberalized its abortion law and women from other states came to NY clinics for safe, legal abortion. She successfully spearheaded a drive to join a hospital and drug workers union and became a delegate to the union assembly. In 1974, she "began to work on issues of women's internalized oppression and empowerment." Since 1991, she has been counseling women disabled by chemical sensitivities and chemical injury. Thibeau was a founder and leader of an all women's bagpipe band (1985). She has three stepchildren. She holds a B.A. from SUNY, Old Westbury (1975), and an M.S.W. from Simmons College (1991). (ABS)

Thom, Doris A. (1920 –) When World War II broke out, Thom took a job with Gilman Engineering in Janesville, WI. She began attending Machinist Local 1266 meetings and in 1941 became the first woman elected to the executive board, as recording secretary. When Thom became pregnant with her second child, she was immediately fired with no opportunity to return. After several years, Thom took a job in the cushion department at the General Motors Automobile Assembly Plant in Janesville, the only section where women were employed. In 1960, she agreed to serve as alternate committee woman for her Local 95 Union, then ran for the executive committee as recording secretary in 1961—another first for a woman. Thom held that position through 1968, during which time she was sent to regional meetings with women from all over the Midwest. There she discovered that women were holding jobs throughout their plants, not kept in just one department. When Thom asked why this was not the case in Janesville, she was told that keeping the women separate was "past practice." But it was 1965 and the Civil Rights Act had passed, initiating the EEOC. Thom contacted both the Wisconsin and federal EEOC and successfully changed the practice at her plant. "I was not very popular then," says Thom. "My first year out in the plant was hell. Now (2004) there are 380 women working in every department of Janesville's G.M. plant, and they comprise nearly one-third of the workforce." In addition, Thom was a founding member of NOW, and was one of five founders of the Blackhawk Community Credit Union in Janesville (1965). She served on the Wisconsin Governor's Commission on the Status of Women (1971–1975), and was president of Rock County (WI) Democratic Women for 15 years. In 2001, Thom, who has three children, received the Catherine Conroy Award honoring Wisconsin women dedicated to the rights of women and labor. Archives: Thom's oral history, recorded in 1990 for The Women of Wisconsin Labor Oral History Project, is at The State Historical Society of Wisconsin, Madison, WI. (ABS)

Thom, Mary L. (1944 –) A writer and editor, Thom was a member of the *Ms.* magazine staff from 1972 – 1991, and was executive editor when she left to write a history of the magazine. She is author of I*nside Ms.: 25 Years of the Magazine and the Feminist Movement* (Henry Holt, 1997) and served as editor of *Letters to "Ms.": 1972 – 1989* (Henry Holt, 1987). Thom is also author of *Balancing the Equation: Where Are Women and Girls in Science, Engineering, and Technology?* which was written for the National Council for Research on Women and published by Prentice Hall in 2001. During her college years (1962

– 1966), Thom was an organizer for civil rights and anti-war activities and served as co-founder of the student action committee. Because Thom attended a women's college, Bryn Mawr, some of this work was focused on feminist issues—for example, making curfew restrictions match those that governed men's college students in the area, and working for pensions and pay raises for domestic workers on campus. Thom earned her B.A. from Bryn Mawr in 1966. Archives: The Sophia Smith Collection, Smith College, Northampton, MA. (ABS)

Thom, Susan Maria – See Loubet, Susan Thom

Thomas, Helen (1920 –) After graduating from Wayne State University in 1942, Thomas, an English major, moved to Washington, D.C., to begin her career in journalism. Struggling to make her mark in an overwhelmingly male-dominated field, Thomas was a copy girl for the *Washington Daily News*. In 1943, she joined UPI and the Washington Press Corps, and in the 1950s, covered desegregation activities at the Department of Justice. Assigned to cover Jackie Kennedy during the 1960 presidential campaign, Thomas reassigned herself as one of three UPI White House correspondents after the election. She became a trailblazer, breaking through barriers for women reporters. Thomas was "one of several women" opening the National Press Club to women in 1971. In 1972, Thomas was the only woman print journalist traveling with President Nixon to China. She traveled around the world several times with Presidents Nixon, Ford, Carter, Reagan, Bush, Clinton, and George W. Bush. Because of her pioneering work, she was known for many years as the First Lady of the Press and Dean of the White House Press Corps. She was White House Bureau Chief for United Press International; the first woman president of the White House Correspondents Association, and the first woman member (1975) and president of the Gridiron Club, a formerly all-male journalists club. In 1974, she published *Dateline: White House* (Macmillan Publishing Company). Thomas is also author of *Thanks for the Memories Mr. President: Wit and Wisdom from the Front Row at the White House* (Simon & Schuster, 2002). The recipient of numerous honorary degrees and awards, including the National Press Club's Fourth Estate Award, she was named a "fellow" in Sigma Delta Chi journalism fraternity. Thomas was inducted into The Michigan Women's Hall of Fame in 1986. (ABS)

Thomas, Marlo (1937 –) An actress, producer, author and pioneering social activist for the women's movement, Thomas created and starred in the landmark situation comedy, *That Girl* (1966 -1971), portraying the first independent working woman on television. In 1974, she co-created *Free To Be…You and Me*, a non-sexist, non-racist entertainment for boys, girls and their parents, which became a record, book and Emmy-winning TV special, and spawned the Emmy-winning sequel, *Free to Be…A Family*

(1988). Born and christened Margaret Julia Thomas in Detroit, MI, to an Italian mother and Lebanese father (entertainer Danny Thomas), she grew up in a show business environment, but briefly turned to academics, graduating from the University of Southern California with a teaching degree. After becoming a television, stage and film star, she turned to social activism, using funds generated by the *Free to Be* series to co-found the Ms. Foundation with her friend, Gloria Steinem. Thomas has starred in more than a dozen TV films, many that have given voice to such important social issues as mental illness (*Nobody's Child*); childhood sexual abuse (*Ultimate Betrayal*); discrimination against homosexuality (*Consenting Adult*); and abuse of the press (*The Lost Honor Of Kathryn Beck*). She is a vice chair of the Museum of Television and Radio (where she created the "She Made It" program, honoring the pioneering women in the TV and radio industries); a board member of the NWPC and The Creative Coalition. She has four Emmys, nine Emmy nominations, a Golden Globe, a Grammy, The George Foster Peabody Award, The William Moses Kuntsler's Racial Justice Award, The Helen Caldicott Award for Nuclear Disarmament, The Thomas Paine Award from the ACLU, and has been inducted into the Broadcasting and Cable Hall of Fame. Thomas is the national outreach director for St. Jude Children's Research Hospital, which was founded by her father in 1962. (ABS)

Thompson, Irene S. (1919 – 2005) was a professor at the University of Florida and served as chair of the University of Florida Commission on the Status of Women (1969 – 1973). She taught the first women's studies course at the university in 1971, and helped found and served as director of the women's studies program (1971 – 1984). As the university's academic equity officer (1975), Thompson initiated the first official study of equity for women. In 1985, she served as chair of the Women's Faculty Association. In 1983, Thompson and her mother (an attorney who passed the bar exam in 1917) and daughter (who teaches history at Syracuse University, including women's studies) were honored by Central NY NOW. Thompson was co-editor (with Patricia Stringer) of *Stepping Off the Pedestal: Academic Women in the South* (Modern Language Association), and co-editor of *The Road Re-Taken: Women Re-Enter the Academy* (Modern Language Association). Thompson, who had one child, earned a B.A., two master's degrees, and an A.B.D. Archives: University of Florida library, Gainesville, FL.

Thorne, Alison Comish (1914 – 2004) helped found the women's studies program at Utah State University, serving as chair of the women's studies committee from 1977 – 1989. She was also involved with the Women's Center and the committee on women and international development, and served on the Utah Commission on the Status of Women (1964 – 1969). Thorne taught at USU from 1964 – 1980s. However, because of anti-nepotism laws (her husband was a faculty member there), she was not allowed to hold a regular faculty position. Thanks to campus feminists, she was promoted to professor emerita in 1985. Thorne's biography, *Leave the Dishes in the Sink: Adventures of an Activist in Conservative Utah*, was published by Utah State University Press in 2002. Thorne received the Utah State University's Distinguished Service Award (1982), Woman of the Year, Utah Chapter of the AAUW (1967), and the Utah Governor's Award for Volunteer Service (1980), and the Women's Achievement Award from the Utah Governor's Commission on the Status of Women (2002). Thorne earned her undergraduate degree from Brigham Young University, and held an M.A. (1935) and Ph.D. (1938) from Iowa State University. Archives: Special Collections & Archives, Utah State University Libraries, Logan, UT.

Thorne, Barrie (1942 –) After hearing two women from Chicago Voice of Women's Liberation speak at a draft resistance conference in Illinois (1969), Thorne returned to Boston and co-founded a women's rap group, which joined with other groups to found Bread and Roses. Thorne was active in Bread and Roses from 1970 – 1971. In 1971, she became an assistant professor of sociology at Michigan State University. In 1973, she and other women succeeded in getting undergraduate women's studies courses approved. Thorne was also active in the Alliance to End Sex Discrimination at MSU, and spoke extensively in Michigan about Title IX and sexism in education. In 1976, she began researching gender relations in schools. Thorne helped form Sociologists for Women in Society; creating the Sex and Gender Section of the American Sociological Association (which she chaired at one point); and serving on the status of women committee of the ASA. Thorne co-edited Language and Sex: Difference and Dominance (Newbury House, 1975, with Nancy Henley); and Language, Gender and Society (Newbury House, 1983, with Cheris Kramarae and Nancy Henley). She also co-edited (with Marilyn Yalom) *Rethinking the Family: Some Feminist Questions* (Longman, 1980), and began researching gender relations among children. In 1987, Thorne became Streisand Professor of Intimacy and Sexuality in the Program for the Study of Women and Men in Society at the University of Southern California, and also professor of sociology (a joint appointment). She chaired SWMS for several years and published *Gender Play: Girls and Boys in School* in 1993. She also co-edited, with Barbara Laslett, *Feminist Sociology: Life Histories of a Movement* (1997). She has (2005) a joint appointment at the University of California, Berkeley, in the women's studies department (which she chairs) and in sociology. She has two children, and holds B.A. from Stanford University (1964), and an M.A. (1967) and Ph.D. (1971) from Brandeis University. Archives: Special Collections, Michigan State University, East Lansing, MI.   (ABS)

Thornton, Eileen (1942 –) A lifetime fighter to improve the educational and economic rights of women and their political opportunities, Thornton joined the New Jersey Federation of Business and Professional Women in the late 1960s, as well as the New Jersey chapter of the WPC. A member of WEAL, she served as board member and later as national president. In that capacity, Thornton was involved in the Economic Equity Act, was involved in passing Title IX, and played a key role in the ratification efforts for the ERA, working with congresswoman Elizabeth Holtzman and ERAmerica. Thornton served as president of the NJ WPC from 1980 – 1982 and from 1994 – 1997. During that time, she helped promote women candidates, developing contacts with the media to get their stories out. With Kathy Brock, she spearheaded a coalition to get more women in statehouse cabinets and other positions, and worked with both parties to develop opportunities for women to be delegates at national nominating conventions. Thornton was also a catalyst for the first woman appointed to the NJ State Supreme Court, Marie Garibaldi. Thornton continues to advance the rights of women in her role as Hamilton (NJ) councilwoman. She holds a B.S. from Rider University. Archives: Center for American Women in Politics, which will be transferred to Douglass College, Rutgers University, New Brunswick, NJ. (ABS)

Threinen, Constance Fuller (1925 –) The great, great niece of Margaret Fuller, Threinen felt herself "a feminist from birth." She joined the LWV after college, and in 1962 was hired by the University of Wisconsin-Extension to arrange continuing education services for women around the state. Says Threinen, "This program played a major role in organizing the women's movement in Wisconsin." Threinen twice served as chair of the Wisconsin Women's Network, and chaired the first state task force on sex stereotyping in the schools. She also served for many years on the legislative committee of the LWV of Wisconsin and has been responsible for its work on women's issues. Now retired from the University of Wisconsin's department of women's education resources, Threinen has three children. She attended Mount Holyoke College and the University of Wisconsin. Archives: Wisconsin State Historical Library, Madison, WI. (ABS)

Thulin, Barbara Wasson (1926 –) A neurologist, Thulin was a founding member and the second president of Denver NOW and a board member of national NOW. The Denver chapter addressed sex discrimination in admissions in the University of Colorado graduate programs. It persuaded the Colorado School of Medicine to admit women in the same ratio as men who applied for admittance. Colorado was the first state in the U.S. where this was accomplished. And because of the chapter's work, the university's law school admitted more women. The chapter demonstrated for the ERA and also worked to pass laws favorable to women. Members testified at hearings and lobbied legislators regarding abortion; a law legalizing abortion was passed in Colorado prior to Roe v. Wade.

Tiefer, Leonore (1944 –) is a theorist, researcher, educator and activist on behalf of women. In 1969, Tiefer came to Colorado State University as an assistant professor, and for the next three years was the only woman in its 27-person psychology department. In 1972, she was joined by Pamela Pearson, who introduced her to women's liberation. Within two years, Tiefer had co-founded the Fort Collins chapter of NOW (1972). She constantly wrote letters to both the town and school newspapers complaining about inequities such as separate job ads for women and men, and assumptions about who could do what and what they should be paid. Tiefer also helped found a Colorado State University Commission on the Status of Women, a staff-faculty-student group that held meetings on such topics as rape treatment services, better lighting on campus, part-time employment opportunities and childcare services. In addition, she initiated a women's faculty caucus at the university that "created a lot of trouble." The caucus conducted surveys of promotion, tenure, salaries and benefits that showed the stark discrepancy between men and women. The author of *Sex Is Not a Natural Act* (Westview Press, 1994), Tiefer holds Ph.D. from the University of California, Berkeley. Archives: Kinsey Institute for Sex, Gender and Reproduction, Indiana University, Bloomington, IL. (ABS)

Tierney, Karline Koenen (1926 –) In 1973, Tierney organized and headed ERA United, a coalition of 100-plus groups supporting ratification in Louisiana. In 1978, she was a co-founder of the LA WPC. In addition, Tierney chaired the Mayor's Commission on the Needs of Women (Baton Rouge, 1973) and served on the board of the city's battered women's shelter, also in the early 1970s. From 1973 – 1975, Tierney served as national chair of AAUW study/action topic, "The 21st Century – Deciding NOW." From 1981 – 1983, she served as director of women's issues, AAUW national board. Tierney, who worked as an environmental chemist for 20 years, earned her B.S. from Nazareth College, Rochester, NY. She has three children. Archives: Center for Research on Women, Newcomb College, New Orleans, LA. (ABS)

Timlin, Catherine (1943 – 1999) In 1970, Timlin was active when NOW's women's center started up in Los Angeles, but she is known for co-writing, with Alice Bennett, the ERA extension, when she was a student at Whittier School of Law in Los Angeles (1977). In 1977, Elizabeth Holtzman introduced the bill calling for an extension of the deadline, which Congress moved from 1979 to 1982. A social worker in the 1970s, Timlin was an officer of both Southern California NOW and Los Angeles NOW. Timlin also helped publish "The Women's Heritage Calendar and Almanac" (1970), a forerunner of many feminist calendars and datebooks to come. She moved to a small town in Northern CA, near Reno, and then went back into social work as a protective services worker. She graduated from Whittier College with a JD.

T

Timmer, Ann (1925 –) A high-school English teacher, Timmer became active in the women's movement as ERA coordinator for the Elmhurst, IL, LWV. After moving to Arizona, she was one of the organizers and first president of the Sun City's chapter of NOW, then served as Arizona NOW state coordinator. She has marched in Phoenix, Denver, Oklahoma City, Philadelphia, New York City, Washington, D.C., and New Orleans for both the ERA and reproductive rights. Timmer also served as Arizona NOW legislative coordinator for four years, lobbying at the state capital. She has three children. (ABS)

Tinker, Bonnie Jeanne (1948 –) An activist and organizer who has worked on health and domestic violence issues, Tinker is executive director of Love Makes a Family, Inc., which provides support and a public voice for lesbian, gay, bi and trans-headed families, and educates people on the need for marriage equality. She was a co-founder of the Red Emma collective in Portland, OR (1971). Members were subsequently active in founding the Portland Women's Health Center, the Portland Women's Book Store and Prescott House (originally a shelter for women coming out of prison). The collective was part of a resurgent women's community in Portland that was referred to as the Southeast Women's Community. In 1972, Tinker and Sharon Keeler informally adopted a baby girl. When her daughter, Connie, turned 18, the adoption was legalized. Says Tinker, "It was one of the earliest lesbian adoptions I know of where the child was raised by out parents." In 1974, Tinker was appointed to the executive committee of the Regional American Friends Service Committee, and served on the women and violence committee of the AFSC in Portland. With the support of the AFSC and others, Tinker helped found Bradley Angle House (1975 – 1978), one of the first shelters for battered women in the U.S., and served as the executive director (1975 – 1978). Tinker was a founder of the National Coalition Against Domestic Violence, and served as the acting chair during the first year (1977). In 1981, Tinker began to actively encourage the Portland Quaker meeting, Multnomah Meeting, to discuss same-sex marriage. The first lesbian wedding was held in 1989. After studying photography (1987) for the purpose of creating a book about the Quaker process surrounding same-sex marriage, Tinker ultimately produced a video, "Love Makes A Family, Lesbian and Gay Families in the Religious Society of Friends." By 1992, Love Makes A Family was organized, and in 1993 was incorporated. From 1993 – 1997, she hosted a talk radio program on AM station KKEY on Love Makes a Family, and in 1997 worked with Love Makes A Family and other groups to found the Oregon Freedom to Marry Coalition. In 2004, Tinker says, she and her partner, Sara Graham, were married "under the care of the Multnomah Monthly Meeting of the Religious Society of Friends with a marriage license issued by Multnomah County." Together since 1977, they have three children. Tinker attended Grinnel College and earned an M.S. from Marylhurst University (1986). Archives: Oregon Historical Society, Portland, OR. (ABS)

Tittle, Carol Kehr (1933 –) After earning a Ph.D. in educational psychology from the University of Chicago in 1965, Tittle wrote a paper, "Studies in Psychological Measurement: Science, Objectivity, and Sex Differences," that marked the beginning of her life work on gender, equity and testing, and test bias and women. The paper was presented in 1971 at the annual meeting of the South Eastern Psychological Association. Tittle, who was very involved with women's groups in various professional associations, especially the American Educational Research Association, organized and chaired a symposium for the 1972 annual meeting of the association titled Women as Equals: Interdisciplinary Perspectives for Educational Research. From that meeting, two groups were formed: one to work within the established structure of the AERA, the SIG Research on Women in Education; and a women's caucus, today (2005) called Women Educators. Tittle served as program chair for the annual AERA meeting of the newly formed SIG in 1973, and chaired the AERA committee on SIGS (1975 – 1977). From 1973 – 1975, Tittle chaired an ad hoc committee on the role and status of women in educational research and development, and was a member of the committee from 1976 – 1978. Made a standing committee in 1980, it published surveys and studies on women in AERA that were reported in a special issue of *Educational Researcher* in October 1980. Tittle was elected member at large of the AERA Council (1983 – 1986), and served on the council executive committee (1985 – 1986). She is author of *Career and Family: Sex Roles and Adolescent Life Plans* (Sage, 1981) and co-author (with Elenor R. Denker) of *Returning Women in Higher Education: Defining Policy Issues* (Prager, 1980). She has published numerous articles in scholarly journals on women and education, and has spoken widely on the topic. From 1987 – 1988, she was president of the National Council on Measurement in Education, and was also president of Division 15 (Educational Psychology) in the APA (1992 – 1993). She has served on the editorial boards of a number of journals, including *Sex Roles*, and on advisory committees, including for the Women's Educational Equity Act Programs and for the defense advisory committee on military testing (1984 – 1987). Since 1986, Tittle has been a professor in the Ph.D. program in educational psychology at the Graduate School of the City University of New York. I Tittle holds a B.A. from the University of Colorado and an M.A. from Ohio State University. (ABS)

Tjosvold, Mary Margaret (1943 –) became a feminist activist in 1969, working in the Twin Cities of Minnesota. Tjosvold organized groups to achieve equal pay for coaches of girls high-school sports; lobbied to get women into administrative positions and underemployed areas in the Minnesota public schools and the University of

(ABS) indicates Approved By Subject

Minnesota; and worked for the equalization of Title IX funds for girls. She was a founder of the Women's Education Action Group and Women Hurling Into Personhood (WHIP), was a member of WEAL and a founding member of Teachers for Change. She served as a member of the Minnesota task force on sexism in education and as chair and founding member of the Minnesota public school task force on sex bias. She spoke on the elimination of sex bias in education, was a protester in various capacities to bring attention to sexism in our society, and marched for the ERA in events around the country. She was also a writer and participant in "Don't Call Me Girl: Amazon Revisited" and a writer and presenter of the slide show "Don't Call Me Girl: Sex Bias in the Minneapolis Public Schools." Active in the civil rights movement of the 1960s, Tjosvold also marched in numerous peace and anti-war demonstrations. She holds a B.S. (1964), M.A. (1975) and Ph.D. (1975) from the University of Minnesota, and an OPM XII from Harvard Business School (1987). (ABS)

Tobias, Sheila (1935 –) An education consultant and university administrator, lecturer and writer, Tobias says that her "self-appointed task within the women's movement was to take on the patriarchy, that is, those institutions dominated by men and excluding (or abusing) women." In 1970, after teaching the first course in women's studies at Cornell, Tobias took a position at Wesleyan for eight years, where she forged a New England network featuring job search and referral, off-the-job training, and national activism in the service of women's studies, affirmative action and gender equity in education. While at Wesleyan, Tobias uncovered "math anxiety," developed a program to fight it, and wrote *Overcoming Math Anxiety* (W.W. Norton, 1978). Tobias has written 11 books on women and their concerns, including *Women, Militarism, and War* (co-authored with Jean B. Elshtain, Press of America, 1990); and *Faces of Feminism: An Activist's Reflections on the Women's Movement* (Westview Press, 1997). She was a founder of the Finger Lakes (NY) chapter of NOW (1969); a member of the Professional Women's Caucus (1967–1970); and in 1970 attended the Congress to Unite Women. She was a co-founder of the Cornell women's studies course and program, and author of the first volume of "Female Studies–I," a compilation of course material (1972) that still (2005) exists. From 1974–1978, she served as publisher of *Alert, Women's Legislative Review*. Tobias was also a member of NOW's LDEF (1974–1978), and a member of VFA (1994 – 1998). She became a VFA board member in 1998, and serves (2006) as executive VP. Tobias holds a B.A. from Radcliffe, and an M.A. and M. Phil. from Columbia University. Archives: Schlesinger Library, Radcliffe Institute, Cambridge, MA. (ABS)

Tobin, Joan Adele (1930 –) A writer and former editor of the South Shore (Long Island, NY) NOW newsletter (1974 – 1975), Tobin entered the women's movement with the publication of her letter to the editor of *Long Island Newsday*, "But Men Consume, Too" (October 8, 1973). Since that time, Tobin has published letters to the editor, news articles, essays, columns and poems of importance to women in publications as diverse as the *International Mensa Journal*, *The New York Times*, *The Hartford Courant*, *New Directions for Women*, *Media Report to Women*, *OWL News*, and New York State and Connecticut state NOW newspapers. Her published work includes "Conditioned to Fear Equality?" an essay published in the South Shore NOW paper (December 1975); "The Folly of Rejecting Feminism," published in *The New York Times* (January 26, 1984); and "A Safety Net Saved Jane Eyre," an essay published in *Spectacle* (Spring/Summer, 1997). In 2002, Tobin was added to the Veteran Feminists of America's Honor Roll of Feminist Writers. Tobin, who has three children, holds a B.A. from Charter Oak State College (1996). (ABS)

Tobolowsky, Hermine (1921 – 1995) While studying law at the University of Texas Law School in the 1940s, Tobolowsky discovered the blatant inequities that women faced, then experienced them herself after graduation. In response, she opened a private practice in San Antonio and devoted her life to advancing the rights of women. In 1957, she became the leader of a statewide campaign for equal legal rights for men and women in Texas, and worked simultaneously on the national ERA. When Texas passed the ERA in 1972, Tobolowsky became known as the Mother of the ERA in Texas. In 1982, the women's law caucus of the University of Texas School of Law established the Hermine Tobolowsky Award in her honor. Her other awards include Top News Shapers in Dallas (1972 and 1974, *Dallas Times Herald*); Texas Woman in History (1976, Texas Federation of Business and Professional Women's Clubs, Inc.); Women Helping Women Award (1979, Dallas Women's Center); and Women Helping Women Award (Soroptimist International). Archives: Southwest Collection/Special Collections Library, Texas Tech University, Lubbock, TX.

Todasco, Ruth Taylor (1931 –) Todasco entered the women's movement in 1971, and by 1972 had started one of the first lay advocate programs in the Chicago area to assist survivors of rape. Awareness of sexism in language as a social force inspired her to propose and edit *The Feminist English Dictionary: An Intelligent Woman's Guide to Dirty Words*, published by Chicago Loop Center YWCA. In 1975 Todasco suggested a second volume, *The New Women's Dictionary: Sharpening the Mother Tongue*, now (2006) a work in progress to be published by Crossroads Books. The dictionary shows the changes in language that have come about as a result of women's struggles and experience. Starting in 1981, Todasco initiated the Tulsa, OK, chapter of the Wages for Housework Campaign and the No Bad Women, Just Bad Laws

Coalition pressing for the human, civil and economic rights of prostitute women. She served several years on the board of Domestic Violence Intervention Services, founding Lay Advocates for Women to monitor how the court was treating women seeking protective orders. She participated in the Wages For Housework delegation to the 1985 United Nations Decade for Women conference in Nairobi, where the resolution calling on governments to count women's work in the GNP was won. In 1989, Todasco moved to work with WFH in Los Angeles, which coordinates the Global Women's Strike/Los Angeles. A multiracial grassroots women's network in over 60 countries, the GWS takes action on International Women's Day and throughout the year under the theme "Invest in Caring, Not Killing." In 1995, Todasco was part of the International Women Count Network delegation to the United Nations World Conference on Women in Beijing, where the decision was won calling on governments to measure and value all unwaged work in satellite accounts of the Gross Domestic Product. Todasco, a Woodrow Wilson Fellow in Philosophy, earned her Ph.D. at Texas Tech in 1963. She continues her involvement with the Global Women's Strike/Los Angeles. (ABS)

Toder, Nancy L. (1948 –) A psychology major at SUNY Buffalo in 1968, Toder was the first researcher in the area of adolescent identity formation to conduct an experiment on college women—not men. The result, "Ego Identity Status and Response to Conformity Pressure in College Women," was published in the *Journal of Personality and Social Psychology* in 1973. After coming out in 1971, Toder joined the first Los Angeles Lesbian Feminist Consciousness Raising Group, which met in the original Women's Center on Crenshaw Blvd. She served as editor of *Lesbian Tide* (1973 – 1975), and in 1973 put together the first all-female dissertation committee on the UCLA campus. At the same time, Toder began a 30-year process of speaking publicly about women's issues, sexuality, lesbianism and prejudice when she taped a TV show for public television on lesbian feminism in 1974. She also co-planned and organized the Lesbian History Exploration, the first national lesbian separatist gathering held in Malibu, CA, in 1975. In 1977, she wrote a groundbreaking article on lesbian sexuality for Ginny Vida's *Our Right to Love*. Says Toder, "As far as I know, this was the first time a lesbian 'expert' [had written] about this subject as opposed to the myriad articles/books written from the outside with their predictable bias and misinformation." When human sexuality became a Continuing Education requirement in CA, Toder became an expert, offering workshops throughout the state. In 1979, Toder wrote "Lesbian Couples: Special Issues" for Betty Berzon's *Positively Gay*, and in 1977 wrote a screenplay, "A Woman's Touch," that became the basis for the lesbian novel *Choices* (Persephone Press, 1980). A keynote speaker at NOW's national conference in 1981, Toder addressed conservative women's fears that NOW's support of les-

bians would jeopardize passage of the ERA. Deciding to become a psychoanalyst in 1987, Toder was part of the first wave of out lesbian and gay therapists to receive analytic training. Toder holds a B.A. from SUNY Buffalo, a Ph.D. from UCLA, and completed her psychoanalytic training at Newport Psychoanalytic Institute. (ABS)

Tolpin, Martha (1939 –) In 1972, Tolpin earned one of the first Ph.D.'s in women's history at Harvard University when she completed her thesis on Darwin's influence on views of feminine character. From 1975 – 1977, she was associate director of New England Higher Education Resource Services and director of academic career advancement workshops. In that capacity, she traveled to colleges and universities across the U.S. running workshops for women graduate students and junior faculty to help them advance their careers in teaching and administration. "Basically," says Tolpin, "I made trouble on behalf of women." She also taught European women's history at Wheaton College. She currently teaches European women's history at Bentley College. There she founded what became the gender issues committee. In addition to her Ph.D., Tolpin holds a B.A. from Barnard (1960) and an M.A. from Radcliffe College (1961). (ABS)

Tomlin, Lily (1939 –) (also known as Mary Jean Tomlin) An award-winning actress (six Emmys, a Grammy, a Writers Guild, two Cable Ace Awards and a Peabody, among others) Tomlin throughout her career has been a staunch supporter of women's rights. She once walked off the "Dick Cavett Show" following sexist remarks by another guest. She has also campaigned for the ERA and for women candidates, including Bella Abzug and Texas Governor Ann Richards, and has supported the rights of gays and lesbians. In addition, Tomlin worked with Women of Hope and Project Home in Philadelphia, Rachel's Women's Center in San Diego, and Rosie's Place in Boston, the first shelter in the U.S. for homeless women. The late comedienne Gilda Radner said of her, "Lily Tomlin is a role model and a change agent. Because of her work, the consciousness of Americans has been raised to the concerns and problems of women in all walks of life." Tomlin was inducted into The Michigan Women's Hall of Fame in 1998.

Topping, Christine – See Milliken, Christine

Torre, Susana (1944 –) organized and curated the first major exhibition of American women architects, and edited the book *Women in American Architecture: A Historic and Contemporary Perspective*. The exhibition, which opened at the Brooklyn Museum in 1977 and traveled across the country and to The Netherlands, and the book were the most visible outcomes of The Archive of Women in Architecture of the Architectural League of New York, which Torre co-founded in 1973. Torre was also a cofounder of *Heresies, A Feminist Journal on Art and Politics*;

was a member of the editorial collectives for *Heresies 2: Patterns of Communications and Space*, and *Heresies 11: Making Room: Women in Architecture*; and served on the editorial board of *Chrysalis* between 1976 – 1978. An architect, critic and educator, Torre was the first woman invited to design a building in Columbus, IN, a town internationally known for its collection of buildings designed by prominent architects. Firehouse #5 (finished in 1987) was the first firehouse designed specifically to integrate women into the firefighting force. The design, which eliminated dorm-style sleeping and promoted bonding in the kitchen rather than the locker room, was adopted nationwide. Torre, who was born in Puan, Buenos Aires, Argentina, has written widely on women and architecture, and served as editor and author of several chapters of *Women in American Architecture: A Historic and Contemporary Perspective* (Whitney Library of Design, 1977). Torre, who has been active in the civil rights, gay rights and the peace and environmental movements, earned her Dipl. Arch. from the School of Architecture and Planning, Universidad de Buenos Aires, Argentina. She has also done post-graduate studies at Columbia University Graduate School of Architecture and Planning. Archives: International Archive of Women in Architecture, Virginia Polytechnic, Blacksburg, VA; and the Avery Library Centennial Drawings Archive, Columbia University, New York, NY.　　　　(ABS)

Torrey, **Jane** (1925 –) was a co-founder of the Southeastern CT chapter of NOW (1970). A professor in the psychology department at Connecticut College for 35 years, Torrey was instrumental in the formation of the program in gender and women's studies there. In honor of her work, the college established the Jane W. Torrey Prize, which is awarded to a senior in gender and women's studies for outstanding work in that field.　　　　(ABS)

Toth, **Emily Jane Fitzgibbons** (1944 –) is a writer about women's lives, activist for civil rights and feminism, and pioneering scholar in women's studies and popular culture. As a Ph.D. graduate student at Johns Hopkins, she wrote for *Women: A Journal of Liberation* (1971 – 1973), joined a CR group, and gave community talks for Baltimore Women's Liberation. With Janice Delaney and Mary Jane Lupton, she wrote about women's secrets and popular culture in *The Curse: A Cultural History of Menstruation* (Dutton, 1976; University of Illinois Press, 1988). She is a founder of NWSA and the Women's Caucus for Popular Culture (1985), whose Emily Toth Award honors the best books in feminist popular culture studies. Toth is responsible for reviving the once-forgotten author Kate Chopin through her writings, including two Chopin biographies and two collections of letters and diaries. She is working on a feature film based on her book *Inside Peyton Place: The Life of Grace Metalious* (Doubleday, 1981; University Press of Mississippi, 2000). Toth also wrote an award-winning feminist historical novel,

Daughters of New Orleans (Bantam, 1983). Since 1997, Toth has been dispensing Ms. Mentor's wisdom in *Ms. Mentor's Impeccable Advice for Women in Academia* (University of Pennsylvania Press, 1997) and in a monthly advice column on the Chronicle of Higher Education's Career Network Web site. Toth is now Robert Penn Warren Professor of English and Women's Studies at Louisiana State University.　　　　(ABS)

Townley, **Windflower** (1948 –) (also known as Annette Townley) Teaching English and drama in NYC in 1971, Townley organized an after-school class using Robin Morgan's book *Sisterhood Is Powerful*. While doing graduate work at the University of Massachusetts in Amherst in 1972, she helped found Everywoman's Center. She went on to co-design and co-coordinate the Feminist Arts Program at EWC (1973 – 1976), which organized women's cultural weeks. She also helped edit and publish *Chomo Uri*, a women's multi-arts magazine, organized the first National Women's Poetry Festival, and taught a feminist writing seminar in poetry. In 1972, she helped create and performed in a women's theater group that became the Amherst Feminist Repertory Company in 1976. Townley performed in feminist and lesbian feminist plays through 1981, and in 1987 helped organize the first lesbian art show in Northampton, MA. A fighter for both women's rights and civil rights, she says one of her favorite memories of feminist organizing is "a Miss World Contest held in Springfield, MA. Bob Hope was the MC and we walked around chanting 'No Hope for Bob Hope.' When Sammy Davis Jr. and his entourage of women showed up, we persuaded him to turn around and go home. He said something to the effect that we were there with him in Selma, and he would be with us." Townley, who has a M.Ed. in English, became a mediator in 1984. She is the executive director of the North Bay Consensus Council and a faculty member in the Conflict Resolution Program at Sonoma State University (CA).　　　　(ABS)

Towns, **Maria T.** – See Mangual, Maria T.

Trachtenberg, **Rebecca** – See Alpert, Rebecca T.

Trahey, **Jane** (1923 – 2000) Trahey was a major donor and on the board of the NOW LDEF. She lectured to professional women's organizations and wrote the book *Jane Trahey on Women & Power: Who's Got It. How to Get It*. Her play "Ring Around the Bathtub" was produced on Broadway in 1972. Her autobiographical book *Life With Mother Superior* was made into the film "The Trouble With Angels." Trahey's novels include *Thursdays Till Nine* and *Pecked to Death by Goslings*. One of the most prominent women in advertising in the 1960s, with campaigns to her credit such as "What Becomes a Legend Most" and "Danskins Are Not Just for Dancing," Trahey was named Advertising Woman of the Year by the American Advertising Federation in 1969.

Traina, Gerri (1936 –) was member of a 1960s NYC CR group formed of women active in anti-Vietnam organizing. Traina made the critical shift from the male Left to the women's movement in Miami during the 1972 Democratic and Republican conventions, where she served as an organizer of the women's march from Flamingo Park to the Convention Center. She then went to Washington, D.C., to run the Washington Area Women's Center, which housed the LDEF, Rape Crisis Center and Feminist Counseling Collective, among other groups. Traina also served as an editor of *Quest: A Feminist Quarterly*, for the duration of its existence (1974 – early 1980s). In the 1980s, Traina helped establish the Washington Area Feminist Federal Credit Union, and served as a founder, board member and eventual executive director of the Washington Area Women's Fund, which helped such members as My Sister's Place, a women's shelter; the Rape Crisis Center; Black Women's Health Collective; a Native American women's group; and others. Traina also served as co-director of the D.C. chapter of The National Congress of Neighborhood Women, and has worked with OWL. Traina earned a B.A. from Hunter College and an M.A. from New York University. (ABS)

Trainor, Patricia Helen (1938 –) A school teacher, multilingual stenographer, systems programmer and a corporate lawyer, Trainor got her first "man's job at a man's pay" as a systems programmer by answering a "Help-Wanted-Male" ad in *The New York Times* in March 1966. When, later in 1966, she read about the formation of NOW in the women's page of *The New York Times*, she immediately wrote to Betty Friedan saying she wanted to join. At NOW's first meeting Trainor was made coordinator of NOW's image committee. At the initial meeting of that committee, desegregating *The New York Times* Help Wanted ads was chosen as a NOW project. In addition to directly approaching *The New York Times*, where the general counsel said "over my dead body" to the idea of integrating the ads, the committee also worked with the EEOC and the New York City Human Rights Commission. That was necessary because EEOC policy, in spite of Title VII making it illegal to discriminate against women, explicitly permitted *The New York Times* policy. All that the EEOC required was a disclaimer printed with the Help Wanted ads stating that gender segregation was only for the convenience of readers and was not meant to discriminate. After two years of negotiations, letters and demonstrations, the New York City Human Rights Commission mandated that all newspapers within its jurisdiction would have to integrate their Help Wanted ads. *The New York Times* printed its first fully-integrated ads on December 1, 1968. Trainor also served as NY NOW board member, VP, treasurer of NY NOW, and treasurer of the NOW LDEF. In 1972 Trainor entered New York University Law School, graduated in 1975, and became a corporate lawyer. (ABS)

Trawick, Mary Atkeson
– See Gibson, Mary Cordelia Atkeson

Triantafillou, Katherine (1950 –) began her advocacy for battered women after graduating from Suffolk Law School in 1975. From 1976 – 1980, she provided legal counsel to Transition House Massachusetts, helping to incorporate the organization and obtain its tax-exempt status. In 1977, she designed and supervised the Transition House Legal Advocacy Program, which trained volunteers and staff to give free legal assistance to battered women, and for many years operated as an unofficial, unpaid 24-hour legal hotline. Triantafillou also wrote the pamphlet "Have You Been Beaten by the Man You Live With?" and *Legal Rights of Battered Women Handbook – How to Use the Law* (1978). With members of the battered women's action committee, Triantafillou wrote the domestic violence legislation known as the Abuse Prevention Act, Chapter 209A of the M.G.L. As a member of the Coalition Against Domestic Violence, she also coordinated the successful legislative strategy that made the law a reality in one year (1978). In 1979, she served as editor of the *Massachusetts Police Institute Training Manual* on the Abuse Prevention Act, and has trained hundreds of police officers on the legal issues and rights of battered women. From 1984 – 1990, she was a member of the Governor's State-Wide Anti-Crime Council and the Battered Women's Working Group. Elected as a Cambridge (MA) city councilor (1994), Triantafillou introduced one of the nation's first municipal programs against domestic violence, the Domestic Violence Free Zone. Triantafillou was the first openly gay person to practice law in Massachusetts. She is a founder and former co-chair of the National Lesbian and Gay Law Association and the Massachusetts Lesbian and Gay Bar Association. Her groundbreaking case, Adoption of Tammy, established the right of unmarried co-habitants to jointly adopt in Massachusetts. (ABS)

Trieff, Selina (1934 –) An artist and teacher, Trieff worked to have women's art included in galleries and museums. As an early member of Women in the Arts and Women's Caucus for Art, Trieff picketed museums in NYC to open up exhibitions to women's work, and also fought to get women faculty into college art departments. Trieff has two children and was active in the peace and civil rights movements. She holds a B.A. from Brooklyn College. Archives: Archives of American Art, Washington, D.C. (ABS)

Tripp, Maggie (1920 –) From 1970 – 1989, Tripp taught women's studies at the New School for Social Research, New York University and Temple University. She also lectured at Smith College, Wellesley, Purdue and Eastern Michigan University on topics such as "The Changing Conscience and Consciousness of Women – Liberation How?" "Take Charge of Your Life and You'll Never Look Back in Anger," and "Legal Tender has no Gender." Under the auspices of the U.S. Information Service, Tripp spoke to university students and politicians in Europe about the changing role of women in the U.S. She served as co-chair of NOW's education committee, lobbied President Carter and others for passage of the ERA, and debated Phyllis Schlafly in Kansas City. She also worked for the Women's Action Alliance. In 1974, Tripp wrote and edited the book *Woman in the Year 2000*. She has two children. Archives: Wellesley Center for Women, Wellesley, MA.   (ABS)

Trocke, Linda – See Weston, Jenna Linda

Troester, Rosalie Riegle – See Riegle, Rosalie

Trugman, Donna – See Henes, Donna

Truitt, Myrna Ruth (1938 –) A retired advertising research director at *Newsweek*, Truitt entered the women's movement in the late 1960s. She was a board member of Boston NOW, taught auto repair as a fundraiser, and helped organize Amelia Earhart Day in Boston for Women's Equality Day. Truitt also demonstrated against Harvard's affirmative action policies. She says: "Harvard's affirmative action plan was not implemented, and they had the nerve to sponsor a national conference on affirmative action!" Truitt holds a B.A. from Georgia State University and an M.B.A. from Boston University.   (ABS)

Tucker, Marna Susan (1941 –) An attorney (senior partner at Feldesman, Tucker, Leifer, Fidell LLP), Tucker was one of a small band of women lawyers in Washington, D.C., in 1970. She became involved in what was then called the Public Interest Law Movement, and was a founding member of the Washington Council of Lawyers, a group dedicated to the goals of the Public Interest Law Movement—one of which was improving the rights of women. She was also a founder of a number of women lawyers' organizations, including The Women's Legal Defense Fund and the Women's Rights Project of the Center for Law and Social Policy. As of this writing, although the names have changed, these are two of the most effective women's rights legal organizations in the country: National Partnership for Women and Families, and the National Women's Law Center. Tucker has been a board member of the later for 30 years. She became active in the ABA in 1972 and worked to improve the status of women in the legal profession. With Brooksley Born, she founded the ABA women's caucus, which was the impetus behind the creation of the Commission on Women in the Profession, an extremely effective body within the ABA for the advancement of women. (Its first chair was Hillary Rodham Clinton.) As the first woman president of the District of Columbia Bar in 1984 and the first woman president of the National Conference of Bar Presidents, Tucker had the opportunity to change the legal profession that once routinely denied women. While president of the D.C. Bar (1984), she was asked by a coalition of women's

organizations to give testimony before the U.S. Senate on the ERA hearings. "While the ERA never became law, we fought the good fight and achieved much through later Supreme Court rulings," she says. Tucker, who practices family law, became involved in the fight against domestic violence. In the ABA, she co-chaired the first commission on violence against women. Later, two successive mayors of the District of Columbia appointed her to chair the Mayor's Commission on Violence Against Women. Tucker, who has two children, holds a B.S. from the University of Texas (1962) and an L.L.B. from Georgetown University Law Center (1965).   (ABS)

Tufts, Eleanor (1927 – 1991) An art historian from Exeter, NH, who ended up chairing the art history department at Southern Methodist University in Dallas, Tufts was a pioneer researcher and lecturer on women artists, past and present. It was while working in the Prado on her dissertation that Tufts, in a pre-computer age, first began making her famous index cards on women artists. Her 1974 book *Our Hidden Heritage: Five Centuries of Women Artists* (Paddington Press) was the first scholarly book to focus on women in the visual arts, causing her to be in demand around the country as a lecturer on what in the early days of feminism was less frighteningly presented as "revisionism." In 1985 she was asked to curate the inaugural exhibition for the new National Museum of Women in the Arts in Washington, D.C. The show, a result of two years of coast-to-coast research assembling 124 works, was American Women Artists 1830 – 1930, and featured 23 sculptures as well as miniatures and paintings. Its opening in April 1987 received much coverage in the national press and on television. Then, over a two-year period, it traveled to The Minneapolis Institute of Arts, The Wadsworth Atheneum in Hartford, the San Diego Museum of Art, and the Meadows Museum of Southern Methodist University. Tufts received a B.S. from Simmons College, an M.A. from Harvard, and a Ph.D. from New York University. Archives: Tufts Archive of Women Artists at Southern Methodist University.

Tully, Mary Jean (1925 – 2003) An "Army brat," Tully was a lecturer in sociology at Long Island University, but living in Westchester, NY, when Westchester NOW was formed in her living room. She became its first VP and edited NOW's first national newsletter, "Do It NOW." Tully also served as president of the Fund for Women's Rights, an organization founded with Betty Friedan to work for the ERA. A founding member (1971) of the NY State NWPC, Tully became finance chair. As president of NOW LDEF (1971 – 1977), she was a pioneer fundraiser for the women's movement, getting the first corporate and foundation grants. When Tully left, the budget had gone from $0 to $600,000. Then, as a founding member and co-chair of the national committee for responsive philanthropy, Tully helped open foundations and corporations to non-traditional funding. Tully served on the

VFA ad hoc procedures committee. She also conceived of and founded the Midlife Institute at Marymount Manhattan College and was director from 1981 – 1986. The Institute, which offered advice and counsel to women in their middle years as they faced major life changes, was the first of its kind in the U.S. In late 1989, Tully established and funded the Tully-Crenshaw Feminist Oral History Project at the Schlesinger Library, Radcliffe College. The project, named in honor of her mother, Maude Gresham Crenshaw, documents the founding and development of NOW through 24 oral histories. Tully was also on the board of VFA, an organization founded in her Manhattan apartment. In latter years, Tully worked pro bono as a development and fund-raising adviser to feminist undertakings. Tully was educated at Stanford University, the University of Chicago and Wayne University (Detroit). She raised five children. Archives: The Schlesinger Library, Radcliffe Institute, Cambridge, MA.

Tunstall, Tricia (1952 –) As an undergraduate at Yale University, Tunstall was a member (1972 – 1975) of both the two main feminist groups in the area: Women vs. Connecticut and Women's Abortion Referral Service (WARS). WARS later became the Women's Health Education Project. Tunstall helped coordinate the initiatives of both WARS and WHEP and also edited the Women vs. Connecticut newsletter for a significant period of time. From 1974 – 1975, she received funding as the health organizer of the group that opened a clinic, Women's Health Services, in 1975. After the clinic opened, Tunstall coordinated the merger of WHEP and Women vs. Connecticut into an umbrella education and advocacy group, Women's Health Education. During her years in New Haven, CT, Tunstall was also involved in various peace efforts, organized a rally on the New Haven Green (1971) in support of Welfare Moms, and helped coordinate strike support efforts when the Yale unionized workers twice went on strike. Tunstall, who earned her B.A. from Yale in 1974, has two children. (ABS)

Turbin, Carole (1942 –) A college professor (1975 – 2002) and fine artist, Turbin marched for reproductive choice in NYC (1967) and later joined one of the NYRF brigades. She also joined women artists' groups at the Woman's Liberation Workshop in Manhattan. In 1971 she went to England, where she met with feminist writers such as Sheila Rowbotham (then writing *Hidden From History, 300 Years of Women's Oppression and the Fight Against It* and *Woman's Consciousness, Man's World*) and Juliet Mitchell. Turbin has taught at SUNY/Stony Brook, Vassar College, Occidental College and SUNY/Empire State College, Old Westbury. She taught and wrote about 19th century working women because she believed that conventional ideas about gender were distortions based on privileged women's lives. Revealing mid-19th century women trade unionists' family and work lives led her to challenge conventional wisdom and formulate new per-

spectives. She is author of *Working Women of Collar City: Gender, Class and Community in Troy, 1864 – 86* (University of Illinois Press, 1992). In the 1990s, Turbin began studying and writing about the social history of fashion and gender. She holds a B.A. from Queens College, CUNY (1964), and an M.A. (1971) and Ph.D. (1978) from the New School for Social Research. Archives: Tamiment Library, New York University, New York, NY. (ABS)

Turner, Doris Sewell (1925 –) In 1950, Turner was rudely introduced to the world of discrimination against women when she married—then lost her job because wives were not allowed to work. She joined the AAUW and began a lifetime's work on women's issues. In 1967, she became president of the Carbondale, IL, branch of the AAUW. In 1969, she attended the meeting of the International Federation of University Women in Karlsruhe, Germany, where she became interested in the problems of women on a global scale. For the next 12 years, she served on the state board of the Illinois division of the AAUW and on its pubic policy committee. Working with other members, she successfully got an equal-rights-for-women statement into the state's proposed new constitution. Turner also served as state chair of AAUW's Equal Right Amendment committee. She coordinated the work of AAUW members with coalition groups, and went to Washington, D.C., to lobby Illinois senators on the extension of the time limit for passage and to attend a strategy session in the office of the U.S. VP. During this time, Turner also served on the board of ERA Illinois, and founded and led the ERA efforts in her state legislative district. In 1975, Turner founded the women's caucus at Southern Illinois University. She served for two years as its chair, and as a member of the board until 1983. For the caucus, Turner edited the university catalog to remove sexist language, identified the names of courses with sexist titles, and wrote guidelines on the use of non-sexist language (which were distributed to all members of the faculty). She also served as a member of the university's women's studies committee. After moving to Arizona in 1983, she became public policy chair and later president of AAUW Arizona. In 1984, Turner attended a conference in New York City on the United Nations Decade for Women, then in 1985 attended the conference in Nairobi. After the conference, she served for five years on the National Women's Conference Committee. In Arizona, Turner has worked on the board, or as a committee member of the LWV, the Arizona Women's Partnership, the Arizona Governor's Leadership Conference, the ERA committee, the Governor's task force on juvenile corrections, the Phoenix AAUW, the Children's Action Alliance, the Phoenix Women's Commission, the Judicial Performance Review Committee and the Northminster Presbyterian Church. Turner holds a B.A. from the University of Illinois and an M.S. from Southern Illinois University. Archives: Law School Library, Southern Illinois University, Carbondale, IL. (ABS)

Turpeau, Anne Brock — served for nine years as a member of the District of Columbia Commission for Women, and as chair from 1976–1979. Under her direction, the commission successfully advanced revisions of the D.C. code that eliminated sexist language in the civil laws of the district. Turpeau also served as the commission's director of a federally funded research project on sexual harassment, and organized a citywide conference on elder abuse. Following the 1977 National Women's Conference in Houston, Turpeau was elected co-chair of the National Women's Conference Continuing Committee, serving for three terms. She is also an emeritus board member. Turpeau was a member of the U.S. delegation to the U.N. Mid-Decade Conference in Copenhagen (1980) and in 1985 attended the End of Decade Conference in Nairobi as a representative of several non-governmental organizations. Turpeau graduated from West Virginia State College, studied journalism at Ohio State University and went to Baltimore, where she became feature editor of the Afro-American Newspapers. After marrying in 1946, Turpeau moved to Washington, D.C., and earned a master's degree in African Studies from Howard University. She has received numerous awards from organizations recognizing her contribution to the community and to women's rights. These include the Southern Christian Leadership Conference; a Washington section of the National Council of Negro Women; the Center City Community Corporation; the D.C. Democratic Women's Club (for fostering political awareness among women); the D.C. Commission for Women, and both the Myrtle Wreath Award from the Washington area chapter of Hadassah and a citation from its national office. (ABS)

Tuttle, Emily Anne (1929 –) (also known as Emily Anne Staples) has worked in Minnesota for almost four decades to advance women's rights. Appointed to the women's advisory committee of the Minnesota Dept. of Human Rights in 1979 by Governor LeVander, Tuttle was named chair in 1969. She was a member of the Interstate Association of Commissions on the Status of Women (1969–1972), and was a founding member, with Arvonne Fraser, of the MN WPC (1971). A member of the executive committee of Minnesotans for the ERA (1973), Tuttle switched political affiliation to the Democrats after the GOP state platform repudiated choice and the ERA (1973). In 1976, Tuttle made a successful run for the Minnesota Senate and became the first woman from the Democratic Farmer Labor Party to serve. A founding member of the Minnesota Women's Economic Roundtable (1977), Tuttle received several appointments during 1977–1980, including HEW Commission on National Health Insurance and White House Conference on Balanced National Growth. In 1992, she was elected to the Hennepin County Board of Commissioners from the 7th district. Describing herself simply as "a community volunteer," Tuttle holds a B.A. from the University of Minnesota and an M.P.A. from Harvard University–John F. Kennedy School of Government. Archives: Minnesota Historical Society, St. Paul, MN. (ABS)

Tyler, Robin (1942 –) With her comedy partner, Pat Harrison, Tyler formed the first feminist comedy team in the 1970s. Harrison and Tyler appeared in numerous demonstrations, including running into the middle of the field at a Raider/Rams football game where they called for more athletic scholarships for women. This action made headlines all over the world. They are credited with changing women from being the object of humor to being the subject of humor. They starred in the Krofft Comedy Hour on ABC. The duo also recorded two feminist comedy albums and produced the first lesbian record (single), Maxine Feldman's "Angry Atthis." In 1978, Tyler became the first openly "lesbian or gay comic," with the release of her solo album Always a Bridesmaid Never a Groom. She also appeared as the first open lesbian on national television in Showtimes Funny Women Comedy Hour in 1979. Tyler made the original call for the first March on Washington for lesbian and gay rights, and produced the main stages for the first, second and third marches on Washington. She produced 25 outdoor women's music and comedy festivals. She was also co-founder of stopdrlaura.com, the group that successfully removed Laura Schlessinger from TV for calling gays a biological error. Tyler is CEO of Robin Tyler Productions International Tours and Cruises for Women. She is also executive director of The Equality Campaign, the organization fighting for same-sex marriage. On February 24, 2004, she and her partner, Diane Olson, through feminist attorney Gloria Allred, became the first couple to sue for marriage equality in California in 2006. (ABS)

Uebelhoer, Joan Daley (1928 –) began her work for women's rights in the mid 1960s at her church in Fort Wayne, IN. Told by the bishop of her diocese that laymen could help distribute Communion, but that women could not assist, Uebelhoer declared herself "on strike against the Catholic Church," and with other likeminded church women formed Fort Wayne Feminists, a group that survives today/2004. The women helped establish women's studies at Indiana/Purdue University, did a sit-in at a local restaurant that had a room reserved for men only, and helped establish the local abortion clinic and provided escorts into the facility. FWF also created Sisterspace, a meeting place for women that later included a bookstore. Uebelhoer, who taught women's studies for 26 years, helped develop a group of women who did cameo portraits of women in history for schools and other groups. In 1974, she ran successfully for county auditor, cheered on and assisted by feminist volunteers. Uebelhoer has also marched for civil rights and gay rights, and been active in the anti-Vietnam War and anti-Iraq war movements. She has five children. (ABS)

Ulku, Kathleen – See Laurila, Kathleen

Underberg, Thelma Arlene (1931 –) A part-time executive director (2005) of NARAL Pro-Choice South Dakota, Underberg became aware of the inequities women faced during more than 25 years in the clerical/secretarial field. A member of CLUW, she helped form the Sioux Falls Association of Educational Secretaries, where she served as a negotiator with the SF School District, always focusing on pay equity for women. In 1973, she joined other women in the fight for the ERA in South Dakota. Later she lobbied against its rescission. In 1975, Underberg joined the SF LWV, became a board member in 1976, and from 1977 – 1978 was part of its Women and Property Study, which looked at South Dakota marriage/divorce laws. She served as president of SF LWV from 1979 – 1980, and has been a member of NARAL since 1980, serving as VP in 1987, 1988 and 1989. Underberg has also been a member of the South Dakota Advocacy Network for Women since its inception (in 2005 serving as secretary), and a member of NWPC since 1977, serving as board chair in 1983. Underberg has three children.   (ABS)

Unger, Doris (1930 –) (also known as Doris Karasov) In 1969, Unger joined a group of women who became the steering committee for the Twin Cities Chapter of NOW. Unger served as the first VP of PR and as such spoke at meetings of other organizations in the area including the Young Presidents Club, women's clubs and business organizations. She participated in the sit-in at Dayton's (department store) to protest the public dining room that was for men only, and assisted other committees working for the ERA and reproductive rights and to end violence against women. She also provided PR seminars at national conventions. In addition, Unger joined the steering committee for the Minnesota WPC and served as treasurer pro tempore. She attended the first national conference in Washington, D.C., and helped plan for the first meeting of the Minnesota women's caucus at Hamline University. Earlier, as an intern at *The Farmer Magazine* (1965 – 1968), Unger wrote "The Changing Role of Women." As a member of San Francisco NOW (1970), Unger provided support for women who wanted to have non-traditional jobs. She also joined Options for Women Over 40 and served on its board for the next 10 years. Unger, who has four children, says they are "the greatest asset the women's movement could have because their lives reflect my efforts as a feminist. My example showed them that a woman's life is not limited by her biology, but only by her own choices." Unger holds a B.A. from the University of Minnesota.   (ABS)

Urich, Beatrice ("Bede") (1917 –) An artist, Urich was one of the founders of the Milwaukee NOW chapter (1968) and the Santa Monica chapter (early 1970s). While in Milwaukee, she was included in the August 1971 *Life* magazine article by Jane Howard ("Is Women's Lib a Dirty Word in Milwaukee?") that set out to prove there were feminists not just in New York and California, but in the Midwest. Later Urich moved to Los Angeles, where she shared a house with Toni Carabillo and Judith Meuli. In Los Angeles she worked at the NOW office and did layouts for the *NOW Times*. Urich was also featured in Jane Howard's book, *A Different Woman* (1973). In both write-ups by Jane Howard, Urich was using her married name of Yaffe. "When I went to California I all of a sudden realized that wasn't my name and I took myself back to my original name of Urich." Urich's art has won many awards and has been included in a number of juried shows. Her work is in many private collections and corporate offices.   (ABS)

Useem, Ruth Hill (1915 – 2003) A graduate of Miami University, Useem entered the graduate program of sociology and anthropology at the University of Wisconsin in 1937, the only woman graduate student at the school. She completed her dissertation in 1947, but was not allowed to attend her graduation because she was pregnant at the time. In the early 1950s, she and her husband traveled to India to study Westerners living there. While Useem's husband studied the men, she studied their wives, determining that the wives experienced significant stress related to their dependent role. Useem's feminist contribution was that she treated the women as serious subjects, and identified stressors directly related to their status as women. In an article on women's education published in 1963, Useem declared that "sex is not only irrelevant but downright dysfunctional for most of the significant roles of modern society." Useem became an expert on the problems faced by families living away from their native country and a passionate advocate of women's and children's rights—especially "third-culture kids," a concept she developed. Archives: University of Wisconsin, Madison, WI.

Usinger, Jane Elizabeth (1951 –) As a student at Purdue University (1969 – 1974), Usinger was a member of various CR groups and Campus NOW, and served as pro-choice discussion leader at the St. Thomas Aquinas (RC Newman) Center. Also a member of Hoosiers for Freedom of Choice, Usinger distributed anti-Phyllis Schlafly literature when Schlafly began distributing anti-feminist literature to Indiana voters before the 1972 elections. Usinger was also involved in placing ads in local and campus newspapers and arranging meetings and group discussions. As a dorm counselor, Usinger held self-defense and other information sessions for university women. She also assisted in arranging out-of-state abortions, and helped raise funds for these trips. As a member of Seattle NOW and BPW and the Rape Relief Clinic (1974 – 1980), she counseled women post-rape, promoted gender-free help-wanted ads, and led a letter campaign to the IRS demanding that the IRS give space on its 1040 forms for women who retained their birth names or used names other than their married names. She began this assault in 1975 and held the course until the 1040 form was revised in the late 1980s. Usinger was involved in Chicago NOW's sexual harassment training (1980–1983), and was a member of NYC NOW's sexual harassment training group (1983–1986). From 1986–1999 she served as a consultant and educator involved in sexual harassment training, created an AIDS training workshop and sexual harassment training workshops, and developed feminist leadership training. In Charleston, SC, she was involved in a children's center for preventing and treating childhood sexual abuse. Usinger is the author of "Man's Role in the Women's Movement," published in the BPW newsletter (1979). Usinger, who holds a B.S. and Ms. Ed. from Purdue University and an M.B.A. from De Paul University, has two children.

Van Beek, Nancy L. – See Lee, Nancy

Van Deren, Audrey B. (1931 –) An early childhood teacher, Van Deren is the co-author of *Sexism in Education*, published by the Emma Willard Task Force in 1971. Prompted by CR groups to join the Twin Cities Female Liberation Group, Van Deren marched for peace as part of a women's group for the first time in Minneapolis, worked to integrate the *Star Tribune*'s help-wanted ads, and served as a spokesperson for women's liberation on television and radio and at local high schools. In 1994, Van Deren self-published four collections of her feminist poetry, *Organic Fondue*.   (ABS)

Van Deurs, Kady – See Kady

Van Gelder, Lindsy Evans (1944 –) A reporter for the *New York Post*, Van Gelder says, "I was the one who first wrote about women's lib, in 1968, after interviewing Robin Morgan on the first planned protest of the Miss America contest." In 1969 she was fired from the *Post* for refusing to allow her byline to be used on stories she thought trivialized women. Another feminist reporter who came to her defense, Bryna Taubman, was also fired, although both were rehired through the insistence of their union. Van Gelder wrote about feminist topics for mainstream newspapers and magazines, and in the late 1960s joined with several other feminist reporters to found Media Women, a group that was active for several years. She was a contributing editor to *Ms.* and covered emerging issues of the time, such as the ERA, battering and childcare. "I tried to write as often as I could on lesbian issues (it was difficult because it made most of our advertisers break out in hives), and I believe I wrote the first piece ever on why we should be fighting for marriage equality." A 1966 graduate of Sarah Lawrence College, Van Gelder has two children.   (ABS)

Van Horn, Edith ("Edie") (1919 – 1998) A major union leader, political activist and organizer for the UAW, Van Horn had set her sights on graduate school and had accepted a position as a graduate assistant at Oberlin College when the United States entered World War II in 1942. She ended up taking a job at the Goodyear Aircraft Corporation and served as a committeeperson in the UAW. She took several other factory jobs and was laid off in 1958. In 1963 she was appointed International Representative in the UAW's Citizenship Dept. In the 1970s her interests turned to women and minorities. She helped found the NWPC and was a charter member of NOW. She was also a member of NAACP and one of the union women who took part in the founding of CLUW in 1973. Van Horn served as CLUW national coordinator and shared the position of Midwest chairperson with Addie Wyatt of the Amalgamated Meat Cutters and Butchers Workmen of North America. In 1975 the NOW Detroit chapter named her Feminist of the Year. In 1981 she became interested in violence against women, particularly as it relates to pornography. Van Horn was later appointed chairwoman of the subcommittee on rape of the City of Detroit's task force on crime. In 1986, her alma mater, Denison University, honored her as the first recipient of its "Women's Week Alumna Award." Says Marley Weiss, "She was a tremendous inspiration to the women of the UAW, the labor movement more broadly, and all the feminist activists in the Detroit metro area in the 1970s and 1980s."

Vasiliades, Mary Christ (1930 –) was a member of the organizing committee for the August 26, 1970 Women's Strike for Equality march on Fifth Ave. in NYC. She also worked on the 1970 demonstration and takeover of the Statue of Liberty. In 1971, Vasiliades again worked on the August 26 march. Vasilides also lobbied for the ERA in Washington, D.C., in 1971 and 1972, and in 1972 joined the *Majority Report* collective, for which she wrote political news and the "Inquiring Feminist" column. Also in 1972, Vasiliades co-chaired workshops at the NYRF rape conference, and ran to be an alternate delegate for Shirley Chisholm's presidential campaign. In 1973, Vasiliades was elected to the board of NY NOW and served for several years. She established the chapter's first rape prevention committee and worked with other women's groups to change rape law and improve the treatment of victims. She also testified for NOW before a NY State committee that was reviewing rape legislation. In 1976, Vasiliades was a volunteer in the NWPC press office at the Democratic National Presidential Convention in NYC. In addition to this work, Vasiliades has done public speaking for NOW, and written several articles about violence against women and the women's movement for *Lady's Circle Magazine, WomanNews, Nichibei* (a Japanese American newspaper) and other publications. In 1980 she had two plays that dealt with women's issues produced off-off Broadway ("Hidden Agenda" and "Graduation Party"), and in 2001 her book *Sappho Rising* was published. Vasiliades holds a B.J. from the University of Missouri (1953). Archives: Tamiment Library, New York University, New York, NY.   (ABS)

Vaught, Wilma L. (1930 –) A brigadier general, USAF (retired), Vaught not only served her country with a distinguished military career, but worked to open doors and opportunities for women in the Armed Forces. Vaught entered the military in 1957. In the early days of the women's movement Vaught worked in management analysis. At the time women comprised less than one percent of the military. The women's movement was in keeping with Vaught's personal beliefs that women should get equal pay, and particularly equal opportunities. Vaught's accomplishments broke many barriers. For example, military regulations forbade women from being deployed with any mission that involved combat until 1991 (on aircraft) and 1993 (on ships). Nevertheless, she was deployed with her bombardment wing to Guam in 1966 during the B22 bombings of Vietnam. and later assigned to Vietnam from October 1968 to October 1969. Vaught was the first Air Force woman to attend the Industrial College of the Armed Forces. She served as chair of NATO Women in the Allied Forces, and was the senior female military representative to the Secretary of Defense's Advisory Committee on Women in the Services. In 1980, she became the first woman in the comptroller career field to be promoted to brigadier general. When she was in positions of influence in the military, Vaught encouraged women and men to seek more education to be qualified for higher positions in the military. Upon her retirement in 1985, Vaught was one of just three female generals in the Air Force and one of seven female generals in the United States Armed Forces. As president of the board of the Women's Memorial Foundation, she helped establish the Women In Military Service For America Memorial (1997). Vaught's awards include the Defense and Air Force Distinguished Service Medals, the Air Force Legion of Merit, the Bronze Star and the Vietnam Service Award (four stars). She was the first woman to command a unit that received the Joint Meritorious Unit Award. Vaught is the recipient of the 1985 Women Who Made a Difference Award, International Women's Forum (1985) and was inducted into the National Women's Hall of Fame (2000). (ABS)

Veith, Patricia – See Alea, Patricia Veith

Vida, Virginia ("Ginny") (1939 –) served as chair of Lesbian Feminist Liberation and VP of the Gay Activist Alliance in the early 1970s, and was media director of the National Gay Task Force (1976 – 1980). As deputy director of the NYC Commission on the Status of Women (1980 – 1991), Vida promoted policy and legislation to improve the lives of women on Welfare in the city and state. She is the editor of *Our Right to Love: A Lesbian Resource Book* (Prentice Hall, 1978), the first comprehensive lesbian anthology of the new wave feminist era, and *The New Our Right to Love* (Simon & Schuster, 1996). The former executive director of the San Francisco Ethics Commission (1980 – 2004), Vida holds a B.A. from the

University of Illinois and an M.A. from New York University. Archives: The Lesbian Herstory Archives, Brooklyn, NY. (ABS)

Vidina, Bette (1940 –) joined NOW in 1969 and remained a member for the next 35 years. She served as membership chair for Chicago NOW, and offered her house whenever it was needed—including putting up the entire California Marching Band when the members were in Chicago for an ERA rally. She also offered her house for use by Jane, the abortion services network, to perform abortions. As a result of her being active in NOW, Vidina quit her job and went to Northwestern University, graduating in 1977 at age 37. "Not afraid of a little action," Vidina was arrested by the Chicago police when she and some colleagues were illegally posting fliers on telephone poles in the middle of the night. (ABS)

Viggiano, Andrea C. (1947 –) (also knows as Andrea Clendining) A fallen-away Catholic at age 18, Viggiano joined a CR group at age 23. "I saw it was in society's interest to keep us separate from one another, because once the boundaries dissolved, the strength and joy of our sharing and bonding was irresistible." An important issue for the group was sexual liberation. In one of her "funniest and most liberating experiences," Viggiano and her CR group, all married, seeking "ownership of their own bodies," went to a Manhattan pharmacist and demanded dildos. A graduate of Montclair (NJ) State College (1969), Viggiano was the first woman field representative hired by a national pharmaceutical company (Leeming-Pacquin, div. of Pfizer, Inc.) to do a "man's job." She was the only woman among 100-plus reps. "The regional manager told me that the only reason he hired me was because of affirmative action." Viggiano also participated in peace and civil rights demonstrations. An English and journalism teacher at Toms River (NJ) high school (2005), Viggiano has three children. (ABS)

Vivas, Marta (1932 – 1984) A member of NYRF (1970 – 1977), Vivas was one of the groups most steady workers—from its early days through the publishing of its final newsletter in 1977. Vivas was a member of one of the original New York Radical Feminists Brigades, West Village #3, whose members in late 1970 established the NYRF newsletter and treasury, and took on the task of answering mail sent to the P.O. box kept open until 1990 as a source for the NYRF Manifesto and CR guide. Vivas was a conference organizer, speaker, CR group organizer and workshop leader. As a member of Women Against Pornography, Vivas helped organize the 1979 conference. She was also part of the August 26, 1980 march and rally in Times Square; was an instructor of women's history extension courses; a lifelong member of NARAL; and a conscientious-objector counselor for the American Friends Service Committee. She was an owner of a film production company, cine arts, which made documentary

(ABS) indicates Approved By Subject

films about contemporary artists, including Louise Nevelson and Salvador Dali, for colleges and universities, and Herstory Films. She was also a founding member of Women Make Movies. From 1960–1984, Vivas worked as an editor on *Art Forum Magazine, Cousteau Almanac*, and the *American Journal of Nursing*. In this capacity, says her son, Wil Zogbaum, she "spent a lot of time encouraging and editing many other women writers."

Vogel, Lise — Growing up in a progressive NYC family, Vogel learned early that "women lack opportunities they deserve, that male chauvinism is wrong and must be challenged, and that I should think of myself as capable and independent." While a graduate student in art history at Harvard University in the early 1960s, Vogel was stirred by the civil rights movement and spent time in 1964 with the SNCC initiative that sent Northern volunteers into black communities to live and work with local activists. In the late 1960s, along with other veterans of the civil rights movement, Vogel moved into the socialist-feminist wing of the women's movement and joined Bread and Roses in Boston. She participated in the early development of feminist scholarship and teaching in both art history and women's history. But "as a radical with a feminist bent I found myself virtually alone in the elite field of art history." Turning to sociology, she obtained a second Ph.D. from Brandeis University and relaunched her academic career. She is the author of *Marxism and the Oppression of Women: Toward a Unitary Theory* (Rutgers University Press, 1993) and *Woman Questions: Essays for Materialist Feminism* (Routledge, 1995). Vogel is a retired professor of sociology at Rider University. (ABS)

Von Dohre, Bev Jo - See Jo, Bev

Vorhauer, Delia Villegas (1940–1992) was the founder of the Hispanic organization Mujeres Unidas de Michigan (Women United from Michigan). As a result of this effort, six of 48 delegates to the 1977 National Women's Conference in Houston were from Mujeres Unidas. A caseworker, teacher and program administrator, Vorhauer was the first Hispanic chair of the Michigan Commission for the Blind. Earlier, while working for the Michigan Department of Education as a higher education consultant, Vorhauer wrote the first Report on Minorities in Higher Education. Known as the Mason Miller Report, it became the standard for reviewing minority enrollment in Michigan colleges and universities. She was inducted into The Michigan Women's Hall of Fame in 1990.

Votaw, Carmen Delgado (1935 –) Born in Humacao, Puerto Rico, Votaw has been a catalyst for Hispanic women's involvement in the women's movement, and represented their causes and interests in numerous organizations. She was president of the D.C. chapter of the National Conference of Puerto Rican Women in the early 1970s, and later served as president of the national organ-

ization. In that capacity, she participated in the ERA efforts. She attended all the United Nations Conferences on Women (Mexico City, Copenhagen, Nairobi, Beijing and NY). From 1964–1981, she was VP of the overseas education fund of the LWV, and worked with women in Latin America in what became the Women in Development Movement. She was very involved with the NWPC and the Coalition for Women's Appointments during the Carter administration, and served on the international committee of the IWY conference held in Mexico City. In 1976, she was appointed by the administration to be the U.S. representative to the InterAmerican Commission of Women of the OAS (1977–1981), and was subsequently elected president (1978 – 1980). She served as chair of the Coalition for Women and Girls in Education (1993 – 1995), defending Title IX and girls' opportunities in education and sports, and as co-chair of the National Women's Conference continuing committee created after the Houston conference. She also chaired the Human Services Forum of the National Assembly of Health and Social Welfare Organizations, and served on the Independent Sector Government Relations Committee. Votaw has written two biographies of Puerto Rican women (published in 1978 and 1995). Votaw was inducted into Maryland's Women's Hall of Fame, and has received awards from the National Conference of Puerto Rican Women, the Cuban American Women's Association, NASA, the Hispanic Heritage Award for Education and the Institute for Women of Color. A board member (2004) of the Congressional Hispanic Caucus Institute, Votaw also received a Mentor Award from the Public Leadership Education Network, and awards from the National Alliance for Partnerships in Equity, the United Nations Association Human Rights Day Recognition, National Council for Hispanic Women, *Hispanic USA Magazine's* Medallion, FEW, Coalition of Federal Hispanic Employee Organizations, Girl Scouts of the USA, and the U.S. Army Seventh Corps Scroll of Appreciation. Votaw, who earned a B.A. from The American University, also received an Honorary Doctorate in the Humanities in 1982 from Hood College for her work on behalf of women's rights. She has three children. Archives: Hood College, Frederick, MD. (ABS)

Wackwitz, Winnie (1925 –) (also known as Winnie Davis Booksh-Wackwitz) helped organize Women for Change in Dallas, TX (1971). In 1972, she was a co-founder of Dallas and Plano, TX, NOW, where she worked on ERA ratification, textbook critiques, the media and the women and sports committee. She is the author of a textbook, *Fantastic Womanhood!* (Winone Publications, 1972), used to teach a course on women's history from the point of view of religion and its historical effect on the status of women in Western civilization. From 1972 – 1973, Wackwitz was writer and editor of *The Feminist Echo*. In addition, she is the author of *Mystery of the Swamp Lights, The Creature of the Lost Bayou* (1998), a collection of adventure stories about a 10-year-old girl written to inspire girls and to show boys that girls can be brave, strong and take leadership. Wackwitz, who has two children, earned a B.A. from Louisiana State University (1953). She also began taking flying lessons in the 1940s, and earned a commercial pilot's license as well as flight instructor rating. Archives: Women's Library, Southern Methodist University, Dallas, TX. (ABS)

Waddle, Roberta (1943 –) A computer technician, environmentalist and feminst, Waddle says she entered the women's movement because "I needed to get out of the house and was pointed to the League of Women Voters and just kept getting in deeper." Waddle led the land planning survey, recycling conference, at Cumberland County LWV (1974 – 1976); and was secretary, North Carolina LWV (1975 – 1976). She was also an organizer of national NOW rallies in 1985, 1986, 1989, 1992 and 1995. Waddle worked to defeat the anti-ERA state incumbent in 1982, and worked to elect the first woman-of-color representative to Congress from North Carolina in almost 100 years, in 1992. Newsletter editor for "Fayetteville NOW" (1987 –) and "NC NOW" (1989 – 1990), she also ran for public office twice and was the first in her family to earn a college degree. Waddle, who has two children, holds a B.S. from Northeast Missouri University (Truman University) in 1965 and an M.S. from Iowa State in 1968.

Wade, Betsy (1929 –) (also known as Elizabeth W. Boylan) worked as a reporter for the *New York Herald Tribune* in the 1950s, but was fired when she became pregnant. Says Wade, "This aligned my politics, although there was no movement I knew of to join to get justice." She then worked for the Scripps-Howard feature syndicate, the Newspaper Enterprise Association. In 1956, Wade was hired by *The New York Times* as its first female copy editor. She worked on the Style section, city copy desk, foreign desk and national desk, and later wrote a travel column. She was active in the Newspaper Guild, and in 1968 became one of the eight trustees for the Guild-Times Pension Fund. This gave Wade an inside look at the disparities in men's and women's salaries and pensions. She was a founding member of CLUW (1974), and in 1974 became a complainant against *The New York Times* before the State Commission Against Discrimination and the U.S. Equal Opportunity Commission. The resulting federal case, Boylan et al v. *The New York Times*, was settled in November 1978, with cash awards and an affirmative action program with goals and timetables. She was president of the Women's Media Group in 1985 and active in JAWS, the Journalism and Women Sympo-sium. Wade, who has two children, earned her A.B. from Barnard College (1951) and her M.S. from Columbia Graduate School of Journalism (1952). Archives: Papers from Boylan v. *The New York Times* are at the Schlesinger Library, Radcliffe Institute, Cambridge, MA. Papers about CLUW and Wade's personal papers as president of Local

3 and an international VP of the Newspaper Guild, AFL-CIO,CLC, are at the Wagner Archives, Bobst Library, Washington Square, New York, NY. (ABS)

Wadlow, Joan (1932 –) A graduate of the University of Nebraska (1953), Wadlow joined its faculty in the 1960s and founded the Women's Studies Center. She also served as president of the advisory committee for the Lincoln, NE, YWCA (1970 – 1971). Wadlow then moved to the University of Wyoming, where she held positions on the faculty and in academic administration. In the latter capacity, she elevated the status of women's studies from a student organization with volunteer faculty assistance to, step by step, a master's degree program. Her career also included serving as provost at the University of Oklahoma. Wadlow retired from her position of chancellor at the University of Alaska, Fairbanks, in 1999. In addition to her undergraduate degree, Wadlow, who has two children, earned a Ph.D. from the University of Nebraska (1963) and was awarded an M.S. from the Fletcher School of Law and Diplomacy (1956) and a certificate from the Graduate Institute of International Studies in Geneva, Switzerland. (ABS)

Wagner, Marion Kathryn (1943 –) A social work professor and executive director, MSW Programs, Indiana University School of Social Work (2005), Wagner was active in the civil rights and peace movements of the 1960s, and in 1972 joined NOW, where she remains (2005) active. She has served as spokesperson for Oregon NOW to Eastern Oregon (1972 – 1975); co-coordinator, ERA Caravan, and coordinator, ERA rally (1976); president of the Indianapolis chapter (1976 – 1978) and member of the Indianapolis board since 1992. She was also IN NOW state coordinator (1978 – 1981); coordinator of the national NOW conference (1982); and a member of the national NOW PAC (1980 – 1983). In addition, Wagner has served several terms on the Indiana board since 1989. Other work in the 1990s forward includes serving on the national nominating committee, the national lesbian rights committee, as Great Lakes regional director, and as chair of the national elections committee. Wagner earned her B.A. from California State University at Los Angeles (1965), her M.S.W. from San Diego State University (1969), and her Ph.D. from the University of Illinois, Urbana/Champaign (1992). (ABS)

Wagner, Mary Anthony (1916 – 2002) A nun, Sister Mary taught in the theology department of the College of Saint Benedict, a college for women, and became director of the Benedictine Institute of Sacred Theology in 1959. Founded to make serious theological studies available to women monastics, BIST later became the Graduate School of Theology at Saint John's University, where Sister Mary served as dean from 1974 – 1980. She also edited the magazine *Sisters Today* from 1958 – 1979. Sister Mary earned a B.A. from St. Louis University, an M.A.

from Catholic University, and a Ph.D. from St. Mary's School of Theology at Notre Dame. Archives: Saint Benedict's Monastery, St. Joseph, MN.

Wagner, Sally Roesch (1942 –) was an organizer of Daughters of the American Revolution II, a group of women associated with California State University, Sacramento (then Sacramento State College) in 1968. DAR II was involved in direct action, such as a protest at a beauty pageant and bridal fair, and organizing on campus. Out of this group the women's studies program at California State University, Sacramento, evolved, as well as a day care center. In 1969, Wagner taught her first women's studies course, Introduction to the Women's Movement. In the next few years, she developed others, including Women in Psychology; Mother, Woman, Person; Violence Against Women; The Politics of Female Sexuality; and Feminist Theory. "Battles with the administration were especially brutal," Wagner recalls. "We were perceived as dangerous, out of control women who presented a real threat to the stability of the college." Wagner participated in sit-ins and a month-long occupation of the campus after Kent State and Jackson State (1970), and was part of an anti-war group, the 7:00 Coalition, which published a newspaper, *The Capitol Outrage*, out of her home. In 1971, Wagner served on the cultural affairs committee of the first International Women's Day celebration, helping to bring a number of speakers to campus. In the summer of 1973, Wagner met her mother's friend, Matilda Jewell Gage, whose grandmother, Matilda Joslyn Gage, had been an early suffragist. Fascinated by Gage's history, Wagner applied to the History of Consciousness Program at the University of California, Santa Cruz, to study the life of Gage, who had been part of the National Woman Suffrage Association leadership with Susan B. Anthony and Elizabeth Cady Stanton. Wagner graduated in 1978, one of the first two women in the country to receive doctorates for work in women's studies. Wagner founded the Matilda Joslyn Gage Foundation in Fayetteville, NY, to bring Gage back to memory. Wagner, who has two children, earned her B.A. (1969) and M.A. (1974) from California State University, Sacramento, and her Ph.D. from the University of California, Santa Cruz (1978). Archives: Special Collections, California State University, Sacramento. (ABS)

Walbot, Virginia (1946 –) A co-organizer of Women at Yale, Walbot organized women in cell biology and produced a newsletter for the group for three years. She also lobbied Margaret Mead to request $50,000 from the American Association for the Advancement of Science to establish an Office of Women. The Office, whose first leader was Janet Brown, eventually expanded to be Diversity in Science and is a major component of the AAAS. A professor, Walbot earned her A.B. from Stanford and her Ph.D. from Yale. Archives: Women's History, University of California, Berkeley, CA. (ABS)

Walker, Alice (1944 –) Novelist, poet, short-story writer, essayist, educator, biographer and editor, Walker wrote her first volume of poetry, *Once* (1968), based on her unplanned pregnancy and abortion while in college. This experience also gave Walker a new sense of herself as a woman, and she "began to understand how alone a woman is, because of her body." Walker became internationally known with the 1982 publication of her novel *The Color Purple*. The search to integrate race and gender issues took a giant step forward when, in a preface to her 1983 collection of essays, *In Search of Our Mother's Gardens*, Walker described women of color as "womanists" rather than feminists. The word womanist, she explained, grew out of the black folk expression, "You acting womanish," which meant that the youngster was engaging in outrageous, audacious or willful behavior. Her novel *Possessing The Secret Joy* (1992) and her collaboration with director Pratibha Parmar on the documentary film "Warrior Marks: Female Genital Mutilation and the Sexual Bind of Women" (1993) both addressed African womanist issues. Walker returned to an American setting with her novels *By the Light Of My fathers Smile* (1998) and *The Way Forward Is A Broken Heart* (2000). Walker was born the last of eight children to sharecroppers in rural Eatonton, GA. At age eight, she was shot in the eye with a BB gun. The family's isolation and poverty meant that the injury went untreated for a week. Walker lost sight in that eye and was disfigured until corrective surgery when she was 14. Walker went on to study at Spelman College in Atlanta (1961 – 1963) and Sarah Lawrence College in Bronxville, NY (1963 – 1965). She has taught at Jackson State University (1968 – 1969) and Tougaloo College (1970 – 1971). She was a Radcliffe Institute fellow (1971 – 1973), and was a lecturer at Wellesley College (1972 – 1973) and at the University of Massachusetts in Boston (1972 – 1973). She is a member of the board of Sarah Lawrence College. Walker was awarded a Guggenheim Fellowship in 1977 – 1978 and the American Book Award and the Pulitzer Prize (1983) for *The Color Purple*.

Walkowitz, Judith Rosenberg (1945 –) A member of a feminist study group at the University of Rochester (1967), Walkowitz completed her dissertation in 1974 under the title "We Are Not Beasts of the Field: Prostitution and the Campaign Against Contagious Diseases Acts, 1869 – 1886." This was later published as *Prostitution and Victorian Society: Women, Class and the State* (Cambridge University Press, 1980), which won the Berkshire Conference Book Prize in 1980. She co-presented (with Daniel Walkowitz) part of her research at the first Berkshire Conference of Women's History (1972). This segment was later published in *Feminist Studies* (Winter/Spring, 1973) and in *Clio's Consciousness Raised: Historical Perspectives on Women*, edited by M. Hartman and L. Banner (Harper and Row, 1974). In 1974, she became one of two history editors of *Feminist Studies*, the first feminist scholarly journal. She served on the program committee of the Berkshire Conference on Women's History (1974 and later) and assumed the presidency (1987–1990). Walkowitz helped organize the women's history program at Rutgers University. In 1990, she founded and organized the women's studies program at Johns Hopkins University. Walkowitz, who has one child, holds a Ph.D. from the University of Rochester.   (ABS)

Wallace, Adriane Ann (1941 –) (also known as Ann Di Leo and Ann Wallace) A Wall Street entrepreneur, Wallace was a 26-year-old stock broker in Denver, CO, in 1967 when she spoke to several men's civic groups, identifying herself as a feminist and urging them to hire women for "men's" jobs. When she moved East in 1968, she joined NY NOW, where she served in various positions, including board member, chair of the legislative and political committee, and vice president. In 1968, given the assignment of resuscitating the Equal Rights Amendment, Wallace first called the NWP and spoke with Alice Paul, who provided encouragement, intelligence on enemies and friends of the ERA, literature, and a current list of women's groups supporting the ERA. Using the names of those groups, Wallace created a letterhead for the Ad Hoc Committee for the ERA; wrote a motivational pamphlet and put it together with packets of ERA background information for all NOW chapters and other feminist groups; and worked with over 100 reporters and editors to encourage them to cover the ERA. In 1969, Wallace's ERA subcommittee, working with Beth Dater, organized a bus trip to Washington, D.C., for constituent lobbying with members of the Senate Judiciary Committee and an all-media ERA press conference. This was the first event of the second wave to lobby for and publicize the ERA. Throughout 1969 and 1970, Wallace's group pressured Congress with letters and demonstrations and gave community talks on the ERA. In 1970, Wallace was approached by senior members of NOW NY about running for president, which she declined because of her Wall Street career and because NY NOW "already had a brilliantly effective president in Ivy Bottini, who was willing to run again." Wallace and 15 other members resigned in protest against the chapter's January 1971 election, which they considered to be unfair and resulted in Bottini's defeat, and against changes in the chapter's leadership and procedures that damaged the legislative and political committee's effectiveness. They explained their reasons in an alternative newsletter titled "NOW... And Then." Later that year, Wallace and Carol Turner coordinated the panel on violence and the women's movement. Wallace continued with her pioneering Wall Street career and in 1983 founded a successful economic advisory firm, which provided publications and services to major investment and financial institutions around the world. (ABS)

Wallace, Michele (1952 –) Describing herself as "inclined to revolutionary politics and radical gestures of one kind or another at least since the seventh grade," Wallace says she became a black feminist at age 18. Reflecting on this in her essay "To Hell and Back: On the Road with Black Feminism in the 60s & 70s," she says, "Some unimaginative types, most persistently in the provinces, continue to believe that a black woman must be brainwashed by white culture in order to voluntarily call herself a feminist. I find it difficult to imagine how women who are not feminists stand themselves." Becoming a black feminist in the 1970s had much to do with Wallace being the daughter of "the ambitious, fiercely militant and driven black artist Faith Ringgold." Wallace was deeply affected by the Miss American protest of 1968. During the 1970s, she accompanied her mother on various feminist art actions, including those at the Museum of Modern Art and the Whitney Museum, and with her co-founded Women Students and Artists for Black Art Liberation. In 1971, Wallace published her first black feminist essay, "Black Women and White Women," in *Women's World* under editor Kathie Sarachild. Wallace was also co-founder, with Pat Mainardi, Irene Peslikis and Marjorie Kramer, of the leftwing publication *Women and Art*. After graduating from City College of New York (1974), Wallace began working as a book review researcher at *Newsweek*. At the same time, she became a founder of the National Black Feminist Organization. Also in 1974, Wallace published two essays in the *Village Voice*: one about being a black feminist, called "Anger in Isolation: A Search for Sisterhood," and the other about growing up as a "black American princess" in the Harlem of the 1950s and 1960s." In 1976, Wallace was an organizer, with poet Pat Jones, Margo Jefferson and Faith Ringgold, of the Sojourner Truth Festival of the Arts, held at the Women's Interarts Center. Wallace later began working on her seminal book *Black Macho and the Myth of the Superwoman*, published in 1979. She is also author of *Invisibility Blues: From Pop to Theory*, which contains a number of her articles published in the 1970s. In 2004, Wallace authored *Dark Designs and Visual Culture*. As of this writing, she is working on *Black Feminist Generations*, a series of photo-essays on her mother, her grandmothers and herself. Archives: Schomburg Collection, Harlem, NY.   (ABS)

Wallace, Simone (1945 –) A bookstore owner and activist, Wallace first explored feminism in the early 1970s at the Los Angeles Women's Center on Crenshaw Blvd., California. There she participated in CR groups and gay-straight dialogues. After coming out, Wallace, with her sister-in-law, Adele Wallace, and a friend, Gahan Kelley, opened Sisterhood Bookstore in West Los Angeles (1972). Sisterhood stayed in business on Westwood Blvd. for 27 years. Like other women's bookstores, Sisterhood was not only a purveyor of books, music and periodicals by and for women, but also a de facto community center where both residents and out-of-town visitors could find information on events and resources in the Los Angeles women's and lesbian communities. It was also a space for authors to give readings of their works. With the advent of large chain bookstores, Sisterhood, like other women's and independent bookstores, fell victim to a successful mission to make these materials widely available. During her time with Sisterhood, Wallace was also active in the Westside Women's Center, the Westside Women's Clinic, the Radical Feminist Therapy Collective, a Jewish Feminist study group, the Fat Underground and the No on 6 Campaign, which helped defeat an anti-gay statewide amendment in 1978. (ABS)

Walsh, Alida (1933 – 2006) A visual artist working in sculpture, film, video and multimedia, Walsh made powerful statements about women—revealing their exploitations and celebrating their history—early in the second wave. In 1968, she was a member of Women Artists in Revolution. She was also in the world's first all-women art exhibition (called X12) in 1970 in New York City, a time when the outside world ignored and laughed at feminist artists. Undaunted, the women proclaimed, "The old game is dead. We will begin again. We have paid our dues in the art world, first as artists and doubly as women." Walsh's best-known works include the 12-foot, 1973 sculpture, Earth Mother Goddess, made of steel, fiberglass and polyester resin, which was exhibited in the 10 downtown loft shows, P.S. 1, and published in the Goddess issue of *Heresies*. Women Bound and Unbound, a multimedia performance utilizing film and four slide projectors beamed onto a dancer moving to music, was funded by the Ms. Foundation and presented at the 1977 National Women's Conference in Houston. In the 1973 Erotic Art Show at the Women's Interart Center, she constructed a nine by twelve-foot bas-relief sculpture and projected a 16mm film, "The Martyrdom of Marilyn Monroe," on the sculpture. A major film, which took her three years to create, is "Happy Birthday, I'm 40." Kate Millett said, "Alida Walsh's film is brave, braver than one is when watching it, braver than a woman has dared to be before. We have all been cowards, and she gives us courage." The award- winning film toured the United States and international festivals. Walsh is one of the founding members of Women Artists Filmmakers Inc. (1973). She served as the executive director of WAF and curator of the programs for 12 years. She studied at the Art Institute in Chicago, received a B.F.A. from Northwestern in 1955 and an M.F.A. from San Diego State University in 1956. She came to New York City in 1958 and studied at the Art Students League. Walsh was an assistant professor at Montclair State University for 26 years. Archives: Donnell Library, New York, NY. (ABS before death)

Walsh, Ruth G. - See Kirsch, Ruth G.

Walton, Jean (1914 –) With three degrees in mathematics —a B.A. from Swarthmore College, an M.A. from Brown University and a Ph.D. from the University of Pennsylvania—Walton arrived at Pomona College in 1949 and stayed for the next 30 years. With an initial appointment as dean of women, she became dean of students during the 1960s, and in the 1970s played a leading role in building women's studies at the college. In 1971 she spent a sabbatical semester driving across the country looking for answers to a basic question: What has been the impact of the new feminist movement on the educational experience of women students? The answers she found to that question were very helpful in her work at the college during the last years before her retirement in 1979. (ABS)

Wandrei, Karin Evon (1953 –) An administrator/therapist/ social worker, Wandrei entered the women's movement in 1972 when she helped develop feminist intervention training at Bay Area (CA) Women Against Rape. Active in the early feminist mental health movement in the San Francisco Bay Area, Wandrei wrote her B.A. thesis on lesbians and therapy (1975) and her doctoral thesis on suicidal women, and worked as a member of the Berkeley/Oakland Women's Union, a socialist-feminist organization. Wandrei earned her B.A., M.S.W. and D.S.W. from the University of California, Berkeley. (ABS)

Wang, Lonny Myers - See Myers, Lonny

Wangen, Nancy Register (1935 –) As a teacher in Minnesota in 1970, Wangen educated people about equal rights and the need for change. She organized and made presentations for numerous civic groups, education associations and institutions, offering information on gender equity, the ERA and civil rights. In 1973 – 1974, she organized a community effort to bring change to local schools by setting up human relations certification classes for teachers and administrators. She was then hired by her local school district to write and implement the first affirmative action plan, addressing gender and racial equity in both employment and curriculum. The plan, written for the Hopkins (MN) School District, was published in a national superintendents journal. From 1974 – 1978, she and Mary Peek traveled throughout Minne-sota to present teacher/administrator workshops in numerous school districts. Peek, a white-haired grandmother, and Wangen, a suburban mom, mystified some residents of rural areas because the two defied stereotypes about feminists. Through subsequent years, Wangen earned a Ph.D. from the University of Minnesota, then worked in college and university administration. She offered university workshops for school administrators and developed training and curriculum materials for the Minnesota Education Association and the Minnesota Department of Education. She is (2006) retired, but continues to do human-rights volunteer work. (ABS)

Ward, Jill (1944 –) became an activist at Mount Holyoke College, where she initiated a campaign that ultimately brought an end to parietal hours. After graduation, she motorcycled through the Middle East and across North

Africa, then spent a year camping in Central America. Upon her return, she went to work as a management-consultant trainee with Arthur Andersen, but quickly realized it was too corporate for her. Her career as a feminist began in 1970 when she took on the role of treasurer and an organizer of the August 26th Women's Strike for Equality march in NYC, a demonstration estimated at 50,000 strong and now seen as a key event in second-wave history. Two years later, Ward used her early experience helping her mother run a family-owned golf and swim club in Lincoln Park, NJ, to open a restaurant in Greenwich Village (NY). Mother Courage, which Ward co-owned with Dolores Alexander, was the first feminist restaurant in the United States. It became a popular meeting place for feminist writers, thinkers and activists from all over the world. She sold the restaurant after seven years "due to a bad case of movement burn out." Ward, who became an ecofeminist in the late 1970s, was arrested in an antinuclear demonstration. After closing Mother Courage, Ward switched careers, and went to work for *Time* magazine, where she was instrumental in securing domestic-partnership benefits for lesbians and gay men, the culmination of a five-year grievance struggle. A copy-desk supervisor, Ward retired in 2001. (ABS)

Ward, Nancy (1926 –) A retired school librarian (2005), Ward spearheaded, with Anne Ewing, the effort in California to make elementary and secondary textbooks portray the contributions and problems of women and minorities, not just those of white males. After reviewing thousands of textbooks in the early 1970s, speaking before innumerable groups, and finally getting the help of the law firm Public Advocates, the two succeeded in forcing the California State Department of Education to comply. Because California was the largest buyer of textbooks in the country, publishers were forced to change the books nationwide. A member of Berkeley NOW, Ward earned her M.A. from the University of California, Berkeley. (ABS)

Ware, Caroline Farrar (1899 – 1990) A historian and scholar of note, Ware taught history at Vassar College and social work at Howard University and American University. She was a member of the President's Commission on the Status of Women (1963), and of the commission's committee on home and community. In addition, Ware attended the NOW organizing conference in Washington, D.C., in October 1966. Although Ware was not initially attracted by the suffragists or feminism, her work in history focused on incorporating industrialism and the experiences of the working classes into the broader picture. This led to her publication of *The Cultural Approach to History* (1940), for which she served as editor, and later *The Early New England Cotton Manufacture*, in which she explored the convergence of manufacturing interests, market conditions, work culture and women's lives. In 1927, Ware married Gardiner Means, but took the highly

unusual step of retaining her own name. In 1979, Ware was honored at a Smith College conference devoted to the history of New England's working class. Archives: Schlesinger Library, Radcliffe Institute, Cambridge, MA.

Ware, Cellestine (1940 –) An African American writer, Ware wrote one of the first books to discuss the connections between the women's movement and black women, *Woman Power: The Movement for Women's Liberation* (Tower Books, 1970). In a chapter discussing the black woman's point of view, she noted how black people had always valued light skin and that "entering the women's movement at this time may seem like a re-entry into the old farce of pretending to be white." She also thought that black feminism would be another attempt by the power structure to divide black men and women. Nevertheless, she revealed how black women felt devalued and degraded in their own culture, being called "black bitches" by men who sought out white women.

Ware, Cynthia Sanborn (1912 – 2002) Born in Tennessee, Ware was a lifelong feminist. She joined the Independent Women's Organization and the League of Women Voters in the 1940s and was active in the NWPC and the LA WPC in the 1960s and 1970s. Ware campaigned for the ERA and joined Planned Parenthood, NARAL and the Reproductive Action League in their fight for reproductive choice. Ware also worked to advance civil rights and became a Democratic Party activist.

Warren, Karen J. (1947 –) Considering herself a street philosopher, Warren has helped facilitate women's-issues book clubs and feminist presentations to nonprofit organizations such as the AAUW. She has taught philosophy to children of all ages, but especially grades one through four, exploring interconnections among feminism and ecology. Since 1972, Warren has initiated innovative courses on women's issues and contemporary moral problems to underserved populations. In 1972, for example, she founded what she believes to be the second high-school philosophy curriculum in the U.S. at Amherst (MA) High School. And in 1974 she taught critical thinking and ethics for both women and men inmates at the Berkshire County House of Corrections (MA). Warren is best known for her pioneering work in ecofeminist philosophy. Her books include *Ecofeminist Philosophy: A Western Perspective on What It Is and Why It Matters* (2000). Warren, who is a professor of philosophy at Macalester College, is (2005) working on a first-of-its-kind textbook that pairs 15 women philosophers with their male contemporaries from the 4th Century B.C.E. to the present. She holds a Ph.D. from the University of Massachusetts, Amherst (1978), and has one child. (ABS)

Warrior, Betsy (1940 –) was a founding member of Cell 16 in 1968. She served as co-author of *Journals of Female*

Liberation (1968 – 1972), and contributed to grassroots public education and CR about discrimination and violence against women, economic exploitation of women, and the international character of women's oppression. Warrior is also co-author of two editions of *Houseworker's Handbook* (1973 – 1975), an analysis of women's economic contribution and economic worth and status, and author of nine editions of *The Battered Women's Directory* (1975 – 1985). In 1976, Warrior facilitated the oldest support group for battered women. The group incorporated feminist consciousness raising, practical information and emotional support. The group continues to exist as of 2005. Warrior, who is self-educated, has been a factory worker and as a librarian. She has supported tenants rights, Welfare rights and civil rights. She has one child. Archives: The Schlesinger Library, Radcliffe Institute, Cambridge, MA; and the Cambridge Women's Center Library, Cambridge, MA. (ABS)

Warshaw, Sandy (1933 –) was an early member of NOW. She facilitated a feminist forum in 1969 and participated in the August 26, 1970, Women's Strike for Equality march on Fifth Ave., New York City. She served on the board of OWL, 1990 – 1996; chaired the NYC chapter from 1989 – 1994, and convened OWL's Northeast Regional Organization in 1987. Warshaw was active in the peace movement, championed community involvement in the NYC public schools during integration battles, and developed parent involvement and empowerment programs for Head Start and day care. A breast cancer survivor (1975), she co-founded SHARE (Self Help for Women with Breast and Ovarian Cancer) in 1977. Warshaw joined Congregation Beth Simchat Torah, NYC's synagogue for LGBT Jews, in 1992; has coordinated feminist programming since 1995, and has been a board member since 1996. From 1999 – 2004, she served as director of policy, education and advocacy for SAGE (Services and Advocacy for GLBT Elders); From 2002 – 2006 she was a board member of the American Society on Aging and co-chair of its LGBT Aging Issues Network (LGAIN). Warshaw was awarded 4th degree black belt in Seido Karate in 2005 at age of 72. She is active in the National Women's Martial Arts Federation and competed in Gay Games 1998 and 2002. In 1994, Warshaw was honored by NYC NOW with the Susan B. Anthony Award. In 1997 she was inducted into the City University of New York Women's Activist Archives. (ABS)

Warshow, Joyce P. (1937 –) Psychologist, teacher and filmmaker, Warshow has been a member of the Association of Women in Psychology since 1973. This grassroots organization helped establish Division 35 (The Psychology of Women) within the APA. Warshow has also been a member of the Association of Gay Psychologists, which brought about the inclusion of Division 44 (The Society for the Psychological Study of Lesbian and Gay Issues) into the APA. In the 1970s, Warshow conducted work-

shops (with Adrienne Smith) for heterosexual therapists working with lesbian clients. From 1973 – 1995, she was a member and then president of the Women's Psychotherapy Referral Service, which matched clients with therapists with a feminist orientation. Its educational program consisted of papers and workshops presented at the New School for Social Research in New York City and other programs sponsored by the New York Commission on the Status of Women. Warshow taught college courses in the 1970s – 1980s, including the psychology of the handicapped and the psychology of women. She facilitated a workshop at an international women's conference in Costa Rica titled What Price Feminist Counseling?, and has conducted sensitivity training for police to help them better understand gays and lesbians. She began a multicultural committee on Long Island (NY) as part of the East End Gay Organization. She co-edited the book *Lesbians at Midlife: The Creative Transition* (1991); and produced and directed two films about older lesbian activists, "Some Ground to Stand On" (1998) and "Hand on the Pulse" (2002) as part of Activist Productions. She is a former board member of the Feminist Therapy Institute and a member of Old Lesbians Organizing for Change and Senior Action in the Gay Environment. Warshow received awards from both EEGO and Legacy for her work. Warshow holds a B.A. from Brooklyn College, an M.A. from New York University and a Ph.D. from Yeshiva University. Warshow studied filmmaking at Women Make Movies, Film and Video Arts, and with Tami Gold at Hunter College. Archives: The Lesbian Herstory Archives, Brooklyn, NY. (ABS)

Washburn, Janey (1933 – 1995) was one of 18 women artists whose works were exhibited at A Lesbian Show, curated by Harmony Hammond in New York City (1978). Washburn's piece dealt with internalized sexism and was composed of the self-deprecating words women use to describe themselves. A Lesbian Show is generally considered to be the first important lesbian art exhibition. Both a painter and writer, she was also part of an early artists support group that met regularly at the Peacock Café in New York City. She later moved to Santa Fe, NM, and became an official member of an Indian tribe.

Washington, Jacquelin E. (1931 –) A pioneer in affirmative action and employment discrimination, Washington was a co-founder in Detroit of New Options Personnel. Organized in the mid 1970s, the company successfully sought both nontraditional trade jobs and management-level jobs for women. After joining NOW in the 1970s, Washington became chair of the minority women's task force. She also served on the NOW LDEF board for 12 years, and as president in 1983. As a result of her decades of feminist activities, Washington came to believe that a source of funding for women's and girl's projects was needed, and so became a co-founder and president of the Sojourner Foundation (1990). Washington, who has three children, earned her B.A. from Fisk University (1951) and her M.S.W. from Wayne State University (1964). (ABS)

Wasserman, Elga Ruth (1924 –) Born in Berlin, Wasserman is a chemist, lawyer, author and lecturer. In 1968, as special assistant to Yale's president, she agreed to oversee the admission of women to Yale College. During that period, she served as adviser to the Women's Action Program of the Department of Health, Education and Welfare, as a member of the advisory committee on the status and education of women of the Association of American Colleges, and as co-founder of HERS. She left Yale in 1973 to enter law school, and later became an outspoken advocate for women's rights, serving on many boards and commissions including the Mayor's Commission on Affirmative Action for the City of New Haven (1980s – 1993), and the Connecticut Judicial Gender Bias Task Force (1988 – 1991). Since 1996, Wasserman has lectured and written about women's issues. In addition to numerous articles, she has published several books, including *Women in Academia: Evolving Policies Toward Equal Opportunities* (Praeger, 1975), for which she served as co-editor; and *The Door in the Dream: Conversations with Eminent Women in Science* (Joseph Henry Press, 2000). Wasserman, who has three children, earned her B.S. from Smith College (1945), her Ph.D. from Radcliffe College (1949) and her J.D. from Yale Law School (1976). Archives: Schlesinger Library, Radcliffe Institute, Cambridge, MA. (ABS)

Waters, Anne Schulherr (1949 –) (also known as Anne Schulherr) Teacher, writer, philosopher and poet, Waters was an organizer of the New Mexico Women's Forum (1975); a member of the original constitutional task force for the National Women Studies Association, for which she wrote the preamble (1978 – 1979); an active member of the Society for Women in Philosophy, Midwest (1979 – 1989); and founder and president of the American Indian Philosophy Association. She assisted in an NEH grant summer seminar at the University of Illinois, Chicago Circle, to develop multicultural materials for use in women's studies courses; and served as faculty in various women studies programs, including those at Washington University in St. Louis (1979 – 1982), The University of New Mexico (1983 – 1984), Purdue University (1985 – 1986), and Texas Woman's University (2000 – 2001). The recipient of the Pergamon Press/NWSA dissertation scholarship in honor of Ruth Bleir, Waters wrote her dissertation on the law, morality and politics of surrogacy, producing the most extensive bibliography on the topic up to 1992. She also served as co-editor of *Hypatia, A Journal of Feminist Philosophy: Indigenous Women in the Americas* (2003), edited *American Indian Thought: Philosophical Essays* (2004) and co-edited *American Philosophies* Anthology (2004). She is editor of Rodopi Press Value Inquiry Book Series

special series on indigenous philosophies of the Americas. Waters, who has raised four children and is an Indigenous American Indian, Seminole Nation, earned her B.A. from the University of New Mexico (1978), her M.A. from Washington University (1982), her Ph.D from Purdue University (1992) and her J.D. from the University of New Mexico (1992). (ABS)

Waters, Chocolate (1949 –) was a co-founder of the Denver, CO, radical women's newspaper *Big Mama Rag*, which first appeared in 1972. A regular contributor of articles and a long-running column, "News From Around the Country" (later changed to "Scraps from Mama's Table"), Waters also served at various times as production manager, distribution manager, features manager, advertising volunteer and, in 1975, editor. When an unfavorable article about *BMR* and its staff appeared in the *Denver Post*, Waters responded with a long prosy poem, "To The Man Reporter from the *Denver Post*," that was widely reprinted and later became the title of Waters' earliest book of poems. That book was one of the first collections of lesbian poetry to be widely distributed and sold in the U.S. Waters is author of two other books of poetry: *Take Me Like a Photograph* (Eggplant Press, 1977) and *Charting New Waters* (Eggplant Press, 1980). By the mid 1970s, Waters had learned how to be a performance poet, "long before the term was popularly used or known. I count this work as a contribution to the women's movement because I performed throughout the United States as a feminist and/or lesbian feminist performance poet," she says. In 1982, Waters moved to New York City, where she continued to perform for women's groups, lesbian/gay groups and others. In addition, she was a featured performer onstage at the lesbian/gay pride march of 1983. Waters earned her B.A. from Lock Haven State University (1971). Archives: The Lesbian Herstory Archives, Brooklyn, NY. (ABS)

Waterstreet, Margaret Grace (1953 –) attended the first feminist meeting in the Quad-Cities (Rock Island and Moline, IL, and Davenport and Bettendorf, IA), which *The Rock Island Argus* covered by printing a photo of the women shown only from the waste down, legs crossed below their skirts. In 1973, Waterstreet became the first woman to graduate with a B.S. in biology from St. Ambrose University (magna cum laude). She helped start a women's honor society there. As a medical student at Northwestern University, she helped form a year-long CR group, and in 1975 joined NOW, working to include the ERA in the Illinois Constitution. From 1978 – 1979, Waterstreet was the first woman manager at Stewart Warner Corp. (automotive parts), and in that capacity incorporated images of women and minorities in its brochures. In 1981, Waterstreet hosted an 11-member OR NOW delegation at her home. She later helped publicize Judy Chicago's The Dinner Party in Chicago, "even though I do not quilt." Waterstreet also organized over 90 volunteers to double the size of The Dinner Party quilt with their contemporary triangular pieces recognizing personal heroines. As a board member of the Women's Advertising Council (1979 – 1981), Waterstreet recruited women members and managed speakers. From 1983 – 1985, she was newsletter editor, University of Chicago Women's Business group, and until she was disabled in 1992, actively hired, promoted and mentored women employees. From 1993 – 2001, Waterstreet periodically handled phone calls for Chicago NOW and organized lobbying trips. She has written 10 feminist plays produced from Los Angeles to NYC. In addition, she has organized support groups for women with health problems. Politically active, Waterstreet has been a board member of Advocates for the Handicapped (1979 – 1982), marched against Anita Bryant for gay rights, demonstrated and wrote letters on behalf of migrant workers, and for 30 years volunteered on feminists' elections campaigns, including Senator Carol Mosley Braun's successful 1992 run. In addition to her B.S., Waterstreet earned an M.B.A. from the University of Chicago (1983). Archives: University of Illinois, Chicago, IL. (ABS)

Watkins, Joan C. – See Casale, Joan Therese

Watkins, Virginia ("Ginny") Smith (1939 –) worked for decades to empower women both as a member of NOW and through her social services career. She convened and served as first president of Des Moines NOW (1970 – 1971). During that time, she established a letter writing campaign for federal childcare legislation, got momentum going for maternity leave, and was chapter fundraiser for the ERA. From 1971 – 1972, Watkins was a founding member of Minnesota WPC, and became secretary and then president of Twin Cities NOW. She served on the women's advisory committee to the Minnesota Department of Human Rights (1973 – 1975) and was elected MN NOW state coordinator (1975 – 1977). In that capacity, she organized NOW chapters in other Minnesota cities and towns, and established the MN NOW legislative program, working on issues such as maternity leave, overhaul of rape legislation and the right to change one's name. In 1977, Watkins was elected to NOW's national board, serving six years. She was elected NOW's Midwest regional director in 1978, serving for five years, and from 1978 – 1979 served as president of the Minnesota Children's Lobby. In 1979, Watkins successfully lobbied for passage of Minnesota's first childcare sliding fee legislation; from 1980 – 1983, she served as a member of NOW's national PAC; and beginning in 1984 began chairing NOW's national employment committee. Watkins, who has two children, is the author of "Can Moral Values Go Too Far?" an article on the need for liberalized abortion law published in *Engage* (1970), a magazine of the United Methodist Church. She is also author of "Women on the Move in Minnesota" (*Response*, 1972), and "Diagnosis Drives Women Crazy" (*New Directions for Women*, 1987). Watkins, who holds a B.A. from Drake University, says her husband, David, took full responsibility for their children on countless weekends and evenings so she could be an active feminist. He was also a charter member of Des Moines NOW, enabling the group to have the necessary 10-person membership. Archives: Minnesota History Center, St. Paul, MN, and University of Iowa Women's Archives, University of Iowa Library, Iowa City, IA. (ABS)

Watson, Susan M. – See Meredith, Susan Rebecca

Wattenberg, Esther (1921 –) In 1956 Wattenberg was the founder and co-president of the Democratic Women's Forum, the progressive faction of the Minnesota Democratic Farmer-Labor Party. In 1965 Watternberg wrote an article entitled "Present But Powerless," regarding women in both political parties. The article received attention locally in Minnesota and became the impetus for improvement of the status of women within parties. Wattenberg was active in major Minnesota feminist organizations during their formative years, including DFL Feminist Caucus, MN WPC, and NOW. A professor from the University of Minnesota, her teaching interests are in the field of children and family social services policies and programs. She has published works on integrated services, paternity issues, kinship care, school-linked services, and children in neglecting families. Archives: Minnesota Historical Society, St. Paul, MN. (ABS)

Wattleton, Faye (1943 –) In 1978, Wattleton became the youngest person and the first woman named president of Planned Parenthood Federation of America, a position she held until 1992. In that capacity, Wattleton is described as having played a critical role in defining the national debate over reproductive rights and health. Wattleton holds a B.S. in Nursing from Ohio State University and an M.S. in Maternal and Infant Care, with certification as a nurse-midwife, from Columbia University. In addition, she has received 12 Honorary Doctoral degrees. Her numerous honors and awards include being named Outstanding Mother by the National Mother's Day Committee, and the Jefferson Award for the Greatest Public Service Performed by a Private Citizen. Wattleton is also the recipient of the Congressional Black Caucus Foundation Humanitarian Award, the Women's Honors in Public Service Award from the American Nurses Association, and the American Humanist Award. Planned Parenthood honored her with its Margaret Sanger Award in 1993; in the same year she was inducted into the National Women's Hall of Fame. In addition, Wattleton was selected by *Money* magazine as "one of five outstanding Americans who project the forces that will shape our lives in the year 2000," and *Ebony* named her as one of the 100 most fascinating black women of the 20th century. In 1996, Ballantine Books published her memoir, *Life on the Line*. (ABS)

Wayne, June Claire (1918 –) is an internationally acclaimed artist who reinvigorated printmaking in the U.S. when, in 1959, she founded the Tamarind Lithography Workshop with funding from the Ford Foundation. Tamarind widely influenced the aesthetic, ethical and economic aspects of all printmaking and provided Wayne with a podium from which her views on the problems of artists could be heard, with special emphasis on women and minority artists. Some of her essays are still used in university curriculae: The best known, she says, is "The Male Artist as Stereotypical Female" (*College Art Journal*, 1973), which has been reprinted in many other publications over the years. In 1973, she wrote and hosted a KCET/PBS TV series on professional problems of visual artists, and about the same time created the Joan of Art seminars, which enabled young feminists to present their works and themselves more effectively in the museum, gallery and teaching sectors of the art world. Rutgers University Press published a definitive *Catalogue Raisonne* of her art in 2005. Wayne is visiting professor of research at Rutgers Center for Innovative Printmaking and Paper. She lives primarily at her Tamarind, Los Angeles studio. Archives: Department of Special Collections, University of California, Los Angeles, CA.   (ABS)

Weathers, Brenda (1936 – 2005) The executive director of Women's Shelter of Long Beach (CA), Weathers was one of the first lesbian/feminists to join the Gay Liberation Front during the year after Stonewall, and helped organize the first lesbian/feminist group within that organization. She marched in the first Gay Pride Parade down Hollywood Blvd., and later helped organize the breakaway of the lesbian/feminists from GLF to an independent organization meeting at the Women's Building in Los Angeles. Weathers also demonstrated with the GLF to end the APA's designation of homosexuality as a mental illness. In addition, she helped support the founding of the first gay community services center in her area, and was later instrumental in changing the center's name to Gay and Lesbian Community Services Center. In 1974, Weathers and Lillene Fifield wrote the grant for the founding of the Alcoholism Center for Women; she then became that agency's founding director. The center, she said, "was the first openly lesbian program to receive federal funds, and for many years held the distinction of winning the largest grant ever given to any GLBT organization." Weathers, who held a B.A. degree, was also active in peace and anti-war movements, and was an early supporter of NOW and the ERA.   (ABS before death)

Weathers, Carolyn Sue (1940 –) began her activism for women and gay rights in 1970, when she participated in a rally in San Francisco's People's Park to celebrate the 50th anniversary of women's suffrage. That year, Weathers protested against the American Psychiatric Association for declaring homosexuality a disease that should be cured by shock aversion therapy. Active with the GLF, Weathers put on workshops on feminist issues for the men of GLF, participated in many of its agit-prop events, and helped develop its Gay Women's Speakers Bureau. Also in 1970, Weathers joined the lesbian feminists at the Women's Center in Los Angeles, working in outreach, giving speeches and "hell-raising throughout the L.A. area." With Kaye Pender (also known as Kate O'Brien), Weathers wrote "The True Story of Lesbianism by Frank Straight," which she read at various conferences, festivals and workshops. In 1974, Weathers set up the first library of the Alcoholism Center for Women (Los Angeles). As a printer at ACW, she produced materials for the 1977 campaign against Anita Bryant and against the Briggs Initiative. In the early 1980s, Weathers was a member of the original Southern California Women for Understanding, and in 1984 was the writer asked by Ann Bradley to inaugurate the Lesbian Writers Series at A Different Light Store in Los Angeles' Silverlake area. She has written and published *Leaving Texas: A Memoir, Shitkickers and Other Texas Stories*, and *Crazy*. In 1986, she co-founded, with Jenny Wren, Clothespin Fever Press, dedicated to publishing books by lesbian writers. The press continued until 1996. Also in 1987, Weathers and Wren formed the Los Angeles Committee to Free Sharon Kowalski. (Kowalski had been severely brain damaged in a car accident and was prevented by her family from seeing her partner, Karen Thompson. In 1989, Thompson was finally awarded legal custody of Kowalski.) A librarian at the Los Angeles Public Library, Weathers holds an M.L.S. degree. Archives: Gay & Lesbian Archives, Los Angeles, CA.   (ABS)

Weaver, Minnie Bruce – See Pratt, Minnie Bruce

Webb, Marilyn Salzman (1942 –) An author, journalist and feminist organizer, Webb was co-organizer and founder of the first women's CR group in Chicago (1966). In 1967, she co-organized the first women's CR group in Washington, D.C., and in 1968 was key organizer of the Sandy Springs Conference. Also in 1968, Webb co-organized the Lake Villa Conference. She was also an original founder of Washington Women's Liberation (1967 – 1968). In 1970, Webb was one of five women (Reggie Siegel, Alice Wolfson, Caroline Nickerson and Judy Spellman) who disrupted the U.S. Senate hearings on the birth control pill. Webb participated in the Jeannette Rankin Brigade, and spoke at (and was loudly jeered by New Left men during) the Counter-Inaugural Demonstration at President Nixon's inauguration. In 1970, Webb was a founder of *Off Our Backs*, a feminist news journal that continues to publish, and she served as a writer and editor. She also co-founded "what may have been the first women's studies program at a college, Goddard College, in 1970," and served as its executive director. In 1975, Webb co-launched Sagaris Institute. She is (2005) distinguished professor of journalism and co-chair of the journalism program at Knox College. Webb, who has one child and three stepchildren, earned her B.A.

from Brandeis, her M.A. from the University of Chicago, and her M.S. from Columbia University.   (ABS)

Webber, Karen – See Mulhauser, Karen

Webb-Vignery, June L. (1937 –) Part of the prototype team assigned to achieve racial balance in the Houston (TX) Independent School District (1967 – 1970), Webb-Vignery became aware of the connection between racism and sexism and "began to search out opportunities to bring change to our society regarding women." In Arizona in 1974, she was selected to participate in the development of the City of Tucson's affirmative action program, and was charged with creating programs for women. In that capacity, she developed the first women-in-management course in the U.S., which was implemented in 1975 through the University of Arizona College of Business, Department of Management. Webb-Vignery subsequently taught the courses (1977 – 1985). She also participated in the University of Arizona's women's studies program curriculum integration project (1981 – 1984), and development of Pima Community Colleges Gender Awareness Program (1986 – 1990). In 1975, Webb-Vignery was appointed to the Arizona Women's Commission by Governor Raul Castro, and chaired the task force on employment to 1980. In 1981, as part of the commission's work, the Arizona Women's Hall of Fame was established and them implemented by Webb-Vignery and Allison Hughes, Tucson Women's Commission. In 1991, Webb-Vignery was co-author, with M. Elizabeth Lynch, of *Everybody's Business: Winning the Workforce 2000 Challenge* (Garland Publications), which focuses on race and gender issues and organizational change. Webb-Vignery has been associated with the Arizona WPC for more than two decades, and in 2003 served as vice chair. In 1991, she received the YWCA's Women on the Move Award, and in 2001 was the recipient of the Mim Morris Women Making History Award from the Arizona WPC. Webb-Vignery, who has four children, holds an A.A., a B.A., an M.A. and a Ph.D.   (ABS)

Weber, Diana Athena (1942 –) A tennis pro, Weber has worked since the 1960s to improve the lives of women and adolescent girls in prisons and after their release. In 1967 she treated and helped women in the court system as a clinical social worker at Jewish Family Services in Philadelphia. After moving to Louisiana in 1969, Weber worked as a volunteer setting up Narcotics Anonymous groups in St. Gabriel Women's Prison in Louisiana, and from the late 1960s into the 1970s, volunteered to obtain jobs for women prisoners upon their release from prison, helping them network and introducing them to the women's movement's philosophy, ideals and values. From 1974 – 1975, Weber voluntarily worked with battered women, teaching them tennis and assertiveness skills. Weber entered the women's movement through the civil rights movement (1969). Working in Mississippi

with the Charles Evers Foundation as a white female volunteer, she helped register many African Americans to vote, going door to door in Canton County and running registration tables at a time when that was an extremely dangerous thing to do. She holds a B.A. from Newcomb College and an M.S. from Southern University.   (ABS)

Weber, Rose Minna (1955 –) An attorney, Weber became radicalized when she was 15 during the Vietnam War. She was a member of the national staff, Women's National Abortion Action Coalition (1970 – 1972); a student negotiator, University of Pennsylvania anti-rape sit-in (1973), when all demands were met; and a founding member, Penn Women's Center (1973). In 1974, Weber was a founder, "Amazon Country," a lesbian feminist radio show, and in 1975 was the first student to graduate from the University of Pennsylvania with a major in women's studies. From 1978 – 1981, she served as co-director, Women's Resources, consultants to women's nonprofits and businesses, and from 1981 – 1985 was executive director, Ars Femina Inc., publishers of women's artwork. Weber earned her B.A. in 1975 and her J.D. in 1996, both from the University of Pennsylvania. She went back to law school at age 38, incurring a large debt, so she could practice public interest law for the rest of her life.   (ABS)

Webster, Sally Beyer (1938 –) was a member of the Heresies Collective, beginning in the mid 1970s, and from 1979 – 1981 served as director of the AIR Gallery in Soho (NY), the first women's alternative gallery. Since 1985, Webster has been a professor of modern and contemporary art history at CUNY. She is the author of *Eve's Daughter/Modern Woman: A Mural by Mary Cassatt* (University of Illinois Press, 2004). Webster, who has two children, also worked with her husband to organize the reading of the names of the soldiers who were killed in Vietnam. This 24-hour, round-the-clock effort was held at Riverside Church in NYC, 1968 – 1969. Webster holds a B.A. from Barnard College, an M.A. from the University of Cincinnati, and a Ph.D. from CUNY.   (ABS)

Weddington, Sarah Ragle (1945 –) Best known as the attorney who successfully argued Roe v. Wade, Weddington is also widely known as a high ranking official in the administration of President Jimmy Carter, where she served as assistant to the President and adviser on women's issues. She also served as general counsel of the United States Department of Agriculture, and later was director of the Texas Office of State-Federal Relations. A pioneering female student of law, woman lawyer and state legislator, she was one of just five women in her law school class. As a student, she was active in a feminist CR group, and later helped establish and do legal work for an abortion referral group (1969), the Women's Liberation Birth Control Information Center. Eventually, this group decided to challenge the Texas abortion law, one of the most stringent in the nation, in court. The group felt strongly that the presenting attorney should be a woman, and Weddington was chosen. Having never done trial work, or even handled a contested case, Weddington was very reluctant, but finally agreed to file the case and donate her time. Roe v. Wade was launched. Victory came on January 22, 1973, when a U.S. Supreme Court majority opinion affirmed the points in Weddington's argument. In 1972, Weddington was elected to the Texas House of Representatives from Austin. As a legislator, she was instrumental in the passage of bills involving a state equal rights amendment, maternity rights for teachers, rape law reform and equal credit. Weddington is (2005) an adjunct professor at the University of Texas, Austin. She serves in a number of volunteer positions, including that of a board member for the Foundation for Women's Resources, which created The Women's Museum: An Institute for the Future. Weddington graduated from McMurry College, earned her law degree from the University of Texas, and holds Honorary Doctorates from McMurry University, Hamilton College, Austin College and Southwestern University. She is the author of *A Question of Choice* (G.P. Putnam and Sons, 1992). (ABS)

Weesner, Katherine Ann (1945 –) (also known as Katherine Ann Betz) was one of four women let go from a computer programming job in the 1960s because her supervisor "wanted a man because he was supporting a family." Told by one of the women that this was against the law, Weesner filed with the EEOC and won, then sued and lost in court. Says Weesner, "This was the first suit for women under the 1964 Civil Rights Act in Minnesota." Weesner then joined Women Against Male Supremacy and began picketing the Minneapolis and St. Paul newspapers to stop their sex-segregated help-wanted ads. Responding to their complaint filed with the Minnesota Human Rights Department, the Minnesota human rights commissioner said publicly that he would "no more accept a complaint from WAMS than he would from the Black Panthers." In a meeting with the Minnesota attorney general, Weesner and the other women explained their case. The next week, the papers announced they were changing their policy and listing all jobs (even the men's jobs) as "Help Wanted." Twin Cities NOW formed shortly after that incident, and Weesner served as its first president. Weesner, who has four children, holds a B.S. degree and is involved in social science research. (ABS)

Weinbaum, Batya Susan (1952 –) was founder (1990s) and, as of 2005, remains editor of *Femspec*, a feminist journal dedicated to creative works in fantasy fiction. She is also author of *The Curious Courtship of Women's Liberation and Socialism* (South End Press, 1978); *Pictures of Patriarchy* (South End Press, 1983); *The Island of Floating Women* (Clothespin Fever Press, 1993); *Leslie F. Stone: A Case Study of Minority Women Writing Popular Culture* (University of Wisconsin Press, forthcoming); and *Islands of Women and Amazons: Representations and*

Realities (University of Texas Press, 2000). Her original work on the role of women in the transition to socialism in the Chinese economy was considered breakthrough. Weinbaum's first works were published in the magazine *Second Wave* (1971). From 1972–1975, she was involved in the women's caucus of Union for Radical Political Economics in NYC. There she served as political education and action coordinator, helping research and publish pamphlets such as "Women in Health" and "The Food Crisis Packet." From 1972–1975, Weinbaum published the photography of women in Chile and Cuba in *Liberation News Service*. Also in the mid 1970s, Weinbaum spoke to groups such as Salsa Soul in NYC, and worked with the women in the Grail and National Council of Churches, organizing economic CR seminars for women. She gave one of the keynote addresses at the Socialist Feminist Conference in Antioch at Yellow Springs (1975). Weinbaum later worked with the group at Michigan Women's Music Festival that initiated The Oasis as an alternative healing space "the year a woman was taken off the land and dropped into a mental hospital." Weinbaum has published numerous articles and poems in *Heresies*, and published on the search for utopia, after visiting women's lands, in the anthology *Mythmakers: Women in Search of Utopia*, edited by Elaine Baruch and Ruby Rohlich (Schocken). In addition, Weinbaum was co-founder, Feminist Mothers and Their Allies task force, NWSA; a member of the women's comprehensive program curriculum committee, Cleveland State University; and initiator of the multicultural task force, initiating a multicultural literature minor, at CSU. She has been a reader/reviewer for *Signs*, *Utopian Studies*, *NWSA Journal*, *Studies in Jewish American Studies*, *Utopian Studies*, *MELUS*. She is (2005) a member of the editorial board of *Women and Judaism*. Weinbaum holds a B.A. from Hampshire College (1976), an M.A. from SUNY Buffalo (1986), and a Ph.D. from the University of Massachusetts (1996). Archives: The Lesbian Herstory Archives, Brooklyn, NY. (ABS)

Weiner, Maurine – See Greenwald, Maurine W.

Weis, Judith Shulman (1941 –) was the convener (1970) of the Essex County (NJ) NOW chapter, serving as VP and then president (1972). She focused the chapter's efforts on employment and education issues. The group challenged the sex-segregated help-wanted ads in the local papers; assisted women with job-related issues; and, after Title IX was passed, filed the first set of complaints about the schools' tradition of tracking boys into shop and girls into home economics. Before the government did anything, all the schools changed their practices so that all students took both shop and home economics. In 1972, when a girl was kicked off the Little League team in Hoboken at the insistence of the national Little League, Weis's group filed charges to the state based on New Jersey Civil Rights law, which had a "public accommodation" section. Because Little League played on park land, not on its own private fields, it was "public accommodation" and NOW won its case. When Little League appealed, NOW won each successive case as it worked its way through the court system. Weis was also involved behind the scenes as a non-tenured faculty member in women faculty discrimination charges at Rutgers University relative to salaries and promotions (early 1970s). "We also won this one and got considerable notice," she says. In addition to this work, Weis, who has two children, has been active in the Sierra Club and has used her science background (marine biology and toxicology) to increase environmental protection and support development of marine reserves. A professor of biology, Weis holds a B.A. from Cornell and an M.S. and Ph.D. from New York University. (ABS)

Weisberg, Ruth (1942 –) An artist who works primarily in painting, drawing and large scale installation, Weisberg was founder of the Women's Caucus for Art in Southern CA in 1975. When the Women's Building was established in Los Angeles in the mid 1970s, she and Judy Chicago had the first show there. In 1979, a Weisberg lithograph was presented to Georgia O'Keefe as part of the National Women's Caucus for Art ceremony honoring O'Keefe at the White House. Weisberg was also the first woman artist to be president of the College Art Association (1990), the largest art association of its kind in the world. Weisberg became dean of fine arts at the University of Southern California in 1995. She is (2005) an active exhibitor and is represented in museum collections including the Metropolitan, the Whitney and the National Gallery. (ABS)

Weisman, Leslie Kanes (1945 –) is (2005) a professor emerita and the former associate dean of the School of Architecture at New Jersey Institute of Technology, which she joined as a founding faculty member in 1975. She began her career as an academic in 1968 at the University of Detroit, where she was the only woman member of the architecture faculty. At the same time, Weisman was involved in founding the Oakland County, MI, chapter of NOW. In 1974, when Weisman was deciding that the stress of not seeing meaningful connections between feminism and architecture was taking too high a toll, she was asked to speak at a conference on women in architecture, the first ever held in the U.S., organized by a group of women architecture students at Washington University in St. Louis. At that conference, she proposed to three other attendees that they start a feminist school of their own. One year later, the first session of The Women's School of Planning and Architecture was held in Biddeford, ME. WSPA became an internationally known and widely acclaimed summer program open to all women studying, working or interested in the environmental design professions and trades. The school was open for six years (1975 – 1981). Says Weisman, "I have discovered that feminist pedagogy is particularly relevant to the field of architecture, because in its making, use and design, the built environment shapes human experience, identity and consciousness, and reinforces assumptions about culture and politics." Weisman was a founding member (1977 – 1981) of Networks: Women in Architecture, NYC; was a founding mother (1977) of the Astraea Lesbian Action Foundation, NYC; and a founding member of North Fork Women for Women Fund, Inc. (1992). Weisman is co-editor, with Diana Agrest and Patricia Conway, of the anthology *The Sex of Architecture* (Harry N. Abrams, 1996), and author of *Discrimination by Design: A Feminist Critique of the Man-Made Environment* (University of Illinois Press, 1992) and numerous other feminist publications. *Discrimination by Design* is considered a primary source in the pioneering field of feminist spatial theory, and has been translated into a Chinese language edition. It has won two awards for contributions to human rights. She holds a B.F.A. and M.A. Archives: The Sophia Smith Collection, Smith College, Northampton, MA. (ABS)

Weiss, Marley S. (1949 –) A law professor, Weiss was one of the first women law faculty members at the University of Maryland School of Law. Earlier, she had been a member of Barnard Women's Liberation (1968 – 1971); served as second woman editor on the *Columbia Daily Spectator* (1970 – 1971); and was the first woman managing editor of the *Columbia Yearbook* (1970 – 1971). At that time, she participated in the *Ladies' Home Journal* sit-in, and as a member of the Barnard College and Columbia University collective, served as co-author for a segment of the *Ladies' Home Journal* summer supplement on feminist issues, published in partial settlement of the sit-in demands. A member of Harvard Women's Law Association (1971 – 1974), Weiss helped lobby the Harvard Law faculty to address women students as "Ms." The group also organized the women students to demand hiring and retention of women tenure-track faculty, more women law students, and more respectful treatment of women students in the classroom. With other leaders of the Women's Law Association, Weiss devised a policy to pool recruitment efforts with black, Latino/a, and Native American student organizations to maximize recruitment of non-white male applicants. The group also pressured the law school placement office to ban law firms that asked women interviewees/applicants about their use of birth control. In 1974, Weiss became first woman attorney in the general counsel's office of the International Union, UAW. From 1975 – 1982, she served as a dissident activist, and later a leader of the Feminist Federal Credit Union, holding various offices including member of the credit committee, member of the board of directors, pro bono general counsel, and VP. In the mid 1970s, she helped organize a fundraiser benefit for Joanne Little and Inez Garcia, both accused of murder for defending themselves against domestic violence. In 1979 – 1984, Weiss filed and litigated on behalf of the UAW a series of pregnancy discrimination cases against each of the Big Three domestic auto manufacturers. In 1983 – 1984, as associate general counsel of the UAW, Weiss filed EEOC charges and later the complaint in federal district court for the case that eventually went to the Supreme Court and established that women could not be excluded from jobs on the basis of actual or potential reproductive health hazards. In 1997, Weiss wrote (in Hungarian) and published in Hungary an article comparing Hungarian sexual harassment law in the workplace to U.S. and European Union law on this subject. Weiss earned her J.D. from Harvard Law School in 1974. (ABS)

Weisstein, Naomi (1939 –) Professor emerita of psychology, SUNY, Buffalo, a Guggenheim Fellow, and a Fellow of the AAAS, Weisstein published over 60 papers on visual cognitive neuroscience in such journals as *Science, Vision Research* and the *Psychological Review.* She also has written extensively on women, psychology, feminism and culture, but is perhaps best known for the essay "Kinder, Kirche, Kuche as Scientific Law: Psychology Constructs the Female" (New England Free Press, 1967). Widely reprinted here and overseas, the article is characterized as having started the discipline of the psychology of women. A lifelong feminist whose militance was sharpened by her experiences in male-dominated science at Harvard, Weisstein counts as her first women's liberation demonstration the "distraction" she held in front of Harvard's Lamont Library, still men-only in 1962. Told that women were barred from the library because they distracted serious scholarship, she and her friends slithered in front of the library windows in skin-tight leotards, playing a clarinet and two tambourines. "Distraction," they shouted. "We'll show you distraction!" In addition, Weisstein was a founder of the Chicago Westside Group (1967), the first independent women's liberation group in the emerging movement, and CWLU (1969). She was organizer of and comedian and keyboardist in the Chicago Women's Liberation Rock Band (1970 – 1973). In 1970, she helped found American Women in Psychology. In 1972 Weisstein was a founder of the women's caucus of the Psychonomic Society, and in 1980 was a founder of a caucus of the Association for Research in Vision and Ophthalmology. Weisstein has also worked as a cartoonist and comic. Her work has appeared in *The Voice of the Women's Liberation Movement* (1968 – 1969), *The New University Conference Newsletter* (1969), and *The Rogers' Spark* (1970). Her comic monologues have appeared in *Cultural Correspondence* (1978), *Pulling Our Own Strings: Women's Humor* (Indiana University Press, 1980), and *National Forum* (1999). Her article "Why We Aren't Laughing Anymore" was the cover story for *Ms.* magazine in 1973. Weisstein holds a B.A. from Wellesley College (1961) and a Ph.D. from Harvard University (1964). Earlier, Weisstein was active in New Haven, CT CORE (1963), Chicago SNCC (1965) and Students for a Democratic Society. Archives: Schlesinger Library, Radcliffe Institute, Cambridge, MA. (ABS)

Weitzman, Lenore J. — is best known for her award-winning book *The Divorce Revolution: The Unexpected Social and Economic Consequences for Women and Children in America* (Free Press, 1985) which led to the passage of 14 new laws in California and influenced national legislation on child support enforcement. Weitz- man was fortunate to be a graduate student in Sociology at Columbia University in the late 1960's when her mentor, William J. Goode, introduced her to Betty Friedan and to the intellectual excitement of analyzing the social structure of gender differences in American society. In 1970 Weitzman was awarded a post-doctoral fellowship at Yale Law School, and was invited to teach in the Yale Sociology Department. She developed the first course on "Women in American Society," which sparked considerable interest because 1970 was the first year that Yale admitted women as undergraduates. Her pioneering multimedia publications on sex-role socialization in picture books and elementary school textbooks, which she co-authored with her students, grew out of that course and became a best seller for the Feminist Press. At the same time, as a post-doctoral fellow at Yale Law School, Weitzman focused on family law and began analyzing the legal structure of marriage and divorce. Other books include *The Marriage Contract: Spouses, Lovers and the Law* (Free Press, 1981), *The Economic Consequences of Divorce: The International Perspective* (co-edited with Mavis Maclean, Oxford, 1991). She analyzed gender in the Holocaust and co-edited *Women in the Holocaust* (Yale, 1998). Weitzman's involvement in feminist organizations includes being a founding member and first VP of Sociologists for Women in Society; a board member of NOW LDEF, where she co-chaired the educational committee with Sheila Tobias; a board member of the Feminist Press; and from 1995 – 2000, chair of the board of Women for Women International. As a professor at the University of California, Stanford University and Harvard University, Weitzman has been a dedicated teacher. In 1990 she was awarded Harvard's Phi Beta Kappa Distinguished Teaching Award. Among her many honors are a Guggenheim Fellowship, membership at the Institute for Advanced Studies, Princeton, and a Fulbright Fellowship in Israel. Weitzman is (2006) the Clarence J. Robinson Professor of Sociology and Law at George Mason University (VA). (ABS)

Welch, Frank Prince (1919 – 2004) A VFA board member, Welch was a founding member of South Shore, Long Island (NY) NOW (1972), and served as treasurer in 1974. He also co-chaired the human sexuality committee, assisted with the monthly newsletter, and was involved in the masculine mystique committee, CR and ERA rallies. Welch also attended the national NOW conventions in 1973, 1974 and 1975. He served as photographer for the Atlantic City NOW national Miss America march (1973), and also attended relevant meetings where women were banned, such as an American Red Cross fundraiser, getting information and photos. A professional photographer who served in the U.S. Navy in WWII as photographer for Camp Peary, VA, Welch was retired from Brookhaven National Laboratories, Long Island. He and his wife, feminist Grace Welch, had three children. In a questionnaire sent to Welch prior to his death, Welch wrote, "I have been honored and happy to be a member of the women's revolution affecting future generations."

Welch, Grace Ripa (1924 –) From 1964 – 1973, Welch was a member of the executive board of the Long Island Advertising Club, serving as chair of women's issues in advertising. After joining Nassau (NY) NOW in the early 1970s, she served as publicity director and member of its executive committee (1970 – 1972). In 1972, Welch was a convener of the Long Island Feminist Coalition and coordinated its first press conference at Hofstra University. The event included an action against the Colonie Hill Convention Center, Hauppauge, and the American Red Cross for sex discrimination in their annual fundraiser. In 1973, Welch was one of nine women and one man (her husband) who founded the South Shore (Long Island, NY) chapter of NOW. She served two terms as president (1974 – 1976). During her tenure, the chapter held the first Human Sexuality Conference on Long Island (Dowling College, 1974), the first assertiveness training classes at the Women's Center, Oakdale, Long Island, and the first masculine mystique committee, facilitating the first co-ed-CR groups; the chapter also held the first CR meeting with editors of *Newsday*, and the first discussion of women's images in advertising at a Long Island Advertising Club general meeting, Plainview, Long Island. Welch ran for the Central Islip school board in 1976, campaigning for equal funds for girls in education and sports as directed by Title IX. Welch's research showed that the sports budget for male students was $43,000, while girls received only $300. From 1976 – 1979, Welch co-chaired the employment committee of South Shore NOW. In 1984 she planned and coordinated the 7th Annual Women & Careers Conference for New Directions Resource Center at Southampton College; and in 1985 planned and coordinated Hauppauge High School's Adult Education Conference for Working Women. Welch was voted Woman of the Year by the Bay Shore chapter of BPW in 1986. She was elected president of Mid-Suffolk NOW in 2004. Welch has three children. Archives: Women's History of Seneca Falls, NY. (ABS)

Welch, Mary-Scott ("Scottie") (1919 – 1995) A writer and editor, Welch was born in Chicago, graduated from the University of Illinois and was in the first group of Waves commissioned by the Navy in World War II. In the 1970s in NYC, she was the coordinator of NOW's rape prevention committee and on the advisory board. She also served on the advisory board of Cornell University's Institute for Women and Work. Welch wrote many articles for E*squire*, *Redbook*, *Ladies' Home Journal* and *Woman's Day*. Welch promulgated the idea of networking as a way for women to advance their careers at a time when the "old boy" network still served men, but women were left to their own devices. In 1980, her book *Networking: The Great New Way for Women to Get Ahead*, was published by Harcourt, Brace, Jovanovich. She was a strong supporter of the VFA and helped in its early organization. She had four children. Archives: Schlesinger Library, Radcliffe Institute, Cambridge, MA.

Wellisch, Karen – See Fishman, Karen

Wellman, Judith (1943 –) was one of the first members of the women's liberation group at the University of Virginia in 1970. Earlier, she was editor of a progressive newspaper, *The Virginia Weekly* (1968 – 1969), and worked on the underground newspaper *The Sally Hemings* (1969 – 1970). Involved in the scholarship of women's history, Wellman was co-founder of a Charlottesville research group in 1970. Wellman was also professor emerita of history at SUNY Oswego, and former park historian at the Women's Rights National Historical Park in Seneca Falls, NY. She is the author of *The Seneca Falls Women's Rights Convention: A Study of Social Networks.* (ABS)

Wells, Nancy M. (1930 –) In 1969, Wells was a member of a CR group in Los Angeles that worked to pass the ERA. She also marched for union women and worked on a curriculum guide for the history of women in labor. In 1973, Wells chaired WEAL, and in 1975 was elected to the board of the National Council of Teachers of English. In addition, she participated in the Comparable Worth project, which sought to change the adage from "Equal Pay for Equal Work" to "Equal Pay for Comparable Work." This, she says, "was an Act to consider more opportunities for women in all occupations and include factors of expertise, energy expended and management qualifications (for housewives to get positions)." While California law stipulated that a married woman needed her husband's, brother's or father's approval to get a credit card, Wells demanded and received a credit card in her own name. Wells was assigned to a textbook assessment committee for California, and "not only read the text, but counted the pictures to ensure that boys making cookies could wear aprons and girls could help paint the house." Wells has also supported women's right to choose, and is involved with Women in Prison committee. Wells, who has two children, earned her B.A. in 1962 and her M.A. in 1975. Still teaching part-time at a local community college (2005), Wells is active in the historical society, is a docent at the local lighthouse, is politically active, and is a volunteer for a quadriplegic. (ABS)

Wells-Roth, Linda (1939 –) Wells-Roth was a member of the Shasta Heights, OH, chapter of NOW from 1972 – 2000. She served as convener/president, CR group leader and chair of the education task force. She joined the founding board of the Cleveland Women's Counseling

Service (1973), serving as chair for the marriage and divorce committee, and on the 24-hour hotline for spouse abuse and rape. In 1976, she coordinated five NOW chapters in New Jersey into Essex County, NJ, NOW, with a central office, hotline, rape support, the first incest assistance in the area, and a major CR task force. Wells-Roth has two children and holds a B.A. (ABS)

Wells-Schooley, Jane (1949 –) served as officer of NOW ERA PAC, as national VP action of NOW (1979 – 1982), and as a board member (1977 – 1979). Wells-Schooley testified before Congress and state legislative bodies, served on the Leadership Conference on Civil Rights, the national committee on pay equity, the national committee for women and girls in education, and the Consumer Advisory Council of the American College of Nurse-Midwives, and was an officer of the national NOW ERA committee. She was national leader and organizer of the July 9, 1978, ERA march in Washington, the largest march in American history for women's rights. A member of the PA NOW board of directors, Wells-Scholley was elected delegate to Democratic National Convention (1980), was a member of the Platform Accountability Commission, Democratic National Committee (1982), and executive director of the PA State Democratic Party (1983). She was also an elected delegate to the 1988 National Democratic Convention. She co-founded the Lehigh Valley Rape Crisis Council and founded the Women's Council of Realtors, Lehigh Valley Chapter. Co-owner of Dutch Springs and the Allentown office of Keller Williams Real Estate in Allentown, Wells-Schooley received the Athena Award-Business Woman of the Year (1991) from the Lehigh Valley Chamber of Commerce, and has received awards for excellence in business and for real estate achievement. She holds a B.A. (1969) and M.A. (1973) from Pennsylvania State University, where she has served on the faculty (1971 – 1977). She was also elected to the board of directors of the National Association of Women Business Owners in the 1980s. Her work has been cited in the Congressional Record, *The New York Times*, *Los Angeles Times* and other media outlets. (ABS)

Wenig, Mary Moers (1926 – 2003) was one of the first women law professors to be heavily involved in women's issues. She began teaching law in 1971, after having practiced law for 20 years in prestigious New York law firms. She left her position at one law firm, where she had served from 1951 – 1957, and a second, where she had served from 1957 – 1960, because they refused to grant maternity leaves. When she joined Skadden, Arps, Slate, Meagher and Flom (1960 – 1971), she was the company's only female lawyer. From 1973 – 1979, she was on the board of the Connecticut Women's Educational and Legal Fund, which she helped found, serving as president for three years. CWEALF was one of the earliest organizations fighting sex-based discrimination and working for women's legal rights. From 1985 – 1991, Wenig was a commissioner on the State of Connecticut Permanent Commission on the Status of Women. A major focus of Wenig's work was marital property reform, to make sure that married women received an equitable share of marital property. Beginning in the mid 1970s, Wenig published and lectured widely on this and other topics relative to women. Wenig received numerous awards, including the Distinguished Service Award, Advocates for the Advancement of Women in Law, from St. John's University School of Law (1976); Distinguished Service Commendation, Connecticut Bar Association Committee on Women (1977); UNA-USA of Connecticut Outstanding Women of Connecticut, Award for Contributions to Equality (1987); University of Bridgeport School of Law, Women's Law Association Honoree (1990); and Greater Bridgeport YWCA Salute to Women Honoree (1990). As a woman, Wenig was an active, pioneer member of numerous honorary associations, especially the American Law Institute and the American College of Trusts & Estate Counsel, and chair of many committees in professional associations of lawyers and law professors. She earned her B.A. from Vassar College (1946) and her J.D. from Columbia University School of Law (1951), where she was editor of the *Law Review*.

Wenkart, Henny (1928 –) is a poet, translator, writer and scholar. Born in Vienna, Austria, Wenkart began her feminist work at Radcliffe College in the mid 1950s in a group that was really consciousness-raising, but before that term was coined. As part of that group, she agitated for and achieved goals for women workers and graduate students in the university, such as the first day care center. She joined NOW as soon as it began in Boston. Her work there included the writing and distribution of a deep questionnaire about the sharing of housework between working couples. In 1980, Wenkart moved to New York, where her work has been with the Feminist Jewish Women's Resource Center. She originated and co-edited the landmark anthology *Which Lilith? Feminist Writers Recreate the World's First Woman* (1998). Since the 1990s, she has been editor of *The Jewish Women's Literary Annual*. In 2005, she was honored by the National Council of Jewish Women, New York. Wenkart, who has three children, earned her A.B. from Pembroke (1949), an M.S. from Columbia (1950), an M.A. from Radcliffe (1957) and a Ph.D. from Harvard (1970). (ABS)

Wenning, Judy (1944 –) Elected as an openly lesbian candidate, Wenning served as president, NYC chapter of NOW, from 1973 – 1974. She developed and chaired the women and sports committee for national NOW, and traveled throughout the country to speak at colleges and to communities and professional groups about the importance of Title IX. Wenning appeared on "The Barbara Walters Show" and "The Phil Donahue Show" to promote passage of Title IX and other issues related to women and sports. Wenning was an active member of NY NOW's education committee, which published a booklet on sexism in education, and was a member of the coordinating committee for the women's march down Fifth Ave., 1971 and 1972. A psychotherapist with a master's degree in counseling and a postmaster's in clinical social work, Wenning has been a board member of the Lambda Legal Defense and Education Fund and was a member of Lesbian Feminist Liberation. She developed and directed the first community-based, multi-service AIDS project in NYC, which served women, men and families.   (ABS)

Werden, Frieda Lindfield (1947 –) (also known as Linda Catherine Samfield and Linda Dunson) is a radio producer and author of "Adventures of a Texas Feminist," published in *No Apologies: Texas Radicals 'Celebrate the '60s* (Eakin Press, 1992); "WINGS," in *Women's Experiences in Media* (Isis International, 1997) and "The Founding of WINGS: A Story of Feminist Radio Survival," in *Women Transforming Communications: Global Intersections* (Sage Publications, 1996). She attended the first women's liberation meeting in Austin, TX, held at the University of Texas Y (1969), and in the early 1970s volunteered as a birth control and abortion counselor. Hired in 1970 by University of Texas Press (then in the midst of a feminist uprising), Werden joined a rap group that became the Austin Women's Organization, which in turn created the Austin Women's Center. In 1972, lawyer Bobby Nelson helped Werden gain one of the first divorces under the new Texas Family Code, and change her name. Werden soon came out and called the first lesbian meeting at the Austin Women's Center. From 1973 – 1975, she joined Carol Stalcup as a founding editor/publisher of *Texan Woman Magazine.* In 1973 – 1974, she produced Longhorn Radio Network's first feminist series, "Women Today." Werden was a board member of Sheila Womack's Austin Woman's Theatre, and produced the first Austin Women's Music Festival (1978). She served as associate curator under Ruthe Winegarten for the Texas Women's History Project (1979 – 1981), and with Margaret Nunley collected and fostered women's art and hosted a Woman's Salon. Living in NY from 1981 – 1983, she wrote non-sexist grammar lessons for textbook publishers, joined the WOW Café, and volunteered for the women's department at WBAI-FM. In New York and Washington, D.C., from 1982 – 1985, she produced docudramas on women writers for NPR, produced women's news for community radio, and with Judie Pasternak convened a women's news caucus at the National Federation of Community Radio Broadcasters conference. In San Francisco (1985 – 1989), Werden co-founded (with Katherine Davenport) the series WINGS: Women's International News Gathering Service, producing it continuously until today (2006). In Austin, TX again (1993 – 2002), Werden worked for Genevieve Vaughan's Foundation for a Compassionate Society, co-produced the cable access television show "Women Today," and helped found Women's Access to Electronic Resources. In 1998, Werden was elected North American representative to the Women's International Network of AMARC (the World Association of Community Radio Broadcasters) and in 2002 became VP for North America. In 2005, she was elected president of the International Association of Women in Radio and TV. From Vancouver, BC, Canada, she works (2006) on feminist radio and media issues. Archives: Center for American History, University of Texas at Austin; audio archive, University of South Florida women's studies department.   (ABS)

Werner, Ella Christine (1899 – 1986) A founder of NOW, Werner was a member of the NWPC, serving as vice chairman and as a member of the endowment fund committee. Among her numerous activities, she was also a founder (1936) of the Washington Criminal Justice Association, and served as a member of its executive committee (1936 – 1961), and as first VP (1944 – 1948). A Soroptimist, she served as Washington president in 1936, as regional governor from 1948 – 1950, and as national treasurer from 1950 – 1952. A graduate of Benjamin Franklin University (1924), Werner was with the War Department from 1918 – 1921.

Wernette, Timothy J. (1947 –) A gender equity specialist since 1985, Wernette gives classroom presentations for faculty/staff development on gender stereotyping/bias, sexual harassment prevention and non-traditional vocational careers. Wernette entered the women's movement in the summer of 1974. From 1976 – 1980, he was a member, Los Angeles Men's Collective. There, he hosted a national anti-sexist men's conference and was involved with anti-rape/violence demonstrations. During that time, Wernette also served as a board member of the National Organization for Men Against Sexism. Since 1981, he has been a member of the Tucson Men's Cooperative. In addition to hosting a national anti-sexist men's conference, Wernette was a volunteer at the Tucson Rape Crisis Center, and also a board member of Tucson Center for Women & Children, a domestic violence center and service organization. He serves (2005) on the board of the Tucson YWCA. Wernette, who has two stepchildren, earned a B.A. from Justin Morrill College, Michigan State University (1969), and an M.A. from the College of Education, Michigan State University (1974).   (ABS)

West, Charlotte (1932 –) An athletics administrator, West has worked tirelessly to improve the conditions and opportunities for women in sports. As president of the Association for Intercollegiate Athletics for Women (1978), she created opportunities for women athletes, coaches and administrators. She was also a Title IX consultant for the federal government, and a Title IX advocate, for 30 years. In addition to this work, West served as coach of a national championship golf team, and has been a member of numerous NCAA committees. As a member of the NCAA certification committee

(1990), she instituted an equity component in the accreditation process for NCAA Division I schools, and as a member of the gender equity committee (1992), she changed NCAA policies and rules to improve the status of and opportunities for college athletes. Archives: University of Maryland, College Park, MD.　　　(ABS)

West, Jayne (1950 –) was a founder of Cell 16, one of the most radical groups in Boston, MA, in 1968. After a narrow escape from men trying to force her into a car on a quiet street near Harvard Square in Cambridge, MA, West, along with Dana Densmore, got serious about martial arts and soon co-founded Ja Shin Do, a school of feminist martial arts (1974). The Korean words mean the Way of Self Belief. She taught in the school until late 1976, then, retiring from teaching and martial arts, turned over the school and the lineage to Densmore. West was a friend of and roommate with Abby Rockefeller, another member of Cell 16 and the martial arts group.

West, Martha Smeltzer (1946 –) (also known as Martha Smeltzer) joined the women's movement in 1967 when she discovered how difficult it was going to be to deliver her baby by natural childbirth and to breast-feed. West attended a Bread and Roses meeting in Boston in 1969, but as a wife and mother felt excluded. That changed in 1970 when she entered Indiana University Bloomington, School of Law. Immediately branded a radical, West became a co-founder of the University of Indiana Law School's women's caucus in 1971. That year, she began working with professor Julius Getman to develop a course on women and the law. The two attended the first conference on such courses, held at Yale University Law School, in 1972. When the course was taught at Indiana University in 1973, West taught the sections on women's history and family law. In addition, West worked as a research assistant for Getman in developing the first affirmative action plan for Indiana University. A member of the Law Review, West wrote her note on "Sex Classifications in the Social Security Benefit Structure," discussing the possible impact of the proposed ERA on the Social Security system. She also participated in a research project that identified all provisions of IN law that would be affected by the ERA. After graduating in 1974, West began a long career focusing on women's rights. She was treasurer of the IN ERA campaign in 1976 and 1977. She became a law professor at the University of California, Davis, in 1982. Since 1996, she has been co-author (with professor Herma Hill Kay) of the law school text *Sex-Based Discrimination* (4th, 5th and 6th editions). She was also on the first gay rights task force at University of California, Davis, 1991 – 1992. West, who has three children, earned her undergraduate degree from Brandeis University (1967).　　　(ABS)

Weston, Jenna Linda (1949 –) (also known as Linda Trocke and Linda Weston) After reading the first issue of *Ms.* magazine in 1971, Weston joined a new women's CR group in St. Joseph, MI. She later joined NOW, and in the mid 1970s attended The Midwest Conference for Women Artists at Oxbow in Saugatuck, MI. Says Weston, "For the first time I met a group of serious, working women artists and saw art that spoke of and to my experiences as a woman." After leaving her marriage and coming out as a lesbian (1977), Weston moved to Grand Rapids (1978) and joined the feminist organization Aradia. There, she was elected to head the Anne Hutchinson task force on natural healing and women's spirituality. The women started a spirituality group, Owabajibi, which met weekly for years. Weston helped publish a monthly newsletter and fine arts/literary quarterly, contributing many articles and drawings. She also regularly contributed written pieces and artwork to national lesbian and feminist publications, including the Lesbian Almanac series, *Trivia, Maize Magazine, WomanSpirit* magazine, *The Woman's Book of Healing* (by Diane Stein) and two feminist tarot decks, *Daughters of the Moon* and *The Amazon Tarot*. Also active in the women's peace movement, Weston participated in Take Back the Night marches, the women's march on the Pentagon and the women's peace encampment in Seneca Falls, NY. Weston also worked at the Michigan Womyn's Music Festival for two years, then in 1985 moved with her partner, Jo, to land they bought in Missouri. The 80-acre farm became a gathering place for many women over the following years, and many Aradians visited and then began to move there. Weston is working on a feminist history of Aradia; initial results were presented at the National Women's Studies Conference, held in New Orleans in 2003. An artist, Weston holds a B.F.A. from Michigan State University, and an M.F.A. from the University of Missouri.　　　(ABS)

Weyand, Ruth (1912 – 1989) was a labor attorney who worked to expand and assure women's rights in the workplace. As an attorney for the International Union of Electrical Workers, Weyand filed General Electric Co. v. Gilbert (1976). The case went to the Supreme Court, which held that pregnancy discrimination was not sex discrimination because if men could get pregnant, they would also be denied paid disability benefits for their pregnancy. The backlash and activism engendered by this case culminated in Congressional enactment of the Pregnancy Discrimination Amendment of 1978, prohibiting discrimination on the basis of pregnancy, childbirth and related medical conditions as encompassed under the prohibition against sex discrimination under Title VII. She was a litigator for the EEOC from 1977 to 1988. To honor Weyand's more than 50 years of work in the areas of equal pay, pension rights and anti-discrimination in the workplace, The Ruth Weyand Award was created by the Association of Women in Communications. It recognizes companies with forward-thinking policies toward women and minorities. Weyand had two children. Weyand received a Ph.B (1930) and a J.D. (1932 from the University of Chicago (1930).

Whitbeck, Caroline Ann (1940 –) In 1970, Whitbeck became co-author (with Carol Christ) of the first model affirmative action program. At that time, Whitbeck was a lecturer and then assistant professor at Yale University. People were asking what affirmative action could possibly mean, says Whitbeck, and "we showed them. For example, remove nepotism rules (which in fact functioned to keep wives, not husbands, in marginal positions; stop sexual harassment (which at the time Yale treated as a personal problem of the offender); and provide high-quality day care." Whitbeck then wrote "The 'Maternal Instinct'" (1972), which she believes was the first feminist philosophy work in English to deal with maternity from inside the experience of maternity. She presented it, "baby in tow," at the first Eastern Society for Women in Phylosophy Conference held at Smith College in 1972. It was "ahead of its time," says Whitbeck, "and so not published until 1975." Whitbeck is also author of "Theories of Sex Difference," which she believes is the first feminist philosophy work in English to address the "masculist" bias in scientific theory. The paper grew out of a very early feminist philosophy course that Whitbeck taught at Yale. It was published in *The Philosophical Forum* in 1974, and reprinted in *Women and Philosophy*, edited by Carol C. Gould and Marx Wartofsky (Perigree Books, 1976) and elsewhere. "The 'Maternal Instinct'" was published in the *Philosophical Forum* in 1975 and reprinted in *Mothering: Essays in Feminist Theory*, edited by Joyce Trebilcot (Rowman & Allanheld, 1984). Whitbeck later shifted her attention to the philosophy of medicine, feminist bioethics and the philosophy of engineering and research ethics, where she continued to address issues of women— as patients and professionals in healthcare, and as scientists and engineers. In 1995, she started the Online Ethics Center for Engineering and Science at MIT. The idea for this Web site grew out of another assignment to create Web pages that would help reduce the barriers to women and minorities in engineering. She continues (2006) to direct the project, which is now known as the National Academy of Engineering Online Ethics Center. Whitbeck, who is (2006) the Elmer G. Beamer – Hubert H. Schneider Professor in Ethics, and adjunct professor in mechanical and aerospace engineering, Case Western Reserve University, holds an A.B. from Wellesley College (1962), an M.A. from Boston University (1965) and a Ph.D. from MIT (1970). Whitbeck has one child and two stepchildren. (ABS)

White, Barbara Anne (1942 –) A professor and writer, White taught the first women's studies course at Northwestern University, Evanston, IL, in 1970. She was also founder of the women's caucus of the Teaching Assistant Association (1970), in Madison, WI. White, who has written numerous scholarly articles on women and women writers, is the author of "Up from the Podium: Feminist Revolution in the Classroom," published in *Female Studies IV: Teaching About Women* (Know Inc., 1971). Her books include *American Women Writers: An Annotated Bibliography of Criticism* (Garland Publishing Co., 1977); *Hidden Hands: American Women Writers, 1790 – 1870, An Anthology* (with Lucy M. Freibert) (Rutgers University Press, 1985); *Growing Up Female: Adolescent Girlhood in American Fiction* (Greenwood Press, 1985); *American Women's Fiction, 1790 – 1870: A Guide to Research* (Garland Publishing Co., 1990); *Edith Wharton: A Study of the Short Fiction* (Macmillan Co., 1991); and *Wharton's New England: Seven Stories and "Ethan Frome"* (University Press of New England, 1995). White, who has one child, earned her B.A. from Cornell University (1964) and her Ph.D. from the University of Wisconsin (1974). (ABS)

White, Juanita — When her adult daughter attended one of the first NOW meetings in Richmond, VA, in the early 1970s, White was fascinated and soon joined. She marched in Washington, D.C., stood vigil at the capitol in Richmond, served as newsletter editor, chaired the women in education task force, and served as both co-coordinator and chair of the reproductive rights task force. She also attended the national NOW convention in Philadelphia in 1975. Born on a farm in Tennessee, White attended Memphis State University, but left to work in an aircraft factory during World War II. She later graduated from a small liberal arts college. In addition to raising her four children, White has been an aircraft inspector, schoolteacher, advertising copy writer, and analyst for a medical care agency.

White, Margita Eklund (1937 – 2002) Born in Sweden, White immigrated to the United States after WWII. She became active in politics and national campaigns, and was among the first wave of women working in significant positions in government. Prior to her death, White, a founder of Executive Women in Government, was collaborating with Barbara Franklin, also a founder of EWG and a former Secretary of Commerce, on an oral history project with the Pennsylvania State University Archives to document the advances made by women in government during the 1970s. The first phase of the project, called *A Few Good Women*, contains 20 oral histories, including White's and those of some other founding EWG members. Regarded as a leader in the broadcast industry, White was appointed assistant director for public information at the United States Information Agency during the Nixon administration (1969 – 1973). She was assistant press secretary and later director, White House Office of Communications, during the Ford administration (1975 – 1976). She was then appointed commissioner of the FCC (1976 – 1979) and later served as director and then vice chair of Radio Free Europe/Radio Liberty, Inc. (1979 – 1982). From 1988 to her retirement in 2001, White was president of the Association for Maximum Service Television Inc., an industry group working on technology policy issues. White graduated from the University of Redlands in California in 1959 and received an M.A. from

Rutgers University in 1960. Archives: Gerald R. Ford Library, Ann Arbor, MI.

Whitehill, Virginia Bulkley (1928 –) says she derived her sense of equity and fairness for women from her suffragist mother. Present at the oral argument before the United States Supreme Court during Roe v. Wade, Whitehill has worked for decades on behalf of women's rights. She was a co-founder of the Dallas Women's Coalition, Women's Issues Network, Dallas Women's Foundation, The Family Place (the first Dallas shelter for battered women), Texans for Motherhood by Choice, Women's Southwest Federal Credit Union, Dallas WPC, Dallas VFA, and WEAL. She has also chaired fundraising events for many of these and other organizations. In addition, she made presentations and served on planning advisory committees to promote women's issues, such as The Women's Museum: An Institute for the Future. Whitehill has served on numerous boards, including the Leaguer of Women Voters of Dallas, NARAL, National Network of Women's Funds, Planned Parenthood of Dallas, Women's Council of Dallas County, and Friends of SMU Libraries (DeGolyer Library Archives of Women of the Southwest). She was an adviser to the YWCA Women's Resource Center and is a sustaining member of the Junior League of Dallas. Her volunteer career has been recognized with numerous awards, including the Association of Women Journalists Woman of Courage Award, the Women's Center of Dallas Women Helping Women Maura Award, the Planned Parenthood Champion of Choice Award, the SMU Women's Symposium Profiles in Leadership Award, The Women's Enterprise Magazine Women of Excellence Award, the American Jewish Congress Woman of Spirit Award, the Women's Council of Dallas County Distinguished Service Award, the Veteran Feminists of America Medal of Honor, and the Texas Women's Political Caucus Good Gal Award. In addition, Whitehill has been honored with the Mount Holyoke College Distinguished Alumna Award and the Dallas LWV Myrtle Bulkley Award for Outstanding Service (named for Whitehill's mother, a suffragist and charter member of the LWV). In 2000, Whitehill was one of 100 distinguished women honored by the Texas Women's Chamber of Commerce as a Woman of the Century. Whitehill, who has two children, graduated from Mount Holyoke College in 1950. Archives: DeGolyer Library, Southern Methodist University, Dallas, TX.   (ABS)

Whitlock, Kay (1949 –) An activist and organizer, Whitlock has contributed to various movements for gender, racial, LGBT, economic and environmental justice, always emphasizing the interconnectedness of these struggles. She was appointed co-chair of NOW's sexuality and lesbian task force by Karen DeCrow after DeCrow was elected president of NOW in 1974. Nancy Boyd was co-chair through 1975, then Whitlock became the sole chair, until 1979, of what was renamed the lesbian rights committee. She also served for several years as a writer/editor for Planned Parenthood, Southeastern Pennsylvania (1977 – 1986), becoming manager of educational resources in 1984. During that time she wrote two booklets that became national bestsellers in sex education literature for teens. Whitlock was a delegate to the 1977 National Women's Conference in Houston and a member of the International Women's Year continuing committee, established under President Carter. From 1998 – 2003, she served as special representative for LGBT issues for the American Friends Service Committee, a Quaker organization working for peace, demilitarization, human rights and social justice. From 2003 – 2006 she was the national representative for LGBT issues for AFSC. Her association with AFSC and its spiritually centered vision of nonviolence was informed by her own spiritual practice in the Tibetan Buddhist tradition. Whitlock is the author of "In a Time of Broken Bones: A Call for Dialogue on Hate Violence and the limitations of Hate Crimes Legislation," an AFSC Justice Vision working paper (2001); the first in a series of LGBT Justice Visions working papers she wrote addressing the structural violence and racial/economic inequities of the U.S. criminal justice system; and AFSC's landmark "Bridges of Respect: Creating Support for Lesbian and Gay Youth" (1988), the first national resource guide for adults working with queer youth.   (ABS)

Whitman, Marina von Neumann (1935 –) An economist, Whitman has served in government, worked with corporations, and taught at universities. At the University of Pittsburgh, where she started in 1963 as an instructor in economics and became Distinguished Public Service Professor of Economics in 1973, she supported women students "who were bucking the opposition of their parents, many of whom at that time felt college was not necessary or even desirable for a girl." Whitman was a member of the President's Council of Economic Advisers in 1972 – 1973, the first woman ever to hold such a position. Beginning in 1973, she also served as an outside or independent director on various corporate boards. She spent 13 years (1979 – 1992) as an executive of General Motors, first as vice president and chief economist and later, starting in 1985, as vice president and group executive for public affairs. In that position, she was the highest-ranking woman in the United States. in the automobile industry at the time. Whitman is (2005) professor of business administration and public policy at the University of Michigan, "a position in which I spend a good deal of time advising/mentoring younger women, both students and faculty." Whitman has written many articles and several books, including *New World, New Rules: The Changing Role of the American Corporation* (Harvard Business School Press, 1999). Whitman, who has two children, earned her B.A. from Radcliffe College and her M.A. and Ph.D. from Columbia University. Archives: Schlesinger Library, Radcliffe Institute, Cambridge, MA.   (ABS)

Whitney, Ruth (1938 –) A university teacher, Whitney is author of *Feminism and Love: Transforming Ourselves and Our World* (Cross-Cultural Publications, 1998). Since 1970, she has been an activist in NOW on the local and state level, wherever she lived. From 1978 – 1982, she worked for national NOW as a field organizer and field director in NOW's ERA campaign in Illinois, Wyoming, South Dakota and Florida. From 1973 – 1978, she was an assistant professor of religion at Rutgers University (Douglass College), which included teaching a women's studies course on women and religion. Whitney was also part of the informal women's studies group that coordinated women's studies at Douglass College and hired the first full-time women's studies teacher. This group also helped organize feminist speakers to come to Douglass. In addition, Whitney served as faculty adviser for a student group called Action Against Rape. During the 1970s, Whitney participated in New York Women Scholars of Religion, a group that met in NYC. Whitney, who holds a B.S., M.A. and Ph.D., has also been active in the civil rights, peace and environmental movements.   (ABS)

Whittington, Virginia ("Ginger") (1931 –) (also known as Ginger Kolasinski and Ginger Karlin) A retired teacher, Whittington was also a freelance writer for the *Youngstown* (OH) *Vindicator* (1979 – 1984), reporting on the ERA and other women's issues. She has been a member of the LWV since 1965, NOW since 1977, and the NWPC. Her membership in LWV included chapters in New Castle, PA, Youngstown, OH, and Chester County, PA. Whittington served as board member (1965 – 1969), and as president of the New Castle chapter (1965 – 1967). A member of NOW in the New Castle, Youngstown and the Philadelphia areas, Whittington served as president of Youngstown NOW (1985 – 1988). She also helped organize escorts for the women's clinic when Operation Rescue and local protestors targeted it on a regular basis. Whittington was a founder of the Youngstown chapter of the NWPC (1994). She also reorganized a defunct chapter in the Philadelphia area in 1999. As president of the NWPC of Pennsylvania, she provided training for women candidates and organized a PAC that contributed several thousand dollars to women candidates. Whittington, who has four children, holds a B.A. from Pennsylvania State University, an M.Ed. from Westminster College, and an M.A. from the University of Pittsburgh.   (ABS)

Wikle, Linda L. (1951 –) was a co-founder of Traverse City (MI) NOW, 1974 – 1975. The chapter started by developing task forces that went into the community and applied for jobs. Finding that the questions the women were asked by potential employers "were deplorable," the group began educating employers about correct hiring practices. Later, after attending state coordinator meetings, Wikle realized that there was a need for an out lesbian to be active on the state level. She volunteered to be affectional preference state task force chair. At the same time, Wikle was part of the group that supported Jeannette Smith, an abused wife accused of murdering her husband. The group raised bail, found Smith a place to live, got some of her belongings back, did fundraisers and sat in court. Smith was eventually found not guilty, and the NOW chapter got a lot of invaluable press exposure. Wikle later attended the first gay rights march on Washington as a representative of NOW, and continued to work on the affectional preference committee endeavoring to break down barriers. In 1981, Wikle became a founding member of Friends North, a gay and lesbian organization in Northern MI. Wikle holds a B.A. and has her own insurance agency. She has three children.   (ABS)

Will, Paulette C. (1944 –) was a member of the DFL Feminist Caucus (1973 – 1978) and served as special events coordinator. In 1976, she worked for the election of Barbara Goldman for Vermont State Senate, and in 1978 worked as office manager in Coral Gables, FL, for the Yes on 2 statewide ERA referendum campaign. From 1989 – 1991, Will generated over $100,000 for the Pro-Choice Fund by developing the fundraising package and funding strategy for high-donor contributors. Will holds a B.A. degree. Archives: Immigration History Research Center, College of Liberal Arts, Minneapolis, MN.   (ABS)

Willems, Marcia – See Suttenberg, Marcia Lee

Willett, Roslyn L. (1924 –) In 1946, Willett was the first female technical executive at Stein, Hall & Co., Inc., named to head technical service and development on food products. In 1949, she was the first female editor hired at McGraw-Hill Publishing Co., and in 1950 was hired as editor of *Diner Magazine*, the only woman applicant in a field of 150 men. Later in 1950, Willett (who had an extremely long commute) pioneered flextime, working in the office three days a week and from home two days a week. She was also the first independent female professional food service consultant in the U.S., and was the first woman to establish a professional PR and marketing firm for industrial equipment, high-tech and medical work, as well as corporate and financial PR. She did all this from a home office so that she could be at home with her new baby. In 1966, Willett joined NOW and helped establish a committee on the image of women. She later provided the American Association of Advertising Agencies and the National Association of Broadcasters with written guidelines for the presentation of women. "They both adopted the guidelines, and the depiction of women as idiots ceased," she says. In 1970, Willett was a member of the steering committee that drafted the bylaws for what became the WPC. She was elected first chair of Women's Political Caucus, Inc. She also developed the first-ever training programs for women who wanted to run for office, with faculty provided by women who were already in office as well as by specialists in communications. In addition, Willett was a keynote speaker and ran workshops on women's issues at colleges such as Sarah Lawrence and other venues. Her essay, "Working Together," was published in *Woman in Sexist Society* (Basic Books, 1971) and remained in print until 2001. Willett was also named to the board of Women Studies Abstracts, was one of the first female activists named to the New York Advisory Council for the Federal Small Business Administration in 1976, and ran seminars for women who wanted to start businesses. Willett, who has one child, earned her B.A. from Hunter College. Archives: Hunter College Archive, New York, NY.   (ABS)

Williams, Alice (1942 –) became a feminist in the early 1970s when, as director of the social work department at Middlesex Hospital in Middletown, CT, she observed the demeaning manner in which the hospital's physicians treated young and vulnerable women (low-income, single, nonwhite) who sought prenatal care. Working with other women, her solution was to launch a family planning clinic operated by volunteer women trained in patient advocacy who would refer women to physicians from out of town. The new clinic opened in 1972. While at Middlesex, and before Roe v. Wade, Williams was part of a network that referred women to out-of-state abortion providers. When she became director of social work at Waterbury (CT) Hospital, Williams developed a program to address the unique needs of women in violent relationships. At the time, the problem was often misdiagnosed or simply overlooked. Programs like these fueled the safehouse movement nationwide. Says Williams, "At the time, I viewed these early activities as just good social work. Now I am proud to be a feminist, to have been engaged in these acts of feminist advocacy, and pledge a lifelong commitment to feminist values."   (ABS)

Williams, Dell (1922 –) joined the women's movement in 1970 when she marched for equality down Fifth Avenue. in New York City. She then joined NYC NOW, participated in many zap actions, and served on the board. In addition, Williams volunteered to act as fundraiser for the chapter. In 1972, Williams was asked by Judy Wenning, president of NYC NOW, to coordinate a conference on women's sexuality. With Laura Scharf as co-coordinator, Williams put together a committee that produced the first Women's Sexuality Conference (1973), with an attendance of over 1,400 women. The success of the conference and her own commitment to the freedom of sexual expression for all women led Williams to open Eve's Garden (1974), "a safe place where women could purchase pleasure-empowering tools and books to celebrate their sexuality." She published her first catalog in September 1974 and opened a retail sexuality boutique in 1978 in NYC. The mail-order catalog has been endorsed by many therapists and sex educators, including Dr. Ruth Westheimer. In 1977, the National Women's Health Coalition gave Williams the Woman of the Year Award for her contributions to women's sexual health. She was in-

cluded in the 1988 edition of *Foremost Women of the Twentieth Century*, as well as being listed in *Who's Who Worldwide* (1944 – 1995). In 1994 Williams received Uncommon Woman Award from the Uncommon Legacy Foundation. In 2002, she was ordained as an Interfaith Minister, and began serving on the board of *Spirituality and Sexuality*, a quarterly. Williams, who studied acting and theater in the early 1940s, joined the Women's Army Corps in 1945 and served as an entertainment specialist. Archives: Human Sexuality Collection, Cornell University, Ithaca, NY.   (ABS)

Williams, Elizabeth Friar (1931 – 1998) after earning a master's degree in psychology from City College of New York, Williams began a private practice as a feminist therapist in 1969. Her book *Notes of a Feminist Therapist* was published in 1976 (Praeger). She later served as editor of *Voices of Feminist Therapy* (Harwood Academic Publishers, 1995) and co-author (with Tina Tessina) of *The 10 Smartest Decisions a Woman Can Make Before 40*. The author of numerous articles on feminist therapy and related topics, Williams moved from the East Coast to San Francisco in 1989, where she taught part time in a graduate program and worked part time as a counselor at a private elementary school.

Williams, Ferne – See Ferne

Williams, Geralyn – See Horton, Geralyn

Williams, Maxine — is an African American woman active in the very early period of Redstockings (circa 1969). In 1970 she wrote *Black Women's Liberation* (NY, Pathfinder Press) with Pamela Newman. She also wrote an article in *The Militant* (July 3, 1970) titled "Why Women's Liberation is Important to Black Women." At that time, she was a member of the New York Young Socialist Alliance and the Third World Women's Alliance.

Williamson, Cris (1947 –) Best known to audiences as a songwriter and musician, Williamson describes herself as "a poet and a scholar." A spiritual seeker in the 1960s, she gravitated toward the hippie culture and sang at anti-Vietnam War demonstrations. In 1964 her first record, The Artistry of Cris Williamson, was released. In 1973, while she was a guest on a radio show, Williamson envisioned a women's record label as a counter to the problems women faced in the music industry. Later that year, a group of activist women formed Olivia Records. Although Williamson was not a co-founder, she did contribute to Olivia's success. In 1975, Olivia produced Williamson's now classic The Changer and the Changed, which has sold over 500,000 copies. Williamson's interactions with the Olivia women raised her consciousness about feminist politics. While her songs were not "specifically gendered," they were embraced by women who responded to the songs' spiritual, comforting and inspiring nature and to the energy that Williamson often communicated during her concerts. Feminist lesbians, especially, "found images of power" in her songs and these became part of the soundtrack of U.S. lesbian culture. Over the decades Williamson has toured in the U.S. and abroad, has sold out Carnegie Hall, and has participated in fundraising efforts for diverse social justice causes, including a benefit produced by Mimi Fariña for a Vietnamese hospital and a concert to save the lesbian Wild Side West Bar in San Francisco. In the 1970s she collaborated with a Women on Wheels project to bring instruments into the California Institute for Women, a state prison. Her support for Native American issues includes helping weavers of Big Mountain and participating in the Water for Life Tour with Bonnie Raitt, Jackson Brown and others. Williamson describes herself as "Trying to thrive outside the box and encourage other women to do the same." She is (2006) traveling on the 30th Year Tour of Changer and the Changed. She also teaches songwriting and continues her search for wisdom through study, action and song/writing. Williamson notes that "The personal is political and the personal should aim to be universal." (ABS)

Williamson, Nancy (1938 –) briefly attended study groups at Cell 16 in Boston (1969) and spoke at many colleges, universities, and community and church groups about the principles of feminism. Williamson also taught feminist studies at Goddard College (1975 – 1976). In early 1970, she was a co-founder of Boston Female Liberation, the group that published *The Second Wave: A Magazine of Female Liberation*. She also published articles about the feminist movement, book and movie reviews, and personal essays in Boston newspapers during the 1970s and 1980s. Two of her essays on Anais Nin appeared in the anthology *Anais Nin: A Book of Mirrors*, edited by Paul Herron (Blue Sky Press, 1996). A psychotherapist in private practice for several decades, Williamson applied feminist principles to her therapy practice. She has one child, and holds a B.A. from Boston University (1967) and an M.Ed. from Suffolk University (1975). Archives: Schlesinger Library, Radcliffe Institute, Cambridge, MA. (ABS)

Willis, Ellen J. (1941 –) A writer and journalism professor, Willis joined NYRW in 1968, and in 1969 became a co-founder, with Shulamith Firestone, of Redstockings. In 1970, Willis organized a women's liberation group in Colorado Springs, where she had gone to work on an anti-Vietnam War project. In 1975, Willis got together with a group of feminist-activist friends who formed a CR group that lasted for 11 years. In 1977, this group met with other women to discuss how to respond to the recently passed Hyde amendment, and formed CARASA. Shortly afterward, some of the women who felt the need for militant action defending abortion specifically formed No More Nice Girls. In 1982, Willis was on the planning committee for the controversial Barnard conference on the politics of sexuality. She is (2005) a member of the discussion group Feminist Futures. Willis has published numerous articles and essays analyzing feminist issues such as the institution of marriage and the family, abortion politics, sexuality, the contradictions of feminist politics, and the relationship of feminism to popular culture and to psychoanalytic and cultural radicalism. Her writings have appeared in many publications and have been reprinted in her three books of cultural commentary: *Beginning to See the Light* (A.A. Knoph, 1981), *No More Nice Girls* (Wesleyan University Press, 1992), and *Don't Think—Smile! Notes on a Decade of Denial* (Beacon Press, 1999). As an editor of *Ms.* (1972 – 1975) and the *Village Voice* (1984 – 1990), she worked with many feminist writers. In addition to this work, Willis took part in the sex debates of the 1980s, defending sexual liberation as a feminist priority and critiquing the anti-pornography movement. Willis has one child. She earned her B.A. from Barnard College in 1962. (ABS)

Willoughby, Sally – See Willowbee, Sally

Willowbee, Sally (1946 –) (also known as Sally Willoughby) helped start a CR group in Philadelphia in the late 1960s – early 1970s, as well as a feminist conference held at the Quaker Meeting Hall in Haddonfield, NJ. In 1971 Willowbee organized an all-women apple-picking crew in Vermont. Four women from the group decided to move to West Virginia, where they lived in a rented house and started building a log cabin on land that was part of the Peacemakers Land Trust. Willowbee moved to Egg Harbor, NJ, in 1973, "where I renovated a chicken coop and became involved in the Stockton College Women's Union." Another group of women in rural Southern New Jersey started a monthly camping group at a Girl Scout camp near Bridgeton, NJ, that met monthly for camp outs, programs and workshops. The group called itself Women of the Sticks. In 1976, Willowbee moved to Los Angeles and became involved in the Women's Building there. Willowbee, who is a cabinetmaker, woodworker and artist, has been involved in the civil rights, peace, gay rights and environmental movements. She holds a B.A. from Kalamazoo College. Archives: The Lesbian Herstory Archives, Brooklyn, NY. (ABS)

Wilson, Barbara Ann – See MacIntyre, Barbara Ann

Wilson, Nellie — was a labor leader and a pioneer defender of women's rights in industrial jobs. As a single mother raising two daughters, Wilson began working at A.O. Smith Corporation in 1943, where she joined the Smith Steelworkers Union. She later became the first "effective" female officer elected to the union, and established the union's first civil rights committee. She also served as director of employment for their Human Resources Development Institute, helping single mothers find employment. Wilson was also active with the Wisconsin AFL-CIO in 1969 and 1970, "when women were considered incapable of doing anything." On behalf of office workers, she and Helen Hensler challenged the state AFL-CIO president at a public meeting to do more for women, "who needed things men didn't need." Wilson was one of the founders of the first civil rights committee and, later, women's committee. After retiring, Wilson founded the Milwaukee Northside AARP Chapter 4035 and was one of the spokespersons for the AARP Minority Affairs Institute. Wilson also founded the only minority chapter of the Wisconsin AARP. She served on the Commission on Aging (1993 – 2000) and chaired its advocacy committee starting in 1996. She is a lifetime member of the NAACP. (ABS)

Wimer, Kathleen (1944 –) In 1970, Wimer challenged and changed the punitive pregnancy leave policy at a major corporation, changing company policy for all who followed. From 1970 – 1971, she helped open the New Haven (CT) Women's Liberation Center, and from 1971 – 1972 helped establish the Rape Crisis Center in New Haven. From 1972 – 1982, she helped sustain a parent cooperative day care center in New Haven, and from 1970 – 1980 developed feminist politics in league with others in the feminist, peace and social justice movements in New Haven. Wimer also was a member of a local feminist theater troupe in New Haven from 1971 – 1973. Wimer, who holds an M.A., has one child. Archives: New Haven Colony Historical Society, New Haven, CT. (ABS)

Winant, Fran (1943 –) was a founding member of the GLF (1969) and Radicalesbians (1971). In 1970, she founded the Lesbian Feminist Small Press, Violet Press, and in 1973 edited and published *We Are All Lesbians: A Poetry Anthology*, the first anthology of lesbian poetry and art published in the U.S. Winant's poetry collections are *Looking at Women* (1971), *Dyke Jacket: Poems and Songs* (1976), and *Goddess of Lesbian Dreams: Poems and Songs* (1980). In 1977, Winant received the New York State Council on the Arts Poetry Award for her gay liberation poetry, which has been widely anthologized. In 1978, she participated in the first show by lesbian artists at a NYC gallery, A Lesbian Show (Greene Street Gallery), and in 1982 her paintings were included in Extended Sensibilities: Homosexual Presence in Contemporary Art, at the New Museum in NYC, the first show of gay/lesbian artists in a major museum. In 1990, Winant received the National Endowment for the Arts Award in painting for her goddess and nature-inspired images. A featured artist in Harmony Hammond's *Lesbian Art in America, 2000*, Winant is also a founding member of early collectives that wrote about lesbian feminist issues, and organized poetry readings and women's dances, self-defense and car repair classes, and a food coop, The Lesbian Food Conspiracy. She holds a B.A. from Fordham University. Archives: The Lesbian Herstory Archives, Brooklyn, NY. (ABS)

Window, Marcia – See Suttenberg, Marcia Lee

Winegarten, Ruthe (1930 – 2004) A tenacious researcher and author, Winegarten was determined that the histories of women, blacks, Jews and Latinos in Texas not be forgotten. She was author or co-author of 18 books, including *Black Texas Women: 150 Years of Trial and Triumph* and *Capitol Women: Texas Female Legislators 1923 – 1999*. Both books won the Liz Carpenter Award given by the Texas State Historical Association. Her first book, *Texas Women's History Bibliography*, was spun off into a second (co-written with Sherry A. Smith and Mary Beth Rogers), *Texas Women: A Celebration of History*. In the 1970s, while researching a thesis paper at the University of Texas, Dallas, Winegarten compiled an oral history of black entrepreneur and activist Annie Mae Hunt. This later became the book, co-written with Hunt, *I Am Annie Mae*. In 1974, Winegarten began working as a research historian for the Texas Women's History Project, founded by former Governor Ann Richards. That work is now a permanent collection at Texas Woman's University in Denton. Winegarten, who had three children, was a member of the LWV, the Jewish Welfare Federation of Dallas and the North Dallas Democratic Women's Club. She earned a B.A. from the University of Texas (1950) and an M.A. from the University of Texas at Arlington.

Winsett, Judy (1943 –) A friend of The Furies collective in Washington, D.C., in the late 1960s, Winsett helped with various projects and attended rallies for feminists and gay rights. A jewelry maker, Winsett and her business partner, Leslie Reeves, began making lesbian jewelry, and, in 1972, opened Lammas Women's Shop, selling women's crafts, their jewelry and women's books. Winsett attended some college, and holds a Horsemaster's degree from the British Horse Society, "having worked my way through a riding school in England." She lives (2005) on a secluded 164-acre mountain farm in West Virginia "with my horses, dogs and cats." (ABS)

Winslade, Ann Garry – See Garry, Ann

Winslow, Barbara (1945 –) (also known as Barbara Joan Slaner) Associate professor of education and women's studies at Brooklyn College of the City University of New York (2005), Winslow was a founding member of Seattle Radical Women (1967), Women's Liberation Seattle (1968), Union WAGE (Alliance to Gain Equity) (1972) and the Coalition of Labor Union Women (1974). In addition, Winslow was a member of Women Against Racism in Detroit (1976) and the Cleveland Council of Labor Union Women (1974 – 1976), and was a founding member of the Reproductive Rights National Network (1979 – 1984), the Cleveland ProChoice Action Committee (1977 – 1984) and the Brooklyn Pro-Choice Network (1984). In England from 1969 – 1970, Winslow was a member of Coventry Women's Liberation, and in London of the

Women's Liberation Workshop. She is a member of the Berkshire Conference of Women Historians and the Coordinating Council for Women in History, and has served on both boards. In addition to this work, Winslow attended "probably the first women's liberation demonstration ever" in Seattle, WA, in 1967—Radical Women's demonstration against a Playboy Bunny. Winslow has participated in demonstrations for abortion rights, against sterilization abuse, for the ERA, for Joan Little, Inez Garcia and Yvonne Wanrow, for farm workers, the Harlan County women's club, and demonstrations for lesbian and gay rights, for Take Back the Night and anti-sweatshop. Winslow, who has two children, holds a B.A., two master's degrees, and a Ph.D. in from the University of Washington, Seattle. She helped found the women's studies programs at both the University of Washington and Seattle Community College, and is the author of *Sylvia Pankhurst: Sexual Politics and Political Activism* (St. Martin's Press, 1996). Archives: Her Seattle papers will go to the University of Washington; her England papers go to the Faucett Library, London; and her other papers will go to the Wisconsin Historical Association. (ABS)

Winstead, Mary Jane (1943 –) (also known as Budda Winstead) In the mid 1960s, Winstead was one of the first VISTA volunteers in New York City. She helped establish a storefront community in the Lower East Side where poor women went for help with housing problems. Winstead also taught English to groups of women and physically walked them through the maze of the NYC Department of Social Services so that they could get the benefits to which they were entitled. In 1968, as director of the Teen and Young Adult Group at Lenox Hill Settlement House, Winstead worked to end discrimination against lesbian and gay social workers. As a member of Radicalesbians, she also spoke regularly at graduate social work seminars at Columbia University. As a black woman, Winstead was aware that the white women's movement in the late 1960s and early 1970s did not speak directly to the needs of the average black woman. Resolved to present herself as a black empowered radical lesbian, Winstead began to speak out against racism and for the liberation of all women. She joined the Gay Liberation Front in the early 1970s, and in 1971 moved to Whiteport, NY, where a house she co-purchased became a meeting place for all women involved in the women's movement. "I believe that it was from our efforts that the women's movement and the visible lesbian community was created in the Hudson Valley," says Winstead. "We helped establish the first women's conference at New Paltz College, and State University of New York, New Paltz, later became one of the first schools to offer a degree in women's studies. In 1972, Winstead started a home-repair business, Working Women, which ran successfully for the next 15 years. In 1973, Winstead helped establish the first women's center in Woodstock, NY. A city planner, Winstead holds a B.A., M.A. and Ph.D. (ABS)

Wiseheart, Susan Elizabeth (1941 –) (also known as Susan Peterson) joined the New Women's Coalition in Grand Rapids, MI, in the early 1970s. As part of her work there, she served on the textbook committee of Grand Rapids Public School System to encourage them to eliminate sexist texts from the classrooms. Wiseheart also served as a primary organizer of a series of CR events held at the local Y. Eventually, the group changed its name to Grand Rapids Feminists, thereby "losing a few nervous members," she says. Wiseheart was very involved with the opening of the Grand Rapids Feminist Center, which shared space with the first women's bookstore. She also published a mimeographed newsletter, "The Grand Rapids Feminist," for a few issues, and was part of an ongoing CR group. In addition, she was active in pro-choice events and once had her car dented "at a Right to Life Rally where I picketed and tried to hold discussions with women coming to attend. I was later bodily removed from a Phyllis Schlafly talk at one of the local colleges." Adds Wiseheart, "Some of us held a meeting to begin the Rape Crisis Team during this time, and we had an unofficial women's crisis line at my house to connect women with services like the RCT and abortion referrals, plus we had an active Welfare Rights organization that I helped support." In 1974, Wiseheart, who held a B.A. at the time, went back to school, eventually graduating with a Bachelor's of Philosophy and a specialization in women's studies from Grand Valley State Colleges. At that time, she was a co-founder of Aradia, a feminist group that evolved into a loose community of feminist women, largely lesbian, who lived near Grand Rapids and then spread out to other states, countries and continents. For about 10 years, she published the newsletter "Practicing Anti-Racism." Wiseheart has been living at Hawk Hill Community Land Trust with a revolving group of lesbians since 1989 and is "still involved in creating alternatives to patriarchy and staying connected with feminist activities." Wiseheart has two children. Archives: The Lesbian Herstory Archives, Brooklyn, NY. (ABS)

Witter, Jean (1927 –) was a member of the board and served one term as president of Pittsburgh NOW. Her major efforts were in legislation. As chair of the Pittsburgh legislation committee, she was able to lead the chapter to get a sex amendment added to the Pennsylvania Human Relations Act (1970). Witter and the other committee members were able to convince their Legislature to introduce bills to amend the Pennsylvania Constitution to include sex. The bill passed by two separately elected legislatures and was approved by the voters. Pennsylvania was the first state to have an ERA in its Constitution (1971). Says Witter, "The Pennsylvania ERA was actually part of the effort to get the ERA in the U.S. Constitution. We sent many mailings from the ERA committee to Congress, to the NOW board and to other organizations. The mailings included information, action sheets, cartoons and petitions." Witter and her committee urged the

Discharge Petition, which representative Martha Griffiths used to get the ERA out of committee. After Witter became an attorney in 1976, she was asked to write an article for the *Women's Rights Law Reporter*. She subsequently published "Extending Ratification Time for the Equal Rights Amendment: Constitutionality of Time Limitations in the Federal Amending Process" in 1978.   (ABS)

Wittner, Judith Ginsberg (1939 –) A mother and "stay-at-home housewife feeling trapped in a role I had never intended to assume," Wittner says, she moved with her family from New York to Chicago in 1968. There she entered graduate school and became involved in community organizing and the peace movement. Wittner met many people who helped her develop her feminist and socialist understandings, and with whom she participated politically. She joined anti-racist work on local housing and worked as a counselor for the underground abortion collective, Jane, that "famously provided thousands of abortions free to Chicago women." In 1971 she was invited to teach women's history and feminist theory classes at Roosevelt University. That year, Wittner and her friends held weekly rap group meetings that attracted scores of women. By 1975, Wittner was studying for a Ph.D. and on her way to an academic career. Wittner, who has two children, is (2005) a professor of sociology at Loyola University in Chicago. She holds a B.A. from Brandeis (1960) and a Ph.D. from Northwestern (1977).   (ABS)

Wolf, Virginia ("Ginny") (1924 – 2004) was a professor of physical education at the University of Idaho from 1964 – 1982. As chair of the University of Idaho's women's caucus, Wolf filed a complaint with the Idaho Human Rights Commission and the Equal Employment Opportunity Commission in 1973 when the university administration hesitated to make changes recommended by the caucus. Rather than have the complaint go through the court system, university president Ernest Hartung and members of the women's caucus negotiated the issues and settled with a Conciliation Agreement, signed on May 8, 1974. That document detailed various actions the university would take regarding gender issues. Wolf was probably the most feared woman on the university campus because she did not hesitate to confront any administrator or university policy that did not treat women equally. In honor of her work, the University of Idaho Women's Center annually awards the Virginia Wolf Distinguished Services Award for Gender Justice to a university faculty or staff member and to a university student. Wolf also convened the Moscow, ID, chapter of NOW in January 1975 and served as its president for two terms. In 1976, Moscow NOW held the first ID NOW conference, and Wolf was elected state coordinator. Archives: University of Idaho Library Special Collections, Moscow, ID.

Wolfe, Leslie R. (1943 –) President of the Center For Women Policy Studies, the first feminist policy research and advocacy institute in the U.S. (founded in 1972), Wolfe worked in government for 10 years to further the rights of women and minorities. From 1973 – 1977, she was deputy director of the Women's Rights Program, U.S. Commission of Civil Rights. There she worked to bring a Congressionally-mandated focus on sex discrimination to the Commission's work, which was the first federal agency to address the combined impact of sexism and racism through studies, civil rights enforcement reports and journals. From 1977 – 1979, Wolfe was special assistant to the assistant secretary for education, U.S. Dept. of Health, Education and Welfare, where she was responsible for civil rights and women's rights issues in education policy. From 1979 – 1983, Wolfe was director, Women's Educational Equity Act Program, U.S. Dept. of Education. There, she directed priority setting and funding to focus on educational equity for women and girls with disabilities and for women and girls of color. She also worked to implement institutional change to ensure women's leadership in education. Wolfe was then fired by the Reagan administration after a campaign launched by the Heritage Foundation, *Conservative Digest* and others. Undaunted, she served as director of NOW LDEF's Project on Equal Education Rights, from 1983 – 1987. There she created new programs to focus on education policy beyond Title IX, and concentrated on sexism-plus-racism perspectives as they affected educational equity. Wolfe earned her B.A. from the University of Illinois (1965), her M.A. from the University of Maryland (1967) and her Ph.D. from the University of Florida (1970).   (ABS)

Wolfson, Alice J. (1941 –) An attorney specializing in policyholder representation against insurance companies, Wolfson focused her feminist work in the area of women's health. She is author of the chapter "Clenched Fist, Open Heart," published in the book *The Feminist Memoir Project: Voices From Women's Liberation*. The chapter recounts, among other things, her efforts to publicize the dangers of the birth control pill, including her part in the disruption of the Nelson pill hearings in the Senate (1969), as well as her particular history in the second wave. In addition to fighting for abortion rights, Wolfson organized the pill hearings in 1970 – 1971 around the issue of informed consent. She was a founder of the National Women's Health Network, and founded and for 10 years worked for the committee to defend reproductive rights of the Coalition for the Medical Rights of Women in San Francisco. From 1969 – 1977, Wolfson was a member of D.C. Women's Liberation. She has two children, one of whom died of leukemia in 1988.   (ABS)

Wolfson, Sharon Deevey – See Deevey, Sharon

Wolfson, Susan Wartur (1938 – 2005) As the third consecutive woman to be president of the Connecticut Bar Association (1991 – 1992), Wolfson appointed the first gender bias committee and later served as chair. Wolfson also served on the Second Circuit Judicial District's committee on gender bias (1994–1998) and on the Connecticut task force on racial bias in the courts. In addition, she was active in formulating and implementing gender-neutral language in legislative developments. In the early 1970s, Wolfson was active in Planned Parenthood and the LWV. During one of her first divorce cases (while in legal practice in New Haven, CT), Wolfson discovered that the husband of her client had secretly had an extension of his wife's telephone installed in his office. Wolfson successfully sued the telephone company and had the illegal line removed. This was a typical example of her ongoing struggle for fairness and gender equity. Wolfson continued her passionate advocacy for women's rights throughout her legal career. She received several awards for her work in helping the poor, and poor women in particular, find legal help. Her honors include the New England Bar Association Public Service Award, the Connecticut Law Tribune Pro Bono Award, the Connecticut Legal Services Distinguished Service Award, and a One Woman Makes a Difference Award from CWEALF. Wolfson, who had two children, earned a B.A. from Barnard College (1959) and a J.D. from the University of Connecticut (1976).

Womendez, Chris (1949 –) (also known as Chris Mendez) was a co-founder, with Cherie Jimenez, Betsy Warrior and Lisa Leghorn, of Transition House, Boston, MA, the first battered women's shelter in New England (1970s). She was co-founder of Finex House, which at its opening was the only wheelchair-accessible women's shelter in the state. Nearly 900 women used the shelters each year. Womendez, who changed her name from Mendez to reflect her commitment to women's issues, is a former battered woman and prostitute. She is a tireless champion of the rights of women who have been in abusive relationships. (ABS)

Wong, Nellie (1934 –) is a poet, teacher, lifelong activist and retired analyst in affirmative action, University of California, San Francisco. She has participated in the feminist, people of color, Asian Pacific American and labor movements since the early 1970s, and remains (2006) active in Radical Women, a socialist feminist organization dedicated to building the leadership of women. Wong was the first organizer for the Women Writers Union (1975), a group that grew out of a struggle of feminists at San Francisco State University who wanted more women faculty and the inclusion of women writers in the curriculum. She also helped organize a conference for International Women's Day that led to the formation of the Caucus for Creative Writing and Literature at the university. Wong is a co-founder of Unbound Feet, a collective of six Asian American women writers, poets and dramatists who performed their work in the late 1970s and early 1980s. She was a delegate to the first U.S. Women Writers' Tour to China (1983), and since the early 1980s has been a keynote speaker at many conferences, including Women

Against Racism, NWSA convention, and Feminist Perspectives and Third World Women. In 1985, Wong taught women's studies at the University of Minnesota. A prize-winning poet, her first poems were published in the mid 1970s in feminist and Asian American publications. Wong is the author of three collections of poetry: *Dreams in Harrison Railroad Park* (1977), *The Death of Long Steam Lady* (1986) and *Stolen Moments* (1997). She has contributed poems and essays to numerous publications, anthologies and journals, and her work is included in *This Bridge Called My Back: Writings By Radical Women of Color*, edited by Cherrie Moraga and Gloria Anzaldua. In addition to this work, Wong worked as an organizer for the Freedom Socialist Party in San Francisco for 15 years and was active in the anti-war and labor movements. Her poem, "Sailing With Memories of Li Wong" was nominated for a Pushcart Prize, best in small press poetry (2005). Archives: Califorinia Ethnic and Multicultural Archives, Davidson Library, University of California, Santa Barbara, CA. (ABS)

Wood, Nancy ("Nan") Farley (1904 – 2003) Wood's work in the women's liberation movement included being a founder of Chicago NOW and serving as national secretary of NOW. She also picketed United Airlines in 1969 because women were not allowed to fly on executive flights between NYC and Chicago; protested men-only restaurants in 1970; and was involved in environmental causes. Born on a farm in Green Ridge, MO, Wood displayed her intelligence early and inspired her father to provide her the opportunity to attend college. By age 12, Wood had read the entire Bible, and, according to her daughter, said she would always be bothered by the way women were treated in the Bible. Wood debated women's right to vote and marched with the suffragists in her high school. She later graduated from Warrensburg Teachers College, and in the 1920s received a master's degree in education from the University of Chicago. During World War II, she taught calculus to U.S. Navy sailors while her husband took care of their five children. Afterwards, Wood was recruited by the FBI to the top-secret Manhattan Project, where she worked on the designs of radiation detectors. In 1949, Wood founded N. Wood Counter Laboratory, which she ran until she was 87 years old.

Wood, Ruth Chloe LaFleur (1919 – 1986) Born in Eunice, LA, Wood attended Louisiana State University and was deeply involved in politics and the civil rights movement. When the Louisiana public schools were ordered to desegregate, she joined OPEN, an organization of parents who petitioned the state legislature to stop local governments from closing down the system to avoid compliance. In 1962 husband Bob Wood's work took the family, which included five children, to NYC, where they lived on Staten Island. But Wood was living the feminine mystique life, and, after reading Betty Friedan's book by that name she moved her family to Greenwich Village

(NYC), the heart of radical feminist action. She became a tireless worker for NY NOW, marched down Fifth Avenue in the Women's Strike for Equality, 1970, was on the organizing committee for the first Conference on Marriage and Divorce, picketed *The New York Times* to desegregate the Want Ads, and held CR groups in her home. Through the 1970s she was active in OWL. In 1984, she moved to New Orleans.

Woods, Harriett F. (1927 – 2007) Civic leader, journalist and television producer, Woods was the first woman elected statewide in Missouri as Lieutenant Governor (1985 – 1989). Earlier, in 1976, she was elected to the Missouri State Senate and re-elected in 1980. She was the second woman in Missouri history elected to that legislative body. As a city council member (1967 – 1976), Woods worked to create a racially open community. She was the first woman appointed to the Missouri Highway Commission (1974); the second woman elected to the board of the National League of Cities (1971); and the second elected a director of the National Conference of Legislators. Woods organized the first women's caucuses in both bodies. As state senator, she led efforts to improve the lives of the elderly and disabled. Woods was chief Senate sponsor of the 1977 resolution to ratify the ERA in Missouri and Senate sponsor of a bill to establish comparable worth. She aired the first campaign commercial in the U.S. declaring support for women's right to choose an abortion (1982). As national NWPC president (1991 – 1995), she helped move a record number of women into elected and appointed office. In 1995, she co-founded the Sue Shear Institute for Women in Public Life. As a journalist and public affairs director of KPLR-TV (1964 – 1974), Woods hired the first woman of color to host a public affairs show. She produced several documentaries, including "Women in Local Government" (1974), and is the author of *Stepping Up to Power: The Political Journey of American Women* (Westview Press, 2000). Woods, who has three children, holds a B.A. from the University of Michigan and an Honorary Doctor of Laws from the University of Missouri, St. Louis and Webster University. Archives: Western Historical Manuscript Collection, Columbia, MO; and NWPC collection at Vassar College, Poughkeepsie, NY. (ABS)

Woods, Laurie (1947 –) organized a newsletter on women's rights/issues while attending Boston University School of Law (1970 – 1973). She wrote articles on women's rights for "Blind Justice," a newsletter of the National Lawyers Guild, from 1970 – 1973, represented battered women in family court cases at MFY Legal Services (1974 – 1979), and developed the first class action lawsuit against the police department on behalf of battered women, forcing the police to arrest batterers (filed in 1976). In addition, Woods established the National Center on Women and Family Law (1979), and helped found the Battered Women's Resource Center in

NYC to give survivors an opportunity to influence policy makers (2000). Woods, who has two children, has also been a peace and civil rights activist. (ABS)

Woodsea, Marilynn – See zana

Woodul, Jennifer (1948 –) entered the women's movement in 1969. Woodul was a member of The Furies in Washington, D.C., "where we dedicated ourselves to woman-identification" in the early 1970s. A part of several actions in the 1970s to support lesbian feminists, Woodul was in the audience at the Second Congress to Unite Women to support the speakers who "came out" as lesbians within the women's movement in the Lavender Menace action. In addition, Woodul co-taught (with Kate Winter) a course on lesbian feminism in America at the University of New Mexico in 1973. Woodul was a founding member of Olivia Records (1974), the first national company to record feminist music. "There we devoted ourselves to women's culture and I learned the astounding power and importance of community," she says. Woodul holds a B.A. from Vassar (1970) and an M.A. from the University of New Mexico (1973). (ABS)

Wright, Doris — was a member of the board of NOW and a militant black feminist. She called a meeting in the spring of 1973 to discuss black women and their relationship with white women. Out of that meeting grew the National Black Feminist Organization, with Wright as a founder. Wright critiqued both black and white male dominance. Her critique of black male dominance evoked allegations of betrayal from many mainstream black leaders. In her article "Angry Notes from a Black Feminist," Wright wrote, "Two minutes in the Movement will prove to you that when it comes to being a member of the female sex, we're all in the same boat."

Wurf, Mildred Kiefer (1928 –) worked with Girls Incorporated from 1972 – 2001, retiring as director of public policy. At Girls Inc., Wurf created an advocacy role for traditional social service organizations, including adoption of policy statements stressing gender equity. She developed links with women's organizations and created the understanding that women should have special ties to "girls," not "children" or "youth," if things were ever to change. Wurf did the first analysis of public and private funding inequities between boys'/men's organizations and girls'/women's organizations. She also developed the Girls Bill of Rights and the mission statement, "To be Strong, Smart and Bold." Wurf has two children and holds an A.B. from the University of California, Berkeley. (ABS)

Wurl, Sheryl Lee (1948 –) (also known as Sheryl Zeman) A minister, chaplain and pastoral educator, Wurl says she has been "hit and spat upon during anti-war activities, called a lesbian when working for women's rights, and referred to as a communist lesbian traitor when on strike or negotiating for decent work conditions." She was a founding member of the Aberdeen, SD, chapter of NOW, where she was a member from 1972–1986. With other members of the chapter, Wurl organized Women's Day celebrations and conducted women's history programs in elementary and secondary schools. She also marched for the ERA, abortion rights and the ERA extension. A member of the Resource Center for Women (1972–1985), she served as board member and officer, including president. Wurl worked with the local YWCA and United Way to develop plans for a shelter for abused women and children (Women's Place), and conducted community education programs on the history of women, images of women in literature and women's rights. Wurl also served as a victim advocate for five years as part of her association with the coalition against domestic violence (mid 1970s). In addition, she participated in community education programs on the prevention of and response to domestic violence, and lobbied the South Dakota Legislature for tougher offender penalties and funding for shelters. She was a founding member of a shelter for abused women and their children, serving as president and volunteer. Wurl also worked with the speaker of the South Dakota House to implement what was termed "the marriage tax" as a major funding source for shelters in South Dakota. In addition, she worked with the White Buffalo Calf Society to help meet the needs of abused Native American women and their children (1970s) and served as a rape victim advocate through the rape task force (1972–1985). In 1973, Wurl designed and taught a class on images of women in literature, the first such high-school curriculum in South Dakota. She also taught this class at the college and community levels. Associated with the Brown County (SD) United Way from 1974–1984, Wurl acted as volunteer, communications committee chair, VP and president. She spearheaded a move to fund Women's Place shelter as the second largest United Way grant in the community. Wurl, who has two children, holds an M.S. and an M.A.   (ABS)

Wyatt, Addie L. (1924 –) has fought for women's rights for over 50 years. She was appointed to the labor legislation committee of the Commission on the Status of Women by Eleanor Roosevelt, was a founding member of NOW, and served as national VP of the National Council of Negro Women. Wyatt was also the first local union president of the United Packinghouse Food and Allied Workers, and then the first woman international VP of the Amalgamated Meat Cutters and Butcher Workmen of North America. In 1975, when she was women's affairs director of the AMBCW, which had 550,000 workers at the time, she fought successfully to eliminate wage differentiation between men and women workers. In 1974, Rev. Wyatt delivered the keynote address at the initial meeting of CLUW, of which she was a co-founder. She retired in 1984 as the international VP and director of the Civil Rights and Women's Dept. of the United Food and Commercial Workers. In 2005, she was honored by Women in Religious Life, Labor and Women's Rights Movements, and received the Alpha Phi Alpha Fraternity Phenomenal Woman in Religion Award.   (ABS)

Wyngaarden, Marjorie Alma (1928 –) was a founding member of the New Jersey Commission on Abortion (1968), the first in the state calling for repeal of abortion laws. Wyngaarden was also a founder of Northern NJ NOW (1970), serving as VP and chair of the speakers bureau and speaking on feminist issues before college groups, all-male organizations and on radio and television. Recognizing the difficulty of contacting NOW members unless their husbands' first names were known, Wyngaarden fought a nearly decade-long battle to make dual-name listing in telephone directories an option. She spoke directly to the companies, commenced a letters-to-the-editor campaign in the state's major newspapers, testified before the New Jersey Public Utilities Commission, wrote legislation requiring such listings, and finally submitted a shareholder proposal at AT&T's 1977 annual meeting. Says Wyngaarden, "AT&T lawyers argued before the SEC against including the proposal in the proxy statement that would be sent to the many thousands of company shareholders. The SEC was about to reject their argument when AT&T relented and, in 1977, permitted dual-name listings in Bell system directories. My activities resulted in desexegrating telephone directories nationwide and opening procedures in SEC rules regarding shareholder proposals." Wyngaarden, who has two children, has also been a member of the ACLU and the Bergen County Democratic Club. She holds an M.P.A. from Harvard University.   (ABS)

X, Laura (1940 –) Since 1969, the "X" of Laura's name has stood for the anonymity of women's stolen history and women having to carry their slave owners' names. She co-founded a SANE chapter at Vassar College, and since 1960 has been involved in the peace, civil rights, educational reform, lesbian, Jewish, socialist, African, Puerto Rican and Mexican movements and music. A Spanish-speaking Head Start teacher in NYC (1960–1961), she moved to Berkeley, CA in 1963, joining the students' non-violent Free Speech Movement (1964), and Women for Peace. After visiting the USSR in 1967, she discovered that the women who sparked the 1917 revolution were celebrating International Women's Day, and that IWD was based on an American event. She called for U.S. celebrations of IWD (11/11/58 Daily Cal). From July 1968, she collected manifestos and letters to the editor from movement women everywhere documenting their dismissal as "bourgeois" for demanding equal rights. In February 1969, enraged by a male professor's remark that it was not worth teaching women's studies because there was not enough material to fill a quarter course, she collected a list of 1,000 historical women and nailed it to the professor's door. She helped organize the first U.S. IWD (March 8) street demonstration since 1947, and called for/aided National Women's History Month activities to be built around IWD. People from 40 countries began sending material for her growing Women's History Library. In April 1969, she and fellow members of Redstockings West published the only national women's liberation newsletter, SPAZM. This became the first women's liberation newspaper, *It Ain't Me Babe* (1970). Firsts from her Women's History Library: the anthology *Masculine/Feminine* (1969); *Women's Songbook* (1971); *Films by and/or about Women* (1972); *Bibliography on Rape* (1973); *Herstory* (821 serial titles); *Women and Law, Women and Health/Mental Health*—nearly one million documents published on microfilm (1974) by the Library, commended by the ALA as the most comprehensive archive of any social protest movement. Laura co-founded the disability rights caucuses of NWSA, NCASA, NCADV. From 1978, she campaigned successfully in 45 states and 20 countries to make marital and date rape a crime, culminating in the unanimous vote against a husband's entitlement to his wife at the 1995 UN Beijing Conference. Microfilmed archives available in 400 libraries/14 countries. (ABS)

Yamada, Mitsuye May (1923 –) supported the ordination of women in the Episcopal Church in 1963. Despite being told in 1964 that she had terminal emphysema, Yamada went back to school and, with daily lung treatments, became a full-time instructor of English and literature in community colleges in California. Told by a lung specialist in 1971 that her "terminal illness" was a misdiagnosis, Yamada says, she suddenly felt free to make some "real" contributions to the women's movement. In 1973, she initiated and coordinated a course at Cypress College for women returning to school. Yamada also changed her standard American literature class to include writings by women and ethnic American writers. In 1975, she participated in the Feminist Press Panel at the IWY regional conference held in Cerritos, CA, and a panel on feminist poets held at the Pacific Coast Regional Conference in San Francisco. Seeing televised images of Vietnam refugees in Tent City at Camp Pendleton, CA, in 1975, Yamada recalled her own experiences in the Japanese internment camp in Idaho during World War II. In response, Yamada went to Tent City twice a week to teach English, seeking out women when they failed to appear because of childcare issues and later creating childcare arrangements in the tent. Her book, *Camp Notes and Other Poems*, was published by Shameless Hussy Press in 1976. In 1977, Yamada organized a women's writers conference in Santa Ana, CA, and served as delegate at large at the National Women's Conference in Houston. She was a founding member of the Asian Pacific Women's Network, and as a founding member of her local Amnesty International USA (1972), helped organize the first Amnesty International meeting of women in Geneva to discuss issues regarding women's rights.

Yamada, who has four children, earned a B.A. from New York University and an M.A. from the University of Chicago. Archives: Special Collections Library, University of California, Irvine, CA. (ABS)

Yankowitz, Nina (1946 –) An artist and graduate of the School of Visual Art, NYC (1969), Yankowitz was a founding member of *Heresies* magazine, a political journal on art and politics. She also took part in many CR groups in the New York City area, and supported actions on behalf of women artists demanding to be exhibited in the male-dominated art world of the 1960s and 1970s. In 1975, she taught a course at Womanschool, a part of Finch College in NYC, based on the question, Is there a female aesthetic? She was invited by Judy Chicago and Arlene Raven to speak and interact with young women artists at the Women's Building in Los Angeles in 1975. She has had her work exhibited nationwide as well as having created numerous public art projects. Yankowitz, who has one child, more recently co-chaired (with Carey Lovelace) a panel called Lone Rangers for the College Art Association in NYC that investigated non-group activist feminist artists from the 1970s. Yankowitz's work is in numerous private and public collections, including the Museum of Modern Art Artist Books Archives and the New Museum Rhizome.org archives. (ABS)

Yard, Molly (1912 – 2005) served as president of NOW from 1987 – 1991. During that time, she organized the 1989 national march for women's lives, one of the largest marches in Washington, D.C., history. Under her leadership, NOW helped defeat the Supreme Court nomination of Robert Bork. Yard was also chair of the Feminist Majority Foundation's task force on women and girls in sports. She was instrumental in passage of the Civil Rights Restoration Act of 1988, which included the reinstatement of Title IX. Born in Shanghai, China, where her parents were Methodist missionaries, Yard was painfully aware of the second-class citizenship of women there. This realization propelled her into a lifetime of civil rights activism. She returned with her family to the U.S. in 1924, and in 1933 graduated from Swarthmore College. From 1935 – 1944, she worked as an administrator and program director for various youth and student organizations, and became a close friend and adviser to Eleanor Roosevelt. Dedicated to civil rights, Yard was the Western PA coordinator for Martin Luther King's "I Have a Dream" march in 1963. She joined Pittsburgh NOW in 1974, and from that point devoted much of her time to ratification of the ERA. Throughout her feminist career, she distinguished herself as a gifted orator. Yard married in 1938, but took the then-unusual step of retaining her birth name. She had three children. Archives: The Sophia Smith Collection, Smith College, Northampton, MA.

Yildiz, Linda Jewell (1939 –) (also known as Linda Jewell) A biologist, Yildiz was living in Niantic, CT, in the late 1960s when she and her friend Judy Pickering began reading everything about feminism that they could get their hands on. They "made a common commitment to change the patriarchal order of things, which we translated into forming a group, then a chapter, which is called Southeastern Connecticut NOW," says Pickering. One of the group's first collective state actions was to integrate the male-only Hawaiian Room, an eating and drinking club located in the State Capitol Building in Hartford. Following the defeat of a bill to ratify the ERA by the CT Legislature (1972), the chapter convened ConnERA, a coalition to work for ratification, in 1973. Yildiz received her B.A. from Radcliffe College (1961), an M.A.T. from Harvard in 1964 and a Ph.D. from the University of New Hampshire (1978). (ABS)

Yorkin, Peg (1927 –) A philanthropist and activist, Yorkin was an elected delegate from California to the National Women's Conference, 1977. She donated to the half million-dollar Edith Bunker Memorial Award to help the ERA, and in 1986 produced NOW's 20th Anniversary Show at the Dorothy Chandler Pavilion in Los Angeles, where she met Ellie Smeal, then president of NOW. This association led to the formation of the Feminist Majority Foundation (1987). In 1991, Yorkin gave $10 million—the largest gift ever donated to a feminist organization—to assure FMF's success. Yorkin, who served as chair of the FMF, also provides funding for numerous women's causes, including the American Film Institute's Directing Women's Workshop, the Rape Foundation, Sojourner Center for Abused Women, NOW, Voters for Choice and feminist political candidates. She has two children. (ABS)

Young, Clarissa M. (1922 – 1979) was hired by the Lansing, MI, police department as a policewoman, the first sworn position available to a woman. In 1951, she became the first female sergeant, and in 1953 the first female lieutenant. In 1962, Young was the first woman in Michigan, and possibly in the nation, to achieve the rank of captain. Young founded Women Police of Michigan in 1968 to address discrimination and harassment of women police officers and to provide training opportunities. Her success with these issues inspired the creation of the Clarissa Young Officer of the Year Award. In addition to her trailblazing for and mentoring of women, Young was responsible for the establishment of what is today called community policing, or the integration of police, schools, communities and social agencies to serve the public. Young was inducted into The Michigan Women's Hall of Fame in 2000.

Young, Velma Nacella – See Taylor, Valerie

Younger, Judith T. (1933 –) was the associate dean of Hofstra University in 1971 when Governor Nelson Rockefeller held a conference on women that included a marriage and divorce workshop. NOW women attending brought the recommendations to Younger, who, with her students and the NOW women, translated the recommendations into appropriate language for the NY State Legislature to act upon. Originally called the Equal Rights Divorce Bill and then the NOW Responsible Divorce Bill, various portions were eventually passed into law, serving as a model for use throughout the country. Younger served as the educational consultant for the brochure, "Your Marriage, the Law and You in New York," published by the Council on Women and the Presbyterian Church in the U.S.A. In 1974, Younger was the keynote speaker at a NY state NOW conference on marriage and divorce. In 1995, Younger was presented (in absentia) with the VFA Medal of Honor as a pioneer in the fight for justice in family law. (ABS)

Youngman, Lenore Louise (1938 –) joined Los Angeles NOW in 1967 and remained active there until 1973. She took many photos of NOW marches that were published in NOW newsletters and books, and helped organize membership and plan meetings. In addition, Youngman worked on the *Woman's Almanac* with Toni Carabillo, Judith Meuli and Cathy Timlin, and was part of a project to hold AT&T accountable for its discriminatory employment practices. Youngman holds a B.S. from the University of Wisconsin. (ABS)

Yusuf, Zulekha (1951 –) Born in Karachi, Pakistan, Yusuf served as president of the National Students Federation (1970) and the Sirsyed College Student Union. She was an organizer of the Mohallah Group in Karachi, which helped abused women to get divorces and educated them about their rights. She was also an active participant in the Pakistani Democratic Women's Association, and organized the Sirsyed Literacy Foundation to help illiterate women. Says Yusuf, "During the regime of Ms. Benazir Bhutto, I wrote 24 episodes for Pakistan TV and also compiled a weekly program on the exploitation of women in Pakistan. As a result, the fundamentalists threatened me and my children, and the whole family was compelled to seek asylum in the U.S. I have also lived in Somalia, where I experienced a difficult kind of torture meted out to women, and have written about it for newspapers." Yusuf, who has two children, holds an M.A. from the University of Karachi, Pakistan. (ABS)

zana (1947 –) (also known as Marilynn Siegel, Marilynn Neel and Marilynn Woodsea) was hired as a women's editor by the *Hot Springs (AR) Sentinel-Record* in 1972, and quickly transformed the dull catch-all lists of wedding announcements and recipes to an award-winning section covering topics such as the ERA, CR groups, sexism, women's clothing and local women in non-traditional jobs. From 1974 – 1976, zana (who uses just the one name, not capitalized) was media coordinator for the Hot Springs chapter of NOW, and was a member of Hot Springs LWV. After moving to San Francisco (1976), zana

Z

became part of the core group that founded the Women's Building of the Bay Area (1978), worked on the publicity committee for the WBBA, and was a member of the San Francisco Women's Centers. She was also a member of the Feminist Writers Guild (1979 – mid 1980s). zana, who came out as a lesbian in 1977, became interested in the lesbian land movement in 1979. In 1980, she settled at Golden Farm in Wolf Creek, OR. In 1981, she became a founding member of the Southern Oregon Women Writers Group, Gourmet Eating Society and Chorus, in which she remained active until 1984. In 1984, she moved to Adobeland, women's land near Tucson, AZ, and lived there until 1991. During that time, she was a founding member of Sister Homelands on Earth, and helped purchase Saguaro Sisterland, also near Tucson, to provide housing for low-income women and women with disabilities. She lived there until 1994. zana began publishing writing and art in lesbian and feminist publications in 1979. In 1983, she published a book of her poetry and art, *herb womon*. Archives: The Lesbian Herstory Archive, Brooklyn, NY. (ABS)

Zarchin, Natalie (1922 –) In 1971, Zarchin began volunteering at the Rap Center at the Berkeley Free Clinic, and in 1972 became co-director. She was then invited to join the Berkeley Feminist Counseling Collective, where she practiced for two years. Zarchin was also active in the Berkeley Women's Health Collective. When that dissolved, she joined Womenrise, where she remained for six years doing feminist counseling, supervision and mediations in the community. During that same time and for 15 years forward, Zarchin led groups for lesbians at the Pacific Center for Human Rights. In 1978, she was hired to help start A Safe Place, a shelter for battered women, where she worked until 1985. Zarchin has also served on the planning committees for West Coast Old Lesbian Conferences (1987 and 1989), and on the steering committee of the San Francisco Bay Area OLOC. In 1994 she became a founding member of Lavender Seniors of the East Bay and has served on the board. She is (2005) a member of the San Francisco Bay Area OLOC steering committee. Zarchin, who has two children, has been active in civil rights, peace and environmental movements. She completed an oral history, recorded by Arden Eversmeyer, Houston, TX, under a grant from Astraea Foundation to interview members of OLOC. (ABS)

Zeitlin, Harriet Brooks (1929 –) A sculptor, fiber artist, painter and fine artist, Zeitlin was active in WomanSpace in Los Angeles in the 1970s, where she exhibited and helped remodel the building. She attended June Wayne's Joan of Art seminars in the early 1970s, and served as president of Artists for Economic Action (1977 – 1979), working to enact legislation to benefit visual artists. Zeitlin was also director of a national program to employ visual artists to create art for public places in Los Angels (CETA Title V1 Art in Public Places, 1977 – 1978). Says

Zeitlin, "I made sure that half of the artists selected were women." The group employed 10 visual artists for a full year and paid each $10,000. In addition, Zeitlin belonged to a group of women visual artists, the LA 9. Zeitlin, who has three children, attended Pennsylvania Academy of the Fine Arts, the University of Pennsylvania, Barnes Foundation, the University of California and Santa Monica College. (ABS)

Zellner, Harriet S. (1944 –) Zellner's first action was protesting the Lent Commission hearings on abortion in NYC with Carol Gerstle and Arlene Waxberg. There Flo Kennedy disrupted the hearings and all of them were thrown out. Kennedy told Zellner, who wanted to form a feminist group at Columbia, to contact Kate Millett. Soon after, in December 1969, Zellner and Millett founded Columbia Women's Liberation. Signs everywhere, including in the women's rest rooms, attracted an "overflow crowd" at the first meeting in Fayerweather Hall. At that meeting it was decided that staff and untenured faculty did not have to speak out publicly, and that nothing said at a meeting would ever leave the room. The group sat in at the university health services to protest Columbia's failure to provide even basic gynecological services to its female students, staff and faculty. It also successfully fought against discrimination in pay between maids and janitors. CWL ceased most of its activities in 1973. Zellner then concentrated on her career and earned her Ph.D. from Columbia in 1975. She joined the Rutgers University faculty where she taught labor economics on the graduate level and, on the undergraduate level, statistics, microeconomics, the economics of discrimination and the economics of income inequality as well as labor economics. She founded Integral Research Inc. in 1979. Zellner serves as an expert economist and statistician in personal injury, wrongful death, wrongful discharge and discrimination cases. In addition to her expert-witness work, Dr. Zellner also directs Integral's on-site Continuing Legal Education division. (ABS)

Zeman, Sheryl – See Wurl, Sheryl Lee

Zenko, Moe – See Sila, Mo

Ziegler, Vicki – See Noble, Vicki Jo

Zill, Anne Broderick (1941 –) In 1973, Zill was a founder of both the Fund for Constitutional Government and the Women's Campaign Fund, Washington, D.C. She served as board chair and board member for many years. In 1978, Zill served as president of the Karen Silkwood Fund, working to raise funds and coordinate the activities of the lawyers, fundraisers and organizers. In 1996, Zill became founder and director of the Center for Ethics in Action, a women's leadership training program that continues today (2005). Zill was president (1987 – 1988) of Women for Meaningful Summits, and was Washington representative for WEDO (1994 – 1996). Zill, who has four children, holds a B.A. from Barnard College and an M.A. from American University. (ABS)

Zimmerman, Anne (1914 – 2003) Born in Montana, Zimmerman was a pioneer in the movement to give nurses more control over their practice and better pay for their work. She served as director of the American Nurses Association's Economic and General Welfare Program (1951 – 1952), for which she received ANA's Shirley Titus Award (1980). From 1954 – 1981 she served as executive administrator of the Illinois Nurses Association, and from 1976 – 1978 was president of the ANA.

Zimmerman, Elaine (1950 –) founded the Berkeley (CA) Women's Center in 1972. To her knowledge, it was the first women's center in Northern California and was used by women for education and employment opportunities, and to find information about displaced homemaker concerns, domestic violence, youth resources, legal issues and women's support groups. The Center, which did not disconnect from older women, women with children, and women who needed economic self-sufficiency skills, partnered with the emerging Alameda County Resource and Referral network, Bananas (going Bananas), for childcare. Zimmerman led public policy efforts, stemming from the work of the Center, to address the growing poverty of women. She worked with sociologist Diana Pearce, who coined the phrase the "feminization of poverty," and the State Legislature's human services committee to hold the first state public hearing in the nation on women's poverty. That began a commitment and partnership between women and California legislators. Zimmerman was appointed by the lieutenant governor to sit on a state Feminization of Poverty Task Force, and also founded the Women's Economic Agenda Project (1981), which addressed women's economic issues across race and class. Zimmerman began to work with Bella Abzug, leading Women USA on the gender gap in parts of California. With the first major gender gap emerging in the early 1980s, Zimmerman began to organize women in the state to vote for their needs. She designed a strategic campaign that linked the negative poverty trend facing women with the positive growing political strength for women in the gender gap. With Oakland organizer Sandy Chelnov, she designed a poster that read "Two out of three adults are female. What if we all were to go to the polls?" The poster traveled the states and the press quickly, and the slogan was put on billboards and postcards. Zimmerman's get-out-the women's-vote campaign resulted in California having the largest turnout of women voters in the 1982 elections. In 1982, women delegates from throughout California attended a conference at the Capitol led by Zimmerman. Policy issues were debated and a legislative agenda was drawn up. Zimmerman was hired by assemblyman Tom Bates to be the senior consultant to the California Assembly Human Services Committee in 1985.

In 1987, she was appointed to staff and lead the first state legislative committee on the family in the nation. Zimmerman organized family hearings throughout the counties in California and drafted, with Sherry Novick and Joan Walsh, the first state legislative report on the changing family. In 1989, Zimmerman was hired to lead a comprehensive children's initiative for the State of Connecticut. She designed a public policy campaign focused on the needs of children from birth to age five. Following this successful campaign, she was selected to be the executive director of the State Commission on Children. In this role, she has facilitated public policy reform in school readiness, literacy, anti-bullying and prevention policy. Zimmerman also designed the Parent Leadership Training Institute, a democracy school for parents teaching both mothers and fathers the civic skills necessary to make change for children, for which she received the *Good Housekeeping* Award for Women in State Government in 2001. The PLTI has been replicated in various cities and states. Following this, Zimmerman designed, with Patrice Nelson of the Center for School Change, an initiative for parents to learn civic skills in order to improve public schools. Zimmerman led a model initiative with Jim Amman, Connecticut State speaker of the house, to invest state dollars in prevention rather than crisis for children. (ABS)

Zimmerman, Libby (1942 –) A social worker, Zimmerman and five other women created a mental health agency in 1973 called Focus, Counseling and Consultation for Women and Their Friends. Based in Cambridge, MA, its goal was to include lesbian and straight women seeking to affirm their lives, work and relationships, and help them resolve painful issues. The agency, now called Focus, Counseling and Consultation, still exists (2005). Earlier, while working on her thesis at the Heller School, Brandeis University (1972), Zimmerman joined a Marxist/feminist study group of women working on their dissertations or other intellectual work. Zimmerman, who has one child, holds both an M.S.W. and Ph.D. (ABS)

Zimmerman, Sophie Frankel (1916 – 2005) After receiving her B.A. degree (at age 57) in 1973, Zimmerman worked for the Feminist Press, addressing teachers at various schools on the importance of women's contributions in history. She also volunteered as a receptionist and hotline worker at an abortion clinic in Deleware, marched in demonstrations for the Equal Rights Amendment, and attended the conference in Albany that selected representatives to go to the International Women's Year conference in Texas. In addition, Zimmerman started a reading group in Glen Cove, NY, that emphasized women's literature. A member of NOW, she was instrumental in starting many CR groups. Zimmerman, who had two children, was also a member of SANE and Mothers for Peace.

Zimmermann, Luba - See Fineson, Luba

Zobel, Jan (1947 –) helped set up the library and organize various groups at the San Francisco Women's Building in the 1970s. She was a prime organizer of Breakaway (1971), an alternative learning center for women, where she taught classes in PR and car repair. She was also part of the lesbian teachers group that formed shortly before John Briggs's California State amendment that would have prohibited lesbians and gay men from being hired as teachers. Zobel, who began taking foster children in 1975, was the first out parent through the San Francisco Dept. of Social Services, and later counseled other lesbians interested in fostering children. About 1977, she and four colleagues (JoAnn Loulan, Marny Hall, Arthur Atlas and Jack Morin) formed Options: An Institute for Lifestyle Education, which offered gay/lesbian sensitivity-training sessions to the doctors at the University of California Medical Center, San Francisco. The first organization of its kind, it also offered conferences and workshops focused on sexuality and mental health issues for lesbians and gay men. In 1974, Zobel began doing lesbian/gay sensitivity trainings through Planned Parenthood. She also spoke at college-level classes on sexuality. "At that time, I considered myself to be a 'professional lesbian' because I spent so much time educating straight people about what it meant to be a lesbian." In 1975, she was trained at UCSF to lead pre-orgasmic groups for women. She and Marny Hall led a group just for lesbians. Zobel attended the first West Coast Quaker Lesbian conference (1977), and was an original member of the People's Yellow Pages Collective (1971 – 1981), which included categories like "gay" and "women's movement." Zobel earned her B.A. from Whittier College and her M.A. from the University of Chicago. (ABS)

Zucker, Barbara M. (1940 –) was a co-founder (with Susan Williams) of AIR Gallery in New York City, the first women's gallery in the United States. Zucker served as a board member of the WCA in NYC, and as chair of the art department at the University of Vermont, where she brought women faculty up to the academic level of their male peers. Zucker introduced women's art history at the university, and curated numerous exhibits at the university art department's Colburn Gallery of women artists, including N. Spero, A. Mendieta, C. Carlson and Lenore Malen. In addition, she has actively supported the ERA and pro-choice. Zucker, who has one child, holds a B.S. from the University of Michigan and an M.A. from Hunter College. (ABS)

Zuckerman, Marilyn (1925 –) A member of Women Strike for Peace (1964 – 1968), Zuckerman participated in demonstrations, leafleting and pressuring congressmen and mayors in both Washington, D.C., and New York City. In 1968, she returned to Sarah Lawrence College as an older student. Her book of poetry, *Personal Effects* (which includes two other poets) was published by Alice James Books in 1976. Zuckerman, who has three chil-

dren, holds a B.A. from Sarah Lawrence and an M.A. from Goddard College. Archives: Women's Archive, Radcliffe Institute, Cambridge, MA. (ABS)

Zwerling, Sandra Chusid (1931 –) Working with the American Jewish Congress and Beth Rocke, Zwerling surveyed 459 employment agencies in four cities in the United States. to determine the extent of discrimination against women (1970s). As a result of this work, 118 agencies were accused by the attorney general of New York of violating federal and state laws barring sex discrimination. As co-coordinator of the NOW conference on marriage and divorce, Zwerling handled all PR and wrote the program and press releases, which resulted in unprecedented local and national coverage. Zwerling also worked with *The New York Times* and *Daily News* to improve the image of women in the media. In addition, Zwerling's writing has appeared in numerous feminist magazines and journals such as *Ms.*, as well as in mainstream publications such as *Family Circle* and *The New York Times*. She had her own radio program in New York, "A Feminist View of the News," and appeared as a feminist representative on radio and television. Zwerling is also a founder of New Yorkers for Women in Public Office (1974). Zwerling, who has two children, is a graduate of the University of Chicago, New York University and the Manhattan School of Music. (ABS)

*Index created by Diane Brenner,
www.dianebrenner.com*

Main entries are indicated in **bold** type.

Main entries are indicated in **bold** type.

D

E

Main entries are indicated in **bold** type.

Main entries are indicated in **bold** type.

Main entries are indicated in **bold** type.

L

Main entries are indicated in **bold** type.

Main entries are indicated in **bold** type.

Main entries are indicated in **bold** type.

Main entries are indicated in **bold** type.

Smith, Ruth, 330, 364
Smith, Sandra L., **432**
Smith, Sherry A., 496
Smith, Sidonie, 6
Smith, Sondra Lou, **432**
Smith-Robinson, Ruby Doris, **432**
Smithson, Rosemary Leitz, **432–433**
Sneierson, Elaine
    See Leeder, Elaine
Snider, Mary Beth
    See Edelson, Mary Beth
Snitow, Ann Barr, 127, **433**
Snortland, Ellen Barbara, **433**
Snyder, Elayne Phyllis, **433–434**
Snyder, Joan, **434**
Snyder, Mary-jane Ryan, **434**
Soares, M.G., 113
Sobieski, Wanda Graham Glenn, **434**
Sogg, Joyce, **434**
Soler, Esta, 2
Solo, Pat
    See Matthews, Patricia Ann
Somer, Carol B., **434**
Somers, Peggy, 237
Sommers, Helen Elizabeth, **434**
Sommers, Letitia ("Tish"), **434**
Sorensen, Jane Forester
    See Lord, Jane Sorensen
Souder, Sandra Silverman, **435**
Sowell, Vickie Jo, 439
Spalding, Elizabeth ("Betty"), **435**
Spannaus, Olive Wise, **435–436**
Specktor, Peggy, **436**
Spencer, Lonabelle Ann ("Kappie"), **436**
Spender, Dale, 263
Spero, Nancy, 334, **436**
Spiegel, Diane Meier
    See Meier, Diane
Spiegel, Martin, 308
Spikes, Eleanor Ruth, **436**
Spillar, Katherine, 71, 311
Spindel, Karen S., **436–437**
Spiotta, Toni, 331
Spitz, Lilly Therese, **437**
Sporazzi, Laura Ponsor, 2
Sprague, Elizabeth ("Beth") Carole, **437**
Spretnak, Charlene, **437**
Springel, Nona
    See Ferdon, Nona Marie
St. George, Katherine, **437–438**
St. James, Margo, 171, **438**
Staats-Westover, Hazel Vivian, **438**
Stacey, Judith, **438**
Stagg, Mary Ellen
    See Capek, Mary Ellen S.
Stamberg, Margie, 317
Stamberg, Susan Levitt, **439**
Stambolian, Janet Beth, **439**
Stanbridge, Barbara, 423
Stanley, Julia *See* Penelope, Julia
Stanley, M. Louise, **439**
Stanley, Mary T., **439**

Staples, Emily Anne
    See Tuttle, Emily Anne
Stapleton, Jean, 58, **439–440**
Star, Aura, **440**
Star, BJ, **440**
Stark, Mavra E., **440**
Stark, Myra, 113
Starr, Vicky, **440**
Staub, Susan, 149
Staudt, Kathleen, **440–441**
Stauffer, Mary Louise
    See Hadditt, Marylou
Steckel, Anita, 307, **441**
Stecker, Vera, **441**
Steele, Carolyn Ann, **441**
Steele, Clelia, **441–442**
Steele, Joanne, **442**
Steere, Helen Weaver
    See Horn, Helen Steere
Stegall, Lael, **442**
Stein, Beverly, **442**
Stein, Judith Ellen, **442–443**
Stein, Linda, **443**
Steinbacher, Roberta, **443**
Steinberg, Mavra *See* Stark, Mavra
Steinberg, Susan
    See Danielson, Susan L.
Steinem, Gloria,
    72, 166, 226, 252, 429, **443–444**
Steingarten, Ellen M.
    See Raintree, Elizabeth
Steingold, Jacqueline, **444**
Steinman, Susan Leibovitz, 199
Stellman, L. Mandy, **444**
Stender, Fay Abrahams, **444**
Stephens, Wanda Brewer, **444–445**
Stern, Beverly Bartko, **445**
Stern, Gwen, **445**
Stern, Mickey, **445**
Stern, Susan, 299, **445**
Stetsenko, Ekaterina, 7
Stevens, May, 55
Stevens, Wilma Theodora, **445–446**
Stevenson, Florence Cozart Byrd, **446**
Stewart, James Brewer, 427
Stickles, Maureen
    See Carrsyn, Maureen Doris
Stiehm, Judith Hicks, **446**
Stille, Darlene, **446**
Stimpson, Catharine Rosalind, **446–447**
Stoltenberg, Susan Irene, **447**
Stonaker, Francesca
    See Benson, Francesca
Stone, Janet, **447**
Stone, Martha, 165
Stone, Merlin, **447**
Stone, Susan, 426
Stoner, Lillian Mary, **447–448**
Stonerock, Linda Sue, **448**
Storch, Marcia L., **448**
Strasser, Susan, 427
Straus, (Arlene) Susan, **448**
Straus, Sandy, **448**

Strauss, Mary Beth
    See Edelson, Mary Beth
Streiker, Premrup, **448**
Striebel, Charlotte Thomas, 16, **448–449**
Stringer, Patricia, 460
Striver, Irene, 314
Strobel, Margaret ("Peg") Ann, **449**
Strober, Myra H., **449**
Strom, Sharon Hartman, **449**
Strothman, Linda Jean, **449–450**
Stuart, David, 128
Stuart, Michelle, 255
Stuermer, Virginia M., 305, **450**
Stuhler, Barbara, **450**
Styers, Aleta Aslani, **450–451**
Suelzle, Marijean, **451**
Summers, Jane Frazer, **451**
Summers, Suzanne Schad, 7
Suneson, Charlene Ida, **451**
Suratt, Judith Hole
    See Hole, Judith
Surgal, Ruth, **451**
Surrey, Paula, **451–452**
Sussman, Diane, 149
Sutherland, Elizabeth
    See Martinez, Elizabeth ("Betita")
Sutherland, Viv, **452**
Suttenberg, Marcia Lee, **452**
Suttles, Donna
    See Pollach, Donna Helen
Swanson, Edith Mays, **452**
Sweet, Ellen Barbara, **452**
Swenson, Norma Meras, **452–453**
Swerdlow, Amy, **453**
Swetkis, D., 443
Swietnicki, Colette A., **453**
Swift, Earlyse, **453**
Swift, Kate, 313, **453–454**
Swigert-Gacheru, Margaretta, **454**
Switzer, Katherine, 343
Syfers, Judith
    See Brady, Judith Ellen
Sykes, Martha, 401
Symon, Mary Louise, **454**
Szekely, Ella, 420
Sznajderman, Suzanne Messing,
    454–455
Szymalak, Nola
    See Claire, Nola

T

Tacha, Athena, **456**
Talkington, Betty M., **455**
Tangeman, Jean Janette
    See Mountaingrove, Jean Janette
Tangri, Sandra Schwartz, 308, **455**
Tanner, Leslie B., **455**
Tatnall, Sally, **455**
Taubman, Bryna, 471
Tavenner, Patricia May, **455**
Tax, Meredith, 15, **455–456**
Taylor, Emily, 419